The Oscar Wilde Encyclopedia

Oscar Wilde in America, 1882

The Oscar Wilde Encyclopedia

by

Karl Beckson

With a Foreword by Merlin Holland

AMS Press
New York

Library of Congress Cataloging-in-Publication Data

Beckson, Karl E., 1926-
    The Oscar Wilde encyclopedia / Karl Beckson : with a foreword by
Merlin Holland.
    (AMS studies in the nineteenth century, ISSN 0196-657X; no. 18)
    Includes bibliographical references and index.
    ISBN 0-404-61498-1
    1. Wilde, Oscar, 1854-1900--Encyclopedias. 2. Authors,
Irish--19th century--Biography--Encyclopedias. 3. Gay men--Great
Britain--Biography--Encyclopedias. I. Title. II. Series.
PR5823.B34 1998
828'.809--dc21
[B]   97-36303
                                                              CIP

All AMS books are printed on acid-free paper that meets the guidelines for
performance and durability of the Committee on Production Guidelines for Book
Longevity of the Council on Library Resources.

AMS Press, Inc.
56 East 13th Street
New York, NY 10003

MANUFACTURED IN THE UNITED STATES OF AMERICA

CONTENTS

ILLUSTRATIONS

ACKNOWLEDGMENTS

For permission to quote from material still under copyright, I am greatly indebted to Merlin Holland, Wilde's grandson, for his generosity and friendship. Without such material, especially Wilde's dazzling letters, the effectiveness of this encyclopedia would have been severely diminished. I am also indebted to him for his contributing the droll foreword to this book and for permission to quote from Vyvyan Holland's *Son of Oscar Wilde* and *Time Remembered*.

I wish to thank the following colleagues and correspondents who graciously read early drafts of various entries in this book and suggested revisions or additions, provided me with important material, suggested new lines of investigation, or responded to queries when I needed assistance in my research: S.V. Baum, Laurel Brake, G.A. Cevasco, Davis Coakley, Pierre Coustillas, Geoff Dibb, Wayne Dynes, J.Z. Eglinton, Fay and Geoffrey Elliott, Bobby Fong, Benjamin Franklin Fisher, Edwin Gilcher, R.A. Gikoski, Hardy Hansen, Joel Kaplan, Norman Kelvin, Clinton Krauss, Mark Samuels Lasner, David Lateiner, Dan H. Laurence, Yvette Louria, Jeremy Mason, Peter McDonald, David Meadows, Frank Miles, Bruce Morris, Michael Murphy, James G. Nelson, Kevin O'Brien, Frances Miriam Reed, Horst Schroeder, Morton Seiden, Rodney Shewan, Ian Small, Claire Sprague, John Stokes, Martha Vogeler, Stanley Weintraub, and Richard Whittington-Egan.

For attending to my many requests for inter-library loan material, I am greatly indebted to the staff at Brooklyn College and at the New York Public Library.

Finally, I owe two deeply felt debts of gratitude to those who worked closely with me in the production of this encyclopedia: first, to James Vandenberg, our compositor, whose expertise and wise judgments resulted in the readability of the printed page; and to Jack Hopper, editor-in-chief at AMS Press, for his encouragement when I first proposed this book, for his scrupulous attention to details in the process of its completion, and for his helpful suggestions in the presentation of the contents.

ALSO BY KARL BECKSON

London in the 1890s: A Cultural History (1993)
Arthur Symons: A Life (1987)
Henry Harland: His Life and Work (1978)

Co-Author

Arthur Symons: A Bibliography (1990), with Ian Fletcher, Lawrence W. Markert, and John Stokes
Literary Terms: A Dictionary, 3rd ed. (1989), with Arthur Ganz

Editor

"I Can Resist Everything except Temptation" and Other Quotations from Oscar Wilde (1997)
Aesthetes and Decadents of the l890s, 2nd ed. (1981)
The Memoirs of Arthur Symons: Life and Art in the 1890s (1977)
Oscar Wilde: The Critical Heritage (1970)
Great Theories in Literary Criticism (1963)

Co-Editor

Oscar Wilde: Poems and Poems in Prose (1998), with Bobby Fong. Vol. 1 of *The Complete Works of Oscar Wilde*, gen. eds. Russell Jackson and Ian Small
Arthur Symons: Selected Letters, 1880-1935 (1989), with John M. Munro
Max and Will: Max Beerbohm and William Rothenstein, Their Friendship and Letters, 1893-1945 (1975), with Mary M. Lago

Foreword

Merlin Holland

Prefaces and Oscar Wilde have never made the easiest of companions. His *Picture of Dorian Gray* was first published in *Lippincott's Magazine* without one, but having engendered hundreds of column inches of vituperation, its author found quite irresistible the temptation to fire another broadside at his critics when it appeared in book form ten months later. "I am curious to see whether these wretched journalists will assail it so ignorantly and pruriently as they did before. My preface should teach them to mend their wicked ways," he wrote to a friend just before publication. If anything it aroused them to even greater indignation, and one of its aphorisms – "There is no such thing as a moral or an immoral book. Books are well written, or badly written. That is all" – was subsequently used as part of Queensberry's defence against Wilde's disastrous libel suit.

More than thirty years later, "Bosie" Douglas went to Nice to see Frank Harris, the publication of whose book *Oscar Wilde: His Life and Confessions* he had prevented in England for a decade with the threat of libel actions. Together the two men composed a new preface to be included in an English edition. It never was. Douglas took the text back to England with him, having told Harris "one truth and twenty lies," as Harris later wrote to my father, and published it separately as a sort of apology. Oscar does not come out well from Bosie's side of the story, but he seldom did. No, prefaces over the years have done him no favours.

This one, though, is different. It is neither defensive nor apologetic but rather an expression of delight that a scholar of Karl Beckson's stature should share a lifetime's study of Wilde and his circle and in a form which will make it the most useful reference work to appear on Wilde since Christopher Millard's *Bibliography* over eighty years ago. I hesitate to use the epithet "useful" since anyone with the smallest knowledge of Wilde will instantly recognize it as one of his least favourite words – the uselessness of anything being, for the most part, directly proportional to its attractiveness as far as he was concerned. Nonetheless, there were instances, notably in his lectures on "The Decorative Arts" and "The House Beautiful" delivered in America in 1882, in which he shows that utility and beauty can travel happily hand in hand. "There is no country in the world where machinery is so lovely as in America," declared the Professor of Aesthetics on his return to England, despite causing a storm of protest with his derogatory remarks about the Chicago water tower while he was there.

On the subject of American books Wilde was no less extreme: with the urchins on the railroad he remonstrated when they sold pirated copies of his poems for ten cents "vilely printed on a kind of grey blotting paper"; to J. M. Stoddart, the publisher of Rennell Rodd's collection of poems, *Rose Leaf and Apple Leaf* (and later of his own *Dorian Gray*), he enthused, "The book is a *chef d'oeuvre* of typography. It is an era in American printing." He then, incidentally, found himself in very hot water with his friend Rodd, not for organising the American publication, which Rodd found sumptuous, but for adding, unsolicited, an effusive dedication to himself and – yes – a preface with which Rodd largely disagreed. Their friendship ceased shortly after.

So now the tables are turned. Oscar Wilde, who once exhorted us "to check, or at least to modify, our monstrous worship of facts," has himself become the subject of an encyclopedia, the perfect challenge to printer, binder, and typographer to marry looks with intellect and prove the very point he was trying to make about art and function. I suspect, too, that once he had recovered from the initial shock he would be forced to concede, however disloyally, that it would be far better demonstrated by the quality of modern American book production than by the sadly falling standards in his home country.

As the current reassessment of Wilde's place in the social and literary history of late nineteenth-century England gathers momentum, so the people, the events, and the facts which seemed merely peripheral thirty years ago, begin to assume a far greater significance. Secondary characters, like pieces restored to a mosaic damaged by time, bring the picture once more to life and we can now appreciate the colour of their contribution to the whole rather than the dull monochrome of footnotes and asides with which we have had to make do in the past. It is a need filled in a perfect and timely fashion by the *Oscar Wilde Encyclopedia*, which will also correct elementary factual errors to which not even Richard Ellmann was immune, in particular, I noticed recently, mistaking both the full names of Sir William Wilde and Oscar's elder brother, Willie. Had it appeared on library shelves in 1994, it might also have saved the embarrassment of a member of the British public who, having attended the unveiling of Oscar Wilde's memorial window in Westminster Abbey's Poets' Corner, consulted *Pears' Cyclopaedia* and wrote to the Dean. "Sir," he protested. "As every schoolboy knows, Oscar Wilde was born in 1856. I enclose a cheque for £25 to have the date on the window altered." Our monstrous preoccupation with facts is obviously alive and well, and as misguided as ever.

However, for all his railing against realism and facts for their own sake (and even against encyclopedias in "The Decay of Lying"), Oscar was not averse to a little borrowing from reference works himself. He plundered the South Kensington Museum handbooks and Ernest Lefébure's work on textiles quite mercilessly for the descriptions of jewels and embroideries and music instruments in Chapter 11 of *Dorian Gray*, though in his defence it must be said that by altering the order of the words he managed to give them a flow which in the original they never had.

Exposing Oscar's peccadillos in this way leaves me with a twinge of remorse which stems from a desire to protect him against what he called "the mere body snatchers of literature." Was it not enough that for six terrible weeks his private life was paraded in all its intimate details before a Britain gloating at his downfall and that he was later stripped to his very soul in prison, without subjecting his works to forensic scrutiny as well? Should we not leave him a few enigmas, an iridescent fancy or two to cover his nakedness? Will we eventually tarnish the glitter of his personality for ever by explaining him away entirely, exchanging a little mystery for a mess of facts?

Certainly it is a danger, but a far greater one threatens. Reputations, like languages, need to be on the move constantly if they are not to grow stale and die, and Oscar Wilde's reputation, at least for the general public, is in grave danger of ossifying into the frivolous lightweight form it has kept for a hundred years. Remaining incomprehensible, as he advised James Whistler to do, is no longer enough to carry him into the next century. The delicate process, which he began on himself in *De Profundis*, of understanding without demystifying, is ours to continue, and it is with the guidance of such as Karl Beckson that we can discover the richness of Wilde's world and start to see some of the greatness which has been too long hidden behind the mask.

Publication of the *Oscar Wilde Encyclopedia* will also give relief to an old friend amongst my books, press-ganged years ago into unusual service – the 1962 edition of Wilde's collected letters. I doubt there is a single Wilde scholar who could deny using its footnotes at one time or another as a convenient source of quick reference to the 1890s. In this vicarious role, I shall now be able to put my own battered copy into honorable retirement, and in its place welcome to my shelves with enthusiasm a work which must surely prove itself indispensable in our rediscovery of one the most charismatic figures of English literature.

INTRODUCTION

In Richard Finneran's *Anglo-Irish Literature: A Review of Research* (1976), Ian Fletcher and John Stokes describe a "clever graduate student" who once observed:

"How can I write anything about Wilde? He is always right about everything." Some have written about Wilde, holding an opposite belief; but more truth subsists in the remark than in the notion that Wilde is insincere, shallow, immoral, irremediably minor. It needs to be said unequivocally that Wilde is a major figure, a master of the moral life. (55)

Though the scholarly authority of Fletcher and Stokes should have ended the case for Wilde's stature as a writer, there remains, on the part of certain critics (the number progressively dwindling), sufficient uncertainty to keep the case open with regard to his reputation, which runs the gamut from minor entertainer to major visionary. Denigrators are sometimes willing to admit that Wilde did, of course, write one important work, *The Importance of Being Earnest*, but that everything else is decidedly "minor." What is remarkable is that Wilde has probably been written about more than most nineteenth-century writers, and in recent years has surpassed, in sheer volume, all but the very greatest writers. Thomas A. Mikolyzk's *Oscar Wilde: An Annotated Bibliography* (1993), for example, lists more than 3,000 articles and books partially or wholly on Wilde, including many plays and novels based on Wilde's life and art. By the early 1990s, academia had produced well over 100 PhD dissertations (listed in Mikolyzk) and countless numbers of MA theses in the United States and abroad either wholly or partially on Wilde. In recent years, these numbers have been steadily growing, an indication of Wilde's current reputation.

This encyclopedia, the first on Wilde to appear, is designed as a guide through the massive amounts of material concerning Wilde's art and life, significant cultural and literary conceptions of his time, and those persons important in his life. In the biographical entries, the focus – as might be expected – is on the relationship of Wilde with the figure who is the subject of the entry. Hence, for the various figures included, I do not survey their lives and works, as would be expected in such works as Sally Mitchell's *The Victorian Encyclopedia* (1991) or G. A. Cevasco's *The 1890s: An Encyclopedia of British Literature, Art, and Culture* (1993).

Each work by Wilde is given a separate entry with bibliographic details of publication for its first appearance and subsequent appearances in revised form as well as its first inclusion in a collected volume. Included is an entry on *De Profundis*, for most critics regard it as a major autobiography rather than a mere letter. In addition, entries are included on the lectures that Wilde delivered on his 1882 tour of America. As carefully reconstructed by Kevin O'Brien, these lectures give us insight into the aesthetic attitudes of the young Wilde. Whenever possible, a work's background and sources are indicated, location of manuscripts is given, and scholarly references listed for further reading. Inevitably, repetition of certain material is unavoidable because of the very nature of an encyclopedia with its separate entries.

I have not included separate entries on Wilde's fictional and dramatic characters since they are handled in the entries on individual works in which they appear. I have, however, included references to characters in the index. Restrictions on space have necessitated the exclusion of any mention of plays, novels, recordings, and videos based on Wilde's works or life. Such material (which would necessitate a second volume) is marginal to the scope and intent of this encyclopedia.

Many poems, some incomplete, that did not appear in Wilde's lifetime are also included here for discussion. In 1976, a privately printed Tragara Press pamphlet had appeared with a number of these poems, but the texts were taken from transcripts prepared by Robert Ross, Wilde's literary executor, rather than from the original holographs. Hence, they have questionable authority. In 1978, Bobby Fong completed a critical edition of Wilde's poems as his PhD dissertation at the University of California (Los Angeles), utilizing Wilde's manuscripts as the basis for the texts (thereby revealing the liberties that Ross took in his transcripts). A scholarly edition of the poems based on Fong's prior work is forthcoming as Vol. 1, *Poems and Poems in Prose*, edited by Bobby Fong and Karl Beckson, of the Oxford English Texts Edition of *The Complete Works of Oscar Wilde*, whose general editors are Russell Jackson and Ian Small.

The number of books on Wilde has proliferated so alarmingly that, as this encyclopedia goes to press, omissions will inevitably occur. However, three volumes should be mentioned here: Jean Gattégno, and Merlin Holland's *Album Oscar Wilde* (Paris, 1996), which contains a biographical account and many unfamiliar illustrations of Wilde and his times; *The Wilde Album* (London, 1997), a quite different version by Merlin Holland; and Andrew McDonnell's *Oscar Wilde at Oxford: An Annotated Catalogue of Wilde Manuscripts and Related Items in the Bodleian Library, Oxford* (1996), a selection of items with illustrations of manuscripts and photographs of Wilde's fellow students.

In a cartoon that appeared in a recent issue of the *Chronicle of Higher Education*, an academic soirée is depicted in progress with an impressive professorial figure standing to one side with authority, his hands clenched behind his back and his determined jaw jutting out in earnest conversation with two others. A woman nearby, perhaps the gentleman's wife, whispers to another woman: "Don't bring up the coming *fin de siècle*. It will only get him talking about Oscar Wilde." Indeed, it is difficult *not* to talk about him since his genius and wit vitalized the late nineteenth century and helped to characterize that unique period in cultural history. Whether or not Wilde was "always right," as the clever graduate student reportedly said, he has inevitably become a mythic tragic figure whose extraordinary success and precipitous fall contain the essential elements of classical tragedy:

> His life was gentle, and the elements
> So mixed in him that Nature might stand up
> And say to all the world, "This was a man!"
> (*Julius Caesar* V.v. 73-75)

KEY TO ABBREVIATIONS

Beckson   Karl Beckson, ed., *Oscar Wilde: The Critical Heritage* (London and New York, 1970).

Beinecke Library   Beinecke Rare Book and Manuscript Library, Yale University.

Berg Collection   Henry W. and Albert A. Berg Collection, New York Public Library.

Borland   Maureen Borland, *Wilde's Devoted Friend: A Life of Robert Ross* (Oxford, 1990).

Clark Library   William Andrews Clark Memorial Library, University of California, Los Angeles.

Dulau   Dulau & Co., *A Collection of Original Manuscripts, Letters, and Books of Oscar Wilde*, Cat. No. 161 (London, 1928)

Ellmann   Richard Ellmann, *Oscar Wilde* (New York, 1988; London, 1987). Since pagination for these editions differs, page references are given for both in this order.

ELT   *English Literature in Transition, 1880–1920.* (Greensboro, North Carolina)

Harris   Frank Harris, *Oscar Wilde* (New York, 1989). Privately printed as *Oscar Wilde: His Life and Confessions* (1916).

Huntington Library   Henry E. Huntington Library, San Marino, California.

Hyde Collection   Mary Hyde (Lady Eccles), Four Oaks Farm, Somerville, New Jersey.

Kohl   Norbert Kohl, *Oscar Wilde: The Works of a Conformist Rebel*, trans. David Henry Wilson. (Cambridge, Eng., 1989).

Letters   *The Letters of Oscar Wilde*, ed. Rupert Hart-Davis (London and New York, 1962).

Lewis and Smith   Lloyd Lewis and Henry Justin Smith, *Oscar Wilde Discovers America, 1882* (New York, 1936; rpt. New York, 1967).

Mason   Stuart Mason (pseud. of Christopher Millard), *Bibliography of Oscar Wilde* (London, 1914; rpt. 1967).

Mikhail   E. H. Mikhail, ed., *Oscar Wilde: Interviews and Recollections*, 2 vols. (London and Totowa, New Jersey, 1979).

Miscellanies (1908)   Vol. 14, *Collected Edition of the Works of Oscar Wilde*, ed. Robert Ross (London, 1908; rpt. 1993).

More Letters   *More Letters of Oscar Wilde*, ed. Rupert Hart-Davis (New York, 1985).

Morgan Library   J. Pierpont Morgan Library (New York).

MS. (pl., MSS.)   An autograph manuscript, or holograph.

N&Q   *Notes and Queries* (Oxford).

PMG   *Pall Mall Gazette* (London).

Reviews (1908)   Vol. 13, *Collected Edition of the Works of Oscar Wilde*, ed. Robert Ross (London, 1908; rpt. 1993).

Rosenbach Library   Rosenbach Museum and Library (Philadelphia).

Ross	Margery Ross, ed., *Robert Ross: Friend of Friends* (London, 1952).
Small	Ian Small, *Oscar Wilde Revalued: An Essay on New Materials and Methods of Research* (Greensboro, North Carolina, 1993).
Texas	Harry Ransom Humanities Research Center, University of Texas (Austin).
TLS	*Times Literary Supplement* (London).
TS. (pl., TSS.)	Typescript.

CHRONOLOGY

1854	16 Oct	Oscar Fingal O'Flahertie Wilde is born at 21 Westland Row, Dublin.
1855		The Wilde family moves to 1 Merrion Square N.
1857	2 Apr	Isola, Oscar's sister, is born.
1864	12-17 Dec	Mary Travers's libel suit against Lady Wilde
1864-71		Attends the Portora Royal School, Enniskillen
1867	23 Feb	Isola dies.
1870	22 Oct	Lord Alfred Douglas, son of the 8th Marquess of Queensberry, is born.
1871-74		Attends Trinity College, Dublin.
1874	17 Oct	Matriculates at Magdalen College, Oxford.
1875	June	Tours Italy with Rev. J. P. Mahaffy, his former Trinity College tutor.
	Nov	First published work in verse, "Chorus of Cloud-Maidens," a free translation of songs from Aristophanes' *The Clouds* in the *Dublin University Magazine*.
1876	19 Apr	Sir William Wilde dies.
	5 July	Achieves a First in Classical Moderations ("Mods").
	Nov	Admitted to 33rd degree of Scottish Masonic rite in the Oxford chapter.
1877	Mar-Apr	Tours Italy and Greece with Rev. Mahaffy.
	?28 Apr	Returns to Oxford, late for the term, to discover that he has been "rusticated" (temporarily expelled).
	13 June	Dr. Henry Wilson, Wilde's half-brother, dies.
	July	First prose work published, a review titled "The Grosvenor Gallery," appears in the *Dublin University Magazine*.
1878	10 June	Wins Newdigate Prize for the poem *Ravenna*.
	26 June	*Ravenna* published on the day when he recites excerpts in the Sheldonian Theatre, Oxford.
	19 July	Achieves a Double First in *Literae Humaniores* ("Greats").
	28 Nov	Awarded the BA degree.
1879	early	Shares rooms at 13 Salisbury Street with the artist Frank Miles until August of 1880.
	7 May	Lady Wilde and her elder son, Willie, leave Dublin to establish a residence in London.
1880	Aug	Moves with Frank Miles to Keats House, Tite Street, Chelsea.
1881	23 Apr	Gilbert and Sullivan's *Patience* opens at the Opera Comique, London.
	June	*Poems* published.
	24 Dec	Sails for New York.
1882	Jan-Oct	Lectures in the USA and Canada.
	27 Dec	Sails from New York to England.
1883	Jan-May	In Paris.
	mid-May	Returns to London.

	2 Aug	Sails for New York
	20 Aug	*Vera; or, The Nihilists* opens and closes in a week.
	11 Sept	Sails for England.
	24 Sept	Begins a sporadic series of lectures until 1885.
	25 Nov	Becomes engaged to Constance Lloyd.
1884	29 May	Marries Constance.
	May-June	Spends honeymoon in Paris and Dieppe.
	24 June	Returns to England.
1885	1 Jan	Moves into 16 Tite Street.
	21 Feb	Becomes a regular reviewer for the *Pall Mall Gazette* until 24 May 1890.
	5 June	Cyril, the Wildes' first child, is born.
1886		Meets Robert Ross at Oxford.
	?5 Nov	Vyvyan, the Wildes' second child, is born.
1887		Robert Ross, a paying guest, stays with the Wildes while his mother travels abroad for three months.
	Nov	Begins editing *Woman's World* (he resigns in October 1889).
1888		Constance Wilde edits *Rational Dress Society Gazette* until 1889.
	May	*The Happy Prince and Other Tales* published.
1889		Meets John Gray.
1890	20 June	*The Picture of Dorian Gray* published in the July issue of *Lippincott's Monthly Magazine*.
1891	26 Jan	*The Duchess of Padua*, under the title of *Guido Ferranti*, is produced in New York and closes in three weeks.
	?24 Apr	*The Picture of Dorian Gray* (revised and expanded) published in book form.
	2 May	*Intentions* (containing "The Decay of Lying," "Pen, Pencil and Poison," "The Critic as Artist," and "The Truth of Masks") published.
	June	Meets Lord Alfred Douglas.
	July	*Lord Arthur Savile's Crime and Other Stories* published. Meets Aubrey Beardsley.
	4 Oct	Willie Wilde marries Mrs. Frank Leslie.
	Nov	*A House of Pomegranates* published.
1892	20 Feb	*Lady Windermere's Fan* opens at the St. James's Theatre.
	26 May	"Author's Edition" of *Poems* published (identical with the 1882 rev. edition of the 1881 publication).
	June	*Salomé* denied a license by Lord Chamberlain for public performance.
	29 July	*Lady Windermere's Fan* ends its run in London.
	Aug-Sept	At work on *A Woman of No Importance*.
1893	22 Feb	*Salomé* published in French.
	19 Apr	*A Woman of No Importance* opens at the Haymarket Theatre.
	10 June	Willie Wilde is divorced by Mrs. Frank Leslie.
	9 Nov	*Lady Windermere's Fan* published.

1894	Jan	Willie marries Lily Lees.
	24 Feb	*Salome* published in English translation by Alfred Douglas with Wilde's revisions and Beardsley's illustrations.
	1 Apr	Marquess of Queensberry threatens to cut off Douglas's allowance if his intimacy with Wilde continues.
	11 June	*The Sphinx* published.
	30 June	Marquess of Queensberry confronts Wilde at his Tite Street home and screams "loathsome threats."
	30 July	Walter Pater dies.
	Aug-Sept	At work on *The Importance of Being Earnest*.
	9 Oct	*A Woman of No Importance* published.
1895	3 Jan	*An Ideal Husband* opens at the Haymarket Theatre.
	15 Jan	Leaves with Douglas for Algiers. Wilde remains until the end of the month.
	27 Jan	Sees Andre Gidé by chance in Blidah, Algeria.
	14 Feb	*The Importance of Being Earnest* opens at the St. James's Theatre.
	28 Feb	Receives the Marquess of Queensberry's calling card at the Albemarle Club, charging that he is "posing" as a sodomite.
	2 Mar	Queensberry arrested for criminal libel and on 9 March is committed for trial.
	23 Mar	At a luncheon, Frank Harris urges Wilde to drop charges against Queensberry. Bernard Shaw, who is present, agrees, but after Douglas appears, Wilde rejects Harris's advice.
	3 Apr	Queensberry's trial begins at the Central Criminal Court (Old Bailey).
	5 Apr	Queensberry is acquitted; Wilde is arrested and imprisoned at Holloway.
	26 Apr	Wilde's first criminal trial begins.
	1 May	Jury unable to agree on a verdict. A new trial is ordered.
	7 May	Released on bail.
	22 May	The second trial begins.
	25 May	Found guilty and sentenced to two years at hard labor. Spends two days at Newgate Prison.
	28 May	Transferred to Pentonville Prison.
	4 July	Transferred to Wandsworth Prison.
	8 Sept	Constance Wilde changes her name and that of her two sons to "Holland."
	20 Nov	Transferred to Reading Prison.
1896	3 Feb	Lady Wilde dies.
	11 Feb	*Salomé* is given a performance by Théâtre de l'Oeuvre (Paris).
	7 July	Charles Thomas Wooldridge, a Royal Horse Guards trooper, is hanged in Reading Prison, the central event in *The Ballad of Reading Gaol*.
	10 Nov	Petitions the Home Secretary for an early release from prison. The petition is denied.

1897	Jan-Mar	Writes *De Profundis*.
	18 May	Transferred to Pentonville Prison.
	19 May	Released. More Adey and Rev. Stewart Headlam are waiting at the gate.
	20 May	Arrives in Dieppe, where he is greeted by Reginald Turner and Robert Ross, to whom he gives the manuscript of *De Profundis*.
	26 May	Moves to Berneval-sur-Mer, some five miles from Dieppe. Receives a procession of visitors.
	?28-29 Aug	Reunited with Alfred Douglas in Rouen.
1898	13 Feb	*The Ballad of Reading Gaol* published.
	18 Feb	Living at the Hôtel de Nice, Paris.
	16 Mar	Aubrey Beardsley dies.
	28 Mar	Moves to Hôtel d'Alsace
	7 Apr	Constance Wilde dies.
1899	Feb	*The Importance of Being Earnest* published.
	13 Mar	Willie Wilde dies.
	18 June	With Douglas at Nogent-sur-Marne.
	July	*An Ideal Husband* published.
1900	31 Jan	Marquess of Queensberry dies.
	10 Oct	Undergoes an ear operation in his hotel room, but the infection leads to cerebral meningitis.
	26 Nov	Turner informs Ross that there is little hope of recovery for Wilde, who, for the next few days, is in a state of delirium.
	30 Nov	Last rites of the Roman Catholic Church are administered by a priest. Wilde dies at 1:50 P.M.
1905	23 Feb	*De Profundis* published in a version drastically cut by Robert Ross.

A

"THE ACTRESS": *See ECHOES*

"ADAM LINDSAY GORDON"
Published: *PMG*, 25 March 1889, 3; rpt. in *Reviews* (1908). An unsigned review of Gordon's *Poems* (1888).

Wilde alludes to himself as a critic who had recently remarked of Gordon "that through him Australia found its first fine utterance in song" (see "Australian Poets"). Wilde now seizes the opportunity to correct himself: "This, however, is an amiable error. There is very little of Australia in Gordon's poetry. His heart and mind and fancy were always preoccupied with memories and dreams of England and such culture as England gave him.... Had he stayed at home he would have done much better work." On the whole, says Wilde, "it is impossible not to regret that Gordon ever emigrated. His literary power cannot be denied, but it was stunted in uncongenial surroundings, and marred by the rude life he was forced to lead. Australia has converted many of our failures into prosperous and admirable mediocrities, but she certainly spoiled one of our poets for us."

Australia, Wilde concludes, certainly contains new material for the poet: "...here is a land that is waiting for its singer. Such a singer Gordon was not. He remained thoroughly English, the best that we can say of him is that he wrote imperfectly in Australia those poems that in England he might have made perfect."

ADEY, WILLIAM MORE (1858-1942)
A translator of Ibsen's *Brand* (1891) under the pseudonym of "William Wilson," More Adey – as he was known – was one of Wilde's closest friends. When Adey first met Wilde is unknown, as is their relationship before the prison years. From Reading Prison, Wilde wrote in March 1896 to Robert Ross to thank Adey for sending books on more than one occasion. In his petition to the Home Secretary in July 1896, Wilde requested permission to have Adey see him at Reading

(before the stipulated time had elapsed to make a visit possible), concerning arrangements with Constance Wilde with regard "to the guardianship, education, and future of their children, and also with regard to financial arrangements connected with their marriage-settlements..." (*Letters* 406). The visit was approved by the Home Secretary. Adey also petitioned the Home Secretary for Wilde's early release from prison (the petition believed, says Hart-Davis, to have been written by Shaw), but before it was sent, the Home Secretary informed Adey that "no grounds, medical or other, exist which would justify him in advising any mitigation of the sentence" (*Letters* 408n1).

During Wilde's imprisonment, Adey was a key figure in attending to various financial matters not only relating to Constance but to other figures as well. Adey, Ross, and other friends had apparently urged Wilde to settle a divorce suit by surrendering – "as a sort of parting-gift" – his "life-interest" (that is, interest derived from an investment of funds). In a letter to Adey on 7 April 1897, Wilde wrote that the interest in question of £150 or £200 a year was "paltry": "My friends seem not to have realised that what I wanted was access to my children, and their affection and my wife's." The divorce settlement would break every "link" with his children. There was, he told Adey, "no link left but my wife's kindness to me" (*Letters* 525).

In a later letter to Ross, Wilde revealed his annoyance with him and Adey over their advice to him at the time of the impending divorce proceedings: "...now that I reflect on your conduct and More Adey's to me in this matter I feel that I have been unjust to that unfortunate young man [Alfred Douglas]" (*Letters* 547). In mid-May 1897, Wilde wrote to Reginald Turner that he was "distressed" by Adey's conduct in spending, without his consent, £150 that was intended to cover the cost of legal expenses. Turner, however, defended both Ross and Adey. Before his release, Wilde asked Adey to read Ross's copy of *De Profundis* and send the original to Alfred Douglas: Ross apparently disregarded Wilde's instructions (see *Letters* 419 and 423n2).

In *De Profundis* Wilde mentions Adey, among others, as one who had given him "comfort, help, affection, sympathy and the like" (*Letters* 495). Anticipating release in late May, Wilde planned to go to a seaside village abroad with both Ross and Adey. On 19 May, Adey was present with Stewart

Headlam to meet Wilde when he was released from Pentonville Prison. Later that afternoon, Adey escorted Wilde to Newhaven for the night boat to Dieppe.

Despite the sporadic resentment that Wilde felt towards Adey, Wilde sent him copies of *The Ballad of Reading Gaol*, *The Importance of Being Earnest*, and *An Ideal Husband*. Several months before his death, Wilde wrote to Ross: "I thought of you, and dear More, and all your generosity and chivalry and sacrifice for me" (*Letters* 829). In the same year, Ross and Adey became partners in the Carfax Gallery, which exhibited the works of such artists as Charles Conder, Max Beerbohm, Augustus John, and William Rothenstein.

AESTHETICISM

In the early 19th century, the literary and artistic Aesthetic Movement, usually associated with Wilde, had emerged on the Continent. Aestheticism contended that art should avoid social, political, or moral instruction, for art was autonomous with its own internal laws; hence, the artist's principal concern was with the perfection of his work. Central to Aestheticism was Kant's view of art as "purposiveness without purpose" (a view shared by other late 18th and early 19th-century German philosophers and writers, such as Schelling, Schiller, and Goethe). The French characterized this view as *l'art pour l'art*, the term first used by Benjamin Constant in his *Journal intime* on 11 February 1804, but not published until 1895. The public first became acquainted with the phrase in Victor Cousin's philosophy lectures delivered in 1818 but not published until 1836. The first known translation of *l'art pour l'art* occurs in an essay by Désiré Nisard on Lamartine in the *Westminster Review* (Jan. 1837), which refers to theories of "art for art's sake" (Findlay 247). In France, Théophile Gautier enunciated the doctrine of *l'art pour l'art* in the preface of his novel *Mademoiselle de Maupin* (1835). In England, such early 19th-century writers as Coleridge, Leigh Hunt, and Arthur Hallam also conceived of art's autonomy, as did Poe in "The Poetic Principle" (1850), which speaks of the "poem written solely for the poem's sake" and the "heresy of the didactic." Such Pre-Raphaelites as Rossetti, Swinburne, and William Morris have often been associated with the Aesthetic Movement (principally because of their concern with beauty of design and their anti-Establishment attitudes), but though they usually avoided didacticism, their art was usually grounded in moral concerns.

In 1862, Swinburne reviewed Baudelaire's *Les Fleurs du mal* by echoing Gautier's earlier aesthetic view: "...a poet's business is presumably to write good verse, and by no means to redeem the age and remould society." However, he did note the moral background to the poems. In his *William Blake* (1868), Swinburne developed his aesthetic view of art at greater length: "Handmaid of religion, exponent of duty, servant of fact, pioneer of morality, she cannot in any way become.... Her business is not to do good on other grounds, but to be good on her own.... Art for art's sake first of all, and afterwards we may suppose all the rest shall be added to her."

The principal figure who helped to shape late 19th-century Aestheticism was, to be sure, Walter Pater, whose *Studies in the History of the Renaissance* (1873) became the "golden book" for such figures as Wilde and Arthur Symons, who referred to it as "the most beautiful book of prose in our literature." Pater's notorious "Conclusion" to *The Renaissance* (as it was titled in later editions) urged his readers "to burn always with [a] hard, gemlike flame" and spoke of the "love of art for art's sake." Though Pater, like the Aesthetes, opposed didacticism in art, he did not rule out the moral effect that art had the capacity to produce. In "Style" (1888), for example, he contended that "good art" becomes "great art" if it devotes itself "further to the increase of men's happiness, to the redemption of the oppressed, or the enlargement of our sympathies with each other...." But Pater's moral aesthetic was generally overlooked by those who were enthralled by the style and intellectual hedonism of *The Renaissance*.

In the late 19th century, Aestheticism incurred much condemnation because of its attitudes towards art, which, for conventional Victorians, was expected to be spiritually uplifting and morally instructive. As a result, *Punch* satirized many of the principal figures associated with Aestheticism, such as Wilde, Whistler, and Swinburne, drawings of whom indicted them for their "too too" and "utter" devotion to Art. Gilbert and Sullivan took up the cry in their delightful *Patience; or Bunthorne's Bride* (1881) by depicting Bunthorne as one who expresses the Pre-Raphaelite preoccupation with medievalism. He is called a "fleshly poet," which suggests Swinburne or Rossetti, both of whom had been attacked by Robert Buchanan in 1871 as members of the "Fleshly School of Poetry." The operetta fixed, perhaps for all time, the image of the Victorian Aesthete when Bunthorne, the self-confessed "aesthetic sham" announces:

I am *not* fond of uttering platitudes
  In stained-glass attitudes.
In short, my mediaevalism's affectation,
Born of a morbid love of admiration!
. . . .
Though the Philistines may jostle, you will rank
  as an apostle in the high aesthetic band,
If you walk down Piccadilly with a poppy or a lily
  in your mediaeval hand.

The legend that Wilde also walked down Piccadilly with a lily in his hand amused him, but he protested: "Anyone could have done that. The difficult thing to achieve was to make people believe that I had done it" (qtd. in Holland 29).

When, in *Patience*, the manly Dragoons strike aesthetic poses to win over the "love-sick maidens," they are converted to the "principles of Aesthetic Art" associated with the "Inner Brotherhood" (that is, the Pre-Raphaelite Brotherhood, of which Rossetti was a member; Swinburne was associated with some in the group). Employing the popular clichés of aesthetic devotion, which focused on life rather than art, the maidens describe the Dragoons as "perceptively intense and consummately utter." Swinburne is often said to have been the model for Grosvenor – Bunthorne's rival – but after the "idyllic poet" reads one of his inane poems, he remarks that there is "not one word...which is calculated to bring the blush of shame to the cheek of modesty" – quite unlike Swinburne's *Poems and Ballads* (1866). Whistler, who regularly exhibited his paintings during the 1870s at the Grosvenor Art Gallery in New Bond Street, is more likely the model for Grosvenor, for he had established himself as a devotee of the basic doctrine of Aestheticism (though he avoided identification as an "Aesthete"). Moreover, the "greenery-yallery, Grosvenor Gallery" is mentioned in one of the operetta's songs sung by Bunthorne, echoing Archibald Grosvenor's name, and a reference in Bunthorne's song about a "Japanese young man, / A blue-and-white young man" presumably alludes to Whistler's immersion in Japanese art and to his well-known collection of blue and white china. Indeed, the influence of such art in his own paintings resulted in his being called, in the 1870s, "the Japanese artist."

Whistler's enunciation of aesthetic doctrine occurs later in his "Ten O'Clock" lecture (1885): namely, that art is "selfishly occupied with her own perfection only – having no desire to teach – seeking and finding the beautiful in all conditions and in all times..." (*The Gentle Art* 136). In a further statement concerning the autonomy of art, he argued: "Art should be independent of all clap-trap – should stand alone, and appeal to the artistic sense of eye or ear, without confounding this with emotions entirely foreign to it, as devotion, pity, love, patriotism, and the like...."

On his American lecture tour in 1882, Wilde incurred much ridicule for his aesthetic costume, which mimicked Bunthorne's, but it also reenforced the idea that Aestheticism was a deliberate joke perpetrated on the public. By the end of that decade, however, Wilde's literary essays, collected in *Intentions* (1891), undertook to rescue the basic principles of Aestheticism. His contention that Aestheticism sought to eliminate moral questions from art emerged as a global struggle, as indicated in a letter written in the summer of 1890 to a friend: "For myself, I look forward to the time when aesthetics will take the place of ethics, when the sense of beauty will be the dominant law of life: it will never be so, and so I look forward to it" (*Letters* 265).

However, in writing *The Picture of Dorian Gray*, Wilde compromised his own position by ending the novel with the self-inflicted death of the wicked Dorian Gray, an end that conformed to conventional expectations concerning the outcome of such a character. As Norbert Kohl suggests, Wilde was a "conformist rebel." For the second version of *The Picture of Dorian Gray* (1891), Wilde added a "Preface," which echoed Gautier: "All art is quite useless." In a letter to an unidentified correspondent, Wilde reiterated the Aesthetic principle:

A work of art is useless as a flower is useless. A flower blossoms for its own joy. We gain a moment of joy by looking at it. That is all that is to be said about our relations to flowers. Of course man may sell the flower, and so make it useful to him, but this has nothing to do with the flower. It is not part of its essence. (*Letters* 292)

Despite this anti-utilitarian statement (implying the rejection of any didactic intent), Wilde indicated his inconsistency throughout his career in adhering to the doctrine of art for art's sake.

Dorian Gray, Wilde argued, was not designed to teach a moral lesson; moreover, it contained elements of Decadence (see entry), which had affinities with Aestheticism. In the 1890s, Kipling condemned what he regarded as an unmanly devotion to aesthetic objects, for many Victorians an indication of "decadence" or "degeneration": in his poem "The 'Mary Gloster,'" (1896), he depicts a dying shipowner who tells his aesthetically inclined son: "For you muddled with books and pictures, an' china an' etchin's an' fans, / And your rooms at college were beastly – more like a whore's than a man's."

References: John Wilcox, "The Beginnings of *L'art pour l'art*," *Journal of Aesthetics and Art Criticism* (June 1953); Vyvyan Holland, *Oscar Wilde: A Pictorial Biography* (1960); L. M. Findlay, "The Introduction of the Phrase 'Art for Art's Sake' into English," *N&Q* (July 1973); Ruth Z. Temple, "Truth in Labelling: Pre-Raphaelitism, Aestheticism, Decadence, Fin de Siècle," *ELT* 17:4 (1974); Linda Dowling, *Aestheticism and Decadence: A Selective Annotated Bibliography* (1977); Ian Fletcher, "Some Aspects of Aestheticism," *Twilight of Dawn: Studies in English Literature in Transition*, ed. O M Brack (1887); Karl Beckson, "The Damnation of Decadence," *London in the 1890s: A Cultural History* (1993).

AHAB AND JEZEBEL

According to André Gide in "Oscar Wilde," *L'Ermitage* (June 1902), Wilde, after his release from prison, planned to write a play that Gide called *Achab et Jésabel* (presumably based on 2 Kings 9:1-10, 30-37), but which, he says, Wilde pronounced as "Isabelle" (indeed, Hart-Davis gives the play the title *Ahab and Isabel* in *Letters* 589n1). Vincent O'Sullivan, a friend in Wilde's post-prison years, recalls in his *Aspects of Wilde* (1936) that Wilde had discussed with him the "projected drama *Isabel*, based on the story of Jezebel in the Bible" (183). Possibly, the prose poem "Jezebel" (itself dubious: see *Echoes*) contains some elements that Wilde might have

used in his projected play. No MSS. exist to indicate that Wilde wrote any part of the play, nor does Wilde mention either title of the "projected drama" in any of his extant letters. Undaunted, the enterprising M. Guillot de Saix proceeded to write and publish the play in "Oscar Wilde et le théâtre. Jézabel. Drame inédit en un acte," *Mercure de France* (1 Nov. 1937) with the announcement below the title of the play: "Essai de reconstitution, par Guillot de Saix, de la dernière pièce imaginée et racontée par Oscar Wilde."

"Αἴλινον, αἴλινον ἐιπέ, Τὸ δ' ἔυ νικάτω" ["Ailinon, ailinon eipe, To d'eu nikato"]

Published: *Dublin University Magazine* 88 (Sept. 1876): 291; rev. with the title "O well for Him" in William MacIlwaine, ed., *Lyra Hibernica Sacra* (Belfast: M'Caw, Stevenson and Orr; London: Geo. Bell & Sons; Dublin: Hodges, Foster, & Figgis, 1878, 2nd ed. 1879), the editor having given the poem a new title from the first line; rpt. in *Poems* (1908) with its present title. The original title – "Tristitiae" – was restored in Methuen's twelfth edition of *Poems*, dated April 1913, but in later reprintings, the present title was restored. The title, a quotation from Aeschylus's *Agamemnon* (458 BC), line 121, reads: "Sing the song of woe, the song of woe, but may the good prevail." Wilde called the passage "a great chaunt" (*Letters* 22). This poem is not listed in Mason.

Throughout his life Wilde expressed compassion for the poor and the oppressed, as he does in this sonnet by alluding to the person who lives "at ease" and with wealth but has never known "The travail of the hungry years, / A father grey with grief and tears, / A mother weeping all alone." But one who has trod "The weary road of toil and strife" is more fortunate, for "from the sorrows of his life" he "builds ladders to be nearer God" (the metaphor derived from Jacob's ladder reaching to heaven in Genesis 28:12).

Manuscript: Dartmouth College has a MS. of the poem entitled "Tristitiae" (printed in Mason 67).

ALEXANDER, GEORGE (1858-1918)

An actor and manager of the St. James's Theatre from 1890 to 1918, Alexander was knighted in 1911 for his distinguished contributions to the British theater. Alexander's aristocratic air, handsome appearance, and personal charm no doubt attracted Wilde when he approached him in 1890 with his *Duchess of Padua*. When Alexander declined the play because the scenery might be too expensive and urged Wilde to write a play of modern life, Wilde agreed when offered a contract with an advance. The result was *Lady Windermere's Fan*. On completing it, Wilde asked Alexander whether he liked it. The actor responded: "Like it is not the word, it is simply wonderful" (qtd. in Ellmann 334/315).

However, they disagreed bitterly on the disclosure of the secret that Mrs. Erlynne, the "fallen woman," is, in fact, Lady Windermere's mother: at first, Wilde had withheld the secret until the last act in order to maintain the suspense and "dramatic wonder" (*Letters* 308). In a letter to the drama critic Clement Scott, Alexander sought his help "if I am still unable to persuade this conceited, arrogant and ungrateful man of his stupidity" (qtd. in Kaplan 64). After the first performance, however, Wilde yielded to Alexander's insistence and revised the play accordingly.

When Wilde completed his third society comedy, *An Ideal Husband*, he wrote to Alexander early in 1894 that he was offering it to another actor-manager:

> I shall always remember with pride and with pleasure the artistic manner in which you produced my first play [*Lady Windermere's Fan*], and the artistic care you showed, down to the smallest detail of production, that my work should be presented in the best manner possible, and it would be a great delight to me to have some other play of mine produced by you at your charming theatre.... (*Letters* 350)

In the summer of 1894, Wilde sent Alexander a scenario of *The Importance of Being Earnest* for his consideration: "You have always been a good wise friend to me..." (*Letters* 359). But convinced that the play was too farcical for a romantic actor like Alexander, Wilde wrote another scenario for him, later to be turned into *Mr. and Mrs. Daventry* by Frank Harris. Despite the different style of acting that he was accustomed to performing on stage, the creation of the role of Jack Worthing in *Earnest* remains one of Alexander's triumphs.

When Wilde was arrested on 5 April 1895, he asked Alfred Douglas to see whether Alexander (along with two others) would provide bail for

him, but Alexander was unresponsive. Nevertheless, after his release from prison, Wilde still felt his indebtedness to him as a result of Alexander's artistic integrity in producing two of his plays so successfully. But when Wilde was at the seaside resort in Napoule in December 1898, he suddenly encountered Alexander on a bicycle, as he wrote to Robert Ross: "He gave me a crooked, sickly smile, and hurried on without stopping. How absurd and mean of him!" (*Letters* 772).

But by the summer of 1900, Wilde had forgotten the slight and greeted Alexander warmly: "It was really a great pleasure to see you again, and to receive your friendly grasp of the hand after so many years." Alexander, who owned the rights to *Lady Windermere's Fan* and *Earnest* when Wilde was declared bankrupt, voluntarily agreed to spread the payment for the plays over a certain period – to which Wilde responded: "...I know it was dictated by sheer kindness and the thoughtfulness of an old friend" (*Letters* 832). Alexander later willed the rights of the plays to Wilde's son, Vyvyan.

References: A. W. E. Mason, *Sir George Alexander and the St. James's Theatre* (1935; rpt. 1969); Barry Duncan, *The St. James's Theatre: Its Strange and Complete History, 1835-1957* (1964); Joel H. Kaplan, "A Puppet's Power: George Alexander, Clement Scott, and the Replotting of *Lady Windermere's Fan*," *Theatre Notebook* 46:2 (1992).

"UN AMANT DE NOS JOURS": *See* **"THE NEW REMORSE"**

"THE AMERICAN INVASION"
  Published: *Court and Society Review* 4 (23 March 1887): 270-71; rpt. in *Miscellanies* (1908). An unsigned article.

Wilde announces that there is "a terrible danger" hanging over Americans in London: "Their future, and their reputation this season, depend entirely on the success of Buffalo Bill and Mrs. Brown-Potter [a former American society figure, now an actress]." Buffalo Bill, Wilde continues, "is certain to draw; for English people are far more interested in American barbarism than they are in American civilization." Denigrating remarks about this "civilization" follow: "The cities of America are inexpressibly tedious. The Bostonians take their learning too sadly; culture with them is an accomplishment rather than an atmosphere.... Chicago is a sort of monster-shop, full of bustle and bores.... Better the Far West, with its grizzly bears and its untamed cowboys, its free, open-air life and its free, open-air manners.... This is what Buffalo Bill is going to bring to London."

Since acting is "no longer considered absolutely essential for success on the English stage," Mrs. Brown-Potter, a "pretty, bright-eyed lady, who charmed us all last June by her merry laugh and her *nonchalant* ways," should be a huge success. Wilde welcomes her, for American women generally are "clever and wonderfully cosmopolitan": "They insist on being paid compliments, and have almost succeeded in making Englishmen eloquent.... They admire titles, and are a permanent blow to Republican principles.... If a stolid young Englishman is fortunate enough to be introduced to them, he is amazed at their extraordinary vivacity; their electric quickness of repartee; their inexhaustible store of curious catchwords." They have, however, "one grave fault – their mothers. Dreary as were those old Pilgrim Fathers, who left our shores more than two centuries ago to found a New England beyond the seas, the Pilgrim Mothers, who have returned to us in the nineteenth century, are drearier still."

The American father, Wilde observes, "is better, for he is never seen in London. He passes his life entirely in Wall Street, and communicates with his family once a month by means of a telegram in cipher. The mother, however, is always with us, and, lacking the quick imitative faculty of the younger generation, remains uninteresting and provincial to the last." In spite of the mother's dullness, the American girl is "always welcome.... [She] can talk brilliantly upon any subject, provided that she knows nothing about it." Of all of the "factors that have contributed to the social revolution of London, there are few more important, none more delightful, than the American invasion."

AMERICAN LECTURE TOUR: *See* LECTURES IN AMERICA, 1882

"THE AMERICAN MAN"

Published: *Court and Society Review* 4 (13 April 1887): 341-43; rpt. in Mason 22-27 (uncollected in the *Collected Edition*, 1908). An unsigned article. In connection with this article, see "The American Invasion" above.

Wilde points to the "curious fact" that, so far as society is concerned, "the American invasion has been purely female in character. With the exception of the United States Minister, always a welcome personage wherever he goes, and an occasional lion from Boston or the Far West, no American man has any social existence in London." Though "his women-folk, with their wonderful dresses, and still more wonderful dialogue, shine in our salons, and delight our dinner-parties," the "poor American man remains permanently in the background, and never rises beyond the level of the tourist." He is often seen "loafing through the street with a carpet bag," taking stock of the products and trying to understand Europe by gazing at the windows. He is Renan's *l'homme sensuel moyen* or Matthew Arnold's "middle-class Philistine." To him, a country's greatness, writes Wilde, consists in its physical size, and he never tires of telling the waiters at his hotel that "the state of Texas is larger than France and Germany put together."

For him, Art has "no marvel, and Beauty no meaning, and the Past no message.... The ruin and decay of time has no pathos in his eyes. He turns away from Ravenna, because the grass grows in her streets, and can see no loveliness in Verona, because there is rust on her balconies. His one desire is to get the whole of Europe into thorough repair." The American man is the "Don Quixote of common sense" because he is so utilitarian that he is "absolutely unpractical." He is consoled for having wasted a day in a picture gallery by turning to the *New York Herald*. After looking at everything and seeing nothing, "he returns to his native land." There, he is "delightful," for the "strange thing about American civilisation is, that the women are most charming when they are away from their own country, the men most charming when they are at home."

American men seem "to get a hold on life much earlier than we do. At an age when we are still boys at Eton, or lads at Oxford, they are practising some important profession, making money in some intricate business." Marriage is one of their "most popular institutions: The American man marries early, and the American woman marries often...." In America, the great success of marriage is due "partly to the fact that no American man is ever idle and partly to the fact that no American wife is considered responsible for the quality of her husband's dinners." Even the American capacity to divorce at will has, "at least the merit of bringing into marriage a new element of romantic uncertainty."

The American man is the "most abnormally serious creature who ever existed.... It is true that when we meet him in Europe his conversation keeps us in fits of laughter," but if he is in his own environment, the observations that provoked laughter in Europe "will fail even to excite a smile. They have sunk to the level of the commonplace truism...and what seemed a paradox when we listened to it in London, becomes a platitude when we hear it in Milwaukee." An English girl would marry him after meeting him, for though "he may be rough in manner, and deficient in the picturesque insincerity of romance, yet he is invariably kind and thoughtful, and has succeeded in making his own country the Paradise of Women. This, however, is perhaps the reason why, like Eve, the women are always so anxious to get out of it."

This article, obviously designed to entertain rather than inform, relies upon its epigrammatic style. Wilde's 1882 lecture tour in America provided not only the experiences but also the prose for "The American Man" as well as his lecture "Impressions of America," first given in England on 10 July 1883.

"AMIEL AND LORD BEACONSFIELD"

Published: Anya Clayworth and Ian Small, "'Amiel and Lord Beaconsfield': An Unpublished Review by Oscar Wilde," *ELT* 39:3 (1996), 284-97.

This incomplete and previously unpublished review, probably written in 1886, deals with three works: Henri-Frédéric Amiel's *Journal intime*, in an English translation by Mrs. Humphry Ward with the title *Amiel's Journal* (1885); and two volumes of Disraeli's letters, both edited by Ralph Disraeli: *"Home Letters": The Letters of Lord Beaconfield, 1830-1831* (1885) and *Lord Beaconsfield's Correspondence with his Sister, 1832-1852* (1886). Clayworth and Small conjecture that the "most likely reason" why Wilde did not complete the review is that Wilde was "simply unable to place [it] (Amiel's *Journal intime* had already been quite widely noticed in the press) and that as a result he simply abandoned it" (284).

Wilde opens his review with the possibility that

Amiel's journal and Disraeli's early correspondence suggest a comparison "between two remarkable literary legacies.... We may call one the diary of Hamlet, and the other the letters of Osric." They were both actors, and "like most actors" they were interested only in themselves. Disraeli, "immensely pleased," performed a "brilliant comedy to a 'pit full of kings,'" and Amiel performed a tragedy "to an empty house and was deeply affected at his own pathos." The singular advantage that Disraeli had over Amiel was that he "did not take himself seriously." Wilde's "strategy," write Clayworth and Small, is to introduce a topic and then, "by use of skillfully selected quotation, he contrasts the personalities of Amiel and Disraeli as they are revealed in their writing" (284). However, the review is burdened by so many quotations that, in the process, the reviewer virtually vanishes. It may have been the strategy itself that discouraged Wilde from completing the review.

Manuscript: The Clark Library has the incomplete MS.

"AMOR INTELLECTUALIS"

Published: *Poems* (1881). The Latin title of this poem, which Wilde probably wrote during his last year at Oxford, means "Intellectual Love."

This sonnet celebrates the aesthetic experiences that the speaker and friend (referred to only as "we") have enjoyed in the various arts. Indeed, the opening line echoes that of Keats's "On First Looking into Chapman's Homer" ("Much have I traveled..."): "Oft have we trod the vales of Castaly / And heard sweet notes of sylvan music blown / From antique reeds to common folk unknown." The friends have experienced not only the nine Muses of Greece but also Sordello's passion (in Browning's *Sordello*), the "honeyed line / Of young Endymion" (in Keats's *Endymion: A Poetic Romance*), "lordly Tamburlaine" (in Marlowe's play), "the seven-fold vision of the Florentine" (Dante's *Divine Comedy*), and "grave-browed Milton's solemn harmonies."

Manuscripts: The Clark Library has two early MS. drafts: one containing lines 1-11 (printed in Mason 308-09); the other containing lines 9-14.

"APOLOGIA"

Published: *Poems* (1881); rev. in (1882).

In this lyric poem, consisting of nine quatrains, the speaker addresses himself to a capricious lover who weaves "that web of pain / Whose brightest threads are each a wasted day." He shall endure, he insists, even though "sorrow dig its grave within my heart." At least, he argues, "I have not made my heart a heart of stone" (a phrase that reappears in "Impression du Matin" and in *The Ballad of Reading Gaol*), nor has he "walked where Beauty is a thing unknown." Echoing Tennyson's "'Tis better to have loved and lost / Than never to have loved at all" in *In Memoriam* (1850), the speaker remarks: "But surely it is something to have been / The best beloved for a little while...." And though passion has fed on his heart, he has "burst the bars, / Stood face to face with Beauty," and taking the line that concludes Dante's *Divine Comedy* ("The Love that moves the sun and the other stars"), he too concludes that he has "known indeed / The Love which moves the Sun and all the stars!" (see "At Verona" for another concluding line that more faintly echoes Dante).

For other poems that depict a beautiful woman's rejection of her suitor, see "Quia Multum Amavi," "Silentium Amoris," "Her Voice," and "My Voice." All of these poems were grouped together in *Poems* (1881), suggesting that they were composed as a sequence within a brief period of time, probably sometime between 1878 and 1881.

ARCHER, WILLIAM (1856-1924)

A leading drama critic of his day and the foremost translator and supporter of Ibsen, Archer was virtually alone (except for Bernard Shaw) in protesting the banning of *Salomé* from the stage in a letter to the editor of the *Pall Mall Gazette* (1 July 1892): Calling the Examiner of Plays in the Lord Chamberlain's Office, Edward Pigott (1826-95), the "Great Irresponsible," Archer writes: "A serious work of art, accepted, studied, and rehearsed by the greatest actress of our time [Sarah Bernhardt], is peremptorily suppressed, at the very moment when the personality of its author is being held up to ridicule, night after night, on the public stage, with the full sanction and approval of statutory Infallibility." Declaring Wilde's talent "unique," Archer continues: "We require it and we appreciate it – those of us, at any rate, who are capable of any sort of artistic appreciation."

Later that month, Wilde wrote to express his gratitude to Archer for his letter in the *Pall Mall Gazette*, "not merely for its very courteous and generous recognition of my work, but for its strong protest against the contemptible official tyranny that exists in England in reference to the drama." Wilde regarded the agreement of the other drama critics to the "tyranny" of such suppression as "perfectly astounding": "The whole affair is a great triumph for the Philistine, but only a momentary one" (*Letters* 319). When *Salomé* was published in French, Archer reviewed it in *Black and White* (11 May 1893). Aware of the influence of Maeterlinck on the play, he perceives "far more depth and body in Mr. Wilde's work than in Maeterlinck's. His characters are men and women, not filmy shapes of mist and moonshine" (rpt. in Beckson).

When, in the same year, *A Woman of No Importance* reached the stage, Archer reviewed it in the *World* (26 April 1893): Though "far from exalting either *Lady Windermere's Fan* or *A Woman of No Importance* to the rank of a masterpiece...we are dealing with works of an altogether higher order than others which we may very likely have praised with much less reserve." Archer claims for Wilde "a place apart among living English dramatists" because of the "keenness of his intellect, the individuality of his point of view, the excellence of his verbal style..." (rpt. in Beckson).

Since he had been "accused of wantonly overrating Wilde," Archer defended himself while reviewing Pinero's *The Second Mrs. Tanqueray* in the *St. James's Gazette* (3 June 1893): Though Pinero's tragedy "stands alone on a still higher plane," Wilde's plays stand above many of Pinero's lesser plays. Wilde is a writer, Archer concludes, of the "first rank" (rpt. in Beckson). Wilde wrote to him in appreciation of his "luminous, brilliant criticism": "...to be criticised by an artist in criticism is so keen a delight, and one so rare in England, that I love our modes of difference" (*Letters* 338).

With the production of *An Ideal Husband*, Archer, writing in the *Pall Mall Budget* (10 Jan. 1895), called it "a highly entertaining play," though he had reservations about Wilde's "epigram-factory" when it "threatens to become all trademark and no substance" (rpt. in Beckson). Reviewing *The Importance of Being Earnest* in the *World* (20 Feb. 1895) before the debacle, Archer calls it "an absolutely wilful expression of an irrepressibly witty personality" (rpt. in Beckson). On 1 May, several days after Wilde's first criminal trial began, the disturbed Archer wrote to his brother:

Really the luck is against the poor British drama – the man who has more brains in his little finger than all the rest of them in their whole body goes and commits worse than suicide in this way. However, it shows that what I hoped for in Oscar could never have come about – I thought he might get rid of his tomfoolery and affectation and do something really fine. (Qtd. in Charles Archer 215-16)

No evidence exists that thereafter Archer and Wilde ever saw each other or exchanged letters, but when *The Ballad of Reading Gaol* appeared, Wilde instructed his publisher to send him a copy.

References: Charles Archer, *William Archer: Life, Work and Friendships* (1931); Thomas Postlewait, *Prophet of the New Drama: William Archer and the Ibsen Campaign* (1986); Peter Whitebrook, *William Archer: A Life* (1993).

"ARISTOTLE AT AFTERNOON TEA"
Published: *PMG*, 16 Dec. 1887, 3; rpt. in *Reviews* (1908). An unsigned review of John Pentland Mahaffy's *The Principles of the Art of Conversation* (1887).

In reviewing a book by his one-time tutor in classics at Trinity College (see entry on Mahaffy), Wilde praises this "social guide without which no *débutante* or dandy should ever dream of going out to dine." After all, in society, "every civilised man and woman ought to feel it their duty to say something, even when there is hardly anything to be said...." On the question of conversation, Mahaffy has not merely followed Aristotle's scientific method, "which is perhaps excusable, but he has adopted the literary style of Aristotle, for which no excuse is possible." There are no anecdotes or illustrations to warn the reader or to dissuade him "in his reckless career." Nevertheless, Wilde warmly recommends the book to readers "who propose to substitute the vice of verbosity for the stupidity of silence." Despite its form and its pedantry, it fascinates and pleases: it is, says Wilde, "the nearest approach, that we know of in modern literature, to meeting Aristotle at an afternoon tea."

Mahaffy, continues Wilde, regards a musical voice as absolutely essential to a pleasing conversationalist. Though some have suggested that a slight stammer provides a "peculiar zest" to conversation, Mahaffy rejects such a view; he is,

moreover, severe on eccentricities, such as a native brogue or artificial catchwords – that is, repetition of phrases. On this point, Wilde entirely agrees:

"Nothing can be more irritating than the scientific person who is always saying *Exactly so*, or the commonplace person who ends every sentence with *Don't you know*, or the pseudo-artistic person who murmurs *Charming, charming*, on the smallest provocation."

Wilde is pleased with Mahaffy's remark, which he quotes: "Even a consummate liar" is a better addition to company than "the scrupulously truthful man, who weighs every statement, questions every fact, and corrects every inaccuracy." The liar, Wilde comments, "at any rate recognizes that recreation, not instruction, is the aim of conversation, and is a far more civilized being than the blockhead who loudly expresses his disbelief in a story which is told simply for the amusement of the company" (Wilde later develops his point in "The Decay of Lying").

At the dinner table, says Wilde, "Nobody, even in the provinces, should ever be allowed to ask an intelligent question about pure mathematics...." Such a question is as inept as one about the state of one's soul, which, says Mahaffy, "many pious people have actually thought a decent introduction to a conversation." As for "prepared or premeditated wit," Mahaffy has contempt for such a device; he tells of a certain college don (Wilde adds: "let us hope not at Oxford or Cambridge") who habitually carried a jest-book in his pocket, referring to it to enliven the conversation.

Since great wits are often cruel and great humorists often vulgar, it is better, says Mahaffy, to "make good conversation without any help from these brilliant but dangerous gifts." The best conversationalists, concludes Wilde, are those with bilingual ancestors, such as the French and the Irish, "but the art of conversation is really within the reach of almost every one, except those who are morbidly truthful, or whose high moral worth requires to be sustained by a permanent gravity of demeanour, and a general dulness of mind."

"ART AND THE HANDICRAFTSMAN"
According to Kevin O'Brien, this lecture, appearing with the above title in *Miscellanies* (1908), "is not really one of Wilde's lectures at all, but a pastiche of manuscript fragments remaining after Robert Ross put together 'The English Renais-

sance.'" In fact, "Art and the Handicraftsman" is closest to the first version of "The Decorative Arts" (31-2).

Manuscripts: The Clark Library has the MS. fragments and TS. versions referred to by O'Brien.

Reference: Kevin O'Brien, "An Edition of Oscar Wilde's American Lectures," PhD diss., University of Notre Dame, 1973.

ART AS RELIGION: *See* RELIGION OF ART

ART FOR ART'S SAKE: *See* AESTHETICISM

"ART IN WILLIS'S ROOMS"

Published: *Sunday Times*, 25 Dec. 1887, 7; rpt. in *Miscellanies* (1908). An unsigned review of Selwyn Image's second lecture on modern art. The first lecture was reviewed by Wilde in the *Pall Mall Gazette* (12 Dec.): see "The Unity of the Arts."

Image apparently accepted a suggestion made by "a friendly critic" (actually Wilde himself) to explain more fully his idea of literary art. In his lecture, Image explained the difference between an ordinary illustration for a book as opposed to such works as Michelangelo's fresco of "The Expulsion from Eden" and Rossetti's "Beata Beatrix." In the examples of Michelangelo and Rossetti, "the artist treats literature as if it were life itself, and gives new and delightful form to what seer or singer has shown us; in the former, we have merely a translation which misses the music, and adds no marvel." As for style, which Image described as "that masterful but restrained individuality of manner by which one artist is differentiated from another," the true qualities "lie in restraint, which is submission to law; simplicity, which is the unity of vision; and severity, for *le beau est toujours sévère*."

The "true artist," Wilde reports Image as saying, is a realist, for he acknowledges "an external world of truth, an idealist for he has selection, abstraction, and the power of individualisation." Wilde remarks, presumably paraphrasing Image but probably in total agreement:

To stand apart from the world of nature is fatal, but it is no less fatal merely to reproduce facts. Art, in a word, must not content itself simply with holding the mirror up to nature, for it is a re-creation more than a reflection, and not a repetition, but rather a new song.

A picture, Image said, is completed when the form and color employed by the artist adequately convey his intention, and, Wilde remarks, "with this definition...[Image] concluded his interesting and intellectual lecture."

"THE ARTIST": *See* "POEMS IN PROSE"

L'ART POUR L'ART: *See* AESTHETICISM

"'AS YOU LIKE IT' AT COOMBE HOUSE"

Published: *Dramatic Review* 1 (6 June 1885): 296-97; rpt. in *Reviews* (1908). A signed review of Shakespeare's play staged by the Pastoral Players, including Lady Archibald Campbell and the theatrical designer Edward William Godwin (see his entry). Coombe House was on the grounds of a hydropathic establishment near Kingston-on-Thames.

Quoting from Swinburne's famous "Sonnet (With a copy of *Mademoiselle de Maupin*)," though without using quotation marks, Wilde refers to that "golden book of spirit and sense, that holy writ of beauty" in which Gautier gives an account of an amateur performance of *As You Like It* in a French country house. The actual presentation at Coombe House, however, was "lovelier still," the play enhanced by "the exquisite charm of the open woodland and the delightful freedom of the open air." Lady Archibald Campbell's Orlando, Wilde writes, was "a really remarkable performance." Praising the production, including its costumes and music, he concludes: "Few things are so pleasurable as to be able by an hour's drive to exchange Piccadilly for Parnassus."

"ATHANASIA"

Published: First published as "The Conqueror of Time" in *Time: A Monthly Miscellany of Interesting and Amusing Literature* 1 (April 1879): 30-31; rev. as "Athanasia" in *Poems* (1881), which omits the final stanza (Wilde's apparent belief that it weakened the poem) but restored in *Poems* (1908), presumably by Robert Ross, then omitted in the 1909 editions and those following. The Greek title means "Immortality." Written around 1878-79, the poem was possibly influenced by Shelley's "The Sensitive Plant" in *Prometheus*

Bound, with Other Poems (1820).

For the first issue of *Time*, Wilde designed his poem to capitalize on the contemporary interest in recent archaeological discoveries in Greece and Egypt, resulting, in his poem, in a fusion of Hellenic and Egyptian allusions to suggest the agelessness of the flower, the central symbol of the poem. Consisting of ten stanzas of six lines each, "Athanasia" tells the story of the "withered body of a girl" brought to "that gaunt House of Art" (presumably the British Museum), but "when they had unloosed the linen band / Which swathed the Egyptian's body, – lo! was found / Closed in the wasted hollow of her hand / A little seed...." Sown in England, it yields "wondrous snow of starry blossoms" and "spread rich odours through our spring-tide air." The beauty of this "flower of Egypt" affects the flora and fauna around it:

For love of it the passionate nightingale
Forgot the hills of Thrace, the cruel king,
And the pale dove no longer cared to sail
Through the wet woods at time of blossoming....

This "bright flower...never feels decay but gathers life / From the pure sunlight and the supreme air." Whereas "we to death with pipe and dancing go," the flower is the "child of all eternity." The stanza that originally concluded the poem and subsequently omitted by Wilde in *Poems* (1881) contains characteristic Victorian discursiveness in pointing to the decline of great civilizations as opposed to the enduring nature of the flower:

The woes of man may serve an idle lay,
Nor were it hard fond hearers to enthral,
Telling how Egypt's glory passed away,
How London from its pinnacle must fall;
But this white flower, the conqueror of time,
Seems all too great for boyish rhyme.

"AT VERONA"

Published: *Poems* (1881).

At the time of his Italian tour in June 1875, Wilde wrote to Lady Wilde from Milan that Dante grew "weary of trudging up the steep *stairs*, as he says, of the *Scaligeri* [the powerful family ruling Verona, Dante punning on the Italian for *stairs*] when in exile at Verona" (*Letters* 9), an echo of Dante's passage in the "Paradiso" (17:59-60). In "At Verona," Wilde recalls Dante's banishment in

1302 from Florence by his political enemies. At Verona, Dante found a haven in the hospitality of Can Grande della Scala, a lord of the city-state and member of the Scaligeri family. Dante, who regarded Can Grande as Italy's redeemer, dedicated the "Paradiso" of the *Divine Comedy* to him. Wilde also drew upon the apocryphal tradition, as expressed in Rossetti's "Dante at Verona," which depicts the levity of those in the Veronese court, including Can Grande, who take Dante's melancholy lightly. Possibly identifying with the Florentine, Wilde dramatizes the dilemma of the artist's alienation in a hostile world, the theme also expressed in his "Theoretikos."

In the sonnet, the speaker is Dante, lamenting his fate in seeking favor with Verona's aristocrats: "How steep the stairs within Kings' houses are / For exile-wearied feet as mine to tread...." He recalls the line from Job (2:9), in which Job's wife urges: "'Curse God and die.'" But Dante consoles himself with the presence of God's love: "...behind my prison's blinded bars / I do possess what none can take away, / My love, and all the glory of the stars" (an echo of the final line of the *Divine Comedy*: see the conclusion of "Apologia" for the exact line from Dante).

Manuscript: The Clark Library has a photocopy of the first page of a notebook, now unlocated, which lists a poem entitled "With Can Grande at Verona," possibly an early version of "At Verona."

AUDIENCES, THEATER: *See* THEATER AUDIENCES IN THE 1890s

"AUSTRALIAN POETS"

Published: *PMG*, 14 Dec. 1888, 2-3; rpt. in *Reviews* (1908). An unsigned review of *Australian Poets, 1788-1888*, ed. Douglas B. W. Sladen (1888).

Wilde notes that the editor of this anthology dedicates it to Edmund Gosse, whose "exquisite critical faculty" is "as conspicuous in his poems as in his lectures on poetry." Wilde notes that, except for Adam Lindsay Gordon, in whom Australia found "her first fine utterance in song" (and whom Wilde reviewed later: see "Adam Lindsay Gordon"), Sladen has chosen an "extraordinary collection of mediocrities...ruthlessly dragged from their modest and well-merited obscurity." Moreover, Wilde remarks, "What strikes one on reading over Mr. Sladen's collection is the depressing provinciality of mood and manner in almost every writer. Page follows page, and we find nothing but echoes without music, reflections without beauty, second-rate magazine verses, and third-rate verses for Colonial newspapers." Perhaps, concludes Wilde, Sladen "will some day produce an anthology of Australian poetry, not a herbarium of Australian verse. His present book has many good qualities, but it is almost unreadable."

"AVE IMPERATRIX"

Published: First appeared as "Ave Imperatrix! A Poem on England" in the *World: A Journal for Men and Women* 13 (25 Aug. 1880): 12-13; rev. as "Ave Imperatrix" with two additional stanzas – the tenth and the fourteenth – in *Poems* (1881) and (1882). The Latin title means "Hail, Empress" (from 1 Jan. 1877, Queen Victoria was officially "Empress of India").

Written around 1879-80, the poem reflects Wilde's preoccupation with the British war in Afghanistan, which had opposed British political influence in the Middle East. In late July 1880, British forces, defending Kandahar, were defeated at the time that Wilde was probably completing his poem or reading proofs.

In the revised version, this poem of 31 quatrains is, at first, a traditional patriotic tribute to the imperial British Empire, as the opening indicates:

Set in this stormy Northern sea,
Queen of these restless fields of tide,
England! what shall men say of thee,
Before whose feet the worlds divide.

In various parts of the world, "the measured roll of English drums" is heard, and "girt and crowned by sword and fire, / England with bare and bloody feet / Climbs the steep road of wide empire."

But midway through this poem, tone and direction change abruptly, for imperial expansionism has resulted in the loss of English lives:

Down in some treacherous black ravine,
Clutching his flag, the dead boy lies....
Pale women who have lost their lord
Will kiss the relics of the slain.

Those who have died are buried in the outposts of the Empire: "not in quiet English fields / are these, our brothers, lain to rest...." The glory of England has been transformed by greed: "What profit now that we have bound / The whole round world with nets of gold.... / Ruin and wreck are at our side...." The poem ends, however, on an ambivalent note, for though "wasted dust" and "senseless clay" are the legacy of Empire, "we wrong the noble dead / To vex their solemn slumber so...." England must go on "up the steep road," yet Wilde's hope is that a new world – "the young Republic," not an imperial Empire – may, "like a sun / "Rise from these crimson seas of war."

Early Reviews: In its review of the American edition of *Poems*, the *New York Times* (14 Aug. 1881) remarked of "Ave Imperatrix": "[Wilde] has written an ode on England such as Tennyson has not and cannot.... [Tennyson] is not capable of grasping the idea of Great Britain and her colonies as one living empire, and pouring out a majestic lament for her dead as [Wilde] has done.... Wilde need not have written but this one poem...to win him respectful hearing wherever people exist who are responsive to what is noble in literature." In the New York *Century Illustrated Monthly Magazine* (Nov.), the reviewer also hailed the poem: "How an Englishman can read it without a glow of pride and a sigh of sorrow is beyond comprehension. Mr. Wilde can comfort himself. 'Ave Imperatrix' outweighs a hundred cartoons of *Punch*."

Manuscripts: Texas has a MS. fragment containing lines 25-32, dated 14 Jan. 1882, written as a presentation copy for the American artist James Edward Kelly (1855-1933), who had completed an etching of Wilde for circulars advertising his American lecture tour. Another MS. fragment of lines 25-29, dated 11 April 1882, is quoted in Sotheby's sale catalogue for 20 July 1989.

"AVE MARIA GRATIA PLENA"

Published: *Irish Monthly* 6 (July 1878): 412, as "Ave Maria Gratia Plena" (Latin: "Hail Mary, full of grace," the Catholic prayer, which continues: "blessed art thou amongst women, and blessed is the fruit of thy womb"); rev. as "Ave! Maria" in *Kottabos* 3 (Michaelmas term 1879): 206; further rev. as "Ave Maria Plena Gratia" in *Poems* (1881) and (1882); rpt. in *Poems* (1908) and succeeding editions with the original title "as being the more correct" (Mason 90 and n).

Inspired by a visit to the Vatican Gallery in 1877 (as indicated in the subscript of the poem's *Irish Monthly* appearance), Wilde had probably seen a painting of the Annunciation, though he confused matters by indicating in *Kottabos* and in *Poems* that the poem had been written in Florence.

In this sonnet, the speaker evokes such figures of Greek mythology as Danae and Semele, who offer spectacular, dramatic moments of "wondrous glory." The moment of the Annunciation, however, is less fraught with violence, as the speaker stands "with wondering eyes and heart... / Before this supreme mystery of Love." The scene before him depicts a kneeling girl with "passionless pale face," the annunciating angel, Gabriel, with a lily (the symbol of the Virgin's purity) in the presence of the Holy Ghost, as indicated by "the white wings of a Dove," often visualized in Annunciation scenes in medieval and Renaissance art.

B

THE BALLAD OF READING GAOL

Written: Shortly after his release on 19 May 1897 from Reading Prison, Wilde began writing the poem at the Chalet Bourgeat, Berneval, near Dieppe. To Robert Ross, he wrote on 22 July that the poem "aims at eternity" (*Letters* 626). On 2 September, publisher Leonard Smithers told Wilde that he had shown the first draft of the poem to Aubrey Beardsley: "...he seemed to be much struck by it. He promised at once to do a frontispiece for it – in a manner which immediately convinced me that he will never do it" (qtd. in Mason 410). On 14 October, Wilde told Reginald Turner that he had finished "the great poem," though to Smithers, he confessed that the "subject is all wrong and [the] treatment too personal." He later told Frank Harris that the poem was "too autobiographical and that *real* experiences are alien things that should never influence one" (*Letters* 708). He continued revising and adding passages to the proofs, including the two final sections, as late as December, convinced that the *Ballad* was his swan song (*Letters* 715).

Published: 13 Feb. 1898, by Leonard Smithers; rpt. in *Poems* (1908). In France, Henry-D. Davray, in collaboration with Wilde, published a French prose translation in the *Mercure de France* (May 1898). The first six English editions (totaling over 5,000 copies) cite the author as "C.3.3.," referring to Wilde's prison cell number. The dedication reads: "In Memoriam / C.T.W. / Sometime Trooper of the Royal Horse Guards. / Obiit H. M. Prison, Reading, Berkshire, / July 7th, 1896." "C.T.W." was Charles Thomas Wooldridge, 30, who was hanged on that day for murdering his wife on 29 March by slashing her throat three times in a jealous rage (though he was remorseful, the jury's strong plea for clemency was rejected by the judge). At exactly eight o'clock on 7 July, the prisoner was led to the gallows in a shed located in the exercise yard. The body was buried in quicklime in an unmarked grave on the prison grounds, the customary procedure for executed felons.

In the first proof sheets, Wilde had included an additional dedication to Robert Ross (though without mentioning his name): "Dedication / When I came out of prison some met me with garments/ and with spices and others with wise counsel / You met me with love." Smithers persuaded Wilde to omit this dedication (Mason 408).

Wilde mistakenly believed that the *Ballad* had a printing of only 400 copies, whereas 800 were printed. However, when Smithers resisted advertising the book, Wilde complained that the publisher was "so fond of 'suppressed' books that he suppresses his own" (*Letters* 705). By May, Wilde was so annoyed with Smithers that he told him: "You are so accustomed to bringing out books limited to an edition of three copies, one for the author, one for yourself, and one for the Police, that I really feel you are sinking beneath your standard in producing a six-penny edition of anything" (*Letters* 736–37). In March 1899, Smithers asked Wilde whether he had any objection to his name appearing on the title page underneath "C.3.3" in parentheses: "I think the time has now come when you should own the 'Ballad'" (qtd. in Mason 422). In the seventh edition, issued on 23 June of that year, Wilde's name appeared on the title page for the first time. In 1899, Benjamin Tucker (New York) issued the first American edition.

The Poem: Wilde adapted the traditional ballad structure in this poem of 109 stanzas, each consisting of six lines with an intricate rhyme scheme. The metre, alternating within each stanza from iambic tetrameter (four metrical feet) to trimeter (three metrical feet), generally resists a metronome beat by its subtle use of additional syllables in a line. As for imagery and subject matter, Wilde's poem was probably inspired by such works as Coleridge's "The Rime of the Ancient Mariner" (1798); Thomas Hood's "The Dream of Eugene Aram" (1829), the story of a repentant murderer; and A.E. Housman's "IX. On moonlit heath and lonesome bank" (concerned with a hanging in prison) in *A Shropshire Lad* (1896), some poems of which Robert Ross recited to Wilde while visiting him at Reading. Though Wilde told Ross that the idea for the *Ballad* came to him while he was in the dock, "waiting for my sentence to be pronounced" (*More Letters* 171), his remark seems designed to refute Alfred Douglas's suggestion that he was the inspiration for the poem.

The poem focuses on the narrator's responses to

the events of the execution and, as William Buckler suggests, the reader's "identification through the narrator with the brotherhood of the damned"; moreover, the narrator's reaction suggests what the trooper himself feels when a prisoner whispers:

> *"That fellow's got to swing"*:
> Dear Christ! the very prison walls
>   Suddenly seemed to reel,
> And the sky above my head became
>   Like a casque of scorching steel....

The autobiographical element enters soon after, a major refrain and theme of the poem suggesting the mystery of Wilde's own self-destructiveness: "The man had killed the thing he loved / And so he had to die. / Yet each man kills the thing he loves..." (this famous line may have been derived from Bassanio's line in *The Merchant of Venice*, IV.i.66: "Do all men kill the things they do not love?"). Though each man does kill the thing he loves, "Yet each man does not die." What occurred to Wilde, the poem suggests, was a fate worse than a felon's shame and death, for his career as an artist was destroyed while he continued to live in disgrace. Yet the narrator and the other prisoners progressively identify themselves with the trooper: "We watched him day by day, / And wondered if each one of us / Would end the self-same way...."

The reality of prison life is often suggested by striking passages, such as the following, in which realism clashes with allegory:

> We sewed the sacks, we broke the stones,
>   We turned the dusty drill:
> We banged the tins, and bawled the hymns,
>   And sweated on the mill:
> But in the heart of every man
>   Terror was lying still.

The lack of compassion from the governor of the prison, H. B. Isaacson (see The Prison Years); the prison physician, Dr. O. C. Maurice; and the Rev. Martin Thomas Friend (1843–1934), who was the prison chaplain from 1872 to 1913, is depicted in the following:

> The Governor was strong upon
>   The Regulations Act:
> The Doctor said that Death was but
>   A scientific fact:

> And twice a day the Chaplain called,
>   And left a little tract.

Occasionally Wilde echoes Coleridge's "Rime" and even his own poem "The Harlot's House," as in the lines describing the "evil sprites," or "phantoms," that "seemed to play" by night:

> About, about, in ghostly rout
>   They trod a saraband:
> And the damned grotesques made arabesques,
>   Like the wind upon the sand!

By allegorizing the experience (and thereby alleviating his own pain), Wilde envisions the morning of the execution as an elaborate drama of abstract forces: "...the Lord of Death with icy breath / Had entered in to kill." By punning on his own name, Wilde identifies with the doomed man near the end of Part III and identifies himself as the narrator, implying that his own transgressions by leading a double life had led to his inevitable punishment, a "death" in life:

> And the wild regrets, and the bloody sweats,
>   None knew so well as I:
> For he who lives more lives than one
>   More deaths than one must die.

The narrator contemplates the pit of lime where the trooper will lie after his execution: "And all the while the burning lime / Eats flesh and bone away...." Yet, anticipating Surrealism, Wilde presents a vision of resurrection:

> Out of his mouth a red, red rose!
>   Out of his heart a white!
> For who can say by what strange way,
>   Christ brings His will to light....

After the hanging, Part IV ends with Wilde's identification with the trooper in lines that were later inscribed on Jacob Epstein's monument (unveiled in 1914) over Wilde's grave in Père Lachaise cemetery, Paris (see The Tomb of Wilde):

> And alien tears will fill for him
>   Pity's long-broken urn,
> For his mourners will be outcast men,
>   And outcasts always mourn.

Though Wilde agreed with Robert Ross's suggestion that the poem should have ended at this point, he remarked that "the propaganda, which I desire to make, begins there" (*Letters* 661).

Part V makes explicit the moral implications of cruel imprisonment, a radical departure from his own previous aesthetic attitudes concerning Art: "...every prison that men build / Is built with bricks of shame, / And bound with bars lest Christ should see / How men their brothers maim." The final section, Part VI, which contains only three stanzas, sums up and repeats the central theme: "And all men kill the thing they love...."

Thus ends Wilde's most impressive didactic poem, another indication that, throughout his career, he could not maintain his aesthetic principles concerning the autonomy of art – that is, art for art's sake – for his moral preoccupations were equally compelling. Indeed, in the *Ballad*, he abandoned any attempt at a coherent style, as he wrote on 8 Oct. 1897, to Ross, who had pointed to the clashes in the poem: "With much of your criticism I agree. The poem suffers under the difficulty of a divided aim in style. Some is realistic, some is romantic: some poetry, some propaganda. I feel it keenly, but as a whole I think the production interesting: that it is interesting from more points of view than one is artistically to be regretted" (*Letters* 654).

Early Reviews: Though many reviewers had the uneasy feeling, as did Wilde, that the disparate elements of the poem threatened its unity, the reviews were nevertheless often favorable. Indeed, Wilde told Ross that "really the Press has behaved very well" (*Letters* 720). Reviewers discreetly omitted Wilde's name despite the fact that presumably everyone knew the author's identity. The anonymous reviewer in the *Athenaeum* (28 Feb. 1898) regarded the *Ballad* as "authentic: hence its worth. The poem is not great, is not entirely trustworthy; but in so far as it is the faithful record of experiences through which the writer – C.3.3. – has passed, it is good literature."

Perhaps the most ascerbic review, unsigned in the *Outlook* (5 March 1898), was written by W.E. Henley, one of Wilde's antagonists. Henley points to echoes from Coleridge and from Thomas Hood, who had provided Wilde with the stanzaic structure and metre: "In matter, it is a patchwork of what is and what is not. Here it is instinct and vigorous with veracity; there it is flushed and

stertorous with sentimentalism. It is carefully written and elaborately designed; yet is it full fifty stanzas too long...."

Calling the description of the night before the execution "sentimental slush – writing for the writing's sake," Henley remarks: "None who reads it can believe in any word of it. It is a blunder in taste, in sentiment, in art; for it is a misstatement of fact. If C.3.3. had been no Minor Poet, but an Artist – !" Despite the "sincerity, veracity, vision even...in this mixty-maxty of differences," the "trail of the Minor Poet is over it all. And when the Minor Poet is at rest, then wakes the Pamphleteer." Henley concedes that the poem has something "worth heeding" about the prison system, but he concludes rather tactlessly: "...let C.3.3 at once proceed to sink the Minor in the Pamphleteer, and make his name honoured among men" (rpt. in Beckson).

The review distressed Wilde, who told Smithers that it was "very coarse and vulgar, and entirely lacking in literary or gentlemanly instinct" (*Letters* 712). In contrast to Henley's review, Arthur Symons's in the *Saturday Review* (12 March 1898) greatly pleased Wilde, who told Smithers that the review was "admirably written, and most...artistic in its mode of approval..." (*Letters* 716). The review celebrates "a great spectacular intellect, to which, at last, pity and terror have come in their own person, and no longer as puppets in a play." And now, "having so newly become acquainted with what is pitiful, and what seems most unjust, in the arrangement of mortal affairs, it has gone, not unnaturally, to an extreme, and taken, on the one hand, humanitarianism, on the other realism, at more than their just valuation in matters of art." As "partly a plea on behalf of prison reform...it is not art," indeed "not really a ballad at all, but a sombre, angry, interrupted reverie," and the "real drama" is that of "'the souls in pain' who tramp around the prison yard...." The symbol of the "obscure deaths of the heart, the unseen violence upon souls, the martyrdom of hope, trust and all the more helpless among the virtues, is what gives its unity" to the poem (rpt. in Beckson).

In the "Literary Notes" of the *Pall Mall Gazette* (19 March 1898), the reviewer, who signed his name as "S. G." (probably the popular playwright Sydney Grundy, who, at the time of the trials, had objected in a letter to the *Daily Telegraph* to the removal of Wilde's name from theater programs and posters at the St. James's Theatre) begins by calling the *Ballad* "the most remarkable poem that has appeared this year." He sees a "curious parallel" between Wilde's work and Kipling's "Danny Deever" in *Barrack-Room Ballads* (1892), which is a "grim lyric...a conspicuously manly piece of work." The *Ballad*, however, "with all its feverish energy, is unmanly" (a term often associated with effeminacy or even homosexuality in the Victorian age). Yet the poem, he concludes, "has beautiful work in it, and touches of a genuine and honourable sympathy for the sorrow of weak things suffering" (rpt. in Beckson).

In the New York *Critic* (June 1899), which identifies C.3.3. as Oscar Wilde at the head of the review, the reviewer points to a revealing passage in the poem in the light of his remark: "The reader who happens to possess the subconsciousness of the artist (who necessarily in great or less degree assumes vicariously the roles he describes), – the reader alone will understand the full force of the asseveration contained in the following...: "And the wild regrets and the bloody sweats, / None knew so well as I." The "objection" to the poem is that it "is a congeries of morbid descriptions..." (rpt. in Beckson). Such objections to the depiction of the prison life encountered in other reviews prompted Wilde to tell Smithers that, for example, the review in the *Daily Chronicle* (15 Feb. 1898) "meant well, but there is more in the poem than a pamphlet on prison-reform" (*Letters* 704).

Manuscripts: A MS. (its whereabouts unknown), containing lines 529–46, is printed in Mason 416. The Clark Library has the TS. of the poem with Wilde's autograph revisions and additions. The Berg Collection has the first printed proofs with corrections in Wilde's hand. The Anderson Galleries auction catalogue, p. 25, for the John B. Stetson sale of 23 April 1920 contains a facsimile of three stanzas (lines 175–92) from an unlocated MS.

References: Abraham Horodisch, *Oscar Wilde's "Ballad of Reading Gaol": A Bibliographic Study* (1954); Garrett Anderson, "What Wilde's Tragic Trooper Never Knew," *Times* (London) (7 July 1980); William Buckler, "Oscar Wilde's *'chant de cygne'*: *The Ballad of Reading Gaol* in Contextual Perspective," *Victorian Poetry* (Autumn/Winter 1990); Leonard Nathan, "The Ballads of Reading Gaol: At the Limits of the Lyric," *Critical Essays on Oscar Wilde*, ed. Regenia Gagnier (1991); Guy

Willoughby, "The Community Restored: Christ in *The Ballad of Reading Gaol*," *Art and Christhood: The Aesthetics of Oscar Wilde* (1993); Seamus Heaney, "Speranza in Reading: On 'The Ballad of Reading Gaol,'" *The Redress of Poetry (1995).*

"BALLADE DE MARGUERITE. (NORMANDE)"

Published: First appeared as "'La Belle Marguerite.' Ballade du Moyen Age" in *Kottabos* 3 (Hilary term 1879): 146–47, the main title taken from the refrain of William Morris's "The Eve of Crécy" in *The Defence of Guenevere and Other Poems* (1858): "*Ah! qu'elle est belle La Marguerite*"; rev. in *Poems* (1881) with the present title. The term *ballade*, which Wilde employs in his title, refers, in Old French verse, to a fixed form, consisting of three eight or 10-line stanzas and a concluding four-line *envoi* ("a sending on the way"). Wilde's poem, of course, does not adhere to this structure.

Dante Gabriel Rossetti's "John of Tours (Old French)" had probably inspired Wilde to employ a similar setting for his poem. When A. H. Miles requested permission to include some of Wilde's poems in *The Poets and the Poetry of the Century* (1891–97), he responded: "You are quite at liberty to make use of the poems you mention, with the exception of 'The Dole of the King's Daughter,' the 'Ballade de Marguerite,' the 'Serenade,' and the 'La Bella Donna [della mia Mente].' These four I do not consider very characteristic of my work" (*Letters* 325).

In the characteristic pseudo-medievalism of Pre-Raphaelite verse, Wilde writes in his poem of knights and fair ladies (in the original version, even the spelling is sometimes archaic, as in *knyghtes*). The poem involves a conversation between the Forester's son, of low estate, and his mother, who warns him, when he expresses the wish to walk by his "Lady's side," that he is "overbold, / A Forester's son may not eat off gold." When he sees mourners walking to the graveyard, his mother attempts to keep the truth from him that the aristocratic Lady, whom he has adored from afar (the convention of courtly love: see discussion in "La Bella Donna della mia Mente"), has died, but he hears a voice "chaunting sweet, / 'Elle est morte, la Marguerite.'" When his mother urges her son to come in "And let the dead folk bury their dead," he responds: "O mother, you know I loved her true: / O mother, hath one grave room for two?"

Manuscript: The Jeremy Mason Collection has a MS. of the poem with Wilde's final revisions.

"LES BALLONS": *See* **"FANTAISIES DÉ-CORATIVES"**

"BALZAC IN ENGLISH"

Published: *PMG*, 13 Sept. 1886, 5; rpt. in *Reviews* (1908). An unsigned review of Balzac's *The Duchess de Langeais and Other Stories* and *César Birotteau* (1886).

Many years ago, Wilde writes, Dickens complained that Balzac was little read in England:

> ...although since then the public has become more familiar with the great masterpieces of French fiction, still it may be doubted whether the *Comédie Humaine* is at all appreciated or understood by the general run of novel readers. It is really the greatest monument that literature has produced in our century, and M. Taine hardly exaggerates when he says that, after Shakespeare, Balzac is our most important magazine of documents on human nature.

Studying men and women as the naturalist studied lions and tigers, Balzac "converted facts into truths, and truths into truth. He was, in a word, a marvellous combination of the artistic temperament with the scientific spirit." The latter he "bequeathed to his disciples; the former was entirely his own." Comparing Zola's *L'Assommoir* and Balzac's *Illusions perdues*, Wilde concludes that the former represents "unimaginative realism" as opposed to the latter's "imaginative reality."

Wilde quotes Baudelaire on Balzac, whose "fictions are as deeply coloured as dreams...." Of course, Balzac was accused of being immoral, adds Wilde: "Few writers who deal directly with life escape that charge." Balzac himself responded to such a charge: "Whoever contributes his stone to the edifice of ideas," he wrote, "whoever proclaims an abuse, whoever sets his mark upon an evil to be abolished, always passes for immoral." The characters' morals in the *Comédie Humaine*, notes Wilde, "are simply the morals of the world around us. They are part of the artist's subject matter; they are not part of his method.... Balzac is essentially universal. He sees life from every point of view.... He feels that the spectacle of life con-

tains its own secret."

Alluding to what was said of Trollope – "that he increased the number of our acquaintances without adding to our visiting list" – Wilde remarks that "after the *Comédie Humaine* one begins to believe that the only real people are the people who have never existed." Balzac's characters have "a fierce vitality about them: their existence is fervent and fiery-coloured" (one of Wilde's favorite phrases). They "dominate our fancy and defy scepticism... It is pleasanter to have the entrée to Balzac's society than to receive cards from all the duchesses in Mayfair."

BARLAS, JOHN (1860–1914)

Born in Burma and educated at New College, Oxford, Barlas published eight volumes of verse between 1884 and 1893 under the pseudonym "Evelyn Douglas." On "Bloody Sunday" (13 Nov. 1887), he participated in the famous Socialist demonstration in Trafalgar Square (Bernard Shaw and William Morris were also present), when, he later wrote, he had "the pleasure of being batoned and floored." This side of Barlas contrasts sharply with the view expressed by a friend, David Lowe, who wrote that he "never saw a man of such exquisite mould. He was like a Greek statue vivified.... He was not only a Greek in form, but a Greek in spirit" (3). To be sure, Wilde took an interest in him. In the summer of 1889, Barlas and Wilde first met at a dinner party in a Soho restaurant. In an unpublished memoir in the Clark Library, Frank Liebich, a popular concert pianist who was present, recalls Wilde jesting with Barlas in a conversation "full of lively trivialities..." (qtd. in McCormack 48).

On 31 December 1891, when Barlas was arrested for shooting outside of the Speaker's House in the Palace of Westminster, he asserted: "I am an anarchist. What I have done is to show my contempt for the House of Commons" (qtd. in *More Letters* 108n1). With a friend of Barlas – Henry Hyde Champion (1859–1928), secretary of the Social Democratic Federation and the publisher of Bernard Shaw's first novel, *Cashel Byron's Profession* (1886) – Wilde went to the Westminster Police Court on 16 January 1892, to post a bond as surety for Barlas's good behavior. En route, Champion informed Wilde that Barlas suffered from the delusion that he was a reincarnated figure from the Bible and believed that others recognized his significance by crossing their hands reverently as he passed. Wilde reportedly said to Champion: "My dear fellow, when I think of the harm the Bible has done, I am quite ashamed of it" (qtd. in Ellmann 308/291).

In response to Barlas's letter of gratitude for the posting of the bond, Wilde wrote: "Whatever I did was merely what you would have done for me or for any friend of yours whom you admired and appreciated. We poets and dreamers are all brothers. I am so glad you are feeling better.... We will have many days of song and joy together when the spring comes, and life shall be made lovely for us, and we will pipe on reeds. I must come and see you soon" (*More Letters* 108). However, despite the close of the letter with "Your affectionate friend," Wilde apparently saw little of Barlas: only one other letter to Barlas has survived, postmarked 4 February 1892, in which Wilde responds to Barlas's request that he sign an application for admission to the British Museum Reading Room (*More Letters* 109).

In a study of Wilde in the *Novel Review* (April 1892), reprinted in a Tragara Press pamphlet in 1978, Barlas observes that "concentration and universality are great gifts not often found together; the gift of the creative artist is not often united in one person with the gift of the sterile critic. Oscar Wilde has both: he can make beautiful things of a distinct type; he can enjoy beautiful things of every type." But it is Wilde's "dagger" – that of paradox – that makes him, says Barlas, a "revolutionist":

No weapon [that is, of paradox] could be more terrible. He has stabbed all our proverbs, and our proverbs rule us more than our kings. Perhaps it is better to say he uses sheet lightning. With a sudden flash of wit he exposes to our startled eyes the sheer cliff-like walls of the rift which has opened out, as if by silent earthquake, between our moral belief and the belief of our fathers. That fissure is the intellectual revolution.

Other than the few casual meetings recorded between Barlas and Wilde, it is possible that they saw each other at a Rhymers' Club gathering, when the afflicted poet became a "guest" for a brief period of time. Wilde's friend and later biographer Robert Sherard reported that one of the Rhymers,

John Davidson, had told him that Barlas was proposing "a fresh act of folly" as soon as his bail expired. Sherard comments in his letter to John Gray: "I do hope that this is not so, as it would be fatal for him. So far he has not done badly, for he has won much sympathy & a number of admirers who have written to me" (qtd. in McCormack 73).

Many of Barlas's remaining years were spent in mental institutions. On 21 June 1898, Davidson responded to a query from Edmund Gosse concerning Barlas's whereabouts:

No; Barlas is not dead. When I last heard of him he was in Gartnavel Asylum, Glasgow. I am afraid there is little chance of his recovery. His face was very handsome, and he was physically strong, but his head was small, and nothing in it to outweigh insanity. (qtd. in Townsend 190n)

Barlas died in Gartnaval Royal Hospital on 15 August 1914.

References: David Lowe, *Barlas: Sweet Singer and Socialist* (1915); J. Benjamin Townsend, *John Davidson: Poet of Armageddon* (1961; rpt. 1978); John Barlas, *Oscar Wilde: A Study* (1978); Jerusha Hull McCormack, *John Gray: Poet, Dandy, and Priest* (1991).

"A BATCH OF NOVELS"
Published: *PMG*, 2 May 1887, ll; rpt. in *Reviews* (1908). Unsigned reviews.

Wilde announces that "of the three great Russian novelists of our time," Turgenev is "by the far the finest artist":

He has that spirit of exquisite selection, that delicate choice of detail, which is the essence of style; his work is entirely free from any personal intention; and by taking existence at its most fiery-coloured moments, he can distill into a few pages of perfect prose the moods and passions of many lives.

Tolstoy's method is "much larger, and his field of vision more extended." Though Tolstoy at first seems to lack "artistic unity of impression," which is Turgenev's chief charm, Tolstoy's work "seems to have the grandeur and simplicity of an epic." Dostoevsky is "not so fine an artist as Tourgenieff [*sic*], for he deals more with the facts than with the effects of life; nor has he Tolstoi's largeness of vision and epic dignity." Nevertheless, he has

> qualities that are distinctively and absolutely his own, such as a fierce intensity of passion and concentration of impulse, a power of dealing with the deepest mysteries of psychology and the most hidden springs of life, and a realism that is pitiless in its fidelity, and terrible because it is true.

(At this point, Wilde alludes to his 1886 review of *Crime and Punishment*, unnoted by Mason, and borrows a sentence from that review: see "A Russian Realistic Romance.")

In turning to Dostoevsky's *Injury and Insult*, translated by Frederick Whishaw (1887), Wilde remarks that this novel is not at all inferior to "that great masterpiece" *Crime and Punishment*: "Mean and ordinary though the surroundings of the story may seem, the heroine Natasha is like one of the noble victims of Greek tragedy: she is Antigone with the passion of Phaedra, and it is impossible to approach her without a feeling of awe." Wilde expresses admiration for Dostoevsky's "subtle objective method" in presenting his characters "by little tricks of manner, personal appearance, fancies in dress...and afterwards by their deeds and words...yet he never explains his personages away...." Since George Eliot's *Adam Bede* and Balzac's *Le Père Goriot*, "no more powerful novel has been written than *Insult and Injury*."

In the remainder of his review, Wilde devotes the equivalent of slightly more than a page to the remaining six novels. W. M. Hardinge's *The Willow-Garth* (1887), he notes, "has a most charming style, and, as a writer, possesses both distinction and grace," his novel combining romance and satire. Rosa Mulholland's *Marcella Grace* (1886) is about modern life in Ireland, "and is one of the best books Miss Mulholland has ever published." In its "artistic reserve...it is an excellent model for all lady-novelists to follow." In her treatment of nature, "she never shrieks over scenery like a tourist."

Proceeding to Constance MacEwen's *Soap* (1886), Wilde remarks that she was once compared to George Eliot and Carlyle, "but we fear that we cannot compete with our contemporaries in these daring comparisons. Her present book is very

clever, rather vulgar, and contains some fine examples of bad French." Concluding rapidly, Wilde departs by citing the final three novels in one sentence: Faucet Street's *A Marked Man* (1887) "shows some power of description and treatment, but is sadly incomplete"; Robert Buchanan's *That Winter Night* (1887) is "quite unworthy of any man of letters"; and Evelyn Owen's *Driven Home* (1887) is "absolutely silly."

BEARDSLEY, AUBREY (1872–98)

As an artist and author, Beardsley achieved fame early in life, when, at the age of 20, he began the arduous commission of illustrating Malory's *Morte Darthur* in a style that revealed not only the influence of decorative Pre-Raphaelitism but also a strikingly new artistic sensibility. In July 1891 at the home of the Pre-Raphaelite artist Edward Burne-Jones, Wilde first met Beardsley, whose face – he later said – was "like a silver hatchet" (Rothenstein 187). Oscar and Constance Wilde impressed Beardsley as "charming people" (Beardsley, *Letters* 22). Robert Ross, who first met Beardsley in February 1892, later recorded his impressions of the young artist:

> Though prepared for an extraordinary personality, I never expected the youthful apparition which glided into the room. He was shy, nervous, self-conscious, without any of the intellectual assurances and ease so characteristic of him eighteen months later when his success was unquestioned.... His face even then was terribly drawn and emaciated. Except in his manner, I do not think his general appearance altered very much in spite of the ill-health and suffering, borne with such unparalleled resignation and fortitude: he always had a most delightful and engaging smile for both friends and strangers. (15)

In 1893, however, Arthur Symons described Beardsley after their first meeting as "the thinnest young man I ever saw, rather unpleasant and affected" (Symons, *Letters* 112n4). By this time, Beardsley had adopted a dandiacal pose as a defensive reaction to his developing fatal illness, tuberculosis; also, as Ellmann suggests, Beardsley had perhaps developed a "more satirical and sinister" style under Wilde's influence (307/290).

When Wilde's French version of *Salomé* was

published in London and Paris by John Lane and Elkin Mathews in late February 1893, Beardsley drew the illustration later titled "The Climax," which depicts Salome in flight while gazing longingly at Iokanaan's decapitated head – "a serious comment," writes Stanley Weintraub, "on the grotesque eroticism of the play" (59). The drawing was intended for the first issue of the *Studio* (April 1893) to accompany Joseph Pennell's article on the artist. Wilde, who had apparently seen the drawing before publication, inscribed a copy of the French version of *Salomé* for Beardsley: "For Aubrey: for the only artist who, besides myself, knows what the dance of the seven veils is, and can see that invisible dance. Oscar" (qtd. in Weintraub 55).

Meanwhile, Ross, who had also seen the drawing before publication, urged Lane to consider it for publication. The result was a commission to have Beardsley provide illustrations for the English translation in the following year. During his friendship with Wilde, Beardsley kept Wilde's autographed photograph over his fireplace. Their relationship, however, underwent radical change when the *Salome* illustrations began to arrive at the Bodley Head. Wilde, increasingly annoyed, perhaps even outraged, at Beardsley's pictures, showed them to the artist and stage designer Charles Ricketts, who disappointed Wilde by praising them. Wilde contended, however, that the illustrations were "too Japanese, while my play is Byzantine," and to another friend, he noted that the illustrations were "like the naughty scribbles a precocious boy makes on the margins of his copybooks" (qtd. in Weintraub 56). Responding to Lane and Wilde's objections to some of the illustrations, Beardsley wrote on a proof that he gave to Frank Harris:

Because one figure was undressed
This little drawing was suppressed.
It was unkind, but never mind,
Perhaps it all was for the best.

(qtd. in Weintraub 71)

By late November 1893, Beardsley was complaining to Ross:

I suppose you've heard all about the *Salomé* row. I can tell you I had a warm time of it between Lane and Oscar and Co. For one week

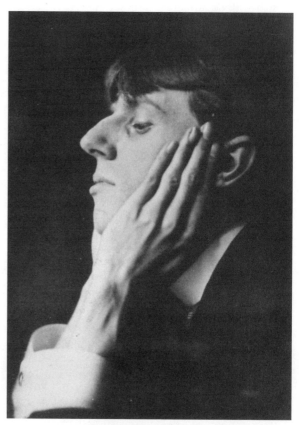

Aubrey Beardsley

the numbers of telegraph and messenger boys who came to the door was simply scandalous. I really don't quite know how matters really stand now.... I have withdrawn three of the illustrations and supplied their places with three new ones (simply beautiful and quite irrelevant). (Beardsley, *Letters* 58)

In the same letter, Beardsley refers to Lord Alfred Douglas and Wilde as "really very dreadful people." His distaste for the two was probably prompted by Wilde's behavior over the translation of the French version of *Salomé*. Hoping to translate it, Beardsley was disappointed when Wilde asked Douglas to undertake it. Mischievously, Beardsley depicted Wilde's bloated face in several of the *Salome* illustrations.

Nevertheless, Wilde's friendship with Beardsley survived the *Salomé* episode, for in February 1894, when the English translation with the illustrations appeared, Wilde took Beardsley to the St. James's Theatre to see Pinero's *The Second Mrs. Tanqueray*. From their box seats, Wilde sent the actress Mrs. Patrick Campbell a note to ask her permission to "come round after Act III" to introduce Beardsley to her: "Mr. Aubrey Beardsley, a very brilliant and wonderful young artist, and like all artists a great admirer of the wonder and charm of your art, says that he must once have the honour of being presented to you.... He has just illustrated my play of *Salome* for me.... His drawings are quite wonderful" (*Letters* 353).

The "Beardsley Boom" suddenly ended in April 1895 with the Wilde debacle. One newspaper featured a misleading headline: "WILDE ARRESTED: YELLOW BOOK UNDER HIS ARM" (actually a French novel, not the periodical). As art editor of the *Yellow Book*, Beardsley was fired principally because of his association with Wilde's *Salome*. (Beardsley wrote to Ada Leverson with levity: "I look forward eagerly to the first act of Oscar's new Tragedy" – Beardsley, *Letters* 82.) When Arthur Symons became editor of the newly founded *Savoy* (the first issue appearing in January 1896), he enlisted Beardsley as the principal illustrator.

During his trials and imprisonment, Wilde did not see or correspond with Beardsley, whose health, progressively deteriorating after 1895, required the milder climate of the Continent. Wilde, however, was concerned about Beardsley's condition, as he wrote to More Adey in September 1896: "Poor Aubrey: I hope he will get all right. He brought a strangely new personality to English art, and was a master in his way of fantastic grace, and the charm of the unreal. His muse had moods of terrible laughter. Behind his grotesques there seemed to lurk some curious philosophy..." (*Letters* 410).

After Wilde's release from prison, Wilde informed Ross that he had met Beardsley by chance in July 1897: "I saw Aubrey at Dieppe on Saturday: he was looking very well, and in good spirits. I hope he is coming out here [Berneval-sur-Mer] tomorrow to dine" (*Letters* 627). Whether Beardsley accepted the invitation is unknown. Wilde again saw Beardsley in August, as he wrote to Reginald Turner: "I have made Aubrey buy a hat more silver than silver: he is quite wonderful in it" (*More Letters* 151).

When the publisher Leonard Smithers showed Beardsley the manuscript of *The Ballad of Reading Gaol* in September 1897, he later told Wilde that Beardsley "seemed to be much struck by it. He

promised at once to do a frontispiece for it – in a manner which immediately convinced me that he will never do it" (qtd. in Mason 410). When, in December, Smithers proposed publishing a new aesthetic periodical to be titled the *Peacock*, he asked Beardsley to act as illustrator and editor. Now devoted to his "Mentor" and patron, André Raffalovich, whose influence resulted in his conversion to Roman Catholicism, Beardsley accepted Smithers's offer only "if it is *quite agreed that Oscar Wilde contributes nothing to the magazine anonymously, pseudonymously or otherwise*" (Beardsley, *Letters* 409). The periodical never materialized.

When Beardsley died on 16 March 1898, at the age of 25, Wilde wrote to Smithers:

I was greatly shocked to read of poor Aubrey's death. Superbly premature as the flowering of his genius was, still he had immense development, and had not sounded his last stop. There were great possibilities always in the cavern of his soul, and there is something macabre and tragic in the fact that one who added another terror to life should have died at the age of a flower. (*Letters* 719)

References: Robert Ross, *Aubrey Beardsley* (1909); *Men and Memories: Recollections of William Rothenstein, 1872–1900* (1931); Henry Maas, J. L. Duncan, and W. G. Good, eds. *The Letters of Aubrey Beardsley* (1970); Stanley Weintraub, "Aubrey and Oscar," *Aubrey Beardsley: The Imp of the Perverse* (1976); Ian Fletcher, *Aubrey Beardsley* (1987); Karl Beckson and John M. Munro, eds., *Arthur Symons: Selected Letters, 1880–1935* (1989); Robert Langenfeld, ed., *Reconsidering Aubrey Beardsley* (1989); Chris Snodgrass, *Aubrey Beardsley: Dandy of the Grotesque* (1995); Mark Samuels Lasner, *A Selective Checklist of the Published Work of Aubrey Beardsley* (1995).

BEATRICE AND ASTONE MANFREDI

According to Small (106), Rodney Shewan (214n55) errs in identifying a manuscript fragment of this unfinished blank verse tragedy with Wilde's unfinished play *The Cardinal of Avignon*.

Manuscript: The Clark Library has a photostat of the MS. fragment, a single leaf, which appears to be a fair copy.

"THE BEAUTIES OF BOOKBINDING"

Reference: Rodney Shewan, *Oscar Wilde: Art and Egotism* (1977).

"THE BEAUTIES OF BOOKBINDING: MR. COBDEN-SANDERSON AT THE 'ARTS AND CRAFTS'"

Published: *PMG*, 23 Nov. 1888, 3; rpt. in *Miscellanies* (1908). An unsigned review of T.J. Cobden-Sanderson's lecture at the Arts and Crafts Exhibition Society's presentation, New Gallery, Regent Street, on 22 November.

In his lecture, Cobden-Sanderson, the bookbinder and printer, remarked: "The beginning of art is man thinking about the universe." Cobden-Sanderson desires, says Wilde, "to give expression to the joy and wonder that he feels at the marvels that surround him, and invents a form of beauty through which he utters the thought or feeling that is in him. And bookbinding ranks amongst the arts." In beautiful bindings, said Cobden-Sanderson, "decoration rises into enthusiasm"; indeed, a beautiful binding is "a homage to genius." It has, says Wilde, its "ethical value, its spiritual effect." And Wilde quotes Cobden-Sanderson: "By doing good work we raise life to a higher plane." In short, said the lecturer as reported by Wilde, "the design must 'come from the man himself ' and express the moods of his imagination, the joy of his soul."

The lecturer (following the lead of William Morris, a founder of the Arts and Crafts Exhibition Society) spoke of

the necessity for the artist doing the whole work with his own hands. But before we have really good bookbinding we must have a social revolution. As things are now, the worker diminished to a machine is the slave of the employer, and the employer bloated into a millionaire is the slave of the public, and the public is the slave of its pet god, cheapness.

Cobden-Sanderson, however, errs in treating bookbinding as an art: it is, Wilde contends,

essentially decorative, and good decoration is far more often suggested by material and mode of work than by any desire on the part of the designer to tell us of his joy in the world...These handicrafts are not primarily expressive arts, they are impressive arts.... The beauty of bookbinding is abstract decorative beauty. It is not, in the first instance, a mode of expression for a man's soul.

Hence, Wilde objects to the attempt to elevate such crafts to the level of poetry, painting, and sculpture since their aim is different: "Between the arts that aim at annihilating their material, and the arts that aim at glorying it, there is a wide gulf."

"BEAUTY, TASTE, AND UGLINESS IN DRESS"

This lecture, given on Wilde's British lecture tour, was apparently the one usually titled "Dress": see Lectures in Britain, 1883–85. No MSS. of this lecture are known to have survived.

BEERBOHM, MAX (1872–1956)

A caricaturist and writer, Beerbohm first met Wilde while a student at Charterhouse School in 1888, probably introduced to him by the actor-manager Herbert Beerbohm Tree, Max's half-brother. The friendship between Beerbohm and Wilde did not develop until early 1893, when Max, while an undergraduate at Merton College, Oxford, attended rehearsals of *A Woman of No Importance* conducted by Tree at the Haymarket Theatre. In April, Beerbohm wrote to his friend Reggie Turner: "I am sorry to say that Oscar drinks far more than he ought: indeed the first time I saw him, after all that long period of distant adoration and reverence, he was in a hopeless state of intoxication.... I think he will die of apoplexy on the first night of the play." After the play opened on 19 April, Beerbohm lamented to Turner: "How the critics attack gentle Oscar." Except for William Archer and A. B. Walkley, "the rest have scarcely tried to write on the play at all. They have simply abused Oscar" (*Letters to Reggie* 35, 38).

Beerbohm's first essay on Wilde and his first published work – "Oscar Wilde" by "An American" – had appeared in the *Anglo-American Times* (25 March 1893). By posing as an outsider, Beerbohm attempts to understand a complex personality: Wilde is an "incomparable wit," the best talker in London, though when he enters a room, "everything must go to the wall; ...he stands on the hearthrug and monopolises the conversation...." Indolent by nature, Wilde possesses "one of the most salient and not the least charming of his qualities" – vanity. Concluding, the speaker regards Wilde as a genius, "a spirit which makes him a perfect type and a personality without flaw" – the final ironic thrust (rpt. in *Letters to Reggie*, Appendix). Wilde read the article in proof, Beerbohm told Turner, and pronounced it "incomparably brilliant," though "he is rather hurt at my reference to *Dorian Gray...*" (*Letters to Reggie* 34). Beerbohm had written: "We have heard the grumble that the idea of an inanimate complicated by an animate personality developed in the story of *Dorian Gray* has been done before."

In August 1893, Beerbohm wrote to his friend the painter Will Rothenstein that he had read Wilde's French version of *Salomé* a second time and that he liked it "immensely": " – there is much, I think, in it that is beautiful, much lovely writing – I almost wonder Oscar doesn't dramatise it" (*Max and Will* 18). Later that year, Beerbohm encountered Wilde's elder brother, Willie, at Broadstairs, Kent, and offered Rothenstein his distasteful reaction, a further indication of Beerbohm's ambivalence towards Wilde: "Quel monstre! Dark, oily, suspecte yet awfully like Oscar: he has Oscar's coy, carnal smile & fatuous giggle & not a little of Oscar's esprit" (*Max and Will* 21). On one occasion in 1893, Beerbohm observed Wilde with his entourage (as he reported in a letter to Robert Ross): "Poor Oscar! I saw him the other day, from a cab, walking with Bosie and some other members of the Extreme Left. He looked like one whose soul has swooned in sin and revived vulgar. How fearful it is for a poet to go to bed and find himself infamous" (qtd. in Ellmann 394n/371n).

In late 1893 or early 1894, Beerbohm wrote another essay on Wilde, "A Peep into the Past," for the first number of the *Yellow Book*, but it never appeared. In his characteristically playful manner of combining fact and fiction to produce multiple ironies, Beerbohm pretends that Oscar Wilde was, at one time, "quite a celebrity.... Once a welcome guest in many of our Bohemian haunts, he lives now a life of quiet retirement in his little house in Tite Street with his wife and his two sons...." The "old gentleman" (Wilde was 39) continues to write; indeed, he "has not yet abandoned his old intention of dramatising *Salome...*" – echoing Beerbohm's letter to Rothenstein. Noting Wilde's first play (that is, his first society comedy, an indication that Max thought little of Wilde's early romantic melodramas), Beerbohm

remarks that, at the curtain call, the "dazed" author had forgotten to extinguish his cigarette, "an oversight that the Public was quick to pardon in the old gentleman" (in fact, some critics were offended when Wilde appeared with a lighted cigarette before the curtain at the conclusion *Lady Windermere's Fan*). The Wilde debacle in 1895 made "A Peep into the Past" unpublishable for a number of years (it finally appeared in 1923).

In April 1894, when the first number of the *Yellow Book* appeared, Beerbohm's essay "A Defence of Cosmetics," an ironic defense of Decadence, created a sensation. This essay was revised and retitled "The Pervasion of Rouge" for *The Works of Max Beerbohm* (1896). Delighted with the essay, Rothenstein told Beerbohm with levity: "...all my friends chuckled over your dear cosmetics as they read & reread them. Oscar, solitary exception, was moved to a torrent of tears, so strong was his emotion" (*Max and Will* 28). To Alfred Douglas, Wilde wrote: "Max on Cosmetics in the *Yellow Book* is wonderful: enough style for a large school, and all very precious and thought-out: quite delightfully wrong and fascinating" (*Letters* 355). Wilde's appreciation of Beerbohm's wise, ironic manner is reflected in his remark: "The gods bestowed on Max the gift of perpetual old age" (qtd. in O'Sullivan 68).

Long before the Wilde trials, as Rupert Hart-Davis remarks, Beerbohm's family "worried because so many of his friends were homosexual – Oscar Wilde, Alfred Douglas, Reggie Turner, Robbie Ross – but, although Max greatly enjoyed their company, there is no scrap of evidence that he ever shared their sexual propensities" (*Letters of Max Beerbohm* xiii). Indeed, Beerbohm often reveals his cautiously satirical view of Wilde in his many cartoons, his literary works, and his letters, both before and after Wilde's trials. In August 1894, in what Hart-Davis calls an "all-too-prophetic joke" concerning a police raid on a male house of prostitution, Beerbohm reports to Turner: "Oscar has at length been arrested for certain kinds of crime. He was taken in the Café Royal (lower room). Bosie [Alfred Douglas] escaped, being an excellent runner, but Oscar was less nimble" (*Letters to Reggie* 97 and n6).

In April 1895, however, when Wilde was actually arrested, Beerbohm was quite distressed, as he reveals in a letter to Ada Leverson from New York: "Poor Oscar! Why did he not go away while he could? I suppose there has *never* been so great a scandal and sensation! Over here the papers have been full of it. We are all so fearfully sorry about the whole thing" (*Letters of Max Beerbohm* 8–9). Later that month, Beerbohm was in the courtroom when Wilde gave his famous speech on "The love that dare not speak its name"; to Turner, he wrote that the speech was "simply wonderful, and carried the whole court right away, quite a tremendous burst of applause" (*Letters to Reggie* 102), though there were apparently also hisses.

During Wilde's imprisonment, Beerbohm published his fanciful tale in the *Yellow Book* (Oct. 1896) titled "The Happy Hypocrite," an apparent parody of *The Picture of Dorian Gray*. (When Wilde's novel had first appeared, Beerbohm wrote "Ballade de la Vie Joyeuse," doggerel verse with little bite, containing the wry observation that hedonists, wearying of defying the moral strictures of St. Paul, sometimes embrace morality: "Even the author of 'Dorian Gray' / Makes for his hero a virtuous mood" – *Max in Verse* 7.) In "The Happy Hypocrite," Beerbohm depicts the wicked Lord George Hell, who, by donning a mask of saintliness, becomes George Heaven, transformed by love – as opposed to Dorian Gray, who is transformed by evil. Wilde's novel had probably suggested the allegory of good and evil in Dorian's remark: "Each of us has Heaven and Hell in him." Indeed, Beerbohm's interest in masks once prompted Wilde to ask Ada Leverson: "When you are alone with him, Sphinx, does he take off his face and reveal his mask?" (Wyndham 119).

Wilde was delighted with "The Happy Hypocrite," which he read after his release from prison in May 1897: "I have just read Max's *Happy Hypocrite*," he told Turner, "beginning at the end, as one should always do. It is quite wonderful, and to one who was once the author of *Dorian Gray*, full of no vulgar surprises of style or incident" (*Letters* 575). To Beerbohm, Wilde wrote that "The Happy Hypocrite," a "wonderful and beautiful story," was obviously inspired by his novel: "The implied and accepted recognition of *Dorian Gray* in the story cheers me. I had always been disappointed that my story had suggested no other work of art in others" (*Letters* 576).

Beerbohm apparently never saw Wilde in prison or after his release – an indication that he had distanced himself further from his former friend. Nevertheless, when the time approached for

Wilde's release, Beerbohm wrote to Robert Ross out of concern about the expected reaction by the press: "Is there any way of getting Oscar out of the country without benefit of journalism? There are sure to be a dozen reporters at the prison gate and they will follow him to the English shore...and they will ask him if he has anything to say to them and so on and so on." Beerbohm suggests a decoy carriage to lure the reporters while another carriage with Wilde would make its way out unobserved: "This sounds rather absurd, I suppose...but surely it is rather important to let Oscar be spared a gang of gaping and offensive pressmen" (Ross 48). In August 1897, Beerbohm heard from France "that that ass Oscar is under *surveillance* – I suppose he is playing the giddy goat. Can't someone warn him to be careful?" (*Letters to Reggie* 120).

On the day after Wilde died, Beerbohm wrote to Turner, who had attended Wilde at his bedside: "I am, as you may imagine, very sorry indeed; and am thinking very much about Oscar, who was such an influence and an interest in my life. Will you please lay out a little money for me in flowers for his grave.... I suppose really it was better that Oscar should die. If he had lived to be an old man he would have become unhappy. Those whom the gods, etc. And the gods *did* love Oscar, with all his faults" (*Letters to Reggie* 137–38). As the drama critic for the *Saturday Review* (having replaced Bernard Shaw in 1898), Beerbohm devoted part of his column on 8 December 1900, to a restrained tribute:

> The death of Mr. Oscar Wilde extinguishes a hope that the broken series of his plays might be resumed.... Despite the number of his books and plays, Mr. Wilde was not, I think, what one calls a born writer. His writing seemed always to be rather an overflow of intellectual temperamental energy than an inevitable, absorbing function. That he never concentrated himself on any one form of literature is a proof that the art of writing never really took hold of him.... But for his death, he might possibly have returned to [playwriting]. And thus his death is, in a lesser degree than his downfall, a great loss to the drama of our day.

In evaluating Wilde's plays, Beerbohm regards all three of the serious comedies as "marred by staginess," particularly *An Ideal Husband*, least so in *A Woman of No Importance*. In the latter play, Wilde "allowed the psychological idea to work itself out almost unmolested, and the play was, in my opinion, by far the most truly dramatic of his plays." As for *The Importance of Being Earnest*, Beerbohm regards it merely as superior to the "every-day farces whose scheme was so frankly accepted in it" (rpt. in Beckson).

In the *Saturday Review* (18 Jan. 1902), Beerbohm reviewed the first revival of *The Importance of Being Earnest* since its premiere in 1895. Clearly, Beerbohm has now gone beyond his previous view of the play as merely a superior farce:

...to me the play came out fresh and exquisite as ever, and over the whole house almost every line was sending ripples of laughter – cumulative ripples that became waves, and receded only for fear of drowning the next line. In kind the play always was unlike any other, and in its kind it still seems perfect. I do not wonder that now the critics boldly call it a classic, and predict immortality. And (timorous though I am apt to be in prophecy) I join gladly in their chorus. (rpt. in *Around Theatres*)

Beerbohm reviewed other Wilde plays, including the first production of *Salome* in England in 1905 and the first production of the incomplete *A Florentine Tragedy* in 1906 as well as a revival of *Lady Windermere's Fan*. Of the latter play, he wrote in the *Saturday Review* (26 Nov. 1904) that it was "incomparable in the "musical elegance and swiftness of its wit" – "a classic assuredly": "Those artificialities of incident and characterisation (irritating to us now, because we are in point of time so near to this play that we cannot discount them) will have ceased to matter. Our posterity will merely admire the deftness of the construction" (rpt. in *Last Theatres*).

When John Middleton Murray, editor of the *Athenaeum*, asked Beerbohm to review the second edition of Frank Harris's *Oscar Wilde: His Life and Confessions* (1918), he declined, having read the first edition in 1916: "...all that raking-up of the old Sodomitic cesspool – the cesspool that was opened in 1895, and re-opened in recent years by various law-suits – seemed to me a disservice

(howsoever well-meant) to poor old O. W.'s memory" *(Letters of Max Beerbohm* 118). For the celebration of Wilde's hundredth birthday in 1954, Vyvyan Holland asked Beerbohm to unveil the London Council County plaque on the house in Tite Street. Pleading that he was "too old to travel" (he was almost 81), Beerbohm sent a tribute to be read at a luncheon after the unveiling: "I suppose there are now few survivors among the people who had the delight of hearing Oscar Wilde talk. Of these I am one." After citing such figures as Henry James, Edmund Gosse, and Swinburne, who were all "splendid" talkers, he remarks: "But assuredly Oscar in *his* own way was the greatest of them all – the most spontaneous and yet the most polished, the most soothing and yet the most surprising" *(Letters of Max Beerbohm* 223n1).

References: Max Beerbohm, *Around Theatres* (1953); J. G. Riewald, *Sir Max Beerbohm: Man and Writer* (1953); Violet Wyndham, *The Sphinx and Her Circle: A Memoir of Ada Leverson* (1963); Beerbohm, *Max in Verse: Rhymes and Parodies*, ed. J. G. Riewald (1963); David Cecil, *Max: A Biography* (1964); *Max Beerbohm's Letters to Reggie Turner*, ed. Rupert Hart-Davis (1964); Beerbohm, *Last Theatres, 1904–1910* (1970); Beerbohm, *A Peep into the Past and Other Prose Pieces*, ed. Rupert Hart–Davis (1972); John Felstiner, *The Lies of Art: Max Beerbohm's Parody and Caricature* (1972); Mary M. Lago and Karl Beckson, eds., *Max and Will: Max Beerbohm and William Rothenstein: Their Friendship and Letters, 1893–1945* (1975); Ira Grushow, *The Imaginary Reminiscences of Sir Max Beerbohm* (1984); Robert Viscusi, *Max Beerbohm, or The Dandy Dante* (1986); Rupert Hart-Davis, ed., *Letters of Max Beerbohm, 1892–1956* (1988); Lawrence Danson, *Max Beerbohm and the Act of Writing* (1989).

"LA BELLA DONNA DELLA MIA MENTE"

Published: This poem first appeared in two parts as "Δηξίθυμον Ἔρωτος Ἄνθος" ("The Rose of Love and with a Rose's Thorns") in *Kottabos* 2 (May 1876) 268–69. The Greek title is from Aeschylus's *Agamemnon*, 720, referring to Helen, "a soul-wounding flower of love" (for Wilde's discussion in a manuscript of an unpublished essay on Greek heroines, written at Oxford between 1874 and 1876, see Mason 91). When revised in *Poems* (1881), the two original parts of the poem were separated: Part I became "La Bella Donna della mia Mente" – from Italian, meaning "The Beautiful Lady of My Memory"; for Part II, see "Chanson."

"La Bella Donna della mia Mente," presents the speaker's conventional sentiments about his "Lady," suggesting, as a source, the poetic conventions of courtly love, as they developed in the late Middle Ages (a knight, worshipping a married aristocratic lady, conducts a secret relationship, which inspires him to noble deeds). For Dante and the poets of the later *dolce stil nuovo*, the "sweet new style" of late medieval love poetry has Platonic significance, the divine beauty of the woman, even in death, inspiring her "lover" to achieve spiritual transcendence of the flesh, as in *The Divine Comedy*.

Wilde's focus, however, is derived from such Pre-Raphaelite poets as Rossetti (whose "Blessed Damozel," in Heaven, is eroticized), William Morris (whose "Praise of My Lady" involves her sensual attraction), and Swinburne (whose living Lady is alluring as a sadistic "Lady of Pain" in "Dolores"). Such sources are apparent in Wilde's opening lines of this lyric poem of eight four-line stanzas:

My limbs are wasted with a flame,
    My feet are sore with travelling,
For, calling on my Lady's name,
    My lips have now forgot to sing.

The speaker enumerates her charms, though the implication that he is speaking of a *femme fatale* progressively emerges as he celebrates his exquisite agony:

        ...O delicate
    White body made for love and pain!
O House of love! O desolate
    Pale flower beaten by the rain!

"LA BELLE GABRIELLE. (FROM THE FRENCH)"

Not published in Wilde's lifetime, this lyric poem was probably written around 1878–79. The main title seems inappropriate for a poem concerned with figures from Greek mythology, but the subtitle implies a source that remains untraced.

Addressing his "Love," the speaker imagines himself with the powers to express his love:

"Love, could I charm the silver-breasted moon / To lie with me upon the Latmian hill..." (The "hill" – actually, a mountain in Greek myth – is where Endymion sleeps eternally in a cave. Wilde also writes of this figure in "Endymion" and in "Nocturne.") Narcissus is also evoked, leaning "to kiss / His laughing double in the glassy stream..." (for Wilde's preoccupation with this figure, see Narcissus and Narcissism). Such experiences would be of little worth, the speaker implies, since he does not have the love that he really craves.

Manuscripts: The Clark Library has the MS. of this poem.

"BEN JONSON"

Published: *PMG*, 20 Sept. 1886, 6. An unsigned review of John Addington Symonds, *Ben Jonson* (1886) in the "English Worthies" series, edited by Andrew Lang; rpt. in *Reviews* (1908).

Wilde compliments Lang for selecting Symonds to write the life of Ben Jonson: "Mr. Symonds, like the author of *Volpone*, is a scholar and a man of letters" as well as a "recognised authority on the Italian Renaissance." Though his book does not contain much new material about Jonson's life, "what is true is of more importance than what is new, appreciation more valuable than discovery." Symonds ranks Jonson "with the giants rather than with the gods, with those who compel our admiration by their untiring energy and huge strength of intellectual muscle, not with those 'who share the divine gifts of creative imagination and inevitable instinct.'"

Wilde disagrees with Symonds's remark that Jonson "'rarely touched more than the outside of character,' that his men and women are 'the incarnations of abstract properties rather than living human beings,' that they are in fact mere 'masqueraders and mechanical puppets.'" Though we do not find the same "growth of character" that we find in Shakespeare, "a ready-made character is not necessarily either mechanical or wooden, two epithets Mr. Symonds uses constantly in his criticism." If, says Wilde, a character is "life-like, if we recognise it as true to nature, we have no right to insist on the author explaining its genesis to us." Mere presentation by a good dramatist can "take the place of analysis, and indeed is often a more dramatic method, because a more direct one."

Symonds's style is "very fluent, very picturesque and very full of colour," though on occasion it is "really irritating. Such a sentence as 'the tavern had the defects of its quality' is an awkward Gallicism...." Symonds, concludes Wilde, has written "some charming poetry, but his prose, unfortunately, is always poetical prose, never the prose of a poet. Still the volume is worth reading, though decidedly Mr. Symonds, to use one of his own phrases, has 'the defects of his quality.'"

"BÉRANGER IN ENGLAND"

Published: *PMG*, 21 April 1886, 5; rpt. in *Reviews* (1908). An unsigned review of *A Selection from the Songs of De Béranger in English Verse*, ed. William Toynbee (1886).

Wilde regrets that the "new democracy does not use poetry as a means for the expression of political opinion. The Socialists, it is true, have been heard singing the later poems of Mr. William Morris, but the street ballad is really dead in England." As a whole, the people are little moved by most modern poetry because it is "so artificial in its form, so individual in its essence and so literary in its style" so that when they have "grievances against the capitalist or the aristocrat they prefer strikes to sonnets and rioting to rondels."

Toynbee's "pleasant little volume" of translations may, says Wilde, "be the herald of a new school," since Béranger had "all the qualifications for a popular poet," for he wrote poems to be sung more than read: "He was patriotic as well as romantic, and humorous as well as humane." After pointing to some awkwardness in the translations ("rapiers," for instance, "is an abominable rhyme to 'forefathers'"), Wilde concludes that "Béranger is not nearly well enough known in England, and though it is always better to read a poet in the original, still translations have their value as echoes have their music."

BERNHARDT, SARAH (1844–1923)

One of the most acclaimed actresses of her time, the French-born Bernhardt made her debut with the Comédie Française in 1862. Her first appearance on the London stage was in May 1879. On her arrival in England, according to legend, Wilde met her with an armful of lilies. In June, when she performed in Racine's *Phèdre*, Wilde was in the audience. On 11 June, his sonnet "To Sarah Bernhardt" (later titled "Phèdre") appeared in the *World*: "How vain and dull our common world must seem / To such a one as Thou...." Other than

a brief meeting in 1883 in a Parisian theater, while Bernhardt was changing her costume backstage, Wilde had little contact with Bernhardt until 1892, when she agreed to act the role of Salomé in French on the London stage. When the play was banned by the Lord Chamberlain, it was published in French in 1893. Reviewing the play, the *Times* (23 Feb.) remarked that *Salomé* was "written for Mme Sarah Bernhardt," prompting Wilde to write to the editor:

> The fact that the greatest tragic actress of any stage now living saw in my play such beauty that she was anxious to produce it, to take herself the part of the heroine, to lend the entire poem the glamour of her personality, and to my prose the music of her flute-like voice – this was naturally, and always will be, a source of pride and pleasure to me....But my play was in no sense of the words written for this great actress. (*Letters* 336)

When Wilde was imprisoned, he wrote to Robert Sherard that he was cheered that Bernhardt "and other great artists are sympathising with me" (*Letters* 390). Facing bankruptcy, Wilde urged Sherard to see whether she would purchase *Salomé*. Sherard later recorded the scene with Bernhardt: "I was delighted at the reception that Madame Bernhardt gave me and at the kind way in which she spoke of 'her good friend,' and deplored the calamity which had befallen him. She wrung her hand, and her wonderful eyes moistened with real emotion" (136). Despite her promise to see what she could do to grant Wilde a loan, she was often out when Sherard called. In the end, she sent nothing.

On 30 December 1899, Wilde saw Bernhardt in Nice performing in Sardou's *La Tosca*. In a letter to Robert Ross, he described his touching reunion with her: "I went round to see Sarah and she embraced me and wept, and I wept, and the whole evening was wonderful" (*Letters* 775). According to Vincent O'Sullivan, Wilde remarked to him in 1899: "The three women I have most admired are Queen Victoria, Sarah Bernhardt, and Lily Langtry. I would have married any one of them with pleasure,' he added, laughing" (18). Wilde's final remark about Bernhardt in his extant letters occurs in early September 1900, when he told his publisher Leonard Smithers: "The only person in the world who could act Salome is Sarah Bernhardt, that 'serpent of old Nile' [*Antony and Cleopatra*, I.v.25], older than the Pyramids" (*Letters* 834). His allusion to Cleopatra was apt, for one of Bernhardt's most famous roles was in Sardou's *Cléopatre* (1890).

References: Robert Sherard, *Oscar Wilde: The Story of an Unhappy Friendship* (1905; rpt. 1970); Vincent O'Sullivan, *Aspects of Oscar Wilde* (1936); John Stokes et al., *Bernhardt, Duse, Terry: The Actress in Her Time* (1983); Ruth Brandon, *Being Divine: A Biography of Sarah Bernhardt* (1991).

"A BEVY OF POETS"

Published: *PMG*, 27 March 1885, 5; rpt. in *Reviews* (1908). Anonymous reviews of Atherton Furlong, *Echoes of Memory* (1884); E. W. Bowling, *Sagittulae: Random Verses* (1885); Mark André Raffalovich, *Tuberose and Meadowsweet* (1885); and *Sturm und Drang* (1885) by an anonymous writer.

Wilde greets these four volumes as "little singers" who are "out before the little sparrows" this spring "and have already begun chirruping." Furlong's "charm is the unsullied sweetness of his simplicity." Indeed, Wilde facetiously cites a poem as "eminently suitable for recitation by children" (presumably not the poet's intent). Such poetry cannot "possibly harm anybody, even if translated into French." But Furlong, Wilde concludes, "must not be discouraged. Perhaps he will write poetry some day." As for the "modest little volume" by Bowling, it contains "delicate little arrows" (the meaning of the Latin title), "for they are winged with the lightness of the lyric, and barbed daintily with satire."

Turning quickly to *Tuberose and Meadowsweet* by Mark André Raffalovich (whom Wilde had apparently not yet met: see Raffalovich, André), Wilde hailed it as "really a remarkable little volume, and contains many strange and beautiful poems." Defending the Decadent nature of the work, he remarks: "To say of these poems that they are unhealthy, and bring with them the heavy odours of the hothouse, is to point neither their defect, nor their merit, but their quality merely." Though not "a wonderful poet," Raffalovich was "a subtle artist in poetry....a boyish master of curious music, and of fantastic rhyme...." Wilde points to Raffalovich's insistence on making "tuberose" a trisyllable, "as if it were a potato blossom, and not a flower shaped like a tiny trumpet of ivory.... And though he cannot pronounce 'tuberose' aright, at least he can sing of it exquisitely."

Wilde briefly noted the anonymous volume *Sturm und Drang*, "a curious but not inartistic combination of the mental attitude of Mr. Matthew Arnold with the style of Lord Tennyson." Pointing to one poem, "Caliban in East London," Wilde praises its considerable power, though the use of the adjective *knockery* is condemned "even in a poem on Whitechapel." In the passage following, Wilde reveals his disenchantment with Swinburne and his admiration of Tennyson:

> The most interesting thing in young poets is not so much what they invent as what masters they follow. A few years ago it was all Mr. Swinburne. That era has happily passed away. The mimicry of passion is the most intolerable of all poses. Now it is all Lord Tennyson, and that is better. For a young writer can gain more from the study of a literary poet than from the study of a lyricist. He may become the pupil of the one, but he can never be anything but the slave of the other.

"THE BIRTHDAY OF THE INFANTA"

Published: First appeared as "The Birthday of the Little Princess" in *Paris Illustré* (Paris, New York, and London) 2 (30 March 1889): 203, 206–07, 209, in French translation in the Paris edition; rpt. as "The Birthday of the Infanta" in *A House of Pomegranates* (1891), the story dedicated to Mrs. William H. Grenfell, mother of the war poet Julian Grenfell (1888–1915). Wilde believed that, in style, it surpassed his other stories (see *Letters* 248).

The Plot: On the twelfth birthday of the Spanish Infanta, nature itself seems to glory in the event by showing its brightest colors. The King orders that the princess may invite any of her young friends not of her own rank to play with her. From the palace window, the melancholy King watches his daughter, thinking of his French Queen, who had died just six months after the princess's birth. Instead of burial, he had the Queen's body embalmed and placed on a tapestried bier in the palace chapel. Each month, the King, in a cloak and with a lantern, goes to the chapel and kneels, clutching her jewelled hands, kissing her cold, painted face and crying in grief: "*Mi reina! Mi reina!* (This scene was undoubtedly inspired, Horst Schroeder suggests, by a similar one in Hugo's poetic drama *Ruy Blas*, 1838.) After the Queen's death, the King refuses to entertain re-marriage, remarking that he is "already wedded to Sorrow, and that though she was but a barren bride he loved her better than Beauty." Because the princess reminds him of his deceased wife, the saddened King withdraws from the window.

In celebration of the Infanta's birthday, a marvellous bull-fight is staged in the arena but "much nicer, the Infanta thought, than the real bull-fight that she had been brought to see at Seville." Some boys prance about on "richly-caparisoned hobbyhorses brandishing long javelins with gay streamers of bright ribands attached to them," while the bull, "made of wicker-work and stretched hide," charges at them. After the "bull" has been decapitated, other entertainments designed to please the Infanta and her guests are a tight-rope walker, Italian puppets in a "semi-classical tragedy," and a juggler and snake charmer that thrill and frighten the children.

The funniest performance is the dancing by a little Dwarf, who had been discovered on the previous day "running wild through the forest." His grotesque appearance and dance delight the children and the Infanta, who fascinates him. Appreciative of his performance and partly in jest, she takes a beautiful white rose from her hair and throws it to the Dwarf, who presses the flower to his "rough coarse lips" and puts his hand on his heart. Retiring for her siesta, she orders that the Dwarf perform another dance afterwards. Having heard of the order, he runs into the garden, "kissing the white rose in an absurd ecstasy of pleasure, and making the most uncouth and clumsy gestures of delight."

The flowers in the garden resent the Dwarf's intrusion into their "beautiful home," the Cactus screaming: "He is a perfect horror! Why, he is twisted and stumpy, and his head is completely out of proportion with his legs." The birds, however, like him, for they had seen him dancing in the forest like an elf after the eddying leaves. Moreover, in the bitter winter, he had shared his bread with them. The Dwarf knows nothing of the flowers' hostility; the most important thing in his life is that the Infanta has given him a white rose

and that she loves him. A child of nature, the Dwarf imagines the Infanta coming to play with him in the forest, where he introduces her to its wonders and dances with her all day long.

Wondering where she is, he enters the palace through a little private door, which leads to a great hall. Wandering through splendid, tapestried rooms, he comes to the magnificently appointed throne room. Caring little for such luxury, he wants to see the Infanta before she goes to the pavilion in order to urge her to come away with him after his dance. He comes to the brightest and most beautiful of the rooms, where he sees a small figure watching him from the other end. When the Dwarf moves, the other figure also moves: "It was a monster, the most grotesque monster he had ever beheld. Not properly shaped, as all other people were, but hunchbacked, and crooked-limbed, with huge lolling head and mane of black hair."

Every gesture and movement that the Dwarf makes, the "monster" also makes. "When the truth dawned upon him, he gave a wild cry of despair, and fell sobbing to the ground." The monster was himself reflected in a mirror (as Kohl writes: "The dwarf gazing into the mirror at a deformed monster has its parallel in Dorian Gray's unveiling of the portrait which shows his bloodstained image, the painted likeness of his soul," 60). Now realizing that everyone has mocked him, he tears the rose to pieces. When the Infanta and her companions come upon the Dwarf beating the floor and sobbing with fury, they all laugh. Suddenly gasping and clutching his side, he falls back and lies still. The Chamberlain informs the Infanta that her "funny little dwarf will never dance again," for his heart is broken. Frowning, she announces: "For the future let those who come to play with me have no hearts."

Reference: Horst Schroeder, "Some Historical and Literary References in Oscar Wilde's 'The Birthday of the Infanta,'" *Literatur in Wissenschaft und Unterricht* 21:4 (1988).

BLACKER, CARLOS (1859–1928)

An Englishman of independent means who lived most of his life abroad, Blacker devoted his life to the study of languages, literature, and comparative religion. Though he apparently never published anything, he corresponded with a wide circle of friends, including Bernard Shaw and Anatole France. His friendship with Wilde may have begun at the time when he apparently invested in the production of *Lady Windermere's Fan*. In a lengthy letter to Blacker from Berneval, dated 12 July 1897, Wilde addresses him as "My dear old Friend":

You were always my staunch friend and stood by my side for many years. Often in prison I used to think of you: of your chivalry of nature, of your limitless generosity, of your quick intellectual sympathies, of your culture so receptive, so refined. What marvellous evenings, dear Carlos, we used to have! (*Letters* 621)

In late July, Wilde was distressed to hear of Constance's spinal disease from Blacker, with whom she was staying in Freiburg; within the week another letter to Blacker reveals Wilde's depression: "I don't mind my life being wrecked – that is as it should be – but when I think of poor Constance I simply want to kill myself." And turning to Blacker, he writes: "I fear we shall never see each other again.... I was made for destruction. My cradle was rocked by the Fates. Only in the mire can I know peace" (*Letters* 628–29). In September, he writes from Naples to explain why he has rejoined Alfred Douglas: "You must not, dear Carlos, pass harsh judgments on me, whatever you may hear. It is not for pleasure that I come here, though pleasure, I am glad to say, walks all round. I come here to try to realise the perfection of my temperament and my soul" (*Letters* 647).

In March 1898, Wilde expresses his gratitude to Blacker for urging Constance to increase her financial allotment to him. When he receives £30, Wilde writes to Blacker: "A thousand thanks for your great kindness. Really you have saved my life for me, for a little at any rate, and your friendship and interest give me hope" (*Letters* 726). When Constance died, Blacker visited Wilde to console him, and when Wilde revealed distress over his financial state and directed urgent appeals to him for assistance, Blacker generally responded.

According to Ellmann, by the end of May 1898 Robert Ross "heard from somebody – Wilde suspected it was Blacker – that authorities were forcing Wilde to leave Paris. Evidently Blacker had disapproved of Wilde's behavior in Paris, which made Wilde think he had spread the 'ca-nard' (563/529). Wilde had become friendly with Walsin-Esterhazy, the spy in the Dreyfus affair who was guilty of treason. Blacker, convinced of Dreyfus's innocence, believed that Wilde had informed the anti-Dreyfusards of Blacker's secret negotiations on behalf of Dreyfus. After an exchange of letters, involving a demand by Blacker that Wilde apologize (a letter that apparently has not survived), their friendship ended.

H. Montgomery Hyde suggests that Wilde's relationship with Douglas after Constance's death was also "one of the factors that caused the breakup of his long-standing friendship with Carlos Blacker." Hyde quotes a portion of Wilde's letter to Ross, dated 27 June 1898 (omitted in the Hart-Davis edition in order to spare Blacker's descendents any pain):

C. Blacker has behaved like a hypocritical ass to me....The comic thing about him is the moral attitude he takes up. To be either a Puritan, a prig, or a preacher is a bad thing. To be all three at once reminds one of the worst excesses of the French Revolution.... He came down to see me about a fortnight ago, inquired affectionately into my financial position, actually wept floods of tears...and left me with violent protestations of devotion.

Then, Wilde adds, Blacker wrote him a "Nonconformist conscience letter" that, morally, he could no longer assist him financially except with advice: "He also added that his wife disapproved of my knowing Bosie!! So Tartuffe goes out of my life" (Hyde 349).

Reference: H. Montgomery Hyde, *Oscar Wilde: A Biography* (1975).

BLOXAM, JOHN FRANCIS (1873–1928)

While an undergraduate at Exeter College, Oxford, Bloxam edited a magazine titled the *Chameleon*, as though to suggest the means of disguising its obvious homosexual orientation. Yet after its first number, with a printing of 100 copies in December 1894, the publishers Gay and Bird announced that it would not continue. Under the pseudonym of "X," Bloxam included his own story titled "The Priest and the Acolyte," depicting love between a priest and his young acolyte, both of whom, having drunk from a poisoned chalice in a suicide pact after their relationship is discovered by the priest's superior, die by embracing on the steps of the altar. Echoes from *The Picture of Dorian Gray* are evident, as in the priest's remark to his superior that "there are sins more beautiful than anything else in the world." Timothy d'Arch Smith writes that Bloxom's story "may perhaps be considered the first piece of English fiction to echo the firmly-founded French syndrome of the 'naughty' priest" (56).

To the *Chameleon*, Alfred Douglas contributed a poem titled "Two Loves," which concludes with the most famous line in homoerotic literature: "I am the love that dare not speak its name." And Wilde, at Douglas's urging, contributed "Phrases and Philosophies for the Use of the Young," which concludes with a line that he later used in *An Ideal Husband*: "To love oneself is the beginning of a life-long romance" (suggesting the homoerotic fable of Narcissus). When the *Chameleon* appeared, Wilde wrote to Ada Leverson:

"The Priest and the Acolyte" is not by Dorian [that is, John Gray]: though you were right in discerning by internal evidence that the author has a profile. He is an undergraduate of strange beauty. The story is, to my ears, too direct: there is no nuance: it profanes a little by revelation: God and other artists are always a little obscure. Still, it has interesting qualities, and is at moments poisonous: which is something. (*Letters* 379).

Bloxam had met Wilde in George Ives's rooms in the Albany, at which time he showed his story to Wilde, who urged him to publish it. In Act II of *The Importance of Being Earnest*, Wilde face-tiously includes a remark by Jack Worthing, who has rented his Belgrave Square house to a Lady Bloxham (slightly altering Bloxam's name), who never appears in the play: "She is a lady consider-ably advanced in years" – to which Lady Bracknell responds: "Ah, nowadays that is no guarantee of respectability of character."

In his libel suit against the Marquess of Queensberry, Wilde was cited in Queensberry's "plea of justification" as one who had joined in publishing the magazine. Though a contributor to the magazine, he denied that he had a hand in its publication. Furthermore, he testified – inaccu-rately – that he had not known of "The Priest and the Acolyte" until its appearance in the *Chame-leon*. When asked for his opinion of the story, Wilde remarked (in a decided but understandable shift of opinion under the circumstances): "I thought it bad and indecent, and I strongly disap-proved of it" (Hyde, *Trials* 104). Bloxam was never called as a witness in any of Wilde's trials.

After graduating from Exeter College a few weeks after Wilde's final trial, Bloxam went on to Ely Theological College, took orders in 1897–98 in the Church of England, and returned to Exeter for his MA in 1901. Following a series of curateships in London, he served as a chaplain in the First World War, and after his discharge, resumed his religious duties in London, becoming vicar in what J. Z. Eglinton calls the "desperate slum of Hoxton" between 1922 and 1927. He apparently did not publish anything after 1894.

References: H. Montgomery Hyde, *The Trials of Oscar Wilde* (2nd. ed., 1962; rpt. 1973); J. Z. Eglinton, "The Later Career of John Francis Bloxom," *International Journal of Greek Love* (Nov. 1966); Brian Reade, ed. *Sexual Heretics: Male Homosexuality in English Literature from 1850 to 1900* (1970); Timothy d'Arch Smith, *Love in Earnest: Some Notes on the Lives and Writings of English "Uranian" Poets from 1889 to 1930* (1970).

BODLEY HEAD

Despite the fact that, in the period between 1887 and 1894, the Bodley Head publishing company issued only about 100 or so books as well as the *Yellow Book* – the periodical that created a sensa-tion – the firm in many ways "summed up the spirit and ideals of that aesthetic milieu that pro-duced not only Wilde and Aubrey Beardsley, but Ernest Dowson, Lionel Johnson, Arthur Symons, and W. B. Yeats as well" (Nelson, *The Early Nineties* v). In short, the Bodley Head was the principal publisher that stimulated early Modernist developments in the late 19th century.

Before the Bodley Head was established in London, Elkin Mathews (1851–1921) had been proprietor of an antiquarian bookstore in Exeter and had planned to issue a "Bodley Library Cata-logue," named after Sir Thomas Bodley, the founder of the famous library at Oxford and a native of Exeter. While still in Exeter, Mathews met John Lane (1854–1925), whose book collec-tion eventually joined that of Mathews when he moved to London in September 1887 and opened the Bodley Head bookshop in Vigo Street, near the Burlington Arcade. Mathews, who had issued some books of local interest while in Exeter, now continued his practice in London; the Bodley Head imprint did not appear, however, on any of his volumes until Richard Le Gallienne's *Volumes in Folio* (1889), which the poet himself helped to design. As Nelson remarks, this first Bodley Head publication "in large part set the tone of later Bodley Head books. As a book of poetry whose binding and typography enhanced its subject and made it a work of art, it sounded the keynote of the Bodley Head productions which followed" (25).

In 1890, Lane, unwilling to resign from his position as a clerk in the Railway Clearing House at Euston Station until the success of the venture was assured, became a silent partner in the firm, though in name only, for several books issued in that year and in 1891 were the result of his active involvement in securing promising manuscripts. By January 1892, Lane abandoned his role of ostensible silent partner and entered the firm officially: he continued as the principal force in discovering new authors and publicizing the company; indeed, his determination to publish the daring *Yellow Book* and the "Keynotes" series of experimental fiction, without the direct involvement of Mathews, eventually created a rift between himself and his more sedate partner that led to the firm's dissolution in late 1894.

In May of 1892, the first Bodley Head book to include the names of Mathews and Lane was Wilde's *Poems* (a reprint of the fifth edition of the 1881 volume, first published by David Bogue) with designs by Charles Ricketts. In accordance with the Bodley Head's practice of issuing limited editions (usually around 500 or fewer copies), often on fine hand-made paper – all based, as Mathews and Lane announced, on "the probable demand for the book" – they purchased the remainder of 220 copies in unbound sheets from Wilde's publisher, whose business had gone bankrupt.

With respect to contracts, as Nelson states, Wilde was "one of the more difficult of the Bodley Head authors," for he was quite knowledgeable concerning business matters; hence, he insisted on contracts that included various provisions "designed to protect his interests fully" (95). Difficulties between Wilde and Lane erupted over the publication of *Salomé*. When Lane heard that a French edition was to be published, he urged Wilde to accept an increase in the number of ordinary copies from 250 to 600 in addition to the Bodley Head imprint in order for Mathews and Lane to have the rights to publish in England. Despite Wilde's agreement, Lane failed to prepare a formal contract. On the eve of publication – that is, on 21 February 1893 – Lane sent Wilde a telegram, indicating his willingness to take the number of copies allotted to him. Exasperated by Lane's "promises, excuses, apologies" over the previous three months, Wilde wrote to him: "...I very nearly struck your name off the title-page of the book, and diminished the edition. As you had advertised it, however, I felt this would have been somewhat harsh and unkind to you" (*Letters* 327).

If Lane's business dealings over the French edition caused Wilde anguish, the English translation in the following year created new problems that involved Lane and now Aubrey Beardsley, whose daring illustrations, particularly the caricatures of Wilde in several of them, were unacceptable to both Lane and Wilde (see Beardsley, Aubrey). At this time, Beardsley was preparing illustrations for the forthcoming *Yellow Book* and, according to Max Beerbohm, showed Wilde the cover design for the first volume. When Max asked what it was, Wilde remarked: "Oh, you can imagine the sort of thing. A terrible naked harlot smiling through a mask – and with ELKIN MATHEWS written on one breast and JOHN LANE on the other" (Beerbohm, *Letters* 94). Beardsley, the art editor, and Henry Harland, the literary editor of the *Yellow Book*, had agreed with Lane that Wilde should not be invited to contribute to the periodical, for he was acquiring an unsavory reputation that might be damaging to its success; moreover, the difficulty that Beardsley and Lane had with Wilde over the illustrations to *Salome* was still fresh in their minds. When the *Yellow Book* appeared in mid-April, even before the reviewers launched a widespread attack on the first number, Wilde gloated to Douglas: "It is dull and loathsome, a great failure. I am so glad" (*Letters* 354).

In November 1893, the Bodley Head published *Lady Windermere's Fan*, issuing the customary 500 cloth copies and 50 copies in a large paper edition. Apparently, there were no difficulties between Wilde and Lane concerning the publication of this play, either with respect to the contract or production. A work that had been contracted for as early as 1892 – *The Sphinx* – was finally published in June 1894. This work, which sold at two guineas for a small-paper copy and five guineas for the large, was the most expensive of the Bodley Head books issued until September of 1894.

In that month, Lane and Matthews agreed to dissolve their partnership: Mathews regarded Lane as "an impossible man to get on with – a man who was simply working for his own hand" (qtd. in Beckson, *Harland* 70). They proceeded to divide the authors whom they had published: Lane took the Bodley Head name to open his premises on the other side of Vigo Street and with him many of the authors whom he had been instrumental in bringing to the firm. Wilde wished to divide his works between the partners, but he was informed by Lane and Mathews (much to his annoyance) that Lane would take them.

One work – the expanded version of *The Portrait of Mr. W.H.* – was still under contract with the Bodley Head, but which of the partners would publish it remained uncertain. The manuscript had remained for more than a year in the hands of Charles Ricketts, who was supposedly preparing illustrations; indeed, at one point Wilde had been willing to cancel the contract on the payment to him of £25, an offer rejected. Lane had informed Wilde that Mathews would not publish the story "at any price" and that he would have to "approve" of it first (qtd. in Small 93). Wilde wrote to both Lane and Mathews: "For the firm to break their agreement with me would be dishonourable, dishonest, and illegal" (*Letters* 366). While negotiations to publish *The Portrait of Mr. W. H.* were still in progress, the final work by Wilde to appear before his arrest was *A Woman of No Importance*, issued by Lane "at the sign of the Bodley Head in Vigo Street" in October 1894 with the customary run of 500 copies.

Wilde's exasperation over *The Portrait of Mr. W. H.* took its form in *The Importance of Being Earnest*, in which he had planned to name two of the servants Lane and Mathews, but for the final version of *Earnest*, Wilde decided to focus on Lane (the greater of the two thorns in his side) by making him Algernon Moncrieff's manservant, whereas Mathews became "Merriman." The correspondence over *The Portrait of Mr. W. H.*, involving all three of the parties, dragged on until

April of 1895, when, during the chaos that ensued after the Wilde debacle, the manuscript of *The Portrait of Mr. W. H.* vanished, only to be discovered many years later and published (see entry).

In the remaining years of the nineties and in the following century, Lane and Mathews each became highly successful publishers: Lane, continuing with the "Keynotes" series of avant-garde fiction, published such writers as Ella D'Arcy, Grant Allen, and Arthur Machen; later, he published such writers as H. G. Wells, Arnold Bennett, and James Joyce, whose *Ulysses* bore the imprint of the Bodley Head. Mathews later published such figures as Yeats, Joyce, and Pound.

References: James G. Nelson, *The Early Nineties: A View from the Bodley Head* (1971); Karl Beckson, *Henry Harland: His Life and Work* (1978); J. W. Lambert and Michael Ratcliffe, *The Bodley Head, 1887–1987* (1987); Rupert Hart-Davis, ed., *Letters of Max Beerbohm, 1892–1956* (1988); James G. Nelson, *Elkin Mathews: Publisher to Yeats, Joyce, Pound* (1989); Margaret Diane Stetz, "Sex, Lies, and Printed Cloth: Bookselling at the Bodley Head in the Eighteen-Nineties," *Victorian Studies* (Autumn 1991).

BOUCICAULT, DION (1820–90)

An Irish-born American playwright who wrote approximately 150 plays and adaptations (the exact number remains in doubt), Boucicault (né Dionysius Boursiquot) is best known for *London Assurance* (1841), written under the pseudonym of "Lee Moreton" when he was 21. On one of his return trips to Dublin in 1861, Boucicault was warmly received by Dr. and Mrs. William Wilde and in later years was a friend of the young Oscar. When Wilde completed the script of *Vera; or, The Nihilists*, he sent it to Boucicault, who responded: "You have dramatic powers but have not shaped your subject perfectly before beginning it." He suggested that "a chain of *incidents*," not merely dialogue, should "lead from one to the other" of the main events in the play (qtd. in Small 96). It has been commonly believed that Boucicault was prepared to direct the play, but George Rowell argues that it was highly unlikely since Boucicault "had commitments in Dublin for late November 1881 and in New York for late December" (99).

In Boston in late January 1882, when the two met, Wilde revealed his difficulties with the management of his American lecture tour. In a letter to a mutual friend, Boucicault wrote:

> He has been much distressed; and came here last night looking worn and thin.... Oscar is helpless, because he is not a practical man of business, so when I advised him to throw over [D'Oyly] Carte, and offered to see him through financially if he did so, he felt afraid. I offered him a thousand pounds or two if he required it, but he says he will play out his contract to April.... There is a future for him here, but he *wants management....*

In a postscript added to his unmailed letter some two weeks later, Boucicault wrote: "I fear that he has no second visit here – those who undertake such enterprises tell me they would not be able to touch him. Still he might make a fair income – if better managed – and if he would reduce his hair and take his legs out of the last century" (qtd. in *Letters* 92–93n3).

In the remaining years of Boucicault's life, there seems to have been little or no contact between him and Wilde. However, Boucicault's son, Darley George (known as "Dot" and "Dion junior"), who had made his debut as actor at the age of 20 in his father's play *Rescued* (1879), maintained the Boucicault connection with Wilde. In a letter dated April 1894, addressed to "My dear old friend Oscar," he wrote from Australia:

> I produce *Lady Windermere's Fan* in about a month's time here – you shall have all the papers, and photographs of the scenes & principal characters forwarded to you. Here's to its success. Why should I write that? A play by Oscar Wilde cannot fail. His name alone is one to conjure with. In the lexicon of his youth there's been no such word as "fail." (qtd. in Small 92)

References: Richard Fawkes, *Dion Boucicault: A Biography* (1979); George Rowell, "The Truth about *Vera*," *Nineteenth Century Theatre* (Winter 1993).

BROOKFIELD, CHARLES (1860–1913)

An actor and author who played a major role in Wilde's downfall, Brookfield was the son of a former royal chaplain and a lady-in-waiting to Queen Victoria. After leaving Cambridge University, he abandoned his intention of becoming a lawyer and became associated with the Haymarket Theatre. Though he wrote several plays that attracted attention, Wilde's brilliant success apparently provoked him to jealousy; as a result, he "conceived a violent hatred of Wilde" (Hyde 88). Whatever the cause, O'Sullivan writes, "There came a time when he could not keep Wilde out of his talk" (93–94). In a musical burlesque titled *The Poet and the Puppets* (1892), Brookfield (and the composer J. M. Glover) parodied *Lady Windermere's Fan* (see Parodies and Satires of Wilde).

Despite his increasing anger towards Wilde, Brookfield accepted a part (as did Charles Hawtrey, who had performed the role of the Poet in Brookfield's parody) in *An Ideal Husband*: "I told [Wilde]," Brookfield said, "that as I did not want to learn many of his lines I would take the smallest part, and took the valet" (qtd. in Hyde 89).

When the Wilde/Queensberry case erupted, Brookfield went about London (assisted, it is believed, by Hawtrey) gathering damaging evidence concerning Wilde's liaison with male prostitutes in order to inform one of Queensberry's private detectives. When Wilde was finally convicted in his second trial, Brookfield and Hawtrey celebrated by entertaining Queensberry at a banquet (Mason 392). In 1912, shortly after Brookfield was appointed Examiner of Plays, some of Wilde's admirers protested at the Prince of Wales's Theatre on 20 February 1912, when Hawtrey revived Brookfield's play *Dear Old Charlie*.

References: Vincent O'Sullivan, *Aspects of Wilde* (1936); H. Montgomery Hyde, *The Trials of Oscar Wilde* (2nd ed. 1962; rpt. 1973).

"THE BURDEN OF ITYS"

Published: *Poems* (1881); rev. in (1882).

This poem consists of 58 stanzas, which, like those in all of the other long poems that appeared in *Poems*, consist of five lines in iambic pentameter, the sixth in heptameter (seven metrical feet). This stanzaic and metrical form is also used in the other long poems in *Poems* (1881): "The Garden of Eros," "Charmides," "Panthea," and in "Humanitad." The poem was written around 1877–78, Wilde's final year at Oxford, alluded to in the final lines, when he was drawn towards Hellenism, the result of his 1877 tour of Greece and Italy. In July 1881, Wilde told Violet Hunt (see entry): "The poem I like best is 'The Burden of Itys' and next to that 'The Garden of Eros.' They are the most lyrical, and I would sooner have any power or quality of 'song' writing than be the greatest sonnet writer since Petrarch" (*Letters* 79).

The Myth: Various Greek myths tell of the slaying of Itys, son of Procne, whose father was Pandion, King of Athens. In gratitude to Tereus, son of Ares, for coming to his assistance in war, Pandion gives him the hand of Procne in marriage. Tereus, falling in love with Philomela, his sister-in-law, rapes her and cuts out her tongue, but she nevertheless reveals the outrage to her sister Procne by weaving a tapestry depicting the act. To punish Tereus, she kills her own son, Itys, boils his corpse, and presents her husband with the gruesome stew. In a rage, Tereus pursues both Procne and her sister Philomela, but the gods transform both women into birds: in the version used by the Roman poets, Philomela becomes a nightingale and Procne a swallow.

The Poem: The speaker contemplates the startling contrasts between the ancient mythic world and the dull world of contemporary Oxfordshire, where the Thames "creeps on in sluggish leadenness, / And from the copse left desolate and bare / Fled is young Bacchus with his revelry." The "burden" of the title implies the role that Itys plays in the grisly tale. Wilde alludes to the myth in the following lines: "Poor mourning Philomel, what dost thou fear? / Thy sister doth not haunt these fields, Pandion is not here, / Here is no cruel Lord with murderous blade...."

In the course of the poem, the speaker alludes to such poets as Swinburne, Rossetti, and Matthew Arnold in lines 151–68, a device by which Wilde celebrates those poets of his private pantheon, particularly Swinburne and Arnold, whose enthusiasm for Greek culture paralleled his. Moreover, the speaker, immersed in the mythic horrors of the past, urges the nightingale to sing of those sorrowful events: "Cry out aloud on Itys!" The speaker then pleads: "Cease, Philomel, thou dost the forest wrong / To vex its sylvan quiet with such wild impassioned song!" The "burden" of Itys is one of a violently erotic past that the son must bear (that is, as the sins of the father, Tereus, are visited upon him). The poem ends with a return to the familiar and comforting prosaic world of academic Oxford:

Magdalen's tall tower tipped with tremulous gold

Marks the long High Street of the little town,
And warns me to return; I must not wait,
   Hark! 'tis the curfew booming from the bell at
     Christ Church gate.

Manuscripts: The Clark Library has two early MSS., consisting of drafts of lines 25-42 and 271-74; the Hyde Collection also has an early draft of lines 217-22, 253-58 , and 293-94.

BURNE-JONES, EDWARD (1833–98)

The Pre-Raphaelite painter Burne-Jones probably met Wilde sometime in the summer of 1881, for in a letter to Violet Hunt, postmarked 22 July, he refers to him as "Mr. Burne-Jones," with whom he was visiting friends (*Letters* 79). In a letter to a correspondent, to whom he sent a photograph of Burne-Jones's water color titled *Spes* (called *Hope* in the letter, a companion-piece to *Temperantia* and *Fides*), Wilde expresses his admiration of the painter's work: "It seems to me to be full of infinite pathos and love.... In so many of Burne-Jones's pictures we have merely the pagan worship of beauty: but in this one I seem to see more humanity and sympathy than in all the others" (*Letters* 52). During the celebrated libel suit that Whistler brought against John Ruskin for denigrating his art, Wilde remained on good terms with Whistler on one side and simultaneously with Ruskin and Burne-Jones on the other.

When Wilde departed for America on his lecture tour, he carried with him various letters of introduction, one of them dated 23 December 1881, from Burne-Jones to Charles Eliot Norton (1827–1908), the American scholar and man of letters: "The gentleman who brings this little note to you is my friend Mr. Oscar Wilde, who has much brightened this last of my declining years....he really loves the men and things you and I love..." (qtd. in *Letters* 123n1).

During the 1880s and early 1890s, Wilde saw Burne-Jones periodically, either at The Grange, where he visited him and composed a poem for his daughter (see "To M. B. J.") or at Thames House, where Wilde and Miles were sharing rooms. According to Penelope Fitzgerald, Burne-Jones wrote in his diary two days before Wilde's arrest that he waited in misery for "the probable ruin of Wilde tomorrow" (261). At the time of Wilde's arrest, Burne-Jones – according to Ellmann – "hoped that Wilde would shoot himself and was disappointed when he did not; but in a few months he relented and expressed sympathy" (479/450).

Fitzgerald writes of Burne-Jones: "To the evidence of the trial he reacted at first with extreme disgust, not because of Wilde's sins of the flesh, but because he had spent £50 a day on boys at the Savoy while his wife was left in difficulties" (261). Nevertheless, in a letter to a friend, Burne-Jones vowed to "speak up for [Wilde] whenever I hear him abused" because he knew of his "many generous actions and the heavy merciless fist of London society" (qtd. in Fitzgerald 262). Generously he loaned Constance Wilde £150 to cover her current expenses.

On 22 February 1896, Burne-Jones wrote in his diary that Constance Wilde, visiting him and his wife at The Grange, had been to Reading Prison to inform Wilde of the death of his mother:

> She says he was changed beyond recognition and they give him work to do in the garden and the work he likes best is to cover books with brown paper – for at least it is books to hold in his hand: but presently the keeper made a sign with his finger, and like a dog he obeyed, and left the room. (qtd. in Ellmann 499/468)

Reference: Penelope Fitzgerald, *Edward Burne-Jones: A Biography* (1975).

"THE BUTTERFLY'S BOSWELL"

Published: *Court and Society Review* 4 (20 April 1887): 378; rpt. in Mason 28–31 (uncollected in *Reviews*, 1908). An unsigned review of Walter Dowdeswell's article in the *Art Journal* (April 1887) on Whistler's life.

Wilde begins with a remark now widely quoted: "Every great man nowadays has his disciples, and it is usually Judas who writes the biography" (in its later incarnation in "The Critic as Artist," Part I, "always" replaces "usually"). Whistler, however, is "more fortunate than most of his *confreres*, as he has found in Mr. Walter Dowdeswell the most ardent of admirers...who gives us an extremely graphic picture of this remarkable artist...." After his Paris successes, "like all true Americans, [Whistler] gravitated towards England...where, according to Mr. Dowdeswell, he discovered the Thames." Wilde commends the author for his "distinct recognition of the complete absence from

Mr. Whistler's work of any alien quality, and of the great service he has rendered to Art by his absolute separation of painting from literature." Wilde denigrates the practice by English painters of "poaching upon the domain of the poets, marring their motives by clumsy treatment, and striving to render, by visible form and colour, the marvel of what is invisible, the splendour of what is not seen."

The "domain of the painter," Wilde continues, "is widely different from the domain of the poet":

> To the latter belongs Life in its full and absolute entirety; not only the world that men look at, but the world that men listen to also; not merely the momentary grace of form, or the transient gladness of colour, but the whole sphere of feeling, the perfect cycle of thought, the growth and progress of passion, the spiritual development of the soul. The painter is so far limited that it is only through the mask of the body that he can show us the mystery of the soul; only through images that he can handle ideas; only through its physical equivalents that he can deal with psychology.

Whistler, however, "has not by any means limited the painter's vision....he has pointed out possibilities of beauty hitherto undreamt of...he has given to Art itself a new creative impulse." Wilde also praises "the rare and exquisite wonder of his work, not its wonder merely, but its width also, its mastery over all chords, its possession of all secrets." Despite Wilde's claim that English painters had poached on the domain of the poets, he praises Whistler's etchings done "with the brilliancy of epigrams, and pastels with the charm of paradoxes, and many of his portraits are pure works of fiction."

"BY THE ARNO"

Published: See "San Miniato" for early publication details for these two poems. "By the Arno" was revised in *Poems* (1881) and (1882).

Consisting of six quatrains, "By the Arno" shifts from spiritual turmoil on reaching San Miniato al Monte, a 12th-century Romanesque church, to an emotional calm in the contemplation of Nature as the speaker, like such Romantics as Shelley and Keats, focuses on the sound of a "lonely nightingale" (an identification of bird and lyrical poet):

"BY THE ARNO"

"The day will make thee silent soon, / O nightin-gale sing on for love!"

Manuscript: See the "San Miniato" entry for details.

C

C.3.3

Wilde's prison number in Reading Prison, referring to Block C, the third cell on the third floor, described in *The Ballad of Reading Gaol*: "Each narrow cell in which we dwell / Is a foul and dark latrine...." When the poem was published, "C.3.3" appeared on the title page without Wilde's name until the seventh edition, issued on 23 June 1899, when his name finally appeared on the title page in square brackets beneath his cell number.

Wilde's Reading Prison Cell

"CAMMA"

Published: *Poems* (1881).

Wilde wrote this sonnet after seeing Ellen Terry as Camma, a priestess of Artemis, in Tennyson's verse play *The Cup* at the Lyceum Theatre (Henry Irving had a leading role). On the day of its opening, 3 January 1881, Wilde wrote to Terry: "I write to wish you *every success* tonight. *You* could not do anything that would not be a mirror of the highest artistic beauty, and I am so glad to hear you have an opportunity of showing us that passionate power which *I know you have*. You will have a great success – perhaps one of your greatest" (*Letters* 74).

Recalling Terry in the play "in the midmost shrine of Artemis /...standing, antique-limbed, and stern" as the goddess's priestess, Wilde prefers to see her in the role of Cleopatra, "That serpent of old Nile [from *Antony and Cleopatra*, I.iv.25], whose witchery / Made Emperors drunken, – come, great Egypt, shake / Our stage with all thy mimic pageants!" He ends by echoing Tennyson's poem "The Lady of Shalott" ("I am half sick of shadows," which is also echoed in Chapter 7 of *The Picture of Dorian Gray*, when Sibyl Vane, rejecting the stage, declares: "I have grown sick of shadows"). In his poem, Wilde envisions himself as Cleopatra's lover: "I am grown sick of unreal passions, make / The world thine Actium, me thine Antony!"

Manuscripts: The Clark Library has two MSS.: one contains early versions of lines 1–7; a second is titled "Helena," several lines of which were incorporated into "Camma." The Huntington Library has the final version of the poem.

CAMPBELL, MRS. PATRICK (1865 – 1940)

The actress known as "Mrs. Patrick Campbell" was born Beatrice Rose Stella Tanner in London of a English father and an Italian mother, whose own father had been a political exile. In 1884, she married Patrick Campbell, with whom she went to South Africa to discover gold. On her return, she became an actress, adopting her husband's name, though friends called her "Stella" and acquaintances called her "Mrs. Pat."

In May 1893, she created a sensation in the title role of Pinero's *The Second Mrs. Tanqueray*. In February 1894, while the play was still in production, Wilde brought Aubrey Beardsley to the St. James's Theatre to see her performance. When Beardsley expressed the wish to meet her, Wilde sent her a note: "...he must once have the honour of being presented to you, if you will allow it. So, with your gracious sanction, I will come round after Act III with him, and you would gratify and honour him much if you would let him bow his compliments to you" (*Letters* 353). Evidently impressed, Beardsley later included his drawing of her – looking quite ethereal – in the first number of the *Yellow Book* (April 1894).

Wilde's relationship with Mrs. Campbell was evidently sporadic and distant. There seems to have been little social contact between the two, but his admiration of her dramatic genius is obvious as late as October 1898, when he insisted that, in the staging of a play he had sketched out (later titled *Mr. and Mrs. Daventry* in Frank Harris's version), Mrs. Campbell would have a leading role. He consequently wrote to a theater manager: "It is understood that you will endeavour to procure... Mrs. Patrick Campbell for the [leading female role]" (*Letters* 762). When *Mr. and Mrs. Daventry* opened in October 1900, Mrs. Campbell performed the role of Mrs. Daventry.

References: Mrs. Patrick Campbell, *My Life and Some Letters* (1922; rpt. 1969); Margot Peters, *Mrs. Pat: The Life of Mrs. Patrick Campbell* (1984).

"THE CANTERVILLE GHOST"

Published: *Court and Society Review* 4 (23 Feb. and 2 March 1887): 183–86 and 207–11; rpt. with the sub-title "A Hylo-Idealistic Romance" in *Lord Arthur Savile's Crime and Other Stories* (1891).

The Plot: Hiram B. Otis, the American minister to Great Britain, has purchased Canterville Chase, reputed to be haunted. The ghost, says Lord Canterville, "has been seen by several living members of my family, as well as by the rector of the parish...." Dismissing such reports, Otis responds that "if there were such a thing as a ghost in Europe, we'd have it at home in a very short time in one of our public museums, or on the road as a show."

When the family (consisting of Mrs. Otis; Washington, the eldest son; Virginia, fifteen years old; and the mischievous male twins, called "The Stars and Stripes") arrives at the house, just seven miles from Ascot, the first disturbing sight is a red stain in the library, the site of Sir Simon de Canterville's murder of his wife in 1575: "The bloodstain," says the old housekeeper, "has been much admired by tourists and others, and cannot be removed." But no sooner has Washington applied a stain remover to the floor with success than "a terrible flash of lightning lit up the sombre room, a fearful peal of thunder made them all start to their feet...." The next morning the blood stain

reappears on the floor. Two more attempts to remove it also fail. The members of the Otis family are now firm believers in the existence of ghosts.

Sometime later, Otis encounters a ghost "in the wan moonlight, an old man of terrible aspect": "...his garments, which were of antique cut, were soiled and ragged, and from his wrists and ankles hung heavy manacles and rusty gyves." Addressing it, Otis says: "I really must insist on your oiling those chains, and have brought you for that purpose a small bottle of the Tammany Rising Sun Lubricator." When Otis retires to his room, the "Stars and Stripes" fling a pillow at the ghost, who flees: "Never, in a brilliant and uninterrupted career of three hundred years, had he been so grossly insulted." The ghost's second appearance occurs when the family hears a "fearful crash" in the hall: a suit of armour had become detached from its stand when he attempted to put it on to thrill the Americans with a vision of a "Spectre In Armour" (possibly derived from Longfellow's ballad "The Skeleton in Armor," 1841).

They find the apparition sitting in a high-backed chair rubbing its knees. The twins immediately direct their peashooters at him while Otis "covered him with his revolver, and called upon him, in accordance with Californian etiquette, to hold up his hands!" With a "wild shriek of rage," the ghost sweeps past them "like a mist." He is now determined to frighten the Otis family by various methods appropriate to ghosts, such as gibbering at the foot of Washington's bed and stabbing himself three times in the throat to the sound of low music.

But when he himself encounters what appears to be a fearful ghost, he flees to his room (the "ghost" turns out to be a joke: "He had been tricked, foiled, and outwitted!"). Though he decides on retribution, he also recognizes that the Otises were "evidently people on a low, material plane of existence, and quite incapable of appreciating the symbolic value of sensuous phenomena." (While emphasizing the parody in Wilde's story of the supernaturalism in the late 18th-century Gothic novel, Kohl also writes of the satirical view of Americans: "Among the features that seem to him typical of the American character are materialism, a predominantly pragmatic way of thinking, no sense of aesthetics, no sense of history, and generally no sense of culture," 65.)

The ghost resolves to give up restoring the blood

stain on the floor. Each of his attempts to frighten the family backfires as various tricks are played on him, such as a heavy jug of water falling on him and soaking him as he flings a door open. When he stops his nocturnal expeditions, the family believes that he has left the house for good.

However, in the Tapestry Chamber, Virginia comes across the ghost, who appears to be in an "extreme depression." In conversation, he tells her that he must rattle his chains and groan through keyholes: "It is my only reason for existing." He accuses her family of being "horrid, rude, vulgar, dishonest," but she responds by accusing him of those very qualities. She offers free passage to America, and "though there is a heavy duty on spirits of every kind, there will be no difficulty about the Custom House, as the officers are all Democrats." But he declines. He informs her that he has not slept for 300 years, and his account of the Garden of Death deeply moves her. He speaks to her of an old prophecy inscribed on the library window: she must weep for him so that the Angel of Death "will have mercy on me" (the witty parody of the traditional ghost story has now turned into an allegorical fairy tale). He then walks with her – despite warnings from figures in the tapestry: "Go back! little Virginia" – through the wainscoting.

With Virginia missing, a search is undertaken without success. Otis and the others return to the house after scouring the countryside, but as the clock strikes midnight, "a dreadful peal of thunder shook the house, a strain of unearthly music floated through the air," and Virginia appears on the landing with "a little casket in her hand." The ghost, she tells everyone, is dead: before he died, he gave her a box of beautiful jewels. She leads them to a low, vaulted room where a chained "gaunt skeleton" has lived out its life. When the "old withered almond-tree miraculously blossoms (a device that Wilde uses in various fairy tales), Virginia murmers, alluding to the murder of his wife: "God has forgiven him." (Rodney Shewan regards Virginia as the "redemptive heroine" who "rescues the Ghost from his purgatory by believing in him and retaining that belief until he can find death," 33.)

Lord Canterville insists that the jewels belong to Virginia. Three years later, she marries the young Duke of Cheshire. On a visit to the Chase, the Duke asks her what happened when Virginia was locked up with the ghost. Without telling her husband, she says: "He made me see what Life is, and what Death signifies, and why Love is stronger than both." (Virginia's marriage, suggests Shewan, achieves a cultural fusion: "the fresh moral vision of the new world redeems the inherited misdeeds of the old...., the pastoral peace of the aristocracy and the moral insight of the Puritan," 35)

Reference: Rodney Shewan, *Oscar Wilde: Art and Egotism* (1977).

"CANZONET"

Published: *Art and Letters* 2 (April 1888): 46–47; rpt. in *Poems* (1908). The title of this poem, consisting of four eight-line stanzas, refers to Wilde's variation on the longer Italian *canzone*, a serious lyric poem written during the late medieval and Renaissance periods by Italian and Provençal poets; the canzonet, however, is a light, airy song of four or five eight-line stanzas.

In the tradition of pastoral verse, the shepherd bids the shepherdess to "pluck a reed / And bid me sing to thee, / For I would feed / Thine ears with melody." Since the pagan world is gone ("Pan is not here, / And will not come again"), none will "divine / Those little red / Rose-petalled lips of thine." The traditional theme is the passage of time and the need to seize the day: "No ivory dryads play, / Silver and still / Sinks the sad autumn day."

THE CARDINAL OF AVIGNON

Wilde wrote a scenario of a play with this title in April 1894, at which time he told Alfred Douglas: "I think of writing *The Cardinal of Avignon* at once. If I had peace, I would do it" (*Letters* 355). The scenario has survived as well as an apparent draft of Act II (see Manuscripts below).

The Plot: The opening curtain reveals the Cardinal alone in his palace, excited at the news that the Pope is near death. "What if they were to elect me Pope?" he says, revealing his ambition. When nobles and princes enter, he obtains their promises of votes after he assures them that he will, upon achieving the papacy, fulfill their personal desires. When they leave, he soliloquizes on the papal office. A beautiful young girl, the Cardinal's ward, enters and upbraids him for his refusal to see her. As Wilde writes, "a very pretty and affectionate scene occurs between them" about love. She informs him that she has plighted her troth to a handsome young man in the Cardinal's court. The Cardinal makes her promise not to reveal their conversation to her lover. When the young girl leaves, the Cardinal is filled with rage and sorrow: "And so my sin of 20 years ago has risen up against me, and come to rob me of the only thing I love." The allusion is to the handsome young man, his son.

In the next scene, which is set in the garden at the rear of the palace, the Cardinal's ward and her betrothed have "a passionate love scene." When he asks whether she has informed the Cardinal of their betrothal, she remains faithful to her promise not to reveal her conversation with the Cardinal; the young man urges her to tell him of their betrothal. A pageant and "a masque of death" appear, thereby alarming the girl that it foreshadows disaster. But the young man assures her that "Death is not for such as you and I." When they part, she drops her glove, which the Cardinal picks up when he sees the young man. Furious, he says to himself, "So they have met."

Determined to keep his son, "the only thing he loves," the Cardinal tells him that, years before, a dying prince had entrusted his two children to the Cardinal's care and that he and his betrothed are those children. He urges the young man "to pluck this impossible love from his heart and also to kill it in the heart of the girl." When the girl enters, the Cardinal reveals that her lover has found that he has made a mistake and that he does not wish to marry her. Wilde writes: "This portion of the play winds up with a powerful scene between the two lovers, the young man rigidly carrying out the promise exacted from him by the Cardinal."

In the third scene, the Cardinal is alone within the palace, repenting his action in dissolving the betrothal. Because he is "desperately in love" with his ward, he doubts whether God will make him Pope. At this moment, trumpets sound, and nobles and princes enter. The Pope has died, and the Cardinal has been elected as the next pope. When the nobles and princes leave, the Cardinal is exultant: "I who was but now in the mire am now placed so high, Christ's Vicar on earth...." When he sends for the young man, he tells him: "What I told you yesterday was simply done to test you. You and your betrothed are no relations. Go, find her and I will marry you to her tonight before I ride away to Rome." Wilde describes what happens at this moment: "...the huge doors at the end

of the hall are thrown open and there enter friars bearing a bier covered with a pall, which they proceed to set down in the centre of the hall, and then exeunt, without speaking a word. Both men intuitively feel who is the occupant of the bier. The young girl has killed herself in despair at the loss of her lover."

The Cardinal (now the Pope), opening the doors, orders the soldiers not to enter until he walks forth again. When he closes the doors, the young man says: "Now I am going to kill you." The Pope will not defend himself but will plead with him, pointing out the sacrilege of murdering a Pope. The young man insists, however, that he must die. The Pope then reveals that he is the young man's father (a scene echoing the revelation at the end of Act III of *A Woman of No Importance* that Gerald Arbuthnot is the son of Lord Illingworth): his murder would now include patricide. But the young man responds that he has no filial feelings. The Pope, going to the bier, draws back the pall and says that he too loved his ward.

The final moments are described as follows by Wilde: "At this the young man runs and flings open the doors and says: 'His Holiness will ride hence tonight on his way to Rome' – The Pope is standing blessing the corpse, and as he does so, the young man throws himself on the bier between the Pope and the corpse and stabs himself." The soldiers, nobles and princes re-enter while the Pope stands blessing both corpses as the curtain falls.

Manuscripts: Dartmouth College has an early version of the scenario of the play, written in 1882. The Clark Library has five leaves, copied in November 1896 by Wilde's friend More Adey from a scenario "sketch" that Wilde had composed in April 1894 but which he apparently abandoned without composing any scenes. The scenario is printed in *Miscellanies* (1908), 313–15; in Mason 583–85; and in Small 120–23. The Taylor Collection at Princeton has the autograph scenario of the play in 15 pages as well as the apparent beginning of Act II in a notebook containing 61 leaves of the unfinished play in Wilde's hand.

CARTE, RICHARD D'OYLY: *See* **LECTURES IN AMERICA, 1882**

CE QUI NE MEURT PAS (WHAT NEVER DIES): See SATYRICON

"'THE CENCI'"

Published: *Dramatic Review* 3 (15 May 1886): 151. A signed review of a production of Percy Bysshe Shelley's *The Cenci* at the Grand Theatre, Islington, on 7 May 1887; rpt. in *Reviews* (1908).

The Shelley Society, writes Wilde, "deserves the highest praise and warmest thanks of all for having given us an opportunity of seeing Shelley's play under the conditions he himself desired for it." Shelley saw that "the essence of the drama is disinterested presentation, and that the characters must not be merely mouthpieces for splendid poetry but must be living subjects for terror and for pity." Shelley wrote of his play: "I have avoided with great care the introduction of what is commonly called mere poetry....the imagery and the passion should interpenetrate one another, the former being reserved simply for the full development and illustration of the latter." Wilde comments: "He fully realises that it is by a conflict between our artistic sympathies and our moral judgment that the great dramatic effects are produced." The Shelley Society, in carrying out the poet's own wishes, "are to be congratulated on the success of their experiment...."

CHAMELEON: *See* **BLOXAM, JOHN FRANCIS**

"CHANSON"

Published: See "La Bella Donna della mia Mente" for details of publication.

"Chanson," a lyric of four stanzas, presents the speaker's vision of his Lady's eternal glory ("For you a House of Ivory," associated with the Virgin Mary) but for the speaker "A narrow bed for me to lie" – that is, the grave: "(Plant lilies at my head)!"

Manuscript: Texas has a presentation MS. of "Chanson," signed by Wilde and re-titled "Lily-Flower," possibly given to the actress Lillie Langtry (see entry), for whom he had written "The New Helen."

"CHARMIDES"

Published: *Poems* (1881); rev. in (1882). The longest poem in the volume, "Charmides" consists of 111 stanzas in three parts, written around 1878–79. On his lecture tour in San Francisco, Wilde was pressed by an interviewer for the *Daily Examiner* (27 March 1882) to name his favorite poem: "Charmides," he reportedly said, was his

"most finished and perfect" (Mikhail 1:62).

Sources: Wilde undoubtedly derived his story from Lucian's *Essays in Portraiture*, 4, which concerns a boy who intrudes upon Aphrodite's temple to embrace the goddess. He later drowns, though other versions say that he leaped from a cliff to his death. Wilde derived the title of his poem from Plato's dialogue *Charmides*. Born into an aristocratic Athenian family, Charmides (d. 403 BC) was Plato's uncle and Socrates' friend. In Plato's dialogue, Socrates describes Charmides as "a marvel of stature and beauty; and all the rest, to my thinking, were in love with him...."

In Part I, Charmides, a Grecian lad, is returning home from Sicily on his galley with "pulpy figs and wine." Reaching harbor, he bathes and dresses, enters the town, approaches the temple unnoticed by the priests, and occupies "some dark retreat." He observes Athena's votaries presenting offerings and prayers. When they leave, the "venturous lad" flings aside the door of the shrine to expose the goddess to his view, thereby violating her sacred enclosure: "From round the temple rolled the clang of arms, / And the twelve Gods leapt up in marble fear, / And the air quaked with dissonant alarums...." When quiet is restored, the lad removes the goddess's cloak. At this point, Wilde issues a warning in a quaint, traditional style: "Those who have never known a lover's sin / Let them not read my ditty...."

The lad embraces the marble goddess and spends the night with her "till overhead the lark of warning flew." At daybreak, he rushes from the temple to a stream in an olive wood, well known to him from childhood: "And down amid the startled reeds he lay / Panting in breathless sweet affright, and waited for the day." Some passing woodmen marvel at his beauty and speculate on his godlike appearance. One of them remarks: "It is Narcissus, his own paramour, / Those are the fond and crimson lips no woman can allure." Another cries: "It is young Dionysos who has hid / His spear and fawnskin by the river side...." The lad pays little attention to the movements and songs of squirrels and birds about him, "for he had seen / The breasts of Pallas and the naked wonder of the Queen." When rain begins falling, he rises, goes to his galley, calls his mates aboard, and leaves the quay.

A "great owl with yellow sulphurous eyes" (Athena's sacred bird) alights on the galley, flaps its wings, and shrieks. Then, suddenly rising from the ocean's edge, the figure of Athena herself "strode across the stretch of sick and shivering sea!" When the lad beholds "those grand relentless eyes," he laughs for joy and cries out, "I come" and leaps "into the chill and churning foam." From heaven, a bright star falls and "a few gurgling bubbles rose where her boy lover sank." The owl flies off with "mocking hoots after the wrathful Queen," and later the pilot tells "how he had seen / Close to the stern a dim and giant form." No one dares speak of Charmides, "deeming that he some evil thing had wrought."

In Part II, A Triton-god has pity on him, however, and carries the boy's drowned body back to "Grecian land, / And mermaids combed his dank and dripping hair...." Some wood-nymphs come across the boy's body on the sand, one of them approaching "who deemed it would not be / So dread a thing to feel a sea-god's arms / Crushing her breasts in amorous tyranny...." She "called him soft names, played with his tangled hair, / And with hot lips made havoc of his mouth...." She continues until sundown, when she urges Charmides to awaken: "Then come away unto my ambuscade / Where clustering woodbine weaves a canopy / For amorous pleasaunce...." Artemis (called by the Romans "Diana"), the virginal goddess of the hunt, sends a "barbed reed" flying into the nymph's breast and "with a bitter cry / On the boy's body fell the Dryad maid, / Sobbing for incomplete virginity." Venus, however, takes up the lovers into the skies in her "bright car," but the maiden dies.

In Part III, the concluding section of only eight stanzas, Charmides is seen lying on the bank of the river Acheron in the mythic Underworld "far from the goodly earth and joyous day." The nymph is reunited with him with renewed passion, and together the lovers will serve Persephone, the goddess of the Underworld and wife of Hades.

Early Reviews: The Cambridge University don Oscar Browning, reviewing *Poems* (1881), remarked in the *Academy* (30 July 1881) that "Charmides" had "music, beauty, imagination, and power; but the story, as far as there is one, is most repulsive. Mr. Wilde has no magic to veil the hideousness of a sensuality which feeds on statues and dead bodies." An unsigned review in the Chicago *Dial* (Aug. 1881) pointed to Wilde's "fondness for Greek themes and treatment – a fondness which is the dominant spirit of the book,

and in which he almost surpasses Swinburne. Suggestive, too, of Swinburne, and of a gross 'fleshly' rather than aesthetic school, are many of the stanzas; others are very beautiful, and most are full of power...." In the Boston *Woman's Journal* (4 Feb. 1882), the author, social reformer, and champion of woman's suffrage T. W. Higginson remarked that if "Charmides" were read aloud to a gathering of women of "high social position...not a woman would remain in the room until the end."

Manuscripts: Three partial MSS. are extant: one in the Huntington Library of lines 511–606; another in the Clark Library of lines 595–98; and the third, a fair copy of lines 607–54 in the Hyde Collection.

"CHATTERTON"

The Clark Library has this unpublished essay in a notebook of some 70 manuscript leaves, a rough draft consisting of notes, clippings from such biographies as Daniel Wilson's *Chatterton: A Biographical Study* (1869), and David Masson's *Chatterton: A Story of the Year 1770* (1874), as well as excerpts from Chatterton's poems, letters, and his will, presumably for the essay announced as forthcoming in the January 1887 issue of the *Century Guild Hobby Horse*; the essay, however, never appeared. Mason prints the introductory section to the essay (13). As a lecture, it was given at Birkbeck College, University of London, on 24 November 1886. Wilde wrote to Herbert Horne (1864–1916), editor of the *Century Guild Hobby Horse*: "To my amazement I found 800 people there! And they seemed really interested in the marvellous boy" (*Letters* 192).

The lecture notes suggest that Wilde regarded Chatterton as one who defied bourgeois values in the quest for Beauty:

Was he [a] mere forger with literary powers or a great artist? The latter is the right view. Chatterton may not have had the moral conscience which is truth to fact – but he had the artistic conscience which is truth to Beauty. He had the artist's yearning to represent and if perfect representation seemed to him to demand forgery he needs must forge. Still this forgery came from the desire of artistic self-effacement. (qtd. in Ellmann 285/268–69)

Ellmann states that Wilde gave "his last reported

lecture" in March 1888 "on a new subject, the poet Chatterton," and that he concluded it with an unpublished poem on him (284–85/268–69). However, there is a triple error here since Wilde had already given a lecture on Chatterton in 1886 (see *Letters* 192n1); he gave it again – with the title "Thomas Chatterton: The Boy-Poet of the Eighteenth Century" – on 7 April 1888 in the Shaftesbury Hall, Bournemouth (see *More Letters* 73n2); and the poem that Wilde concluded the March 1888 lecture with was not by Wilde but by Dante Gabriel Rossetti, who published it in *Ballads and Sonnets* (1881).

Reference: Roger Lewis, "A Misattribution: Oscar Wilde's 'Unpublished Sonnet on Chatterton,'" *Victorian Poetry* (Summer 1990).

"A CHEAP EDITION OF A GREAT MAN"

Published: *PMG*, 18 April 1887, 5; rpt. in *Reviews* (1908). An unsigned review of Joseph Knight's *Life of Dante Gabriel Rossetti* (1887) in the "Great Writers" series.

Wilde's opening reveals his attempt to renovate the reputation of a figure who exerted a strong influence on the late 19th-century Aesthetes: "Formerly we used to canonise our great men; nowadays we vulgarise them. The vulgarisation of Rossetti has been going on for some time past with really remarkable success, and there seems no probability at present of the process being discontinued." Obviously, Knight's popular biography is herewith set up for attack. Yet Wilde restrains himself by first acknowledging that the book is "much better than that of predecessors in the same field. His book is on the whole, modestly and simply written; whatever its other faults may be, it is at least free from affectation of any kind." But, says Wilde, it is "just the sort of biography Guildenstern might have written of Hamlet" (that is, a work by a devious "friend" who pretends friendship).

The "whole scheme and method of the book," Wilde continues with surgical precision, is "radically wrong":

Rossetti's was a giant personality, and personalities such as his do not easily survive shilling primers. Sooner or later they have inevitably to come down to the level of their biographers, and in the present instance nothing could be more absolutely commonplace than

the picture Mr. Knight gives us of the wonderful seer and singer whose life he has so recklessly essayed to write.

Wilde regrets that such a "shallow and superficial biography as this should ever have been published." A "true artist," he states, "reveals himself so perfectly in his work, that unless a biographer has something more valuable to give us than idle anecdotes and unmeaning tales, his labour is misspent and his industry misdirected."

Such biographies "rob life of much of its dignity and its wonder, add to death itself a new terror, and make one wish that all art were anonymous." Rossetti lived apart, Wilde contends, from the gossip and "tittle-tattle of a shallow age." He never "trafficked with the merchants for his soul, nor brought his wares into the market-place for the idle to gape at. Passionate and romantic though he was, yet there was in his nature something of high austerity. He loved seclusion, and hated notoriety...." Returning to his allusion to Guildenstern, Wilde quotes Hamlet: "'Though you can fret me, yet you cannot play upon me,' says Hamlet to his false friend, and even so might Rossetti speak to those well-intentioned mediocrities who would seem to know his stops...."

"THE CHILD-PHILOSOPHER"

Published: *Court and Society Review* 4 (20 April 1887): 379–80; rpt. in Mason 31–34 (uncollected in *Reviews*, 1908). An unsigned article on Mark Twain's review in the New York *Century Magazine* (April 1887) of Caroline B. LeRow's *English as She is Taught* (1887).

LeRow's book reports errors, writes Wilde, "by the interesting pupils of the American Board-Schools [that] are not mistakes springing from ignorance of life or dulness of perception; they are, on the contrary, full of the richest suggestion, and pregnant with the very highest philosophy." He cites such "luminous definitions" as the following: "*Republican*, a sinner mentioned in the Bible"; "*The Constitution of the United States*, that part of the book at the end that nobody reads"; and "*Plagiarist*, a writer of plays." The latter, Wilde suggests, "is the most brilliant thing that has been said on modern literature for some time."

Even women, "most complex of all modern problems, are analyzed with a knowledge that in Europe is confined to poets and dandies. 'They make fun of boys,' says the child-philosopher, 'and then turn round and love them.'" Wilde concludes with a tribute to Mark Twain, who "deserves our warmest thanks for bringing to light the true American genius. American patriots are tedious, American millionaires go bankrupt, and American beauties don't last, but the schoolboy seems to be eternally delightful...."

"THE CHILDREN OF THE POETS"

Published: *PMG*, 14 Oct. l886, 5; rpt. in *Reviews* (l908). An unsigned review of *The Children of the Poets: An Anthology from English and American Writers of Three Centuries*, ed. Eric S. Robertson (1886).

Calling the idea of this book "exceedingly charming," Wilde notes, "As children themselves are the perfect flowers of life, so a collection of the best poems written on children should be the most perfect of all anthologies." However, the book is "not by any means a success," for many of the best child-poems are excluded. Wilde cites a number of examples of these "sins of omission," such as Matthew Arnold's "To a Gipsy Child," Edgar Allan Poe's "Annabel Lee," a "little lyric full of strange music and strange romance," and Blake's "The Little Girl Lost." The "gravest omission," however, is that no poem by Robert Herrick appears, yet "no English poet has written of children with more love and grace and delicacy," such as in "Ode on the Birth of Our Saviour" and his "many lovely epitaphs on children...exquisite works of art, simple, sweet and sincere." Excluding Herrick is the equivalence of "an English garden without its roses and...an English woodland without its singing birds." Though an "industrious compilation," it is not an anthology or even a selection of the best works, for "it lacks the discrimination and good taste which is the essence of selection...."

"A CHINESE SAGE"

Published: *Speaker: A Review of Politics, Letters, Science, and the Arts* 1 (8 Feb. l890): l44–46; rpt. in *Reviews* (l908). A signed review of *Chuang Tzŭ: Mystic, Moralist, and Social Reformer*, trans. Herbert A. Giles (1889). In *The Artist as Critic: Critical Writings of Oscar Wilde* (1969), Richard Ellmann errs in identifying Chuang Tzŭ as Confucius (221).

Citing Chuang Tzŭ's writings as "the most caustic criticism of modern life," Wilde assumes that the "spread of popular education has no doubt made the name of this great thinker quite familiar to the public, but for the sake of the few and over-cultured," he believes that he should identify him and present a brief outline of his philosophy. After his obligatory identification of this philosopher (c. 369–c. 286 BC), Wilde remarks that Chuang Tzŭ "spent his life preaching the great creed of Inaction, and in pointing out the uselessness of all useful things" (here, as Isobel Murray has written, Wilde perceives certain parallels with Aestheticism):

To resolve action into thought, and thought into abstraction, was his wicked transcendental aim. Like the obscure philosopher of early Greek speculation, he believed in the identity of contraries; like Plato, he was an idealist, and had all the idealist's contempt for utilitarian systems; he was a mystic like Dionysius, and Scotus Erigena, and Jacob Böhme, and held, with them and with Philo, that the object of life was to get rid of self-consciousness, and to become the unconscious vehicle of a higher illumination.

But, Wilde continues, Chuang Tzŭ was "something more than a metaphysician and an illuminist. He sought to destroy society, as we know it, as the middle classes know it; and the sad thing is that he combines with the passionate eloquence of a Rousseau the scientific reasoning of a Herbert Spencer." This "curious thinker" looked in retrospect to a Golden Age "when there were no competitive examinations, no wearisome educational systems, no missionaries, no penny dinners for the people, no Established Churches, no Humanitarian Societies, no dull lectures about one's duty to one's neighbour, and no tedious sermons about any subject at all."

Moreover, Tzŭ believed that all forms of government were wrong, unscientific, because they sought to change man's natural environment; hence, they were immoral because, by obstructing individual development, they produced the "most aggressive forms of egotism...." Wilde alludes to the social reformers who preach "salvation from the ills that they and their system had caused": "The poor Social Reformers! 'They know not shame, nor what it is to blush,' is the verdict of

Chuang Tzŭ upon them."

Who, asks Wilde, is the "perfect man," according to Chuang Tzŭ, and what is his "manner of life"? The perfect man "does nothing beyond gazing at the universe.... His mental equilibrium gives him the empire of the world. He is never the slave of objective existences. He knows that, 'just as the best language is that which is never spoken, so the best action is that which is never done.'" Moreover, the perfect man is not troubled about moral distinctions: "All this is of course excessively dangerous, but we must remember that Chuang Tzŭ lived more than two thousand years ago, and never had the opportunity of seeing our unrivalled civilisation." Wilde regards him as "one of the Darwinians before Darwin. He traces man from the germ, and sees his unity with nature."

Chuang Tzŭ's doctrine of the uselessness of all useful things, says Wilde, "would not merely endanger our commercial supremacy as a nation, but might bring discredit upon many prosperous and serious-minded members of the shop-keeping classes.... And what would be the fate of governments and professional politicians if we came to the conclusion that there is no such thing as governing mankind at all?" As a "dangerous writer," Chuang Tzŭ is "obviously premature, and may cause a great deal of pain to many thoroughly respectable and industrious persons."

Clearly, Wilde's own individualism and subversiveness found resonances in Chuang Tzŭ's philosophic outlook on life and culture. Though Chuang Tzŭ "would be disturbing at dinner-parties, and impossible at afternoon teas," one presumes that Wilde's narcissism would resist the Chinese sage's observation that the "'perfect man ignores self" and "the true sage ignores reputation" but perhaps endorse the observation that "the divine man ignores action." (Isobel Murray contends that it would "of course be absurd to see anything in the review as an instance of Chuang Tzŭ's influencing Wilde," 4.)

Reference: Isobel Murray, "Oscar Wilde's Absorption of 'Influences': The Case History of Chuang Tzŭ," *Durham University Journal* (Dec. l97l).

"CHOIR BOY"

This uncompleted lyric poem, unpublished in Wilde's lifetime, was probably written during Wilde's first years at Magdalen College, Oxford.

Every day, the speaker, who is the choir boy, sings praises to God: "And they say that my voice mounts higher, / Than even a bird can sing – " His voice, divinely inspired, reaches "the heavens blue, / Up through the vaulted ceiling / To where God sits out of view." The poem stops abruptly in the final line of the fourth stanza in which an uncompleted comparison is made involving a portrait of St. Michael "painted upon the wall, / With his golden glory of backblown hair, / White as a lily, and tall – "

The presence of the lily image suggests not St. Michael, the Protector of the Church Militant, but St. Gabriel, God's Chief Messenger, who informs the Virgin of her forthcoming birth to Jesus, as told in Luke 1:26–31. In art, this Annunciation scene usually includes images of lilies, symbolizing purity and chastity, either held by Gabriel or visible in vases. Wilde has apparently conflated the two archangels, both associated with the Virgin. The person to whom St. Michael in the portrait is compared is not mentioned but presumably it is the choir boy. The archangel "Is not so lovely to the view / His lips are not so red, / His eyes are not such wells of blue...."

Manuscript: The Clark Library has a MS. of the poem.

"CHORUS OF CLOUD-MAIDENS"

Published: *Dublin University Magazine* 86 (Nov. l875): 622; rpt., rev. as "Nubes" ("Clouds") in Alfred William Pollard, ed., *Odes from the Greek Dramatists* (1890) and, with the current title, in *Poems* (1908). Written around 1874–75, during Wilde's first year at Magdalen College, Oxford, this translation from Aristophanes's *Clouds* (423 BC), which satirizes Socrates as a sophist corrupting the youth with his absurd new learning, is Wilde's earliest published work. Its metrical and verbal facility reveals Wilde's considerable poetic talent at this early age.

CHRIST AND CHRISTIANITY

From his prison cell at Reading, Wilde wrote to Alfred Douglas in *De Profundis*: "Christ's place indeed is with the poets. His whole conception of Humanity sprang right out of the imagination and can only be realised by it. What God was to the Pantheist, man was to him. He was the first to conceive the divided races as a unity" (*Letters* 477). Christ, Wilde writes, was "the precursor of the Romantic movement in life," for Romantic art – an integrated structure as opposed to "the dull lifeless mechanical systems that treat people as if they were things" – was for him "the proper basis of actual life" (*Letters* 484–85). Commenting on this view, Guy Willoughby writes:

Wilde's powerfully imaginative Jesus embodies a commitment to the community at large, and to an expanded organic view of self and society that derives from aesthetic appreciation, rather than moral instinct.... Wilde's work, *in toto*, celebrates the human power to imagine and to impose order, however fleetingly, on experience; his rereading of Jesus as a definitive model for the new aesthetics – as a quintessential artist-in-life – is the key to his thought. (15–16, 18)

In short, "instead of rejecting Christianity, Wilde modified it to suit his own needs and, consequently, brought to Christianity the same kind of aesthetic impulse he brought to the spheres of politics and ethics" (Quintus 514). Wilde's view of Christ, Willoughby contends, is, like Matthew Arnold's, "synonymous with that ideal man of culture." Wilde also "shares Arnold's concern with the mythopoeic and imaginative value of religion" (53).

Before Wilde's imprisonment, "The Soul of Man under Socialism" expressed his most comprehensive view regarding Christ and Christianity. In this essay, Wilde contends that individualism will be the condition of self-realization, the outcome of socialism, "assisted by Christianity, if men desire that; but if men do not desire that, it will develop none the less surely." As "Know thyself" was the great imperative of the ancient world, "the message of Christ was simply 'Be thyself.' That is the secret of Christ." Leading a Christ-like life involves being "perfectly and absolutely" oneself, and, as John Allen Quintus adds, Wilde's hope is that "humanity will come to appreciate beauty and live intensely" (517). Thus, for Wilde, the "true meaning of Christ is to inspire the individual to realize, through his or her own particular genius, the aspirations of the Greeks to self-perfection" (Willoughby 59).

In developing the relationship between pain, individualism, and Christianity, Wilde asserts in "The Soul of Man under Socialism" that a "Nihilist who rejects all authority because he knows authority to be evil, and who welcomes all pain, because through that he realises his personality, is a real Christian." Yet, he remarks, "pain is not the ultimate mode of perfection. It is merely provisional and a protest." In this essay, Christ is not a redeemer or "living God," nor is he motivated by a "divine calling." As Quintus observes, the moral of the essay "nevertheless fully complements the spirit of a religion that holds individual conscience over community consciousness, that favors spiritual integrity over material gain, and that looks on people of all ranks with equanimity and sympathy" (518). At the end of his essay, Wilde shifts his position in regarding "Individualism" as the "new Hellenism," as though to offer a positive conclusion to his unorthodox view of Christ and Christianity.

In many of Wilde's other works – such as "The Doer of Good," "The Selfish Giant," "The Young King," and "The Nightingale and the Rose" – Christ or Christlike figures appear as redemptive figures or as those who cannot save others. In the long poem "Humanitad," Christ symbolizes "the divinity inherent in mankind," again as a symbolic embodiment of individualism, but in *The Sphinx*, the speaker reveals his sexual fantasies before his embrace of Christianity, bidding the Sphinx to leave him: "Go thou before, / And leave me to my crucifix." In *The Ballad of Reading Gaol*, Christianity is portrayed as a forgiving religion, and Christ, Quintus remarks, is "a compassionate and forgiving god whose mercy far surpasses mankind's" (522); indeed, Christ is more orthodox in this ballad than he is in Wilde's essays or in *De Profundis*, in which Wilde asserts that Christ's "morality is all sympathy, just what morality should be" (*Letters* 485).

In contending that the secret of life is suffering, Wilde concludes that, if our world was "built out of Sorrow, it has been by the hands of Love.... Pleasure is for the beautiful body, but Pain is for the beautiful Soul" (*Letters* 474). In his radical view of Christian doctrine, Wilde believed that Christ was not, as Quintus remarks, the incarnated "Son of God who cautioned against sin," but "the son of Man who knew frailty and forgave it" (525). In an age of skepticism, in which ideals are sought, "the theological or ethical validity of Jesus gives way to the aesthetic," Willoughby states in characterizing Wilde's New Hellenism, "which means that [Christ] represents one means among many of ordering and expressing the complex energies of the self..." (61).

References: John Allen Quintus, "Christ, Christianity, and Oscar Wilde," *Texas Studies in Literature and Language* (Winter 1991); Guy Willoughby, *Art and Christhood: The Aesthetics of Oscar Wilde* (1993); Ronald Schuchard, "Wilde's Dark Angel and the Spell of Decadent Catholicism," *Rediscovering Oscar Wilde*, ed. C. George Sandulescu (1994).

CLARKE, SIR EDWARD: *See* **THE TRIALS, 1895**

"THE CLOSE OF THE 'ARTS AND CRAFTS': MR. WALTER CRANE'S LECTURE ON DESIGN"

Published: *PMG*, 30 Nov. 1888, 3; rpt. in *Miscellanies* (1908). An unsigned review of the concluding lecture at the Arts and Crafts Exhibition Society's presentation, New Gallery, Regent Street, by Walter Crane, the first president of the society. (For Wilde's other reviews of lectures in the series, see the index under the society's name.)

For the closing lecture, Walter Crane was "greeted last night by such an enormous audience that at one time the honorary secretary became alarmed for the safety of the cartoons, and many people were unable to gain admission at all." Crane began by speaking of the "two fields" of art, "aspect and adaptation": the designer was principally concerned with the latter, "his object being not literal fact but ideal beauty. With the unstudied and accidental effects of Nature the designer had nothing to do. He sought for principles, and proceeded by geometric plan and abstract line and colour."

As for naturalism, "we must remember that we see not with our eyes alone but with our whole faculties. Feeling and thought as part of sight." On a blackboard, Crane drew the naturalistic oak tree as the landscape painter might have painted it, then the decorative oak tree as the designer might have envisioned it. He showed that each of these artists looks for different things, that the designer "always makes appearance subordinate to decorative motive." The two approaches are analogous to "naturalistic presentation that the imaginative language of the poetic drama bears to the language of real life."

Much bad art, said Crane, comes from the attempt of one art to borrow from another. As Wilde reports this point: "We have sculptors who try to be pictorial, painters who aim at stage-effects, weavers who seek for pictorial motives, carvers who make Life and not Art their aim...." (At this time, Wilde himself was writing poems as though they were Whistlerian paintings with such titles as "Symphony in Yellow" and "Nocturne.") Crane then turned to Socialism, "very sensible and very quietly put," observes Wilde, who paraphrases Crane's insistence that "Art depends on Life. We cannot get it from machines. And yet machines are only bad when they are our masters."

Wilde, disagreeing with Crane's underestimate of Japanese art, regards the Japanese as decorative artists, not as naturalists:

It is true that they are often pictorial, but by the exquisite finesse of their touch, the brilliancy and beauty of their colour, their perfect knowledge of how to make a space decorative without decorating it (a point on which Mr. Crane said nothing, though it is one of the most important things in decoration), and by their keen instinct of where to place a thing, the Japanese are decorative artists of a high order.

Wilde concludes by praising the society's lectures: "Their influence for good can hardly be overestimated."

COLLECTED EDITION OF THE WORKS OF OSCAR WILDE

Published: According to Mason (459), the first six volumes of the *Collected Edition* were issued on 13 February 1908, by Methuen & Co. (London), the next five on 13 March, and the last two on 15 October. The twelfth volume, containing *The Picture of Dorian Gray*, was issued by Charles Carrington (Paris) on 16 April and added to the Methuen edition. (The 1911 volume of *The English Catalogue of Printed Books* erroneously lists the Methuen edition simply as *Works*, published between 1907 and 1909.)

Mason calls the Methuen edition, edited by Robert Ross, "The First Collected Edition," though none of the volumes contains such a designation. Moreover, the designation is misleading since a collected edition had already appeared in 1907 in 15 volumes, published by A. R. Keller & Co. (London and New York) with an introduction by Richard Le Gallienne. However, this edition is unsatisfactory and unreliable: one volume, for example, contains the translation of Barbey d'Aurevilly's *What Never Dies*, erroneously attributed to Wilde; another volume claims to be the unexpurgated version of *De Profundis*, translated from the German, but it is obviously only a portion of it; another volume contains the story "The Priest and the Acolyte" but now identified as having been written by John Francis Bloxom, the editor of the *Chameleon*, where it first appeared; and another volume contains stories and essays by Lady Wilde.

The authorized 1908 Ross edition had, on the other hand, the assistance of Stuart Mason and has remained the standard edition of Wilde's works, each volume of which is herewith listed (see separate entries for each title): 1 *The Duchess of Padua*; 2 *Salome, A Florentine Tragedy, Vera; or, The Nihilists*; 3 *Lady Windermere's Fan*; 4 *A Woman of No Importance*; 5 *An Ideal Husband*; 6 *The Importance of Being Earnest*; 7 *Lord Arthur Savile's Crime and Other Prose Pieces*; 8 *Intentions* and *The Soul of Man [under Socialism]*; 9 *Poems*; 10 *A House of Pomegranates, The Happy Prince and Other Tales*; 11 *De Profundis* [with additional letters]; 12 *The Picture of Dorian Gray*; 13 *Reviews*; 14 *Miscellanies*; [15 *For Love of the King*, added by Methuen in 1922, subsequently exposed by Mason as a fraudulant work].

Dawsons of Pall Mall (London) issued a facsimile reprint of this edition in 1969, and in 1993, Routledge issued a reprint of the edition (*For Love of the King* included), with the addition of Mason's *Bibliography of Oscar Wilde*.

"COMMONPLACE BOOK" and "NOTEBOOK KEPT AT OXFORD"

Published: *Oscar Wilde's Oxford Notebooks: A Portrait of Mind in the Making*, eds. Philip E. Smith II and Michael S. Helfand (New York and Oxford: Oxford University Press, 1989).

The notebooks reveal Wilde's extensive reading in the works of such thinkers as Plato, Aristotle, Kepler, Hume, Kant, Hegel, John Stuart Mill, Herbert Spencer, and T. H. Huxley as well as such literary figures as Aristophanes, Marlowe, Shakespeare, Milton, Wordsworth, Shelley, Swinburne, Browning, and John Addington Symonds. In their

preface, Smith and Helfand propose that their lengthy critical essay and the notebooks that follow it

describe and present a far different Oscar Wilde than the dandy, aesthete, and homosexual who has become a myth for modernist sensibilities. The Wilde of the notebooks is a precocious Victorian humanist, an Oxford undergraduate studying in the *Literae Humaniores* program and later, a postgraduate competing for a faculty position at Oxford, immersed in a year's research and writing for the Chancellor's English Essay Prize of 1879. He studies a number of controversies which concerned contemporary intellectuals; for instance, evolution and human descent, historical criticism, and the opposition of philosophical idealism and materialism.

Manuscripts: The Clark Library has the notebook titled "Commonplace Book," of 133 pages with 2 inserted smaller pages. It is likely that he wrote most of the entries in this notebook in 1878–79, though some may have been written earlier. Also at the Clark Library is the "Notebook Kept at Oxford, Containing Entries Dealing Mostly with Philosophical, Historical, and Literary Subjects," which consists of 84 pages. This notebook may have entries written as early as 1874, when Wilde entered Oxford, and as late as 1879. As Smith and Helfand write: "Neither was intended for publication, and both contain mostly quotations and paraphrases of other writers, along with Wilde's own analytical and descriptive comments, jottings, and fragmentary drafts" (1).

"COMMON SENSE IN ART"

Published: *PMG*, 8 Jan. 1887, 5; rpt. in *Reviews* (1908). An unsigned review of John Collier's *A Manual of Oil Painting* (1886).

"At this critical moment in the artistic development of England," Wilde begins, "Mr. John Collier [an English portrait painter] has come forward as the champion of common sense in art." Collier's qualities are of "a solid, indeed we may say a stolid order; he is thoroughly honest, sturdy, and downright...." According to Collier, "this art of painting is a very simple thing indeed.... It consists merely in 'the representation of natural objects on a flat surface by means of pigments.' There is nothing, he tells us, 'so very mysterious' in it after all." Wilde calls Collier's view "obviously pure common sense, and it is clear that art-definitions of this character can be comprehended by the very meanest capacity, and indeed may be said to appeal to it." As for suitable subjects for art, Collier divides them into two kinds, ancient and modern, as Wilde describes them: "Modern are more healthy than ancient subjects," but since picturesqueness is more pictorial than the commonplace, the painter should go to the "rural poor" and for pathos to the London slums. For ancient subjects, he should go to Greek and Roman mythology; if he is "a mediocre painter," he should go to the Old Testament, "a recommendation [Wilde adds] that many of our Royal Academicians seem to have already carried out." This review was clearly written with tongue in cheek, particularly when Wilde discusses the arrangement, according to Collier, with a sitter's relations before the painter begins the picture: "If they want a profile, he must do them a profile; if they require a full face, he must give them a full face, and he should be careful also to get their opinion as to the costume the sitter should wear, and 'the sort of expression he should put on.' 'After all,' says Mr. Collier pathetically, 'it is they who have to live with the picture.'"

CONDER, CHARLES (1868–1909)

An artist whose reputation rests on his designs for fans and for water colors painted on silk, Conder lived much of his life in France, where he studied painting. When he first met Wilde is unknown, but in June 1897, after Wilde's release from prison, Conder went to Berneval-sur-Mer to dine with him. Conder was often in Wilde's company during that summer. Wilde, who admired his work, called him "a sort of Corot of the sunlight" (*Letters* 621), but he underestimated Conder's capacity to handle his own affairs: "Dear Conder! With what exquisite subtlety he goes about persuading someone to give him a hundred francs for a fan, for which he was fully prepared to pay three hundred!" (*Letters* 592n2). John Rothenstein writes that although Conder "was too unreliable and disorderly in his habits to be good at business, he was far from indifferent to the financial aspect of his art, and the notion of making a fortune by selling his pictures possessed him early" (148).

In May 1898, Wilde remarks to Robert Ross that

Conder – "very vague and mist-like" – is in Paris (*Letters* 734). Arthur Symons, who had invited Conder to contribute to the *Savoy*, recalls the quality in Conder that puzzled Wilde: "His conversation was never wonderful; he was often silent; he loved to hear others talk; he rarely said anything that was really original" (185). Later in May, Wilde writes to Ross that he and Conder had, at Wilde's insistence, dined at an inexpensive restaurant: "...this was the only occasion I managed to make him economise at all" (*Letters* 739). On another occasion, Wilde visited Conder at Chantemerle in late September 1898. Conder wrote to a friend that Wilde was "much more serious than when we saw him in Dieppe – very depressed at times poor fellow. He says with so much sorrow [that] he can never go into society again and feels I think that he is rather old for the volatile poets of the '*quartier*'" (qtd. in Ellmann 567/533). When Wilde died, Conder's name was on the wreath that Robert Ross placed on the grave.

In his final years, Conder suffered from mental illness. When he was taken to Brighton on one occasion, Arthur Symons describes Conder's disturbed reaction: "...he gets violent, begins to rave, raves for forty-eight hours, without food, till the blood drops from his mouth, he is reduced to a skeleton, turns almost green" (188). After being confined in various sanatoriums, he died on 9 April 1909.

References: John Rothenstein, *The Life and Death of Conder* (1938); Karl Beckson, ed., *The Memoirs of Arthur Symons: Life and Art in the 1890s* (1977).

CRIMINAL LAW AMENDMENT ACT: *See* LABOUCHERE, HENRY

"THE CRITIC AS ARTIST"

Published: First appeared as "The True Function and Value of Criticism; With Some Remarks on the Importance of Doing Nothing: A Dialogue" in *Nineteenth Century* 28 (July and Sept. 1890): 123–47 (Part I) and 435–59 (Part II); rev. as "The Critic as Artist" with the subtitle "With Some Remarks upon the Importance of Doing Nothing" for Part I and with the subtitle "With Some Remarks upon the Importance of Discussing Everything" for Part II in *Intentions* (1891).

Isobel Murray notes that the original title of this essay implies that Wilde was responding to

"THE CRITIC AS ARTIST"

Mathew Arnold's essay "The Function of Criticism at the Present Time" in *Essays in Criticism: First Series* (l865), in which criticism is defined as "the endeavour...to see the object as in itself it really is"; Wilde is particularly opposed to Arnold's conventional attitude that "the critical power is of lower rank than the creative." Murray also suggests that the names of the two figures in Wilde's dialogue – Gilbert and Ernest – are not idly employed: "'Gilbert' immediately recalls Sir William Schwenk Gilbert, author of the *Bab Ballads* and librettist of the Gilbert and Sullivan operas [particularly *Patience*, which satirizes Aestheticism], a master of extravaganza and satirical nonsense. 'Ernest' is doomed by his name to be the loser here: Wilde consistently preached the Importance of *not* being Earnest" (*Oscar Wilde* 598–99).

The Dialogue: Part I is set in the library of a house in Piccadilly overlooking Green Park. While Gilbert is at the piano, Ernest, somewhat amused, mentions a volume of reminiscences that he has found on his friend's table: "They are generally written by people who have either entirely lost their memories, or have never done anything worth remembering...." In life, says Gilbert, "egotism is not without its attractions. When people talk to us about others they are usually dull. When they talk to us about themselves they are nearly always interesting...." Ernest turns to the question of the use of criticism: "Why cannot the artist be left alone, to create a new world if he wishes it, or, if not, to shadow forth the world which we already know...? ...Why should those who cannot create take upon themselves to estimate the value of creative work? What do they know about it? If a man's work is easy to understand, an explanation is unnecessary...." Gilbert completes Ernest's sentence: "And if his work is incomprehensible, an explanation is wicked."

Gilbert regards Robert Browning as a great poet: though "he turned language into ignoble clay, he made from it men and women that live. He is the most Shakespearean creature since Shakespeare. If Shakespeare could sing with myriad lips, Browning could stammer through a thousand mouths.... The only man who can touch the hem of his garment is George Meredith. Meredith is a prose Browning, and so is Browning [for the source of this droll remark, see Horst Schroeder in References below]. He used poetry as a medium for writing in prose." Ernest contends that in "the best

days of art there were no art-critics," and citing the artists of ancient Greece, he argues that "there were no silly art congresses bringing provincialism to the provinces and teaching the mediocrity how to mouth. By the Ilyssus, my dear Gilbert, there were no tedious magazines about art, in which the industrious prattle of what they do not understand." Gilbert's riposte is that the Greeks were

a nation of art-critics.... For, after all, what is our primary debt to the Greeks? Simply the critical spirit. And, this spirit, which they exercised on questions of religion and science, of ethics and metaphysics, of politics and education, they exercised on questions of art also, and, indeed, of the two supreme and highest arts, they have left us the most flawless system of criticism that the world has ever seen.... Life and Literature, life and the perfect expression of life.

Having discussed Aristotle's *Poetics* ("one perfect little work of aesthetic criticism") and Plato's dialogues ("it is as a critic of Beauty that Plato is destined to live"), Gilbert concludes: "Whatever, in fact, is modern in our life we owe to the Greeks. Whatever is an anachronism is due to mediaevalism. It is the Greeks who have given us the whole system of art-criticism....the material they criticised with most care was, as I have already said, language.... If the Greeks had criticised nothing but language, they would still have been the great art-critics of the world. To know the principles of the highest art is to know the principles of all the arts" (Wilde's conviction concerning the aesthetic unity of the arts). While conceding that the Greeks were a nation of art critics, Ernest feels "a little sorry for them. For the creative faculty is higher than the critical. There is really no comparison between them." Gilbert argues, however, that without the "critical faculty, there is no artistic creation at all, worthy of the name." (Here, Gilbert launches one of the major themes of the essay.)

Matthew Arnold, Gilbert continues, defined literature as a "criticism of life," not a very felicitous expression, but "it showed how keenly he recognised the importance of the critical element in all creative work." Without self-consciousness, there is no fine art, and "self-consciousness and the critical spirit are one." Focusing on the individual creator, Gilbert argues that "the longer one studies life and literature, the more strongly one feels that behind everything that is wonderful stands the individual, and that it is not the moment that makes the man, but the man who creates the age."

In discussing the nature of action, Gilbert remarks: "What is termed Sin is an essential element of progress. Without it the world would stagnate, or grow old, or become colourless. By its curiosity Sin increases the experience of the race. Through its intensified assertion of individualism, it saves us from monotony of type" (Wilde repeated such ideas, in much the same phraseology, in his essay "The Soul of Man under Socialism"). "Self-denial is simply a method by which man arrests his progress, and self-sacrifice a survival of the mutilation of the savage...."

Returning to the relationship between art and criticism, Gilbert again contends that the latter is itself an art. Indeed, criticism is, he says, both "creative and independent." That is, criticism is "no more to be judged by any low standard of imitation or resemblance than is the work of poet or sculptor. The critic occupies the same relation to the work of art that he criticises as the artist does to the visible world of form and colour, or the unseen world of passion and of thought." When Ernest asks whether criticism is really a creative art, Gilbert answers that "criticism [is] a creation within a creation.... I would say that the highest Criticism, being the purest form of personal impression, is in its way more creative than creation, as it has least reference to any standard external to itself, and is, in fact, its own reason for existing...." Then, adopting the aesthetic of impressionism, Gilbert argues that the highest criticism is "the record of one's own soul. It is more fascinating than history, as it is concerned simply with oneself.... It is the only civilised form of autobiography, as it deals not with the events, but with the thoughts of one's life...with the spiritual moods and imaginative passions of the mind." The critic's "sole aim," then, is "to chronicle his own impressions."

Echoing Arnold's remark that "the proper aim of Criticism is to see the object as in itself it really is," Gilbert calls such an aesthetic "a very serious error, and takes no cognisance of Criticism's most perfect form, which is in its essence purely subjective, and seeks to reveal its own secret and not the secret of another. For the highest Criticism deals with art not as expressive but as impressive purely."

Citing Pater's famous description in *Studies in the History of the Renaissance* of Leonardo's *Mona Lisa*, referred to by Pater as *La Gioconda* – "She is older than the rocks among which she sits; like the vampire, she has been dead many times, and learned the secrets of the grave" – Gilbert asks whether anyone cares that Pater has put into the portrait something that the painter never dreamed of: "And so the picture becomes more wonderful to us than it really is, and reveals to us a secret of which, in truth, it knows nothing...." Criticism, then, "treats the work of art simply as a starting-point for a new creation." In summarizing Gilbert's view concerning the nature of criticism, Ernest alters Arnold's definition of criticism: "...the primary aim of the critic is to see the object as in itself it really is not: that is your theory, I believe?"

Gilbert affirms Ernest's remark, adding that "the critic reproduces the work that he criticises in a mode that is never imitative, and part of whose charm may really consist in the rejection of resemblance, and shows us in this way not merely the meaning but also the mystery of Beauty, and, by transforming each art into literature, solves once for all the problem of Art's unity." With this remark, Part I concludes.

Part II begins with Ernest's determination to continue his dialogue with Gilbert on the critic and criticism by asking whether the critic is sometimes a "real interpreter." Gilbert responds with the proviso that the critic can choose to be an interpreter by passing from his "synthetic impression of the work of art as a whole, to an analysis or exposition of the work itself, and in this lower sphere, as I hold it to be, there are many delightful things to be said and done. Yet his object will not always be to explain the work of art. He may seek rather to deepen its mystery, to raise round it, and round its maker, that mist of wonder which is dear to both gods and worshippers alike."

Gilbert insists, however, that the critic must also be learned in the history of the literature he is involved with, providing, as an example, the fact that the critic must learn Shakespeare's "true position in the history of European drama and the drama of the world." Moreover, "only by intensifying his own personality" can the critic interpret the personality and work of others: "If you wish to understand others you must intensify your own individualism." Here, Wilde extends the concept of "the critic" to include, for example, the actor and musician, who interpret the written word or composition through gesture, voice, or performance to reveal the playwright's or the composer's meaning. And since, Gilbert argues, "art springs from personality," from the "meeting of the two [that is, the creator of a work of art and its "critic" or "interpreter" – actor, singer, etc.] comes right interpretative criticism." As civilization progresses, he continues, and it becomes more "highly organized, the elect spirits of each age, the critical and cultured spirits, will grow less and less interested in actual life, and *will seek to gain their impressions almost entirely from what Art has touched.* For Life is terribly deficient in form" (Wilde's argument in "The Decay of Lying").

Responds Ernest: "Must we go, then, to Art for everything?" The expected reply: "For everything. Because Art does not hurt us. The tears that we shed at a play are a type of the exquisite sterile emotions that it is the function of Art to awaken.... But the sorrow with which Art fills us both purifies and initiates, if I may quote once more from the great art-critic of the Greeks [Aristotle's *Poetics*]. It is through Art, and through Art only, that we can realize our perfection; through Art, and through Art only, that we can shield ourselves from the sordid perils of actual existence."

When Ernest charges that such notions imply that "all art is immoral," Gilbert expounds a central doctrine of Aestheticism: "...emotion for the sake of emotion is the aim of art, and emotion for the sake of action is the aim of life, and of that practical organization of life that we call society. Society, which is the beginning of and basis of morals, exists simply for the concentration of human energy...to ensure its own continuance and healthy stability...." Contemplation, Gilbert argues, is "the gravest sin of which any citizen can be guilty" in society, whereas "in the opinion of the highest culture it is the proper occupation of man." Ernest asks: "We exist, then, to do nothing?" To which Gilbert responds: "It is to do nothing that the elect exists."

Gilbert then expresses one of the central ideas of the essay concerning the contemplative life, "the life that has for its aim not *doing* but *being*" (an idea that Isobel Murray traces to Chuang Tzŭ;

indeed, Wilde had enthusiastically reviewed a book on this Chinese philosopher: see "The Chinese Sage"). Gilbert proceeds beyond *being* to *becoming* as the aim of life, for that is "what the critical spirit can give us.... We might make ourselves spiritual by detaching ourselves from action, and become perfect by the rejection of energy.... For action of every kind belongs to the sphere of ethics. The aim of art is simply to create a mood."

In turning to the relationship between objective and subjective work, Gilbert argues that it is one of "external form merely," for "All artistic creation is absolutely subjective." He cites Corot's remark that the landscape that he looked at was "but a mood of his own mind." The "most objective form," Gilbert insists, is "the most subjective in matter" – from which idea follows one of Wilde's most famous epigrams: "Man is least himself when he talks in his own person. Give him a mask, and he will tell you the truth." In talking about the critic's sincerity, Gilbert insists that the "true critic" will always be sincere in his "devotion to the principle of beauty, but he will seek for beauty in every age and in each school...." Then Gilbert utters a remark that also appears in Chapter 11 of *The Picture of Dorian Gray*: "What people call insincerity is simply a method by which we can multiply our personalities."

Extending his argument from Art to life, Gilbert regards "Form" as everything: "It is the secret of life. Find expression for a sorrow, and it will become dear to you." Returning to Art, he continues: "...it is Form that creates not merely the critical temperament, but also the aesthetic instinct that reveals to one all things under their conditions of beauty."

In considering the future of criticism, Gilbert deplores the current state of literature: "He who would stir us now by fiction must either give us an entirely new background, or reveal to us the soul of man in its innermost workings." He cites Kipling in a famous judgment of his *Plain Tales from the Hills*: "...one feels as if one were seated under a palm-tree reading life by superb flashes of vulgarity." Further, Kipling is "a genius who drops his aspirates.... He is our first authority on the second-rate, and has seen marvellous things through keyholes...."

In summing up the significance of criticism, Gilbert contends that "by concentration, [criticism] makes culture possible," an idea that he acknowledges in Matthew Arnold. Adopting an extreme aesthetic position, however, Gilbert declares: "To discern the beauty of a thing is the finest point to which we can arrive. Even a colour-sense is more important, in the development of the individual, than a sense of right and wrong." Having attained "that perfection of which the saints have dreamed, the perfection of those to whom sin is impossible," Gilbert envisions a mode of thought and passion that can do the soul no harm. Finally, he concludes that the "Critical Spirit and the World-Spirit are one." A person possessing this spirit will look out "upon the world and know its secret. By contact with divine things, he will become divine. His will be the perfect life, and his only."

Early Reviews: See *Intentions*.

Manuscripts: The Hyde Collection has drafts of the original essay, and the Clark Library has the complete revised MS. in 152 leaves with its original title.

References: Isobel Murray, "Oscar Wilde's Absorption of 'Influences': The Case History of Chuang Tzŭ," *Durham University Journal* (Dec. 1971); Edward Watson, "The Critic as Artist," *ELT* 27:3 (1984); William Buckler, "Building a Bulwark against Despair: The Critic as Artist,'" *ELT* 32:3 (1989); Zhang Longxi, "The Critical Legacy of Oscar Wilde," *Texas Studies in Literature and Language* (Spring 1988), rpt. in Regenia Gagnier, ed., *Critical Essays on Oscar Wilde*, (1991); Horst Schroeder, "The Robert Browning Passage in Oscar Wilde's 'The Critic as Artist,'" *English Language Notes* (Sept. 1994); Lawrence Danson, "The Critic as Artist," *Wilde's Intentions*: *The Artist in His Criticism* (1997).

"CYPRIOTS OR FOLK MAKING FOR MALTA"

Not published in Wilde's lifetime, this fragmentary poem of 26 lines was probably written at the same time that Wilde was at work on *Ravenna* – that is, around 1877–78, for both poems have similar passages.

The opening two lines ("Like a flame-bearded beacon seen from far / By storm-vexed sailors...") are almost identical with lines in *Ravenna* (142–43). This lengthy Homeric simile, employing the imagery of rescue by "some God / Pitying their fortunes landward turns their prow," is completed by the lines "So bright and welcome is thy face to me, / Constrained to wander on a stormier deep / Than is the wild Atlantic." The fragment ends by the speaker's resolve not to lie "in some sick port.../ Where rat and rot and scurvy may creep in" but to "launch / Into the white-plumed battle of the waves / And seek new land...."

Manuscript: The Clark Library has a notebook containing this poem with an early draft of *Vera; or, The Nihilists*, completed in 1880.

D

"LA DAME JAUNE"

Not published in Wilde's lifetime, this lyric poem (its title meaning "The Yellow Lady") is related to, though not identical with, two other Wilde poems, "Remorse: (A Study in Saffron)" and "Symphony in Yellow," the dominant color in all three associated with Decadence (see entry), here capitalized to suggest the avant-garde's new aesthetic.

This poem of three quatrains describes a young lady undressing, attention paid by the speaker, among other things, to the color harmonies, such as "her jonquil-coloured gown." In the second stanza, "She loosed her lemon-satin stays, / She took a carven ivory comb, / Her hair crawled down like yellow foam...." Her thick locks, "like a mass / Of honey" drips from the pin, each "separate hair" like the thin "gold thread within a Venice glass."

Manuscript: A MS. of the poem is quoted in the auction catalogue of the American Art Association for the sale of John Quinn's library, 8–9 February 1927.

DANDYISM

Though the term *dandy* is traceable to the late 18th century, its current meaning in literary discourse is more closely associated with the idea as it developed in England, then in France, extending from the elegantly dressed George "Beau" Brummell (1778–1840) in the early 19th century to the aesthetically philosophical poses of such figures as Wilde and Max Beerbohm at the end of the century. Brummell was devoted to the perfection of self, and his "arrogant superiority" – as Ellen Moers writes – was an "affirmation of the aristocratic principle" that opposed bourgeois mediocrity (17).

Ironically, Brummell, a bourgeois "gentleman" as dandy, who dominated Regency society, displayed his superiority over an aristocracy in decline. As a wit, Brummell revealed the witlessness of others. Brummell's influence pervades such novels as Disraeli's *Vivian Grey* (1826) and

Bulwer-Lytton's *Pelham; or the Adventures of a Gentleman* (1828); in France, where anglomania was already prominent, *le dandysme* achieved a widespread following as well as a different form after Brummell fled there in 1816 to escape payment of debts.

In *Du Dandysme et de Georges Brummell* (1845), "the pivotal work upon which the history of the dandy tradition turns" (Moers 256), Jules Barbey d'Aurevilly (1808–89) regards dandyism as "a complete theory of life" that "springs from the unending struggle between propriety and boredom" in a declining society: "Accordingly, one of the consequences and principal characteristics...of Dandyism is always to produce the unexpected, that which could not logically be anticipated by those accustomed to the yoke of rules" (31–33). Like all dandies, Barbey continues, Brummell "preferred astonishing to pleasing," but "his indolence forbad his being lively, for to be lively is to be excited; to be excited is to care about something, and to care about anything is to shew oneself inferior" (56). Barbey's "original" conception of the dandy, writes Moers,

> is to make dandyism available as an intellectual pose. The dandy is equated with the artist; society thus ought to pay him tribute. Brummell is indeed the archetype of all artists, for his art was one with his life. His achievements in costume and manner were living masterpieces.... Brummell was born to rule, and he ruled with insulting wit and cruel irony....Barbey points out that the dandy's distinction, almost his responsibility, is his abhorrence of uniformity, mediocrity and vulgarity (263–64)

Finally, Barbey writes that the dandy embodies "twofold and multiple natures, of an undecidedly intellectual sex, their Grace...heightened by their Power, their Power by their Grace; they are the hermaphrodites of History, not of Fable, and Alcibiades [the Athenian general and statesman, who appears as Socrates's would-be seducer in Plato's *Symposium*] was their supreme type, among the most beautiful of the nations" (78).

Proceeding from Brummell's importance in the development of 19th-century intellectual dandyism and Barbey's seminal essay on its principles, Baudelaire emerged as perhaps the century's most important theorist of dandyism. Théophile Gautier, who knew him, observed that, in his aristocracy of spirit and severity of dress, Baudelaire "was a dandy lost in Bohemia, but preserving his rank and his manners and that cult of self which characterizes the man imbued with the principles of Brummell" (qtd. in Moers 273). His indulgence in alcohol and opium were, as Moers writes, "justified by the elevation of Boredom to the status of an all-powerful divinity.... Disgust with the commonness of a middle-class world was at the root of his aesthetic of control" (274–75).

In *Le Peintre de la vie moderne* (1863), Baudelaire developed the idea that life and art were inseparable and that, in addition to pose and gesture, modernity in art is manifest by the depiction of modern dress, clothes revealing its own "moral and spiritual nature." In the section in praise of cosmetics ("Éloge du maquillage"), Baudelaire argues that modernity in art is also concerned with artifice – that which improves on nature – for "All that is beautiful and noble is the result of reason and calculation.... Evil is done effortlessly and naturally by fate; the good is always the product of some art."

In another section of his work ("Le Dandy"), Baudelaire develops his conception of the pure dandy, who, in his superiority to the artist, is the embodiment of modernity. The dandy conceals his abhorrence of 19th-century vulgarity and mediocrity under a mask of disdain while focusing on achieving elegance with such artistic control that he transforms himself into something original. The dandy, then, confronts a doomed society with the challenge of superiority: "Dandyism," Baudelaire wrote, "is the last burst of heroism in the midst of decadence" – by which he meant, ironically, the rise of democracy. Against the optimism of the age, he insisted on original sin, and against the sentimentality in popular art, he "posited a dandyism of despair" (Moers 283). Indeed, he regarded dandyism as "a kind of religion."

By the 1890s, dandyism had become fused with Decadence, for artifice in manner and artifice in art were now inseparable: as Moers remarks, dandyism involved the "worship of the town and the artificial; grace, elegance, the art of the pose, sophistication and the mask. The wit of epigram and paradox was called upon to confound the bourgeois" (288). In his "Phrases and Philosophies for the Use of the Young," for example, Wilde wrote: "The first duty in life is to be as artificial as possible," ignoring Baudelaire's remark that virtue was the product of artifice. But while adopting certain elements of the dandiacal tradition, Wilde also radically transformed others. The neophyte dandy Dorian Gray, who eventually commits murder, "looked," we are told, "on evil simply as a mode through which he could realize his conception of the beautiful" – a rejection of Baudelaire's insistence on original sin. The dandiacal Lord Henry, clearly contemptuous of vulgarity and sentimentality, likewise rejects bourgeois morality: self-absorbed, he regards Dorian as his creation, whom he does not fully know or understand.

In his plays, Wilde created dandies whose destiny was not only to maintain a pose of superiority but also to involve themselves directly in the action of the plot rather than existing, as does Lord Henry, in mere idleness. At the same time, Wilde developed his unique form of dandyism, based, as Arthur Ganz observes, on the idea that the "secret" of art lay in "the achievement of perfect form": "He took form, the basis of art, turned it into a philosophy of life in which esthetics replaces ethics and introduced it into his plays cloaked with the elegance and wit of nineteenth-century dandyism" (43). Thus, his dandies employ aesthetic judgments precisely when audiences expect moral judgments, as when the female dandy in *An Ideal Husband*, Mabel Chiltern, objects to a remark concerning the idleness of the dandiacal Lord Goring: "Why, he rides in the Row at ten o'clock in the morning, goes to the Opera three times a week, changes his clothes at least five times a day, and dines out every night of the season. You don't call that leading an idle life, do you?" In the course of the play's action, Lord Goring not only employs wit to triumph over dullards but also acts to save Sir Robert Chiltern from the wicked Mrs. Cheveley.

In *A Woman of No Importance*, the villainous Lord Illingsworth, convinced that someday the dandy will achieve power (echoes of Brummell and Disraeli), reveals his belief to his illegitimate son: "A man who can dominate a London dinner-table can dominate the world. The future belongs to the dandy. It is the exquisites who are going to rule." Indeed, in *The Importance of Being Earnest*, the "exquisites" in Wilde's play are all touched by the spirit of dandyism: even the arch-Philistine Lady Bracknell employs, on a number of occasions, aesthetic (or, at least, anti-Philistine) judgments rather than moral judgments, for as Gwendolen remarks, "In matters of grave importance, style, not sincerity, is the vital thing." Because the pervasive dandiacal wit throughout the play makes it unique, it is "a kind of dandiacal Utopia, a world of perfect form" (Ganz 49).

References: Jules Barbey d'Aurevilly, *Of Dandyism and of George Brummell*, trans. Douglas Ainslie (1897; rpt. as *Dandyism*, 1988); Ellen Moers, *The Dandy: Brummel to Beerbohm* (1960); Arthur Ganz, "The Meaning of *The Importance of Being Earnest*," *Modern Drama* (May 1963); Domna Stanton, *The Aristocrat as Art: A Study of the Honnête Homme and the Dandy in 17th- and 19th-Century French Literature* (1980); Regenia Gagnier, "Dandies and Gentlemen," *Idylls of the Marketplace: Oscar Wilde and the Victorian Public* (1986); Jessica Feldman, *Gender on the Divide: The Dandy in Modernist Literature* (1993).

DAVRAY, HENRY-D. (1873–1944)

A French journalist, translator, and author who reviewed books in English for the *Mercure de France*, Davray was, wrote Wilde, "a charming fellow besides being a good English scholar" (*Letters* 647). When Davray expressed his admiration for *The Ballad of Reading Gaol*, Wilde responded around 1 March 1898 that he was "touched and gratified" by his appreciation and that he would like him to translate it, "for no French man of letters can render English as you can..." (*Letters* 709). When arrangements were completed for Davray to undertake the translation, Wilde offered to help with it: "Of course, there are many words, relating to prison life, for which the proper French *prison* equivalents must be found: words that, though not *argot*, are still *technical*. I am always free, so pray let me know when I can see you, on the completion of the poem" (*Letters* 713).

Writing to Robert Ross late in March 1898, Wilde told him that he had gone over the translation with Davray: "It is a very difficult thing to translate, as, unluckily and oddly, Davray has never been in prison, so knows nothing of prison-terms" (*Letters* 727). In April, Wilde sent him a list of suggested revisions for the proofs and expressed his great satisfaction with the transla-

tion: "C'est admirablement fait, par un admirable et parfait artiste" (*Letters* 729). The translation appeared in the May issue of *Mercure de France* and in book form that autumn.

Wilde and Davray maintained their friendship after the appearance of the translation. In the *Revue blanche* (1 May 1899), Davray's translation of five poems in prose appeared. On the day of Wilde's death, Davray attended the funeral at Bagneux cemetery. In 1928, he published *Oscar Wilde: La Tragédie finale*, which is not, as the title suggests, a coherent narrative; rather, the book contains miscellaneous sections of random reminiscences, discussion of Wilde's correspondence, and a lengthy account of the discredited *For Love of the King*, attributed to Wilde.

DEATH OF WILDE

Since Wilde's death on 30 November 1900, the circumstances surrounding his reported conversion to Roman Catholicism on his death bed and the reputed cause of his death have been subjects of uncertainty and disagreement. Rev. Edmund Burke, in his account of Wilde's last hours, draws upon the papers of Father Cuthbert Dunne (1869–1950), the Irish-born priest attached to the Passionist Church, St. Joseph's in Paris, who had ministered to Wilde. After Wilde's death, Father Dunne entered into the register of St. Joseph's the following, dated 29 November: "To-day Oscar Wilde, lying *in extremis* at the Hôtel d'Alsace, 13 Rue des Beaux-Arts, Paris, was conditionally baptised by me. He died the following day, having received at my hands the Sacrament of Extreme Unction." Wilde's attraction to Roman Catholicism dates from his student days at Oxford, and Rev. Burke quotes part of an interview granted by Wilde to John Clifford Millage, Paris correspondent of the *Daily Chronicle* about three weeks before he died:

"He turned to religious subjects," says Millage, "and muttered most savagely: 'Much of my moral obliquity is due to the fact that my father would not allow me to become a Catholic. The artistic side of the Church and the fragrance of its teaching would have cured my degeneracies. I intend to be received before long.'" Concluding his report, which was written a few days after Wilde's death, Millage observed: "Oscar Wilde tried to articulate the prayers which accompany Extreme Unction and his death-bed was one of repentence." (Burke 39)

More than once, Wilde had informed his close friend and later literary executor Robert Ross that he wished to become a Catholic, but Ross – himself a Catholic – advised his friend to wait. Of this advice, Wilde reportedly said: "I wish indeed to enter the Catholic Church, but at every approach I make, Robert Ross stands at the door like an angel with a flaming sword and drives me away" (qtd. in Burke 39). Ross, present with Father Dunne during the last hours, wrote to Adela Schuster on 23 December 1900, to inform her that he had followed Wilde's wish to have a priest attend to him in his final moments and that Wilde was conscious during this time:

When I went for the priest to come to his death bed he was quite conscious and raised his hand in response to questions and *satisfied* the priest Father Cuthbert Dunn of the Passionists. It was the morning before he died and for about 3 hours understood what was going on (and knew I had come from the South in response to a telegram), that he was given the last sacraments. (*Letters* 859)

Rev. Burke quotes Father Dunne's own account:

[Wilde] was unable to articulate but endeavoured to recite the acts of Faith, etc., suggested, and showed signs of a sincere conversion.... As the man was in a semi-comatose condition, I did not venture to administer Holy Viaticum [Holy Eucharist when given to one in danger of death]; still, I must add that he could be roused and was roused from this state in my presence. When roused, he gave signs of being inwardly conscious.... Indeed I was fully satisfied that he understood me when told that I was about to receive him into the Catholic Church and gave him the Last Sacraments.... And when I repeated close to his ear the Holy Names, the Acts of Contrition, Faith, Hope and Charity, with acts of humble resignation to the Will of God, he tried all through to say the words after me. (40–41)

Father Dunne had visited Wilde several times to console him, when he observed him closely. Writes Rev. Burke: "...what [Father Dunne] saw confirmed his first impression that, although the power of speech had failed, Oscar Wilde still retained a large measure of consciousness and coherence" (41). When Wilde died at two o'clock in the afternoon on 30 November, Ross sent Father Dunne a note informing him of the end. Father Dunne's account concludes with the conviction that Wilde "turned to God for pardon and for the healing grace of the Sacraments in the end, and died a child of the Catholic Church" (qtd. in Burke 43).

The cause of Wilde's death, according to Ellmann, was the result of an advanced stage of syphilis, originally contracted when Wilde was a student at Oxford, reportedly from a woman prostitute (92/89). Ellmann's "view of Wilde's medical history" relies on statements by Reginald Turner and Robert Ross, the certificate of the doctor in charge during Wilde's final illness, as well as Arthur Ransome's *Oscar Wilde* (1912) and Frank Harris's *Oscar Wilde: His Life and Confessions* (1916), both books attributing Wilde's death to syphilis (Ellmann 92n/88n).

A major problem in Ellmann's assertion is that, when Wilde died, he would have reached the tertiary stage of syphilis (which Ransome mentions as the source of Wilde's meningitis, though he omits it in his second edition). The tertiary stage – more than 25 years after the alleged initial infection – usually manifests itself in skin lesions, tumors in subcutaneous tissue and in internal organs, with possible paralysis, blindness, or psychosis. None of these symptoms was reported by the doctors in attendance, nor was syphilis mentioned: the recorded diagnosis was "encephalitic meningitis" (Ellmann 582/547).

In disputing Ellmann's view, Merlin Holland remarks that cerebral meningitis, a "classic complication arising from a disease or inflammation of the middle ear," had been treated some weeks before Wilde's death. Holland adds:

There is no mention of syphilitic meningitis and even if there had been, according to one modern venereologist, such a diagnosis probably would not have been worth the paper it was written on. Tertiary syphilis is characterised by the slow atrophy of certains parts of the body, not by the inflammatory symptoms and high fever from which Wilde was suffering. (35)

Alluding to two discussions of Wilde's alleged syphilis by doctors in two respected medical journals, Holland concludes: "While exercising caution in making posthumous diagnoses they and other modern doctors have expressed serious doubts that syphilis was the cause of Wilde's death" (34).

References: Edmund Burke, "Oscar Wilde: The Final Scene," *London Magazine* (May 1961); Macdonald Critchley, "The Death of Oscar Wilde," *British Medical Journal* 1 (1988); Merlin Holland, "What Killed Oscar Wilde?," *Spectator* (24/31 Dec. 1988); Macdonald Critchley, "Oscar Wilde's Fatal Illness: A Mystery Unshrouded," *Encyclopedia Britannica Medical and Health Annual* (1990); J. B. Lyons, "The Death of Oscar Wilde: A Post-Mortem," *What Did I Die Of?* (1991); J. B. Lyons, "Oscar Wilde's Final Illness," *Irish Studies Review* 11 (1995).

DECADENCE

The term *decadence* (with a lower-case "d") has, for centuries, implied a "falling away" from a standard of artistic and moral excellence (the meaning adopted by Victorian Establishment critics). However, in late 19th-century France and Britain, Decadence (as capitalized by recent critics) implies a new aesthetic vision with its own integrity. It had its origins in France in the 1830s, when writers, reacting to Romanticism, transformed the pejorative meanings of decadence (as used to characterize declining civilizations of the past) into a startling term of positive value. As Koenraad W. Swart writes of these early Decadents, who developed the new aesthetic:

Their unconventional and partly perverse mentality, repudiating traditional morality, rejecting all social restraints, defying society, and taking a morbid delight in corruption, obviously constituted a radical reversal of almost all earlier attitudes towards historical decline. It was this consciously adopted ideology of Satanism, individualism, and estheticism that formed the most important legacy of French Romanticism to the so-called Decadent movement in literature at the end of the nine-

teenth century. (77)

In writing of the subject matter and themes associated with Decadence in 19th-century France, Ruth Z. Temple refers to

preferences in subject matter – which reflect the artist's situation and his beliefs – the city, the man-made, the artificial in preference to the natural (*le fard* [make-up], patchouli [a penetrating perfume]), what is sordid or trivial rather than what is obviously beautiful or good. Preferences in theme, such as boredom raised to the intensity of spleen (*le mal fin-de-siècle*), disorientation in an alien world.... (220)

Verlaine's sonnet on weariness, "Langueur" (1883), extends its significance to cultural history: "Je suis l'Empire à la fin de la décadence...."

Such works as Gautier's novel of perverse sexuality, *Mademoiselle de Maupin* (1835), Baudelaire's "Praise of Cosmetics" (1863), and Huysmans's *A Rebours* (1884) – which R. K. R. Thornton calls "the Bible of Decadence" (21) – celebrate artifice (rather than Nature, as the Romantics had done) and depict states of mind at variance with bourgeois proprieties. The use of cosmetics, symbolizing a rejection of nature, as in Baudelaire, was not an exclusively 19th-century phenomenon, for in ancient Rome, as L. P. Wilkinson writes, cosmetics "were considered in strait-laced circles to be a shade unhealthy or improper," for among the Classical writers, the prevailing opinion was that "nature is right and art is wrong." Ovid, however, defended cosmetics in his prologue to the *Medicamina faciei femineae* (ca. 1 BC).

Max Beerbohm also defended cosmetics – albeit ironically and playfully – in his "Defence of Cosmetics" in the *Yellow Book* (April 1894), reprinted as "The Pervasion of Rouge" in his *Works of Max Beerbohm* (1896). In response to attacks on the essay, he published a letter to the editor in Volume II of the *Yellow Book* (July 1894) in order to extend his facetiousness further. In the process, he approaches a good definition of Decadence:

There are signs that our English literature has reached that point, when, like the literatures of all the nations that have been, it must fall at length into the hands of the decadents. The qualities that I tried in my essay to travesty – paradox and marivaudage, lassitude, a love of horror and all unusual things, a love of argot and archaism and mysteries of style – are not these displayed, some by one, some by another of les jeunes écrivains? Who knows but that Artifice is in truth at our gates and that soon she may pass through our streets?

Following Baudelaire in giving expression to the superiority of artifice, Wilde in "The Decay of Lying" wrote: "Art is our spirited protest, our gallant attempt to teach nature her proper place." Indeed, Wilde wittily contended, Nature imitates Art far more than Art imitates Nature. (Ovid had long before advanced this idea while describing a grotto of Diana in the Actaeon section of Book III in the *Metamorphoses*.) Wilde was also influenced by Huysmans's *A Rebours*, which, he admitted in his first trial, was the "novel without a plot" mentioned in Chapter 10 of *The Picture of Dorian Gray*, which depicts Dorian Gray's fascination with the "passions and modes of thought that belonged to every century except his own."

In the *Harper's New Monthly Magazine* (Nov. 1893), Arthur Symons's "The Decadent Movement in Literature" challenged Establishment critics for their condemnation of Decadence by contending that Symbolism and Impressionism were "two main branches" of the Decadent Movement (a more coherent "movement" in France than in England, for *les décadents* had published their own periodical, *Le Décadent* in 1886). By a transvaluation of values intended to startle readers, he wrote that Decadence

has all the qualities that mark the end of great periods, the qualities that we find in the Greek, the Latin, decadence: an intense self-consciousness, a restless curiosity in research, an over-subtilizing refinement upon refinement, a spiritual and moral perversity. If what we call the classic is indeed the supreme art – those qualities of perfect simplicity, perfect sanity, perfect proportion, the supreme qualities – then this representative literature of to-day, interesting, beautiful, novel as it is, is really a new and beautiful and interesting disease. Healthy we cannot call it, and healthy

it does not wish to be considered. (rpt. in Beckson, *Aesthetes* 135–36)

Paul Verlaine, Symons writes, has achieved the "ideal of Decadence": "To fix the last fine shade, the quintessence of things; to fix it fleetingly; to be a disembodied voice, and yet the voice of a human soul...." As Temple remarks: "These are not random words but the heart of the matter...(219).

Because Decadence insists on the autonomy of art, it is often identified with Aestheticism, but the former is the dark side of the latter. The British Decadents were devoted to Pater's *Studies in the History of the Renaissance* (1873), which focused on the "fascination of corruption" (the phrase occurring in the chapter on Leonardo da Vinci). In the preface, Pater speaks of "that subtle and delicate sweetness which belongs to a refined and comely decadence." Devoted to Pater's work on the Renaissance, Wilde (according to Yeats) said that it was his "golden book; I never travel anywhere without it; but it is the very flower of decadence: the last trumpet should have sounded the moment it was written" (qtd. in Yeats 87). Such an artificially colored prose style associated with Decadence, Linda Dowling writes, was "an attempt to save something from the wreck" of an immanent cultural crisis in the 19th century: "...the idea that written language, the literary tongue of the great English writers, was simply another dead language in relation to living speech" (xv).

Dandyism, though it has been associated with Aestheticism, is more often regarded as a self-conscious pose of the Decadent, whose boredom or indifference dominates his reaction to life. In Wilde's plays his dandies may pose, but they do act when necessary. In "Phrases and Philosophies for the Use of the Young," Wilde reveals the nature of such a pose: "The first duty in life is to be as artificial as possible. What the second duty is no one has as yet discovered." In his narcissistic devotion to self, the dandiacal Dorian Gray exhibits the entire range of Decadent perversity: distorting Lord Henry's hedonistic philosophy, Dorian "looked on evil simply as a mode through which he could realize his conception of the beautiful." His *taedium vitae* – his weariness of life, a characteristic Decadent motif – results in his ironic, grotesque death.

In Wilde's *Salome* – the only truly Decadent/Symbolist play in fin-de-siècle England – the eponymous character evokes shudders with her sexual perversity, and the dialogue – written in an unnatural, incantatory style – reveals French Decadent/Symbolist influences. Such elements of Decadent subject matter and themes – present in various degrees in earlier Romanticism, Impressionism, and Symbolism – were all absorbed and developed in the early 20th century as aspects of Modernism.

References: A. E. Carter, *The Idea of Decadence in French Literature, 1830–1900* (1958); L. P. Wilkinson, *Ovid Surveyed* (1962); Koenraad W. Swart, *The Sense of Decadence in Nineteenth-Century France* (1964); *The Autobiography of W. B. Yeats* (1965); Jerome H. Buckley, "The Idea of Decadence," *The Triumph of Time* (1966); John M. Munro, *The Decadent Poetry of the Eighteen Nineties* (1970); Ruth Z. Temple, "Truth in Labeling: Pre-Raphaelitism, Aestheticism, Decadence, Fin-de-Siècle," *ELT* 17:4 (1974); Linda Dowling, *Aestheticism and Decadence: A Selective Annotated Bibliography* (1977); Ian Fletcher, ed., *Decadence and the 1890s* (1979); Karl Beckson, ed., *Aesthetes and Decadents of the 1890's* (1981); R. K. R. Thornton, *The Decadent Dilemma* (1983); Patricia Clements, "Wilde: The True Brotherhood of the Arts," *Baudelaire and the English Tradition* (1985); Linda Dowling, *Language and Decadence in the Victorian Fin de Siècle* (1986); Murray Pittock, *Spectrum of Decadence: The Literature of the 1890s* (1993); Karl Beckson, "The Damnation of Decadence," *London in the 1890s: A Cultural History* (1993); Matthew Sturgis, *Passionate Attitudes: The English Decadents of the 1890s* (1995); David Weir, *Decadence and the Making of Modernism* (1995).

"THE DECAY OF LYING"

Published: *Nineteenth Century* 25 (Jan. 1889): 35–56, with the subtitle "A Dialogue"; rev., with the subtitle "An Observation" in *Intentions* (1891).

In *De Profundis*, Wilde recalled that the "idea, title, treatment, mode, everything was struck out" for "the first and best of all my dialogues" at a dinner with Robert Ross in a little Soho cafe (*Letters* 428). Wilde told the poet and essayist Violet Fane that his dialogue was "meant to bewilder the masses by its fantastic form; *au fond* it is of course serious" (*Letters* 236); however, it is no more "fantastic" in form than Plato's dialogues, which obviously provided Wilde with the model.

To the poet and journalist W. H. Pollock, he wrote that "the public so soon vulgarise any artistic idea that one gives them that I was determined to put my new views on art, and particularly on the relations of art and history, in a form that they could not understand, but that would be understood by the few who, like yourself, have a quick artistic instinct" (*Letters* 236). And to Kate Terry, the actress and elder sister of Ellen Terry, Wilde alluded to his dialogue: "I have blown my trumpet against the gate of dullness..." (*Letters* 237).

The Dialogue: The two speakers, Cyril and Vivian (named after Wilde's two children, the younger one's name, however, spelled "Vyvyan"), are in the library of a country house in Nottinghamshire. Cyril, coming in through the open window from the terrace, urges Vivian not to remain all day in the library but to join him in lying on the grass, smoking cigarettes, and enjoying Nature. Revealing, with relief, that he has "entirely lost that faculty," Vivian proceeds to develop a central idea in the dialogue – the superiority of Art to Nature (a concept central to artistic Decadence):

> My own experience is that the more we study Art, the less we care for Nature. What Art really reveals to us is Nature's lack of design, her curious crudities, her extraordinary monotony, her absolutely unfinished condition. Nature has good intentions, of course, but, as Aristotle once said [in the *Poetics*], she cannot carry them out.... Art is our spirited protest, our gallant attempt to teach Nature her proper place.

Vivian's preference for Art, the product of the creative imagination, extends to the daring conclusion characteristic of the dandiacal Wilde: "Egotism itself, which is so necessary to a proper sense of human dignity, is entirely the result of indoor life. Out of doors one becomes abstract and impersonal. One's individuality absolutely leaves one."

Vivian reveals that he is publishing an article titled "The Decay of Lying: A Protest," which celebrates "the temper of the true liar, with his frank, fearless statements, his superb irresponsibility, his healthy, natural disdain of proof of any kind!" – in short, the artist. The article is designed for the "elect," whom Vivian describes as "The Tired Hedonists...a club to which I belong. We are supposed to wear faded roses in our button-holes when we meet, and to have a sort of cult for Domitian" (the Roman emperor noted for his cruelty). Wilde's arch humor, his pose of ennui, and the Decadent icon of faded roses are closely related to his advocacy of the green carnation for the "elect" (as Ellmann remarks, "With a hint of decadence, the painted flower blended art and nature," 365/345).

Vivian then begins reading his article to Cyril: it is critical, clearly, of the French Naturalists and the Zola disciple who may be found at the Bibliothèque Nationale or the British Museum "shamelessly reading up his subject. He has not even the courage of other people's ideas, but insists on going directly to life for everything.... The loss that results to literature in general from this false ideal of our time can hardly be overestimated. People have a careless way of talking about a 'born liar,' just as they talk about a 'born poet.' But in both cases they are wrong. Lying and poetry are arts – arts, as Plato saw, not unconnected with each other...." (In *The Republic*, Book X, Socrates condemns poetry for its "imitation" of an "imitation" – the shadows in this world that copy transcendent reality.) A young man, starting out in life with "a natural gift for exaggeration," falls prey to

careless habits of accuracy, or takes to frequenting the company of the aged and the well-informed...and in a short time he develops a morbid and unhealthy faculty of truth-telling, begins to verify all statements made in his presence, has no hesitation in contradicting people who are much younger than himself, and often ends by writing novels which are so like life that no one can possibly believe in their probability....if something cannot be done to check, or at least to modify, our monstrous worship of facts, Art will become sterile, and Beauty will pass away from the land.

Among many authors who are guilty of "this modern vice," Vivian cites Robert Louis Stevenson, whose novel *The Black Arrow* is "so inartistic as not to contain a single anachronism to boast of, while the transformation of Dr. Jekyll reads dangerously like an experiment out of the *Lancet* [the British medical journal].... Mr. Henry James writes fiction as if it were a painful duty, and wastes upon

mean motives and imperceptible 'points of view' his neat literary style...." As for Zola's novels, his work is "entirely wrong from beginning to end, and wrong not on the ground of morals, but on the ground of art...." His characters have

their dreary vices, and their drearier virtues. The record of their lives is absolutely without interest.... In literature we require distinction, charm, beauty, and imaginative power.... We have mistaken the common livery of the age for the vesture of the Muses, and spend our days in the sordid streets and hideous suburbs of our vile cities when we should be out on the hillside with Apollo.

As to the "popular cry of our time" – that is, "Let us return to Life and Nature; they will recreate Art for us" – Vivian contends: "One touch of Nature may make the whole world kin, but two touches of Nature will destroy any work of Art" (the first part of this statement is taken almost verbatim from Whistler's "Ten O'Clock" lecture). When "Life gets the upper hand, and drives Art out into the wilderness," that, says Vivian, is the "true decadence, and it is from this that we are now suffering." In Shakespeare, we can see "the beginning of the end":

It shows itself by the gradual breaking-up of the blank-verse in the later plays, by the predominance given to prose, and by the over-importance assigned to characterisation. The passages in Shakespeare – and they are many – where the language is uncouth, vulgar, exaggerated, fantastic, obscene even, are entirely due to Life calling for an echo of her own voice, and rejecting the intervention of beautiful style....

Facts are "usurping the domain of Fancy, and have invaded the kingdom of Romance. Their chilling touch is over everything. They are vulgarising mankind."

Vivian insists that Nature itself is a creation of the imagination in a mocking passage that Wilde includes in the revised version of the dialogue – that is, he imitates Whistler's vision of the transforming imagination in the "Ten O'Clock" lecture, which depicts "the evening mist [that] clothes the riverside with poetry, as with a veil, and the poor buildings lose themselves in the dim sky, and the tall chimneys become campanili, and the warehouses are palaces in the night, and the whole city hangs in the heavens and fairy-land is before us...." Wilde's passage begins:

> Where, if not from the Impressionists, do we get those wonderful brown fogs that come creeping down our streets, blurring the gas-- lamps and changing the houses into monstrous shadows? To whom, if not to them and their master [that is, Whistler], do we owe the lovely silver mists that brood over our river, and turn to faint forms of fading grace curved bridge and swaying barge? The extraordinary change that has taken place in the climate of London during the last ten years is entirely due to a particular school of Art.

Nature, Vivian insists, is our creation: "It is in our brain that she quickens to life. Things are because we see them, and what we see, and how we see it, depends on the Arts that have influenced us.... At present, people see fogs, not because there are fogs, but because poets and painters have taught them the mysterious loveliness of such effects."

When Cyril remarks that surely Art expresses the "temper of its age, the spirit of its time, the moral and social conditions that surround it, and under whose influence it is produced," Vivian denies this view vehemently: "Art never expresses anything but itself. This is the principle of my new aesthetics.... No great artist ever sees things as they really are. If he did, he would cease to be an artist...." Vivian cites the example of Japanese as represented in art: they are, he argues, "the deliberate self-conscious creation of certain individual artists.... The actual people who live in Japan are not unlike the general run of English people; that is to say, they are extremely commonplace.... In fact the whole of Japan is a pure invention."

In summarizing his aesthetic doctrines, Vivian concludes that "all bad art comes from returning to Life and Nature, and elevating them into ideals. Life and Nature may sometimes be used as part of Art's rough material, but before they are of any real service to art they must be translated into artistic conventions.... As a method Realism is a complete failure.... The final revelation is that Lying, the telling of beautiful untrue things, is the proper aim of Art."

Manuscripts: The Berg Collection has an incomplete MS. version, titled "On the Decay of Lying." The Hyde Collection also has a fragmentary MS. of the essay. The original, complete MS., according to Mason (123), consisted of 54 folios, given by Wilde to Frank Richardson. It was subsequently sold at Sotheby's in 1910; and again sold at Sotheby's in 1934.

References: William Buckler, "Wilde's 'Trumpet Against the Gate of Dullness': 'The Decay of Lying,'" *ELT* 33:3 (1990); Lawrence Danson,"The Decay of Lying," *Wilde's Intentions*: *The Artist in His Criticism* (1997).

"THE DECORATIVE ARTS" (first version)

Published: First appeared in Kevin O'Brien, "An Edition of Oscar Wilde's American Lectures," PhD diss. (University of Notre Dame, 1973), 99–130. In *Miscellanies* (1908), Ross erroneously titles the truncated version of Wilde's lecture (which is taken from only one newspaper, the *New York Daily Tribune*) as "House Decoration," which was given as a special lecture in Philadelpia (10 May), New York (11 May), and Boston (2 June). Ross took the text (with some emendations) from "Decorative Art in America" in Richard Butler Glaenzer's volume of Wilde's writings, *Decorative Art in America: A Lecture by Oscar Wilde, Together with Letters, Reviews, and Interviews* (New York, 1906). In fact, as O'Brien reveals, this text is a combination of two lectures that Wilde gave on his lecture tour in 1882: the second version of "The Decorative Arts" and "The House Beautiful."

The first version of "The Decorative Arts" was initially given on 13 February 1882, in Chicago. This became Wilde's principal lecture after he stopped giving "The English Renaissance" in the first month of his lecture tour, though portions were taken from the latter for "The Decorative Arts." O'Brien traces the permutations that "The Decorative Arts" went through in Wilde's apparent attempt to vary the lectures on his arduous tour of the United States and Canada.

The Lecture: Wilde begins by announcing that he will inform the audience of what England is doing "to search out in every city those men and women who have power of design, the knowledge and love of noble color and of imagination, and of the schools that we have given them, the work we have done already, and the work we propose to do." What the English wish to do, Wilde assures his audience, is "to produce among people by the means of beautiful surroundings that artistic temperament without which there is no creation of art, there is no understanding of art, there is not even an understanding of life, for, as the life of a nation is, so will its art be...." The current artistic movement is a reaction against the

> empty, conventional workmanship, the lax execution of previous poetry and painting, showing itself in the work of such men as Rossetti and Burne-Jones, by a far greater splendor of color, a far more intricate wonder of design than English imaginative art has shown before; and above all, and more than this, it has been the first movement which has brought the handicraftsman and the artist together in loving brotherhood as they were in the days of Grecian art, which is the keynote of all artistic and beautiful creation.

Wilde assures his audience that "the art we want is the art based on all the inventions of modern civilization, and to suit all the needs of nineteenth century life." Machinery, for example, should be reverenced "when it does its proper work, when it relieves man from ignoble and soulless labor" (an idea advanced by William Morris), but Wilde adds, "Let us have no machine-made ornament at all; it is all bad and worthless and ugly." American workmen should have the "bright and novel surroundings that you can yourself create. Stately and simple architecture for your city, bright and simple dress for your men and women, and streets clean enough for them to walk across without being soiled – those are the conditions of a real artistic movement...."

In addition to providing a beautiful external world, a school of design should be established in each city, a "stately and noble building full of the best examples of the best art of the world." While visiting an American school of design, Wilde observed a student painting a "romantic moonlight landscape on a large round dish," while another student covered a set of dinner plates with a series of sunsets "of the most remarkable imagination." He disapproved of such work: "Let them take canvas or paper for such work but not clay or china. They are merely painting the wrong subject on the wrong material.... One doesn't want to eat

one's clams off a harrowing sunset."

Wilde is convinced that the best art flourishes in republics: "We do not want the rich to possess more beautiful things, but the poor to create more beautiful things, *for every man is poor who cannot create*." He urges his audience to make the subject of art "all that is noble in men and women, the stately in your lakes and mountains, the beautiful in your flowers and in your life. [At this point, Wilde borrows several paragraphs from his first lecture, "The English Renaisssance."] We want to see you possess nothing in your house that has not given delight to its maker, and does not give delight to its user; we want to see you create an art made by the hands of the people, for all art to come must be democratic, coming to all alike and hovering about, low and high, in unconscious existence."

Manuscripts: The Clark Library has an incomplete TS. of 15 leaves with Wilde's autograph revisions. Ross gave his version of this typescript the erroneous title of "Art and Handicraftsman" in *Miscellanies* (1908) by adding other MS. fragments now in the Clark Library, one of which belongs to "The House Beautiful."

"THE DECORATIVE ARTS" (second version)

Published: First appeared in Kevin O'Brien, "An Edition of Oscar Wilde's American Lectures," PhD diss. (University of Notre Dame, 1973), 133–61; rpt. in O'Brien, *Oscar Wilde in Canada: An Apostle for the Arts* (Toronto: Personal Library, 1982), 151–65. O'Brien reconstructed the lecture from over 60 newspaper accounts. This second version – which Wilde began writing soon after he wrote "The House Beautiful" – evolved through various permutations during his 1882 lecture tour, when, in March and April, he lectured in Utah, Colorado, Missouri, Kansas, Iowa, and Ohio (see Lectures in America).

By June, "The Decorative Arts" had achieved its final version, though Wilde continued making changes while in Eastern Canada, where he concluded his tour on 13 October. As O'Brien writes of this second version, which develops many of the same ideas as those in the first version: "...the ideas are better filtered through Wilde's own observations, personal experiences, and aesthetic tastes. It thus is more informal, witty, definite, and more like the Wilde one would expect to hear on a lecture tour" ("An Edition" 132).

The Lecture: Wilde begins by informing his audience that he does not wish to present any abstract definition of beauty:

...you can get along very well without philosophy if you surround yourselves with beautiful things; but I wish to tell you of what we have done and are doing in England to search out those men and women who have knowledge and power of design, of the schools of art provided for them, and the noble use we are making of art in the improvement of the handicraft of our country.

Art, Wilde continues, is "no mere accident of existence which men may take or leave, but a very necessity of human life...." As to what art Americans should devote themselves in the United States, Wilde suggests that instead of talking of "that higher order of imaginative art of the poet and the painter," he will devote his lecture to decorative art, "the art that will hallow the vessels of everyday use, exerting its influence in the simplest and humblest of homes." As to the term "decorative art," Wilde offers some clues to its meaning (much of the following borrowed from William Morris's essay "The Unity of Art"):

To progress in the decorative arts, to make chaste and elegant patterns of carpet or wall paper, even the little wreath of leaf or vine traced around the margin of cups we drink out of, requires more than mere machine work: it requires delicacy of hand, cultivated taste, and nobility of character. For the mark of all good art is not that the thing is done exactly or finely, for machinery may do as much, but it is worked out with the tender, appealing vitality of the workman's heart and head.

"Give," Wilde continues, "the workman noble designs, dignify and ennoble his work, and through this, his life." The poet or painter will create whether the world acclaims or denigrates his work: "he has his own world and is independent of his fellow men, but the ordinary handicraftsman is almost entirely dependent upon your pleasure and opinion and upon the influences which surround him for his knowledge of form and color." Consequently, it is crucial that he be "supplied with the noble productions of original minds so that he may acquire that artistic temperament without which there is no creation of art...."

Because of advances made during the last five years in the various branches of the decorative arts, Wilde expects to see England "take her place once again as the foremost of all nations in the cultivation and development of art and the encouragement of those who love to perpetuate in their handiwork the beauties about them." He complains, however, that the 19th century "has been marked by more dishonest workmanship and has produced more rubbish than any that preceded it." One article of furniture, for example – the cast iron American stove – is notable for its "absolutely horrid ugliness." Furniture that is simple in design and "honestly made" does not "depreciate in value as does our modern furniture." Those artisans who have lost their love for good work have been dishonest and hypocritical in their workmanship, and their "so–called works of art...are unpunished crimes." Art, Wilde contends, will do more than

make our lives joyous and beautiful; it will become part of the new history of the world and a part of the brotherhood of man; for art, by creating a common intellectual atmosphere between countries might, if it could not overshadow the world with the silvery wings of peace, at least make men such brothers that they would not go to slay one another for the whim or folly of some king or minister as they do in Europe, for national hatreds are always strongest where culture is lowest.

Here Wilde pleads the case for utilitarian, moralistic art radically different from his occasional excursions into art for art's sake – a confrontation, so to speak, of the influence of Ruskin and Morris as opposed to Gautier and Whistler.

Manuscript: The Clark Library has a fragment with the erroneous title assigned as "Art and the Handicraftsman."

DE PROFUNDIS

Written: January–March 1897 in Reading Prison. The governor of the prison, Major J. O. Nelson, wrote to the Prison Commissioners to explain how Wilde's letter to Lord Alfred Douglas was handled: "Each sheet was carefully numbered before being issued and withdrawn each evening at locking and placed before me in the morning with the usual papers." Hart-Davis, however, doubts that the procedure was rigidly enforced: "Careful study of the MS. makes this statement hard to believe, and I suspect that Major Nelson had been much more considerate to Wilde than his official position allowed him to admit to his superiors" (*Letters* 424n). The letter was not posted from the prison: on 2 April, Nelson wrote to the Prison Commission to inquire whether the letter might be sent out. The response was that it was not possible but that it could be kept and given to Wilde on his release. (For the disposition of the MS., see Manuscripts below).

Published: On 23 February 1905, Methuen & Co. issued this letter in book form, drastically cut by Robert Ross to less than half the length of the original MS. with all references to Douglas, including the salutation "Dear Bosie," removed. Before the English edition appeared, an authorized translation in German by Dr. Max Meyerfeld had been published serially in Berlin in *Die Neue Rundschau*, (Jan.–Feb. 1905), which contained more of the original text than the English version.

According to Hart-Davis, the Methuen director E. V. Lucas, himself a noted critic, suggested the title for Wilde's letter (*Letters* 423n2) – presumably derived from Psalm 130, which begins "Out of the depths," the meaning of the Latin *De Profundis*. Wilde had written facetiously to Ross that the letter was "indeed...an Encyclical Letter, and as the Bulls of the Holy Father are named from their opening words, it may be spoken of as the *Epistola: In Carcere et Vinculis*" (*Letter: In Prison and in Chains)*: see *Letters* 513. A letter from Lucas to Ross confirms the likelihood that both were involved in editing the letter, Lucas perhaps in an advisory capacity: "You are very kind; but please don't suggest payment. I really like to think it possible to do something for your friend" (Ross 88).

With "additional matter," *De Profundis* (including four letters to Ross from Reading Prison and two letters previously published by Wilde in the *Daily Chronicle* on Warder Martin and prison reform) was reprinted, in a slightly enlarged version, as Volume 11 of the *Collected Edition* (1908). In the "Prefatory Dedication" to Dr. Meyerfeld, Ross remarks that the title *De Profundis*, "against which some have cavilled, is, if you will remember from *our* correspondence, my own." In 1913 further material from the original MS. of *De Profundis* was added in a limited edition published in New York. In 1949, Vyvyan Holland published Ross's typed copy, erroneously describing it as the "first complete and accurate version." Finally, Hart-Davis's 1962 edition of Wilde's letters contained a reliable transcription of *De Profundis* from the original autograph MS. in the British Museum.

The Letter: Though the intent of this prison letter is clearly one of reconciliation with Douglas, it is also Wilde's elaborate accusation that his lover was a destructive element in their "ill-fated and most lamentable friendship" that "ended in ruin and public infamy for me, yet the memory of our ancient affection is often with me, and the thought that loathing, bitterness and contempt should for ever take that place in my heart once held by love is very sad to me...." Aware that what he writes will wound Douglas's "vanity to the quick," Wilde hopes that his letter will kill that vanity. He recalls his first important encounter with Douglas, who had been threatened with blackmail over his homosexual adventures and who had appealed to Wilde for help: "The gutter and the things that live in it had begun to fascinate you. That was the origin of the trouble in which you sought my aid, and I, so unwisely according to the wisdom of this world, out of pity and kindness gave it to you."

Charging Douglas and himself with a fatal lack of self-knowledge, Wilde remarks that the "real fool, such as the gods mock or mar, is he who does not know himself. I was such a one too long. You have been such a one too long. Be so no more. Do not be afraid. The supreme vice is shallowness. Everything that is realised is right." (These themes, which permeate the letter, reveal the influence of Emerson, says Isobel Murray, who cites Wilde's request for Emerson's *Essays* in July 1896, so "he had them to hand as he wrote," 206n39.) Writing in "this dark cell in convict clothes, a disgraced and ruined man," Wilde blames himself for "allowing an unintellectual friendship, a friendship whose primary aim was not the creation and contemplation of beautiful things, to entirely dominate my life."

Douglas, says Wilde, did not understand that an artist, "especially such an artist as I am, one, that is to say, the quality of whose work depends on the intensification of personality, requires for the development of his art the companionship of ideas, and intellectual atmosphere, quiet, peace, and solitude." Wilde charges him with the "absolute ruin of my Art...." (Yet Wilde's most important plays, including his masterpiece, *The Importance of Being Earnest*, were written after he met Douglas. Though Wilde may have lost some control over his personal life, the turbulence of his relationship with Douglas did not constrict Wilde's artistic energy or the incisive wit that informs his plays.) Characterizing Douglas, he writes: "Your insistence on a life of reckless profusion: your incessant demands for money: your claim that all your pleasures should be paid for by me whether I was with you or not: brought me after some time into serious monetary difficulties...." He estimated that between the autumn of 1892 and the date of his imprisonment, he spent more than £5000 while with Douglas, aside from the bills he incurred. "It was," Wilde says, "the triumph of the smaller over the bigger nature. It was the case of that tyranny of the weak over the strong...."

At the "one supremely and tragically critical moment of all my life," Wilde continues, "on the one side there was your father [the Marquess of Queensberry] attacking me with hideous cards left at my club, on the other side there was you attacking me with no less loathsome letters." Soon Wilde was pressured, at Douglas's urging, to take out a "ridiculous warrant" for Queensberry's arrest on the charge of libel (the Marquess referred to Wilde as a "posing Somdomite," misspelling the offensive word on a card, presumably in his haste): "Between you both I lost my head" (the image of another martyr, as he had dramatized in *Salome*). Reflecting on his time in prison, Wilde regards the past, with its "throbs of pain" as the "record of bitter moments," which is all one can think about: "Suffering – curious as it may sound to you – is the means by which we exist, because it is the only means by which we become conscious of existing; and the remembrance of suffering in the past is necessary to us [that is, those in prison] as the warrant, the evidence, of our continued identity."

Wilde reveals his own illusions concerning the role that Douglas would play in their relationship: "I thought life was going to be a brilliant comedy, and that you were to be one of many graceful figures in it. I found it to be a revolting and repellent tragedy...." Nevertheless, Wilde remains convinced that Douglas loves him. During those two and a half years "during which the Fates were weaving into one scarlet pattern the threads of our divided lives you really loved me. Yes: I know you did." But Douglas's hatred of his father and the consequences in Wilde's life indicated a "terrible lack of imagination, the one really fatal defect of your character...." When he received the "obscene threats and coarse violences" in a letter from Queensberry, who was determined to rescue his son from the corrupt (and presumably corrupting) older man, Wilde "saw at once that a terrible danger was looming on the horizon of my troubled days...."

At the time of his trials, Wilde said to himself: "*At all costs I must keep Love in my heart. If I go into prison without Love what will become of my soul?*" He also reveals that he could have saved himself at either trial, "though not from shame indeed but from imprisonment," by showing that the three most important witnesses for the Crown had been "carefully coached" by Queensberry and his solicitors and that they would have been dismissed by the Judge. In his attempt to account for the disaster of his life (initially blaming himself, then shifting the blame to Douglas), Wilde now focuses on Queensberry and his position in society: "I am here for having tried to put your father into prison.... Your father completely turned the tables on me, and had *me* in prison, has me there still. That is why there is contempt felt for me. That is why people despise me."

What follows are some of the most often-quoted passages in the letter on Wilde's estimate of his own significance in late Victorian culture:

I was a man who stood in symbolic relations to the art and culture of my age.... The gods had given me almost everything. I had genius, a distinguished name, high social position, brilliancy, intellectual daring: I made art a philosophy, and philosophy an art: I altered the minds of men and the colours of things: there was nothing I said or did that did not make people wonder: I took the drama, the most objective form known to art, and made it as personal a mode of expression as the lyric or the sonnet, at the same time that I widened its range and enriched its characterisation: drama, novel, poem in rhyme, poem in prose, or subtle or fantastic dialogue, whatever I touched I made beautiful in a new mode of beauty.... I treated Art as the supreme reality, and life as a mere mode of fiction: I awoke the imagination of my century so that it created myth and legend around me: I summed up all systems in a phrase, and all existence in an epigram. (*Letters* 466)

But now, in his prison cell, Wilde claims that if he realizes what he has suffered, society should also realize what it has done to him. On either side, bitterness should be abandoned. He recalls that, when in Wandsworth Prison (before being transferred to Reading), he was determined to commit suicide on the day when he left prison, but that "evil mood passed away" when he made up his mind to live. Sorrow is now his "new world.... I now see that sorrow, being the supreme emotion of which man is capable, is at once the type and test of all great Art. What the artist is always looking for is that mode of existence in which soul and body are one and indivisible: in which the outward is expressive of the inward: in which Form reveals."

Wilde's contemplation of the significance of sorrow leads him to an extensive discussion of Christ, the "precursor of the romantic movement in life," with whom he identifies himself as a martyr. The idea of a "young Galilean peasant imagining that he could bear on his own shoulders the burden of the entire world" is, to Wilde, "almost incredible." Even now, those "who are dumb under oppression" discover that through Christ "the ugliness of their sins is taken away and the beauty of their sorrow [is] revealed to them." Christ's life, declares Wilde, is the "most wonderful of poems": nothing in Greek tragedy can parallel the pity and terror of his drama. Indeed, nothing in Dante or Shakespeare can equal the "sheer simplicity of pathos wedded and made one with sublimity of tragic effect" in the last act of Christ's Passion.

In another moment of identification, Wilde calls Christ "the supreme Individualist...the first in History." His creed was not "to live for others as a definite self-conscious aim." Wilde's identification with Christ is further implied in his quotation from the Book of the Prophet Isaiah (53:3): "He is despised and rejected of men, a man of sorrows and acquainted with grief...." Christ's message is that "*every* moment should be beautiful," Philistinism being "simply that side of man's nature that is not illumined by the imagination...."

In discussing the notions of self-realization and of self-knowledge, Wilde remarks that "two of the most perfect lives I have come across in my own experience" are the lives of the French Symbolist poet Paul Verlaine and of the anarchist and author Prince Kropotkin, "both of them men who passed years in prison: the first, the one Christian poet since Dante, the other a man with the soul of that beautiful white Christ that seems coming out of Russia." Alluding to his own imprisonment, Wilde recalls that in his first year he did "nothing else, and can remember doing nothing else, but wring my hands in impotent despair, and say 'What an ending! What an appalling ending!'...." But with a new governor of Reading Prison, he can now say, "What a beginning!"

Returning to those events that led to his disaster, Wilde recalls that people thought it "dreadful of me to have entertained at dinner the evil things of life, and to have found pleasure in their company. But they, from the point of view through which I, as an artist in life, approached them, were delightfully suggestive and stimulating. It was like feasting with panthers. [This well-known phrase has been traced by Timothy d'Arch Smith and Horst Schroeder to Balzac's *Illusions perdues*, trans. H. J. Hunt, 1971, p. 312: "...I feel as if I were supping with lions and panthers...."] The danger was half the excitement." His life had been "full of perverse pleasures and strange passions."

Approaching the end of this letter, Wilde expresses his belief that "behind all this Beauty" of the visible world there is "some Spirit hidden of which the painted forms and shapes are but modes of manifestation, and it is with this Spirit that I desire to become in harmony. I have grown tired of the articulate utterances of men and things. The Mystical in Art, the Mystical in Life, the Mystical in Nature – this is what I am looking for...." What follows is the repudiation of Decadent artifice and ideology in his return to Nature, for

Society, as we have constituted it, will have no place for me, has none to offer; but Nature, whose sweet rains fall on unjust and just alike, will have clefts in the rocks where I may hide, and secret valleys in whose silence I may weep undisturbed.... she will cleanse me in great waters, and with bitter herbs make me whole. (*Letters* 510)

Early Reviews: From their reading of the 1905 version, many reviewers were convinced that

Wilde was a repentant sinner. In an unsigned review in the *TLS* (24 Feb.), E. V. Lucas, who had seen the entire MS., nevertheless concluded that "here and there it makes a sweet and reasonable contribution to the gospel of humanity." Such titles of reviews as "A Book of Penitence" (*Bookman*, April) and "A Soul's Awakening" (*Inquirer*, 12 Aug.) were commonplace. In France, André Gide confessed that he could not read the work without tears (*L'Ermitage*, 15 Aug.).

In *Vanity Fair* (2 March), however, Max Beerbohm questioned whether the book was "indeed a heartcry": "Nothing seemed more likely than that Oscar Wilde, smitten down from his rosy-clouded pinnacle, and dragged through the mire, and cast among the flints, would be *diablement changé en route*. Yet lo! he was unchanged. He was still precisely himself. He was still playing with ideas, playing with emotions.... And sorrow was turned to joy by the 'lord of language.'" Beerbohm is most delighted by the "mastery of prose." No modern writer, except for Ruskin in his prime, writes Beerbohm, "has achieved through prose the limpid and lyrical effects that were achieved by Oscar Wilde" (rpt. in Beckson).

In the Vienna *Neue Freie Presse* (23 April), Shaw, agreeing with Beerbohm, wrote that

no other Irishman had yet produced as masterful a comedy as *De Profundis*. In spite of the unspeakable horrors of the circumstances under which this work was written, it stimulated me to laughter more than any other of Wilde's works. The man was so completely unbroken, so untouched by misery, hunger, punishment, and shame; he was so consummately successful and sincere in his magnificent attitude of doleful superiority – in the face of a society which had behaved so weakly, narrowly, and unjustly toward the great man – that pity and sentimentality would amount to weakmindedness and bad taste, and one is moved to rejoice over the kind of unsurpassable genius that he was. (rpt. in *The Matter with Ireland*)

In a letter to Ross (dated 13 March 1905), Shaw calls *De Profundis* "really an extraordinary book, quite exhilarating and amusing as to Wilde himself, and quite disgraceful and shameful to his stupid tormentors. There is pain in it...but no real

tragedy, all comedy. The unquenchable spirit of the man is magnificent.... It annoys me to have people degrading the whole affair to the level of sentimental tragedy" (rpt. in Beckson). The New York *Critic* (Nov.) remarked that *De Profundis* "has done a good deal to reinstate Wilde in public opinion, not as a man, perhaps, but as a writer."

Manuscripts: On 19 May 1897, the day of his release, the entire letter was given to Wilde, who told Robert Ross in Dieppe on 20 May to have two copies typed (one for Wilde and one for Ross) and to give the original MS. to Douglas. Ross later insisted that he sent Douglas one of the typed copies: in a libel suit against Arthur Ransome for remarks made about him in *Oscar Wilde: A Critical Study* (1912), Douglas admitted that he had received a copy, but apparently believing that Ross had sent him excerpts from Wilde's letter, he threw it into the fire. Later, however, he always denied having received it. Ross bequeathed the second typed copy to Wilde's son, Vyvyan Holland. This copy was, however, different from the original MS., which Ross had deposited in the British Museum in 1909 with the stipulation that it be sealed for 50 years. In addition to this MS., there are TSS. in the British Library, the Clark Library ("Extracts of *De Profundis*" – prepared by Stuart Mason), and in the Ross Collection in the Bodleian Library (Oxford).

References: Bernard Shaw, "Oscar Wilde," *The Matter with Ireland*, eds. Dan H. Laurence and David H. Greene (1962); W. H. Auden, "An Improbable Life," *Oscar Wilde: A Collection of Critical Essays*, ed. Richard Ellmann (1969); Harvey Kail, "The Other Half of the Garden: Oscar Wilde's *De Profundis* and the Confessional Tradition," *Prose Studies, 1800–1900* (June 1979); H. Montgomery Hyde, "The Riddle of *De Profundis*," *Antigonish Review* (Summer 1983); Bruce Bashford, "Oscar Wilde as Theorist: The Case of *De Profundis*," *ELT* 28:4 (1985); William Buckler, "Oscar Wilde's Aesthetic of the Self: Art as Imaginative Self-Realization in *De Profundis*," *Biography* (Spring 1989); Isobel Murray, ed., *"The Soul of Man" and Prison Writings* (1990); Timothy d'Arch Smith and Horst Schroeder, "Feasting with Panthers," *N&Q* (June 1995).

"DÉSESPOIR"

Published: Not published in Wilde's lifetime, this poem (its title meaning "Despair") appeared in

Poems, vol. 1 of Methuen's second *Collected Edition* (1909). In the same year, John W. Luce & Co. (Boston) issued the "hitherto unpublished" texts of "Désespoir" and "Pan. Double Villanelle" to secure the American copyright (see Mason 492), these poems included in *Poems*, vol. 1 of Luce's 1910 publication of the collected works, which Mason calls the "Ross Edition."

The octave of this sonnet expresses conventional views of seasonal change involving death and renewal: "The seasons mend their ruin as they go...." Inevitably, the leafless trees will be renewed and "this grey land grow green with summer rain...." The sestet, however, turns to human existence: "...whose bitter hungry sea / Flows at our heels, and gloom of sunless night / Covers the days which never more return?" The intense experiences of ambition and love are soon lost and in their place we "only find delight / In withered husks of some dead memory."

Manuscripts: The Clark Library has Mason's personal interleaved copy of his bibliography, in which, opposite p. 91, he transcribed an early MS. version of this poem titled "Tacitus senescimus annis" (from Ovid's *Fasti* 6:771, meaning "We grow old with silent lapse of years"). Texas has a later MS. of the poem with the present title.

"THE DEVOTED FRIEND"

Published: *The Happy Prince and Other Tales* (1888).

The Plot: One morning an old Water-rat observes some little ducks swimming in the pond, urged on by their mother, who advises: "You will never be in the best society unless you can stand on your heads" (one of Wilde's devices by which he introduces social satire into seemingly innocuous tales, thereby creating a clash of diverse modes of discourse). But the little ones ignore their mother since "they did not know what an advantage it is to be in society at all." In conversation with the understanding mother, the Water-rat remarks that he has never been married: "Love is all very well in its way, but friendship is much higher."

A Linnet sitting in a tree and having overheard the conversation tells a story of a devoted friend: "Once upon a time...." (the traditional beginning of a fairy tale as opposed to Wilde's avoidance of such a device in his own fairy tales; the Water-rat had asked whether the Linnet's story was about

him: "If so, I will listen to it, for I am extremely fond of fiction"). The story concerns honest little Hans, whose most devoted friend is big Hugh the Miller, a rich man who, when passing Hans's garden, plucks flowers or fruits: "Real friends should have everything in common," he says. Smiling, Hans is proud of having a friend with such noble sentiments.

In the winter, Hans suffers not only from hunger and cold but also from loneliness, for Hugh, who never visits him, says that "when people are in trouble they should be left alone and not be bothered by visitors." That is his idea of friendship. When his youngest son offers to give Hans half of his porridge and show him his white rabbits, Hugh scolds him: "I really don't know what is the use of sending you to school. You seem not to learn anything." Hans, he said, would grow envious, and envy is "a most terrible thing." Also, Hans might ask for some flour on credit, but "flour is one thing, and friendship is another, and they should not be confused."

With the winter over, Hugh visits Hans, who is happily working in his garden. When Hans tells him that he was half-afraid that Hugh had forgotten him, his devoted friend responds: "Hans, I am surprised at you; friendship never forgets." As proof of his noble idea, Hugh offers to give him his old wheelbarrow in exchange for a plank of wood for his own barn, in need of repair as is the wheelbarrow. Hugh notes that there is not enough wood to repair the wheelbarrow: "...but, of course, that is not my fault." Hugh also expects Hans to fill his large basket with Hans's flowers (Hans now has none left to buy back his silver buttons, which he had sold to stay alive during the winter).

The next day, Hugh asks his friend to carry a sack of flour to the market for him. Despite other chores, Hans agrees, fearful of being regarded as unfriendly. Returning home exhausted, Hans remains in bed when Hugh arrives and complains of his friend's laziness: "Anyone can say charming things and try to please and to flatter, but a true friend always says unpleasant things, and does not mind giving pain." When he asks Hans to repair his barn roof, Hans, though busy, agrees when Hugh reminds him that he will be giving him his wheelbarrow. Having completed the repair, Hans is now faced with another request: to drive Hugh's sheep to the mountain on the next day. Hans, afraid to say anything, not only undertakes this chore but other ones as well, reminding himself of the promised wheelbarrow, "an act of [Hugh's] pure generosity."

On a stormy night, Hugh knocks at his door to ask Hans to go for a doctor, for his son has fallen off a ladder. Again, Hugh mentions the wheelbarrow: "...it is only fair that you should do something for me in return." Hugh refuses to give Hans his new lantern since he fears that something may happen to it. After three hours, Hans reaches the doctor's house. Returning home, Hans loses his way, falls into a bog, and drowns. Hugh walks at the head of the procession at Hans's funeral, later mentioning that his wheelbarrow, intended for Hans, is now in such poor condition that he cannot sell it. "I will certainly take care not to give away anything again. One always suffers for being generous." That is the end of the story, says the Linnet, who seems indifferent to Hugh. The Water-rat says: "It is quite evident then that you have no sympathy in your nature."

"DINNERS AND DISHES"

Published: *PMG*, 7 March 1885, 5; rpt. in *Reviews* (1908). An unsigned review of "Wanderer" (unidentified), *Dinners and Dishes* (1885), described by Mason as "a series of articles (mostly reprinted from *Vanity Fair*), dealing with the ethics of gastronomy in various countries" (135).

Wilde cites Baudelaire at the opening of this review: "A man can live for three days without bread, but no man can live for one day without poetry, was an aphorism of Baudelaire's: you can live without pictures and music, but you can't live without eating, says the author of *Dinners and Dishes*: and this latter view is no doubt the more popular." Somewhat facetiously, he declares cookery to be an art: "are not its principles the subject of South Kensington lectures, and does not the Royal Academy give a banquet once a year?" Since the coming democracy will insist on feeding the population "penny dinners," the burning or bad seasoning of the "national meal" might result in a "dreadful revolution." While he strongly recommends the book, Wilde notes "something depressing about the coloured lithograph of a leg of mutton."

Wilde agrees with the author that "the tyrant of the English kitchen is shown in her proper light," for "the British cook is a foolish woman, who should be turned, for her iniquities, into a pillar of that salt which she never knows how to use." Praising the delicacies of Boston and New Orleans, particularly when these are obtained at the famous New York restaurant Delmonico's [where he dined when he was in New York during his 1882 lecture tour], Wilde remarks that "the two most remarkable bits of scenery in the States are undoubtedly Delmonico's and the Yosemite Valley, and the former place has done more to promote a good feeling between England and America than anything else has in this century."

"THE DISCIPLE": *See "POEMS IN PROSE"*

"THE DOER OF GOOD": *See "POEMS IN PROSE"*

"THE DOLE OF THE KING'S DAUGHTER. (BRETON)"

Published: *Dublin University Review* 87 (June 1876): 682–83, with the title "The Dole of the King's Daughter. (For a Painting)," the archaic word *dole* meaning "grief" or "lamentation"; rev. in *Poems* (1881) with the present subtitle.

This poem of eight four-line stanzas reflects the influence of the Pre-Raphaelites, particularly of Dante Gabriel Rossetti, whose "The Blessed Damozel" depicts the eponymous figure with three lilies in her hand and seven stars in her hair. Wilde also employs such a familiar medieval setting with archaic diction and ecclesiastical symbolism:

Seven stars in the still water,
  And seven in the sky;
Seven sins on the King's daughter,
  Deep in her soul to lie.

A *femme fatale*, she is responsible for the deaths of seven admirers; as a result, the blood on her hand is reflected in the lilies, "flecked with red." There is one now "who loves her true," but he prepares for the worst: "He hath duggen a grave by the darksome yew."

Manuscripts: The Berg Collection has an untitled MS. containing lines 17–32 (printed in Mason 66), and the State University of New York at Buffalo has a complete MS. of the poem.

DOUGLAS, LORD ALFRED (1870–1945)

In his prison letter, *De Profundis*, Wilde refers to Douglas (or "Bosie," a name derived from his childhood name "Boysie") as descending from the "mad, bad line" of an eccentric, dissolute, and sometimes self-destructive family. Some of Douglas's closest family members certainly give such an impression: For example, Alfred's uncle, Lord James Douglas, was a manic-depressive who slashed his throat in a hotel room; Alfred's grandfather, the 7th Marquess of Queensberry, was found dead with a double-barrelled gun at his side, probably a suicide; Alfred's eldest brother, Viscount Drumlanrig, was also a suspected suicide despite an inquest finding that he was the victim of an accidental explosion of his gun, which occurred at the time that he was facing exposure over a homosexual relationship with the future prime minister, Lord Rosebery, whose secretary he was.

In his early years, Douglas suffered, he later wrote, because his father, the 8th Marquess of Queensberry (see entry), took little interest in his children:

> My mother's spoiling would not have harmed me if my father had been a real father, and had ever taken half as much interest in his children as he did in his dogs and horses. As it was, I scarcely ever saw him.... All through my childhood and youth the shadow of my father lay over me, for though I loved him, and had indeed a quite absurd admiration for his supposed heroic qualities, I could not be blind to his infamous treatment of my mother, even long before she was driven to divorce him, which took place when I was sixteen. (*Autobiography* 16)

At the age of 14, Douglas was sent to Winchester (he had preferred Eton, but his father decided otherwise); homesick, he sent letters to his mother addressed "My own Darling." After four years at Winchester (where, he said, he had lost his innocence), he proceeded to Magdalen College, Oxford. There, he did little work towards a BA degree other than publishing his first serious poem, titled "Autumn Days," in the *Oxford Magazine* and editing the *Spirit Lamp*, an undergraduate periodical, between November 1892 and June 1893.

Either in late June or early July 1891, Wilde (then 37) was introduced to Douglas (then 21) in Tite Street by Lionel Johnson (see entry), a mutual friend of Douglas at Oxford (not his cousin, as Ellmann states: 414/391). In a second meeting,

according to Douglas, Wilde made homosexual advances, which he resisted, as he did for the ensuing six or nine months before yielding to Wilde's desire. But looking back, Douglas did not charge Wilde with "corrupting" him:

> Even before I met Wilde I had persuaded myself that "sins of the flesh" were not wrong, and my opinion was of course vastly strengthened and confined by his brilliantly reasoned defence of them, which may be said to have been the gospel of his life.... [A]t that time [I was] a frank and natural pagan, and he was a man who believed in sin and yet deliberately committed it, thereby obtaining a doubly perverse pleasure.... Inevitably, I assimilated his views to a great extent. (*Autobiography* 76–77)

While at Oxford, Douglas indulged in homosexual acts with boys, which led to his being blackmailed in the spring of 1892. In *De Profundis*, Wilde alludes to Douglas's "begging" him "in a most pathetic and charming letter" to assist him in the matter. Douglas's father heard of the suppressed scandal from Sir George Lewis, a lawyer and personal friend, whom Wilde had turned to on behalf of Douglas. At the end of the summer term of 1893, Douglas left Oxford without a degree, a disappointment to his divorced parents.

In the fall of 1893, Douglas completed an English translation of *Salomé*, which displeased Wilde, who revised it. Douglas, however, disowned it in anger (see *Salome*). By early 1894, in response to his mother's concern about his association with Wilde, Douglas wrote: "I am passionately fond of him and he of me. There is nothing I would not do for him and if he dies before I do I shall not care to live any longer" (qtd. in Hyde, *Biography* 51). Douglas's association with Wilde had repercussions beyond his immediate family: Having learned of the association, Sir Philip Currie, the British ambassador in Constantinople, refused to accept Douglas as an honorary attaché.

At this time, as Wilde later said, the Marquess of Queensberry began his "first attack" on him. Wilde had been having lunch at the Café Royal with Douglas when Queensberry, who suddenly appeared as though to satisfy his curiosity, was invited to join them. The experience so provoked Queensberry that he wrote to his son that his

Wilde and Douglas, ca. 1893

"intimacy with this man Wilde" must either cease or his income would end: "I am not going to try and analyse this intimacy, and I make no charge; but to my mind to pose as a thing is as bad [as] to be it [the prelude to his famous card charging Wilde as a posing sodomite]. With my own eyes I saw you both in the most loathsome and disgusting relationship as expressed by your manner and expression. Never have I seen such a sight as in your horrible features. No wonder people are talking as they are." Replying, Douglas sent his father a telegram: "WHAT A FUNNY LITTLE MAN YOU ARE" – to which Queensberry responded in his own manner: "You impertinent young jackanapes. I request that you will not send such messages to me by telegraph" (qtd. in Hyde, *Biography* 54–55). Wilde later told Douglas that the "the commonest street-boy" would have been ashamed to have sent such a telegram (*Letters* 446).

While Douglas was in Algeria, his father attempted to disrupt the opening night's performance of *The Importance of Being Earnest*. On receiving a telegram from his brother Percy informing him of the incident, Douglas left immediately for London. By the end of February, when he arrived at his club, Wilde had been handed Queensberry's famous calling card. Wilde first turned to Robert Ross, who advised that he ignore the card, but Douglas urged Wilde to have his solicitor arrange for Queensberry's arrest on the charge of criminal libel. Thus began the process of Wilde's three trials: the first as prosecutor of Queensberry, the remaining two as defendant (see The Trials, 1895). Douglas was determined to appear in the witness box against his father in order to expose the pretense that Queensberry was, as H. Montgomery Hyde remarks,

outwardly pretending to be a solicitious father trying to save his son, whereas in fact he had behaved like an inhuman brute towards every member of his family. Bosie did not appreciate – indeed he never grasped the point as long as he lived – that such evidence as this had nothing to do with the issue to be decided at the trial, and that, even if he did go into the witness box, he would never be permitted to give it. (*Biography* 78–79)

As the trial proceeded, Wilde's counsel urged him to drop his suit against Queensberry, who sent a message to Wilde: "If the country allows you to leave, all the better for the country! But if you take my son with you I will follow you wherever you go and shoot you!" (qtd. in Hyde, *Biography* 81). Meanwhile, Wilde wrote a letter to the editor of the *Evening News* explaining why he had agreed to drop the charges against Queensberry: "It would have been impossible for me to have proved my case without putting Lord Alfred Douglas in the witness-box against his father. Lord Alfred Douglas was extremely anxious to go into the box, but I would not let him do so" (*Letters* 386).

During this time, when Wilde was at the Cadogen Hotel in Sloane Street with Ross and Reginald Turner, Douglas went to see his cousin George Wyndham, M.P., to ask whether Wilde's arrest was inevitable; Wyndham said it was. Then, when Bosie returned to the hotel to discover that Wilde had been taken into custody, he followed Wilde's directions to ask various people to post bail. George Alexander and Lewis Waller, at whose theaters Wilde's plays were being performed, both refused. Constance Wilde's cousin Adrian Hope also refused.

Douglas was not permitted to see Wilde that evening at the Bow Street jail. During the following days, a preliminary hearing was held and a trial date set. Though it was widely believed that Douglas would also be arrested, George Wyndham wrote to his father, the Hon. Percy Wyndham, that there was "no case against Bosie," and friends had urged him to go abroad for one or two years: "Bosie took it very well. He thought I was going to ask him to go at once, and began by saying that nothing on earth would make him leave London until the trial was over. You may be sure that nothing will: he is quite insane on the subject" (qtd. in Hyde, *Biography* 84). Nevertheless, Wilde's counsel, Edward Clarke, urged Douglas to go abroad since his presence might prejudice Wilde's chance of an acquittal. Douglas agreed only if Wilde approved. Douglas's last visit to Wilde, in Newgate Prison adjoining the Old Bailey, occurred on 23 April. On the following morning, he left for France.

After Wilde's conviction and sentence to two years at hard labor, Douglas sent a petition to Queen Victoria, appealing to her to pardon Wilde, "unjustly convicted by the force of prejudice; a victim not to the righteous indignation of abstract justice but rather to the spite and unscrupulous cunning of another man, the Marquess of Queensberry, whose son I have the misfortune to be" (qtd. in Hyde, *Aftermath* 203). At Windsor, the Queen's private secretary prevented the petition from reaching her and sent it to the Home Secretary, who replied with a formal letter of rejection to Douglas in Rouen.

Wilde's displeasure with Douglas occurred over an article that the *Mercure de France* had asked Douglas to write on the Wilde affair. In the article, he had planned to include some incriminating letters previously used in the trials. News of Douglas's intent reached Wilde, who was "much annoyed." Wilde then asked Robert Sherard to prevent the article's publication. When the periodical asked Douglas to omit the letters, he refused; hence, the article never appeared (the MS. is at Princeton).

In an attempt to reconcile himself with Wilde, Douglas wrote to More Adey, who was reportedly soon going to visit Reading Prison:

> If only you could make him understand that though he is in prison he is still the court, the jury, the judge of my life and that I am waiting hoping for some sign that I have to go on living. There is nobody to play my cards in England, nobody to say anything for me, and Oscar depends *entirely* on what is said to him, and they all seem to be my enemies....

In this letter, Douglas protests that he has suffered more than Wilde: "The only thing that could make his life bearable is to think that he is suffering for me because he loved me, and if he doesn't love me I can't live and it is so utterly easy to die.... Tell him that I know I have ruined his life, that everything is my fault, if that pleases him." Adey, however, had seen Wilde before the letter arrived; hence, he urged Douglas "to show the love which I know you have for him by the most difficult of all things – *waiting*" (qtd. in Hyde, *Biography* 94–95).

When Wilde's release from prison approached, Constance Wilde's solicitor wrote to More Adey on 10 May 1897, to inform Wilde

> how absolutely fatal to him any further intercourse with Lord Alfred Douglas will be: apart from the fact that Lord Alfred Douglas

is a "notoriously disreputable companion" Lord Queensberry has made arrangements for being informed if his son joins Mr. Wilde and has expressed his intention of shooting one or both. (qtd. in Hyde, *Biography* 104)

Though Wilde's letters to Douglas after his release were subdued, by 4 June they were affectionate: "Of course I love you more than anyone else. But our lives are irreparably severed, as far as meeting goes. What is left to us is the knowedge that we love each other, and every day I think of you, and I know you are a poet, and that makes you doubly dear and wonderful." But their meeting was now out of the question since Queensberry represented a threat to both of them if he created a scandal: "...it would utterly destroy my possible future and alienate all my friends from me" (*Letters* 595, 613). Douglas, however, was accusing Ross and Adey of collusion with Constance Wilde so that she would withdraw her allowance of £150 if he and Wilde met. Ross urged Douglas to provide Wilde with the same amount and "then let Oscar choose which he likes" (qtd. in Hyde, *Biography* 107).

At the end of August, Wilde and Douglas were finally reunited, though only briefly, in Rouen. Later, Douglas wrote: "Poor Oscar cried when I met him at the station. We walked about all day arm in arm, or hand in hand, and were perfectly happy" (*Autobiography* 152). They agreed to meet again in Naples in six weeks. Meanwhile, Wilde wrote to him from Berneval: "Everyone is furious with me for going back to you, but they don't understand us. I feel that it is only with you that I can do anything at all. Do remake my ruined life for me, and then our friendship and love will have a different meaning to the world" (*Letters* 637). When Constance received news of Wilde's meeting with Douglas, she cut off his weekly allowance, though she later restored it.

With his father's death, Douglas inherited £15,000 (the sum of 8,000 immediately). Ross suggested that Douglas give £2,000 to Wilde, but he refused; however, he sent Wilde regular checks for various sums – between £10 and £125 – as indicated in his pass-book for 1900. At the end of that year, when Wilde was near death, Douglas was shooting in Scotland; hence Turner, at Wilde's bedside, had no address; Ross, who had been in Menton, informed Douglas on 1 December, but it was too late. When he did arrive, he paid for the funeral expenses.

In the years following, Douglas's history includes a marriage in 1902 to the poet Olive Custance (1874–1944), a contributor to the *Yellow Book* and author of four volumes of verse. After ten years of their marriage, they separated (the result of her father's interference with respect to their only son), but they continued a friendly relationship. The memory of Wilde, however, was constant in his life.

In 1907, Douglas became the editor (and then proprietor) of the *Academy*, a literary publication, which he sold in 1910 after a series of legal problems in the courts (indeed, his life was filled with suits – generally on grounds of libel – either brought by him or against him; the most notable was a case of criminal libel involving Winston Churchill, resulting in Douglas's incarceration for six months).

When Arthur Ransome's *Oscar Wilde: A Critical Study* (1912) appeared, Douglas sued the author for libel over certain passages in *De Profundis*, which had been omitted by Ross in the published version. The entire letter was read aloud in court when Douglas insisted that he had never received a copy despite Ross's assertion that one had been sent to him in 1897 (whatever was sent – whether the entire letter or excerpts – Ross, in a statement prepared for his solicitors, said that Douglas had told him and Wilde that he had thrown the typescript almost immediately into the fire). The jury found that the passages published from *De Profundis* were true. In the second edition, Ransome removed the passages out of consideration for Douglas.

In 1914, Douglas's *Oscar Wilde and Myself*, most of it written by his former assistant editor of the *Academy*, Thomas William Hodgson Crosland (1865–1924), was inspired by Douglas's defeat in the *De Profundis* trial, for much of the book expresses outrage over Wilde's "lies" in his prison letter and Ross's alleged role in failing to send Douglas a copy. Crosland's style is vituperative and insulting, as in his description of Wilde as "this big fat man" and in his denigration of Wilde as an artist. In later years, Douglas repudiated the book. In 1912, Crosland, who had a pathological hatred of Wilde, published *The First Stone: On Reading the Unpublished Portions of Oscar Wilde's "De Profundis,"* a free verse diatribe,

which begins: "Thou, / The complete mountebank, / The scented posturer, / The flabby Pharisee /... The whining convict / And Prince of Hypocrites...." In *The Autobiography of Lord Alfred Douglas* (1929), which is principally about his relationship with Wilde, the tone is much less disparaging and the praise of Wilde as man and writer more abundant. Finally, in *Oscar Wilde: The Summing Up* (1940), Douglas's awareness that this work on the subject would be his final estimate of his friend subdued some of his lingering resentments, though he was also concerned with his self-image: "I have, as I hope is well known, nothing but abhorrence for homosexuality..." (17). Furthermore, he was not reluctant to make some harsh judgments: he calls Frank Harris's biography of Wilde, for example, "an ignoble and pornographic book" (135). At the end of *The Summing Up*, Douglas pays his final tribute to Wilde: "He had, as Shaw truly says, an unconquerable gaiety of soul which ever sustained him, and, while he had lost the faculty of writing, he retained to the last his inimitable supremacy as a talker" (138).

References: *The Autobiography of Lord Alfred Douglas*, 2nd ed. (1931; rpt. 1970); H. Montgomery Hyde, *Oscar Wilde: The Aftermath* (1963); Brian Roberts, *The Mad Bad Line: The Family of Lord Alfred Douglas* (1981); Mary Hyde, ed., *Bernard Shaw and Alfred Douglas: A Correspondence* (1982); H. Montgomery Hyde, *Lord Alfred Douglas: A Biography* (1984); David Eakin, "In Excelsis: Wilde's Epistolary Relationship with Lord Alfred Douglas," *Twilight of Dawn: Studies in English Literature in Transition*, ed. O M Brack (1987).

DOWSON, ERNEST (1867–1900)

A poet, novelist, and short story writer, Dowson was born into a comfortable middle-class family, his father the owner of a dry dock in Limehouse. As a boy, Ernest, having spent much time in southern France in the company of his father, developed considerable proficiency in the language. After a brief attendance, from 1886 to 1888, at Queen's College, Oxford, he left without a degree and joined his father's firm in 1889. As a result of his acquaintance at Oxford with the poet Lionel Johnson, now living in London, Dowson became part of the circle that in May 1890 established the Rhymers' Club. Probably in the same year, he met Wilde, who occasionally attended meetings, but they did not establish a friendship until the time of Wilde's trials and the post-prison years on the Continent.

In April and May 1895, none of Dowson's extant letters mentions Wilde's trials, but in May he visited Wilde, who was on bail before his final trial, and in June 1896, he alludes to Wilde in a letter to Arthur Moore, Dowson's collaborator on two novels, as "that poor victim of English hypocrisy" having to live through "his torture" (Dowson, *Letters* 369). In France at the time, Dowson also wrote to Constance Wilde to inform her of the "enthusiasm" with which the Parisian audience at the Théâtre de l'Oeuvre responded to the first production of *Salomé* on 11 February 1896: "It is astonishing how different the feeling about him is in Paris to what it is in London" (Dowson, *Letters* 343).

After Wilde's release from prison in May 1897, Dowson spent much time with him in Dieppe, where Wilde had gone directly from England. On 5 June 1897, Wilde wrote to him from Berneval-sur-Mer: "Cher Monsieur le Poète, It was most kind of you coming to see me, and I thank you very sincerely and gratefully for your pleasant companionship and the many gentle ways by which you recalled to me that, once at any rate, I was a Lord of Language, and had myself the soul of a poet" (*Letters* 597). Around 10 June, Dowson wrote to a friend about Wilde's "enormous joy in life just at this moment.... He was in wonderful form, but has changed a good deal – he seems of much broader sympathies, much more human & simple. And his delight in the country, in walking, in the simplicities of life is enchanting" (Dowson, *Letters* 384). On 16 June, Wilde invited him again to Dieppe: "Why are you so persistently and perversely wonderful?" (*Letters* 612). Later that month, they spent their days together, and after they parted once again, Wilde wrote around 30 June: "Tonight I am going to read your poems – your lovely lyrics [probably in *Verses*, 1896] – words with wings *you* write always. It is an exquisite gift, and fortunately rare in an age whose prose is more poetic than its poetry" (*Letters* 619).

At about this time, Yeats heard a "wonderful tale" from Dowson concerning his adventure with Wilde in Dieppe. When Dowson "pressed upon [Wilde] the necessity of acquiring 'a more wholesome taste,'" they pooled their financial resources and proceeded to the appropriate place, accompan-

Dowson at Oxford

nied by a cheering crowd. At their destination, Dowson and the crowd waited in the street until Wilde emerged. To Dowson, he whispered, "The first these ten years, and it will be the last. It was like cold mutton" – then he added aloud so that the crowd could hear, "But tell it in England, for it will entirely restore my character" (*Autobiography* 219).

After some additional meetings, Dowson last saw Wilde in June 1899. After Dowson died on 23 February 1900, aged 32, Wilde told the publisher Leonard Smithers how "greatly distressed" he was over such a sudden death:

Poor wounded wonderful fellow that he was, a tragic reproduction of all tragic poetry, like a symbol, or a scene. I hope bay-leaves will be laid on his tomb, and rue, and myrtle too, for he knew what love is. He was a sweet singer, with a note all the lovelier because it reminds us of how thrushes sang in Shakespeare's day. If he is not yet laid to rest or unrest, do put some flowers for me on his grave. (*Letters* 816)

References: *The Autobiography of W. B. Yeats* (1938; rpt. 1965); Mark Longaker, *Ernest Dowson,*

3rd ed. (1967); Desmond Flower and Henry Maas, eds., *The Letters of Ernest Dowson* (1967).

DOYLE, ARTHUR CONAN (1859–1930)

A novelist and short story writer, Doyle was practicing medicine at Southsea, Portsmouth, when he published his first Sherlock Holmes story, *A Study in Scarlet* (1887). He first met Wilde on 30 August 1889 at a dinner party in the Langham Hotel given by Joseph M. Stoddart (1845–1921), managing editor of *Lippincott's Magazine* (Philadelphia), who was planning to inaugurate an English edition of the periodical with an English editor and English contributors, the London publisher to be Ward, Lock. In his memoirs, Doyle recalls that "golden evening" when Wilde was enthusiastic about *Micah Clarke* (1889), which Doyle had recently published. Wilde's conversation left an "indelible impression" on him:

He towered above us all, and yet had the art of seeming to be interested in all that we could say. He had delicacy of feeling and tact, for the monologue man, however clever, can never really be a gentleman at heart. He took as well as gave, but what he gave was unique.... I should add that never in Wilde's conversation did I observe one trace of coarseness of thought, nor could one at that time associate him with such an idea. (73)

As a result of that evening, Doyle and Wilde each promised to write stories for *Lippincott's*, eventually published as *The Sign of Four*, the second Holmes story, and *The Picture of Dorian Gray*. Doyle's novel, which appeared in February 1890, features Thaddeus Sholto, who, Samuel Rosenberg suggests, is

a superaesthete who talks like Oscar Wilde and who even has several physical features which clearly identify him as the man whom Conan Doyle called "the champion of aestheticism." The obviously effeminate and effete Sholto reveals himself as a caricature of Wilde with his opening remarks: "Pray step into my sanctum. A small place...but furnished to my liking, an oasis of art in the howling desert of London." (171)

The description of Thaddeus Sholto also closely approximates that of Wilde, according to his contemporaries: "Nature had given him a pendulous lip, and a too visible line of yellow and irregular teeth, which he strove feebly to conceal by constantly passing his hand over the lower part of his face."

The impression that Wilde made on Doyle, Rosenberg suggests, found expression in various characters, including Holmes himself, who became progressively more epigrammatic in some of Doyle's other Sherlock Holmes stories. In "The Red-Headed League," for example, an effeminate Duncan Ross (Robert Ross?) and John Clay (John Gray?) appear – echoing the names of two of Wilde's close friends. Complicating the associations is the fact that "Duncan Ross" is the alias of a character named William Morris! Roden contends that Doyle "profited from study of Wilde's dialogues such as 'The Decay of Lying' and 'The Critic as Artist' whose views are at various times adopted or refuted by Holmes, notably in the opening of 'A Case of Identity.' Wilde's hand beckons Sherlock Holmes into the 'nineties" (xxv).

When *Dorian Gray* appeared, Doyle wrote to give Wilde his impressions of the novel. In his reply – only a portion of which has survived – Wilde wrote: "I throw probability out of the window for the sake of a phrase, and the chance of an epigram makes me desert truth. Still I do aim at making a work of art, and I am really delighted that you think my treatment subtle and artistically good" (*Letters* 291–92). Years later, Doyle saw Wilde on only one other occasion:

...he gave me the impression of being mad. He asked me, I remember, if I had seen some play of his which was running. I answered that I had not. He said, "Ah, you must go. It is wonderful. It is genius!" All this with the gravest face. Nothing could have been more different from his early gentlemanly instincts. I thought at the time, and still think, that the monstrous development which ruined him was pathological, and that a hospital rather than a police court was the place for its consideration. (74)

After Wilde's death, Doyle published "The Adventure in the Empty House" (1903), which depicts an attempt by Holmes to foil his own murder by having a wax image of himself – a second self like Dorian Gray and his painting – sculpted by *Oscar* Meunier. Rosenberg – too ingenious for words – includes, in his many parallels, the projected murderer who is the Irish "*wild beast*," an outcast whose name is Sebastian Moran, the initials "S.M." evoking Wilde's pseudonym, "Sebastian Melmoth," adopted after his release from prison (180–81).

In the 1920s, Doyle, who had an abiding interest in psychic phenomena – he had attended seances as early as 1879 and was an investigator for the Society for Psychical Research in 1894 – was convinced that Wilde's alleged communication with a medium in 1923 and 1924 was geniuine and that Wilde had written an entire play through her. Some scripts published by the medium, Mrs. Hester Travers Smith (later Dowden), contain Wilde's alleged remarks, sometimes reminiscent of those in his writings. For example: "Being dead is the most boring experience in life. That is, if one excepts being married or dining with a schoolmaster." Doyle wrote to Mrs. Smith to congratulate her on her success: "I think that the Wilde messages are the most final evidence of continued personality that we have.... If you are in contact you might mention me to him – I knew him – and tell him that if he would honour me by coming through my wife who is an excellent automatic writer, there are some things which I should wish to say" (qtd. in Beckson, "Psychic Messages" 40). Apparently, Wilde declined to communicate with him through Mrs. Doyle.

In her *Psychic Messages from Oscar Wilde* (1924), Mrs. Smith published all of her communications with the ghostly Wilde, the most striking of which is his alleged comment on Joyce's *Ulysses*: "It is a singular matter that a countryman of mine should have produced this bulk of filth" (39). Doyle, whose review of the book appeared in the London *Daily News* (16 April 1924), wrote to her: "Wilde is in purgatory – to reduce his condition to popular terms – & will stay there until he gets over the frame of mind he shows in his script. By the way he shocked me once by saying to me that his play [*The Importance of Being Earnest*] was 'a perfect thing' which he repeats, I see, in his script" (qtd. in "Psychic Messages" 41). Doyle never doubted that Mrs. Smith had actually communicated with Wilde's spirit.

References: Arthur Conan Doyle, *Memories and Adventures* (1924); Samuel Rosenberg, *Naked is the Best Disguise: The Death and Resurrection of Sherlock Holmes* (1975); Karl Beckson, "Psychic Messages from Oscar Wilde: Some New A. Conan Doyle Letters," *English Language Notes* (Sept. 1979); Jon Lellenberg, *The Quest for Sir Arthur Conan Doyle* (1987); Christopher Roden, intro. to Doyle's *The Sign of Four* (1993).

"DRESS": *See* **"BEAUTY, TASTE, AND UGLINESS IN DRESS"**

THE DUCHESS OF PADUA

Written: Wilde began writing the play in 1882 and completed it in March 1883 for the American actress Mary Anderson. According to an agreement reproduced in Mason, Wilde would receive $1,000 on signing the agreement and $4,000 on Anderson's "acceptance and approval of the said tragedy" (327). However, when Wilde sent the completed play to her from Paris, she refused it, convinced that it would not please a modern audience (presumably because of its Renaissance setting, its echoes from Shakespeare, and its blank verse).

Published: The British Library has one of only 4 extant copies of 20 privately printed facsimiles of the signed manuscript containing 57 leaves, dated 15 March 1883, with Wilde's handwritten corrections (see Mason 326–27). The title page, which cites the work as "Op. II" (presumably, the second *dramatic* opus after *Vera*), contains no date; the subtitle of the play is "A Tragedy of the XVI Century," and the statement "Written in Paris in the XIX Century" also appears on the title page, though most of the play was written in America and in England. The first publication occurred in Volume 1 of the *Collected Edition* (1908), with a dedicatory letter "To A. S." (see Schuster, Adela), signed by Robert Ross.

In July 1898, while in Paris, Wilde expressed little admiration for his own play. He told Ross, who had apparently made some disparaging remarks about it: "You are quite right. *The Duchess* is unfit for publication – the only one of my works that comes under that category. But there are some good lines in it" (*Letters* 757). Despite this later judgment, earlier he had intended to publish it in a Bodley Head edition, but his imprisonment in 1895 resulted in cancellation of the project (Mason 331n).

Produced: 26 January 1891 at the Broadway

Theatre in New York with the title *Guido Ferrante*. In a letter to the actor-manager Lawrence Barrett (1838–91) late in 1890, Wilde had proposed to alter the title "so as to preserve the secret of authorship perfectly" (*More Letters* 92). But there may have been a secondary consideration: that is, to emphasize the role acted by Barrett (the role of Beatrice was performed by Minna Gale). Though Wilde had been "anxious to have the play judged entirely on its own merits" (*Letters* 283) – hence the omission of his name in the playbill – he later placed a paragraph revealing his authorship in the 6 February issue of the *Daily Telegraph* (London). However, the American reviewers already knew or suspected that Wilde was the author. The twenty-first performance ended the run on 14 February.

Sources: In addition to the obvious influence of Shakespeare and of Elizabethan/Jacobean revenge tragedy (particularly in the latter's florid rhetoric and conventional plotting though without the multi-scene fluidity of such drama), Victor Hugo – whom Wilde had met in Paris in 1883 – was another significant source. In a typical plot in Hugo's dramas, such as *Hernani* (1830) and *Lucrèce Borgia* (1838), a young nobleman has been raised without knowledge that he has been deprived of his rightful succession to power. When he discovers this injustice, he vows revenge. Attracted to a woman who is associated with the villain (in Hugo's *Angelo*, his wife), the hero broods endlessly on such lofty ideals as duty, honor, and love. In the final act, the tragedy results in multiple deaths on stage, including those of the hero and heroine. Wilde leaves little doubt that he has borrowed, for example, from Hugo's *Lucrèce Borgia*, for the first names of some of the minor characters in that play and in Wilde's are identical (Maffio, Jeppo, and Ascanio).

Furthermore, a significant influence as well as the source of some elements of Wilde's plot was undoubtedly Shelley's *The Cenci* (1819), which has a Renaissance setting with a story advancing revolutionary ideals (when the Lord Chamberlain banned it, the Shelley Society presented a private performance in 1886). As Katharine Worth suggests: "Shelley was a key figure in Wilde's pantheon and *The Cenci* expressed most of the sentiments the two writers had in common, including passionate devotion to freedom" (40).

The Plot: In Act I, Guido Ferrante, accompa-

nied by his travelling companion Ascanio, arrives in Padua from Perugia to meet a friend of his father, whom Guido had never known. Impatient, he decides to leave the meeting place just as Count Moranzone appears. (Prose dialogue at this point shifts to blank verse for the remainder of the play except for the beginning of Act IV, where ordinary citizens discuss the trial, and at the beginning of Act V, where common soldiers engage in dialogue.) The Count, Wilde told Mary Anderson, was "the incarnate image of vengeance: the bird of evil omen; the black spectre of the past moving like Destiny through the scene" (*Letters* 137). Moranzone reveals that Guido is the son of Lorenzo, "the Prince of Parma and the Duke / Of all the fair domains of Lombardy / Down to the gates of Florence." Lorenzo was lured by Giovanni Malatesta, "that foul adulterous Lord of Rimini," into a "treacherous ambush" and murdered on the public scaffold. Lorenzo's closest friend had betrayed him.

This execution occurred before Guido's birth, his mother having died after her premature delivery. Moranzone arranged to have Guido raised by a vassal. The man who "sold" Lorenzo, says the Count, is yet alive. When Guido vows to kill him, the Count urges that he "sell" the seller in his turn: "I will make you of his household, you will / At the same board with him, eat of his bread – " Then, when the "time is ripe – " The Count, however, cannot trust Guido to control his impulses, for his "hot young blood / Undisciplined nature, and too violent rage / Will never tarry for this great revenge." Guido, however, promises to follow the Count's counsel. When Guido wishes to know the identity of his father's murderer, Moranzone responds with an allusion to the imminent entrance of the Duke of Padua with his courtiers, implying that the Duke will be Guido's object of revenge. When the Duke enters moments later, Moranzone says to Guido: "The man to whom I kneel / Is he who sold your father! mark me well."

Moranzone introduces Guido to the Duke as his sister's son and requests a place for him at court. The Duke offers Guido some Machiavellian advice on how to conduct himself in the world:

So be not honest: eccentricity
Is not a thing should ever be encouraged....
See thou hast enemies,
Else will the world think very little of thee,

It is its test of power; yet see you show
A smiling mask of friendship to all men,
Until you have them safely in your grip,
Then you can crush them.

In an aside, Guido remarks: "O wise philosopher! / That for thyself dost dig so deep a grave." When the Duke, welcoming Guido to his "household," offers him his hand to kiss, Guido "starts back in horror, but at a gesture from Count Moranzone, kneels and kisses it." When the Duke withdraws with his entourage, Guido says: "So the Duke sold my father; / I kissed his hand." Moranzone urges Guido to separate himself from Ascanio in order to concentrate on his revenge.

Alone, Guido pledges himself to God "that punishest all broken oaths," to "forswear / The noble ties of honourable friendship.... / All love of women, and the barren thing / Which men call beauty...." This is no sooner said than the cathedral organ peals and a stately woman comes down the steps under a canopy attended by four pages in scarlet. Her eyes and Guido's meet: as she leaves the square, she turns to look back at him. When he asks who she is, a citizen responds: "The Duchess of Padua!"

Act II opens in the state apartment, its walls hung with rich tapestries depicting the festive procession of Venus and the Graces (a symbolic representation of what will later be the central theme of love and passion in the play). From the streets below, the shouts from a mob can be heard: "Death to the Duke!" Leaning on Guido's arm, the Duke enters, an indication that the young man has achieved considerable favor at court. When told that there are 2,000 people shouting below, the Duke (like one of Wilde's later dandies employing aesthetic rather than moral judgments) remarks:

I fear
They have become a little out of tune,
So I must tell my men to fire on them.
I cannot bear bad music!

Provoking the Duke's extreme anger, the Duchess places herself between the soldiers and the mob in order to prevent a massacre. She then appears before the Duke, "followed by a crowd of meanly dressed Citizens" to plead on their behalf not only for better food and water but also for less taxation. In response, the Duke, addressing himself to the

Cardinal, who is present, argues:

Why should I change their state,
Or meddle with an all-wise providence,
Which has apportioned that some men should
  starve
And others surfeit?
I did not make the world.

When all appeals to the Duke fail, Beatrice informs those in the crowd that her treasurer shall share 100 ducats among them. With scorn, the Duke commands her to remain within the palace: "I am grown weary of your airs and graces...." The Duke leaves, leaning on Guido's arm.

The Duchess remains brooding on how the seemingly good Guido could be such a confidant of her intolerable husband. When Guido returns, he not only vows his service to her but also confesses his love to her, the Duchess responding with her own avowal of love. As they embrace, she perceives Moranzone observing the scene. Soon, a servant enters with a silk-wrapped package for Guido: it is a dagger decorated with two leopards, a sign that the time for revenge has arrived. Beatrice, who had left the room momentarily, now returns to find Guido in a different mood. A "barrier," he tells her, has arisen between them. To her consternation, he informs her that they must part. Distraught, Beatrice resolves on suicide that night. Moranzone enters, dressed in symbolic black, looking for Guido. When Beatrice accuses him of separating her from Guido, Moranzone tells her that Guido does not love her and that she will never again see him. When she asks what his name is, the Count responds: "Revenge!"

Act III opens in a corridor of the Duke's palace. On the bottom step of a staircase leading to the Duke's chamber sits a masked, black-robed figure. As a storm with thunder and lightning rages outside, Guido enters the corridor through a window, having ascended it with a rope ladder. Challenging the seated figure, Guido learns that it is Moranzone, who removes his mask and says: "Thy murdered father laughs for joy to-night." But when he informs Guido of a plan by which to escape from Padua after the Duke is killed, Guido reveals that he will not kill him. Though Moranzone refers to Guido as "God's minister of vengeance," the younger man responds that "God hath no minister but his own hand."

As for his oath, Guido is determined to break it. He intends to lay the dagger on the Duke's breast as he sleeps with a note revealing who "held him in his power / And slew him not: this is the noblest vengeance / Which I can take." He could have performed the act at the time when Moranzone had first told him of the Duke's treachery, but now he is incapable of murdering in cold blood. Guido argues that his own father would never have crept, like a thief by night, to stab an old man in his bed.

While this argument goes on between Guido and Moranzone, groans are heard from the Duke's bedroom, but they place no importance on the sounds. After the Count makes his last appeal to Guido to exact vengeance on the Duke, he leaves through the window by means of the ladder. Guido then kneels to call upon his father's spirit to appear and to approve of his decision not to kill the Duke. When the spirit does not appear, Guido takes out the letter and dagger that he will place on the Duke's body while he sleeps. When Beatrice appears dressed all in white, Guido interprets her presence as a symbolic manifestation of divine approval of his decision:

> O white and spotless angel of my life,
> Sure thou hast come from Heaven with a
>   message
> That mercy is more noble than revenge?

When Beatrice is assured of Guido's love, she says that she must leave for Venice, where "They will not think of looking for me there." After he tells her that he will follow her "across the world," he says that he wishes to leave his letter and dagger in the Duke's chamber. But Beatrice informs him that she has killed the Duke, believing him to be the "barrier" that Guido had spoken of (the Duchess lapsing into familiar lines modeled after Lady Macbeth's):

> I did not think he would have bled so much,
> But I can wash my hands in water after;
> Can I not wash my hands? Ay, but my soul?

Horrified, Guido recoils from her bloody hands, but she insists that she has done the deed for his sake. Guido responds that she has killed his love for her: "...when you stabbed him / You stabbed Love with a sharp knife to the heart. / We cannot meet again." When he bids her be gone, she throws herself on her knees, pleading with Guido to kill her if love between them is no longer possible. When Guido remains firm, Beatrice concludes that "when men love women / They give them but a little of their lives, / But women when they love give everything." As the storm outside increases in intensity, Guido orders her away. But no sooner is she gone than he realizes his cruelty. As he calls out to her, the noise of soldiers is heard, then Beatrice's voice: "This way went he, the man who slew my lord." The Duchess, surrounded by servants bearing torches, appears at the top of the staircase and points to Guido, who is seized. A soldier removes the dagger from Guido's hand and shows it to the Captain of the Guard.

Act IV opens on the following day in the Court of Justice, where some citizens await the beginning of Guido's trial. When Moranzone enters, he inquires who the prisoner is: a citizen informs him that it is Guido Ferrante who is to be tried. In an aside, Moranzone remarks: "Yet it is strange he should have killed the Duke, / Seeing he left me in such different mood." When he learns that the Duchess had pointed Guido out and that the Duke was killed with the Duchess's dagger, Moranzone sees something "strange in this," something of a "mystery about this." The Lord Justice and other judges enter, then the Duchess, who takes her seat on the throne above the judges.

When Guido is charged with the Duke's murder, he refuses to respond to the charge. When the Lord Justice begins to pass the sentence of "swift Death," Moranzone interrupts him to inquire what proof exists of Guido's guilt. The Lord Justice cites the dagger taken from Guido's blood-stained hands, but Moranzone approaches the Duchess: "Saw I not such a dagger / Hang from your Grace's girdle yesterday?" Shuddering, she makes no answer. Approaching Guido, Moranzone whispers to him: "She did it! Nay, I see it in her eyes." But Guido assures him that he himself killed the Duke: "My father is avenged." Moranzone, however, disbelieves him, for had Guido committed the deed, his father's dagger, not the Duchess's, would have been found in his hands. Meanwhile, the Duchess glares at the two of them. When Moranzone threatens to unmask her, Guido appeals to the Lord Justice to reveal the name of the Duke's murderer. Beatrice forbids him to speak, but the Lord Justice cites the law that permits the accused to defend himself.

The Duchess insists that a "most vile traitor" to the state is an exception to the law. When the judges retire to examine the statutes, the Duchess tells Guido that he will die with his secret. When the Lord Justice returns, he announces that because Guido is "alien born, not Paduan, / Nor by allegiance bound unto the Duke," he has the "right of public utterance / Before the people and the open Court." The Duchess, demanding to see the statute, tears the page out of the volume and orders a horse for a an immediate journey to Venice. The Lord Justice, however, forbids her to leave until the trial is completed. Offended, the Duchess challenges his authority, but the Lord Justice has the doors closed to her. He then turns an hourglass upside side, indicating the amount of time granted to Guido to explain his case. He describes in detail how he killed the "treacherous villain" who had betrayed his father (the dagger, he says, he had found by chance in the chamber). Guido is condemned to death. As he is led off, the Duchess stretches out her arms and rushes down the stage, shouting "Guido! Guido!" She then faints.

Act V opens in a dungeon, where Guido is asleep while five soldiers are playing dice and discussing the Duchess's failed attempt to secure a pardon for him. Since Guido is of noble blood, he has the choice of taking poison, a goblet of which has been placed on a table near him. When the Duchess enters, disguised, and shows a ring (revealing her rank), the soldiers leave. She contemplates the poison: "...I must die; / I have been guilty, therefore I must die. / He loves me not, and therefore I must die." As the execution bell begins to peal, she drinks the poison. Guido, awakening, is unaware that the Duchess will shortly die. She informs him that he must dress in her cloak and mask so that he may leave disguised, the signet ring providing passage from the prison. Horses near the prison are waiting to take him to Venice. But he declines her offer, reaffirming his love for her and refusing to permit her to die for him.

As the Lord Justice, the Headsman with his axe, and monks bearing candles are seen through the grated windows proceeding down the corridor, Guido takes up the goblet but discovers that it is empty, the Duchess confessing that she has already drunk the poison. What follows is a Wagnerian ending: Guido and the Duchess profess their mutual love at great length as the monks begin to chant outside. There is always time, however, for

a last-minute borrowing from *Hamlet* as the Duchess is dying: "The cold meats of my husband's funeral feast / Are set for you; this is a wedding feast." Shortly thereafter, echoes from *Macbeth* again resound:

> ...Oh, do you think that love
> Can wipe the bloody stain from off my hands,
> Pour balm into my wounds, heal up my hurts,
> And wash my scarlet sins as white as snow?

They kiss just as the Duchess is in her final death agony: she "leaps up in a dreadful spasm of death, tears in agony at her dress, and finally, with face twisted and distorted with pain, falls back dead in a chair." Guido seizes her dagger and kills himself. As Katharine Worth suggests, the image of the Duchess dead in her chair and Guido "lying dead across her," as Wilde's stage directions indicate, form a secular *Pieta* (46). Wilde concludes the play, its mood consistently religious, with these final stage directions: "The Lord Justice rushes forward and drags the cloak off the Duchess, whose face is now the marble image of peace, the sign of God's forgiveness."

Early Theater Reviews: The reviewer in the *New York Times* (27 Jan. 1891), regarding Wilde's play as "better than the ordinary," cites the oath of vengeance entered into by Guido as "a reminder of a dozen almost forgotten tragedies, but there are some passages full of the fire of eloquence. The rhythm is there, if there is not much in the matter." There are, the reviewer continues, "a number of well-imagined and skilfully wrought scenes" in the play, and "many passages that must have been written in a glow of excitement." Though "a competent authority" is cited as attributing the play to Wilde later in the review, the reviewer alludes to "the author, whoever he is" (rpt. in Beckson).

In the *New York Daily Tribune* (27 Jan.), the "eagerly attentive, and often kindly responsive audience" at the Broadway Theatre responded "at certain telling points...with earnest applause." The blank verse is "always melodious, often eloquent, and sometimes freighted with fanciful figures of rare beauty." However, it is "less a tragedy, however, than a melodrama – by which is meant a drama of situation. To this ingredient everything is moulded and sacrificed." The reviewer concludes that the "radical defect of the work is insincerity" (a term frequently used in the late 19th century to characterize a degree of artifice, as indicated in the remark that follows: "No one in it is natural...."). The reviewer, remarking that the authorship has not been disclosed, reveals that several years ago the play was called *The Duchess of Padua*: "The author of it is Oscar Wilde" (rpt. in Beckson).

The reviewer in the *New York Herald* (27 Jan.) reported that "there was no doubt at all about the interest roused last night or the enthusiasm it at times created." Though not "a perfect play," it is "a good, strong, moving and effective play." He asks whether it "would have been written had William Shakespeare not created *Macbeth* and *Romeo and Juliet*," since it is full of scenes recalling them: "The plagiarism now and then is flagrant, but enough originality shines through the plot to make it interesting." The reviewer concludes by judging the performances as "unsatisfying": Barrett was "stilted," Gale "artificial," and the rest of the cast "feeble."

Manuscripts: According to Ross's prefatory note to Volume 1 of the *Collected Edition*, the original MS. of the play was stolen from Wilde's home in Tite Street in April 1895, at the time of the sale of Wilde's effects. Possibly, the MS. of 226 leaves, the final draft of the play with printers' marks (implying that the privately printed edition of 20 prompt copies was set from this MS.), now in the Fay and Geoffrey Elliott Collection, is that mentioned by Ross. The Clark Library has a MS. of 122 leaves, an earlier version of the play with many revisions in Wilde's hand. Eight leaves, possibly a portion from the Clark MS., were sold at the Anderson Galleries (New York) in 1924, and two leaves were sold at Christie's (New York) in 1981. The Taylor Collection at Princeton has a portion of the scenario of *The Duchess of Florence*, which became *The Duchess of Padua*, in addition to two pages from an apparent early draft of the play; the Hyde Collection also has a portion of a MS.

References: Alan Johnson, "The Italian Renaissance and Some Late Victorians," *Victorian Newsletter* (Fall 1969); Katharine Worth, *Oscar Wilde* (1983).

E

"EARLY CHRISTIAN ART IN IRELAND"

Published: *PMG*, 17 Dec. 1887, 3; rpt. in *Reviews* (1908). An unsigned review of Margaret Stokes's *Early Christian Art in Ireland* (1887).

Wilde welcomes Stokes's "useful little volume," for there had been a "want of a good series of popular handbooks on Irish art." He alludes to his father's work, such as *Memoir of G. Béranger and his Labours in the Cause of Irish Art and Antiquities* (1880), as "being somewhat too elaborate for the ordinary student." Though Stokes is not original, "it is unfair to look for originality in primers, and the charm of the illustrations fully atones for the somewhat heavy and pedantic character of the style."

Early Christian art in Ireland, in its rudest forms, says Wilde, returns us to the simplicity of the primitive Christian Church, "while to the period of its highest development we owe the great masterpieces of Celtic metal-work." On the whole, the book is "wonderfully well illustrated, and the ordinary art-student will be able to get some useful suggestions from it." Though Stokes hopes for "a revival of a native Irish school in architecture, sculpture, metal-work, and painting...," it may be questioned whether the peculiar forms characteristic of Irish ornamentation could be made at all expressive of the modern spirit." Still, says Wilde, there are aspects of beauty in ancient Irish art that could be instructive to the modern artist.

Though the value of the illuminations in the Book of Kells, "as far as their adaptability to modern designs and modern materials goes, has been very much over-rated," in certain artifacts, such as brooches, pins, and clasps, there is an untouched area for the modern goldsmith. "Now that the Celtic spirit has become the leaven of our politics, there is no reason why it should not also contribute something to our decorative art."

"EASTER DAY"

Published: *Waifs and Strays: A Terminal Magazine of Oxford Poetry* 1 (June 1879): 2; rev. in *Poems* (1881).

In mid-May 1877, Wilde sent a version of this poem to former Prime Minister Gladstone shortly after the statesman received Wilde's "On the Recent Massacres of the Christians in Bulgaria." In his accompanying letter, Wilde wrote: "The idea of *your* reading anything of mine has so delighted me, that I cannot help sending you a second sonnet" (see *Letters* 37–38).

This sonnet envisions the Pope, who, "Like some great god," wears "three crowns of gold...high upon his head" – a reference to the papal tiara – and is "borne upon the necks of men" – that is, in a formal procession. The scene of such splendor in Rome is contrasted with the suffering of Jesus, "who wandered by a lonely sea, / And sought in vain for any place of rest." (Wilde has clearly retreated from his attraction to Roman Catholicism as a result of his exposure to Hellenism.)

Manuscripts: The Clark Library and the British Library have MSS. of this poem, written in the spring of 1877 (but not in Rome, as Wilde indicates, since on Easter Day he was in Brindisi en route to Greece: see "Impression de Voyage").

ECHOES

This privately printed twelve-page pamphlet, undated (the British Library catalogue suggests the possibility of 1890), consists of four "poems in prose" – "The Poet," "Jezebel," "The Actress," and "Simon of Cyrene" – written down by Gabrielle Enthoven (1868–1950), the collector and theater historian who was Wilde's friend. Inserted into the pamphlet, which Enthoven presented to the British Museum in 1948, are two letters both addressed to G. E. Oldman, Principal Keeper of Printed Books. In one dated 19 March 1948, Enthoven states that Wilde used to tell her stories, and sometimes she wrote them down after he had left. "A friend," she says, printed five or six copies of the stories for her (sometime between 1890 and 1893, according to the other letter, undated, from Enthoven to Oldman).

However, since no evidence exists that Wilde had a hand in the printing of *Echoes*, the attribution of these works to Wilde remains doubtful. A complicating factor occurred in January, April, July, and October of 1912, when the same four stories (with only very minor differences) appeared in the *Mask: A Quarterly Journal of the Art of the Theatre* (Florence, Italy), edited by the scene designer and writer Gordon Craig. Each is described as "An Unpublished Story by Oscar Wilde" and each is preceded with the following note: "This story was told by Wilde to Miss Aimée Lowther when a child and written out by her. A few copies were privately printed but this is the first time it has been given to the public." Lowther (1871–1935), an actress, was a friend of Enthoven.

Vyvyan Holland included these poems in prose in Appendix C of his *Son of Oscar Wilde* (1954), noting that he had received a copy of these prose poems from an unnamed "lady": "When I came of age, I met a lady whom my father had known as a girl; she who had gone straight home after he had been fascinating her and some of her friends with his stories, and had written them down exactly as he had told them, so far as she could from memory" (42–43). Hart-Davis notes that it was indeed Lowther who gave Holland the prose poems (*Letters* 809n3).

EDWARD, PRINCE OF WALES (1841–1910)

Edward, who became King Edward VII after Queen Victoria's death in 1901, had a great love of the theater as well as the other arts. At the opening of the Grosvenor Gallery on 1 May 1877, Wilde appeared when Edward, Gladstone, Ruskin, and Henry James were also present. In the following year, Edward asked to meet Wilde, observing epigrammatically: "I do not know Mr. Wilde, and not to know Mr. Wilde is not to be known" (qtd. in Ellmann 128/123). He was soon a regular visitor, with various writers and artists, to the aesthetically decorated Thames House, which Wilde and Frank Miles shared. He even bought Miles's portrait *The Flower Girl*. Since Edward was then having an affair with Lillie Langtry, he was no doubt interested in Miles's drawings of the actress.

When F. C. Burnand, editor of *Punch*, amused audiences at the Prince of Wales Theatre in February 1881 with his play *The Colonel*, which satirized Aestheticism and Wilde, Edward was so impressed that he urged the Queen to see it in a command performance at Balmoral. Later that year, Wilde's hope for a production of his *Vera; or, The Nihilists* failed to materialize. Wilde scholars have generally agreed that, probably at the request of the Prince of Wales or those close to him, the production was withdrawn because its subject matter – the assassination of a czar – might be discomforting to his wife, the sister of the new czarina. New evidence, however, indicates that Wilde was unable to find the required financial support for the production (see *Vera; or, The Nihilists*).

When Wilde's society dramas established his fame as a playwright, Edward attended at least three of them. He approved of *Lady Windermere's Fan*. In the following year, he was delighted with *A Woman of No Importance* and reportedly said to Wilde: "Do not alter a single line." To which the playwright responded: "Sire, your wish is my command," which was followed by a later comment: "What a splendid country where princes understand poets" (qtd. in Ellmann 382/360). Edward also attended the premiere of *An Ideal Husband*, its plot involving corruption in high places – of particular interest, one presumes, to the prince.

"ELEUTHERIA"

The section title for the first eight poems in *Poems* (1881), meaning "freedom."

"ENDYMION. (FOR MUSIC)"

Published: *Poems* (1881).

Source: The Greek myth of Endymion has many variants, one identifying him as the son of Aethlius (who himself was Zeus' son), another as the son of Zeus himself. The best-known account is concerned with Endymion's relationship with Selene, the moon-goddess. When Selene first beholds Endymion, usually portrayed as a shepherd of great beauty, she falls in love with him and then seduces him. Acceding to Selene's request, Zeus grants Endymion one wish; when he chooses eternal sleep, he remains young forever. The most notable adaptation of the myth is Keats's poem *Endymion: A Poetic Romance* (1818).

In Wilde's poem of three fourteen-line stanzas, "Endymion" is set in traditionally pastoral, mythic Greece. The speaker throughout is the shepherd's lover who awaits his return: "O rising moon! O Lady moon! / Be you my lover's sentinel, / You cannot choose but know him well...." When she complains that Endymion has not returned, she accuses the moon: "False moon! False moon! O waning moon! / Where is my own true lover gone...?" The poem ends with her awareness of betrayal: "Ah! thou hast young Endymion, / Thou hast the lips that should be kissed!" (This final line is echoed in Wilde's "Nocturne," an early version of "Endymion.")

Manuscript: The Clark Library has a MS. fragment of the poem, lines 29–42.

"ENGLISH POETESSES"

Published: *Queen: The Lady's Newspaper and Court Chronicle* 84 (8 Dec. 1888): 742–43; rpt. in *Miscellanies* (1908).

Wilde begins with the announcement:

England has given to the world one great poetess, Elizabeth Barrett Browning. By her side Mr. Swinburne would place Miss Christina Rossetti, whose New Year hymn he describes as so much the noblest of sacred poems in our language, that there is none which comes near it enough to stand second.... Much as I admire Miss Rossetti's work, her subtle choice of words, her rich imagery, her artistic *naïveté*, wherein curious notes of strangeness and simplicity are fantastically blended together, I cannot but think that Mr. Swinburne has, with noble and natural loyalty, placed her on too lofty a pedestal. To me, she is simply a very delightful artist in poetry.

Alluding to Mrs. Browning, Wilde accounts for her superior gift as a poet: "Beyond [Christina Rossetti's work] and above it are higher and more sunlet heights of song, a larger vision, and an ampler air, a music at once more passionate and more profound, a creative energy that is born of the spirit, a winged rapture that is born of the soul, a force and fervour of mere utterance that has all the wonder of the prophet, and not a little of the consecration of the priest."

Wilde compares Mrs. Browning with the "great Aeolian poetess," Sappho, "undoubtedly a far more flawless and perfect artist" who "stirred the whole antique world more than Mrs. Browning ever stirred our modern age. Never had Love such a singer." He turns from Sappho to "one whose song still remains to us as an imperishable glory to our literature; to her who heard the cry of the children from dark mine and crowded factory, and made England weep over its little ones; who, in the feigned sonnets from the Portuguese, sang of the spiritual mystery of Love...." In envisioning her view of the poet's mission, Wilde writes that the poet was

to utter Divine oracles, to be at once inspired

prophet and holy priest.... She was a Sibyl delivering a message to the world, sometimes through stammering lips, and once at least with blinded eyes, yet always with the true fire and fervour of lofty and unshaken faith, always with the great raptures of a spiritual nature.... Indeed, Mrs. Browning is the wisest of the Sibyls, wiser even than that mighty figure whom Michael Angelo has painted on the roof of the Sistine Chapel at Rome..., for she realised that, while knowledge is power, suffering is part of knowledge.

As for her influence, Wilde attributes the "really remarkable awakening of woman's song that characterises the latter half of our century in England. No country has ever had so many poetesses at once." It would be impossible, Wilde contends, to list all of the women of the time who have "tried lute and lyre," but he does mention a dozen by name (the only ones who are likely to be known to the late 20th-century reader, however, are Alice Meynell and Edith Nesbit, famous for her children's stories, not her verse).

Wilde then presents a brief historical survey of English poetesses, beginning (so he believes) with the 15th-century Abbess Juliana Berners and ending with Emily Brontë, "whose poems are instinct with tragic power, and seem often on the verge of being great." Since Mrs. Browning's day, Wilde concludes, "our woods have become full of singing birds, and if I venture to ask them to apply themselves more to prose and less to song, it is not that I like poetical prose, but that I love the prose of poets."

"THE ENGLISH RENAISSANCE"

Published: *Miscellanies* (1908), which conflates early and final versions. (This lecture is also known as "The English Renaissance of Art.") The "final version" is in Kevin O'Brien's PhD diss., "An Edition of Oscar Wilde's American Lectures" (University of Notre Dame, 1973). Wilde gave the lecture during the first month of his 1882 lecture tour of the United States and Canada – that is, between 9 January and 9 February – continually revising it as he lectured in various Eastern cities. After complaints in the press that the lecture was boring, Wilde

immediately set to work, to improve the lecture, and by the time it reached the final version a month later, he had shortened it from two hours to an hour and a half by cutting out the flabby parenthetical paragraphs and by doing away with much of the French Revolution and other theoretical material. He improved the tone by making the whole lecture more informal and colloquial, but more significantly, he added to the decorative art, Ruskin-Morris school, that was tucked away at the back of the first version. (O'Brien, *Canada* 35)

The Lecture: Wilde begins by informing his audience that he will not attempt an abstract definition of beauty; rather, he will express the

general ideas which characterise the great English Renaissance of art in this century, to discover their source...and to estimate their future.... I call it our English Renaissance because it is indeed a sort of new birth of the spirit of man, like the great Italian Renaissance of the fifteenth century, in its desire to produce a type of general culture, its desire for a more gracious and comely way of life, its passion for physical beauty, its exclusive attention to form, its seeking for new subjects for poetry, new forms of art, new intellectual and imaginative enjoyments, and I call it our romantic movement because it is our most recent expression of beauty.

The two "forms of the human spirit" are the Hellenic and the romantic, which "may be taken as forming the essential elements of our conscious intellectual traditon, of our permanent standard of taste." In art and politics, there is but "one origin for all revolutions, a desire on the part of man for a nobler form of life, for a freer method and opportunity of expression." Such a "sensuous and intellectual spirit" central to this English Renaissance cannot be isolated from the "progress and movement and social life of the age that has produced it," for any attempt would sap it of its true vitality and possibly "mistake its true meaning."

In its "passionate cult of pure beauty, its flawless devotion to form, its exclusive and sensitive nature," it is to the French Revolution "that we must look for the most primary factor of its pro-

duction, the first condition of its birth, that great revolution of which we are all the children...." Rousseau summoned humanity back to the "golden age that still lies before us and preached a return to nature" while Goethe and Scott brought romance "back again from the prison she had lain in for so many centuries...."

Central to the English Renaissance is a "love of definite conception" and "clearness of vision... [which] lies at the base of all noble, realistic and romantic work as opposed to colorless and empty abstractions of our own eighteenth-century poets and of the classical dramatists of France, or of the vague spiritualities of the German sentimental school." For the artist, "there is no escape from the bondage of the earth, there is not even the desire of escape." He is the only "true realist; symbolism, which is the essence of the transcendental spirit, is alien to him." In Keats, one senses the

beginning of the artistic renaissance of England. Byron was a rebel and Shelley a dreamer, but in the calmness and clearness of his vision, his perfect self-control, his unerring sense of beauty, and his recognition of a separate realm for the imagination, Keats was the pure and serene artist, the forerunner of the Pre-Raphaelite school, and so of the great romantic movement of which I am to speak.

Though Blake had "claimed for art a lofty spiritual mission," his remoteness in poetry and painting and "the incompleteness of his technical powers" precluded any direct influence on other poets. The "absolute incarnation" of the "artistic spirit of this century" is first found in Keats.

Wilde then briefly gives an account of the founding and aims of the Pre-Raphaelite Brotherhood, among whom he cites Dante Rossetti, Holman Hunt, and Millais. They were, to be sure, objects of satire, "that usual homage which mediocrity pays to genius, doing here, as always, infinite harm to the public, blinding them to what is noble and beautiful...." These men brought to the "regeneration of English art" a desire for a "deeper spiritual value to be given to art, as well as a more decorative value." Preeminently, their art indicated a return to nature, to draw and paint "nothing but what they saw, they would try and imagine things as they really happened."

From Oxford came two young men, Edward

Burne-Jones and William Morris, the first of whom replaced the realism of the early days with a "more exquisite spirit of choice, a more faultless devotion to beauty," while to Morris "we owe poetry whose perfect precision and clearness of word and vision has not been excelled in the literature of our country, and by the revival of the decorative arts, he has given to our individualized romantic movement the social idea and social factor also."

Wilde remarks that the "absolute distinction of the artist" is not "his capacity to feel nature so much as his power in rendering it." Advancing the idea of art for art's sake, central to the concept of Aestheticism, Wilde remarks: "Art never harms itself by keeping aloof from the social problems of the day. Rather, by so doing it more completely realizes for us that which we desire, for to most of us the real life is the life we do not lead, and thus remaining more true to the essence of its own perfection...." The true artist will admit nothing "into the secure and sacred house of Beauty" that is "disturbing or that gives pain, nothing that is debatable, nothing about which men argue." If he does indulge in discussion of the social problems of his day, such subjects will be handled, "as Milton nobly expressed it, with his left hand, in prose and not in verse, in a pamphlet and not in a lyric."

Wilde borrows directly from Pater's famous remark concerning art in "The School of Giorgione" (1877), reprinted in *The Renaissance* (3rd. ed., 1888), which contends, "*All art constantly aspires towards the condition of music.*" Without acknowledging his source, Wilde continues: "...music is the art in which form and matter are always one, the art whose subject cannot be separated from the method of its expression, the art which most completely realizes the artistic ideal, and is the condition to which all the other arts are constantly aspiring."

In developing the ideal of Aestheticism, Wilde contends that "it is not an increased moral sense, an increased moral supervision that your literature needs." What follows is a passage that Wilde later repeated almost verbatim in the "Preface" to *The Picture of Dorian Gray* (1891): "Indeed, one should never talk of a moral or an immoral poem; poems are either well written or badly written, that is all." Proceeding with this aesthetic principle, Wilde argues that "any element of morals or implied

reference to a standard of good and evil in art is often a sign of a certain incompleteness of vision, often a note of discord in the harmony of an imaginative creation, for all good work aims at a purely artistic effect."

Again turning to Pater's Renaissance studies, Wilde echoes the "Conclusion" (which he will raid again later in the lecture): "Love art for its own sake, and then all things that you need will be added to you....the secret of life is in art." (For the other American lectures, see "The Decorative Arts," "The House Beautiful," and "Irish Poets and Poetry of the Nineteenth Century.")

Manuscripts: The Huntington Library has an incomplete MS. of this lecture delivered at Chickering Hall, New York, on 9 January 1882, some 89 folio sheets with autograph corrections and deletions. The Clark Library has MS. fragments of the lecture and a TS. corrected by Wilde.

Reference: Kevin O'Brien, *Oscar Wilde in Canada* (1982).

"L'ENVOI"

Published: As the introduction to Rennell Rodd's *Rose Leaf and Apple Leaf* (Philadelphia: J. M. Stoddart & Co., 1882) 11–28; rpt. in *Miscellanies* (1908). Wilde had arranged for the publication of the volume, which had previously been published in London as *Songs in the South* with a dedication to Rodd's father. In addition to the change in title, Wilde replaced the existing dedication with a new one of his own devising (see Rodd, Rennell). After publication of the book, Rodd wrote to Stoddart that he was "not over pleased at the way in which I find myself identified with much that I have no sympathy with.... There is one thing in it that has annoyed me excessively, and had I had a proof I should not have allowed it to stand. The dedication is too effusive.... I want to have it removed from all copies that go out for the future" (qtd. in Mason 185).

Beginning his "L'Envoi" (a "sending off" of his friend's volume), Wilde alludes to the principal subject of his 1882 American lecture tour:

Amongst the many young men in England who are seeking along with me to continue and to perfect the English Renaissance...there is none whose love of art is more flawless and fervent, whose artistic sense of beauty is more subtle and more delicate – none, indeed, who is dearer to myself – than the young poet whose verses I have brought with me to America....

Wilde associates Rodd's poems with what Keats called the "sensuous life of verse" and with "the scheme and symphony of the colour...so that the ultimate expression of our artistic movement in painting has been, not in the spiritual visions of the Pre-Raphaelites, for all their marvel of Greek legend and their mystery of Italian song, but in the work of such men as Whistler and Albert Moore, who have raised design and colour to the ideal level of poetry and music."

Echoing Walter Pater's dictum – "All art constantly aspires towards the condition of music" – in order to advance the notion of art for art's sake, Wilde comments that "music is the art in which form and matter are always one – the art whose subject cannot be separated from the method of its expression; the art which most completely realises for us the artistic ideal, and is the condition to which all the other arts are constantly aspiring" (a passage taken from Wilde's lecture "The English Renaissance"). In short, art does not deal with inspiring messages or moral instruction but with "the primary importance of the sensuous element in art, this love of art for art's sake, is the point in which we of the young school have made a departure from the teaching of Mr. Ruskin...."

Wilde praises Ruskin as the "Master indeed of the knowledge of all noble living and of the wisdom of all spiritual things....it was he who by the magic of his presence and the music of his lips taught us at Oxford that enthusiasm for beauty which is the secret of Hellenism...." Ruskin had "filled some of us, at least, with the lofty and passionate ambition to go forth into far and fair lands with some message for the nations and some mission for the world, and yet in his art criticism, his estimate of the joyous element of art, his whole method of approaching art, we are no longer with him; for the keystone to his aesthetic system is ethical always."

With respect to symbolism, Wilde contends that, in looking at a work of art, we should not be "dreaming of what it symbolises, but rather loving it for what it is. Indeed, the transcendental spirit is alien to the spirit of art" (yet later in his play *Salome*, Wilde strove for the aesthetic effects associated with the Symbolist Movement). Wilde states that design and colour are "enough to stir the most divine and remote of the chords which make music in our soul, and colour, indeed, is of itself a mystical presence on things, and tone a kind of sentiment."

After discussing some of Rodd's poems, Wilde returns to his view of art and of the life of the imagination. Again echoing Pater, Wilde contends that the artist will remain aloof from "discordant despair of doubt or the sadness of a sterile scepticism." Rather, he will be "always curiously testing new forms of belief....and searching for experience itself, and not for the fruits of experience."

Manuscript: The Fay and Geoffrey Elliott Collection has the MS. of this essay.

EPSTEIN, JACOB: *See* **THE TOMB OF WILDE**

"E TENEBRIS"

Published: *Poems* (1881); rev. in (1882), the Latin title meaning "Out of Darkness." Wilde probably wrote this poem in the spring of 1877, at a time when his religious impulses resulted in such poems as "Urbs Sacra Aeterna" and "Easter Day."

In this sonnet, the speaker expresses the need for spiritual succour: "Come down, O Christ, and help me!" Complaining that his heart is "as some famine-murdered land / Whence all good things have perished utterly," the speaker is convinced that his soul "in Hell must lie / If I this night before God's throne should stand." But the poem ends with the conviction (clearly, one of faith) that he will "behold, before the night," Jesus's "wounded hands, the weary human face."

F

"FABIEN DEI FRANCHI"

Published: *Poems* (1881); rev. in (1882). In the fourth edition in 1882, Wilde dedicated this poem "To My Friend Henry Irving," who had performed the roles of both Louis and Fabien dei Franchi in *The Corsican Brothers* by Dion Boucicault. Adapted from Alexandre Dumas *père*'s novel of murder and revenge, in which Fabien kills the murderer of his brother, the play was performed at the Lyceum Theatre from 18 September 1880 to 9 April 1881.

In this sonnet, Wilde describes the elements of the popular melodrama that Irving had successfully revived:

> The silent room, the heavy creeping shade,
> The dead that travel fast, the opening door,
> The murdered brother rising through the floor,
> The ghost's white fingers on thy shoulders
>   laid....

Such Gothic theatricialism is "well enough," says Wilde, but, addressing Irving, "thou wert made / For more august creation!" He suggests that such roles as Lear, Romeo, and Richard III would be more fitting: "Thou trumpet set for Shakespeare's lips to blow!"

Manuscript: The Huntington Library has the MS.

"THE FAITHFUL SHEPHERD"

Published: Karl Beckson and Bobby Fong, "A Newly Discovered Lyric by Oscar Wilde," *TLS*, 17 Feb. 1995, 9.

This pastoral poem is set in the idealized world mythically known as Arcadia, though, initially, the founder of the tradition, Theocritus, depicted a world based on Sicilian peasants (see "Theocritus"). The artificial pastoral world that developed after Theocritus expressed a yearning for an irretrievable past. In such a world, faithfulness to a lover is paramount, the source of Wilde's title, which appears in many traditional pastorals, such as John Fletcher's *The Faithful Shepherdess* (1608) and Battista Guarini's *Il Pastor Fido* (1590), meaning *The Faithful Shepherd*.

Written for an acquaintance, Wilde's poem appears on one side of a MS., a note to "My dear Jack Capel" on the reverse side, which includes a postscript: "something old-fashioned – for the spinet." John Mais Capel (b. 1862) had published *Six Songs* (London, 1889), consisting of musical settings for poems by Poe, Tennyson, and Byron. Wilde's allusion to the spinet suggests that possibly he hoped that Capel would set "The Faithful Shepherd" to music, hence the choice of a lyric with refrains, such as the roundelay. Perhaps because Capel, between 1892 and 1909, was associated with many London productions as actor, conductor, composer, or music director for plays by such playwrights as Jerome K. Jerome, Henry Arthur Jones, Brandon Thomas, and Ibsen, he was too preoccupied to provide a musical setting for Wilde's poem or perhaps, after composing settings for poems by Poe, Tennyson, and Byron, Capel regarded Wilde's as less inviting.

In his lyric, Wilde observes the conventions of pastoral verse, including a lament by a shepherd or shepherdess when either is not present. The unnamed shepherd loves his Phillis, one of the conventional names for shepherdesses in pastoral verse. Her absence ("But my love is far away") provides the speaker with the traditional motif of yearning for her return. The poem also has the musical qualities that Wilde may have thought would attract Capel's interest. The first two stanzas end with the refrain: "So I sing ah: well-a-day"; the third stanza concluding: "Roundelay, a roundelay, / I will sing a roundelay."

Manuscript: Johns Hopkins University has the MS.

"FANTAISIES DÉCORATIVES"

Published: *Lady's Pictorial* (Christmas Number, 1887): 2–3, with a full-page illustrated border for each of the poems in black by J. Bernard Partridge; rpt., without the illustrations, in *Poems* (1908).

From the mid to the late 19th century, the oriental "craze" among writers and artists – especially for Japanese artifacts – was the result of such collectors as Rossetti and particularly Whistler, whose paintings make use of such decorative objects, though often the women are occidental. Perhaps because of his admiration of Whistler,

Wilde employs Japanese settings in "Fantaisies Décoratives." Writing to the artist John Bernard Partridge (1862–1945), who illustrated some of Wilde's poems in the *Lady's Pictorial*, Wilde suggested that his two poems be set on a full page and that the "decorative design" be "around them and through them":

Perhaps, as the girl under the rose tree is Japanese, the children who are playing with the balloons should be Japanese also. They would give a unity to the composition. Round the verses of the first poem should be fluttering rose leaves, and round the verses of the second the balloons should float, the children holding the strings from the side of the page. (*Letters* 206)

The published illustration depicts an oriental woman in a kimono standing near a tea house, behind which an oriental man peers. In "Les Ballons," the children are not oriental.

Part I, "Le Panneau" suggests a Japanese panel (the meaning of the title), the first stanza depicting the color harmony favored by the Aesthetes:

With pale green nails of polished jade
  Pulling the leaves of pink and pearl
  There stands a little ivory girl
Under a rose-tree's dancing shade.

The printed version, revised, moves this stanza to the end of the poem with the first stanza echoing the final one in a slightly different form.

For Part II, "Les Ballons" (which contains four quatrains as opposed to eight in "Le Panneau"), Wilde revised the first stanza of another MS. titled "Impression de Paris: Le Jardin des Tuileries" (see Mason 78), now in the Huntington Library. "Les Ballons" is a striking anticipation of later Imagist poetry because of its non-discursive focus on clearly defined, suggestive images with relaxed cadences, the alliteration intensifying the lines, as in the opening stanza:

Against these turbid turquoise skies,
  The light and luminous balloons
  Dip and drift like satin moons,
Drift like silken butterflies.

The balloons "Reel with every windy gust," rising and reeling like dancing girls, "Each with coy fantastic pose, / Each a petal of a rose / Straining at a gossamer string." The poem concludes with the final image of the balloons in the trees:

Then to the tall trees they climb,
  Like thin globes of amethyst,
  Wandering opals keeping tryst
With the rubies of the lime.

Manuscripts: For "Le Panneau," the Berg Collection has MS. jottings of this poem – versions of lines 1–8 and 21–32 – with the title "Impression Japonais: Rose et Ivoire" (printed in Mason 102). Also, Mason prints fragmentary early versions of lines 1–8 and 21–24 with the title "Symphonie en Rose" (103). For "Les Ballons," the Huntington Library has a MS. (of an early version of "Le Jardin des Tuileries"), which has lines 1–4 of the present poem. An early MS. of "Le Panneau" (cited above as printed in Mason 103) contains lines 1–8 of the present poem. The close connections of these MSS. suggest that Wilde had one poem in mind when he composed them during his 1883 stay in Paris.

"A FASCINATING BOOK"

Published: *Woman's World* 2 (Nov. 1888): 53–56; rpt. in *Reviews* (1908). A signed review ("By the Editor" – that is, Wilde) of Ernest Lefébure's *Embroidery and Lace: Their Manufacture and History from the Remotest Antiquity to the Present Day*, trans. Alan S. Cole (1888). This book, Mason notes (223), provided Wilde with his description of embroidery in Chapter 11 of *The Picture of Dorian Gray*.

Wilde calls Alan Coles's "carefully-edited translation" of Lefébure's history of embroidery and lace as "one of the most fascinating books that has appeared on this delightful subject." The work has "not merely an important historical value, but as a handbook of technical instruction...of the greatest service by all needle-women." Wilde is convinced, like Cole, that the productions of embroidery should be placed on the same level with those of painting, engraving and sculpture, "though there must always be a great difference between those purely decorative arts that glorify their own material and the more imaginative arts in which the material is, as it were, annihilated, and absorbed into the creation of a new form."

Lefébure's work reveals that current English artists in embroidery are "merely carrying out certain old traditions of Early English art." Pope Innocent IV, Wilde notes, greatly admired the splendid vestments worn by the English clergy in 1246, and ordered similar articles from Cistercian monasteries in England. In alluding to the influence of Oriental art on Western decorative arts, Wilde remarks:

In Byzantium the two arts met – Greek art, with its intellectual sense of form, and its quick sympathy with humanity; Oriental art, with its gorgeous materialism, its frank rejection of imitation, its wonderful secrets of craft and colour, its splendid textures, its rare metals and jewels, its marvellous and priceless traditions.

Currently, Wilde continues, "We are beginning now to dye by Oriental methods, and the silk robes of China and Japan have taught us new wonders of colour-combination, and new subtleties of delicate design."

During the 15th century, a household of means retained "the services of an embroiderer by the year. The preparation of colours also, whether for painting or for dyeing thread and textile fabrics, was a matter which, M. Lefébure points out, received close attention from the artists of the Middle Ages." Early in the 16th century, books of embroidery designs appeared, and because of their success French, German, Italian, Flemish, and English publishers "spread broadcast books of design made by their best engravers."

After the Revolution ruined much of the lace industry, Napoleon encouraged the manufacture of lace and restored the "old rules about the necessity of wearing point-lace at Court receptions. A wonderful piece of lace, powdered over with devices of bees, and costing 40,000 francs, was ordered." Lefébure concludes with a remark concerning machine-made lace: "It would be an obvious loss to art," for a machine cannot do what a hand does. Art is absent "where formal calculation pretends to supersede emotion," where intelligence that guides handicraft is absent. Wilde concurs in these "admirable remarks, and with them we take leave of this fascinating book...."

FASHION AND THEATER

The importance of fashion on the London stage in the 1890s was the result of several developments at the time: in such theaters as the Haymarket, the Criterion, and the St. James's, leading actresses functioned as the equivalent of "living mannequins" for fashionable dressmakers and provided audiences with a standard for suitable public attire. An indication that the theater anticipated as well as reflected current fashion may be seen in the remark by Florence Alexander, who was in charge of women's costumes at the St. James's Theatre, where her husband, George Alexander (see entry), was the actor-manager: "I was rather 'extreme' with clothes on stage, for in those days people went to see the St. James's plays *before* ordering a new gown" (qtd. in A. E. W. Mason 233).

Fashion also functioned as a means of symbolizing themes and of overcoming resistance from audiences. When the producer of Henry Arthur Jones's *The Liars* (1897) at the Criterion Theatre objected to a too-explicit verbal expression of moral decay, the theater engaged a dressmaker to create risqué costumes, the visual equivalent. With the prominence of Ibsen's plays in the 1890s, the problem of presenting such challenging theater to audiences accustomed to sentimental drama was partly overcome, as Kaplan and Stowell write, with "smart gowns and chic accessories" (3).

In a letter to the *Daily Telegraph* in February 1891, Wilde, who had for years been concerned with the ugliness of male dress (see "More Radical Ideas upon Dress Reform"), cited the color of the costume worn by the actor Charles Wyndham in Dion Boucicault's *London Assurance* as the possible

basis for a new departure, not in the style, but in the colour of modern evening dress.... Freedom in such selection of colour is a necessary condition of variety and individualism of costume, and the uniform black that is worn now, though valuable at a dinner-party, where it serves to isolate and separate women's dresses, to frame them as it were, still is dull and tedious and depressing in itself.... (*Letters* 283).

In his plays, Wilde reacted to such conventions by creating dandies whose passion was precise attention to ties, waistcoats, and buttonholes – all designed to discomfort sober Victorian gentlemen on stage and in the audience. In *An Ideal Husband*, for example, Lord Goring changes his buttonhole three times a day in order to emphasize his dandiacal superiority to those involved in less imaginative and less aesthetic pursuits.

Women's dress, to be sure, offered more opportunities for variety and innovation, for dramatic characters, such as the adventuress or the puritan wife, could be "turned into 'fashion statements' that cut provocatively across moral and generic bounderies." Containing both an adventuress (Mrs. Erlynne) and a puritan wife (Lady Windermere), *Lady Windermere's Fan* provided the fashionable audience with a mirror in which it could see its own sophistication and elegance while, for the pit and gallery patrons, the opportunity "to watch with voyeuristic relish an intimacy between stage and stalls..." (Kaplan and Stowell 13).

Wilde's ironic stage direction for Mrs. Erlynne's first appearance – "*very beautifully dressed and very dignified*" – is a radical departure from the theatrical cliché of the "fallen woman," whose costume and demeanor would be expected to reflect her fallen state. In Act IV, Mrs. Erlynne rejects the idea of repentence for her past life by informing Lord Windermere that it is "quite out of date. And besides, if a woman really repents, she has to go to a bad dressmaker, otherwise no one believes in her."

Commenting on the production of *A Woman of No Importance*, "Florence," the fashion critic for the *Sketch*, regarded Hester Worsley's gown of white, veiled by silver-spangled tulle (a fine silk net), as "in itself...pretty, but somehow...hardly suited to the stately, puritanical Hester" (qtd. in Kaplan and Stowell 25), for, in Act II, Hester denounces fashionable society as "shallow, selfish, foolish...a dead thing smeared with gold." The gown's fabric, "glistening and shimmering with every movement," seemed inappropriate as a stage image in association with Hester's stern puritanism; hence, the reviewer in the *Sporting Times* (23 April 1893) remarks that "sermons and silk and satin gowns are incompatible." But the irony of the paradox undermines the self-righteous homilies by "the Puritan in white muslin" – apparently Wilde's intent. As for Mrs. Arbuthnot's two severe black gowns, "Florence" pronounced them "appropriate to a betrayed woman," as conventionally represented on the popular stage. However, the color and severity were also associated with dandiacal dress as well as with mourning apparel – an irony

when accompanied by a low neckline and form-fitting bodice, the erotic effect noted by Lord Illingworth.

In *An Ideal Husband*, Lady Chiltern (whose stern morality reminds one of Hester Worsley) was dressed, to undermine her severity, in "silks, diamonds, and rich brocades" (Kaplan and Stowell 28), the discrepancy noted by the *Queen* (12 Jan. 1895), which described her as "a paragon of correct principle, [who] nevertheless dresses enchantingly." The adventuress, Mrs. Cheveley, incurred the hostility of some critics, the *Lady's Pictorial* (12 Jan.) calling her "vulgar...undignified" and the *Illustrated Sporting and Dramatic News* (12 Jan.) regarding her as "overdressed," though, in the play, Lord Goring remarks in Act II: "Well, she wore too much rouge last night, and not quite enough clothes. That is always a sign of despair in a woman." However, her cloak of black and red satin – in which she visits Lord Goring on a late-evening call – was greeted with general approval by the fashion critics. But the most provocative costume that she wears – in Act I, an evening dress of emerald-green satin adorned with images of six dead swallows – prompted the *Sketch* to urge fashionable women "to make a stand against this veritable massacre of the innocents." Other periodicals also found Mrs. Cheveley's gown distasteful, the *Queen* (12 Jan.) regarding the dead birds as "an insignia of vice": "we have little doubt of the lady's character."

References: A. E. W. Mason, *Sir George Alexander and the St. James's Theatre* (1935); Joel H. Kaplan and Sheila Stowell, *Theatre and Fashion: Oscar Wilde to the Suffragettes* (1994).

"A FEW MAXIMS FOR THE INSTRUCTION OF THE OVER-EDUCATED"

Published: *Saturday Review of Politics, Literature, Science and Art* 78 (17 Nov. 1894): 533–34. Mason does not list the publication of these anonymous maxims. Hart-Davis remarks that these maxims "have never been included in the Wilde canon, but they certainly belong there" (*Letters* 378n4).

These 19 aphorisms contain many of Wilde's characteristically subversive ideas, as in the first one: "Education is an admirable thing. But it is well to remember from time to time that nothing that is worth knowing can be taught." And in denigrating utilitarian attitudes, Wilde remarks: "It is a very sad thing that nowadays there is so little useless information." A suggestive aphorism that may have provoked shock for some but laughter for others then follows: "To be really mediaeval one should have no body. To be really modern one should have no soul. To be really Greek one should have no clothes." The central theme, perhaps, of all of these aphorisms is concerned with advancing the image of dandyism: "Dandyism is the assertion of the absolute modernity of Beauty."

Wilde composed 35 other aphorisms, which were also intended for the *Saturday Review* but which appeared instead in the *Chameleon* (1894): See "Phrases and Philosophies for the Use of the Young."

"FIELD, MICHAEL": KATHERINE BRAD-LEY (1846–1913) and EDITH COOPER (1862–1914)

The collaboration of Katherine Bradley and her niece Edith Cooper, who published, as "Michael Field," resulted in many volumes of poems and verse plays, only one of which was ever produced. The two seem to have first met Wilde at an "At Home" held by the American poet and journalist Mrs. Louise Chandler Moulton (1835–1908) on 21 July 1890. Bradley (the "Michael" of the two) recognized Wilde and later recorded her impressions:

> He has a brown skin of coarse texture, insensitive surface and no volcanic blood fructifying it from within – powerful features, a firm jaw and fine head – with hair that one feels was much more beautiful some years ago.... The whole face wears an aspect of stubborn sense, and the aesthete is discovered simply by the look of well-being in the body (soul, take thine ease!).... But the dominant trait of that face is the humour – humour that ridicules and gently restrains the wilfulness, the hobby-horse passion, the tendency to individualism, of the rest of the man. (*Works* 135)

On another occasion when Michael Field visited Wilde, they were received by Constance: "The afternoon goes on in a dull fashion till Oscar enters. He wears a lilac shirt and heliotrope tie, a great primrose pink – very Celtic combination, ma foi! His large presence beams with the 'Heiterkeit'

[gaiety] of a Greek God that has decended on a fat man of literary habits" (*Works* 138–39). On another occasion, Wilde met them with considerable coldness, according to the journal entry written by Michael:

> ...I put out my hand, which he takes (afar off) and never addresses a single word to me after. I have not often seen such rudeness – he is not of the men who can be rude offensively and yet escape.... We were not well dressed, as the day had begun with rain – we do not belong to the fashionable world – so Oscar rolls his shoulders toward us. (*Works* 139–40).

In August 1890, Wilde acknowledged their gift of *The Tragic Mary*, which, he writes, "is closer to flesh and blood than the Mary of Swinburne's *Bothwell* [1865]..." (*Letters* 272). When the Independent Theatre was planning to produce their prose drama titled *A Question of Memory* on 27 October 1893, at the Opera Comique in London, Wilde offered suggestions to both of them:

> Tell Grein [manager of the Independent Theatre] to select only *young* actors – there are possibilities of poetry and passion in the young – and picturesqueness also, a quality so valuable on the stage. Shun the experienced actor; in poetic drama he is impossible. Choose graceful personalities – young actors and actresses who have charming voices – that is enough.
>
> I look forward to listening to your lovely play recited on a rush-strewn platform, before a tapestry, by gracious things in antique robes, and, if you can manage it, in gilded masks. (*Letters* 345)

After seeing the play, Wilde wrote that their third act was "quite admirable – a really fine piece of work – with that touch of terror our stage lacks so much" (*Letters* 346).

Michael Field's published journal (containing excerpts from the many holograph journals in the British Library) does not include any comments on the Wilde debacle. In 1906, the two saw *A Florentine Tragedy*, which was "vulgar and unconvincing and cannot bear the weight of Oscar's rhetoric. I begin to wonder what we came forth to see." However, when *Salome* followed on the same program, the journal records their delight: "At once, what we came for. Eastern luxury in moonlight. A picture painted by Titian or Delacroix...no, only by Ricketts himself. Never has the stage been so wonderfully used.... The whole play is full of harmony and 'leit motifs,' of evocations, and all this character is brought out by gesture and timbre of voice" (*Works* 250).

References: T. & D. C. Sturge Moore, eds., *Works and Days: From the Journal of Michael Field* (1933); Chris White, "'Poets and lovers evermore': The Poetry and Journals of Michael Field," *Sexual Sameness: Textual Differences in Lesbian and Gay Writing*, ed. Joseph Bristow (1992).

"A FIRE AT SEA"

Published: *Macmillan's Magazine* 54 (May 1886): 39–44; rpt. in Owen Dudley Edwards, ed., *The Fireworks of Oscar Wilde* (1989). This Ivan Turgenev story, states an accompanying note, "is said to have been a real incident in the novelist's life, dictated by him in French three months before he died." Though Wilde's name as translator does not appear, Mason based the attribution in his bibliography on a letter from *Macmillan's Magazine* to him, dated 8 November 1912, citing the translation, "which appears to have been written by Oscar Wilde" – quoted in *The Library of William Andrews Clark, Jr.: Wilde and Wildeiana*, eds. Robert Ernest Cowan and William Andrews Clark, Jr. (1924), 3:50.

Manuscript: Texas has an incomplete signed MS. of the translation with the first five pages missing.

FIRST COLLECTED EDITION OF THE WORKS OF OSCAR WILDE (1908): *See COLLECTED EDITION*

"THE FISHERMAN AND HIS SOUL"

Published: *A House of Pomegranates* (1891), with illustrations by Charles Ricketts for each story. "The Fisherman and His Soul" is dedicated to H. S. H. Alice, Princess of Monaco (1858–1925), born Alice Heine, a grandniece of the poet Heinrich Heine. The widow of the Duc de Richelieu, she married Prince Albert Honoré Charles of Monaco in 1889. She was widely known as a patron of the arts.

Sources: Wilde probably drew inspiration from Hans Christian Andersen's tale "The Little Mermaid" or from an Old Danish ballad, "The Deceived Merman," the source of Matthew Arnold's poem "The Forsaken Merman" (1849), which, of course, Wilde knew. In the latter work, which is concerned with the conflict between religious and pagan values, Arnold's figure yearns for his wife, who has deserted him because she complains that her "kinsfolk pray / In the little grey church on the shore to-day. / 'Twill be Easter-time in the world – ah me! / And I lose my poor soul, Merman, here with thee."

The Plot: Every evening a young Fisherman goes out to sea to cast his nets into the water. On one evening, they contain a beautiful young Mermaid fast asleep. When he clasps her in his arms, she cries out in terror and tries to escape. Weeping, she pleads to be released, for she is the only daughter of an aged king. The Fisherman, however, agrees to release her if she promises to come and sing to him when he calls to her; in that way, the fish, who delight to hear the song of the seafolk, will fill his nets. Swearing an oath, she promises to do as he bids. When the Fisherman releases her, she sinks into the water, "trembling with a strange fear."

On every evening, the Fisherman calls to the Mermaid, who appears and sings her "marvellous song." After he catches the fish that approach to hear her song, the Mermaid "would sink down into the sea, smiling at him." With each passing day, her voice becomes sweeter to his ears; indeed, he forgets his nets and neglects his boat. On one evening, he calls to her: "Little Mermaid, little Mermaid, I love thee. Take me for thy bridegroom, for I love thee." Shaking her head, she responds: "Thou hast a human soul. If only thou would'st send away thy soul, then could I love thee." Pondering what use his soul is to him, the Fisherman decides to send it away: "You shall be my bride," he cries to the Mermaid. But neither he nor the Mermaid knows how to separate the body from the soul.

On the next morning, the Fisherman sees a priest to ask him how he can send his useless soul away. Distressed, the priest protests that "the soul is the noblest part of man, and was given to us by God that we should nobly use it." He urges the Fisherman to think no more of this matter, "for it is a sin that may not be forgiven. And as for the Sea-folk, they are lost, and they who would traffic with him are lost too." The Fisherman, however, insists that his soul is useless if it stands between him and his love. The priest, he cries, does not know what he says: "For her body I would give my soul, and for her love I would surrender heaven" (the Faust theme, to be repeated in *The Picture of Dorian Gray*, which also dramatizes the divided self). The priest, refusing to bless him, drives him from his door. When he offers to sell his soul to some passing merchants, they mock him, insisting that it is of no use to them. Puzzled, the Fisherman recalls that the priest had said that "the soul is worth all the gold in the world."

Next, the Fisherman sees a witch, who will show him how to send his soul away if he dances with her. On that night, he must come to the top of the mountain. During the full moon, the Fisherman climbs the mountaintop, and at midnight witches fly in for the event. During the wild dance, the Fisherman notices "a man dressed in a suit of black velvet, cut in the Spanish fashion" (clearly the Devil in the guise of Don Juan). When the Fisherman is called to worship, he makes the sign of the cross and calls upon the holy name. Instantly, the witches scream and fly away. But the Fisherman holds fast to the witch who had promised to tell him how to send his soul away. She tells him: "What men call the shadow of the body is not the shadow of the body, but is the body of the soul. Stand on the sea-shore with thy back to the moon, and cut away from around thy feet thy shadow, which is thy soul's body, and bid thy soul leave thee, and it will do so."

When the witch departs, the Fisherman's Soul pleads with him not to send him away, particularly without a heart. The Fisherman replies: "My heart is my love's." With that, he cuts away his shadow and frees himself of his soul (enter here the theme of the *Doppelgänger*, or the double). The Soul tells him that each year he will return to this place and call to him: "It may be that thou wilt have need of me." A year later, the Soul returns to tell the Fisherman of his strange adventures in the Middle East (these lengthy accounts provide Wilde with the opportunity to paint scenes with color harmonies). The Soul has acquired a Mirror of Wisdom, which he has hidden, but if the Fisherman allows him to re-enter his body, he will be wiser than the wise men. "Love is better than Wisdom, and the little Mermaid loves me," says the Fisherman and plunges into the sea.

In the second year, the Soul returns to tell him of his further adventures: He has acquired a Ring of Riches, which can make the Fisherman richer than all the kings in the world. However, the Fisherman again protests that love is better than riches and plunges into the sea. In the third year, the Soul again tells the Fisherman of his exotic adventures, particularly of a dancing girl who performs only a day's journey away. Recalling that the Mermaid had no feet and could not dance, the Fisherman agrees to accompany the Soul to see the dancer. Walking towards the shore, the Fisherman holds out his hands and the Soul, with "a great cry of joy," runs to meet him and enter into his body. But the first city they come to is not the city where the dancer performs. The Soul urges the Fisherman to steal a silver cup in the Street of the Jewellers and hide it. Far from the city the Fisherman flings the cup away: "Why did'st thou tell me to take the cup and hide it, for it was an evil thing to do?" In the next city, the Soul tells the Fisherman to strike a child. But after leaving the city, the Fisherman again asks why the Soul told him to strike the child, "for it was an evil thing to do."

On the third day, they come to another city, but it is apparently not where the dancer performs. A merchant offers to take the Fisherman to his home for the night. Before dawn, the Soul awakens him and instructs him to murder the merchant and take his gold. The merchant, however, awakens and cries to the Fisherman: "Dost thou return evil for good, and pay with the sheddding of blood for the kindness that I have shown thee?" But at the instigation of the Soul, the Fisherman strikes the merchant and flees with nine purses of gold.

Far from the city, the Fisherman asks why he was urged to slay the merchant and take his gold: "Surely thou art evil....all that thou hast made me to do I hate. Thee also I hate." But the Soul responds that since he was sent away without a heart, "I learned to do all these things and love them." The Fisherman accuses the Soul of having tempted him and of having led him into sin. When the Soul suggests that they spend the gold on pleasure, the Fisherman, refusing to abide by the Soul's wishes, tramples on the gold.

Taking his little knife with the handle of green viper's skin, he attempts to cut from his feet the shadow of the body that is the body of the Soul. But he is unsuccessful. Aware that he is now possessed by an evil, he weeps bitterly. He is now determined to return to the sea and inform the Mermaid of the evil he has done. But the Soul tempts him by offering to take him to see dancing girls of Samiris, "who dance in the manner of all kinds of birds and beasts." The Fisherman, however, resists temptation by returning to the city from which they had started, "so great was the power of love that was within him." He calls to the Mermaid, who does not answer. Mocking him, the Soul offers to take him to the Valley of Pleasure. Again, the Fisherman resists the Soul. He builds a house of wattles in the cleft of the rock, where he lives for a year, calling on the Mermaid to appear to him. But she never does.

After a year has passed, the Soul decides to tempt the Fisherman with good since his love is stronger than evil. He urges the Fisherman to go forth with him to mend the ills of this world. But resisting, the Fisherman calls to the Mermaid. At the end of the second year, the Soul pleads with the Fisherman to permit him to enter his heart so that he may be "one with thee even as before." But though the Fisherman agrees, the Soul cannot enter, for his heart is encompassed with love.

When a great mourning sound comes from the sea, the Fisherman rushes to the shore, only to find the body of the dead Mermaid. He grieves over the corpse, then confesses his evils to it. The Soul urges the Fisherman to flee for his safety since the sea is threatening. But he says to the Mermaid that "Love is better than wisdom, and more precious than riches." His love has abided with him despite the evils he had committed. "Now that you art dead, surely I will die with thee also." Knowing that the end is near, he kisses the cold lips of the Mermaid, and when his heart breaks, the Soul finds an entrance "and was one with him even as before. And the sea covered the young Fisherman with its waves."

The next morning the Priest, going to bless the sea, reaches the shore, where he sees the drowned Fisherman with the dead little Mermaid clasped in his arms. He refuses to bless the "accursed" seafolk and has the bodies removed to the Field of the Fullers (who gather or pleat cloth), where no sign is to be set above them "that none may know the place of their resting. For accursed were they in their lives...." In the third year, the Priest enters the chapel on a holy day and notices the altar covered with strange flowers, which came from the corner of the Fullers' Field. At dawn, he goes to the shore and blesses the sea and all the things in God's world, and the people were filled with "joy and wonder." But never again do flowers of any kind grow in the corner of the Fullers' Field, the field remaining barren as before, nor do the Sea-folk come into the bay, for "they went to another part of the sea."

Manuscripts: The Bibliotheca Bodmeriana (Cologny-Geneva) has an incomplete 40-page MS., beginning with p. 4, with some gaps. The Clark Library has four MS. pages, apparently a corrected fair copy.

Reference: Guy Willoughby, "Toward a New Aestheticism: Christ's Vision in *A House of Pomegranates*," *Art and Christhood: The Aesthetics of Oscar Wilde* (1993); Christopher S. Nassaar, "Andersen's 'The Shadow' and Wilde's 'The Fisherman and His Soul': A Case of Influence, *Nineteenth-Century Literature* (Sept. 1995).

FITCH, CLYDE (1865–1909)

America's most successful playwright at the turn of the century, Fitch wrote 36 original plays and 26 adaptations of novels and foreign plays in addition to directing many of his own plays and overseeing the scenery and costumes. In a letter to a friend, Fitch recalls that, in the mid-1880s, when Whistler and Wilde quarrelled, "I stuck to the Wildes, & so do not visit Whistler anymore & seldom see him" (MS., dated 13 June 1892, New York Public Library). The only surviving Wilde letter to him – which Hart-Davis dates as possibly September 1890, when Fitch's first play, *Beau Brummell*, was a success in New York – begins with "Dear Clyde." Wilde is "sorry" that Fitch has left London and that he will miss him: "When you return we must make merry over a flagon of purple wine, and invent new tales with which to charm the world." Wilde had inscribed in a copy of *The Happy Prince and Other Tales*: "Clyde Fitch from his friend Oscar Wilde. Faëry-stories for one who lives in Faëry-Land. Sept. '90" (*Letters* 275 and n3).

The Clark Library has "several effusive letters from Fitch to Oscar," writes Gary Schmidgall, who quotes from them, the first a letter from Fitch after he had read "The Portrait of Mr. W. H.": addressing Wilde as "You precious maddening man," Fitch calls the story "*great* – and *fine*": "*I* believe in Willie Hughes." He closes: "Invent me a language of love. *You* could do it." Another letter,

Schmidgall writes, "suggests infatuation that goes beyond mere hero-worship":

> Oh! you adorable creature! You *are* a great genius. And oh! such a sweet one. Never was a genius so sweet so adorable.... And I – wee I – i am allowed to loose the latchet of yr shoe. Am bidden tie it up – and I do, in a *lover's knot!*.... You are my sight, and sound, and touch. Yr love is the fragrance of a rose – the sky of a summer – the wing of an angel – the cymbal of a cherubim. (qtd. in Schmidgall 178)

Another letter goes further: "*Nobody* loves you as *I* do. When you are here I dream. When you are away I awake....you great, *great* man. Make me what you will but only keep me yours forever. Clyde" (qtd. in Schmidgall 178).

Such letters might suggest a long-lasting relationship between the two playwrights, but the correspondence seems to have come to an abrupt end before the time of the trials. Early in 1895, Max Beerbohm wrote to Ada Leverson from New York that he had met Fitch, "a rather nice man here" who was "at one time a friend of Oscar.... I think they must have quarreled, as Clyde Fitch always speaks very charitably of Oscar" (qtd. in Schmidgall 18ln). In 1897, however, Fitch wrote to Wilde with a suggestion on publishing *The Ballad of Reading Gaol* in America. But no other correspondence is known to exist. Fitch seems to have maintained a discreet distance from the condemned Wilde. In 1901, Fitch's play, *The Last of the Dandies*, about Count D'Orsay, may have been inspired, in part, by the death of Wilde in the previous year.

References: Montrose J. Moses and Virginia Gerson, eds., *Clyde Fitch and His Letters* (1924) ; Gary Schmidgall, *The Stranger Wilde: Interpreting Oscar* (1994).

A FLORENTINE TRAGEDY

Written: In *De Profundis*, Wilde recalled that in 1893 he had conceived and almost finished this one-act "tragedy" in verse (*Letters* 427). In February 1895, he intended to send the actor-manager George Alexander "the vital parts" of the play (*Letters* 383), an indication that Wilde had not yet completed it. While in prison, Wilde wrote to More Adey on 25 September 1896: "I have tried to remember and write down the *Florentine Tragedy*: but only bits of it remain with me, and I find that I cannot invent: the silence, the utter solitude, the isolation from all humane and humanising influences, kills one's brain-power..." (*Letters* 410).

In June 1897, after his release from prison, Wilde told Robert Ross that he was "determined" to complete the play (*Letters* 591). From Dieppe in September, he wrote to Ross that he was going to Rouen "to try to rewrite my *Love and Death – Florentine Tragedy*" (*Letters* 638), but then from Naples in October, he told Ross: "Tomorrow I begin the *Florentine Tragedy* (*Letters* 649), presumably to rewrite it. Apparently, Wilde never completed the play, which seems modeled after Alfred de Musset's *proverbes dramatiques*, brief dialogues with a dramatic reversal at the end to illustrate a moral point.

Produced: On 10 June 1906, the Literary Theatre Society at King's Hall gave a private performance of the play, the opening scene of some 200 lines of blank verse written by one of its members, the poet and critic T. Sturge Moore (1870–1944). The first public performance of the play was given by the New English Players at the Cripplegate Institute, Golden Lane, on 28 October 1907.

Published: The surviving fragment of the play (without the opening scene by Moore) first appeared in Volume 2 of the *Collected Edition* (1908). A Russian translation had appeared in *Viessy* (Moscow) 4 (Jan. 1907): 17–38.

The Plot: Moore's opening scene is laid in a tapestried upper room leading to a balcony in an old Florentine house. Maria, the servant, is telling her mistress, Bianca, of a conversation with Sir Guido Bardi (the name derived from Guido Ferrante and Taddao Bardi in Wilde's *The Duchess of Padua*), the conversation having taken place in the palace "in a painted hall! – / Painted with naked women on the walls...." He was complaining that Bianca had returned a purse of 50,000 crowns: "Come, name the sum that will buy me grace of her." Bianca had never opened the purse. Maria also repeats part of the conversation in which she told Guido what Bianca had asked about his appearance and dress. Guido had asked whether Bianca had a lover "beside that old / Soured husband or is it him she loves, my God!" Maria told him that Bianca "might like to love, / If she were loved by one who pleased her well." Guido then informed Maria to tell her mistress that he would pass by her balcony and that she should "throw down some favour...."

Guido arrives below at that moment, when she throws down a ribbon weighted with a brooch. Almost immediately, she has second thoughts: "But if! Ah if! he is a wandering bee, / Mere gallant taster, who befools poor flowers...." When she shows him in, she inquires whether he is interested in purchasing velvets, silks, or brocades. She assumes that the 50,000 crowns that he sent was for her husband's Lucca damask. Guido offers 100,000, to which Bianca responds that her husband, Simone, would sell everything in the house for such a sum. "Would he sell everyone?" he asks. Her response is that Simone values women at less than half the price of his goods. Finally, Guido says: "It is thyself, Bianca, I would buy." She refuses him by saying that she has already been bought and sold in marriage in that "common market." Simone had spoken to her of love while in her father's ear he made the gold "clink."

Guido expresses his sense of shame over his own attempt to buy her. He urges the "witty, divine Bianca" to dispute no more but "sup with the moon / Like Persian princes, that, in Babylon / Sup in the hanging gardens of the king." Wittily, they talk of love and of Simone's indifference to her beauty. Guido urges her to "escape from out this dismal life / As a bright butterfly breaks a spider's web, / And nest with me among those rosy bowers...." But as he speaks these lines, a noise is heard on the stair: it is Simone returning home. As the door opens, they "separate guiltily" (thus ends Moore's portion).

In Wilde's fragment, which begins at this point, the merchant Simone, burdened under a heavy pack, returns home to discover that she has a visitor – possibly, he believes, a kinsman or cousin. He gives the impression that he is surprised. Bianca informs him that the visitor is Sir Guido Bardi, the son of the "great Lord of Florence" whose towers Simone sees from his casement every night. Guido assures Simone that Bianca has welcomed him "with such sweet courtesies / That if it be her pleasure, and your own, / I will come often to your simple house." Indeed, he will also "charm her loneliness" when Simone is abroad. Simone thanks Guido from his "heart's core" for the honored guest's attentions to his wife,

repeating the word *honest* to suggest its opposite.

Simone offers to show Guido his goods – silks, velvets, damasks – in order to make a sale. When Simone remarks that his house "with everything" it contains is Guido's, the nobleman inquires: "What if I asked / For white Bianca here?" Simone assures him that she is "not worthy of so great a Prince." Simone then directs conversation to the woolen trade, then to politics, but his wife objects that he is tiring their "most gracious guest." When Simone withdraws, Bianca tells Guido that she hates her husband "body and soul": "Oh, would that Death might take him where he stands!"

Having overheard her mention of death, Simone alludes to adultery, directing a barbed remark to Guido, who, he says, does not know the world: "*You* are too single and too honourable." When Simone withdraws again, Bianca and Guido speak as lovers: at dawn he will return to take her from her husband. When Simone returns, Guido announces his departure, but Simone directs the conversation to a time when a robber sought to take his pack-horse from him: "Who filches from me something that is mine, / ...Perils his soul and body in the theft / And dies for his small sin."

Simone then wonders whether his sword is better tempered than Guido's. A challenge is issued: Guido now has the opportunity to dispose of the troublesome husband. Urged on by Bianca, who tells her lover to kill him, Guido fights and wounds Simone, who nevertheless overpowers his rival by seizing him by the throat. Guido protests that if he dies, there will be no successor and France will "fall upon the city." But Simone, ignoring Guido's pleas for a priest, kills him. Bianca (as the stage direction indicates) approaches Simone "as one dazed with wonder and with outstretched arms": "Why / Did you not tell me you were so strong?" To which Simone responds in the final line of the fragment: "Why / Did you not tell me you were beautiful?" He then kisses her on the lips.

Early Theater Review: Reviewing the private performance by the Literary Theatre Society in the *Saturday Review* (16 June 1906), Max Beerbohm remarks that *A Florentine Tragedy* and *Salome*, also performed on the program, indicate "anew to us how much was lost to dramatic art in the downfall and death of the great artist who composed them." In discussing the plot, Beerbohm interprets the ending as the justification for the one-act play:

"And now comes the ending for the sake of which, I take it, the play was written – the germ of psychological paradox from which the story developed itself backwards." The final speech by Simone "is certainly a daring invention. Is the paradox a sound one? I think so. It is not unnatural that the merchant, having won his bride with money, should not have appreciated her at her full human value until he had won her by more primitive, more human means." Beerbohm concludes his review with his "sole objection to the paradox" – that is, "the placing of it":

> No play – no work of art whatsoever – ought to finish on a top note. We ought never to be left gasping, at the fall of the curtain. The paradox that I have examined ought to have been led up to, so that its meaning would have been plain when the curtain fell. It ought to have been a summing-up, not a challenge. Mr Wilde's sure artistic sense here failed him, for once. (rpt. in *Last Theatres*)

Manuscripts: In a preface to a separate edition of the play (Boston, 1908), Ross said that he had succeeded in rescuing some loose MS. pages from Wilde's study in April 1895, the time of his arrest; when Ross arranged them, he recognized that they comprised part of *A Florentine Tragedy*. Later, the well-known actor Edward Smith Willard (1853–1915) informed him that he had a TS. of the play, which Wilde had sent him, presumably to solicit his opinion. Ross's fragment and Willard's TS. began at the same place, suggesting that Wilde had never written the opening scene; however, the Hyde Collection has a MS. portion of what is apparently that scene. Furthermore, fragments of a MS., apparently of the opening scene, are printed in Mason 464–65. Texas has an early sketch of this uncompleted play in a notebook, and the Clark Library has two MSS. of five and thirteen leaves, containing a scenario, notes, dialogue, and stage directions.

References: Alan Johnson, "The Italian Renaissance and Some Late Victorians," *Victorian Newsletter* (Fall 1969); Max Beerbohm, *Last Theatres, 1904–1910* (1970), intro. by Rupert Hart-Davis.

"FLOWER OF LOVE"

A half-title added to the last poem of *Poems* (1882) as a gloss for the Greek title ΓΛΥΚΥΠΙΚΡΟΣ ΕΡΩΣ ("GLUKUPIKROS EROS").

"FLOWERS OF GOLD"

This section title appears in *Poems* (1882) for ten poems.

FOR LOVE OF THE KING: A BURMESE MASQUE

Published: *Hutchinson's Magazine* (Oct. 1921) and in the New York *Century* 103 (Dec. 1921): 225–42; added as Volume 15 (1922) to the *Collected Edition* (1908).

The "Introductory Note," which is a letter to Mrs. Mabel Chan Toon, née Cosgrave (b. 1872) attributed to Wilde, states that this masque was written in 1894 "as a personal gift to the author's friend and friend of his family...." Mrs. Chan Toon's husband, the letter reveals, was the nephew of the King of Burma and a barrister of the Middle Temple. To William Andrews Clark, the collector of Wilde MSS. and books and founder of the Clark Library, Vyvyan Holland wrote on 26 November 1923: "There appears to be no doubt whatever of the authenticity of the MS. [of *For Love of the King*]. My father was a great friend of the lady in question [Mrs. Chan Toon] and had a good deal of correspondence with her" (qtd. in *The Library of William Andrews Clark* 3:11).

However, on 20 July 1925, Stuart Mason wrote to the publisher Walter Hutchinson after examining the MS. of the play: "I accuse Mrs. Wodehouse Pearse [formerly Mrs. Chan Toon] of faking the document known as 'For Love of the King' and passing it off as the work of Oscar Wilde, well knowing it to be a forgery, and thereby obtaining money by false pretenses from yourself and other publishers." Mason included this and other letters by him on the subject in an undated, privately printed pamphlet titled *Who Wrote "For Love of the King"?* Wilde scholars have concurred with Mason that *For Love of the King* is indeed a spurious work.

References: *The Library of William Andrews Clark: Wilde and Wildeana*, eds. Robert Ernest Cowan and William Andrews Clark (1924); George Sims, "Who Wrote *For Love of the King*? Oscar Wilde or Mrs. Chan Toon?" *Book Collector* (Autumn 1958).

"THE FOURTH MOVEMENT"

Added as a section title for eight poems in the list of Contents in *Poems* (1882).

"A FRAGMENT FROM THE 'AGAMEM-NON' OF AESCHYLOS"

Published: *Kottabos* 2 (Hilary Term 1877): 320–22; rpt. in *Poems* (1908). Written around 1876–77.

This translation, of lines 1140–73 from the *Agamemnon*, consists of three choruses and three soliloquies by Kasandra (as Wilde spells her name), the prophetess whose visions are ignored as the result of Apollo's curse for her rejection of his advances. Wilde provides a summary of the plot below his title.

FREEMASONRY

Alleged to have had its roots in antiquity, Free-masonry – officially known as the Free and Accepted Masons – is the largest secret fraternal order in the world. No central Masonic authority exists; instead, autonomous jurisdictions exist among national organizations, called "grand lodges." Elaborate symbolic ceremonies and rituals using the traditional instruments of the stone-masons – such as the square, level, and compass – are central to the customs that have provided continuity through the centuries. Liberal and democratic, the Masons are expected to have faith in God and to use a holy book appropriate to each Mason's religion. However, since the papal bull of Pope Clement XII (1738), the Roman Catholic Church has forbidden Catholics to join Masonic lodges because of their anti-clericalism.

Practicing stonemasons and cathedral workmen in the 14th century may have formed the first groups of Masons in England and Scotland. In 1717, the Grand Lodge in London marked the beginning of the dissemination abroad of the order, particularly within the British Empire. When cathedral building began to decline in the late Middle Ages, prospectve members who were not stonemasons were invited to join, a policy that exists to this day (indeed, at least 13 American presidents, including George Washington, have been Masons). In 1700 there were six lodges in England, and by 1723, there were 30. The bylaws – as written in *Anderson's Constitutions* (1723) – of the Grand Lodge of England, the oldest surviving Masonic lodge, outline the ideals of religious tolerance and loyalty to local government, including the ideal of political compromise.

When Wilde was in his second term at Oxford, one of his fellow students, J. E. C. Bodley, urged him to join the Apollo Lodge at the university, in which he was received on 23 February 1875. (Wilde's father was also a Mason: in 1841–42, he was Worshipful Master of the Shakespeare Lodge in Dublin.) Bodley has recorded Wilde's reaction to the Masonic properties: "Wilde was as much struck with their gorgeousness as he was amazed at the mystery of our conversation" (qtd. in Ellmann 40/39). The Masons' costume (the Apollo Lodge, alone of the British lodges, still requires it), consisting of knee breeches and tail coat, white tie, silk stockings, and pumps, perhaps inspired Wilde with the idea for his Aesthetic dress on his lecture tour. Wilde rose through the next "degrees" within the lodge to the 2nd on 24 April and the 3rd, as Master Mason, on 25 May. In the following year, he elected to join the Apollo Rose-Croix Chapter of the lodge, which had an interest in the occult.

By 3 March 1877, having attained to the 33rd degree and having sponsored four new Magdalen students as new Masons, Wilde wrote to a college friend: "I have got rather keen on Masonry lately, and believe in it awfully – in fact would be awfully sorry to have to give it up in case I secede from the Protestant Heresy" (*Letters* 30). Wilde's attraction to the Roman Catholic Church prompted him, in the same letter, to confess: "...I get so wretched and low and troubled that in some desperate mood I will seek the shelter of a Church which simply enthrals me by its fascination."

In his first play, *Vera; or, The Nihilists* (1880), Wilde employs Masonic ritualism in depicting a Nihilist meeting at the beginning of Act I. The dialogue begins when the President of the conspirators, equivalent to the Worshipful Master of the Masons, asks the question: "What is the word?" The conspirators answer with the more appropriate responses suitable to the play. When his *Poems* (1881) appeared, Wilde designed the title page, which depicts a papal tiara above a Masonic rose with a Latin tag surrounding both: *Sub hoc signo vinces* (Under this sign thou shalt conquer). Ellmann comments: "The tiara and the rose invoke the two dispensations, Catholic and pagan, as well as their possible reconciliation in Freemasonry" (140/136).

The Roman Catholic Robert Ross, who disap-

"FROM SPRING DAYS TO WINTER"

proved of Freemasonry, had apparently raised the question after Wilde's release from prison of whether he had met any Freemasons at Reading. According to Ross, Wilde responded:

> Yes, it was very terrible. As I was walking round the yard one day I noticed that one of the men awaiting trial was signalling to me by masonic signs. I paid no attention until he made me the sign of the widow's son which no mason can ignore. He managed to convey a note to me. (*Letters* 565)

The prisoner, "quite mad, poor fellow," wanted Wilde to help him petition for his release.

"FROM SPRING DAYS TO WINTER. (FOR MUSIC)"

Published: *Dublin University Magazine* 87 (Jan. 1876): 47; rpt. in *Poems* (1908). Written around 1874–75.

This lyric poem follows the familiar conventions of spring as the time of blossoming love and winter as the time of death of the beloved one. The speaker, joyously recalling the spring "when leaves were green," thrills at the first sight of his love: "O perfect vision of delight...." The final stanza describes winter when "the tree is grey" with snow, his love now dead. The speaker lays a dove with broken wings at her grave and, echoing Swinburne's "Fragoletta" ("O broken singing of the dove!"), concludes: "Ah, Love! ah, Love! that thou wert slain – / Fond Dove, fond Dove return again!" The dove, traditionally symbolizing peace and purity, depicts the spiritual presence of the Holy Ghost in various biblical passages (as in John 1:32). The bird is also associated with St. Benedict, who saw the soul of his dead sister ascend to Heaven in the form of a dove.

G

"THE GARDEN OF EROS"

Published: *Poems* (1881). Written around 1877–78, this poem contains 46 six-line stanzas in iambic pentameter, the stanzaic form derived from the *Venus and Adonis* of Shakespeare, but, unlike him, Wilde lengthens the concluding line of each stanza to seven metrical feet. As in "The Burden of Itys" (see entry), which Wilde regarded with "The Garden of Eros" as his "most lyrical" poems, the present effusion, with its allusions to such poets as Keats, Shelley, Swinburne, Morris, and Rossetti, suggests his literary aspirations.

Using a familiar trope, the speaker contemplates the "heart of June" and looks forward to "autumn time, the season's usurer." In contemplating the various flowers in the garden – many, like the "amorous flower," associated with Eros – the speaker proposes to his beloved to sing, in the pastoral tradition, of the great loves of the mythic past, including Helen: "And if my flute can breathe sweet melody, / We may behold Her face who long / Dwelt among men by the Aegean sea...."

The speaker then moves from physical love to the love of the "Spirit of Beauty" (see Tite Street House, where Wilde had Shelley's phrase inscribed in his library). The speaker alludes to "the boy who loved thee best": that is, Keats, who "sleeps in silent rest / Beneath the Roman walls..." – that is, in the Protestant Cemetery (see "The Grave of Keats"). He next alludes to Byron without naming him: "...him at least thy love hath taught to sing," one who died in the hope that "The grand Greek limbs of young Democracy / Rise mightily like Hesperus and bring / The great Republic!" The poet William Morris, "with soft and sylvan pipe," brought "from the far and flowerless fields of ice...fair flowers to make an earthly paradise" – an allusion to Morris's popular poem *The Earthly Paradise* (1868–70) and his use of Scandinavian mythology. Next, Dante Gabriel Rossetti is named "Whose double laurels burn with deathless flame / To light thine [i.e., Beauty's] altar; He too loves thee well...."

In the modern world, "all romance has flown"

because of science:

> ...what if we
> Have analysed the rainbow, robbed the moon
>   Of her most ancient, chastest mystery,
> Shall I, the last Endymion, lose all hope
> Because rude eyes peer at my mistress through
>   a telescope!

The speaker asks whether science can "assuage / One lover's breaking heart? what can it do / To make one life more beautiful, one day....?" The Darwinian world is evoked in Wilde's characterization of "Natural Warfare and insensate Chance": "...let them, if they can... / Create the new Ideal rule for man! / Methinks that was not my inheritance...." The poem ends with an affirmation that Nature has more significance than science brings to it, for as the sun rises, the speaker exclaims:

> ...it is the God! for love of him
> Already the shrill lark is out of sight....
> Ah! there is something more in that bird's flight
>   Than could be tested in a crucible!

Manuscripts: The Clark Library has a draft of line 175. The American Art Association catalogue (7–8 May 1928) quotes a MS. of lines 127–32.

GIDE, ANDRÉ (1869–1951)

At the age of 22, Gide, who first met Wilde (then 37) in Paris on 29 November 1891, and saw him often during the next few weeks, was enormously impressed:

> His manner and appearance were triumphant.... All London was soon to rush to see his plays. He was rich, he was great, he was handsome, he was loaded with happiness and honours. Some compared him to an Asiatic Bacchus, others to some Roman Emperor, and others again to Apollo himself – in short, he was resplendent. (*Oscar Wilde: A Study* 22)

On one evening, after they had dined, Wilde told him of his tale of Narcissus, later published as "The Disciple" in "Poems in Prose." In December, Gide's *Traité du Narcisse* (*Treatise of the Narcissus*) was privately printed, most of it written before he met Wilde. The attraction of both writers to the myth reveals their own self-absorbed personalities. On 23 December, the novelist and dramatist Jules Rénard (1864–1900) recorded in his journal that Gide was in love with Wilde; citing Gide's letters and journals, Ellmann suggests that Wilde had "spiritually seduced" him (354/334).

Gide wrote to Paul Valéry (1871–1945) that Wilde was "religiously contriving to kill" what remained of his soul "because he says that in order to know an essence, one must eliminate it: he wants me to miss my soul. The measure of a thing is the effort made to destroy it. Each thing is made up only of its emptiness...." After Wilde's departure from Paris in late December 1891, Gide stopped writing letters for several days. On 24 December, he revealed to Valéry the aftermath of Wilde's stunning impact on him: "Please forgive my silence: since Wilde, I hardly exist any more" (*Self-Portraits* 90, 92). He subsequently destroyed several pages of his journal covering the period spent with Wilde. In unpublished notes, he describes Wilde as "always trying to instil in you *a sanction for evil*" (qtd. in Delay 291).

On 1 January 1892, Gide recorded in his journal that his association with Wilde had done him "nothing but harm": "In his company I had lost the habit of thinking. I had more varied emotions, but had forgotten how to bring order into them." Wilde's professed abandonment of commonplace Christian morality, with its injunction on mortifying the flesh, had a profound effect on Gide: indeed, in *The Picture of Dorian Gray*, Lord Henry Wotton's hedonistic view – "Nothing can cure the soul but the senses, just as nothing can cure the senses but the soul" – was to provide Gide, who read the novel in 1895, with a new aesthetic and ethical system – the "new Hellenism" – as Ellmann suggests, "by turning sacred things inside out to make them secular, and secular things inside out to make them sacred" (361/340–41).

In May 1894, Gide met Wilde and Douglas by chance in Florence; on 28 May, he wrote to his mother that Wilde "has aged [he was 39] and is ugly, but still an extraordinary storyteller" (qtd. in *Letters* 354n2). In his autobiography, *Si le grain ne meurt* (*If It Die*), Gide tells the story of his encounter with Wilde in late January 1895 while in Blida, Algiers, where English homosexuals sought willing boys. He discovered that Wilde and Lord Alfred Douglas were registered in the same hotel

he was just leaving. Gide's first impulse was to avoid their company, for the rumors of Wilde's indiscretions were as well known in Paris as they were in London. Yet his curiosity seemed to draw him to Wilde and his companion.

As Jean Delay suggests, Gide regarded Wilde and Douglas as figures superior to plebeian existence:

> The luxury with which the aesthete [Wilde] and Douglas surrounded themselves, their insolence, their extravagance, their provocations, and their pretensions of being patricians above the laws and morals of the plebs seemed, for a time, to the son of the conventional economical Mme. Gide, to be the "higher immorality" toward which he had been aiming but to which he had not yet dared aspire. (437–38)

Gide, however, now noted that Wilde's light-hearted manner had changed, for he talked of the Marquess of Queensberry's attacks on him as the prelude to a tragic destiny. As Justin O'Brien remarks: "Gide listened to him with a mingling of amazement, admiration, and fear" (*Portrait* 119).

On 28 January 1895, Gide, writing to his mother about his meeting with Wilde, refers to him as "that terrible man, the most dangerous product of modern civilization" and two days later told her of Wilde's famous remark that Gide repeated in his later works: "I have put my genius into my life; I have put only my talent into my works" (*Correspondance* 587, 590). Wilde and Gide were now in Algiers, while Douglas (after quarrelling with Wilde) went off with a boy to Biskra. Though Gide maintained secrecy over his own sexual preference, Wilde observed his fascination with an Arab boy playing a flute in a café. When Wilde asked Gide directly whether he wanted the boy, he responded, "in the most choked of voices," that he did. This confession, O'Brien contends, "marked an important step in Gide's moral liberation" (*Portrait* 119).

At the time of Wilde's trials, Gide asked his mother to send him "all the press cuttings" that were available to her about "the scandalous case brought against Wilde" by Queensberry (*Correspondance* 639), and after Wilde's conviction, Gide read *The Picture of Dorian Gray*, which the prosecutor had used to discredit Wilde in court. By

December 1895, some seven months after Wilde's imprisonment, petitions were circulating in London and Paris to reduce his sentence. Many of the most distinguished writers, including Zola, refused to sign, but Gide consented.

After his release from prison in May 1897, Wilde read Gide's *Les Nourritures terrestres* (*The Fruits of the Earth*), a celebration of the life of sensations, the character named Ménalque depicted as an ironic echo of Wilde (Ménalque reappears in *L'Immoraliste*, 1902). Wilde wrote to Douglas that *Les Nourritures terrestres* did not "fascinate" him: "The egoistic note is, of course, and always has been to me, the primal and ultimate note of modern art, but *to be an Egoist one must have an Ego....* But I love André personally very deeply, and often thought of him in prison..." (*Letters* 590).

When the "most charming" Gide visited him in late June at Berneval (*Letters* 617), Wilde described the ordeal of prison, insisting that the experience had completely changed him and that he had rid himself of bitterness. As Gide was leaving, Wilde praised *Les Nourritures terrestres* as "very good...but promise me you will never write a capital *I* again.... In art, you see, there is no first person" (*Oscar Wilde: A Study* 73).

In December 1898, Gide published his closet drama, *Philoctète*, on a tragic figure associated with the siege of Troy. Gide depicts the plight of the wounded warrior, whose "foul wound" from a snakebite has resulted in his unjust abandonment on an island – the symbolic analogy, Yvette Louria suggests, of Wilde's similar ordeal involving society's condemnation of his homosexuality (a "foul wound" that repels others), followed by imprisonment and suffering. Just as Philoctète's Nietzschean will enables him to rise above adversity to achieve virtue, so too, as Gide hoped during his visit to Berneval in 1897, Wilde might regenerate himself.

After his Berneval visit, Gide saw Wilde only twice more: once, by chance, at a café, when he gave him some money, and the final time by arrangement. On this latter occasion, Gide expressed his disappointment that Wilde had not written a play since his release, but Wilde replied: "One should not reproach someone who has been *struck.*" When Wilde died on 30 November 1900, Gide, in Biskra, regretted his inability to attend the funeral but later published his tribute, "Oscar Wilde: In Memoriam," in *L'Ermitage* (June 1902),

translated by Stuart Mason in 1905 as *Oscar Wilde: A Study*, some of which later reappeared in *Si le grain ne meurt* (1924). In his tribute to Wilde, Gide presents versions (or perhaps, more accurately, echoes) of several of Wilde's poems in prose – "The Disciple," "The Master," "The Doer of Good," and "The House of Judgment" – which had appeared in 1893 and 1894 (see "Poems in Prose").

Contending that "*nearly everything [Gide] has written about Oscar Wilde is pure fake*" (5), Robert Sherard attacked him in *André Gide's Wicked Lies about the Late Oscar Wilde* (1933), expanded as *Oscar Wilde: Twice Defended* (1934). In a letter included in the volume, Alfred Douglas also charged that "André Gide's story about Oscar and myself in *Si le grain ne meurt* is a mass of lies and misrepresentations" (44–45). James D. Griffin, who has studied the evidence, concludes that Gide's writings on Wilde (though they imply a closer friendship than is warranted by the facts) reveal "a keen observer [whose] accounts are of inestimable value" (170). Griffin quotes a letter to Gide from Douglas, who wrote after he had read *Si le grain ne meurt*: "Supposing that what you say about my immoral conduct 35 years ago is true, still what a frightful cad you must be to reveal to the world secrets which were confided to you by a man who was your friend & who never injured you by thought word & deed!" Griffin regards Douglas's letter as "more useful as corroboration than as a refutation of Gide's book. The thrust of the argument is not so much that Gide has *lied*, as that he has violated Douglas' *trust*" (167).

For many years, Gide read books on Wilde, often voicing displeasure with their misunderstanding of Wilde's profusion of masks. On 29 June 1913, for example, he writes in his journal that Arthur Ransome's *Oscar Wilde: A Critical Study* (1912), while generally good, "fails to show to what degree the plays *An Ideal Husband* and *A Woman of No Importance* are revelatory – and I was about to say confidential – despite their apparent objectivity" (later in this day's entry, Gide remarks that the "greatest interest" of Wilde's plays "lies between the lines"). Alluding to his own study of Wilde, Gide concedes that he was "not altogether just to [Wilde's] work" and turned up his nose at it "too readily – I mean before having known it sufficiently": "As I think it over I wonder at the good grace with which Wilde listened to me when, in Algiers, I criticized his plays (very impertinently it seems to me today). No impatience in the tone of his reply, and not even a protest...."

When André Maurois published a study of Wilde in his *Études anglaises* (1927), Gide wrote in his journal on 1 October that he objected to Maurois's view of Wilde's aestheticism, which, Gide wrote, assumes "that Wilde's way of life was a dependence on his aestheticism and that he merely carried over into his habits his love of the artificial":

I believe quite on the contrary that this affected aestheticism was for him merely an ingenious cloak to hide, while half revealing, what he could not let be seen openly; to excuse, provide a pretext, and even apparently motivate; but that very motivation is but a pretense. Here, as almost always, and often even without the artist's knowing it, it is the secret of the depths of his flesh that prompts, inspires, and decides....

Gide also contends that Wilde's plays, "reveal, besides the surface witticisms, sparkling like false jewels, many oddly revelatory sentences of great psychological interest. And it is for them that Wilde wrote the whole play – let there be no doubt about it.... Wilde made up his mind to make of falsehood a work of art."

References: André Gide, *Oscar Wilde: A Study*, trans. Stuart Mason (1905); *If It Die: An Autobiography*, trans. Dorothy Bussy (1935); Justin O'Brien, trans. and ed., *The Journals of André Gide, 1889–1939*, 3 vols. (1947–49); Yvette Louria, "Le Contenu Latent du *Philoctète* Gidien," *French Review* (April 1952); Justin O'Brien, *Portrait of André Gide* (1953); Jules Rénard, *Journal, 1887–1910* (1960); Jean Delay, *The Youth of André Gide*, trans. June Guicharnaud (1963); Robert Mallet, ed., and June Guicharnaud, trans., *Self-Portraits: The Gide/Valéry Letters, 1890–1942* (1966); Richard Ellmann, "Corydon and Ménalque," *Golden Codgers* (1973); James D. Griffin, "The Importance of Being Spurious: Gide's 'Lies,' a Forged Letter, and the Emerging Wilde Biography," *Journal of Modern Literature* (March 1983); André Gide, *Correspondance avec sa mère, 1880–1895*, ed. Claude Martin (1988); Patrick Pollard, *André Gide: Homosexual Moralist* (1991); Jonathan Dollimore, "Wilde and Gide in Algeria,"

Sexual Dissidence (1992); Jonathan Fryer, *André and Oscar: Gide, Wilde and the Gay Art of Living* (1997).

"ΓΛΥΚΥΠΙΚΡΟΣ ΕΡΩΣ" ("GLUKUPIKROS EROS")

Published: *Poems* (1881); rev. in (1882). The Greek title, which comes from Sappho (fragment 81), means "Bittersweet Love." In the fourth edition of *Poems* (1882), "Flower of Love" became the half-title for this poem.

In this lyric poem of 15 stanzas composed of rhyming couplets, the speaker blames not his love for some unspecified fault, for it was his. Had he not been made of "common clay," he would have "climbed the higher heights unclimbed yet." This metaphor leads to a vision of Dante, with whom the speaker identifies: "I had trod the road which Dante treading saw the suns of seven circles shine..." (recalling "Purgatory" in the *Divine Comedy*). Continuing his pleasing fantasy of how he might have achieved greatness as a poet, the speaker next evokes Keats, who had "lifted up his hymenaeal curls from out the poppy-seeded wine, / With ambrosial mouth had kissed my forehead, clasped the hand of noble love in mine."

Turning to his loved one, he boasts that two young lovers "lying in an orchard would have read the story of our love." Implying that, in fact, his love is over, he goes on: "Yet I am not sorry that I loved you – ah! what else had I a boy to do...." Rudderless, the two of them had drifted "athwart a tempest"; but, after all, "Desire shudders into ashes, and the tree of Passion bears no fruit." Concluding that the experience of love is better than the achievement of the poet, the poem ends: "I have found the lover's crown of myrtle better than the poet's crown of bays."

For other poems depicting the parting of lovers, see "Roses and Rue," "Her Voice," and "My Voice."

GODWIN, EDWARD WILLIAM (1833–86)

A theatrical designer and architect, Godwin (who, for nine years, beginning in 1866, lived with Ellen Terry and fathered two children) redesigned a house – named Keats House – in Tite Street for Wilde and Frank Miles (see entry), who moved in August 1880. In the summer of 1884, when Wilde leased another Tite Street house – a four-story dwelling with a basement – after his marriage, he engaged Godwin to design the interior as well as the furniture (see Tite Street House). The many extant letters to Godwin reveal Wilde's distress over the details and over the bills submitted by the workmen through the latter half of 1884. On 19 December, Wilde implores him: "The house *must* be a success: do just add the bloom of colour to it in curtains and cushions" (*Letters* 166). Wilde was finally pleased with Godwin's furniture designs and his ideas for transforming a conventional Victorian house into the "house beautiful."

Like Wilde, Godwin was interested in transforming fashion: in 1884, he published *Dress and Its Relation to Health and Culture*, which Wilde mentioned in a letter to the *Pall Mall Gazette* after lecturing on "Dress" on 1 October 1884. Godwin's book, published for the International Health Exhibition, was, Wilde remarked, "an important fact because it makes almost any form of lovely costume perfectly practicable in our cold climate. Mr. Godwin, it is true, points out that the English ladies of the thirteenth century abandoned after some time the flowing garments of the early Renaissance in favour of a tighter mode, such as northern Europe seems to demand" (*Letters* 162–63).

When Wilde published "Shakespeare and Stage Costume" in 1885 (revised as "The Truth of Masks") and published a review of Godwin's production in 1886 of *Helena in Troas* (see entry), he expressed his appreciation of Godwin's career in the theater, particularly for his extensive research in order to design costumes and sets with historical accuracy in order to achieve unity on stage. Indeed, Godwin was "one of the most artistic spirits of this century in England." As John Stokes has written:

> Godwin's position in the Aesthetic milieu was absolutely central but hidden.... The lectures on interior decoration and dress reform that Wilde delivered on his sensational tour of America in 1881 [actually, 1882] were largely based, unacknowledged, on the teachings of Godwin, who was perhaps too scholarly and professional (or, more likely, too notorious) to receive much publicity himself. (46)

References: Dudley Harbron, *The Conscious Stone: The Life of Edward William Godwin* (1949); H. Montgomery Hyde, "Oscar Wilde and His Architect," *Architectural Review* (March 1951); John Stokes, "An Aesthetic Theatre: The Career of E. W. Godwin," *Resistible Theatres: Enterprise and Experiment in the Late Nineteenth Century* (1972).

GONCOURT, EDMOND DE (1822–96)

A French novelist, historian, and memoirist, Goncourt attracted Wilde's interest by his *La Faustin* (1882) because of its central conflicts between art and life involving an actress modelled after Bernhardt and Rachel. As a possible influence on *The Picture of Dorian Gray*, writes Ellmann: "Sibyl loses her powers as an actress by falling in love, reversing La Faustin's behavior" (229/217).

According to Goncourt's excerpts from his journal in *L'Echo de Paris* (17 Dec. 1891), Wilde met him in 21 April 1883, when, after having sent a copy of his *Poems*, he received an invitation from Théodore Duret (1838–1927), the art critic, to accompany him on a visit to Goncourt. Responding, Wilde writes to Duret that Goncourt is "one of the greatest masters of modern prose, and his novel *Manette Salomon* [1867] is a masterpiece" (*More Letters* 53). After another meeting on 5 May, Goncourt, writes Ellmann, disparaged Wilde in his journal "as a homosexual ('*au sexe douteux*')" but quoted some of his impressions of America (230/218). He also referred to what Wilde had said about Swinburne – that he was "a flaunter of vice." Wilde quickly responded to clarify what he had meant by the phrase (see Swinburne, Algernon).

From Holloway Prison on 13 April 1895, Wilde informed Robert Sherard that he had received messages from various artists who sympathized with him: one was from Goncourt. In March 1897, Wilde asked More Adey to send him, among many other books, the latest volume of Goncourt's *Journal*. In April, he wrote to Robert Ross that he was planning to present some books to the prison library, among them about a dozen novels, adding that they "would please the few who do not care about Goncourt's journal" (*Letters* 521).

"A GOOD HISTORICAL NOVEL"

Published: *PMG*, 8 Aug. 1887, 3; rpt. in *Reviews* (1908). An unsigned review of Stephen Coleridge's *Demetrius* (1887).

Wilde observes that "most modern Russian

novelists look upon the historical novel as a 'faux genre,' a sort of fancy-dress ball in literature, a mere puppet-show, not a true picture of life," despite the fact that their Russian history is replete with such "wonderful scenes and situations, ready for dramatist or novelist to treat of...." As the background for his "strange tale," Coleridge makes use of sixteenth-century Russia; though the novel is remote in time, Wilde argues, "distance of time, unlike distance of space, makes objects larger and more vivid." The modern realistic school offers "little artistic pleasure" because the common things of contemporary life have a "mist of familiarity that often makes their meaning obscure." Realistic novelists "exaggerate the importance of facts, and underrate the importance of fiction."

In this novel – depicting a young lad of unknown parentage who is brought up in a Polish noble's household – Demetrius is discovered to be the son of Ivan the Terrible. Yet, despite all the evidence pointing to his legitimacy, he turns out not to be the true Demetrius: "He is deceived himself, and he deceives others." Because Coleridge is "a young writer of great ability and culture," *Demetrius* remains "one of the most fascinating and delightful novels that have appeared this season."

"THE GOSPEL ACCORDING TO WALT WHITMAN"

Published: *PMG*, 25 Jan. 1889, 3; rpt. in *Reviews* (1908). An unsigned review of Whitman's *November Boughs* (1889). Wilde begins by quoting Whitman:

No one will get at my verses who insists upon viewing them as a literary performance, or as aiming mainly towards art and aestheticism. "Leaves of Grass" has been chiefly the outcropping of my own emotional and other personal nature – an attempt from first to last to put a *Person*, a human being...fully and truly on record. I could not find any similar personal record in current literature that satisfied me.

In these words, says Wilde, Whitman gives us "the true attitude we should adopt towards his work...." *November Boughs*, published in the "winter of the old man's life," reveals to us, not indeed a soul's tragedy, for its last note is one of joy and hope and

noble and unshaken faith in all that is fine and worthy of such faith, but certainly the drama of a human soul, and puts on record with a simplicity that has in it both sweetness and strength the record of his spiritual development...."

Whitman's "strange mode of expression" may be seen in *November Boughs*, the "result of deliberate and self-conscious choice. The 'barbaric yawp,' which he sent over 'the roofs of the world' so many years ago [in *Leaves of Grass* (1855)], and which wrung from Mr. Swinburne's lips such lofty panegyric song and such loud clamorous censure in prose [an allusion to Swinburne's "To Walt Whitman in America" in *Songs before Sunrise* (1871) and his article "Whitmania" in the *Fortnightly Review* (August 1887)], appears here in what will be to many an entirely new light. For in his very rejection of art Walt Whitman is an artist.... There is much method in what many have termed his madness, too much method indeed some may be tempted to fancy."

Wilde notes that, beyond "moods and motives" of his verse, Whitman reveals "the lofty spirit of a grand and free acceptance of all things that are worthy of existence": "...really great poetry," Whitman urges, "is always the result of a national spirit, and not the privilege of a polished and select few" (a view at variance with much that Wilde himself would express in the following year in "The Critic as Artist"). Such, says Wilde, are the views in the opening essay of *November Boughs*, titled "A Backward Glance o'er Travel'd Roads"; other essays in this "fascinating volume" are on Burns and Tennyson, for whom Whitman "has a profound admiration; some on actors and singers; others on native Indians and Western slang as well as on the poetry of the Bible and on Lincoln. But Whitman is "at his best when he is analyzing his own work, and making schemes for the poetry of the future. Literature to him has a distinctly social aim. He seeks to build up the masses by 'building up grand individuals.'" Whitman, concludes Wilde, has

a largeness of vision, a healthy sanity, and a fine ethical purpose. He is not to be placed with the professional *littérateurs* of his country, Boston novelists, New York poets, and the like. He stands apart, and the chief value of his work is in its prophecy, not in its performance.... He is a factor in the heroic and spiritual evolution of the human being.

Thus, Wilde acknowledges Whitman's morality of art, thoroughly at odds with his own belief in art for art's sake, the central doctrine of Aestheticism.

GOSSE, EDMUND (1849–1928)

A poet, critic, biographer, and translator of Ibsen's plays, Gosse did not have a close relationship with Wilde. They first met at a masquerade party given by the painter Lawrence Alma-Tadema (1836–1912) and his wife in 1881. Before the party took place, Gosse wrote to his friend, the sculptor William Hamo Thornycroft (1850–1925), that Wilde was "the only person who refuses to come masked! The Tademas think this most conceited of him and beg that everyone will tease him as much as possible." Introduced to Gosse, Wilde expressed his pleasure in meeting him. Gosse replied: "I was afraid you would be disappointed." Wilde responded: "Oh no, I am never disappointed in literary men, I think they are perfectly charming. It is their works I find so disappointing" (qtd. in Thwaite 211).

In the following year, Gosse expressed his scorn in his private correspondence toward Wilde's flamboyant behavior on his American lecture tour. To the American poet E. C. Stedman (1833–1908), Gosse reported that he had received articles from America about Wilde's tour:

A stinking nosegay, but a medicinal one, which will be of very great use in concocting a Brew or Purge which is in preparation for the animal on his return to these shores. Seriously, he has lost more friends in going to America than all his previous vagaries cost him.... I myself have suffered in the cause of Oscar. I refused to allow any contributions of mine to appear in a book of sonnets [*Sonnets of Three Centuries*, edited by T. Hall Caine in 1882] if Wilde, who had wormed his way into the book, were not ejected. Ejected he was, but I got heaps of abuse, which however is now turning, I find, to something like approbation. (*Transatlantic,* 89–90)

Despite his reaction in 1882, Gosse probably renewed his acquaintance with Wilde at a meeting of the Society of Authors in Willis's Rooms in March 1887, when Gosse presented a lecture on "The Profession of Authorship." In the following month, Wilde was invited by the executive secretary, J. S. Little, to join the society as a Fellow, to which status he was elected on 17 July. In the following year, Wilde complained to Little of Gosse's "gross mismanagement" in arranging a banquet, though, unknown to Wilde, Gosse had little to do with the seating arrangements (*Letters* 221–22).

In October 1888, Wilde was nominated for membership in the prestigious Savile Club, 31 members of which supported the nomination, including Rider Haggard, Henry James, Walter Besant, George Macmillan, W. E. Henley, and Gosse (a marked change in his attitude perhaps because of Wilde's recent publications). However, Wilde was never elected because of opposition – in which case, as the rules provided, a candidate's nomination was set aside indefinitely. In late 1892, Wilde's appreciation of Gosse's support of his status in the literary world was expressed in a letter to Robert Ross: Gosse, in reviewing William Watson's volume of poems *Lachrymae Musarum* in the *New Review* (Dec. 1892), urged Watson to omit "one piece" in the second edition:

To peck at one another is not the business of humming-birds and nightingales [see Watson's doggerel in the entry on *Salomé*].... Mr Oscar Wilde (with whom I seldom find myself in agreement) is an artist, and claims from his fellow-artists courteous consideration.

Wilde was pleased, as he told Ross, to receive "so graceful a recognition from so accomplished a man of letters. As a rule, journalists and literary people write so horribly, and with such gross familiarity, and virulent abuse, that I am rather touched by any mention of me that is graceful and civil" (*Letters* 323).

In 1893, perhaps hopeful that Gosse might review his latest work, Wilde sent him a copy of the French version of *Salomé,* writing that it was his "first venture to use for art that subtle instrument of music, the French tongue. Accept it as a slight tribute of my admiration of your own delicate use of English" (*Letters* 331). What Gosse's reaction was is unknown. In December of that year, Wilde sent him a copy of the published version of *Lady Windermere's Fan,* to which Gosse responded that "the brilliant merit [of the play] is only enhanced by the absence of stage disturbance. I have just read it through, & I think more highly of it than ever" (qtd. in Small 84). At the time of the Wilde debacle, Gosse could not ignore its impact, for Ross was a friend of the Gosse family. On 17 May 1895, he wrote to him: "The recent intolerable events have vexed my soul – mainly (I confess) on your account, my regard for you turning what would else (perhaps) have been comedy, or satiric drama, into pure tragedy" (qtd. in Thwaite 359).

When Ross issued a new edition of *De Profundis* (1908), which contained further portions of Wilde's prison letter, he sent a copy to Gosse, who responded: "They are in themselves picturesque, and they aid us in estimating the character of Wilde. To that character I am afraid I shall always feel instinctively hostile." A repressed homosexual, Gosse expressed his "passion" for "more and more personal liberty...almost a fanaticism with me": "Less and less can I endure the idea of punishing a man – who is not cruel – because he is unlike other men.... Perhaps poor Wilde (who alas! was in life so distasteful to me) may come to be honoured as a proto-martyr to freedom, now he is in his grave." Commenting on the prison letters that Ross included with *De Profundis*, Gosse writes that they "put Wilde in a better, more human, less ridiculous light than anything else that he wrote. Here is, for once, a man speaking, with real pity, real indignation, real pain. What I principally hated about him, poor creature, was not at all his vices, but his unreality" (Ross 146–47).

In March 1910, Gosse's final judgment of Wilde as a writer occurs in a letter to André Gide, whose expanded memoirs of Wilde had just appeared:

There has been a great deal of folly written about Wilde. I like the complete sanity of your picture. Of course he was not a "great writer." A languid romancier, a bad poet, a good (but not superlatively good) dramatist, – his works, taken without his life, present to a sane criticism, a mediocre figure. But the man consistent, extraordinary, vital even to excess, and his strange tragedy will always attract the consideration of the wise. (*Correspondence* 53)

References: Linette Brugmans, ed., *The Correspondence of André Gide and Edmund Gosse,*

1904–28 (1959); Paul Mattheisen and Michael Millgate, eds., *Transatlantic Dialogue: Selected American Correspondence of Edmund Gosse* (1965); Ann Thwaite, *Edmund Gosse: A Literary Landscape, 1849–1928* (1984).

GRAHAM, ROBERT BONTINE CUNNINGHAME (1852–1936)

A Scottish poet, travel writer, author of short stories and essays, a Socialist, and Member of Parliament (1886–92), Graham had apparently met Wilde by the late 1880s, when, in a letter to Mrs. Graham, Wilde wrote: "Give my love to your delightful and dangerous husband" (*More Letters* 84). The relationship between Graham and Wilde seems to have been casual, for no exhange of letters is known to have occurred until 1898. At the time of Wilde's trials, however, Graham wrote to Will Rothenstein:

Courage, he has no courage at all. There were three things & three only he could have done.
1. Commit suicide.
2. Take the train to San Sebastian (where there is no extradition treaty).
3. Stand up in the dock & defy the world & say (if he thought so) he had done no wrong, & that the Judge, the jury, the court & everyone were hypocrites.
He did neither. [Then] where is the courage.

A few days later, he again wrote to Rothenstein: "Poor Oscar, one cannot help being very sorry for him.... He seems a kind hearted & generous fool & a mere baby in the ways of the world" (qtd. in Watts and Davies 135).

When Graham – who had spent time in prison for his part in the "Bloody Sunday" riots in Trafalgar Square, November 1887 – received a copy of *The Ballad of Reading Gaol*, he wrote a "charming letter" to Wilde in appreciation (*Letters* 706). In response, Wilde wrote that, in late February 1898, he had read Graham's article on prison life in the *Saturday Review* (19 June 1897), and, using the metaphor that both had known as literal fact, he wished that they "could meet to talk over the many prisons of life – prisons of stone, prisons of passion, prisons of intellect, prisons of morality, and the rest. All limitations, external or internal, are prison-walls, and life is a limitation" (*More Letters* 165). Though Wilde asked Graham to see him in

Paris in the spring of that year, there is no evidence that the two ever met.

In late February 1905, when the *Saturday Review* sent *De Profundis* to Graham for review, he wrote to Robert Ross: "It is a dreadful thing to read; but I am glad he never repented. How one hates penitents. His old humour peeps out.... Now I know that most people who will do so, will refer to the 'great change in his point of view' etc. I shall write, for in his unchanging point of view, I see his greatness" (Ross 94). In his review (4 March 1905), Graham wrote that, though most people recalled Wilde's wit, humour, brilliance, literary triumphs, and his fall, he most remembered Wilde's "great kindliness...the greatest quality in man." Knowing at first hand the experience of prison, Graham asserts: "Few books in any language, treating of prisons and of prison life, are comparable with this. The book is beautiful in all its misery, and worth a million of the dishonest self-revelations of the men who write about their souls as if their bodies were mere pillow-cases" (rpt. in Beckson).

Reference: Cedric Watts and Laurence Davies, *Cunninghame Graham: A Critical Biography* (1979).

"THE GRAVE OF KEATS"

Published: *Irish Monthly* 5 (July 1877), 478, as "Heu Miserande Puer" (translated as "Ah, child of pity...," from Virgil's *Aeneid*, 6:882), concluding Wilde's essay "The Tomb of Keats"; rev. in the *Burlington* 1 (Jan. 1881): 35, with the present title; further rev. in *Poems* (1881).

The genesis of this poem occurred in 1877, when Wilde visited the Protestant Cemetery in Rome, Keats's burial site, an event he describes in "The Tomb of Keats":

As I stood beside the mean grave of this divine boy, I thought of him as of a Priest of Beauty slain before his time; and the vision of Guido's St. Sebastian came before my eyes as I saw him at Genoa, a lovely brown boy, with crisp, clustering hair and red lips, bound by his evil enemies to a tree, and though pierced by arrows, raising his eyes with divine, impassioned gaze towards the Eternal Beauty of the opening heavens. And thus my thoughts shaped themselves to rhyme....

David Hunter-Blair, a college friend, who accompanied Wilde to the Vatican for an audience with Pope Pius IX, later recalled that, as they passed the Protestant Cemetery, Wilde "would not be dissuaded from alighting at the cemetery and prostrating himself on the turf to venerate the grave of John Keats." This additional detail, omitted by Wilde in his own account, suggests the length to which he worshipped the Religion of Art (he had not prostrated himself before the Pope).

This central myth of Aestheticism, with its need to have martyrs and Priests of Beauty, is given expression by Wilde in the opening lines of his poem: "Rid of the world's injustice, and his pain, / He sleeps at last beneath God's veil of blue." St. Sebastian serves as the prototype of Keats, who, erroneously, was believed to have met an early death because of adverse reviews of his work: "The youngest of the martyrs here is lain, / Fair as Sebastian, and as early slain" (Sebastian, an officer in the Praetorian guards, a favorite of the Emperor Diocletian, was slain ca. 300 AD when discovered to be a Christian). As Ellmann remarks, St. Sebastian was "the favorite saint among homosexuals" (71/68). On his release from prison, Wilde took the name of "Sebastian Melmoth" as his alias in France.

Manuscripts: The Houghton Library at Harvard has a MS. titled "Keats' Grave," which is printed in *Letters* 42. A facsimile of a MS. in the Anderson Galleries catalogue of the John B. Stetson sale (23 April 1920, p. 43) is printed in Mason 11; another facsimile appeared in the American Art Association – Anderson Galleries catalogue (13–14 Nov. 1935, p. 252), the autograph copy of the poem sent to Keats's niece, Emma Speed (1823–83): see *Letters* 109.

Reference: David Hunter-Blair, "Oscar Wilde As I Knew Him," *In Victorian Days and Other Papers* (1939), partially rpt. in Mikhail 1:3–11.

"THE GRAVE OF SHELLEY"

Published: *Poems* (1881). The poem was probably written when Wilde visited Rome in March 1877 (see, also, "The Grave of Keats").

In this sonnet, Wilde recalls the "Gaunt cypress-trees [that] stand round the sun-bleached stone" of Shelley's grave in the Protestant Cemetery in Rome. In the "still chamber of yon pyramid" (the monument, within sight of the cemetery, was erected to memorialize Caius Cestius, a

Roman magistrate who died around 30 BC), "Surely some Old-World Sphynx lurks darkly hid, / Grim warder of this pleasaunce of the dead." The poem concludes with the image of Shelley "within the womb / Of Earth, great mother of eternal sleep," though Wilde suggests that a "restless tomb" would be sweeter for Shelley "In the blue cavern of an echoing deep...."

Manuscripts: An early version of this poem is printed in Mason 309–10. The Jeremy Mason Collection has the MS. of this version and the autograph fair copy, facsimiles of which are included in Jeremy Mason's privately printed pamphlet *Oscar Wilde and the Grave of Shelley* (Edinburgh: Tragara Press, 1992), with his introduction and notes.

GRAY, JOHN (1866–1944) and ANDRÉ RAFFALOVICH (1864–1934)

A poet, critic, and playwright, Gray rose from a working-class background, through arduous self-education, to the position of clerk in the Foreign Office Library. He apparently first met Wilde in the summer of 1889 at a supper party in a Soho restaurant. In an unpublished memoir in the Clark Library, Frank Liebich, a popular concert pianist who was present, recalls that the poet John Barlas (see entry), a known homosexual, "had hinted rather vaguely, of the (alleged) intimacy between Wilde and Gray, so that I was really more curious about the latter, an extraordinarily good-looking youth...but severely conventional in both speech and behaviour" (qtd. in McCormack 49).

In the same year, Gray made the acquaintance of Charles Ricketts and Charles Shannon (see entry), to whose periodical, the *Dial*, Gray contributed a fairy tale, "The Great Worm," inspired by Wilde's *The Happy Prince and Other Tales* (1888). In 1889, while in Brittany, Gray was moved to convert to Roman Catholicism, which he formalized in February 1890, followed, as McCormack states, by "a deliberate lapse, a kind of apostasy *à rebours* during the years 1890–92" (34).

During this period, he assumed the first name of "Dorian" after Wilde's novel, signing at least one letter to Wilde in this manner; friends, moreover, referred to him as "Dorian" in their correspondence (Wilde's use of the name "Gray" for the beautiful young hero of his novel no doubt led those in Wilde's circle to the inevitable conclusion). To a correspondent on 5 February 1891,

Lionel Johnson described a meeting of the Rhymers' Club, which Gray attended: "I have made great friends with the original of Dorian: one John Gray, a youth in the Temple, aged thirty [he was actually 25], with the face of fifteen" (qtd. in Ellmann 308/291).

In the early 1890s, Gray maintained an intimate relationship with Wilde, the precise nature of which remains conjectural. They were seen together at such places as the Café Royal and at meetings of the Rhymers' Club. Indeed, Bernard Shaw regarded Gray as one of Wilde's "abject disciples" (*Autobiography* 250). As a result of Gray's association with Wilde, the popular newspaper, the *Star* (6 Feb. 1892), noted on its front page that Gray was "said to be the original Dorian of the same name. Mr. Gray, who has cultivated his manner to the highest pitch of languor yet attained, is a well-known figure of the Playgoers' Club, where, though he often speaks, he is seldom heard." Annoyed by such unwelcome publicity (for to be named, McCormack suggests, as "Wilde's 'protégé' or as the original of 'Dorian Gray' was the equivalent of being named Wilde's lover," 84), Gray took steps to sue for libel. The amused Ernest Dowson, writing to his fellow Rhymer Victor Plarr of Gray's action, remarks: "This will be droll" (Dowson, *Letters* 225). Within nine days, however, the paper apologized for its remarks after complimenting Gray on his "graceful verse" translation of Théodore de Banville's one-act play *Le Baiser*, scheduled for production by the Independent Theatre Society. Then, the paper continued:

> ...we are told that some people have taken quite seriously a suggestion which appeared in this column a few days since that Mr. Gray was the prototype of Mr. Oscar Wilde's Dorian Gray. The risks of the New Humour could not have a more unfortunate illustration than the acceptance as serious of a statement that a skilful young literary artist of promise like Mr. Gray could possibly be the original of the monstrous Epicurean of Mr. Wilde's creation, and we greatly regret the erroneous impression that has been produced. (qtd. in McCormack 83)

After another reference in a newspaper to his discipleship to Wilde – this time in the *Daily*

Telegraph, which, less than a week following the *Star*'s remarks, alluded to Wilde and Gray as the "literary and dramatic godfather of a youth" who was his *protégé* – Gray apparently asked Wilde to respond to the paper's allegation. Wilde wrote to the editor on 19 February that his acquaintance with Gray was "extremely recent [an obvious inaccuracy], and that I sought it because he had already a perfected mode of expression both in prose and verse. All artists in this vulgar age need protection certainly." But Gray, he continues, has no such need, "nor, indeed, would he accept it" (*Letters* 311–12). By late 1892, McCormack contends, Gray's "revolt" against his recently adopted faith, "a self-conscious cultivation of 'sin' symbolized by his life as 'Dorian' Gray, precipitated a spiritual crisis that was not entirely resolved until Gray decided to enter the priesthood" (34).

By November 1892, Gray was in an agitated state, perhaps induced by his aborted relationship with Wilde and by the death of his father (despite Gray's callous remark about the death to Pierre Louÿs: "I am well pleased with the loss" – qtd. in McCormack 97). In any event, he had an apparent mental and physical breakdown. Ellmann writes that, late in that year, Gray told Louÿs that he was thinking of committing suicide: "Douglas's ascendency over Wilde was pre-emptive and Gray felt jilted" (391/369). An indication of Gray's state of mind may be inferred from the story that he wrote during these months, "The Person in Question," which depicts the central character's eerie experience of encountering his double – which "pictured for Gray," McCormack contends, "as if in a mirror, not only what he *might* become, but what, in fact, he *had* become" (102). The tale, unpublished during his lifetime, was undoubtedly inspired by *The Picture of Dorian Gray* at a time when John Gray's "double life was falling apart" (98).

In December 1892, Gray's crisis drew to him a rescuing figure who would provide comfort and the monetary means whereby Gray could recover: André Raffalovich, a Russian émigré Jew whose wealthy parents had settled in Paris a year before his birth, had embarked for Oxford University when he was 18 but soon abandoned his intention to study. Attracted to London, he not only began publishing critical articles, poems, and fiction but also meeting many prominent men of letters in his "At-Homes." When he first met Wilde is unknown, but a remark attributed to him by Vincent O'Sullivan – that Raffalovich "came to London with the intention of opening a salon and succeeded in opening a saloon" (92) – has often been cited by hostile writers as an example of Wilde's bad taste.

When Raffalovich published his second volume of poems, *Tuberose and Meadowsweet* (1885), Wilde reviewed it on 27 March in the *Pall Mall Gazette* (see "A Bevy of Poets"). Praising it as a "remarkable little volume," Wilde pointed to Raffalovich's insistence in making *tuberose* a three-syllable word, adding: "...though he cannot pronounce 'tuberose' aright, at least he can sing of it exquisitely." Annoyed, Raffalovich sent a letter to the editor (his letter appearing on 30 March) that Shelley, among others, had regarded *tuberose* as a three-syllable word. Wilde responded with his own letter signed "The Critic Who Had to Read Four Volumes of Modern Poetry," which appeared in the paper on 1 April. Wilde good-humoredly defended his own preference for the two-syllable word. (When the *Pall Mall Budget* reprinted the review on 3 May, Wilde's objection to *tuberose* was omitted.)

Raffalovich was probably first introduced to Wilde by Whistler in the mid-1880s. Such a likelihood has a foundation in McCormack's remark: "Within a short time after his arrival in London [that is, in 1882], Raffalovich had established himself as a kind of professional guest of such celebrities as Browning, Whistler..." (46). In Raffalovich's novel *A Willing Exile* (1890), Wilde and his circle of young men are depicted as dandies with implications of homoeroticism:

Cyprian was, or seemed to be, intimate with countless young or youngish men; they were all curiously alike. Their voices, the cut of their clothes, the curl of their hair, the brims of their hats, the parties they went to.... Affectation characterised all these men, and the same sort of affectation.... Cyprian's cult for his own looks...increased instead of diminished. He lived with people who talked much about beauty.... His clothes much occupied him; he was never tired of discussing male fashions....

Meetings between Wilde and Raffalovich, presumed to be few, apparently ceased as the latter's friendship with John Gray intensified. In

GRAY, JOHN and ANDRÉ RAFFALOVICH

1893, Gray's *Silverpoints* was published by the Bodley Head (initially, Wilde had arranged to underwrite the costs, but he subsequently withdrew from the contract). In its unusual format, designed and decorated by Charles Ricketts, the gold flame motif on the green cover of the narrow, slender volume has symbolic significance, as G. A. Cevasco writes: "The green and gold have special meaning, for in virtually each poem of the twenty-nine making up the volume, there is some allusion to nature or plants; but as though to imply the superiority of art over nature, the gold pattern dominates the green color" (47). The text printed in italics with extremely wide margins contains some of the most notable Decadent poems of the 1890s, such as "The Barber" and "Mishka" (indeed, after becoming a priest, Gray bought copies of the book at every opportunity in order to remove them from circulation).

During these years, Gray and Raffalovich, himself a homosexual, collaborated on several plays, none of which achieved success. In 1896, the year that Raffalovich converted to Roman Catholicism, he also published, in France, *Uranisme et Unisexualité*, a historical, psychological, and moral treatise on homosexuality. As P. W. J. Healy remarks:

> It is significant that both events took place in the same year; he came to terms with his sexuality and his religious nature together. In fact, the one resolution could not have been made in isolation from the other. His sexuality required the context of his faith for it to have any meaning. (57)

In his treatise, Raffalovich contends that homosexuality and heterosexuality are two legitimate expressions of sexuality; hence, he rejects the notion that homosexuality is either pathological or criminal. *Uranisme et Unisexualité* includes an essay that he had published in Paris in 1895: *L'Affaire Oscar Wilde*, which establishes his view of Wilde:

> When I accuse [Wilde] of criminality, I am no longer concerned with the sexual acts he has been blamed for, but with the role that he has played, the influence he has exerted and used so badly, the youthful dandies he has led astray, and the vices that he has encouraged so

much. (qtd. in Kohl 357n245)

Raffalovich cites Wilde's egoism as the cause of his disaster: Wilde was the victim of himself, of society, and of his friends. Hence, Raffalovich urges chastity for the invert and public acceptance of homosexuality. Without the support of the Church, he contends, chastity will be difficult to achieve.

In May 1897, he joined the Little Oratorians, a pious group that visited the ill; a year later he joined the Third Order of St. Dominic, taking the name of Sebastian, after the martyred saint whom late 19th-century homosexuals preferred (Wilde also took the name after his release from prison). In 1898, Gray left for Rome to study at the Scots College for the priesthood, and in 1902, he became curate at St. Patrick's Church, Edinburgh. When he became rector in 1907, Raffalovich, who had also taken residence in the city, generously contributed to the building of a new church. Their close friendship endured for the remainder of their lives.

Over the years, Gray continued to write and publish both verse and prose. His striking novel, *Park: A Fantastic Story* (1932), probably resulted from his reading of such works as William Morris's *News from Nowhere* and H. G. Wells's *The Time Machine* in their visions of the future (Cevasco 127). One of the characters in *Park*, Cevasco points out, is named "A Ra" (presumably Raffalovich), who dedicates an oratory to St. Sebastian (130).

Though Gray understandably refrained from writing about Wilde, Raffalovich, under the pseudonym of "Alexander Michaelson," published an essay on Wilde in 1927, which reflects the chaste, austere life that Raffalovich had lived since his conversion and that no doubt influenced his view of Wilde in these later years: "Much as I grew to dislike him, I cannot remember his ever giving me bad advice. It is to his credit that he never did me any harm, and perhaps also to mine that for years I detested him and his presence, and the traces of his influence." While attending a play with Wilde, Raffalovich reports that, after the first act, an acquaintance approached him and, pointing to Wilde, warned: "That is a man you must not know."

After having read Rachilde's *Monsieur Vénus*, Wilde once talked to Raffalovich "for several hours about the more dangerous affections.... It must have been soon after that his wife Constance, who had always befriended me, estranged us. She said to me: 'Oscar says he likes you so much – that you have such improper talks together.'" In time, Raffalovich grew increasingly "furious": "I was innocent of what I called improper talks. I had listened eagerly to his wit and wisdom and experience, to his store of unusual stories.... Never again did I speak with him without witnesses." Though Raffalovich attended the première of *The Importance of Being Earnest*, he recalled that he could not sit through the entire play.

As for "the third and fourth acts of Oscar's tragedy – the trial and verdict and the prison," Raffalovich writes: "I must confess my approval of the verdict." Having wished to attend one of the trials, he was about to enter the courtroom, when "a handsome youthful policemen" stopped him and said, "It is no place for you, Sir; don't go in" (at this time, Raffalovich had not yet converted to Roman Catholicism). Raffalovich responded: "'Thank you; you are right,' and went away" (Michaelson, 108-12).

References: Vincent O'Sullivan, *Aspects of Wilde* (1936); Brocard Sewell, ed., *Two Friends: John Gray and André Raffalovich: Essays Biographical and Critical* (1963); Desmond Flower and Henry Maas, eds., *The Letters of Ernest Dowson* (1967); Alexander Michaelson, "Oscar Wilde," *Blackfriars* (Nov. 1927), rpt. in Brocard Sewell, *Footnote to the Nineties: A Memoir of John Gray and André Raffalovich*, Appendix III (1968); Stanley Weintraub, ed., *Shaw: An Autobiography, 1856–1898* (1969); P. W. J. Healy, "*Uranisme et Unisexualite*: A Late Victorian View of Homosexuality," *New Blackfriars* (Feb. 1978); Ruth Z. Temple, "The Other Choice: The Worlds of John Gray, Poet and Priest," *Bulletin of Research in the Humanities* (Spring 1981); G. A. Cevasco, *John Gray* (1982); Brocard Sewell, *In the Dorian Mode: A Life of John Gray* (1983); Alan Anderson, ed., *A Friendship of the Nineties: Letters between John Gray and Pierre Louÿs* (1984); Jerusha Hull McCormack, *John Gray: Poet, Dandy, and Priest* (1991).

"GREAT WRITERS BY LITTLE MEN"

Published: *PMG*, 28 March 1887, 5; rpt. in *Reviews* (1908). Unsigned reviews of Eric S. Robertson's *Life of Henry Wadsworth Longfellow* and Hall Caine's *Life of Samuel Taylor Coleridge*

– both published in 1887.

Robertson's *Longfellow*, Wilde writes, is a "most depressing book." No one "survives being overestimated, nor is there any surer way of destroying an author's reputation than to glorify him without judgment and to praise him without tact." Though Longfellow was "one of the first true men of letters America produced," Wilde contends that his poems do not call for "intellectual analysis or for elaborate description or, indeed, for any serious discussion at all."

No one reading *Evangeline* would, like Robertson, be reminded of Homer's or Virgil's line: "Where lies the advantage of confusing popularity with poetic power?" If Walter Scott, the publisher of this volume in the "Great Writers" series, "imagines that work of this kind is 'original and valuable' he has much to learn." When Robertson "tells us that Poe's 'loftiest flights of imagination in verse...rise into no more empyreal realm than the *fantastic*,' we can only recommend him to read as soon as possible the marvellous lines 'To Helen,' a poem as beautiful as a Greek gem and as musical as Apollo's lute."

Hall Caine's *Coleridge* has nothing of the "spiritual progress of the man's soul.... The magic of that wonderful personality is hidden from us by a cloud of mean details, an unholy jungle of fact, and the 'critical history' promised to us by Mr. Walter Scott in his unfortunate preface is conspicuous only by its absence." Carlyle, Wilde remarks, "once proposed in jest to write a life of Michael Angelo without making any reference to his art, and Mr. Caine has shown that such a project is perfectly feasible."

The real events of Coleridge's life are not his walking tours but his "thoughts, dreams and passions, his moments of creative impulse, their source and secret, his moods of imaginative joy, their marvel and their meaning...." It is said that "every man's life is a Soul's Tragedy" (here, Wilde echoes the title of Browning's verse drama *A Soul's Tragedy*, 1846). Coleridge's was such, and "though we may not be able to pluck out the heart of his mystery, still let us recognise that mystery is there.... So mediocre is Mr. Caine's book that even accuracy could not make it better."

"GREEK WOMEN"

The Clark Library has an unpublished typescript prepared by Robert Ross from the original MS., which remains unlocated.

GREEN CARNATION

In the 1890s, the image of the green carnation emerged as a symbol of Decadence – as Ellmann suggests, the "painted flower blended art and artifice" (365/345). Furthermore, it has been said (though evidence remains obscure) that the flower was a Parisian symbol of homosexuality. In his "Pen, Pencil and Poison," Wilde had remarked that the poisoner and writer Thomas Griffiths Waine-wright had "that curious love of green, which in individuals is always the sign of a subtle artistic temperament, and in nations is said to denote a laxity, if not a decadence, of morals." At a produc-tion of John Gray's translation of Théodore de Banville's *Le Baiser*, staged by the Independent Theatre Society at the Royalty Theatre, the *Star* (4 March 1892) reported that Wilde was present with "a suite of young gentlemen all wearing the vivid dyed carnation which has superseded the lily and sunflower."

In *Time Was: Reminiscences* (1931), W. Graham Robertson, the scene designer of *Lady Winder-mere's Fan*, tells the doubtful story that Wilde requested that the actor portraying Cecil Graham wear a green carnation in his lapel on stage; at the same time, he asked, according to Robertson, that the young members "of his own entourage in the audience also sport green carnations in their lapels." (Joseph Bristow, in turn, attempts to make an amusing story even more amusing by stating that green carnations "were distributed to all the men in the audience," 20.)

If Wilde had wished to create a sensation, as Robertson implies, there was oddly no reaction among the drama critics reporting the evening's events, nor has anyone present at the première confirmed in memoirs or letters that Robertson's account has any accuracy. Surely, Frank Harris, who attended the première, would have capitalized on the event in his 1916 biography of Wilde, but he is silent on the matter. Wilde may have suggested, with his customary facetiousness, that the charac-ter Cecil Graham wear a green carnation, a little joke that Robertson, some 40 years later, converted into a mythic event. Hesketh Pearson's popular biography of Wilde in 1946 repeats the tale, which, in turn, Ellmann's biography enshrines as though established fact. At the première of *Lady Winder-mere's Fan*, Henry James noted that Wilde did

wear a "metallic blue carnation" – that is, blue green – but he makes no mention of anyone else

Beardsley's "The Woman in the Moon"

wearing the artificial flower in the theater. The satirist Ada Leverson recalls that Wilde also wore a green carnation at the première of *The Impor-tance of Being Earnest* (Wyndham 114).

In 1892, Richard Le Gallienne opened his attack on Decadence and the green carnation in "To the Reader," the introductory poem in his *English Poems*. Contending that the English nightingale was no longer heard in contemporary poetry, Le Gallienne directed the reader's attention to the "new voice" in French poetry that "once was of the spheres": "And not of thee [the English nightin-gale] these strange green flowers that spring / From daisy roots and seem to bear a sting." It was said that a shop in the Burlington Arcade provided Decadents with dyed carnations daily. Le Gallienne concluded that the color green, in its "more complex forms," implied something "not quite good, something almost sinister...though in its simple form, as we find it in outdoor nature, it is innocent enough," but the green of the Aesthete (more accurately the Decadent) does not suggest innocence:

There will always be wearers of the green carnation, but the popular vogue which green has enjoyed for the last ten or fifteen years is probably passing. Even the aesthete himself would seem to be growing a little weary of its indefinitely divided tones. (79–80)

Not one easily dissuaded from employing his personal symbol, Wilde alludes to the strange green flower in *Salome*. When Salome promises the Young Syrian that she will "let fall...a little flower, a little green flower," if he permits her to see Iokanaan, she reveals her own symbol of perverse, forbidden desire. In Beardsley's mocking illustration titled "The Woman in the Moon," the single flower next to Wilde's bloated face in the moon – one is readily convinced – is a stylized green carnation, though, satirically, ashen white in the black and white drawing.

In 1894, Robert Hichens published his first novel, *The Green Carnation*, the most brilliant satire of Decadence in the 1890s. Homosexual himself, Hichens had met Alfred Douglas and Reginald Turner while in Egypt, and on returning to London had seen Wilde at the Café Royal. In his autobiography, he states that he met Wilde only four or five times and that "there was never, so far as I was aware, a shadow between us. All my meetings with him were happy ones.... I saw not merely the wit and the humorist but the deeply serious and imaginative Oscar" (66). He also recalls that, at the première of a play (unidentified), Wilde and an entourage of "ultra-smart youths," all decorated with green carnations, strolled in slowly some ten minutes after the play had begun (somewhat improbable: Wilde would not have distracted a theater audience in such a manner): "Next day all London was talking about the green carnations, and I had got the title for a book which I began to write almost immediately..." (69–70).

Regardless of Hichens's questionable recall, *The Green Carnation* accurately captures the verbal mannerisms of Wilde in the character named "Esmé Amarinth" (from *amaranth*, which the *Oxford English Dictionary* defines as "an imaginary flower that never fades" and as "a genus of plants with coloured foliage"). Described by Hichens as a hulking figure who dresses for elaborate effect and wears a green carnation, Amarinth utters such witticisms as Hichens may have actually heard Wilde utter: "How splendid to die with a paradox upon one's lips!" In a characteristic passage in Chapter 11, Amarinth speaks with the wit and paradox of Wilde's dandies:

"I am going to sit up all night with Reggie, saying mad scarlet things, such as George Meredith loves, and waking the night with silver silences.... Come, Reggie, let us go to the smoking-room, since we are left alone. I will be brilliant for you as I have never been brilliant for my publishers. I will talk to you as no character in my plays has ever talked.... Let me be brilliant, dear boy, or I feel that I shall weep for sheer wittiness, and die, as so many have died, with all my epigrams still in me."

A young woman newly arrived in London questions the significance of the curiously colored flower:

"I only saw about a dozen [green carnations] in the Opera House to-night, and all the men who wore them looked the same. They had the same walk, or rather waggle, the same coyly conscious expression, the same wavy motion of the head.... It is a badge of some club or some society, and is Mr. Amarinth their high priest? They all spoke to him, and seemed to revolve round him like satellites around the sun."

"My dear Emily, it is not a badge at all. They wear it merely to be original."

"And can they only be original in a button-hole way? Poor fellows."

As the novel opens, Lord Reggie (a thinly disguised Alfred Douglas, with an added thrust at his friend Reggie Turner), in a moment of narcissistic self-admiration parodying *The Picture of Dorian Gray*, is seen preparing to leave: "He slipped a green carnation into his evening coat, fixed it in its place with a pin, and looked at himself in the glass, the long glass that stood near the window of his London bedroom. The summer evening was so bright that he could see his double clearly...." He looks "astonishingly young," we are told, for "his sins keep him fresh." Losing interest in Lord Reggie, Lady Locke complains: "...if you could be like a man, instead of like nothing at all in heaven or earth except that dyed flower, I might perhaps care for you in the right way. But your mind is artificially coloured: it comes from the dyer's. It is a green carnation; and I want a natural blossom to wear in my heart."

Wilde was evidently amused by the novel, but because of its homoerotic suggestions, it apparently also provoked some anxiety. In a telegram to Ada Leverson, Wilde referred to himself as Esmé Amarinth and to Douglas as Lord Reggie: "The doubting disciple [Hichens] who has written the false gospel is one who has merely talent unrelieved by any flashes of physical beauty" (*Letters* 373). Because *The Green Carnation* was published anonymously, journalists attributed it to Ada Leverson. Wilde assured her that she had been "deeply wronged": "But there are many bits not unworthy of your brilliant pen.... Hichens I did not think capable of anything so clever" (*Letters* 373). Wilde contradicted the *Pall Mall Gazette*'s assertion that *he* was the author of *The Green Carnation*: "I invented that magnificent flower. But with the middle-class and mediocre book that usurps its strangely beautiful name I have, I need hardly say, nothing whatsoever to do. The flower is a work of art. The book is not" (*Letters* 373).

By early 1895, with the fourth printing, Hichens's name appeared on the title page, and at the time of Wilde's trials, the publisher William Heinemann withdrew the novel with Hichens's consent, both convinced that to offer it for sale under the current circumstances was improper. Thus ended the episode of *The Green Carnation* and apparently Wilde's relationship with Hichens. Yet Wilde had not forgotten the satire directed at him in the novel: in a typescript of the original four-act version of *The Importance of Being Earnest* owned by George Alexander (now in the Harvard Theater Collection), Wilde had added a passage, subsequently removed, in which Lady Brancaster (the name later changed to "Lady Bracknell") alludes to having been given a copy of *The Green Carnation*, which, she says, "seems to be a book about the culture of exotics.... It seems to be a morbid and middle-class affair" (Berggren 190).

References: Richard Le Gallienne, "The Boom in Yellow," *Prose Fancies*, Second Series (1896); *Yesterday: The Autobiography of Robert Hichens*

(1947); Violet Wyndham, *The Sphinx and Her Circle* (1963); Stanley Weintraub, "Introduction" to *The Green Carnation* (1970); *The Definitive Four-Act Version of "The Importance of Being Earnest,"* ed., Ruth Berggren (1987); *"The Importance of Being Earnest" and Related Writings* (1992), ed., Joseph Bristow.

"THE GROSVENOR GALLERY" (1877)

Published: *Dublin University Magazine* 90 (July 1877): 118–26; rpt. in *Miscellanies* (1908). A notice of the first exhibition, which opened on 1 May 1877, at the gallery established by Sir Coutts Lindsay.

Wilde notes that the intent of the new Grosvenor Gallery was to eliminate the "difficulties and meannesses of 'Hanging Committees'" and

exhibit to the lovers of art the works of certain great living artists side by side: a gallery in which the student would not have to struggle through an endless monotony of mediocre works in order to reach what was worth looking at; one in which the people of England could have the opportunity of judging of the merits of at least one great master of painting, whose pictures had been kept from public exhibition by the jealousy and ignorance of rival artists.

Entering the West Gallery, Wilde describes the allegorical painting titled *Love and Death* by George F. Watts and concludes: "Except on the ceiling of the Sistine Chapel in Rome, there are perhaps few paintings to compare with this in intensity of strength and in marvel of conception. It is worthy to rank with Michael Angelo's *God Dividing the Light from the Darkness*."

Next to this work are five pictures by John Everett Millais, three of them portraits of the Duke of Westminster's three daughters: "These pictures do not possess any particular merit beyond that of being extremely good likenesses." Over these portraits hangs a picture of a seamstress, "pale and vacant-looking, with eyes red from tears and long watchings in the night, hemming a shirt. It is meant to illustrate [Thomas] Hood's familiar poem ["The Song of the Shirt"]. As we look on it, a terrible contrast strikes us between this miserable pauper-seamstress and the three beautiful daughters of the richest duke in the world, which breaks

through any artistic reveries by its awful vividness." Nevertheless, Wilde regards these pictures
as inferior to Millais's *Home at Bethlehem* and the
portrait of John Ruskin, which is at Oxford.

Wilde next comments on eight paintings by
Lawrence Alma-Tadema, whose "accurate drawing
of inanimate objects...makes his pictures so real
from an antiquarian point of view, and of the
sweet subtlety of colouring which gives to them a
magic all their own." One, which represents
Roman girls bathing in a marble tank, has a "very
perfect" color of the limbs in the water. "It is
wonderful," Wilde remarks, "what a world of
atmosphere and reality may be condensed into a
very small space, for this picture is only about
eleven by two and a half inches." Alma-Tadema's
most ambitious picture is *Phidias Showing the
Frieze of the Parthenon to his Friends*; there is,
however, "a want of individuality among the
connoiseurs clustered around Phidias, and the
frieze itself is very inaccurately coloured." This
painter, concludes Wilde, is "more at home in the
Greco-Roman art of the Empire and later Republic
than he is in the art of the Periclean age."

The "most abused pictures in the whole Exhibition" are the "'colour symphonies' of the 'Great
Dark Master,' Mr. Whistler...." Wilde cites *Nocturne in Black and Gold: The Falling Rocket* and
Nocturne in Blue and Silver, among others. The
first represents "a rocket of golden rain, with green
and red fires bursting in a perfectly black sky, two
large black smudges on the picture standing, I
believe, for a tower which is in 'Cremorne Gardens' and for a crowd of lookers-on" (this is the
famous picture that Ruskin intemperately attacked
– "I have seen and heard, much of Cockney impu-
dence before now; but never expected to hear a
coxcomb ask two hundred guineas for flinging a
pot of paint in the public's face" – a charge that
prompted Whistler to sue for libel). The other
"nocturne" (later known as *Nocturne in Blue and
Gold: Old Battersea Bridge*) depicts a rocket
"breaking in a pale blue sky over a large dark blue
bridge and a blue and silver river. These pictures
are certainly worth looking at for about as long as
one looks at a real rocket, that is, for somewhat
less than a quarter of a minute."

Wilde alludes to Whistler's *Arrangement in
Black, No. 3* as

apparently some pseudonym for our greatest

living actor, for out of black smudgy clouds
comes looming the gaunt figure of Mr. Henry
Irving, with the yellow hair and pointed beard,
the ruff, short cloak, and tight hose in which
he appeared as Philip II in Tennyson's play
Queen Mary.... The figure is life-size, and,
though apparently one-armed, is so ridicu-
lously like the original that one cannot help
almost laughing when one sees it.

Two other life-size portraits of two young ladies,
"evidently caught in a black London fog...look like
sisters, but are not related probably, as one is a
Harmony in Amber and Black, the other only an
Arrangement in Brown." Wilde cites "one really
good picture" that Whistler had on display in the
entrance hall: "a portrait of Mr. Carlyle" (Whistler's title: *Arrangement in Grey and Black, No.
2*): "The expression on the old man's face, the texture
and colour of his grey hair, and the general sympathetic treatment, show Mr. Whistler to be an artist
of very great power when he likes."

Other artists are briefly commented on in the
remainder of this notice, among them Sir Coutts
Lindsay, William Holman Hunt, Albert Moore,
Spencer Stanhope, Edward Burne-Jones, Walter
Crane, Alphonse Legros, and Frederick Leighton.
Concluding, Wilde notes that

Sir Coutts Lindsay, in showing us great works
of art, will be most materially aiding that
revival of culture and love of beauty which in
great part owes its birth to Mr. Ruskin, and
which Mr. Swinburne, and Mr. Pater, and Mr.
Symonds, and Mr. Morris, and many others,
are fostering and keeping alive, each in his
own peculiar fashion.

"THE GROSVENOR GALLERY" (1879)

Published: *Saunders' Irish Daily News* 90 (5
May 1879): 5; rpt. in *Miscellanies* (1908).

In his second notice of an exhibition at the
Grosvenor Gallery, Wilde begins by contrasting it
with the yearly exhibition at the Royal Academy,
which "may be said to present us with the general
characteristics of ordinary English art at its most
commonplace level," whereas at the Grosvenor
"we are enabled to see the highest development of
the modern artistic spirit as well as what one might
call its specially accentuated tendencies." The most
impressive works in the exhibition are Edward

Burne-Jones's *Annunciation* and his four pictures illustrating the Greek legend of Pygmalion – "works of the very highest importance in our aesthetic development as illustrative of some of the more exquisite qualities of modern culture."

Wilde also praises the work of George F. Watts, the "extraordinary width and reach of whose genius were never more illustrated than by the various pictures bearing his name which are here exhibited. His *Paolo and Francesca* and his *Orpheus and Eurydice* are creative visions of the very highest order of imaginative painting; marked as it is with all the splendid vigour of nobly ordered design...." Turning to Whistler, "whose wonderful and eccentric genius is better appreciated in France than in England," Wilde mentions his "very wonderful picture" entitled *The Golden Girl* and one of his etchings titled *The Little Forge*, "entirely done with the dry point," which possesses "extraordinary merit."

Alluding to the recent Ruskin/Whistler litigation (in which the jury awarded Whistler a farthing for damage to his reputation: see "The Grosvenor Gallery" notice for 1877 above), Wilde notes that Whistler was not deterred from exhibiting some more "arrangements in colour," one of which titled *Harmony in Green and Gold*, "an extremely good example of what ships lying at anchor on a summer evening are from the 'Impressionist point of view.'"

Among other painters whom Wilde briefly notes are Johnston Forbes-Robertson and Eugene Benson, "one of the most cultured of those many Americans who seem to have found their Mecca in modern Rome...." In his final paragraph, Wilde alludes to a projected notice reserved for the "wonderful landscapes" of Cecil Lawson, "who has caught so much of Turner's imagination" as well as a consideration of the works of Herkomer, Tissot, Alphonse Legros, and others of the "modern realistic school," but he did not write it.

H

"'HAMLET' AT THE LYCEUM"

Published: *Dramatic Review* 1 (9 May 1885): 227; rpt. in *Reviews* (1908). A signed review of Henry Irving's revival of the play at the Lyceum Theatre, which had opened on Saturday, 2 May, the role of Ophelia performed by Ellen Terry.

Wilde remarks that he had "rarely witnessed such enthusiasm as that which greeted on last Saturday night the two artists I have mentioned" (Irving and Terry had just returned from a tour in America). Irving is a "great actor" because he brings to the stage the two qualities "which we in this century so much desire, the qualities of personality and of perfection." Irving's "exquisite grace of gesture and clear precision of word" have replaced what many, some years ago, believed – that Irving's personality "overshadowed" his art.

If the role of Hamlet, Wilde writes, is a challenge to perform, that of Ophelia is "the more difficult part" because she has "less material by which to produce her effects." Ellen Terry, however, combines "her infinite powers of pathos and her imaginative and creative faculty" in such lines as those when she lies to Hamlet that her father is at home. "This," says Wilde, "I thought a masterpiece of good acting, and her mad scene was wonderful beyond all description." Among those who maintained a high standard of acting was George Alexander, whose "brilliant" performance as Laertes prompted Wilde to observe that "Mr. Alexander is an artist from whom much will be expected, and I have no doubt he will give us much that is fine and noble." (Alexander later created the role of Jack Worthing in *The Importance of Being Earnest*.)

"A HANDBOOK TO MARRIAGE"

Published: *PMG*, 18 Nov. 1885, 6; rpt. in *Reviews* (1908). An unsigned review of *How to Be Happy though Married: Being a Handbook to Marriage* (1885). The anonymous author – identified on the title page only as "A Graduate in the University of Matrimony" – was the Rev. Edward J. Hardy, an assistant master at Portora Royal School, which Wilde had attended from 1864 to 1871.

"In spite of its alarming title," begins Wilde, "this book may be highly recommended to every one. As for the authorities he quotes, they are almost numberless, and range from Socrates down to Artemus Ward." The anonymous author "may be regarded as the champion of the married life." Wilde alludes to Archbishop Richard Whately, who defined woman as "'a creature that does not reason and pokes the fire from the top,' but since his day the higher education of women has considerably altered their position." In our day, says Wilde, "it is best for a man to be married, and men must give up the tyranny in married life which was once so dear to them, and which, we are afraid, lingers still, here and there." This book, strongly recommended, is "a complete handbook to an earthly Paradise" and the "Baedeker of bliss."

"THE HAPPY PRINCE"

Published: *The Happy Prince and Other Tales* (1888). In mid-July 1888, Wilde told the publisher Leonard Smithers that "The Happy Prince" was "an attempt to treat a tragic modern problem in a form that aims at delicacy and imaginative treatment: it is a reaction against the purely imitative character of modern art..." (*Letters* 221). Early in 1897, Wilde wrote in his prison letter to Lord Alfred Douglas that "The Happy Prince" was one of those works that "foreshadowed and prefigured" his downfall (*Letters* 475).

The Plot: On a tall column above the city stands the statue of the Happy Prince, gilded with thin leaves of fine gold, two bright sapphires for his eyes, and a large red ruby on his sword-hilt. He serves as a model for children: "The Happy Prince never dreams of crying for anything," says a mother to her child. The Charity Children remark that he looks like an angel.

Flying over the city, a Swallow, whose friends have gone to Egypt, has remained behind, for he was in love with a beautiful Reed. His courtship of her had lasted all summer; he tired of her, however, and flew away. Now, having arrived in the city, he sees the statue on the column and rests between its feet. A drop of water falls on him, then two more. He discovers that the Prince's eyes are filled with tears. The Prince tells the Swallow that, when he was alive, he lived in a palace, "where sorrow is not allowed to enter." Around the garden was a protective wall, but, he says, "I never cared to ask what lay beyond it, everything about me was so beautiful." But now, set high on a column, he can see "all the ugliness and all the misery" of the city.

He can see a poor house where a seamstress works, her little boy lying ill. When the Prince instructs the bird to take the ruby from his sword-hilt and bring it to the woman, the Swallow pleads that his friends are waiting for him in Egypt. However, the Swallow agrees to remain for one night and be the Happy Prince's messenger. The bird flies with the precious stone, drops it on the woman's table, flies around the feverish boy to cool his forehead, and returns to the Happy Prince feeling quite warm despite the cold: "This is because you have done a good action," says the Prince.

The next day, the Prince, again asking the Swallow to remain another night, tells him that he can see a young man in a garret trying to write a play, but he is too cold and hungry to continue. The Prince instructs the Swallow to pluck out one of his sapphire eyes and take it to the young man (an act of "self-annihilation," Guy Willoughby suggests, as the Happy Prince "distributes his body literally among his subjects, as Jesus did symbolically at the Last Supper. But for the fin-de-siècle altruist, the parallel is filled with irony," 25). When the young playwright discovers the rare sapphire on his desk, he exclaims: "I am beginning to be appreciated.... Now I can finish my play."

On the following day, the Prince asks the Swallow to remain another night. Despite his insistence that he must leave, the bird agrees to follow the Prince's order to pluck out his other eye and give it to a poor little match-girl who has let her matches be ruined. The Swallow tells the Prince, now blind, that he will remain with him always. The bird relates stories of exotic places he has been to, but the Prince responds that "more marvellous than anything is the suffering of men and of women." He instructs the Swallow to fly over the city, then tell him what he has seen. The bird returns to tell the Prince of the dispossessed and hungry. Hearing of such misery, the Prince instructs the Swallow to strip him of his gold leaf and give it to the poor: "The living always think that gold can make them happy."

Though the weather turns colder, the Swallow does not leave the Prince; he loves him too much.

Sensing his end, the bird tells the Prince that he is going to the "House of Death": he kisses the Prince on his lips and falls down dead at his feet. At that moment, the Prince's leaden heart cracks: "It certainly was a dreadfully hard frost." Because the statue, divested of jewels, now looks shabby, it is pulled down, for it is "no longer useful," says an art professor.

The statue is melted in a furnace, but the heart remains untouched by the fire; it is thrown on a dust-heap where the dead Swallow is lying. The scene shifts to Heaven, where God instructs one of His angels to bring him the "two most precious things in the city." The Angel brings Him the leaden heart and the dead bird. In His garden of Paradise, God announces that "this little bird shall sing for evermore, and in my city of gold the Happy Prince shall praise me."

References: David Monaghan, "The Literary Fairy-Tale: A Study of Oscar Wilde's 'The Happy Prince' and 'The Star-Child,'" *Canadian Review of Comparative Literature* (Spring 1974); Robert K. Martin, "Oscar Wilde and the Fairy Tale: 'The Happy Prince' as Self-dramatization," *Studies in Short Fiction* (Winter 1979); Maria Edelson, "The Language of Allegory in Oscar Wilde's Tales," *Anglo-Irish and Irish Literature: Aspects of Language and Culture,* Vol. 2, eds. Birgit Bramsbäck and Martin Croghan (1988); Carol Tattersall, "An Immodest Proposal: Rereading Oscar Wilde's 'Fairy Tales'," *Wascana Review* (Spring/Fall 1991); Guy Willoughby, "Jesus as a Model for Selfhood in *The Happy Prince and Other Tales*," *Art and Christhood: The Aesthetics of Oscar Wilde* (1993).

THE HAPPY PRINCE AND OTHER TALES

Published: May 1888 by David Nutt (London) and Roberts Brothers (Boston), dedicated to Carlos Blacker (see entry). For this volume, Jacomb Hood contributed the head-pieces, tail-pieces, and other decorations; Walter Crane provided three full-page illustrations. In mid-June 1888, Wilde told the poet and playwright George Kersley that his fairy tales, "studies in prose," were put "for Romance's sake into a fanciful form: meant partly for children, and partly for those who have kept the childlike faculties of wonder and joy, and who find in simplicity a subtle strangeness" (*Letters* 219).

Contents: [See the individual entries:] The

Happy Prince – The Nightingale and the Rose – The Selfish Giant – The Devoted Friend – The Remarkable Rocket.

Early Reviews: Before reviews appeared in the press, Walter Pater sent a letter of appreciation, dated 12 June: "The Happy Prince" and "his companions," he wrote, are "delightful." The "whole, too brief, book abounds with delicate touches and pure English" (Pater, *Letters* 132). A brief, unsigned notice in the *Universal Review* (June), possibly written by the editor, Harry Quilter (who was unsympathetic to Aestheticism and who had previously attacked Wilde as an exemplar of the unmanly "Gospel of Intensity") pronounced the stories as a revelation of "Mr. Oscar Wilde's genius at its best" and recommended the volume for its "literary craftsmanship." A brief, unsigned notice in the *Athenaeum* (1 September) was equally commendatory: "The gift of writing fairy tales is rare, and Mr. Oscar Wilde shows that he possesses it in a rare degree....not unworthy to compare with Hans Christian Andersen, and it is not easy to give higher praise than this" (rpt. in Beckson).

An unsigned piece in the *Saturday Review* (20 Oct.), written by Robert Ross's elder brother, Alexander Galt Ross, argued that, since children "do not care for satire" and since the "dominant spirit of these stories is satire – a bitter satire differing widely from that of Hans Andersen" – the audience for Wilde's volume "will assuredly not be composed of children." The "quality of bitterness," however, will not "repel the reader," for Wilde "always contrives to leave us at the end of every tale with a very pleasant sensation of the humorous" (rpt. in Beckson). The *Christian Leader* (3 July 1890), while commenting on *The Picture of Dorian Gray*, just published, referred to *The Happy Prince and Other Tales* as the "cleverest book of fairy tales that has been issued in his generation from the British press."

References: *Letters of Walter Pater,* Lawrence Evans, ed. (1970); John Allen Quintus, "The Moral Prerogative in Oscar Wilde: A Look at the Fairy Tales," *Virginia Quarterly Review* (Autumn 1977); Jack Zipes, "Inverting and Subverting the World with Hope: The Fairy Tales of George MacDonald, Oscar Wilde, and L. Frank Baum," *Fairy Tales and the Art of Subversion* (1983); Maria Edelson, "The Language of Allegory in Oscar Wilde's Tales," *Anglo-Irish and Irish Liter-ature: Aspects of Language and Culture*, Vol. 2, eds. Birgit Bramsbäck and Martin Croghan (1988); Guy Willoughby, "Jesus as a Model for Selfhood in *The Happy Prince and Other Tales*," *Art and Christhood: The Aesthetics of Oscar Wilde* (1993).

"THE HARLOT'S HOUSE"

Published: *Dramatic Review* 1 (11 April 1885): 167; rpt. in *Poems* (1908). Wilde wrote the poem in the spring of 1883 in Paris after returning from his lecture tour of America.

The transformation of the harlots into "wire-pulled automatons," a "clockwork puppet," and "a horrible marionette" suggests the late 19th-century Decadent devotion to artifice. Though similar imagery was available to Wilde in two of his favored authors – Gautier's dancing skeletons in "Bûchers et tombeaux," *Émaux et camées* (1835); Baudelaire's dance of death in "Danse Macabre" and "Les Métamorphoses du vampire," *Les Fleurs du mal* (1857) – his poem remains an original rendition of Decadent motifs. Poe's poem "The Haunted Palace" in his story "The Fall of the House of Usher" ("And travellers now within that valley, / Through the red-litten windows see / Vast forms that move fantastically / To a discordant melody") may also have provided inspiration for "The Harlot's House."

The Poem: The speaker and a companion, walking down a moonlit street, observe dancing shadows on the window blind of a brothel. The image of the dead "dancing with the dead" suggests the archetype of the *danse macabre*, revealing the speaker's moral vision, as does the line "Sometimes a clock-work puppet pressed / A phantom lover to her breast." The speaker's beloved, drawn by the sensual rhythms of the music and the dance, leaves his side. At this point, Wilde allegorizes her and renders her as an abstraction: "Love passed into the house of Lust." The brothel musicians have been playing "Treues Liebes Herz" ("The Heart of True Love"), an ironic accompaniment to the beloved's impulsive action (Wilde's identification of the composer as "Strauss" is apparently a misattribution). When the tune suddenly turns false, Wilde ends the poem with a simile of questionable effect: "And down the long and silent street, / The dawn, with silver-sandalled feet, / Crept like a frightened girl."

Echoes of this poem recur in *The Picture of Dorian Gray* early in Chapter 16 as Dorian makes his way to an opium den: "Most of the windows were dark, but now and then fantastic shadows were silhouetted against some lamp-lit blind. He watched them curiously. They moved like monstrous marionettes, and made gestures like live things." Later, in *The Ballad of Reading Gaol*, some of these images reappear in Part III: "...the damned grotesques made arabesques, / Like the wind upon the sand! / With the pirouettes of marionettes, / They tripped on pointed tread."

Manuscripts: The Clark Library has a draft of the poem, containing lines 1–11 and 19–36 (printed in Mason 56–58). The Hyde Collection also has a MS. written – apparently from memory because of its many errors – for Douglas Ainslie (1865–1948), a diplomat, poet, and translator of Benedetto Croce. A facsimile of this MS. was printed in Sotheby's auction catalogue, titled *English Literary History*, item 113, dated 10–11 July 1986.

References: J. D. Thomas, "The Composition of Wilde's 'The Harlot's House,'" *Modern Language Notes* (Nov. 1950); Bobby Fong, "Wilde's 'The Harlot's House,'" *Explicator* (Spring 1990).

HARRIS, FRANK (1856–1931)

An Irish-born short story writer, playwright, novelist, and controversial biographer of Shakespeare, Wilde, and Shaw, Harris was best known in the 1890s as the editor of the *Fortnightly Review* and the *Saturday Review*. He apparently first met Wilde in 1884 in a society drawing room, then saw him at a theater, and at various other social gatherings. Though Alfred Douglas said that Wilde always avoided Harris, they were apparently good friends.

At first, however, as Harris recalls in his autobiographical *Oscar Wilde: His Life and Confessions* (1916; rpt. 1989), Wilde's appearance "was not in his favour; there was something oily and fat about him that repelled me. Naturally being British-born and young I tried to give my repugnance a moral foundation; fleshly indulgence and laziness, I said to myself, were written all over him." Periodically referring to him as "driven by an inordinate vanity" and as "colossally vain," Harris regarded Wilde's monologues in company as consisting of epigrams "almost mechanically constructed of proverbs and familiar sayings turned upside down." On being introduced to him, Harris disliked the limp handshake as well as Wilde's "flabby, greasy" hands. He also noted that

Wilde was "over-dressed rather than well-dressed." With his height of over six feet and his broad build, he looked like "a Roman Emperor of the decadence" (53–54).

Soon, however, the brilliant talk, the "extraordinary charm in his gaiety, and lightning-quick intelligence" made Harris forget Wilde's "repellant physical peculiarities." Indeed, within ten minutes Harris confessed to himself that he liked him. Yet in accounting for Wilde's early success, Harris does not attribute it to Wilde's literary achievements; rather, he points vaguely to "'sexual inverts,' who looked to the brilliancy of his intellect to gild their esoteric indulgence. This class in England is almost wholly recruited from the aristocracy and the upper middle-class that apes the 'smart set.' It is the inevitable product of the English boarding school and University system" (63).

Nevertheless, in writing about *The Picture of Dorian Gray*, Harris recalls a note that he sent to Wilde congratulating him on its appearance: "Other men have given us wine; some claret, some burgundy, some Moselle; you are the first to give pure champagne. Much of this book is wittier even than Congreve and on an equal intellectual level: at length, it seems to me, you have justified yourself" (70). In *Salome*, however, Harris saw only "student work, an outcome of Oscar's admiration for Flaubert and his 'Hérodias,' on the one hand, the 'Les Sept Princesses,' of Maeterlinck on the other.... One can only say that *Salome* confirmed Oscar's growing reputation for abnormal viciousness" (76–77).

At the first night of *Lady Windermere's Fan*, Harris told a theater critic, who had asked for his opinion after just one act: "...so far it is surely the best comedy in English, the most brilliant, isn't it?" Though, thought Harris, "the humour was often prepared, the construction showed a rare mastery of stage-effect. Oscar Wilde had at length come into his kingdom" (83). Following his success, Wilde revealed "a new tone in him of arrogance and disdain....his new intimacy with Lord Alfred Douglas, coming on the top of his triumph as a playwright, was lending him aggressive self-confidence.... I regretted the change in him and was nervously apprehensive" (98).

As the "threatening cloud" approached, Harris tried to warn Wilde of the "unpleasant stories" that were circulating about his behavior, but Wilde remained seemingly indifferent, attributing such stories to envy and malice. When the Queensberry affair reached the point of litigation, Harris urged Wilde to leave England rather than undertake legal action against the marquess for libel. Wilde asked Harris whether he would be willing to testify that *The Picture of Dorian Gray* was "not immoral." Harris readily agreed, but he sensed disaster.

Throughout his biography, he depicts himself as one of Wilde's staunchest supporters – "Wilde's offense was pathological and not criminal and would not be punished in a properly constituted state" (150) – and he regarded himself as one of his potential saviors. Indeed, after Wilde's release from prison, Harris, in urging him to resume his writing to restore himself within the literary world, remarks: "If he could be saved, I was determined to save him" (267). Wilde was appreciative of Harris's assistance during his ordeal in prison: in *De Profundis*, he cites Harris, among other friends, as one who gave him "comfort, help, affection, sympathy and the like" (*Letters* 495).

In depicting Wilde as a genius made victim by the English, Harris seizes every opportunity to demean those who destroyed him:

Alas, the English are pedants, as Goethe saw; they think little of literary men or of merely spiritual achievements. They love to abide by rules and pay no heed to exceptions, unless indeed the exceptions are men of title or great wealth, or "persons of importance" to the Government.... The man of genius in Great Britain is feared and hated in exact proportion to his originality, and if he happens to be a writer or a musician he is despised to boot. The prejudice against Oscar Wilde showed itself virulently on all hands. (139)

Yet the English flocked to the theaters to see and applaud his plays.

When Harris wished to write a "sane and liberal view" for his own paper, the *Saturday Review*, which he also edited, he was dissuaded from doing so for fear that the paper would be "ruined": "I had no wish to minimise [Wilde's] offence. No one condemned unnatural vice more than I, but Oscar Wilde was a distinguished man of letters; he had written beautiful things, and his good works should have been allowed to speak in his favour" (148). After Wilde's first criminal trial, which

ended in a hung jury, he was released on bail. Harris dramatizes an outing with Wilde at a restaurant: responding to Harris's optimism concerning the re-trial, Wilde said: "'Oh, Frank,' he said, 'you talk with passion and conviction, as if I were innocent.' 'But you are innocent,' I cried in amaze, 'aren't you?' 'No, Frank,' he said, 'I thought you knew that all along'" (167).

It seems inconceivable that Harris did not know – or at least suspect – that, in fact, Wilde was not "innocent" since Harris knew the various players in the drama. There is, indeed, the problem of credibility in his biography, which is principally a series of lengthy dialogues in quotation marks, skillfully structured as though fiction: these dialogues reveal the fallen Wilde while enhancing Harris as his willing savior, as in the incident when Harris urges Wilde to flee to France on a steam yacht that awaited him in the Thames. Harris has some penetrating observations that explain Wilde's incapacity to return to his writing after his release from prison:

...whenever he met a kindred spirit, he absolutely revelled in gay paradoxes and brilliant flashes of humour. But he was at war with himself, like Milton's Satan always conscious of his fall, always regretful of his lost estate and, by reason of this division of spirit, unable to write. Perhaps because of this he threw himself more than ever into talk. (241)

Wilde had his own evaluation of Harris, who, he said, "had no feelings. It is the secret of his success. Just as the fact that he thinks that other people have none either is the secret of the failure that lies in wait for him somewhere on the way of Life." In the same letter to More Adey, Wilde alludes to promises, principally financial, made by Harris and then concludes: "The Frank Harrises of life are a dreadful type. I hope to see no more of them" (*Letters* 538–39). To Robert Ross, Wilde complained that Harris made "gorgeous offers of his cheque-book to any extent I required and then sent a verbal message to say he had changed his mind..." (*Letters* 543). A week later, however, Wilde wrote to thank Harris for his "great kindness...for the lovely clothes, and for the generous cheque. You have been a real good friend to me, and I shall never forget your kindness..." (*Letters* 566). In short, Wilde's oscillating view of Harris during the final years was more the result of Wilde's desperation rather than Harris's unreliability. As Hart-Davis comments: "Harris had many faults, but lack of generosity to Wilde was not one of them" (*Letters* 837n3). Despite the instabilities of their relationship, Wilde dedicated *An Ideal Husband* (1899) to Harris.

In his biography, Harris generally writes with high praise of Wilde's achievements: for example, he regards *The Ballad of Reading Gaol* as "beyond all comparison the greatest ballad in English; one of the noblest poems in the language" (230); *The Importance of Being Earnest* has "its own place among the best of English comedies. But Oscar Wilde has done better work than Congreve or Sheridan" (320). As for Wilde himself, he was, concludes Harris, the wittiest man he had ever known.

References: Frank Harris, *My Life and Loves*, ed. John F. Gallagher (1963); Philippa Pullar, *Frank Harris: A Biography* (1976); Stanley Weintraub, ed., *The Playwright and the Pirate: Bernard Shaw and Frank Harris: A Correspondence* (1982).

HEADLAM, STEWART (1847–1924)

An Anglican clergyman, a Fabian socialist, and editor of the *Church Reformer* (1884–95), the Rev. Headlam wrote of the spiritual benefits of the theater, especially the ballet, which he called "poetry in motion" (a phrase that Bernard Shaw used in *Immaturity*, an early novel unpublished until 1930). After he established the Church and Stage Guild in 1879 to bring together music-hall performers and church members, Headlam was deprived of his curacy in the East End. In a lecture on the function of the stage, specifically with reference to the aesthetic beauty of ballet, he challenged the clergy "to face the fact whether they think the human body an evil thing or the temple of the Holy Ghost" (22).

Though Headlam had known Wilde only slightly before the trials, he acted as surety by posting a bond of £1,225 – half of the total amount – to enable Wilde to be released on bail after his first criminal trial. For his generosity, a hostile group menaced Headlam outside of his Bloomsbury house. Later, in the *Church Reformer* (1 June 1895), Headlam defended his action by arguing that the press and the public had exhibited their prejudice against Wilde before the trial had begun:

"I was a surety, not for his character, but for his appearance in Court to stand his trial.... My confidence in his honour and manliness has been fully justified by the fact that (if rumour be correct), notwithstanding strong inducements to the contrary, he stayed in England and faced his trial."

During the second criminal trial, Headlam met Wilde at the home of Ada Leverson to escort him to the court, and in the evening accompanied him on his return. In September 1896, Headlam was prepared to sign a petition drawn up by More Adey for a remission of Wilde's sentence at Reading Prison, but the Home Office informed Adey before signatures could be collected that "no grounds, medical or other, exist which would justify [the Home Secretary] in advising any mitigation of the sentence" (*Letters* 408n1).

In preparation for Wilde's release from prison, Headlam and More Adey arranged for Wilde's immediate departure from England. At 6:15 a.m. on 19 May 1897, they were present at Pentonville Prison in the north of London (where Wilde had been transferred the night before from Reading Prison). They proceeded to Headlam's house in Bloomsbury, where Wilde changed his clothes and had breakfast. In the late afternoon, he left Headlam's house in Adey's company for Newhaven and arrived in Dieppe by night boat at 4:00 a.m. Thereafter, Wilde and Headlam apparently did not exchange letters or see each other again. When *The Ballad of Reading Gaol* appeared, Wilde arranged to have a copy sent to him.

References: Stewart Headlam, *The Function of the Stage: A Lecture* (1889); F. G. Bettany, *Stewart Headlam: A Biography* (1926); T. H. Gibbons, "The Reverend Stewart Headlam and the Emblematic Dancer: 1877–1894," *British Journal of Aesthetics* (Oct. 1965).

"HEART'S YEARNINGS"

Not published in Wilde's lifetime, this poem appeared in Davis Coakley's *Oscar Wilde: The Importance of Being Irish* (Dublin: Town House, 1994), 217–18.

The Greek epigraph, translated as "Love of the Impossible," has its source in the Greek proverb – "to desire impossible things is a disease of the soul" – attributed to Bias, one of the Seven Sages, by Diogenes Laërtius in his *Lives of the Eminent Philosophers* (I.v.86). The epigraph also appears with its French equivalent in Part I of "The Critic as Artist": "...that *Amour de l'Impossible*, which falls like a madness on many who think they live securely and out of reach of harm, so that they sicken suddenly with the poison of unlimited desire, and in the infinite pursuit of what they may not obtain, grow faint and swoon or stumble." The idea also appears in Chapter 7 of *The Picture of Dorian Gray*, in which Dorian (like Gautier's D'Albert in *Mademoiselle de Maupin*) is stirred by the "passion for impossible things." See, also, *Letters* 185. Horst Schroeder has suggested that Wilde derived the juxtaposition of the Greek and French phrases for "Love of the impossible" from John Addington Symonds's *Studies of the Greek Poets* (1873), 292–93.

In Wilde's lyric poem of eight five-line stanzas, the speaker complains that "the world is all too drear, / To shape my sorrow to a tuneful strain...." His saddened soul is "out of tune with time" – a traditional metaphor of emotional disharmony, as in Ophelia's observation that Hamlet is "out of tune and harsh" (III.i.l59). "Nor," says the speaker in the poem, "have I care to set the crooked straight...." Rather, he will sit and wait "Until the opening of the Future's Mystic Gate." Weary of the "busy throng / That chirp and chatter in the noisy street," he will "sit alone and sing no song / But listen for the coming of Love's feet." He tells his breaking heart that Love "comes apace," but he is mistaken, for he asks, "Why does Love tarry in his flight / And not come near for my heart's delight – " All he can hear is "the sighing of the breeze / That makes complaint in a sweet under-tune" – indeed, an echo of his own yearning.

Manuscripts: The Clark Library has a note-book, dating from 1873, that Wilde used when a student at Trinity College, Dublin, in which he wrote a version of lines 1–5 of this poem. A facsimile of a signed MS. of "Heart's Yearnings" appeared in a Sotheby Parke-Bernet catalogue listing items from the library of Gordon A. Block, Jr., for sale on 29 January 1974, possibly the same MS. – as reported in *TLS*, 4 July 1986, 747 – offered by Sotheby in their 10/11 July 1986 auction.

Reference: Horst Schroeder, "A Graeco-French Collocation in 'The Critic as Artist,'" *N&Q* (March 1993).

"HÉLAS!"

Published: *Poems* (1881) as the introductory poem (meaning "Alas!"), printed entirely in italics.

This sonnet, with its anti-Victorian attitudes towards the notion of manliness, duty, and work, suggests an indebtedness to Pater's "Conclusion" to his *Studies in the History of Renaissance* (1873). To appreciate the passing of every choice moment – "for that moment only" – Pater urges, "Not the fruit of experience, but experience itself, is the end": "While all melts under our feet, we may well grasp at any exquisite passion, or any contribution to knowledge that seems by a lifted horizon to set the spirit free for a moment.... What we have to do is to be forever curiously testing new opinions and courting new impressions...." (This famous passage was adapted by Wilde for a speech by Lord Henry Wotton in *The Picture of Dorian Gray*, Chapter 2.)

Initially, Wilde's poem adopts Pater's view by employing the familiar Romantic image of the stringed instrument, such as Coleridge's aeolian harp: "To drift with every passion till my soul / Is a stringed lute on which all winds can play." But Wilde also evokes the troubling question of moral responsibility: "Is it for this I have given away / Mine ancient wisdom, and austere control?" Indeed, "idle songs for pipe and virelay... / ...but mar the secret of the whole." The final lines sum up the moral dilemma posed in the poem, for the speaker (the persona, one senses, for Wilde himself) had had the capacity in the past to strike "one clear chord to reach the ears of God": "Is that time dead? lo! with a little rod / I did but touch the honey of romance – / And must I lose a soul's inheritance?"

These final suggestive lines are derived from the Bible (I Samuel 14:43), where Jonathan, the son of Saul, the valiant fighter against the Philistines, says to his father, whose order not to eat before a battle he inadvertently disobeyed: "I did but taste a little honey with the end of the rod that *was* in mine hand, *and*, lo, I must die." Wilde, it should be noted, eroticizes the passage by substituting "I did but touch the honey of romance...." Moreover, Jonathan's relationship with David involves one, the Bible indicates, "passing the love of women." At his trial, Wilde defended "The love that dare not speak its name" by citing the "great affection of an elder for a younger man as there was between David and Jonathan, such as Plato made the very basis of his philosophy."

Pater, quoting the biblical passage in his essay

on Winckelmann, adds: "It has sometimes seemed hard to pursue that life [that is, one of Christian asceticism] without something of conscious disavowal of a spiritual world." For Pater, Jonathan's speech characterizes "the artistic life, with its inevitable sensuousness." In "Hélas!," Wilde's anxiety over spiritual loss because of his pursuit of pleasure is prominent in Wilde's works from his Oxford years to Reading Prison; as Ellmann suggests, though Wilde "practiced self-indulgence, it was never without remorse" (139/133).

Manuscript: Princeton has a MS. of the poem, which includes Wilde's instructions to print it in italics.

"'HELENA IN TROAS'"

Published: *Dramatic Review* 3 (22 May 1886): 161–62; rpt. in *Reviews* (1908). A signed review of E. W. Godwin's production of Sophocles's play at Hengler's Circus on 17 May. (See Godwin, E. W.)

Wilde regards Godwin's production as "the most perfect exhibition of a Greek dramatic performance that has as yet been seen in this country." The use of the arena of a circus provided Godwin with the proper orchestra for the chorus's song and dance. Describing Godwin's design for the altar of Dionysos, the house of Paris, and the battlements of Troy, Wilde remarks:

No nation has ever felt the pure beauty of mere construction so strongly as the Greeks, and in this respect Mr. Godwin has fully caught the Greek feeling....the historical accuracy that underlies the visible shapes of beauty that he presents to us is not by any means the distinguishing quality of the complete work of art. This quality is the absolute unity and harmony of the entire presentation....

Classical drama, says Wilde, is an "imaginative, poetic art, which requires the grand style for its interpretation, and produces its effects by the most ideal means. It is in the operas of Wagner, not in popular melodrama, that any approximation to the Greek method can be found." To have shown other artists "a dream of form in days of thought" and to have permitted Philistines "to peer into Paradise" is what Godwin's production has accomplished.

HELLENISM

Published: Tragara Press (Edinburgh, 1979). Wilde wrote this essay when he was an undergraduate at Oxford in the summer of 1877. He had spent Easter in Greece with his former tutor in classics at Trinity College, Dublin, Rev. J. P. Mahaffy (see entry), whose influence turned him away from an attraction to Roman Catholicism.

The Essay: The various peoples of Greece, Wilde contends, demonstrated a "great unity of spirit" despite the fact that they were widely dispersed and "socially and politically disunited." The effect was to make them "natural allies." Beyond their common language, Wilde argues, there was a strong bond – "a community of religious sentiments and festivals." Their honoring of such gods as Zeus, Apollo, and Poseidon resulted in the celebrated games, which "brought all Hellas together." Such games were, in reality, "great religious festivals uniting all men through the feeling of common worship and sympathy and common amusement."

Reverence for the Oracle and Temple at Delphi was "one of the strongest feelings in the Greek mind, and the habit of listening respectfully to the advice of the Oracle often produced unanimity of aims amongst men not accustomed to obey the same political superior." Another significant point uniting the Greeks was "the community of manners and character." In no Greek city was there human sacrifice, physical mutilation, sale of countrymen and children as slaves, polygamy, or unlimited obedience to one ruler, such as existed in contemporary Egypt and Persia. The "independence of sovereignty of each city" was "one of the fundamental notions of the Greek mind." Such attitudes "saved the Greeks from the mediocre sameness of thought and feeling which seems always to exist in the cities of great empires."

Wilde devotes much of his essay to Sparta, which exercised "a strict and tyrannical supervision over the private life of the citizen." The general effect of such a political system produced "a great monotony and sameness of character among its citizens, and to crush all personal individuality." Nevertheless, there was great admiration for Sparta among the Greeks. Though "exceedingly cunning and unscrupulous, harsh, and overbearing when in possession of power," the Spartans had a "high culture": they appear to have been "exceedingly fond of music, vocal and instrumental, of recitations and dinner-parties and good wine and the society of women." But compared to the "great intellectual glories of Athens," they "show meanly."

Manuscripts: The Clark Library has a TS. prepared by Robert Ross from the original MS., as well as an earlier fragment of six MS. pages. The Hyde Collection has a substantial portion of the original MS. The Tragara Press publication involves a collation of the existing MSS. and the Ross TS. (the Tragara edition erroneously cites this TS. as having been prepared by Mason).

HENLEY, WILLIAM ERNEST (1849–1903)

A poet, critic, and dramatist, who, Yeats recalls, "grew into a violent unionist and imperialist" (83), Henley was the editor of various periodicals, including the *Scots Observer*, later titled the *National Observer*. Wilde reportedly said in 1898:

Have you noticed that if a man has once been an editor he can always be an editor? The fact that a paper has a way of dying when he is on it is of the smallest importance. He is in demand before the corpse is buried. Here is Henley. He kills the *Scots Observer*. Hey presto! He is made editor of the *New Review*. Then the *New Review* dies. (qtd. in Chesson 379)

When Henley and Wilde first met is unknown, but in a letter written in late 1888, Wilde agreed to have lunch with him at the exclusive Savile Club, though, he wrote: "...I am afraid that I shall be like a poor lion who has rashly intruded into a den of fierce Daniels" (*Letters* 224). Henley was one of some 31 members who supported Wilde's candidacy, but he was not elected. At this time, Wilde was reading Henley's *A Book of Verses* for a review in *Woman's World* (Dec.1888). In his letter to Henley, Wilde wrote facetiously: "I have decided that a great deal of it is poetry, and that, of the rest, part is poesy, and part..." (Wilde left his sentence incomplete). Nevertheless, he praised the volume: see "A Note on Some Modern Poets." Though he expected Henley to "roar like the Bull of Bashan" (Psalms 22:12–13), Wilde thought it "very complimentary" (*Letters* 229). In November, Henley wrote in appreciation to Wilde for his review of *A Book of Verses*.

In July 1889, when "The Portrait of Mr. W. H."

appeared in *Blackwood's Edinburgh Magazine*, an unsigned notice in the *Scots Observer* (6 July) prompted Wilde to write to Henley:

To be exiled to Scotland to edit a Tory paper in the wilderness is bad enough, but not to see the wonder and beauty of my discovery of the real Mr W. H. is absolutely dreadful. I sympathise deeply with you, and can only beg you to return to London where you will be able to appreciate a real work of art. The Philistines in their vilest forms have seized on you. I am so disappointed. (*Letters* 248)

When *The Picture of Dorian Gray* appeared in July 1890, Wilde conducted an ongoing debate with the reviewer and various correspondents in the *Scots Observer*, which had condemned the novel as "discreditable" to its author and recommended that the "sooner he takes to tailoring (or some other decent trade) the better for his own reputation and the public morals." Henley did not participate in the exchange of letters, though he undoubtedly inspired his staff to attack Decadence, of which he had grown exceedingly intolerant. Wilde was apparently convinced that Henley was either the author of the review or the letters to the editor signed "H," for he wrote to the publisher John Lane, who was then issuing Wilde's 1892 volume of poems: "No book of mine...ever goes to the *National Observer*. I wrote to Henley to tell him so, two years ago. He is too coarse, too offensive, too personal, to be sent any work of mine" (*Letters* 318).

Despite his apparent rancor towards Henley, Wilde consoled him on the death of his six-year-old daughter in February 1894: "I hope you will let me come down quietly to you one evening and over our cigarettes we will talk of the bitter ways of fortune, and the hard ways of life. But, my dear Henley, to work, to work; that is your duty; that is what remains for natures like ours" (*Letters* 352). In the following year, at the time of Wilde's downfall, Henley's *National Observer* (6 April 1895) published a gloating attack:

There is not a man or woman in the English-speaking world possessed of the treasure of a wholesome mind who is not under a deep debt of gratitude to the Marquess of Queensberry for destroying the High Priest of the

Decadents. The obscene imposter, whose prominence has been a social outrage ever since he transferred from Trinity Dublin to Oxford his vices, his follies, and his vanities, has been exposed, and that thoroughly at last.

Yeats recalled Henley's remark: "Why did he do it? I told my lads to attack him and yet we might have fought under his banner" – though under which banner Yeats does not say (88).

Wilde's lingering ambivalence towards Henley manifests itself in a brief description written in 1897 at the request of the painter Will Rothenstein for his forthcoming *English Portraits* (1898):

He founded a school, and has survived all his disciples. He has always thought too much about himself, which is wise; and written too much about others, which is foolish. His prose is the beautiful prose of a poet, and his poetry the beautiful poetry of a prose-writer.... He is never forgotten by his enemies, and often forgiven by his friends. He has added several new words to the language, and his style is an open secret. He has fought a good fight, and has had to face every difficulty except popularity. (*Letters* 631)

Though the note was to be printed anonymously, Rothenstein decided that he could not accept it. Writing to Rothenstein, Max Beerbohm thought that the lines had "some witty things in them – 'an open secret' is lovely – but they were rather too antithetical and unfriendly – and too obviously written by Oscar" (*Max and Will* 36).

When *The Ballad of Reading Gaol* appeared, Henley wrote in the *Outlook* (5 March 1898) that "the trail of the Minor Poet is over it all. And when the Minor Poet is at rest, then wakes the Pamphleteer." Henley questions whether what prisoner C.3.3 says about the prison system is true: "'Tis not for us to say. But if it be, let C.3.3 at once proceed to sink the Minor in the Pamphleteer, and make his name honoured among men." Distressed by the review, Wilde wrote to the publisher Leonard Smithers that "it is very coarse and vulgar, and entirely lacking in literary or gentlemanly instinct. He is so proud of having written *vers libres* on his scrofula [in *In Hospital*] that he is quite jealous if a poet writes a lyric on his prison" (*Letters* 712). Wilde decided not to respond to the review: "Be-

sides," he told Smithers, "there are only two forms of writers in England, the unread and the unreadable. Henley belongs to the former class" (*Letters* 716).

References: Wilfred Hugh Chesson, "A Reminiscence of 1898," *Bookman* (New York) (Dec. 1911), rpt. in Mikhail 2:379; Jerome H. Buckley, *William Ernest Henley: A Study in the "Counter-Decadence" of the 'Nineties* (1945; rpt. in 1971); *The Autobiography of W. B. Yeats* (1965); Mary M. Lago and Karl Beckson, eds., *Max and Will: Max Beerbohm and William Rothenstein, Their Friendship and Letters, 1893–1945* (1975).

"'HENRY THE FOURTH' AT OXFORD"

Published: *Dramatic Review* 1 (23 May 1885): 264–65; rpt. in *Reviews* (1908). A signed review of the University Dramatic Society's production at the Town Hall, Oxford, on 15 May.

Affording Wilde an opportunity to praise Oxford as "the most beautiful thing in England" ("nowhere else are life and art so exquisitely blended, so perfectly made one"), the production of *Henry IV* was "in every way worthy of that lovely town, that mother of sweetness and light." Oxford, he muses, "makes the earth lovely to all who dream with Keats; she opens high heaven to all who soar with Shelley...." Turning to the play, Wilde regards those who consider that Shakespeare is "more for the study than for the stage" are mistaken, for he wrote his plays to be acted. Indeed, only through the actor's art can the many "beauties" of his plays be adequately conveyed.

In the Oxford production, the "archaeological accuracy" of the costumes yielded dramatic value: "As the knights and nobles moved across the stage in the flowing robes of peace and in the burnished steel of battle we needed no dreary chorus to tell us what age or land the play's action was passing....and the delicate harmonies of colour struck from the first a dominant note of beauty which added to the intellectual realism of archaeology the sensuous charm of art." In such plays of bygone times, "there is always this peculiar charm, that they combine in one exquisite presentation the passions that are living with the picturesqueness that is dead." With the "modern spirit" in an "antique form," the remoteness of the form can be made "a method of increased realism."

Wilde concludes with the view that a fusion of realism and romance (in the late 19th century, regarded as antithetical) would approximate Shakespeare's attitude towards the ancient world: "This is the attitude we in this century should adopt towards his plays.... For while we look to the dramatist to give romance to realism, we ask of the actor to give realism to romance."

"HER VOICE"

Published: *Poems* (1881). "Her Voice" and "My Voice" (see entry) were apparently one poem entitled "A Farewell," which was originally so listed in the table of contents of the manuscript from which *Poems* was set.

In this lyric poem of six seven-line stanzas, the speaker addresses her beloved, reminding him that "it was here I trow / I made that vow, / Swore that two lives should be like one...." It was, she asserts, a vow for eternity. In a shift from "love" to "friend," she now declares that "those times are over and done, / Love's web is spun." The tone is elegiac, as in "We have lived our lives in a land of dreams! / How sad it seems." But "seems" undercuts the professed depth of feeling. Declaring that "love is never lost," she muses that since "ships tempest-tossed / Will find a harbour in some bay, / And so we may." They must kiss again and part in sadness:

> I have my beauty, – you your Art,
> Nay, do not start,
> One world was not enough or two
> Like me and you.

For other poems forming a sequence with this one, see "Apologia."

Manuscript: The Clark Library has a TS. of three stanzas titled "It Is for Nothing," prepared by Robert Ross from a MS., an early draft of "Her Voice."

"HEU MISERANDE PUER": *See* "THE GRAVE OF KEATS"

HICHENS, ROBERT: *See* GREEN CARNATION

HOLLAND, CYRIL (1885–1915)

Wilde's elder son provided him with the name for one of the speakers in his dialogue "The Decay of Lying," which appeared when Cyril was only three and a half. As his younger brother, Vyvyan

Holland, has written, Cyril was the "favorite of both my father and my mother. He was stronger and healthier than I; he excelled at games, even as a small boy, whereas I took little interest in them" (*Son* 35). When he was nine, Cyril was sent to a preparatory school for the Navy, a rather stern place where the boys had to make their own beds and empty the slops. However, he was there for only a year before his father's downfall and disgrace.

In *De Profundis*, Wilde recalled, at the time of his arrest:

> ...I could not bear the idea of being separated from Cyril, that beautiful, loving, loveable child of mine, my friend of all friends, my companion beyond all companions, one single hair of whose little golden head should have been dearer and of more value to me than, I will not merely say you [Alfred Douglas] from top to toe, but the entire chrysolite of the whole world.... [*Othello* V.ii.145] (*Letters* 453)

After his arrest, Wilde was never to see either Cyril or Vyvyan again. In 1895, the boys were sent abroad to shield them from the scandal. When they returned to England in 1898, Cyril was sent to Radley School, where he excelled in athletics, and in 1903 he enrolled at the Royal Military Academy at Woolwich. Though he saw little of his brother from the time they returned to England, they corresponded frequently through the years.

When Wilde died in November 1900, Robert Ross wrote a letter of consolation to Cyril, who answered:

> I hope that at his death he was truly penitent; I think he must have been if he joined the Catholic Church and my reverence for the Roman Church is heightened more than ever. It is hard for a young mind like mine to realise why all the sorrow should have come on us, especially so young.... It is of course a long time since I saw father but all I do remember was when we lived happily together in London.... I only hope that it will be a lesson for me and prevent me from falling into the snares and pitfalls of this world. (qtd. in *Son* 133–34)

Cyril later wrote to Ross in appreciation of his

loyalty to his father: "The more I experience of life in all its sordid vulgarity and mediocrity, in all its cowardice and egoism, the more I realize the nobility of your conducts" (Ross 244).

After graduating from Woolwich, Cyril entered the Army. As Vyvyan Holland later wrote, "He was not popular with his brother officers, who considered him pompous and intolerant. He would not join the small talk of the mess, mostly scandal or about sport. And they could not understand anyone who spent his ordinary leave in traveling about Europe, studying architecture and visiting art galleries instead of hunting, shooting, yachting, or fishing" (*Son* 123). In June 1914, Cyril wrote to his brother from India that, with respect to the family name, he was determined

to wipe that stain away; to retrieve, if may be, by some action of mine, a name no longer honoured in the land. The more I thought of this, the more convinced I became that, first and foremost, I must be a *man*. There was to be no cry of decadent artist, of effeminate aesthete, of weak-kneed degenerate.... I ask nothing better than to end in honourable battle for my King and Country. (qtd. in *Son* 121–22)

In India at the beginning of the First World War, Cyril, willing to sacrifice his years of seniority, arranged for a transfer to an Indian cavalry regiment that had been ordered to France. However, plans were changed: his own regiment in the Royal Field Artillery was ordered to France, where he was killed by a German sniper on 9 May 1915, during the second battle for Neuve Chapelle, just a few miles away from his brother, also an officer in the Royal Field Artillery. In his will, Cyril bequeathed to Ross one-half share of Wilde's literary estate, the other half to Vyvyan (who had earlier sold his share to his brother).

Reference: Vyvyan Holland, *Son of Oscar Wilde* (1954).

HOLLAND, VYVYAN (1886–1967)

Wilde's second son was christened "Vyvyan Oscar Beresford," though his parents – according to Rupert Hart-Davis – preferred the spelling "Vivian" (as in one of the speakers' names in Wilde's dialogue "The Decay of Lying"). Holland, however, preferred the spelling given at his christening (*Letters* 211n3). Having grown up in the

Wildes' residence in Tite Street, Chelsea, Holland later recalled the many visitors to the house, among them John Singer Sargent, John Ruskin, Mark Twain, Robert Browning, Algernon Swinburne, and Ellen Terry.

Before the trials in 1895, Holland remembers those "happy years" when he and his elder brother Cyril "adored" their father:

...he was a hero to us both. He was so tall and distinguished and, to our uncritical eyes, so handsome.... He was a real companion to us, and we always looked forward eagerly to his frequent visits to our nursery.... He would go down on all fours on the nursery floor, being in turn a lion, a wolf, a horse, caring nothing for his usually immaculate appearance. (*Son* 41)

When the "storm broke" on the Wilde family in April 1895, Constance Wilde decided that, because her two sons could no longer remain at their schools, both Cyril and Vyvyan should be sent to the Continent with a French governess, an exile that lasted more than three years. While in Switzerland with their mother and her brother, Otho Lloyd, the two boys were informed that they must forget the name of Wilde since the family would henceforth be known as "Holland," an old family name from their mother's side. Moreover, "Vyvyan" would now be spelled "Vivian" and "Oscar Beresford" dropped. However, as Holland later wrote, "The thought that at any moment an indiscreet remark or a chance encounter with someone from our former lives might betray us was a sword of Damocles constantly hanging above our heads" (*Son* 80).

In April 1898, shortly before her death in Genoa (having undergone an operation for a spinal injury suffered earlier), Constance Wilde wrote to Vyvyan: "Try not to feel harshly about your father; remember that he is your father and that he loves you. All his troubles arose from the hatred of a son for his father, and whatever he has done he has suffered bitterly for" (qtd. in *Son* 112). With her death, Vyvyan returned to London, escorted by a priest from Monaco (thenceforth to be taken care of by his mother's aunt), and Cyril, now 13, arrived unescorted several days later from his school in Heidelberg.

Vyvyan Holland recalls that, when he was

eleven (that is, in 1897), he did not know the nature of his father's offenses (though Cyril had discovered the truth). Constance Wilde's family tried to eradicate all memory of Oscar Wilde by telling Vyvyan that his father was dead and that his achievements were of no significance. Vyvyan's misery was so intense over such deception that, at one point, he lay down in the snow and wanted to die.

Vyvyan resumed his schooling at Stonyhurst College, Lancashire, while Cyril was sent to Radley School. They were to see little of each other from then on, though they corresponded frequently. Certain incidents occurred that puzzled Vyvyan: "Once more I felt that everyone's hand was against me, and I began to think that there must be something monstrous about my family that caused me always to be in disgrace" (*Son* 135). When Wilde died in November 1900, the Rector of Stonyhurst summoned Vyvyan to his office to inform him that his father had died: "But," he said, "I thought he died long ago." The "surprise, the perplexity, the shock" were too much for him, and he broke down in tears.

When Vyvyan was 16, he read Robert Sherard's *Oscar Wilde: The Story of an Unhappy Friendship* (1902) and discovered the truth. He was so "depressed," he writes, that he decided not to read any other books about his father, a resolution that he maintained for many years. In 1905, now 19, he became a student at Trinity Hall, Cambridge University, to qualify for a degree in law. (At this time, when he began reading his father's works, his admiration of his father's literary achievement increased steadily.) Tiring of the law, he left two years later.

Before Vyvyan was 21, Robert Ross, who had no idea where Wilde's two sons were, finally met him. At this time, Vyvyan was still fearful of discovery and ridicule over his father's "disgrace." He later wrote: "I do not try to defend my father's behavior, but I do think that the penalties inflicted upon him were unnecessarily severe. And by that I do not only mean the prison sentence; I mean the virtual suppression of all his works and the ostracism and insults which he had to endure during the few remaining years of his life" (*Son* 180). At their first meeting, Ross was accompanied by two of Wilde's closest friends, Max Beerbohm, and Reginald Turner – "a highly emotional meeting," Holland later recalled. On the following day, Ross wrote to him:

I regret very much that I was not allowed to see both you and Cyril in the years that have intervened since the tragedy which has darkened your life and about which I know you yourself must feel so bitterly. I believe that I could have made your childhood happier, and it would have made me happier too to know that you realised how fond and devoted I was to you both, because you were the sons of my greatest friend and the most distinguished man of letters in the last years of the last century. (qtd. in *Son* 145)

Ross provided the needed friendship and trust by bringing him into contact with Wilde's old friends and progressively into the wider literary and artistic world. As a result, the old fears diminished in the company of the many illustrious figures who admired Wilde's genius. The guarded secret of his relationship to Oscar Wilde, maintained by his mother's family, was now no longer possible.

When Holland reached the age of 21, Ross gave him "a magnificent dinner party" in Kensington, where he shared a house with another of Wilde's inner circle, More Adey. Attending were such figures as Henry James, Ronald Firbank (whom Holland had known at Cambridge), the painter Will Rothenstein, Reginald Turner, Charles Ricketts, Charles Shannon, and Cyril Holland. His friends now included Henry James, Max Beerbohm, Thomas Hardy, Arnold Bennett, and H. G. Wells, whom he saw frequently. When Wilde's *Collected Works* appeared in 1908, a dinner was given to celebrate Ross as its editor. Of the more than 200 guests, such luminaries as Edmund Gosse, H. G. Wells, William Archer, George Alexander, and Laurence Binyon attended in addition to the Holland brothers – the elder sitting between Rothenstein and the noted critic E. V. Lucas (who, it is said, had suggested the title *De Profundis* to Ross for Wilde's prison letter), the younger sitting next to Somerset Maugham.

On 20 July 1909, Holland accompanied Ross to witness the re-interring of Wilde's remains from Bagneux Cemetery to Père Lachaise in Paris (where Jacob Epstein's monument over the gravesite created a controversy: see The Tomb of Wilde). Now, at the age of 22, Holland resumed his study of law with the aim of becoming a barrister; at the same time, he wrote poetry and short stories, secretly wishing that he could write like his admired father, but, he later wrote, "I was not destined to do so" (*Time* 17). After being called to the bar in 1912, he practiced briefly. When, in 1913, he married Violet Craigie, the daughter of an Army officer, Ross inserted an announcement in the *Times* that Holland was the son of Oscar Wilde. "The 'Family,'" Holland later wrote, "were furious, and I received a terrible letter from my ex-Guardian, accusing me of deliberately undoing all the good work they had done in obliterating Oscar Wilde from my mind and person" (*Time* 65).

With the outbreak of the First World War, Holland entered the Army as a second lieutenant in the Interpreters Corps but was soon informed that no more interpreters were needed; he then transferred to the Royal Field Artillery, in which his brother had served for eight years. At the second battle for Neuve Chapelle, the death of Cyril from a sniper's bullet was a "bitter blow" to Holland, who was only a few miles away: "The last link with Tite Street and the spacious days had snapped" (*Time* 84). Just before the end of the war, Holland read in a Parisian newspaper that Robert Ross, his "greatest friend," had died suddenly: "...I felt that another of the strings that bound me to life had snapped" (*Time* 102). Shortly thereafter, Holland learned that his wife, Violet, had been seriously injured in a fire; before he could reach her from France, she expired.

With the end of the war, Holland – wounded once and mentioned in several dispatches for his bravery under fire – was awarded the Order of the British Empire when he was discharged in 1919. He then embarked on a career as a translator, author, and editor. From 1925 to 1928, he edited a series of 12 French romances of the 18th century for Chatto & Windus, and over the years, he translated fiction and non-fiction from French, German, Spanish, and Italian. Among his notable translations into English were several French novels by Julian Green and a life of Stalin by Henri Barbusse. He also translated and edited several of his father's works: a new translation of *Salomé*; an edition of the expanded version of *The Portrait of Mr. W. H.* (the MS. of which had been discovered in 1920); an edition of *De Profundis*; and a reconstruction of the original four-act version of *The Importance of Being Earnest*. He also wrote the introduction to a one-volume edition of the *Complete Works*, and he published *Oscar Wilde: A Pictorial Biography*.

At the beginning of the Second World War, Holland was offered a position as a translator and editor for the BBC, a post he held for six years. In September 1943, he married Thelma Besant, an Australian, who gave birth in December 1945 to their only child, Merlin (who became a publisher, a dealer in glass and ceramics, and a writer; his son, Lucian, was born in 1979). In 1947, Holland and his wife left for Australia and New Zealand, where Mrs. Holland had been invited to give lectures on fashionable dress in 19th-century Australia. As a result of the acclaim that greeted *Son of Oscar Wilde* (1954), Holland received hundreds of appreciative letters from friends and strangers. In the "Foreword" to a 1988 reissue of the autobiography, Merlin Holland writes that his father had, "as it were, laid to rest the bitter memory of those early years by the cathartic effect of recording them for posterity."

In 1966, Vyvyan Holland published a sequel to *Son of Oscar Wilde*, the narrative of which ends in 1909. In *Time Remembered*, he concludes with the quiet contentment of a man who has lived life to the fullest: "If I ever feel depressed, I contemplate my blessings one by one and say that I am a happy man, that I have no quarrels with fate, which has almost overwhelmed me at times, but which has, in the end, left me, as it were, washed up on the shores of time, in the warm sunlight" (190–91). In the following year, his amusing final book, *An Explosion of Limericks*, was issued just a day before he died at the age of 80.

References: Vyvyan Holland, *Son of Oscar Wilde* (1954) and *Time Remembered*: *After Père Lachaise* (1966).

HOMOSEXUALITY: *See* **URANIANS**

"THE HOUSE BEAUTIFUL"

Published: Kevin O'Brien, "'The House Beautiful': A Reconstruction of Oscar Wilde's American Lecture," *Victorian Studies* 17 (1974): 395–418; rpt. in O'Brien's *Oscar Wilde in Canada: An Apostle for the Arts* (Toronto: Personal Library, 1982), Since there are no extant MSS. of this lecture, O'Brien has reconstructed it from many newspaper reports published during Wilde's American tour in 1882.

After he first gave this lecture as "Interior and

Exterior House Decoration" on 11 March in Chicago, Wilde changed the title to "The House Beautiful" when he gave it in California in April. He subsequently delivered it at least 15 times (particularly on those occasions when he gave a second lecture in the same city), the last on 13 October in Saint John, New Brunswick, Canada. O'Brien writes that "The House Beautiful" was "perhaps Wilde's most effective lecture in America. Practical, colloquial, and witty, it received the best reviews from newspaper critics, and had he made it the main lecture of his tour, he may have deflected much of the suspicious criticism he received for the antic poses he adopted outside the lecture hall..." (*Victorian Studies* 401). Between 1883 and 1885, Wilde lectured on "The House Beautiful" intermittently in England, Scotland, and Ireland.

Until O'Brien's reconstruction of "The House Beautiful," the establishment of a reliable text for this lecture had been problematic. In 1906, Richard Glaenzer included a lecture with the same title as that of his edition of Wilde's writings, *Decorative Art in America*, but he used an incomplete report of Wilde's lecture given on 11 May in New York, the title given as "Art Decoration: The Practical Application of the Principles of the Aesthetic Theory to Exterior and Interior House Decoration, with Observations Upon Dress and Personal Ornaments." In *Miscellanies* (1908), Robert Ross included a lecture with the title "House Decoration," adding a subtitle identical with that given by Glaenzer for "Art Decoration," both containing passages from "The House Beautiful." Like Glaenzer, Ross also used the incomplete newspaper report of the 11 May lecture, and like Glaenzer, he was unaware that "The House Beautiful" was a different lecture.

The Lecture: (In San Francisco and Montreal, Wilde prefaced his lecture for a matinee audience of women with a paragraph contending that the "decorative arts have flourished most when the position of women was highly honored, when women occupied that place on the social scale which she ever ought to do.... It has been from the desire of women to beautify their households that decorative art has always received its impulse and encouragement. Women have natural art instincts, which men usually acquire only after long special training and study, and it may be the mission of the women of this country to revive decorative art into

honest, healthy life.") In urging those in his audience to build and decorate their houses "more beautifully," Wilde does not ask that large sums be spent, "as art does not depend in the slightest degree upon extravagance or luxury, but rather the procuring of articles which, however cheaply purchased and unpretending, are beautiful and fitted to impart pleasure to the observer as they did to the maker."

As an example of how genius can "glorify" stone, metal, and wood, he cites a 2,000-year-old little clay urn in an art museum that is "more artistic than all dreadful silver centerpieces of modern times, with their distorted camels and electroplated palm trees." He also urges his audience to "seek out your workmen and educate them to higher views of their relation to art, and reveal to them the possibilities of their callings"; only then will American art improve. He charges that Americans "do not honor the handicraftsman sufficiently, and do not recognize him as [they] should," for "all art must begin with the handicraftsman, and you must reinstate him into his rightful position, and thus make labor, which is always honorable, noble also" (the influence of William Morris is obvious here).

The "first necessity" in decoration, says Wilde, is that "any system of art should bear the impress of a distinct individuality." The pervasive influence of Morris and Ruskin is manifest in Wilde's urging his audience:

Have nothing in your house that has not given pleasure to the man who made it and is not a pleasure to those who use it. Have nothing in your houses that is not useful or beautiful; if such a rule were followed out, you would be astonished at the amount of rubbish you would get rid of. Let there be no sham imitations of one material in another, such as paper representing marble, or wood painted to resemble stone, and have no machine-made ornaments.

Wilde frowns on carpets for the floor: "ordinary red brick tiles make a warm and beautiful floor, and I prefer it to the geometrically arranged tiles of the present day." As for pictures, he is adamant that "no picture should be placed where you have not time to sit down and reverence and admire and study it." Furthermore, Wilde remarks, "Have none of those gloomy horrors, stuffed animals or stuffed birds, in the hall, or anything else under glass cases."

In discussing the use of color for rooms, Wilde cites the "great fault" in America concerning decoration – namely, "the entire want of harmony or a definite scheme in color." Alluding to Whistler's "Peacock Room" (now in the Freer Gallery in Washington, D.C.), Wilde regards it as "the finest thing in color and art decoration that the world has known since Correggio painted that wonderful room in Italy where the little children are dancing on the walls; everything is of the colors in peacock's feathers, and each part so colored with regard to the whole that the room, when lighted up, seems like a great peacock tail spread out."

Referring to the "aim of all art" as "simply to make life more joyous," Wilde urges his audience to

have such men as Whistler among you to teach you the beauty and joy of color. When he paints a picture, he paints by reference not to the subject, which is merely intellectual, but to color. I was speaking to Mr. Whistler once, before a great critic, of what could be done with one color. The critic said that he did not think that anybody could paint a picture with but a single color, including, of course, in various tones. Mr. Whistler undertook to do without any color, and the critic chose white as the color offering fewest tones; Mr. Whistler painted his beautiful "Symphony in White," which you no doubt have imagined to be something quite bizarre.

Wilde points out that Whistler's painting has "infinitely more value than horrible pictures of historical scenes; here are no extensive intellectual schemes to trouble you and no metaphysics, of which we have had quite enough in art.... I doubt not that our Aesthetic Movement has given to the world an increased sense of the value of color, and that in time a new science of the art of dealing in color will be evolved."

After praising Queen Anne furniture, "made by refined people for refined people," Wilde returns to the question of pictures, in most American homes "dull, commonplace, and tawdry. Poor pictures are worse than none." Pictures should be hung "from a ledge under the frieze and should be

hung also on the eyeline; the habit in America of hanging them up near the cornices struck me as irrational at first; it was not until I saw how bad the pictures were that I realized the advantage of the custom." Neither should photographs of paintings be hung on walls – "they are libels on great masters; there is no way to get a worse idea of a painter than by a photograph of his work."

The final three paragraphs take up the matter of the relation of art to morals. For one devoted to the Aesthetic Movement, Wilde's remark that art "fosters" morality is somewhat startling because of his advocacy (on occasion, at least) of art for art's sake. Wilde contends that, since science denies the soul and the spiritual nature of man and "when commerce is ruining beautiful rivers and magnificent woodlands and the glorious skies in its greed for gain, the artist comes forward as a priest and prophet of nature to protest, and even to work against the prostitution or the perversion of what is lofty and noble in humanity and beautiful in the physical world...."

"HOUSE DECORATION": *See* **"THE HOUSE BEAUTIFUL"** and **"THE DECORATIVE ARTS"**

"THE HOUSE OF JUDGMENT": *See* **"POEMS IN PROSE"**

A HOUSE OF POMEGRANATES
Published: November 1891 by James R. Osgood, McIlvaine & Co. (London); and early in 1892 by Dodd, Mead & Co. (New York). The dedication is to Wilde's wife, Constance (each story has an additional dedication). The volume was designed and decorated by Charles Ricketts and Charles Shannon.

Contents: [See the separate entries:] The Young King – The Birthday of the Infanta – The Fisherman and His Soul – The Star-Child.

Early Reviews: The anonymous reviewer in the *Pall Mall Gazette* (30 Nov.) regarded the "ultra-aestheticism" of the pictures and the "rather 'fleshly' style" of Wilde's writing – "something between a 'Swinburnian ecstasy' and the catalogue of a high art furniture dealer" – as unsuitable for children: "...the more natural among them would certainly prefer Hansel and Grethel's sugar-house to any amount of Mr. Wilde's 'rich tapestries' and 'velvet canopies.'" Wilde's diction, the reviewer insisted, "seems to us hardly suitable to children" (rpt. in Beckson). Responding to the review, Wilde wrote to the editor of the *Pall Mall Gazette*: "Now in building this *House of Pomegranates* I had about as much intention of pleasing the British child as I had of pleasing the British public.... No artist recognises any standard of beauty but that which is suggested by his own temperament" (*Letters* 302).

Having read the letter to the *Pall Mall Gazette*, the anonymous reviewer in the *Athenaeum* (6 Feb. 1892) remarked that Wilde "has been good enough to explain, since the publication of his book, that it was intended neither for the 'British Child' nor for the 'British Public,' but for the cultured few who can appreciate its subtle charms." In Wilde's work, the reviewer continues, "there is too much straining after effect and too many wordy descriptions, but at the same time there is a good deal of forcible and poetic writing scattered through its pages.... It is, perhaps, as well that the book is not meant for the 'British Child'; for it would certainly make him scream, according to his disposition, with terror or amusement" (rpt. in Beckson).

References: John Allen Quintus, "The Moral Prerogative in Oscar Wilde: A Look at the Fairy Tales," *Virginia Quarterly Review* (Autumn 1977); Maria Edelson, "The Language of Allegory in Oscar Wilde's Tales," *Anglo-Irish and Irish Literature: Aspects of Language and Culture*, Vol. 2, eds. Birgit Bramsbäck and Martin Croghan (1988); Carol Tattersall, "An Immodest Proposal: Rereading Oscar Wilde's 'Fairy Tales,'" *Wascana Review* (Spring/Fall 1991); Guy Willoughby, "Toward a New Aestheticism: Christ's Vision in *A House of Pomegranates*," *Art and Christhood: The Aesthetics of Oscar Wilde* (1993).

HOUSMAN, LAURENCE (1867–1959)

A poet, playwright, novelist, artist, and memoirist, Housman (the brother of A. E. Housman) wrote to Allan Wade on 12 November 1954: "When Wilde came out of jail I sent him a copy of my book *All-Fellows* [*: Seven Legends of Lower Redemption*, 1896], hoping that he would find in it something to suit his condition. Presently I got a letter from him saying: 'By the same post that brought me your book of *All Fellows* I received from your brother A. E. H. a copy of his poems, *A Shropshire Lad* [1896]. So you two brothers have between you given me a taste of that rare thing

called happiness.' I think those are almost the exact words" (qtd. in *Letters* 713n1).

On 9 August 1897, Wilde wrote to Laurence Housman in appreciation of his *All-Fellows*, a "beautiful book": "Your prose is full of cadence and colour, and has a rhythmic music of words that makes that constant appeal to the ear, which, to me, is the very condition of literature." Citing the "mysticism" of several of the "legends," which touched him "very deeply," Wilde writes: "...while they are of course dramatic, still one is conscious – as one should be in all objective art – of one personality dominating their perfection all through. The whole book, with its studied and imaginative decorations and its links of song, is a very lovely and almost unique work of art" (*More Letters* 152). Wilde's letter, with its formal greeting – "Dear Mr. Housman" – indicates that they were not close friends. Housman recalls that, at a friend's house, he first met Wilde, who was then "at the height of fame and success and I an unknown beginner [presumably in the early 1890s], still undecided whether to be book-illustrator or author" (*Echo* 13). Their subsequent friendship was principally epistolary.

In August 1897, in another letter to Housman, Wilde defends *A Shropshire Lad* against the criticism of Ricketts and Shannon (see their entry), who cannot "see the light lyrical beauty of your brother's work, and its grace and delicate felicity of mood and music." Wilde also remarks that he is completing "a poem [*The Ballad of Reading Gaol*], terribly realistic for me, and drawn from actual experience, a sort of denial of my own philosophy of art in many ways" (*More Letters* 153).

When *The Ballad* appeared early in 1898, Wilde ordered a copy to be sent to Housman, who responded favorably. Appreciative of Housman's praise, Wilde writes: "I thank you very much for all you have said to me about *The Ballad*: it has greatly touched me. I quite hold with you on all you say about the relation of human suffering to art; as art is the most intense mode of expression, so suffering is the most real mode of life, the one for which we are all ultimately created" (*More Letters* 167).

In December 1898, Wilde again wrote to Housman (this time "My dear Housman"), thanking him "not merely for your kindness, but for your charming letter. Style is certainly part of your character: your soul has beautiful curves and colours." Mentioning that Frank Harris was taking him to Napoule, near Cannes, Wilde writes of the sea, sun, and perfumes of southern flowers: "...perhaps these may tune my soul to some note of beauty" (*Letters* 771). Despite such hope, Wilde remarked to Housman in Paris in September 1899 in the company of friends:

> I told you that I was going to write something: I tell everybody that. It is a thing one can repeat each day, meaning to do it the next. But in my heart – that chamber of leaden echoes – I know that I never shall. It is enough that the stories have been invented, that they actually exist; that I have been able, in my own mind, to give them the form which they demand. (*Echo* 34)

Housman recalls that Wilde was "incomparably the most accomplished talker I had ever met" (*Echo* 15).

In 1900, Housman (the youngest of a group frequenting the Café Royal, including Shaw and Harris) carried funds donated by members of the circle on several trips to Paris to pay Wilde's rent and settle his debts but did not entrust any money to him. After such journeys, Housman reported to the group at the Café Royal (Graves 131–32).

References: Laurence Housman, *Echo de Paris: A Study from Life* (1923); Richard P. Graves, *A. E. Housman: The Scholar-Poet* (1979).

HOWE, JULIA WARD (1819–1910)

American reformer and author, best known for her "Battle Hymn of the Republic" (1861), Howe invited Wilde for lunch at her home when he was in Boston for three days before giving a lecture at the Music Hall on 31 January 1882. Howe noted in her diary that Wilde was "delightful, simple, sincere, and very clever." After his lecture, she gave a party for him, following which she recorded in her diary: "We all think him a man with genuine enthusiasm and with much talent" (qtd. in Clifford 227). Several days later, the anti-slavery reformer and advocate of woman's suffrage Thomas Wentworth Higginson (1823–1911) attacked Wilde in the *Woman's Journal* (4 Feb. 1882) by declaring his poems "prurient," adding:

> Women are as distinctively recognized as the guardians of the public purity as are the clergy of the public morals. Yet when a young man comes among us whose only distinction is that he has written a thin volume of very mediocre verse, and that he makes himself something very like a buffoon for notoriety and money, women of high social position receive him at their houses and invite guests to meet him; in spite of the fact that if they were to read aloud to the company his poem of "Charmides," not a woman would remain in the room until the end. (rpt. in Beckson)

Responding to Higginson's harsh judgments, Howe wrote a letter to the *Boston Transcript* (16 Feb.), in which she contended:

> To cut off even an offensive member of society from its best influences and most humanizing resources is scarcely Christian in any sense.... Mr. Wilde is a young man in whom many excellent people have found much to like. Among his poems are some which judges as competent as Colonel Higginson consider to have much merit.... When he shall leave our shores I shall be glad to have him carry with him the remembrances of a fair hearing and of generous interest in which the shortcomings of his youth shall have been temporarily set out of sight and the best promise and possibility of his manhood cherished and promoted. (qtd. in Lewis and Smith 121)

Wilde sent her a note: "Your letter is noble and beautiful. I have only just seen it, and shall not forget ever the chivalrous and pure-minded woman who wrote it" (*Letters* 122n2). To Joaquin Miller (1837–1913), the American poet, playwright, and journalist, Wilde referred to Higginson as "this scribbling anonymuncule in grand old Massachusetts who scrawls and screams so glibly about what he cannot understand.... This apostle of inhospitality, who delights to defile, to desecrate, and to defame the gracious courtesies he is unworthy to enjoy..." (*Letters* 98). Later that year, Wilde planned on visiting Howe at her summer house in Newport, Rhode Island: "When you are present, the air is cosmopolitan and the room seems to be full of brilliant people. You are one of those rare persons who give one the sense of creating history as they live" (*More Letters* 47).

In 1887, when he became the editor of the

Woman's World, Wilde invited Howe to contribute to the periodical:

> Some account of the remarkable development of the intellectual life of women in America would be most interesting, though as one of the leaders in the movement you may perhaps feel some difficulty about such a subject.... The position taken up by the women of America in the matter of slavery, of education, of social morals, of culture, of religion, and of politics, is one of the most interesting possible as a subject for an article.... (*Letters* 199)

In another letter, Wilde suggested that she write an article on Concord with sketches of Thoreau, Emerson, Louisa May Alcott, and Margaret Fuller – "to whom Venus gave everything except beauty, and Pallas everything except wisdom" (*Letters* 213) – but she did not contribute to *Woman's World*. Their correspondence seems to have ended during this time, and Howe's name never reappears in his subsequent extant letters. In her *Reminiscences, 1819–1899*, published in 1899, she makes no mention of Wilde, an omission that speaks volumes.

References: Deborah Pickman Clifford, *Mine Eyes Have Seen the Glory: A Biography of Julia Ward Howe* (1979).

"HUMANITAD"

Published: *Poems* (1881); rev. in (1882).

This poem contains 73 stanzas, each consisting of six lines. The title may have been inspired by Whitman's "Libertad" in *Leaves of Grass* (1855), and the sentiments expressed in Wilde's poem – a devotion to humanity's inherent nobility, now in a state of decay – were probably influenced by Swinburne's *Songs before Sunrise* (1871), in which "The Hymn of Man" exalts humanity's divinity: "Glory to Man in the highest! for Man is master of things."

Though Wilde's poem begins with conventional nature imagery ("It is full winter now: the trees are bare"), there is an abrupt shift to the personal voice of a speaker:

> There was a time when any common bird
> Could make me sing in unison, a time
> When all the strings of boyish life were stirred
> To quick response or more melodious rhyme

By every forest idyll....

Wondering whether he or nature has changed, he concludes that nature is the same: "...'tis I who seek / To vex with sighs thy simple solitude...." He yearns for wisdom, and – echoing Pater's urging in the "Conclusion" to *Studies in the History of the Renaissance* (1873) "To burn with [a] hard, gem-like flame" – he declares: "To burn with one clear flame, to stand erect / In natural honour, not to bend the knee / In profitless protestations...." He has abandoned Venus, for "her fond and subtle-fashioned spell / Delights no more, though I could win her dearest citadel." Science does not attract him as a means of achieving distinction. At one point in his meditation, he exclaims: "O for one grand unselfish simple life / To teach us what is Wisdom!"

The age lacks ideals, and "if one star / Flame torch-like in the heavens the unjust / Swift daylight kills it," even for such a liberator as Italy's Giuseppe Mazzini, one of Swinburne's heroes. The speaker, deploring the poverty that "Creeps through our sunless lanes and with sharp knives / Cuts the warm throats of children stealthily," concludes that "we are wretched men / Unworthy of our great inheritance!" Again, "austere Milton" is evoked as a symbol of England's former greatness (as in Wilde's "To Milton"), whereas all has fallen into decay (Wilde employs such allegorical figures as Anarchy, Ignorance, Greed as examples of such decline).

The England of old is evoked in a phrase recalling Wordsworth's "Ode: Intimations of Immortality" ("...there hath passed away a glory from the earth"): "The unchanged hills are with us: but that Spirit hath passed away." The speaker yearns for the return of universal unity (similar to Wilde's sentiments in "Panthea"):

> To make the Body and the Spirit one
> With all right things, till no thing live in vain...
> . . . .
> All separate existences are wed
> Into one supreme whole, whose utterance
> Is joy, or holier praise!

The acute awareness of present misery overwhelms the speaker, who concludes: "Nay, nay, we are but crucified, and though / The bloody sweat falls from our brows like rain, / Loosen the nails – we shall come down I know.../... we shall be whole again...."

Manuscript: The Hyde Collection has a MS. of lines 109–14 from the poem.

HUNT, VIOLET (1862–1942)

A novelist whose father, Alfred William Hunt (1830–96), was a Pre-Raphaelite landscape painter and whose mother, Margaret Raine Hunt (1831–1912), was a successful novelist, Violet Hunt wrote in a fragment of a projected book to be titled *My Oscar* that she probably met Wilde in 1879, shortly after his arrival in London, at the home of William Bell Scott (1811-90), the painter. In her diary, Violet recalls that she "gained the friendship of Oscar Wilde, which quite turned my head at the time..." (qtd. in Secor 398). When he rented rooms in Thames House with the artist Frank Miles (see entry), Mrs. Hunt and Violet were visitors along with other writers and artists. His letter to her mother in March 1880 alludes to "the sweetest Violet in England" (*Letters* 64). In July, Wilde and Miles moved to Keats House in Tite Street, closer to the Hunts, who became constant visitors. Later that year, he sent Violet the final stanza of his poem "Ave Imperatrix," which, he hoped, her father's "wonderful radicalism would be appeased by my first attempt at political prophecy" (*Letters* 68).

When Wilde's *Poems* (1881) appeared, he sent Violet a copy. Her response – that the poems were "beautiful" – moved Wilde to send her a grateful reply at a time when the volume was being attacked for its derivativeness:

> In an age like this when Slander, and Ridicule, and Envy walk quite unashamed among us, and when any attempt to produce serious beautiful work is greeted with a very tornado of lies and evil-speaking, it is a wonderful joy, a wonderful spur for ambition and work, to receive any such encouragement and appreciation as your letter brought me, and I thank you for it again and again. (*Letters* 79)

Before Wilde left London for his American lecture tour, he saw Violet weekly. In her diary, she later recorded: "I believe that Oscar was really in love with me..." (qtd. in Belford 43). In later years, she insisted in her memoirs, *The Flurried Years* (1926), that she had "as nearly as possible

escaped the honour of being Mrs. Wilde" (168). She also alluded to her escape in her autobiographical novels: in *Their Lives* (1916), for example, Hunt appears as Christina Radmall and Wilde as Philip Wynyard, who, "sick of all these dressed-up affected women who make up to him," is prepared to ask Mr. Radmall for her hand, but Wynyard is reluctant to proceed because her family has no money.

When Wilde was in the process of assuming the editorship of *Woman's World* (as it was later titled), he hoped that Violet would contribute a poem to it, but she never did. By the late 1880s, Violet saw Wilde not as a young conqueror but a cynical dandy with "courteous manners and splendid sins" (qtd. in Secor 399). As she became noted for her novels, which she began publishing in 1894, her circle of friends included Henry James, Arnold Bennett, D. H. Lawrence, and Ford Madox Hueffer (later Ford) – regarding herself as Ford's "self-proclaimed wife," an affair that lasted from 1909 to 1914 (Secor 397).

References: Robert Secor, "Aesthetes and Pre-Raphaelites: Oscar Wilde and the Sweetest Violet in England," *Texas Studies in Literature and Language* (Fall 1979); Joan Hardwick, *An Immodest Violet: The Life of Violet Hunt* (1990); Barbara Belford, *Violet* (1990).

I

AN IDEAL HUSBAND

Written: Wilde began work on the play in the summer of 1893 at Goring-on-Thames (from which he derived the name of Lord Goring) and completed most of it in the autumn and winter in rooms rented in St. James's Place. John Hare (1844–1921), the actor-manager of the Garrick Theatre, rejected it because of his dissatisfaction with Act IV. Wilde then sent the typescript to the actors Lewis Waller (1850–1915) and H. H. Morell (1865–1916) at the Haymarket Theatre. After they decided to produce the play, rehearsals began in December 1894.

Produced: The play opened on 3 January 1895 and ran for 124 performances, the principal roles performed by the following actors: Charles H. Hawtrey as Lord Goring, Lewis Waller as Sir Robert Chiltern, Julia Neilson as Lady Chiltern, Maude Millet as Mabel Chiltern, Florence West as Mrs. Cheveley, and Fanny Brough as Lady Markby. (In New York, the play premièred on 12 March.) On 6 April, the day after Wilde's arrest, the play completed its final performance at the Haymarket, then transferred to Charles Wyndham's Criterion Theatre (such an arrangement had no connection with the Wilde affair, for Herbert Beerbohm Tree, the actor-manager at the Haymarket, was expected to return from an American tour in early April, when he would resume his management of the theater). Wyndham informed Waller that Wilde's name, which had been removed from the placards on 5 April, had to appear as the author if *An Ideal Husband* continued at the Criterion. Waller agreed. The play ran from 13 to 27 April.

Published: July 1899 by Leonard Smithers, rpt. in the *Collected Edition*, Vol. 5 (1908). The title page does not name Wilde as the author but "By the author of Lady Windermere's Fan." The dedication reads: TO / FRANK HARRIS / A SLIGHT TRIBUTE TO / HIS POWER AND DISTINCTION / AS AN ARTIST / HIS CHIVALRY AND NOBILITY / AS A FRIEND. For this version of the play, Wilde added a number of new passages and cut others – indeed, more additions than omissions. A distinctive addition was a series of more elaborate stage directions, particularly in the extended descriptions of the principal characters, including, for example, the color of a character's hair and other such physical details. Russell Jackson remarks that Wilde was "joining in the movement towards the effective presentation of plays for the reading public – Shaw, Pinero and Jones made similar efforts" (129). In March 1899, while suggesting to Smithers the proper layout for the text of *An Ideal Husband*, Wilde remarked: "I really think it reads the best of my plays" (*More Letters* 181).

Sources: Alexandre Dumas *fils*, the source for many adaptations in late 19th-century English drama, provided Wilde with the material for more than one of his plays. In the case of *An Ideal Husband*, Act III of Dumas *fils*'s *L'Ami des femmes* (1864) has some of the elements that Wilde borrowed and adapted: the heroine, separated from her husband, writes a note to an admirer: "Come tomorrow. All I ask is to believe you." The usual confusion – in which the husband believes that the letter is intended for him – results in a reconciliation, the characteristic conclusion to the "well-made play" in which a theatrical device, such as a letter, usually intercepted by another character, determines the course of the outcome. Wilde, to be sure, adds sufficient ironic twists and turns to the plot so that his borrowings do not diminish his achievement.

Arthur Wing Pinero's *The Cabinet Minister* (1890) may have provided Wilde with some additional elements of the plot: an unscrupulous financier blackmails the wife of a cabinet minister, who is deeply in debt, into disclosing secret information about the government's decision on a canal project, which enables him to make a fortune on the stock exchange. Wilde's basic plot also reflects events occurring in January 1893 in Paris, when a suit was brought against the directors of the Compagnie du Canal Interocéanique, accused of exploiting shareholders' funds. During the trial, implications of political corruption were divulged.

In addition, early reviewers recognized Victorien Sardou's *Dora* (1877) as another probable source for Wilde's basic plot: instead of a character being accused of stealing an important dispatch, as in Sardou, Sir Robert Chiltern is charged with selling a state secret. The intrigue of blackmail, inevitable in such a plot, also finds echoes in *An Ideal Husband*, but this element, commonplace in late 19th-century melodrama, does not account for the wit and ingenuity of Wilde's play.

The Plot: Act I opens in the Grosvenor Square home of Sir Robert Chiltern, a rising politician (Under-Secretary for Foreign Affairs at the age of 40), and his wife, Gertrude, who are hosts at a reception. The stage directions describe a large 18th-century French tapestry on the staircase wall representing the Triumph of Love (a central theme of the play). One of the guests, Lady Markby, is accompanying a friend, Mrs. Cheveley, whom Lady Chiltern recognizes, to her discomfort, as a former fellow student. Clearly, Mrs. Cheveley, who has been living in Vienna for many years, also has dandiacal cleverness and wit.

When Sir Robert asks her why she has returned to London, she replies that she had wished to meet him and to ask him to undertake a task for her. Lord Goring enters before Mrs. Cheveley has the opportunity to proceed further. The stage directions describe Lord Goring as 34, with "a well-bred, expressionless face. He is clever, but would not like to be thought so. A flawless dandy, he would be annoyed if he were considered romantic." After some social conversation, Mrs. Cheveley and Sir Robert leave, and Goring "saunters" over to Mabel Chilton (Sir Robert's sister), a dandy who characteristically avoids moral judgments in favor of aesthetic ones. Goring and Mabel, who clearly engage in an exalted flirtation, cherish the effective riposte. When Mabel protests that he is always telling her of his bad qualities, Goring responds that she knows only half of them, that the others are "quite dreadful": "When I think of them at night I go to sleep at once." But she delights in his bad qualities: "I wouldn't have you part with one of them."

As conversation moves from group to group, Sir Robert and Mrs. Cheveley find themselves able to continue their previous conversation. She raises the question of the Argentine Canal Company, which he believes is a "commonplace Stock Exchange swindle," though Mrs. Cheveley believes it to be a "brilliant, daring speculation." Sir Robert informs her that he has sent a special commission to inquire into the matter privately: the works have hardly begun, and the money, already subscribed, seems to have vanished. On the advice of a mutual friend, Baron Arnheim, now deceased, Mrs.

Cheveley had invested "very largely" in the project. Wishing to change the subject, Sir Robert offers to show her his Corots in the music room, but she prefers to talk business rather than see "silver twilights or rose-pink dawns."

Sir Robert, however, has no advice for her except to invest in less dangerous affairs. "The success of the Canal," he remarks, "depends, of course, on the attitude of England, and I am going to lay the report of the Commissioners before the House tomorrow night." She urges him not to do so for his own interest as well as hers. He must withdraw the report on the grounds that the Commissioners "have been prejudiced or misinformed, or something." Moreover, he must inform the House of Commons that the government will reconsider the question and that the canal, if completed, will be of "considerable international value.... A few ordinary platitudes will do. In modern life nothing produces such an effect as a good platitude." If he follows her suggestions, she will pay him "very handsomely." He is shocked by her offer, but she insists that he, like any man of the world, has his price: "Everybody has nowadays. The drawback is that most people are so dreadfully expensive."

At this, he rises indignantly to escort her to her carriage, but she detains him by touching his arm with her fan: "I realize that I am talking to a man who laid the foundation of his fortune by selling to a Stock Exchange speculator a Cabinet secret.... I know the real origin of your wealth and your career, and I have got your letter, too." The letter, written three days before the government announced its own purchase, was addressed to Arnheim, telling him to buy Suez Canal shares (presumably at a much lower price). Despite Sir Robert's attempt to explain away his action, Mrs. Cheveley calls it a swindle: "Let us call things by their proper names." She is willing to sell him the letter, the price for which is his public support of the Argentine scheme. If he refuses, he will be ruined by her exposure of his secret in the press. Rather than do her bidding, he offers her any sum of money she wishes. However, her threat to destroy his career convinces him that he has no choice. Commenting on the contention of some late 19th-century critics that Wilde had exaggerated the corruption in high places, Alan Bird writes:

What the public of Wilde's day did not know

was that Disraeli had been forced to borrow money from the Rothschilds in order to finance the government's purchase of Suez Canal shares and that this deal must certainly have strengthened the hands (and enlarged the funds) of the dealers in these and related shares. And this furtive financial intrigue had taken place only twenty years or so before *An Ideal Husband* had been written. (144–45)

After Mrs. Cheveley departs, Mabel Chiltern and Lord Goring discover a diamond brooch on the sofa (the conventional device of an object in the "well-made play" that will now direct the plot). Placing the brooch in his breast pocket, he asks Mabel not to mention its discovery to anyone (he had given the brooch to someone years before). When she departs, Lady Chiltern discusses Mrs. Cheveley with Goring, particularly the Argentine Canal project and her husband's moral probity: "She is incapable of understanding an upright nature like my husband's!"

When Goring leaves, Lady Chiltern remarks that Mrs. Cheveley had told her that Sir Robert would support the Argentine Canal project, but she warns him that, at school, Mrs. Cheveley was "sent away for being a thief." Sir Robert tells her that he was mistaken about the Argentine Canal. His talk of private and public life as "different things" and of the need for compromise in political life puzzles and disturbs her. She refers to her husband as a moral ideal for her and for the rest of the world. When she asks him whether there is in his life "any secret dishonour or disgrace," he assures her that there is nothing disgraceful in his past life. She expects him, then, to inform Mrs. Cheveley that he cannot support "this scandalous scheme of hers."

After he writes a letter, Lady Chiltern reads it and has it sent to Mrs. Cheveley's hotel. She affirms her love for him for having "brought into the political life of our time a nobler atmosphere." After she leaves, Sir Robert instructs the servant to put out the lights. The stage direction concluding the act reads: "The only light there is comes from the great chandelier that hangs over the staircase and illumines the tapestry of the Triumph of Love."

Act II opens in the morning room of Sir Robert's house: Lord Goring is lounging in an armchair while Sir Robert stands in front of the fireplace "in

a state of great mental excitement and distress," for he has revealed his dilemma to his visitor concerning his career and his marriage. When he succumbed to Baron Arnheim's suggestion that certain state documents be divulged, Sir Robert received £110,000 from him, and after his becoming a member of the House of Commons, the baron gave him financial advice that in less than five years resulted in Sir Robert's increasing his wealth three-fold. Having been born poor and, at the age of 21, yearning for wealth and power when he encountered Baron Arnheim, Sir Robert remarks, "I remember having read somewhere, in some strange book, that when the gods wish to punish us they answer our prayers." In order to pacify his conscience, he has distributed twice the amount given to him by Arnheim to public charities.

Sir Robert is determined that he will "fight the thing out," but when Goring advises him to tell his wife the whole story, Chiltern insists that to tell her would kill her love for him. When he asks how he can defend himself against Mrs. Cheveley, Goring informs him that he was once engaged to be married to her, but he has no idea of how to proceed. Chiltern decides to send a cipher telegram to the embassy in Vienna to inquire whether there is "some secret scandal she might be afraid of."

When Lady Chiltern enters, he leaves shortly to write some letters, enabling her to speak with Goring about Mrs. Cheveley. However, she is more concerned with her husband's secrets: "He has no secrets from me, and I don't think he has any from you." Goring responds with more meaning for the audience than for Lady Chiltern: "He certainly has no secrets from me." Goring then prepares her for the possibility of full disclosure of her husband's dilemma: "...I have sometimes thought that...perhaps you are a little hard in some of your views on life.... In every nature there are elements of weakness, or worse than weakness." He assures her that she can trust him; indeed, he urges her to come to him for any assistance she may need.

After he leaves, Lady Markby and Mrs. Cheveley arrive, the latter inquiring about a diamond brooch that she may have left behind. Lady Markby (whose imperious manner and dandiacal speeches anticipate Lady Bracknell in *The Importance of Being Earnest*) is one who, says Mrs. Cheveley, "Talks more and says less than anybody I ever met. She is made to be a public speaker."

When Lady Markby leaves, the tensions intensify when Lady Chiltern informs Mrs. Cheveley that "for many reasons any further acquaintance between us during your stay in London is quite impossible." Mrs. Cheveley responds: "...I have always detested you. And yet I have come here to do you a service." But Lady Chiltern remarks that she has saved her husband from "that service." Mrs. Cheveley then reveals the truth: that Sir Robert is "himself fraudulent and dishonest," that she and he are well paired, indeed closer than friends, that the "same sin" binds them. Lady Chiltern orders her to leave; at that moment, Sir Robert enters from behind and hears his wife's final words. Mrs. Cheveley gives them both until the next day at noon or "the whole world shall know the origin of Robert Chiltern."

After Mrs. Cheveley leaves, Lady Chiltern, in a fury over the shocking disclosure of her husband's fraudulent past, charges him with having worn a mask all of those years: "A horrible, painted mask!" Her ideal – once "pure, noble, honest, without stain" – has sold himself "to the highest bidder!" Sir Robert attempts to justify himself by accusing her of harboring a false idealism that has ruined his life. True love, he says, should pardon.

Act III opens in the library of Lord Goring's house. Phipps, the butler, is arranging newspapers on the writing table. Wilde's stage directions describe the butler as a characteristic dandy: "He is a mask with a manner.... He represents the dominance of form." When Phipps's counterpart, Lord Goring, enters, he engages in such witty conversation with his butler that one is reminded of the epigrams that Wilde had previously published as "Phrases and Philosophies for the Use of the Young," including the one uttered by Goring at the beginning of Act III: "To love oneself is the beginning of a life-long romance." Wilde's supreme narcissistic dandy provides the model for his butler, wittily transformed into a male Echo (see Narcissus and Narcissism).

Phipps hands him a letter in a pink envelope, which contains Lady Chiltern's handwriting: "I want you. I trust you. I am coming to you. Gertrude." Concluding that she has found out everything, Goring decides that he will make her stand by Sir Robert. When Lord Caversham enters, Goring instructs Phipps that a lady is expected and that she should be shown into the drawing room. Moments later the bell rings and Mrs. Cheveley (not Lady Chilton, as Goring had expected) is shown in. Alone, she recognizes on the writing table the handwriting on the pink envelope as Lady Chilton's. She reads the letter, then slips it under a blotting-book when Phipps returns and retires into the drawing room, but she re-opens the door in order to fetch the letter. When she hears the voices of Goring and his father approaching, she withdraws.

When Sir Robert enters, he announces to Goring that his wife has discovered everything, thanks to Mrs. Cheveley. Word from Vienna is that there is nothing known that is detrimental to her reputation and that the greater portion of Baron Arnheim's immense fortune had been left to her. Distraught, Sir Robert sees his career and his marriage destroyed. Suddenly, on hearing the sound of a falling chair in the next room, he concludes that someone has overheard every secret of his life, but Goring insists that no one is there. Nevertheless, Sir Robert must see for himself. When he returns, he is furious with Goring, who (believing that the lady is Lady Chilton) swears on his honor that the lady is "stainless and guiltless of all offense" to Sir Robert. Declaring that the "corrupt and shameful" lady, whom he does not name, is Goring's mistress, he leaves.

Mrs. Cheveley, "looking radiant and much amused," enters and offers to give Sir Robert's incriminating letter to Goring if he marries her (he had sometime ago proposed to her but withdrew his proposal because of her flirtation with Lord Mortlake). He refuses her proposal, accusing her of desecrating the word *love* and degrading Sir Robert by informing Lady Chiltern of his past. When she mentions the diamond brooch, Goring goes to his writing table and takes it out of the drawer. She is delighted to have it back. Suddenly clasping it on her arm, he informs her that he knows that she had stolen it from his cousin.

When she attempts to remove the bracelet, she cannot unclasp it. He threatens to call the police if she does not surrender Chiltern's letter. Defeated, she submits, gives him the letter, which he immediately burns. But when Goring turns his back to pour some water, she steals Lady Chiltern's letter, which she had placed under the blotting-book. As she prepares to leave, she tells Goring that she has Lady Chiltern's "love letter" written to him and that she will send it to Sir Robert. Before Goring can reach her to force it from her, she rings the bell to summons Phipps.

The setting for Act IV is the same as that for Act II, the morning room in Sir Robert's house. Looking rather bored, Lord Goring is standing by the fireplace. His father enters and informs his son that Chiltern has denounced the Argentine Canal scheme brilliantly in the House of Commons. Their conversation again turns to Goring's prospects for marriage, Lord Caversham suggesting that he propose to Mabel Chiltern. At that moment, she enters, and shortly thereafter Caversham leaves. Left alone, Goring proposes to Mabel, who is obviously delighted.

When Lady Chiltern enters, Mabel withdraws to the conservatory, leaving Goring to discuss Mrs. Cheveley with her. What had happened in the previous act (the burning of Sir Robert's letter and the theft of Lady Chilton's letter to Goring) is rehearsed; now the problem involves the interception of Lady Chiltern's letter before her husband sees it. But soon Sir Robert, entering with the letter in his hand, assumes that it is addressed to him. Lady Chiltern informs him that his incriminating letter has been destroyed. He is overjoyed, but he is now convinced that he should retire from public life. His wife agrees: "It is your duty to do that." But he is uncertain: "It is much to surrender." Lord Caversham arrives with a letter from the Prime Minister informing Sir Robert that, because of his "high character, high moral tone, high principles," he is to have the vacant seat in the Cabinet.

But Sir Robert sees his wife looking at him "with her clear, candid eyes." Declining the appointment, he reiterates his intention to retire at once. When his wife concurs, he withdraws to write his letter of refusal. Caversham can only assume that both of them suffer from hereditary idiocy and withdraws into the conservatory. Alone with Lady Chiltern, Goring accuses her of thrusting a tragedy on her husband (that Mrs. Cheveley had also attempted) by agreeing to his resignation. Goring now reveals sentiments that one would expect from a conventional Victorian, not a dandy, an indication that inconsistency in characterization was an attempt to escape from commonplace melodrama: "A man's life is of more value than a woman's. It has larger issues, wider scope, greater ambitions. A woman's life revolves in curves of emotions. It is upon lines of intellect that a man's life progresses."

When Sir Robert enters with his letter of refusal, his wife tears it up, offering the same argument concerning a man's life that Goring had offered. She forgives her husband's indiscretion when he was a youth. Overcome, he embraces her and expresses gratitude to Goring for all he has done. Misunderstandings are quickly cleared up; as a result, Sir Robert gives his consent to Goring to marry Mabel. When all depart, Sir Robert asks his wife: "Gertrude, is it love you felt for me, or is it pity merely?" She responds: "It is love, Robert. Love, and only love. For both of us a new life is beginning." (Bird comments that "it is not the triumph of love [recalling the rich tapestry depicting that theme in Act I] we witness in the drama but the triumph of money, ambition and corruption," 150.)

Early Theater Reviews: In general, the reviews were decidedly mixed in judging Wilde's play. In the *Pall Mall Gazette* (4 Jan.), H. G. Wells (in an unsigned review) regards the play, in many ways, as "diverting, and even where the fun is not of the rarest character the play remains interesting." Whereas the common man begins in innocence, remarks Wells, Wilde is, "so to speak, working his way to innocence, as others work towards experience – is sloughing his epigrams slowly but surely, and discovering to an appreciative world, beneath the attenuated veil of his wit, that he, too, has a heart."

However, after *Lady Windermere's Fan* and *A Woman of No Importance*, the play is "decidedly disappointing," Wells concludes:

> It may be this melodramatic touch, this attempt at commonplace emotions and the falling off in epigram, may be merely a cynical or satirical concession to the public taste. Or it may be something more, an attempt to get free from the purely clever pose, that merely epigrammatic attitude, that has been vulgarized to the level of the punster. But, taking it seriously, and disregarding any possibly imaginary tendency towards a new width of treatment, the play is unquestionably very poor. (rpt. in Beckson).

In the *Pall Mall Budget* (10 Jan.), William Archer, more favorably disposed than Wells in his estimate of the play, writes of this "highly entertaining play" that "we all enjoyed very nearly as much as [Wilde] himself did." Archer, devoting much space to a consideration of Sir Robert Chiltern's moral dilemma, concludes: "It may be a mistake to hold a man disabled by his past from doing service to the State; but this man is disabled by his present. The excellent Sir Robert proves himself one of those gentlemen who can be honest so long as it is absolutely convenient, and no longer....."

As for the play as a whole, Archer regards it as "a very able and entertaining piece of work, charmingly written, wherever Mr. Wilde can find it in his heart to sufflaminate [that is, to obstruct] his wit. There are several scenes in which the dialogue is heavily overburdened with witticisms, not always of the best alloy....[and] there are times when the output of Mr. Wilde's epigram-factory threatens to become all trademark and no substance" (rpt. in Archer's *The Theatrical "World" of 1895* [1896] and in Beckson).

In the *Saturday Review* (12 Jan.), Bernard Shaw praised the play in a characteristically Shavian manner by opening with the remark that Wilde's new play is "a dangerous subject, because he has the property of making his critics dull":

They laugh angrily at his epigrams.... They protest that the trick is obvious, and that such epigrams can be turned out by the score by any one lightminded enough to condescend to such frivolity. As a far as I can ascertain, I am the only person in London who cannot sit down and write an Oscar Wilde play at will. The fact that his plays, though apparently lucrative, remain unique under these circumstances, says much for the self-denial of our scribes. In a certain sense Mr. Wilde is to me our only thorough playwright. He plays with every thing: with wit, with philosophy, with drama, with actors and audience, with the whole theatre.

Wilde's "subtle and pervading levity" in his play, Shaw continues, "all the literary dignity of the play, all the imperturbable good sense and good manners with which Mr. Wilde makes his wit pleasant to his comparatively stupid audience, cannot quite overcome the fact that Ireland is of all countries the most foreign to England, and that to the Irishman...there is nothing in the world quite so exquisitely comic as an Englishman's seriousness."

The Englishman, moreover, is "shocked, too, at the danger to the foundations of society when seriousness is publicly laughed at. And to complete the oddity of the situation, Mr. Wilde, touching what he himself reverences, is absolutely the most sentimental dramatist of the day."

The modern note is struck, says Shaw, in Sir Robert's "assertion of the individuality and courage of his wrongdoing as against the mechanical idealism of his stupidly good wife, and in his bitter criticism of a love that is only the reward of merit." Shaw's only criticism of the mechanics of Wilde's "stage illusion" is the question why Mrs. Cheveley, while hiding in Goring's room, knocks down a chair (rpt. in Shaw's *Our Theatres in the Nineties* [1932] and in Beckson).

In the *Speaker* (12 Jan.), A. B. Walkley also praised the play in such a manner that, at first, it seems to be rave review: "...a strepitous [that is, noisy], polychromatic, scintillant affair, dexterous as a conjurer's trick of legerdemain, clever with a cleverness so excessive as to be almost monstrous and uncanny, [that] was received with every token of success." Though the significance of Wilde's success is that there is "promise for the future," Walkley is convinced that the play "will not help the drama forward a single inch, nor – though that is a comparatively unimportant matter – will it, in the long run, add to Mr. Wilde's reputation." Nevertheless, Walkley delights in Wilde's "dexterity, his dancing rhythms, his orchestral bass."

Despite the commonplace nature of the plot and the tricks associated with the "well-made play," such as the incident with the bracelet and the two stolen letters (even Sardou, he says, "has tired of these kleptodramatics"), Walkley concludes that "by dint of sheer cleverness," Wilde keeps one "continually amused and interested," yet after remarking that the play "presents at least one pleasant and human character, everybody's friend save his own," he ends with the startling judgment that "the fact remains that Mr. Wilde's work is not only poor and sterile, but essentially vulgar" (rpt. in Beckson).

In the *Illustrated London News* (12 Jan.), Clement Scott, who had written a negative review of *Lady Windermere's Fan*, begins with an obvious parallel between *An Ideal Husband* and Sardou's *Dora*. But, as Scott remarks, "a play is never less interesting to the ordinary playgoer because something in it has been done before.... It is to me quite clear that the mere fact that Mr. Oscar Wilde's play suggests something else does not in the least interfere with its success – a success that is naturally increased by the author's method and trick of talk. In fact, Oscar Wilde is the fashion. His catch and whimsicality of dialogue tickle the public." Scott ends his review with characteristic denigration not only of Wilde's wit but also of the audience: "There is scarcely one Oscar Wildeism uttered in the new Haymarket play that will bear one minute's analysis, but for all that they tickle the ears of the groundlings, and are accepted as stage cleverness" (rpt. in Beckson).

The American critic and novelist William Dean Howells, reviewing the New York production of *An Ideal Husband* in *Harper's Weekly* (30 March), writes that the play is "not only an excellent piece of art, but an excellent piece of sense...." Yet, he remarks, "the play left me with some very grave misgivings as to the usefulness of the moral problem in the drama. That is, it gave me question whether it could well be made the chief interest of a play; for there is great danger that it may be falsely solved, or else shirked, which is nearly as bad." Howells believes that the subordinate people of the plays [Jones's *The Case of Rebellious Susan* and *An Ideal Husband*] gave him the feeling of character, and that he cared for the hero and heroine because of what happened to them, or through them, "and not because they were interesting persons except as the actors made them so. They were working out a problem, and so busy in doing it that they had no time for being" (rpt. in Beckson).

Manuscripts: The British Library has a MS. draft of four acts – including two drafts of Act II – with the original title *Mrs. Cheveley* and TSS. of a later version with autograph corrections. The British Library also has a TS., dated 2 Jan. 1895, the licensing copy submitted to the Lord Chamberlain's office. The Clark Library has notebooks containing the original fragmentary draft of the play – as well as a separate draft of Act IV in addition to TSS. and proofsheets of the book publication in 1899, with revisions and additions. The Harvard Theater Collection has a corrected TS. of the play with the title changed to *The Foolish Journalist* – as Russell Jackson suggests, "possibly so as to conceal the play's title until the appropriate time for public announcements" (128). The Morgan Library has a TS. of Act III with

extensive revisions in Wilde's hand. The New York Public Library at Lincoln Center has a TS., with stage directions, presumably written by Daniel Frohman, who produced the play in New York. The Lewis Collection at Texas Christian University (Fort Worth) has Wilde's incomplete revised TS. of a printer's copy used to set type for the 1899 publication of the play – in addition to some 35 pages in Wilde's hand (see Lich's article below).

References: Alan Bird, *The Plays of Oscar Wilde* (1977); *An Ideal Husband*, ed. Russell Jackson, in *Two Society Comedies*, eds. Ian Small and Russell Jackson (1983); Glen Lich, "'Anything But a Misprint': Comments on an Oscar Wilde Transcript," *South Central Review* (Summer 1986); Peter Raby, *Oscar Wilde* (1988); Kerry Powell, "*An Ideal Husband*: Resisting the Feminist Police," *Oscar Wilde and the Theatre of the 1890s* (1990); Joseph Bristow, "Dowdies and Dandies: Oscar Wilde's Refashioning of Society Comedy," *Modern Drama* (Spring 1994); Karl Beckson, "Narcissistic Reflections in a Wilde Mirror," *Modern Drama* (Spring 1994).

THE IMPORTANCE OF BEING EARNEST

Written: August – November 1894, principally in Worthing, Sussex, a seaside resort (hence the main character's name, Jack Worthing) and London. In a typescript of a letter discovered by Peter Raby among the uncatalogued material at the Clark Library, Wilde initially outlined the plot of *Earnest*, probably in late July, to George Alexander, the actor-manager of the St. James's Theatre. Many of the elements of the final version are already present in the outline, including what Wilde called the "double life" of the guardian (later called "Jack Worthing"; indeed, the earliest title for the play was *The Guardian*). The names of the other characters in the scenario are different from the stage version except for Miss Prism, the governess, who has, says Wilde in the scenario, matrimonial "designs on the guardian" – this portion of the plot was later dropped. The entire handbag incident involving Miss Prism was added later.

When he concluded a draft of *Earnest*, he told Alfred Douglas: "My play is really very funny: I am quite delighted with it" (*Letters* 362). An indication of Wilde's labor over the play is revealed by Ruth Berggren in her edition: "As Wilde revised the play, he was concerned about pacing, characterization, and conventionality. He trimmed scenes, he tightened speeches, and he polished his prose. He edited his work ruthlessly, sacrificing epigram after epigram to keep plot and dialogue moving" (25). Around 24 October, Wilde sent the first typewritten copy of the completed play to Alexander, explaining that it was called *"Lady Lancing* [with the subtitle *A Serious Comedy for Trivial People*] on the cover: but the real title is *The Importance of Being Earnest* [the subtitle later changed to *A Trivial Comedy for Serious People*]" (*Letters* 376). Wilde did not want the "real title" to be known before the opening of the play in order to conceal the "Earnest" pun in the final line.

Alexander, who had commissioned Wilde to write the play, rejected the four-act version. But after the disastrous opening and sudden death of Henry James's *Guy Domville* at the St. James's Theatre, Alexander needed an immediate replacement. He suggested that Wilde compress Acts II and III of his play into a single act so that a shorter play would permit the staging of a curtain-raiser. When Wilde objected, Alexander proceeded to cut a major scene in which the solicitor Gribsby threatens to arrest Algernon Moncrieff, Jack's friend, who is masquerading as Ernest, for non-payment of a debt. Jack, however, rescues him by providing the money. The roles of Miss Prism, the Rev. Chasuble, and Algernon were also reduced to enlarge Alexander's role as Jack Worthing.

Weeks before the opening, Wilde and Ross invented an interview for the *St. James's Gazette* (18 Jan. 1895) to publicize the play and to suggest the means by which it could be understood: "That we should treat all the trivial things of life very seriously, and all the serious things of life with sincere and studied triviality" (rpt. in Mikhail 1:250). Asked by an interviewer before the opening whether the play would be a success, Wilde responded: "My dear fellow, you have got it all wrong. The play *is* a success. The only question is whether the first night's audience will be one" (qtd. in A. E. W. Mason 78).

Produced: 14 February 1895 at the St. James's Theatre. (The curtain raiser was Langdon Elwyn Mitchell's *In the Season*.) In addition to Alexander, the cast for the major roles in *Earnest* consisted of Allan Aynesworth as Algernon Moncrieff, Irene Vanbrugh as Gwendolen Fairfax, Evelyn Millard as Cecily Cardew, Rose Leclercq

as Lady Bracknell, H. H. Vincent as the Rev. Chasuble, and Mrs. George Canninge as Miss Prism. The audience was, as Wilde had hoped, a great success, for Allan Aynesworth recalled that in his 53 years on the stage, he could not remember a similar triumph: "The audience rose in their seats and cheered and cheered again" (qtd. in Beckson 21). In his dressing room, Alexander asked Wilde: "Well, wasn't I right? What did you think of it?" Pleased and amused, Wilde responded: "My dear Aleck, it was charming, quite charming. And, do you know, from time to time I was reminded of a play I once wrote myself, called *The Importance of Being Earnest*" (qtd. in A. E. W. Mason 79).

After Wilde's arrest on 5 April, the play remained in production until 8 May, its 83rd performance – his name, however, removed from the placards and programs. Alexander insisted that the closing of *Earnest* had resulted in a loss of £300. In New York, Charles Frohman produced the play at the Empire Theatre on 22 April, but a combination of factors, such as the Wilde scandal, a mediocre production, and lackluster reviews, resulted in meagre audiences; the play lasted little more than a week.

Published: February 1899 by Leonard Smithers with the sub-title *A Trivial Comedy for Serious People*, without Wilde's name; instead, as Wilde preferred, the following appears on the title page: "By the author of *Lady Windermere's Fan*." The dedication is to Robert Ross: "In Appreciation / In Affection." In preparing the play for publication, Wilde made numerous revisions of the acting version. The play was reprinted in the *Collected Edition*, Vol. 6 (1908). The "Definitive Four-Act Version," edited by Ruth Berggren, appeared in 1987. The typescript of this version (including the later excised scene in the draft of Act II, in which the lawyer Gribsby appears in order to have Algernon imprisoned for ignoring his debts), intended for Frohman's New York production, was shelved when Wilde's revised three-act version replaced it. After Frohman's death when the *Lusitania* was torpedoed in 1915, the original four-act version remained in private hands until the New York Public Library acquired it in 1953 shortly before its owner, R. H. Burnside, died.

Sources: As in other of his plays, Wilde borrowed theatrical devices from the French well-made play, with its secrets and use of stage props (in *Earnest*, the handbag) to move the plot to its resolution. In addition, he apparently borrowed elements of plot and character from Alfred de Musset's popular play *Il ne faut jurer de rien* (1848), a type of *comédie-proverbe* in which farcical intrigue and witty proverbs include the use of the title in the final line of the play, as in *Earnest*. Wilde also knew of Menander, the ancient Greek dramatist responsible for the profusion of misplaced baby plots in subsequent literature (Wilde had won the Berkeley Gold Medal at Trinity College, Dublin, for his essay on August Meineke's edition of the *Fragmenta Comicorum Graecorum* [1841], which included the extant fragments by Menander).

W. S. Gilbert's *Engaged* (1877) also seems to have exerted an important influence on Wilde's play, particularly in the scene in which the two young women, at first bubbling over with affection, become hostile when they discover that one has married the other's fiancé. In the same play, a character appears on stage in mourning (the stage directions similar to those describing Jack Worthing's appearance in *Earnest*) in anticipation of a friend's suicide. Gilbert's advice to the cast of *Engaged* indicates a probable source of the acting style essential to an effective performance of *Earnest*:

> It is absolutely essential to the success of this piece that it should be played with the most perfect earnestness and gravity throughout. There should be no exaggeration in costume, make-up, or demeanour; and the characters, one and all, should appear to believe, throughout, in the perfect sincerity of their words and actions. Directly the actors show that they are conscious of the absurdity of their utterances the piece begins to drag. (qtd. in Booth 330)

Kerry Powell has revealed that a farce by "W. Lestocq" (the pseudonym of William Lestocq Wooldridge [d. 1920]) and E. M. Robson (d. 1932) titled *The Foundling* (1894), a success at the time that Wilde was writing *Earnest*, was also a likely source since the plots of both plays have some remarkable parallels: for example, in *The Foundling*, the 25-year-old orphan, confronted by the mother of the woman he wishes to marry, contemplates christening to resolve the problem of his birth. When he concludes that a middle-aged woman is his long-lost parent, he embraces her and cries "Mother!" – as does Jack Worthing in *Earnest* – which, however, has the wit and ingenuity lacking in *The Foundling*. Nevertheless, says Powell, some of the dialogue indicates Wilde's borrowings (122). Powell also cites another borrowing by Wilde from a recent successful farce at the Comedy Theatre by F. C. Philips and Charles Brookfield (see entry), titled *Godpapa* (1891), in which the hero, Reggie, concocts an imaginary illness of an acquaintance named Bunbury, in order to pursue pleasure while leading – as do Algernon and Jack in *Earnest* – a double life (127).

The Plot: In Act I, Jack Worthing, visiting the London flat of Algernon Moncrieff, is announced by Lane, the servant, as "Ernest." (Jack assumes the identity in town of an imaginary younger brother with a reputation for profligacy in order to escape from responsibilities in the country, where he lives. As Katharine Worth remarks, this "existential farce" is "a play of mirror images in which ordinary, everyday life can still be glimpsed through the comic distortions imposed upon it," 154.) Algernon, whose cousin, Gwendolen Fairfax, Jack wishes to marry, discovers the secret of his friend's double life (in Algernon's flat, Jack had left his cigarette case, which is inscribed "From little Cecily with her fondest love to her dear Uncle Jack").

Jack reveals that, as an orphan, he had been adopted by a Mr. Thomas Cardew, who had named him in his will as the guardian of his granddaughter, Cecily, but he refuses to give Algernon his country address. In turn, Algernon confesses to his own double life by revealing his devotion to an imaginary invalid named Bunbury, who lives in the country and whom he dutifully visits whenever his friend's "illness" worsens in order to escape from painful social obligations. Though Algernon believes that knowing Bunbury is useful in marriage, Jack intends to "kill off" his other identity, Ernest, if Gwendolen accepts him.

Gwendolen now arrives with her overbearing mother, Algernon's Aunt Augusta, Lady Bracknell. Left alone with Jack, Gwendolen professes her love for him because his name is Ernest (he consequently decides to be christened with that name). Lady Bracknell returns to interview Jack when she discovers that he is engaged to Gwendolen. In one of the most celebrated scenes in English drama, Jack responds to Lady Bracknell's question concerning his family by disclosing that he has "lost" both his parents – to which she responds: "Both? To lose one parent may be regarded as a misfortune – to lose *both* seems like carelessness."

He explains that he was found by Mr. Thomas Cardew in a handbag in the cloak room of the Victoria Station. She advises him "to try and acquire some relations as soon as possible, and to make a definite effort to produce at any rate one parent, of either sex, before the season is quite over," for she and Lord Bracknell would never dream of allowing their only daughter "to marry into a cloak-room, and form an alliance with a parcel." Until then, she forbids the marriage. After Lady Bracknell and Gwendolen leave, Algernon and Jack discuss how "Ernest" can be disposed of. Gwendolen suddenly enters to inform Jack that their marriage seems unlikely because of her mother's objections. When she asks Jack for his country address, Algernon writes it on his cuff and later informs Lane, his butler, that he is going Bunburying on the following day.

In Act II, Miss Prism, the governess and tutor, is giving a German lesson to Cecily Cardew in the garden of Manor House, Woolton, Hertfordshire, when the Rev. Chasuble enters and is persuaded to take a stroll with Miss Prism. When Algernon, posing as Ernest, arrives, Cecily is taken aback when he insists that he is not Jack's "wicked" brother: "If you are not, then you have certainly been deceiving us all in a very inexcusable manner. I hope you have not been leading a double life, pretending to be wicked and being really good all the time. That would be hypocrisy." They go into the house as Miss Prism and the Rector return.

Jack, dressed in funereal black, arrives and announces that his brother Ernest has died in Paris. He then asks the Rector to arrange a christening that afternoon. To everyone's surprise and joy, Cecily greets Jack with the news that Ernest, his brother, is within. Left alone with Cecily, Algernon expresses his love for her and proposes marriage; he is startled to learn that they have been "engaged" for the last three months, all of which is recorded in her diary. When they pledge their undying love for each other, Algernon is also now determined to be christened "Ernest," for Cecily informs him that "there is something in that name that seems to inspire absolute confidence" (the mirror image of Gwendolen's similar determination to marry someone named Ernest).

When Gwendolen arrives, she and Cecily are at first cordial, but when they discover that they are both engaged to Ernest, they bristle with hostility. Algernon and Jack's appearance ends misunderstanding, but new complications begin: neither Algernon nor Jack is Ernest, and the young women are drawn to each other when they discover that they have both been misled.

In Act III, the dandiacal world of the play, in which all the characters, including the servants, speak not with moral earnestness but with aesthetic ardor, is suggested by Gwendolen's remark to Cecily when Algernon seeks reconciliation: "In matters of grave importance, style, not sincerity is the vital thing." Lady Bracknell, discovering that her nephew Algernon is engaged to Cecily, questions Jack about the financial condition of his ward. When Jack discloses that she has £130,000 in the Funds, Lady Bracknell gives her blessing. However, Cecily, according to Mr. Cardew's will, will not come of age until she is 35. Moreover, Jack will not approve of the marriage unless Lady Bracknell agrees to his marriage to Gwendolen.

When the Rector announces that all is ready for the christening, he casually mentions Miss Prism's name – at which point Lady Bracknell demands to see her. Miss Prism, it appears, was responsible – some 28 years ago when employed by Lord Bracknell – for inadvertently depositing Jack in a handbag and the MS. of her three-volume novel of "more than usually revolting sentimentality" (as Lady Bracknall recalls) in the perambulator. Jack produces the very handbag that had been left at the Victoria Station; learns from Lady Bracknell that he had been named after his father, a general; leafs through the Army lists for the past 40 years; and discovers to his joy that *Ernest* is his actual name and that Algernon is his brother. All is brought to a happy conclusion as each couple, including Miss Prism and the Rev. Chasuble, embraces. Jack finally realizes "for the first time in [his] life the vital Importance of Being Earnest."

Early Theater Reviews: In general, the London production of *Earnest* impressed most of the critics. In the *Pall Mall Gazette* (15 Feb.), H. G. Wells, in an unsigned review, recalled that, though *An Ideal Husband* was "fairly bad," he "anticipated success." *Earnest*, he can now report, was "indeed as new a new comedy as we have had this year.... To the dramatic critic especially who leads a dismal life, it came with a flavour of rare holiday." Wells noted the play's Gilbertian quality but with "that wit that is all [Wilde's] own": "This time we must congratulate him unreservedly on a delightful revival of theatrical satire" (rpt. in Beckson).

In the *World* (20 Feb.), William Archer wrote that *Earnest* was "delightful to see, it sends wave after wave of laughter curling and foaming round the theatre.... What can a poor critic do with a play which raises no principle, whether of art or morals, creates its own canons and conventions, and is nothing but an absolutely wilful expression of an irrepressibly witty personality?" Such a play "imitates nothing, represents nothing, means nothing, is nothing, except a sort of *rondo capriccioso*, in which the artist's fingers run with crisp irresponsibility up and down the keyboard of life." To classify the play as "farce," Archer insists, is

far too gross and commonplace a word to apply to such an iridescent filament of fantasy. Incidents of the same nature of Algy Moncrieff's "Bunburying" and John Worthing's invention and subsequent suppression of his scapegrace brother Ernest have done duty in many a French vaudeville and English adaptation; but Mr. Wilde's humour transmutes them into something entirely new and individual.

Worthing's entrance in black to announce the "death" of Ernest while the audience knows that Algernon, masquerading as Ernest, is meanwhile making love to Cecily requires a "born playwright" to produce a "'sudden glory' of laughter" that fills the theater (rpt. in Archer's *The Theatrical "World" of 1895* [1896] and in Beckson).

The anonymous reviewer – actually the owner and editor Henry Labouchere – in *Truth* (21 Feb.) confesses to being amused, noting that Wilde's play is "as full of echoes as Prospero's isle – echoes of Marivaux, echoes of Meilhac, echoes of Maddison Morton, echoes of William Schwenk Gilbert and George Bernard Shaw.... But the very fact that Mr. Wilde's inspiration can be traced to so many sources proves that he can owe very little to any of them...." Like other reviewers, Labouchere senses that the "chief reason why the St. James's piece proves so amusing is because it is so completely dominated by its author....all the *dramatis personae*, from the heroes down to their butlers, talk pure and undiluted Wildese." The reviewer

predicts that "the public taste for 'Oscarisms' is not likely to be a lasting one.... It may pass, as the cult of the lily has passed, and the *mode* of the green carnation. Indeed, I am not sure that Mr. Edison could not, if he gave his mind to it, design an apparatus for turning out 'Oscarisms' automatically. We might put our pennies in the slot, press a button, and draw out 'Wilde' paradoxes on tape by the yard" (rpt. in Beckson).

In the *Speaker* (23 Feb.), the prominent critic A. B. Walkley, one of Wilde's staunchest defenders who regarded *Earnest* as the culmination of Wilde's development as a dramatist, announces that Wilde has "'found himself,' at last, as an artist in sheer nonsense....and better nonsense, I think, our stage has not seen." Unlike other farces on the English stage, *Earnest*, Walkley observes, excites laughter that is "absolutely free from bitter afterthought. Mr. Wilde makes his personages ridiculous, but...he does not ridicule them." A perceptive remark by Walkley (anticipating the Theater of the Absurd in the next century) is that "the conduct of the people in itself is rational enough; it is exquisitely irrational in the circumstances. Their motives, too, are quite rational in themselves; they are only irrational as being fitted to the wrong set of actions. And the result is that you have something like real life in detail, yet, in sum, absolutely unlike it" (rpt. in Beckson).

To be sure, there were dissenters. In the *Saturday Review* (23 Feb.), Bernard Shaw found *Earnest* amusing, but he argued that, "unless comedy touches me as well as amuses me, it leaves me with a sense of having wasted my evening. I go to the theater to be moved to laughter, not to be tickled or bustled into it; and that is why, though I laugh as much as anybody at a farcical comedy, I am out of spirits before the end of the second act, and out of temper before the end of the third, my miserable mechanical laughter intensifying these symptoms at every outburst." There is, Shaw admits, "plenty of this rib-tickling: for instance, the lies, the deceptions, the cross purposes, the sham mourning.... These could only have been raised from the farcical plane by making them occur to characters who had, like Don Quixote, convinced us of their reality and obtained some hold on our sympathy." Moreover, the play lacked humanity – an element that Shaw preferred in his own social and political drama (rpt. in Shaw's *Our Theatres in the Nineties*, vol. 1 [1932] and in

Beckson).

For the second edition of Frank Harris's *Oscar Wilde: His Life and Confessions* (1918), Shaw contributed "My Memories of Oscar Wilde," which was appended to the end of the second volume. He extended his opinion of *Earnest*: "Clever as it was, it was [Wilde's] first really heartless play. In the others the chivalry of the eighteenth century Irishman and the romance of the disciple of Théophile Gautier...not only gave a certain kindness and gallantry to the serious passages and to the handling of women, but provided that proximity of emotion without which laughter, however irresistible, is destructive and sinister. In *The Importance of Being Earnest* this had vanished; and the play, though extremely funny, was essentially hateful" (rpt. in Richard Ellmann, ed., *Oscar Wilde: A Collection of Critical Essays* [1969]).

The anonymous reviewer in *Theatre* (1 March) was probably Clement Scott, the editor, who had been particularly distressed when Wilde appeared before the curtain at the end of *Lady Windermere's Fan* with a cigarette in hand. Calling *Earnest* "frivolous," he regards the play as having been written by "an author who caters for the less intelligent section of the public" (rpt. in Beckson). In *Punch* (25 March), the inevitable parody appeared, written by Wilde's friend Ada Leverson. Titled "The Advisability of Not Being Brought Up in a Handbag: A Trivial Tragedy for Wonderful People," the brief sketch includes a new character, Mr. Dorian (borrowed from Wilde's novel), of whom Aunt Augusta says to Algernon: "Mr. Dorian has a beautiful nature. And it is *such* a blessing to think that he was not brought up in a handbag, like so many young men of the present day."

The reviewers of the New York production were generally unimpressed. In the *New York Herald* (23 April), the writer, noting that Wilde's name was on the program, remarked that the audience was not a large one. As for the play, it had "none of the bustle and grotesquerie of farce." The reviewer in the *New York Times* (23 April), who did not mention Wilde as the author, remarked that the audience was "fairly appreciative." As for Wilde's epigrammatic wit, the reviewer voiced the familiar complaint concerning Wilde's dialogue: "It almost seems that it could be no great triumph of ingenuity of this sort but simple manipulation of

a crank." The drama critic William Winter for the *New York Daily Tribune*, who had little appreciation for Wilde's work, declined to review the play. The *Sun* (23 April) published the rare review that praised the New York production: "The audience did not give the smallest indication that it knew or cared anything about the playwright, further than to appreciate the fact that he had written an exceedingly clever piece."

Early Book Review: In contrast to the numerous reviews of the stage production, the publication of *Earnest* in 1899 was virtually ignored by the press. Wilde told Ross: "I am sorry my play is boycotted by the press, particularly for Smithers's sake; he has shown great pluck in bringing it out at all. However I hope some of the faithful, and all the elect, will buy copies" (*Letters* 782). There was a brief anonymous review in the weekly publication *Outlook* (18 March), which hailed the play for adding to the "gaiety of nations in more permanent form" but did not mention Wilde by name:

> ...it is the work of an immensely clever man playing the fool in so sustained and resolute a manner as to make the work of a piece. Hence, its partial failure as comedy, and its entire success as farce. Comedy, we believe, should have its serious moments; but here the wise face behind the grin is nowhere visible, and the author runs sad risk of being himself confounded with the characters he makes ridiculous. But for this one and certainly large defect, we are inclined to be grateful for "The Importance of Being Earnest."

The reviewer, focusing on the scene in Act I in which Lady Bracknell questions Jack, regards the dialogue as "excellent comedy," but the "remaining dialogue is so often witty that we overlook a great deal of its wrong-headedness. The author's pose is so extreme that the spice of truth that should inevitably give piquancy to satire is frequently lacking. The wit then becomes more cold than spontaneous."

Manuscripts: The Clark Library has the TS. of a letter to George Alexander with the early scenario of the play and a notebook containing Wilde's earliest jottings of notes and dialogue. The Arents Tobacco Collection of the New York Public Library has MSS. of Acts I and II, and the British Library has the remainder of the play – that is, Acts III and IV. Also in the Arents Collection is the recently acquired three-act TS. of the play, once in the possession of the New York producer Charles Frohman, who apparently had the version prepared for the New York production. The Arents Collection also has a TS. of Acts I, III, and IV as well as Wilde's revised TS. prepared for the 1899 edition. The New York Public Library at Lincoln Center has a TS. of the four-act version of the play (dated 31 Oct. 1894), also once in Frohman's possession. The British Library has the licensing copy of the play with the title *Lady Lancing: A Serious Comedy for Trivial People*. The Harvard Theater Collection has George Alexander's TS. (a prompt copy of the play) with his autograph revisions. Texas has the page proofs, revised by Wilde, of the 1899 edition.

References: A. E. W. Mason, *Sir George Alexander and the St. James's Theatre* (1935; rpt. 1969); Arthur Ganz, "The Meaning of *The Importance of Being Earnest*," *Modern Drama* (May 1963); Charles B. Paul and Robert D. Pepper, "The Importance of Reading Alfred: Oscar Wilde's Debt to Alfred de Musset," *Bulletin of the New York Public Library* (Dec. 1971); Michael Booth, ed., *English Plays of the Nineteenth Century*, vol. 3 (1973); William Green, "Oscar Wilde and the Bunburys," *Modern Drama* (March 1978); Russell Jackson, ed., *The Importance of Being Earnest* (1980); Katharine Worth, *Oscar Wilde* (1983); John Glavin, "Deadly Earnest and Earnest Revived: Wilde's Four-Act Play," *Nineteenth-Century Studies* 1 (1987); Harold Bloom, ed., *Oscar Wilde's "The Importance of Being Earnest"* (1988); Kerry Powell, "The Importance of Being at Terry's," *Oscar Wilde and the Theatre of the 1890s* (1990); Peter Raby, "The Making of *The Importance of Being Earnest*," *TLS* (20 Dec. 1991); Peter Raby, "The Origins of *The Importance of Being Earnest*," *Modern Drama* (Spring 1994); Karl Beckson, "Narcissistic Reflections in a Wilde Mirror," *Modern Drama* (Spring 1994); Joseph Donohue and Ruth Berggren, eds., *Oscar Wilde's "The Importance of Being Earnest": The First Production* (1995); Peter Raby, "*The Importance of Being Earnest": A Reader's Companion* (1995).

"IMPRESSION: LE RÉVEILLON"

Published: First appeared as an early version (lines 13–24) of "Lotus Leaves" in *Irish Monthly* 5 (Feb. 1877): 133–35; rev. with its new title (its sub-title suggesting, in painting, a dramatic effect of light against a dark background, as in the Italian term *chiaroscuro*) in *Poems* (1881).

In this "impression," inspired by French Impressionism, the attempt to capture fleeting images is suggested by its first stanza:

> The sky is laced with fitful red
> The circling mists and shadows flee,
> The dawn is rising from the sea,
> Like a white lady from her bed.

A "long wave of yellow light / Breaks silently on tower and hall," waking into flight "some fluttering bird, / And all the chestnut tops are stirred, / And all the branches streaked with gold." In the late 19th century, the elimination of discursiveness (mention of science, religion, or morality) in impressionistic verse eventually led to such developments in the early 20th century as Imagism and Vorticism, manifestations of Modernism.

Manuscript: The Clark Library has an early draft of "Lotus Leaves," lines 1–4 and 9–12 (printed in Mason 83–84).

"IMPRESSION DE PARIS: LE JARDIN DES TUILERIES": *See* "LE JARDIN DES TUILERIES"

"IMPRESSION DE VOYAGE"

Published: First appeared as "Hellas! Hellas!" in the Boston *Pilot* 40 (28 July 1877): 4; rev. as "Impression de Voyage" in *Waifs and Strays: A Terminal Magazine of Oxford Poetry* 1 (March 1880): 77; further rev. in *Poems* (1881), the title given as "Impression du Voyage" but in the further revised *Poems* (1882), the "de" is restored in the title. In the original publication, Wilde indicated that the poem was written in Katakolo, on the west coast of the Peloponnesian peninsula in April 1877, when Wilde traveled to Greece with his former teacher at Trinity College, Dublin, the classical scholar John Mahaffy (see entry).

In this sonnet, Greece – "the flower-strewn hills of Arcady" – is the destination. The images of sea and ship are accompanied by the "ripple of girls' laughter at the stern, / The only sounds," but by sundown, with "a red sun upon the seas," the speaker exclaims: "I stood upon the soil of Greece at last!"

Manuscript: The Berg Collection has the MS.

"IMPRESSION DU MATIN"

Published: First appeared as "Impression de Matin" in *World: A Journal for Men and Women* 14 (2 March 2 1881): 15; rev. as "Impression du Matin" in *Poems* (1881).

The title of this poem may have been inspired by the English title of Claude Monet's painting *Impression: Sunrise*, which, when exhibited in 1874, prompted a hostile critic to christen the work of the new Parisian school with the term *impressionisme*. The first lines of Wilde's poem borrow Whistler's title for one of his most famous paintings, *Nocturne in Blue and Gold: Old Battersea Bridge*. Whistler had mentioned this painting at the libel trial brought by him in 1878 against the art critic John Ruskin, who had impugned his artistic integrity. The jury awarded Whistler a farthing (one fourth of a penny), implying that his reputation had suffered little. Nevertheless, the trial permitted Whistler to publicize his "nocturnes," "harmonies," and "symphonies." In 1879, Wilde wrote of Whistler's *Harmony in Green and Gold* as an "extremely good example of what ships lying at anchor on a summer evening are from the 'Impressionist point of view'": see *Miscellanies* (1908), 27.

The poem begins: "The Thames nocturne of blue and gold / Changed to a Harmony in grey" (another borrowing from Whistler's *Harmony in Grey: Chelsea in Ice*, ca. 1864). But a Whistlerian yellow fog comes "creeping down" to effect an aesthetic transformation with its shadows: "St. Paul's / Loomed like a bubble o'er the town." The final lines, however, depart radically from the color harmony of the opening stanzas with the depiction of a prostitute, who provides a comforting moral for Victorian readers, an indication that Wilde's aestheticism was difficult to maintain without modification: "But one pale woman all alone... / Loitered beneath the gas lamps' flare, / With lips of flame and heart of stone."

Manuscript: The Beinecke Library has a MS. version, dated January 1891, of only three stanzas (apparently written from memory) with the title "To My Friend Luther Munday," which appeared in facsimile in the *Picture Magazine* 5 (Feb. 1895): 101 (printed in Mason 176). The poem, originally in the Lyric Club Guest Book, was removed when the club was disbanded. Munday (1857–1922), a theatrical producer and director, was secretary of the Lyric Club (1887–93). The poem facing "Impression du Matin" in the guest book was "In the Garden," which became part of "Impressions: I. Le Jardin."

"IMPRESSIONS: I. LE JARDIN. II. LA MER"

Published: *Our Continent* (Philadelphia) 1 (15 Feb. 1882): 9; rpt. in *Poems* (1908). On 4 January 1882, the London *World* published a cablegram that presumably had been sent to Richard D'Oyly Carte before Wilde left for America: "Will Wilde write poem, twenty lines, terms guinea a line; *subject – sunflower or lily*, to be delivered on arrival to order of – – " (qtd. in Mason 125). "Le Jardin," consisting of three quatrains, is the poem made "to order," with its allusions to the lily and sunflower, the Aesthete's emblematic flowers.

In Part I, "Le Jardin" (which the *St. Moritz Post* in Switzerland published, with a few minor differences, as "Autumn" in its Special Christmas Number in 1888), Wilde borrows the term *impression* from the French Impressionist painters of the 1870s and 1880s to depict the fleeting autumnal effects on "the lily's withered chalice" and the "gaudy leonine sunflower," which "Hangs black and barren on its stalk," concluding with the roses that "lie upon the grass / Like little shreds of crimson silk."

In Part II, "La Mer," the sea has been stormy and "A wild moon in this wintry sky / Gleams like an angry lion's eye / Out of a mane of tawny clouds." The steersman at the wheel "Is but a shadow in the gloom." The "shattered storm has left its trace / Upon this huge and heaving dome...." In both poems, the exclusive focus on imagery and the avoidance of discursiveness or truths drawn from nature for the enlightenment of Victorian readers suggest anticipations of Imagism in the early 20th century, particularly in the final image of "thin threads of yellow foam / Float on the waves like ravelled lace."

Manuscripts: The Hyde Collection has a draft of "Le Jardin" (printed in Mason 124, 126). A facsimile of a MS. (the poem now titled "Autumn") appeared in Sotheby's auction catalogue (New York, dated 1 Oct. 1980). The Jeremy Mason Collection has a fair copy version with the title "In the Garden" (dated Jan. 1891). For its provenance, see the MS. section of "Impression du Matin."

"IMPRESSIONS: I. LES SILHOUETTES II. LA FUITE DE LA LUNE"

Published: *Pan* 1 (23 April 1881): 4; rev. in *Poems* (1881) and in (1882). For details on the first publication of "La Fuite de la Lune," see "Lotus Leaves."

Like other "impressions" by Wilde, these poems draw inspiration from the French Impressionists of the l870s and l880s (see "Impression du Matin"); at the same time, they indicate a turning away from Victorian discursiveness (often, the teaching of moral precepts). Anticipating early 20th-century Imagism, these poems focus exclusively on the images as perceived by the speaker.

Part I, "Les Silhouettes," presents images associated with the sea: the moon, "like a withered leaf," is "blown across the stormy bay" and "Etched clear upon the pallid sand / Lies the black boat." But in the final stanza, the focus shifts to a scene reminiscent of the painting, Jean François Millet's *The Sower* (1850):

And overhead the curlews cry,
Where through the dusky upland grass
The young brown-throated reapers pass,
Like silhouettes against the sky.

In Part II, "La Fuite de la Lune" ("The Flight of the Moon"), there is, to "outer senses," peace: "A dreamy peace on either hand, / Deep silence in the shadowy land" except for the cry of "some lone bird disconsolate" (a characteristic Romantic device of fusing bird with poet). The moon is now enveloped by silence, but

...suddenly the moon withdraws
Her sickle from the lightening skies,
And to her sombre cavern flies,
Wrapped in a veil of yellow gauze.

Manuscripts: For Part I, the Clark Library has an untitled MS. of lines 1–8 (printed in Dulau 7); the Bibliotheca Bodmeriana (Cologny-Geneva) has a MS. of this poem with the title "Impression du Soir" but without lines 5–8; the Hyde Collection has a MS. of the complete poem. For Part II, Dartmouth College has a MS. titled "Le Crépuscule" (printed in Mason 85–86), a transformed new poem derived from Part III of "Lotus Leaves" (see Mason 81). In turn, "Le Crépuscule" was revised and published as "Impressions. II. La Fuite de la Lune" in *Pan*. The Hyde Collection has a MS. containing further revisions of "La Fuite de la Lune" after its first appearance.

"IMPRESSIONS DU THÉÂTRE"

A section title for six poems in *Poems* (1881).

IMPRESSIONS OF AMERICA

Published: March 1906 by Keystone Press (Sunderland, England), a limited edition of 500 copies edited by Mason, who also provided an introduction. (This lecture is also known as "Personal Impressions of America.") The dedication, to a friend of Robert Ross and collector of Wilde material, reads as follows: "TO / WALTER LEDGER: / PIGNUS AMICITIAE" (Latin for "Assurance of Friendship").

In his introduction, Mason briefly outlines Wilde's lecture tour of America in l882 (see Lectures in America). On his return to England in 1883, Wilde delivered his lecture on America in various cities in this year and in the following two years (see Lectures in Britain). Instead of the knee-breeches and velvet jacket that he wore in many appearances in America, Wilde appeared in ordinary evening dress and carried an orange-coloured silk handkerchief in his breast pocket.

The Lecture: On arriving in America, Wilde was initially impressed by the fact that, "if the Americans are not the most well-dressed people in the world, they are the most comfortably dressed," unlike the English, who are too often seen "in close contact with rags." Also, Wilde noticed that everybody in America "seems in a hurry to catch a train. This is a state of things which is not favourable to poetry or romance. Had Romeo or Juliet been in a constant state of anxiety about trains..., Shakespeare could not have given us those lovely balcony scenes...." Furthermore, because America is the "noisiest country that ever existed" one is not awakened by nightingales but by steam whistles. Since all Art "depends upon exquisite and delicate sensibility," the musical faculty will ultimately be adversely affected.

As for the cities, they cannot be compared with such beautiful English places as Oxford, Cambridge, Salisbury, or Winchester, which are "lovely relics of a beautiful age." Still, here and there, there is a "good deal of beauty" in American cities "but only where the American has not attempted to create it. Where the Americans have attempted to produce beauty they have signally failed." The manner in which the Americans have applied science to modern life is apparent in New York. Unlike England, where an inventor is regarded almost as a "crazy man," America honors its inventors, and the "shortest road to wealth" is the reward for ingenuity in applying science to the "work of man." The result is that there is "no country in the world where machinery is so lovely as in America." Until he saw the water-works at Chicago, Wilde had not realized the "wonders of machinery; the rise and fall of the steel rods, the symmetrical motion of the great wheels is the most beautifully rhythmic thing I have ever seen" (the tone throughout the lecture is, to be sure, facetious).

Wilde was disappointed, he remarks, with Niagara Falls: "Every American bride is taken there, and the sight of the stupendous waterfall must be one of the earliest, if not the keenest, disappointments in American married life." The most beautiful area in America is the West, which requires a six-day journey in a train drawn by "an ugly tin-kettle of a steam engine." San Francisco, he believes, is a "really beautiful city," and China Town, populated by Chinese labourers, "is the most artistic town I have ever come across. The people – strange, melancholy Orientals, whom many people would call common, and they are certainly very poor – have determined that they will have nothing about them that is not beautiful." In a restaurant he visited, he found them drinking tea out of china cups "as delicate as the petals of a rose-leaf, whereas at the gaudy hotels I was supplied with a delf cup an inch and a half thick."

Salt Lake City has only two noted buildings, one being the Tabernacle, which looks like a soup-kettle but is decorated with religious subjects in the "native spirit of the early Florentine painters, representing people of our own day in the dress of the period side by side with people of Biblical history who are clothed in some romantic costume." From Salt Lake City, he traveled to the Rocky Mountains, where he saw Leadville, Colorado, the "richest city in the world." It also has the "reputation of being the roughest, and every man carries a revolver." Since he expected miners in his audience, he lectured to them on the ethics of Art and read passages from Benvenuto Cellini's autobiography, with which they seemed "much delighted," but he was "reproved" for not having

brought Cellini with him: "I explained that he had been dead for some little time, which elicited the enquiry 'Who shot him?'"

When he arrived at the theater to deliver his lecture, he was told that just before his arrival two men "had been seized for committing a murder, and in that theatre they had been brought on to the stage at eight o'clock in the evening, and then and there tried and executed before a crowded audience. But I found these miners very charming and not at all rough." Wilde found the knowledge of Art "so infinitesimal" west of the Rocky Mountains that an art patron, who had been a miner, sued the railroad company for damages because the plaster cast of the Venus de Milo arrived without the arms.

The young American men are "pale and precocious, or sallow and supercilious, but American girls are pretty and charming – little oases of pretty unreasonableness in a vast desert of practical common-sense." The men, he notes, are "entirely given to business; they have, as they say, their brains in front of their heads." In America, poverty is a "necessary accompaniment to civilisation. There at any rate is a country that has no trappings, no pageants and no gorgeous ceremonies." He did see two processions: "...the Fire Brigade preceded by the Police, the other was the Police preceded by the Fire Brigade."

Every male is allowed to vote when he reaches the age of 21, Wilde notes, and Americans are "the best politically educated people in the world." Wilde concludes with the remark that it is "well worth one's while to go to a country which can teach us the beauty of the word FREEDOM and the value of the thing LIBERTY."

Manuscript: The Huntington Library has Wilde's autograph notes in outline form on 12 leaves (given the title "Lecture Notes on America" by the library cataloguer), which follow the subject order of the lecture.

"IN THE FOREST"

Published: *Lady's Pictorial* (Christmas Number, 1889): 9; rpt. in *Poems* (1908). The illustration by John Bernard Partridge (see "Fantaisies Décoratives") depicts a toga-clad figure who is crowned with laurel and holding a lyre while gazing at a boy dressed in a leopardskin dancing in the woods.

In this lyric poem, set at twilight, the speaker is

startled, for there "Flashes my Faun!" Singing and dancing through the copse, the Faun evades the speaker: "...I know not which I should follow, / Shadow or song!" He appeals to the Hunter to snare the Faun's shadow and to the Nightingale to catch the Faun's song, "Else moonstruck with music and madness / I track him in vain!"

Manuscript: Martin Birnbaum, in *Oscar Wilde: Fragments and Memories* (1920), 11, quotes an untitled MS. of this poem (with slight differences in the final two lines from the published version), inscribed in a copy of *Intentions* and presented to Clyde Fitch (see entry). The volume remains unlocated.

"IN THE GOLD ROOM: A HARMONY"

Published: *Poems* (1881); rev. in (1882).

The title of this poem, which consists of three six-line stanzas, alludes to many of Whistler's paintings, which he often titled "harmonies," but Wilde was probably inspired by Whistler's *The Music Room* (1860) – later retitled *Harmony in Green and Rose* – and by *At the Piano* (1859) and *A Harmony of Yellow and Gold: The Gold Girl* (1876), the settings of which are suggested in the poem: "Her ivory hands on the ivory keys / Strayed in a fitful fantasy...." The gold room harmonizes with the pianist's gold hair, but Wilde introduces suggestive erotic Swinburnian imagery where Whistler had focused on color effects:

And her sweet red lips on these lips of mine
Burned like the ruby fire set
In the swinging lamp of a crimson shrine,
Or the bleeding wounds of the pomegranate....

The final image appears in other early Wilde poems.

Manuscripts: The Clark Library has Mason's personal interleaved copy of his bibliography, in which the poem is transcribed (opposite p. 307) from an unidentified MS. Some variations of a MS., unlocated, are printed in Mason 307. In Francis Edwards's sale catalogue, No. 355, for October 1915, p. 72, the poem is quoted from an "original" MS.

INTENTIONS

Published: 2 May 1891, by James R. Osgood McIlvaine & Co. (London) and by Dodd, Mead & Co. (New York).

Contents: [See separate entries for each work:] The Decay of Lying – Pen, Pencil, and Poison – The Critic as Artist, Part I and II – The Truth of Masks.

Early Reviews: The anonymous reviewer in the *Pall Mall Gazette* (12 May), after a lengthy discourse on the "Paradise of Dainty Paradoxes" through which a reader must wander in Wilde's volume, writes that, "whatever else it may be, [Wilde's] book is entertaining. He has every qualification for becoming a popular Pater." Aside from stylistic mannerisms, "there is much excellent matter in Mr. Wilde's dialogues and essays. His criticisms are often just and sometimes luminous; his wit, except where we smell the formula, is very pretty indeed." The reviewer concludes: "He has written a fascinating, stimulating book, with more common sense in it than he would perhaps care to be accused of" (rpt. in Beckson).

In the *Athenaeum* (6 June), the reviewer is annoyed by the volume's "showy paradoxes," but Wilde "succeeds in proving that he has something to say, and it is a pity that he should think, or find, it necessary to resort to the tricks of the smart advertiser in order to attract attention to his wares." Like others during Wilde's career, the reviewer regards Wilde's wit as a mere reversal of some well-established truth. Of the various essays, "The Decay of Lying" is "by the far the cleverest" (rpt. in Beckson).

In the *Speaker* (4 July), Arthur Symons, one of Wilde's most perceptive critics at the time, writes that Wilde is "too witty to be taken seriously":

A passion for caprice, a whimsical Irish temperament, a love of art for art's sake – it is in qualities such as these that we find the origin of the beautiful farce of aestheticism, the exquisite echoes of the *Poems*, the subtle decadence of *Dorian Gray*, and the paradoxical truths, the perverted common sense, of the *Intentions*.

Though Wilde, says Symons, has "gained a reputation for frivolity," he has "always been serious in the reality of his devotion to art. The better part of his new book is simply a plea for the dignity, an argument for the supremacy, of imaginative art." In the essays of *Intentions*, Wilde is "at his best, to our thinking, when he is most himself – an artist in epigram...."

Closing with a touch of facetiousness, Symons acknowledges Wilde's self-transformation, evident in the volume under review:

After achieving a reputation by doing nothing, he is in a fair way to beat his own record by real achievements. He is a typical figure, alike in the art of life and the art of literature, and, if he might be supposed for a moment to represent anything but himself, he would be the perfect representative of all that is meant by the modern use of the word Decadence. (rpt. in Beckson).

In the *Academy* (4 July), a friend and admirer of Wilde, Richard Le Gallienne, writes that

Mr. Wilde's worship of beauty is proverbial, it has made a latter-day myth of him before his time; and yet, at least in these essays, his gift of comic perception is above it, and, rightly viewed, all his "flute-toned" periods are written in the service of the comic muse.... I, for one, take Mr. Wilde very seriously as a creator of work which gives me much and various new pleasure: he is so absolutely alive at every point, so intensely practical....

Wilde is "wittier than is quite fair in a man of his nationality," Le Gallienne writes, and "he often writes prose that one loves to say over for mere pleasure of ear – his own literary touchstone." *Intentions*, Le Gallienne concludes, is "delightful reading," especially for its humor, "and if I have failed to do [the essays] justice, it is but a proof of Mr. Wilde's paradox that it is impossible to do justice to anything we care about" (rpt. in Beckson).

Reference: R. J. Green, "Oscar Wilde's *Intentions*: An Early Modernist Manifesto," *British Journal of Aesthetics* (Autumn 1973); Lawrence Danson, *Wilde's Intentions: The Artist in His Criticism* (1997).

"INTENTIONS: APHORISMS ON ART"

The Bibliotheca Bodmeriana (Cologny-Geneva) has this one-page MS. signed by "Sebastian Melmoth," Wilde's adopted pseudonym after his release from prison. The first aphorism states: "The duty we owe to history is to rewrite it."

IRELAND AND ENGLAND, WILDE ON THE RELATIONSHIP BETWEEN

As Davis Coakley writes on a widely perceived misconception concerning Wilde's relationship to Ireland,

The fact that Wilde left Ireland in his early twenties and returned only on two occasions has been used to argue that the writer rejected his native country. Wilde's exile, however, unlike that of James Joyce, was not designed to be symbolic. Wilde rarely returned to Ireland for the simple reason that his father had died and his mother had moved to London, and as a consequence the family base was no longer in Dublin. (2)

Moreover, Coakley writes, Wilde's distancing himself from "traditional Irish themes for his inspiration" was partly attributable to his wish to avoid writing "stage Irish" plays, popular in his day. Nevertheless, Wilde was a supporter of Irish causes despite the fact that his allegiances rarely surfaced except in his unsigned reviews and in some of his American lectures in 1882.

During that time, Wilde openly professed his support of Home Rule, though with increasing fame and stature as a man of letters, he generally avoided expressing his political sentiments concerning Ireland. On 5 March 1882, he reportedly said in the course of a lecture on "The English Renaissance," delivered in Milwaukee, that he was "strongly in sympathy" with Parnell's parliamentary movement for Irish Home Rule (qtd. in Lewis and Smith 215). He embraced what Lady Wilde had said: "...Parnell is the man of destiny. He will strike off the fetters and free Ireland, and throne her as queen among the nations" (qtd. in Ellmann 127/122). On St. Patrick's Day in the St. Paul Opera House, Wilde spoke for ten or fifteen minutes to a "huge crowd" of Hibernians, telling them that "when Ireland gains her independence, its schools of art and other educational branches will be revived and Ireland will regain the proud position she once held among the nations of Europe" (qtd. in Lewis and Smith 226).

On 6 April 1882, the San Francisco *Examiner* reported that on the previous evening, Wilde averred, in the course of his lecture on "Irish Poets and Poetry of the Nineteenth Century," that the "English conquest destroyed [Irish] art, but could not destroy the poetry of the Celtic people, as that was something beyond the reach of the sword, and vandal hand of the conquering Saxon.... The poetry of the Irish people, he claimed, ever kept alive the fires of patriotism in the hearts of the Irish people."

In an anonymous article in the *Pall Mall Gazette* (17 Feb. 1887), titled "The Poets and the People" (see entry), Wilde turned on Swinburne, a poet he had greatly admired, who in "The Commonweal: A Song for Unionists" (*Times*, 1 July 1886), had attacked the Irish for their agitation for Home Rule. He was, wrote Wilde, one "who has hitherto posed as the poet of freedom, and even licence – some would say licentiousness – when he does turn his attention to practical affairs does his best to abuse and dishearten a nation that is heroically struggling against the injustice of centuries and panting for national freedom."

In a review signed "O.W." in the *Pall Mall Gazette* (13 April 1889) of J. A. Froude's *The Chiefs of Dunboy* (see "Mr. Froude's Blue Book"), Wilde asserts that the English occupation of Ireland has been "one of the great tragedies of modern Europe," and in official publications, England has given to the world "the history of her shame." Wilde concludes that "as a record of the incapacity of a Teutonic to rule a Celtic people against their own wishes, [Froude's] book is not without value."

References: Oscar Wilde, *Irish Poets and Poetry of the Nineteenth Century*, ed. Robert D. Pepper (1972); Davis Coakley, *Oscar Wilde: The Importance of Being Irish* (1994); Declan Kiberd, "Wilde and the English Question," *TLS* (l6 Dec. 1994); Neil Sammells, "Rediscovering the Irish Wilde," *Rediscovering Oscar Wilde*, ed. C. George Sandulescu (1994); Richard Pine, *The Thief of Reason: Oscar Wilde and Modern Ireland* (1995).

IRISH POETS AND POETRY OF THE NINETEENTH CENTURY

Published: Book Club of California (San Francisco, 1972), ed. Robert D. Pepper. The title page indicates that this lecture, delivered in Platt's Hall, San Francisco, on 5 April 1882, has been edited from Wilde's MS. and reconstructed, in part, from contemporary newspaper accounts. See, also, Michael J. O'Neill, "Irish Poets of the Nineteenth Century: Unpublished Lecture Notes of Oscar Wilde," *University Review* (Dublin) 1 (Spring 1955): 29–33.

The Lecture: According to the report of the lecture in the *Chronicle*, Wilde began with remarks concerning the effect of the "English occupation" of Ireland:

...we have had no national art in Ireland at all, and there is not the slightest chance of our having it ever until we get that right of legislative independence so unjustly robbed from us; until we are really an Irish nation – a nation for whose constitutional liberty Henry Grattan [member of the Irish Parliament, opposed to union with Britain] lived and died. There is, however, one art which no tyranny can kill and no penal laws can stifle, the art of poetry – an art which is one of the supreme triumphs of the race to which we belong....

The opening portion of the extant MS. appears to continue from this point: Wilde speaks of a time when the poets in Ireland were honored by being allowed to wear four colors in their dress, whereas the peasantry were allowed to wear only one color; moreover, poets were encouraged to wear whatever kind of clothes thought to be attractive, "a state of things which I am sure I would wish to see revived for the benefit of modern poets." From "those idyllic days down to the evil times when the bards lurked with the outlaws in forest glen and mountain cave, and lit with the fire of enthusiasm the hearts of the weak or hurled at the oppressor their indomitable scorn, the poets were the lifeblood and heart-blood of Irish life."

Wilde then discourses on the Celtic imagination (drawing upon Matthew Arnold's *On the Study of Celtic Literature*, 1867), an imagination, Wilde states, to which "we owe nearly all the great beauties of modern literature," such as the spirit of modern romance, style in literature, the use of rhyme (a Celtic invention), as well as "those chords of penetrating passion and melancholy which swept over Europe with the publication of Macpherson's *Ossian* [1765] and whose echo still lingers in the work of every poet of our day." Wilde contends that such poets as Byron and Keats were influenced by this work; moreover, Tennyson drew upon the Celtic romances for his epic poem *The Idylls of the King*. William Morris, a Celt by birth, "infused the Celtic sentiment into his treatment of the old Greek legends of his

Earthly Paradise so exquisitely that they seem quite new to us, and just before I left England Mr. Burne-Jones, another Celt, was beginning the designs for a great picture from the Arthurian cycle."

Wilde alludes to the men of the Young Ireland movement, particularly to Charles Gaven Duffy, one of his friends in London: "...the poets amongst them were men who had made their lives *noble poems also*, men who had not merely written about the sword but were ready to bear it.... The greatest of them all and one of the best poets of this century in Europe was, I need not say, Thomas Davis" – from whose works Wilde read selections. "But of all the remarkable literary figures of this time none was so wonderful in genius as Clarence Mangan – the Edgar Allan Poe of our country, whose romantic life and wretched death are among the many tragedies of literature." Wilde then read a passage from one of Mangan's works as he did from the works of various other Irish writers, including Aubrey de Vere and Lady Wilde ("Speranza").

Celtic poetic genius, Wilde remarks, "never flags or wearies; it is as sweet by the groves of California as by the groves of Ireland, as strong in foreign lands as in the land which gave it birth.... The Saxon took our lands from us and left them desolate, we took their language and added new beauties to it" (here the MS. ends). The San Francisco newspaper, the *Call*, adds a postscript to the material in the MS. that Wilde had observed that "of the three great races comprising the foundation stock of America, Saxon, Teuton, and Celtic races, the latter were incomparably the most artistic." Because San Francisco was always so generous to the cause of Ireland, Wilde was pained that this city had no library of Irish literature; he urged that a museum of Irish art be established there.

Manuscript: The Hyde Collection contains the MS. of 34 leaves in two exercise books, apparently, as Pepper notes, "fragments, perhaps rough drafts, of the completed lecture" (25).

IRVING, HENRY (1838–1905)

The most celebrated Shakespearean actor of his day, Irving (the stage name of John Henry Brodribb) performed the role of Macbeth in December 1876, when Wilde was in the audience. In November 1879, Wilde and John Ruskin (see entry) went to see Irving as Shylock. Ruskin, who

knew Irving, may have introduced Wilde to him on this occasion. In *Poems*, Wilde included a sonnet "Fabien dei Franchi" (see entry); which describes Irving's virtuoso performance in Dion Boucicault's *The Corsican Brothers* (1880). In the fourth edition of *Poems* (1882), Wilde added the dedication "To My Friend Henry Irving."

In a letter to a correspondent during his American lecture tour in 1882, Wilde alluded to Irving as one of his "heroes" (*Letters* 105). In his 1885 review "'Hamlet' at the Lyceum" (see entry), Wilde called Irving's performance "that combination of poetic grace with absolute reality which is so eternally delightful."

In late December 1888, Wilde wrote to congratulate Irving on his "magnificent production" and his "magnificent performance" in *Macbeth* at the Lyceum Theatre with Ellen Terry as Lady Macbeth. Wilde cites the murder scene and banquet scene as "two of the finest, most imaginative bits of acting I have ever seen. They were instances of the highest *style*, and of the most subtle psychological insight and the true temper of tragedy never left you all through the play" (*Letters* 235).

In "The Soul of Man under Socialism" – of all places – Wilde praises Irving's acting style:

With his marvellous and vivid personality, with a style that has really a true colour element in it, with his extraordinary power, not over mere mimicry but over imaginative and intellectual creation, Mr. Irving, had his sole object been to give the public what they wanted, could have produced the commonest plays in the commonest manner, and made as much success and money as a man could possibly desire.

Irving's object, Wilde continues, is "to realise his own perfection as an artist, under certain conditions and in certain forms of Art." Wilde seized the moment by sending Irving a letter, in which he mentions the essay and stresses the point that "there is an audience for a poet inside a theatre, though there is no or but a small audience for a poet outside a theatre." He then asks Irving to produce *The Duchess of Padua*, if only for one performance: "You know that you have no warmer and sincerer admirer than myself, and your theatre has always been to me the one link between our stage and our literature" (*Letters* 286). But Irving declined the invitation, as he had when Wilde had previously sent him a copy of *Vera; or, The Nihilists*.

In 1892, at the time that *Salomé* was officially banned from the stage by the Examiner of Plays, the Select Committee on stage censorship had been conducting hearings on the issue: Henry Irving, among other prominent figures in the theater, spoke strongly in favor of censorship.

Reference: Madeleine Bingham, *Henry Irving and the Victorian Theatre* (1978)

ISAACSON, HENRY BEVAN: *See* PRISON YEARS, 1895–97

"ITALIA"

Published: According to Mason – in a note opposite p. 177 of his personal interleaved copy of his 1914 bibliography, in the Clark Library – this poem first appeared as "To Italy" in the Boston *Pilot* in 1877, yet it remains unlocated, for the available issues in that year are in fragmentary condition. In *Poems* (1881), the title is "Italia."

In this sonnet, Wilde deplores the fallen state of Italy (echoed in "Sonnet on Approaching Italy"), despite its new unity as a nation in 1870: "Ay! fallen, though the nations hail thee Queen / Because rich gold in every town is seen..." (The rhyming words *Queen*, *seen*, and *green* are also present in Wilde's "Urbs Sacra Aeterna," which takes up a similar theme of anti-clericalism in modern Italy.) Wilde urges Italy to look southward, "where Rome's desecrated town / Lies mourning for her God-anointed King! / Look heaven-ward! shall God allow this thing?" The archangel Raphael, one of seven who stand before God, is evoked: he "shall come / And smite the Soiler with the sword of pain."

IVES, GEORGE (1867–1950)

A self-described "evolutionary anarchist," Ives was also a poet and penologist who, around 1893, founded a secret homosexual society, the Order of Chaeronea, the name taken from the town in ancient Greece where, in the late 19th century, the remains were found of an elite corps of 150 pairs of male lovers who died in 338 BC in a battle against Philip II of Macedon. Chosen from noble families and bound together by loyalty to Thebes, these lovers were known as the Sacred Band. Ives's Order adopted rituals, insignia, and codes

suggestive of Masonic orders, though it remains unclear how widespread the Order of Chaeronea was among late Victorian homosexuals, for, writes John Stokes, "the mixture of portentousness and evasion in the diaries makes it extremely difficult to determine just how the Order operated and who belonged to it..." (68). The diaries consist of 122 volumes in the Ransom Humanities Center of the University of Texas (Austin).

Born of aristocratic parents, the illegitimate Ives was educated at Cambridge and lived most of his life in London. Like other Uranians, Ives yearned for a society in which homosexuals would have the freedom to live as they wished. After he and Wilde met at the Authors' Club in June 1892, Ives later recorded in his diary: "...of course the leader of the aesthetic movement is very interesting to meet, for it is, so far as I know, a great change for Art in the age and one with which I have always been in full sympathy. Our meeting was quite droll and romantic, and would be pronounced far-fetched in a play but such meetings are not new to me or to W."

The difference between the two was obvious when later that year Ives read, for the first time, *The Picture of Dorian Gray*: "It seems very brilliant as far as I have gone..., but though admiring the acting and cold cutting cynicism I am not of it... – yet I have a Cause: I feel an instrument and in that above the weakness of my nature – ah, the world is a terrible school." In August of 1892, he mentions Wilde in his diary as well as the art of Edward Carpenter and Whitman: "Well, the Cause must be served and followed by all sorts of men, each to work in their particular sphere; the issue and the hope is great enough to bind even the most heterogeneous society, and if only organised, which we have never been before, we shall go on to victory." Carpenter was not a member of the Order, nor is there evidence that Wilde joined.

After dining with Wilde at the Savoy in October 1893, Ives recorded his impressions, apparently unable to grasp Wilde's paradoxical wit or to delight in his flamboyant nature: "A teacher [that is, Wilde], he either cannot or will not give the key to his philosophy, and till I get it I can't understand him. He seems to have no purpose, I am all purpose. Apparently of an elegant refined nature and talented as few men are, brilliant as a shining jewel, yet he teaches many things which cannot be held and which are so false as not even to be dangerous." Nevertheless, Ives maintained cordial relations with Wilde, who was often invited, along with Lord Alfred Douglas, to his homosexual menage at E4, the Albany (which is mentioned as Jack Worthing's London address in the early version of *The Importance of Being Earnest*, presumably intended as an in

side joke among friends, but before the opening, Wilde changed the number to B4, though an obvious and appropriate homophone).

When Ives first met Douglas through Wilde in 1893, he thought him charming but reckless: "I want him to change his life, for his own good, but especially for the Cause, which is sacred to us both." By 1894, after Douglas had edited the homoerotic Oxford periodical the *Spirit Lamp* and had contributed to the similarly oriented under-graduate periodical the *Chameleon* (which in-cluded Douglas's poem "Two Loves," with its best-known line: "I am the love that dare not speak its name"), Ives recorded in his journal: "If Bosie has really made Oxford homosexual, he has done something good and glorious" (qtd. in Ellmann 386/364).

On 6 April 1895, the day after Wilde's arrest, Ives contemplated suicide in his diary for the first time, gazing at the barrel of his revolver with the "little messenger" within: "What ar[t] thou, such a little thing, but it is thine to save me from the force of all the State.... Thanks little minister, remain patiently until I call for thee, it may be soon or not for many years, God knows...." When Wilde gave his celebrated speech on "The love that dare not speak its name" at his first criminal trial, Ives copied it from the report in the *Daily Telegraph* and recorded in his diary on 5 May 1885 that Wilde was "a man who sticks to his colours," one of "the great of the earth." Ives thought of visiting him in prison, but he decided that the "whole affair would have been painful and more or less impru-dent for me and no use for the victim" (27 Aug. 1895). In a letter to Robert Sherard, a mutual friend, Wilde said that he was "greatly touched at hearing of [Ives's] desire to come and see me.... He is such a good fellow and so clever" (*Letters* 407).

After Wilde was released from prison, Ives sent him his anonymous book of prison poems, *A Book of Chains* (1897). In a letter to Robert Ross, Wilde noted the lack of an inscription: "His caution is amusing. He means well, which is the worst of it" (*Letters* 673). In March 1898, Wilde thanked him for ordering *The Ballad of Reading Gaol* and

responded to what Ives apparently had said in a previous letter: "Yes: I have no doubt we shall win, but the road is long, and red with monstrous martyrdoms. Nothing but the repeal of the Crimi-nal Law Amendment Act would do any good" (*Letters* 721).

In February 1900, Ives sent Wilde his third volume of poems, *Eros' Throne*, which drew the following from its recipient: "...it's powerfully written. Of course it lacks style, but between Truth and Style there is a *désaccord*, unless one is a poet. The ideas in the book are excellent, but the mode of presentation lacks charm. The book stimulates but does not win one" (*Letters* 816). With Wilde's death, Ives wrote tersely in his diary on 1 December 1900: "Oscar Wilde, victim and martyr, died yesterday in Paris," and on the follow-ing day, he added: "The greatest tragedy of the whole nineteenth century makes me pause and think. But there is no justice in the world I have seen, that the land is full of tears I know: we must leave to time and evolution and then our day will come."

On 23 February 1905, the publication date of *De Profundis*, Ives read the heavily edited version and confided to his diary: "Oscar *meant* well, to all. He had not the gift of responsibility, he could not estimate consequence, he was all Art, and all Emotion, and I looked up to him as to a superman (and do still, while utterly disagreeing with his written philosophy, and even with his life, on many sides)."

References: George Ives, *Man Bites Man: The Scrapbook of an Edwardian Eccentric*, ed. Paul Sieveking (1980); John Stokes, "Wilde at Bay: The Diaries of George Ives," *Oscar Wilde*: *Myths, Miracles, and Imitations* (1996).

J

JAMES, HENRY (1843–1916)

The American novelist, playwright, critic, and short story writer first met Wilde on 21 January 1882, in a Washington, D.C., drawing room when the latter – dressed in his costume of knee breeches and velvet jacket in imitation of Bunthorne in Gilbert and Sullivan's *Patience* – was on his lecture tour of America. James wrote to Isabella Stewart Gardner that Wilde was "repulsive and fatuous" (*James Letters* 2:372) and, to another correspondent, an "unclean beast" (qtd. in Edel 3:31). When, at this meeting, James expressed his longing for London, Wilde perceived his provincialism: "Really! You care for *places*? The world is my home" (qtd. in Edel 3:31).

The more flamboyant Wilde, who spoke respectfully of the more subdued James, nevertheless said in "The Decay of Lying" (1889) that the American novelist wrote fiction "as if it were a painful duty, and wastes upon mean motives and imperceptible 'points of view' his neat literary style, his felicitous phrases, his swift and caustic satire." James, on the other hand, regarded Wilde's theatrical personality as "cheap" with little evidence of artistic accomplishment (qtd. in Edel 4:43).

Clearly, as Edel observes, "They had no common bonds of temperament; and they represented two diametrically opposed attitudes toward life and the imagination. If Wilde insisted on putting his talent into his art and his genius into his life (as he later told André Gide), Henry James did exactly the opposite" (4:43). (Nevertheless, in October 1888, James supported Wilde's unsuccessful candidacy for membership in the exclusive Savile Club.) In *The Tragic Muse* (1890), the aesthete Gabriel Nash, drawn from James's perception of 19th-century Aestheticism, is based, in part, on Wilde, though Whistler and Walter Pater have also been suggested as sources for the composite character. When James's novel was being serialized, Wilde was writing *The Picture of Dorian Gray*: both novels have magic portraits that mirror the inner states of the characters. Though James's influence is possible, Kerry Powell has revealed that "magic-picture mania" was widespread in the popular fiction of the day.

By 1892, James, who had begun writing plays in 1890, was hoping to succeed in the theater at the time that Wilde's *Lady Windermere's Fan* was produced. Having attended the première, James wrote to a friend on 23 February that the play struck him

> as a mixture that will run..., though infantine to my sense, both in subject and in form. As a drama it is of a candid and primitive simplicity.... In short it doesn't, from that point of view, bear analysis or discussion. But there is so much drollery – that is, "cheeky" paradoxical wit of dialogue, and the pit and gallery are so pleased at finding themselves clever enough to "catch on" to four or five of the ingenious – too ingenious – *mots* in the dozen, that it makes them feel quite "*décadent*"...and they enjoy the sensation as a change from the stodgy.

Continuing with his brief analysis of *Lady Windermere's Fan*, James remarks: "There is of course absolutely no characterization and all the people talk equally strained Oscar – but there is a 'situation' (at the end of Act III) that one has seen from the cradle, and the thing is conveniently acted." Alluding to Wilde's curtain call, when he appeared with a lighted cigarette in his hand to the annoyance of some reviewers, James reports that the

> "impudent" speech at the end was simply inevitable mechanical Oscar – I mean the usual trick of saying the unusual – complimenting himself and his play.... The tone of the virtuous journals makes me despair of our stupid humanity. Everything Oscar does is a deliberate trap for the literalist, and to see the literalist walk straight up to it, look straight at it and step straight into it, makes one freshly avert a discouraged gaze from this unspeakable animal. (*James Letters* 3:372–73)

James wrote to another correspondent that "the unspeakable one" was wearing "a metallic blue carnation" (that is, blue-green) in his curtain speech, which, James said, was "stupid," for Wilde only said that "he judged the audience felt the play to be nearly as charming as he did" (qtd. in Edel 4:45). Though Wilde's popular success and theatrical mannerisms obviously irritated James, whose own plays were either unproduced or unacclaimed, he wrote down some of Wilde's epigrams that he liked, such as "Yes, London is all sad people and fogs. I don't know whether fogs produce the sad people, or the sad people produce the fogs."

When James heard of Wilde's next play, *A Woman of No Importance* (1893), he was worried because it had a fallen woman and her illegitimate son as characters similar to those in his own unproduced comedy *Tenants*. When he saw Wilde's play, he called it "a piece of helpless puerility" (qtd. in Edel 4:46). However, says Edel, James had

> fidgeted uneasily as Oscar Wilde's newest epigrams burst from the stage like well-timed firecrackers.... The play did not have the soothing effect James had expected. Perhaps no play existed which could alleviate the panic Henry James felt. The newest success of Oscar Wilde seemed alarmingly to spell his own doom. (71–72)

On 5 January 1895, instead of attending the opening at the St. James's Theatre of his own play, *Guy Domville*, James, "too nervous to do anything else," went to see *An Ideal Husband*, which had been greeted favorably by audiences and drama critics. To his brother, William, he wrote that its apparent success gave him the "most fearful apprehension":

> The thing seemed to me so helpless, so crude, so bad, so clumsy, feeble and vulgar, that as I walked away across St. James's Square to learn my own fate, the prosperity of what I had seen seemed to me to constitute a dreadful presumption of the shipwreck of *Guy Domville*; and I stopped in the middle of the Square, paralyzed by the terror of this probability – afraid to go on and learn more. "How *can* my piece do anything with a public with whom *that* is a success?"

Indeed, James told his brother that *Guy Domville* had failed: when he appeared for the curtain call, the gallery exploded with jeers and catcalls while the audience in the more expensive seats applauded; the play was "whisked away," he said, after 31 performances "to make room for the triumphant Oscar" – that is, for the première of *The Importance of Being Earnest* on 14 February (*James Letters* 3:514). As for *Earnest*, James wrote to his brother that he believed it was "a great success – and with his two roaring successes [the other, of course, was *An Ideal Husband*] running now at once he must be raking in the profits" (qtd. in Edel 4:88).

Three days after Wilde's arrest on 5 April 1895, James told Edmund Gosse that the case was "hideously, atrociously dramatic and really interesting," though it also had "a sickening horribility":

> But the *fall* – from nearly twenty years of a really unique kind of "brilliant" conspicuity (wit, "art," conversation – "one of our two or three dramatists, etc.") to that sordid prison-cell and this gulf of obscenity over which the ghoulish public hangs and gloats – it is beyond any utterance of irony or any pang of compassion! He was never in the smallest degree interesting to me – but this hideous human history has made him so – in a manner. (*James Letters* 4:9–10)

James's anxiety-filled reaction to Wilde's "fall" (he told friends that it was "a very squalid tragedy, but still a tragedy" – quoted in Edel 4:122) was activated, perhaps, by his own repressed homosexuality.

At the time of Wilde's first criminal trial, which began on 26 April, James wrote to Edmund Gosse that there might be hope for "the wretched Wilde" in "the fearful exposure of his (of the prosecution's) little beasts of witnesses. What a nest of almost infant blackmailers!" (qtd. in Edel 4:129). And to his brother, William, James wrote that "the squalid violence of [Wilde's fall] gives him an interest (of misery) that he never had for me – in any degree – before. Strange to say I think he may have a 'future' – of a sort – by reaction – when he comes out of prison – if he survives the horrible sentence of hard labour that he will probably get" (qtd. in Edel 4:129).

Though he believed that Wilde's sentence of two years was too severe, he refused to sign a petition for his early release circulated by Stuart Merrill (see entry) among French and English writers in

December 1895. James sent word through a friend that the petition would have no effect on the authorities, "in whose nostrils the very name of Zola" – who did not sign the petition but who had often been called in Britain a French *décadent* – "is a stench, and that the document would only exist as a manifesto of personal loyalty to Oscar by his friends, of which [James] was never one" (qtd. in Ellmann 493/463). James believed that Wilde could be helped by quiet pressure on the Home Office rather than by public petitions.

As though following his own advice, James discussed Wilde's imprisonment with a Member of Parliament (probably R. B. Haldane), who was a member of the Commission for Penal Reform and who visited Wilde in prison. In November 1895, James wrote to the French novelist Alphonse Daudet that he had heard from the M.P. that Wilde was in a deep depression, that he had been physically ill, and that some improvement in his circumstances might occur. Also, Wilde revealed no wilful resistance or capacity for recuperation. If such were the case, James added, "what masterpiece might he yet produce!" (qtd. in Edel 4:130). The Wilde case, Edel contends, had for James "opened the way to greater frankness," as in his short novel *Maisie* (1897), for "he could now deal with sex more directly in his work" (4:180).

After Wilde's release from prison in 1897 and his death in 1900, James said that Wilde had returned to "the abominable life he had been leading" and that his death was "miserable" (qtd. in Edel 5:278). In the years following, James went to the theater to see *Earnest* in September 1909 and *Lady Windermere's Fan* in October 1911. Writing to Edith Wharton, James told her of "the doddering rococo and oh so flat 'fizz' now of *Lady Windermere's Fan*!" (*James Letters* 4:588).

References: Leon Edel, *Henry James*, Vols. 3–4 (1962–72); Leon Edel, ed., *Henry James Letters*, Vols. 2–4 (1975–84); Kerry Powell, "Tom, Dick, and Dorian Gray: Magic-Picture Mania in Late Victorian Fiction," *Philological Quarterly* (Spring 1983); Leon Edel and Lyall H. Powers, eds., *The Complete Notebooks of Henry James* (1987); Richard Ellmann, "Henry James Among the Aesthetes," *a long the riverrun: Selected Essays* (1988).

"LE JARDIN": *See* **"IMPRESSIONS: I. LE JARDIN. II. LA MER"**

"LE JARDIN DES TUILERIES"

Published: Margaret S. Tyssen Amherst, ed., *In a Good Cause: A Collection of Stories, Poems, and Illustrations* (London: Wells Gardner, Darton & Co., 1885), 83, issued for the benefit of the North-Eastern Hospital for Children (later the Queen's Hospital for Children, Bethnal Green); this volume was also published by E. & J.B. Young & Co. (New York). The poem was reprinted in *Poems* (1908).

Printed entirely in italics, this poem, consisting of five quatrains, is accompanied by an illustration at the foot of the page by Laura Troubridge (1853–1929), later Mrs. Adrian Hope, whose husband was the cousin of Constance Wilde (see entry).

In Wilde's lyric, images of people on the promenade of the Tuileries gardens in Paris yield to those of children who run "Like little things of dancing gold" (obviously Wilde tailored the poem to the volume in which it appeared). When they climb up "the black and leafless tree," the poet chastises its barrenness: "...if I were you, / And children climbed me, for their sake / Though it be winter I would break / Into spring blossoms white and blue!" The event recalls Wilde's fairy tale "The Selfish Giant."

Manuscripts: The Huntington Library has a MS. version, dated June 1885, with the title "Impression de Paris: Le Jardin des Tuileries," the first stanza of which was revised and used as the opening of "Les Ballons," Part II of "Fantaisies Décoratives" (see Mason 103). The Berg Collection also has a proof of the poem with an autograph note to the editor of *In a Good Cause* (though a correction to line 5 was never made).

JEBB, R. C., ON GREEK HISTORY AND LITERATURE: A REVIEW

Published: *Athenaeum*, 4 Sept. 1880: 301–02. An unsigned review of an article by the Cambridge classicist R. C. Jebb in the *Encyclopaedia Britannica* (Vols. X and XI) on Greek history and literature. According to Ellmann (600n9/563n9), the review was only partially written by Wilde: from "Mr. Jebb's article," at the beginning of the third paragraph, through the seventh paragraph, ending with "modern Athens." Ellmann has a typographical error for the year (1879 instead of 1880), which, however, is correctly given in the notes. This review is not listed in Mason, nor has it been reprinted.

Jebb was "a *bête noire* of Mahaffy [Wilde's former tutor at Trinity College, Dublin]," says Ellmann, "who had conducted a long controversy with him in 1876 and 1877, and Wilde shared his old tutor's dislike" (107/103). Wilde acknowledges that Jebb rightly states the facts of the Persian war, "though to say that Themistocles was ostracized for intriguing with the Persians is not merely inaccurate, but a complete misrepresentation of the peculiar character of ostracism – a punishment never inflicted on any definite accusation, and least of all for high treason." Other aspects of the subject, Wilde insists, are either ignored or slighted: "There is thus, on the one side, a want of broad general views on the relation of Greek history to modern, and, on the other important facts are often neglected.... It is impossible not to feel that such omissions as these [which Wilde cites in detail] detract much from the value of Mr. Jebb's brilliant article."

Wilde has qualified praise for Jebb's discussion of ancient Greek literature, particularly his "excellent remarks on the Greek consciousness of the artistic value of the different dialects and metres as instruments of literary expression, but, on the whole, it is slight and sketchy." Wilde notes that, among the Greek writers of comedy, Menander is not mentioned (Wilde had won a prize at Trinity College, Dublin, for an essay on a Greek anthology, which included Menander), nor is there mention of the "exquisite poem of 'Hero and Leander,' which has been eternally enshrined in our own literature by Marlowe."

JEZEBEL: *See AHAB AND JEZEBEL*

JOHNSON, LIONEL (1867–1902)

While an undergraduate at New College, Oxford, the poet and critic Johnson first met Wilde in February 1890; at this time, Wilde was visiting Walter Pater, at Brasenose College. To a friend, Johnson reported on 18 February that Wilde "discoursed, with infinite flippancy, of everyone...laughed at Pater: and consumed all my cigarettes. I am in love with him" (qtd. in *Letters* 255n). Later that year, Johnson composed a poem in Latin praising *The Picture of Dorian Gray*, beginning: "Benedictus sis, Oscare!" In such lines (here translated) as "He avidly loves strange loves and fierce with Beauty, he plucks strange flowers,"

Johnson grasps the Decadent subtext of the novel (qtd. in Ellmann 324n/306n).

After graduation in 1890, Johnson took rooms in a building in Fitzroy Street, which housed the offices and studios of the Century Guild of Artists and embarked on a career as a reviewer for various publications. The writers and artists who frequented the house included poets, such as Yeats and Ernest Rhys, who, with other poets, founded the Rhymers' Club, the meetings of which Wilde occasionally attended. In early 1891, Johnson introduced Lord Alfred Douglas (a close friend at Oxford, not a cousin, as Ellmann states, 324/306) to Wilde in a visit to his Tite Street home. Douglas recalls Johnson as "a delightful fellow, though exceedingly eccentric," in later years an alcoholic. While at Oxford, he would "discourse in the most brilliant way" until five in the morning rather than go to bed.

Douglas recalls that "one of the griefs of [Johnson's] later years [was] that he had introduced me to Wilde..." (57–58). In 1892, Johnson wrote a poem titled "The Destroyer of a Soul": later, he revealed that Douglas was the "soul" and that Wilde was the "destroyer." The poem, with the dedication "To _____" (that is, Wilde), begins, "I hate you with a necessary hate" and proceeds to the revealing lines:

> Mourning for that live soul, I used to see;
> Soul of a saint, whose friend I used to be:
> Till you came by! a cold, corrupting, fate.

In 1892, Yeats, who regarded Johnson as his closest friend until the mid-1890s, drew him into the newly founded Irish Literary Society because of a claim that he had distant Irish relatives and because of his newly adopted Roman Catholicism: he was, said Yeats, "our theologian" who presumably would defend the society against detractors. In London, Dublin, and Belfast, Johnson gave lectures on Irish poets and novelists. Yeats recalls Johnson's striking appearance: "He was very little, and at first glance he seemed but a schoolboy of fifteen" (*Autobiography* 149). In 1894, the year in which Johnson published *The Art of Thomas Hardy*, one of the earliest books on Hardy's fiction, he wrote his best-known poem, "The Dark Angel," which depicts the intense inner struggle, some critics believe, against his homoerotic impulses:

I fight thee, in the Holy Name!
. . . .
Do what thou wilt, thou shalt not so,
Dark Angel! triumph over me:
Lonely, unto the Lone I go,
Divine, to the Divinity.

At the time of Wilde's trials, Yeats received a letter from Johnson "denouncing Wilde with great bitterness. He had 'a cold scientific intellect'; he achieved a 'sense of triumph and power, at every dinner-table he dominated, from the knowledge that he was guilty of that sin which, more than any other possible to man, would turn all those people against him if they but knew.'" Yeats replied that he "regretted Wilde's downfall," and because Johnson, like most others, believed that Wilde was a martyr, Yeats said that "tragedy might give his art a greater depth," though Johnson believed that Wilde "would produce, when it was all over, some comedy exactly like the others, writing from an art where events could leave no trace" (*Autobiography* 189, 192–93).

As Johnson's alcoholism consumed him, he withdrew periodically from others into what Yeats called his "mythic phase." In one of his best-known poems, "Mystic and Cavalier" (1894), the tragic elements of his life are dramatized, as in the startling opening: "Go from me: I am one of those, who fall." Indeed, he did fall – from a cerebral hemorrhage on 29 September 1902, when, at the age of 35, he collapsed and never regained consciousness.

References: *The Autobiography of Lord Alfred Douglas* (2nd ed., 1931; rpt. 1970); Raymond Roselieb, "Some Letters of Lionel Johnson," PhD diss., University of Notre Dame (1954); *The Autobiography of W. B. Yeats* (1965).

"A 'JOLLY' ART CRITIC"

Published: *PMG*, 18 Nov. 1886, 6; rpt. in *Reviews* (1908). An unsigned review of Harry Quilter's *Sententiae Artis: First Principles of Art for Painters and Picture Lovers* (1886).

In the *World* (17 Nov.), the day before Wilde's adverse review appeared, Whistler had attacked his "arch-enemy" Harry Quilter, the well-known journalist and author of several books, three of them on art. In condemning, as he often did, the conventional and unimaginative exhibitions mounted by the Royal Academy, Whistler took the opportunity to ridicule both Quilter and Wilde (the latter of the two often accused by Whistler of plagiarizing his aesthetic principles): "I am naturally interested in any effort made among your Painters to prove they are alive – but when I find, thrust in the van of your leaders, the body of my dead 'Arry [Quilter], I know that putrefaction alone can result. When, following 'Arry, there comes an Oscar, you finish in farce, and bring upon yourselves the scorn and ridicule of your confreres in Europe.... With 'Arry and Oscar you have revenged the Academy."

Wilde begins his review by alluding to Quilter as the "apostle of the middle classes": "There is a healthy bank-holiday atmosphere about this book which is extremely pleasant. Mr. Quilter is entirely free from affectation of any kind. He rollicks through art with the recklessness of the tourist and describes its beauties with the enthusiasm of the auctioneer." Seizing the opportunity to jab Whistler in their on-going publicly staged verbal duals, Wilde associates Whistler with Quilter, an odd couple indeed: "After listening so long to the Don Quixote of art, to listen once to Sancho Panza is both salutary and refreshing." Wilde selects from *Sententiae* various quotations designed, obviously, to discredit Quilter's wisdom about art, such as the "jubilant" observation: "Paint firm and be jolly," and the "purely autobiographical" remark that "Few of us understand what it is that we mean by Art."

Wilde finds that Quilter's manner is as "interesting" as his matter: "He tells us that at this festive season of the year, with Christmas and roast beef looming before us, 'Similes drawn from eating and its results occur most readily to the mind.' So he announces that 'Subject is the diet of painting,' that 'Perspective is the bread of art,' and that 'Beauty is in some way like jam.'" Since Quilter regards sculpture as "Painting's poor relation," he hardly discusses the plastic arts, but on painting "he writes with much vigour and joviality." In Gainsborough, Quilter sees "a plainness almost amounting to brutality," while in Sir Joshua Reynolds, the chief qualities are "vulgarity and snobbishness." Wilde comments acidly: "It is obviously unnecessary for us to point out how luminous these criticisms are, how delicate in expression."

With respect to "the general principles of art," Wilde continues with ironic disdain, "Mr. Quilter writes with equal lucidity.... [He] does his best and bravely faces every difficulty in modern art, with the exception of Mr. Whistler. Painting, he tells us, is 'of a different quality to mathematics,' and finish in art is 'adding more fact'!" In his running attack on Quilter, Wilde quotes *Sententia* No. 351: "'There is nothing furnishes a room like a book-case, *and plenty of books in it*.' How cultivated the mind that thus raises literature to the position of upholstery and puts thought on a level with the antimacassar!"

Wilde points to misquotations and misspelled names ("quite bravely and sincerely making mess after mess from literature, and misquotes Shake-speare, Wordsworth, Alfred de Musset Mr. Mat-thew Arnold, Mr. Swinburne, and Mr. Fitzgerald's *Rubaiyat*"), concluding: "On the whole, the book will not do. We fully admit that it is extremely amusing and, no doubt, Mr. Quilter is quite earnest in his endeavours to elevate art to the dignity of manual labour, but the extraordinary vulgarity of the style alone will always be sufficient to prevent these *Sententiae Artis* from being anything more than curiosities of literature."

Quilter responded to this review in a lengthy letter to the *Pall Mall Gazette* (23 Nov.), in which he pointed out at least twenty-five misquotations by the anonymous reviewer: "...and on the strength of these proceeds to ridicule and condemn the author he has mangled." The *Pall Mall Gazette*, however, in a lengthy editorial commentary, defended Wilde's critical objections to Quilter's book.

K

"KEATS' SONNET ON BLUE"

Published: *Century Guild Hobby Horse* 1 (July 1886): 83–86; rpt. in *Miscellanies* (1908). The original MS. of Keats's sonnet was presented to Wilde by Mrs. E. K. Speed (1823–83), the daughter of George Keats, the poet's brother. While in Louisville, Kentucky, on his lecture tour in 1882, Wilde met Mrs. Speed.

Wilde mentions that in his Louisville lecture – on the mission of art in the nineteenth century – he quoted Keats's "Sonnet on Blue" as an example of color harmonies. After presenting his lecture, a middle-aged lady approached him and introduced herself as Mrs. Speed, who invited him to examine the Keats MS. On the following day, he examined not only the MS. but also Keats's letters to her father, some of which at that time were unpublished. Several months later, Mrs. Speed offered to present Wilde with the MS., a facsimile of which he included in his article on Keats.

The "psychological interest" in the MS., Wilde writes, "shows us the conditions that preceded the perfected form, the gradual growth, not of the conception but of the expression, and the workings of that spirit of selection which is the secret of style." Wilde devotes most of this brief article to the published and unpublished versions of the poem and the variants between them.

L

LABOUCHERE, HENRY DU PRÉ (1831–1912)

A Radical Member of Parliament for Northampton, 1880–1906, Labouchere was the owner and editor of the popular newspaper *Truth*, which he began publishing in 1877. Around 1880, he and Wilde apparently first met. When Wilde was preparing to leave England on his lecture tour of America, Labouchere wrote in *Truth* (22 Dec. 1881): "Mr. Wilde – say what one may of him – has a distinct individuality, and, therefore, I should fancy that his lectures will attract many who will listen and look." As Wilde's tour proceeded, Labouchere wrote favorably of the American reception and mused that Wilde's aestheticism could counteract American materialism. In St. Louis, Wilde called him "the best writer in Europe, a remarkable gentleman" (qtd. in Ellmann 156/149). In March 1882, Wilde mentioned in a letter that Labouchere – in addition to Whistler and Henry Irving – was one of his "heroes" (*Letters* 105).

However, when Wilde returned to England and lectured on "Impressions of America" at Prince's Hall in July 1883, Labouchere was less impressed. In *Truth* (18 July), he complained that the word *lovely* had been used 43 times, *beautiful* 26 times, and *charming* 7 times. On the following day, *Truth* published a lengthy article titled "Exit Oscar," which referred to Wilde at Oxford as the "epicene youth" and in America as an "effeminate phrasemaker... lecturing to empty benches." Significantly, *Truth* reported, Prince's Hall was only half full. Wilde allegedly responded: "If it took Labouchere three columns to prove that I was forgotten, then there is no difference between fame and obscurity" (qtd. in Ellmann 240/226).

Before the summer of 1885, Labouchere had revealed no concern about male homosexuality. He himself – a witty, bohemian man with a love of the theater – was not above having affairs with actresses, behavior that did not, however, result in his tolerance towards a different sexual orientation from his own. His action in the House of Commons in 1885 had a devastating effect on Wilde: in that year, his introduction of Article XI of the Criminal Law Amendment Act, the law under which Wilde was convicted, was passed by a sparsely attended House of Commons on the night of 7 August:

> Any male person who, in public or private, commits, or is a party to the commission of, or procures or attempts to procure the commission by any male person of, any act of gross indecency with another male person, shall be guilty of a misdemeanor, and being convicted thereof shall be liable at the discretion of the court to be imprisoned for any term not exceeding two years, with or without hard labour.

The amendment concerning homosexual activities in public or private was, in fact, unrelated to the central intent of the act: to protect women and girls with respect to the age of consent, to suppress brothels, and "other purposes" – the result of revelations by W. T. Stead in his articles on prostitution titled "Maiden Tribute of Modern Babylon," which began on 6 July 1885, in the *Pall Mall Gazette*. When Stead informed Labouchere, as the bill was about to be discussed in open committee, that homosexuality had become widespread in London, Labouchere hastily introduced Article XI. Had such an addition been introduced at any other time, it would probably have been ruled out of order, but the wish by members of the House to discontinue meetings in order to concentrate on the imminent General Election resulted in hasty readings of the bill. Moreover, Labouchere's original section called for only one year in prison; the additional year was added in open committee. Soon, the law was dubbed the "Blackmailers' Charter." In 1967, the Criminal Law Amendment Act was repealed by the passage of the Sex Offenses Act, which decriminalized mutually consenting private homosexual acts over the age of 21.

When *The Importance of Being Earnest* opened, Labouchere wrote in *Truth* (21 Feb. 1895) that the play was "undoubtedly amusing," though it was "full of echoes" of several other playwrights, including Bernard Shaw: "But I have no doubt in my own mind that the chief reason why the St. James's piece proves so amusing, is because it is so completely dominated by its author." But, he adds, the "public taste for 'Oscarisms' is not likely to be a lasting one.... The days of the 'Paradox *à la* Wilde' may be numbered. It may pass, as the cult of the lily has passed, and the *mode* of the green carnation" (rpt. in Beckson).

During and after the trials, Labouchere's *Truth* was hostile towards Wilde. For example, when Alfred Douglas wrote a letter to *Truth* denouncing Labouchere as "quite bigoted" and deploring "the cruelty and prejudice" that resulted in Wilde's plight as well as the charge that Douglas was a "coward," Labouchere printed a portion of the letter and responded to it: "Certainly this exceptional moralist has the courage of his opinions but, these opinions being what they are, it is to be regretted that he is not afforded an opportunity to meditate on them in the seclusion of Pentonville [Prison]" (qtd. in *Letters* 450n1). When Wilde was convicted, Labouchere believed that the sentence of two years at hard labor was insufficient:

As I had drafted it the maximum sentence was seven years. The then Home Secretary and Attorney-General, both most experienced men, suggested to me that in such cases convictions are always difficult and that it would be better were the maximum to be two years. Hence the insufficiency of the severest sentence that the law allows. In view of the mischief that such a man does, the sentence he has received compares but lightly with those almost every day awarded for infinitely less pernicious crimes. (qtd. in Pearson 242–43)

References: Hesketh Pearson, *Labby: The Life and Character of Henry Labouchere* (1937); F. B. Smith, "Labouchere's Amendment to the Criminal Law Amendment Bill," *Historical Studies* (Oct. 1976); Jeffrey Weeks, *Between the Acts: Lives of Homosexual Men, 1885–1967* (1991).

LADY WINDERMERE'S FAN

Written: Encouraged by the actor-manager George Alexander, who was negotiating for the lease of the St. James's Theatre, Wilde agreed to write a comedy (further encouraged by Alexander's advance of £100 in July 1890 for rights to the play). But Wilde delayed, to Alexander's reported consternation, until the summer of 1891, when a draft was composed while Wilde was vacationing at Lake Windermere (hence, the name of his leading characters, a practice he also em-

ployed in his other society comedies). Wilde's original title was *A Good Woman*, which he changed before the première performance to *Lady Windermere's Fan.*

Responding to an unidentified correspondent after the New York opening, Wilde explained his view of Mrs. Erlynne's dilemma in the play:

The psychological idea that suggested to me the play is this. A woman who has had a child, but never known the passion of maternity (there are such women), suddenly sees the child she has abandoned falling over a precipice. There wakes in her the maternal feeling – the most terrible of all emotions.... She rushes to rescue, sacrifices herself, does follies – and the next day she feels "This passion is too terrible. It wrecks my life.... Let me go away. I don't want to be a mother any more." And so the fourth act is to me the psychological act, the act that is newest, most true. (*Letters* 331–32)

Produced: The play opened at the St. James's Theatre on 20 February 1892, and ran until 29 July. After a brief tour, it returned to London, where it re-opened on 31 October and ran until 30 November for a total of 197 performances. The leading roles were performed by George Alexander as Lord Windermere, Lily Hanbury as Lady Windermere, Nutcombe Gould as Lord Darlington, and Marion Terry (sister of Ellen) as Mrs. Erlynne. At the conclusion of the play, Wilde appeared before the curtain with a cigarette in his hand and a blue-green carnation in his buttonhole to inform the audience, as reported by Alexander:

Ladies and gentlemen: I have enjoyed this evening *immensely*. The actors have given us a *charming* rendering of a *delightful* play, and your appreciation has been *most* intelligent. I congratulate you on the *great* success of your performance, which persuades me that you think *almost* as highly of the play as I do myself. (qtd. in Ellmann 366/346)

In New York, the play opened at Palmer's Theatre on 6 February 1893, with Maurice Barrymore (father of Ethel, John, and Lionel) as Lord Darlington, and closed on 15 April.

Published: 9 November 1893, with the title

Lady Windermere's Fan: A Play about a Good Woman by Elkin Mathews and John Lane at the Sign of the Bodley Head, London; rpt. in the *Collected Edition* (1908), Vol. 3. The dedication reads: "TO / THE DEAR MEMORY / OF / ROBERT EARL OF LYTTON / IN AFFECTION / AND / ADMIRATION." Edward Robert Bulwer, first Earl of Lytton (1831–91), was the only son of the popular novelist Edward Bulwer-Lytton (1803–73). As "Owen Meredith," he wrote much poetry while serving as Viceroy of India, 1876–80, and Ambassador to France, 1887–91. At the time of Lytton's death, Wilde wrote that he and Lytton during the past year had become "very great friends.... He was a man of real artistic temperament. I had grown to be very fond of him..." (*Letters* 299). When preparing the play for publication, Wilde returned to earlier MSS. for not only individual lines but also for entire speeches that he had omitted from earlier versions. "As a consequence," Ian Small writes, "the published play is longer, and has more characters, than any of the drafts" (*Fan* xxx).

Sources: As his principal sources, Wilde turned to Dumas *fils*'s *Françillon* (1887) and *L'Etrangère* (1876), particularly the plot involving an adventuress in the latter Dumas play, in which Mrs. Clarkson is the equivalent of Wilde's Mrs. Erlynne, though the differences are more striking than the similarities between the two plays. Another possible source for part of the plot is Jules Lemaître's *Revoltée* (1889), in which a divorced woman, assumed by her daughter to be dead, intervenes to save her from a similar fate that she herself had suffered. The mother unmasks herself to the daughter as her mother; in *Lady Windermere's Fan*, however, Mrs. Erlynne maintains her secret.

While French *boulevard* drama was an important source of material for Wilde's plays, Peter Raby argues that Wilde's comedy has "stronger affinities with the English than with the French tradition," particularly in the use of various devices of Restoration comedy, which provided Wilde with the organization and themes that

belong to a tradition which stretches back, by way perhaps of Boucicault's *London Assurance* [1841], to Sheridan, and before him to Congreve, Vanbrugh and Etherege. The relationships between the sexes, the problems of reconciling private with public morality, love

with marriage (and property), the conflict between wit and sentiment – these carry the flavour of the Restoration as surely as does the apparatus of intercepted letters, well- or ill-intentioned gossip, discovered objects and concealments behind curtains. (86)

The Plot: Act I, which takes place in the morning-room of Lord Windermere's house in present-day London, finds Lady Windermere arranging roses in preparation for her birthday party that evening. When Lord Darlington calls on her, he admires the fan that is lying on a table. She refers to it as a birthday gift from her husband (she is twenty-one). As they have tea, she reveals her annoyance with Darlington, who had been paying her "elaborate compliments" on the previous evening at a Foreign Office party. (Despite two years of marriage and the mother of a young child, she remains a prim young lady.) As one of Wilde's dandies, Darlington responds with a facetious pun: "Ah, nowadays we are all of us so hard up, that the only pleasant things to pay *are* compliments." He urges her to take him seriously: the world, he says, takes only those who pretend to be good seriously. She assumes that he takes her to be a Puritan. Indeed, brought up like one, she regards life as a sacrament: "Its ideal is Love. Its purification is sacrifice." But Darlington, as a dandy, is merely amused by such ideals.

He then asks her, in a hypothetical manner, whether a wife, married only two years, should "console herself" when her husband "suddenly becomes the intimate friend of a woman of – well, more than doubtful character, is always calling upon her, lunching with her, and probably paying her bills....?" (He is, of course, alluding to Mrs. Erlynne.) Such a wife, she responds, would be as "vile" as her husband. Their conversation leads to the double-standard of men's sexual morality, much discussed in the late 19th century. Darlington asks her: "Do you think that there should be the same laws for men as there are for women?" She responds: "Certainly!" When Darlington remarks that life is "too complex a thing to be settled by these hard and fast rules," Lady Windermere admits of no exceptions. He calls her "a fascinating Puritan," a judgment he cannot avoid: "I can resist everything except temptation." (This best known of Wildean paradoxes is recycled in altered form in *A Woman of No Importance*, Act

III.)

Also calling on Lady Windermere are the Duchess of Berwick and her daughter, Lady Agatha Carlisle. After the Duchess refuses to introduce her daughter to Darlington because of his presumed wickedness, he departs with a warning to Lady Windermere: "It is dangerous to reform anyone." The Duchess raises the issue of Mrs. Erlynne, who, she says, is "absolutely inadmissible into society. Many a woman has a past, but I am told that she has at least a dozen, and that they all fit." (In late-19th century drama, "Mrs." – as in Shaw's *Mrs. Warren's Profession* and Pinero's *The Second Mrs. Tanqueray* – usually indicated a fallen woman attempting to re-enter society.)

The Duchess reveals that Lord Windermere has been the talk of society because of his visits to Mrs. Erlynne, as reported by the Duchess's two nieces who live across the street. Furthermore, "this terrible woman" has "got a great deal of money out of somebody, for it seems that she came to London six months ago without anything at all to speak of, and now has this charming house in Mayfair, drives her ponies in the Park every afternoon and all – well, all – since she has known poor dear Windermere." The Duchess suggests the standard remedy for such situations: "Just take him abroad, and he'll come back to you, all right." However, Lady Windermere remains skeptical of the Duchess's story concerning Lord Windermere's unfaithfulness.

When her visitors leave, Lady Windermere recalls Lord Darlington's allusion to Mrs. Erlynne. She goes to her husband's desk to see whether he has written checks for huge sums in Mrs. Erlynne's name. She finds no evidence in the bank book, but suddenly she notices a second book "private – locked!" She cuts the cover from the book and discovers, to her horror, such sums as £600, £700, and £400 withdrawn in Mrs. Erlynne's name. Shortly after she flings the book to the floor, her husband enters and notices it. Objecting to her right to cut open his bank book, he insists that she has misinterpreted his behavior concerning Mrs. Erlynne. However, she regards his relationship with Mrs. Erlynne as adulterous, she herself "stained" and "degraded."

When Lady Windermere asks whether there was a Mr. Erlynne – "or is he a myth?" – he responds that he died many years ago; she once had been "honoured, loved, respected. She was well born,

she had position – she lost everything – threw it away...." Now, she wishes to be restored to society, and, says Lord Windermere, "she wants you to help her." At this, Lady Windermere is shocked. He then asks her to invite her to that evening's party: "She wants you to receive her once." Mrs. Erlynne, he continues, regards Lady Windermere as "a good woman – and that if she comes here once she will have a chance of a happier, a surer life than she has had. She will make no further effort to know you." Adamantly, she refuses his request. Nevertheless he will invite her.

Picking up the fan that he had given her as a birthday present (the theatrical device of the fan, like other objects, often letters, drawn from the French conventions of the "well-made play"), she issues a threat: "If that woman crosses my threshold, I shall strike her across the face with it." If he wishes to avoid a scandal, he must inform Mrs. Erlynne that she is forbidden to come to the party. When he refuses, she leaves in anger, and Lord Windermere speaks the curtain line: "My God, what shall I do? I dare not tell her who this woman really is. The shame would kill her." The stage direction follows: "*Sinks down into a chair and buries his face in his hands.*"

Prior to the première, Alexander urged Wilde to suggest the mother-daughter relationship of Mrs. Erlynne and Lady Windermere early in the play instead of at the end of Act IV, for a late disclosure would mislead the audience for most of the play. Clement Scott, the critic for the *Daily Telegraph*, with whom Alexander had been corresponding on the "great strife" between himself and Wilde, pressed the actor to insist on the revision: "Not a moment should be lost in writing in these important lines if future audiences are not to be irritated.... Further obstinacy in such a matter would be suicidal" (qtd. in Kaplan 6l). After the first performance of the play, Wilde conceded that Alexander was correct and that Clement Scott's review of the play in the *Daily Telegraph* on 22 February – clearly designed to assist Alexander in his disagreement with Wilde – was persuasive. Wilde consequently made the appropriate changes for the second performance so that the audience was given a strong hint in Act I and full disclosure by Act II so that Mrs. Erlynne's motivation for her behavior was now clear.

The setting for Act II is again Lord Windermere's house though this time in the drawing-room, where a band is heard playing in the adjoining ballroom. The room is crowded with guests, whom Lady Windermere is receiving before they enter the ballroom. After an Australian, Mr. Hopper, and Lady Agatha go within, the Duchess of Berwick asks Lady Windermere to have a word with her, but the distractions of people entering the drawing room prevent any conversation. Lord Augustus, who is intrigued by Mrs. Erlynne, approaches Lord Windermere to inquire about her: "Do you think she will ever get into this demmed thing called Society? Would you introduce her to your wife?"

Meanwhile, Lady Windermere is holding her fan, as though in preparation for Mrs. Erlynne's arrival. She tells Lord Darlington that she wants a friend that night: "I didn't know I would want one so soon." He responds with delight: "I knew the time would come some day." Mrs. Erlynne's entrance is then announced: she is, as Wilde describes her, "very beautifully dressed and very dignified." Lady Windermere clutches at her fan, then lets it drop to the floor; she bows coldly to Mrs. Erlynne, who, the stage direction states, "bows to her sweetly in turn, and sails into the room" – her obvious moment of triumph.

Mrs. Erlynne urges Lord Windermere to introduce her to some of the women. As she speaks with Lord Augustus, Lord Windermere says to his wife: "How pale you are!" She responds: "Cowards are always pale!" Meanwhile, Mrs. Erlynne is holding forth with wit and intelligence, as she observes about Lady Jedburgh's nephew, who is in politics: "He thinks like a Tory and talks like a Radical, and that's so important nowadays." Wilde shifts the conversation among the women to those curious about Mrs. Erlynne. One of them, for example, says: "I have heard the most shocking things about her. They say she is ruining poor Windermere. And Lady Windermere, who goes in for being so proper, invites her!" As the women pass into the ballroom, Lady Windermere and Lord Darlington enter from the terrace. Distraught, she calls Mrs. Erlynne's arrival "monstrous, unbearable": "I feel that every woman here sneers at me as she dances by with my husband." He knows that she cannot live with a man who treats her as Lord Windermere has treated her: "You would feel that the look in his eyes was false, his voice false, his touch false, his passion false." She asks him to be her friend, but no friendship is possible, he insists, between men and women.

Confessing his love for her, he now urges her to leave the house that night instead of "dragging out some false, shallow, degrading existence that the world in its hypocrisy demands." But she says that she lacks the courage; perhaps her husband will return to her. Disappointed, Lord Darlington says that she is "just the same as every other woman.... You would endure anything rather than break with one blow this monstrous tie." When she refuses again, he announces that he is leaving England on the following day and that she will never see him again. After he departs, the Duchess enters and praises Mrs. Erlynne: "Of course, she must be all right if *you* invite her. A most attractive woman, and has such sensible views on life."

As the guests leave, Mrs. Erlynne and Lord Windermere enter, unaware that Lady Windermere is nearby. Mrs. Erlynne informs Windermere that she will accept Lord Augustus's proposal of marriage and that she expects Windermere to make her "a handsome settlement." She suggests £2500 a year, which she will tell Lord Augustus was left to her by a distant relative. They exit onto the terrace while Lady Windermere, now furious at what she has overheard, is determined to leave the house for Lord Darlington; before she departs, she writes a letter to her husband and in a soliloquy declares: "It is he who has broken the bond of marriage – not I. I only break its bondage." When Mrs. Erlynne returns, she discovers that Lady Windermere has left the house and has left a letter for her husband. A sudden awareness of the situation disturbs her: "No, no! It would be impossible! Life doesn't repeat its tragedies like that!"

She tears the letter open and reads it: "Oh, how terrible! The same words that twenty years ago I wrote to her father! and how bitterly I have been punished for it! No; my punishment, my real punishment is tonight, is now!" When Lord Windermere enters, Mrs. Erlynne, crushing the letter in her hand, pretends that Lady Windermere has retired with a headache and that she has left word not to be disturbed. As they speak, the letter falls from Mrs. Erlynne's hand. As she asks for it, he notices his wife's handwriting, but Mrs. Erlynne says that it is merely an address. When he leaves, she wonders how she can save her child: "The daughter must not be like the mother... A moment may ruin a life. Who knows that better than I." Lord Augustus enters to ask her whether she has decided to accept his proposal, but she instructs him to take Lord Windermere down to his club and keep him there as long as possible.

Act III opens in Lord Darlington's rooms, where Lady Windermere is standing by the fireplace and waiting for Darlington's arrival. In a lengthy monologue, she assumes that her husband has read her letter and that, because he has not come for her, is "entrammelled by this woman – fascinated by her – dominated by her." Though she brings nothing to Darlington but "lips that have lost the note of joy," she decides to leave England with him. But then she reverses herself and decides to return to her husband. At that moment, Mrs. Erlynne enters, urging her to return to Lord Windermere: "You are on the brink of ruin....my carriage is waiting at the corner of the street." But Lady Windermere is now reminded that it is unthinkable "to live under the same roof" as her husband, who, she believes, is having an affair with Mrs. Erlynne. But Mrs. Erlynne reveals that Lord Windermere has never read the letter intended for him, for she herself read it to save Lady Windermere from the "abyss" into which she is falling. She throws the letter into the fire, and she promises, if Lady Windermere returns to her husband, never to see either one of them again. The money she has received was not through love, she says, but "in contempt. The hold I have over him–."

She attempts to justify her behavior by insisting that Lord Windermere's love is not to be cast away, that he is "guiltless of all offence." She warns Lady Windermere of the consequences of sin; indeed, Mrs. Erlynne speaks of her own life: "You don't know what it is to fall into the pit, to be despised, mocked, abandoned, sneered at – to be an outcast!" When she ends her speech with an appeal to Lady Windermere's child, Lady Windermere breaks down in tears and pleads to be taken home. When voices are heard, Mrs. Erlynne tells Lady Windermere to hide behind a curtain and slip out when she gets a chance. Recognizing Lord Augustus's voice, Mrs. Erlynne, in distress, sees that she is now lost unless she leaves before Augustus and the others enter. Darlington, Windermere, Augustus, and two minor characters, Dumby and Cecil Graham, who now enter, speak with the cynical assurance of dandyism (for example, Dumby remarks: "In this world there are only two tragedies. One is not getting what one wants, and the other is getting it").

Darlington, the dandy in Act I, becomes the sentimental lover in Act III. Their conversation leads to a discussion of Mrs. Erlynne that prompts Windermere to say: "You must leave Mrs. Erlynne alone. You don't really know anything about her, and you're always talking scandal against her." When the morality of men arises, Darlington utters one of Wilde's most famous but uncharacteristically sentimental lines: "...we are all in the gutter, but some of us are looking at the stars." When Darlington calls Dumby and Graham cynics, one asks him what a cynic is. The response is perhaps the most quoted line in the play: "A man who knows the price of everything and the value of nothing" (a remark that had appeared in slightly different form in Chapter 4 of *The Picture of Dorian Gray*). Graham, amused by Darlington's moralizing, points to a fan, indicating that a woman is present in his rooms. When Windermere recognizes the fan, he confronts Darlington, who is surprised by his friend's indignation but assumes that the woman is Lady Windermere. When Windermere rushes to a moving curtain, Mrs. Erlynne is discovered while Lady Windermere slips from behind the curtain and leaves the room unnoticed. Mrs. Erlynne apologizes for taking the fan by mistake.

The setting for Act IV is the same as that for Act I. Lady Windermere, lying on the sofa, wonders what happened after she left Darlington's rooms: "Perhaps she [Mrs. Erlynne] told them the true reason of her being there, and the real meaning of that – fatal fan of mine...." She is convinced that Mrs. Erlynne has revealed her presence in Darlington's rooms. When Windermere enters, he kisses her. He suggests that they go to their country house, but she tells him that she must see someone (obviously Mrs. Erlynne) before leaving. The butler interrupts to say that Mrs. Erlynne has called to leave Lady Windermere's fan, which she had taken by mistake. Lord Windermere insists that he should see her first, but Mrs. Erlynne enters, offering apologies for her "silly mistake" and announcing that she will be living abroad again, for the English climate does not suit her. When she asks Lady Windermere for a photograph of herself and her child, an opportunity presents itself for a final conversation between Mrs. Erlynne and Lord Windermere while Lady Windermere is upstairs in search of a suitable photograph.

The secret of Mrs. Erlynne's relationship to Lady Windermere is finally made explicit when Lord Windermere remarks "that the mother whom she was taught to consider as dead, the mother whom she has mourned as dead, is living – a divorced woman, going about under an assumed name, a bad woman preying upon life, as I know you now to be – rather than that, I was ready to supply you with money to pay bill after bill, extravagance after extravagance, to risk what occurred yesterday, the first quarrel I have ever had with my wife." Citing her presence in Lord Darlington's house, he calls her "a worthless, vicious woman" and denies her right to claim Lady Windermere as her daughter, for she had abandoned both husband and child for a lover.

When Lord Windermere mentions that she began "blackmailing" him when she learned that her daughter had married someone rich, she hates the word but admits to the act. She also remarks that she prefers Lady Windermere to "cherish the memory of [her] dead, stainless mother. Why should I interfere with her illusions?" When Lord Windermere expresses his horror at her cavalier attitude towards morality, Mrs. Erlynne responds: "...what consoles one nowadays is not repentance, but pleasure. Repentance is quite out of date." Windermere is determined to tell his wife the truth about Mrs. Erlynne, but she counters this impulse cleverly: "If you do, I will make my name so infamous that it will mar every moment of her life. It will ruin her and make her wretched."

When Lady Windermere returns with the photograph, she acknowledges that Mrs. Erlynne had saved her last night and that she intends to inform her husband of the truth, but Mrs. Erlynne urges her to remain silent as payment of her debt to her. Preparing to leave, Mrs. Erlynne asks to have the fan, which has the name "Margaret" on it, the same name that both women have. Lord Augustus enters in time to escort Mrs. Erlynne to her carriage. Her final moment consists of a look back at Lady Windermere (the stage direction reads: "*Their eyes meet*"). Then she exits. Moments later, Augustus returns to inform the Windermeres that Mrs. Erlynne "has explained everything!"

Believing that their individual secrets have been exposed, the Windermeres are horrified, but Mrs. Erlynne has invented still another story that, not having found Augustus at his club, she had gone to Darlington's rooms looking for him. Furthermore,

she consents to Augustus's marriage proposal provided they "live entirely out of England." The Windermeres are relieved, Lord Windermere remarking that Augustus is "certainly marrying a very clever woman!" Lady Windermere concludes the play with her remark that Augustus is "marrying a very good woman!" (Joseph Bristow comments that the play "does not struggle either to reform or to punish [Mrs. Erlynne] so that the moral system of the drama can be easily resolved," 58).

Early Theater Reviews: Reviewers generally praised *Lady Windermere's Fan*, acknowledging the fact that, although Wilde had made use of the conventions of the French "well-made play" – as expected in the late 19th-century English theatre – he had nonetheless provided a new and refreshing theatrical experience. A.B. Walkley, who became one of Wilde's supporters, wrote in the *Speaker* (27 Feb. 1892): "Here is a gentleman who devotes brilliant talents, a splendid audacity, an agreeable charlatanry and a hundred-Barnum-power of advertisement, to making a change in old customs and preventing life from being monotonous. He does this in innumerable ways – by his writings, his talk, his person, his clothes, and everything that is his. He has aimed at doing it in his play, *Lady Windermere's Fan*, and has been, to my mind, entirely successful."

Though the play, Walkley contends, has a thin plot, "often stale," and "full of faults," it is "a good play, for it carries you along from start to finish without boring you for a single moment." As for "sparkling dialogue on the stage," he contends that no other playwright in the 19th century has written with such brilliance; moreover, the play "breaks long-established laws of the theatre...with light-hearted indifference." As for its style, Walkley points to Disraeli and the "Age of the Dandies. And a very delightful style, too! Meretricious, you say? Oh, yes! undeniably meretricious. But mere-tricious wit is better than the usual jog-trot, philistine stupidity of the stage. Anything for a change..." (rpt. in Beckson).

The anonymous reviewer in *Black and White* (27 Feb.) also believed that the play was "exceedingly diverting" despite its "weatherworn" situations: "But paradox is the thing, not the play. The Great God Paradox has his impassioned prophet in Mr. Wilde and all Mr. Wilde's puppets chant his litany. It has a quaint effect to find, in this Cloud-

Cuckoo-Town of Mr. Wilde's, all its inhabitants equally cynical, equally paradoxical, equally epigrammatic.... Once accept the conditions of the game, and the fantastic becomes the familiar" (rpt. in Beckson).

In the *Academy* (5 March), Frederick Wedmore concludes that Wilde's "boldnesses of conception" are such that, on the whole, there is much to enjoy: "The play, if not a revelation, is a pleasure...." Wedmore focuses on the characterization of Mrs. Erlynne, which reveals Wilde's refusal to cater to those in the audience who expect to see her either repentant or punished: "The dramatist bent upon conciliation would have made her repentant; Mr. Wilde does nothing of the kind. He recognises the nature of the woman, and is faithful to the formula that the leopard does not change her spots" (rpt. in Beckson).

Like Wedmore, the anonymous reviewer in the *Westminster Review* (April) agrees that Wilde is "nothing unless brilliant and witty." Precisely because of the play's profusion of cynicism and wit, the reviewer is "inclined to think that a drama conceived on the lines of *Lady Windermere's Fan*, though successful for once, should not be attempted too often, for really, clever and entertaining as it undoubtedly is, it is scarcely a play at all!" Though the reviewer finds illogical characterization in the work – such as Lady Windermere, "a good moral woman" who deserts her husband "because of the mere gossip of a scandalmongering old lady" – he praises the dialogue as "exquisitely funny...satirical without being aggravating to the audience.... To anyone interested in plays we certainly say, if you have not yet been to see it, go at once" (rpt. in Beckson).

There were, to be sure, reviewers who were considerably less impressed by the play. In the *Illustrated London News* (27 Feb.), Clement Scott – a vigorous opponent of Ibsen and the model for the Philistine critic named Cuthbertson in Shaw's *The Philanderer* (1898) – devoted a lengthy opening paragraph to his own indignant reaction to Wilde's appearance on stage after the conclusion of the play with a cigarette in his hand and a green carnation in his buttonhole. As for the play, he imagines Wilde saying: "I can only write for people as they are, not for people as they ought to be. I will prove to you by my play that the very instinct of maternity – that holiest and purest instinct with women – is deadened in the breasts of

our English mothers." Scott goes on to condemn Wilde's play as cynical in undermining virtue and goodness. He concludes by quoting Wilde: "To be intelligible is to be found out." Then he remarks as though Wilde were speaking: "'I have never since I left Oxford and won the Newdigate with my poem on "Ravenna" been wholly intelligible. And I have never been found out.' Thus might argue Mr. Oscar Wilde in his own defence. Meanwhile, society at large will rush to see his play" – a judgment of rare accuracy by Scott (rpt. in Beckson).

Like Scott, Justin McCarthy (a novelist, historian, and Member of Parliament) wrote a notably negative review in *Gentleman's Magazine* (April). He recalls a recent novel in which a character "always has Art upon his lips because he had so little in his soul. Mr. Wilde has called his play a work of art. That of course it is not, could not be. Mr. Wilde is many things needless to enumerate, but he is not an artist. His utterances upon art must be regarded with a delicate disdain" (rpt. in Beckson).

The reviewer of the American production reported in the *New York Times* (7 Feb. 1893) that the play was "welcomed with noisy demonstrations, and the comedy was liked." The play, he wrote, was "clever and interesting, if neither profound nor particularly wise." Still, it was "witty and entertaining throughout."

Manuscripts: The British Library has an early, incomplete MS., considerably different from the published version, as well as the licensing TS. submitted to the Lord Chamberlain's office. The Morgan Library has a MS. of an early draft of Act III. Magdalen College, Oxford, has a TS. of Acts I and II titled *A Good Woman*, later used in the subtitle, with many penciled corrections and additions by Wilde. Texas has TSS. of the play with the title *A Good Woman*, one dated 15 November 1892 by the typewriting office for submission as a licensing copy to the Lord Chamberlain's office. The Clark Library has an early MS. draft of the play and two TSS., one of which is titled *Lady Windermere's Fan*, the other titled *A Good Woman*.

References: Alan Bird, *The Plays of Oscar Wilde* (1977); Ian Small, ed., *Lady Windermere's Fan* (1980); Katharine Worth, *Oscar Wilde* (1983); Peter Raby, *Oscar Wilde* (1988); Kerry Powell, "*Lady Windermere's Fan* and the Unmotherly Mother," *Oscar Wilde and the Theatre of the 1890s* (1990); Joel H. Kaplan, "A Puppet's Power: George Alexander, Clement Scott, and the Replotting of *Lady Windermere's Fan*," *Theatre Notebook* 46:2 (1992); Joseph Bristow, "Dowdies and Dandies: Oscar Wilde's Refashioning of Society Comedy," *Modern Drama* (Spring 1994).

LANE, JOHN: *See* BODLEY HEAD

LANGTRY, LILLIE (1853–1929)

The actress Lillie Langtry – born Emily Charlotte Le Breton on the island of Jersey, the daughter of Rev. Corbet Le Breton, Dean of Jersey – married Edward Langtry in 1874 and soon moved to the fashionable Belgravia section of London. Widely accepted in society as the most beautiful woman of her time, Langtry was painted by Whistler, Burne-Jones, Frederick Leighton, and John Everett Millais, whose portrait *The Jersey Lily* provided her with the epithet (but caused confusion over the spelling of her adopted Christian name). Frank Miles (see entry), who had drawn her many times, introduced her to Wilde in the summer of 1877. In her memoirs, Langtry recalled her first sight of Wilde:

The plainness of his face was redeemed by the splendour of his great, eager eyes.... To me he was always grotesque in appearance, although I have seen him described by a French writer as "beautiful" and "Apollo-like." ...He had one of the most alluring voices that I have ever listened to, round and soft, and full of variety and expression.... (83)

In July 1879, Wilde hailed Langtry as "The New Helen," the title of his poem that appeared in *Time* (in her memoirs, Langtry errs in citing the *World* as its first appearance), then revised it for his *Poems* (1881). Drawing a parallel in the poem between the actress and Helen of Troy (which Yeats would later do with another actress, Maud Gonne), Wilde later reportedly said: "Yes, it was for such ladies that Troy was destroyed, and well might Troy be destroyed for such a woman" (qtd. in Ellmann 111/107). The poem reveals his worship of Langtry's beauty: "Yet care I not what ruin time may bring / If in thy temple thou wilt let me kneel." Referring to her as the "Lily of love, pure and inviolate," Wilde calls her a "Tower of ivory,"

both flower and tower symbols of purity and strength associated with the Virgin Mary. When *Poems* appeared, Wilde sent her a copy with the inscription: "To Helen, formerly of Troy, now London" (qtd. in *Letters* 65n3). In her memoirs, Langtry included the text of "The New Helen" in its entirety (*Days* 86–89).

At this time, Wilde had been acting as Langtry's secretary, advisor, and apparently tutor, as an undated letter from her indicates:

Of course I'm longing to learn more Latin but we stay here [near Plymouth] till Wednesday night so I shan't be able to see my kind tutor before Thursday.... I wanted to ask you how I should go to a fancy ball here, but I chose a soft black Greek dress with a fringe of silver crescents and stars, and diamond ones in my hair and on my neck, and called it Queen of Night. (qtd. in *Letters* 66n3)

In time, however, Langtry probably found Wilde a somewhat officious attendant, for she had attracted the attention of the Prince of Wales (the Prince's nephew, Louis of Battenberg, was the father of her only child, Jeanne Marie, born in 1881).

Despite her relationship with the Prince of Wales, Wilde continued to amuse and instruct her; indeed, rumors circulated that every day he would present her with a lily. He also urged her, in view of her beauty, to become an actress, thereby dashing cold water on Frank Miles's suggestion that she undertake a market garden of hardy flowers, then an undeveloped industry. The "well-meaning Frank," Wilde allegedly argued, would "compel the Lily to tramp the fields in muddy boots" (qtd. in *Days* 136).

Subsequently, Wilde introduced her to Henriette Labouchere, the wife of the M.P. and editor of *Truth* (later responsible for the passage of Article XI of the Criminal Law Amendment Act, under which Wilde was later convicted and imprisoned: see Labouchere, Henry). Mrs. Labouchere, formerly an actress, was training people for the stage: she and Langtry acted in a two-character one-act play in November 1881. Langtry, with the moral support of the Prince of Wales, soon established herself as a talented, though not gifted, actress.

On his lecture tour of Canada in October 1882, Wilde reportedly said in an interview conducted in Halifax, Nova Scotia: "I would rather have discovered Mrs Langtry than have discovered America" (qtd. in O'Brien 128). When Langtry, in her first American stage appearance, acted the leading role in Tom Taylor's *An Unequal Match*, Wilde reviewed her performance in the *New York World* (7 Nov. 1882), under the title "Mrs. Langtry" (see entry). Celebrating Langtry's beauty, which he referred to as "Greek," Wilde writes: "It is Greek because the lines which compose it are so definite and so strong, and yet so exquisitely harmonized that the effect is one of simple loveliness purely...." During Langtry's second American tour in 1883, Wilde wrote to her in mid-December of that year: "...I am really delighted at your immense success.... You have done what no other artist of your day has done, invaded America a second time and carried off new victories" (*Letters* 154). In the same letter, Wilde informs her of his engagement.

After his marriage to Constance Lloyd in 1884, he understandably saw less of Langtry, but in 1891 he offered her the role of Mrs. Erlynne (Langtry later insisted that Wilde wrote *Lady Windermere's Fan* for her: see *Days* 93), but at the age of 39, she declined, protesting that she could not portray a mother with a grown-up daughter. Langtry was in the audience when the play opened on 20 February 1892. At the time of the Wilde trials, Ellmann remarks, "Even Lillie Langtry talked against him..." (436/409). Furthermore, Ellmann asserts, though she "pretended in later life that she had sent him money in his last years, she did not" (586/551).

References: Lillie Langtry, *The Days I Knew* (1925); Pierre Sichel, *The Jersey Lily: The Story of the Fabulous Mrs. Langtry* (1958); Noel B. Gerson, *Lillie Langtry: A Biography* (1972); Kevin O'Brien, *Oscar Wilde in Canada* (1982).

"LATIN UNSEEN"

The Morgan Library has an autograph MS. of translations made by Wilde while an undergraduate at Oxford of Tacitus's *Annals* 3:26 and Lucretius's *De Rerum Natura* 4:749–76; the third section of this MS. appears to have been written as a university examination. Wilde gave the title to this MS.

"LECTURE TO ART STUDENTS"

Published: *Miscellanies* (1908). Robert Ross prefaces the lecture with a note: "Delivered to the Art students of the Royal Academy at their Club in Golden Square, Westminster, on June 30, 1883. The text is taken from the original manuscript."

Wilde begins by declining to give an abstract definition of beauty (in this, he follows his mentor, Walter Pater) since artists "seek to materialise it in a form that gives joy to the soul through the senses.... Nothing, indeed, is more dangerous to the young artist than any conception of ideal beauty: he is constantly led by it either into weak prettiness or lifeless abstraction...." Wilde also contends that such an expression as "English art" is as meaningless as "English mathematics": "Art is the science of beauty, and Mathematics the science of truth" (the separation of beauty from "truth" is characteristic of late 19th-century Aestheticism).

Wilde also denies that there is "any such thing as a school of art": "There are merely artists, that is all." Histories of art, he argues, are "quite valueless...unlessness you are seeking the ostentatious oblivion of an art professorship." Wilde urges the students to avoid archaeology altogether, for it is "merely the science of making excuses for bad art.... How worthless archaeology is in art you can estimate by the fact of its being so popular. Popularity is the crown of laurel which the world puts on bad art. Whatever is popular is wrong."

Wilde returns to an earlier point concerning the uselessness of knowing the "relations of the artist to his surroundings, by which I mean the age and country in which he is born": "All good art...has nothing to do with any particular century; but this universality is the quality of the work of art.... And what, I think, you should do is to realise completely your age in order completely to abstract yourself from it: remembering that if you are an artist at all, you will be not the mouthpiece of a century, but the master of eternity...." He cautions the students that anyone who advises them to make art representative of the nineteenth century is advising them to produce "an art which your children, when you have them, will think old-fashioned."

"But," Wilde continues, "you will tell me this is an inartistic age, and we are an inartistic people, and the artist suffers much in this nineteenth century of ours. Of course he does. I, of all men, am not going to deny that." There has never been an artistic age or people since the world began, Wilde contends. The "sign of a Philistine age is the cry of immorality against art," a cry raised by the

Athenians, for example, against every great poet and thinker of the time – Aeschylus, Euripides, and Socrates. Indeed, one of the "most important questions of modern art" is concerned with the relations of the artist to the external and "the result of the loss of beautiful surroundings": "...and there is no point on which Mr. Ruskin so insists as that the decadence of art has come from the decadence of beautiful things; and that when the artist can not feed his eye on beauty, beauty goes from his work.... Without a beautiful national life, not sculpture merely, but all the arts will die."

Raising the question of whether the artist needs "beautiful surroundings" in order to create, Wilde is convinced that they are not essential:

Indeed, to me the most inartistic thing in this age of ours is not the indifference of the public to beautiful things, but the indifference of the artist to the things that are called ugly. For, to the real artist, nothing is beautiful or ugly in itself at all. With the facts of the object he has nothing to do, but with its appearance only, and appearance is a matter of light and shade, of masses, of position, and of value.

The artist, then, does not deal with the "real condition" of the object but with the "effects of nature." Under certain conditions, a beautiful object may appear ugly; likewise, an ugly object may look beautiful. Wilde insists that the artist does not copy beauty but creates it in art by watching and waiting for it in nature. Like the dramatist who has only virtuous people as characters in his play, the artist who "paints nothing but beautiful things... misses one half of the world."

Wilde cites Whistler as one "living amongst us who unites in himself all the qualities of the noblest art, whose work is a joy for all time, who is, himself, a master of all time." (At this point, the remaining two pages of the text are apparently incomplete, for there are indications of discontinuity.) Raising the question "What is a picture?" Wilde responds with the notion of art for art's sake: "Primarily, a picture is a beautifully coloured surface, merely, with no more spiritual message or meaning for you than an exquisite fragment of Venetian glass or a blue tile from the wall of Damascus. It is, primarily, a purely decorative thing, a delight to look at.... Art should have no sentiment about it but its beauty, no technique

except what you cannot observe.... A picture has no meaning but its beauty, no message but its joy."

LECTURES IN AMERICA, 1882

Wilde's American lecture tour had its unforeseeable origins when the impresario Richard D'Oyly Carte (1844–1901) produced Gilbert and Sullivan's latest work, *Patience; or Bunthorne's Bride*, at the Opera Comique in London in April 1881. A satire of the Aesthetes, whose ostentatious love of beauty had been satirized in George Du Maurier's cartoons for *Punch*, the operetta presents Bunthorne, the "Fleshly Poet," a composite depiction of Swinburne and Rossetti. Both poets had been attacked in 1871 by the critic and poet Robert Buchanan as prominent members of the so-called "Fleshly School of Poetry." Wearing knee breeches, silk stockings, an Eton collar, long hair, and fondly gazing at lilies and sunflowers, Bunthorne characterizes himself with the current clichés associated with the popular view of Aestheticism as

A most intense young man,
A soulful-eyed young man,
An ultra-poetical, super-aesthetical
Out-of-the-way young man.

And in confessing his pretended love of fashionable Pre-Raphaelitism, with its poetic vision of the Middle Ages, he reveals:

I am *not* fond of uttering platitudes
In stained-glass attitudes.
In short, my medievalism's affectation
Born of a morbid love of admiration!

Wilde's legendary walk down Piccadilly with a poppy or lily in his "medieval hand" and dressed in Bunthorne's costume inevitably became associated with the operetta. Frank Harris either invented or enshrined the image in his biography of Wilde: "He began to go abroad in the evening in knee breeches and silk stockings wearing strange flowers in his coat..." (38). Vyvyan Holland, Wilde's son, reports his father's remark in protesting the story of his famous walk: "Anyone could have done that; the difficult thing to achieve was to make people believe that I had done it" (29). Lady Ottoline Morrell recalls that, as a young girl, she saw Wilde at the première of *Patience* with a large sunflower in his buttonhole in a rush to greet Whistler, who was sitting resplendently in a box near the stage (82).

In September 1881, D'Oyly Carte brought *Patience* to New York, where it opened at the Standard Theatre to rave reviews. According to Colonel W. F. Morse, his American business manager, the success of the operetta "indicated the public would be still further interested in the personality of the man who was said to be the leading light of the new gospel of art and the time was opportune." D'Oyly Carte and Morse had managed the lecture tour of Archibald Forbes, the famed British war correspondent, for five successful months in the United States, and this, too, was "taken as a good omen for the success of another English lecturer" (Morse 74).

Besides the obvious desire to capitalize on the American success of *Patience*, D'Oyly Carte wished to associate Wilde in the public mind with the operetta, which he knew would inevitably fall victim to the theater pirates who had already staged unauthorized versions of *The Pirates of Penzance* (there being no international copyright protection in existence). Thus, the mutual benefit and increased income that Wilde and *Patience* could confer upon each other undoubtedly fired D'Oyly Carte's entrepreneurial imagination.

The idea of Wilde's tour had not, however, originated with either D'Oyly Carte or with Morse. As Morse writes, it had been suggested one afternoon in September 1881 by a "lady well known in English and American newspaper circles as a writer upon the current society topics of the day on both sides of the water" (74). The unnamed lady was Mrs. Frank Leslie, director of the publishing business founded by her late English-born husband and editor of *Frank Leslie's Lady's Magazine* (later, she married Oscar's brother, Willie: see entry). Having suggested to Morse the possibility of a series of lectures by Wilde and having received a favorable response, she cabled to ask Wilde whether he would consider a series of 50 readings in America. He immediately replied: "Yes, if offer good" (Morse 75).

Within a short time, business details were concluded: D'Oyly Carte agreed to pay all tour expenses and give Wilde one-third of box-office receipts. Wilde cabled that he planned to leave for New York aboard the S.S. *Arizona* on 24 December 1881. Without benefit of Baedeker (a guide to

the United States did not appear until 1892), Wilde departed from Liverpool with a copy of his play, *Vera; or, The Nihilists*, in his travelling bag, hopeful for a production that would launch his career as a dramatist. He also brought letters of introduction secured from James Russell Lowell, poet and American ambassador to Britain, who had reviewed Wilde's *Poems* favorably in the *Atlantic Monthly* (Jan. 1882).

Wilde regarded his tour as a mission on behalf of the Aesthetic Movement and saw himself as the embodiment of the Aesthetic Ideal – one that, in dress and manner, proclaimed the urgent necessity of cultivating a sense of beauty in an increasingly industrialized world. He also presumed that converting himself into a theatrical spectacle could lead to financial rewards. Even before his departure for America, London newspapers were attacking him, one referring to him as the "Great Prophet," who is "not much of a prophet in his own country, Ireland, and not much of a poet in this" (qtd. in Ellmann 156/149). *Punch* bid Wilde a belated adieu in its issue of 4 February 1882, by publishing a huge cartoon, "Ariadne in Naxos; Or, Very Like a Wail," depicting a grieving figure in flowing dress, barefoot on the beach, waving to the *Arizona*, which heads into the sunset (in the Greek myth, Ariadne awakens to see Theseus, her lover, on a ship vanishing over the horizon).

Because the *Arizona* arrived late in the evening in New York on 2 January, quarantine was cleared on the following morning. When a customs officer asked whether he had anything to declare, Wilde allegedly responded, "Nothing, nothing but my genius." The officer's less well-known response – perhaps also apocryphal – was at least as witty: "That, sir, is a commodity which does not require protection in the United States" (qtd. in Ervine 100). To celebrate Wilde's arrival, the *Daily Graphic* published welcoming verse (would-be poets across the country would also fill local newspapers with such doggerel):

> Hail to thee! hail to thee!
> Now come from o'er the sea,
>   Hail, Oscar Wilde!
> Hail to thy manly form
>   And thy aesthetic norm
> Unbowed by wave or storm,
>   Poesy's child.

Receptions and dinners were extended to Wilde even before his first lecture at Chickering Hall, and newspaper reporters recorded his clever remarks in countless interviews. But editorial writers were quick to condemn D'Oyly Carte's exploitation of Wilde and Wilde's exploitation of the public. The *New York Herald* (4 Jan.), for example, wrote that *Patience* was more delightful than its imitation: Wilde would merely introduce "a new aesthetic pose" to ladies – that of a "limp and clinging aesthete." The *Brooklyn Daily Eagle* (4 Jan.), citing dandyism and effeminacy as signs of a country's decline, remarked: "It is just possible that [aestheticism] may be a sign of decaying intellectual and social strength, and if so we trust that it will not make as many devotees in America as it has done in England."

Wilde's first lecture on 9 January impressed neither the journalists nor the audience. On the following morning, the *New York Times* reported that Wilde's lecture was delivered in a "sepulchral voice" that varied little in intonation, a complaint echoed by newspapers throughout the tour, and that the audience seemed restless, a number of auditors departing before the end. The *Daily Graphic*, calling Wilde "one of the cleverest mountebanks of the age," insisted that the lecture "was not worth going ten yards for."

Despite the press's hostility, Wilde reported to the actor Norman Forbes-Robertson on 15 January that he was enjoying "great success" and that he was "torn in bits by Society. Immense receptions, wonderful dinners, crowds wait for my carriage. I wave a gloved hand and an ivory cane and they cheer.... Rooms are hung with white lilies for me everywhere" (*Letters* 86–87). In the course of his tour, he met such notables as Whitman, Longfellow, Oliver Wendell Holmes, and Henry James, who found Wilde "a fatuous fool, tenth-rate cad" and "an unclean beast" (see entry). On occasion, Wilde was ignored by social luminaries, such as Mrs. Henry Adams, who refused to receive him in her home.

On 31 January, according to Morse, Wilde enjoyed "perhaps the most pronounced personal victory" he was to achieve on the tour (80). Shortly before eight o'clock in the evening at the Music Hall in Boston, a Harvard delegation of 60 students, dressed in Wilde's aesthetic garb – knee-breeches, short jackets, Eton collars, immense cravats, each student gazing intently at a sunflower

(presumably artificial) – marched in stained-glass attitudes to their seats in the first rows. At their appearance, the audience rose to applaud the students' ingenuity. Rarely to be outdone, Wilde, having heard of the planned entrance, entered the stage *not* in aesthetic costume but in long trousers, a dress coat, and a vest. Gazing down with an amused smile at the undergraduates clutching their sunflowers, he remarked that he was glad to be in Boston and that he saw about him "signs of an aesthetic movement." The audience burst into prolonged laughter and applause. With an audible sigh, Wilde then added: "But save me from my disciples."

Initially, Wilde had agreed to lecture for the first three months of 1882, but his success was such that he consented, despite fatigue and disappointingly small audiences in some towns, to extend the tour an additional seven months. Despite difficult travelling conditions with little respite from continued ridicule on the part of the American press, which distressed him, he appeared in over 100 cities and towns, travelled through the Northeast, the Midwest, the South, the West, and several cities in Canada to deliver about 125 lectures. In the small towns, attendance at his lecture was sparse, though in or near the large cities he had correspondingly larger audiences; in his first lecture in New Orleans (16 June), for example, between 600 and 700 were in the audience; ten days later at Spanish Fort, several miles from New Orleans, Wilde drew 1,000 listeners (the price of tickets reduced to 25 cents). In most cases, tickets for Wilde's lectures sold at $1 or $1.50 and gallery seats at 50 cents. The gross profits for the American lecture tour were almost $22,000, Wilde's share amounting to over $6,100.

He relied on three principal lectures (see separate entries): "The English Renaissance," "The Decorative Arts" (sometimes titled "Decorative Art"), and "The House Beautiful," though all underwent revision during the course of the tour, Wilde sometimes presenting truncated versions or incorporating portions from one lecture into another or even changing titles. In addition, he lectured at least once on "Irish Poets and Poetry of the Nineteenth Century" (5 April). For Wilde's reaction to the Americans whom he encountered on the tour, see "Impressions of America."

Schedule of Lectures, January-October, 1882

Wilde sometimes used one lecture, with revisions,

for many stage appearances, then shifted to another, as indicated below.

January

9   Chickering Hall, New York, New York: "The English Renaissance" (revised extensively during the first month of the tour)

17   Horticultural Hall, Philadelphia, Pennsylvania

23   Lincoln Hall, Washington, D.C.

25   Lincoln Hall, Baltimore, Maryland

27   Music Hall, Albany, New York

31   Boston Music Hall, Massachusetts

February

1   Peck's Opera House, New Haven, Connecticut

2   Opera House, Hartford, Connecticut

3   Brooklyn Academy of Music, Brooklyn, New York

6   City Opera House, Utica, New York

7   Grand Opera House, Rochester, New York

8   Academy of Music, Buffalo, New York

11*   Central Music Hall, Chicago, Illinois: "The House Beautiful"

13   Central Music Hall, Chicago, Illinois: "The Decorative Arts"

16   Old Academy, Fort Wayne, Indiana

17   Detroit Music Hall, Michigan

18   Case Hall, Cleveland, Ohio

21   Masonic Temple, Louisville, Kentucky: "The English Renaissance"

22   English's Opera House, Indianapolis, Indiana: "The Decorative Arts"

23   Grand Opera House, Cincinnati, Ohio

25   Mercantile Library Hall, St. Louis, Missouri

27   Opera House, Springfield, Illinois

March

1   Opera House, Dubuque, Iowa

2   Rockford, Illinois

3   Aurora, Illinois

4   Racine, Wisconsin

5   Grand Opera House, Milwaukee, Wisconsin

6   Joliet, Illinois

7   Jacksonville, Illinois

8   Decatur, Illinois

9   Peoria, Illinois

10   Bloomington, Illinois

11   Central Music Hall, Chicago, Illinois: "Interior and Exterior Decoration of Houses" (in April, revised and retitled as "The House Beautiful")

15   Academy of Music, Minneapolis, Minnesota: "The English Renaissance"

16   Opera House, St. Paul, Minnesota

20   Academy of Music, Sioux City, Iowa

21   Boyd's Opera House, Omaha, Nebraska: "The Decorative Arts"

27   Platt's Hall, San Francisco, California: "The English Renaissance"

28   Armory Hall, Oakland, California.

29   Platt's Hall, San Francisco, California: "The Decorative Arts"

30*   Armory Hall, Oakland, California

31   Congregational Church, Sacramento, California

April

1   Platt's Hall, San Francisco, California: "The House Beautiful"

3   California Theater, San Jose, California: "The English Renaissance"

4   Mozart Hall, Stockton, California

5   Platt's Hall, San Francisco, California: "Irish Poets and Poetry of the Nineteenth Century"

8   Sacramento, California: "The House Beautiful"

11   Salt Lake Theatre, Salt Lake City, Utah: "The Decorative Arts"

12   Opera House, Denver, Colorado

13   Tabor Grand Opera House, Leadville, Colorado

14   Opera House, Colorado Springs, Colorado

15   Opera House, Denver, Colorado: "Interior and Exterior House Decoration"

17   Coates Opera House, Kansas City, Missouri

18   Tootle's Opera House, St. Joseph, Missouri: "The Decorative Arts"

19*   New Opera House, Leavenworth, Kansas

20   Crawford's Opera House, Topeka, Kansas

21   Liberty Hall, Lawrence, Kansas

22   Corinthian Hall, Atchison, Kansas

24   Lincoln, Nebraska

25   Fremont, Iowa

26   Des Moines, Iowa

27   Opera House, Iowa City, Iowa

28   Cedar Rapids, Iowa

29   Rock Island, Iowa

May

3   Comstock Opera House, Columbus, Ohio: "The English Renaissance"

4   Harrisburg, Pennsylvania

8   Freehold, New Jersey

9   Newark, New Jersey

10*   Horticultural Hall, Philadelphia, Pennsylvania: "House Decoration" (a truncated version of "The Decorative Arts")

11   Wallack's Theatre, New York, New York: "Decorative Art in America"

12*   Lee Avenue Baptist Church, Brooklyn, New York

15   Queen's Hall, Montreal, Quebec: "The Decorative Arts"

16   Grand Opera House, Ottawa, Ontario

18   Music Hall, Quebec City, Quebec

20   Queen's Hall, Montreal, Quebec: "The House Beautiful"

22   Opera House, Kingston, Ontario

23   City Hall Auditorium, Belleville, Ontario

25   Grand Opera House, Toronto, Ontario

26   Stratford Opera House, Brantford, Ontario

27   Pavilion of the Horticultural Gardens, Toronto, Ontario

29   City Hall Auditorium, Woodstock, Ontario

30   Grand Opera House, Hamilton, Ontario

31   Wesleyan Ladies' College, Hamilton, Ontario: "The Relation of Art to Other Studies"

June

2   Globe Theatre, Boston, Massachusetts: "The Decorative Arts"

11   Grand Opera House, Cincinnati, Ohio

12   Leubrie's Theatre, Memphis, Tennessee

14* Opera House, Vicksburg, Virginia

16   Grand Opera House, New Orleans, Louisiana

19   Pavilion, Galveston, Texas

21   Turner Opera Hall, San Antonio, Texas

23   Gray's Opera House, Houston, Texas

26   Spanish Fort, Louisiana: "The House Beautiful"

28   Frascati Amusement Park, Mobile, Alabama

29   McDonald's Opera House, Montgomery, Alabama: "Decorative Art"

30   Springer Opera House, Columbus, Georgia

July

3   Rolston's Hall, Macon, Georgia

4   DeGive's Opera House, Atlanta, Georgia

5   Savannah Theatre, Savannah, Georgia

6   Augusta, Georgia

7   Academy of Music, Charleston, South Carolina

8* Opera House, Wilmington, North Carolina

10   Van Wyck's Academy of Music, Norfolk, Virginia

11   Richmond Theatre, Richmond, Virginia

15   Casino, Newport, Rhode Island

August

9   Gould Hall, Ballston Spa, New York

10   Congress Hall Ballroom, Saratoga, New York

16   Long Beach Hotel, Long Beach, New York

September

26   Low's Grand Opera House, Providence, Rhode Island

27* Music Hall, Lynn, Massachusetts: "Decorative Art in America"

28   Music Hall, Pawtucket, Rhode Island

29   North Attleboro, Massachusetts

October

3   Opera House, Bangor, Maine: "The Decorative Arts"

4   City Hall Auditorium, Fredericton, New Brunswick, Canada

5   Mechanics' Institute, Saint John, New Brunswick

6   Academy of Music, Amherst, Nova Scotia

7   YMCA Hall, Truro, Nova Scotia

9   Academy of Music, Halifax, Nova Scotia

10   Academy of Music, Halifax, Nova Scotia: "The House Beautiful"

11   Market Hall, Charlottetown, Prince Edward Island

12   Ruddick's Hall, Moncton, New Brunswick

13   Mechanics' Institute, Saint John, New Brunswick [the final lecture of his American tour]

*Location or date differs from Ellmann's list (187-91/178-81)

References: W. F. Morse, "American Lectures," *The Writings of Oscar Wilde*, Vol. l5, Chapter IV (1907); Frank Harris, *Oscar Wilde* (1916; rpt. 1989); Lloyd Lewis and Henry Justin Smith, *Oscar Wilde Discovers America* (1936; rpt. 1967); John Flan-agan, "Oscar Wilde's Twin City Appearances," *Minnesota History* (March 1936); Hubert Hoeltje, "The Apostle of the Sunflower in the State of the Tall Corn," *Palimpsest* (June 1937); Lois Foster Rodecape, "Gilding the Sunflower: A Study of Oscar Wilde's Visit to San Francisco," *California Historical Society Quarterly* (June 1940); Carl Uhlarik, "Oscar Wilde in Omaha," *Prairie Schooner* (Spring 1940); Rose Snider, "Oscar Wilde's Progress Down East," *New England Quarterly* (March 1940); Lowry Charles Wimberly, "Oscar Wilde Meets Woodberry," *Prairie Schooner* (Spring 1947); Francis Roellinger, Jr., "Oscar Wilde in Cleveland," *Ohio State Archaeological and Historical Quarterly* (April 1950); St. John Ervine, *Oscar Wilde: A Present Time Appraisal* (1952); Madeleine Stern, *Purple Passage: The Life of Mrs. Frank Leslie* (1953); Robert Herron, "Have Lily, Will Travel: Oscar Wilde in Cincinnati," *Bulletin of the Historical and Philosophical Society of Ohio* (July 1957); Owen Peterson, "Aesthetic Apostle: The Southern Lecture Tour of Oscar Wilde," *Southern Speech Journal* (Winter 1960); Vyvyan Holland, *Oscar Wilde: A Pictorial Biography* (1960); Robert Gathorne-Hardy, ed., *Ottoline: The Early Memoirs of Lady Ottoline Morrell* (1963); Norman Alford, "Oscar Wilde in Texas," *Texas Quarterly* (Summer 1967); Elizabeth Shafer, "The Wild, Wild West of Oscar Wilde," *Montana: The Magazine of Western History* (Spring 1970); Oscar Wilde, *Irish Poets and Poetry of the Nineteenth Century*, ed. Robert Pepper (1972); John Spalding Gatton, "The Sunflower Saint: Oscar Wilde in Louisville," *Filson Club Historical Quarterly* (Jan. 1978); John Davenport Neville, "Oscar Wilde: An Apostle of Aestheticism in the Old Dominion," *Virginia Cavalcade* (Fall 1978); Robert Luttrell McBath and J. O. Baylen, "'Oh, the Patriots, the Patriots!': Oscar Wilde, Georgia, and the Fourth of July," *Atlanta Historical Journal* (Spring 1980); Charles Cagle, "Oscar Wilde in Kansas," *Kansas History* (Winter 198l); Robert Pepper, "San Jose Greets

Oscar Wilde: April Third 1882," *San Jose Studies* (Spring 1982); Kevin O'Brien, *Oscar Wilde in Canada* (1982); Mary Ellis, "Improbable Visitor: Oscar Wilde in Alabama, 1882," *Alabama Review* (Oct. 1986); Terry Meyers, "Oscar Wilde and Williamsburg, Virginia," *N&Q* (Sept. 1991).

LECTURES IN BRITAIN, 1883–85

Unlike Wilde's American lecture tour, his British series of lectures, as Geoff Dibb observes, "is probably the least documented activity of his adult life" (*Wildean* Vol. 3). Moreover, the texts of Wilde's lectures are "virtually unknown" (see individual entries). Though it is sometimes possible to gain a general idea of their contents by examining newspaper reports, such lectures as those on dress may be revised versions with altered titles, a practice he used in his American lecture tour.

After Wilde returned to London in May 1883 from his American tour – having first lived lavishly for three months in Paris – Colonel W. F. Morse, his tour manager in America, suggested a similar tour of Britain. On 18 August, Morse wrote to Wilde: "I can foresee a good season's work and fair prices – not large" (qtd. in *Letters* 15ln2). Reduced to near penury, Wilde readily agreed.

Schedule of Lectures, 1883-85

Two lectures listed on the same day indicate those given in matinee and evening performances; single lectures on succeeding days at the same location are indicated by hyphenated dates. Wilde's shift in lecture topics from city to city is also indicated. Several lectures given in June and July are here listed before the actual tour began on 24 September 1883.

June, 1883

30　Golden Square, Westminster (to art students of the Royal Academy at their club): "Lecture to Art Students"

July

10　Prince's Hall, Piccadilly: "Impressions of America" (sometimes titled "Personal Impressions of America")

26　Margate and Ramsgate.

27　Southampton

28　Brighton

30　Southport

September

24　Town Hall, Wandsworth

October

8　Free Trade Hall, Manchester

25　Lecture Hall, Derby

26　Stephenson Memorial Hall, Chesterfield, " The House Beautiful"

November

2　Exeter

9-10　Theatre Royal, Bournemouth: "Impressions of America" and "The House Beautiful"

22-24　Gaiety Theatre, Dublin: "The House Beautiful and " Personal Impressions of America"

December

10　Claughton Music Hall, Birkenhead (near Liverpool): "Personal Impressions of America"

18　The Theatre, Worcester: "The House Beautiful"

21　Crystal Palace, Norwood (London)

January, 1884

21-22　Firth College, Sheffield: "The House Beautiful" and "Impressions of America"

23　Queen Street Assembly Rooms, Huddersfield

26　Dean Clough Institute, Stannary, Halifax: "The House Beautiful"

29　Town Hall, Harrogate: "Personal Impressions of America"

30　Stephenson Memorial Hall, Chesterfield, "Impressions of America"

31　Grand Saloon, Fine Art Exhibition, York: "The House Beautiful" and "Personal Impressions of America"

February

1　Londesborough Rooms, Scarborough: "Impressions of America"

11　Albert Hall, Leeds: "The House Beautiful" and "Impressions of America"

13　Public Hall, Cockermouth, Cumberland: "Impressions of America"

14　Mechanics Institute, Bradford

18　County Hall, Carlisle: "The House Beautiful"

22　Temperance Hall, Ulverston

March

5　Crystal Palace: "Impressions of America"

?　Greenock: "The Value of Art in Modern Life"

April

26　East End, London: "Art for Schools"

October

1　Ealing: "Dress"

6　Liverpool

9　Fine Art Exhibition Hall (Yorkshire Fine Art and Industrial Exhibition), York: "The Value of Art in Modern Life" and "Dress"

10　Town Hall, Harrogate: "Dress"

15　Lesser Victoria Room, Clifton (near Bristol): "Dress" (two lectures)

November

5　Town Hall, Stoke-on-Trent: "The Value of Art in Modern Life"

[ca. 11 Nov.]　Birmingham [?]

December

3   Mechanics Institute, Bradford: "Dress"
4   Albert Hall, Leeds: "Beauty, Taste and Ugliness in "Dress"
7   Glasgow
11   Southport
13   Carlisle: "Dress"
19   Glasgow
20   Queen Street Hall, Edinburgh: "Dress" and "The Value of Art in Modern Life"
21   St. Andrew's Hall, Glasgow: "Dress: Artistic Dress and Modern Dress"

According to Ellmann (262/247), Wilde undertook 21 lectures in Ireland, Dec. 1884 - Jan.1885, including the following:

January, 1885

5-6 Gaiety Theatre, Dublin: "Dress" and "The Value of Art in Modern Life"
14   Clonmel
17   Dundalk
18   Tyne Theatre, Newcastle, "Dress"

Wilde returned to England to deliver lectures (titles not known) in the following cities – including those in Wales and Scotland towards the end of his tour:

23   Huddersfield
24   King's Lynn
25   Lincoln
28   Gainsborough

[In Ellmann's listing, the 30 Jan. lecture in Chesterfield occurred not in 1885 but 1884.]

February

1   Scarborough, then Darlington and Falkirk
27   Chesterfield (?), then (dates uncertain) on to Stockton, Maryport, Cockermouth, Ulverston, Sunderland, Leicester

March

7   Leamington, then Cheltenham
10   Wolverhampton
11   Walsall
12   Leicester
14   Northampton, then Colchester, Ipswich, Yarmouth, Norwich, Bury St. Edmunds, Cardiff, Swansea
31   Newport, then Appleton, Birmingham, Peterborough, Edinburgh

After the end of his tour, Wilde gave the same two lectures in the following cities:

November

8   Theatre Royal, North Shields
9   Assembly Hall, Sunderland
10   Town Hall, Newcastle: "The Mission of Art in the Nineteenth Century"

Reference: Geoff Dibb, "Oscar Wilde's Lectures in West Yorkshire," *Wildean*, Vols. 3–4 (1993–94).

LE GALLIENNE, RICHARD (1866–1947)

A poet, critic, novelist, and memoirist, Le Gallienne first saw Wilde on 10 December 1883, at the Claughton Music Hall in Birkenhead, near Liverpool, where Richard's father, John Gallienne, secretary to a brewery company, took him to hear Wilde lecture on "Personal Impressions of America." The younger Gallienne (who later added "Le" to his name) was "enraptured," write his biographers: "So much of this engaging person's teaching appeared to justify and encourage his own ambitions to burn with a hard, gem-like flame.... Already as he left the hall Richard could see the path he had to tread. Wilde's was the star he must follow, and follow it he would" (Whittington-Egan and Smerdon 45–46).

In September 1887, Le Gallienne met Wilde in London and sent him a copy of his first volume of verse, *My Ladies' Sonnets*, which was, Wilde wrote, a "charming little printed edition" (*Letters* 209). While in London in June 1888, Le Gallienne, having spent three days with Wilde, wrote to John Lane of the Bodley Head: "But Oscar Wilde, sweet 'Fancy's child,' how can I write of him to-night?, of all his dear delightful ways thro' three sweet summer nights & days; suffice it I have never yet more fascinating fellow met, and O! how sweet he was to me is only known to R. Le G" (qtd. in Nelson 20). After having been invited to Wilde's Tite Street home in March 1889, Le Gallienne sent him MSS. of his poems, which commemorated their meetings or the appearance of one of Wilde's works. When Le Gallienne's *George Meredith: Some Characteristics* (1890) appeared, Wilde wrote to praise it as

a wonderful book, full of exquisite intuitions, and bright illuminating thought-flashes, and swift, sudden, sure revelations.... I knew the book would be excellent, but its fine maturity amazes me; it has a rich ripeness about it.... I want so much to see you: when can that be? Friendship and love like ours need not meetings, but they are delightful. I hope the laurels are not too thick across your brow for me to kiss your eyelids. (*Letters* 277)

Le Gallienne, who became a member of the Rhymers' Club in 1890 or 1891, probably saw Wilde (not a member but a "guest") at a few meetings, when they were held at members' homes.

LE GALLIENNE, RICHARD

By January 1892, Le Gallienne had achieved importance among the Rhymers, for he was not only reviewing widely in London newspapers and periodicals but he was also the chief reader of MSS. for the Bodley Head, which would publish the Rhymers' anthologies as well as volumes by individual poets associated with the club.

On 20 February 1892, Le Gallienne and his wife attended the première of *Lady Windermere's Fan* at the St. James's Theatre. Wilde had sent him tickets with a note: "Dear Poet, Here are two stalls for my play. Come, and bring your poem to sit beside you" (*Letters* 310). However, Le Gallienne found the play

> rather disappointing.... Not original enough for Oscar. But, of course, it was more the man than the play – which was full of laughable bits of "Oscar." He came before the curtain afterwards and the audience would have a speech.... He thanked the audience for their kind appreciation – they seemed, he said, to have enjoyed his play almost as much as he had enjoyed it himself. You know his style.... He certainly has the most consummate "cheek" of anyone I know. (qtd. in Whittington-Egan and Smerdon 182–83)

However, in reviewing Wilde's *Poems* (1892) in the *Daily Chronicle* (23 May 1892), Le Gallienne remarks that

> no person in earnest about his pleasures will deny that the volume, as a whole, gives one a sense of a new personality. Indeed,...it is a curious fact that a book so full of echoes [which previous critics particularly noted from such poets as Swinburne and Rossetti] should bring so unmistakeable an impression of an original temperament. Mr. Wilde is certainly more original in his "quotations" than most people are in their "originality."

As "Logroller," Le Gallienne reviewed Wilde's French version of *Salomé* in the *Star* (22 Feb. 1893), noting the Symbolist influence and prophetically anticipating the operatic version by Richard Strauss: "It seems built to music. Its gradual growth is exactly like the development of a theme in music" (qtd. in *More Letters* 120n3). Wilde responded:"... how pleased I am that you,with your

Richard Le Gallienne

fluid artistic temperament, should have glided into the secret of the soul of my poem, swiftly, surely, just as years ago you glided into my heart.... I rejoice to think that to you has my secret been revealed, for you are the lover of beauty, and by her much – perhaps over-much – loved and worshipped" (*More Letters* 120–21).

By the summer of that year, however, the poet Theodore Wratislaw (1871–1933) recalls that he and Wilde discussed Le Gallienne's recently published *English Poems*, which contains a prefatory poem attacking French Decadence in English art ("strange green flowers," suggesting green carnations) and a satirical poem titled "The Décadent to His Soul." Wilde, says Wratislaw, "expressed his wonder as to the object of Le Gallienne's onslaught and seemed taken aback when I said that it was undoubtedly himself. He was silent for a moment or two and then remarked: 'Well! it has always seemed to me that the finest feature of a fine nature is treachery.'" Wilde explained that, "to a sensitive nature, the burden of gratitude must be over-whelming, and it was therefore part of the fineness of the debtor's character that he should find it necessary to betray his benefactor" (*Oscar Wilde* 14–15).

By the mid-1890s, Wilde and Le Gallienne apparently ceased their correspondence, nor is there any evidence that they saw each other again. During the Wilde trials, Le Gallienne persuaded John Lane of the Bodley Head, who had considered withdrawing Wilde's books, "that Oscar was much too good a writer to drop even now, whatever the Philistines...had to say about it" (qtd. in Whittington-Egan and Smerdon 282). Nevertheless, when Le Gallienne was preparing his *Retrospective Reviews* (2 vols., 1896) for publication by the Bodley Head, no reviews of Wilde's books were included, presumably a consequence of the Wilde scandal.

In February 1900, some 10 months before Wilde died, Le Gallienne published a novel, *The Worshipper of the Image*, which Whittington-Egan and Smerdon call "an unwholesome little book, palely reflecting all the melodramatic stage properties of the decadence," prompting "oft-quoted criticism of Le Gallienne's work as 'largely Wilde-and-water'" (362). With Wilde's passing, Le Gallienne wrote: "Poor Oscar! his death made a dark day for me. I shall never forget him. He was a great original personality say what they will, and I believe time will confirm his value" (qtd. in Whittington-Egan and Smerdon 403).

In 1907, the New York publisher A. R. Keller & Co. issued an unauthorized 15-volume collected edition of Wilde's works with Le Gallienne's introduction, which points to the fusion in Wilde's writings of the love of beauty and the sense of comedy:

It was as though Keats and Sheridan had been reincarnated in one man. One might add Beau Brummell, and one gains a rough generalization of the complexity that was Oscar Wilde.... Not that he was so eminent as any of these in their own special characteristic; but it was the combination of all three in one man, plus his own extraordinary individuality, that made him so original a figure....

While living in New York, Le Gallienne was asked to write a new version of *Salome*, but, as he wrote in a letter, "the theme was too much Oscar's own, and my writing another play upon it would seem too much like a piece of cheap opportunism..." (qtd. in Whittington-Egan and Smerdon 427). On

looking back in *The Romantic '90s*, Le Gallienne delights in Wilde's wit, but he is nevertheless critical of Wilde's effect on the doctrine of Aestheticism, the memoirs providing an opportunity for a final estimate of his former friend:

Oscar Wilde popularized, and indeed somewhat vulgarized, as he perhaps to a degree misunderstood, and certainly dangerously applied, the gospel of beauty and "ecstasy" which Pater taught with hierarchical reserve and with subdued though intense passion and colour of words. (55)

References: Le Gallienne, *The Romantic '90s* (1925; rpt. 1951, intro. by H. Montgomery Hyde); Richard Whittington-Egan and Geoffrey Smerdon, *The Quest of the Golden Boy: The Life and Letters of Richard Le Gallienne* (1962); James G. Nelson, *The Early Nineties: A View from the Bodley Head* (1971); Theodore Wratislaw, *Oscar Wilde: A Memoir*, foreword by Sir John Betjeman; intro. and notes by Karl Beckson (1979).

"THE LETTERS OF A GREAT WOMAN"

Published: *PMG*, 6 March 1886, 4–5; rpt. in *Reviews* (1908). An unsigned review of *Letters of George Sand*, translated and edited by Raphael Ledos de Beaufort (1886).

At the outset of this review, Wilde announces, "Of the many collections of letters that have appeared in this century few, if any, can rival for fascination of style and variety of incident the letters of George Sand...." When the letters reach 1831, the year in which Sand separated from her husband and during which she entered into Parisian life, "the interest becomes universal, and the literary and political history of France is mirrored in every page." Her letters, Wilde notes, "reveal to us not merely the life of a great novelist, but the soul of a great woman, of a woman who was one with all the noblest movements of her day, and whose sympathy with humanity was boundless absolutely."

Touching on Sand's adoption of the dandy's ideology, Wilde also stresses Sand's humane inclinations: "For the aristocracy of intellect she had always the deepest veneration, but the democracy of suffering touched her more. She preached the regeneration of mankind, not with the noisy ardour of the paid advocate, but with the enthusiasm of the true evangelist. Of all the artists of this century she was the most altruistic; she felt every one's misfortunes except her own."

Sand's letters from 1850 reflect her literary interests: she discusses realism with Flaubert and playwriting with Dumas *fils*. Wilde writes of Sand's "protests with passionate vehemence against the doctrine of 'L'art pour l'art.' 'Art for the sake of itself is an idle sentence,' she writes; 'art for the sake of truth, for the sake of what is beautiful and good, that is the creed I seek.'" Since Wilde was devoted not only to the notion of "art for art's sake" but also to the Victorian injunction that art should serve useful, moral ends, he questions Sand's aesthetic attitudes: "Perhaps she valued good intentions in art a little too much, and she hardly understood that art for art's sake is not meant to express the final cause of art but is merely a formula of creation; but, as she herself had scaled Parnassus, we must not quarrel at her bringing Proletarianism with her. For George Sand must be ranked among our poetic geniuses."

Sand, Wilde observes, did not admire realism, "in M. Zola's acceptation of the word." To her, art was "a mirror that transfigured truths but did not represent realities." She could not, therefore, "understand art without personality" – hence her opposition to Flaubert's approach to fiction, as she writes to him: "...as soon as you handle literature, you seem anxious, I know not why, to be another man, the one who must disappear, who annihilates himself and is no more. What a singular mania!"

Wilde obviously agrees with her when she says to Flaubert that "the worth of our productions depends entirely on our own." She thought that Flaubert was much too preoccupied with form, about which her "excellent observations" are "perhaps her best piece of literary criticism": "You consider the form as the aim, whereas it is but the effect.... We are only moved by that which we ardently believe in." Yet her "too dominant personality," Wilde remarks, was apparently "the reason of the failure of most of her plays. Of the drama in the sense of disinterested presentation she had no idea, and what is the strength and life blood of her novels is the weakness of her dramatic works."

LEVERSON, ADA (1862–1933)

A noted satirist and later a novelist, Leverson (née Beddington) was born into a cultured, pros-

perous family living in a Hyde Park Square mansion. A promising marriage at the age of 19 to Ernest Leverson, 31, the son of a prosperous diamond merchant, soon turned disagreeable, particularly when she discovered that Ernest had an illegitimate daughter who was being raised in a Paris convent. His fondness for gambling led her to turn to other men for consolation and companionship. In 1891 she was corresponding with George Moore and sending him some of her writings. She apparently began meeting him secretly, concerned, she told him, about being discovered: "I am not afraid of death but I am of scandal, of which I have a special horror. The idea of being talked about is one of which I have a weak terror" (qtd. in Wyndham 23).

She first met Wilde probably in late February 1892 at a party: "She and Oscar Wilde were attracted to one another immediately, and thus began one of the deepest and most influential friendships of Ada's life" (Speedie 33). He called her "the wittiest woman in the world," and she later wrote in her memoir that "Oscar was the most generous man I have ever met..." (qtd. in Wyndham 122). He was so fond of sending wires to his friends to announce social gatherings that she facetiously planned to edit a volume titled *The Collected Telegrams of Oscar Wilde*. When she wrote a parody of *Dorian Gray* for *Punch* (15 July 1893) titled "An Afternoon Party," in which such figures as Lady Windermere, Salome, Lord Henry Wotton, Mrs. Tanqueray (of Pinero's play), and Nora (of Ibsen's *Doll's House*) are guests, Wilde called it "brilliant, as your work always is," adding: "It is quite tragic for me to think how completely *Dorian Gray* has been understood on all sides!" (*Letters* 343).

In his letters and telegrams, he called her "the Sphinx of Modern Life" or simply "Dear Sphinx" (his story "The Sphinx without a Secret" had appeared in 1887). In 1894, she wrote a satire of Wilde's poem *The Sphinx* for *Punch* (21 July), titled "The Minx," a comic interview between the Sphinx and the Poet. The editor of *Punch*, Francis Cowley Burnand (1836–1917) apparently regarded Leverson's satire as so successful that he wrote cautiously to her: "...I don't want to *revive* any 'cult' of *him* – it seems for the general public the 'craze' which this illustrates is a bit out of date" (qtd. in Speedie 63).

Nevertheless, in the 12 January 1895 issue,

Burnand published another Leverson parody, "Overheard Fragment of a Dialogue," which mimics Wildean wit in a comic dialogue between Lord Goring (of *An Ideal Husband*) and Lord Illingworth (of *A Woman of No Importance*), as in the following: "If one tells the truth, one is sure sooner or later to be found out" (an epigram that had appeared in Wilde's "Phrases and Philosophies for the Use of the Young"). Before the Wilde trials, Leverson's Wildean parody of *The Importance of Being Earnest* appeared as "The Advisability of Not Being Brought up in a Handbag: A Trivial Tragedy for Wonderful People" in *Punch* (2 March 1895). Wilde thought the title "quite charming" (*Letters* 383).

Leverson attracted such artists and writers to her home as John Gray, Max Beerbohm, Charles Conder, Walter Sickert, Aubrey Beardsley, Charles Ricketts, John Singer Sargent, and, of course, Wilde and Lord Alfred Douglas. When Robert Hichens's brilliant satire of Wilde and Douglas, *The Green Carnation*, appeared anonymously in 1894, Leverson was believed to be its author. Wilde assured her that the novel contained "many bits not unworthy of your brilliant pen..." (*Letters* 373). Leverson, who attended the première of *The Importance of Being Earnest*, recalled that Wilde was wearing a green carnation – as though to reenforce his connection with Hichens's novel.

After Wilde was released on bail after his first criminal trial, Ada and Ernest Leverson welcomed him into their home when no hotel would accept him as a guest and when Wilde's only alternative was to stay with his brother and mother. Indeed, Ernest lent Wilde a large sum of money and assisted him in his business affairs, but after his release from prison, Wilde accused him – unjustifiably, writes Speedie – of withholding money.

When Wilde was brought to Stewart Headlam's home after being released from Pentonville Prison, the Leversons arrived, Ada recalling that Wilde entered the drawing room "with the dignity of a king returning from exile." (Wyndham 121). In the following year, she visited him in Paris, and when *The Ballad of Reading Gaol* appeared, Wilde sent her an inscribed copy: "To the Sphinx of Pleasure from the Singer of Pain." Her loyalty was steadfast to the year of his death. Despite his quarrel with her husband, Wilde never wavered in his affection for her.

After her separation from Ernest (in 1902, he emigrated to Canada with his illegitimate daughter, where he lived until his death in 1922), Ada published six successful novels between 1907 and 1916, written with the epigrammatic, paradoxical wit that Wilde had admired. She remained devoted to the memory of Wilde in articles and in her last published work, *Letters to the Sphinx from Oscar Wilde* (1930), whose contents are cut or altered.

References: Violet Wyndham, *The Sphinx and Her Circle: A Memoir of Ada Leverson* (1963); Charles Burkhart, *Ada Leverson* (1973); Julie Speedie, *Wonderful Sphinx: The Biography of Ada Leverson* (1993).

"LIBERTATIS SACRA FAMES"

Published: *World: A Journal for Men and Women* 13 (10 Nov. 1880): 15; rev. in *Poems* (1881), further rev. in (1882). This sonnet, with its Latin title meaning "The Sacred Hunger for Liberty," was probably written in late 1880, at a time when Russian revolutionaries were carrying out acts of terrorism in protest against the repressive rule by Emperor Alexander II, who escaped an explosion in February 1880 in the dining room at the Winter Palace when dinner was not served at the customary hour. Wilde's *Vera; or, The Nihilists*, inspired by such events, was written in September 1880.

On his lecture tour in 1882, Wilde responded to an interviewer's question in San Francisco concerning his politics: "If you would like to know my political creed, read the sonnet 'Libertatis Sacra Fames'" (*Daily Examiner*, 27 March 1882 – rpt. in Mikhail 1:62). See "Sonnet to Liberty" for Wilde's response to the same reporter's query concerning this sonnet.

In "Libertatis Sacra Fames," Wilde alludes to his being nurtured in democracy and liking "best that state republican / Where every man is Kinglike and no man / Is crowned above his fellows...." Yet such a political system invites "clamorous demagogues [who] betray / Our freedom with the kiss of anarchy." The "rule of One, whom all obey" is therefore better, for those who "Plant the red flag upon the piled-up street / For no right cause" create a reign in which "Arts, Culture, Reverence, Honour, all things fade / Save Treason and the dagger of her trade, / Or Murder with his silent bloody feet."

Manuscript: The Clark Library has an untitled early MS. consisting of jottings (printed in Dulau

8).

"LITERARY AND OTHER NOTES"

Published: *Woman's World* 1 (Nov. 1887): 36–40; rpt. in *Reviews* (1908). Signed reviews ("By the Editor").

Wilde opens with the remark that Princess Christian's translation of the *Memoirs of Wilhelmine* (1887) is "a most fascinating and delightful book. The Margravine and her brother, Frederick the Great, were, as the Princess herself points out in an admirably written introduction, 'among the first of those questioning minds that strove after spiritual freedom' in the last century." They had studied the English philosophers and were "roused to enthusiasm" by Voltaire and Rousseau. Wilde quotes further from the introduction: "In the eighteenth century began that great struggle of philosophy against tyranny and worn-out abuses which culminated in the French Revolution. The noblest minds were engaged in the struggle, and, like most reformers, they pushed their conclusions to extremes, and too often lost sight of the need of a due proportion in things."

In the preface to *Women's Voices: An Anthology* (1887), Mrs. William Sharp writes that the "idea of making this anthology arose primarily from the conviction that our women-poets had never been collectively represented with anything like adequate justice...and that at least some fine fugitive poetry could be thus rescued from oblivion." The collection, says Wilde, is "certainly extremely interesting, extending, as it does over nearly three centuries of our literature." Included is "A Song" by Mrs. Aphra Behn, "the first English woman who adopted literature as a profession" and Emily Brontë, "whose poems are instinct with tragic power and quite terrible in their bitter intensity of passion, the fierce fire of feeling seeming almost to consume the raiment of form." Included, also, is George Eliot, "whose poetry," Wilde remarks, "is too abstract, and lacks all rhythmical life; Mrs. Carlyle, who wrote much better poetry than her husband, though this is hardly high praise; and Mrs. Browning, the first really great poetess in our literature." Among the contemporary writers is Christina Rossetti, "some of whose poems are quite priceless in their beauty."

Wilde turns next to Margaret Woods's *A Village Tragedy* (1887), which he calls "one of the most powerful and pathetic novels that has recently appeared." Parallels to "this lurid little story" may be found in Dostoevsky or Guy de Maupassant: "Not that Mrs. Woods can be said to have taken either of these great masters of fiction as her model, but there is something in her work that recalls their method; she has not a little of their fierce intensity, their terrible concentration, their passionless yet poignant objectivity." The plot involves "a romance of modern Arcadia – a tale of the love of a farm-labourer for a girl who, though slightly above him in social station and education, is yet herself also a servant on a farm." Though the novel "lays bare to us the mere misery of life, it suggests something of life's mystery also."

"LITERARY AND OTHER NOTES"

Published: *Woman's World* 1 (Dec. 1887): 81–85; rpt. in *Reviews* (1908). Signed reviews ("By the Editor").

Wilde remarks that Lady Bellair's *Gossips with Girls and Maidens Betrothed and Free* (1887) contains "some very interesting essays, and a quite extraordinary amount of useful information on all matters connected with the mental and physical training of women," managing "very cleverly to steer a middle course between the Charybdis of dulness and the Scylla of flippancy." Quoting from a section on "What to Avoid," such as "Entertaining wild flights of the imagination, or empty idealistic aspirations," Wilde comments: "I am afraid that I have a good deal of sympathy with what are called 'empty idealistic aspirations'; and 'wild flights of the imagination' are so extremely rare in the nineteenth century that they seem to me deserving rather of praise than of censure."

Turning to Constance Naden's *A Modern Apostle and Other Poems* (1887), Wilde admires its "culture in its use of language, courage in its selection of subject-matter." In summarizing the plot – "a young clergyman who preaches Pantheistic Socialism in the Free Church of some provincial manufacturing town, converts everybody, except the woman he loves, and is killed in a street riot" – Wilde concludes that the story is "exceedingly powerful, but seems more suitable for prose than for verse." He then proceeds to enunciate some aesthetic principles:

It is right that a poet should be full of the spirit of his age, but the external forms of modern life are hardly, as yet, expressive of that spirit. They are truths of fact, not the truths of the imagination, and though they may give the poet an opportunity for realism, they often rob the poem of the reality that is so essential to it. Art, however, is a matter of result, not of theory, and if the fruit is pleasant, we should not quarrel about the tree.

Naden's work is "distinguished by rich imagery, fine colour, and sweet music, and these are things for which we should be grateful, wherever we find them. She deserves," concludes Wilde, "a high place among our living poetesses."

Phyllis Browne's *Mrs. Somerville and Mary Carpenter* (1887) – a biography of Mrs. Somerville, a mathematician, scientist, and translator – forms part of a series of volumes called "The World's Workers" (a biography of Florence Nightingale is included). Wilde notes that Mrs. Somerville's bust is in the hall of the Royal Society, and a woman's college at Oxford is named after her. "Yet," says Wilde, "considered simply in the light of a wife and a mother, she is no less admirable; and those who consider that stupidity is the proper basis for the domestic virtues, and that intellectual women must of necessity be helpful with her hands, cannot do better than read Phyllis Browne's pleasant little book...." Mrs. Somerville's scientific knowledge did not "warp or dull the tenderness and humanity of her nature," Wilde continues, for she had a great love for birds and animals. She vigorously tried to get the Italian Parliament to pass a law for the protections of animals, and she once said: "We English cannot boast of humanity so long as our sportsmen find pleasure in shooting down tame pigeons as they fly terrified out of a cage" – a remark, says Wilde, "with which I entirely agree."

Bound in the same volume is a biography of Mary Carpenter (the educator who established schools and instituted educational reforms), also written by Phyllis Browne. Carpenter, "one of the practical, hardworking saints of the nineteenth century," carried on "her work of rescue and reformation...under great difficulties." There is, however, something "a little pathetic," says Wilde, "in the attempt to civilise the rough street-boy by means of the refining influence of ferns and fossils, and it is difficult to help feeling that Miss Carpenter rather overestimated the value of elementary education. The poor are not to be fed on

facts...."

Wilde turns to May Laffan's *Ismay's Children* (1887) by the "clever authoress of that wonderful little story *Flitters, Tatters, and the Counsellor*, a story which delighted the realists by its truth, fascinated Mr. Ruskin by its beauty, and remains to the present day the most perfect picture of street-arab life in all English prose fiction." The scene of *Ismay's Children* is Ireland, the plot involving a dramatic and ingenious young Irishman who runs off with Ismay, a "pretty, penniless governess, and is privately married to her in Scotland." After both characters die, the remainder of the novel is devoted to the fortunes of the children. The book's chief interest, says Wilde, "lies in the little lifelike sketches of Irish character with which it abounds....and for pure fidelity and truth to nature, nothing could be better than the minor characters in *Ismay's Children*."

With reviews of books completed, Wilde turns to his "notes," the first of which focuses on women's fashions (a topic that increasingly absorbed him). Much had been written at this time concerning "rational dress," which would enable women to dress comfortably. On the subject of tight lacing, Wilde remarks: "To begin with, the waist is not a circle at all, but an oval; nor can there be any greater error than to imagine that an unnaturally small waist gives an air of grace, or even of slightness, to the whole figure."

Wilde notes that Mrs. Dinah Craik, the author of *John Halifax, Gentleman* (1886), had published an article on the English stage before her death in 1887. Of current drama, Wilde remarks:

...for my own part, I must acknowledge that I see more vulgarity than vice in the tendencies of the modern stage; nor do I think it possible to elevate dramatic art by limiting its subject-matter.... As far as the serious presentation of life is concerned, what we require is more imaginative treatment, greater freedom from theatric language and theatric convention. It may be questioned, also, whether the consistent reward of virtue and punishment of wickedness be really the healthiest ideal for an art that claims to mirror nature.

"LITERARY AND OTHER NOTES"

Published: *Woman's World* 1 (Jan. 1888): 132–36; rpt. in *Reviews* (1908). Signed reviews

"LITERARY AND OTHER NOTES"

("By the Editor").

Wilde begins by hailing Madame Adelaide Ristori's *Etudes et Souvenirs* (1887) as "one of the most delightful books on the stage that has appeared since Lady Martin's charming volume on the Shakespearian heroines" (*On Some of Shakespeare's Female Characters*, 1885). He continues with the oft-repeated observation that "actors leave nothing behind them but a barren name and withered wreath; that they subsist simply upon the applause of the moment; that they are ultimately doomed to the oblivion of old play-bills; and that their art, in a word, dies with them, and shares their own mortality." Wilde rejects the notion that acting is "simply a mimetic art," for such a view "takes no account of its imaginative and intellectual basis." While the actor's personality passes away, the "artistic method of a great actor survives. It lives on in tradition, and becomes part of the science of a school." A case in point is the continuing influence of David Garrick on current actors, "far stronger than that of [Sir Joshua] Reynolds on our painters of portraits...."

Turning to Elizabeth Rachel Chapman's *The New Purgatory and Other Poems* (1887), Wilde calls it "a very remarkable little volume," adding:

It used to be said that women were too poetical by nature to make great poets, too receptive to be really creative, too well satisfied with mere feeling to search after the marble splendour of form. But we must not judge of woman's poetic power by her achievements in days when education was denied to her, for where there is no faculty of expression no art is possible.

Wilde proceeds with his discussion to a consideration of Elizabeth Barrett Browning, "the first great English poetess" and "an admirable scholar," who, in such a work seemingly "most remote from classical life," *Aurora Leigh*, reveals the "fine literary influence of a classical training." Since her time, education has become "not the privilege of a few women, but the inalienable inheritance of all; and, as a natural consequence of the increased faculty of expression thereby gained, the women poets of our day hold a very high literary position." Wilde has reservations, however, about the women poets of his time:

Curiously enough, their poetry is, as a rule, more distinguished for strength than for beauty; they seem to love to grapple with the big intellectual problems of modern life; science, philosophy and metaphysics form a large portion of their ordinary subject-matter; they leave the triviality of triolets to men, and try to read the writing on the wall, and to solve the last secret of the Sphinx. Hence Robert Browning, not Keats, is their idol.

Declaring Elizabeth Chapman as a probable disciple of Browning, Wilde perceives his influence on her verse: she has "caught something of his fine, strange faith." But, he continues, "true originality is to be found rather in the use made of a model than in the rejection of all models and masters."

Following this notice on Chapman, Wilde presents a brief survey of the 19th-century novel as a preface to his review of Lady Augusta Noel's *Hithersea Mere* (1887). In France, the one great genius, Balzac, "invented the modern method of looking at life," and one great artist, Flaubert, is the "impeccable master of style." Almost all of contemporary French fiction, Wilde contends, may be traced to their influence. In England, however, there have been no schools "worth speaking of":

The fiery torch lit by the Brontës has not been passed on to other hands; Dickens has influenced only journalism; Thackeray's delightful superficial philosophy, superb narrative power, and clever social satire have found no echoes; nor has Trollope left any direct successors behind him – a fact which is not much to be regretted, however,...admirable though Trollope undoubtedly is for rainy afternoons and tedious railway journeys...."

Wilde's evaluations of 19th-century British novelists achieves something of a climax in his famous attack on George Meredith, most of which reappears in "The Decay of Lying":

As for George Meredith, who could hope to reproduce him? His style is chaos illumined by brilliant flashes of lightning. As a writer he has mastered everything, except language; as a novelist he can do everything, except tell a story; as an artist he is everything, except articulate. Too strange to be popular, too individual to have imitators, the author of *Richard Feverel* stands absolutely alone....

However, says Wilde, "some signs of a school" are currently apparent: "This school is not native, nor does it seek to reproduce any English master. It may be described as the result of the realism of Paris filtered through the refining influence of Boston. Analysis, not action is its aim; it has more psychology than passion, and it plays very cleverly upon one string, and this is the commonplace" (clearly, Wilde is describing the influence of Zola's Naturalism on such American novelists as Henry James and William Dean Howells).

Turning to Lady Augusta Noel's novel, Wilde regards it as "a reaction against this school": "An industrious Bostonian would have made half a dozen novels out of it, and have had enough left for a serial." She is content to bring her characters to life rather than dissect them: "...she suggests rather than explains, and she does not seek to make life too obviously rational." The most delightful character in the novel is Hilary Marston, "a little woodland faun, half Greek and half gipsy...terribly out of place in a drawing-room...." With Lady Augusta Noel's "charming and winning style," and her admirable descriptions of nature, her book is "one of the most pleasantly-written novels that has appeared this winter."

Wilde finds the "same lightness of touch and grace of treatment" in Alice Corkran's *Margery Merton's Girlhood* (1887). Intended for young people, the story can be read with pleasure by all readers, and "its rejection of the stronger and more violent passions of life is artistic rather than ascetic." The eponymous character is raised by an old aunt in Paris, whose educational theory is founded on Darwin and the wisdom of Solomon, but it results in disaster when it is put into practice. Margery's development and "the various attempts she makes to give dream its perfect form is extremely interesting.... Mr. Ruskin in prose, and Mr. Browning in poetry, were the first who drew for us the workings of the artist soul, the first who led us from the painting or statue to the hand that fashioned it, and the brain that gave it life. They seem to have made art more expressive for us, to have shown us a passionate humanity lying behind line and colour. Theirs was the seed of this new literature...."

Wilde proceeds to Emily Pfeiffer's *Women and Work* (1887), a collection of "most interesting essays on the relation to health and physical development of the higher education of girls, and the intellectual or more systematised effort of woman." With her admirable prose style, Pfeiffer deals with the economic problem and the arguments of physiologists; she also produces "some very valuable statistics from America, where the influence of education on health has been most carefully studied. Her book is a most important contribution to the discussion of one of the great social problems of our day."

"LITERARY AND OTHER NOTES"
Published: *Woman's World* 1 (Feb. 1888): 180–84; rpt. in *Reviews* (1908). Signed reviews ("By the Editor") of books published in 1887.
Wilde hails *Canute the Great* by Michael Field (the pseudonym of Katherine Bradley and Edith Cooper: see their entry), as "a really remarkable work of art." The author has

borrowed from modern science the idea that in the evolutionary struggle for existence the true tragedy may be that of the survivor. Canute, the rough generous Viking, finds himself alienated from his gods, his forefathers, his very dreams. With centuries of Pagan blood in his veins, he sets himself to the task of becoming a great Christian governor and lawgiver to men; and yet he is fully conscious that, while he has abandoned the noble impulses of his race, he still retains that which in his nature is most fierce or fearful.

Noting that it is sin, not suffering, that purifies Canute, Wilde quotes from the drama: "Be not afraid; / I have learnt this, sin is a mighty bond / 'Twixt God and man." This "strange and powerful conception" is strong and subtle, and "almost every character in the play seems to suggest some new psychological problem." The verse is "essentially characteristic of our modern introspective method, as it presents to us, not thought in its perfected form, but the involutions of thought seeking for expression." However, Wilde points to

something harsh, abrupt, and inartistic in such a stage-direction as "Canute strangles Edric, flings his body into the stream, and gazes out." It strikes no dramatic note, it conveys no picture, it is meagre and inadequate. If acted it might be fine, but as read, it is unimpressive.

In the same volume, *The Cup of Water* has, Wilde writes, "certainly more beauty" than *Canute the Great* though it may have less power. Based on an idea for a story in Rossetti's notebook, the play involves a young king who falls passionately in love with a peasant girl who gives him a cup of water, but he marries instead a lady of noble birth. Wilde regards the "distinguishing qualities" of Field's verse as "those swift touches of nature and sudden flashes of thought."

Turning to Frances Martin's *Life of Elizabeth Gilbert*, Wilde judges it as "an extremely interesting book." Born in the early 19th century, Elizabeth Gilbert, the daughter of the principal of Brasenose College, Oxford, lived at a time when

kindly and intelligent men and women could gravely implore the Almighty to "take away" a child merely because it was blind; when they could argue that to teach the blind to read, or to attempt to teach them to work, was to fly in the face of Providence; and her whole life was given to the endeavour to overcome this prejudice and superstition; to show that blindness, though a great privation, is not necessarily a disqualification; and that blind men and women can learn, labour, and fulfill all the duties of life.

Before her death, Gilbert could "point to large and well-appointed workshops in almost every city of England where blind men and women are employed.... The whole story of her life is full of pathos and of beauty. She was not born blind, but lost her sight through an attack of scarlet fever when she was three years old." Wilde commends to his readers Martin's sympathetic biography of "one of the remarkable women of our century."

Calling Louise Chandler Moulton "one of the most graceful and attractive of all American poetesses," Wilde praises her "pleasant volume of social essays," *Ourselves and Our Neighbours.* With a "very light literary touch," Moulton discusses important modern problems – "from Society rosebuds and old bachelors, down to the latest fashions in bonnets and in sonnets.... The best chapter in the book is that entitled 'The Gospel of

Good Gowns,' which contains some very excellent remarks on the ethics of dress," such as "Let women delight our eyes like pictures, be harmonious as music, and fragrant as flowers, that they also may fulfil their mission of grace and of beauty."

Warring Angels, writes Wilde about this anonymous work, is "very sad and suggestive,...a truthful picture of men and women as they are." Darwin "could not have enjoyed it, as it does not end happily." Though, says Wilde, we are

often told that we are a shallow age, yet we have certainly the saddest literature of all the ages, for we have made Truth and not Beauty the aim of art, and seem to value imitation more than imagination. This tendency is, of course, more marked in fiction than it is in poetry. Beauty of form is always in itself a source of joy; the mere *technique* of verse has an imaginative and spiritual element; and life must, to a certain degree, be transfigured before it can find its expression in music. But ordinary fiction, rejecting the beauty of form in order to realise the facts of life, seems often to lack the vital element of delight, to miss that pleasure-giving power in virtue of which the arts exist.

This volume is not simply "a specimen of literary photography," for it has a "marked distinction of style, a definite grace and simplicity of manner."

Mrs. De Courcy Laffan's *A Song of Jubilee and Other Poems* "contains some pretty, picturesque verses." The author, known by the pseudonym of "Mrs. Leith Adams," is a well-known novelist and short story writer. Moving quickly to the next book under review, Wilde writes that Bella Duffy's *Life of Madame de Staël* contains "nothing absolutely new...but this was not to be expected" since the subject's papers and letters have either been destroyed or successfully concealed. However, this biography has "the excellent quality of condensation, and gives us in less than 200 pages a very good picture of Madame de Staël and her day." De Staël "gave our literature no form, but she was one of those who gave it a new spirit, and the romantic movement owes her no small debt."

The reprint of John Evelyn's *Life of Mrs. Godolphin*, Wilde continues, is a "welcome addition to the list of charming library books." Margaret

Godolphin, one of the Queen's maids of honor at the court of Charles II, was "distinguished for the delicate purity of her nature, as well as for her high intellectual attainments."

"LITERARY AND OTHER NOTES"

Published: *Woman's World* 1 (March 1888): 229–32; rpt. in *Reviews* (1908). Signed reviews ("By the Editor").

Wilde calls the *Memoirs of an Arabian Princess* (1888) by Princess Ruete of Oman and Zanzibar "a most interesting account of her life." Having married a German and having lived in Germany for many years, she writes "in a very simple and unaffected manner.... Her book throws a great deal of light on the question of the position of women in the East, and shows that much of what has been written on this subject is quite inaccurate.... All through her book the Princess protests against the idea that Oriental women are degraded or oppressed...."

Margaret Oliphant's *Makers of Venice* (1887–88), Wilde remarks in his next notice, is "an admirable literary *pendant* to the same writer's charming book on Florence [*Makers of Florence*, 1876]," a city "full of memories of the great figures of the past." But Venice evokes not the makers of the "marvellous city, but rather of what they made." We know, says Wilde,

that Dante stood within the red walls of the arsenal, and saw the galleys making and mending, and the pitch flaming up to heaven; Petrarch came to visit the great Mistress of the Sea, taking refuge there, "in this city, true home of the human race," from trouble, war and pestilence outside; and Byron, with his facile enthusiasms and fervent eloquence, made his home for a time in one of the stately, decaying palaces, but with these exceptions no great poet has ever associated himself with the life of Venice. She had architects, sculptors and painters, but no singer of her own.

Mabel Robinson's novel *The Plan of Campaign* (1887–88), notes Wilde, is a "very powerful study of modern political life.... Miss Robinson dissects, describes, and discourses with keen scientific insight and minute observation. Her style, though somewhat lacking in grace, is, at its best, simple and strong." After this brief paragraph, Wilde

moves briskly to Harriet Waters Preston's *A Year in Eden* (1886), "a chronicle of New England life...full of the elaborate subtlety of the American school of fiction." Her prose is "admirable," and the minor characters are "wonderfully lifelike and true" (such is Wilde's rather tepid response).

Turning to *The Englishwoman's Year-Book* (1888), Wilde notes the "extraordinary amount of useful information on every subject connected with woman's work." In the 1831 census, no occupation by women was specified except that of domestic service; in 1881, women's occupations numbered 330, the most prominent being domestic service, school teaching, and dressmaking; fewer were involved in banking, gardening, and science-related fields. The *Year-Book* mentions stockbroking and conveyancing "as professions that women are beginning to adopt."

The final book under review is *Rachel and Other Poems* (1887), by "I.S.," "a rather remarkable little volume in its way." Quoting some lines, Wilde notes the "Tennysonian echoes" in the author's "attractive verses." Other than the judgment that the title poem has "strong lines and good images," Wilde devotes little space to this volume.

"A LITERARY PILGRIM"

Published: *PMG* (17 April 1886): 5; rpt. in *Reviews* (1908). An unsigned review of Gaston Boissier's *Nouvelles Promenades Archéologiques: Horace et Virgile* (1886).

Though antiquarian books, says Wilde, are generally "extremely dull reading," an exception is to be found in Boissier's volume: "M. Boissier is a most pleasant and picturesque writer, and is really able to give his readers useful information without ever boring them, an accomplishment which is entirely unknown in Germany, and in England is extremely rare." Wilde focuses on Boissier's theory concerning the location of Horace's Roman villa, and, after the invention of printing, the profession of literature as a source of income. Since there was no copyright protecting books, patrons took the place of publishers: "The Roman patron, in fact, kept the Roman poet alive, and we fancy that many of our modern bards rather regret the old system." In his discussion of Virgil, Boissier claims that his descriptions of nature have "an absolute fidelity of detail." Though the landscape is "now covered with thriving manufactories and stucco villas, and the 'bird-haunted forest' through which the Tiber flowed into the sea has long since disappeared... the general character of the Italian landscape is unchanged...."

"THE LITTLE SHIP"

Not published in Wilde's lifetime, this poem of eight quatrains recalls a ship that the speaker and his love, when a little girl, had built as a "childish toy." The little ship was launched on the pond, and the speaker named it after her: "And for want of the bottle of wine love / We christened it with the dew." Her doll was placed on board with "a cargo of chocolate cream, / But the little ship struck on a cork love / And the doll went down with a scream!" That was 40 years ago, and now her hair is silver grey; they sit in old armchairs and watch their children play. If the poem is touchingly sentimental, it now introduces a startling element of reality:

> And I have a wooden leg love
> And the title K.C.B.
> For bringing her Majesty's Fleet love
> Over the stormy sea.

In his reverie, the speaker returns once more to the past: "I've never forgotten the ship love / I made as a childish toy...."

Manuscript: The Clark Library has the MS., probably written during Wilde's Oxford years.

"LONDON MODELS"

Published: *English Illustrated Magazine* 6 (Jan. 1889): 313–19, with 15 engravings from drawings by Harper Pennington (1855–1920), who, in 1881, painted a full-length portrait of Wilde (now in the Clark Library); rpt., without illustrations, in *Miscellanies* (1908).

"Professional models," Wilde begins, "are a purely modern invention. To the Greeks, for instance, they were quite unknown." The class of people "whose sole profession is to pose" is the "direct creation of Academic Schools." Now, every country has these professionals except America. In such cities as New York and Boston, a good model is "so great a rarity that most of the artists are reduced to painting Niagara and millionaires." In Europe, there are many models, the best of them being Italian. The English models "form a class entirely by themselves": "They are not so picturesque as the Italian, nor so clever as the

French, and they have absolutely no tradition, so to speak, of their order." Usually, the model today is a pretty girl, from about twelve to twenty-five years of age, who knows nothing about art, cares less, and is merely anxious to earn seven or eight shillings a day without much trouble. English models rarely look at a picture, and never venture on any aesthetic theories. In fact, they realise very completely Mr. Whistler's idea of the function of an art critic, for they pass no criticisms at all.... They merely desire that the studio shall be warm, and the lunch hot, for all charming artists give their models lunch.

Such models are intellectual Philistines, but "physically they are perfect – at least some are. Though none of them can talk Greek, many can look Greek, which to a nineteenth-century painter is naturally of great importance.... Their observations are the only *banalités* heard in Bohemia." They usually marry well, says Wilde; sometimes they marry the artist for whom they pose: "For an artist to marry his model is as fatal as for a *gourmet* to marry his cook: the one gets no sittings, and the other gets no dinners."

Among male models, the "true Academy" type is one who is thirty, "rarely good looking, but a perfect miracle of muscles. In fact he is the apotheosis of anatomy, and is so conscious of his own splendour that he tells you of his tibia and his thorax, as if no one else had anything of the kind." Acrobats and gymnasts bring to a painter's art "an element of swiftness of motion and of constant change that the studio model necessary [*sic*] lacks. What is interesting in these 'slaves of the ring' is that with them Beauty is an unconscious result not a conscious aim.... A good acrobat is always graceful, though grace is never his object."

In discussing the artificial effect produced by a painter who has "pretty people" constantly posing for him, Wilde comments: "...when art becomes artificial it becomes monotonous. Outside the little world of the studio, with its draperies and its *bric-à-brac*, lies the world of life with its infinite, its Shakespearean variety." But, Wilde concludes, we cannot blame the models for the artist's inadequacies. The English models are "a well-behaved and hard-working class, and if they are more interested in artists than in art, a large section of the public is in the same condition, and most of our modern exhibitions seem to justify its choice."

"LORD ARTHUR SAVILE'S CRIME"

Published: *Court and Society Review* 4 (11, 18, and 25 May 1887): 447–50, 471–73, and 495–97; rev. in *Lord Arthur Savile's Crime and Other Stories* (1891), the binding designed by Charles Ricketts. In its magazine appearance, the story's subtitle was "A Story of Cheiromancy," palmistry having come into fashion; in revised form, the subtitle became "A Study of Duty."

On several occasions, Wilde consulted a "fortune teller," a Mrs. Robinson, well known to fashionable society, whom he referred to as "the Sibyl of Mortimer Street" (*Letters* 358). In March 1895, he wrote to Ada Leverson that he and his wife, Constance, had been to the "Sibyl Robinson," who "prophesied complete triumph [in Wilde's libel case against the Marquess of Queensberry] and was most wonderful" (*Letters* 385). After his arrest on 5 April, he wrote to Leverson from Holloway Prison: "Why did the Sibyl say fair things?" (*Letters* 389). Later that month, Constance, in a letter to Mrs. Robinson, asked what was to become of her husband "who has so betrayed and deceived me and ruined the lives of my darling boys? Can you tell me anything?" (*Letters* 389n1).

The Plot: At the last reception before Easter, Lady Windermere (a name that Wilde would use again in *Lady Windermere's Fan*) is hostess to a crowd including six cabinet ministers, violent radicals, and Royal Academicians "disguised as artists." She confesses to the Duchess of Paisley that she cannot live without her cheiromantist, Mr. Septimus R. Podgers, "who comes to see my hand twice a week regularly." Podgers reads the Duchess's hand as well as those of some other guests. "Filled with an immense curiosity to have his own hand read," Lord Arthur asks Lady Windermere whether Podgers would read his palm. But when Podgers looks at Lord Arthur's right hand, he grows pale and remains silent, shaken by what he has seen. When he also examines Lord Arthur's left hand, his face becomes "a white mask of horror."

Aware of Podgers's "strange signs of agitation," Lord Arthur has a sense of dread, a "sickening sense of coming evil." He has lived "the delicate and luxurious life of a young man of birth and fortune, a life exquisite in its freedom from sordid care, its beautiful boyish insouciance; and now for the first time he became conscious of the terrible mystery of Destiny, of the awful meaning of Doom." He confronts Podgers and demands the truth of what he had seen. (Kohl, who calls this work a "gem of black humour," sees the description of Lady Windermere's *soirée* and the "pointed, epigrammatic dialogue of the characters" as the equivalent world of *Dorian Gray* and the social comedies, 63.)

Part II opens after Lord Arthur, in a frenzy of fear, has learned what his palm had revealed to Podgers: "Murder! that is what the cheiromantist had seen there. Murder!" Wandering through the London streets, he comes across a notice offering a reward for information leading to the arrest of a man suspected of murder: "Perhaps, some day, his own name might be placarded on the walls of London." The next morning, as he contemplates a photograph of Sybil Merton (the name anticipates the names of two characters in *The Picture of Dorian Gray*: Sibyl Vane and Hetty Merton): "He felt that to marry her, with the doom of murder hanging over his head, would be a betrayal like that of Judas...." The marriage must be postponed: "...he had no right to marry until he had committed the murder.... Life to him meant action, rather than thought." (Wilde parodies the detective story in reverse, Kohl writes, for Lord Arthur is not searching for a criminal but attempting to become one. The central paradox is that Lord Arthur uses such venerated Victorian concepts as "duty" and "sacrifice" to justify, Kohl writes, "a totally immoral deed [that] becomes in itself a morally neutral action," 63.)

But who should his victim be? "Not being a genius, he had no enemies...." He makes a list of friends and relatives who would be suitable. After careful consideration, he selects his second cousin on his mother's side, the elderly, sickly Lady Clementina Beauchamp, whom he is fond of. He decides that the poison aconitine (wolf's-bane), swift and deadly, would be the best means of disposing of her. When he visits her, he presents her with a capsule of the poison in an attractive silver *bonbon* box, informing her that it contains a "cure" for her illness. When she assures him that she will take the "American medicine" at the first sign of an attack, Lord Arthur leaves the house "with a feeling of immense relief." That night, he tells Sybil that their marriage must be postponed, for he is "in a position of terrible difficulty, from which neither honour nor duty would allow him to recede."

Lord Arthur goes to Venice to spend a fortnight with his brother, Lord Surbiton. While there, he studies the daily obituary columns in the *Times* for news of Lady Clementina's death. Finally, when a telegram informs him that she is dead, he returns immediately to London, only to discover that the old lady had died of a heart attack and that the poison remained untouched: "The shock of the discovery was almost too much for him. He flung the capsule into the fire, and sank on the sofa with a cry of despair." His marriage to Sybil would now have to be postponed a second time since duty required him to dispose of someone. His uncle, the Dean of Chichester, becomes the chosen victim, and dynamite is the preferred device with which to dispatch him. He consults with a Russian Count, suspected of being a Nihilist agent, for advice on where to obtain the appropriate "machine." Lord Arthur is directed to a German in Soho, who suggests sending an "explosive clock" – ideal, since the Dean, a collector of clocks, would welcome such a "present."

For days, there is nothing in the newspapers about an explosion killing the Dean. Lord Arthur then learns from a letter written by the Dean's daughter that the clock, sent by an "unknown admirer," struck twelve on the next morning with "a whirring noise, a little puff of smoke came from the pedestal of the figure, and the goddess of Liberty fell off, and broke her nose on the fender!" Removed to the schoolroom, it "does nothing but have small explosions all day long." In despair, Lord Arthur is "oppressed with the sense of the barrenness of good intentions, of the futility of trying to be fine." After spending some time at his club, he wanders down to the Thames Embankment, where he sits until two in the morning. Walking towards Blackfriars, he sees Podgers leaning over the parapet. Approaching, he lifts him up and into the Thames. Several days later, Lord Arthur reads a newspaper account of the "Suicide of a Cheiromantist." He rushes from the club to tell Sybil that they will be married as soon as possible.

In the final section of the story, the wedding takes place, performed by the Dean of Chichester, and some years later two children are born. On a visit by Lady Windermere, Lady Arthur informs her that her husband believes in cheiromancy (Lady Windermere had called Podgers "a dreadful imposter"). When Lord Arthur appears, he remarks that he owes all of his happiness to cheiromancy – that is, Sybil. "What nonsense!" cries Lady Windermere as the story ends.

LORD ARTHUR SAVILE'S CRIME AND OTHER PROSE PIECES: *See below*

LORD ARTHUR SAVILE'S CRIME AND OTHER STORIES

Published: July 1891 by James R. Osgood, McIlvaine & Co.; and in New York by Dodd, Mead & Co.; rpt. as *Lord Arthur Savile's Crime and Other Prose Pieces* (1908), which includes "The Portrait of Mr. W. H.," "Poems in Prose," and "The Rise of Historical Criticism."

Contents: [See individual entries:] Lord Arthur Savile's Crime – The Sphinx without a Secret – The Canterville Ghost – The Model Millionaire (and the "other prose pieces" in the 1908 edition).

Early Reviews: The reviewers were divided in judging this volume. The anonymous reviewer in the *Graphic* (22 Aug. 1891) remarked: "As pure farce – and what can be better than farce at its best? – it deserves to live.... The stories...are excellent, and their author is to be congratulated on having introduced an entirely new and original ghost to the world – no slight feat in these days" (rpt. in Beckson).

However, William Sharp, the Scottish journalist, biographer, and poet who published under the pseudonym of "Fiona Macleod," insisted in the *Academy* (5 Sept.) that the four stories "will not add to their author's reputation." Despite what Sharp regarded as its "florid style and shallow sentiment," *The Picture of Dorian Gray* was a work with "at least a certain cleverness; this quality, however, is singularly absent in at least the first three of these tales." The best of the group, he believed, was "The Model Millionaire," though it is sometimes spoiled, as are the other stories in the volume, "by such commonplace would-be witticisms as 'the poor should be practical and prosaic,' [and] 'it is better to have a permanent income than to be fascinating'" (rpt. in Beckson).

In the *United Ireland* (26 Sept.), W. B. Yeats sees in Wilde's "life and works an extravagant Celtic crusade against Anglo-Saxon stupidity. 'I labour under a perpetual fear of not being misunderstood,' he wrote...and behind this barrier of misunderstanding he peppers John Bull with his peashooter of wit, content to know there are some few who laugh with him." After praising Wilde's previous works, Yeats states that Wilde's volume of stories "disappoints me a little, I must confess." He found the lead story "amusing enough" but other stories had "a quaint if rather meagre charm" or "unworthy of more than a passing interest...." Yeats concludes by remarking that Wilde, Shaw (in whom he recognized the same spirit: "making merry among the things of the mind"), and Whistler ("half an Irishman also, I believe") "keep literary London continually agog to know what they will say next" (rpt. in Beckson).

"THE LORGNETTE"

Published: *Court and Society Review* 5 (14 Sept. 1887): 249–50; rpt. in Mason, 41–47 (uncollected in *Reviews*, 1908). Unsigned reviews of Shakespeare's *The Winter's Tale* at the Lyceum Theatre; George Manville Fenn and J. H. Darnley's *The Barrister* at the Comedy Theatre; and Robert Buchanan's *The Blue Bells of Scotland* at the Novelty Theatre.

The Winter's Tale, writes Wilde, "belongs to that great third period in [Shakespeare's] artistic development – the period of noble and purifying reconciliation, of serene and solemn peace." These works, including *Cymbeline* and *The Tempest*, "are great dramas as well as great poems – wonderful pageants no less than wonderful plays." Praising the actress Mary Anderson (who had declined to perform in his unsuccessful play, *Vera; or, The Nihilists* in 1883), Wilde writes that, in the role of Hermione, she was "stately, dignified, and womanly." She also performed the role of Perdita: "Nothing has been seen in London for a long time more charming than the slight, graceful girl dancing with shepherds at the sheep-shearing...." However, Wilde concludes, "it is not the actors we go to see but the play. The best actor cannot add to Shakespeare, nor the worst take away from him." In *The Winter's Tale* we find "the resolution of the discords of life. The dissonance to which we owe the tragedies, with all the mystery of their misery, has now become a harmony. Reconciliation is Shakespeare's last word."

Turning to Fenn and Darnley's *The Barrister*, Wilde characterizes it as "something between a

practical joke and a pantomime. The dialogue, moreover, lacks "wit, style, and smartness. Mr. Pinero need not tremble for his laurels: up to this he has no rival." Nevertheless, the audience was "immensely delighted, and the play on its first night [6 Sept.] went capitally...." There is, Wilde notes, a "marked resemblance to 'Cox and Box' [a one-act opera by Arthur Sullivan] in some of the situations," and, in the spirit of farce, every room has five or six doors, the characters rushing in and out, misunderstanding each other, and falling exhausted on sofas. Such actions "distribute a gentle air of lunacy over life."

The third production under review, Buchanan's *The Blue Bells of Scotland*, employs a conventional subject that has "served poet, playwright, and novelist again and again; but, treated with freshness and vigour, it will never fail to awake popular sympathy so long as human nature remains recognisably the same. It is the old tale of man's selfishness and woman's trust...." The characters are admirably drawn, and "a great deal of curious and interesting lore about queer and interesting people" contribute to the play's effectiveness.

"LOTUS LAND"

Not published in Wilde's lifetime, this poem appeared in Bobby Fong, "Oscar Wilde: Five Fugitive Poems," *ELT* 22:1 (1979): 7–8.

While a student at Oxford in the late 1870s, Wilde sent this sonnet to Robert Yelverton Tyrrell, Fellow of Trinity College, Dublin, and editor of *Kottabos*, but it never appeared there. Wilde's trip to Greece in April 1877 probably provided the stimulus for the poem. The MS. is signed "O.F.O'F.W.W." (a rare instance when he signed a work with his full name: Oscar Fingel O'Flahertie Wills Wilde, dropped after 1879). The postscript "Illaunroe" refers to the Wilde family's fishing and hunting lodge on Lough Fee, in County Galway, where Wilde presumably completed the poem in the summer of 1877.

Wilde's poem was obviously inspired by Tennyson's "The Lotos-Eaters" (a variant spelling) and by Homer's *Odyssey*, both of which depict the effect of lotus land on Odysseus's weary crewmembers on their way home after the end of the Trojan War. Odysseus recorded that the lotuseaters gave his crew "the lotus to taste. Now whosoever of them did eat of the honey-sweet fruit of the lotos had no more wish to bring tidings nor to come back, but there he chose to abide...forgetful of his homeward way" (9:82–97).

"Lotus Land" follows Tennyson's poem in its imagery suggestive of a retreat into a dream world free of moral responsibility, though Wilde adds an erotic element as well:

> The sultry noon is amorous for rain;
>   The golden bee, the lily's paramour,
>   Sleeps in the lily-bell, which doth allure
> And bind its lovers with a honied chain....

The sestet of the sonnet continues this thematic development: "O sad, and sweet, and silent! surely here / A man might dwell apart from troublous fear...." But in the final lines, Wilde intrudes upon such seclusion from the world with an awkward allusion to the declaration of war by Serbia against Turkey on 30 June 1876 (since July 1875, the Serbs had supported the revolt in Herzegovina and Bosnia against Turkish rule), and on 2 July, Montenegro joined Serbia as an ally: "...you say / That there is War in Europe on this day? / Red War and Ravenous? Can this be so!"

Manuscript: The Berg Collection has the MS. of the poem.

"LOTUS LEAVES"

Published: *Irish Monthly* 5 (Feb. 1877): 133–35. Under the title, Wilde included an epigraph of four lines in Greek from Homer's *Odyssey* (4:195–98) in which Peisistratus speaks of Odysseus's apparent death and Telemachus's grief: "I count it indeed no blame to weep for any mortal who has died and met his fate. Yea, this is the only due we pay to miserable mortals, to cut the hair and let a tear fall from the cheeks."

Divided into five parts, "Lotus Leaves" was partially reprinted in a revised version in *Poems* (1881), the following parts revised as separate poems: Part II newly titled as "Impression. Le Réveillon" and Part III as "Impressions. II. La Fuite de la Lune." Before its appearance in *Poems* (1881), Part III, with the title "La Fuite de la Lune," had appeared as the second of two "Impressions" in *Pan* 1 (23 April 1881). The remaining parts of "Lotus Leaves" (Parts I, IV, and V) appeared in *Poems* (1908) with the original title without the numbering of the parts.

The death of Wilde's father in April 1876, as implied by the epigraph from the *Odyssey*, may

have inspired this elegiac poem. In early July of that year, Wilde wrote to his Oxford friend William Ward (1854–1932): "I think that God has dealt very hardly with us. It has robbed me of any real pleasure in my First, and I have not sufficient faith in Providence to believe it is all for the best – I know it is not. I feel an awful dread of going home to our old house, with everything filled with memories" (*Letters* 15–16). For his poem, Wilde used the stanzaic form in Tennyson's *In Memoriam* (1850), an elegy that he greatly admired (*Letters* 21). "Lotus Leaves" opens with the characteristic elegiac tone:

> There is no peace beneath the noon. –
>   Ah in those meadows is there peace
>   Where, girdled with a silver fleece,
> As a bright shepherd, strays the moon?

The speaker turns to nature for solace: the willow whispers that "death is but a newer life, / And that with idle words of strife / We bring dishonour on the dead." He lays a garland of flowers on the grave "where He lies": "What joy I had to sit alone / Till evening broke on tired eyes." In the last lines, he rejects the capacity of "murmuring tree or song of bird" to provide him with the strength to overcome grief:

> ...such idle dreams belong
>   To souls of lesser depth than mine;
>   I feel that I am half divine;
> I know that I am great and strong.

Manuscripts: The Clark Library has a MS., a working draft of miscellaneous passages (printed in Mason 83–84). Dartmouth College has a MS., titled "Selene," which contains three quatrains, a later draft of the first part of "Lotus Leaves" (also printed in Mason 85–86).

"LOUIS NAPOLEON"

Published: *Poems* (1881). Louis Napoleon was the only son of the deposed Napoleon III, who, after losing the throne in 1870, during the Franco-Prussian War, settled in England with his family. After attending the Royal Military Academy at Woolwich, Louis – then 23 – fought with the British Army in the Zulu War of 1879. On 1 June, while on a reconnaissance mission, he was killed in a surprise attack. News of his death, which ended all hope in France of a Bonapartist restoration, reached England on 20 June.

In this elegy, consisting of four quatrains, Wilde alludes to Napoleon I as the "Eagle of Austerlitz" (in Czechoslovakia), where he achieved his greatest victory in 1805 by defeating the Russian and Austrian armies (as described in Tolstoy's *War and Peace*). Wilde laments that Louis, "Poor boy! " will not "ride in state through Paris in the van / Of thy returning legions...." Instead, France, free and republican, "Shall on thy dead and crownless forehead place / The better laurels of a soldier's crown...." The soul of Louis would not be dishonoured to inform Napoleon I, "the mighty Sire of thy race," that "France hath kissed the mouth of Liberty, / And found it sweeter than his honied bees" and that "the giant wave Democracy / Breaks on the shores where Kings lay couched at ease."

LOUŸS, PIERRE (1870–1925)

A French poet and novelist, Louÿs (his surname modeled after his family name, Louis) first met Wilde in November 1891, when the younger writer was at the beginning of his career. Louÿs had already published some poems in literary magazines and had founded a poetry review, *La Conque* (among the contributors in the eleven issues that appeared were Mallarmé, Verlaine, Moréas, Gide, and Valéry in addition to Louÿs himself). Soon after their first meeting, Wilde sent him the MS. of *Salomé* for his reaction (during his stay in Paris in November and December of 1891, Wilde wrote most or all of the play); Wilde had previously asked Stuart Merrill and Adolphe Retté for their reactions. Louÿs's interlinear comments and suggestions for revision are in the final MS. draft now in the Rosenbach Library; for the most part, Wilde accepted Louÿs's corrections in French idiom.

When *Salomé* was published in February 1893, it was dedicated "*A mon Ami* / PIERRE LOUŸS." Louÿs's facetious response to the dedication – a "trivial jest," Wilde called it – prompted him to write to Louÿs: "Is the enclosed really all that you have to say to me in return for choosing you out of all my friends to whom to dedicate *Salome*? I cannot tell you how hurt I am.... Had you wired '*Je vous remercie*' it would have been enough" (*Letters* 334–35).

During the following two years, Louÿs visited England twice, each time meeting Wilde. On his initial visit in June 1892, Louÿs dined with Wilde almost daily during the first three weeks and met many of his friends. Wilde also introduced him to Sarah Bernhardt, whom Louÿs had worshipped. Though Louÿs was, at first, charmed by the refined manners of Wilde's friends, when he returned to England in 1893 he was critical of their morals.

The incident over *Salomé* obviously had little effect on their friendship, for Louÿs travelled to London to attend the première performance on 19 April 1893 of *A Woman of No Importance*, which he called "a play of no importance" (qtd. in Clive, "Chronicle" 384n3). He remained in London for only a few days, during which time he felt distress over the affair openly conducted between Wilde and Lord Alfred Douglas; since, states Clive, Louÿs regarded homosexuality as "repugnant," he later provoked a quarrel with Wilde over his flagrant behavior that, in effect, ended their friendship ("Chronicle" 369).

When Wilde was arrested in April 1895, Louÿs found himself in an embarrassing situation: he had written a French sonnet based on an erotic letter written by Wilde to Douglas that had been used by male prostitutes for purposes of blackmail and that achieved notoriety in Wilde's libel case against the Marquess of Queensberry: "...those red rose-leaf lips of yours should have been made no less for music of song than for madness of kisses" (*Letters* 326). Because Louÿs's signed sonnet had appeared in an Oxford undergraduate magazine, the *Spirit Lamp* (4 May 1893), edited by Douglas, the poem gave the impression that Louÿs had assisted Wilde in his attempt to diminish the letter's value to the blackmailers. Below the title, "Sonnet," a passage cites its inspiration: "A letter written in prose poetry by M. Oscar Wilde to a friend, and translated into rhymed poetry by a poet of no importance." Louÿs's friends, however, dismissed the significance of the episode, treating it merely as a joke.

In 1896, Wilde wrote to More Adey from prison that Louÿs had told him, some three years before, that he had "to choose between his friendship and my fatal connection with A.D. I need hardly say I chose at once the meaner nature and the baser mind" (*Letters* 410). And in *De Profundis*, Wilde assured Douglas: "When I compare my friendship with you to my friendship with such still younger men as John Gray and Pierre Louÿs I feel ashamed. My real life, my higher life was with them and such as they" (*Letters* 426). Wilde was delighted that Louÿs had made "a great name for himself" with the publication of his historical novel *Aphrodite* (1896), which created a sensation in France. Despite their quarrel, Wilde regarded Louÿs as "most cultivated, refined, and gentle" (*Letters* 410).

References: H. P. Clive, "Pierre Louÿs and Oscar Wilde: A Chronicle of Their Friendship," *Revue de Littérature Comparée* (July-Sept. 1969) and *Pierre Louÿs (1870–1925): A Biography* (1978).

"LOVE SONG"

Not published in Wilde's lifetime, this lyric poem was written when Wilde was at Oxford.

In a world subject to disasters, the speaker asserts that, when his "Love" and he are together, "What matter what men may say?" Indeed, what does Death and sorrow matter "When kisses are sweetest, and lips are red?" No matter whether the speaker is "only the idlest singer / That ever sang by a desolate sea," for he knows that "Love is a god, and fair, / And if death and derision follow after, / The only god worth a sin and a prayer." And what matter if political injustices occur, "if prison and palaces crumble," or if Kings fall "when over the sound of the cannon's rumble / The voice of my Lady is clear and sweet?" The allusion to "my Lady" evokes the medieval conventions of courtly love. For the background of this idea, see "La Bella Donna della mia Mente."

Manuscripts: The Clark Library has two MSS., one titled "Love Song," the other untitled, both of which have only portions of the poem.

LUGNÉ-POE, AURÉLIEN (1869– 1940)

A French actor-manager (once a worker in a gas factory), Lugné-Poe, who performed the role of Herod, produced *Salomé* in its première performance on 11 February 1896 at the Théâtre de l'Oeuvre (Paris) while Wilde was still in prison. On 10 March, Wilde asked Robert Ross to send a word of thanks to Lugné-Poe: "...it is something that at a time of disgrace and shame I should be still regarded as an artist. I wish I could feel more pleasure.... However, please let Lugné-Poe know that I am sensible of the honour he has done me" (*Letters* 399). In February 1897, anticipating his release from prison, Wilde authorized Lugné-Poe to represent him in France: "To be represented by so distinguished a poet charms me" (*Letters* 418).

In May, a few days after his release on the 19th, Wilde invited Lugné-Poe to have breakfast with him in Dieppe; on 25 May, they met, after which Wilde wrote to More Adey: "...I was quite charmed with him: I had no idea he was so young, and so handsome" (*Letters* 567). In a letter to Alfred Douglas in June, Wilde hoped to write a play, "religious in surroundings and treatment of subject" (possibly the never-to-be-written *Ahab and Isabel* or *Pharaoh*, as he told André Gide), which might be produced by Lugné-Poe in Paris, not London, in order to rehabilitate himself through art (see *Letters* 589). Wilde's hope that Lugné-Poe would provide him with sufficient funds to live on in Paris when his projected "religious" play was written never materialized. Whether the two saw much of each other after their breakfast in Dieppe is unknown.

Reference: Gertrude Jasper, *Adventure in the Theatre: Lugné-Poe and the Théâtre de l'Oeuvre to 1899* (1947).

M

"M. CARO ON GEORGE SAND"

Published: *PMG*, 14 April 1888, 3; rpt. in *Reviews* (1908). An unsigned review of Elmé Marie Caro's *George Sand*, trans. Gustave Masson (1888).

Wilde characterizes this book as "the biography of a very great man from the pen of a very lady-like writer...." As for M. Caro, the late professor at the Sorbonne,

> Having never done anything remarkable he was naturally elected a member of the Academy, and he always remained loyal to the traditions of that thoroughly respectable and thoroughly pretentious institution. In fact, he was just the sort of man who should never have attempted to write a life of George Sand, or to interpret George Sand's genius.

Continuing in this manner – that of a determined depreciation of M. Caro's abilities – Wilde refers to the biographer as "too feminine to appreciate the grandeur of that large womanly nature, too much of a *dilettante* to realise the masculine force of that strong and ardent mind. He never gets at the secret of George Sand, and never brings us near to her wonderful personality."

As evidence of Caro's incapacity to appreciate Sand's genius, Wilde remarks that the biographer "looks on her simply as a littérateur, as a writer of pretty stories of country life, and of charming, if somewhat exaggerated romances. But George Sand was much more than this." Wilde quotes Matthew Arnold's essay on Sand in *Mixed Essays* (1879): "We do not know George Sand unless we feel the spirit which goes through her work as a whole." Wilde adds: "With this spirit, however, M. Caro has no sympathy," for, as Wilde paraphrases Caro's views, "Sand's doctrines are antediluvian, her philosophy is quite dead, and her ideas of social regeneration are Utopian, incoherent, and absurd. The best thing for us to do is to forget these silly dreams.... Poor M. Caro! This spirit, which he treats with such airy flippancy, is the very leaven of modern life. It is remoulding the world for us, and fashioning our age anew."

Though Caro believes that the novel "must be allied either to poetry or to science," Wilde responds with the observation that Caro seems not to have been aware that philosophy is "one of its strongest allies. In an English critic such a view might possibly be excusable. Our greatest novelists, such as Fielding, Scott, and Thackeray, cared little for the philosophy of their age. But coming, as it does, from a French critic, the statement seems to show a strange want of recognition of one of the most important elements of French fiction." But what Ruskin and Browning did for England, Sand accomplished for France: "She invented an art of literature."

"MADONNA MIA"

Published: *Poems* (1881). For the permutations of this poem, see "Wasted Days." Since Wilde transformed the original poem into two quite separate works, "Madonna Mia" is discussed here. Wilde's title is probably borrowed from Swinburne, whose "Madonna Mia" had appeared in *Poems and Ballads* (1866).

In this sonnet, the "lily-girl" (possibly another celebration of Lillie Langtry, as in "The New Helen" and in "O Golden Queen of life and joy") was "not made for this world's pain, / With brown, soft hair close braided by her ears" and on whose pale cheeks "no love hath left its stain." Though he praises her, he lacks the boldness "to kiss her feet," and, suggestive of Pre-Raphaelite verse, he envisions himself as Dante "when he stood with Beatrice / Beneath the flaming Lion's breast, and saw / The seventh Crystal, and the Stair of Gold."

MAGDALEN COLLEGE, OXFORD

On 17 October 1874, a day after his 20th birthday, Wilde matriculated at St. Mary Magdalen, pronounced "Maudele'n" – and sometimes comically as "Maudlin" – since its founding in 1458. Because of unstable political conditions, the process of erecting buildings and establishing college regulations did not begin until 1474. By 1576, endowments made Magdalen the wealthiest college at Oxford, but Christ Church College later surpassed it. H. Montgomery Hyde, who, as a student at Magdalen, occupied Wilde's rooms, writes: "With its spacious grounds, which included a deer park, and its noble tower, from the top of which the choristers intoned a Latin hymn on May Day, Magdalen was considered by many to be the university's loveliest college" (15).

At the time of its founding, Magdalen College established a demyship (or scholarship) for each of thirty scholars (the term *demy*, or demi, originally meaning half of the provisions granted to Fellows). On entering the college, Wilde received such a demyship – £95 per annum for up to five years. In June 1876, Wilde took his Classical Honour Moderations, written examinations called "Mods," the first of two public examinations for the BA degree, in which he received a "First." When he did not appear for the beginning of the Easter term on 4 April 1877 (he had requested a ten-days' leave because he had gone abroad, but by 26 April he had not returned), the college authorities resolved

that Mr. Wilde having absented himself during this term up to the present time without permission, be not allowed to reside for the Easter and Trinity Term, and that he be deprived of the emoluments of his Demyship for the half-year ending Michaelmas 1877; and that he be informed that unless he return punctually on the appointed day of October Term, 1877, with an amount of work prescribed by his tutor satisfactorily prepared, the officers will consider whether he shall retain his Demyship. (qtd. in Ellmann 77/74)

In short, Wilde was – in Oxford terminology – "rusticated," that is, temporarily dismissed, "sent down" from the college "into the country" for a specified length of time as punishment. As the result of a convincing letter, the college officers modified the fine on 4 May from £47/10/0 to £26/15/0, provided that the work for his tutor was satisfactory. But when Wilde failed to submit such work, he presented such convincing arguments (presumably as to his financial difficulties) that the college officers did not impose further penalties.

In June 1878, Wilde took his final examinations, called "Schools" or "Greats," in the schools of the Faculty of *Literae Humaniores*. He then underwent a *viva voce* (or oral examination on his written examinations) and was awarded a "Double First." In June, also, Wilde won the prestigious Newdigate Prize for poetry with *Ravenna*, parts of which he recited in the Sheldonian Theatre on 26

June. Sir Roger Newdigate of University College had established the annual prize in 1806, though the many restrictions on length and subject matter were removed after 1827. The best known of Oxford prizes, the Newdigate had been awarded, before Wilde, to such figures as John Ruskin (1839), Matthew Arnold (1843), and John Addington Symonds (1860).

References: H. Montgomery Hyde, *Oscar Wilde: A Biography* (1975); Christopher and Edward Hibbert, eds., *The Encyclopedia of Oxford* (1988).

"MAGDALEN WALKS"

Published: *Irish Monthly* 6 (April 1878): 211; rev. in *Poems* (1881), and further rev. in (1882). The Boston *Pilot* (8 June 1878) changed the title when the poem appeared there to "Primavera" ("Springtime"), perhaps because American readers would not have known what "Magdalen" referred to.

To a friend, Wilde wrote on 13 May 1878 what his intent was in writing the poem (in the following decade, his devotion to nature would be abandoned for the superiority of the artifice of art):

I have tried, in the metre as well as the words, to mirror some of the swiftness and grace of the springtime. And though I know but too well that in this, like in everything that I do, I have failed, yet after all Nature lies out of the reach of even the greatest masters of song. She cannot be described, she can only be worshipped: and there is more perfection of beauty, it seems to me, in a single white narcissus of the meadow than in all the choruses of Euripides, or even in the *Endymion* of Keats himself. (*Letters* 51)

In the opening of this poem of five quatrains, the imagery is that of the awakening spring, its movement suggested by the racing white clouds and the hurrying thrush. The conventional image of birds "singing for joy of the Spring's glad birth" and the woods "alive with the murmur and sound of Spring" leads to "some tale of love" that is whispered among the trees. The poem, however, introduces no humans; it ends with the continued movement in nature: "The kingfisher flies like an arrow, and wounds the air." In its focus on imagery, the poem departs from conventional Victorian aesthetics, which insisted on moral instruction of some kind or the depiction of humanity's nobler aspects in confronting nature.

MAHAFFY, JOHN PENTLAND (1839–1919)

An important influence on Wilde during his three years (1871–74) at Trinity College, Dublin, the Rev. Mahaffy, Professor of Ancient History and later Provost, was Wilde's tutor from the beginning. During his first two years, Wilde excelled in classics more impressively than Mahaffy had done during *his* student years there by winning two of the highest honors available: a Foundation Scholarship and the Berkeley gold medal for his achievement in Greek. Mahaffy is said to have urged Wilde, with obvious facetiousness, to leave Trinity College: "Go to Oxford, my dear Oscar: we are all much too clever for you over here" (qtd. in Stanford and McDowell 39). Wilde departed with Mahaffy's good will: in the preface to the first edition of Mahaffy's *Social Life in Greece* (1874), which contained a frank discussion of Greek homosexuality, the author thanked "Mr. Oscar Wilde of Magdalen College, Oxford" for "having made improvements and corrections all through the book."

In June 1875, when Wilde was in Florence by himself, he met Mahaffy, who had embarked on "a grand tour of the classical world" with a Cambridge undergraduate whose father had engaged Mahaffy to act as guide. Mahaffy invited Wilde to join them in visiting some northern Italian cities. First, they visited Venice: whereas Wilde thought that San Marco was a "most gorgeous" church, Mahaffy "later compared it disparagingly with the Parthenon and instanced Saint Mark's portal as an example of 'the tawdriness which affects the decadence of a great style'" (Stanford and McDowell 31). Leaving the party after a visit to Milan, Wilde, short of funds, returned to England, while Mahaffy and his companion embarked from Naples for Athens.

In August 1876, Mahaffy invited Wilde to assist him in the reading of proofs of his *Rambles and Studies in Greece* (1876) at his seaside house in Dublin on the Hill of Howth. In a letter to an Oxford friend early in August, Wilde wrote: "I am with that dear Mahaffy every day" (*Letters* 22). In the spring of 1877, Wilde accompanied Mahaffy on "a fateful journey to Greece" (Stanford and McDowell 40), "fateful" because Wilde's increas-

ing interest in Roman Catholicism would be undermined by Mahaffy's enthusiasm for Greek culture. Including George Macmillan (1855–1936), of the publishing firm and later a founder of the Hellenic Society, the party was destined for Genoa, where Wilde was planning to leave Mahaffy and Macmillan for Rome.

In a letter to his father, Macmillan wrote on 28 March that Wilde, "being very impressionable," was en route to Rome "in order to see all the glories of the religion which seems to him the highest and the most sentimental. Mahaffy is quite determined to prevent this if possible, and is using every argument he can to check him" (*More Letters* 25). Wilde wrote to an Oxford friend on 27 April: "I never went to Rome at all! What a changeable fellow you must think me, but Mahaffy my old tutor carried me off to Greece with him to see Mykenae and Athens" (*Letters* 34).

As a result, Wilde wrote to his tutor at Magdalen College to explain why he would not be back at the beginning of term: "...seeing Greece is really a great education for anyone and will I think benefit me greatly, and Mr. Mahaffy is such a clever man that it is quite as good as going to lectures to be in his society" (*Letters* 35). On the same day that Wilde wrote this letter, Mahaffy wrote to his wife:

> We have taken Oscar Wilde with us, who has of course come round under the influence of the moment from Popery to Paganism, but what his Jesuit friends will say, who supplied the money to land him at Rome, it is not hard to guess. I think it is a fair case of cheating the Devil. (qtd. in Stanford and McDowell 41)

When Wilde returned to Oxford, he was "rusticated" – that is, "sent down" for the rest of the term "for being the first undergraduate to visit Olympia," he said many years later (qtd. in Stanford and McDowell 42). Wilde wrote to an Oxford friend that Mahaffy was "*raging!* I never saw him so indignantly angry: he looks on it almost as an insult to himself" (*Letters* 36).

Though it has been said that Wilde derived his conversational brilliance from Mahaffy and though Wilde himself told Frank Harris that his old tutor was "a really great talker in a certain way" (24) – the qualification, however, is significant – Stanford and McDowell have concluded: "No very clear influence has been adduced" to warrant the conclusion that Mahaffy significantly shaped Wilde's epigrammatic skill (80). Mahaffy's influence on Wilde in the direction of Hellenic devotion inevitably resulted – as one might expect – in the student's judgment of his former teacher.

In 1887, Wilde published an anonymous review in the *Pall Mall Gazette* of Mahaffy's *Greek Life and Thought* (see "Mr. Mahaffy's New Book"), in which such phrases as "somewhat pedantic," "rather awkward," and "inaccurate" occur in addition to "a certain cheap popular value," though Wilde also calls certain sections "very pleasant indeed," even "excellent." Still, the critical daggers reveal Wilde's need to judge his former tutor from a new position. In December, he also reviewed Mahaffy's *The Principles of the Art of Conversation* (see "Aristotle at Afternoon Tea"), in which, write Stanford and McDowell, Wilde "adopted a different attitude, not that of one scholar castigating another, but more like that of someone trying to be kind to a less gifted friend....its tone of condescension may have stung his old tutor more painfully than the outright attack on his classical book" (82–83).

Despite these reviews, Mahaffy attended one of Wilde's plays – probably *A Woman of No Importance* – and wrote to congratulate him. Wilde replied to his "charming letter, all the more flattering to me as it comes not merely from a man of high and distinguished culture, but from one to whom I owe so much personally, from my first and my best teacher, from the scholar who showed me how to love Greek things. Let me sign myself, in affection and admiration, your old pupil and your old friend..." (*Letters* 338). When Wilde was arrested and Mahaffy heard of the accusations, he asked, "Were they young boys?" After hearing the reply, he never wanted to hear Wilde's name again (Stanford and McDowell 87). He later refused to sign a petition to the Home Secretary for Wilde's early release. However, he reportedly said to a Dublin writer: "Despite his extravagant garb and effeminate way..., I rather liked Wilde... (Griffin 68).

References: Gerald Griffin, *The Wild Geese* (1938); W. B. Stanford and R. B. McDowell, *Mahaffy: A Biography of an Anglo-Irishman* (1971).

MALLARMÉ, STÉPHANE (1842–98)

The French Symbolist poet Mallarmé and Wilde met in Paris on 24 February 1891 in the former's flat in the rue de Rome at one of Mallarmé's famous Tuesday evening receptions. At that meeting, Mallarmé presented Wilde with a copy of his translation of Poe's *The Raven*, which had appeared in 1875 with illustrations by Manet. On the following day, Wilde wrote (addressing him as "Cher Maître") to thank him for the "magnifique symphonie en prose" (*Letters* 288). Wilde praises Mallarmé for having made prose and poetry one and the same thing, unlike the separation of prose and poetry in England. Ellmann remarks that, in February, Wilde was writing the preface, emphasizing symbolism (a "bow" to Mallarmé), to be published in the book version of *The Picture of Dorian Gray* (335/316).

At the end of October in that year, Wilde, in Paris for two months, sent Mallarmé a copy of *The Picture of Dorian Gray* with the inscription "A Stéphane Mallarmé, Hommage d'Oscar Wilde, Paris, '91." In the accompanying letter, written in early November, Wilde expressed admiration for Mallarmé's "noble et sévère art" (*Letters* 297). In Paris at the time and soon to leave, Whistler warned Mallarmé of the imminent Tuesday visit of Wilde, whom he would have denounced before the Frenchman's disciples had he the time. Whistler also sent a comic telegram to Mallarmé just moments before Wilde's arrival to warn Mallarmé and his disciples and to hide the pearls (see Ellmann 337/318). On 10 November, Mallarmé responded to Wilde's gift of *The Picture of Dorian Gray* by citing the human elements within a "perverse atmosphère de beauté" – a miraculous accomplishment in his novel (qtd. in Ellmann 338).

In March 1893, in response to his having received a copy of *Salomé* in French, Mallarmé wrote to Wilde: "I marvel that, while everything in your *Salomé* is expressed in constant, dazzling strokes, there also arises, on each page, the unutterable and the Dream" (qtd. in Ellmann 375n/354n) – those qualities associated with Symbolist literature.

Reference: H. P. Clive, "Oscar Wilde's First Meeting with Mallarmé," *French Studies* (April 1970).

MARBURY, ELIZABETH (1856–1933)

A leading American literary agent twice decorated by the French government for representing French authors, Marbury first met Wilde during his American lecture tour in 1882. Her recollection of her first impressions of Wilde is characteristic of most who met him: "Like many others I fell under the thrall of his gifts as a conversationalist..." (*Crystal* 97). When *Lady Windermere's Fan* was produced in Boston on 23 January 1893, she was already acting as his agent: in a letter to Michael Field, dated by Hart-Davis as "late October 1893," Wilde writes that Marbury "manages all my plays" (*Letters* 346).

When Wilde completed *A Woman of No Importance*, Marbury urged him to undertake another lecture tour of America: "Of course if you do not care to lecture in this country again, there is no more to be said. Although you may be sure that such a tour in New York, Boston, Philadelphia and Chicago would mean a very large amount of money for you." She also urges that he be in New York for the première performance of his new play on 11 December at the Fifth Avenue Theatre: "Your presence here would do more to advance the success of the production than anything else" (MS., 10 Nov. 1893, Clark Library). But Wilde declined the idea of another lecture tour and of attending the première of his play.

In her autobiography, Marbury regards *De Profundis* as Wilde's "masterpiece." Despite her "crystal ball" image in the title, her vision of the past is often inaccurate: for example, she believed that *The Ballad of Reading Gaol* was written in prison. At the time that he completed the *Ballad*, Wilde told his publisher, Leonard Smithers, that Marbury, "a brilliant, delightful woman," had his "full confidence" in handling its American publication (*Letters* 668). Smithers asked her to obtain the best American price for the *Ballad*, with or without Wilde's name. On 13 January 1898, she responded: "Nobody here seems to feel any interest in the poem, and this morning I received from the [*New York*] *Journal* their final offer, which, alas, is only $100" (qtd. in Mason 416). In her memoirs, however, she states that an offer was made for $250 from the *New York World*. Nevertheless, the poem did not appear in any American newspaper.

Reference: Elizabeth Marbury, *My Crystal Ball* (1923).

"THE MASTER" : *See* "POEMS IN PROSE"

MELMOTH, SEBASTIAN

When Wilde was released from prison in May 1897, he adopted the pseudonym of "Sebastian Melmoth" at the suggestion of Robert Ross, the name derived from St. Sebastian, the favorite martyred saint of late 19th-century homosexuals, and from the hero of the Gothic novel *Melmoth the Wanderer* (1820) by Charles Robert Maturin (1782–1824), Wilde's great-uncle. In 1892, Ross and More Adey had written the "introduction and life" to a new edition of the novel. Ross later wrote that Wilde was "amused at the idea" of taking the names of the martyr and wanderer (Ross 33). By October of 1897, however, he wrote to Ernest Dowson: "I have retaken my own name, as my incognito was absurd" (*Letters* 667). Nevertheless, he soon resumed the pseudonym, which he used in registering at the hotel in Paris, where he died.

MERRILL, STUART (1863–1915)

Born in America, a poet associated with the French Symbolists, Merrill lived much of his life in Paris and wrote in French. The son of a New York lawyer and a French Huguenot mother, Merrill was raised in Paris, where his father was the legal adviser to the American legation. In the mid-1880s, he returned to America to attend the Columbia University Law School, after which he returned to France. In 1890, on a visit to London, Merrill met Wilde, but their relationship was casual rather than close. Nevertheless, in November 1895, Merrill attempted to secure signatures from the leading French men of letters for a petition addressed to Queen Victoria for Wilde's early release from prison, but many – including Zola, Sardou, and Daudet – declined to sign it.

In 1896, the Théâtre de l'Oeuvre (founded by Aurélien Lugné-Poe in 1891 to protest the quality of plays at commercial theaters) produced Wilde's *Salomé*. Merrill, who was the stage manager, was one of several friends who read the draft of the play and presumably suggested corrections of the French. Since Wilde wrote French as he spoke it, many expressions, perhaps striking when spoken in conversation, would be ineffective on the stage. Wilde asked Robert Ross to write to Merrill to say how gratified he was about the performance of *Salomé*.

After his release from prison, Wilde saw Merrill several times in July 1897. For example, he mentions to Alfred Douglas that Merrill, "charming and sympathetic," was living only three miles from Dieppe (*Letters* 620). In May 1898, Wilde dined with Merrill, who had asked the actors and actresses from the play they had seen to join them. When *An Ideal Husband* was published, Wilde included Merrill among others who would receive copies.

At the time of Wilde's death, Merrill wrote a tribute to him in *La Plume* (15 Dec. 1900), in which he eulogized his friend, who had withstood the disasters of his life – the loss of his family and the humiliation of imprisonment:

At last he is at peace. Before his body I ask the wits and the hypocrites to lay down their arms. This man has paid his debts in full.... We are especially unjust in sexual matters, and without much consideration we label what is often only a wretched illness as a moral perversion that must be punished. Thus the unsoundness of mind from which Oscar Wilde suffered outweighed, according to public opinion, an entire life of exalted thought, honest hard work, and noble feelings. (rpt. in Mikhail 2:467)

In his later memoir, written in 1912 and translated in 1954, Merrill recalled that Wilde, in 1890, displayed no pose or arrogance: "I maintain my assertion that there was nothing either in his conduct or even in his conversation which could give rise to the least suspicion.... I was never inclined to believe the accusations brought against him before his trial." At the time of Wilde's illness and death, Merrill was confined to bed with influenza – hence, he writes, "I assisted neither at Wilde's last moments nor at his funeral.

Reference: "Some Unpublished Recollections of Stuart Merrill," prefatory note by H. Montgomery Hyde, *Adam International Review*, Nos. 241–43 (1954), rpt. in Mikhail 2:468–70.

MILES, FRANK (1852–91)

The artist best known for his acclaimed drawings of Lillie Langtry, Miles first met Wilde in 1876. On 4 June, Lord Ronald Gower (1845–1916), a sculptor, politician, and art critic, accompanied Miles to be introduced to Wilde at Oxford. Gower wrote in his diary: "...I made the acquaintance of young Oscar Wilde, a friend of Miles's. A pleasant cheery fellow, but with his long-haired head full of nonsense regarding the Church of Rome. His room filled with photographs of the Pope and of Cardinal Manning" (370). In early July, Wilde and Gower stayed for a week at the Miles home in Bingham, where Frank's father was a rector.

Ellmann remarks that the tall, blond, and pleasant Miles "probably hovered on the edges" of homosexuality "as might be inferred from the great interest taken in him by Lord Ronald Gower" (59/57). Brian Reade refers to Gower as "a notorious homosexual, one of the models for Lord Henry Wotton in *The Picture of Dorian Gray*" (25). When Gower adopted a young man named Frank Hird, Wilde reportedly warned a friend: "Gower may be seen but not Hird" (qtd. in Ellmann 54n/52n). But, Ellmann states, though the intimate relationship between Gower and Miles remains puzzling, "More suspect was [Miles's] intimacy with young girls" (110/16).

By the autumn of 1879, Wilde and Miles were sharing rooms on Salisbury Street, off the Strand. Wilde named it "Thames House" because of its view of the river. Lillie Langtry recalls that the house was "a very ghostly mansion, with antique staircases, twisting passages, broken down furniture, and dim corners" (58). In the midst of the untidy house, the rooms occupied by Wilde and Miles were decorated with blue china and lilies. In December, Miles – despite his confession to Lillie Langtry that he was almost color blind – was awarded the Turner silver medal by the Royal Academy for his painting of an ocean coast. By August 1880, Wilde and Miles had moved to No. 1 Tite Street, Chelsea, the house named by them as "Keats House." Miles was appointed artist-in-chief of *Life*, which ran a series of his portraits of prominent society figures.

In 1881 when Wilde's *Poems* appeared, Miles's father warned his son that the volume was wicked; indeed, Miles's mother had cut out a poem that she regarded as dangerous (presumably "Charmides"), and Canon Miles wrote to Wilde:

As to morality I can't help saying Frank ought to be clear – he has, I believe, often argued with you. Our first thought of course must be of him and his good name and his profession. If in sadness I advise a separation for a time it is not because we do not believe you in character to be very different to what you suggest in your poetry, but it is because you do not see the risk we see in a published poem that, which makes all who read it say to themselves, "this is outside the province of poetry," "it is licentious and may do a great harm to any soul that reads it." (qtd. in Ellmann 148/141-42)

When Miles revealed the contents of the letter, Wilde demanded to know whether his friend would yield to his father's wishes. Dependent upon his father's financial support, Miles had no alternative. Wilde left the house as soon as he could pack his things.

After Canon Miles's death in 1883, Frank became seriously disturbed, as indicated in the incoherence of a letter he wrote to the wife of the artist George Boughton (1833–1905): "Tell George I have given up his idea and Oscars – and Jimmy [Whistler] long long ago – that art is for art's sake and if it is good, [if some] unfortunate accident happens of its doing some harm to somebody why it is the artist's fault" (qtd. in Ellmann 149/142). In 1887, he was placed in Brislington asylum near Bristol, where he died four years later.

References: Lord Ronald Gower, *My Reminiscences* (rev. 1895); Lillie Langtry, *The Days I Knew* (1925); Brian Reade, ed., *Sexual Heretics: Male Homosexuality in English Literature from 1850 to 1900* (1970).

"MINER AND MINOR POETS"

Published: *PMG*, 1 Feb. 1887, 5; rpt. in *Reviews* (1908). Unsigned reviews of books published in 1886.

Wilde remarks that "one is sometimes tempted to wish that all art were anonymous" when the conditions under which art is created are "treated as qualities of the work of art itself.... Yet there are certain forms of art so individual in their utterance, so purely personal in their expression, that for a full appreciation of their style and manner some knowledge of the artist's life is necessary" (indeed, later biographers and critics of Wilde were destined to treat his own art as autobiography).

Joseph Skipsey's *Carols from the Coal-Fields, and Other Songs and Ballads*, Wilde writes, has "intense human interest and high literary merit," and the accompanying biographical account of the author is useful since his life and poems are "too indissolubly wedded to be ever really separated."

At the age of seven, the poet had worked in the pitch dark coal pits between 12 and 16 hours a day. Self-taught, he read the Bible, some of its chapters learned by heart. For more than 40 years, he labored in the "coal dark underground" before becoming the caretaker of a Board school in Newcastle-upon-Tyne.

Following this brief biographical account, Wilde turns to the miner's verse, which has "directness" and "natural grace." Skipsey "possesses something of Blake's marvellous power of making simple things seem strange to us, and strange things seem simple." However, the poems are "extremely unequal," but, at their best, "full of sweetness and strength." In addition to his affinity with Blake, Skipsey has a "spiritual kinship" with Burns in the "fine careless rapture in his laughter." Finally, says Wilde, "In these latter days of shallow rhymers it is pleasant to come across some one to whom poetry is a passion, not a profession."

F. B. Doveton's *Sketches in Prose and Verse*, Wilde proceeds, "belongs to a different school." With his "amazing versatility," he composes an elegy on the death of Jumbo (the famous circus elephant who, in 1885, was killed in a collision with a freight train in Canada), a poem "quite up to the level of the subject." Wilde's facetiousness is decidedly arch: "...we like him least when he is amusing, for in his merriment there is but little melody, and he makes his muse grin through a horse-collar." When Doveton is serious, he has "completely mastered the most approved poetical phraseology" ("the 'welkin rings' upon the smallest provocation"). However, concludes Wilde, "we fear that he will never produce any really good work till he has made up his mind whether destiny intends him for a poet or for an advertising agent...."

Turning to J. Ashby-Sterry's *The Lazy Minstrel*, Wilde notes that this poet has "set himself to discover the poetry of petticoats and seems to find much consolation in the fact that, though art is long, skirts are worn short.... He is capable of penning a canto to a crinoline, and has a pathetic monody on a mackintosh." Moreover, the latest French fashions "stir him to a fine frenzy.... He writes rondels on ribands, lyrics on linen and lace...." Despite this critical *tour de force*, Wilde concedes that the poet is "often dainty and delicate, and many of his poems are full of sweet music and pretty conceits."

"THE MODEL MILLIONAIRE"

MISCELLANIES: See *COLLECTED EDITION*

"THE MODEL MILLIONAIRE"

Published: *World: A Journal for Men and Women* 26 (22 June 1887): 18–19; rpt. with the subtitle "A Note of Admiration" in *Lord Arthur Savile's Crime and Other Stories* (1891).

Source: Adeline Tintner reveals that Wilde's story was inspired by an anecdote current in Europe about Baron James Mayer de Rothschild (1792–1868), a French member of the famous banking family. As told in Virginia Cowles's *The Rothschilds: A Family of Fortune* (1973), the painter Eugène Delacroix (1798–1863) asked Rothschild to pose as a beggar as he had "exactly the right, hungry expression." A young artist, serving as Delacroix's assistant, was so moved by the "beggar" that he slipped him a franc. The next day, one of Rothschild's servants arrived with a gift for the young artist: 10,000 francs – the "interest and compound interest" on the original franc (97). Tintner errs, however, in citing the *Woman's World* as the periodical in which Wilde's story appeared.

The Plot: Hughie Erskine, who is intellectually "not of much importance," has never made a brilliant or ill-natured remark in his life. "Wonderfully good-looking," he is popular with both men and women; however, "he had every accomplishment except that of making money." He and Laura Merton, the daughter of a retired colonel, are deeply and passionately in love, but her father refuses to consider their marriage unless Hughie comes up with £10,000.

On visiting his friend, Alan Trevor, an accomplished painter, Hughie finds him completing a painting of a life-size picture of a beggar, who is standing on a raised platform, "a wizened old man, with a face like wrinkled parchment, and a most piteous expression." "What an amazing model!" whispers Hughie, who asks how much a model gets for a sitting. A shilling, Trevor replies, but for the painting he expects two thousand guineas. The model, Hughie says laughing, should receive a percentage. On Trevor's leaving the studio on some business, the old beggar rests on a wooden bench. Moved by the beggar's pitiful condition, Hughie slips a sovereign into his pocket. On Trevor's return, Hughie leaves, "blushing a little at what he had done."

That night, encountering the painter at the Palette Club, Hughie asks him whether he has completed the picture. The beggar, Trevor says, was quite taken with Hughie and wanted to know what his income was and what his prospects were. When Hughie offers to give the beggar some of his old clothes, Trevor insists that the beggar looks "splendid" in his rags: "What you call rags I call romance. What seems poverty to you is picturesqueness to me....our business is to realise the world as we see it, not to reform it as we know it."

Hughie is startled when Trevor informs him that the "beggar" is one of the richest men in Europe and that he knows about the relentless colonel, Laura, and the £10,000. His wish to be painted as a beggar is a whim: *"La fantaisie d'un millionnaire!"* Trevor bursts into laughter at Hughie's confession that he had given the millionaire a sovereign: "He'll invest your sovereign for you, pay you the interest every six months, and have a capital story to tell after dinner." On the next morning, Baron Hausberg's man arrives to present Hughie with a wedding present from "an old beggar": a check for £10,000. At the wedding breakfast, after the Baron makes a speech, Trevor, the best man, remarks: "Millionaire models are rare enough, but, by Jove, model millionaires are rarer still!"

Manuscript: Christie's (New York) sale catalogue for 20 November 1992 listed a signed MS. of 28 leaves, dated 11 December 1886, with Wilde's deletions and revisions.

Reference: Adeline Tintner, "A Rothschild Anecdote as a Source for Oscar Wilde's 'The Model Millionaire,'" *N&Q* (Jan.-Feb. 1977).

"A MODERN EPIC"

Published: *PMG*, 13 March 1885, 11-12; rpt. in *Reviews* (1908). An unsigned review of W. G. Wills's *Melchior* (1885).

Wilde questions whether an epic poem of more than 5,000 lines is "a form of art...most suited to our century." Alluding to Poe's contention that "no poem should take more than an hour to read," Wilde concludes that "a work of art is to be estimated by its beauty, not by its size." Wills's poem (involving a mystic and musician who goes mad but is restored to his reason when he kills the woman he adores in a paroxysm of rage) has "beauty of a rich and lofty character." Wilde praises the fusion of such elements as "the picturesque vision of the painter," the "psychology of the novelist," and the "playwright's sense of dramatic situation": "'Melchoir' is not a piece of poetic writing merely, it is that very rare thing, a poem."

The poem's "artistic use of that scientific law of heredity, which has already strongly influenced the literature of this century," is to be seen, Wilde suggests, in "the dreadful Rougon-Macquart family with whose misdeeds M. Zola is never weary of troubling us." *Melchior* is "a fine imaginative treatment of many of the most important modern problems, notably of the relation of life to art."

"MODERN GREEK POETRY"

Published: *PMG*, 27 May 1885, 5; rpt. in *Reviews* (1908). An unsigned review of *Greek Lays, Idylls, Legends, etc.,* trans. E. M. Edmonds (1885).

Wilde's epigrammatic opening, with its effective use of alliteration in the second sentence, establishes his view of one aspect of modern Greece: "Odysseus, not Achilles, is the type of the modern Greek. Merchandise has taken precedence of the Muses, and politics are preferred to Parnassus." But "by the Illissus there are sweet singers; the nightingales are not silent in Colonos; and from the garden of Greek nineteenth-century poetry Miss Edmonds has made a very pleasing anthology." With characteristic facetiousness, Wilde notes: "Even when translated into English, modern Greek lyrics are preferable to modern Greek loans." In the spirit of the pastoral poet Theocritus, the "flutes of the sheepfold are more delightful than the clarions of battle. Still, poetry played such a noble part in the Greek War of Independence that it is impossible not to look with reverence on the spirited war-songs that meant so much to those who were fighting for liberty...."

MODJESKA, HELENA (1840–1909)

A tragic actress, Modjeska was born in Poland and emigrated to the United States in 1876, where she triumphed in productions of *Romeo and Juliet* and Scribe's *Adrienne Lecouvreur*. In January 1880, she was in London, where she was welcomed to fashionable social gatherings, which Wilde attended when she recited from plays. She inquired about Wilde of various people: "What has he done, this young man, that one meets him everywhere? Oh yes, he talks well, but what has he

done*? He has written nothing, he does not sing or paint or act – he does nothing but talk. I do not understand" (qtd. in Stokes 25). She made her debut at the Court Theatre in May 1880 in a new version of Dumas *fils*'s *La Dame aux Camélias*.

Though the friendship between Wilde and Modjeska was brief, they managed to collaborate in "translating" Modjeska's dream poem into English, "Sen Artistry; or The Artist's Dream" (see entry), subsequently published. She also asked Wilde to adapt "some play" for her, as he told the actor Norman Forbes-Robertson: "...we have not yet settled what – probably *Luisa Miller*" (*Letters* 71), the title derived from Verdi's opera (1849), based on Schiller's *Kabale und Liebe* (1782). Nothing came of the idea. After an extensive tour in England and the Continent, she returned to America, where she performed the role of Nora in *A Doll's House* in 1883, the first production of an Ibsen play in the United States.

Reference: John Stokes, "Helena Modjeska in England," *Women and Theatre* 1 (1992).

"THE MOON IS LIKE A YELLOW SEAL"

Not published in Wilde's lifetime, this untitled lyric poem was apparently written in Paris in 1883, after Wilde's American lecture tour ended. The two quatrains reflect the influence of French Impressionist painting as well as Whistler's paintings in their concern with images without an implied narrative or moral; however, more significant is Wilde's anticipation of early 20th-century Imagist poetry in its exclusive concern with hard, clear images (in contrast to the muted images in Impressionist painting).

The striking similies of the moon "like a yellow seal / Upon a dark blue envelope" and the River Seine lying "Like a black sword of polished steel" is followed, as the poem ends, with the images of fluttering "white or crimson" carriages rolling homeward. Equally striking is that, after the initial three iambic lines, the metre shifts radically when the image of the "dim Seine" is depicted; then, at the end the original rhythm is restored.

Manuscripts: The Huntington Library has a MS., on the reverse side of which is "Le Jardin des Tuileries" (see Mason 78–79). The Anderson Galleries auction catalogue for the sale of the John C. Tomlinson library on 17–18 January 1928, item 568, offered a MS. of this poem among other jottings.

MOORE, GEORGE (1852–1933)

An Irish novelist, dramatist, critic, and poet, Moore maintained a cautious distance from Oscar Wilde, whose flamboyance and brilliant wit apparently overwhelmed the less demonstrative Moore. Early in his career, Moore sent him a copy of his second (and final) volume of verse, *Pagan Poems* (1881), with a simple inscription, "To Oscar Wilde / with the author's compliments," an indication that Moore sought the approval and presumably the re-acquaintance of another Irishman whose star was rising: according to Joseph Hone, they had known each other as children (24). No evidence exists that Wilde responded to Moore's overture.

Wilde never commented, in either review or letter, on any of Moore's major works, such as *A Mummer's Wife* (1885) and *Esther Waters* (1894), unsympathetic as he was with realism and Zola-esque Naturalism. The relationship between the two writers was recalled by Vincent O'Sullivan, who asked Wilde if he knew Moore: "Know him? I know him so well that I haven't spoken to him in ten years" (87). Though both subscribed to the general notion of Aestheticism, with its doctrine of art for art's sake, and moved in similar circles, Moore never reviewed any of Wilde's works, and, in his massive autobiography, *Hail and Farewell* (1911–14), he mentions Wilde only once in passing.

In his private correspondence with the drama critic William Archer, however, Moore was unrestrained in judging Wilde. After seeing *A Woman of No Importance* in May 1893, Moore wrote to Archer that the play was "definitely beneath contempt.... I find in Wilde neither good thinking nor good writing" (MS., British Library). In June, Moore again attacked the play in another letter to Archer: "Honestly *A Woman of No Importance* is in my opinion as worthless a piece of work as I have ever witnessed.... Yet you say that Oscar Wilde is the first of English dramatists" (MS., British Library).

In his biography of Wilde, Frank Harris reports only one conversation with Wilde about Moore. To Harris's remark that Moore was "popular enough," Wilde responds facetiously:

Popular, Frank, as if that counted. George Moore has conducted his whole education in public. He had written two or three books before he found out there was such a thing as English grammar. He at once announced his discovery and so won the admiration of the illiterate. A few years later he discovered that there was something architectural in style, that sentences had to be built up into a paragraph, and paragraphs into chapters and so on. Naturally he cried this revelation, too, from the housetops.... I'm much afraid, Frank, in spite of all his efforts, he will die before he reaches the level from which writers start. It's a pity because he has certainly a little real talent. (278–79)

In February 1899, Wilde told Reginald Turner that Max Beerbohm's caricature of Moore in the *Daily Chronicle* (30 Jan. 1899), depicting him as a tipsy Irish peasant with a shillelagh, was a "masterpiece...it is a most brilliant and bitter rendering of that vague formless obscene face." He also urged Turner to place *The Importance of Being Earnest* (just published) among his "nicest books, not near anything by [Robert] Hichens or George Moore" (*Letters* 778).

In 1918, after the publication of the American edition of his biography of Wilde, Harris invited Moore to comment on it for the American issue of *Pearson's Magazine* (March 1918), which Harris was editing. Moore noted that Harris

would put [Wilde] in the first class as a writer and I should put him in the third or fourth. It is not a long time since I read a book of his called *Intentions*, and it seems to me very thin and casual, without depth, therefore, unoriginal....He had a certain dramatic gift, he moves his characters deftly and his dialogue is not without grace...and superficial enough to attract audiences.... I do not think that anybody would have troubled about him if the Marquis of Queensbury [*sic*] had not written him a post card.... (rpt. in Beckson)

References: Joseph Hone, *The Life of George Moore* (1936); Vincent O'Sullivan, *Aspects of Wilde* (1936).

"MORE RADICAL IDEAS UPON DRESS REFORM"

Published: *PMG*, 11 Nov. 1884, ll–12; rpt. in *Miscellanies* (1908). Wilde had delivered a lecture on "Dress" at Ealing on 1 October, which resulted in letters to the editor (see Wilde's response in *Letters* 161–63).

Wilde begins by alluding to the correspondence printed in the *Pall Mall Gazette* on the subject of his lecture on dress: "It shows me that the subject of dress reform is one that is occupying many wise and charming people, who have at heart the principles of health, freedom, and beauty in costume...." Responding to a letter from a reader who had suggested an ideal costume for a man, Wilde regards a l7th-century doublet as an easier garment to wear than a coat and waistcoat and, "if buttoned from the shoulder, far warmer also"; furthermore, "tails have no place in costume, except on some Darwinian theory of heredity...."

A drawing included by a reader in his letter to the editor provokes Wilde's comment that the hat and boots are all "wrong": "Whatever one wears on the extremities, such as the feet and head, should, for the sake of comfort, be made of a soft material, and for the sake of freedom should take its shape from the way one chooses to wear it, and not from any stiff, stereotyped design of hat or boot maker." Moreover, the crown, says Wilde, is far too high, for it diminishes the stature of a small person, "in the case of any one who is tall...a great inconvenience when one is getting in and out of hansoms and railway carriages...." As for boots, the drawing indicates that they are made of stiff leather, whereas they should be made of soft leather to permit "perfect freedom for walking...." In general, Wilde rejects the style of dress proposed in the drawing: "There is not a single rule of right costume which is not violated in it, for it gives us stiffness, tightness and discomfort instead of comfort, freedom and ease."

"There is," Wilde is convinced, "a divine economy about beauty; it gives us just what is needful and no more, whereas ugliness is always extravagant; ugliness is a spendthrift and wastes its material," and in the reader's drawing, "ugliness, as much in costume as in anything else, is always the sign that somebody has been unpractical." Beauty, he continues, is "the sign always of the rightness of principles, the mystical seal that is set upon what is perfect, and upon what is perfect only."

Wilde concludes with comments upon what many late 19th-century feminists had preferred – the divided skirt – which he would prefer to see an adaptation of, but if it is to be "of any positive value, it must give up all idea of 'being identical in

appearance with an ordinary skirt....'" Finally, Wilde establishes a basic principle for women's dress: "...every right article of apparel belongs equally to both sexes, and there is absolutely no such thing as a definitely feminine garment." (For other entries on fashion and costume, see "Fashion and Theater," "The Relation of Dress to Art," and "The Truth of Masks.")

Manuscript: The Clark Library has a fragment of six leaves from an early draft of this article.

William Morris, 1895

MORRIS, WILLIAM (1834–96)

A poet, painter, printer, designer and manufacturer of wallpaper and furniture, and Socialist, Morris met Wilde at a garden party early in 1881 (presumably not their first meeting), when Morris, "boiling with indignation," as described by Philip Henderson, approached a group: "The press ignores me," he angrily exclaimed. "There's a conspiracy of silence about my book." Quickly Wilde retorted: "Why not join it, Morris?" (228). Wilde's familiarity in addressing the much-older Morris with such a tactless remark undermines the credibility of the report. On 31 March of that year, after this alleged incident, Morris, wrote to his wife, alluding to Wilde, who was just beginning to be satirized in *Punch*: "I must admit that as the devil is painted blacker than he is, so it fares with O. W. Not but what he is an ass: but he certainly is clever too" (Morris, *Letters* 2:38). Wilde's admiration for Morris is expressed in his poem "The Garden of Eros" (1881), in which the "Spirit of Beauty" is expressed by such poets as Keats, Swinburne, Rossetti, and

> Morris, our sweet and simple Chaucer's child,
>   Dear heritor of Spenser's tuneful reed,
> With soft and sylvan pipe has oft beguiled
>   The weary soul of man in troublous need,
> And from the far and flowerless fields of ice
> Has brought fair flowers meet to make an earthly
>   paradise.

One of Morris's most popular works, *The Earthly Paradise* (1868–70), consists of tales drawn from Greek mythology and Scandinavian saga literature, utilizing Chaucerian metres.

In January 1882, while lecturing in New York on "The English Renaissance," Wilde cited Morris as one who was

> substituting for a simpler realism of the earlier days a more exquisite spirit of choice, a more faultless devotion to beauty, a more intense seeking for perfection: a master of all exquisite design and of all spiritual vision.... The visible aspect of modern life disturbs him not: rather it is for him to render eternal all that is beautiful in Greek, Italian, and Celtic legend. To Morris we owe poetry whose perfect precision and closeness of word and vision has not been excelled in the literature of our country, and by the revival of the decorative arts he has given to our individualised romantic movement the social idea and the social factor too....

Further in the lecture, Wilde called Morris "the greatest handicraftsman we have had in England since the fourteenth century." Decoration, "the worker's expression of his joy in work," provided the "opportunity of expressing his own individuality." Wilde recalled what Morris once said to him: "I have tried to make each of my workers an artist,

and when I say an artist I mean a man." In 1885, however, Wilde was quite critical of the decorative value of Morris's wallpapers, as he remarks to William A. S. Benson, an architect and designer-craftsman:

> They seem to me often deficient in real beauty of colour: this may be due as you say to his workmen, but Art admits of no excuses of that kind. Then as regards the design, he is far more successful with those designs which are meant for textures which hang in folds, than for those which have to be seen flat on a stretched material: a fact which may be due to the origin of many of his patterns, but which is a fact still.

In a postscript to this letter, Wilde remarks: "How can you see socialism in *The Early Paradise*? If it is there it is an accident not a quality – there is a great difference" (*Letters* 174–76).

In the 1880s, both Morris and Wilde, as Zelda Austen has written,

> were active in the movement for aesthetic reform; both lectured, edited periodicals and busied themselves more in public affairs than in imaginative writing.... In them we see the dual nature of Victorian England toward the close of the nineteenth century. Morris spent the eighties in an exhausting effort to change a world grown impossibly ugly and unjust; Wilde, in posturing, public performances, social games, and a hidden life that "dared not speak its name." (102)

Between 1887 and 1889, Wilde published laudatory reviews in the *Pall Mall Gazette* of two of Morris's works (including his two-volume translation of the *Odyssey*) as well as of two lectures given at the Arts and Craft Exhibition in 1888: see entries on "Mr. Morris's *Odyssey*," "Mr. Morris's Completion of the *Odyssey*," "Mr. William Morris's Last Book" (on *The House of the Wolfings*), "Mr. Morris on Tapestry," and "Printing and Printers." In his only known surviving letter to Morris, written early in 1891, Wilde thanks him profusely for having sent him what is probably the utopian fantasy *News from Nowhere*:

> How proud indeed so beautiful a gift makes

me. I weep over the cover which is not nearly lovely enough, not nearly rich enough in material, for such prose as you write.... I have always felt that your work comes from the sheer delight of making beautiful things: that no alien motive ever interests you: that in its singleness of aim, as well as in its perfection of result, it is pure art, everything that you do.... I have loved your work since boyhood: I shall always love it. (*Letters* 290–91)

There was apparently no other communication between Wilde and Morris in the early 1890s. In "My Memories of Oscar Wilde," which appeared in Frank Harris's *Oscar Wilde: His Life and Confessions* (1918), Bernard Shaw remarks that Morris, "when he was dying slowly, enjoyed a visit from Wilde more than from anybody else." This story had been long regarded as an invention (Shaw told Hesketh Pearson that the source of the story was Morris's daughter, May), for in 1896 – the year of Morris's death – Wilde was in Reading Prison. William Ruff suggests, however, that, since Morris in 1894 had become physically feeble, Shaw used the phrase "dying slowly" to characterize Morris's decline; hence, Wilde may very well have visited him before the ordeal of the trials in 1895.

References: Philip Henderson, *William Morris: His Life, Work, and Friends* (1967); William Ruff, "Shaw on Wilde and Morris: A Clarification," *Shaw Review* (Jan. 1968); Zelda Austen, "The Grasshopper and the Ant: Oscar Wilde and William Morris in the Eighties," *Journal of Pre-Raphaelite Studies* (Nov. 1983); *The Collected Letters of William Morris*, Vol. 2, ed. Norman Kelvin (1987); Fiona MacCarthy, *William Morris: A Life for Our Time* (1994).

MR. AND MRS. DAVENTRY

The Scenario: In August 1894, while at work on *The Importance of Being Earnest*, Wilde sent George Alexander, the actor-manager at the St. James's Theatre, a scenario of a play, the first act of which he summarized as follows:

A man of rank and fashion marries a simple sweet country girl – a lady – but simple and ignorant of fashionable life. They live at his country place and after a time he gets bored with her, and invites down a lot of fashionable

fin-de-siècle women and men. The play opens by his lecturing his wife on how to behave – not to be prudish, etc. – and not to mind if anyone flirts with her.... The guests arrive, they are horrid to the wife, they think her dowdy and dull. The husband flirts with Lady X. Gerald [one of the guests] is nice and sweet and friendly to the wife. (*Letters* 360)

In outlining the remaining three acts of this untitled play, Wilde depicts a compromising situation involving Lady X and the husband, whose wife has witnessed their indiscretion. The husband implores Gerald to use his influence in seeking his wife's forgiveness. However, the wife refuses Gerald's urging by confessing her love for him: "You have made me love you. You have no right to hand my life over to anyone else. All this self-sacrifice is wrong, we are meant to live. That is the meaning of life." She succeeds in having Gerald take her away with him.

Three months later, a duel between the husband and Gerald having been arranged, the husband appeals to his wife for reconciliation, but she refuses, expressing her wish for her husband's death in the duel because "the father of my child must live." After the husband leaves, a pistol shot is heard: he has killed himself. Having waited for the husband to appear for the duel, Gerald, unaware of his suicide, calls him a coward. "No," she answers, "not at the end. He is dead. We must love one another devotedly now." Wilde concludes his scenario: "Curtain falls with Gerard and the wife clinging to each other as if with a mad desire to make love eternal." Thus, Katharine Worth observes, the scenario ends "in the triumphant self-emancipation of the wife. *A Doll's House* type of triumph, but more complete, for Wilde's heroine acquires a lover as well as her freedom" (185).

Commenting on the scenario, Wilde told Alexander that he believed it was "extremely strong":

I want the sheer passion of love to dominate everything. No morbid self-sacrifice. No renunciation. A sheer flame of love between a man and a woman. That is what the play is to rise to – from the social chatter of Act I, through the theatrical effectiveness of Act II, up to the psychology with its great *dénouement* in Act III, till love dominates Act IV and accepts the death of the husband as in a way its proper right, leaving love its tragedy, and so making it a still greater passion. (*Letters* 361–62)

In June 1900, in a letter to Frank Harris, Wilde alluded to his title for the play as *Love Is Law* and to their "collaboration" in writing it, though Wilde apparently sold performing rights or options to the play to several other people, including the publisher Leonard Smithers, before and during his negotiations with Harris (*Letters* 829 and n4). In a letter to Harris on 26 September, Wilde acknowledged receiving £175 from him (as well as one-fourth share of the profits from the play), assigning him "full rights to deal with said plot and scenario" as Harris chose. Wilde now alluded to the title as *Her Second Chance* (*Letters* 836).

Production: When the staging of *Mr. and Mrs. Daventry* was announced, Harris proceeded to buy out those to whom Wilde had sold options or had assigned rights. The play opened at the Royalty Theatre on 25 October 1900, with Mrs. Patrick Campbell and Fred Kerr in the title roles. Like all other London theatres, the Royalty suspended performances on 22 January 1901, for two weeks of mourning when Queen Victoria died. The theater re-opened on 5 February, but the production closed on 23 February for a total of 116 performances.

Early Theatre Reviews: In general, the reviewers were hostile, charging that Harris had written a play more appropriate for Paris than for London. In the *Daily Telegraph* (26 Oct. 1900), W. L. Courtney called the play "always thin, never forcible, and frequently vulgar. To emphasize the latter quality is needless, for what Mr. Harris has to tell us is vulgar in its very essence.... Why not call this play 'The Adulterers' and hang the conventions?" In the *Times* (26 Oct.), A. B. Walkley alluded to the screen scene in Act II as "the prominent thing" in the play – "that catastrophic sofa": "If the scene is not absolutely indecent, it goes as near to indecency as anything we remember on the contemporary stage. So also does the dialogue. There is a certain joke about the object of ladies in dressing which is quite unprintable."

Unlike most of the other reviewers, who wrote adverse reviews, Max Beerbohm, in the *Saturday Review* (3 Nov.), had some praise to offer despite his criticism of Harris's lack of sophistication as a playwright. Beerbohm devotes much of his review to Harris's penchant for stage soliloquies that inform the audience what it already knows and for "irrelevant" comic servants ("he throws into his second act a comic English cook, into his third act a comic Irish valet, and into his fourth act a comic German waiter"). Moreover, says Beerbohm, Harris errs in placing the climax in the second act instead of at the end of the third.

Despite such deficiencies, the character of Mr. Daventry, writes Beerbohm, is "admirably drawn. It sets Mr. Harris very far above the level of ordinary dramatists, and does much to atone for his faults in technique." As for Mr. Daventry's suicide, Beerbohm notes that "the critics all exclaim that this is an unlikely action. It is not so. It is subtly right. He shoots himself because he cannot bear the idea that his wife should live with a man who is not her husband. By suicide he opens for her the way to matrimony. Stupid to the last, he regards that as her salvation" (rpt. in *More Theatres*, 1969).

On 4 November, Bernard Shaw wrote to Harris that the play was

good and successful (which is not always the same thing) in exact proportion as it is Frank Harris. Before the curtain went up George Moore informed me that I should see at a glance that the whole play was by Oscar Wilde. What I did see was that this was George's honest opinion, because you have undoubtedly amused yourself by writing some imaginary conversations on Wilde's lines.... (193)

Published: In 1954, a French reconstruction of Wilde's unfinished play, titled *Constance*, was published by Guillot de Saix, who, in the introduction, tells the story of how he received a draft of Wilde's play from the actress Mrs. Cora Brown Potter. When Potter and Saix met on the Riviera, she could not produce the draft but promised to leave it in her will for him. When she died before the Second World War, Saix received the draft of the play and collaborated with Henri de Briel on the reconstruction of the four-acts. The original English copy was allegedly destroyed at the end of the war by members of the resistance movement who, suspecting that Briel was a collaborator, entered his apartment and disposed of the MS.

The French reconstruction differs considerably

from Wilde's scenario, sent to George Alexander in 1894, though the Daventrys appear in both. The major change is that the French version involves a radically different ending in Act IV: instead of Daventry's suicide, he is killed by a crazed clergyman, whose wife had been the object of Daventry's attentions. Ian Fletcher and John Stokes, in their extensive review of research on Wilde, regard Guillot de Saix's various "reconstructions" of stories, prose poems, and plays attributed to Wilde as "eccentric activities" (60).

In the introduction to the first publication of *Mr. and Mrs. Daventry* (1956), H. Montgomery Hyde remarks that Wilde had "provisionally" given his play the title of *Mr. and Mrs. Daventry*, but "it appears that Wilde really intended to call it *Constance*, after his wife, who was an essentially 'good' woman like the Mrs. Daventry in the play" (11). Ellmann also refers to the title *Constance* – the play so named, he suggests, because Wilde's wife was kind "in putting up with his thralldom to [Lord Alfred] Douglas" (521/489). Nowhere, however, either in his extant letters or in his extant MSS. does Wilde ever mention the titles *Mr. and Mrs. Daventry* or *Constance*.

Manuscript: The Enthoven Collection in the Victoria and Albert Museum (London) has the complete acting version, which H. Montgomery Hyde discovered and published.

References: T. H. Bell, "Oscar Wilde's Unwritten Play," *Bookman* (New York) (Apr. – May 1930); Henri de Briel and Guillot de Saix, "La Dernière Pièce d'Oscar Wilde: *Constance*," *Les Oeuvres libres* (Oct. 1954); Bernard Shaw, *Collected Letters, 1898–1910*, ed. Dan H. Laurence (1972); Ian Fletcher and John Stokes, "Oscar Wilde," *Anglo-Irish Literature: A Review of Research*, ed. Richard Finneran (1976); Katharine Worth, *Oscar Wilde* (1983).

"MR. BRANDER MATTHEWS'S ESSAYS"

Published: *PMG*, 27 Feb. 1889, 3; rpt. in *Reviews* (1908). An unsigned review of Brander Matthews's *Pen and Ink: Papers on Subjects of More or Less Importance* (1889). (Throughout the *PMG* review, "Matthews" was spelled with a single "t" but corrected in *Reviews*, 1908.)

"If you want to have your book criticized favourably, give yourself a good notice in the preface," Brander Matthews (critic and professor of literature at Columbia University) gives as the "golden rule" for authors in what Wilde calls "an amusing essay on the art of preface-writing." Following his own advice, Matthews calls his own volume "the most entertaining, the most interesting, the most instructive book of the decade." While some of the essays on non-literary subjects are amusing and even clever, Wilde regards those essays on literature and literary subjects "sadly to seek." Matthews's essay on the ethics of plagiarism, for example, is "extremely dull and commonplace."

Wilde focuses on Matthews's remark that Austin Dobson's verse "has not the condensed clearness nor the incisive vigor of Mr. [Frederick] Locker's." Comments Wilde: "Nobody who lays claim to the slightest knowledge of literature and the forms of literature should ever bring the two names into conjunction. Mr. Locker has written some pleasant *vers de société*, some tuneful trifles in rhyme admirably suited for ladies' albums and for magazines. But to mention Herrick and Suckling and Mr. Austin Dobson in connection with him is absurd." Matthews, concludes Wilde, should confine himself to his "clever journalistic articles on Euchre, Poker, bad French and old jokes."

"MR. FROUDE'S BLUE BOOK"

Published: *PMG*, 13 April 1889, 3; rpt. in *Reviews* (1908). This review of James Anthony Froude's *The Two Chiefs of Dunboy* (1889) is signed "O. W."

Wilde alludes to "blue books" (so-called because parliamentary reports and other official publications have blue wrappers), which are "generally dull reading, but Blue Books on Ireland have always been interesting. They form the record of one of the great tragedies of modern Europe. In them England has written down her indictment against herself, and has given to the world the history of her shame." England's rule of Ireland in this century has been accompanied by "stupidity that is aggravated by good intentions."

Froude's novel describes a society that no longer exists, but "an entirely new factor has appeared in the social development of the country, and this factor is the Irish-American, and his influence. To mature its powers...the Celtic intellect has had to cross the Atlantic.... What captivity was to the Jews, exile has been to the Irish. America and American influence has educated them. Their first practical leader is an Irish-American" (an allusion, undoubtedly, to Charles Stewart Parnell, the Irish Nationalist leader in the drive for Home Rule: his mother was American, but he was of English stock and educated in England).

While Froude's book has "no practical relation to modern Irish politics and does not offer any solution of the present question, it has a certain historical value. It is a vivid picture of Ireland in the latter half of the eighteenth century, a picture often false in its lights and exaggerated in its shadows...." Froude, Wilde observes, admits to the martyrdom of Ireland, but he regrets that it was never completely carried out. Colonel Goring, the hero of the novel, suppresses "every fine national aspiration" with the words *Law* and *Order* on his lips.

If Froude intended his book to assist the Tories in solving the Irish question, "he has entirely missed his aim," for the Ireland he depicts has vanished, but, concludes Wilde, "as a record of the incapacity of a Teutonic to rule a Celtic people against their own wishes his book is not without value. It is dull, but dull books are very popular at present...."

"MR. HENRY O'NEILL, ARTIST"

Published: *Saunders's News-Letter*, 29 Dec. 1877; rpt. in Owen Dudley Edwards, "Oscar Wilde and Henry O'Neill," *Irish Book* 1 (Spring 1959): 11–18. Unlisted in Mason's bibliography, this article appeared anonymously: Rosa Mulholland Lady Gilbert's *Life of Sir John Gilbert* (1905) prints a letter from Wilde to Gilbert, revealing his authorship of the article on O'Neill (1798–1880), "the unfortunate author of the 'Irish Crosses'" (see *Letters* 49 and n3).

Wilde's purpose is to focus attention on O'Neill's appeal for "pecuniary assistance":

The circumstances of this case are so peculiarly mournful that we think it right to make them fully known to the public, in order that an Irishman of genius, and of heroic devotion to his art, may be rescued from undeserved want; nor can we do better than Mr. O'Neill's own account of his life, as he tells it plainly and simply in his appeal....

After O'Neill's appeal is reproduced in full – emphasizing his abandonment of a promising career to devote his life to Irish antiquities and the financial difficulties involved in publishing his studies – Wilde resumes his account of O'Neill's "simple story of a very noble but unfortunate life." O'Neill's major work, *The Sculptured Crosses of Ancient Ireland*, Wilde writes, "must always rank among the very finest productions of modern Irish art. The pictures of the various crosses are not only perfectly accurate, even in the minutest detail of ornamentation, but are drawn with sympathy and love and humility which are the three great essentials of the work of the true artist."

Ill-health, remarks Wilde, in addition to the "fatal apathy of the public in appreciating genius and the narrow jealousy of an antiquarian clique," has resulted in poverty and distress in O'Neill's old age: "It remains for the Irish public to make reparation for past injustice. Ireland is under a debt to Henry O'Neill. He has benefitted his country, in rescuing her from the imputations of barbarism in early ages, and he has a right to ask for assistance."

"MR. MAHAFFY'S NEW BOOK"

Published: *PMG*, 9 Nov. 1887, 3; rpt. in *Reviews* (1908). An unsigned review of John Pentland Mahaffy's *Greek Life and Thought: From the Age of Alexander to the Roman Conquest* (1887). The Rev. Mahaffy was Professor of Ancient History at Trinity College, Dublin, and Wilde's tutor, with whom he toured Italy and Greece (see his entry).

Wilde announces that this "disappointing" book, while "extremely interesting," treats its subject in a manner "unworthy of a scholar." Mahaffy's efforts "to degrade history to the level of the ordinary political pamphlet of contemporary party warfare" is, says Wilde, "depressing," though it might please the Unionists, those opposed to Home Rule. Mahaffy's treatment of the Hellenic world as though it were "'Tipperary Writ Large'" reveals

an amount of political bias and literary blindness that is quite extraordinary. He might have made his book a work of solid and enduring interest, but he has chosen to give it a merely ephemeral value, and to substitute for the scientific temper of the true historian the prejudice, the flippancy, and the violence of the platform partisan.

Mahaffy's "prejudice against the Greek patriots," Wilde continues, is unequaled except for "those few fine Romans who, sympathizing with Hellenic civilization and culture, recognized the political value of autonomy and the intellectual importance of a healthy national life. He mocks at what he calls their 'vulgar mawkishness about Greek liberties,' their 'anxiety to redress historical wrongs,' and congratulates his readers that this feeling was not intensified by the remorse that their own forefathers had been the oppressors." Such passages contain much "silliness and bad taste."

When he turns to art, Mahaffy "cannot help admitting that the noblest sculpture of the time was that which expressed the spirit of the first great *national* struggle...." Mahaffy condemns what he considers the "shallow society tendencies of the new comedy, and misses the fine freedom of Aristophanes, with his intense patriotism, his vital interest in politics, his large issues, and his delight in vigorous national life." Nevertheless, the few chapters that deal with the Greek social life and thought are "very pleasant reading indeed." However, Wilde does object to Mahaffy's view of Menander's social comedy, the aim of which, "no less than in Sheridan, is to mirror the manners, not reform the morals of its day, and the censure of the Puritan, whether real or affected, is always out of place in literary criticism, and shows a want of recognition of the essential distinction between art and life."

On the whole, Mahaffy's book, though drawing readers to an important historical period in Greece, has "marred the value of some of his remarks on literature by a bias that is quite as unmeaning" as his "foolish partisan bias" in discussing Greek politics. Not only does Mahaffy "miss the true spirit of the historian, but he often seems entirely devoid of the temper of the true man of letters." Despite his brilliance at times, he lacks "reasonableness, moderation, style, and charm. He seems to have no sense of literary proportion...." Wilde closes with the observation that the book will not add to Mahaffy's reputation "either as a historian, a critic, or man of taste."

"MR. MORRIS ON TAPESTRY"

Published: *PMG*, 2 Nov. 1888, 6; rpt. in *Miscellanies* (1908). An unsigned review of William Morris's lecture, "Carpet and Tapestry Weaving,"

at the Arts and Crafts Exhibition at the New Gallery, Regent Street, on 1 November.

Morris, writes Wilde, "delivered a most interesting and fascinating lecture" with the aid of small practical models of the two looms that are used for carpet and tapestry weaving. He also spoke at length about dyes. A 14th-century Flemish tapestry and a "superb" Persian carpet some 250 years old hung at the back of the platform. Pointing out the carpet's loveliness, Morris showed

how it combined the great quality of decorative design – being at once clear and well defined in form – each outline exquisitely traced, each line deliberate in its intention and its beauty – and the whole effect being one of unity, of harmony, almost of mystery, the colours being so perfectly harmonized together, and the little bright notes of colour being so cunningly placed either for tone or for brilliancy.

The "keynote of tapestry," as Wilde reports Morris, "the secret of its loveliness, was the complete filling up of every corner and square inch of surface with lovely and fanciful and suggestive design." The great Gothic tapestries depict forest trees rising in various places one above the other, "each leaf perfect in its shape and colour and decorative value, while in simple raiment of beautiful design knights and ladies wandered in rich flower-gardens...."

As for the use of tapestries in the modern age, Morris asserted that "we were richer than the Middle Ages, and so should be better able to afford this form of lovely wall-covering, which for artistic tone is absolutely without rival." The "perfect unity between the imaginative artist and handicraftsman" thus exists in the "new and delightful form" with the aid of the loom. Commercialism, "with its vile god cheapness, the callous indifference to the worker, its innate vulgarity of temper, is our enemy," says Morris as reported by Wilde. "We must sacrifice something of our luxury," Wilde remarks, then quotes Morris: "We cannot have riches and wealth both." A choice must be made between them.

"MR. MORRIS'S COMPLETION OF THE ODYSSEY"

Published: *PMG*, 24 Nov. 1887, 3; rpt. in

Reviews (1908). An unsigned review of William Morris's translation of *The Odyssey of Homer*, Vol. 2 (1887). See Wilde's review of the first volume, "Mr. Morris's Odyssey."

In bringing the "great romantic epic of Greek literature to its perfect conclusion," Morris has provided a version that "will always be a true classic amongst our classical translations." In Wilde's review of the first volume, he remarked that Morris was sometimes "far more Norse than Greek, nor does the volume that now lies before us make us alter that opinion." The metre selected by Morris also "misses something of [Homer's] dignity and calm. Here, it must be admitted, we feel a distinct loss, for there is in Homer not a little of Milton's lofty manner...." Nevertheless, "how really admirable is this whole translation!" Its faithfulness to the original is "far beyond that of any other verse-translation in our literature...a fine loyalty of poet to poet."

Wilde regards Morris's use of archaic words in his translation as "amply justified upon historical grounds," for Homer also employed language sometimes difficult to his contemporaries. Alexander Pope, in trying to put Homer into "the ordinary language of his day" (as well as into heroic couplets), produced a result that Wilde obviously disapproves of. Morris, on the other hand, "uses his archaisms with the tact of a true artist, and to whom indeed they seem to come absolutely naturally.... Homer is never quaint, but of old-world romance, and old-world beauty, which we moderns find so pleasurable, and to which the Greeks themselves were so keenly sensitive."

"MR. MORRIS'S LAST BOOK"
Published: *PMG*, 2 March 1889, 3; rpt. in *Reviews* (1908). An unsigned review of William Morris's *A Tale of the House of the Wolfings and All the Kindreds of the Mark* (1889).

Morris's volume, says Wilde, "is a piece of pure art workmanship from beginning to end, and the very remoteness of its style from the language and ordinary interests of our day gives to the whole story a strange beauty and unfamiliar charm." Written in blended prose and verse, the tale is concerned with the House of the Wolfings in their fight against the Roman legions then advancing into Germany. Wilde notes that it may be described "as an attempt to return by a self-conscious effort to the conditions of an earlier and a fresher age.... From some such feeling came the Pre-Raphaelite movement of our own day....":

[Morris's] fine harmonies and rich cadences create in the reader...something of the temper of romance and by taking him out of his own age place him in a truer and more vital relation to the great masterpieces of all time. It is a bad thing for an age to be always looking in art for its own reflection. It is well that, now and then, we are given work that is nobly imaginative in its method, and purely artistic in its aim.

Morris, Wilde states, "has always preferred romance to tragedy, and set the development of action above the concentration of passion. His story is like some splendid old tapestry crowded with stately images and enriched with delicate and delightful detail.... It is the whole presentation of the primitive life that really fascinates." Concluding after lengthy passages quoted to illustrate the work's "narrative power" and "beauty of the verse," Wilde welcomes "in days of uncouth realism and unimaginative imitation...a work of this kind."

"MR. MORRIS'S ODYSSEY"
Published: *PMG*, 26 April 1887, 5; rpt. in *Reviews* (1908). An unsigned review of William Morris's translation of *The Odyssey of Homer*, Vol. 1 (1887). See Wilde's review of the second volume, "Mr. Morris's Completion of the Odyssey."

Wilde begins with an acknowledgment of Morris's stature: "Of all our modern poets Mr. William Morris is the one best qualified by nature and by art to translate for us the marvellous epic of the wanderings of Odysseus. For he is our only true story singer since Chaucer." He has, moreover, "all the Greek's joy in the visible aspect of things, all the Greek's sense of delicate and delightful detail, all the Greek's pleasure in beautiful textures...." Added to all of this, Morris has the "true temper of high romance, the power to make the past as real to us as the present, the subtle instinct to discern passion, the swift impulse to portray life."

Of all the English translations of the *Odyssey*, Morris's is "the most perfect and the most satisfying." Here, Wilde states, we have a true work of art, a rendering not merely of language into language, but of poetry into poetry, and though the new spirit added in the transfusion may seem to many rather Norse than Greek, and perhaps at times more boisterous than beautiful, there is yet a vigour of life in every line, a splendid ardour through each canto, that stirs the blood while one reads like the sound of a trumpet, and that, producing a physical as well as a spiritual delight, exults the senses no less than it exalts the soul.

In no sense is Morris's version literary, Wilde writes, for "it seems to deal immediately with life itself...."

"MR. PATER'S IMAGINARY PORTRAITS"

Published: *PMG*, 11 June 1887, 2–3; rpt. in *Reviews* (1908). An unsigned review of Walter Pater's *Imaginary Portraits* (1887).

Wilde characterizes Pater's work as the embodiment of the "aim of those who are artists as well as thinkers in literature" – that is, "to convey ideas through the medium of images." The four "Imaginative Portraits," as Wilde refers to them, form a "series of philosophic studies, in which philosophy is tempered by personality...." The "most fascinating" of these studies is that of Sebastian van Storck, "the young grave Dutch philosopher, who is charmingly drawn. He is attracted to the "ideal of an intellectual disinterestedness, separating himself more and more from the transient world of sensation, accident, and even affection, till what is finite and relative becomes of no interest to him, and he feels that as Nature is but a thought of his, so he himself is but a passing thought of God."

In "Denys l'Auxerrois," suggested by a figure in old tapestries at Auxerre (in northern France; a center of learning in the 9th century), Pater "has fashioned a curious mediaeval myth of the return of Dionysus among men, a myth steeped in colour and passion and old romance, full of wonder and full of worship, Denys himself half animal and half god, making the world mad with a new ecstasy of living...." The story, notes Wilde, "symbolizes the passion of the senses." The passion for "the imaginative world of art" is the basis of "Duke Carl of Rosenmold," the eponymous character wishing "to amaze and to bewilder." He dies on the night of his marriage to a peasant girl, "the

very failure of his life lending him a certain melancholy grace and dramatic interest."

As an "intellectual impressionist," Pater does not

weary us with any definite doctrine, or seek to suit life to any formal creed. He is always looking for exquisite moments, and, when he has found them, he analyzes them with delicate and delightful art, and then passes on, often to the opposite pole of thought or feeling, knowing that every mood has its own quality and charm, and is justified by its mere existence.

As for Pater's style, "it is curiously ascetic." Indeed, asceticism is the "keynote of Mr. Pater's prose; at times it is almost too severe in its self-control, and makes us long for a little more freedom." Yet "what wonderful prose it is, with its subtle preferences, its fastidious purity, its rejection of what is common or ordinary!"

Pater, concludes Wilde,

is our greatest artist in prose; and though it may be admitted that the best style is that which seems an unconscious result rather than a conscious aim, still in these latter days, when violent rhetoric does duty for eloquence, and vulgarity usurps the name of nature, we should be grateful for a style that deliberately aims at perfection of form...and that sets before itself an ideal of grave and chastened beauty.

"MR. PATER'S LAST VOLUME"

Published: *Speaker* 1 (22 March 1890): 319–20; rpt. in *Reviews* (1908). A signed review of Walter Pater's *Appreciations, with an Essay on Style* (1889). Having read the review "with very great pleasure," Pater sent Wilde a note, dated 22 March, praising his "pleasantly written, genial, sensible, criticism..." (Pater, *Letters* 109).

"When," begins Wilde, "I first had the privilege – and I count it a very high one – of meeting Mr. Walter Pater, he said to me, smiling,"

"Why do you always write poetry? Why do you not write prose? Prose is so much more difficult." It was during my undergraduate days at Oxford, days of lyrical ardour and of studious sonnet-writing; days when one loved the exquisite intricacy and musical repetitions of the ballade, and the villanelle with its linked long-drawn echoes and its curious completeness; days when one solemnly sought to discover the proper temper in which a triolet should be written; delightful days, in which, I am glad to say, there was far more rhyme than reason.

Wilde reveals that, at the time, he did not comprehend what Pater "really meant," and it was only when he had carefully studied "his beautiful and suggestive essays" in *Studies in the History of the Renaissance* (1873) that he fully realized what a "wonderful self-conscious art the art of English prose-writing" really was or might be made to be: "Carlyle's stormy rhetoric, Ruskin's winged and passionate eloquence, had seemed to me to spring from enthusiasm rather than from art. I do not think I knew then that even prophets correct their proofs." Pater's essays became for Wilde "the golden book of spirit and sense, the holy writ of beauty" – here, Wilde quotes, without attribution, from Swinburne's "Sonnet (With a copy of *Mademoiselle de Maupin*").

Turning to *Appreciations*, Wilde praises it as

an exquisite collection of exquisite essays, of delicately wrought works of art – some of them being almost Greek in their purity of outline and perfection of form, others mediaeval in their strangeness of colour and passionate suggestion, and all of them absolutely modern, in the true meaning of the term modernity. For he to whom the present is the only thing that is present, knows nothing of the age in which he lives. To realise the nineteenth century one must realise every century that has preceded it, and that has contributed to its making....

The "most interesting and certainly the least successful" of the essays is "Style," which, says Wilde, is "too abstract. A true artist like Mr. Pater is most felicitous when he deals with the concrete, whose very limitations give him finer freedom, while they necessitate more intense vision." Despite Wilde's reservations concerning the essay, he responds favorably to the "high ideal...contained in these few pages! How good it is for us, in these days of popular education and facile journalism, to

be reminded of the real scholarship that is essential to the perfect writer...." Retreating from his initial judgment that the essay is "too abstract," Wilde remarks that, in Pater's hands, the subject "becomes very real to us indeed, and he shows us how, behind the perfection of a man's style, must lie the passion of a man's soul."

As for Pater's writing, Wilde remarks that the "architecture of the style becomes richer and more complex, the epithet more precise and intellectual" as his career progresses so that Pater's long, complex sentences "come to have the charm of an elaborate piece of music, and the unity of such music also." Of the essays on Shakespeare, Pater writes with "grace of expression and delicate subtlety of thought and phrase." On Wordsworth, Pater's essay has "a spiritual beauty of its own." Quoting from it, Wilde selects the famous passage that had such an influence on him: "That the end of life is not action but contemplation – *being* as distinct from *doing* – a certain disposition of the mind: is, in some shape or other, the principle of all the higher morality.... To treat life in the spirit of art is to make life a thing in which means and ends are identified: to encourage such treatment, the true moral significance of art and poetry."

Concluding, Wilde remarks that if imaginative prose is "really the special art of this century, Mr. Pater must rank amongst our century's most characteristic artists.... The age has produced wonderful prose styles, turbid with individualism, and violent with excess of rhetoric. But in Mr. Pater, as in Cardinal Newman, we find the union of personality with perfection."

"MR. SWINBURNE'S LAST VOLUME"

Published: *PMG*, 27 June 1889, 3; rpt. in *Reviews* (1908). An unsigned review of Algernon Charles Swinburne's *Poems and Ballads*, Third Series (1889).

By way of approaching the book under review, Wilde surveys Swinburne's career:

Mr. Swinburne once set his age on fire by a volume [*Poems and Ballads*, First Series, 1866] of very perfect and very poisonous poetry. Then he became revolutionary, and pantheistic [in *A Song of Italy*, 1867, and *Songs before Sunrise*, 1871], and cried out against those who sit in high places both in heaven and on earth.... Then he retired to the nursery, and wrote poems about children of a somewhat over-subtle character [in *Tristram and Other Poems*, 1882]. He is now extremely patriotic, and manages to combine with his patriotism a strong affection for the Tory party. He has always been a great poet. But he has his limitations, the chief of which is, curiously enough, an entire lack of any sense of limit.

Wilde complains, furthermore, that Swinburne's verse is "nearly always too loud for his subject. His magnificent rhetoric, nowhere more magnificent than in the volume that now lies before us, conceals rather than reveals. It has been said of him, and with truth, that he is a master of language, but with still greater truth it may be said that Language is his master. Mere sound often becomes his lord. He is so eloquent that whatever he touches becomes unreal." Noting the limitations in Swinburne's imagery, Wilde writes that he "has wearied us with his monotony. 'Fire' and 'Sea' are the two words ever on his lips." Again, quoting from "A Word with the Wind," Wilde comments: "Verse of this kind may be justly praised for the sustained strength and vigour of its metrical scheme. Its purely technical excellence is extraordinary. But is it more than an oratorical *tour de force*? Does it really convey much?"

Swinburne, Wilde continues, "puts his clarion to the lips of Spring and bids her blow, and the Earth wakes from her dreams and tells him her secret. He is the first lyric poet who has tried to make an absolute surrender of his own personality, and he has succeeded. We hear the song, but we never know the singer.... Force and Freedom form [Nature's] vague message. She deafens us with her clangours." But in the volume under review, Swinburne has not lost his fascination for romantic ballads in Border dialect, and this last volume contains "some very splendid examples of this curious artificial kind of poetry." Wilde concludes after offering some excerpts from the variety of poems in the volume: "Certainly 'for song's sake' we should love Mr. Swinburne's work, cannot indeed help loving it, so marvellous a music-maker is he. But what of the soul? For the soul we must go elsewhere."

"MR. SYMONDS' HISTORY OF THE RENAISSANCE"

Published: *PMG*, 10 Nov. 1886, 5; rpt. in *Reviews* (1908). An unsigned review of John Addington Symonds's *Renaissance in Italy: The Catholic Reaction* (1886), the final two volumes of his seven-volume work.

"In his previous volumes," Wilde comments, "Mr. Symonds had regarded the past rather as a picture to be painted than as a problem to be solved. In these two last volumes, however, he shows a clearer appreciation of the office of history. The art of the picturesque chronicler is completed by something like the science of the true historian, the critical spirit begins to manifest itself, and life is not treated as a mere spectacle, but the laws of its evolution and progress are investigated also." Symonds's desire to portray the Renaissance "under dramatic conditions still accompanies Mr. Symonds." Indeed, remarks Wilde, "he hardly realises that what seems romance to us was harsh reality to those who were engaged in it."

Symonds has "something of Shakespeare's sovereign contempt of the masses. The people stir him very little, but he is fascinated by great personalities." In the Renaissance, men "appreciated the aristocracy of intellect, but with the democracy of suffering they had no sympathy." Turning to particular aspects of the narrative, Wilde finds the story of Giordano Bruno's betrayal and martyrdom powerfully told, and the account of Ignatius Loyola and the rise of the Society of Jesus "extremely interesting."

On Symonds's discussion of 16th-century poetry, Wilde admits to being sometimes wearied by "the continual application to literature of epithets appropriate to plastic and pictorial art. The conception of the unity of the arts is certainly of great value, but in the present condition of criticism it seems to us that it would be more useful to emphasize the fact that each art has its separate method of expression." (In this view of the arts, Wilde follows Pater, but soon he would follow Whistler in writing such poems as "Symphony in Yellow.")

From poetry, Symonds moves to painting and music with a "most interesting description of the gradual steps by which the Italian genius passed from poetry and painting to melody and song, till the whole of Europe thrilled with the marvel and mystery of this new language of the soul." In disagreeing with Symonds's explanation of why

"MR. SYMONDS' RENAISSANCE"

England did not develop in music as did Italy and Germany, Wilde charges that the lack of development "must be ascribed to other causes than 'the prevalence of Puritan opinion.'"

Wilde concludes by congratulating Symonds on the completion of his history: "It is a most wonderful monument of literary labour, and its value to the student of Humanism cannot be doubted." Symonds's learning has "not made him a pedant; his culture has widened, not narrowed, his sympathies, and though he can hardly be called a great historian, yet he will always occupy a place in English literature as one of the remarkable men of letters in the nineteenth century."

"MR. WHISTLER'S TEN O'CLOCK"

Published: *PMG*, 21 Feb. 1885, 1–2; rpt. in *Miscellanies* (1908). A signed review of Whistler's lecture at Prince's Hall, Piccadilly, on 20 February at the unusual hour of 10 p.m.

Noting that this was Whistler's first public appearance as a lecturer, Wilde reports that Whistler spoke for more than an hour with "really marvelous eloquence on the absolute uselessness of all lectures of the kind." The audience, "a fashionable assemblage" that no doubt recalled "many charming invitations to wonderful private views," seemed "somewhat aghast and not a little amused at being told that the slightest appearance among a civilised people of any joy in beautiful things is a grave impertinence to all painters; but Mr. Whistler was relentless, and, with charming ease and much grace of manner, explained to the public that the only thing they should cultivate was ugliness, and that on their permanent stupidity rested all the hopes of art in the future."

Whistler stood there, "a miniature Mephistopheles, mocking the majority! He was like a brilliant surgeon lecturing to a class composed of subjects destined ultimately for dissection, and solemnly assuring them how valuable to science their maladies were, and how absolutely uninteresting the slightest symptoms of health on their part would be." Those in the audience were obviously delighted when Whistler told them "how vulgar their dresses were, or how hideous their surroundings at home...." Whistler's "arrows, barbed and brilliant," were launched "with all the speed and splendour of fireworks" at the "archaeologists, who spend their lives in verifying the birthplaces of nobodies, and estimate the value of a work of art by its date or its decay; at the art critics who always treat a picture as if it were a novel, and try and find out the plot; at dilettanti in general and amateurs in particular...."

Whistler spoke, in a "passage of singular beauty," of the artistic value of "dim dawns and dusks, when the mean facts of life are lost in exquisite and evanescent effects, when common things are touched with mystery and transfigured with beauty, when the warehouses become as palaces and the tall chimneys of the factory seem like campaniles in the silver air" (a passage that Wilde would imitate in "The Decay of Lying"). After arguing that only a painter could properly judge painting and expressing a "pathetic appeal to the audience not to be lured by the aesthetic movement into having beautiful things about them," Whistler bowed to the audience "which he had succeeded in completely fascinating by his wit, his brilliant paradoxes, and, at times, his real eloquence."

Taking issue with Whistler's attitude towards beautiful surroundings, Wilde remarks:

That an artist will find beauty in ugliness, *le beau dans l'horrible*, is now a commonplace of the schools, the *argot* of the atelier, but I strongly deny that charming people should be condemned to live with magenta ottomans and Albert-blue curtains in their rooms in order that some painter may observe the side-lights on the one and the values of the other.

In addition, Wilde disagrees with Whistler's contention that only a painter can judge painting: "I say that only an artist is a judge of art; there is a wide difference...." Only when the painter becomes an artist do the "secret laws of artistic creation" reveal themselves to him, for "there are not many arts, but one art merely – poem, picture and Parthenon, sonnet and statue – all are in their essence the same, and he who knows one knows them all. But the poet is the supreme artist, for he is the master of colour and of form, and the real musician besides, and is lord over all life and all arts...."

Despite – or perhaps because of – his disagreements with Whistler, Wilde regards the lecture as a masterpiece that will be known "not merely for its clever satire and amusing jests" but also for "the pure and perfect beauty of many of its passages." Convinced that Whistler is "one of the very greatest masters of painting," Wilde concludes archly: "And I may add that in this opinion Mr. Whistler himself entirely concurs."

"MRS. LANGTRY"

Published: *New York World*, 7 Nov. 1882, 5; rpt. as "Mrs. Langtry as Hester Grazebrook" in *Miscellanies* (1908). A review of Lillie Langtry's American debut in Tom Taylor's *An Unequal Match* on 6 Nov. 1882, at Wallack's Theatre in New York.

Wilde's laudatory notice of Langtry compares her "marvellous beauty" with the images on "the best Greek gems, on the silver coins of Syracuse, or among the marble figures of the Parthenon frieze...." In her performance of the role of Hester Grazebrook in the opening scene of the play, Langtry mingled "classic grace with absolute reality which is the secret of all beautiful art, of the plastic work of the Greeks and of the pictures of Jean François Millet equally." Wilde regards her "wonderful face" as

the pervading image of its type [in] the whole of our modern art in England. Last century it was the romantic type which dominated in art, the type loved by Reynolds and Gainsborough.... This type degenerated into mere facile prettiness in the hands of lesser masters, and, in protest against it, was created by the hands of the Pre-Raphaelites a new type, with its rare combination of Greek form with Florentine mysticism.

As for certain elements in the production of the play, Wilde praises Hester Grazebrook's dresses, the masterpiece being the last, "a symphony in silver-grey and pink, a pure melody of colour which I feel sure Whistler would call a *Scherzo*...." The scenery, "prepared in a hurry," was nevertheless "very good indeed," except for the drawing-room scene: "The heavy ebony doors are entirely out of keeping with the satin panels; the silk hangings and festoons of black and yellow are quite meaningless in their position and consequently quite ugly." With respect to scene painting, a scene, Wilde argues, is "primarily a decorative background for the actors, and should always be kept subordinate, first to the players, their dress, gesture, and action; and secondly, to the funda-mental principle of decorative art, which is not to imitate but to suggest nature."

"MY VOICE"

Published: *Poems* (1881). Apparently part of a poem titled "A Farewell" but divided into two separate poems: see "Her Voice." In this lyric poem of three quatrains, the speaker responds to his loved one's pronouncement that "those times" when they exchanged vows "are over and done": "We took our hearts' full pleasure – / You and I, / And now the white sails of our ship are furled...." Sorrow has made his "young mouth's vermilion" pale, but "this crowded life" has been little more to her than the sound of a lute or the "subtle spell / Of viols, or the music of the sea / That sleeps, a mimic echo, in the shell."

For this poem as part of a sequence, see "Apologia."

N

NARCISSUS and NARCISSISM

The most significant mythological figure who appears in Wilde's works and who is central to his sensibility, Narcissus – in Ovid's version of the myth in *Metamorphoses* – has been throughout the centuries a figure emblematic of self-destructive homoerotic desire. After Narcissus rejects Echo, the young woman who persists in her love for him, he gazes into a pool and sees an image of a beautiful young man. Consumed with passion, he is unaware that it is his own reflection. When he discovers that the image is his own, he nevertheless remains transfixed with longing for it until he perishes on the bank of the pool. A flower – named after him – blooms on the site of his symbolic resurrection. In his Tite Street home, Wilde had a bronze statuette of Narcissus on his mantelpiece as though to confirm his identification with the self-absorbed figure: In "The Critic as Artist," Part I, Gilbert remarks: "...the heavy eyelids of my bronze Narcissus are folded in sleep."

In *An Ideal Husband*, the theme of narcissistic self-love is openly expressed by Lord Goring, the dandy who announces at the beginning of Act III in admiration of his own appearance: "To love oneself is the beginning of a life-long romance," an epigram that Wilde had earlier included in his "Phrases and Philosophies for the Use of the Young." In Act II, Goring insists that "everyone has some weak point. There is some flaw in each of us." Then strolling over to the fireplace, he gazes at himself in a mirror to confirm his idealized self: "My father tells me that even I have faults. Perhaps I have. I don't know." Like Lord Goring, Wilde's other dandies in his society plays are obsessed by self-admiration and self-idealization: Lord Illingworth, in *A Woman of No Importance*, responds to a question asking what he had been doing lately that astonished him: "I have been discovering all kinds of beautiful qualities in my own nature." To be sure, Wilde could not depict, in the Victorian theater, the full implications of narcissistic homoeroticism, though some critics have suggested that it exists in the subtexts of his works.

In *The Picture of Dorian Gray*, Narcissus is the central symbolic figure involving doubling – Dorian and his portrait as mirror images. When Lord Henry examines the portrait, he declares that Dorian is a Narcissus, and when the painter Basil Hallward asks Dorian whether he appreciates the painting, the enthralled young man responds: "Appreciate it? I am in love with it, Basil. It is part of myself. I feel that." In Chapter 8, after Sibyl Vane's suicide, Dorian discovers a change in his portrait and recalls that once "in boyish mockery of Narcissus, he had kissed, or feigned to kiss, those painted lips that now smiled so cruelly at him." The episode involving Dorian and Sibyl thus mimics the Narcissus and Echo myth, one of disastrous disunity. As Jeffrey Berman remarks of Ovid:

> The richness of [his] myth is inexhaustible. Narcissus dramatizes not only the cold, self-centered love that proves fatally imprisoning, but fundamental oppositions of human existence: reality / illusion, presence / absence, subject / object, unity / disunity, involvement/ detachment. (1)

In *Salome*, narcissistic doubling occurs in a different manner between Salome – who embodies an extreme of lust – and Iokanaan – who embodies the extreme of asceticism. The Young Syrian describes Salome as "a narcissus trembling in the wind," an image foreshadowing her inevitable death. The extremes meet at the end of the play when Salome, in Beardsley's illustration of surrealistic flight, "The Climax," holds the bloody head of Iokanaan before her: the two faces are remarkably similar, suggesting the Narcissus myth in which the two figures reflect, as mirror images, each other's desires.

Herod's self-deception occurs in a speech focusing on mirrors – narcissistic symbols – after Salome demands Iokanaan's head: "...I will look at thee no more. One should not look at anything. Neither at things, nor at people should one look. Only in mirrors is it well to look, for mirrors do but show us masks." As Miyoshi has observed: "...for the writers of the nineties – as for the Romantics – introspection, mirror-gazing, is a sanctioned activity. For the world, wear your mask; for a true glimpse of yourself, consult your mirror"

(311). But since Herod cannot admit his own lust, he sees only a mask in the mirror.

Though Wilde himself had a strong strain of narcissistic self-admiration in his personality, he also had the capacity to see its potential absurdity. In his story "The Remarkable Rocket," Wilde depicts the irony of a narcissist's self-glorification and ultimate self-extinction after the rocket rises into the sky and explodes but, unnoticed by anyone, falls to earth as a mere stick. Earlier, the rocket had remarked: "I am always thinking about myself, and I expect everybody else to do the same." Only the goose, on whose back the stick has fallen and who rushes into the water, takes notice but not of the "great sensation" that the rocket believes it has achieved but of the fact that it will soon be raining.

In *The Importance of Being Earnest*, all of the characters are self-idealized figures existing in a dandiacal utopia, in which, as Gwendolen remarks, "style, not sincerity, is the vital thing." On first meeting Cecily, Algernon is instantly absorbed by her, for she is "in every way the visible personification of absolute perfection." Into her diary (another symbolic mirror reflecting the writer's narcissistic self-idealization), Cecily delights in inscribing her "absolute perfection." The final unity, which develops out of the disunity between Jack and Algernon, occurs when they discover that they are brothers after all rather than self-created reflections of "Ernest" and when Gwendolen and Cecily are united with the two brothers – one truly Ernest, the other merely his pretended reflection.

References: Louise Vinge, *The Narcissus Theme in Western European Literature up to the Early Nineteenth Century* (1967); Masao Miyoshi, *The Divided Self: A Perspective on the Literature of the Victorians* (1969); Jerome Kavka, "Oscar Wilde's Narcissism," *Annual of Psychoanalysis* 3 (1975); Jeffrey Berman, *Narcissism and the Novel* (1990); Antonio Ballesteros Gonzalez, "The Mirror of Narcissus in *The Picture of Dorian Gray*," *Rediscovering Oscar Wilde*, ed. C. George Sandulescu (1994); Karl Beckson, "Narcissistic Reflections in a Wilde Mirror," *Modern Drama* (Spring 1994); Steven Bruhm, "Taking One to Know One: Oscar Wilde and Narcissism," *English Studies in Canada* (June 1995).

NELSON, MAJOR JAMES OSMOND: *See* **PRISON YEARS, 1895–97**

"A NEW BOOK ON DICKENS"

Published: *PMG*, 31 March 1887, 5. An unsigned review of Frank T. Marzials's *Life of Charles Dickens*; rpt. in *Reviews* (1908).

Wilde praises Marzials's biography as "brightly and cleverly written, admirably constructed, and gives a most vivid and graphic picture of that strange modern drama, the drama of Dickens's life.... We are really brought close to the man with his indomitable energy, his extraordinary capacity for work, his high spirits, his fascinating, tyrannous personality." To Wilde, Dickens's bitterness towards his father and mother is understandable, but his caricatures of them for the "amusement of the public, with an evident delight in his own humour," presents a "curious psychological problem."

Though "good novelists are much rarer than good sons," Wilde observes,

> the fact remains that a man who was affectionate and loving to his children, generous and warm-hearted to his friends, and whose books are the very bacchanalia of benevolence, pilloried his parents to make the groundlings laugh, and this fact every biographer of Dickens should face and, if possible, explain.

Marzials, however, has not faced the fact, for a "popular series [the "Great Writers"] is bound to express popular views, and cheap criticisms may be excused in cheap books."

Nevertheless, Wilde admires Marzials's "cleverness with which he passes over his hero's innumerable failures." Some of these failures occur when Dickens attempts to be serious: "...he succeeds," Wilde remarks, "only in being dull." And when Dickens "aims at truth he reaches merely platitude." Moreover, he was "never able even to satirise: he could only caricature...."

Concluding, Wilde notes that Marzials "expresses his belief that a century hence Dickens will be read as much as we now read Scott, and says rather prettily that as long as he is read 'There will be one gentle and humanising influence the more at work among men,' which is always a useful tag to append to the life of any popular author." Avoiding the question of Dickens's "immortality," Wilde hopes that future authors do not model their style upon his, and as for "the gentle and humanising influence," Wilde remarks: "This is taking

Dickens just a little too seriously."

"A NEW CALENDAR"

Published: *PMG*, 17 February 1887, 5; rpt. in *Reviews* (1908). Unsigned review of *Days of the Year: A Poetic Calendar from the Works of Alfred Austin*, ed. "A.S." (Mrs. William Sharp), with an introduction by William Sharp (1887).

Wilde begins this review with a droll observation:

> Most modern calendars mar the sweet simplicity of our lives by reminding us that each day as it passes is the anniversary of some perfectly uninteresting event. Their compilers display a degraded passion for chronicling small beer, and rake out the dust heap of history in an ardent search after rubbish.

The "new calendar" under review, however, makes every day "beautiful for us by means of an elegant extract from the poems of Mr. Alfred Austin...and though it would be dangerous to make calendars the basis of Culture, we should be all very much improved if we began each day with a fine passage of English poetry."

As criticism, the introduction, Wilde complains, is "not of much value, but as an advertisement it is quite excellent." On the whole, however, Sharp "has attempted an impossible task. Mr. Austin [in 1896, appointed poet laureate] is neither an Olympian nor a Titan, and all the puffery...cannot set him on Parnassus. His verse is devoid of all real rhythmical life; it may have the metre of poetry, but it has not often got its music...."

"THE NEW HELEN"

Published: *Time: A Monthly Miscellany of Interesting and Amusing Literature* 1 (July 1879): 400–02; rev. in *Poems* (1881); further rev. in (1882). The internal evidence suggests that Wilde wrote this poem of 100 lines, probably around 1878–79, with the acclaimed actress Lillie Langtry in mind (see entry). In her copy of *Poems* (1881), Wilde wrote: "To Helen, formerly of Troy, now of London" (*Letters* 65n3).

In this lyric poem, as in "Serenade. (For Music)," Wilde employs the myth of the Trojan War: The "New Helen" of the l9th century has the capacity, as did the mythic Helen, to create discontent (Yeats was later to exploit this parallel but

with Maud Gonne in mind rather than Lillie Langtry). The speaker pleads: "The lotus-leaves which heal the wounds of Death / Lie in thy hand; O be thou kind to me...." Having lost "all hope and heart to sing," he casts aside the possibility of ruin "if in thy temple thou wilt let me kneel." Concluding, he addresses the New Helen in grandiose apostrophes: "Lily of love, pure and inviolate! / Tower of ivory! red rose of fire! / Thou hast come down our darkness to illume...."

NEW JOURNALISM: *See* NEWSPAPERS AND PERIODICALS

"NEW NOVELS"

Published: *PMG*, 28 Oct. 1886, 4–5; rpt. in *Reviews* (1908). Unsigned reviews of books published in 1886.

Beginning with a novel titled *Astray*, by Charlotte M. Yonge, Mary Bramston, Christabel Coleridge, and Esmé Stuart, Wilde remarks: "It has taken four people to write it, and even to read it requires assistance. Its dulness is premeditated and deliberate and comes from a laudable desire to rescue fiction from flippancy." Though the story, "not uninteresting," involves a young doctor who attempts to "build up a noble manhood on the ruins of a wasted youth," the method of presenting it by an interminable sequence of long letters and extracts from diaries is "extremely tiresome": "It contains the rough material for a story, but is not a completed work of art.... We fear that too many collaborators are like too many cooks and spoil the dinner." Nevertheless, there are "certain solid qualities" in the novel, which "one can with perfect safety recommend to other people."

Of Rhoda Broughton's prose style in *Betty's Visions*, Wilde observes that "she at least possesses that one touch of vulgarity that makes the whole world kin." And alluding to Broughton's attendance at meetings of the Psychical Society "in search of copy," he concludes that "mysticism is not her mission, and telepathy should be left to Messrs. Myers and Gurney" (Frederick W.H. Myers, poet, and Edmund Gurney, psychologist, important figures in the founding of the Society for Psychical Research in 1882). Her "true sphere," Wilde continues, is Philistia, to which she should return, for "she knows more about the vanities of this world than about this world's visions...."

"NEW NOVELS"

Wilde devotes much space to summarizing the plot of Mrs. Alfred Hunt's *That Other Person*, an indication, perhaps, that little interested him in this novel of love and sacrifice. At the end of a lengthy paragraph, however, he focuses on the "most attractive character in the book, strangely enough... Mr. Godfrey Daylesford," who "has married not for love but for ambition and is rather severely punished for doing so." Though he is very weak, he is also very charming: "So charming indeed is he, that it is only when one closes the book that one thinks of censuring him.... Such a character has at any rate the morality of truth about it. Here literature has faithfully followed life." And concluding this rather routine review, Wilde observes that Mrs. Hunt writes in "a very pleasing style, bright and free from affectation. Indeed, everything in her work is clever except the title."

The plot of Margaret Roberts's *A Child of the Revolution* involves an adopted child – inevitably of noble birth – whose parents have died in the Reign of Terror. When the child has grown to womanhood, the "father," an ardent Republican, discovers that she is the daughter of his enemy. "This," writes Wilde, "is a noble story, but the workmanship, though good of its kind, is hardly adequate to the idea. The style lacks grace, movement and variety.... Seriousness, like property, has its duties as well as rights, and the first duty of a novel is to please."

Ernest Eckstein's *Aphrodite*, "a romance of ancient Hellas," cares more, Wilde remarks, for its "backgrounds" than for its figures. However, the author tells the story "very well, and his hero is made of flesh and blood." Its tone reminds Wilde of the late Greek novels: "Indeed, it might be one of the lost tales of Miletus. It deserves to have many readers and a better binding."

"NEW NOVELS"

Published: *Saturday Review* 44 (20 Aug. 1887): 264; rpt. in *Reviews* (1908). Unsigned reviews of books published in 1887.

Though, writes Wilde, "teutonic fiction, as a rule, is somewhat heavy and very sentimental," E. Werner's *Her Son*, "excellently translated" by Christina Tyrrell, "is really a capital story, and would make a capital play." After summarizing the plot, involving "a war of character, a clash of personalities," Wilde judges the novel as "full of movement and life, and the psychology of the characters is displayed by action, not by analysis, by deeds, not by description.... It has truth, passion, and power, and there are no better things than these in fiction."

On the other hand, J. Sale Lloyd's *Scamp* "depends on one of those foolish misunderstandings that are the stock-in-trade of second-rate novelists.... There are endless pages of five o'clock tea-prattle, and a good many tedious characters. Such novels as *Scamp* are possibly more easy to write than they are to read." Conversely, Wilde regards Sophie Veitch's *James Hepburn* as "not a mere chaos of conversation, but a strong story of real life, and it cannot fail to give Miss Veitch a prominent position among modern novelists." Hepburn is a minister who, says Wilde, "presides over a congregation of pleasant sinners and serious hypocrites." The story is "exceedingly powerful, and there is no extravagant use of the Scotch dialect, which is a great advantage to the reader."

The title page of *Tiff* informs us, notes Wilde, that it was written by the author of *Lucy; or, a Great Mistake*, "which seems to us a form of anonymity, as we have never heard of the novel in question. We hope, however, that it was better than *Tiff*, for *Tiff* is undeniably tedious." The plot involves a beautiful girl who has many lovers but who loses them and an ugly girl with one lover, whom she keeps. The dullness of *Tiff*, Wilde concludes, is "quite remarkable."

"THE NEW PLAY"

Published: *Court and Society Review* 4 (13 April 1887), 357; rpt. in Mason, 27–28 (uncollected in *Reviews*, 1908). An unsigned review of William Gillette's *Held by the Enemy*, produced for a Saturday matinee performance at the Princess's Theatre on 2 April 1887; a second performance, which Wilde saw, was presented on the following Saturday evening, 9 April.

"American actors," notes Wilde, "have always been more popular in London than American plays.... So the success of an absolutely American play [written by the popular American actor William Gillette, famous for his stage portrayal of Sherlock Holmes] is extremely interesting, and it is very much to be regretted that, as far as the hero's part is concerned, 'Held by the Enemy' is not better acted." In this brief notice, much of it devoted to the acting, Wilde declares the play "a very powerful tragedy, sandwiched between two comedy acts, and contains one of the best situations in the whole of modern dramatic literature."

"THE NEW PRESIDENT"

Published: *PMG*, 26 Jan. 1889, 3; rpt. in *Reviews* (1908). An unsigned review of Wyke Bayliss's *The Enchanted Island* (1889).

Bayliss, the new president of the Royal Society of British Artists, has "just given his gospel of art to the world," writes Wilde. His predecessor also had a gospel of art, but "it usually took the form of an autobiography. Mr. Whistler [president from 1886 to 1888] always spelt art, and we believe still spells it, with a capital 'I.' However, he was never dull. His brilliant wit, his caustic satire, and his amusing epigrams, or perhaps we should say epitaphs on his contemporaries, made his views on art as delightful as they were misleading and as fascinating as they were unsound." Bayliss, on the other hand, is "rather tedious." Whistler "never said much that was true, but the present President never says anything that is new, and if art be a fairy-haunted wood or an enchanted island, we must say that we prefer the old Puck to the fresh Prospero."

Wilde continues this review with additional remarks about Whistler: "Admirable as are Mr. Whistler's fireworks on canvas [an allusion to his *Nocturne in Black and Gold: The Falling Rocket* (1878), which precipitated the famous libel suit against John Ruskin for his disparaging remarks], his fireworks in prose are abrupt, violent, and exaggerated." Bayliss, Wilde contends, "is as much Mr. Whistler's superior as a writer, as he is his inferior as a painter and an artist." Bayliss's sonnets at the end of the book, however, are "almost as mediocre as the drawings that accompany them." Moreover, Bayliss's discourses on art are "very commonplace and old fashioned":

What is the use of telling artists that they should try and paint Nature as she really is? What Nature really is, is a question for metaphysics, not for art. Art deals with appearances, and the eye of the man who looks at Nature, the vision in fact of the artist, is far more important to us than what he looks at. There is more truth in Corot's aphorism, that a landscape is simply the "mood of a man's mind" than there is in all Mr. Bayliss's laborious disquisitions on naturalism.

Bayliss's only original suggestion is that the House of Commons should select an important event from contemporary history and "hand it over to the artists, who are to choose from among themselves a man to make a picture of it." However, if William Frith's *Marriage of the Prince of Wales* is an example of "healthy historic art, the less we have of such art the better." Bayliss is "a pleasant picturesque writer, but he should not speak about art. Art is a sealed book to him."

"THE NEW REMORSE"

Published: First appeared as "Un Amant de Nos Jours" ("A Lover in Our Time") in the *Court and Society Review* 5 (13 Dec. 1887): 587 (Mason 47 prints this version); rev. as "The New Remorse" in the Oxford *Spirit Lamp* 2 (6 Dec. 1892): 97 (when Lord Alfred Douglas was its editor); rpt. in *Poems* (1908).

In *The Autobiography of Lord Alfred Douglas* (2nd. ed.,1931; rpt. 1970), Douglas remarks that six months after first meeting Wilde in early 1891, he received the presentation holograph of the sonnet "The New Remorse." The original MS., of course, had been written and published several years before Wilde met Douglas, who nevertheless remarks of the presentation copy: "Anyone who takes the trouble to read it carefully will see that it shows clearly that the 'familiarities'...had not then begun" (75).

In the poem, the "new remorse" is oddly portrayed, for this sonnet moves from the speaker's awareness of sin ("The sin was mine; I did not understand") to a vision of Christ as Savior (though not for the speaker) with elaborate imagery characteristic of late 19th-century homoerotic verse, as in the following:

Who is this
Who cometh in dyed garments from the
    South?
It is thy new-found Lord, and he shall kiss
    The yet unravished roses of thy mouth,
And I shall weep and worship, as before.

"NEWS FROM PARNASSUS"

Published: *PMG* (12 April 1886): 5; rpt. in *Reviews* (1908). Unsigned reviews of books published in 1886.

Beginning with G. F. Armstrong's *Stories of Wicklow*, Wilde observes that "most modern Irish poetry is purely political, and deals with the wickedness of the landlords and the Tories, but Mr. Armstrong sings of the picturesqueness of Erin, not of its politics." He "very charmingly" tells of the "magic of its mists and the melody of its colour." Armstrong also "carefully observes the rules of decorum, and, as he promises his readers in a preface, keeps quite clear of 'the seas of sensual art.' In fact, an elderly maiden lady could read this volume without a blush, a thrill, or even an emotion."

The second volume of John A. Goodchild's *Somnia Medici* lacks Armstrong's "literary touch," but his volume has "a remarkable quality of forcible and direct expression." He seems, says Wilde, "to be an ardent disciple of Mr. Browning, and though he may not be able to reproduce the virtues of his master, at least he can echo his defects very cleverly." Though Goodchild's verse is often "harsh and rugged," it is on the whole "clever and interesting."

Proceeding to H. E. Keene's *Verses,* Wilde regards the poet as "a pleasant rhymer, as rhymers go,...though we strongly object to his putting the Song of Solomon into bad blank verse.... We wish he would not write sonnets with fifteen lines....as bad a monstrosity as a sonnet in dialogue. The volume has the merit of being very small, and contains many stanzas quite suitable for valentines."

W. G. Hole, "apparently a very young writer," has work "full of crudities," defective syntax, and questionable grammar. Yet the one poem, "Procris," in *Procris and Other Poems*, has the "true poetic ring." The "richness and variety of its metaphors, the music of its lines, the fine opulence of its imagery, all seem to point to a new poet": "...if he will cultivate the technique of his craft a little more we have no doubt but that he will someday give us work worthy to endure" (the eight more books of poems published by Hole did not fulfill Wilde's hope).

NEWSPAPERS AND PERIODICALS: WILDE'S CONTRIBUTIONS

From his initial publications (the earliest dated 1875, a translation of songs from Aristophanes' *The Clouds*) in the *Dublin University Magazine: A Literary and Political Journal*, the *Irish Monthly: A Magazine of General Literature*, and in *Kottabos* (the publication of Trinity College, Dublin),

Wilde contributed prose and verse to a variety of newspapers and periodicals through much of his career. After his graduation from Oxford, he was clearly a "name," as is indicated in a letter from Edmund Yates (1831–94), the popular playwright, novelist, and comic versifier, who had founded the Liberal *World: A Journal for Men and Women* in 1874. To Willie Wilde, Yates wrote in January 1879: "I wish you would put me *en rapport* with your brother the Newdigate man, of whom I hear so much and so favourably" (qtd. in Mason 226). A skillful editor who remained with the *World* until his death, Yates also attracted to its pages William Archer as its drama critic in 1884 and Bernard Shaw as its art critic in 1889.

To the *World*, between 1879 and 1891, Wilde contributed poems that obviously appealed to Yates's theatrical interests: "To Sarah Bernhardt," "Queen Henrietta Maria," and "Portia" (the two latter poems celebrating Ellen Terry's roles on stage), "Ave Imperatrix! A Poem on England" and "Libertatis Sacra Fames" (two poems on his political creed), and "Impression du Matin" (inspired by Whistler's "nocturnes" but ending with moral condemnation of the prostitute "With lips of flame, and heart of stone"). In addition, Wilde's story, "Lady Alroy" (later retitled as "The Sphinx without a Secret") and the amusing "The Model Millionaire" also appeared in the publication. The *World* is also noted for the comic feud over serious aesthetic principles conducted in letters to the editor, most of them from Whistler at the expense of Wilde.

In the *Nineteenth Century* (May 1887), Matthew Arnold characterized recent developments in the British press as the "New Journalism," a term that W. T. Stead (1849–1912), editor of the *Pall Mall Gazette*, had previously used in essays he published in the *Contemporary Review* (May and Nov. 1886). Arnold wrote that the New Journalism was

> full of ability, novelty, variety, sensation, sympathy, generous instincts; its one great fault is that it is *featherbrained*.... Well, the democracy...is disposed to be, like this journalism, featherbrained; just as the upper class is disposed to be selfish in its politics, and the middle class narrow.... (qtd. in Baylen 367)

For 30 years, Arnold was the practitioner of "what by implication was the 'Old' Journalism, whose long-term project was to elevate journalistic practice into 'criticism' and thus to the authority of literature" (Brake, *Subjugated* 83).

In 1883, when Stead became the editor of the *Pall Mall Gazette*, he wrote in his private journal that his "mission was to labour...[for] the social regeneration of the world" (qtd. in Baylen 369). Arnold withdrew as a contributor when Stead proceeded to transform the paper into an instrument for a new style of campaigning and investigative partisan journalism. In July 1885, Stead exposed the white slave traffic in a week-long sensational series of articles titled "Maiden Tribute of Modern Babylon," which resulted in sales reaching 100,000 copies but which also resulted in his two-month imprisonment as a result of his purchase, with the help of the Salvation Army, of a child virgin for purposes of prostitution to expose the shocking manner in which it could be done. His crusading zeal stimulated the passage of the Criminal Law Amendment Act in that year, which raised the age of consent for young women to 16, but which included – at Stead's suggestion to Henry Labouchere (see his entry) – the infamous Article XI, criminalizing private, mutually consenting homosexual acts between adults, which resulted in Wilde's imprisonment.

The one-penny daily *Pall Mall Gazette*, a London evening paper founded in 1865 by Frederick Greenwood (also its editor), was, from its beginnings, a publication with literary interests: indeed, its title was taken from the fictitious journal – "written by gentlemen for gentlemen" – in Thackeray's *Pendennis* (1850). Among its early contributors were George Eliot, Anthony Trollope, John Ruskin, and Matthew Arnold. Though Stead transformed the paper into an instrument for sensational exposés and political causes, he retained something of its original intent to acquaint educated readers with the latest literary publications. From its Conservative beginnings, the *Pall Mall Gazette* became, under Stead, openly Liberal/Radical, though many of the eminent writers published by Greenwood continued to contribute under the new dispensation as the leading literary and political paper of the cultured class.

As the ongoing object of *Punch*'s satires and parodies, Wilde undoubtedly attracted Stead's attention as one who would be suitable to review for the *Pall Mall Gazette*. Wilde seized the opportunity to express his political and literary views in many of his more than 80 reviews and articles that appeared in the paper between 1885 and 1890. Because Stead supported the Liberal position on Home Rule for Ireland, he published Wilde's attack on English rule in Ireland in a signed review of J. A. Froude's *The Two Chiefs of Dunboy* (see "Mr. Froude's Blue Book"). The records of English rule, writes Wilde, "form...one of the great tragedies of Modern Europe. In them England has written down her indictment against herself, and has given to the world the history of her shame."

In Wilde's various departures in the *Pall Mall Gazette* from his previous devotion to art for art's sake – later again championed in *Intentions* – "The Gospel According to Walt Whitman" (see entry) was a spirited defense of the American poet against current criticism: "...there is a largeness of vision, a healthy sanity, and a fine ethical purpose...." More striking is Wilde's "The Poets and the People" (see entry), which asserts that the time has come "when poets should exercise their influence for good, and set fairer ideals before all than the mere love of wealth on one side and the desire to appropriate wealth on the other." Wilde never adhered rigidly to the principle of art for art's sake: his anonymous reviews in the *Pall Mall Gazette* permitted him to express his belief in the morality of art without fear of being accused of apostasy.

Some of Wilde's most important contributions were to the *Fortnightly Review*, founded in 1865 and first edited by the critic G. H. Lewes, who had been living outside of marriage with George Eliot. As one of the founders remarked, the *Fortnightly* "would be neither conservative nor liberal, neither religious nor freethinking, neither popular nor exclusive – but we would let any man who had a thing to say...speak freely." Frank Harris (see entry), later Wilde's most influential early biographer, became the editor in 1886 for the next eight years. The *Fortnightly* "was particularly noteworthy for the high quality of its creative and critical literature: almost every distinguished English writer and critic of the day was among [Harris's] contributors" (Houghton 180). Harris boasted that, in his first year, he had doubled the circulation of the periodical.

Wilde contributed the daring biographical study of the poisoner and writer Thomas Griffiths Wainewright in "Pen, Pencil and Poison" as well as "The Soul of Man under Socialism," the "Preface to 'Dorian Gray,'" and "Poems in Prose."

Harris's wish to attract attention to the *Fortnightly* and his personal friendship with Wilde were probably major factors in Wilde's appearance in the periodical. One wonders what Harris's reaction was to the passages on the press in "The Soul of Man under Socialism," where Wilde remarks, "In old days men had the rack. Now they have the press.... We are dominated by journalism." More denigrating, of course, and perhaps directed to Harris himself is the remark: "The fact is, that the public have an insatiable curiosity to know everything, except what is worth knowing. Journalism, conscious of this, and having tradesmanlike habits, supplies their demands."

At the time that Wilde was contributing to the *Fortnightly Review*, he was also contributing major critical essays to the *Nineteenth Century*: "Shakespeare and Stage Costume" (later revised as "The Truth of Masks"), "The Decay of Lying," and two parts of "The True Function and Value of Criticism" (later retitled as "The Critic as Artist"). One of the most popular monthlies of the time, the *Nineteenth Century* had, from its founding in 1877, attracted such leading writers to its pages as Whitman, Gladstone, Swinburne, and Beatrice Webb – an indication of its Liberal stance.

In his biography of Wilde, Harris writes that the contributions to the *Fortnightly* and *Nineteenth Century* enabled Wilde to reach "the topmost height of the culture of his time and was now able to say new and interesting things." His critical essays in *Nineteenth Century* and the *Fortnightly* – subsequently published in *Intentions*, which codified his aesthetic principles – "had about them the stamp of originality. They achieved a noteworthy success with the best minds, and laid the foundation of his fame" (67).

Wilde's greatest involvement in a periodical was his editing of the monthly *Woman's World*, which Cassell and Co. had begun publishing in November 1886 under the title *Lady's World: A Magazine of Fashion and Society*. In the 1880s, Cassell was one of the leading publishers of respectable popular monthlies and weeklies, such as *Cassell's Family Magazine* and *Cassell's Saturday Journal*. Clearly, the *Lady's World* – as its title implied – was designed for a more limited audience. Its stated intent was to display "by means of Coloured Plates and Wood Engravings executed in the highest style of art" the "latest styles of Dress adopted by the leaders of Society" in London,

Paris, Vienna, and Berlin. Moreover, news of the "doings of Society at home and abroad" was also planned as well as "At Home" articles on society notables "with a pictorial account of their homes and surroundings" – in short, the lifestyles of the rich and famous.

By the spring of 1887, however, the magazine was clearly not selling well, for the publishers were negotiating with Wilde to assume the editorship with the intent of giving the publication a new direction. The choice of Wilde was undoubtedly based on his notoriety and his lectures on the decorative arts, on dress, and on beautifying homes. In addition, by moving in fashionable social circles, he could attract the support of influential society women. As Simon Nowell-Smith writes, Wilde

> entered into the reconstruction [of the magazine] with enthusiasm; criticized, with tact, the features that he wished to see removed; proposed a more high-minded approach to the sex (the magazine must deal not merely with what women wear but with what they think and feel); listed likely contributors of literary or social fame; sought out the most influential of these not only in London and Paris but in Oxford and Cambridge ("We must have the Universities on our side"); advised on the avoidance of extravagance, and of vulgarity, in illustration. (149)

Because of the ambiguities of the term *lady* – which Wilde regarded as having a "certain taint of vulgarity" as well as being "extremely misleading" (*Letters* 203) – and because of the prominence of the "Woman Question" as the late-19th century feminist movement gathered strength, Wilde insisted that the magazine – which was "too feminine, and not sufficiently womanly" (*Letters* 194) – be re-named the *Woman's World*. This change in name (suggested by the popular novelist Mrs. Dinah Craik) implied, as Laurel Brake writes, "a significant move from the world of the 'lady' to that of 'woman,' a word associated at the time with 'commonness,' suffrage, and higher education..." (*Subjugated* 128). At first, the Cassell directors resisted the suggestion but finally acceded to Wilde's wishes.

The prospectus in the October 1887 issue of *Lady's World* announced the changes in title and editorship for November. It also listed a number of such well-known writers who would contribute as Olive Schreiner, Marie Corelli, and Mathilde Blind; the novelist "Ouida" and the writer of children's stories Edith Nesbit contributed as well as Wilde's mother, Lady Wilde, and his wife, Constance. Articles were generally signed (unlike those in the *Lady's World*) to emphasize the prominence of the contributors. To the publisher George Macmillan, Wilde wrote in October: "I am going to make literary criticism one of the features of the *Woman's World*, and to give special prominence to books written by women" (*More Letters* 70).

In addition, Wilde persuaded some well-known male writers to contribute – one of them, Arthur Symons (see entry), contributed his first essay on a major figure in the Symbolist Movement, Villiers de l'Isle Adam, which appeared after Wilde left the magazine – for, said Wilde, "artists have sex but art has none." Such artists as Walter Crane, Dante Rossetti, and Charles Ricketts provided designs and illustrations, associating the Aesthetic Movement with the publication. Finally, Wilde himself contributed a number of reviews and "literary notes" to various issues, emphasizing women writers (see index under *Woman's World*), but for many months in 1888 and 1889, he contributed nothing.

Though Wilde was determined, as he told Wemyss Reid, general manager of Cassell's, to make the publication the "first woman's paper in England," his enthusiasm progressively flagged over the next few months. Wilde's assistant editor, Arthur Fish (1860–1940), has written that, initially, Wilde was punctual at eleven o'clock each Tuesday and Thursday at the editorial office, but he began arriving later and leaving earlier until his appearances amounted to "little more than a call." Fish later wrote that on those occasions when Wilde seemed unenthusiastic, he "would sink with a sigh into his chair, carelessly glance at his letters, give a perfunctory look at proofs or make-up, ask 'Is it necessary to settle anything today?' put on his hat and with a sad 'Good morning,' depart again." When more cheerful, usually in the springtime, "there would be a smiling entrance, letters would be answered with epigrammatic brightness, there would be a cheery interval of talk when the work was accomplished, and the dull room would brighten under the influence of his great personality."

Fish regarded *Woman's World* as the "finest magazine with an exclusive appeal to women that has ever been published. Its editor secured a brilliant company of contributors...and the high level of literary contents has never been attained by any publication of its kind." Articles were not merely on the subjects of fashion but often were devoted to distinguished women, historical events, and women's suffrage. Wilde, says Fish, always expressed "his entire sympathy with the views of the writers and revealed a liberality of thought with regard to the political aspirations of women that was undoubtedly sincere" (18).

Nevertheless, the sales, never high, began to decline. When prodded by the publishers, Wilde contended that his non-literary notes – principally chit-chat about society women – should be written by a woman and that literary reviews should be anonymous. By the end of his first year as editor, the publishers believed that more space should be devoted to dress and fashion; Wilde apparently conceded, for the November 1888 number contained a lengthy review by him of a book devoted to the history of embroidery and lace (subsequently drawn on in Chapter 11 of *The Picture of Dorian Gray*). As time passed, a number of those who had promised to contribute articles failed him. In October 1889, Cassell's decided to terminate publication of the magazine.

Before publishing *Dorian Gray*, which created a storm of critical protest, Wilde had contributed the daring story "The Portrait of Mr W. H." in *Blackwood's Edinburgh Review* in 1889. Frank Harris later wrote that the story "did Oscar incalculable injury. It gave his enemies for the first time the very weapon they wanted.... Oscar seemed to revel in the storm of conflicting opinions which the paper called forth" (69). But Harris apparently confused the reaction to *Dorian Gray* with this story, for there is no evidence that reviewers launched an attack at all comparable to that on Wilde's novel: Yates's *World* (10 July) published an anonymous review calling the subject of the story a "very unpleasant one," told in a "peculiarly offensive manner"; but other reviews do not go even this far. Since Wilde had not been contributing any of his signed prose and verse to the *World* since 1887, Yates may have decided to publish the unfavorable review as the means of dissociating himself from the now offensive Wilde. The publication of the first version of *Dorian Gray* in

Lippincott's Magazine in London and Philadelphia (July 1890) may have strengthened the conviction of many that Wilde had tested his audience in "The Portrait of Mr W.H." and that, without a substantial adverse reaction, he was encouraged to suggest more overtly the homoeroticism of Basil Hallward, the painter.

In 1892–93, when Alfred Douglas became editor of the undergraduate *Spirit Lamp: An Aesthetic and Critical Magazine* at Oxford, he reprinted Wilde's "Un Amant de Nos Jours," which had appeared in the *Court and Society Review* (13 Dec. 1887) with its opening line: "The sin was mine; I did not understand." The poem, with its new title, "The New Remorse," is elusive in defining the speaker's experience. Wilde also contributed two poems in prose – "The House of Judgment" and "The Disciple" – in succeeding issues. In Douglas's hands, the publication was homosexually oriented (as perhaps the term *Aesthetic* in the subtitle was intended to suggest).

More daring was the Oxford-inspired *Chameleon: "A Bazaar of Dangerous and Smiling Chances*," edited by an undergraduate (see Bloxam, John Francis), which appeared in February 1894 in its first and only number. At Douglas's urging, Wilde contributed a list of 25 epigrams, "Phrases and Philosophies for the Use of the Young," albeit as offensive to respectable sensibilities as *Dorian Gray*. The periodical contained some overtly homosexual contributions, one of which, Bloxam's "The Priest and the Acolyte," was printed under the pseudonym of "X." Bloxam had shown the story of the priest's love for his youthful acolyte to Wilde, who urged him to publish it. (One wonders whether Wilde's presence in this periodical was a factor in his exclusion from the *Yellow Book*, which issued its first number in April.)

At the trials, the notorious story was the subject of several questions – as was "Phrases and Philosophies for the Use of the Young" – which the prosecutor directed to Wilde. Wilde's contributions to the *Chameleon*, which also contained Alfred Douglas's "Two Loves," ending with the most famous line in homosexual literature – "I am the love that dare not speak its name" – indicated Wilde's increasing indiscretion when he was at the summit of his career.

References: Arthur Fish, "Oscar Wilde as Editor," *Harper's Weekly* (4 Oct. 1913); Simon Nowell-Smith, *The House of Cassell, 1848–1958* (1958); J. O. Baylen, "The 'New Journalism' in Late Victorian Britain," *Australian Journal of Politics and History* (Dec. 1972); Walter E. Houghton, ed., *Wellesley Index to Victorian Periodicals, 1824–1900* (1972); Alvin Sullivan, ed., *British Literary Magazines: The Victorian and Edwardian Age, 1837–1913* (1984); Laurel Brake et al., eds., *Investigating Victorian Journalism* (1990); Laurel Brake, "The Old Journalism and the New" and "Oscar Wilde and *The Woman's World*," *Subjugated Knowledges* (1994); Isobel Murray, "Wilde as Editor: A Hidden Manifesto in *The Woman's World*," *Journal of the Eighteen Nineties Society* 21 (1994).

"THE NIGHTINGALE AND THE ROSE"

Published: *The Happy Prince and Other Stories* (1888).

The Plot: A student is lamenting his inability to find a single rose in his garden for a young lady who has promised to dance with him at the prince's ball – that is, provided he presents her with red roses. The nightingale, having heard his lamentation, concludes: "Here at last is a true lover." Though the lizard, the butterfly, and the daisy believe that it is ridiculous to weep over a rose, the nightingale "understood the secret of the student's sorrow...and thought about the mystery of Love." Flying to a rose-tree, she asks for a red rose in exchange for her sweetest song. But the tree, which has only white roses, tells the bird to fly to his brother for a red rose. This the nightingale does, but the tree, which has only yellow roses, suggests that she fly to his brother beneath the student's window for a red rose.

Because the tree with red roses has suffered from winter's frost, he consequently has none. When the nightingale asks how she may obtain a red rose, the tree informs her that there is one way, but it is so "terrible" that he dares not tell her. She insists, however, that she is not afraid (here, Wilde employs the traditional device of the Test in myth and fairy tales). The tree explains: "...you must build it out of music by moonlight, and stain it with your own heart's-blood. You must sing to me with your breast against a thorn. All night long you must sing to me, and the thorn must pierce your heart, and your life-blood must flow into my veins, and become mine." The nightingale decides that "Love is better than Life, and what is the heart of

244

a bird compared to the heart of a man?"

She flies to the student to inform him that he will have his red rose if he promises to be a "true lover." But the student cannot understand the nightingale's message: "...she is like most artists; she is all style, without any sincerity" (a line variously used by Wilde, most notably at the beginning of Act III of *The Importance of Being Earnest*, when Gwendolen says: "In matters of grave importance, style, not sincerity is the vital thing"; the student obviously holds the conventional Victorian view of art that sincerity is essential in the creation of a work of art). The student is convinced that the nightingale "would not sacrifice herself for others. She thinks merely of music, and everybody knows that the arts are selfish."

But when the moon rises, the nightingale flies to the rose-tree and sings all night while pressing her breast against a thorn. As a result, there blossoms a "marvellous rose, petal following petal, as song followed song." The tree urges the bird to press closer to the thorn before the day comes in order to complete the rose, for "only a nightingale's heart's-blood can crimson the heart of a rose." At this point in the story, when the nightingale presses closer against the thorn, Wilde puns on his own name to suggest his identification with the bird, emblematic of the self-sacrificing Romantic artist: "Bitter, bitter was the pain, and wilder and wilder grew her song, for she sang of the love that is perfected by death." The tree tells the nightingale to look at the red rose, but she lies still "in the long grass, with a thorn in her heart" (the sacrificial act, the piercing thorn, the nightingale as singing poet, and the creation of a red rose combine the Christ motif with that of the artist as martyr, associated with the Religion of Art: see entry).

Opening his window, the student discovers the red rose in the tree, plucks it, and runs to the young lady's house. But she tells the student: "...the Chamberlain's nephew has sent me some real jewels, and everybody knows that jewels cost far more than flowers." With disgust, the student throws the rose into the road, where it is crushed by a cart. "What a silly thing Love is," he says. It is not half as useful as Logic, for it does not prove anything...." Like the young lady, a confirmed Utilitarian incapable of knowing the value of either love or art, he returns to his room and begins reading "a great dusty book."

In May 1888, Wilde wrote about this fairy tale in a letter to Thomas Hutchinson, a headmaster of a school in Northumberland and the author of *Ballades and Other Rhymes of a Country Bookworm* (1888), which parodies one of Wilde's poems: "[The student] seems to me a rather shallow young man and almost as bad as the girl he thinks he loves. The nightingale is the true lover, if there is one. She, at least, is Romance, and the student and the girl are, like most of us, unworthy of Romance.... I like to fancy that there may be many meanings in the tale, for in writing it I did not start with an idea and clothe it in form, but began with a form and strove to make it beautiful enough to have many secrets and many answers" (*Letters* 218).

Reference: Guy Willoughby, "Jesus as a Model for Selfhood in *The Happy Prince and Other Tales*," *Art and Christhood: The Aesthetics of Oscar Wilde* (1993).

"NOCTURNE"

Not published in Wilde's lifetime, this lyric poem was probably written around 1877–78. "Nocturne" is an early version of Wilde's longer poem "Endymion" (see entry), but the earlier poem is considerably different in its form and expression. For Whistler's use of the musical term *nocturne*, see "Impression du Matin."

The poem's Classical pastoral setting is suggested by such artifice as the "moon hath spread a pavilion of silver and amethyst" and the refrain concluding five of the six quatrains, which alludes to the beautiful young shepherd Endymion (for the mythic source, see Wilde's "Endymion"): "But where is young Endymion, / Where are the lips that should be kissed?" Though "She keeps the lingering lover's tryst," Endymion is in Acheron – another name for the mythic Underworld of the dead, ruled by Proserpine and Hades, her husband – as the final quatrain concludes the poem:

Ah down in moonless Acheron
    Pale Proserpine is glad, I wist:
For there is young Endymion,
There are the lips that should be kissed.

Manuscripts: The Clark Library has three MSS.: one with jottings; another a draft with the present title; and a third containing lines 21–24.

"A NOTE ON SOME MODERN POETS"

Published: *Woman's World* 2 (Dec. 1888): 108–12; rpt. in *Reviews* (1908). Signed reviews ("By the Editor") of books published in 1888.

Wilde opens his review of W. E. Henley's *A Book of Verses* with a quotation from one of the poems: "'If I were king,' says Mr. Henley, in one of his most modest rondeaus,"

> Art should aspire, yet ugliness be dear;
> Beauty, the shaft, should speed with wit for
>   feather;
> And love, sweet love, should never fall to sere,
>   If I were king.

These lines, says Wilde, "contain, if not the best criticism of his own work, certainly a very complete statement of his aim and motive as a poet." Henley seeks to find

> new methods of expression and has not merely a delicate sense of beauty and a brilliant, fantastic wit, but a real passion also for what is horrible, ugly, or grotesque. No doubt, everything that is worthy of existence is worthy also of art – at least one would like to think so – but while echo or mirror can repeat for us a beautiful thing, to render artistically a thing that is ugly requires the most exquisite alchemy of form, the most subtle magic of transformation.

Some of these poems are like "bright, vivid pastels; others like charcoal drawings, with dull blacks and murky whites; others like etchings with deeply-bitten lines, and abrupt contrasts, and clever colour-suggestions. In fact, they are like anything and everything, except perfected poems – that they certainly are not." Judging them as "preludes, experiments, inspired jottings in a note-book," Wilde points to the absence of rhyme, which, he says, "gives architecture as well as melody to verse," but in his rejection of rhyme, Henley has "abdicated half his power. He is a *roi en exil* who has thrown away some of the strings of his lute; a poet who has forgotten the fairest part of his kingdom."

Henley's unrhymed rhythms, Wilde remarks, "form very dainty designs, from a typographical point of view," but they are a "series of vivid, concentrated impressions, with a keen grip of fact,

a terrible actuality, and an almost masterly power of picturesque presentation. But the poetic form – what of that?" Passing on to Henley's use of French fixed forms, such as the rondel and rondeau, Wilde quotes from the "Ballade of a Toyokuni Colour-Print," which keeps "all the wilful fantastic charm of the original." Indeed, alluding to the various fixed forms used by Henley, Wilde exclaims: "How brilliant and fanciful this is!"

Wilde is impressed by the "humane personality that stands behind both flawless and faulty work alike, and looks out through many masks, some of them beautiful, and some grotesque, and not a few misshapen.... There is something wholesome, virile and sane about the man's soul." As though suggesting a Whitmanesque influence in this verse, Wilde concludes that Henley is "made to sing along the highways, not to sit down and write. If he took himself more seriously, his work would become trivial."

William Sharp, on the other hand, "takes himself very seriously." The "most interesting part" of his *Romantic Ballads and Poems of Phantasy* is his preface, which charges, as Wilde paraphrases it, that we are "far too cultured, and lack robustness." Sharp remarks that there are "those amongst us who would prefer a dexterously-turned triolet to apparently uncouth measures...." Wilde cannot imagine anyone preferring "a dexterously turned triolet to a fine imaginative ballad, as it is only the Philistine who ever dreams of comparing works of art that are absolutely different in motive, in treatment, and in form." If, he continues, "English Poetry is in danger – and, according to Mr. Sharp, the poor nymph is in a very critical state – what she has to fear is not the fascination of dainty metre or delicate form, but the predominance of the intellectual spirit over the spirit of beauty."

Wilde then provides a rapid survey of poetic developments during the 19th century and the condition of poetry at the end of the century:

> Lord Tennyson dethroned Wordsworth as a literary influence, and later on Mr. Swinburne filled all the mountain valleys with echoes of his own song. The influence to-day is that of Mr. Browning. And as for the triolets, and the rondels, and the careful study of metrical subtleties, these things are merely the signs of a desire for perfection in small things and of

the recognition of poetry as an art. They have had certainly one good result – they have made our minor poets readable, and have not left us entirely at the mercy of geniuses.

But, says Wilde, Sharp believes that everyone is "far too literary: even Rossetti is too literary. What we want is simplicity and directness of utterance; these should be the dominant characteristics of poetry. Well, is that quite so certain?" Wilde believes that such characteristics are appropriate for the drama; poetry, on the other hand, has "many modes of music; she does not blow through one pipe alone.... Simplicity is good, but complexity, mystery, strangeness, symbolism, obscurity even, these have their value.... A new romantic movement" is at hand, says Sharp, and " 'many of our poets, especially those of the youngest generation, will shortly turn towards the "ballad" as a poetic vehicle....' "

A. Mary F. Robinson has also written a preface to her *Poems, Ballads, and a Garden Play*, but, says Wilde, it is not serious; neither does it propose "any drastic change or any immediate revolution in English literature." Her poems have the "charm of delicate music and graceful expression; but they are, perhaps, weakest where they try to be strong, and certainly least satisfying where they seek to satisfy.... She should never leave her garden, and as for her wandering out into the desert to ask the Sphinx questions, that should be sternly forbidden to her.... What has she to do with shepherdesses piping about Darwinism and 'The Eternal Mind'? "

The final book for consideration is Dinah Craik's *Poems*, published posthumously, which Wilde characterizes as having "a pathetic interest as the artistic record of a very gracious and comely life." Her best poems, written in blank verse, "remind one that prose was her true medium of expression" (she was the author of the popular novel *John Halifax, Gentleman*, 1856). The poems chronicle "the moods of a sweet and thoughtful nature, and though many things in it may seem somewhat old-fashioned, it is still very pleasant to read, and has a faint perfume of withered rose-leaves about it."

"NOTEBOOK KEPT AT OXFORD": *See* **"COMMONPLACE BOOK"**

O

"O GOLDEN QUEEN OF LIFE AND JOY!"

Not published in Wilde's lifetime, this lyric poem was probably written between 1878 and 1880.

As still another tribute to the acclaimed actress Lillie Langtry (allusions to Wilde's association of Langtry – "O Lily without blot or stain!" – with the mythical Helen of Troy recall Wilde's "The New Helen"), the poem contains echoes of another poem about Helen, titled "Serenade. (For Music)," particularly in line 31 ("This is the Queen of life and joy"). Nevertheless, the two poems are quite distinct. The present poem was apparently an early portion of Wilde's "Endymion. (For Music)," which underwent considerable revision.

In "O Golden Queen..." – a lyric of five quatrains – the speaker reveals that he has "loved in vain" a woman who holds "all the keys of life." When "the glad pulse of youth is low," he pleads, "O Helen! Helen! mingle some / Divine nepenthe [a narcotic] for my woe."

Manuscript: The Clark Library has an untitled MS. of the poem.

"'OLIVIA' AT THE LYCEUM"

Published: *Dramatic Review* 1 (30 May 1885): 278; rpt. in *Reviews* (1908). A signed review of W.G. Wills's play, based on an episode in Oliver Goldsmith's *The Vicar of Wakefield* (1766) and revived by Henry Irving at the Lyceum Theatre on 27 May 1885. (Wilde had briefly adopted the name of "Wills" from a family connection with substantial landowners of that name – the playwright W.G. Wills was a member of the family.)

Wilde questions whether it is an "advantage for a novel to be produced in a dramatic form." In the case of a George Meredith novel, with its "psychological analysis," it would "probably lose by being transmuted into the passionate action of the stage." Nor does Zola's *formule scientifique* gain anything at all by theatrical presentation." But Goldsmith sought simply to please readers, not "to prove a theory; he looks on life rather as a picture to be painted than as a problem to be solved; his aim is to create men and women more than to vivisect them; his dialogue is essentially dramatic, and his novel seems to pass naturally into the dramatic form."

There is, Wilde remarks, "something very pleasurable in seeing and studying the same subject under different conditions of art. For life remains eternally unchanged; it is art which, by presenting it to us under various forms, enables us to realise its many-sided mysteries, and to catch the quality of its most fiery-coloured moments" (the latter phrase, one that often appears in Wilde's poetry and prose, reveals his Paterian orientation). Originality, then, is not one of subject, Wilde observes, but one of "treatment": "It is only the unimaginative who ever invents. The true artist is known by the use he makes of what he annexes, and he annexes everything."

With this in mind, Wilde judges Wills's play as "a very exquisite work of art," containing "tenderness" and "power, neither losing the charm of the old story nor forgetting the condition of the new form." Though the play has been written in prose, "it is a poem, and while a poem it is also a play." Wilde also praises the acting of Ellen Terry, "a really great artist," who brings to any role "the infinite charm of her beauty, and the marvellous grace of her movements and gestures." Henry Irving's portrayal of Dr. Primrose, "carefully elaborate in detail, was full of breadth and dignity." Wilde closes with the observation that the Lyceum under Irving's management has become "a centre of art. We are all of us in his debt."

"O LOVED ONE LYING FAR AWAY"

Not published in Wilde's lifetime, this lyric poem was probably written after 19 April 1876, when Wilde's father, Sir William Wilde, died. Wilde's use of Tennyson's *In Memoriam* stanza (see "Lotus Leaves"), with its elegiac theme, and the echo in line 3 of "O Loved one..." from another Wilde elegy, "Requiescat," line 13, reinforce the likelihood that "O Loved one..." is associated with Sir William's death.

This poem of six quatrains asks whether "coffin board and heavy stone / Turn godlike man to senseless clay?" The speaker notes "how mean we must appear / When looked on by the holy dead!" Such fancies arise for the speaker, who is burdened with grief: "...where thou didst think me strong / And foolish where you feigned me wise."

Because of such grief, he feels himself "No better than a broken reed / Less stable than the shifting sand" and ends by crying in vain with each setting sun: "What have I done / This day for immortality?"

Manuscript: The Beinecke Library has an untitled MS. of this poem, a facsimile of which appeared in Donald G. Wing, "The Katherine S. Dreier Collection of Oscar Wilde," *Yale University Library Gazette* (Oct. 1953).

"ON THE SALE BY AUCTION OF KEATS' LOVE LETTERS"

Published: First appeared as "Sonnet. On the Recent Sale by Auction of Keats' Love Letters" in the *Dramatic Review* 2 (23 Jan. 1886): 249; rpt. in William Sharp, ed., *Sonnets of This Century* (London: Walter Scott, 1886), 252, as "On the Sale by Auction of Keats' Love Letters," and with the same title in *Poems* (1908). A letter to William Sharp (1855–1905), the Scottish poet who published under the pseudonym of "Fiona Macleod," contains the poem, the text of which appeared in Elizabeth Sharp's *William Sharp (Fiona Macleod): A Memoir* (1910), 115–16, rpt. in *Letters* 182–83 (where "Keats's" appears in the title).

Keats's letters to Fanny Brawne, written 1819–20, are particularly poignant, for he was suffering from tuberculosis, which doomed him to an early death. Present throughout the auction at Sotheby's on 2 March 1885, when the letters were sold, Wilde purchased several of them. The opening lines of the poem identify Keats as Endymion (after the mythological figure of whom Keats had written): "These are the letters which Endymion wrote / To one he loved in secret...." But the "brawlers of the auction mart / Bargain and bid for each poor blotted note...." Wilde draws a parallel between the death of Keats (a martyr in the Religion of Art: see entry) and the death of Jesus, when some soldiers "began / To wrangle for mean raiment, and to throw / Dice for the garments of a wretched man, / Not knowing the God's wonder, or His woe."

Manuscripts: Three MSS. are extant: one in the Rosenbach Library (dated March 1, 1885), titled "Sonnet. On the Sale by Auction of Keats' Love-Letters"; another, in the Hyde Collection, which has Wilde's letter, postmarked 11 Aug. 1890, in which the untitled poem appears (printed in *More Letters* 90). The addressee is F. Holland Day

(1864–1933), the American publisher and collector of Keatsiana. A facsimile of a MS. appeared in a Sotheby auction catalogue, dated 10–11 March 1952. The Mark Samuels Lasner Collection has a MS. of the poem with the present title.

Reference: Brooks Wright, " 'On the Sale by Auction of Keats' Love Letters': A Footnote to Wilde's Sonnet." *Keats-Shelley Journal* (Winter 1958).

"ONE OF MR. CONWAY'S REMAINDERS"

Published: *PMG*, 1 Feb. 1886, 5; rpt. in *Reviews* (1908). An unsigned review of Hugh Conway's *The Cardinal Sin* (1886). "Hugh Conway" was the pseudonym of Frederick John Fargus.

The "concoction of a modern crime novel," Wilde states, "is a more important ingredient than culture." Conway knows this to be true, though for "cleverness and ingenuity of construction he cannot be compared to M. [Emile] Gaboriau [whose detective, M. Lecoq, anticipated Sherlock Holmes], that master of murder and its mysteries; still he fully recognised the artistic value of villainy." In summarizing the plot at great length, Wilde concludes that "if to raise a goose skin on the reader be the aim of art, Mr. Conway must be regarded as a real artist," though he calls the work under review "a crude novel of a common melodramatic type." Its style is "painful" as well as "slipshod and careless." As an example, Wilde quotes the description of a honeymoon as "*a rare occurrence in any one person's life*," which he regards as "amusing." Wilde concludes: "The nineteenth century may be a prosaic age, but we fear that, if we are to judge by the general run of novels, it is not an age of prose."

"ONE OF THE BIBLES OF THE WORLD"

Published: *PMG*, 12 Feb. 1889, 3; rpt. in *Reviews* (1908). An unsigned review of *The Kalevala: The Epic Poem of Finland*, trans. John Martin Crawford (1889).

The *Kalevala* was described by William Morris as one of "The Bibles of the World," ranking as a national epic with such works as the Homeric poems and the *Nibelungenlied*. Crawford's translation, writes Wilde, is "sure to be welcomed by all scholars and lovers of primitive poetry." The *Kalevala*, "one of the world's great poems," is not accurately described as an epic, for it lacks the "central unity of a true epic, in our sense of the word." More properly, it is a collection of folksongs and ballads. "The gods are those of air, water, and forest, the highest being the sky-god Ukko, who is 'The Father of the Breezes,' 'The Shepherd of Lamb Clouds'...." In all things, visible and invisible, a divine presence exists. The poem itself has as distinguishing characteristics "its wonderful passion for nature and for the beauty of natural objects."

O'SULLIVAN, VINCENT (?1868–1940)

The American novelist, poet, and short story writer came to know Wilde and his circle shortly before 1895. After Wilde's release from prison, O'Sullivan visited him at Berneval on 8 August 1897, then dined with him on two other occasions. To Ernest Dowson, Wilde wrote of O'Sullivan on 18 August: "I *now* like him. At first I loathed him" (*Letters* 632). When O'Sullivan's volume of poems *The Houses of Sin* (1897) reached Wilde, he wrote to its publisher Leonard Smithers: "...I think the poems better than his former ones [*Poems*, 1896] – more concentrated in motive, better thought-out, more fully realised, but in what a midnight his soul seems to walk! And what maladies he draws from the moon!" (*Letters* 692).

Despite a bad beginning, the friendship between Wilde and O'Sullivan continued to improve. In his autobiographical *Aspects of Wilde* (1936), O'Sullivan, recalling Wilde's wish to rejoin Alfred Douglas in Naples, remarks that he paid for Wilde's trip: "It is one of the few things I look back on with satisfaction. It is not every day that one has the chance of relieving the anxiety of a genius and a hero" (180). In one of only two letters to O'Sullivan that have survived, Wilde wrote from Naples on 19 October 1897 that he looked forward "with the greatest pleasure" of seeing him again. He was "deeply touched" by O'Sullivan's defense – in the smoking room of the Authors' Club – of Wilde's resumption of his relationship with Douglas (*Letters* 660).

O'Sullivan's view of Wilde as a writer is curiously contradictory in his public statements: in 1918, for example, he sent a letter to Frank Harris, the editor of *Pearson's Magazine* (New York), replying to George Moore's letter to Harris in the March issue. There, Moore declared that Wilde was a writer "in the third or fourth class and, therefore, not worth troubling about...." O'Sulli-

van's response, in the April issue, gives the erroneous impression that Wilde could not sustain his interest in a work; hence, he had to work in haste to complete it: "...he would only do the thing which could be got over quickly.... I suppose he never spent longer than six weeks over anything he ever wrote. *Salomé*, he told me, was written between luncheon and twelve o'clock at night." O'Sullivan then declares Wilde "a great writer: he had it in him, if he had taken thought and time to purge himself of certain vulgarities, to be much greater" (rpt. in Beckson).

But in *Aspects*, O'Sullivan seemingly reverses himself in judging Wilde not as a writer of the "first order." Nevertheless, he is valued by many, writes O'Sullivan, "not for his wit, but for *De Profundis* and *The Ballad of Reading Gaol*, fruits of his passion. He developed into that great tragic figure known in every part of the earth, whose cruel fate will be sorrowed by thousands for long years to come" (41). Later in his *Aspects*, O'Sullivan asserts that it was Wilde's "personality, not his literature, that carried him through" and that the "impulse to write was never with him the primary impulse" (161, 163). O'Sullivan regards Alfred Douglas, as a poet, to be "superior" to Wilde and prefers Douglas's "way of writing English prose" to Wilde's: "His prose is not gorgeous and decorated as Wilde's is..." (8).

Though O'Sullivan admits that he "never cared much for Wilde's writings taken as a collection" (4), his *Aspects* is designed to lift Wilde "out of the miasmas which still float round his name and place him frankly and clearly where he ought to be: in the history of English Literature" (vi). O'Sullivan insists that "the legend of Wilde's last years ebbing out in squalor and destitution and abandonment should be discarded," for Wilde "had more money at his disposal than many of the young French writers and painters of that time" (33, 43). However, in 1932, O'Sullivan recalled in a letter to A. J. A. Symons that Wilde's former French friends, such as Marcel Schwob and Stuart Merrill, were constantly beseeching him "to get Wilde's English friends to make him realize that he was ruining what sympathy was left for him among the Parisians by shewing himself drunk on the Boulevards in such a place as 'The Calasaya' Bar with sodomist outcasts..." (*Some Letters* 7).

In estimating Wilde the playwright, O'Sullivan asserts that Wilde's plays were derived from "a

French school long out of fashion," and his "peculiar form of wit...had imitators, but no predecessors" (7). O'Sullivan remarks that Wilde had "only a small number of ideas in his plays":

> He disliked hypocrisy in social intercourse, he glorified individualism, he denied the moral right of the community to sacrifice the life of any member of it.... He resigned himself to be the amuser from fear of being the bore. In this he was wrong; he wronged himself, and he deprived his plays of a permanent element. For just at that time the drama of ideas was coming into vogue in England, and Wilde lost the chance of being a pioneer. He left it to Bernard Shaw, and to Archer with his translations from Ibsen. (10–11)

Wilde continued seeing O'Sullivan until mid-1900, when he wrote in the final letter mentioning him to Robert Ross: "I dined with Vincent O'Sullivan last night: he was really very pleasant, for one who treats life from the standpoint of the tomb" (*Letters* 830).

References: Robert Sherard, *Oscar Wilde: The Story of an Unhappy Friendship* (1905; rpt. 1970); *Some Letters of Vincent O'Sullivan to A. J. A. Symons*, intro. by Alan Anderson (1975).

"OUIDA'S NEW NOVEL"

Published: *PMG*, 17 May 1889, 3; rpt. in *Reviews* (1908). An unsigned review of Ouida's *Guilderoy* (1889). "Ouida" was the pseudonym of Marie Louise de la Ramée.

"Ouida," begins Wilde, "is the last of the romantics":

> She belongs to the school of Bulwer Lytton and George Sand, though she may lack the learning of the one and the sincerity of the other. She tries to make passion, imagination, and poetry, part of fiction. She still believes in heroes and in heroines. She is florid, and fervent, and fanciful. Yet even she, the high-priestess of the impossible, is affected by her age.

Guilderoy, "an elaborate psychological study of modern temperaments," expresses "much of the tone and temper of the society of our day." The book, a study of the peerage from "a poetical point of view," is an "amazing romance...a resplendent picture of our aristocracy."

Wilde devotes much of his review to a summary of the plot and lengthy quotations, though he also points out that Ouida "believes that the proper rulers of a country like ours are the aristocrats. Oligarchy has great fascination for her. She thinks meanly of the people and adores the House of Lords...." Ouida, concludes Wilde, "is fond of airing a smattering of culture, but she has a certain artistic insight into things, and though she is rarely true, she is never dull." Despite its faults, "which are great, and its absurdities, which are greater," *Guilderoy* "is a book to be read."

"OUR BOOK SHELF"

Published: *PMG*, 12 April 1887, 5; rpt. in *Reviews* (1908). Unsigned reviews.

Ernest von Wildenbruch's *The Master of Tanagra*, translated by Baroness von Lauer (1886), presents "an exceedingly pretty picture of the bright external side of ancient Greek life, and tells how a handsome young Tanagrian left his home for the sake of art, and returned to it for love's sake – an old story, no doubt, but one which gains a new charm from its new setting." The historical characters, such as Praxiteles and Phryne, seem "less real," Wilde writes, than imaginary characters, "but this is usually the case in all novels that would recreate the past for us, and is a form of penalty that Romance has often to pay when she tries to blend fact with fancy, and to turn the great personages of history into puppets for a little play."

In *Molière et Shakespeare* (1887), Paul Stapfer has "no hesitation in placing the author of *Le Misanthrope* by the side of the author of *Hamlet*." To him, Shakespeare's comedies seem "somewhat wilful and fantastic; he prefers Orgon and Tartuffe to Oberon and Titania [in *A Midsummer Night's Dream*], and can hardly forgive Beatrice [in *Much Ado about Nothing*] for having been 'born to speak all mirth, and no matter.'" Wilde remarks that Stapfer may not realize that "it is as a poet, not as a playwright, that we love Shakespeare in England." Nevertheless, his book is "full of interesting suggestion, many of his remarks on literature are quite excellent, and his style has the qualities of grace, distinction, and ease of movement."

The same cannot be said for Joseph Cundall's *Annals of the Life of Shakespeare* (1886), which is "dull though well-meaning." What is unknown about Shakespeare is "a most fascinating subject, and one that would fill volumes, but what we do know about him is so meagre and inadequate that when it is collected together the result is rather depressing." Moving on rapidly, Wilde praises Allan Ramsay's *Poems* (1886) as always "delightful reading, except when he tries to write English and to imitate Pope." Indeed, his songs "might rank beside those of Burns." J. Logie Robertson's preface to "this attractive little edition" tells the story of Ramsay's life well, and "gives us a really capital picture of Edinburgh society in the early half of the last century."

Arabella Shore's *Dante for Beginners* (1886) is "a sort of literary guide-book," which can do "no possible harm to Dante, which is more than one can say of many commentaries on the *Divine Comedy*." Mary Phillimore's *Studies in Italian Literature* (1887), a "much more elaborate work," displays "a good deal of erudition. Indeed, the erudition is sometimes displayed a little too much, and we should like to see the lead of learning transmuted more often into the gold of thought."

"OUR SOUL IS LIKE A KITE"

Published: First appeared in a letter written by W. T. Mercer, titled "The Aesthetic Gospel: A Profession of Faith and an Unpublished Poem by Oscar Wilde" in the *New York Daily Tribune*, 23 Jan. 1882, 5. Mercer was introduced to Wilde in London "through the kindness of William Morris" and apparently interviewed him early in January 1882 after his first lecture in New York. At this time, he gave Mercer an untitled poem, which, he said, "partly illustrates my views on the longing of the soul for the beautiful and unattainable." Bobby Fong reprinted the poem in his "Oscar Wilde: Five Fugitive Poems," *ELT* 22:1 (1979): 10. Mason does not list the work, nor does Ross include it in the *Collected Edition* (1908).

The poem, consisting of five three-line stanzas, expresses the Romantic aspiration to a transcendent, eternal world, as in Shelley's *Prometheus Unbound* (1820), Shelley's heroine Asia providing the model: "My soul is like an enchanted boat," the means by which escape is possible from the temporal world. Wilde's first lines, "Our soul is like a kite, / That soars with ease to heavenly height," employ air rather than water as the means of transcendence. Yet the speaker in Wilde's poem is acutely aware of the "link" that binds him to his earthly life as well as that which "links [him] with heavenly heights" as he aspires "toward infinity." Our soul, caught in flight between heaven and earth, "longs for new life, / Breaks the frail thread by constant strife, / Now ceases in unending flight."

"OXFORD NOTEBOOK": *See* "COMMONPLACE BOOK"

OXFORD UNIVERSITY: *See* MAGDALEN COLLEGE, OXFORD

P

"PAN. DOUBLE VILLANELLE"

Published: First appeared as "Pan. – A Villanelle," consisting of six stanzas, in *Pan* l (25 Sept. 1880): 15; rev., with the addition of a second part, in *Poems*, Vol. 1 of the second *Collected Edition* (1910), which Mason calls the "Ross Edition" authorized for John Luce & Co. (Boston). In 1909, Luce had issued, separately, the "hitherto unpublished" texts of "Désespoir" and "Pan. Double Villanelle" to secure the American copyright (see Mason 492). In England, Methuen had included both poems in *Poems* (1909).

The form of the villanelle consists of five three-line stanzas, or tercets, with a concluding quatrain, the entire poem employing just two rhymes. In the late 19th century, such poets as Austin Dobson and Edmund Gosse revived the villanelle, among other Old French fixed forms – the word *villa* indicating its pastoral origins.

In Part I, the contrast between the glorious mythic, pastoral world of Pan and dreary contemporary London provides the central theme of lost innocence: "O goat-foot God of Arcady! / This modern world is grey and old, / Ah what remains to us of Thee?" The Thames is "dull and dead," "the winds are chill and cold," and "many an unsung elegy / Sleeps in the reeds our rivers hold...."

In Part II, the speaker urges Pan to leave the hills of Arcady: "This modern world hath need of Thee." Puritanical England, personified by "grave-browed Milton," lacks "some stronger lay." The poem ends with a renewed call to Pan to "blow some Trumpet loud and free, / And give thine oaten pipe away, / Ah leave the hills of Arcady!"

Manuscripts: The Berg Collection has the MS. of the final form of "Pan: Double Villanelle," whereas the Clark Library has only early jottings for the poem, and Texas has the early version titled "Pan: A Villanelle," which had appeared in *Pan*.

"LE PANNEAU": *See* "FANTAISIES DÉCORATIVES"

"PANTHEA"

Published: *Poems* (1881); rev. in (1882). This poem consists of 30 stanzas, each with six lines. Wilde apparently took the title from the Oceanid named "Panthea," who represents the concept of faith (the name perhaps derived from *pantheism*) in Shelley's *Prometheus Unbound* (1820).

The opening lines have an urgency reminiscent of Pater's "Conclusion" to his *Studies in the History of the Renaissance* (1873): "Nay, let us walk from fire unto fire, / From passionate pain to deadlier delight, – / I am too young to live without desire...." A Romantic, the speaker is convinced that "to feel is better than to know, / .... One pulse of passion – youth's first fiery glow, – / Are worth the hoarded proverbs of the sage." Thus, he urges his companion: "Vex not thy soul with dead philosophy, / Have we not lips to kiss with, hearts to love and eyes to see!" The gods themselves "have sick and wearied grown / Of all our endless sins, our vain endeavour / For wasted days of youth to make atone...."

The speaker then expresses the weariness "of this sense of guilt, / Wearied of pleasure's paramour despair, / Wearied of every temple we have built": "For man is weak; God sleeps: and heaven is high: / One fiery-coloured moment: one great love; and lo! we die." Pater's focus on living for the passing moment with aesthetic intensity ("to burn always with this hard, gemlike flame") is evident behind these lines. Wilde then presents a Wordsworthian vision of universal unity, of a spiritual presence that binds all things, by using metaphors from science:

> With beat of systole and of diastole
>   One grand great life throbs through earth's
>   giant heart,
> And mighty waves of single Being roll
>   From nerveless germ to man, for we are part
> Of every rock and bird and beast and hill,
> One with the things that prey on us, and one
>   with what we kill.

These lines (and others in Wilde's poem) recall "Tintern Abbey," in which Wordsworth speaks of "A motion and a spirit, that impels / All thinking things, all objects of all thought, / And rolls through all things." Evolutionary theory also informs Wilde's view of nature: "We who are godlike now were once a mass / Of quivering purple...." Death itself is part of the grand scheme ("Nothing is lost in nature, all things live in Death's despite"), and again borrowing from Wordsworth (this time from "My Heart Leaps Up"), Wilde exclaims: "How my heart leaps up / To think of that grand living after death / In beast and bird and flower... ."

Finally, in alluding to the recently formulated second law of thermodynamics (theorizing that solar energy is constantly diffused in the universe), Wilde questions whether "the light [has] vanished from our golden sun" and declares: "Rather new suns across the sky shall pass, / New splendour come unto the flower, new glory to the grass." (These lines are deftly lifted from Wordsworth's "Ode: Intimations of Immortality": "Though nothing can bring back the hour / Of splendour in the grass, of glory in the flower.") Concluding, Wilde proclaims with the conviction of a Neo-Platonist that "We shall be / Part of the mighty universal whole, / And through all aeons mix and mingle with the Kosmic Soul!"

Manuscripts: Two incomplete MSS., probably written around 1879–80, have survived: one, with lines 1–120, is in the Hyde Collection; the other, with lines 121–38, is in the Huntington Library.

PARADOX

Commonly defined as a self-contradictory statement that contains a truth contrary to received opinion, paradox is a central element of Wilde's epigrammatic style. In the earliest analysis of Wildean paradox, published in 1895, Ernest Newman (later Wagner's biographer) contended that the "one thing the British Philistine cannot understand...is a paradox":

A paradox is simply the truth of the minority, just as a commonplace is the truth of the majority.... For example, everyone knows what Art is, and everyone knows what it is to be immoral; but if a thinker says "Art is immoral" [said by Wilde in "The Critic as Artist"], the new synthesis puzzles them, and they either call it a paradox, or say the writer is immoral. In reality, he is doing just what they cannot do; he can see round corners and the other side of things....he can give to ordinary things a quality that they have not, and place them in worlds that never existed. We ordinary beings can see objects in three dimen-

sions only; a good paradox is a view in the fourth dimension. (196)

Newman offers other examples of his thesis, such as "Sin is an essential element of progress" ("The Soul of Man under Socialism"), "All bad art comes from returning to life and nature" ("The Decay of Lying"), and "I can believe anything, provided that it is quite incredible" (*The Picture of Dorian Gray*). The experience of hearing or reading such paradoxes causes us, says Newman, "to rise from the perusal of them with a self-conscious wisdom that we had not before. We become wise, and know it: and that is the only sort of wisdom worth having." Indeed, as one character remarks in *Dorian Gray*: "...the way of paradoxes is the way of truth."

Not only did Wilde exhibit genius in creating witty paradoxes that are still quoted today but he also made the paradox an essential principle of his aesthetic philosophy. As Ellmann writes:

His paradoxes would be an insistent reminder of what lay behind the accepted or conventional. "A Truth in art is that whose contradictory is also true," he would declare in "The Truth of Masks." This was the great lesson which his immersion in various movements had taught him, first about art, then about life.... As a result, Wilde writes his works out of a debate between doctrines rather than out of doctrine. (99/95)

Wilde's dandies (see dandyism) employ paradox, Kohl suggests, to distance themselves from the Philistines (thereby demonstrating dandiacal superiority) and to satirize their bourgeois preoccupations or, as in the case of Lord Goring in *An Ideal Husband*, to disguise his moral involvement in the central conflicts of the play. Hence, Goring's change from his presumed "intellectual detachment, so typical of the aesthetic attitude," to a "committed protagonist in Act III reveals a certain incongruity between the demands of the plot and the feasibility of the dandy figure" (217–18). Kohl perceives a parallel in the central paradox of Wilde's life and work: namely, that Wilde is a "conformist rebel," one who accepts the moral idealism of his age while provoking and challenging its basic assumptions and principles in accordance with his "aesthetic individualism" (67).

References: Ernest Newman, "Oscar Wilde: A Literary Appreciation," *Free Review* (1 June 1895), rpt. in Beckson; Rolf Breuer, "Paradox in Oscar Wilde," *Irish University Review* (Autumn-Winter, 1993).

PARODIES AND SATIRES

In 1880, the artist and satirist George Du Maurier (1834–96) began satirizing the Pre-Raphaelites, who were popularly believed to be Aesthetes in their devotion to beauty (the former, however, did not uniformly accept the doctrine of art for art's sake, whereas the latter regarded the doctrine as central to Aestheticism). On 14 February of that year, two cartoon figures made their debut in *Punch*: Jellaby Postlewaite, the poet (who resembles Swinburne) and Maudle, the painter (who may represent Rossetti, Swinburne's Pre-Raphaelite associate). Wilde became the object of Du Maurier's satire as early as 30 October 1880, in possibly the first cartoon featuring him (though the figure depicted was obviously not intended as an exact likeness): titled "The Six-Mark Tea-Pot," two figures speak while admiring the object:

> *Aesthetic Bridegroom*: It is quite consummate, is it not!
> *Intense Bride*: It is indeed! Oh, Algernon, let us live up to it! [allegedly said by Wilde at Oxford]

In time, various male aesthetic figures depicted in *Punch* became increasingly effeminate in attitude and appearance as an indication of their exclusive devotion to art and beauty – regarded by many Victorians with some suspicion and hence appropriate for ridicule. By 12 February 1881, Maudle had taken on the more obvious appearance of Wilde. In a conversation with Mrs. Brown, whose son wishes to be an artist and who insists that he must be something, Maudle responds: "Why should he be anything? Why not let him remain for ever content to exist beautifully?"

On 7 May 1881, *Punch* published a cartoon titled "Let Us Live Up to It," showing a figure holding the aforementioned teapot; a week later *Punch* included a poem titled "The Grosvenor Gallery" (where Whistler exhibited his paintings and where Wilde often appeared); the second stanza employs the fashionable aesthetic jargon of the day:

> ...many a maiden will mutter,
> When OSCAR looms large on her sight,
> "He's quite too consummately utter,
> As well as too utterly quite."

When Wilde's *Poems* appeared in June, *Punch* (25 June), ever vigilant, published "O. W." as No. 37 in the series "Punch's Fancy Portraits," depicting Wilde's unmistakable likeness in the midst of a sunflower with the following doggerel below, presumably a critical judgment of the poems:

> Aesthete of Aesthetes!
> What's in a name?
> The poet is WILDE,
> But his poetry's tame.

Satirical cartoons and poems by various *Punch* writers and artists appeared through the 1880s with references to such figures as "Oscuro Wildegoose," "Ossian Wilderness," and "Mr. Wilde Hoskar." On his lecture tour of the United States and Canada in 1882, he was similarly satirized from coast to coast. Since he appeared, at least initially, on the lecture platform aesthetically dressed like Bunthorne in Gilbert and Sullivan's *Patience* (an instance of what Wilde would later contend was life imitating art), he was believed to have been the inspiration for the character, but Bunthorne and Grosvenor were most likely modeled after Swinburne, Rossetti, and Whistler: see Lectures in America, 1882. As for the widely circulated story that he had "walked down Piccadilly with a poppy or a lily in his medieval hand," Wilde remarked: "To have done it was nothing, but to make people think one had done it was a triumph" (*New York World*, 8 Jan. 1882).

Shortly after *Lady Windermere's Fan* achieved success, a parody of the play with the title *The Poet and the Puppets*: A Travestie Suggested by "*Lady Windermere's Fan*" was produced on 19 May 1892, written by Charles Brookfield (see entry), with the assistance of the actor Charles Hawtrey, who was made up to resemble Wilde, and with music composed by James Mackey Glover, later director of music at the Drury Lane Theatre, 1893–1920. The title was taken from the publication of a letter to the editor of the *Daily Telegraph*, in which Wilde objected to the report that he had asserted in a speech given at the Play-goers' Club on 7 February that "the stage is only a frame furnished with a set of puppets." The newspaper titled his letter "Puppets and Actors" (see *Letters* 310 and n).

After he had heard of the burlesque, according to Glover's *Jimmy Glover: His Book* (1911), Wilde implored the Examiner of Plays in the Lord Chamberlain's office to have the script read to him by the authors. In one passage, the Poet sings a song that ends:

> ...the fact remains still,
> A fact I've proclaimed since a child,
> That it's taken, my dears, nearly two thousand years
> To make Oscar O'Flaherty – Wilde.

Though he objected to the use of his full name, he agreed to the use of "O'Flaherty." The line was consequently changed: "To make Neighbour O'Flaherty's child."

In the parody, the Poet informs the audience: "While at Oxford I took every prize and I shook / The whole College from attic to basement," and echoing one of Wilde's bright remarks, the Poet states: "The greatest pleasure in life is to be misunderstood." And the famous witticism in Wilde's play is also echoed by one of the characters: "The one thing that I can't resist [is] temptation." The Poet is working on a parodic plot "about a wise child who doesn't know her own mother" – alluding to Wilde's Lady Windermere and her mother, Mrs. Erlynne, both of whom in the parody are called "Lady Winterstock" and "Mrs. Earlybird." The Poet finally agrees to sign a promise not to write another play, though he does not adhere to his pledge.

While hearing the parody, Wilde was reportedly effusive with his praise: "Delightful!" and "It's exquisite!" But on leaving, he remarked with less than complete delight: "I felt, however, that I have been – well – Brookfield, what is the word? – what is the thing you call it in your delightful epigrammatic Stage English? eh? Oh yes! delightfully spoofed" (qtd. in Hawtrey 227).

In May 1894, an Oxford undergraduate work appeared in blank verse titled *Aristophanes at Oxford: O. W.* by three authors under the collective pseudonym of "Y. T. O." – derived from the final letters of their last names: Leopold Charles

Amery (1873–1955), later a Member of Parliament and journalist; Francis Wrigley Hirst (1873–1953), later editor of the *Economist*; and Henry Alford Antony Cruso (whose obscurity continues to embrace him). In the preface, the authors express their dislike of *The Picture of Dorian Gray*, *Salome*, the *Yellow Book*, and "the whole of the erotic, lack-a-daisical, opium-cigarette literature of the day.... We confess straightway that our Oscar Wilde is mainly a creation of our own fancy."

The tale begins when two Maudlin [i.e., Magdalen] College students, punting on the Cherwell, encounter the shades of Socrates, Thucydides, and Aristotle, much to their distaste. When the Greeks go upstream, Oscar Wilde appears, singing in a canoe while reclining on cushions and smoking a gold-tipped cigarette. His exotic dialogue is crammed with allusions to near-Eastern cities, such as Samarcand and Usbekhan. Wilde is pressed into helping to dispose of the Greeks by merely talking. The dull plot plods onwards until Wilde bursts out:

> Oh! Oh! Salome! bring me some smelling salts
> In a silver-lacquered bottle gemmed with beryl.
> An epigram! my spirit-lamp [alluding to Alfred Douglas's Oxford periodical] for an epigram!
> I faint! I die!....
> Ye spirits of Hedonism! help your priest!

Later, an echo surfaces from the preface to *The Picture of Dorian Gray*: "All art is useless, therefore so am I."

In June 1894, George Slythe Street (1867–1936) published a satire of Decadence titled *The Autobiography of a Boy*, with suggestions that Wilde may have been the principal model, though Decadence and Pre-Raphaelitism in general provided inspiration. Associated with the anti-Decadents on the staff of the *National Observer*, edited by W. E. Henley (see main entry), Street creates a Wildean figure called "Tubby," who, with a "reputation for wickedness," was, at Oxford in his first year, "a severe ritualist, in his second an anarchist and an atheist, in his third wearily indifferent to all things...." In September 1894, the most brilliant satire of Wilde appeared in Robert Hichens's novel *The Green Carnation*, the title symbolizing the artifice of Decadence (for further discussion, see green carnation). Because the novel appeared anonymously, the reviewers assumed, from its close approximation to Wilde's prose style, that he was the author.

Another close approximation of Wilde also occurs in a novel (and a play) by Robert Buchanan and Henry Murray titled *The Charlatan* (1895). In 1871, Buchanan had attacked Swinburne and Rossetti in a notorious essay titled "The Fleshly School of Poetry." Now Buchanan was attacking what he presumably believed to be the heir to those Pre-Raphaelite poets. In the work, Mervyn is depicted as the "Apostle of the New Culture" (the term, by the 1890s, suggesting homosexuality), who moves "languidly," speaks in paradoxes, and remains indifferent to all things. At one point, an impatient young woman says to him: "At college you had the aesthetic scarlatina, and babbled about lilies, and sunflowers, and blue china."

In the 90s, even Wilde's friends satirized him: In December 1893 or early 1894, Max Beerbohm, still an Oxford undergraduate, wrote a satire describing Wilde as though a forgotten relic of the past, titled "A Peep into the Past," designed for the first number of the *Yellow Book*, but it did not appear there (see Beerbohm, Max). In addition, over the years, during and after Wilde's death, Beerbohm caricatured Wilde in many drawings. Another friend, Ada Leverson (see entry) wrote parodies of Wilde's works for *Punch*, her final one (on 2 March 1895) titled "On the Advisability of Not Being Brought Up in a Handbag: A Trivial Tragedy for Wonderful People," a parody of *The Importance of Being Earnest*. Wilde was delighted.

References: Charles Hawtry, *The Truth at Last* (1924); Leonée Ormond, *George Du Maurier* (1969).

PATER, WALTER (1839–94)

The critic and historian, best known for his influential study, *Studies in the History of the Renaissance* (1873), Walter Pater was a Fellow at Brasenose College, Oxford, when Wilde first read his study in the autumn of 1874, during his first term at Magdalen College. Pater's impact on Wilde may be gauged by his remark in *De Profundis*, which refers to Pater's *Studies* as "that book which has had such a strange influence over my life" (*Letters* 471). The obvious influence of Pater's *Studies* on Wilde occurs in *The Picture of Dorian Gray*, in which Lord Henry urges Dorian in Chapter 2 to live to the fullest, for one's youth is transient:

Time is jealous of you, and wars against your lilies and your roses. You will become sallow, and hollow-cheeked, and dull-eyed.... Ah! realize your youth while you have it. Don't squander the gold of your days.... Live! Live the wonderful life that is in you! Let nothing be lost upon you. Be always searching for new sensations. Be afraid of nothing.... A new Hedonism – that is what our century wants.

The famous "Conclusion" of Pater's *Studies* had inspired Wilde, who interpreted Pater's urging as an amoral quest, though Pater, as in the following, had focused on the effect of "experience" on the "spirit":

Not the fruit of experience, but experience itself, is the end.... How shall we pass most swiftly from point to point, and be present always at the focus where the greatest number of vital forces unite in their purest energy? To burn always with this hard, gemlike flame, to maintain this ecstasy, is success in life.... While all melts under our feet, we may well grasp at any exquisite passion, or any contribution to knowledge that seems by a lifted horizon to set the spirit free for a moment....

Yeats later recalled that Wilde mentioned *Studies*, perhaps facetiously, as "my golden book; I never travel anywhere without it; but it is the very flower of decadence: the last trumpet should have sounded the moment it was written" (87). Indeed, in *Intentions*, Wilde wrote that Pater was "on the whole, the most perfect master of English prose now creating amongst us...."

On 24 July 1877, Pater first wrote to Wilde in response to a letter and a review of the Grosvenor Gallery exhibition (1 May) that the young Oxford student had sent him: Pater called the notice "excellent....it makes me much wish to make your acquaintance, and I hope you will give me an early call on your return to Oxford." Wilde's notice, he continues, "shows that you possess some beautiful, and for your age quite exceptionally cultivated, tastes, and a considerable knowledge also of many beautiful things" (Pater, *Letters* 24–25). Their correspondence during Wilde's final year at Oxford suggests that he saw Pater several times.

Wilde's first opportunity to review one of Pater's works occurred in 1887, when he wrote about

Imaginary Portraits in the *Pall Mall Gazette* (11 June). This brief review (see "Mr. Pater's Imaginary Portraits") summarizes each of the portraits, then judges the book as "singularly attractive.... He does not weary us with any definite doctrine, or seek to suit life to any formal creed. He is always looking for exquisite moments, and when he has found them, he analyzes them with delicate and delightful art...."

In 1888, Pater wrote to Wilde after reading *The Happy Prince and Other Tales* to tell him how "delightful" he had found "him and his companions." "The Selfish Giant" was "certainly...perfect in its kind. Your genuine 'little poems in prose,' those at the top of pages 10 and 14, for instance, are gems, and the whole, too brief, book abounds with delicate touches and pure English" (Pater, *Letters* 85).

In 1890, Wilde reviewed Pater's *Appreciations* in the *Speaker* (22 March) under the title "Mr. Pater's Last Volume" (see entry). This lengthy review, glowing with praise, concludes: "...in Mr. Pater, as in Cardinal Newman, we find the union of personality with perfection. He has no rival in his own sphere, and he has escaped disciples." Writing to Wilde, Pater expressed his "very great pleasure" in reading the review, whose prose was "pleasantly written, genial, sensible criticism...": "How friendly of you to have given so much care and time to my book, in the midst of your own work in that prose of which you have become so successful a writer" (Pater, *Letters* 109).

When *The Picture of Dorian Gray* appeared in *Lippincott's Magazine* (20 June 1890), Pater may have been reluctant to review it – possibly because of his own homoerotic impulses – when the reviews attacked it as "unmanly," suitable for "outlawed noblemen and perverted telegraph boys" (who figured in a recent scandal involving a male brothel). When the second version appeared with excisions and revisions, Pater could now review the somewhat less daring novel in the *Bookman* (Nov. 1891) in appreciation of Wilde's favorable review of *Appreciations*.

Pater wrote the most penetrating account of the novel at the time: though Wilde's writing reflected "something of an excellent talker" and, in his use of paradox, the continuity of "the brilliant critical work of Matthew Arnold," Pater also perceived that Wilde's "clever" book "seems to set forth anything but a homely philosophy of life for the middle-class – a kind of dainty Epicurean theory rather – yet fails, to some degree, in this....":

A true Epicureanism aims at a complete though harmonious development of man's entire organism. To lose the moral sense therefore, for instance, the sense of sin and righteousness, as Mr. Wilde's heroes are bent on doing so speedily, as completely as they can, is to lose, or lower organisation, to become less complex, to pass from a higher to a lower degree of development. As a story, however, a partly supernatural story, it is first-rate in artistic management....

Levey has written that, in his review, Pater "had singled out the character of Lord Henry Wotton for surprisingly strong moral disapproval (possibly displeased, or alarmed, by Wotton's echoes of his own earlier hedonism) and he may even have surmised that there was gathering around Wilde far greater opprobrium than he himself had endured" (20). Dorian Gray, "a quite unsuccessful experiment in Epicureanism, in life as a fine art, is...a beautiful creation," writes Pater, who then draws "a very plain moral" from the novel "to the effect that vice and crime make people coarse and ugly." Pater concludes that the work "may fairly claim to go with that of Edgar Poe, and with some good French work of the same kind, done, probably, in more or less imitation of it" (rpt. in Beckson).

Wilde may have met Pater in January 1890, and except for some brief notes from Pater, their correspondence apparently ceased during the few remaining years left to the Oxford don. Levey contends that the paradoxical Pater – who once said, "It doesn't matter what is said as long as it is said beautifully" (qtd. in Levey 83) – provided a model for Lord Henry Wotton in *The Picture of Dorian Gray*: "For the younger, much bolder and far more compulsively fluent [Wilde], Pater must have seemed in possession of a gift he had totally failed to exploit" (Levey 119).

Ellmann notes that Wilde later criticized the style of Pater's *Renaissance* work as too studied, lacking "the true rhythmical life of words," and when Pater died, Wilde (according to Max Beerbohm) queried, "Was he ever alive?" According to Robert Ross, writes Ellmann, Wilde later "disparaged Pater as man, as writer, and as an influence..." (52/50). But given Wilde's unpredictable facetiousness, such reports may be unreliable. Other accounts – in addition to what Wilde had written about Pater – indicate his devotion to him. For example, in an "interview" in the *St. James's Gazette* (18 Jan. 1895), Wilde said that "the only writers who have influenced me are Keats, Flaubert, and Walter Pater" (rpt. in *More Letters* 195), and in a memoir of a meeting with Wilde in 1898 written by the critic and novelist Wilfred Hugh Chesson (1870–1952) and published in the *Bookman* (Dec. 1911), Wilde told him, in referring to the small size of a series of books: "It is unjust to a good style to print it on a tiny page. Imagine turning Pater over rapidly. It is violence" (rpt. in *More Letters* 207).

References: *The Autobiography of W. B. Yeats* (1965); Lawrence Evans, ed., *Letters of Walter Pater* (1970); Michael Levey, *The Case of Walter Pater* (1978); Laurel Brake, *Subjugated Knowledges* (1994); Denis Donoghue, *Walter Pater: Lover of Strange Souls* (1995).

"PEN, PENCIL AND POISON"

Published: *Fortnightly Review* 45 (Jan. 1889): 41–54, with the subtitle "A Study"; rev., with the subtitle "A Study in Green" in *Intentions* (1891). Wilde's biographical essay on Thomas Griffiths Wainewright (who published under the name of "Janus Weathercock"), writes Jonathan Curling, "brought no new facts to his study...but he was the first writer to regard Wainewright as a man, not a monster, and to omit the pious reprobations with which all the other authors hitherto had justified themselves" (10).

Sources: Wilde made use of W. Carew Hazlitt's edition of Wainewright's *Essays and Criticisms* (1880) and the biographical essay included by Hazlitt. A less significant source was Thomas de Quincey's essay "Charles Lamb." As Ian Small writes, Wilde's "reliance upon Hazlitt is enormous, and on occasions Wilde repeats Hazlitt's essay almost verbatim" (62). Horst Schroeder reveals a further source for Wilde's essay: Alexander Gilchrist's *Life of William Blake* (new and enlarged edition), 2 vols. (London, 1880). Verbal echoes from Gilchrist found their way into the Wainewright essay when Wilde revised it for his *Intentions*. Lawrence Danson suggests that Wilde's essay draws upon such works as Swift's *A Modest Proposal* ("most strongly") and De Quincey's "On

Murder Considered as One of the Fine Arts" ("more distantly"): "...the reader's job is to invert the initial shocking assumption, that there is no significant difference between art and murder" (88).

The Study: Wilde begins his biographical "memoir" of Lamb's friend, Wainewright (1794– 1852), with the observation that much reproach has been directed

against artists and men of letters that they are lacking in wholeness and completeness of nature. As a rule this must necessarily be so. That very concentration of vision and intensity of purpose which is the characteristic of the artistic temperament is in itself a mode of limitation. To those who are preoccupied with the beauty of form nothing else seems of much importance.

There have been exceptions, as Wilde points out: Rubens served as an ambassador, and Milton as Latin secretary to Cromwell. Wainewright was not only a poet and painter, an art critic, an antiquarian, a prose writer, "an amateur of beautiful things, and a dilettante of things delightful, but also a forger of no mean or ordinary capabilities, and as a subtle and secret poisoner almost without rival in this or any age."

Tracing Wainewright's childhood and young manhood to his enlistment in the army, Wilde reveals his subject's disillusionment with barrack-life and with the dissipation among his companions, which "failed to satisfy the refined artistic temperament of one who was made for other things." The editor of *London Magazine*, "struck by the young man's genius," commissioned him to write a series of articles on artistic subjects, which he undertook under a series of pseudonyms, such as "Janus Weathercock" and "Van Vinkvooms," – "grotesque masks," says Wilde, "under which he chose to hide his seriousness or to reveal his levity. A mask tells us more than a face. These disguises intensified his personality." (Kohl suggests that Wilde's fascination with Wainewright "must have been the double life of painter and murderer, writer and forger that attracted the attention of a man who also led two lives...," 118.) Lamb referred to Wainewright as "kind, light-hearted... whose prose is 'capital.'"

Wainewright progressively moved in artistic

circles, startling the town as a dandy by wearing beautiful rings, a cameo breast-pin, and pale lemon-colored gloves: "This young dandy sought to be somebody, rather than to do something. He recognised that Life itself is an art, and has its modes of style no less than the arts that seek to express it." Wainewright's work was not without interest: William Blake reportedly stopped before one of his pictures in the Royal Academy and judged it to be "very fine." Appreciative of the "value of beautiful surroundings," Wainewright never wearied of describing his rooms, decorated with exquisite works of art. He had, says Wilde, that "curious love of green, which in individuals is always the sign of a subtle artistic temperament, and in nations is said to denote a laxity, if not a decadence of morals" (a foreshadowing of Wilde's interest in the green carnation: see entry).

As an art critic, Wainewright "concerned himself primarily with the complex impressions produced by a work of art, and certainly the first step in aesthetic criticism is to realise one's own impressions" (an approach advocated by Walter Pater in his preface to *Studies in the History of the Renaissance*, 1873). Wainewright "never lost sight of the great truth that Art's first appeal is neither to the intellect nor to the emotions, but purely to the artistic temperament...." He admired Turner and Constable "at a time when they were not so much thought of as they are now, and saw that for the highest landscape art we require more than 'mere industry and accurate transcription.'" He sought for the qualities of "composition, beauty and dignity of line, richness of colour, and imaginative power,'" of which he wrote: "I hold that no work of art can be tried otherwise than by laws deduced from itself...." He was one of the first, writes Wilde, "to develop what has been called the art-literature of the nineteenth century, that form of literature which has found in Mr. Ruskin and Mr. Browning its two most perfect exponents."

Wilde now comes to the aspect of Wainewright's life that most fascinates him: his career as "one of the most subtle and secret poisoners of this or any age." His first victim was his uncle in order to gain possession of Linden House. In the following year, he poisoned his wife's mother and his "lovely" sister-in-law, who had been insured by Wainewright and his wife for about £18,000 "in various offices." After a complicated series of events, a verdict was given in the insurance companies'

favor. He next convinced the father of a young lady that had interested him to insure his life for £3,000, then dropped some crystals of strychnine into his coffee at dinner. Wainewright's intent was not only to acquire the money but also to revenge himself on one of the insurance companies that had won a verdict against him. (The precise number of victims at Wainewright's hands remains unknown.)

After living in Paris for several years, he returned to England in pursuit of a woman he loved and was arrested on a charge of forgery, committed some 13 years before. While in Newgate Prison, he was visited by various men of letters, including Charles Dickens, who based his hero in the story "Hunted Down" on Wainewright. From Newgate, he was sent to Van Diemen's Land, Tasmania, with 300 other convicts. His "love of art, however, never deserted him"; he did sketching and portrait painting, and "his conversation and manners seem not to have lost their charm."

Refused a "ticket-of-leave" in 1844, he lived on until 1852, when he died of apoplexy. His crimes, Wilde comments, "seem to have had an important effect upon his art. They gave a strong personality to his style, a quality that his early work certainly lacked." Though Wainewright's biographer believes that his love of art was a mere pretense, Wilde regards such a view as shallow: "The fact of a man being a poisoner is nothing against his prose." Art, concludes Wilde, has not forgotten Wainewright: in addition to Dickens, Bulwer-Lytton based his character of Varney in *Lucretia* (1846) on the poisoner: "...it is gratifying to note that fiction has paid some homage to one who was so powerful with 'pen, pencil and poison.' To be suggestive for fiction is to be of more importance than a fact."

Early Reviews: In the *Speaker* (4 July 1891), Arthur Symons noted that Wilde's essay on Wainewright "suffers from the lack of intrinsic interest in its subject. A pretentious affected writer does not become interesting merely because he commits a murder" (rpt. in Beckson). In the *Academy* (4 July), Richard Le Gallienne writes that Wilde has "unearthed [Wainewright's] curious history, made selections from his criticism, and then set his own epigram, diamond-wise, in the midst of a biographical essay. Various readers solemnly add to their historical knowledge, discuss the strange character of the man, study his criticism; but Mr. Wilde sits and watches his epigram sparkling far within. About Wainewright he cares far less than the reader, about his own epigram – far more" (rpt. in Beckson).

The American essayist and biographer Agnes Repplier writes in the *North American Review* (Jan. 1892) that "Pen, Pencil and Poison" is "visibly lacking in sincerity [a common criticism of Wilde's writings]. The author plays with his subject very much as his subject, 'kind, light-hearted Wainewright,' played with crime, and in both cases there is a subtle and discordant element of vulgarity.... This 'study in green' contains, however, some brilliant passages, [such as] 'The domestic virtues are not the true basis of art, though they may serve as an excellent advertisement for second-rate artists'" (rpt. in Beckson).

References: Jonathan Curling, *Janus Weathercock: The Life of Thomas Griffiths Wainewright, 1794–1847* (1938); Ian Small, "Intertextuality in Pater and Wilde," *ELT*, Special Series, No. 4 (1990); William Buckler, "Antinomianism or Anarchy? A Note on Oscar Wilde's 'Pen, Pencil and Poison,'" *Victorian Newsletter* (Fall 1990); Horst Schroeder, "A Source for 'Pen, Pencil and Poison,'" *N&Q* (Sept. 1994); Lawrence Danson, "Pen, Pencil and Poison," *Wilde's Intentions: The Artist in His Criticism* (1997).

PÈRE LACHAISE TOMB: *See* **THE TOMB OF WILDE**

PERSONAL IMPRESSIONS OF AMERICA: *See IMPRESSIONS OF AMERICA*

PHARAOH

Wilde apparently did not proceed beyond the title of this projected play, which he alludes to in a letter on 1 October 1897, to Robert Ross: "Tomorrow I begin the *Florentine Tragedy*. After that I must tackle *Pharaoh*" (*Letters* 649).

"PHÈDRE"

Published: First appeared as "To Sarah Bernhardt" in the *World: A Journal for Men and Women* 10 (11 June 1879): 18; rev. as "Sara [*sic*] Bernhardt" in *Biograph and Review* 4 (Aug. 1880): 135; further rev. as "Phèdre" in *Poems* (1881). In *Poems* (1908), Robert Ross added "To Sarah Bernhardt" as the dedication.

In *Woman's World* (Jan. 1888), Wilde wrote:

"For my own part, I must confess that it was not until I heard Sarah Bernhardt in *Phèdre* that I absolutely realised the sweetness of the music of Racine." On 2 June 1879, she had appeared in Racine's *Phèdre* at the Gaiety Theatre in a Comédie Française production, acting in the role of the heroine passionately in love with her stepson.

In his sonnet, Wilde expresses admiration of Bernhardt by alluding to a vision of greatness in a world of dullness: "How vain and dull this common world must seem / To such a One as thou, who should'st have talked / At Florence with Mirandola, or walked / Through the cool olives of the Academe...." Associating her with the mythic world of ancient Greece, the speaker concludes: "Ah! surely once some urn of Attic clay / Held thy wan dust, and thou hast come again / Back to this common world so dull and vain...."

Manuscript: The Huntington Library has a MS. of the poem titled "Sara [*sic*] Bernhardt," the reverse side of which has "Phèdre," probably written at the time of her performance in the play.

"PHRASES AND PHILOSOPHIES FOR THE USE OF THE YOUNG"

Published: *Chameleon: "A Bazaar of Dangerous and Smiling Chances"* 1 (Dec. 1894): 1–3; rpt. in *Miscellanies* (1908). Alfred Douglas had asked Wilde, "as a personal favour," to write something for the undergraduate Oxford periodical, the *Chameleon* (the subtitle borrowed from Robert Louis Stevenson). To please him, Wilde sent "a page of paradoxes destined originally for the *Saturday Review*" (*Letters* 441). These 35 aphorisms (augmenting those titled earlier in the *Saturday Review*, 17 November 1894, as "A Few Maxims for the Instruction of the Over-Educated,") include some of Wilde's most famous remarks. A central concept of Decadence and dandyism appears first: "The first duty in life is to be as artificial as possible. What the second duty is no one has as yet discovered." Associated also with Decadence and dandyism is the suggestion of the green carnation, appropriate for the homosexually oriented *Chameleon*: "A really well-made buttonhole is the only link between Art and Nature." In impugning the Victorian piety of "sincerity," Wilde offered: "In all unimportant matters, style, not sincerity, is the essential. In all important matters, style, not sincerity, is the essential" – the approximate line later spoken by Gwendolen at the beginning of Act III of *The Importance of Being Earnest*, as is the line later spoken by the dandiacal Lord Goring at the beginning of Act III of *An Ideal Husband*: "To love oneself is the beginning of a life-long romance."

Manuscripts: The Clark Library has two MS. fragments of these aphorisms.

THE PICTURE OF DORIAN GRAY

First Published Version: *Lippincott's Monthly Magazine* 46 (July 1890): 3–100 (the issue was released on 20 June). The entire novel appeared in this one issue. The magazine was published by Ward, Lock & Co. in London; by J.B. Lippincott & Co. in Philadelphia.

Second Published Version: 24(?) April 1891 by Ward, Lock & Co. (London, New York, and Melbourne). Mason (343) cites this uncertain date, whereas *The English Catalogue of Printed Books, 1890–1897* cites May 1891. For this second version, Wilde used the printed sheets of the Lippincott version to make extensive revisions; he generally accepted the revisions that J.M. Stoddart, the editor, had made without consulting Wilde. For the second version, Wilde added six new chapters – 3, 5, 15, 16, 17, and 18 – as well as the "The Preface" (the latter previously published in the *Fortnightly Review*, March 1891), which presents his aesthetic principles in epigrammatic form, presumably his reaction to the critical onslaught on the first version. The new chapters give greater complexity and development to the plot, particularly that involving Sibyl Vane and the quest for vengeance by her brother, James. Wilde divided Chapter 13 of the first version into two chapters (19 and 20) for the second version, which now contains a total of 20 chapters as opposed to the 13 chapters in the first version.

Sources: Dorian Gray's wish to remain young while his portrait ages is principally derived from the various legends of Faust, who pledges his soul to the Devil for youth, power, and knowledge. Another source is the ancient myth of Narcissus, who falls in love with his own image in the pool and dies from his self-love, best known in Ovid's *Metamorphoses*. The combination of dandiacal wit and a mysterious portrait that, as Stanley Weintraub remarks, "undergoes enigmatic physical changes" in Disraeli's *Vivian Grey* (1825) anticipates *Dorian Gray* (Wilde had named his younger

son "Vyvyan," 23–24). Kerry Powell has written of the "magic-picture mania" in many popular late 19th-century novels with such titles as *The Veiled Picture*, *The Picture's Secret*, and *His Other Self*, which undoubtedly provided Wilde with the central idea of the *Doppelgänger* for his own novel. The most notable of these "magic-picture" novels, Henry James's *The Tragic Muse* (1890), involves an aesthete whose portrait fades as he himself fades from the story.

As Isobel Murray writes, the popularity of Stevenson's *The Strange Case of Dr. Jekyll and Mr. Hyde* (1885), which depicts the secrecy of the divided self, may have provided Wilde with further impetus for his own novel; other critics have cited such works as Poe's "The Oval Portrait," Balzac's "Peu de Chagrin," and Charles Maturin's *Melmoth the Wanderer* (by Wilde's great-uncle) as further possibilities for Wilde's inspiration. The list of possible sources, including Wilde's own stories – "The Portrait of Mr W. H.," involving a mysterious portrait in the context of a homoerotic tale, and "The Fisherman and His Soul," involving a divided self – continues to grow alarmingly, but Wilde's novel remains a unique achievement, the alleged "sources" bearing only remote resemblances to Wilde's work.

The Preface: First published separately in the *Fortnightly Review* (March 1891), this listing of statements, in no discernible order, confirms Wilde's devotion to art for art's sake – a concern with aesthetic perfection rather than with utilitarian value. The final statement in "The Preface" is thus central to Wilde's aestheticism: "All art is quite useless" (this statement, like others at the end of this preface, is drawn from Gautier's preface to *Mademoiselle de Maupin*, 1835).

Whatever moral ideas are found in a work of art, Wilde suggests, are to be regarded merely as subject matter, not as the justification for the work: "Vice and virtue are to the artist materials for an art." Furthermore, "The moral life of man forms part of the subject-matter of the artist, but the morality of art consists in the perfect use of an imperfect medium. No artist desires to prove anything.... No artist has ethical sympathies.... Thought and language are to the artist instruments of an art." The intent, consequently, of the work is not moral instruction but an aesthetic experience; hence, "There is no such thing as a moral or an immoral book. Books are well written, or badly written. That is all."

Wilde's aesthetic principle "To reveal art and conceal the artist is art's aim" has been interpreted by some critics as inconsistent with the novel, for the painter, Basil Hallward, refuses to exhibit his portrait of Dorian Gray because it is too self-revelatory; Wilde later admitted that his novel reflected his own quest for pleasure, which is "foreshadowed and prefigured" in "the note of Doom that like a purple thread runs through the gold cloth of *Dorian Gray*" (*Letters* 475). Ellmann contends that this preface "flaunted the aestheticism that the book would indict" and that "Wilde the preface-writer and Wilde the novelist deconstruct each other" (315/297).

Taking issue with Ellmann's latter statement, William Buckler remarks that "it assumes either that Wilde had a purpose in writing the novel that represented a rejection on moral grounds of all his labors as a critic both before and after *Dorian Gray* or that his novel got away from him and asserted a thesis that he could not or did not suppress." It is clear, however, that "Wilde knew just what he was doing and suggests, further, that if he had intended anything like what Ellmann asserts, he would have used that fact against his critics" (139–40).

As for Ellmann's contention that the novel depicts the "tragedy of aestheticism" (315/297), Buckler argues that the story's central "tragedy" is the "inevitable consequence, not of aestheticism, but of an ugly, self-deceiving, all-devouring vanity that leads the protagonist to heartless cruelty, murder, blackmail, and suicide" (140). Buckler concludes that, since Wilde "certainly knew" that Dorian was capable of only "creative mediocrity," it is unlikely that he intended him "to be taken as a serious, credible, impressive spokesman for art or aestheticism" (169).

The Plot: The opening chapter, which takes place in the studio of the painter Basil Hallward, depicts the young Lord Henry Wotton smoking an "opium-tinted cigarette" while lying on a divan and watching Hallward, who is contemplating a full-length portrait of "a young man of extraordinary personal beauty." When Lord Henry urges him to exhibit it in the Grosvenor Gallery, Hallward assures him that he does not intend to send it anywhere: "I have put too much of myself into it." Disagreeing, Lord Henry contrasts the painter's "rugged strong face" with the beauty of the subject

in the painting, who is a "young Adonis...a Narcissus" (the latter myth suggesting the homoerotic subtext of the novel; see entry: Narcissus). When Hallward reveals the name of Dorian Gray, he confesses that he had not intended to, that he had grown to love secrecy.

When they go out into the garden and Lord Henry presses his friend to explain why he refuses to exhibit his painting, Hallward echoes the Narcissus motif: "...every portrait that is painted with feeling is a portrait of the artist, not of the sitter." He is afraid that he has revealed the secret of his own soul. He then speaks of first seeing the "fascinating" Dorian at a society party, the narration of which indicates Hallward's homoerotic attraction and reaction: When their eyes met, a "curious sensation of terror" came over him. He felt that he was "on the verge of a terrible crisis" in his life.

Dorian has provided Hallward with inspiration with "all the spirit that is Greek. The harmony of soul and body...." Musing about Hallward's remark about art, Lord Henry observes that in the "wild struggle for existence, we want to have something that endures" (the first appearance of the word *wild*, which – with the use of *wilder* and *wildly*, some 34 instances in the novel – reveals Wilde's autobiographical signature, a device also employed in many of his other works).

In Chapter 2, Dorian is seated at the piano as Lord Henry and Hallward enter from the garden. Introduced to him, Lord Henry studies the "wonderfully handsome" Dorian carefully. When Dorian mounts the dais with the "air of a young Greek martyr," Hallward resumes work on his portrait. In conversation concerning good and bad influences while Dorian is posing as Hallward's model, Lord Henry contends that "all influence is immoral," for the "aim of life is self-development. To realize one's nature perfectly – that is what each of us is here for." The "Hellenic ideal" would make us forget all of the "maladies of mediaevalism," the "self-denial that mars our lives."

Lord Henry continues with lines that would be recycled in later works: "The only way to get rid of a temptation is to yield to it. Resist it, and your soul grows sick with longing for the things it had forbidden to itself...." Momentarily confused, Dorian senses that Lord Henry's ideas "seemed to him to have come really from himself." A "secret chord" that had never before been touched was now "vibrating and throbbing to curious pulses."

Wearying of maintaining the pose, Dorian relaxes in the garden, "feverishly drinking in [the] perfume" of lilac blossoms. Joining him, Lord Henry remarks: "You are quite right to do that. Nothing can cure the soul but the senses, just as nothing can cure the senses but the soul." Fascinated by Lord Henry, Dorian is also fearful, for suddenly "there had come some one across his life who seemed to have disclosed to him life's mystery."

In a passage partly echoing – but also distorting – Walter Pater's "Conclusion" to *Studies in the History of the Renaissance* (1873), Lord Henry urges Dorian to live life to the fullest before he becomes "sallow, and hollow-checked, and dull eyed":

Ah! realize your youth while you have it.... Live! Live the wonderful life that is in you! Let nothing be lost upon you. Be always searching for new sensations. Be afraid of nothing.... A new Hedonism – that is what our century wants. You might be its visible symbol.

At that point, Hallward completes the portrait. Dorian, standing before it and recalling Lord Henry's "terrible warning" of the brevity of youth, has a "revelation" of his own beauty:

How sad it is! I shall grow old, and horrible, and dreadful. But this picture will remain always young.... If it were only the other way! If it were I who was to be always young, and the picture that was to grow old! For that – for that – I would give everything! ...I would give my soul for that!

Distressed by Dorian's reaction to the completed portrait, Hallward attempts to destroy the canvas, but Dorian seizes the knife and flings it away: "It would be murder!" He more than appreciates the painting; he enacts the role of Narcissus: "I am in love with it, Basil. It is part of myself."

As Chapter 3 begins, Lord Henry is visiting his uncle, Lord Fermor, who provides his nephew with information on Dorian's family tragedy: the beautiful Lady Margaret Devereux had run off with a penniless subaltern in a foot regiment. A few months after their marriage, he was killed in an apparent plot instigated by Lady Margeret's father, Lord Kelso. She died within the year, leaving the infant Dorian in the care of her father. Lord Henry departs, reviewing the story and contemplating his own effect on Dorian: "He would seek to dominate him – had already, indeed, half done so."

In Chapter 4, while visiting Dorian, Lord Henry utters one of his notable epigrams that reappears in Act III of *Lady Windermere's Fan:* "Nowadays people know the price of everything and the value of nothing." Dorian reveals to Lord Henry that he is in love with an actress, Sibyl Vane – "a genius." He attributes this experience to Lord Henry: "You filled me with a wild desire to know everything about life." On one evening, Dorian's "passion for sensations" impelled him to "go out in search of some adventure." In "great monstrous London," with its "sordid sinners and its splendid sins," undoubtedly there was something in store for him. As Lord Henry had said, "the search for beauty [was] the real secret of life."

He tells Lord Henry that, in a sordid part of the city, he had passed by an "absurd little theatre," into which he entered: He was startled by the actress performing the role of Juliet. He returned night after night to see her perform in other Shakespeare plays. On the third night, he was introduced to Sibyl, who called him "Prince Charming." He invites Lord Henry and Hallward to accompany him to see Sibyl perform Shakespeare. Returning home from an evening out, Lord Henry learns from a telegram that Dorian is now engaged to her.

At the opening of Chapter 5, Sibyl expresses her joy to her mother concerning her love for Dorian. Her brother, James, who will soon be departing for Australia, walks with her through the park while questioning her about a "gentleman" who has been going backstage every night to speak with her. James had urged his mother to watch over her in his absence. To Sibyl, James issues a warning: "He means you no good." She insists that she loves him, but Jim vows to kill him should any harm come to her.

At the opening of Chapter 6, Dorian, Lord Henry, and Hallward dine, then prepare to depart for the theater. Dorian talks about his engagement, convinced that one of his guardians, Lord Radley, is "sure to be furious." As though uttering prophecy, Dorian remarks to his friends: "When you see Sibyl Vane, you will feel that the man who could wrong her would be a beast, a beast without a heart...." As Chapter 7 opens, the three friends arrive at the theater. Some 15 minutes after the curtain rises, Sibyl appears on stage "amidst an extraordinary turmoil of applause, but she speaks Juliet's lines "in a thoroughly artificial manner." Dorian turns pale, and his friends remain silent. "She was a complete failure." Even the "common uneducated" audience disapproves and greets her with "a storm of hisses." Lord Henry says: "She is quite beautiful, Dorian, but she can't act."

When Lord Henry urges Dorian to leave, he decides to remain. After the seemingly interminable performance ends with the theater almost empty, Dorian rushes behind the scenes into the green room. Sibyl, standing alone "with a look of triumph on her face," is smiling "over some secret" of her own. She explains that, before knowing him, acting was the "one reality" of her life: "It was only in the theatre that I lived.... I believed in everything." Accusing her of throwing away her gifts, he regards her now as "shallow and stupid." He vows never to see her again: "You have spoiled the romance of my life...."

After wandering until dawn through the sordid streets, he returns home. As he turns the handle of the door to his bedroom, he glances at Hallward's portrait of him in the library and "started back as if in surprise": "...the face appeared to him to be a little changed.... One would have said that there was a touch of cruelty in the mouth," but he sees no such expression in his own face (his incapacity to perceive his cruelty is the beginning of Dorian's disintegration rather than expansion of personality that Lord Henry had urged).

He then recalls what he had said in Hallward's studio: that he wished to remain young while the portrait grew old and that "the face on the canvas [would] bear the burden of his passions and his sins..." (in point of fact, Dorian does not mention this last wish in Chapter 2). The change in the portrait, he concludes, is only an illusion brought on by his "troubled senses." The picture "would be to him the visible emblem of conscience.... He would go back to Sibyl Vane, make her amends, marry her, try to love her again.... He had been selfish and cruel to her."

In Chapter 8, on the next morning, Dorian removes the screen that he had placed before the picture, "a visible symbol of the degradation of sin." He writes a "passionate letter" to Sibyl, "imploring her forgiveness and accusing himself of madness." Completing the letter, he feels for-

given. But when Lord Henry arrives with the news that Sibyl is dead, Dorian accuses him of telling a "horrible lie." Lord Henry informs him that she was found lying in her dressing room, having swallowed "something by mistake, some dreadful thing they use at theatres." He advises Dorian not to get himself mixed up in the case, but Dorian is convinced that he has murdered her. He reflects, however, that life goes on. As for Sibyl Vane, Lord Henry urges Dorian to regard her "lonely death in the tawdry dressing-room simply as a strange lurid fragment from some Jacobean tragedy...." Lord Henry's speech touches a responsive chord in Dorian, who admits that he had felt the same way about Sibyl.

After Lord Henry leaves, Dorian rushes to the screen to see whether any further changes have occurred in the portrait, but no, it remains the same. As though to underscore Wilde's autobiographical signature of "wild joys and wilder sins," the homoerotic myth of Narcissus occurs again: "Once, in boyish mockery of Narcissus, he had kissed, or feigned to kiss, those painted lips that now smiled so cruelly at him.... This portrait would be to him the most magical of mirrors. As it had revealed to him his own body, so it would reveal to him his own soul."

At the beginning of Chapter 9, Hallward is shown in while Dorian is having breakfast. He is aghast at Dorian's indifference to Sibyl's death and his epigrammatic responses to Hallward's distress. But Dorian assures him that, if he had arrived yesterday "at about half-past five, perhaps, or a quarter to six," he would have found him in tears. "To become a spectator of one's life, as Harry [Lord Henry] says, is to escape the suffering of life."

The painter, noticing the screen, asks Dorian to remove it so that he may see his portrait, but Dorian warns him that if the screen is touched, their friendship is over. At this point, Dorian recalls that Lord Henry had learned of Hallward's reason for not wishing to exhibit the painting, but when Dorian asks the painter what his "secret" was, Hallward responds: "Have you noticed in the picture something curious?" With "wild startled eyes," Dorian cries out, "Basil!" But Hallward was not referring to the change in the portrait but to its revelation of his own homoeroticism. Relieved that Hallward is unaware of the change in the portrait, Dorian nevertheless refuses to permit him to see it.

In Chapter 10, Dorian opens the door of the schoolroom at the top of the house, which was his playroom as a child and his study until four years before (a symbolic return to the innocence of the past). He decides to cover the painting with "a purple satin coverlet" and move it to this room. He regrets that he had not told Hallward the true reason "why he wished to hide the picture away...." He acknowledges that Hallward's love for him "had nothing in it that was not noble and intellectual. It was not that mere physical admiration of beauty that is born of the senses and that dies when the senses tire. It was such love as Michelangelo had known, and Montaigne, and Winckelmann, and Shakespeare himself" (another version of this passage was spoken by Wilde in his first criminal trial as a defendant when the prosecutor asked him to explain "the love that dare not speak its name" – the famous line from Lord Alfred Douglas's poem "Two Loves": see The Trials, 1895).

Dorian's attention is now drawn to a "yellow book" (that is, a yellow paper-covered French novel), the "strangest book that he had ever read," which Lord Henry had sent him. This book has some echoes from Huysmans's *A Rebours* (1884), which Wilde revealed had particularly influenced him. What interests Dorian in this novel is that the "life of the senses was described in the terms of mystical philosophy [a characteristic element of Decadent/Symbolist literature].... It was a poisonous book." When he joins Lord Henry at the club, Dorian blames the book's fascination for his being late.

In Chapter 11, Dorian returns home from "one of those mysterious and prolonged absences" and stands before his portrait with a mirror, "looking now at the evil and aging face on the canvas, and now at the fair young face that laughed back at him from the polished glass." The contrast quickens his sense of pleasure, and he grows "more enamoured of his own beauty, more and more interested in the corruption of his own soul...."

In his own "delicate scented chamber," or in the sordid room of a tavern near the docks, where he went incognito, he would think of the "ruin he had brought upon his soul...." Yet he believed (as did the late Victorian Aesthetes) that "life itself was the first, the greatest, of the arts, and for it all the other arts seemed to be but a preparation." Dandyism – "an attempt to assert the absolute modernity of beauty" – fascinated him. He wished "to elaborate some new scheme of life that would have its reasoned philosophy and its ordered principles, and find in the spiritualizing of the senses its highest realization." Dorian recalls Lord Henry's prophecy that a New Hedonism would "recreate life" and "save it from that harsh uncomely puritanism that is having, in our own day, its curious revival."

The New Hedonism provides Dorian with a vision of a renewed world: "...in his search for sensations that would be at once new and delightful, and possess that element of strangeness that is so essential to romance, he would often adopt certain modes of thought that he knew to be really alien to his nature, abandon himself to their subtle influences...." (The Decadent vision, here suggested, comes increasingly to dominate Dorian, making this a pivotal chapter.) Dorian is also attracted to the Roman Catholic communion and particularly to its ritualism (his aesthetic rather than spiritual reactions imply a devotion to the Religion of Art: see entry).

But, echoing Pater, Dorian never "fell into the error of arresting his intellectual development by any formal acceptance of creed or system.... He knew that the senses, no less than the soul, have their spiritual mysteries to reveal." Like Huysmans's Des Esseintes, Dorian immerses himself in exotic sensations (at this point, Wilde's language grows increasingly esoteric with numerous historical allusions, particularly of Renaissance Italy, a characteristic of literary Decadence): he collects, for example, primitive instruments from all parts of the world – "things of bestial shape and with hideous voices" – which he plays.

Dorian also collects elaborate embroideries and reads of the great ages of the past when the art flourished (Wilde used material from a book on embroidery and lace, which he had reviewed for *Woman's World*: see "A Fascinating Book"). Dorian also has a "special passion" for ecclesiastical vestments, as indeed for everything connected with church services. But at the top of the house, the portrait "showed him the real degradation of his life." He is now reluctant to leave the house for long periods, for he "hated to be separated from the picture that was such a part of his life"; he is fearful that during his absence someone might discover his secret. "Curious stories" about him begin to circulate: he has been seen fighting with foreign sailors "in a low den" in Whitechapel, and he is said to consort with thieves. At his club, members avoid him or whisper rumors about him. But his "charming boyish smile" and "infinite grace" seem to confirm his innocence. He remains immersed in – indeed "poisoned" by – the strange novel that Lord Henry had sent him. Distorting Lord Henry's urging to subject himself to all aspects of experience in order to develop his personality, Dorian reveals his confusion, ultimately his impulse to self-destruction: "There were moments when he looked on evil simply as a mode through which he could realize his conception of the beautiful."

In Chapter 12, Dorian, who is now 38, encounters Hallward in Grosvenor Square on a foggy night. Hallward informs Dorian that "the most dreadful things are being said" against him in London. Hallward then asks him, "Why is your friendship so fatal to young men?" Dorian responds by charging that he cannot be responsible for the disasters that others bring on themselves. Hallward wonders whether he really knows Dorian; he would have to see his soul. Dorian responds with a "bitter laugh of mockery": "You shall see it yourself, to-night!" When Hallward urges him to deny such stories as he has heard, Dorian invites him to accompany him upstairs.

Chapter 13 opens with the ascent to the schoolroom, Wilde providing some conventions of Gothic fiction: the lamp casts "fantastic shadows on the wall and staircase," and a "rising wind" makes some of the windows rattle. When Dorian tears the curtain from the portrait, Hallward reacts with "an exclamation of horror" when he sees "in the dim light the hideous face on the canvas grinning at him...." Nevertheless, he recognizes it as his painting. He recalls that Dorian had said that he had destroyed the painting, but Dorian responds: "'I was wrong. It has destroyed me.... Each of us has Heaven and Hell in him, Basil,' cried Dorian with a wild gesture of despair."

Hallward urges him to kneel and pray with him, but Dorian suddenly has "an uncontrollable feeling of hatred" for him. Glancing "wildly around," he notices a knife, which he seizes and plunges into the "great vein behind the ear," stabbing him repeatedly. Locking the door of the room and descending to the hall, Dorian takes his cloak and hat, lets himself out of the house, and then pretending to have just arrived home, rings the door-bell. When the valet opens the door, Dorian asks whether anyone has called for him. Using this device, he is convinced that no one will know that he and Hallward were in the house at the same time.

The following morning, at the beginning of Chapter 14, Dorian has sent a note to Alan Campbell, once a "great" friend, who has studied chemistry and who can dispose of Hallward's corpse. When Campbell arrives, he tells Dorian that he had never intended to enter his house again, but because of Dorian's urgent summons, it was a "matter of life and death." Dorian tells him that he must change the dead man seated at a table at the top of the house "into a handful of ashes." When Dorian confesses to the murder, Campbell refuses to help him, but Dorian then writes something on a piece of paper, reads it over twice, folds it carefully, and pushes it across the table. As Campbell reads it, his face becomes "ghastly pale" and he falls back in his chair (the reader is never told what Dorian has written).

Eventually, Campbell agrees to dispose of the body. On taking Campbell to the upstairs room, Dorian notices that the exposed painting has a "loathsome red dew that gleamed, wet and glistening, on one of the hands, as though the canvas had sweated blood.... How horrible it was!" Hours later, Campbell returns to the library to inform Dorian that he is finished: "And now good-bye. Let us never see each other again." Appreciatively, Dorian says: "You have saved me from ruin, Alan. I cannot forget that."

In the evening at Lady Narborough's social gathering, which opens Chapter 15, Dorian wonders at his calm demeanor and "for a moment felt keenly the terrible pleasure of a double life." Among the guests is Mrs. Erlynne, a "pushing nobody, with a delightful lisp and Venetian-red hair" (Wilde later employed the name for the "fallen woman" in *Lady Windermere's Fan*). Another guest, named Ernest Harrowden, is described as one of those "who have no enemies, but are thoroughly disliked by their friends" (the celebrated remark, according to Yeats, that Wilde used to characterize Bernard Shaw, on whom see entry).

In Chapter 16, Dorian, lying back in a hansom as it proceeds to an opium den in the dock area, recalls Lord Henry's remark when they had first met nearly 20 years before: "'To cure the soul by means of the senses, and the senses by means of the soul.' Yes, that was the secret." At this stage in his deterioration, having previously devoted himself to aesthetic sensations derived from art, he now embraces ugliness as the "one reality" because "it made things real." When the hansom pulls up in front of a shabby building, Dorian notices a young man when he enters one of the rooms: it is Adrian Singleton, one of Dorian's friends who have come to bad ends. Dorian looks at the "grotesque things that lay in such fantastic postures on the ragged mattresses. The twisted limbs, the gaping mouths, the staring lustreless eyes, fascinated him.... They were better off than he was. He was prisoned in thought."

A woman engages Dorian in conversation, but he ignores her until he offers her a few coins. As he leaves, she shouts after him: "Prince Charming is what you like to be called, ain't it?" A drowsy sailor, leaping to his feet and looking "wildly" round, rushes out after him, seizes him, and thrusts him against a wall, charging that he had destroyed Sibyl Vane's life; as her brother, he will now kill him. But Dorian, by his unchanged appearance, convinces him that he is a mere youth of 20. After Dorian leaves, the woman tells James that it has been almost 18 years "since Prince Charming made me what I am.... They say he has sold himself to the devil for a pretty face." When James rushes to the corner of the street, Dorian has already vanished.

At the beginning of Chapter 17, a week later in the conservatory at Selby Royal, Dorian's country house, he is entertaining guests at tea-time. Suddenly, a groan and a dull thud are heard from the far end of the conservatory: Dorian has fainted on the tiled floor. When he comes to in the drawing-room, to which he had been carried, he asks Lord Henry whether he is safe there: he remembers that he saw James Vane's face pressed against the conservatory window, watching him.

On the next day, as Chapter 18 opens, Dorian remains in his own room, "sick with a wild terror of dying, and yet indifferent to life itself." He fears the thought of "being hunted, snared, tracked down...." On the third day, he leaves his room, has breakfast, and joins the shooting party in the park. When one of the guests shoots a hare, two cries are then heard – that of the hare and that of a man. In the ensuing confusion, Dorian is convinced that the accidental death of the man in the thicket is an omen.

Back at the house, Dorian is filled with terror until the head-keeper informs him that the dead man is unknown to him, though he appears to be a sailor. Dorian goes to see the corpse, which turns out to be Jim Vane's. He now knows that he is safe. Dorian later informs Lord Henry in Chapter 19: "I have a new ideal, Harry. I am going to alter. I think I have altered" (another irony related to Dorian's extraordinary change in his portrait). He tells Lord Henry that he has "spared somebody," a young girl in the village named Hetty Merton, who was quite "beautiful and wonderfully like Sibyl Vane": "We were to have gone away together this morning at dawn. Suddenly I determined to leave her as flowerlike as I had found her."

Lord Henry, however, regards Dorian's noble act, from the moral point of view, as a grave error: "Well, the fact of having met you, and loved you, will teach her to despise her husband, and she will be wretched." When Dorian asks what has been going on in town, Lord Henry mentions Hallward's disappearance, his own divorce, and Alan Campbell's suicide. After musing about these matters, Lord Henry asks Dorian how he has retained his youthful appearance: "You must have some secret. I am only ten years older than you are, and I am wrinkled, and worn, and yellow.... Ah, Dorian, how happy you are! What an exquisite life you have had! You have drunk deeply of everything.... Life has been your art."

In Chapter 20, on returning home from an evening out with Lord Henry, Dorian contemplates some of his friend's remarks, such as the impossibility of anyone changing one's nature: "He felt a wild longing for the unstained purity of his boyhood...." He recalls a letter he received from someone who had loved him: "The world is changed because you are made of ivory and gold. The curves of your lips rewrite history." But he loathes his own beauty: "...flinging the mirror on the floor," he crushes it under his heel (the end of the Narcissus myth as a subtext in the novel). But when he removes the purple hanging from the portrait, he cries out in "pain and indignation," for he can see no change, "save that in the eyes there was a look of cunning and in the mouth the curved wrinkle of the hypocrite. The thing was still loathsome – more loathsome, if possible, than before...." He believes that he has spared Hetty Merton because of his vanity: "In hypocrisy he had worn the mask of goodness."

The only evidence that could be used against him was the painting, which had been his conscience: it must be destroyed. Seizing the knife that he had used to kill Hallward, he stabs the picture with it (in the first version, he slashes the canvas from the top to the bottom; in the second version, he stabs the picture in the heart). A great cry is heard throughout the house by the servants and in the street below.

When the servants break in through the window, they see on the wall "a splendid portrait of their master as they had last seen him, in all the wonder of his exquisite youth and beauty. Lying on the floor was a dead man, in evening dress, with a knife in his heart. He was withered, and loathsome of visage. It was not till they had examined the rings that they recognized who it was." (Thus ends, as Joyce Carol Oates writes, "one of the strongest and most haunting of English novels," 5.)

Early Reviews: In general, Wilde's novel received a negative, sometimes abusive, critical reception. An unsigned review, titled "A Study in Puppydom," written by Samuel Jeyes in the *St. James's Gazette* (20 June 1890) is typical: "The writer airs his cheap research among the garbage of the French *Décadents* like any drivelling pedant, and he bores you unmercifully with his prosy rigmaroles about the beauty of the Body and the corruption of the Soul" (rpt. in Beckson). In response, Wilde dispatched four letters to the editor of the periodical; each was disputed by Jeyes (maintaining his anonymity). In the letter appearing on 27 June, Wilde contended, somewhat facetiously, that the public would find that the novel "is a story with a moral":

All excess, as well as all renunciation, brings its own punishment.... Yes; there is a terrible moral in *Dorian Gray* – a moral which the prurient will not be able to find in it, but which will be revealed to all whose minds are healthy. Is this an artistic error? I fear it is. It is the only error in the book. *(Letters* 259)

In the *Daily Chronicle* (30 June), the reviewer launches his attack at the outset: "Dulness and dirt are the chief features of *Lippincott's* this month." There is, in Wilde's novel, something that is "unclean, though undeniably amusing." The reviewer continues:

It is a tale spawned from the leprous literature of the French *Décadents* – a poisonous book, the atmosphere of which is heavy with the mephitic odours of moral and spiritual putre-- faction – a gloating study of the mental and physical corruption of a fresh, fair and golden youth, which might be horrible and fascinating but for its effeminate frivolity, its studied insincerity, its theatrical cynicism, its tawdry mysticism, its flippant philosophisings, and the contaminating trail of garish vulgarity.... (rpt. in Beckson)

W. E. Henley's *Scots Observer* (5 July) published an anonymous review, written, says Rupert Hart-Davis, by a member of the staff, Charles Whibley, who used the pseudonym of "Thersites." Whibley wrote: "Why go grubbing in muck-heaps? The world is fair, and the proportion of healthy-minded men and honest women to those that are foul, fallen, or unnatural is great." Though the novel is "ingenious, interesting, full of cleverness, and plainly the work of a man of letters, it is false to art – for its interest is medico-legal...[and] false to morality – for it is not made sufficiently clear that the writer does not prefer a course of unnatural iniquity to a life of cleanliness, health and sanity" (rpt. in Beckson).

Even John Addington Symonds, himself a homosexual, took exception to the novel, which Wilde had sent him. To his future literary executor, Horatio Brown, he wrote on 22 July:

It is an odd and very audacious production, unwholesome in tone, but artistically and psychologically interesting. If the British public will stand this, they can stand anything. However, I resent the unhealthy, scented, mystic, congested touch which a man of this sort has on moral problems. (Symonds, *Letters* 3:477; rpt. in Beckson)

In *Lippincott's Monthly Magazine* (Sept. 1890), Julian Hawthorne, son of the novelist, wrote a review for the very magazine in which Wilde's novel appeared (presumably, it was expected to praise rather than condemn); indeed, as expected, Hawthorne says that it is a work that "everybody will want to read. It is a story strange in conception, strong in interest, and fitted with a tragic and ghastly climax." However, Hawthorne tempers his praise with the reservation that Dorian Gray, as a character study, is not "adequately realised and worked out." If he had been, the novel "would have been remembered after more meritorious ones were forgotten" (rpt. in Beckson).

Fewer reviews appeared when the second version was published. However, two are noteworthy: In the *United Ireland* (26 Sept. 1891), W. B. Yeats regarded *Dorian Gray*, "with all its faults of method," as a "wonderful book." For Walter Pater's review – the most insightful of the early reactions to the novel – see his entry.

Manuscripts: The Morgan Library has the entire MS. of the 1890 version; in addition, it has a copybook MS. of 10 pages of Chapter 5. The Clark Library has the TS. of the Morgan Library MS. with autograph revisions as well as a draft of 23 leaves of Chapter 3 from the 1891 version with many corrections and alterations and a single leaf from Chapter 5 of the 1891 version. In his *Inquiry into Oscar Wilde's Revisions of "The Picture of Dorian Gray"* (1988), Donald Lawler proposes the hypothesis that before these versions, Wilde had written a complete first draft, now lost, of the novel. From his examination of the Morgan Library MS., Lawler surmises that Wilde made copying errors while preparing a "fair copy" from what was probably a heavily corrected first draft. The Berg Collection has a corrected MS. of what Wilde first titled as Chapter 13 for the second version; then, as the novel grew, he changed the chapter number to 14 and finally to 15. The MS. of Chapter 16, consisting of 19 leaves, once in the collection of the composer Jerome Kern, was offered at Sotheby's (New York) on 4 December 1996.

References: Jacob Korg, "The Rage of Caliban," *University of Toronto Quarterly* (Oct. 1967); Herbert Schueller and Robert Peters, eds., *The Letters of John Addington Symonds* 3 (1969); Lewis Poteet, "*Dorian Gray* and the Gothic Novel," *Modern Fiction Studies* (Summer 1971); Isobel Murray, "Some Elements in the Composition of *The Picture of Dorian Gray*," *Durham University Journal* (June 1972); Donald Lawler and Charles Knott, "The Context of Invention: Suggested Origins of *Dorian Gray*," *Modern Philology* (May 1976); Joyce Carol Oates, "Wilde's Parable of the Fall," *Contraries: Essays* (1981); Kerry Powell, "Tom, Dick, and Dorian Gray: Magic-Picture Mania in Late Victorian

Fiction," *Philological Quarterly* (Spring 1983); Karl Beckson, "Wilde's Autobiographical Signature in *The Picture of Dorian Gray*," *Victorian Newsletter* (Spring 1986); Isobel Murray, "The Strange Case of Dr. Jekyll and Oscar Wilde," *Durham University Journal* (June 1987); Donald Lawler, ed., *The Picture of Dorian Gray* [both versions] (1988); William Buckler, "*The Picture of Dorian Gray*: An Essay in Aesthetic Exploration," *Victorians Institute Journal* (1990); Stanley Weintraub, "Disraeli and Wilde's Dorian Gray," *Cahiers Victoriens et Edouardiens* (Oct. 1992); Isobel Murray, "Oscar Wilde in his Literary Element: Yet Another Source for *Dorian Gray*?" *Rediscovering Oscar Wilde*, ed. C. George Sandulescu (1994).

"PLEASING AND PRATTLING"

Published: *PMG*, 4 Aug. 1886, 5; rpt. in *Reviews* (1908). Unsigned reviews of books published in 1886.

Sixty years ago, Wilde writes, Sir Thomas Lauder's historical romance *The Wolfe of Bandenoch* was very popular (its present incarnation is in the sixth and final edition): "To us its interest is more archaeological than artistic, and its characters seem merely puppets parading in fourteenth-century costume." Nowadays, Wilde states, few people have the time to read a novel requiring a glossary to explain archaic words: "In a novel we want life, not learning.... Still, there is a healthy spirit of adventure in the book, and no doubt many people will be interested to see the kind of novel the public liked in 1825."

G. M. Robins's *Keep My Secret*, by contrast, is "quite modern both in manner and in matter": the heroine has tried to murder someone when she was a small girl, and the intended victim made her promise to keep her action a secret. At the end, the novel "gets too melodramatic in character [the heroine is blackmailed by "a fascinating and unscrupulous uncle, and is nearly burned to death in the secret chamber of an old castle"], and the plot becomes a chaos of incoherent incident, but the writing is clever and bright..., yet makes no demands at all upon the intellect."

Mrs. Henry Chetwynd's *Mrs. Dorriman* contains "a new type of widow. As a rule in fiction widows are delightful, designing, and deceitful; but Mrs. Dorriman is not by any means a Cleopatra in crepe." The widow, in fact, is a "bore." The book "can be read without any trouble, and was probably written without any trouble also. The style is prattling and pleasing." In George Curzon's *Delamere*, plot is not new: the widow discovers that the estates belong not to her son but to her niece, a secret that the widow never reveals. The son and niece eventually marry to end the story happily. Curzon has a "clever style, and though its construction is rather clumsy the novel is a thoroughly interesting one."

In *A Daughter of Fife*, Amelia Barr tells the story of the love of a young artist for a Scotch fishergirl. Character sketches are "exceptionally good," particularly that involving a fisherman who abandons his nets to preach the gospel, "and the heroine is quite charming till she becomes civilised." The book, "a most artistic combination of romantic feeling with realistic form," has pleasant descriptions of Scotch scenery...." T. W. Speight's *A Barren Title*, in Wilde's briefest notice of these six novels, presents an "impoverished earl who receives an allowance from his relations on condition of his remaining single, being all the time secretly married and the father of a grown-up son. The story is improbable and amusing."

Finally, Wilde criticizes the "ordinary English novelists" of his day for their lack of "concentration of style":

Their characters are far too eloquent, and talk themselves to tatters. What we want is a little more reality and a little less rhetoric...we wish that they would talk less and think more.... We wander aimlessly through a very wilderness of words in search of one touch of nature. However, one should not be too severe on English novels; they are the only relaxation of the intellectually unemployed.

POEMS (1881)

Published: June 1881 by David Bogue (London) and by Roberts Brothers (Boston). According to the contract (reproduced in Mason 283), Wilde paid for all costs related to its publication. The initial printing of 750 copies provided stock for three editions, a new title page printed for each. The first edition used 250 copies of the initial printing; the second and third editions in 1881 used 250 copies each (Mason 282). The title page of the volume contains an emblem, designed by Wilde, showing a papal tiara above a Masonic rose enclosed in an oval, bearing the saying "*Sub hoc signo vinces*" ("Under this sign thou shalt conquer"), the tiara and rose symbolizing Catholicism and paganism "as well as their possible reconciliation in Freemasonry" (Ellmann 140/134): see entry on Freemasonry. In January 1882, Bogue issued fourth and fifth editions, 250 copies printed for each edition with additional revisions. When Bogue declared bankruptcy, the Bodley Head reissued the fifth edition: see *Poems* (1892).

Early Reviews: Wilde sent copies to such figures as Robert Browning, Matthew Arnold, W. E. Gladstone, Algernon Swinburne, and Edmond de Goncourt with the hope, presumably, of their reviewing it. None of those mentioned here wrote a review. At the hands of several reviewers, the volume underwent either ridicule or condemnation, as in *Punch*'s satirical cartoon – see Parodies and Satires.

When the librarian of the Oxford Union Society asked Wilde for a presentation copy of *Poems*, he responded with a signed volume, dating his gift on 27 October 1881. However, at a meeting of the Union on 3 November, a member (Oliver Elton, later a critic and historian of English literature) condemned it as a pastiche of other writers' works:

It is not that these poems are thin – and they *are* thin: it is not that they are immoral – and they *are* immoral: it is not that they are this or that – and they *are* all this and all that: it is that they are for the most part not by their putative father at all, but by a number of better-known and more deservedly reputed authors. They are in fact by William Shakespeare, by Philip Sidney, by John Donne, by Lord Byron, by William Morris, by Algernon Swinburne, and by sixty more.... (qtd. in Ellmann 146/140)

After an intense debate and two separate votes by members of the Society as to whether Wilde's volume should be accepted, it was rejected (see *More Letters* 36n2). Wilde informed the Society's librarian: "My chief regret indeed [is] that there should still be at Oxford such a large number of young men who are ready to accept their own ignorance as an index, and their own conceit as a criterion of any imaginative and beautiful work" (*More Letters* 36).

Wilde asked the Cambridge University don Oscar Browning, with whom he was on very friendly terms, to review the book: "Books so often fall into stupid and illiterate hands that I am anxious to be really criticised: ignorant praise or ignorant blame is so insulting" (*Letters* 77). Browning's review in the *Academy* (30 July 1881) calls the poems "the product of a fresh, vigorous mind, dowered with a quick perception of the beauties of nature, with a command of varied and musical language...." Concluding, Browning remarks: "...we lay down this book in the conviction that England is enriched with a new poet" (rpt. in Beckson).

In America, during Wilde's lecture tour, the reviews were often similar in tone to those in Britain. In the Boston *Women's Journal* (4 Feb. 1882), the prolific author, social reformer, and champion of women's suffrage T. W. Higginson remarked on the "unmanly" quality of the verse:

> Women are as distinctively recognized as the guardians of the public purity as are the clergy of the public morals. Yet when a young man comes among us whose only distinction is that he has written a thin volume of very mediocre verse, and that he makes himself something very like a buffoon for notoriety and money, women of high social position receive him at their houses and invite guests to meet him.... We have perhaps rashly claimed that the influence of women has purified English literature. When the poems of Wilde and Whitman lie in ladies' boudoirs, I see no evidence of the improvement. (rpt. in Beckson)

The journalist and author Ambrose Bierce unleashed an amusing attack on Wilde as "that sovereign of insufferables" in an unsigned column titled "Prattle" in the San Francisco *Wasp* (31 March 1882), which reveals a widespread attitude towards Wilde and his *Poems*:

> ...this gawky gowk has the divine effrontery to link his name with those of Swinburne, Rossetti and Morris – this dunghill he-hen would fly with eagles. He dares to set his tongue to the honored name of Keats. He is the leader, quota'a, of a *renaissance* in art, this man who cannot draw – of a revival in letters, this man who cannot write! This littlest and looniest of a brotherhood of simpletons,

whom the wicked wits of London, haling him dazed from his obscurity, have crowned and crucified as King of the Cranks, has accepted the distinction in stupid good faith and our foolish people take him at his word. (rpt. in Beckson)

The Chicago *Dial* (August 1881), however, called Wilde's poems "remarkable," adding: "...there is something in this young man from Dublin not discovered by the caricaturist of *Punch*...if we are to have more of this Aesthete's philosophy it is desirable by all means to have it in the form of his poetry" (rpt. in Beckson).

Manuscript: The Huntington Library has a MS. title page and an epigraph intended for but not used in *Poems*; on the title page, a statement in Wilde's hand appears: "mes premiers vers sont d'un enfant, mes seconds d'un adolescent" (see Mason 285); the next page contains a quotation from Keats's letter to his friend, the author John Hamilton Reynolds (9 April 1818): "I have not the slightest feel[ing] of humility towards the Public – or to anything in existence – but the eternal Being, the Principle of Beauty, and the Memory of great Men."

References: Averil Gardner, "'Literary Petty Larceny': Plagiarism in Oscar Wilde's Early Poetry," *English Studies in Canada* (March 1982); Jerome H. Buckley, "Echo and Artifice: The Poetry of Oscar Wilde," *Victorian Poetry* (Autumn/Winter 1990); Merlin Holland, "Plagiarist, or Pioneer?" *Rediscovering Oscar Wilde*, ed. C. George Sandulescu (1994).

POEMS (1892)

Published: 26 May 1892 by Elkin Mathews and John Lane, the Bodley Head. This was an "author's edition" of the remaining 220 copies of the fifth edition of *Poems* (1882), issued by David Bogue (who had gone bankrupt). Charles Ricketts provided a new title page. In all other respects, the fifth edition and this Bodley Head edition are identical.

POEMS (1908): *See COLLECTED EDITION*

"POEMS IN PROSE"

Published: *Fortnightly Review* 54 (July 1894): 22-29. Of the six "poems in prose" ("The Artist," "The Doer of Good," "The Disciple," "The Master," "The House of Judgment," and "The Teacher of Wisdom"), two had been previously published, in somewhat different versions, in the *Spirit Lamp*: "The House of Judgment" (Vol. 3, 17 Feb. 1893) and "The Disciple" (Vol. 4, 6 June 1893). All six were reprinted in *Lord Arthur Savile's Crime and Other Prose Pieces* (1908).

The prose poem, which utilizes certain poetic devices, such as highly figurative expression and intense rhythms but without conventional stanzaic or metrical patterns, has been called an "oxymoron" and "a hyphenated transgeneric form." Vista Clayton has traced its beginnings in France as a new literary form to the early 18th century, when "revolutionaries" attacked the neo-classical rules governing the various genres; the result was an increasing focus on the prose poem by such writers as Montesquieu, Rousseau, and, in the 19th century, by Chateaubriand and Baudelaire, who, in his *Petit poèmes en prose* (1849), acknowledges Bertrand's *Gaspard de la nuit* (1842) as a significant work in the development of the genre. The English poets, of course, had their own sources of inspiration, such as the evocative King James translation of the Bible and Blake's ironic prose poem, *The Marriage of Heaven and Hell* (1792).

Utilizing an allegorical, pseudo-biblical style, Wilde portrays in "The Artist" the creative desire "to fashion an image of *The Pleasure that abideth for a Moment*," not merely to provide a transient pleasure but a permanent, enduring work out of bronze, a paradox inherent in any work of art. The only bronze the Artist can find in the world is that which he had used in fashioning an image of *The Sorrow that endureth for Ever*, which he had set "on the tomb of the one thing he had loved in life." From this bronze, he fashions in the "great furnace" an image of *The Pleasure that abideth for a Moment*: furnace and fire are thus the symbolic instruments of the creative imagination. In *De Profundus*, Wilde cites this poem in prose as one of several works that "foreshadowed and prefigured...the note of Doom" in his life *(Letters* 475-76).

"The Doer of Good" is the story of Jesus's encounter with those recipients of his miraculous cures or forgiveness who now live for pleasure and sin. He finally comes upon a young man, who tells him why he is weeping: "...I was dead once and you raised me from the dead. What else should I do but weep?" Thus, those who ostensibly bene-

fitted from Jesus's miraculous powers ironically charge him with creating their sorrows. As a result, acts of charity may be futile, unlike the outcome in "The Happy Prince." A more trenchant observation is expressed by Gilbert in "The Critic as Artist," Part I: "It is well for his peace that the saint goes to his martyrdom. He is spared the sight of the horror of his harvest."

In "The Disciple," the pool that Narcissus had gazed into until he died has turned from a cup of sweet waters into a cup of salt tears. The Oreads come to give comfort to the pool, which, unaware of Narcissus's beauty, has its own narcissistic preoccupation: "...I loved Narcissus because, as he lay on my banks and looked down at me, in the mirror of his eyes I saw ever my own beauty mirrored." Thus, Wilde achieves an ironic effect by reversing the myth. As Willoughby remarks, "selfish motives...often lie behind discipleship" and "it is often oneself, the parable implies, that one is really admiring in the act of worship...(96)."

Joseph of Arimathea, in "The Master," encounters a young man weeping in the Valley of Desolation. He has "wounded his body with thorns and on his hair had he set ashes as a crown": "It is not for Him that I am weeping, but for myself," he tells Joseph, for he has performed miracles similar to those by Jesus. "And yet they have not crucified me." The "Master," therefore, is not Jesus but the young man, who, filled with pride, regrets that he has not been exalted by being crucified. Wilde's parable "inscribes, in short, a misunderstanding of the genuine requirements of Christian imitation. Real discipleship involves imagination, selflessness, and courage; false discipleship...is characterized by self-gratification, like that of the pool" in "The Disciple" (Willoughby 97).

When Man comes naked before God in "The House of Judgment," he is confronted with a litany of his evil life. But when God tells him that he will go into Hell, Man responds that God cannot do that "because in Hell have I always lived," for hedonism and selfishness have plunged him into despair. When God tells him that he will be sent to Heaven, Man responds that He cannot send him "because never, and in no place, have I been able to imagine it."

Isobel Murray (635) suggests a partial source for this poem in prose from a legend in Lady Wilde's *Ancient Legends, Mystic Charms, and Superstitions of Ireland* (1887; rpt. 1925). In "The Priest's

Soul," the priest, filled with pride, argues "that there was no Purgatory, and then, no Hell, and then no Heaven, and then no God." When an angel informs him that his death is imminent, the priest pleads to be sent to Heaven, or at least Purgatory; the angel responds: "You must go straight to Hell." But the priest retorts: "I denied Hell also, so you can't send me there either" (34-5).

"The Teacher of Wisdom" tells the story of a religious teacher's sorrow despite his success in winning converts and disciples, for "he had given to others the perfect knowledge of God...and his faith was leaving him by reason of the number of those who believed in him." He becomes a hermit when his disciples turn from him because he will not speak of God. When he saves a robber from sin by imparting to him his knowledge of God, the Hermit falls upon the ground and weeps, but Jesus raises him up and says: "Before this time thou hadst the perfect knowledge of God. Now thou shalt have the perfect love of God."

Manuscript: Princeton has an incomplete MS. of "The Master."

References: Vista Clayton, *The Prose Poem in French Literature of the Eighteenth Century* (1936); *Oscar Wilde*, ed. Isobel Murray (1989); Guy Willoughby, "The *Poems in Prose*," *Art and Christhood: The Aesthetics of Oscar Wilde* (1993).

"THE POET": *See ECHOES*

"POETICAL SOCIALISTS"
Published: *PMG*, 15 Feb. 1889, 3; rpt. in *Reviews* (1908). An unsigned review of Edward Carpenter, ed., *Chants of Labour: A Song-Book of the People* (1889) with designs by Walter Crane.

Wilde recalls that Stopford Brooke (a one-time clergyman within the Church of England who became a Unitarian minister after he rejected the miracles sanctioned by the established Church) said that Socialism and the socialistic spirit "would give our poets nobler and loftier themes for song, would widen their sympathies and enlarge the horizon of their vision, and would touch with the fire and fervour of a new faith lips that had else been silent, hearts that but for this fresh gospel had been cold." Whether art gains from contemporary events Wilde is not certain, but certainly Socialism, he acknowledges, "starts well equipped," for she has her poets and painters as well as orators and clever writers: "If she fails it will not be for

lack of expression. If she succeeds, her triumph will not be a mere triumph of brute force."

Wilde notes the "curious variety" of occupations held by the contributors to Carpenter's volume, the "wide differences of social position that exist between them, and the strange medley of men whom a common passion has for the moment united" (a draper, a porter, two late Eton masters, two bootmakers, an ex-Lord Mayor of Dublin, a steel worker, an authoress, among others). "And when we mention that Mr. William Morris is one of the singers and that Mr. Walter Crane has designed the cover and frontispiece of the book, we cannot but feel that...Socialism starts well-equipped."

As for the songs in the volume, Carpenter refers to some of them in his preface as "purely revolutionary; others are Christian in tone; there are some that might be called merely material in their tendency, while many are of a highly ideal and visionary character." To this, Wilde comments that such a varied selection is promising:

It shows that Socialism is not going to allow herself to be trammelled by any hard-and-fast creed, or to be stereotyped into an iron formula.... She has the attraction of a wonderful personality, and touches the heart of one and the brain of another, and draws this man by his hatred of injustice, and his neighbour by his faith in the future, and a third, it may be, by his love of art, or by his wild worship of a lost and buried past. And all of this is well. For to make men Socialists is nothing, but to make Socialism human is a great thing.

The poems that have been set to music, however, are not of "any very high literary value": "They are rough, direct, and vigorous, and the tunes are stirring and familiar. Indeed, almost any mob could warble them with ease."

"POETRY AND PRISON"
Published: *PMG*, 3 Jan. 1889, 3; rpt. in *Reviews* (1908). Unsigned review of Wilfrid Blunt's *In Vinculis* (1889). Wilde's review of Andrew Lang's *Grass of Parnassus: Rhymes of Old and New* (1888), which also appeared under the heading of "Poetry and Prison," was, says Mason, "inadvertently omitted in Methuen's volume of *Reviews*, 1908, and is here [that is, in Mason's bibliography]

reprinted for the first time" (157–59).

Blunt, a supporter of Irish nationalism, was imprisoned for two months, the experience having had, says Wilde, "an admirable effect" on him as a poet. His latest book "stirs one by its fine sincerity of purpose, its lofty and impassioned thought, its depth and ardour of intense feeling." In his preface, Blunt states: "Imprisonment is a reality of discipline most useful to the modern soul, lapped as it is in physical sloth and self-indulgence. Like a sickness or a spiritual retreat it purifies and ennobles; and the soul emerges from it strong and more self-contained."

The opening sonnets, composed in Galway prison, are "full of things nobly conceived and nobly uttered...intensely personal in expression." Wilde quotes from a "very fine" sonnet: "A prison is a convent without God – / Poverty, Chastity, Obedience / Its precepts are...." By sending Blunt to gaol, Arthur Balfour (Chief Secretary of Ireland) "has converted a clever rhymer into an earnest and deep-thinking poet. The narrow confines of the prison-cell seem to suit the sonnet's 'scanty plot of ground,' and an unjust imprisonment for a noble cause strengthens as well as deepens the nature."

In his review of Lang's *Grass of Parnassus*, Wilde begins facetiously: "Whether or not Mr. Andrew Lang should be sent to prison is another matter. We are inclined to think that he should not, except as a punishment for writing sonnets to Mr. Rider Haggard. His gay pleasant Muse, with her dainty if somewhat facile graces, her exquisite triviality, and her winsome irresponsible manner, would probably gain very little from such a dreary exile." Prison, says Wilde, is for "souls stronger than the soul revealed to us in the charming whisperings and musical echoes of the 'Grass of Parnassus.'" Nevertheless, Wilde writes, this is a "very fascinating little volume, in its way, and possesses many delicately-carved 'ivories of speech,' to borrow one of Mr. Pater's phrases." Though the translation of Rémy Belleau's poem on April is excellent, Wilde is less enthusiastic over Lang's own verse. Such a volume should not have been published in winter: "It is made for summer. On a lazy June evening no more delightful companion could be found than a poet who has the sweetest of voices and absolutely nothing to say."

"POETRY OF THE PEOPLE"

Published: *PMG*, 13 May 1886, 5; rpt. in *Reviews* (1908). An unsigned review of Countess Evelyn Martinengo-Cesaresco's *Essays in the Study of Folk-Songs* (1886).

Because folklore is often studied from the point of view of comparative mythology, Wilde welcomes this "delightful" book that deals with the subject "simply as literature." The folk-tale is "the father of all fiction, as the Folk-song is the mother of all poetry, and in the games, the tales, and the ballads of primitive people it is easy to see the germs of such perfected forms of art as the drama, the novel, and the epic." Though "the highest expression of life" is not to be found in "popular songs however poetical of any nation but in the great masterpieces of self-conscious Art," it is sometimes pleasant "to leave the summit of Parnassus to look at the wild flowers in the valley, and to turn from the lyre of Apollo to listen to the reed of Pan."

Folk songs, Wilde says, are still to be heard: "The Sicilian shepherd has not yet thrown his pipe aside, and the children of modern Greece sing the swallow-song through the villages in springtime...." This popular poetry is highly imaginative, taking its inspiration from nature and abounding in "realistic metaphor and in picturesque and fantastic imagery." Occasionally, in the poems in the extreme South "one meets with a curious crudity of realism, but as a rule the sense of beauty prevails." Quoting songs from Corsica and Roumania ("Gold and pearls my vessel lade" and "Sleep my daughter, sleep an hour"), Wilde remarks that "we hardly know what poems are sung to English babies, but we hope they are as beautiful as these two. Blake might have written them."

"THE POETS AND THE PEOPLE"

Published: *PMG*, 17 Feb. 1887, 4; rpt. in Mason 146–48 (uncollected in *Reviews*, 1908). An anonymous article signed "By One of the Latter." Wilde took the opportunity to publish this commentary on the utilitarian value of poetry. The *Pall Mall Gazette*, a paper edited by the Radical W. T. Stead, would presumably be opposed to art for art's sake.

Wilde recognizes the need, at this time "in our national history" for the "creation of a spirit of enthusiasm among all classes of society, inspiring men and women with that social zeal and the spirit of self-sacrifice which can save a great people in the throes of national misfortune." He alludes to "tirades of pessimism" that require "little intellectual effort." To inspire people with "hope and courage, to fill them with a desire after righteousness and duty" requires intelligence and feeling. In what would be expected of a Victorian reformer rather than a fin-de-siècle Decadent, Wilde asks a burning question: "Who, in the midst of all our poverty and distress, that threatens to become intensified, will step into the breach and rouse us to the almost superhuman effort that is necessary to alter the existing state of things?"

Before Wilde would attend a meeting of the Fabian Society at the invitation of Bernard Shaw in 1888 and subsequently write his essay on "The Soul of Man under Socialism" (1891), his reformist zeal was manifest in this article, which calls upon the poets to provide the inspiration that he mentions at the beginning:

When the poor are suffering from inherent faults of their own, and the greediness of capitalists, and both are in danger of suffering still more from causes over which they have but partial control, surely the hour has come when the poets should exercise their influence for good, and set fairer ideals before all than the mere love of wealth and ostentatious display on one side and the desire to appropriate wealth on the other.

But, says Wilde, the "inspiring ode or ballad" is not heard that reaches the "hearts of the people or touches the consciences of capitalists." When the need of "a truly great poet" is required "in this hour of national trial," none is found in the columns of newspapers. One (here Wilde alludes to Tennyson's *Locksley Hall Sixty Years After*, 1886) "gives us a strong melancholy pessimism that has achieved no higher results than increasing the poet's fortune...."

Another (Swinburne in "The Commonweal: A Song for Unionists" in the *Times*, 1 July 1886, which attacks the Irish on their agitation for Home Rule), "who has hitherto posed as the poet of freedom, and even licence – some would say licentiousness – when he does turn his attention to practical affairs does his best to abuse and dishearten a nation that is heroically struggling against the injustice of centuries and panting for national freedom."

And what, queries Wilde, "shall be said of the conduct of one who in the eyes of many is esteemed the greatest of living poets [that is, Browning]? He, at the hour when his country requires inspiration and encouragement, prostitutes his intelligence to the production of a number of unwieldy lines that to the vast majority of Englishmen are unintelligible jargon." Wilde condemns Browning for his lack of music and for a lack of "simple language that the people can understand." Indeed, even "the efforts of a society of intellectual pickaxes cannot discover what his words really mean." Since Browning is living in the 19th century, he has, says Wilde, no excuse for "banging his intellectual tin kettle while a fourth part of his fellow-countrymen are struggling against poverty, and are weighed down by the gloomy outlook towards the future." His recent poetry has no passage that can "stir the pulses of any man or women, or create a desire to lead a higher, a holier, and a more useful life in the breast of the indifferent average citizen."

The struggle to survive is such that "all that is idealistic and beautiful" is in danger of being "crushed out of us by the steam engine and the manipulations of the Stock Exchanges." Focusing again on Browning, Wilde asks whether anything can "induce him to make an earnest endeavour to help the people out of their difficulties and to make their duty plain." Though he may be "a man of genius," for whom the language of the common people is inadequate for his thoughts, the humblest writer in the poets' corner of a provincial paper, "who is aiming in his own honest way to set his fellows straight," has a greater right to the title of "poet."

Wilde concludes this extraordinary essay (radically different from the essays that he will soon publish and become part of his *Intentions*, a volume arguing that art is autonomous): "The people are suffering, and are likely to suffer more; where is the poet who is the one man needful to rouse the nation to a sense of duty and inspire the people with hope?"

"THE POETS' CORNER"

Published: *PMG*, 27 27 Sept. 1886, 5; rpt. in *Reviews* (1908). Unsigned reviews of *Low Down: Wayside Thoughts in Ballad and Other Verse* by "Two Tramps" (identities unknown) and H.C.

Irwin's *Rhymes and Renderings*, both published in 1886.

Wilde begins with the observation: "Among the social problems of the nineteenth century the tramp has always held an important position, but his appearance among the nineteenth-century poets is extremely remarkable." The tramp's "mode of life" is not, however, "at all unsuited to the development of the poetic faculty," for he presumably possesses "that freedom of mood which is so essential to the artist...." *Low Down* has "every fantastic variation of type, and the pages range in colour from blue to brown, from grey to sage green, and from rose pint to chrome yellow...." The poetry by the "Two Tramps," however, is disappointing, for it reveals instances of plagiarism: "From highway robbery and crimes of violence, one sinks gradually to literary petty larceny.... On the whole, the volume, if it is not quite worth reading, is at least worth looking at."

Irwin's verse, on the other hand, "finds music for every mood, and form for every feeling." Despite the fact that Irwin is a "fervent admirer" of Matthew Arnold, he is "in no sense of the word a plagiarist. Throughout the volume, Henry Crossly Irwin, of the Bengal Civil Service, provides "good work": "...the descriptions of Indian scenery are excellent...and [the] monstrous beasts, strange flowers and fantastic birds are used with much subtlety for the production of artistic effect."

"THE POETS' CORNER"

Published: *PMG*, 8 March 1887, 5; rpt. in *Reviews* (1908). Unsigned reviews.

Wilde begins with his characteristic facetiousness (and his determination to consign mediocre works to oblivion) by recalling that "a little schoolboy was once asked to explain the difference between prose and poetry. After some consideration, he replied, 'blue violets' is prose, and 'violets blue' is poetry. The distinction, we admit, is not exhaustive, but it seems to be one that is extremely popular with our minor poets." Wilde cites examples from Elise Cooper's *The Queen's Innocent, with Other Poems* (1886) of such "unnecessary and awkward inversions." The most delightful poem in the whole volume, he concludes hastily, is "a little lyric called 'April,' which is like a picture set to music."

Constance E. Dixon's *The Chimneypiece of Bruges and Other Poems* (1886), its title poem a narrative in blank verse, tells the story of a young artist unjustly convicted of his wife's murder. On the prison's chimneypiece, he spends his life carving the story of his love and suffering: "There are some pretty things in the book, and a poet without hysterics is rare." Dawson Burns's *Oliver Cromwell* (1887) is "a pleasant panegyric on the Protector, and reads like a prize poem by a nice sixth-form boy."

The Circle of Saints (1886) by "K.E.V." (who remains unidentified) contains a series of poems on the saints, each poem prefaced by a brief biography. Though it "does not display much poetic power,...it is a thoroughly well-intentioned book and eminently suitable for invalids." Edward Foskett's *Poems* (1886) is "very serious and deliberate." He has apparently "forgotten to insert the rhymes in his sonnet to Wordsworth; but, as he tells us elsewhere that 'Poesy is uninspired by Art,' perhaps he is only heralding a new and formless form." Wilde then quickly disposes of John Thomas Barker's *The Pilgrimage of Memory* (1886), which "suffers a good deal by being printed as poetry, and Mr. Barker should republish it at once as a prose work."

In *Errata* (1886), G. Gladstone Turner, remarks Wilde, "believes that we are on the verge of a great social cataclysm, and warns us that our *cradles* are even now being rocked by *slumbering volcanoes*!" We hope that there is no truth in this statement, and that it is merely a startling metaphor introduced for the sake of effect, for elsewhere in the volume there is a great deal of beauty which we should be sorry to think was doomed to immediate extinction." J.M.W. Schwartz's *Nivalis* (1886), a five-act tragedy in blank verse, evokes Wilde's remark that "most plays that are written to be read, not to be acted, miss that condensation and directness of expression which is one of the secrets of true dramatic diction, and Mr. Schwartz's tragedy is consequently somewhat verbose. Still it is full of fine lines and noble scenes."

"THE POETS' CORNER"

Published: *PMG*, 30 May 1887, 5; rpt. in *Reviews* (1908). Unsigned reviews.

Wilde refers to *The Discovery and Other Poems* (1886) by "Glenessa" – who remains unidentified – as the author's "most ambitious work," a poetic drama about the Garden of Eden. Though the subject, says Wilde, is "undoubtedly interesting," the "execution can hardly be said to be quite worthy of it." Wilde quotes some inane dialogue between Adam and Eve, which seems "to belong rather to the sphere of comedy than to that of serious verse." Impatiently, Wilde proceeds to Edwin Ellis Griffin's *Vortigern and Rowena: A Dramatic Cantata* (1887), a work about the Britons and Danes: "It is charmingly printed, and as a libretto for music quite above the average."

Wilde devotes slightly more space to the next work, *The Poems of Madame de la Mothe Guyon*, ed. Rev. A. Saunders Dyer (1887): "As truly religious are resigned to everything, even to mediocre poetry, there is no reason at all why Mme. Guyon's verses should not be popular with a large section of the community." The editor has added a "pleasing preface about this seventeenth-century saint whose life was her best, indeed her only true, poem."

J. Pierce, Wilde moves on, "has discovered a tenth muse [in his *Stanzas and Sonnets*, 1887], and writes impassioned verses to the Goddess of Chess...." Pierce does, however, have other subjects. In turning to the next book under review, Wilde refers to its author, Clifford Harrison, who is "well known as the most poetic of all our reciters, but as a writer himself of poetry he is not so famous." His *In Hours of Leisure* (1887) "contains some charming pieces," though his rhymes are not always felicitous: "Those who have Keats' genius may borrow Keats' cockneyisms, but from minor poets we have a right to expect some regard to the ordinary technique of verse." When Harrison writes about nature, "he is certainly pleasing and picturesque, but as a rule he is over-anxious about himself...."

The next volume, *AEonial* (1885), published anonymously by John Nott Peykenott, evokes Wilde's facetiousness: "The daily increasing class of readers who like unintelligible poetry should study 'AEonial.'" Its qualities include the "very fantastic, very daring, crowded with strange metaphor and clouded by monstrous imagery....he hardly realizes that an artist should be articulate." Wilde briefly disposes of James Ross's *Seymour's Inheritance* (1885) as "a short novel in blank verse.... On the whole it is very harmless both in manner and matter...." Unlike Ross's work, E.H. Brodie's *Lyrics of the Sea* (1887) "are spirited and manly, and show a certain freedom of rhythmical movement, pleasant in days of wooden verse."

"THE POETS' CORNER"

Published: *PMG*, 20 Jan. 1888, 3; rpt. in *Reviews* (1908). Unsigned reviews.

Wilde recalls that a "cynical critic once remarked that no great poet is intelligible, and no little poet worth understanding, but that otherwise poetry is an admirable thing. This, however, seems to us a somewhat harsh view of the subject. Little poets are an extremely interesting study. The best of them have often some new beauty to show us, and though the worst of them may bore, yet they rarely brutalize." Turning to the first of the works under review, Rev. Frederick Langbridge's *Poor Folks' Lives* (1887), Wilde decides that it is a volume "that could do no possible harm to anyone." Displaying a "healthy, rollicking...tone of feeling, an almost unbounded regard for the converted drunkard," these poems also reveal "a strong sympathy with the sufferings of the poor."

Those, however, who prefer "pseudo-poetical prose to really prosaic poetry will wish that Mr. [George] Dalziel had converted most of his [poems in *Pictures in the Fire*, 1886] into leaders for the *Daily Telegraph*...." In F. Harald Williams's *Women Must Weep* (1887), the first poem vigorously attacks those "wicked and misguided people who believe that Beauty is its own reason for existing, and that Art should have no other aim but her own perfection":

Why do they patch, in their fatal choice,
    When at secrets such the angels quake,
But a play of the Vision and the Voice? –
    Oh, it's all for Art's sake.

Wilde concludes: "...we cannot but think that Professor Harald Williams is happier in his criticism of life than he is in his art criticism."

Alexander Buchan's blank verse drama, *Joseph and His Brothers* (1887), "may be said to possess all the fatal originality of inexperience." Because Buchan has attempted, as he said, to put the "language of real life into the mouths of the speakers," the central characters are, says Wilde, tedious, and the Chorus of Ancients is much worse. These "ideal spectators" spend their time uttering solemn platitudes "that with the aged pass for wisdom." Concludes Wilde: "It is a curious thing that when minor poets write choruses to a play they should always consider it necessary to adopt the style and language of a bad translation."

Wilde moves on to *God's Garden* (1887) by "Heartsease" (who remains unidentified), a "well-meaning attempt to use nature for theological and educational purposes. It belongs to that antiquated school of thought that, in spite of the discoveries of modern science, invites the sluggard to look at the ant, and the idle to imitate the bee." The worst thing, says Wilde, that "man can make of Nature is to turn her into a mirror for his own vices...." Wilde presses on with Cyrus Thornton's *Voices of the Street* (1887), the title of which puzzles him. In this volume, the verse is "graceful and melodious, and some of his lines...have a pleasant Tennysonian ring," as in: "And the wise old Roman bondsman saw no terror in the dead – / Children when the play was over, going softly home to bed."

Mrs. Horace Dobell, having published sixteen volumes of poetry and determined to publish two more, declares that she composed most of the poems "in the neighbourhood of the sea, between the hours of ten and two o'clock." If so, Wilde ruminates, this seems to have been a disadvantage for the purpose of inspiration, as the illustrative lines from *In the Watches of the Night* (1887) indicate:

Were Anthony Trollope and George Eliot
Alive – which unfortunately they are not –
As regards the subject of "quack-snubbing,"
   you know,
To support me I am sure they hadn't been
   slow –

"THE POETS' CORNER"

Published: *PMG*, 15 Feb. 1888, 2–3; rpt. in *Reviews* (1908). Unsigned reviews.

J. C. Heywood's *Salome* (1887) "seems to have thrilled the critics of the United States," but, Wilde comments, "the best that one can say of it is that it is a triumph of conscientious industry. From an artistic point of view, it is a very commonplace production indeed, and we must protest against such blank verse as the following":

From the hour I saw her first, I was entranced,
Or embosomed in a charmed world,
   circumscribed
By its proper circumambient atmosphere,
Herself its centre, and wide pervading spirit.

Wilde proceeds quickly to William Griffiths's

Sonnets and Other Poems (1887), the poems of which are "very simple," a good thing but since they are sentimental, "not quite so good." His verse is "full of pretty echoes of other writers, but in one sonnet he makes a distinct attempt to be original, and the result is extremely depressing": "Earth wears her gaudiest robe, by autumn spun, / Like some stout matron who of youth has run / The course...."

In turning to Francis Prevost's *Fires of Green Wood* (1887), Wilde observes that imitators of Browning "are, unfortunately, common enough, but imitators of Mr. and Mrs. Browning combined are so very rare that we have read [Prevost] with great interest." Despite "ingenious caricatures" of Mrs. Browning's "Aurora Leigh" and Mr. Browning's poems, "there are some good poems, or perhaps we should say some good passages in Mr. Prevost's volume." Concludes Wilde: "We have no doubt that some day Mr. Prevost will be able to study the great masters without stealing from them" (an odd remark in view of Wilde's own borrowings in his early verse).

John Cameron Grant, Wilde tells us, has christened himself "England's Empire Poet" and "lest we should have doubts upon the subject, tells us that he 'dare not lie,' a statement which in a poet seems to show a great want of courage." Wilde quotes lines from Grant's *Vauclin and Other Verses* (1887) that "would thrill any Tory tea-party in the provinces": "Ask the ruined Sugar-worker if he loves the foreign beet – / Rather, one can hear him answer, would I see my children eat – " The hymn to the Union Jack, Wilde continues, "would make a capital leaflet for distribution in boroughs where the science of heraldry is absolutely unknown, and the sonnet on Mr. Gladstone is sure to be popular with all who admire violence and vulgarity in literature."

Regarding W. Evans's *Caesar Borgia* (1888), Wilde pronounces it "a very tedious tragedy." The other poems in the volume are "comparatively harmless, though it is sad to find Shakespeare's "Bacchus with pink eyne" reappearing as "pinky-eyed Silenus." Moving rapidly, Wilde turns to the anonymous volume *The Cross and the Grail* (1887), which, compared to "real poetry," contains verses that are "'as water unto wine,' but no doubt this was the effect intended." The illustrations, he remarks, are "quite dreadful, especially one of an angel appearing to a young man from Chicago who seems to be drinking brown sherry."

Juvenal in Piccadilly (1888) by "Oxoniensis" and *The Excellent Mystery: A Matrimonial Satire* (1887) by Lord Pimlico are "two fierce social satires, and, like most satires, they are the product of the corruption they pillory." The first enables readers to fill in the names of the victims: "Must _____bluster, _____ give the lie, / _____wear the night out, _____ sneer!" The other volume is "much better. It is full of clever epigrammatic lines, and its wit fully atones for its bitterness."

In the final volume, James Aitchison's *The Chronicle of Mites* (1887) is a mock-heroic poem depicting the inhabitants of a decaying cheese "who speculate about the origin of their species and hold learned discussions upon the meaning of Evolution." Wilde calls this "cheese-epic" a rather "unsavoury production" and unleashes a barb that has been widely quoted: "...the style is, at times, so monstrous and so realistic that the author should be called the Gorgon-Zola of literature" (Wilde's pun on the famous blue cheese from the Italian town of Gorgonzola, near Milan, by combining the monstrous Gorgon of Greek myth with Zola, the "realistic" novelist).

"THE POETS' CORNER"

Published: *PMG*, 6 April 1888, 3; rpt. in *Reviews* (1908). Unsigned reviews.

Alfred Hayes's *David Westren* (1888), a narrative poem in Tennysonian blank verse, is "a sort of serious novel set to music," writes Wilde. "Somewhat lacking in actuality," its picturesque style contributes to this effect, "lending the story beauty but robbing it of truth. Still it is not without power...." The hero is a young clergyman of the "muscular Christian school." But eventually like Job, "he cries out against the injustice of things, and his own personal sorrow makes him realise the sorrow and misery of the world.... Mr. Hayes states the problem of life well, but his solution is sadly inadequate...": the clergyman is left "preaching platitudes to a village congregation."

Rennell Rodd, a former friend of Wilde, had broken with him over the publication of a book of verse in 1882: see entry on Rodd for Wilde's judgment of *The Unknown Madonna and Other Poems* (1888). James Ross's "The Wind" in *The Wind and Six Sonnets* (1888) is "a rather gusty ode, written apparently without any definite

scheme of metre, and not very impressive, as it lacks both the strength of the blizzard, and the sweetness of Zephyr." Moving onwards, Wilde turns to Isaac Sharp's *Saul of Tarsus* (1888), in some respects, says Wilde, a "fine poem," as illustrated by "two strong, simple verses": "Saul of Tarsus, silently, / With a silent company, / To Damascus' gates drew nigh...." The spirit of the entire poem is "dignified and stately. The rest of the volume, however, is disappointing."

George Mackenzie's *Highland Daydreams* (1887), on the other hand, "could not possibly offend any one." Though rather "old-fashioned," such is usually the case "with natural spontaneous verse. It takes a great artist to be thoroughly modern. Nature is always a little behind the age." Charles Nash's *The Story of the Cross* (1888) versifies the Gospel narratives, revealing the poet, as he says of himself, as "a humble soldier in the army of Faith." Though Nash hopes that his volume may "invigorate devotional feeling especially among the young," Wilde responds by doubting that readers of any age could admire paraphrases of biblical passages. Wilde concludes that the "worst work is always done with the best intentions, and that people are never so trivial as when they take themselves very seriously."

"THE POETS' CORNER"

Published: *PMG*, 24 Oct. 1888, 5; rpt. in *Reviews* (1908). Unsigned reviews of books published in 1888.

Wilde regards Ian Hamilton's title poem in *The Ballad of Hádji and Other Poems*, about a "wonderful Arab horse that a reckless hunter rides to death in the pursuit of a wild boar," as "undeniably clever." There are, however, throughout the volume curious mixtures of good and bad passages. To say, Wilde remarks, that the sun kisses the earth "'with flame-moustachoed lip' is awkward and uncouth, and yet the poem in which the expression occurs has some pretty lines.... Pruning, whether in the garden or in the study, is a most healthy and useful employment."

Charles Catty's *Poems in the Modern Spirit* is dedicated to the memory of Wordsworth, Shelley, Coleridge, and Keats – "a somewhat pompous signboard," says Wilde, "for such very ordinary wine." As for "The Secret of Content," Wilde concludes that Catty has written "a very tedious blank verse poem...but which certainly does not convey that secret to the reader. It is heavy, abstract, and prosaic, and shows how intolerably dull a man can be who has the best intentions, and the most earnest beliefs." When, however, Catty "does not take himself quite so seriously, there are some rather pleasing things."

Turning to John Todhunter's title poem in *The Banshee and Other Poems*, Wilde remarks that "part of his poem reads like a translation of an old Bardic song, part of it like rough material for poetry, and part of it like misshapen prose. It is an interesting specimen of poetic writing, but it is not a perfected work of art. It is amorphous and inchoate...." Wilde, insisting that "rhyme gives architecture as well as melody to song," quotes a passage without rhyme but with archeological interest, though with "no artistic value at all." The few brief poems at the end of the volume, however, "are worth all the ambitious pseudo-epics that Mr. Todhunter has tried to construct out of Celtic lore."

According to the preface written by Professor Thomas Danleigh for *Poems of the Plains and Songs of the Solitudes*, Thomas Brower Peacock, an American poet, is "entitled to be called the Laureate of the West." The preface, Wilde remarks facetiously, is "the most amusing part of the book, but the poems also are worth studying." The opening lines of "The Vendetta," for example, deserve mention: "When stars are glowing through day's gloaming glow, / Reflecting from ocean's deep, mighty flow, / At twilight...." The first line, says Wilde, is "certainly a masterpiece, and indeed the whole volume is full of gems of this kind."

In *Holiday Recreations and Other Poems*, Alexander Skene Smith has a "placid, pleasant way of writing, and indeed his verses cannot do any harm, though he really should not publish such attempts at metrical versions of the Psalms [from *The Book of Common Prayer*]. According to Wilde, the late George Morine once wrote to a friend: "I study Poetry simply as a fine art by which I may exercise my intellect and purify and elevate my taste." His *Poems* contains "the record of his quiet literary life." The poems are "often distinguished by a grave and chastened beauty of style, and their solemn cadences have something of the 'grand manner' about them.... We hope that this little book will meet with the recognition that it deserves."

"THE POETS' CORNER"

Published: *PMG*, 16 Nov. 1888, 2–3; rpt. in *Reviews* (1908). Unsigned reviews of books published in 1888.

Wilde begins his reviews with the observation that "a few years ago some of our minor poets tried to set Science to Music, to write sonnets on the survival of the fittest, and odes to Natural Selection. Socialism, and the sympathy with those who are unfit, seem, if we can judge from Miss [Edith] Nesbit's remarkable volume [*Lays and Legends*], to be the new themes of song, the fresh subject-matter for poetry." The change, Wilde remarks, has advantages: "Scientific laws are at once too abstract and too clearly defined, and even the visible arts have not yet been able to translate into any symbols of beauty the discoveries of modern science."

The etchers and painters find in poverty and misery suitable subjects, and poets have "admirable opportunities of drawing vivid and dramatic contrasts between the purple of the rich and the rags of the poor." From Nesbit's volume "comes not merely the voice of sympathy, but also the cry of revolution" (Nesbit was a member of the Fabian Society, which did not advocate such radical tactics): "The graves we will dig for our tyrants we bore with too much and too long." Wilde, however, prefers her "gentler moods" and her "delicate ear for music."

The popular American poet David Foster, says Wilde, "has read Hawthorne, which is wise of him, and imitated Longfellow, which is not quite so commendable." His "Rebecca the Witch" in *Rebecca the Witch and Other Tales*, a story of colonial Salem, is written in the metre of "Hiawatha" and "conceived in the spirit of the author of *The Scarlet Letter*. The combination is not very satisfactory, but the poem, as a piece of fiction, has many elements of interest." As for his other works, "we cannot recommend the definitely comic poems. They are very depressing."

Moving briskly to *Poems and Songs* by John Renton Denning, Wilde observes that his poems "show an ardent love of Keats, and a profligate luxuriance of adjectives," as in the following lines: "And I will build a bower for thee, sweet, / A verdurous shelter from the noonday heat, / Thick rustling ivy, broad and green, and shining, / With honeysuckle creeping up and twining...." This, says Wilde, "is the immature manner of *Endymion* with a vengeance, and is not to be encouraged," though Denning sometimes writes with "wonderful grace and charm."

Joseph McKim's "little book," *Poems*, has at least one poem, "William the Silent," which is written in the "spirited Macauley style," as in "Awake, awake, ye burghers brave! shout, shout for joy and sing." Wilde concludes hastily: "Some people like this style." Turning to Mrs. Horace Dobell's 17th volume of verse, *In the Watches of the Night*, Wilde observes that she "seems very angry with everybody, and writes poems to 'A Human Toad,' with lurid and mysterious footnotes such as 'Yet some one, *not* a friend of—— *did*! on a certain occasion of a glib utterance of calumnies, by ——! at Hampstead.'" Wilde ends his brief notice: "Here indeed is a Soul's Tragedy" (the title of Browning's 1846 drama, used by Wilde to suggest facetiously, no doubt, the degradation of poetry).

In his preface to *Poems*, James Kelly states: "In many cases I have deliberately employed alliteration, believing that the music of a line is intensified thereby." Wilde responds with the observation that alliteration is "one of the many secrets of English poetry, and as long as it is kept a secret it is admirable." Kelly, he continues, "uses it with becoming modesty and reserve, and never suffers it to trammel the white feet of his bright and buoyant muse." His sonnets, however, are "too narrative, too diffuse, and too lyrical.... It is a pity that Mr. Kelly has included the poems written before the age of nineteen. Youth is rarely original."

The Rev. Clarence Walworth's title, *Andiator-octè*, is "a word borrowed from the Indians, and should, we think, be returned to them as soon as possible." The "most curious" poem in his book is called "Scenes at the Holy Home": "Jesus and Joseph at work! Hurra! / Sight never to see again, / A prentice Deity plies the saw, / While the Master ploughs with the plane." Such poems, states Wilde, were popular in the Middle Ages, "when the cathedral of every Christian country served as its theatres. They are anachronisms now, and it is odd that they should come to us from the United States. In matters of this kind we should have some protection."

"THE POETS' CORNER"

Published: *PMG*, 30 March 1889, 3; rpt. in *Reviews* (1908). Unsigned reviews.

Facetiously, Wilde alludes to George Denman (Judge of the High Court of Justice) in his opening remark: "Judges, like the criminal classes, have their lighter moments, and it was probably in one of his happiest and certainly in one of his most careless moods that Mr. Justice Denman conceived the idea of putting the early history of Rome into doggerel verse for the benefit of a little boy of the name of Jack." The preface to Denman's *The Story of the Kings of Rome in Verse* (1889) explains that Jack is under six years of age. "Poor Jack!" Wilde expostulates. It is "sad to think of the future career of a boy who is being brought up on bad history and worse poetry.... If Jack goes to the bad, Mr. Justice Denman will have much to answer for."

Wilde then turns "after such a terrible example from the Bench," to E. Cooper Willis's *Tales and Legends in Verse* (1889), a work "somewhat boisterous in manner [but] very spirited and clever." After a brief quotation from Willis, Wilde proceeds to the next volume, *The Poetry of South Africa* (1889), ed. Alexander Wilmost, from which he mentions and quotes Duncan Moodie and Thomas Pringle with little enthusiasm: "The South African poets, as a class, are rather behind the age. They seem to think that 'Aurora' is a very novel and delightful epithet for the dawn. On the whole, they depress us." Then, Wilde very briefly notices Louis Tylor's *Chess: A Christmas Masque* (1888), in which the characters, who sing and converse, are taken from the chess board: "The silliness of the form makes it an absolutely unreadable book."

Determined to get through the remaining volumes, Wilde comments briefly on David Williamson's *Poems of Nature and Life* (1888), which contains poems "as orthodox in spirt as they are commonplace in form. A few harmless heresies of art and thought would do this poet no harm. Nearly everything that he says has been said before, and said better." Next, Amand Müllner's *Guilt* (1889) is, says the translator John Cockle, a masterpiece of "German fate-tragedy," prompting Wilde to comment: "His translation...does not make us long for any further acquaintance with the school." With meritorious haste, Wilde moves on to *The Circle of Seasons* (1889) by "K. E. V." (who remains unidentified). This work, a series of hymns and verses for the various seasons, is a well-meaning but "somewhat tedious book." The poem that begins "Lord, in the inn of my poor worthless heart / Guests come and go; but there is room for Thee" has merit, and, says Wilde, "might be converted into a good sonnet. The majority of the poems, however, are worthless."

Lord Henry Somerset's *Songs of Adieu* (1889), "marred by their excessive sentimentality of feeling, and by the commonplace character of their weak and lax form," contains nothing new. Somerset, says Wilde, "has too much heart and too little art to make a good poet, and such as he does possess is devoid of almost every intellectual quality, and entirely lacking in any intellectual strength. He has nothing to say, and says it." Cora Davis's *Immortelles* (1888) is disposed of hastily as Wilde alludes to a "delightful passage" (referring to Egypt's "colossal statues, whose barbaric story / The caustic pens of erudition still record...."), "which will be appreciated by all Egyptologists."

"THE POETS' CORNER"

Published: *PMG*, 24 June 1889, 3; rpt. in *Reviews* (1908). Unsigned reviews of books published in 1889.

Wilde opens with a startling question: "Is Mr. Alfred Austin [in 1896 named the poet laureate] among the Socialists? Has somebody converted the respectable editor of the respectable *National Review*? Has even dulness become revolutionary? From a poem in Mr. Austin's last volume [*Love's Widowhood and Other Poems*], this would seem to be the case." The poem in question, "Two Visions," which was begun in 1863 and revised in 1889, may be regarded as "fully representative of Mr. Austin's maturer views," despite the "somewhat lumbering and pedestrian verses." But, says Wilde, Austin has other moods, "and perhaps he is at his best when he is writing about flowers. Occasionally he wearies the reader by tedious enumerations of plants, lacking indeed reticence, and tact, and selection in many of his descriptions, but as a rule he is very pleasant when he is babbling of green fields" (in *Henry V*, II.iii., the dying Falstaff is said to have "babbl'd of green fields").

William James Linton's fame as a wood-engraver has, writes Wilde, "somewhat obscured the merits of his poetry.... As a poet [in his *Poems and Translations*], Mr. Linton is always fanciful, with a studied fancifulness, and often felicitous with a chance felicity.... There is a pleasant flavour about his verse. It is entirely free from violence and from

vagueness, those two besetting sins of so much modern poetry" (for Wilde's attack on such "sins," see "Poets and the People"). As for Heloise Durant's *Dante: A Dramatic Poem*, Wilde disposes of it in a lengthy quotation, then concludes: "The play is well meant, but it is lumbering and heavy, and the blank verse has absolutely no artistic merit."

Wilde proceeds to Alfred Perceval Graves's *Father O'Flynn and Other Irish Lyrics*, most of which is written in dialect. For English readers, notes are appended, "in which the uninitiated are informed that 'brogue' means a boot, that 'mavourneed' means my dear, and 'astore' is a term of affection." It is, concludes Wilde, "a very dreary production, and does not 'lighten and brighten' us a bit. The whole volume should be called 'The Lucubrations of a Stage Irishman.'" The final volume, the anonymously published *The Judgment of the City*, is "a sort of bad Blake. [The anonymous author] has every form of sincerity, except the sincerity of the artist, a defect that he shares with most of our popular writers."

"A POLITICIAN'S POETRY"

Published: *PMG*, 3 Nov. 1886, 4–5; rpt. in *Reviews* (1908). An unsigned review of the Earl of Carnarvon's translation of *The Odyssey of Homer*, Books I–XII (1886).

"Although," writes Wilde, "it is against etiquette to quote Greek in Parliament, Homer has always been a great favourite with our statesmen.... For as the cross-benches form a refuge for those who have no minds to make up, so those who cannot make up their minds always take to Homeric studies." In Lord Carnarvon's case, "the love of literature alone has produced this version of the marvellous Greek epic, and to the love of literature alone it appeals." Wilde approves of the translator's use of blank verse, which "undoubtedly gives the possibility of a clear and simple rendering of the original." On the other hand, the ten-syllable line "brings but a faint echo of the long roll of the Homeric hexameter, its rapid movement and continuous harmony." Nevertheless, there are pleasing qualities in Lord Carnarvon's translation, though "it may not contain much subtlety of melody...." It is not quite Homer, concludes Wilde, "but no translation can hope to be that, for no work of art can afford to lose its style or to give up the manner that is essential to it."

"PORTIA"

Published: *World: A Journal for Men and Women* 12 (14 Jan. 1880): 13; rev. in *Poems* (1881). In *Poems* (1908), this sonnet is included under the section heading "Sonnets Written at the Lyceum Theatre."

On 28 November 1879, Wilde saw Ellen Terry perform the role of Portia in Henry Irving's production of *The Merchant of Venice* at the Lyceum Theatre. In the poem, "No woman Veronese looked upon / Was half so fair as thou whom I behold." Alluding to the famous trial scene in the play, Wilde concludes his sonnet: "O Portia! take my heart: it is thy due: / I think I will not quarrel with the Bond."

Manuscript: The Huntington Library has the only extant MS. The dedication to Ellen Terry, which appears in the MS., was included in the version published in *Poems* (1908).

PORTORA ROYAL SCHOOL

In February 1864, at the age of nine, Oscar was sent to Enniskillen, County Fermanagh, 100 miles northwest of Dublin, to attend Portora Royal School. Reputed to be an excellent Royal school – one of four in Ireland – Portora, located on a hill, had a view of the town and of a ruined castle. Surrounding the school building and for over 60 acres, the grounds stretched along the Lough Erne, ideal for rowing, bathing, fishing, and ice skating. Of its academic achievements, Davis Coakley writes: "Most of the students... were the sons of colonial officials, landed gentry, clergy and professional people. Over the years it educated many students who subsequently gained distinction. Samuel Beckett was a student there in the twentieth century" (77).

For its approximately 100 boarders and 50 day pupils, the curriculum included English, classics, mathematics, and French; optional subjects were German and Italian. In addition, religious instruction was essential, and attendance was required at the boys' respective Protestant churches. The liberal headmaster, William Steele, who had been educated at Trinity College, Dublin, and who led Portora for 34 years, admitted Catholic pupils after he was appointed headmaster in 1857.

At Portora, Oscar was reserved and somewhat distant. A classmate recalls: "He had, I think, no very special chums while at school. I was perhaps as friendly with him all through as anybody....

Willie Wilde was never very familiar with him, treating him always, in those days, as a younger brother" (qtd. in Coakley 80). Nevertheless, Oscar seemed to be a prodigy to the other students, for he read with extraordinary speed and excellent retention.

Anticipating his achievements at Trinity College and later at Oxford, Oscar won the school's Gold Medal for his mastery of classical Greek. As another classmate later recalled: "In the *viva voce* which was on the *Agamemnon* of Aeschylus he simply walked away from us all" (qtd. in Coakley 83). He also won the Carpenter Greek Testament Prize, and in his final year, he was awarded a Royal scholarship to Trinity College, Dublin. As Coakley concludes: "Portora played a crucial role in Wilde's development and its importance in this respect has been greatly underestimated. It was an ideal environment for a child with an interest in culture, and it complemented the influence of his home" (83).

Reference: Davis Coakley, "Portora Royal School," *Oscar Wilde: The Importance of Being Irish* (1994).

"THE PORTRAIT OF MR W. H."

First Version: In a letter sent to William Blackwood around the end of April 1889, Wilde offered him a story for *Blackwood's Magazine* on the subject of Shakespeare's sonnets titled "The Portrait of Mr W. H.," containing "an entirely new view on the subject of the identity of the young man to whom the sonnets are addressed" (*Letters* 243). Horst Schroeder, who has written the most thorough studies of the work, suggests that Wilde had probably written the story early in 1889, though Ellmann, without citing his source, alludes to evidence that Wilde had been at work on the story in October 1887 (296/279).

Published: *Blackwood's Edinburgh Magazine* 146 (July 1889): 1–21, pre-publication copies having been sent out to the press on 24 June; rpt. in *Lord Arthur Savile's Crime and Other Prose Pieces* (1908).

Second Version: Soon after publication of the story, Wilde wrote to Blackwood: "What would you say to a dainty little volume of 'Mr W. H.' by itself? I could add to it, as I have many more points to make, and have not yet tackled the problem of the 'dark woman' at the end of the sonnets" (*Letters* 247). Apparently, Blackwood urged him to expand the story; by early autumn of 1889, Wilde had substantially completed the longer version, though he continued working on it sporadically, but information is lacking on the successive stages of the writing, which involved revisions of the first version (in its ultimate printed form, the story is more than twice the length of the *Blackwood's Magazine* version). In *Recollections of Oscar Wilde* (1932), Charles Ricketts recalled that Wilde had asked him in the autumn of 1889 to paint "a small Elizabethan picture" of Mr W. H. to be used as the frontispiece for his book (28–30) and that Wilde read the longer version of the story to him several days later (35).

Apparently, in late 1889, either Blackwood or another publisher declined to publish the work. When, in May 1893, John Lane and Elkin Mathews of the Bodley Head proposed to publish it, a draft of an agreement was drawn up, its final form signed by Wilde on 3 August. However, publication of *The Portrait of Mr W. H.* was delayed probably because of the uneasiness that Lane and Mathews felt about the story (moreover, by September 1894, they were in the process of dissolving their partnership). When Wilde informed Lane "to let Mr Mathews have 'Mr W.H.'" (*Letters* 365), Lane replied on 7 September 1894 that Mathews would not publish it "at any price" and that neither would he unless he approved of it first (*More Letters* 125).

Wilde's arrest and trials in April and May 1895 ended all hope of publishing *The Portrait of Mr W. H.* The MS., said to have been returned to Wilde by Lane on the day of his arrest (5 April), disappeared when his home in Tite Street was besieged by the public at the 24 April auction of his books and MSS. In July 1920, the "lost" MS. surfaced in the hands of the British-born publisher Mitchell Kennerley (1878–1950), once an employee of Lane, who, in 1896, had sent him to open and direct the New York branch. The *New York Post* (20 June 1921) reported Kennerley's account of the discovery:

> There is no doubt now that Wilde gave the MS. to a literary friend, and asked him to prepare it for the printer, for it was in the home of this friend, who died, that the lost script was found. The surviving sister of this literary friend came across the yellowed package of folio pages only last July, and being in

doubt as to their significance, they were sent to Mr. Kennerley, who straightway recognized their import.

The "literary friend" was Frederick Chapman, Lane's office manager, who, while Lane was in America, was in charge of the Bodley Head at the time of Wilde's trials. Schroeder, however, questions how the MS. could have lain in Chapman's private desk, completely forgotten and unnoticed for more than 25 years, even when he moved into his new home in Middlesex in 1900 (*Annotations* 76).

Published: July 1921 by Mitchell Kennerley (New York) in a limited edition of 1,000 copies, "now first printed from the original enlarged MS. which for twenty-six years has been lost to the world." In September, Vyvyan Holland arranged with Duckworth & Co. (London) to have 10 copies printed to insure the British copyright. In 1923, Doubleday & Co (New York) included the second version in Volume 6 of its *Complete Works*; rpt. in W. H. Wise & Co.'s "Connoisseurs' Edition" of the *Complete Works* (New York, 1927).

In England, an edition of 1,500 copies appeared on 30 October 1958, when Methuen & Co. issued the second version, edited and introduced by Vyvyan Holland, in a text of 90 pages. Its next incarnation, in November 1966, finally reached a wide readership in Britain in a one-volume *Complete Works of Oscar Wilde*, introduced by Holland and published by Collins.

The Plot: In Part I, the narrator, after dining with his friend Erskine, is talking about literary forgeries, particularly those by Thomas Chatterton. His "so-called forgeries," the narrator insists, "were merely the result of an artistic desire for perfect representation." To censure the artist for such a forgery was "to confuse an ethical with an aesthetical problem."

Alluding to "a young man" who committed a forgery in order to prove "a strange theory about a certain work of art," Erskine shows the narrator a full-length portrait of a young man in 16th-century costume with his hand on a book, a boy "of quite extraordinary personal beauty, though evidently somewhat effeminate." It is the portrait of Mr W. H., Erskine tells him, and the book is inscribed "To The Onlie Begetter of These Insuing Sonnets." The narrator claims that Mr W. H. is Lord Pembroke, who, with Shakespeare and Mrs Mary

"THE PORTRAIT OF MR W. H."

Fitton (a maid of honor to Queen Elizabeth), are the three personages in the sonnets: the effeminate young man in the portrait, he insists, is not at all like Pembroke.

Erskine tells the narrator of his friend Cyril Graham, whom he had known at Eton and at Cambridge: "...he was the most splendid creature I ever saw, and nothing could exceed the grace of his movements, the charm of his manner." At school, the effeminate Graham had played female leads in Shakespeare's plays. The friendship continued after both had left school. One day, Graham revealed that "he had at last discovered the true secret of Shakespeare's Sonnets....[he] had found out who Mr W. H. really was." Graham explained his intricate theory, involving biographical details with key passages from the sonnets, which, says Erskine, eliminated Pembroke as Mr W. H. Likewise, he disposed of the other leading contender, the Earl of Southampton.

Graham then asked Erskine to clear his mind of all preconceptions: "Who was that young man of Shakespeare's day who, without being of noble birth or even of noble nature, was addressed by him in terms of such passionate admiration that we can but wonder at the strange worship, and are almost afraid to turn the key that unlocks the mystery of the poets's heart? Who was he whose physical beauty was such that it became the very cornerstone of Shakespeare's art...?"

The art alluded to by Shakespeare ("Thou art all my art") is the dramatist's art: Mr W. H. "was surely none other than the boy-actor for whom he created Viola and Imogen, Juliet and Rosalind, Portia and Desdemona, and Cleopatra herself." His name was Will, or Willie, Hughes, whose name Shakespeare punned on in sonnets 135 and 143 as well as the surname in sonnet 20 ("A man in hew [i.e., hue], all *Hews* in his controwling"), the puns significantly italicized and capitalized in the original printing of these sonnets. The argument, says Erskine, converted him at once, though Willie Hughes's name does not appear in the list of actors printed in the First Folio of 1623.

But sonnet 86, Graham assured him, indicates that Willie had left Shakespeare's company earlier. (Ellmann suggests that the story of Willie Hughes had personal significance for Wilde, who "imagined Shakespeare, a married man with two children like himself [actually, Shakespeare had three children], captivated by a boy as he had been by

[Robert] Ross" [297–98/281]. "Indeed," Wilde told Ross, "the story is half yours, and but for you would not have been written.... Now that Willie Hughes has been revealed to the world, we must have another secret" [*Letters* 247].)

Before such a discovery could be published, Erskine suggested that he and Graham search church registers and archives to find independent evidence of Willie Hughes's existence. After several weeks, no trace of the boy actor could be found. Later, Graham informed him that he was able to establish not only Willie's existence but also his identity as Mr W. H. He had discovered an Elizabethan chest, within which was the portrait that Erskine had shown to the narrator. The initials "W. H." were carved on a panel of the chest, and the portrait had the name "Master Will. Hews." It was, says Erskine, an obvious forgery, though he did not suspect it at the time. By chance, he discovered that an artist had done this portrait of Mr W. H. for Graham. Confronted by Erskine, Graham assured him: "I did it purely for your sake. You would not be convinced in any other way. It does not affect the truth of the theory." Furious, Erskine charged that Graham never believed in his own theory; otherwise, he would not have resorted to the forgery.

The next morning, Graham killed himself with a revolver, "a sacrifice," he informed Erskine in a letter, "to the secret of the Sonnets." He entrusted the theory to Erskine, who in presenting it to the world, would "unlock the secret of Shakespeare's heart." But Erskine has refused to carry out Graham's wishes because "it is a perfectly unsound theory." The narrator, insisting that the theory is the "only perfect key" to the sonnets and that Graham is "the most splendid of all the martyrs of literature," resolves to give the theory to the world despite Erskine's warning that it would be laughed at.

In Part II, Wilde dispenses with the narrative of the story for an elaborate discussion, by the narrator, of the sonnets with further "evidence" of Willie Hughes's presence: indeed, every day he seems to discover "something new, and Willie Hughes became to me a kind of spiritual presence, an ever-dominant personality." As for Shakespeare's devotion to Willie, the narrator remarks: "I did not care to pry into the mystery of his sin or of the sin, if such it was, of the great poet who had so dearly loved him." In this second version, Wilde adds a lengthy discussion of the actor's and the dramatist's art as well as the influence of Neo-Platonism on the Renaissance:

>...we can [then] understand the true meaning of the amatory phrases and works with which friends were wont, at this time, to address each other. There was a kind of mystic transference of the expressions of the physical sphere to a sphere that was spiritual, that was removed from gross bodily appetite, and in which the soul was Lord.

Also new in the second version is an extensive discussion of, among other figures, Michelangelo, who "addressed himself to the worship of intellectual beauty," and John Addington Symonds's interpretation of "the Platonic conception of love as nothing if not spiritual, and of beauty as a form that finds its immortality within the lover's soul" – Wilde's elevation of the ultimate significance of homosexual love to an empyrean sphere. "It was no wonder, then," says the narrator, "that Shakespeare had been stirred by a spirit that so stirred his age.... In Willie Hughes, Shakespeare found... the visible incarnation of his idea of beauty, and it is not too much to say that to this young actor, whose very name the dull writers of his age forgot to chronicle, the Romantic Movement of English Literature is largely indebted."

In the first version, Part III, which concluded the story, there is a brief section of several pages in which the narrator confesses to Erskine that he has become indifferent to the whole subject of Willie Hughes's identity ("Perhaps, by finding perfect expression for a passion, I had exhausted the passion itself"). When the narrator goes to see Erskine to apologize for a hasty letter, Erskine tells him that he is more than ever convinced of Graham's theory (in short, as the narrator's passion wanes, Erskine's increases). Two years later, a letter from Erskine, now in France, confesses his failure to verify the Willie Hughes theory, and just as Graham "had given his life for this theory, he himself had determined to give his own life also to the same cause." But Erskine, the narrator discovers, has died not at his own hand but from consumption. He has left the "fatal portrait" of Willie Hughes for the narrator, who concludes his story: "...when I look at it, I think that there is really a great deal to be said for the Willie Hughes theory of Shakespeare's Sonnets."

In the second version, Part III continues the narrator's account of his quest for Willie Hughes. When he discovers that no one has ever written a history of the English boy actors of the 16th and 17th centuries, he decides to undertake the task himself. "The Puritans," says the narrator, "with their uncouth morals and ignoble minds, had of course railed against them, and dwelt on the impropriety of boys disguising as women, and learning to affect the manners and passions of the female sex." This section, like Part II of the second version, is more a historical and critical discussion rather than a fictive narration.

In Part IV, the narrator becomes absorbed with sonnets 127–152, "that deal with the dark woman who, like a shadow or thing of evil omen, came across Shakespeare's great romance, and for a season stood between him and Willie Hughes." Like Part III, this part of the story abandons narration in favor of expository discussion. In dating the sonnets from internal evidence, the narrator concludes that, by 1594, Shakespeare "had been cured of his infatuation for the dark lady, and had already been acquainted for at least three years with Willie Hughes." The playwright Christopher Marlowe, however, lured the boy actor away from the Globe Theatre to play Gaveston in *Edward II*: "...for the second time Shakespeare is separated from his friend." (The concluding pages of this section had been, in the first version, the end of Part II.)

In Part V, the narrator reveals how his absorption in the Willie Hughes story has revealed his own hidden impulses: in a passage suggesting Wilde's awareness of the submerged life of the unconscious, the narrator observes that the "secret soul" had "senses that quickened, passions that came to birth, spiritual ecstasies of contemplation, ardours of fiery-coloured love. It was we who were unreal, and our conscious life was the least important part of our development." The sonnets "had suddenly explained to me the whole story of my soul's romance."

The rest of this part is a revision of Part III of the first version, as given above. Additions include the narrator's new-found knowledge about himself: "Had I touched upon some secret that my soul desired to conceal?" The story concludes with a new passage in which the narrator meditates on Erskine's attempt to keep the Willie Hughes theory alive: "Martyrdom was to me merely a tragic form of scepticism, an attempt to realise by fire what one had failed to do by faith. No man dies for what he knows to be true. Men die for what they want to be true, for what some terror in their hearts tells them is not true."

Reviews of the First Version: Though Harris remarked that Wilde's story not only "set everyone talking and arguing" but also did him "incalculable injury," his enemies having used it "unscrupulously and untiringly with the fierce delight of hatred" (69), the available evidence fails to substantiate Harris's claim. Most reviewers saw nothing morally offensive in the story. A notable exception, perhaps, was W. E. Henley's unsigned review in the *Scots Observer* (6 July 1889), which covertly alludes to Wilde's story by saying that the July number of *Blackwood's* was "particularly good...with the exception of one article which is out of place...." Clearly annoyed, Wilde wrote to Henley:

> To be exiled in Scotland to edit a Tory paper in the wilderness is bad enough, but not to see the wonder and beauty of my discovery of the real Mr W.H. is absolutely dreadful. I sympathise deeply with you, and can only beg you to return to London where you will be able to appreciate a real work of art. The Philistines in their vilest forms have seized on you. (*Letters* 248)

More openly critical, however, was an anonymous review in the *World* (10 July), which found the subject "very unpleasant, and it is dilated upon in...a peculiarly offensive manner: a rapture on 'the golden hair; his tender, flower-like grace; his dreamy, deep-sunken eyes; his delicate, mobile limbs, and white, lily hands,' of a play-acting boy, is scarcely what one would have expected in [*Blackwood's*]."

Because of Wilde's reputation as a poseur (his "sincerity" was consequently always in question), the review in the *St. James's Gazette* (27 June) questioned "how far he takes himself seriously. He carries his irony very far indeed in his new theory of Shakespeare's Sonnets." Likewise, the review in the *Pall Mall Gazette* (29 June) was uncertain whether Wilde "really" believed in the Willie Hughes theory or whether he had his tongue in cheek. And the *Tablet* (20 July) queried: "The question remains – is Mr. Wilde joking?"

Mason (6) identifies Andrew Lang as the author of a review that appeared in the *Saturday Review* (29 June). Lang reveals that the Willie Hughes theory was not "absolutely original" since the 18th-century Shakespearean scholar Tyrwhitt had advanced it earlier. Quoting the suggestive passage describing the "ambiguous young man," Lang offers an alternative theory, which parodies both Wilde's story and the current theory that Francis Bacon was the author of Shakespeare's plays: the sonnets were "of course" written by Bacon to Shakespeare. Because the critical reception of Wilde's story achieved prominence without abuse, Blackwood told Wilde on 9 July: "I hope you have been pleased with the reaction your story has had, and on the whole I think it has taken well" (*Letters* 246n4).

Reviews of the Second Version: In New York, the reviewer for the *Nation* (31 Aug. 1921) preferred to read the story as fiction, "a charming story, adorned with dainty erudition, presented with a nice fictive art, written in a graceful, insinuating style, and rounded out with a whimsical conclusion that draws the teeth of the narrative's apparent seriousness." Wilde's friend, the poet Richard Le Gallienne, now residing in New York, wrote in *Bookman* (Oct.) that he was intrigued by "the mystery in the Sonnets," which were "sufficiently romantic" with the "elements of a beautiful" and "complex literary adventure."

The reviewer for the New York *Dial* (Sept.), Arthur Hooley, who published under the pseudonym of "Charles Vale," concluded that the story, "not a masterpiece," nevertheless had some "masterly touches in it" and "many rememberable things," yet, he remarks, "It is a shadowy portrait, after all, that Wilde has sketched so carefully; he could not make it vital." The reviewer contends that Wilde has missed "a sense of bigger personalities and larger issues than he has painted in The Portrait."

In New Orleans, a review by the poet Michael Monahan in the *Double-Dealer* (Nov.) hailed Wilde as "the Great Fantastic in his most plausive and fascinating vein of paradox – not seriously deceiving us for a moment, but always enthralling and delighting us...." Despite his reservation about the "perversity" of the "dark lady" section, he nonetheless calls it "brilliant." In Vyvyan Holland's edition in 1958, the story entranced the poet and translator Hilary Corke in the *Listener* (4 Dec.), who called it "a sparkling piece of work in the ninetyish manner," while the anonymous reviewer in the *Times Literary Supplement* (21 Nov.) remarked that the story had a "remarkable interest as an imaginative study."

Manuscript: The expanded version of the story – consisting of 105 pages, partly of printed pages from *Blackwood's Magazine* (with revisions and additions) and partly of MS. pages – is in the Rosenbach Library.

References: Horst Schroeder, *Oscar Wilde, "The Portrait of Mr W. H.": Its Composition, Publication and Reception* (1984) and *Annotations to Oscar Wilde, "The Portrait of Mr W. H."* (1986); Bruce Bashford, "Hermeneutics in Oscar Wilde's 'The Portrait of Mr W. H.," *Papers on Language and Literature* (Fall 1988); William Buckler, "The Agnostic's Apology: A New Reading of Oscar Wilde's 'The Portrait of Mr W. H.,'" *Victorian Newsletter* (Fall 1989); William Cohen, "Willie and Wilde: Reading *The Portrait of Mr W. H.,*" *South Atlantic Quarterly* (Winter 1989); Patrice Hannon, "Aesthetic Criticism, Useless Art: Wilde, Zola, and 'The Portrait of Mr W. H.,'" *Critical Essays on Oscar Wilde*, ed. Regenia Gagnier (1991); Robert J. G. Lange, "The Provenance of Oscar Wilde's *The Portrait of Mr W. H.*: An Oversight?" *N&Q* (June 1995); Lawrence Danson, "The Portrait of Mr W. H.," *Wilde's Intentions: The Artist in His Criticism* (1997).

"'PRIMAVERA'"

Published: *PMG*, 24 May 1890, 3; rpt. in *Reviews* (1908). An unsigned review of *Primavera: Poems* by Four Authors (Laurence Binyon, Manmohan Ghose, Stephen Phillips, and Arthur Cripps).

"In the summer term," Wilde begins, "Oxford teaches the exquisite art of idleness, one of the most important things that any University can teach, and possibly as the first-fruits of the dreaming in grey cloister and silent garden, which either makes or mars a man, there has just appeared in that lovely city a dainty and delightful volume of poems by four friends." Of the four authors, Wilde cites Manmohan Ghose first as of "particular interest," for he was born in India of purely Indian parentage, brought up entirely in England, and excelled in "literary attainments" at Christ Church, Oxford. His poems, says Wilde,

"show us how quick and subtle are the intellectual sympathies of the Oriental mind, and suggest how close is the bond of union that may some day bind India to us by other methods than those of commerce and military strength." Quoting a passage from one of Ghose's songs, Wilde perceives Keats's temper and Matthew Arnold's moods: "...what better influences could a beginner have?" Wilde errs in his prediction, however, that Ghose "ought some day to make a name in our literature."

Stephen Phillips, who, says Wilde, performed the role of the Ghost in *Hamlet* at the Globe Theatre with "dignity and elocution," has a "more solemn Muse" than that of Ghose. A lengthy quotation follows from his best work, "Orestes," which reveals the influences of Milton and Greek tragedy: "...what better influences could a young singer have?" Arthur Cripps, disposed of quickly, "is melodious at times," and Laurence Binyon, "Oxford's latest Laureate," having won the coveted Newdigate Prize (as Wilde had won it earlier), "shows us in his lyrical Ode on Youth that he can handle a difficult metre dexterously...." *Primavera*, Wilde concludes, is "a pleasant little book.... charmingly 'got up,' and undergraduates might read it with advantage during lecture hours."

"PRINTING AND PRINTERS: LECTURE AT THE 'ARTS AND CRAFTS'"

Published: *PMG*, 16 Nov. 1888, 5; rpt. in *Miscellanies* (1908). An unsigned review of Emery Walker's lecture on "Letterpress, Printing and Illustration" on 15 Nov. at the Arts and Crafts Exhibition Society's presentation, New Gallery, Regent Street.

Wilde praises Walker's "admirable" lecture," which included a series of "most interesting specimens of old printed books and manuscripts displayed on the screen by means of the magic-lantern...." Walker explained the different kinds of type and displayed specimens of old block-printing, still used in China, that preceded movable type. He spoke of Aldus, the first publisher of cheap books, and he exhibited a page of a copy-book written by Vicentino, "the great Venetian writing master," and made suggestions on how to avoid "slanting writing."

Latin, Walker contended, was a better language to print than English since the "tails of the letters did not so often fall below the line." The type used by the *Pall Mall Gazette*, Wilde remarks, was, "we are glad to say, rightly approved of." As for illustrations, Walker pleaded for "true book-ornament as opposed to the silly habit of putting pictures where they are not wanted, and pointed out that mechanical harmony and artistic harmony went hand in hand." Wilde concludes: "...we hope that some of the publishers in the audience will take [Walker's suggestions] to heart."

PRISON YEARS, 1895–97

On 25 May 1895, at the Old Bailey, Wilde was sentenced to two years at hard labor. Of the intent of such punishment, H. Montgomery Hyde has written:

> The deterrent object of imprisonment had been officially laid down as "hard labour, hard fare, and a hard bed." Evidence given by a variety of witnesses before a recent Home Office Committee on Prisons had shown that two years imprisonment with hard labour, involving solitary cellular confinement, with its attendant laborious and largely useless work in the shape of the treadwheel [pumping water or grinding grain], the crank [turning the handle in a cylindrical metal drum] and oakum picking [separating loose fibers in old rope used in caulking seams of wooden ships], which had to be performed on a poor and inadequate diet, were calculated to break a man in body and spirit. (2)

After a month of turning the crank or treadmill, prisoners were generally given less arduous labor, such as sewing mail bags, making mats, or picking oakum in their cells – as described in *The Ballad of Reading Gaol*: "We turn the crank or tear the rope, / Each in his separate Hell...." The latter work was useless since iron ships had long since replaced most wooden ones.

Moreover, no provision was made to reduce a sentence for good behavior on the part of the convict, who was confined to a poorly ventilated cell for 23 hours a day under primitive sanitary conditions. Insomnia inevitably resulted from sleeping on a plank bed, "an instrument of torture" (Hyde 2). Visitors – each permitted only 20 minutes – and outgoing or incoming letters were possible only once every three months. Other than the Bible, a prayer book, and hymn book, books were not allowed for the first three months of

imprisonment; then, the convict could borrow one book a week from the prison library, stocked with commonplace theological works selected by the prison chaplain. Of these conditions, Wilde wrote on 23 March 1898, to the editor of the *Daily Chronicle* in order to urge reforms when a prison bill was before the House of Commons:

> The present prison system seems almost to have for its aim the wrecking and the destruction of the mental faculties.... Deprived of books, of all human intercourse, isolated from every humane and humanising influence, condemned to eternal silence, robbed of all intercourse with the external world, treated like an unintelligent animal, brutalised below the level of any of the brute-creation, the wretched man who is confined in an English prison can hardly escape becoming insane. (*Letters* 724)

After being sentenced on Saturday, 25 May 1895, Wilde spent the weekend in a jail adjacent to the Old Bailey, then transferred on Monday to Pentonville Prison in North London (where his weight was recorded as just under 14 stone – or about 195 pounds – and his height over six feet). In June, Wilde's first visitor was R. B. Haldane (1856–1928), a Liberal M.P. who was a member of the Gladstone Committee, charged with reviewing prison administration; his visit to Pentonville was probably prompted by a newspaper report that Wilde had developed serious mental problems, a report subsequently found baseless. A casual acquaintance of Wilde in former days, Haldane arranged to have books, including Pater's *The Renaissance*, sent to him as well as writing materials to encourage his resumption of artistic work. During his first visit, according to Haldane, Wilde burst into tears, though he soon became cheerful – amused, apparently – when told that *Madame Bovary* was unlikely to be sanctioned by the prison.

On 4 July 1895, Wilde was transferred from Pentonville to Wandsworth Prison, located south of the Thames. Why he was transferred is not entirely clear, since it seemed to have been the intention of the authorities to have Wilde serve out his sentence at Pentonville, but Hyde surmises that Sir Evelyn Ruggles-Brise (1857–1935), the enlightened Chairman of the Prison Commission, and

Haldane "had considerable confidence in the Chaplain at Wandsworth...on whom they could rely to keep a particular eye on [Wilde]" (18).

This prison, however, was not much of an improvement. Wilde later wrote that he "longed to die. It was my one desire" (*Letters* 471). But it was at Wandsworth that a fellow prisoner – in a famous incident – whispered to Wilde "in the hoarse prison-voice men get from long and compulsory silence" during the exercise period in the prison yard: "*I am sorry for you: it is harder for the likes of you than it is for the likes of us*" (*Letters* 495) – an act of kindness that moved Wilde, who had encountered little sympathy since his imprisonment. Unaccustomed to speaking without moving his lips, a skill learned by the other prisoners, he responded: "No, my friend, we all suffer alike." Because he wished to spare his fellow prisoner any punishment, Wilde informed the prison governor, when brought to him by a warder, that he had begun the conversation; hence, he was confined in a dark cell up to three days on bread and water (Hyde 20 and n2).

The first visitor in late August to see Wilde after the initial three months in prison was Robert Sherard (see entry), his future biographer, whose "chivalry and courage" on Wilde's behalf was remembered with "pride and gratitude" (*Letters* 407). On leaving the prison, Sherard, who was approached by a newspaper reporter, said that he "was much struck by [Wilde's] courage and resignation, though his punishment weighs terribly upon him," and Sherard later informed the *Daily Chronicle* that Wilde was "insufficiently fed" and was "suffering greatly from sheer want of nourishment" (qtd. in Hyde 26).

Indeed, Wilde now weighed approximately 167 pounds, a loss of about 28 pounds since he had left Pentonville Prison in June. The doctor at Wandsworth consequently recommended increasing his diet. When Ruggles-Brise and the other Prison Commissioners sent the Superintending Medical Officer of Prisons to examine Wilde, they found "no evidence of despondency. On the contrary, the prisoner is adjusting himself in a sensible manner to his new environment, and seems to have no difficulty in reconciling himself to the inevitable" (qtd. in Hyde 27).

Hyde, however, writes: "The truth is that Wilde was a consummate actor and was in fact much nearer a breakdown than appeared to the two doctors" (28). Ten days after facing the ordeal of being brought before the public in the Bankruptcy Court on 24 September and after suffering from semi-starvation, diarrhoea, and sleeplessness, Wilde collapsed on the floor of the prison chapel. After Sherard visited him in the infirmary, he wrote to More Adey (see entry): "He is a perfect wreck and says he will be dead before long" (qtd. in Hyde 33).

The fear of insanity prompted officials in the Home Office to dispatch two specialists from the Broadmoor Criminal Lunatic Asylum to examine Wilde, who, they concluded, was not suffering from a "mental derangement" and who would benefit from open-air activities, such as gardening, and more suitable indoor activity, such as bookbinding, in another prison outside of London. At the same time, articles that were currently appearing in the *Daily Chronicle* and in the French press critical of Wilde's treatment at Wandsworth may have convinced the Home Office to follow the specialists' recommendations and transfer him to Reading Prison.

On 20 November (not the 21st, as Ellmann states: see Hyde 40n2), Wilde underwent "the single most humiliating experience of Wilde's prison life" during his transfer to Reading (Ellmann 495/465). Forced to stand on the center platform at Clapham Junction in convict dress and handcuffs "for the world to look at," Wilde recalls being "surrounded by a jeering mob" (*Letters* 491). Reading Prison, a fortress-like building of red brick with battlements, was a small county prison able to house 192 men and 29 women. Its governor, Henry B. Isaacson (1842–1915), who had retired as a lieutenant-colonel in the Royal Marines, was a stern administrator under whose rule Wilde would spend eight months. Borrowing a phrase from Tennyson's "Lucretius" (1868), Wilde later described Isaacson as a "mulberry-faced Dictator": "...a great red-faced bloated Jew who always looked as if he drank, and did so" (*Letters* 676). But Isaacson was not a Jew – an error undoubtedly inspired by his name – but a Christian, the son of the Rev. Stuteville William Isaacson, Rector of Bradfield St. Clare, Suffolk.

Ellmann writes that Isaacson was "flattered at Haldane's preference for Reading over Wandsworth" and that Isaacson had addressed his staff: "A certain prisoner is about to be transferred here, and you should be proud to think the Prison Commissioners have chosen Reading Gaol as the one most suitable for this man to serve the remainder of his sentence in" (496/465). Despite his negative reaction to the governor, Wilde was assigned to work in the garden and act as the "schoolmaster's orderly." Thus, he was free of the hard, manual labor that most prisoners were required to perform.

In a letter to More Adey after a visit to Wilde, Robert Ross also described Isaacson as "a Jew, tall and not unlike the head master of a public school. He at first was haughty and impatient, but became quite polite and amiable after a few minutes." Concerned about Oscar's mental condition and general heath, Ross got "nothing" out of Isaacson concerning Wilde's physical condition, though he was favorably impressed by the governor (Ross 43). Frank Harris, reporting Isaacson's boast that he was "knocking the nonsense out of Wilde," believed that the governor was "almost inhuman" (qtd. in Hyde 41–42). To André Gide, Wilde wrote that Isaacson was "very harsh because he was entirely lacking in imagination" (65).

In July 1896, Major J. O. Nelson, who succeeded Isaacson, administered the prison in a more humane manner, which prompted Wilde to refer to him as "this new personality that has altered every man's life in this place" (*Letters* 488); later, Wilde called him "the most Christ-like man I ever met" (*More Letters* 200). In his last months in prison, Wilde struck up a friendship with Warder Thomas Martin, who wrote his reminiscences of Wilde – "The Poet in Prison" – included as Chapter 17 in Sherard's 1906 biography, which is dedicated to him, one who "proved himself the true friend of an unhappy man." Despite Martin's inflated rhetoric, his compassion and admiration for Wilde are evident:

What the Poet was before he went to prison I care not. What he may have been after he left prison I know not. One thing I know, however, that while in prison he lived the life of a saint, or as near that holy state as poor mortal can ever hope to attain.... Farewell, brave heart! May your sleep be as peaceful as your smile. May the angels hover around your tomb in death as they hovered around your tomb in life.

Shortly after his release from prison, Wilde read of Martin's dismissal for giving some sweet biscuits to a hungry child in the prison; he immediately sent a lengthy letter to the *Daily Chronicle* (see *Letters* 568–74) in protest and detailed the inhumane treatment of children in prison as he had observed it – a protest that was instrumental in helping to bring about prison reform.

Shortly before his release on 19 May 1897, Wilde told More Adey that Nelson was "most sympathetic about my going out and full of kindness... (*Letters* 533). At the end of May, from Berneval-sur-Mer, Wilde wrote to Nelson with "*affectionate* gratitude" for his "kindness and gentleness" to him in prison, and "for the real care that you took of me at the end, when I was mentally upset and in a state of very terrible nervous excitement." He concludes by asking Nelson to allow him to sign himself, "once at any rate in life, your sincere and grateful friend" (*Letters* 580–81).

When *The Ballad of Reading Gaol* appeared in 1898, Robert Ross, at Wilde's direction, sent a copy to Nelson, who responded with the literary judgment that the poem was "not worthy of the writer's best effort. It is a terrible mixture of good bad and indifferent.... I fear he is too sensitive and may I say in confidence of too unstable and morbid a nature. Let us hope we shall someday see something really worthy of so brilliant and so unique a pen" (Ross 50).

In July 1899, Wilde also sent Nelson a copy of the first publication of *An Ideal Husband*; if he responded, his letter to Wilde has not survived. When *De Profundis* appeared in February 1905, Nelson wrote to thank Ross for having sent him a copy: "I think it one of the grandest and saddest efforts of a truly penitent man. One has to read but little to recognize what literature has lost in the death of a man like poor Oscar Wilde" (Ross 95).

References: André Gide, *Oscar Wilde*, trans. Stuart Mason (1905); R. B. Haldane, *An Autobiography* (1929); H. Montgomery Hyde, *Oscar Wilde: The Aftermath* (1963); Karl Beckson, "Oscar Wilde and the 'Almost Inhuman' Governor of Reading Gaol," *N&Q* (Aug. 1983).

PROUST, MARCEL (1871–1922)

The French novelist and critic, best known for his *Remembrance of Things Past* (English trans., 1922–31), Proust moved in fashionable Parisian society during the 1890s. The portrait painter Jacques-Émile Blanche introduced Wilde to Proust at the home of Mme Arthur Baignères, whose grandsons gave an account to Philippe Jullian of the relationship between the two writers (the grandsons having learned of it from their grandfather). At their initial meeting, Wilde was impressed by Proust's enthusiasm for English literature and particularly by his intelligent questions concerning Ruskin and George Eliot.

Wilde accepted Proust's invitation to dine in the Boulevard Haussmann apartment, but the evening began awkwardly, for Proust was detained. When he arrived out of breath, Proust asked his servant, "Is the English gentleman here?" The servant informed him that Wilde had arrived but almost immediately thereafter went to the bathroom and was still there. Proust rushed to the door: "Mr. Wilde are you ill?" Wilde emerged "majestically": "No, I am not in the least ill. I thought I was to have the pleasure of dining with you alone, but they showed me into the drawing- room. I looked at the drawing-room and at the end of it were your parents, my courage left me. Goodbye, dear Monsieur Proust, goodbye...." Proust learned from his parents that Wilde had made an unpleasant comment concerning the furnishings in the drawing-room: "How ugly your house is" (Jullian 241–42), but this report depicts Wilde so crudely that it undermines itself.

In April 1894, on his final visit to Paris, Wilde dined with Proust at the home of Mme. Arman de Caillavet, where, writes George Painter, "the two men eyed one another...with a complex curiosity" (208–09). They apparently never met again, nor are there any letters known to have been exchanged between them. Painter contends that Wilde "failed to impress Proust: yet perhaps Wilde's glorying in his vice may have taken some effect in that spring of 1894. Possibly there is a little of Wilde in Charlus," the baron in *Remembrance* (209). In the volume of *Remembrance* titled *Cities of the Plain*, Proust alludes to Wilde in a passage concerning the secret lives of homosexuals and the consequences of discovery, a dilemma with which Proust himself was preoccupied: "Their honour precarious, their liberty provisional, lasting only until the discovery of their crime; their position unstable, like that of the poet one day feted in every drawing-room and applauded in every theatre in London, and the next driven from every lodging, unable to find a pillow upon which to lay his head...." (638).

References: George Painter, *Proust: The Early Years* (1959); Philippe Jullian, *Oscar Wilde*, trans. Violet Wyndham (1969); Proust, *Remembrance of Things Past*, trans. C. K. Scott Moncrieff and Terence Kilmartin, Vol. 2 (1981).

Q

"QUANTUM MUTATA"

Published: *Poems* (1881). The Latin title of the poem means "How Much Changed." Probably written after 1877, this sonnet is a response to the Disraeli government's non-interventionist policy toward the Turkish atrocities against the Christian rebels in Bulgaria in 1877, a policy politically motivated by the fear of possible Russian expansion in the Balkans if Turkey's strength were challenged. These events resulted not only in "Quantum Mutata" but also in Wilde's "Sonnet on the Massacre of the Christians in Bulgaria."

The speaker recalls that at one time in Europe long ago "no man died for freedom anywhere, / But England's lion leaping from its lair / Laid hands on the oppressor!" Even the Pope, in his painted portico, "Trembled before our stern ambassadors." But now "from such high estate / We have thus fallen": the wealth of Empire – "Luxury / With barren merchandise piles up the gate" – dominates England instead of noble thoughts and deeds. The mention of Milton in the final line echoes Wilde's lament over England's decline in his sonnet "To Milton."

"QUEEN HENRIETTA MARIA"

Published: *World: A Journal for Men and Woman* 11 (16 July 1879): 18, with an added subtitle: "(*Charles I, act iii*)"; rev. in *Biograph and Review* 4 (Aug. 1880): 135, and in *Poems* (1881), the subtitle removed. In *Poems* (1908), Robert Ross included the dedication "To Ellen Terry," the poem also included under the section heading "Written at the Lyceum Theatre," which had appeared in a MS. (see Mason 227).

The stimulus for this sonnet occurred when Wilde saw a revival of W. G. Wills's *Charles I* at the Lyceum Theatre on 27 June 1879 with Ellen Terry as the queen. Later, she wrote: "Some people thought me best in the camp scene in the third act.... I was proud of it myself when I found that it had inspired Oscar Wilde to write me this lovely sonnet" (*The Story of My Life*, 1908, 181).

Wilde recalls the image of Terry on stage "In the lone tent, waiting for victory, / She stands with eyes marred by the mists of pain, / Like some wan lily overdrenched with rain." With characteristic self-plagiarism, Wilde used the opening lines of the slightly revised sestet ("O hair of gold! O crimson lips! O face / Made for the luring and the love of man!") in Act V of his play *The Duchess of Padua* (1883).

Manuscript: The Huntington Library has a MS. of the poem.

QUEENSBERRY, MARQUESS OF (1844–1900)

The unstable John Sholto Douglas was the 8th Marquess of Queensberry (after the Second World War, the 10th Marquess was ruled to be the 11th Marquess, a previous heir to the title having been passed over because he was "an idiot from birth," hence the ensuing confusion in biographical accounts citing John Sholto Douglas as the 9th Marquess, whereas during his lifetime he was referred to, of course, as the 8th Marquess). The father of Lord Alfred Douglas, he played the role of nemesis in the disaster of Wilde's life and career. Douglas's vilification of his father as "an inhuman brute" presents one aspect of Queensberry's enigmatic personality, but Brian Roberts (whose composite biography of the Douglas family borrows the phrase from Wilde's *De Profundis* for the title of his book, *The Mad Bad Line*) reveals other aspects of Queensberry that have often been overlooked.

At the age of 21, for example, he was disturbed by the report of the disappearance of his younger brother Francis (1847–65), who was in the party that first scaled the Matterhorn. He rushed off to Switzerland, but once there, he refused to wait for a search party but trudged into the snow-laden foothills of the Matterhorn at night without any previous experience of mountain climbing and without proper clothing or equipment; as a result, he was found early the next morning half frozen in the snow. For years, he brooded over his brother's loss: out of this tragedy emerged a long blank-verse poem titled *The Spirit of the Matterhorn* (privately printed in 1881), which expressed his vision of nature's "eternal cycle."

A free-thinker, Queensberry served as president of the British Secular Union while pursuing his lifelong interest in boxing and in horse racing. With an old Cambridge friend, John Graham

Chambers, a founder of the Amateur Athletic Club, he traveled to America to study the rules of boxing. When Chambers subsequently drew up new rules and submitted them to Queensberry for his approval, Chambers, "it seems, insisted on [the rules] being known simply as 'The Queensberry Rules'.... From the outset the intention had been to make boxing more respectable and what, in Victorian England, could be more respectable than a nobleman's name?" (Roberts 56). To his credit, Queensberry never pretended to have had a hand in their actual formulation. Many of Queensberry's supporters contended that honesty – brutal though its expression may have been – was one of his admirable traits.

In the late 1880s and early 1890s, a series of disturbing events undoubtedly contributed to Queensberry's increasingly erratic behavior. In 1887, he wife divorced him on the grounds of adultery (he was a notorious philanderer). His eldest son Francis (1867–94), who had taken a position as secretary to Lord Rosebery, the foreign minister, whom Queensberry suspected (with apparent cause) of being a homosexual, was killed in what was reported to be a hunting accident though rumored to be a suicide. Another son, Percy (1868–1920), later the 9th Marquess of Queensberry, married the daughter of an impoverished clergyman, to whom the 8th Marquess characteristically wrote abusive letters. Queensberry himself had remarried, but the girl was thought to be only 16; an annulment followed. On 1 April 1894, Queensberry, determined either to save or destroy his son and humiliate Wilde, sent Alfred a lengthy letter, which called his relationship with Wilde "loathsome and disgusting" (qtd. in Ellmann 417–18/394).

Queensberry's obsessions and exhibitionistic bravado make sense in view of his disappointments and various family disasters – which go back at least to the 7th Marquess of Queensberry (1818–58), who was found shot on the grounds of his Scottish estate, again under suspicious circumstances. In a notable public embarrassment that occurred during the Wilde trials, Queensberry attacked his son Percy on the street, resulting in both their arrests. So notorious were certain members of the family that a newspaper remarked that they "enjoy an almost unique reputation for eccentricity."

Queensberry's most eccentric action was planned but never executed: at the première of *The Importance of Being Earnest* on 14 February 1895, he appeared at the St. James's Theatre clutching vegetables in what Wilde referred to as a "grotesque bouquet" – possibly carrots and turnips to suggest Wilde's sexual preference. Presumably, Queensberry was planning to fling the bouquet on stage when Wilde appeared before the curtain at the end of the play. What else he had in mind is unknown but possibly a charge that Wilde was a sodomite. Disrupting a theatrical performance was nothing new to Queensberry, for on 14 November 1882, Queensberry had shouted during a performance of Tennyson's play *The Promise of May*, charging that it distorted freethinking views (Ellmann has the wrong title and date: see 388/366).

Having heard of Queensberry's intent to disrupt the première, Wilde had the theater surrounded by 20 policemen to prevent his entrance. Wilde later told Alfred Douglas that Queensberry "prowled about for three hours, then left chattering like a monstrous ape" (*Letters* 383). On 18 February, Queensberry left the famous calling card with the porter of the Albemarle Club (who handed it to Wilde 10 days later), charging that Wilde was "posing" as a sodomite. Wilde's agony and fall had begun: see entries on Douglas and The Trials, 1895.

Reference: Brian Roberts, *The Mad Bad Line: The Family of Lord Alfred Douglas* (1981).

"QUIA MULTUM AMAVI"

Published: *Poems* (1881). The Latin title means "Because I Have Loved Much," probably derived from Swinburne's "Quia Multum Amavit" in *Songs before Sunrise* (1871).

In this lyric poem, the speaker compares his experience when he first saw his "dear Heart" with that of a "young impassioned priest" on first taking from out of "the hidden shrine / His God imprisoned in the Eucharist" and eating the bread and drinking the "dreadful wine." One "Feels not such awful wonder as I felt / When first my smitten eyes beat full on thee...." Yet the "dear Heart" has not returned such idolatry or love; thus the speaker is "sorrow's heritor," a "lackey in the House of Pain." Nevertheless, despite remorse, he is "most glad" to have loved.

For the poems forming a sequence with this one, see "Apologia."

R

RAVENNA

Written: While en route to Greece in March and April of 1877, Wilde visited Ravenna, which fortuitously was the topic later announced in the *Oxford University Gazette* (12 June 1877) for the following year's Newdigate Prize competition: the poem was required to be written in heroic couplets – that is, two rhyming lines in iambic pentameter. In writing his poem in March 1878 (and submitted anonymously, as required, on 31 March, the deadline for submissions), Wilde borrowed and adapted a number of lines from many of his own previously published poems, a practice he habitually employed throughout his career both in prose and verse. As winner of the competition, he received £20 for his poem, excerpts of which he read at an academic convocation in the Sheldonian Theatre at Oxford on 26 June 1878. Previous winners of the Newdigate Prize included John Ruskin (1839), Matthew Arnold (1843), and John Addington Symonds (1860).

Published: 26 June 1878 by Thomas Shrimpton & Son (Oxford). The pamphlet of 16 pages has "Newdigate Prize Poem" on the cover; rpt. in *Poems* (1908).

Wilde dedicated the poem "To my friend George Fleming," the pseudonym of the novelist Julia Constance Fletcher (1858–1938), who had met Wilde in the spring of 1877 in Rome and whose *Mirage* (1877) has a character named Claude Davenant, a young Oxford poet, an enthusiast of Greek paganism and an Aesthete reminiscent of Wilde: "He wore his hair rather long, thrown back, and clustering about his neck like the hair of a mediaeval saint" (see *Letters* 46n). In the auction of Wilde's possessions in 1895, Fleming's novel was among the books offered for sale.

Consisting of seven parts totalling 332 lines, *Ravenna* opens with the announcement that the author had visited the city exactly one year before he submitted his prize poem. After many lines on the Ravenna spring (with an abundance of conventional observations of nature's rebirth), the speaker sees "that Holy City rising clear, / Crowned with crown of towers!" Recalling the historic figures of the past when he sees "the lone tombs where rest the Great of Time" (in 402 AD, the Roman emperor Honorius made Ravenna the capital of the Western Empire, and under the Ostrogoth kings, it was the capital in the later 5th and 6th centuries), the speaker lapses into commonplace sentiment: "...and again / We see that Death is mighty lord of all, / And king and clown to ashen dust must fall." Dante's tomb (the principal reason, perhaps, for Wilde's visit to the city), "his place of resting, far away / From Arno's yellow waters," leads to images of exile and pain: "Yet this dull world is grateful for thy song." This section ends with Wilde's final tribute: "O mightiest exile! all thy grief is done: / Thy soul walks now beside thy Beatrice; / Ravenna guards thine ashes: sleep in peace."

Byron is also recalled, one who lived there "in love and revelry" but who roused himself when "Greece stood up to fight for Liberty, / And called him from Ravenna: never knight / Rode forth more nobly to wild scenes of fight!" And Wilde, wishing to redeem Byron from a lingering reputation as a dissolute immoralist in order, perhaps, to discomfort the dons who sat listening in the Sheldonian Theatre, announces that

> ...England, too, shall glory in her son
> Her warrior-poet, first in song and fight.
> No longer now shall Slander's venomed spite
> Crawl like a snake across his perfect name,
> Or mar the lordly scutcheon of his fame.

Concluding, Wilde evokes the renewed cities of Italy, since 1870 a unified nation, but laments the condition of Ravenna: "But thou, Ravenna, better loved than all, / Thy ruined palaces are but a pall / That hides thy fallen greatness!" Yet the speaker envisions renewal also in this "much-loved city." With many adieus, he takes his leave from this "poet's city.... / Where Dante sleeps, where Byron loved to dwell."

READING PRISON: *See* **PRISON YEARS, 1895–97**

"THE RELATION OF DRESS TO ART"

Published: *PMG*, 28 Feb. 1885, 4; rpt. in *Miscellanies* (1908). The subtitle of this article is "A Note in Black and White on Mr. Whistler's

Lecture" (see also "Mr. Whistler's Ten O'Clock").

In "one of the most valuable passages" in Whistler's "Ten O'Clock" lecture – "Art seeks and finds the beautiful in all times, as did her high priest Rembrandt, when he saw the picturesque grandeur of the Jews' quarter of Amsterdam, and lamented not that its inhabitants were not Greeks" – Wilde perceives that the painter, or the true artist, "does not wait for life to be made picturesque for him, but sees life under picturesque conditions always – under conditions, that is to say, which are at once new and delightful.... That, under certain conditions of light and shade, what is ugly in fact may in its effect become beautiful, is true; and this, indeed, is the real *modernité* of art...."

Turning to the subject suggested by his title, Wilde remarks that he hardly thinks that "pretty and delightful people will continue to wear a style of dress as ugly as it is useless and as meaningless as it is monstrous, even on the chance of such a master as Mr. Whistler spiritualising them into a symphony or refining them in a mist. For the arts are made for life, and not life for the arts." And alluding to Whistler's lecture, Wilde questions whether Whistler has always been true to his dogma "that a painter should paint only the dress of his age and of his actual surroundings: far be it from me to burden a butterfly with the heavy responsibility of its past: I have always been of opinion that consistency is the last refuge of the unimaginative: but have we not all seen, and most of us admired, a picture from his hand of exquisite English girls strolling by an opal sea in the fantastic dresses of Japan?"

Wilde insists that "where there is loveliness of dress, there is no dressing up." Were the national attire "delightful in colour, and in construction simple and sincere..., then would painting be no longer an artificial reaction against the ugliness of life, but become, as it should be, the natural expression of life's beauty." All the arts would benefit "through the increased atmosphere of Beauty by which the artists would be surrounded and in which they would grow up. For Art is not to be taught in Academies. It is what one looks at, not what one listens to, that makes the artist." The "real schools" should be the streets. Whistler, in pointing out that "the power of the painter is to be found in his powers of vision, not in his cleverness of hand, has expressed a truth which needed expression, and which, coming from the lord of form and colour, cannot fail to have its influence."

RELIGION OF ART

As the cultural historian Jacques Barzun has written, the Religion of Art – that is, the use of sacred imagery for aesthetic purposes, the capacity of art "to evoke the transcendent," the work of art as redemptive, and the role of the artist as priest, saint, and visionary – is the source of our present ideas and attitudes towards art today; indeed, "the present age as a whole assumes without question that man's loftiest mode of expression is art" (39). Such figures as Goethe, Schiller, Kant, and Hegel were, writes Barzun, the Religion of Art's "first apostles" during the Enlightenment of the late 18th century:

> Its deism and atheism, its skepticism and materialism left many earnest souls seeking an outlet for piety, a surrogate for the *infâme* church that had been discredited.... Like Rousseau they started from man's kinship with nature, his perception of beauty, and his notion of the ideal. The desire to grasp all three in one fused experience leads to art as supreme spiritual fulfillment.... (26)

The Religion of Art, prominent among writers, painters, and composers throughout the 19th century, provided the means of achieving "the effects of religious fervor – enthusiasm, awe-struck admiration, raptures and devoutness. Great artists constituted the Communion of Saints" (Barzun 27). In Wagner's story "Death in Paris" (1841), for example, a dying German musician is one of these martyred saints who have died in the cause of Art:

> I believe in God, Mozart, and Beethoven, and likewise their disciples and apostles; I believe in the Holy Spirit and the truth of the one, indivisible Art; I believe that this Art proceeds from God, and lives within the hearts of all illuminated men.... I believe that through this Art all men are saved, and therefore each may die for Her of hunger.... Amen!

In *The Doctor's Dilemma* (1906), Bernard Shaw – a "perfect Wagnerite" – depicts the dying artist Louis Dubedat, who exclaims the creed of the Religion of Art with its dogma of redemption: "I believe in Michael Angelo, Velásquez, and Rembrandt, in the might of design, the mystery of colour, the redemption of all things by Beauty everlasting, and the message of Art that has made these hands blessed. Amen. Amen."

Such a view of the artist differs radically from that of Carlyle, who believed that the religious vision of the artist (the Romantic poet as prophet) could be the handmaid of stability for Victorian culture, though he distrusted the "dandiacal sect" of alienated artists hostile to bourgeois society. Ruskin's aesthetic vision, important to Wilde, was also ultimately religious in his conception of art, the purpose of which was to inculcate spiritual values. As Hilary Fraser remarks, "Arnold's position was an even more complicated one than Ruskin's, for he was not only saying with the early Ruskin, 'Religion is Morals' and 'Art is Morals,' but saying with Pater and Wilde that 'Religion is Art,' and that Hebraism ['strictness of conscience'] should be making way for Hellenism ['spontaneity of consciousness']" (182).

In the 19th century, such figures as Poe, Baudelaire, Mallarmé, and Rimbaud, who had either lost their religious faith or had unsettling doubt as the result of scientific materialism, embraced the Religion of Art as a suitable substitute for a lost sacred order in a world incapable of providing spiritual comfort. In his autobiography, W. B. Yeats reveals that such scientists as T. H. Huxley and John Tyndall had deprived him of the "simple-minded religion" of his childhood. For him, the alternative was not atheism but art, which held the promise of regenerating his spiritual life: "I had made a new religion, almost an infallible church of poetic tradition.... I had even created a dogma" (77). Yeats consequently studied the occult, like others before him, and experimented with magic in order to affirm the eternal world, from which he drew image and symbol for his art. In his apocalyptic essay "The Autumn of the Flesh" (1898), later retitled "The Autumn of the Body," he writes that a new age is at hand, for the arts have the capacity to restore the lost world of spirit: "The arts are, I believe, about to take upon their shoulders the burdens that have fallen from the shoulders of priests, and to lead us back upon our journey by filling our thoughts with the essences of things, and not with things" ("Autumn" 191–93).

Arthur Symons, Yeats's friend and major interpreter of the French Symbolists, wrote at the end of his "Introduction" to *The Symbolist Movement in Literature* (1900) that literature, "in speaking to us intimately, so solemnly, as only religion had hitherto spoken to us...becomes itself a kind of religion, with all the duties and responsibilities of the sacred ritual." Like Symons, many writers employed the image of the poet as priest presiding over the Mystery of Transubstantiation in the process of re-spiritualizing the Word. In his essay on Rimbaud, Symons suggests the analogy of the work of art with the Eucharist, the artist's imagination equivalent to the priest's transforming power: "Is it not tempting...to worship the golden chalice in which the wine has been made God, as if the chalice were the reality, and the Real Presence the symbol?"

Nineteenth-century Aesthetes had also provided themselves with appropriate martyrs (for example, Keats, of whom legend said that he had died after receiving adverse reviews of his verse), the destiny of such figures dramatizing the indifference of society to art. Yeats's story "The Crucifixion of the Outcast" (1897) raises the conflict to mythic dimensions in its depiction of an unsympathetic abbot (symbolizing the Established Church in its fear that art may be subversive) and a wandering bard (who, like Christ, is crucified at the top of a hill, another Calvary). As Symons remarks in *The Symbolist Movement in Literature*: "It is the poet against society, society against the poet, a direct antagonism." One of Wilde's early poems "The Grave of Keats" depicts the poet as the "youngest of the Martyrs... / Fair as Sebastian, and as early slain" (St. Sebastian was taken as Wilde's model when he adopted the name after his release from prison). In his essay "The Tomb of Keats," which concludes with the poem on Keats, Wilde calls him "a Priest of Beauty slain before his time."

In some of Wilde's fairy tales, the Religion of Art plays a significant role in the lives of the various characters. "The Nightingale and the Rose," for example, depicts the sacrifice/ martyrdom of the nightingale in the creation of a "work of art" – here, the rose (the nightingale in Romantic literature recalls, in particular, Keats's "Ode to a Nightingale," the surrogate for the artist). In "The Young King," the eponymous character discovers in his loneliness that "the secrets of art are best learned in secret, and that Beauty, like Wisdom, loves the lonely worshipper." He is seen kneeling in "real adoration before a great picture that had just been brought from Venice, and that seemed to herald the worship of some new gods."

In Chapter 11 of *The Picture of Dorian Gray*, Dorian briefly enacts his devotion to the Religion of Art in his aesthetic rather than religious attraction to Roman Catholic ritual, stirred as he was by the "sacrifice" and beauty implicit in the sacred Mass:

He loved to kneel down on the cold marble pavement and watch the priest, in his stiff flowered dalmatic, slowly and with white hands moving aside the veil of the tabernacle, or raising aloft the jewelled, lantern-shaped monstrance with that pallid wafer that at times, one would fain think, is indeed the *"panis caelestis,"* the bread of angels, or, robed in the garments of the Passion of Christ, breaking the Host into the chalice.... But he never fell into the error of arresting his intellectual development by any formal acceptance of creed or system....

In "The Cultured Faun" (1891), Lionel Johnson parodies the novel's depiction of Dorian as a Decadent with "just a dash of the dandy" in his self-indulgence in the "exquisite adoration of suffering":

Here comes in a tender patronage of Catholicism: white tapers upon the high altar, an ascetic and beautiful young priest, the great gilt monstrance, the subtle-scented and mystical incense,...the splendor of the sacred vestments. We kneel at some hour, not too early for our convenience, repeating the solemn Latin, drinking in those Gregorian tones, with plenty of modern French sonnets in memory, should the sermon be dull. But to join the Church! Ah, no! better to dally with the enchanting mysteries.... (111)

Later, in *A Portrait of the Artist as a Young Man* (1914), Joyce reaffirmed the sacred role of the artist in presenting Stephen Dedalus (his first name recalling the first Christian martyr, who was accused of blasphemy) as "priest of eternal imagination, transmuting the daily bread of experience into the radiant body of everliving life." The image of the artist as a member of an alienated elite is presented by Joyce as the "God of creation, [who] remains within or behind or beyond or above his handiwork, invisible, refined out of existence, indifferent, paring his fingernails." Such, then, was the mythology of Aestheticism, which – associated with Decadence and Symbolism – was to become central to the mainstream of Modernism.

References: W. B. Yeats, "The Autumn of the Body," *Essays and Introductions* (1961); *The Autobiography of W. B. Yeats* (1965); Maurice Beebe, "Art as Religion," *Ivory Towers and Sacred Founts: The Artist as Hero in Fiction from Goethe to Joyce* (1964); Jacques Barzun, "The Rise of Art as Religion," *The Use and Abuse of Art* (1973); Karl Beckson, "A Mythology of Aestheticism," *ELT* 17:4 (1974); Lionel Johnson, "The Cultured Faun," *Aesthetes and Decadents of the 1890s*, 2nd ed., Karl Beckson (1981); Hilary Fraser, "Aestheticism: Walter Pater and Oscar Wilde," *Beauty and Belief: Aesthetics and Religion in Victorian Literature* (1986).

"THE REMARKABLE ROCKET"

Published: *The Happy Prince and Other Tales* (1888).

The Plot: The King's son, who had waited for a year for his bride, a Russian princess, is about to be married. The elaborate celebration in the Great Hall even includes a flute performance by the King and fireworks. At the stand where the Royal Pyrotechnist has put everything in place, the fireworks begin talking among themselves. The Catherine Wheel complains that "Romance is dead," while the "very remarkable Rocket," impressed with himself and speaking "as if he were dictating his memoirs," insists that, if anything happened to him on that night, the Prince and Princess "would never be happy again, their whole married life would be spoiled." He claims that the "only thing that sustains one through life is the consciousness of the immense inferiority of everybody else, and this is a feeling that I have always cultivated." Later, he says: "I am always thinking about myself, and I expect everybody else to do the same." (In *An Ideal Husband*, Lord Goring, also expressing his narcissistic self-admiration, remarks: "To love oneself is the beginning of a life-long romance.")

At midnight, the King commands the Royal Pyrotechnist to begin the fireworks display, which lights up the sky. The Rocket, however, who had been weeping over the mere possibility of some disaster occurring to the Prince and Princess, can not go off at all because the gunpowder is too wet. On the next day, a workman throws the "bad rocket" over the wall into a ditch. A brief conversation with a Frog occurs, prompting the Rocket to conclude that the Frog was "very ill-bred": "I hate people who talk about themselves, as you do, when one wants to talk about oneself, as I do."

A Duck, who also engages him in conversation, is struck by the Rocket's remark that he can "fly up into the sky and come down in a shower of golden rain." The Duck sees no usefulness in doing that, but the Rocket answers "in a very haughty tone of voice": "My good creature, I see that you belong to the lower orders. A person of my position is never useful. We have certain accomplishments, and that is more than sufficient" (another anti-Victorian sentiment by Wilde, the dandy). The Rocket concludes that "hard work is simply the refuge of people who have nothing whatever to do." He avoids domesticity, for it "ages one rapidly, and distracts one's mind from higher things." When the Duck leaves, the Rocket sinks a little deeper into the mud and begins to think about "the loneliness of genius."

Two boys approach, pile sticks together, and put the Rocket at the top. He is delighted: "I know that I shall go much higher than the stars, much higher than the moon, much higher than the sun." Up in the sky, he explodes, but no one sees him, not even the boys, who are sound asleep. The Rocket's stick falls to earth, landing on the back of a Goose, who exclaims: "Good heavens! It is going to rain sticks," and she rushes into the water. The Rocket's final words end the story: "I knew I should create a great sensation," and he goes out.

On the publication of *The Happy Prince and Other Tales*, Pater wrote to Wilde, praising the volume, particularly the "wise wit" of "The Remarkable Rocket" (Pater, *Letters* 85).

Manuscript: Texas has a TS. with Wilde's corrections of a French translation.

"REMORSE: (A STUDY IN SAFFRON)"

Not published in Wilde's lifetime, this lyric poem appeared in Bobby Fong, "Oscar Wilde: Five Fugitive Poems," *ELT* 22:1 (1979): 13. Fong states that the poem was written on a card, the reverse side of which contains the words: "Written for me by Oscar Wilde in exchange for an autograph Sonnett [*sic*] of Paul Verlaine. 10 November 1889. GE." – probably Mrs. Gabrielle Enthoven (see *Echoes*).

The ambivalent eroticism in this poem, as Fong suggests, may be the result of the "latent sexual conflicts" that were brought "to the fore" by Wilde's marriage in 1884. The speaker's frankness in the early lines is counterpointed against the implication of the title: "I love your body when it lies / Like amber on the silken sheets." Indeed, he loves everything about the apparent object of his desire, including her "honey-coloured hair / That ripples to your ivory hips." The concluding lines reinforce the "remorse" of the title, which suggests the speaker's perverse delight in his apparent rejection by his loved one: "But most of all, my love! I love / Your beautiful fierce chastity!"

Manuscripts: The Clark Library has two MSS.: an untitled early draft of three stanzas (printed in Dulau 13) and the presentation copy to "GE" cited above. In 1961, the Clark Library privately printed a facsimile of the card presented to "GE" with a note by Majl Ewing (copies of which were presented as mementoes of a visit to the library by members of the Grolier Club in New York).

REPUTATION, LITERARY

At the conclusion of his magisterial biography, Richard Ellmann sums up his final estimate of Wilde as though speaking to posterity:

> His work survived as he had claimed it would. We inherit his struggle to achieve supreme fictions in art, to associate art with social change, to bring together individual and social impulse, to save what is eccentric and singular from being sanitized and standardized, to replace a morality of severity by one of sympathy. He belongs to our world more than to Victoria's. Now, beyond the reach of scandal, his best writings validated by time, he comes before us still, a towering figure, laughing and weeping, with parables and paradoxes, so generous, so amusing, and so right. (589/554–55)

Yet Wilde's literary reputation remains less than certain, and its long and complicated history has inevitably included his personal life as well as his literary career. In the late 19th century, critics judged Wilde, as one might expect, by the narrow criterion of Victorian aesthetics, now generally held in disrepute: that is, a work's "sincerity." In "The Critic as Artist," Wilde disputed the legitimacy of such a standard in judging the value of any work of art: "A little sincerity is a dangerous thing. All bad poetry springs from genuine feeling." Insincerity, in fact, was central to the creation of art, he contended in *The Picture of Dorian Gray*, for it was "merely a method by which we multiply our personalities" – the idea of the mask, which Yeats adopted for his own poetics. The poet Francis Thompson, writing to a friend in 1890, reveals the characteristic Victorian bias in judging Wilde: "A witty, paradoxical writer, who, nevertheless, *meo judicio*, will do nothing permanent because he is in earnest about nothing" (44). Did Wilde, one wonders, title his greatest, most "insincere," and most artificial play *The Importance of Being Earnest* in order to discomfort the critics over his *lack* of earnestness?

As for the morality of a work of art, the Aesthetic Movement, in which Wilde was prominent, was devoted to combating such a standard of judgment, for art had its own unique integrity whereas morality, as a standard of judgment, was concerned with behavior, not works of the imagination. Hence, because of his advocacy of art for art's sake, Wilde was often the subject of attack or ridicule. Those who supported aesthetic doctrine did not deny that morality, as a subject, could be part of a work of art, but, as Arthur Symons insisted, the work itself could not be condemned as either "moral" or "immoral." Wilde expressed the point succinctly in the "Preface" to *Dorian Gray*: "There is no such thing as a moral or an immoral book. Books are well written, or badly written. That is all." Because of the narrow Victorian biases concerning the value of art, critics regarded Wilde as less than a reliable guide to morality and spiritual enlightenment.

From the time of his first volume of poems, *Poems* (1881), *Punch* (25 June) focused on Wilde as an object of hilarity by publishing an illustration depicting Wilde's head at the center of an aesthetic sunflower, accompanied by the following:

> Aesthete of Aesthetes!
> What's in a name?
> The poet is WILDE,
> But his poetry's tame.

The general consensus among reviewers was that Wilde had imitated other poets so that, as the *Athenaeum* (23 July) contended, there was no "distinct message" from the "apostle of the new worship" of beauty. The lack of sincerity, as the *Saturday Review* (23 July) complained, was the "great fault of all such writing as this...." The American reviewers, however, reacted favorably, the *Century* (Nov.), for example, citing "Ave Imperatrix": "How an Englishman can read it without a glow of pride and sigh of sorrow is beyond comprehension. Mr. Wilde can comfort himself. 'Ave Imperatrix' outweighs a hundred cartoons of *Punch*." Yet Wilde would soon reject patriotic verse as inartistic and focus on art free of such discourse.

After his American lecture tour in 1882, which resulted in considerable acclaim and expected ridicule principally because of his aesthetic costume, Wilde witnessed the failure of his first produced play, *Vera; or, The Nihilists*, which closed in New York within a week, *Punch* (1 Sept. 1883) noting that it was "Vera Bad." In contrast to this setback, Wilde's *The Happy Prince and Other Tales* was a veritable triumph, the *Universal Review* (June 1888) stating that the volume "shows Mr. Oscar Wilde's genius at its best." The critical reception resulted in good sales, which even helped *Poems* in the United States, where Roberts Brothers of Boston issued three printings between 1888 and 1894.

The publication of the first version of *The Picture of Dorian Gray*, however, created a critical storm because of its homoerotic subtext, implied in various reviews but not identified as such. The *St. James's Gazette* (24 June 1890) cited the novel's "esoteric prurience," adding: "The writer airs his cheap research among the garbage of the French *Décadents* like any drivelling pedant," hoping – somewhat facetiously – that the Vigilance Society would not prosecute the book. Wilde joined in the debate over the morality of the novel, but he was outnumbered by the number of the reviews (Wilde estimated some 200) that expressed disapproval. Certainly, he had achieved notoriety.

In the following year, Wilde's second play, *The Duchess of Padua*, in a New York production, was not well received, its "insincerity" again raised as a battle cry. Shortly thereafter, the appearance of Wilde's essays in critical theory, *Intentions*, provoked some reviewers to denigrate his paradoxical wit, but Arthur Symons wrote in an unsigned review in the *Speaker* (4 July 1891) that Wilde "has gained a reputation for frivolity which does injustice to a writer who has at least always been serious in the reality of his devotion to art" – a rare comment at the time. *Intentions*, however, did win over some reviewers, such as the one in the *Pall Mall Gazette* (12 May), who praised the book as "fascinating, stimulating...with more common sense in it than [Wilde] would perhaps care to be accused of."

With his society drama *Lady Windermere's Fan*, Wilde began a series of dramatic triumphs that pleased audiences if not always the drama critics, who, to be sure, were critical of his paradoxical wit, which seemed to undermine the drama. Nevertheless, Wilde was cheered by the support of some of the leading critics, such as A. B. Walkley, who, in the *Speaker* (27 Feb. 1892) regarded its "brilliant talk" as "entirely successful." In that year, Wilde was distressed by the decision of the Lord Chamberlain's Examiner of Plays not to license his *Salomé* because it portrayed biblical characters (and possibly because of its shocking perversity).

Nevertheless, in the following year, *A Woman of No Importance*, though it ran for a month less than *Lady Windermere's Fan*, drew high praise from the leading critic and translator of Ibsen, William Archer, who in the *World* (26 April 1893), contended that Wilde's dramatic work "stands alone... on the very highest plane of modern English drama," but he noted that Wilde's "pyrotechnic wit" was "one of the defects of his qualities." Indeed, even Walkley in the *Speaker* (29 April) confessed that Wilde's witty paradoxes were beginning to tire him by their sheer number despite the playwright's "true dramatic instinct."

Wilde's final plays, *An Ideal Husband* and *The Importance of Being Earnest* were staged early in 1895 just a month apart. The former received high praise from Archer, Walkley, Shaw, and William Dean Howells, despite what Archer called Wilde's "epigram-factory." Even *Punch* (2 Feb. 1895), which was more respectful as Wilde's career progressed, called *An Ideal Husband* an "unmistakable success." In New York, most of the critics regarded it as Wilde's best play thus far. When *The Importance of Being Earnest* opened shortly after *An Ideal Husband*, Wilde was almost universally lauded for his masterpiece. The actor Allan Aynesworth, who created the role of Algernon Moncrieff, told Hesketh Pearson: "In my 53 years

of acting, I never remember a greater triumph than the first night of *The Importance of Being Earnest*. The audience rose in their seats and cheered and cheered again" (qtd. in Pearson 257). The critics agreed, though Shaw had reservations in the *Saturday Review* (23 Feb. 1895): "I cannot say that I greatly cared for *The Importance of Being Earnest*. It amused me, of course; but unless comedy touches me as well as amuses me, it leaves me with a sense of having wasted my evening." Nevertheless, audiences flocked to Wilde's plays in the West End, the extraordinary event of Wilde's having two major theatrical successes at the same time.

But in April, Wilde's world came to an end. Archer, wrote to his brother a few days after Wilde's first criminal trial began:

Really the luck is against the poor British drama – the man who has more brains in his little finger than all the rest of them in their whole body goes and commits worse than suicide in this way. However, it shows that what I hoped for in Oscar could never have come about – I thought he might get rid of his tomfoolery and affectation and do something really fine. (qtd. in Charles Archer 215–16)

Wilde's imprisonment and subsequent self-exile on the Continent resulted in his final work, *The Ballad of Reading Gaol*, one that Arthur Symons praised in the *Saturday Review* (12 March 1898) as a "very powerful piece of writing," indicating an "extraordinary talent." The poem sold remarkably well, requiring the publisher to issue several editions; in the seventh edition, Wilde's name appeared on the title page for the first time beneath his cell block number, C.3.3., which had identified the author.

With Wilde's death, many obituaries remained unappreciative of his achievement, the *Pall Mall Gazette* (1 Dec. 1900) remarking that Wilde's plays were "full of bright moments but devoid of consideration as drama"; the *Literary World* (7 Dec.) noted that the "names of Mr. Wilde's works were at one time almost household words in literary circles, but they have fallen into obscurity since his disappearance from society." In Dublin, the leading literary periodical, *Irish Monthly*, carried no notice of Wilde's death. In France, however, Henry-D. Davray, who had translated

The Ballad of Reading Gaol, wrote in the *Mercure de France* (Feb. 1901) that Wilde was "a pure artist and a great writer," and Stuart Merrill, the American poet who lived much of his life in France, remarked in *La Plume* (15 Dec. 1900) that Wilde was the "most unfortunate man of our times.... Let the work of Oscar Wilde appear to us henceforth in the serene beauty of anonymity."

In 1905, the publication of the prison letter titled *De Profundis*, cut drastically by Robert Ross, gave the impression to many that Wilde had repented. Reviews appeared with such titles as "A Soul's Awakening" and "A Book of Penitence," but Shaw wrote to Ross that the work was "all comedy," that there was no fundamental change in Wilde despite the many cuts in the text. Nevertheless, the public reaction to Wilde was probably more sympathetic as the result of Ross's edition since Wilde's love affair with Alfred Douglas was entirely omitted.

On 1 December 1908, at a dinner in Robert Ross's honor on the publication of the *Collected Edition*, which he had edited, Ross recalled that, in 1901, an official at the Court of Bankruptcy assured him, when Wilde's creditors had received about three shillings on the pound, that "Wilde's works were of no value; and would never command any interest whatever...." Ross emphasized that Wilde's "regenerated reputation was made in Germany" (indeed, Wilde was generally regarded there as one of the three greatest British writers, the other two being Shakespeare and Byron). The royalties from productions of Wilde's plays in Germany, principally *Salomé*, together with receipts from *De Profundis*, paid off not only all of the English creditors by mid-1906 but also those in France "in accordance with Wilde's last wishes" (Ross 154).

However, the biographical approach to Wilde, which predominated at the time of his death as a result of the sensationalism associated with his disgrace and imprisonment as well as his genius for paradox and theatrical style, gathered momentum through the early 20th century. Richard Le Gallienne's introduction to *The Complete Works of Oscar Wilde* (New York, 1907) was characteristic: "The writings of Oscar Wilde, brilliant and even beautiful as they are, are but the marginalia, so to say, of a striking fantastic personality."

When Wilde's plays were revived, his popularity again soared. In a letter to Ross on 5 December 1909, about the production of *The Importance of Earnest* at the St. James's Theatre, the actor-manager George Alexander wrote: "You will be glad to hear that dear *E* has really caught on: we had splendid houses yesterday....how this would have pleased him!" (Ross 173). Moreover, early in the 20th century, translations of Wilde's works began to appear in virtually every European country as well as in Japan, China, and the Middle East.

In his widely influential study, *The Eighteen Nineties* (1913), Holbrook Jackson devotes a chapter to Wilde, which begins with a consideration of his enigmatic personality:

> The singularity of Oscar Wilde has puzzled writers since his death quite as much as it puzzled the public during the startled years of his wonderful visit to these glimpses of Philistia; for after all that has been written about him we are no nearer a convincing interpretation of his character than we were during the great silence which immediately followed his trial and imprisonment.

Because Jackson's initial approach is biographical, like that of other critics and literary historians at the time, the serious and scholarly examination of Wilde's literary works would be impeded by the primary interest in his character, as though it were the key to an understanding and judgment of his achievement. In his discussion of Wilde's works, Jackson inevitably returns to personality, as in the following passage, which echoes Gide's memory of Wilde, who said that he had put only his talent into his art and his genius into his life:

> With many writers, perhaps the majority, it requires no effort to forget the author in the book, because literature has effectually absorbed personality, or all that was distinctive of the author's personality. With Oscar Wilde it is otherwise. His books can never be the abstract and brief chronicles of himself; for, admittedly on his part, and recognisably on the part of others, he put even more distinction into his life than he did into his art. (rpt. in Beckson)

In the 1920s, caution among the English concerning Wilde's stature as a writer persisted, as in the judgment of E.T. Raymond in the *Outlook* (4 Dec. 1920):

...those who would pass by this ill-starred man of genius because of the event which interrupted his career as a writer would be acting almost as foolishly as the absurd people (mostly Germans) who on the same account yield him a perverse and irrational homage. Wilde was not only important in himself; he was still more important as the representative of a mood still to some extent with us, but extraordinarily prevalent in the latter years of the nineteenth century. Of this mood he was in letters the only able English representative.

And Archer, whose admiration of Wilde's genius surpassed that of other late 19th-century drama critics, remarked in *The Old Drama and the New* (1923) that the continued popularity of Wilde in Germany must "be taken largely as a political demonstration – a wilful glorification of a man whom England cast out." By 1954, James Laver wrote in a British Council monograph that though Wilde had a "permanent niche" in literary history, his reputation has remained problematic: "On the continent of Europe his reputation stands as high as ever it did, and his name is probably, after Shakespeare's, the best known in English letters. Englishmen are inclined to think this estimate exaggerated..." (7).

Despite the passage of time and the gradual movement away from a biographical approach to Wilde to a critical assessment of his literary achievement, periodically there has been retrogression in the writing about Wilde. In 1970, Bernard Bergonzi echoed what Wilde had said to André Gide and what Richard Le Gallienne had contended in his 1907 introduction to the collected works: "...[Wilde] is difficult to place in literary history, since, as he admitted, he devoted his genius to his life rather than his art." Wilde, "a tragic celebrity with relatively slender talents," produced work "largely derivative" (24). The focus on the life at the expense of the art is also central to Morley Sheridan's popular biography, *Oscar Wilde* (1976), which intends "to show that Oscar's own life was indeed the greatest of all theatrical productions" (10).

With the appearance of Ellmann's biography, Wilde's stature as a major writer confirmed the judgments of some previous writers, such as Ian Fletcher and John Stokes, who, in their 1976 survey of Wilde scholarship, wrote: "He is more than a figure in the dense literary history of Britain; he is a figure in world culture, as both hero and victim" (48). At the opening of his biography, Ellmann writes: "Oscar Wilde: we have only to hear the great name to anticipate that what will be quoted as his will surprise and delight us. Among the writers identified with the 1890s, Wilde is the only one whom everyone still reads" (xv/xiii). In the *Observer* (4 Oct. 1987), Anthony Burgess, in reviewing the biography, writes that Wilde "has been considered minor, and his art still tends to be overshadowed by the scandal of his life," yet Burgess agrees with Ellmann's estimate of Wilde's stature ("the great name"): "These epithets are just. No one glitters as Wilde does...."

In an attempt to dispel "The Myth of Wilde" (focused on his tragic fall, as Ellmann's biography does, though not exclusively), Ian Small writes in *Oscar Wilde Revalued* (1993) that the enormous number of books, articles, and reviews that have been published on Wilde reveals that "few writers have achieved the distinction of having had so much ink spilled on their behalf. By the same token, however, virtually no major writer in English has been so badly treated for so long by the academic and non-academic critical industries alike" (1). Though the amount of such material on Wilde has continued "to grow inexorably," writes Small, "in the last fifteen years the *nature* of writing about Wilde has changed almost beyond recognition." A new "de-mythologized" Wilde has emerged in recent publications in "gender studies, women's studies, textual scholarship, or theatre history":

Wilde becomes the epitome of the new type of professional writer at the turn of the century, concerned with the unglamorous business of self-promotion, negotiating with publishers, cultivating potential reviewers, and constantly polishing his work.... The "new" Wilde is preoccupied with issues such as authority, gender, identity, and prison reform; he is seen as thoroughly and seriously engaged with some of the most contentious intellectual issues of his day. (3)

The "newness" of Small's Wilde may be somewhat exaggerated, but it is unquestionably true that Wilde continues to be, as Fletcher and Stokes remarked in 1976, "a figure in world culture" –

that is, a major writer central to the development of early Modernism in the late 19th century and a notable influence in its later manifestations.

Wilde's stature achieved official recognition on 14 February 1995 – the 100th anniversary of the première of *The Importance of Being Earnest* – when a window was dedicated to him in the Poets' Corner in the south transept of Westminster Abbey, where Chaucer, Dryden, Browning and Tennyson are buried and where such figures as Shakespeare, Milton, Blake, Wordsworth, Keats, Shelley, Byron, Dickens, the Brontë sisters, Thackeray, Hardy, Kipling, and T. S. Eliot have memorials of one kind or another acknowledging their contributions to the nation.

References: Hesketh Pearson, *The Life of Oscar Wilde* (1946); Walter Nelson, *Oscar Wilde in Sweden and Other Essays* (1965); John Evangelist Walsh, ed., *The Letters of Francis Thompson* (1969); Bernard Bergonzi, "Fin de Siècle," *The Turn of the Century: Essays on Victorian and Modern English Literature* (1973); Ian Fletcher and John Stokes, "Oscar Wilde," *Anglo-Irish Literature: A Review of Research*, ed. Richard Finneran (1976), and its supplement, *Recent Research in Anglo-Irish Writers* (1983); Agustin Coletes, "Oscar Wilde en España, 1902–1928," *Cuaderno de Filologia Inglesa* (1985); Walter Nelson, *Oscar Wilde from "Ravenna" to "Salome": A Survey of Contemporary English Criticism* (1987); Roy Rosenstein, "Re(dis)-covering Wilde for Latin America," *Rediscovering Oscar Wilde*, ed. C. George Sandulescu (1994).

"REQUIESCAT"

Published: *Poems* (1881); rev. in (1882).

Written: Wilde noted that this poem (its Latin title meaning "May She Rest") was written at Avignon some seven years after his sister, Isola, died on 23 February 1867, less than two months before her 10th birthday. Wilde, who was 12 at the time of her death, later made regular visits to her grave: Isola's doctor recalled that Wilde's "lonely and inconsolable grief" sought relief in "long and frequent visits to his sister's grave in the village cemetery" (qtd. in Mason 295).

Sources: Critics have noted the similarity of Wilde's lyric poem to Thomas Hood's "The Bridge of Sighs" (1844), as in the lines: "Take her up tenderly / Lift her with care; / Fashion'd so slenderly, Young, and so fair!" Another possible inspiration may have been Matthew Arnold's "Requiescat" (1853): "Strew on her roses, roses, / And never a spray of yew! / In quiet she reposes; / Ah, would that I did too!"

In its quiet simplicity, Wilde's lyric poem embodies his deep sense of loss:

> Tread lightly, she is near
> Under the snow,
> Speak gently, she can hear
> The daisies grow.

Her "bright golden hair" is tarnished with rust: "She that was young and fair / Fallen dust." The final lines – "All my life's buried here, / Heap earth upon it" – are reminiscent of another untimely death of a young girl, that of Ophelia in *Hamlet*. When she is lowered into her grave, the mourning Laertes leaps in after her: "Now pile your dust upon the quick and dead..." (V.i.251).

When compiling *A Book of Irish Verse* (1895), W. B. Yeats asked Wilde for permission to include "Requiescat." Wilde responded: "I don't know that I think 'Requiescat' very typical of my work" (*Letters* 365). Though Wilde suggested other poems, Yeats included only "Requiescat."

Manuscript: The Clark Library has a MS. of the poem.

REVIEWS (1908): *See COLLECTED EDITION*

RICKETTS, CHARLES (1866–1931) and CHARLES SHANNON (1863–1937)

The costume and stage designer, painter, sculptor, and book illustrator Charles Ricketts and his lifelong friend and companion – the wood engraver, lithographer, and painter Charles Shannon – were living in a small semi-detached house once owned by Whistler in a Chelsea cul-de-sac called "The Vale" when Wilde met them in May 1889. On first meeting Ricketts, Wilde remarked in a letter that he had found him "very cultured and interesting" (*Letters* 249). In the summer of that year, Ricketts and Shannon issued the first number of the *Dial: An Occasional Publication* (1889–97), which reflected the influence of French Symbolist art and literature. Ernest Dowson called the periodical "that mad, strange art review" (Dowson, *Letters*, 169).

By the beginning of the 1890s, The Vale had become, on Friday evenings, the gathering place of artists and writers, Wilde among them. According to J. G. P. Delaney, Wilde was at his best in Ricketts's brilliant, witty company, and according to Wilde's friend, the artist and writer W. Graham Robertson, Ricketts "had modelled himself so much upon Oscar – voice and speech sometimes [were] identical.... I suppose Oscar had made such a tremendous impression upon Ricketts when they first met and the imitation followed unconsciously" (qtd. in Delaney 57).

In 1889, Wilde had asked Ricketts to paint a small picture of Willie Hughes in the Elizabethan style as the frontispiece to an enlarged book edition of "The Portrait of Mr W. H." Wilde regarded the picture as "quite wonderful" (Shannon had designed the frame for it), and he promised to "come round and enjoy the company of the Dialists..." (*Letters* 250). The volume, however, never appeared in Wilde's lifetime (see the MS.'s subsequent history in the main entry). After Wilde's arrest, Ricketts's picture was sold at the auction held in Tite Street on 24 April 1895.

Throughout the 1890s, Ricketts and Shannon designed, either singly or together, almost all of Wilde's books: Ricketts designed the title-page and binding of *The Picture of Dorian Gray*, *Poems* (1892), and *The Sphinx* as well as the binding of *Intentions* and *Lord Arthur Savile's Crime and Other Stories*. Together Ricketts and Shannon designed and illustrated *A House of Pomegranates*. Shannon designed the binding of *Lady Windermere's Fan*, *A Woman of No Importance*, *An Ideal Husband*, and *The Importance of Being Earnest*.

When *A House of Pomegranates* appeared, the reviewer in the *Speaker* (28 Nov. 1891) confused the work of Ricketts and Shannon. Wilde wrote to the editor that Shannon was the "drawer of dreams" and that Ricketts was "the subtle and fantastic decorator," having designed the binding, the title-page, and the decorations in the text. Indeed, Ricketts had designed the entire book, having selected type and having placed the ornamentation while Shannon provided four illustrations. The reviewer's objection to Ricketts's cover was countered by Wilde, who responded that both he and Ricketts admired it "immensely" (*Letters* 300). However, when *The Sphinx* was in production, Wilde told Ricketts: "...your drawings are not of your best. You have seen them through your intellect, not your temperament" (qtd. in Ricketts,

Wilde 38).

At the time of Wilde's arrest and trials, Ricketts was deeply perturbed, dreading the possibility that he might himself become involved in the tragedy. In his diary in 1916, he wrote:

I believe the crash of his scandal affected his contemporaries to a degree unknown to younger people. Not only did eminent men, his seniors, do nothing, but several friends behaved badly, Sarah Bernhardt, for instance, Degas, Gosse, and I believe Burne-Jones. Meredith was brutal and Morris indifferent....it is only with men of my age, whose career was actually affected by the crash, that the story shows itself as a tragic event, in which the fiber of the nation seemed of poor quality. Personal friends of Oscar's who had positions to maintain may have passed unpleasant moments, and still remember this. (qtd. in Delaney 96).

But since Ricketts, though also homosexual, had never been associated with homosexual circles – indeed, he disapproved of such groups – he had little to fear, though, as Delaney remarks, Ricketts "must have felt keenly the humiliation and vindictiveness that Wilde had suffered" (97).

On 10 May 1897, fewer than ten days before Wilde was released from Reading Prison, Ricketts visited him, but before he was scheduled to make the visit, Wilde wrote to More Adey, who questioned whether Ricketts should be present when Adey and Ross were discussing personal matters with Wilde. To Adey, Wilde wrote that Ricketts had applied often to visit him: "...it was not for me to refuse a kindly offer from an artist of whom I am very fond, but I think that after half-an-hour I will ask Ricketts to leave us together to talk business... (*Letters* 534). After Ricketts's visit, Wilde told Ross: "...I was wrong to have Ricketts present: he meant to be cheering, but I thought him trivial: everything he said, including his remark that he supposed time went very fast in prison (a singularly unimaginative opinion, and one showing an entirely inartistic lack of sympathetic instinct), annoyed me extremely" (*Letters* 541). At the time of Wilde's release, Ricketts contributed £100 to a fund for Wilde, a contribution that he preferred to remain anonymous, but Ross repaid him in later years out of the Wilde estate. After leaving Reading Prison, Wilde looked forward to seeing Ricketts and Shannon in August 1897 at Berneval.

When *The Ballad of Reading Gaol* appeared, Wilde had a copy sent to Ricketts (though, curiously, not to Shannon), and when the "author's edition" of 99 signed copies (the third edition) appeared, it had Ricketts's leaf design stamped in gold on the purple and white linen cover. However, Wilde thought little of it: in a letter to his publisher Leonard Smithers, who had wanted to use Ricketts's design in a future edition, Wilde wrote in May 1898: "I don't know what you mean by talking of Ricketts's 'design,' and the advisability of using it. A badly-drawn leaf flung casually on a cover is not a design at all. It is a mistake – nothing more" (*Letters* 733).

Apparently, Wilde saw little of Ricketts and Shannon in the final years of his life, though there was correspondence between them concerning Wilde's publications. In June 1900 at the Paris Exhibition, Wilde saw Shannon's self-portrait, which, he informed Ross, was "the most beautiful modern picture.... I have gone several times to see it" (*Letters* 829). When news of Wilde's death reached Ricketts, he wrote in his diary:

I feel too upset to write about it, and the end of that Comedy that was realy [*sic*] Tragedy. There are days when one vomits one's nationality, when one regrets that one is an Englishman.... I know that I have not realy felt the fact of his death. I am merely wretched, tearful, stupid, vaguely conscious that something has happened that stirs up old resentment and the old sense that one is not sufficiently reconciled to life & death. (qtd. in Delaney 143)

Ross informed More Adey that, inside the funeral wreath, he had tied the names of "those who had shown kindness to [Wilde] during or after his imprisonment": Ricketts's and Shannon's were among them (qtd. in *Letters* 856).

After seeing a production of *An Ideal Husband* in September 1905, Ricketts wrote in his diary:

Oscar was always better than he thought he was, and no one in his lifetime was able to see it, including my clairvoyant self. It is astonishing that I viewed him as the most genial, kindly, and civilized of men, but it never entered my head that his personality was the

most remarkable one that I should ever meet, that in intellect & humanity he is the largest type I have come across. (qtd. in Delaney 143)

In the same year, Ricketts completed a bronze statuette titled *Silence* which he regarded as his memorial to Wilde (see Delaney 273 for a photograph of the statuette, now in the Clark Library).

On 10 June 1906, the Literary Theatre Society produced *A Florentine Tragedy* and *Salome*, the costumes and sets designed by Ricketts. In the *Saturday Review* (16 June), Beerbohm praised Ricketts's costumes and sets for *Salome* as "dramatically appropriate – just enough conventionalised to be in harmony with the peculiar character of the play" (rpt. in *Last Theatres*), and the critic Roger Fry, writing to a friend, reported that Ricketts "did the staging with ideas of colours that surpassed belief. I've never seen anything so beautiful on the stage" (1:267).

References: Charles Ricketts, *Oscar Wilde: Recollections* (1932); T. Sturge Moore and Cecil Lewis, eds., *Self-Portrait: Taken from the Letters and Journals of Charles Ricketts* (1939); Max Beerbohm, *Last Theatres, 1904–1910* (1970); Roger Fry, *Letters*, 2 vols., ed. Denys Sutton (1972); Stephen Calloway and Paul Delaney, *Charles Ricketts and Charles Shannon: An Aesthetic Partnership* (1979); J. G. P. Delaney, *Charles Ricketts: A Biography* (1990).

"A RIDE THROUGH MOROCCO"

Published: *PMG*, 8 Oct. 1886, 5; rpt. in *Reviews* (1908). An unsigned review of Hugh Stutfield's *El Maghreb: 1200 Miles' Ride through Morocco* (1886).

Stutfield, writes Wilde, has "feasted with sheikhs and fought with robbers, lived in an atmosphere of Moors, mosques and mirages, visited the city of the lepers and the slave-market of Sus, and played loo [a card game] under the shadow of the Atlas Mountains." His book, "delightful reading," does not bore the reader with platitudes. The Moorish language is "so guttural that no one can ever hope to pronounce it aright who has not been brought up within hearing of the grunting of camels, a steady course of sneezing being, consequently, the only way by which a European can acquire anything like the proper accent."

The Moors are "the masters of a beautiful

country and of many beautiful arts, but they are paralyzed by their fatalism and pillaged by their rulers.... Freedom of thought has been killed by the Koran, freedom of living by bad government." If, in the "general scramble for Africa," the French obtain sovereignty over Morocco, Stutfield predicts that British supremacy over the Straits will vanish. There is no doubt, remarks Wilde, that "in Morocco England has interests to defend and a mission to pursue, and this part of the book should be carefully studied."

"THE RISE OF HISTORICAL CRITICISM"

Published: Part I was "privately printed" by the Sherwood Press (Hartford, Conn.) in 1905; rpt. with Parts II and III in *Lord Arthur Savile's Crime and Other Prose Pieces*, Volume 7 of the *Collected Edition* (1908); the concluding section, Part IV, having been discovered by Robert Ross, first appeared in *Miscellanies* (1908).

In a note preceding Part IV, Ross remarks that this essay was written for the Chancellor's English Essay Prize at Oxford in 1879, the subject being "Historical Criticism among the Ancients." The prize was not awarded. Mason comments that the original MS. of Wilde's essay was "one of the many which disappeared (or, in this case, possibly was sold) at the time of the sale of Wilde's effects at Tite Street, Chelsea, on April 24, 1895" (470).

The Essay: Part I begins with the thesis that historical criticism "nowhere occurs as an isolated fact in the civilisation or literature of any people. It is part of that complex working towards freedom which may be described as the revolt against authority." History and the spirit of historical criticism may be found among the Hellenic branch of the Indo-Germanic race: "...among that wonderful offshoot of the primitive Aryans, whom we call by the name of Greeks and to whom, as has been well said, we owe all that moves in the world except the blind forces of nature." Doubt in the realm of religion occurs first, then in secular matters. Historical criticism in the sacred and secular spheres is, says Wilde, essentially a manifestation of the same spirit. He will proceed by examining the succession of writers in chronological order within both spheres.

In Part II, Wilde initiates a discussion of the intellectual development of the Greeks, who, at an early period, introduced speculation within the "domain of revealed truth, when the spiritual ideas of the people" could no longer be content by "lower, material conceptions of their inspired writers," and when they found it "impossible to pour the new wine of free thought into the old bottles of a narrow and a trammelling creed." Their ancestors had left them "the fatal legacy of a mythology stained with immoral and monstrous stories which strove to hide the rational order of nature in a chaos of miracles...." Plato rewrote history with a "didactic purpose, laying down certain ethical canons of historical criticism. God is good; God is just; God is true; God is without the common passions of men. These are the tests to which we are to bring the stories of the Greek religion." Religions, Wilde notes,

> may be absorbed, but they never are disproved, and the stories of the Greek mythology, spiritualised by the purifying influence of Christianity, reappear in many of the southern parts of Europe in our own day. The old fable that the Greek gods took service with the new religion under assumed names has more truth in it than the many care to discover.

In Herodotus, "rightly hailed as the father of history," we discover "not merely the empirical connection of cause and effect, but that constant reference to Laws, which is the characteristic of the historian proper." The great conceptions which unify his work are those that "even modern thought has not yet rejected":

> The immediate government of the world by God, the nemesis and punishment which sin and pride invariably bring with them, the revealing of God's purpose to His people by signs and omens, by miracles and by prophecy; these are to Herodotus the laws which govern the phenomena of history....

Though Herodotus recognized that history is a matter of evidence, in many instances he accepts "supernatural influences as part of the ordinary forces of life": "Compared to Thucydides, who succeeded him in the development of history, he appears almost like a mediaeval writer matched with a modern rationalist." Herodotus, for example, envisions the fall of Troy as the result of God's avenging hand "desiring to manifest unto men the mighty penalties which always follow upon mighty sins." Thucydides, on the other hand, "either sees not, or desires not to see" in the story of Troy the "finger of Providence, or the punishment of wicked doers." The fall of the city is "the result of a united military attack consequent on a good supply of provisions." Unlike Herodotus, who "wrote to illustrate the wonderful ways of Providence and the nemesis that falls on sin," Thucydides has "no creed to preach, no doctrine to prove." His object was to reveal those laws of history in order to illuminate the future.

At the end of this section, Wilde advances his earliest formal statement on the separation of art from ethics:

> History, no doubt, has splendid lessons for our instruction, just as all good art comes to us as the herald of the noblest truth. But, to set before either the painter or the historian, the inculcation of moral lessons as an aim to be consciously pursued, is to entirely miss the true motive and characteristic of both art and history, which is in the one case the creation of beauty, in the other the discovery of the laws of evolution in progress.

In Part III, Wilde regards the philosophical treatises of Plato and Aristotle, "these two great thinkers," as major stages in the progress of historical criticism, not only in "Plato's endeavours to purge sacred history of its immorality by the application of ethical canons at the time when Aristotle was beginning to undermine the basis of miracles by his scientific conception of law, but with reference to these two wider questions of the rise of civil institutions and the philosophy of history." Of these two thinkers, Aristotle's theory of the origin of society is "much wider," says Wilde, than that of Plato: "They both rest on a psychological basis, but Aristotle's recognition of the capacity for progress and the tendency towards a higher life, shows how much deeper his knowledge of human nature was."

In Part IV, which resumes a discussion of the historical writings of Thucydides, Wilde acknowledges the significant point that this historian "is ready to admit the variety of manifestations which external causes bring about in their workings on the uniform character of the nature of man." Nevertheless, though Thucydides dwells on the effects of peace and war, there is "no real analysis

of the immediate causes and general laws of the phenomena of life, nor does Thucydides seem to recognise the truth that if humanity proceeds in circles, the circles are always widening." In Plato, Wilde finds the "first explicit attempt to found a universal philosophy of history upon wide rational grounds" – that is, Plato created history by the deductive method in order "to discover the governing laws of the apparent chaos of political life."

In citing an important passage in Aristotle's *Poetics*, which "may be said to mark an era in the evolution of historical criticism," Wilde observes that Aristotle's method is

> essentially historical though by no means empirical.... He too was the first to point out, what even in our own day is incompletely appreciated, that nature, including the development of man, is not full of incoherent episodes like a bad tragedy, that inconsistency and anomaly are as impossible in the moral as they are in the physical world, and that where the superficial observer thinks he sees a revolution the philosophical critic discerns merely the gradual and rational evolution of the inevitable results of certain antecedents.

If Thucydides "ignored the supernatural," Polybius "rationalised" it. Plutarch "raises it to its mystical heights again, though he bases it on law. In a word, Plutarch felt that while science brings the supernatural down to the natural, yet ultimately all that is natural is really supernatural." Greek philosophy, Wilde notes, began and ended in scepticism: "the first and the last word of Greek history was Faith." The conservative attitude of the Romans towards tradition prevented "any rise of that spirit of revolt against authority...." Thus their religion "became as it were crystallised and isolated from progress at an early period of its evolution."

Manuscripts: The Clark Library has two MS. notebooks containing Parts II and III of the essay.

ROBINS, ELIZABETH (1862–1952)

An American-born actress and writer who was in the forefront of the "Ibsen campaign" to transform late 19th-century drama, Robins met Wilde at a social gathering within the first week after arriving in England at the beginning of September 1888. Her recently published memoir of Wilde (from the extensive Robins papers in the Fales Library, New York University), written around 1950, reveals her appreciation of his efforts on her behalf despite the disappointing results:

> He was then at the height of his powers and fame and I utterly unknown on this side of the Atlantic. I could do nothing for him; he could and did do everything in his power for me. He introduced me to Beerbohm Tree and others, encouraged me to cancel an American engagement and try my fortunes here.... (103–04)

Though busy with his own work, says Robins, Wilde gave his "valuable opinion on play, production and acting...and even came to see me in plays which were not at all in his line...."

One of those plays was Frances Hodgson Burnett's *The Real Little Lord Fauntleroy*, adapted from her novel and produced in January 1889. Wilde regarded the play as "second-rate and provincial," but in a letter to Robins, who appeared in her first major role on the English stage, he wrote: "...you have definitely asserted your position as an actress of the first order.... Your future on our stage is assured" (*More Letters* 79). In the following year, Robins confided to her diary her distress over *The Picture of Dorian Gray*: "...vile & revolting & not interesting in any way – Oh Mr. Wilde! Mr. Wilde!" (qtd. in Powell, "Theatre of the Future" 231). But in her memoir, she is more restrained in remarking that she "disliked" the novel.

In a letter to Robins in late March 1891, Wilde requested a stall seat at the Vaudeville Theatre for the matinee performance on 20 April of the first English production of Ibsen's *Hedda Gabler* with Robins in the leading role, the production staged by Robins and Marion Lea (1861–1944), also an American actress and an Ibsen enthusiast. To Robins, he wrote: "It is a most interesting play, nor could there be any [better] exponent of its subtlety and tragedy than yourself" (*Letters* 290). After seeing the performance, he asked for a box or two stall seats to see her "great performance again. It is a real masterpiece of art" (*Letters* 291).

On 18 February 1893, Wilde wrote to express his regret to Robins that he would be unable to see the première of the first English production of *The Master Builder* on 20 February, but he wished "the amazing Hedda every possible success. I count

Ibsen fortunate in having so brilliant and subtle an artist to interpret him" (*Letters* 330). In May and June of that year, Robins performed in 12 Ibsen plays at the Opera Comique in London, financed by subscribers who would receive shares of the profits. Those shares were later returned to present Robins with a gift of a silver tea-service. In a letter enclosing his check, Wilde wrote that she was "a very imaginative artist, who has done very real work. The English stage is in her debt" (*Letters* 351).

As Kerry Powell remarks, "Robins attacked the exploitation of women as the chief evil of Victorian theatre, recognizing that to end it would mean structural change in the institution itself" ("Theatre of the Future" 226). The 19th-century theater was dominated by the actor-managers who regarded drama as a marketable commodity rather than a form of artistic expression and who believed that women could not write for the stage. In a diary entry for 17 May 1892, Robins records a meeting with Wilde over tea and cigarettes, when they discussed their "visions of the Theatre of the Future" (Fales Library). In her memoir of Wilde, she writes:

> In 1892 I recall his laughing summary of a discussion with me: "Well, we've had a profitable time – we've built a theatre, written several plays and founded a school!"
>
> I told him that anyone with all those ideas about the Theatre ought to give them to the world in practical, permanent form. He should sketch a working plan, wake people up to the need and value of a Theatre on non-commercial lines. He promised to "speak for it" at a Dinner, shortly to be held, and then to crystallize the subject in an essay.

But, to Robins's disappointment, Wilde did not fulfill her expectations. As Powell observes of Wilde: "More than Robins, certainly, he entered into the economy of the theatre as it was, working within the established framework rather than against it" ("Theatre of the Future" 234).

In the 1890s, Robins published several novels and had a play produced by the Independent Theatre Society. Though she made her last stage appearance in 1902, she continued writing unproduced plays (except for the suffragette work of 1907, the highly successful *Votes for Women*) and several unpublished novels. In one of her early unpublished works, "The Coming of Women," Wilde is thinly disguised as a writer who doesn't write because, as he says, he is "horribly indolent...so engrossed with idleness I'm afraid I can't spare time to work" (qtd. in Powell, "Theatre of the Future" 229) – possibly her exasperation with Wilde, who had been enthusiastic about the Theatre of the Future. In her memoir, she recalls her final meeting with Wilde ("unwholesome looking...as if he were stuffed with spices and caviar") and the ordeal of his trials, which left a profound impression on her:

> My poignant share of suffering in the tragic crisis of his life was none the less bitter for being obscure. I had seen him at his height, and his fall was shattering not to him alone. It is difficult even at this long distance of time to look back at the days of his fiercely lime-lit trial, with its aftermath of solitary imprisonment and degrading exile. (111)

References: Elizabeth Robins, *Both Sides of the Curtain* (1940); "'Oscar Wilde: An Appreciation': An Unpublished Memoir by Elizabeth Robins," ed. Kerry Powell, *Nineteenth Century Theatre* (Winter 1993); Kerry Powell, "Oscar Wilde, Elizabeth Robins, and the Theatre of the Future," *Modern Drama* (Spring 1994); Joanne Gates, *Elizabeth Robins, 1862–1952* (1994); Angela John, *Elizabeth Robins: Staging a Life, 1862–1952* (1995).

RODD, JAMES RENNELL (1858–1941)

A poet, biographer, historian, British ambassador to Italy (1908–19), and in 1933 elevated to the peerage as Lord Rennell of Rodd for his distinguished diplomatic career, Rodd first met Wilde in 1878 while both were students at Oxford, but since they were in different colleges and their ages differed by four years, Rodd recalls in his memoirs that he "hardly saw him" (9). However, Wilde went on a trip to Belgium with Rodd and his family in the summer of 1879, and they travelled on the Continent together in the following summer. When Rodd graduated from Balliol College in 1880, having failed to get a first in "Greats," Wilde wrote early in December: "I wish you had got a First....still, a Second is perhaps for a man of culture a sweeter atmosphere than the chilly Causcasus of an atheistical First" (*More Letters* 33–34). Just as Wilde had won the Newdigate Prize in 1878, Rodd won the prize in 1880 for a poem on Sir Walter Raleigh.

When Wilde published his *Poems* (1881), Rodd later recalled: "I had endeavoured but in vain to induce him to eliminate one or two passages which violated my own sense of taste. They revealed his ability, his command of language and feeling for colour. But there was artificiality in the longer and more recent poems.... There was more power behind him than he really used" (22). During this time, Rodd saw much of "that brilliant but unhappy man" in Chelsea, where Rodd associated not only with Wilde but also with Whistler and Burne-Jones.

Early in 1882, when Wilde was on his American lecture tour, Rodd wrote to him:

> Well, you seem to be having amazing fun over there. We all feel a little jealous. And then your statements are amazing, of course, but you mustn't assert yourself so positively.... I wish I could have been with you when you went to see Walt Whitman. It must have been charming. (qtd. in Ellmann 173/165)

In his memoirs, however, Rodd writes that he warned Wilde "of the harm which I felt he was doing to himself by his extravagant performances in America" (25) – rpt. in Mikhail 1:113.

When he left England, Wilde had carried a volume of Rodd's recently published *Songs in the South*, which he hoped to have published in America. Early in 1882, Wilde sent the volume from Cincinnati to the publisher J. M. Stoddart, and by May he proposed a new title, *Rose Leaf and Apple Leaf* – these arrangements apparently agreed to by Rodd. The book was issued in a limited edition of 175 copies in brown ink on one side of transparent paper with interleaved blank sheets of apple-green paper, the ordinary edition printed in black on white paper.

When the book appeared in late July, Wilde congratulated Stoddart, calling it "a *chef d'oeuvre* of typography," the beginning of "an era in American printing" (*Letters* 124). In October, Rodd received copies of the book with the dedication written by Wilde, who used the phrase "heart's brother" from Rodd's poem "By the South Sea," containing the suggestive line "We two alone in the world, no other":

TO
OSCAR WILDE –
"HEART'S BROTHER" –
THESE FEW SONGS AND MANY SONGS
TO COME.

Rodd was perturbed, fearful of possible misinterpretation (he had just begun his career in the Foreign Office). Moreover, he was also troubled by Wilde's "L'Envoi" (see entry), which hailed Rodd as his disciple. Rodd attempted, without success, to have the dedication removed.

Having read a review in the *Saturday Review* (4 Nov. 1882) of the Rodd publication, Swinburne wrote in a fury to the poet and critic Theodore Watts (later, Watts-Dunton) about "Oscar Wilde's young man – the Hephaestion of that all-conquering Alexander? Really these fools are enough to make one turn Wesleyan – if only one were fool enough on one's own part – and contribute prose only to the Methodist's Magazine from henceforward" (*Swinburne Letters* 4:312).

The unfortunate event contributed to the eventual falling out between Rodd and Wilde, for when Wilde returned to London in 1883, they quarreled, Rodd later attributing the end of their friendship to Wilde's "Olympian attitude as of one who could do no wrong...." As a result, they "parted in anger and did not meet again" (25). To Robert Sherard, Wilde sent a copy of *Rose Leaf and Apple Leaf*, written by "the true poet, and the false friend" (*Letters* 144).

In the *Pall Mall Gazette* (6 April 1888), Wilde reviewed Rodd's *The Unknown Madonna and Other Poems* (1888) with no trace of resentment over Rodd's break with him: "Mr. Rodd looks at life with all the charming optimism of a young man, though he is quite conscious of the fact that a stray note of melancholy, here and there, has an artistic as well as a popular value...." By no means, however, is this review a "puff" for an old friend (despite some words of praise), for Wilde is critical of Rodd's occasional awkwardness and repetition as well as the "excessively tedious" lines in one poem, which is "somewhat too abstract and metaphysical." Despite Rodd's bitterness, his later memories of Wilde are appreciative of "this daring and gifted personality [who] brought me nearer to emancipation from convention" (22).

References: J. Rennell Rodd, *Social and Diplomatic Memories, 1884–1893* (1922); Cecil Y. Lang, ed., *The Swinburne Letters*, Vol. 4 (1960).

"ROME UNVISITED"

Published: First appeared as "Graffiti d'Italia (Arona. Lago Maggiore)" in *Month and Catholic Review* 9 (Sept. 1876): 77–78; rpt. in the *Pilot* (Boston) on 23 Sept. 1876, Wilde's first published work in America; rev. as "Rome Unvisited" in *Poems* (1881); further rev. in (1882). For an account of Wilde's travels in Italy with his former tutor at Trinity College, Dublin, see Mahaffy, John Pentland.

In this four-part poem, the poet, having returned home ("my pilgrimage is done"), writes this tribute to Holy Rome ("Roma, at thy feet / I lay this barren gift of song!"). Various sites are evoked, including a vision of papal grandeur:

O joy to see before I die
   The only God-anointed King,
   And hear the silver trumpets ring
A triumph as He passes by!

In the final part, the poet turns to his own preoccupations with the passage of time: "The cycles of revolving years / May free my heart from all its fears, / And teach my lips a song to sing." That song, presumably, is one inspired by religious faith, symbolized by his catching the torch "while yet aflame" so that he may call upon "the holy name / Of Him who now doth hide His face" (this final line derived from Psalm 30:7–8: "...thou didst hide thy face, and I was troubled").

Manuscripts: The Huntington Library has an early draft of "Graffiti d'Italia: II. Arona. July 10th 1875," written after Wilde's first trip to Italy (printed in Mason 113–15). The Hyde Collection has a draft of four stanzas, lines 45–56 (printed in Mason 115–16), which appear in a letter to an unidentified correspondent in *More Letters* 23.

"ROSA MYSTICA"

A section title in *Poems* (1881) for 14 poems, many of them inspired by Wilde's travels in Italy and his attraction to Roman Catholicism.

"ROSES AND RUE"

Published: *Society* (Summer Number: "Midsummer Dreams") June 1885: 25; rev. as "To L.L."

(Lillie Langtry) in *Poems* (1908), which contains two additional stanzas at the beginning of the poem. Later printings of *Poems* (from Dec. 1911) restore the original title, "Roses and Rue," with "To L.L." as the dedication.

Recalling a lost love, the speaker in this poem reveals an elegiac, melancholy reaction to his memories, sometimes bitter: "How these passionate memories bite / In my heart as I write!" Shattered by the memory of his love's painful departure, he recalls her biting words: "'You have only wasted your life' – / (Ah! there was the knife!)." He admits that he has wasted his boyhood, "But it was for you, / You had poets enough on the shelf, / I gave you myself!" In the brief final part, he is resigned in this internalized dialogue. If his heart must break, he concludes, "It will break in music, I know, / Poets' hearts break so." But he finds it "strange" that he was not told (or indeed had not read Blake) that "the brain can hold / In a tiny ivory cell / God's Heaven and Hell."

Manuscripts: An incomplete MS. is printed in Mason 205–06. Mason erroneously believed that "Roses and Rue" was an early draft of "To L. L.," which had appeared in *Poems* (1908), but the former is the later version. The Hyde Collection has the complete MS. titled "To L. L." with Wilde's final revisions, later incorporated in "Roses and Rue."

ROSS, ROBERT BALDWIN (1869–1918)

As one of Wilde's closest friends, Ross was instrumental not only in assisting his friend's Estate in paying off remaining debts but also in editing the 14-volume edition of Wilde's *Collected Edition* (1908). Born of Canadian parents (his father a lawyer and politician, Speaker of the Senate, 1869; his mother the daughter of Robert Baldwin, a prominent politician who was Premier of Upper Canada, 1842–43), Ross was educated in England as his father had wished. He was placed in a school in Surrey until 1882, then entrusted to a tutor, who took the young boy on cultural visits to European cities.

The precise date when "Robbie" first met Wilde is unknown. The often-repeated notion that Ross was "the first boy" to corrupt Wilde is doubtful, for Borland writes that there is "certainly no direct evidence" to support such a view: "...the mere fact that a proposition is frequently repeated does not substantiate its credibility" (18). In 1887, when his

mother was travelling abroad, Ross became a paying guest at the Wildes' Tite Street home. Other than that brief stay of three months, their relationship involved only intermittent contact for the next ten years (indeed, Wilde did not introduce Ross to Lord Alfred Douglas until 1893).

In October 1888, he arrived at King's College, Cambridge, to begin his formal university studies, but after an unhappy year there and after quarreling with his mother and sister over his homosexuality (the disclosure of which resulted in his not being welcome at home), Ross left for Edinburgh to work for W. E. Henley on the *Scots Observer*. He soon returned to London and accepted the post of assistant editor of the Society of Authors' magazine titled *Author*, probably on the recommendation of his elder brother, Alex, a critic, who had been Honorary Secretary of the society from 1885 to 1889. Thenceforth, he associated with such figures at the Society as Arthur Conan Doyle, Rudyard Kipling, and John Addington Symonds.

In July 1893, Ross apparently became sexually involved with a sixteen-year-old son of a "military gentleman," an incident that involved Alfred Douglas and another boy, whose charge that Ross had seduced him three times was, said Ross, "an absolute fabrication" (Borland 35). Ross's close friend, More Adey (see entry), managed to have any possible criminal charges dropped. After a brief stay with his brother in Davos, Switzerland, and a trip to Canada, Ross was back in London as the disaster involving Wilde and Douglas's father, the Marquess of Queensberry, was about to take center stage. When Queensberry left the infamous calling card at Wilde's club, Wilde's first impulse was to write to Ross, asking for his wise counsel: "My whole life seems ruined by this man.... I don't know what to do.... I mar your life by trespassing ever on your love and kindness" (*Letters* 384). As Borland remarks: "...when Wilde's and Douglas's love-affair ended in the fires of hell it was inevitable that Ross would rise like a phoenix from the ashes" (42).

Douglas believed that his father must be sued for criminal libel, but Ross urged Wilde to ignore Queensberry's insult that he was "posing" as a sodomite and withdraw from the struggle between Douglas and his father. Characteristically, Douglas persuaded Wilde to go with him to Monte Carlo, much to Ross's distress over their apparent indifference to the crisis. When the case against

Queensberry collapsed (see The Trials, 1895), Ross urged Wilde to flee the country to France, which had no extradition treaty with England, but he was determined to remain. With Wilde's arrest on 5 April 1895, Ross, with his usual foresight, went to Wilde's Tite Street home (Mrs. Wilde and the children had left to stay with relatives), broke into his study, and carried off an unspecified number of manuscripts. On the advice of his family, Ross left for Calais to avoid possible implication in the Wilde debacle, a most difficult decision, Borland states, for "it went against everything he believed in to desert a friend in need" (47). In a memoir written around 1913, Ross wrote:

My relatives were naturally distressed at my connection with a very disgraceful scandal. My name had appeared in the papers as being with Wilde when he was arrested. In consequence I was obliged to leave some of my clubs. My mother promised that if I would go abroad for a few weeks she would contribute to the expenses of Wilde's defence, which she did; and that she would assist Lady Wilde... which she did until Lady Wilde's death.... (qtd. in Hyde 84–85)

Coincidentally, Wilde's conviction on 25 May occurred on Ross's twenty-sixth birthday: their lives would be further linked in other ways in the years to come.

When Queensberry petitioned to institute bankruptcy proceedings against Wilde, Ross was present at one of the public hearings when Wilde was brought from prison between two policeman, as described in De Profundis: "...Robbie waited in the long dreary corridor, that before the whole crowd, whom an action so sweet and simple hushed into silence, he might gravely raise his hat to me, as handcuffed and with bowed head I passed him by. Men have gone to heaven for smaller things than that" (Letters 459). In December 1895, when Ross joined Douglas in Italy, the relationship between the two was undergoing a radical change because of Wilde's increasing confidence in Ross's judgment and because of Ross's visits to comfort Wilde in prison.

In April 1897, just weeks before his release from prison, Wilde authorized Ross to act on his behalf as his literary executor, a burden that he carried

and discharged with distinction. On 20 May, after leaving prison, Wilde arrived in Dieppe, where he was greeted by Ross and Reginald Turner. Wilde gave Ross his prison letter addressed to Douglas (later titled De Profundis) with instructions to have two copies made, the original to be given to Douglas. Ross, however, sent Douglas one of the copies. (Though Douglas denied that he had ever received it, he later admitted in the Arthur Ransome libel trial that he had destroyed the copy without reading it.) Eventually, Wilde and Douglas achieved reconciliation despite all that Ross did to discourage it. With Wilde's death in 1900, Ross wrote to Adela Schuster, a mutual friend (see entry): "Among his many fine qualities he showed in his later years was that he never blamed anyone but himself for his own disasters" (qtd. in Letters 862).

On his return to London in 1901, Ross acquired the Carfax Gallery in Bury Street, St. James's, which became an important site for exhibitions, particularly of the work of Max Beerbohm and Aubrey Beardsley (in 1909, he published an illustrated monograph on Beardsley). Douglas, his anger increasing over the years towards Ross, referred to the gallery as "Robbie's unsuccessful little picture shop" (Borland 85). However, the "little picture shop" contributed to Ross's growing reputation as an art dealer and critic. In 1905, Ross published De Profundis in a drastically expurgated edition with all references to Douglas omitted. Douglas reviewed it unsympathetically in the Motorist & Traveller (1 March 1905), an indication of his alienation from his former lover. The publication of De Profundis had the effect of further dividing Ross and Douglas, the consequences of which later resulted in bitter legal struggles.

By 1906, the Oscar Wilde Estate, legally bankrupt, was finally free of debt, and by 1908, Ross, with copyright control over most of Wilde's writings, edited the Collected Edition. A dinner in Ross's honor was held on 1 December at the Ritz Hotel to celebrate not only his editing of the collected works but also his assistance to the Oscar Wilde Estate in helping to pay off lingering debts by pursuing publishers who had not paid copyright fees. More than 200 guests attended, including Cyril and Vyvyan Holland, Wilde's two sons whom Ross had finally met for the first time since they were small children. Douglas declined to attend, principally, he told Ross, because there were at least 20 people at the dinner with whom Wilde was not on speaking terms at the time of his death.

In 1912, while writing art reviews for the *Morning Post*, Ross was appointed Assessor of Pictures and Drawings for the Board of the Inland Revenue, requiring visits to great estates to estimate the value of art for the purpose of death duties. In the following year, Ross found himself at the center of a libel suit brought by Douglas against Arthur Ransome, who, Douglas charged, had made some offensive remarks about him in his *Oscar Wilde: A Critical Study* (though Douglas's name is never mentioned). Because Ross had shown Ransome the unpublished sections of *De Profundis*, he was required to provide Ransome's counsel with a copy to be read aloud in court to support the Plea of Justification. The jury subsequently found no basis in Ransome's book to support Douglas's charge.

The publication of Douglas's *Oscar Wilde and Myself* (1914), which was, in fact, written by Thomas Crosland, his former erratic assistant editor of the *Academy* and a hater of Wilde, convinced Ross that he had grounds for a writ of libel. Equally determined to undermine Ross's status in society, Crosland had recently sent Ross a letter demanding that he resign as Wilde's literary executor and issue a public statement that he had erred in restoring Wilde's reputation. The conspiracy of Douglas and Crosland to disgrace Ross involved their hiring of a private investigator to have Ross's letters stolen to reveal incriminating evidence of his sexual affairs and to link Ross with a convicted male prostitute known to Christopher Millard ("Stuart Mason," Wilde's bibliographer).

When, in March 1914, Ross filed a charge of criminal libel against Douglas and issued writs against both him and Crosland for conspiracy and perjury, the two were in France: the arrogant Crosland, however, returned in April to face arrest on the charges. Douglas and Crosland's attempt to impugn Ross emerged during the magistrate's hearing prior to the trial at the Old Bailey: When, for example, the male prostitute was released from prison, he was urged to sign a statement that he had had sexual relations with Ross, but he refused, insisting that the statement was untrue. In June, the trial began, the jury hearing Crosland's condemnation of Wilde's works as "most dangerous." Undoubtedly, the association of Wilde's name with

Ross and Millard had a significant effect on the jury's perception of Ross's presumed innocence. The jury found Crosland not guilty.

During the war, Ross gave Frank Harris assistance in the writing of his Wilde biography, which paid tribute to Wilde's "devoted friend" in Chapter 26: "It became the purpose of his life to pay his friend's debts, annul his bankruptcy and publish his books in a suitable manner, in fine to clear Oscar's memory from obloquy while leaving to his lovable spirit the shining raiment of immortality." In 1917, Ross accepted the offer of Trustee of the Tate Gallery, a position he had particularly desired. These final years were not without renewed attempts by Douglas to vilify his name, but on 5 October 1918, Ross died, apparently in his sleep, of heart failure. His will stipulated that his ashes be placed in Wilde's monument in Père Lachaise cemetery, in which, at Ross's request, a special chamber had been designed by Jacob Epstein (see entry). Fearful of Douglas's fury, Ross's relatives delayed fulfilling his request until 30 November 1950, on the fiftieth anniversary of Wilde's death and safely after Douglas's.

Reference: H. Montgomery Hyde, *Lord Alfred Douglas: A Biography* (1984).

ROTHENSTEIN, WILLIAM (1872–1945)

A painter, educator, and writer who was knighted in 1931, Rothenstein probably first met Wilde when he was brought to Rothenstein's studio in Paris by a mutual friend in December of 1891. Wilde's first extant letter to Rothenstein indicates their initial meeting: "I send you my novel [*The Picture of Dorian Gray*], with my best wishes. It was a great pleasure to see you last night, and it will be a great pleasure to see you tomorrow" (*Letters* 302–03). Rothenstein did not like *Dorian Gray*, which, he believed, had borrowed much from Huysmans's *A Rebours* (*Men* 124).

He later recalled that he was "not at all attracted by Wilde's appearance.... His hands were fat and useless looking, and the more conspicuous from a large scarab ring he wore. But before he left I was charmed by his conversation, and his looks were forgotten." After that meeting, Rothenstein recalled that Wilde "talked of me as a sort of youthful prodigy; he was enthusiastic about my pastels. He introduced me to Robert Sherard, to Marcel Schwob, and to Rémy de Gourmont...." Wilde impressed Rothenstein as "not only an unique talker and story-teller...but he had an extraordinarily illuminating intellect. His description of people, his appreciation of prose and verse, were a never-failing delight. He seemed to have read all books, and to have known all men and women." Though Wilde was affected in manner, it was "an affectation which, so far as his conversation was concerned, allowed the fullest possible play to his brilliant faculties" (*Men* 86–87).

With the success of *A Woman of No Importance*, Rothenstein recalled that Wilde

had been rather apologetic about his first play [*Lady Windermere's Fan*]; as though to write a comedy were rather beneath a poet. When I saw it I thought, on the contrary, here is the genuine Wilde, making legitimate use of the artifice which was, in fact, natural to him; like his wit, indeed, in which his true genius lay. (*Men* 132–33)

In May 1893, Wilde wrote to comment on one of Rothenstein's drawings of Alfred Douglas that he had commissioned: "The lovely drawing is complete in itself. It is a great delight to me to have so exquisite a portrait of a friend done by a friend also, and I thank you very much for letting me have it" (*Letters* 340). Facetiously titled "The Editor of the *Spirit Lamp* at work," the drawing depicts Douglas reclining in an armchair (see *Letters*, facing p. 351). Rothenstein recalled Douglas as "an erratic but most attractive person, defiant of public opinion, generous, irresponsible and extravagant" (*Men* 147).

After Wilde's release from prison, Rothenstein offered "to come over if he cared to see any of his old friends..." (*Men* 308). Wilde wrote facetiously to Robert Ross that Rothenstein was "organising a Pilgimage to the Sinner this week" (*Letters* 604). Wilde replied to Rothenstein that he looked forward with "real delight" to seeing him:

...you will be pleased to know that I have not come out of prison an embittered or disappointed man. On the contrary: in many ways I have gained much. I am not really ashamed of having been in prison....but I *am* really ashamed of having led a life unworthy of an artist.... I know simply that a life of definite and studied materialism, and a philosophy of

appetite and cynicism, and a cult of sensual and senseless ease, are bad things for an artist: they narrow the imagination, and dull the more delicate sensibilities. (*Letters* 604)

When Wilde saw him in Dieppe, Rothenstein noted that he looked "surprisingly well, thinner and healthier than heretofore. He was happy at Berneval, he assured me, full of plans for the future.... He seemed to have lost none of his old wit and gaiety" (*Men* 311).

In August 1897, Wilde submitted, at Rothenstein's request, a brief note on W. E. Henley, which Rothenstein had planned to include in his *English Portraits* (1898). Wilde's droll note – including such remarks as "He is never forgotten by his enemies, and often forgiven by his friends" and "his style is an open secret. He has fought a good fight, and has had to face every difficulty except popularity" (qtd. in *Letters* 631) – expressed Wilde's paradoxical style; hence, Rothenstein decided, at Max Beerbohm's urging, to reject it. Beerbohm had written to Rothenstein: "I am much amused by your difficulty with Sebastian [Wilde's pseudonym]. I thought his lines had some witty things in them – "an open secret" is lovely – but they were rather too antithetical and unfriendly – and too obviously written by Oscar" (*Max and Will* 36). Beerbohm wrote the note on Henley instead.

Rothenstein's "difficulty" with Wilde did not end their friendship: When Wilde included his friend among those to whom he sent copies of *The Ballad of Reading Gaol*, Rothenstein sent an appreciative letter that touched Wilde deeply: "Your letter has given me more pleasure, more pride, than anything has done since the poem appeared" (*Letters* 707). In the remaining years, Rothenstein visited Wilde when he was in Paris. In the autumn of 1899, he also brought the youthful Augustus John (1878–1961) to meet Wilde and spend time over a ten-day period with him. John recalled that the "distinguished reprobate...a great man of inaction" was a "big and good-natured fellow with an enormous sense of fun, impeccable bad taste, and a deeply religious apprehension of the Devil." Awed by Wilde's wit and distressed by the deference of the audience (which included Rothenstein's wife and the painter Charles Conder), John was at a loss as to how to respond: "I could think of nothing whatever to say. Even my laughter sounded hollow" (qtd. in Holroyd 95). Nevertheless, Wilde was much taken by "the charming Celtic poet in colour" (*Letters* 811).

On one of his last visits to Paris in 1900, Rothenstein and his wife invited Wilde to dinner in an open-air restaurant, which had a small orchestra. Rothenstein recalls his annoyance with Wilde: "He chose a table near the musicians; he liked being near the music, he said; but during dinner it was plain that he was less interested in the music than in one of the players." Rothenstein resolved not to see him again, but in a chance encounter on the boulevard on another occasion, he "saw at once that [Wilde] knew we had meant to avoid him. The look he gave us was tragic, and he seemed ill, and was shabby and down at heel" (*Men* 361–62). Nevertheless, they joined him for a drink, but Wilde's gaiety was unconvincing. They never saw him again.

References: *Men and Memories: Recollections of William Rothenstein, 1872–1900* (1931); Robert Speaight, *William Rothenstein: The Portrait of an Artist in His Time* (1962); Michael Holroyd, *Augustus John: A Biography* (1974); Mary M. Lago and Karl Beckson, eds., *Max and Will: Max Beerbohm and William Rothenstein, Their Friendship and Letters, 1893–1945* (1975).

"THE ROUT OF THE R. A."

Published: *Court and Society Review* 4 (27 April 1887): 390; rpt. in Mason 34–37 (uncollected in *Miscellanies*, 1908). An anonymous review of Harry Furniss's exhibition at the Gainesborough Gallery. Furniss, a well-known illustrator and caricaturist whose work appeared in *Punch* and the *Illustrated London News*, parodied the styles of various members of the Royal Academy.

The annual attacks, Wilde writes, on the Royal Academy "with which we are all so familiar, and of which most of us are so tired, have, as a rule, been both futile and depressing..... It is always a sorry spectacle when the Philistines of Gath go out against the Philistines of Gaza; so we are delighted to find there has risen up, at least, a young and ruddy David to slay this lumbering Goliath of middle-class art." Furniss's "brilliant wit and clever satire" has routed the Royal Academicians, writes Wilde, but the final encounter will soon take place when the Royal Academy of Art exhibits in Burlington House "under the patronage of the British public and under the protection of the

British policeman." Furniss, Wilde continues, has attempted to show the Academicians "the possibilities of real beauty, and wonder, and pleasure that lie hidden in his work." In his satire of the noted classicist Sir Lawrence Alma-Tadema, Furniss has included the archeological detail "so dear" to Alma-Tadema, an industrious painter. However, the "one thing that was wanting in Mr. Tadema's work has been added, the passionate interest in human life, and the power to portray it."

As for Sir Frederick Leighton, president of the Royal Academy, Furniss has provided a satire in "Pygmalion and Galatea in the Lowther Arcadia," which has "all that wax-doll grace of treatment" that is so characteristic of the president's best work. Furniss reveals that the "one thing lacking in the [Royal Academicians] is a sense of humour, and that, if they would not take themselves so seriously, they might produce work that would be a joy, and not a weariness to the world. Whether or not they will profit by the lesson, it is difficult to say, for dulness has become the basis of respectability, and seriousness the only refuge of the shallow." For his service to English art, Furniss's gallery "will be remembered as the most brilliant criticism upon the British school that has been made in this century."

RUSKIN, JOHN (1819–1900)

An art critic and essayist concerned with the effect of industrialism on life and the arts, particularly architecture, Ruskin was Slade Professor of Fine Arts at Oxford University, 1870–78, at the time that Wilde was an undergraduate. He attended Ruskin's lectures on Florentine art in the autumn of 1874 at the University Museum. During one of them, Ruskin reminded the students that he had begun a project several months before to construct a flower-bordered country road in Ferry Hinksey, where there had been a swampy lane. Wilde enthusiastically volunteered to help, even adding, with facetious braggadocio, that he had the honor of filling "Mr. Ruskin's especial wheelbarrow" and of being instructed by the great man himself in skillfully maneuvering it from place to place (qtd. in Ellmann 49/48). Ruskin rewarded his students by inviting them to breakfast. As Ellmann remarks, "The roadbuilding fostered Wilde's conviction that art had a role to play in the improvement of society" (50/48).

But before Wilde graduated from Oxford, the

influence of Walter Pater would turn him in another direction: the evangelical moralism of Ruskin would yield to the aesthetic self-indulgence of Pater. "For Wilde," writes Ellmann, "the two [had] stood like heralds beckoning him in opposite directions" (51/50). Nevertheless, Wilde's friendship with Ruskin would provide gratifying memories in later years. In November 1879, he and Ruskin attended a performance by Henry Irving as Shylock.

When in America on his lecture tour, Wilde arranged to have Rennell Rodd's poems published and wrote a preface, titled "L'Envoi," which he described as "signifying my new departure from Mr. Ruskin and the Pre-Raphaelites, and marks an era in the aesthetic movement" (*Letters* 96). Back in England, Wilde delivered a lecture in 1884 on "The Value of Art in Modern Life," citing Ruskin as one of the greatest men that England had ever produced, but he also rejected Ruskin's basic method of judging a painting "by the number of noble and moral ideas that he found in it" (qtd. in Ellmann 262/247). Nevertheless, Wilde maintained friendly relations with his former teacher, even asking him, in 1886, to be the godfather of his second son, Vyvyan, but Ruskin declined because of age. When Wilde sent him a copy of *The Happy Prince and Other Tales* (1888), he enclosed an appreciative letter:

...the dearest memories of my Oxford days are my walks and talks with you, and from you I learned nothing but what was good. How else could it be? There is in you something of prophet, of priest, and of poet, and to you the gods gave eloquence such as they have given to none other, so that your message might come to us with the fire of passion, and the marvel of music, making the deaf to hear, and the blind to see. I wish I had something better to give you, but, such as it is, take it with my love. (*Letters* 218)

In the early 1890s, Ruskin's mental illness and progressive isolation ended Wilde's contact with his former mentor. One can only imagine what Ruskin's reaction was to the Wilde scandal in 1895.

References: Joan Evans, *John Ruskin* (1954); John D. Rosenberg, *The Darkening Glass: A Portrait of Ruskin's Genius* (1961).

"A RUSSIAN REALISTIC ROMANCE"

Published: *PMG*, 28 May 1886, 5. An unsigned review of Dostoevsky's *Crime and Punishment*, trans. Frederick Whishaw, unlisted in Mason and uncollected in *Reviews* (1908).

John Stokes has identified this review as Wilde's on the evidence of a passage in one of Wilde's later reviews: see "A Batch of Novels." There, Wilde reviews Dostoevsky's *Injury and Insult*, in the course of which he writes: "Some time ago we had occasion to draw attention to his marvellous novel 'Crime and Punishment'...." Some sentences in both reviews are virtually identical: for example, in his review of *Injury and Insult*, Wilde alludes to the scene in *Crime and Punishment* where "in the haunt of impurity and vice a harlot and an assassin meet together to read the story of Lazarus and Dives, and the outcast girl leads the sinner to make atonement for his sin" – lifted almost verbatim from his 1886 review.

Since Wilde had an aversion to French Naturalism (later in "The Decay of Lying," he alludes to the "dreary vices" and "drearier virtues" of Zola's characters), he launches an attack on the publisher Vizetelly & Co., who should not have "polluted the fair name of Dostoeffsky by including 'Crime and Punishment' among their series of unclean romances which they borrow from the French. Between the Russian novelist and the obscene brood of pseudo-realists which roosts in the *Cloaca maxima* of France there is a great gulf fixed." Wilde praises three Russian novelists – Turgenev, Tolstoy, and Dostoevsky – as "men of ideal aims, of a strange sweetness of soul, and of a subtle personal fascination, compared with which the personalities of the so-called realists are but as satyrs to angels." The three Russians were men "whose thought is a distinctly purifying, inspiring, ennobling element in European literature."

In alluding to Raskolnikoff, the central character of *Crime and Punishment*, Wilde quotes a passage from the novel that foreshadows his own view of the poisoner and writer Thomas Griffiths Wainewright in his 1889 study, "Pen, Pencil and Poison": "...he has fled the society of men; has brooded over many social questions; has written an article in a social paper on crime, in which he declares that crime, though it is punishable in ordinary men and women, is permitted to extraordinary beings." Dostoevsky's novel, Wilde concludes, is "one of the most interesting and curious psychological studies of modern fiction." Stokes suggests that the Russian novelist "may have played a part in the construction of the great Aesthete's antinomous pose."

Reference: John Stokes, "Wilde on Dostoevsky," *N&Q* (June 1980).

S

LA SAINTE COURTISANE; OR, THE WO-MAN COVERED WITH JEWELS

Written: According to Wilde in *De Profundis*, most of the play had been written by December 1893 (*Letters* 427), but by the time of Wilde's trials in 1895, he had not, apparently, completed it.

Published: *Miscellanies* (1908).

Sources: The obvious source is Flaubert's *La Tentation de Saint Antoine* (1874), the setting of which provided Wilde with the model for his play. In Flaubert, the Queen of Sheba, like Wilde's courtesan, is a "woman covered with jewels." An additional source may have been Anatole France's *Thaïs* (1890), which depicts how the eponymous character, a dancer, actress, and courtesan, is converted by a religious hermit, who, like the central figure in Wilde's play, comes from a monastery in Thebes. After he converts her and succeeds in urging her to enter a convent, he himself is damned for his erotic fantasies provoked by the sensuous Thaïs.

The Plot: The stage directions suggest a symbolic landscape in keeping with the play:

> The scene represents a corner of a valley in the Thebaid [the area around Thebes, the ancient city on the upper Nile]. On the right hand of the stage is a cavern. In front of the cavern stands a great crucifix. On the left, sand dunes. The sky is blue like the inside of a cup of lapis lazuli. The hills are of red sand. Here and there on the hills there are clumps of thorns.

Two men are speaking of a beautiful woman wondrously clad (their dialogue containing the hypnotic rhythms and repetitions also used by Wilde in *Salome*): "Who is she? She makes me afraid. She has a purple cloak and her hair is like threads of gold. She must be the daughter of the Emperor." The second man believes that she is one of the gods, who should not leave their temples. The woman, named Myrrhina, asks them whether "the beautiful young hermit, he who will not look on the face of woman," dwells there. She also asks why the two men do not look at her. The first man says that she is covered with "bright stones," which dazzle their eyes.

When she is told that the hermit dwells in the cavern, the second man informs her that a white unicorn lived in the cave, and when it saw the hermit, it knelt down and worshipped him (the medieval myth of the unicorn, which could be tamed only by a virgin). Myrrhina asks whether the hermit sows or reaps, whether he catches fish in a net, whether he weaves linen on a loom, or whether he ploughs the land. The second man responds: "He being a very holy man does nothing." She orders them to tell the hermit that one who comes from Alexandria desires to speak with him, but they dare not tell him, for he is at prayer.

She herself calls into the cave to the hermit, named Honorius. In a lengthy speech, Myrrhina speaks of her desirability and of those who have been attracted to her. She also beseeches him to come with her: "I will clothe you in a tunic of silk.... I will clothe you in hyacinth and put honey in your mouth. Love – " But the hermit interrupts her: "There is no love but the love of God.... The body is vile, Myrrhina." She begins to say "The beauty....," to which the hermit adds that "The beauty of the soul increases till it can see God. Therefore, Myrrhina, repent of thy sins." (Kohl remarks, "One is struck immediately by the similarity between the Myrrhina/Honorius motivation and that of Salome/Iokanaan. Both pairs embody the contrast between sensuality and the spirit, earthly pleasure and religious asceticism," 309.)

What follows is an evident gap in the MS., for the hermit now says that the scales have fallen from his eyes and that he now sees what he had not seen before: "Take me to Alexandria and let me taste of the seven sins." But now she tells him that, because she has repented of her sins, she refuses to accompany him to Alexandria; indeed, she warns him not to go. In the final section (separated from the preceding by an ellipsis) she curses her beauty for what it has done, and curses the wonder of her body "for the evil that it has brought upon you." The hermit, having asked her why she had come into the valley with her beauty, asks: "Why didst thou tempt me with words?" The final line suggests the dramatic reversal and moral point of the play (as in the *proverbe dramatique* of *A Florentine Tragedy*): "That thou shouldst see

Sin in its painted mask and look on Death in its robe of Shame."

Manuscript: On 9 April 1895, from Holloway Prison, Wilde wrote to Ross to go to Tite Street in order to obtain "a black book containing *La Sainte Courtisane...*" (*Letters* 390). Ross gave the MS. notebook to Ada Leverson, who, he wrote, went to Paris after Wilde's release from prison in 1897 to give it to him: "Wilde immediately left the manuscript in a cab. A few days later he laughingly informed me of the loss, and added that a cab was a very proper place for it" (*Miscellanies* xiii). A different version of the loss occurs in a letter from Leverson to the publisher Grant Richards, who wanted to issue the play: "...poor O.W. left 'The Woman Covered with Jewels' with *me* while he was away for two years! I returned the MS. to More Adey to take to Paris: and Bobbie [Ross] tells me it was left in a cab in Paris: & never found!" (qtd. in Speedie 116). The Clark Library has the notebook containing the MS. of the play, which differs considerably from the published version (see Small 146-49).

References: Epifanio San Juan, *The Art of Oscar Wilde* (1967); Alan Bird, *The Plays of Oscar Wilde* (1977); Julie Speedie, *Wonderful Sphinx: The Biography of Ada Leverson* (1993).

SALOME: A TRAGEDY IN ONE ACT

Written: Before leaving for Paris in late October 1891, Wilde had breakfast with friends, one of whom, the poet Wilfred Scawen Blunt (1840-1922), later wrote in his diary on 27 October: "...Oscar told us he was writing a play in French to be acted in the Français" (1:72). During his stay in Paris in the final months of 1891, Wilde worked on *Salomé*, the resulting legends of which are as numerous as his biographers: the principal account is that he first told the plot to French friends at lunch, then, on returning to his rooms, dashed off the play in a few hours in a blank notebook that happened to be lying on a table; another account is that he wrote the play in English, then translated it into French with the assistance of friends. A persistent element in these legends is that Wilde's French was apparently not adequate to the task, though André Gide insisted that Wilde knew French "admirably" (perhaps meaning "for an Irishman"). What is certain is that *Salomé* was written in French and corrected by such friends as Stuart Merrill and Adolphe Retté. Before the

French version was published, Marcel Schwob and Pierre Louÿs corrected some grammatical errors on the final proofs. In an interview in the *Pall Mall Budget* (30 June 1892), Wilde responded to the question of how he came to write the play in French:

My idea of writing the play was simply this: I have one instrument that I know that I can command, and that is the English language. There was another instrument to which I had listened all my life, and I wanted once to touch this new instrument to see whether I could make any beautiful thing out of it. (rpt. in Mikhail 1:188)

In an article in the *Morning Post* (8 Dec. 1910), Robert Ross emphatically stated that *Salomé* was

not written for Madame Sarah Bernhardt. It was *not* written with any idea of stage representation. Wilde did *not* "write the play in English," nor afterwards "re-write in French, because he could not get it acted in English".... *Salomé* was written in Torquay in the winter of 1891-92. The initial idea of treating the subject came to him some time previously, after seeing in Paris a well-known series of Gustave Moreau's pictures inspired by the same theme.... Wilde's confusion of Herod Antipas (Matthew XIV.1) and Herod the Great (Matthew II.1) and Herod Agrippa the first (Acts XII.23) is intentional. He follows a mediaeval convention of the mystery plays. There is no attempt at historical reconstruction.... (rpt. in Ross 122-23)

The Aborted London Production: In June 1892, rehearsals were underway in French at the Palace Theatre with Sarah Bernhardt in the leading role when Edward Pigott, Examiner of Plays in the Lord Chamberlain's office, refused to licence the play, presumably because it contained biblical characters (a traditional policy since the Protestant Reformation to prevent Catholic mystery plays from being staged); undoubtedly, the Examiner was also shocked by Salomé's sexual perversity. Outraged by the ban, Wilde announced his intention of staging the play in France and of becoming a French citizen. Wilde's critics responded with glee: William Watson, for example, wrote "Lines to Our New Censor" for the *Spectator* (9 July 1892):

> And wilt thou, Oscar, from us flee,
> And must we, henceforth, wholly sever?
> Shall thy laborious *jeux-d'esprit*
> Sadden our lives no more for ever?

To such doggerel, Wilde responded: "There is not enough fire in William Watson's poetry to boil a tea-kettle" (qtd. in Mikhail 1:230).

Published: In French on 22 February 1893, by Elkin Mathews and John Lane of the Bodley Head (London) and by the Librairie de l'Art Indépendant (Paris). *Salomé: Drame en un Acte* contains a title-page design by the Belgian artist Félicien Rops (1833-98), who had also illustrated the works of Baudelaire, Péladan, and Barbey d'Aurevilly. The illustration depicts a Satanic woman with angelic wings and a fish tail, the Latin caption reading "NON HIC PISCIS OMNIUM" (see Mason 371), translatable as "This is not the fish of everyone" (or, more colloquially, "This is not everyone's cup of tea"). Since Rops was best known for his explicit sexual depictions, the fish may suggest an obscene allusion, as in Shakespeare's "groping for trouts in a peculiar river" in *Measure for Measure* (I.ii.90). How Rops became associated with the publication of the play remains unknown (Wilde apparently did not know him personally). Wilde's dedication for this French version of *Salomé* reads: *"A mon Ami / PIERRE LOUŸS."*

On 24 February 1894 (Mason has 9 February), Mathews and Lane issued an English translation with eleven celebrated illustrations, a title page, and cover design by Aubrey Beardsley, who endured the objections of both Lane and Wilde to some of the drawings (Wilde claimed that they were "too Japanese while my play is Byzantine"). In a letter to Robert Ross, who had urged Wilde to permit the young artist to illustrate the play, Beardsley alludes to the "*Salomé* row": "I can tell you I had a warm time of it between Lane and Oscar and Co. For one week the numbers of telegraph and messenger boys who came to the door was simply scandalous.... I have withdrawn three of the illustrations and supplied their places with three new ones (simply beautiful and quite irrelevant)" (Beardsley, *Letters* 58). Although Wilde regarded the illustrations as "cruel and evil,

and so like dear Aubrey," he told the actress Mrs. Patrick Campbell that they were "quite wonderful" (*Letters* 353).

The dedication of the English version reads:

> TO MY FRIEND
> LORD ALFRED BRUCE DOUGLAS
> THE TRANSLATOR OF MY PLAY

That Douglas's name as translator does not appear on the title page indicates Wilde's dissatisfaction with the translation; indeed, he made numerous revisions in Douglas's version. In his prison letter to Douglas – *De Profundis* – Wilde recalls the difficulty between them over the translation: "...new scenes occurred, the occasion of them being my pointing out the schoolboy faults of your attempted translation of *Salome*. You must by this time be a fair enough French scholar to know that the translation was as unworthy of you, as an ordinary Oxonian, as it was of the work it sought to render" (*Letters* 431-32).

In his *Autobiography* (1929; 2nd. ed., 1931), Douglas defended his translation, to which, he said, he "devoted a great deal of time and careful work." He recalled that, when Wilde rejected it, Beardsley offered to undertake a translation since "he thoroughly understood the spirit of the play." Douglas contends that Beardsley translated the play after Wilde acceded to Beardsley's request to undertake the translation, which Wilde declared "utterly hopeless," but there is no evidence that Beardsley either began or completed a translation. Douglas then writes: "I told Oscar that if my translation was any use to him he could use it, and that anything in it he did not like he could alter. But I added that if he altered it, it would no longer be my translation, and that in that case it would not be advisable for my name to appear as the translator." Though Wilde made only "a few alterations," Douglas refused to claim it as his translation: "I think my own translation, as a matter of fact, was much better!" (160n1).

First Productions: On 11 February 1896, while Wilde was still in Reading Prison, *Salomé* was produced in Paris by Aurélien Lugné-Poe (see entry), director of the avant-garde Théâtre de l'Oeuvre, with Lina Muntz as Salomé and Lugné-Poe as Herod. In Berlin, Max Reinhardt, who established his reputation with his production of *Salomé*, supervised a private performance of the play on 15 November 1902 at the Kleines Theater, a production that also established Wilde's considerable reputation in Europe (indeed, *Salomé*, it has been said, "staggered even Berlin" in public performances during the next four years). The first London production, the first of several private ventures, was staged by the New Stage Club on 10 and 13 May 1905, at the Bijou Theatre, Bayswater, with Millicent Murby as Salome and Robert Farquharson (the stage name of Robin de la Condamine) as Herod. The first public performance of the play in England finally occurred in 1931 at the Lyceum Theatre.

In 1906 at the Astor Theater in New York, the Progressive Stage Society performed the play with little success. Richard Strauss's opera, which uses a shortened version of Wilde's play as the libretto, created a sensation in its 9 December 1905 Dresden première by its musical setting, which emphasized the Decadent mood of the play. When the director of the Metropolitan Opera presented a dress rehearsal for 1,500 guests on a Sunday morning, 22 January 1907, the clergy was so outraged, as was the Metropolitan board of directors, that the opera was not performed again there for twenty years.

Sources: The most direct source for Wilde's play is, of course, the Bible – Matthew 14:1-12 and Mark 6:14-29 – particularly the latter account, which is the more elaborate version of the story from which Wilde took the line spoken by Herod after Salome's dance: "Whatsoever thou shalt ask of me, I will give it thee, unto the half of my kingdom." The legend of Salome had fascinated writers and painters on the Continent throughout the 19th century (even Wilde's elder brother, Willie, had written a Salome poem).

To be sure, Wilde had read Huysmans's *A Rebours* (1884), particularly Chapter 5, in which Gustave Moreau's painting of Salomé – regarded by Huysmans as "the accursed Beauty exalted above all other beauties...the monstrous Beast" – is described as dancing before Herod; Huysmans describes a second painting depicting her reaction to Iokanaan's severed head. These paintings no doubt suggested to Wilde her central role in the story, unlike the biblical Salome, who merely follows her mother's wishes. In Chapter 14 of *A Rebours*, Mallarmé's "Hérodiade" is quoted, undoubtedly a further stimulus to Wilde.

For a structural model, Wilde probably turned to Théophile Gautier's *Une Nuit de Cléopâtre* (1838), a tale of a satiated Cleopatra, who, suffering from ennui, takes on a handsome lover, dances for him at a feast, and has him killed the next morning. Mario Praz identifies Cleopatra and Salome as femmes fatales, associated with late 19th-century Decadence. Another model for parts of the plot was probably Flaubert's "Hérodias" in *Trois Contes* (1877).

For the construction of dialogue, however, Maurice Maeterlinck, the "Belgian Shakespeare," was the obvious inspiration, for his incantatory, repetitive style suggesting mysterious worlds, both material and spiritual, as in *La Princesse Maleine* (1889), provided Symbolist resonances for *Salomé*. Indeed, the opening scene of Maeterlinck's play also provided the basic setting for Wilde's play: *La Princess Maleine* is set in a garden outside of a royal banquet hall, in which a feast takes place. Two officers are discussing certain ominous signs that have been observed in the sky. As Alan Bird has written: "...the pauses, the silences and the repetitions which Wilde introduced and exploited have become the basic technical weapons of the modern theatre, particularly in the plays of Pinter and Beckett" (86). Furthermore, as Peter Raby suggests, "Maeterlinck's insistent use of colour, sound, dance, visual description and visual effect offered Wilde a theatrical vocabulary more complete and more innovative than anything the London stage could demonstrate" (105).

The Plot: The setting is the great terrace in Herod's palace, set above the banqueting hall. At the back is an old cistern, surrounded by a wall of green bronze. The moon (the central, unifying symbol in the play) is shining "very brightly." Narraboth, the young Syrian captain of the guard, is speaking to a page about Salome, the daughter of Queen Herodias and the step-daughter of Herod, Tetrarch of Judaea. The stylized dialogue, as we have seen, derives principally from Maeterlinck: "Look at the moon. How strange the moon seems! She is like a woman rising from a tomb. She is like a dead woman." The voices of Jews arguing over their religion are heard from the banqueting hall below. But the attention of the Syrian captain focuses on Salome: "How beautiful is the Princess Salome tonight!" The page utters a warning of things to come: "You are always looking at her. You look at her too much. It is dangerous to look at people in such fashion.

Something terrible may happen."

Against a background of talk by a Nubian, a Cappadocian, and two soldiers concerning gods in one country who demand sacrifice, the Romans who have driven the gods out of another, and the Jews who "worship a God that one cannot see," the voice of the prophet Iokanaan (or John the Baptist) rises from the cistern: "After me shall come another mightier than I" – an obvious prophecy of the coming of Christ (as Raby has written, Iokanaan is "the voice of the Apocalypse, ushering in the last days of the world," 109). Herod, who had imprisoned his own brother in that same place for twelve years in order to possess his brother's wife, Herodias, eventually had him strangled. When the prophet condemned them both for incest, Herod placed him in the cistern, forbidding anyone to see him or speak with him. When the Syrian captain notices that Salome is leaving the banquet table looking very troubled, the page warns him again not to look at her. Disturbed over Herod's constant looking at her "with his mole's eyes under his shaking eyelids," Salome calls Herod's behavior strange, but she senses his lust.

Salome speaks of the moon (which, in the play, becomes increasingly associated with her): "She is cold and chaste. I am sure she is a virgin...." When she hears Iokanaan announcing that the "Son of Man is at hand," she wishes to speak with the prophet, but when she orders the soldiers to bring him forth, they refuse. Approaching the Syrian captain, she urges him to do her bidding, but he too alludes to the Tetrarch's order not to raise the cover of the cistern. But the persistent Salome tells him: "Thou wilt do this thing for me, Narraboth, and tomorrow when I pass in my litter beneath the gateway of the old-sellers I will let fall for thee a little flower, a little green flower" (Wilde's suggestion of the green carnation, symbol of Decadence, here indicative, as the play proceeds, of her perverse, unnatural desire).

The captain, yielding to Salome's seductive wiles, orders the prophet to be brought forth. When Iokanaan appears, he speaks indirectly of Herod, though Salome and the young Syrian are unaware of the allusion. Salome is increasingly fascinated by his body as well as his voice: "He is like a thin ivory statue.... I am sure he is chaste, as the moon is...." But he refuses to know who she is. When she reveals herself as the daughter of Herodias, he condemns her mother, who "hath

filled the earth with the wine of her iniquities...."

When she bids him speak again, he urges her to "seek out the Son of Man." Salome wishes to know who the Son of Man is: "Is he as beautiful as thou art, Iokanaan?" He responds by alluding to "the beating of the wings of the angel of death" in the palace. But Salome's desire becomes shockingly evident: "I am amorous of thy body, Iokanaan!" When he rejects her, she turns on him in fury: "Thy body is hideous. It is like the body of a leper." Instead, she focuses her desire on his hair: "It is of thy hair that I am enamoured, Iokanaan. Thy hair is like clusters of grapes.... Suffer me to touch thy hair." Rejected again, she calls his hair "horrible...covered with mire and dust." Finally, she craves his mouth.

Her obsession with the prophet drives the young Syrian to kill himself; when he falls between Salome and Iokanaan, she is too self-absorbed to note what has happened, and the prophet is too repelled by her perverse desire. Addressing her as the "daughter of adultery," he says that only one can save her: "It is He of whom I spake. Go seek Him. He is in a boat on the sea of Gaililee, and He talketh with His disciples." Ignoring what he says, Salome continues to express her desire. Calling her "accursed," the prophet descends into the cistern.

Herod, Herodias and all the court enter, inquiring where Salome is. Herod, echoing the lines spoken by the young Syrian captain at the beginning of the play, alludes to the moon as "a mad woman" seeking for lovers. He soon discovers that he has slipped in blood – an "ill omen," he believes. He then becomes aware of the Syrian's corpse. The wind then rises, which, to Herod, sounds like the beating of wings (an echo of the earlier image associated with the angel of death). The voice of Iokanaan is again heard: "Behold the time is come!" When Herodias asks Herod why he has not delivered the prophet to the Jews, a debate ensues among them concerning the possibility of Iokanaan (or any man) having seen God since the prophet Elias; they also debate the nature of the miracles attributed to the Messiah. The voice of Iokanaan announces that "the Saviour of the world" is making his way upon the mountains.

From this point on in the play, Herod obsessively gazes at Salome. Herod now wishes (then commands) Salome to dance for him, but she disobeys his order. But Herod promises to give her whatever she wishes, even half of his kingdom, if she will dance for him. When Salome requires him to swear an oath, Herod complies. (Wilde here modifies the biblical story in Mark by having Salome insist, *before she dances*, that Herod grant her whatever she wishes.) Slaves bring perfumes and the seven veils to Salome, whose sandals are removed. Though Herodias urges Salome not to dance for Herod, the dance proceeds.

Herod is delighted when Salome completes her performance. When he asks what Salome wishes, she begins: "I would that they presently bring me in a silver charger [as Beardsley pictures it, a large, flat dish] – " But before she completes her request, Herod interrupts, laughing at what will presumably be a modest wish rather than half his kingdom. Salome continues: "The head of Iokanaan." (In Mark 6:24, when Salome asks her mother what she should ask of Herod, Herodias says: "The head of John the Baptist.") Herodias is delighted, but Herod, who is horrified, offers her (in what Katharine Worth calls "three sumptuous arias," echoing "the triple pattern of Salome's ritualistic pleading with Iokanaan," 68) half of his kingdom, then precious jewels, white peacocks, anything but her request for the prophet's head.

But Salome insists that he has pledged an oath to her. Increasingly disturbed, Herod argues that Iokanaan is a holy man: "It may be that this man comes from God.... If he die also, peradventure some evil may befall me." When his pleas fall on deaf ears, he gives his ring of death to the soldier, who bears it to the executioner. Then, as Wilde's stage directions indicate, a "huge black arm, the arm of the Executioner, comes forth from the cistern, bearing on a silver shield the head of Iokanaan. Salome seizes it. [In Matthew 14:11 and Mark 6:28, she gives the head to Herodias.] Herod hides his face with his cloak. Herodias smiles and fans herself. The Nazarenes fall on their knees and begin to pray."

Possessing the prophet's head, Salome addresses it: "Ah! thou wouldst not suffer me to kiss thy mouth, Iokanaan. Well! I will kiss it now. I will bite it with my teeth as one bites a ripe fruit...." This lengthy speech concludes with her profession of love: "Oh, how I loved thee! I love thee yet, Iokanaan. I love only thee.... I am hungry for thy body...." Herod calls her "monstrous," but Herodias is "well pleased."

Herod orders the torches extinguished: "Hide the moon! Hide the stars! Let us hide ourselves in our palace, Herodias. I begin to be afraid." As he climbs the staircase, he hears the ecstatic voice of Salome: "Ah! I have kissed thy mouth, Iokanaan, I have kissed thy mouth." At that moment, "a ray of moonlight falls on Salome and illumines her." Herod, turning around and seeing Salome, cries out: "Kill that woman!" (This ending is not found in either biblical or literary sources usually cited by critics.) Soldiers rush forward and crush Salome beneath their shields. Thus, Wilde's fusion of color, dance, musical language, spectacle, and symbolism ends. As Katharine Worth remarks, *Salome* is "the first triumphant demonstration of the symbolist doctrine of total theatre" in England (73).

Early Critical Reception: In reviewing the published French edition of *Salomé*, the critic in the *Times* (23 Feb. 1893) called it "an arrangement in blood and ferocity, morbid, *bizarre*, repulsive, and very offensive in its adaptation of scriptural phraseology to situations the reverse of sacred" (rpt. in Beckson). In the *Pall Mall Gazette* (27 Feb.), the reviewer confessed to hearing various voices of other writers, such as Gautier (particularly in *Une Nuit de Cléopatre*), Maeterlinck ("the jugglery with the moon's resemblances, the short, repeated sentences in the phrase-book manner"), and expecially Flaubert: "If Flaubert had not written *Salammbô*, if Flaubert had not written *La Tentation de Saint Antoine* – above all, if Flaubert had not written *Hérodias*, *Salomé* might boast an originality to which she cannot now lay claim. She is the daughter of too many fathers. She is a victim of heredity. Her bones want strength, her flesh wants vitality, her blood is polluted. There is no pulse of passion in her" (rpt. in Beckson).

In *Black and White* (11 May) William Archer notes that Wilde's method of creating dialogue – "the brief melodious phrases, the chiming repetitions, the fugal effects beloved by the Belgian poet" – may be borrowed from Maeterlinck: "I am quite willing to believe, if necessary, that the two artists invented their similar devices independently, to meet a common need; but if, as a matter of fact, the one has taken a hint from the other, I do not see that his essential originality is thereby impaired. There is far more depth and body in Mr. Wilde's work than in Maeterlinck's." Archer senses the pathology in Salomé as in Ibsen's famous heroine when he remarks: "Salomé is an oriental Hedda Gabler; and who could portray such a character in the hues of radiant health?" (rpt. in Beckson).

In the New York *Critic* (12 May), the anonymous reviewer vented his inflamed spleen:

The downward course of a certain current in English literature and art has probably not reached an end in Oscar Wilde's *Salomé*. Someone will, doubtless, arise who shall be as incoherent as Blake, as hysterical as Rossetti, as incapable of decent reserve as Swinburne, and as great a humbug as Wilde. But it is doubtful whether the latter's cleverness in patching up sham monsters can go much farther.

The reviewer notes that Wilde has borrowed Maeterlinck's "trick of repeating stupid phrases until a glimpse of meaning seems almost a flash of genius." However, he does concede that Wilde "adds something of his own..." (rpt. in Beckson).

Early Theater Reviews: In 1896, the French critics were divided on Wilde's achievement. In *Gil Blas* (13 Feb.), Léon Bernard-Derosne wrote that the play's repetitive lines were monotonous and hence lacked dramatic power. In the *Revue bleue* (15 Feb.), Jacques du Tillet tempered his response with doubt concerning its essential inspiration: "I do not know exactly what name would be suitable to the work of M. Oscar Wilde. Play, poem, reverie? It is not without value.... I am not wholly convinced that these enumerations, these roars of a rutting beast, and also those philosophic 'resumes' are good poetry.... [Wilde] seems to me rather an adroit man of letters than an inspired poet." However, Jean de Tinan, in the *Mercure de France* (March) hailed Wilde "with all the enthusiasm of admiration multiplied by indignation." He praised Lugné-Poe for producing the play.

Reviewing the first London production of *Salome*, the critic for the *Daily Chronicle* (11 May 1905), though sympathetic to Wilde, saw little to praise in the play: "If only the dazzling and unfortunate genius who wrote *Salome* could have seen it acted as it was yesterday at the little Bijou Theatre! One fears, if he had, he would have found that little phrase of his – 'the importance of being earnest' – a more delicately true satire than ever upon our sometimes appalling seriousness.... Altogether, beneath this pall of solemnity on the

one hand and lack of real exaltation on the other, the play's beauties of speech and thought had practically no chance whatever." The scenes between Salome and Iokanaan, he continues, were performed "solemnly, dreamily, phlegmatically," and Robert Farquharson presented Herod as "a semi-grotesque portrait of one of the late Roman emperors."

In the *Saturday Review* (13 May), Max Beerbohm also lamented the acting and staging, though he believed that "not even the best acting and the best stage-management could make this play so good to see as it is good to read. Of course, I do not mean that 'Salome' has less dramatic than literary fibre. Mr. Wilde was a born dramatist – a born theatrist, too." Through what Beerbohm calls the play's "note of terror," well struck in the opening lines, "slowly the action advances, step by step, to the foreknown crisis...it is mainly through this very slowness, this constant air of suspense, that the play yields us the tragic thrill."

Nevertheless, says Beerbohm, "it is not a good play for the stage. It is too horrible for definite and corporeal presentment. It should be seen only through the haze of our imagination." When we see Salome kissing the dead lips of Iokanaan, "when we have it illustrated to us in sharp detail by a human being – then we suffer something beyond the rightful tragic thrill: we suffer qualms of physical disgust." By having Salome bring the head "briskly down to the footlights, and in that glare delivered to it all her words and kisses," the production at the Bijou not only "intensified our physical disgust, but also...destroyed all our illusion" (rpt. in Beerbohm, *Around Theatres*, 1953).

In 1906, the Progressive Stage Society of New York produced the play in a matinee performance at the Astor Theatre, briefly described in the *New York Daily Tribune* (16 Nov.) as "a repulsive composition...written by that vulgar dramatist the late Oscar Wilde," the reviewer regarding it as "decadent stuff, and unworthy of notice." The reviewer in the *New York Times* (16 Nov.) reported "little applause" for the play, though the audience "showed that it was impressed by the daring and grewsome [*sic*] finale which was given the well-known tale.... Whether Wilde's play is not a trifle too strong meat for the public to enjoy is a fair question."

Manuscripts: The MSS. of *Salomé* were written in French, and corrections were apparently made over a long period of time. The Bibliotheca Bodmeriana (Cologny-Geneva) has an early draft of 100 leaves bound in a notebook. Texas also has an early draft (dated Nov. 1891, Paris) in Wilde's hand. The Rosenbach Library has the final fair copy in two notebooks with Louÿs's interlinear corrections and suggestions for revision, particularly in Wilde's use of the subjunctive. Wilde accepted only the grammatical corrections. According to Rupert Hart-Davis, the *Salomé* MS. in the Berg Collection is a forgery, probably by Fabian Lloyd, Wilde's nephew by marriage (*Letters* 306n). Apparently, the Clark Library also has a forgery (Small 106).

References: Adolphe Retté, *Le Symbolisme: anecdotes et souvenirs* (1903); Wilfrid Scawen Blunt, *My Diaries: Part One, 1888 to 1900* (1919); Clyde de L. Ryals, "Oscar Wilde's 'Salomé,'" *N&Q* (Feb. 1959); Mario Praz, *The Romantic Agony* (1933); Nicholas Joost and Franklin Court, "*Salomé*, the Moon, and Oscar Wilde's Aesthetics," *Papers on Language and Literature* (Fall 1972); Rodney Shewan, *Oscar Wilde: Art and Egotism* (1977); Alan Bird, *The Plays of Oscar Wilde* (1977); Elliot Gilbert, "'Tumult of Images': Wilde, Beardsley, and *Salomé*," *Victorian Studies* (Winter 1983); Graham Good, "Early Productions of Oscar Wilde's *Salomé*," *Nineteenth Century Theatre Research* (Winter 1983); Katharine Worth, *Oscar Wilde* (1983); Robert Schweik, "Oscar Wilde's *Salomé*, the Salomé Theme in Late European Art, and a Problem of Method in Cultural History," *Twilight of Dawn: Studies in English Literature in Transition*, ed. O M Brack, Jr. (1887); Peter Raby, *Oscar Wilde* (1988); Kerry Powell, "*Salomé*, the Censor, and the Divine Sarah," *Oscar Wilde and the Theatre of the 1890s* (1990); Robert Schweik, "Congruous Incongruities: The Wilde-Beardsley 'Collaboration,'" *ELT* 37:1 (1994); Joseph Donohue, "*Salomé* and the Wildean Art of Symbolist Theatre," *Modern Drama* (Spring 1994); William Tydeman and Steven Price, *Wilde: Salome* (1996).

SALTUS, EDGAR (1855-1921)

An American poet, novelist, and essayist, Saltus apparently first met Wilde in Delmonico's restaurant in New York early in January 1882, when Wilde was on his lecture tour of America. Saltus's memoir, *Oscar Wilde: An Idler's Impression* (1917), has vivid images of Wilde, such as his appearance at Delmonico's: "He was dressed like a mountebank. Without, at the entrance, a crowd had collected. In the restaurant people stood up and stared. Wilde was beautifully unmoved" (14). While talking about his play, *Vera; or, The Nihilists*, Wilde mentioned that he had been offered a $5,000 advance – "mere starvation wages," he said. As for certain revisions requested by the manager, Wilde responded: "'But who am I to tamper with a masterpiece?' – a jest which afterward he was too generous to hoard" (14-15).

In early September 1890, while Saltus – a less extravagant Decadent than Wilde – was visiting London, Wilde praised one of Saltus's books – unnamed – which he found "strange...so pessimistic, so poisonous and so perfect. You have given me that *nouveau frisson* [new shudder] I am always looking for" (*Letters* 275). According to a letter from Saltus to Carl Van Vechten, dated 19 February 1918 (MS., Yale), Saltus's *Mary Magdalen* (1891) "purportedly originated in a conversation with Oscar Wilde in which both Saltus and Wilde agreed to write a work containing the figure of Salome; their common inspiration was Flaubert's *Hérodias*" (Sprague 101). When Wilde completed *Salomé*, he read the MS. to Saltus, who applauded as well as shuddered. Wilde remarked: "It is only the shudder that counts" (qtd. in Saltus 22).

After Wilde's release from prison, Saltus saw him in Paris: "...to my regret, he looked like a drunken coachman, and [I] told him how greatly I admired the 'Ballad,' – that poem which tells of his life, or rather of his death, in jail." Laughing, Wilde said: "It does not seem to me sufficiently vécu [lived]" (qtd. in Saltus 23-24). Wilde, said Saltus, was

a third rate poet who occasionally rose to the second class but not once to the first. Prose is more difficult than verse and in it he is rather sloppy. In spite of which, or perhaps precisely on that account, he called himself lord of language.... In talk he blinded and it is the subsiding wonder of it that his plays contain.... For assuming his madness, one must also admit his genius and the uninterrupted conjunction of the two might have produced brilliancies such as few bookshelves display. Therein is the tragedy of letters. (24-25)

Reference: Claire Sprague, *Edgar Saltus* (1968).

"SAN MINIATO"

Published: First appeared as Part I of "Graffiti d'Italia: I. San Miniato (June 15)" in *Dublin University Magazine* 87 (March 1876): 297-98; rev. as "San Miniato" in *Poems* (1881). See "By the Arno," originally Parts II and III of "Graffiti d'Italia."

Wilde wrote "San Miniato," consisting of four quatrains, after his visit to San Miniato monastery in Florence in mid-June 1875: "See, I have climbed the mountain side / Up to this holy house of God...." In a state of spiritual turmoil, the speaker pleads with the Virgin Mary: "My heart is weary of this life / And over-sad to sing again." The poem ends with an address by the speaker to divinity to intercede on his behalf "ere the searching sun / Show to the world my sin and shame."

Having read the poem, Lady Wilde wrote to Oscar that it *"looks* and reads *perfect* – musical and poetic – the evident spirit of a Poet Natural in it," but she disliked the final line, particularly the word *shame*, for it was not "highly poetical." She would have used a different word, she said, that "expressed moral weakness" (qtd. in Melville 127).

Manuscript: The Hyde Collection has a MS. titled "San Miniato (June 15th)," containing versions of lines 1-4, as well as lines 1-4 and 9-24 of "By the Arno" (printed in Mason 64).

Reference: Joy Melville, *Mother of Oscar: The Life of Jane Francesca Wilde* (1994).

"SANTA DECCA"

Published: *Poems* (1881); rev. in (1882). Wilde indicated that he wrote the poem on his visit to the Greek island of Corfu (where Santa Decca, a mountain now called Mt. Pantokrator, is located) during his trip to Greece in 1877.

This sonnet initially appears to celebrate the passing of the Greek gods, a view perhaps inspired by Elizabeth Barrett Browning's "The Dead Pan" in *Poems* (1844), which envisions Christ's sacrifice as ending the "vain false gods of Hellas." Yet Wilde harbors regret over the fact that "The Gods are dead: no longer do we bring / To grey-eyed Pallas crowns of olive-leaves!" In effect, Christianity has supplanted Paganism: "Great Pan is dead, and Mary's son is King" (in the headnote to her poem, Mrs. Browning cites the legend that, at the hour of Christ's death, "a cry of 'Great Pan is dead!' swept across the waves in the hearing of certain mariners, – and the oracles ceased"). The speaker addresses his "Love": there may be "in this sea-tranced isle" some god "chewing the bitter fruit of memory" lying "hidden in the asphodel." He urges his beloved to flee from the god's anger but then pauses in wonder as though hoping to catch a glimpse of an ancient relic: "The leaves are stirring: let us watch awhile."

Manuscript: The Huntington Library has a MS. of the poem.

SARONY, NAPOLEON (1821-96)

Known as "The Napoleon of Photography," Sarony succeeded Matthew Brady as the best-known photographer of late 19th-century America. Born in Quebec of an Austrian father and French mother, Sarony arrived in New York in 1836 and later became a lithographer. By 1864, he began his career as a photographer of the famous, particularly of those in the theater. A flamboyant "eccentric little man" just over five feet tall, Sarony sought unusual poses from his subjects against backgrounds and props that characterized their personalities. On his photomounts, he had his name printed in a red swirl and emblazoned it on his studio building in Union Square. For certain celebrities, he offered large sums of money for their willingness to pose: to Sarah Bernhardt, he reportedly gave $1,500 and to Lillie Langtry the huge sum of $5,000.

When Wilde was in New York at the beginning of his lecture tour in 1882, his manager, Colonel Morse, chose Sarony to create a series of poses that could be used to publicize the tour. Sarony dispensed with the customary charge in view of the opportunity to enhance his reputation as Wilde's photographer. Dancing about with his customary red fez perched atop his head, Sarony was delighted at the prospect of photographing the young Aesthete: "A picturesque subject, indeed!" he cried out when Wilde arrived.

Sarony first took a picture of Wilde wearing a sealskin cap, then bareheaded in his long trousers and fur-trimmed coat with a white cane, then lying recumbent on a settee in his knee breeches, then, in a series of famous poses, in his knee breeches against a decorative background with a classical dado. At that time, subjects had to maintain a pose lasting from 15 seconds to a full minute (indeed, Sarony had designed a rigid frame for his subjects to stand against or sit in so that they could keep their bodies still). As Wilde held each pose, Sarony would "turn and stare out of the window in rapt silence while an assistant took the picture" (Lewis and Smith 39). In fact, assistants also developed the pictures.

Before Wilde left America, he returned to Sarony's studio to pose with his new close-cropped Neronian haircut in imitation of Nero's bust in the Louvre (a photograph at the University of Texas of Wilde's new coiffure appears in Small 10). Wilde told Robert Sherard that his "Neronian coiffure" amazed London: "Nobody recognizes me, and everybody tells me I look young: that is delightful, of course" (*Letters* 148).

Reference: Ben L. Bassham, *Theatrical Photographs of Napoleon Sarony* (1978).

SATIRES OF WILDE: *See* **PARODIES AND SATIRES**

SATYRICON

This erotic work by Petronius Arbiter (d. AD 65), allegedly translated by Wilde, is clearly a false attribution perpetrated by the publisher, Charles Carrington, who, on issuing this volume in Paris in 1902, pasted the following "Important Notice" over his own name on the title page: "The present translation was done directly from the original Latin by 'Sebastian Melmoth' (Oscar Wilde)." The implication is that Wilde translated the work after his release from prison, but no evidence exists that Wilde translated anything in the final three-and-a half years of his life. In his 1909 Paris edition of *The Picture of Dorian Gray*, Carrington appended a notice following the text that the *Satyricon* and Barbey d'Aurevilly's *What Never Dies*, also issued in 1902, "have been attributed quite erroneously" to Wilde, hence "no longer offered *as authentic productions* of the talented author of DORIAN GRAY, albeit the Parisian publisher was led to believe, from their brilliancy and thoroughness, that they really were the work of the one time SEBASTIAN MELMOTH."

Reference: Rod Boroughs, "Oscar Wilde's Translation of Petronius: The Story of a Literary Hoax," *ELT* 38:1 (1995).

SCHUSTER, ADELA (d. 1941)

The daughter of a wealthy Frankfurt banker, Adela Schuster, whom Wilde probably met late in 1892, was one of his closest friends and generous benefactors. Playfully, Wilde called her "Miss Tiny" because of her considerable size or the "Lady of Wimbledon," where her family had a large villa. In February 1893, after she read *Lady Windermere's Fan*, she wrote to Wilde: "It so enchanted and electrified me...it is admirable, it is perfect" (qtd. in Schmidgall 290).

According to Frank Harris, Wilde told him that, at the time of his second trial, "a very noble and cultured woman, a friend of both of us, Miss S—, a Jewess by race tho' not by religion, had written to him asking if she could help him financially, as she had been distressed by hearing of his bankruptcy, and feared that he might be in need." When Wilde outlined what his expenses might be, Schuster sent him a check for £1,000, "assuring him that it cost her little even in self-sacrifice and declaring that it was only inadequate recognition of the pleasure she had through his delightful talks" (Harris 169).

Schuster maintained contact with Wilde while he was in prison through his close friend More Adey (see entry). In his letter to Wilde in late September 1896, Adey quoted Schuster's remark: "Could not Mr. Wilde now write down some of the lovely tales he used to tell me? ...I think the mere reminder of some of his tales may set his mind in that direction and stir the impulse to write" (qtd. in *Letters* 407–08n2). Wilde responded to her wish in his letter to Adey: "I was greatly touched by the extract from the letter of the Lady of Wimbledon. That she should keep a gracious memory of me, and have trust or hope for me in the future, lightens for me many dreadful hours of degradation or despair" (*Letters* 410). In November of that year, Wilde asked Robert Ross to send "whatever of remembrance and reverence she will accept, to the Lady of Wimbledon, whose soul is a sanctuary for those who are wounded, and a house of refuge for those in pain" (*Letters* 415).

In *De Profundis*, Wilde recalls a discussion on the subject of sorrow with Schuster, who is alluded to but not named as "one of the most beautiful personalities I have ever known: a woman, whose sympathy and noble kindness to me both before and since the tragedy of my imprisonment have been beyond power and description: one who has really assisted me...to bear the burden of my troubles more than anyone else in the whole world has..." (*Letters* 474). After his release from prison, Wilde expressed his concern to More Adey that a letter sent to Schuster may have gone astray, for he did not want to appear "ungrateful...to that gracious and wonderful personality" (*Letters* 615).

No evidence exists that Wilde saw Schuster after his release, but he had a copy of *The Importance of Being Earnest* sent to her. For his funeral, she sent a wreath, and at the head of Wilde's coffin, Ross placed a wreath of laurels inscribed "A tribute to his literary achievements and distinction" with the names of "those who had shown kindness to him during or after his imprisonment," Schuster's among them (see *Letters* 856); on 23 December 1900, Ross sent a lengthy account to her of Wilde's final months (see *Letters* 858-63).

In including *The Duchess of Padua* in the *Collected Edition* (1908), Ross dedicated it to Schuster, to fulfill a wish by Wilde to express his gratitude for her "infinite kindness" (*Letters* 757n1). When Harris published his biography in 1916, the loyal Schuster took exception to Harris's characterization of Wilde and wrote to tell him. Harris quoted her in a letter to Ross: "Miss Schuster objects, and rightly, to my saying that Oscar was very cold and hard and incapable of friendship" (qtd. in Schmidgall 291).

Reference: Gary Schmidgall, *The Stranger Wilde: Interpreting Oscar* (1994).

SCHWOB, MARCEL (1867-1905)

A French Symbolist writer and journalist, Schwob – "a young lion of the day" (Ellmann 346/326) – guided Wilde to the various Parisian literary salons in late 1891. In his journal, Schwob recorded his impressions of Wilde: "While he ate – and he ate little – he never stopped smoking opium-tainted Egyptian cigarettes. A terrible absinthe-drinker, through which he got his visions and desires" (qtd. in Ellmann 346/327).

Having requested permission to translate Wilde's fairy tale "The Selfish Giant" into French, Schwob published it in *L'Echo de Paris* (27 Dec. 1891) and dedicated a story of his own, "Le Pays bleu," to Wilde in 1892. In December of that year, when Wilde was seeing the proofs of the French version of *Salomé* through the press, Schwob agreed to read them and revise any grammatical solecisms. Appreciative of Schwob's friendship and help,

Wilde dedicated *The Sphinx* to him.

At the time of Wilde's arrest, however, Schwob – like many of Wilde's presumed supporters – abandoned his former friend when his name was linked with Wilde's. In an article in *Le Figaro littéraire* (13 April 1895), Jules Huret mentioned Schwob as one of Wilde's intimate friends: "A furor resulted. Schwob sent his seconds to meet Huret's seconds, and was angry when they accepted Huret's explanation" (Ellmann 458/430).

Reference: Pierre Champion, *Marcel Schwob et son temps* (1927).

"A SCOTCHMAN ON SCOTTISH POETRY"

Published: *PMG*, 24 Oct. 1887, 3; rpt. in *Reviews* (1908). An unsigned review of John Veitch's *The Feeling for Nature in Scottish Poetry*, 2 vols. (1887).

Wilde takes issue with Veitch's view of the primitive attitude towards nature: The "open-air feeling," Wilde believes, seems comparatively modern. The "modern Wordsworthian," he remarks, "desiring to make man one with Nature, finds in external things 'the symbols of our inner life, the workings of a spirit akin to our own.'" The earliest "Nature-myths tell us, not of man's 'sensuous enjoyment' of Nature, but of the terror that Nature inspires. Nor are darkness and storm regarded by the primitive man as 'simply repulsive,' they are to him divine and supernatural things, full of wonder, and full of awe." As for the influence of cities, it is because of them that "we owe the love of the country."

Wilde alludes to many early Scottish poets about whom Veitch "writes with fine judgment and delicate feeling, and even his admiration for Burns has nothing absolutely aggressive about it." Veitch's judgment and taste are "as a rule, excellent, and his book is, on the whole, a very fascinating delightful contribution to the history of literature."

"SCULPTURE AT THE 'ARTS AND CRAFTS'"

Published: *PMG*, 9 Nov. 1888, 3; rpt. in *Miscellanies* (1908). An unsigned review of George Simonds's lecture, "Sculpture," at the Arts and Crafts Exhibition Society's presentation in the New Gallery, Regent Street, on 8 November.

Simonds's lecture, Wilde remarks, was "at once too elementary and too elaborately technical. The ordinary art-student, even the ordinary studio-loafer, could not have learned anything from it, while the 'cultured person,' of whom there were many specimens present, could have but felt a little bored at the careful and painfully clear descriptions given by the lecturer of very well-known and uninteresting methods of work." Simonds described clay and wax modelling, plaster and metal casting, bas-reliefs and "working in the round," and how to use such instruments as the drill, the wire, and the chisel. He even exhibited some works of sculpture.

What Simonds's lecture lacked, Wilde continues, were ideas, such as the "artistic value of each material; of the correspondence between material or method and the imaginative creative faculty seeking to find expression; of the capacities for realism and idealism that reside in each material; of the historical and human side of the art he said nothing.... He never once brought his subject into any relation either with art or with life." Wilde notes that William Morris, in the previous week, while lecturing on the technical processes of weaving, "never forgot that he was lecturing on an art" (see entry: "Mr. Morris on Tapestry"). Wilde concludes by "regretting the extremely commonplace character" of Simonds's lecture: "If a man lectures on poets he should not confine his remarks purely to grammar."

"SEE! THE GOLD SUN HAS RISEN"

Not published in Wilde's lifetime, this incomplete lyric of five stanzas utilizes the ballad stanza and rhyme scheme (*abab*) in giving expression to romantic love. Introducing his own device for structuring each quatrain, Wilde separates the fourth line from the previous three as a refrain but nonetheless rhymes it with the second line.

The first three stanzas trace the time of day with allusions to parts of the body, as in the light of the sky: "Is it only the light of thine eyes?" The final lines suggest sacramental transfiguration in the image of the sun "Turning my blood to wine, / As we lie by a stream and the warm soft grass / Ah Sweet! 'tis my body and thine."

Manuscript: The Clark Library has the MS. of this poem.

"THE SELFISH GIANT"

Published: *The Happy Prince and Other Tales* (1888). Shortly after its publication, Walter Pater

wrote a letter of appreciation on having received a copy of the volume, citing "The Selfish Giant" as "certainly perfect in its kind" (Pater, *Letters* 85). Wilde told his publisher, Alfred Nutt, that Pater had written him "a wonderful letter about my prose, so I am in high spirits" (*Letters* 219).

The Plot: On their way home from school, the children often play in the Giant's large, lovely garden. "How happy we are here!" they cry. After being away for seven years, the Giant returns and sees the children playing in his garden. When he demands what they are doing there, they flee. He immediately builds a high wall around his garden and posts a notice: "Trespassers will be prosecuted." Shut out, the children, with nowhere to play, recall how happy they had been in the garden.

When the spring comes, the Giant's garden looks as though it were still winter. Even the birds refuse to sing because the children are gone. The Giant cannot understand why his garden has remained frozen white. As the seasons pass without a change in the garden, Autumn refuses to yield any "golden fruit" because, as she says, the Giant is "too selfish." One morning, when he hears a linnet's song coming from his garden, the Giant believes that spring has finally arrived. Leaping from his bed, he sees that the children have crept into the garden through a hole in the wall and are sitting on the branches of the trees. Pleased, the trees have blossomed, and the birds and flowers are equally delighted. In the far corner of the garden, however, it is still winter. A small boy is crying bitterly, for he cannot reach the branches of a tree.

His heart melting, the Giant says: "How selfish I have been!" He resolves to put the boy on top of the tree, then knock down the wall to transform his garden into a children's playground "for ever and ever." When the children see the Giant, they flee once again from the garden, which suddenly looks as though it were winter again. The small boy, however, does not run; the Giant lifts him to the top of the tree, whereupon it bursts into blossoms, the birds alighting in it to sing their songs. The boy, flinging his arms about the Giant's neck, kisses him. When the other children run back to the garden, it is spring again. The Giant knocks down the wall; people on their way to market note that he is playing with the children in "the most beautiful garden they had ever seen."

When the Giant asks the children one day where the small boy is, none of them knows, nor do they know who he is. With the passing years, the Giant grows very old and feeble, unable to play with the children: "I have many beautiful flowers, but the children are the most beautiful flowers of all." On one winter morning, he notices, to his astonishment, that in the far corner of his garden a tree is covered with blossoms, its branches all golden with silver fruit; underneath it stands the small boy whom he had loved. When he comes close, however, he is angered by the wounds caused by nails in the boy's hands and feet, demanding to know who has injured him (Wilde's characteristic device of introducing crucifixion imagery in "non-Christian" contexts). The boy, however, says that they are "the wounds of Love." Suddenly filled with awe, the Giant kneels before the "little child," who tells him: "You let me play once in your garden, to-day you shall come with me to my garden, which is Paradise." When the children return that afternoon, they discover the dead Giant lying under the tree "all covered with white blossoms."

Reference: Michael Kotzin, "'The Selfish Giant' as Literary Fairy Tale," *Studies in Short Fiction* (Fall 1979).

"SEN ARTYSTY; OR, THE ARTIST'S DREAM"

Published: Clement Scott, ed., *Routledge's Christmas Annual: The Green Room Stories by Those Who Frequent It* (London: George Routledge & Sons, 1880) 66-68, with the subscript: "By Madame Helena Modjeska (Translated from the Polish by Oscar Wilde)"; rpt. in *Poems* (1908) without the subscript.

Since Wilde knew no Polish, he was obviously guided by the actress Helena Modjeska (see entry), whose "dream" (the Polish text remains unlocated) resembles those in her *Memories and Impressions* (1910). Wilde told the theatre critic Clement Scott (1841-1904) that he had read the translation to the actress (around September 1880): "...she was good enough to say beautiful things about it, so she was satisfied fully." After hearing from Scott, Wilde wrote to him again: "...whatever beauty is in the poem is due to the graceful fancy and passionate artistic nature of Madame Modjeska. I am really only the reed through which her sweet notes have been blown: yet slight as my own work has been, and of necessity hasty, I thank you very much for your praise..." (*Letters* 69).

The poem depicts the artist's dream (recalling Keats's "The Fall of Hyperion": "Fanatics have their dreams...."), which occurs in the spring when "The pure air was soft, / And the deep grass I lay on soft as air." Though the "whole world / Seemed waking to delight," the artist's "soul was filled with leaden heaviness: / I had no joy in Nature...." The poem reflects artistic Decadence in its rejection of nature as the source of inspiration, as it had been for the Romantics. Thus, the speaker continues:

The bright bird
Sang out of tune for me, and the sweet flowers
Seemed but a pageant, and an unreal show
That mocked my heart....

The artist resists a fiery angel's advice to accept the beauties of nature, and the poem proceeds with an image of the artist as martyr, complete with the transformation of her laurel wreath into a crown of thorns, an image of a Christ-like artist in addition to a pun on Wilde's own name: "With wild hands / I strove to tear it from my bleeding brow, / But all in vain...."

Manuscript: The Clark Library has two untitled MSS.: one is a rough draft of lines 1-40 (printed in Mason 187-88); the other contains jottings from line 20 to the end (printed in Dulau 4-8).

"A 'SENTIMENTAL JOURNEY' THROUGH LITERATURE"

Published: *PMG*, 1 Dec. 1886, 5; rpt. in *Reviews* (1908). An unsigned review of Roden Noel's *Essays on Poetry and Poets* (1886).

Calling Noel's volume "undoubtedly interesting...not merely through its eloquence and earnestness, but also through the wonderful catholicity of taste that it displays," Wilde regards the author's "sobriety" with approval. The best essay, "The Poetic Interpretation of Nature," claims that what Ruskin calls the "'pathetic fallacy of literature' is in reality a vital emotional truth." Wilde also agrees with Noel's severe repudiation concerning the preference of sound to sense in poetry, but Noel is

guilty of a much graver sin against art when, in his desire to emphasize the meaning of Chatterton, he destroys Chatterton's music [by using a modernized text].... Nineteenth-century restorations have done quite enough harm to English architecture without English poetry being treated in the same manner, and we hope that when Mr. Noel writes again about Chatterton he will quote from the poet's verse, not from a publisher's version.

"The fault of this book," Wilde states, "is that it tells us far more about [Noel's] own personal feelings than it does about the qualities of the various works of art that are criticized. It is in fact a diary of the emotions suggested by literature, rather than any real addition to literary criticism.... [W]e wonder what Keats would have thought of a critic who gravely suggests that *Endymion* is 'a parable of the development of the individual soul.'"

Furthermore, Noel has "a curious habit of classing together the most incongruous names and comparing the most incongruous works of art." Wilde offers examples, among them the following: "What is gained by telling us that...Edgar Allan Poe, Disraeli, and Mr. Alfred Austin are artists of note whom we may affiliate on Byron, and that if Sappho and Milton 'had not high genius, they would be justly reproached as sensational'?" With respect to occasional indelicacies of expression in Noel's essays, Wilde observes that "though indignation may make a great poet, bad temper always makes a poor critic." The "best we can say" of Roden's book is that "it is a Sentimental Journey through Literature, the worst that any one could say of it is that it has all the merits of such an expedition."

"SERENADE. (FOR MUSIC)"

Published: First appeared as "To Helen. (Serenade of Paris)" in *Pan* ("Musical Supplement") 1 (8 Jan. 1881), consisting of two stanzas; rev. in five stanzas with the present title in *Poems* (1881).

The Greek myth of Helen and Paris, the son of Priam, King of Troy, involves love and betrayal, for Helen, wife of Menelaus, King of Sparta, falls in love with Paris and both flee to Troy (though the myth also has variants, such as the abduction of Helen by Paris); thus begins the ten-year Trojan War. Wilde's poem depicts the dramatic moment when Paris serenades Helen in order to lure her from her bed: "My Tyrian galley waits for thee. / Come down! the purple sail is spread, / The watchman sleeps within the town." When Helen appears, Paris is ecstatic: "It is my own dear Lady true /

With golden hair and lily hand! / O noble pilot, steer for Troy...." See "O Golden Queen of life and joy!" for its relationship to this poem."

Manuscript: A facsimile of a fragmentary MS. containing lines 1-8 appeared in the Maggs Bros. Ltd. sale catalogue 1157 (1993).

"'SERMONS IN STONES' AT BLOOMS-BURY"

Published: *PMG*, 15 Oct. 1887, 5; rpt. in *Miscellanies* (1908). An unsigned review with the subtitle "The New Sculpture Room at the British Museum."

Wilde hails "some of the wonderful treasures so long immured in the grimy vaults of the British Museum," now on exhibition in the new Sculpture Room. The philosopher, preacher, practical man of the world and "even the Philistine himself cannot fail to be touched by these 'sermons in stone' [*As You Like It*, II.i.17], with their deep significance, their fertile suggestion, their plain humanity." The tombstones exhibited reveal how the Greeks and Romans regarded death: "Here is one of two ladies of Smyrna, who were so remarkable in their day that the city voted them honorary crowns; here is a Greek doctor examining a little boy who is suffering from indigestion...." Roman art differs, for it depicts "vigorous and realistic portraiture, and deals with pure family life far more frequently than Greek art does. They are very ugly, these stern-looking Roman men and women, whose portraits are exhibited on their tombs, but they seem to have been loved and respected by their children and their servants."

In addition to these tombstones, there are "most fascinating examples of Roman decorative art under the Emperors," the most impressive being a bas-relief marriage scene. There are also "delightful friezes of children," one depicting them playing on musical instruments, another showing them at play with Mars' armor, which is "full of fancy and delicate humour." It is not difficult "to see whence the Renaissance sprang, and to what we owe the various forms of Renaissance art."

"SHAKESPEARE ON SCENERY"

Published: *Dramatic Review* 1 (14 March 1885): 99; rpt. in *Reviews* (1908).

In addressing himself to the question of Shakespeare's view of scenery, Wilde cites the chorus in *Henry V*, in which Shakespeare complains of the smallness of the stage for a large historical pageant so that few supers are available to play the soldiers, and horses are unable to be brought on stage. Indeed, says Wilde, Shakespeare is "constantly protesting against the two special limitations of the Elizabethan stage – the lack of suitable scenery, and the fashion of men playing women's parts...." Shakespeare probably felt hampered at the necessity of interrupting the play so that an actor could explain to the audience a scene change or designate the stage as the deck of a ship in a storm. In addition, placards and descriptions provided other means of establishing the setting of a scene.

Yet audiences prefer to see rather than be told: "...the modern dramatist, in having the surroundings of his play visibly presented to the audience when the curtain rises, enjoys an advantage for which Shakespeare often expresses his desire." The use of "self-explanatory scenery enables the modern method to be far more direct," to produce "an artistic temperament in the audience, and to produce that joy in beauty for beauty's sake, without which the great masterpieces of art can never be understood...." However, an excessive number of properties can crowd the stage: "Properties kill perspective. A painted door is more like a real door than a real door is itself, for the proper conditions of light and shade can be given to it." Therefore, the scene-painter needs to be restored "to his proper position as an artist...."

SHAW, GEORGE BERNARD (1856-1950)

The Irish playwright, critic, novelist, and Socialist came to know Wilde's family through his sister Lucy, "a very attractive girl who sang beautifully [and] who had met and made some sort of innocent conquest of both Oscar and Willie" (*Playwright* 30). Shaw made his first visit to Lady Wilde's "at home" in Park Street, London, in November 1879; at one of these social affairs, Shaw met Wilde, who, he recalled,

> came and spoke to me with an evident intention of being specially kind to me. We put each other out frightfully; and this odd difficulty persisted between us to the very last, even when we were no longer mere boyish novices and had become men of the world with plenty of skill in social intercourse. I saw him very seldom [Shaw recalled possibly between six and twelves times from first to

> last], as I avoided literary and artistic coteries like the plague.... (*Playwright* 30)

Shaw later wrote that "Oscar was an overgrown man, with something not quite normal about his bigness: something that made [the writer] Lady Colin Campbell [1857-1911], who hated him, describe him as 'that great white caterpiller.' ...I have always maintained that Oscar was a giant in the pathological sense, and that this explains a good deal of his weakness" (*Playwright* 34).

Perhaps at Shaw's invitation, Wilde attended a meeting of the Fabian Society on 6 July 1888, in Willis's Rooms, to hear the artist Walter Crane speak on "The Prospects of Art under Socialism." On the following day, the evening newspaper the *Star* reported:

> Mr. Crane believed that art would revive under these new socialistic conditions. Mr. Oscar Wilde, whose fashionable coat differed widely from the picturesque bottle-green garb in which he appeared in earlier days, thought that the art of the future would clothe itself not in works of form and colour but in literature.... Mr. Shaw agreed with Mr. Wilde that literature was the form which art would take....

Robert Ross later "surprised" Shaw by telling him that it was the response to Crane's talk that "moved Oscar to try his hand at a similar feat by writing 'The Soul of Man under Socialism'" (*Playwright* 31).

Shaw's account of his difficulty in socializing with Wilde reveals the dilemma of two dominant personalities with different moral visions attempting to establish a casual friendship. In a review published in *United Ireland* (26 Sept. 1891) of *Lord Arthur Savile's Crime and Other Stories*, Yeats, who also found Shaw difficult to deal with, alluded to him – without naming him – as a "cold-blooded Socialist," of whom, according to Yeats, Wilde said that "he has no enemies, but is intensely disliked by all his friends." Wilde had first used this celebrated remark – unrelated to Shaw – in Chapter 15 of the second version of *The Picture of Dorian Gray*, where Ernest Harrowden is described as "one of those middle-aged mediocrities so common in London clubs who have no enemies, but are thoroughly disliked by their friends...." This often-quoted and often-revised remark reappears in somewhat different form in the writings of Shaw and others. In a letter to Ellen Terry on 25 September 1896, Shaw gave his own version: "Oscar Wilde said of me 'An excellent man: he has no enemies; and none of his friends like him'" (*Collected Letters: 1874-1897*, 668; see, also, *1911-1925*, 8).

Wilde and Shaw exchanged books and letters, perhaps as a means of maintaining their distance from each other. When *Lady Windermere's Fan* was published in early 1893, Wilde sent an inscribed copy to Shaw: "Op. 1 of the Hibernian School, London '93" (*Letters* 339n2). Stanley Weintraub writes that the "joke was more than half in earnest since the two were the first Irish playwrights in decades to make a major impact upon the London theater" ("Hibernian School" 30). When the French version of *Salome* was published, Wilde sent Shaw a copy "in purple raiment" as a reciprocal gesture for Shaw's presentation to him of his *The Quintessence of Ibsenism*, about which Wilde wrote:

...your little book on Ibsenism and Ibsen is such a delight to me that I constantly take it up, and always find it stimulating and refreshing: England is the land of intellectual fogs but you have done much to clear the air: we are both Celtic, and I like to think that we are friends.... (*Letters* 332)

When, for some reason, Wilde's play was delayed in the mails, Shaw wrote:

Salomé is still wandering in her purple raiment in search of me; and I expect her to arrive a perfect outcast, branded with inky stamps, bruised by flinging from hard hands into red prison [i.e., post office] vans, stifled and contaminated by herding with review books....

In the same letter, Shaw informs Wilde that he will soon be sending him a copy of *Widowers' Houses*, which he expects Wilde to find "tolerably amusing": "Unfortunately I have no power of producing beauty: my genius is the genius of intellect, and my farce is derisive brutality. Salomé's purple garment would make Widowers' Houses ridiculous; but you are precisely the man to appreciate it on that account." Shaw, who had seen *Lady Windermere's Fan*, urges Wilde to "follow up hard on that trail; for the drama wants building up very badly; and it is clear that your work lies there" (*Theatrics* 8-9)

When *Widowers' Houses* appeared in May 1893, Shaw sent a copy to Wilde, who hailed it as

Op. 2 of the great Celtic School [Op. 3, *A Woman of No Importance*, was enjoying a great success in the theater]. I have read it twice with the keenest interest. I like your superb confidence in the dramatic value of the mere facts of life. I admire the horrible flesh and blood of your creatures, and your preface is a masterpiece – a real masterpiece of trenchant writing and caustic wit and dramatic instinct. I look forward to your Op. 4 [*The Philanderer*]. As for Op. 5 [*An Ideal Husband*], I am lazy, but am rather itching to be at it. (*Letters* 339 and n2)

Shaw habitually defended Wilde against his critics, as though enacting the myth of two imaginative Irishmen besieged by the unimaginative, puritanical English. In a letter to Lady Colin Campbell, who had succeeded Shaw as art critic of the *World* and who disliked *A Woman of No Importance*, Shaw wrote in May 1893 that she was wrong to "rail thus at Oscar" and that Wilde's epigrams were far superior to the "platitudes" of other dramatists:

There are only two literary schools in England today: the Norwegian school and the Irish school. Our school is the Irish school; and Wilde is doing us good service in teaching the theatrical public that "a play" may be a playing with ideas instead of a feast of sham emotions.... No, let us be just to the great white caterpillar: he is no blockhead and he finishes his work, which puts him high above his rivals here in London.... (*Theatrics* 10)

In 1895, when critics attacked *An Ideal Husband*, Shaw counter-attacked in the *Saturday Review* (12 Jan.): the critics, he argued, assumed that Wildean "epigrams can be turned out by the score by any one lightminded enough to condescend to such frivolity. As far as I can ascertain, I am the only person in London who cannot sit down and write an Oscar Wilde play at will.... In a certain sense Mr. Wilde is to me our only thorough playwright. He plays with everything: with wit, with philosophy, with drama, with actors and audience, with the whole theatre" (rpt. in *Our Theatres* and in Beckson).

In reviewing *The Importance of Being Earnest* in the *Saturday Review* (23 Feb. 1895), Shaw was less impressed, though he was "amused" by the play despite his reservations: "...unless comedy touches me as well as amuses me, it leaves me with a sense of having wasted my evening" (rpt. in *Our Theatres* and in Beckson). Shaw denigrates farce – despite his description of the "rib-tickling" nature of *Earnest* – as compared to the emotional and intellectual capacity of comedy to serve social issues. Later, Shaw expressed his belief that *Earnest*, "clever as it was," was Wilde's "first really heartless play," seemingly a "potboiler" that represented "a real degeneracy produced by his debaucheries. I thought he was still developing; and I hazarded the unhappy guess that The Importance of Being Earnest was in idea a young work written or projected long before..." (*Playwright* 32).

Responding to Max Nordau's *Degeneration* (1895), with its hostile attack on Wilde in the chapter on the Aesthetes and Decadents, Shaw defended him in a lengthy open letter to the New York anarchist publication *Liberty* (12 July) with the witty title "A Degenerate's View of Nordau"; revised, it appeared as *The Sanity of Art* (1908). Despite the press's attitude towards Wilde, who was often treated as a "witty trifler," Shaw later wrote that he took Wilde "seriously and with scrupulous good manners. Wilde on his part also made a point of recognizing me as a man of distinction by manner, and repudiating the current estimate of me as a mere jester."

When Wilde was arrested, Shaw's impulse was "to rally to him in his misfortune, and my disgust at 'the man Wilde' scurrilities of the newspapers was irresistible." Shaw's view of Wilde's "perversion" was that it did not imply "any general depravity or coarseness of character" (*Playwright* 33). Shaw was convinced that "never was there a man less an outlaw than [Wilde]" (qtd. in Holroyd 3:192). In 1940, Shaw wrote to the editor of the *TLS* that "Oscar Wilde, being a convinced pederast, was entirely correct to his plea of Not Guilty; but he was lying when he denied the facts; and the jury, regarding pederasty as abominable, quite

correctly found him Guilty" (rpt. in *Agitations* 316).

After Wilde's imprisonment, Shaw drafted a petition to the Home Secretary for an early release and showed it to Willie Wilde. Although Shaw and the Rev. Stewart Headlam (who had provided bail for Wilde during the trials) were prepared to sign it, Shaw warned Willie that it would be "of no use, as we were two notorious cranks, and our names alone would make the thing ridiculous and do Oscar more harm than good" (*Playwright* 33). When the petition received little support, it was dropped.

In July 1895, Shaw began writing a new play, later titled *You Never Can Tell*, which would – as Weintraub writes – "have something of Wilde in it, emanating from the very heartless play that Shaw had disliked and responding to Shaw's own sense of [*Earnest*'s] chilly mechanicalness" ("Hibernian School" 49). Echoing *Earnest*, Shaw's play depicts a similar search for a father, who, however, is found in a dentist's office. Other echoes occur, as in the figure of Mrs. Clandon, who is another Lady Bracknell. But, says Weintraub, the most convincing evidence that Shaw was influenced by *Earnest* is that "the wordplay on *earnestness* is too pervasive to be coincidence" (51).

Though the press adopted a policy of not mentioning Wilde during his imprisonment, Shaw alluded to him in several drama reviews. In the *Saturday Review* (17 Oct. 1896), for example, while judging a minor play, Shaw remarked on the superiority of Wilde's comedies: "...Mr. Wilde has creative imagination, philosophic humour, and original wit, besides being a master of language" (rpt. in *Our Theatres*). When the *Academy* (6 Nov. 1897) suggested the founding of an academy of letters and listed forty possible nominees as "Immortals," Shaw protested in a letter to the editor on 13 November that the "only dramatist, besides Mr. Henry James, whose nomination could be justified is Mr. Oscar Wilde" (H. G. Wells also proposed Wilde for the academy, which never materialized).

When *The Ballad of Reading Gaol* was published, Wilde sent Shaw an inscribed copy from Paris, but their relationship had ended with the trials. In 1905, when Wilde's prison letter appeared as *De Profundis* in a cut version, Robert Ross sent a copy to Shaw, who wrote to thank him:

It is really an extraordinary book, quite exhilarating and amusing as to Wilde himself, and quite disgraceful & shameful to his stupid tormentors. There is pain in it, inconvenience, annoyance, but no unhappiness, no real tragedy, all comedy. The unquenchable spirit of the man is magnificent: he maintains his position & puts society squalidly in the wrong – rubs into them every insult & humiliation he endured – comes out the same man he went in – with stupendous success. (*Collected Letters: 1898-1910*, 521)

To the end of his life, Shaw continued to be intrigued by Wilde and his work. In *Man and Superman* (1903), for example, a character offers a bright saying: "There are two tragedies in life. One is to lose your heart's desire. The other is to gain it." Wilde had provided Shaw with the witty pattern in *Lady Windermere's Fan*: "In this world there are only two tragedies. One is not getting what one wants, and the other is getting it." Katharine Worth has suggested that Wilde's aphorisms in "The Soul of Man under Socialism" could be the "raw material (perhaps they were) for The Revolutionist's Handbook which Tanner flourishes in *Man and Superman*" (10). Tanner's reaction to Violet Robinson's presumed motherhood echoes Jack Worthing's reaction to Miss Prism's similar state in *Earnest*. In *Major Barbara* (1905), Shaw's imperious Lady Britomart is remarkably like Wilde's Lady Bracknell, and Andrew Undershaft is a self-possessed munitions maker who, as an embodiment of the Life Force, expresses his social vision in witty, mysterious paradoxes – a transformation of a Wildean dandy into a Shavian hero.

In 1918, Shaw contributed to Frank Harris's *Oscar Wilde: His Life and Confessions* a preface titled "My Memories of Oscar Wilde" (actually, a letter, to which Harris added the title and edited the contents), and in 1938, Shaw edited Harris's biography with the assistance of Lord Alfred Douglas, who provided comments on the work. During this time, Shaw wrote to Douglas: "I think Wilde took you both [Harris and Douglas] in by the game he began to amuse himself [with] in prison: the romance of the ill treated hero and the cruel false friend. Once you see the character of this make-believe, all his lies and your imaginary crimes become merely comic" (*Collected Letters: 1926-1950*, 489). When Shaw completed his editing of the biography, he wrote to Douglas: "...I

George Bernard Shaw in 1888

agreed with all your notes and made no attempt to improve on them.... I hope its publication will do you a service as shewing for the first time that the Queensberry affair was your tragedy and, comparatively, Wilde's comedy" (*Collected Letters: 1926-1950*, 500).

Just months before his death in 1950, Shaw wrote to the playwright St. John Ervine to offer his harsh judgment of Wilde's greatest play, a judgment not substantively different from his 1895 review:

> Do not let yourself be trapped into the silly cliché that The Importance is Wilde's best play. It's a mechanical cat's cradle farce without a single touch of human nature in it. It is Gilbert and Sullivan minus Sullivan. The other plays – except, of course, the boyish [Duchess of] Padua – have the conventional woman-with-a-past plot of their day; and the feeling of which they are full is a bit romantic: but the characters are all human, and their conversation the most delightfully brilliant in the annals of the English stage, knocking Congreve and Sheridan into a cocked hat. (*Collected Letters: 1926-1950*, 871)

In the same letter, Shaw finally concedes that he had borrowed from *The Importance of Being Earnest*: "I was present at all the Wilde first nights, and enjoyed them intensely, except The Importance, which amused me by its stage tricks (I borrowed the best of them) but left me unmoved and even a bit bored and quite a lot disappointed."

References: Bernard Shaw, *Our Theatres in the Nineties*, 3 vols. (1932); Shaw, "Oscar Wilde," *The Matter with Ireland*, eds. Dan H. Laurence and David H. Greene (1962); Shaw, *Collected Letters*, 4 vols., ed. Dan H. Laurence (1965-1988); Stanley Weintraub, ed., *The Playwright and the Pirate: Bernard Shaw and Frank Harris, a Correspondence* (1982); Katharine Worth, *Oscar Wilde* (1983); Shaw, *Agitations: Letters to the Press, 1875-1950*, eds. Dan H. Laurence and James Rambeau (1985); Michael Holroyd, *Bernard Shaw*, 3 vols. (1988-91); J. L. Wisenthal, "Wilde, Shaw, and the Play of Conversation," *Modern Drama* (Spring 1994); Karl Beckson, "Oscar Wilde's Celebrated Remark on Bernard Shaw," *N&Q* (Sept. 1994); Shaw, *Theatrics*, ed. Dan H. Laurence (1995); Stanley Weintraub, "'The Hiber-nian School': Oscar Wilde and Bernard Shaw," *Shaw's People* (1996).

"SHE STOLE BEHIND HIM WHERE HE LAY"

Unpublished in Wilde's lifetime, this incomplete lyric consists of eight quatrains.

The young lady, tired from the dance, says to a young man: "I loved you all the while, / Rough Colin is a clumsy clout" – the traditional rustic name used in such works as John Skelton's *Collyn Clout* (1521) and Edmund Spenser's "Colin Clouts Come Home Again" (1595). Despite the young man's seeming indifference, she presses her point with an inelegant, perhaps facetious comparative: "You are more dear to me / Than are the fat lambs of my flock." Her wish to attract his attention, however, results in his flight, she following: "But ere he closed the sheepfold door / The gold-haired child crept in behind." The fragment ends with an image of the moon, which "leaned down with naked arms of gold."

Manuscripts: The Clark Library has four MS. leaves containing jottings of this poem.

SHERARD, ROBERT (1861-1943)

The author of 34 books, including 14 novels, Sherard (whose mother was Wordsworth's grand-daughter) is best known as the author of five books wholly or partly on Oscar Wilde and as one of Wilde's inner circle of friends before and after the criminal trials of 1895. In his lengthy career as a journalist, he published investigative reports, which were compiled by going under-cover to experience the social problems at first hand in such books as *The White Slaves of England* (1897), on the white-lead works at Newcastle-on-Tyne, and *The Child Slaves of Britain* (1905).

In March of 1883, Sherard first met Wilde in Paris – both, writes Kevin O'Brien (4), "ambitious young writers looking forward to fame and glory." "On that first night in Paris," Sherard wrote in *The Real Oscar Wilde* (1915), "[Wilde] appeared to me one of the most wonderful beings that I had ever met, and it seemed to me that there was no prize which the world offers to endeavour and genius...to which he might not aspire" (rpt. in Mikhail 1:119). In 1881, Sherard left New College, Oxford, soon after matriculating because of conflict with his father, a clergyman, over Robert's poor attendance at chapel and his failure in the qualifying examinations. On the Continent, he dropped the family surname, "Kennedy," and went first to Naples, where he had several adventures, including love affairs and at least one duel.

Later, Wilde amused Sherard by using his name for one of Dorian's ancestors in Chapter 11 of *The Picture of Dorian Gray*: Sir Anthony Sherard, the "lover of Giovanna of Naples [who] bequeathed him some inheritance of sin and shame," a veiled allusion, perhaps, to Robert Sherard's being wounded in the duel with a Neapolitan "for ogling his girl friend" (O'Brien 5). Sherard also spent a year at the University of Bonn studying Sanscrit and law before leaving for Paris to begin his literary career. There, Sherard managed to obtain an invitation for Wilde to a soirée conducted by Victor Hugo.

After leaving Paris, Wilde wrote extravagant letters to the heterosexual, handsome Sherard, as in the following: "Your letter was as loveable as yourself.... As for the dedication of your poems [*Whispers*, 1884], I accept it: how could I refuse a gift so musical in its beauty, and fashioned by one whom I love so much as I love you?" (*Letters* 146). But, says O'Brien, Sherard was "not alarmed" by such expressions of affection, though once Wilde embraced and kissed him, for he "never did understand Wilde's sexuality, and his books are full of his dithering in trying to explain it away." Years later, Sherard recalled (though perhaps with doubtful innocence), "I never had the faintest idea that my looks attracted him" (qtd. in O'Brien 7).

When Wilde was in Paris in late 1891 at work on *Salomé*, Sherard conducted him with two other friends, Stuart Merrill and Will Rothenstein, to a thieves' cellar, where, as Max Beerbohm later described the incident that Rothenstein witnessed, "they mixed freely with the company – mostly cut-throats":

> Sherard, as is his wont, got drunk and frightful and rising from his chair assumed an attitude of defence, saying in a loud voice that anyone who attacked Mr. Oscar Wilde would have to reckon with *him* first. "Hush, Robert, hush!" said Oscar, laying a white hand of plump restraint upon Sherard's shoulder, "hush, you are defending me at the risk of my life!" (Beerbohm 87)

Despite such gallantry, Sherard fell from grace when, in November 1894, he attempted to interview Wilde but who, at Christmas dinner, told him that gossip was "not for publication." Crushed, Sherard left the house, as he later wrote in *Oscar Wilde: The Story of an Unhappy Friendship* (1902), "grieved to think that the end was coming of a friendship which had for many years been the joy and the pride of my life" (117-18). But when Sherard heard of Wilde's trial against Queensberry, he sent a telegram offering his assistance, and when Wilde was arrested on 5 April 1895, he proclaimed his support among those in the British community in Paris who had responded with condemnation.

When Wilde asked him from Holloway Prison to see whether Sarah Bernhardt would buy the copyright of *Salomé* for £400 or lend him that amount, Sherard pursued the actress but without success. Appreciative, Wilde wrote to him: "You good, daring reckless friend!... I suppose Sarah is hopeless; but your chivalrous friendship – your fine, chivalrous friendship – is worth more than all the money in the world" (*Letters* 391). Sherard left for London when Wilde was released from jail on bond after his first criminal trial resulted in a hung jury. Though Sherard wished to attend to his friend's needs, his impetuousness in trying to get Wilde to flee the country only succeeded in creating anxiety in those around him. When his sentence was announced at the end of the second trial, Wilde asked the judge: "And I? May I say nothing, my lord?" Wilde was forbidden to speak, at which point Sherard leaped to his feet to utter he knew not what, but Ernest Dowson restrained him. Sherard left the court in a depressed state. He later wrote that his own life was finished.

Deciding to remain in England, Sherard took rooms near Wandsworth Prison, where Wilde was temporarily housed, and was the first to visit him there in August. Interviewed after the visit, Sherard irritated Wilde's friends by saying that he had tried and failed to get others to accompany him to the prison. This attempt to establish himself as Wilde's chief defender was a stance that Sherard adopted for the rest of his life. His first skirmish was with Alfred Douglas. When Sherard, at Wilde's direction, stopped Douglas's attempt to publish some of Wilde's letters in France, Douglas threatened to shoot him "like a dog" if anything he did resulted in Douglas's loss of Wilde's friendship. Sherard also urged Wilde's wife, Constance, to remain loyal despite her family's wish for a divorce.

Though Sherard continued visiting Wilde in 1896 and 1897 when he was transferred to Reading Prison, he was not among those who met Wilde on his release on 19 May 1897; Wilde, however, invited him to Berneval. But the end of their "unhappy friendship" was signaled by Sherard's disapproval of Wilde's reunion with Douglas in Naples in September and, as Wilde told Sherard, for attacking him "behind [his] back" (particularly painful to Wilde since the attack occurred at the Authors' Club): "...you expose yourself to rebuke and contempt, and of course I hear all about it" (*Letters* 660). (Vincent O'Sullivan defended Wilde by rebuking Sherard: see entry on O'Sullivan.) When *The Ballad of Reading Gaol* appeared, Wilde sent Sherard an inscribed copy "In Memory of an old and noble friendship."

Sherard's increasing alcoholism, which accompanied his growing financial difficulties, was a concern of all who knew him. In Paris with Wilde and Douglas in a chance meeting at a bar during the Zola trial in February 1898, the unsteady Sherard attacked a customer after shouting "Down with the Jews!" but he was duly throttled. After another incident in the same bar, when Sherard insisted on reciting *The Ballad of Reading Gaol* at the top of his voice, Wilde told Robert Ross: "Poor Robert, he really is quite insane.... Years ago he was a very good and dear fellow" (*Letters* 747-48). Sherard last saw Wilde after Ernest Dowson's death (Sherard had cared for him during the last six weeks of Dowson's life), but at the time of Wilde's final illness and his funeral, Sherard was living in Catford while preparing another exposé, *The Cry of the Poor* (1901).

His long life after Wilde's death included several books on Wilde, such as the first biography, *The Life of Oscar Wilde* (1906), in which Douglas is never named, Wilde's homosexuality is never mentioned, and Wilde's unconventional or aberrant behavior is attributed to "epileptiform fits" or "madness." Wounded by Bernard Shaw's praise of the Frank Harris biography, which assumes the role of Wilde's heroic defender, Sherard published *Oscar Wilde Twice Defended from André Gide's Wicked Lies and Frank Harris's Cruel Libels* (1934) and *Bernard Shaw, Frank Harris and Oscar Wilde* (1937) – the former an attack on

Gide's autobiography, *If It Die* (1926), the latter an attack on Harris's biography, which presents Wilde, Sherard contends, as "the squalid hero of a pornographic book" (52).

In 1938, Shaw responded in a preface to an edition of Harris's Wilde biography by remarking that Sherard's book was "frantic" and that Sherard was "the champion hurricane fighter of the Wilde fans" (x). Sherard's attack on Harris, says Shaw, gives the "exhilarating impression of a man who lives in a permanent rage...." Ever the warrior, even at the age of 78, Sherard attempted a rejoinder with *Ultima Verba* but could not find a publisher.

References: Max Beerbohm, *Letters to Reggie Turner*, ed. Rupert Hart-Davis (1964); Kevin O'Brien, "Robert Sherard: Friend of Oscar Wilde," *ELT* 28:1 (1985).

"SHOULD GENIUSES MEET?"

Published: *Court and Society Review* 4 (4 May 1887): 413-14; rpt. in Mason 37-40 (uncollected in *Miscellanies*, 1908). An unsigned review of a lecture by Courtland Palmer, an American social radical and president of the Nineteenth Century Club in New York.

Wilde notes the "spiritual advantages to be derived from the spectacle of geniuses arguing in the presence of people in evening dress" – the subject of Palmer's address. When the "prophets and pioneers of thought" stand face to face in such dress, "misunderstanding becomes impossible, and misrepresentation a thing of the past." Holding his audience spellbound, Palmer

described how, under the auspices of his useful society, the American believer had fraternized with the American atheist, how the Anarchist, the Socialist, and the Individualist had met without murder, and separated without suicide; how the Wagnerites and the worshippers of Mozart, the artists and the Philistines, the priests of beauty, and the pedants of duty, had settled their differences with charming courtesy, and with sweet reasonableness preached their separate creeds....

Palmer urged that a society similar to his own be founded in London "and not to forget the refining influence of the presence of people in evening dress."

Wilde proceeds in his review to envision such a "Talking Club," which might seem "to some the beginning of a new reign of terror, in which the wisdom of silence will be forgotten, and the dignity of culture have to give place to the shrill voice of chatter...." The only objection that Wilde foresees in such a club is that writers and thinkers "love solitude, and seek quiet, and are hardly to be tempted from their libraries, even by the prospect of meeting people in evening dress."

In the case of Ruskin and Whistler (who sued the former for having written that he "never expected to hear a coxcomb ask two hundred guineas for flinging a pot of paint in the public's face"), the painter "had to submit to the decision of an incompetent tribunal, to plead before a judge who knew nothing of nocturnes, and a jury to whom Symphonies were a rock of offence." Wilde is convinced that though Whistler would undoubtedly be present at a talking club, "armed to the teeth with brilliant epigram and barbed with clever caustic jest, we hardly think that Mr. Ruskin would have... troubled himself to play the prize-fighter to a gallery of Impressionists."

Writers and thinkers, however, prefer "to fight their battles on paper, and to make their repartees through the medium of pen and ink." If geniuses were to meet, "something of the dignity of the literary calling will probably be lost, and it is perhaps a dangerous thing for a country to be too eloquent."

"SILENTIUM AMORIS"

Published: *Poems* (1881). The Latin title means "The Silence of Love."

In this lyric poem of three six-line stanzas, the speaker, in a troubled state because of his "stormy passions," complains that his lover's beauty makes his lips fail, "And all my sweetest singing out of tune." The "excess of Love" has made his love "dumb" (nevertheless, he writes his poem about his inability to express himself, a convention beloved by poets). He pleads, however, that his eyes reveal why he is silent and his lute is unstrung:

Else it were better we should part, and go
Thou to some lips of sweeter melody,
And I to nurse the barren memory
Of unkissed kisses, and songs never sung.

For other poems forming a sequence with this one, see "Apologia."

"SIMON OF CYRENE": *See ECHOES*

"SIR CHARLES BOWEN'S *VIRGIL*"

Published: *PMG*, 30 Nov. 1887, 3; rpt. in *Reviews (1908).* An unsigned review of Sir Charles Bowen's *Virgil in English Verse: Eclogues and Aeneid I-VI* (1887).

Though Wilde remarks that Bowen's translations are "hardly the work of a poet," they are "charming" versions, combining "the fine loyalty and learning of a scholar with the graceful style of a man of letters...." On the whole, these translations are "extremely pleasant" to read, and if they do not "absolutely mirror Virgil," they evoke "many charming memories of him."

After discussing Bowen's choice of a form of the English hexameter (that is, lines of six metrical feet), Wilde remarks: "To any English metre that aims at swiftness of movement rhyme seems to be an absolute essential...." As examples, Wilde quotes lengthy passages from the fifth *Eclogue* and the fourth and sixth books of the *Aeneid*. Wilde concludes by congratulating Bowen on his "success."

"SIR EDWIN ARNOLD'S LAST VOLUME"

Published: *PMG*, 11 Dec. 1888, 3; rpt. in *Reviews* (1908). An unsigned review of Sir Edwin Arnold's *With Sa'di in the Garden; or, The Book of Love* (1888).

In this unfavorable review, Wilde begins by observing that "writers of poetical prose are rarely good poets. They may crowd their lines with gorgeous epithet and resplendent phrase,...may abandon themselves to highly coloured diction and rich luxuriance of imagery, but if their work lacks the true rhythmical life of verse, all their efforts are of very little avail." For journalistic purposes, "Asiatic" prose may be useful, but "Asiatic" poetry should be discouraged. Indeed, Wilde continues, poetry requires "far more restraint than prose. Its conditions are more exquisite. It produces its effects by more subtle means. It is, in one sense, the most self-conscious of all the arts, as it is never a means to an end, but always an end in itself."

Sir Edwin Arnold, Wilde pronounces, "is not a poet. He is simply a poetical writer – that is all." The scene of the story takes place in a mosque next to the Taj-mahal, where a scribe, two singing girls with an attendant, and an Englishman (Arnold himself) pass the night reading the chapter of Sa'di on love, accompanied by music and dance. The best parts of the book, says Wilde, are the descriptions of the Taj, "extremely elaborate," and the translations from Sa'di. Sir Edwin "suffers of course from the inevitable comparison that one cannot help making between his work and the work of Edward Fitzgerald [best known for his translation of the *Rubáiyát of Omar Khayyám*, 1859], and certainly Fitzgerald could never have written such a line as 'utterly wotting all their innermosts'...."

Regrettably, Arnold's book is written in "what really amounts to a sort of 'pigeon English,'" such as the attendant's response: "*Achcha! Achcha!*" This is not "local colour" but "a sort of local discoloration":

It does not bring the Orient more clearly before us.... We are sorry that a scholar and a man of culture like Sir Edwin Arnold should have been guilty of what is really an act of treason against our literature.... As it is, Sir Edwin Arnold has translated Sa'di and some one must translate Sir Edwin Arnold.

SMITHERS, LEONARD (1861-1907)

A publisher and dealer in rare and second-hand books as well as in the fine arts, Smithers had been a solicitor in Sheffield before settling in London in 1891 to found a publishing firm with a partner, the printer H. S. Nichols. Sometimes inaccurately referred to as a dealer in pornography (books such as *Teleny; or, The Reverse of the Medal* were rare on his list, which included *Magister Adest*, a volume by a community of nuns), Smithers had a keen eye for the unusual, the imaginative, and the avant-garde, which led him to commission Beardsley's illustrations for editions of *The Rape of the Lock*, *Mademoiselle de Maupin*, and *Lysistrata* and to publish Max Beerbohm's first volume of collected drawings as well as the poems of Ernest Dowson, Arthur Symons, and Oscar Wilde.

Vincent O'Sullivan recalled that Smithers once said, "I'll publish anything that the others are afraid of" (102), but though daring as a publisher, he also acquired a reputation for treating his authors badly. Symons referred to him, perhaps facetiously, as his "cynical publisher...with his diabolical monocle"

(*Memoirs* 183), but others, such as Wilde and Dowson, were, at least at one time, appreciative of Smithers's generosity. When Beardsley was fired from the *Yellow Book* after Wilde's arrest, Smithers launched the *Savoy*, the only truly British avant-garde periodical of the 1890s, for which Symons, the editor, recruited Beardsley – probably on Smithers's suggestion – as its principal illustrator.

The first exchange of letters between Wilde and Smithers occurred as early as 1888, when the Sheffield solicitor wrote a complimentary letter to the author of *The Happy Prince and Other Tales*. Thanking him for his "charming letter," Wilde was "glad to think that 'The Happy Prince' has found so sympathetic an admirer, so gracious a lover" (*Letters* 221). No further correspondence between the two is known to exist until after Wilde's release from prison. Their first meeting occurred in Dieppe, probably in late July 1897, when Ernest Dowson, who was staying with Wilde, introduced him to Smithers. Dowson later wrote to a friend: "...they have struck up an alliance" (Dowson, *Letters* 390). In August, Smithers sent a parcel of books to Wilde, who much appreciated the gesture. Describing Smithers in a letter to Reginald Turner, Wilde wrote:

His face, clean-shaven as befits a priest who serves at the altar whose God is Literature, is wasted and pale – not with poetry, but with poets, who, he says, have wrecked his life by insisting on publishing with him. He loves first editions, especially of women: little girls are his passion. He is the most learned erotomaniac in Europe. He is also a delightful companion, and a dear fellow, very kind to me. (*Letters* 630-31)

By late August, when he completed a partial draft of *The Ballad of Reading Gaol*, Wilde asked Smithers to have it typewritten, an indication that they had already decided on publication. Robert Ross, later Wilde's literary executor, acted as his agent in dealing with Smithers, of whom he once said: "You always knew where you were with him, you knew he would cheat you and he always did" (qtd. in Borland 62). By late November 1897, Ross wrote to Smithers: "...I have ceased to be on intimate terms with Oscar Wilde or to enjoy his confidence in business or any other matter." The falling out with Wilde resulted when Alfred Douglas charged that Ross "tried to prevent any considerable sum being obtained for the poem" (qtd. in *Letters* 688n1). Wilde immediately informed Smithers that Ross was mistaken (*More Letters* 160-61).

The unpredictable Smithers was the object of ambivalent responses from Wilde, who had been asking Smithers for an advance of £20, but the publisher had not responded. To Dowson, Wilde wrote that Smithers was "personally charming, but at present I simply am furious with him, and intend to remain so, till he sends me the money" (*Letters* 656). Regardless of Wilde's hostility towards Smithers, Wilde praised him on the occasion of Beardsley's death in March 1898:

I quite understand how you feel about poor Aubrey. Still, you, and you alone, recreated his art for him, gave him a new and greater position, and for such generous and enthusiastic service to art and to an artist you will have your reward in Heaven: at least you will never have it in this world. (*More Letters* 170)

When, in January 1899, Wilde received a copy of Ben Jonson's *Volpone* with Beardsley's illustrations, he wrote to Smithers that it was "a very fine issue," though the illustrations were not up to those for *Salome*. Facetiously, Wilde alludes to the meaning of the name "Volpone" – a clever, devious fox: "The play is, I suppose, by you" (*More Letters* 177). In February, when Smithers published *The Importance of Being Earnest*, Wilde complained to Ross that the play was being "boycotted by the press" – that is, scarcely reviewed: "...I am sorry...particularly for Smithers's sake; he has shown great pluck in bringing it out at all" (*Letters* 782). In July, Smithers issued *An Ideal Husband*. In the same year, severe illness prevented Smithers from attending to business matters, possibly accounting for the darker tone that Wilde's letters to Smithers take on when they plead for money, as in one written in late July: "It is extraordinary what an amount of suffering you cause me" (*Letters* 807).

By mid-1900, Smithers was facing imminent financial ruin, as Wilde implies in a letter to Ross: "I am horrified about Smithers. It really is too bad" (*Letters* 829). On 18 September, Smithers filed for bankruptcy. During these months, Wilde was involved in the complicated business of selling options to various people, including Smithers, for the scenario of a new play later titled *Mr. and Mrs. Daventry*. By this time, Wilde's relationship with Smithers was deteriorating. In a letter dated 20 November (just ten days before his death), Wilde expressed amazement that Frank Harris had permitted Smithers to blackmail him over some matter connected with the disputed scenario: "...Smithers was at that time [presumably two or three years before] a great friend of mine, and in his case, as later on in yours, I considered the word of a friend adequate" (*Letters* 843).

In order to survive, Smithers turned to pirating Wilde's works. After Wilde's death, he announced or issued, sometimes under various bogus imprints, such works as *Lord Arthur Savile's Crime*, and *Phrases and Philosophies for the Use of the Young* (see Mason 539-40, 542). Though Smithers had claimed ownership of the copyrights, Ross denied the allegation. In 1903 and 1905, Smithers also issued unauthorized editions of *Lady Windermere's Fan* and *A Woman of No Importance*. Smithers's final years, often shrouded in mystery, involved constant moves, presumably to escape arrest over his debts and piracies. In a 1906 *Academy* article, Ross called Smithers "the most delightful and irresponsible publisher" that he ever knew (qtd. in Borland 108).

On 19 December 1907, Smithers was found dead in a small bare room in Fulham, his end attributed by some writers to an overdose of drugs, although his death certificate indicates cirrhosis of the liver. His nine years of publishing had resulted, as George Sims remarks, in issuing "some of the most important books of the period" (39).

References: Vincent O'Sullivan, *Aspects of Wilde* (1936); George Sims, "Leonard Smithers: A Publisher of the Nineties," *London Magazine* (Sept. 1956); Desmond Flower and Henry Maas, eds., *The Letters of Ernest Dowson* (1967); Karl Beckson, ed., *The Memoirs of Arthur Symons: Life and Art in the 1890s* (1977).

"SOME LITERARY NOTES"
Published: *Woman's World* 2 (Jan. 1889): 164-68; rpt. in *Reviews* (1908). Signed reviews ("By the Editor") of books published in 1888.

Wilde recalls his article "English Poetesses," published in the *Queen* (8 Dec. 1888), in which he urges "women of letters" to turn their attention "somewhat more to prose and somewhat less to poetry." Women, he writes, seem to possess "just what our literature wants – a light touch, a delicate hand, a graceful mode of treatment, and an unstudied felicity of phrase." The English want a writer who will duplicate in prose what Madame de Sévigné did for France. As for George Eliot's style, it was "far too cumbrous, and Charlotte Brontë's too exaggerated." There are in contemporary England, however, women who are "charming letter-writers, and certainly no book can be more delightful reading than Mrs. [Janet] Ross's *Three Generations of English Women: Memoirs and Correspondence of Susannah Taylor, Sarah Austin, and Lady Duff Gordon....*" The most interesting correspondence in the volume is by Sarah Austin and those who wrote to her. One of her correspondents was Henri Beyle (Stendhal), who, Wilde writes, may be the "greatest of French novelists." Beyle wrote to Austin: "It seems to me that except when they read Shakespeare, Byron, or Sterne, no Englishman understands '*nuances*'; we adore them."

Turning to Lady Lindsay, Wilde judges her *Caroline* to be her "best work. It is written in a very clever modern style, and is as full of *esprit* and wit as it is of subtle psychological insight. Caroline is an heiress, who, coming downstairs at a Continental hotel, falls into the arms of a charming, penniless young man." Noting that the novel appears in one volume, Wilde comments that the

> influence of Mudie on literature, the baneful influence of the circulating library, is clearly on the wane. The gain to literature is incalculable. English novels were becoming very tedious with their three volumes of padding – at least, the second volume was always padding – and extremely indigestible.

Following this brief review, Wilde raises the question: "What are the best books to give as Christmas presents to good girls who are always pretty, or to pretty girls who are occasionally good?" Wilde notes some books recently sent to him by publishers that are the "best and the most pleasing": Randolph Caldecott's *Gleanings from the "Graphic,"* "a most fascinating volume full of sketches that have real wit and humour of line"; Alice Corkran's *Meg's Friend,* "one of our most delicate and graceful prose-writers in the sphere of

fiction, and one whose work has the rare artistic qualities of refinement and simplicity"; Sarah Doudney's *Under False Colours,* "an excellent story"; Florence Montgomery's *The Fisherman's Daughter,* "a tale with real charm of idea and treatment"; Mrs. Mary Louisa Molesworth's *The Third Miss St. Quentin* and *A Christmas Posy* "from the same fascinating pen, and with delightful illustrations of Walter Crane." Rosa Mulholland's *Giannetta* and Agnes Giberne's *Ralph Hardcastle's Will* "are also admirable books for presents...."

Wilde also notes that the "prettiest, indeed the most beautiful, book from an artistic point of view is undoubtedly Mr. Walter Crane's *Flora's Feast.* It is an imaginative Masque of Flowers, and as lovely in colour as it is exquisite in design.... It is, in its way, a little masterpiece, and its grace and fancy, and beauty of line and colour, cannot be over-estimated." Wilde concludes this series of reviews with observations concerning Sheridan's *Here's to the Maiden of Bashful Fifteen,* illustrated by Alice Havers and Ernest Wilson.

There is, Wilde contends, "a danger of modern illustration becoming too pictorial. What we need is good book-ornament, decorative ornament that will go with type and printing, and give to each page a harmony and unity of effect." Japanese art, he states, is both decorative and pictorial, but it has "the most wonderful delicacy of touch" and there is "an intimate connection between their art and their handwriting or printed characters." English practice should be "to discover some mode of illustration that will harmonise with the shapes of our letters."

"SOME LITERARY NOTES"

Published: *Woman's World* 2 (Feb. 1889): 221-24; rpt. in *Reviews* (1908). Signed reviews ("By the Editor").

After describing the contents of *Fairy and Folk Tales of the Irish Peasantry* (1888) at length, Wilde concludes that W.B.Yeats "has certainly done his work very well. He has shown great critical capacity in his selection of the stories, and his little introductions are charmingly written. It is delightful to come across a collection of purely imaginative work, and Mr. Yeats has a very quick instinct in finding out the best and the most beautiful things in Irish folklore."

By way of leading into a review of Violet Fane's

"SOME LITERARY NOTES"

The Story of Helen Davenant (1888-89), Wilde remarks that the "wittiest writer in France at present is a woman. That clever, that *spirituelle grande dame*, who has adopted the pseudonym 'Gyp' [Comtesse de Martel de Janville], has in her own country no rival. Her wit, her delicate and delightful *esprit*, her fascinating modernity, and her light, happy touch, give her a unique position in that literary movement which has taken for its object the reproduction of contemporary life." The only work in England that can be compared with Gyp's is Fane's *Edwin and Angelina Papers*. Her *Helen Davenant* is "as earnestly wrought out as it is cleverly conceived. If it has a fault, it is that it is too full of matter." In addition to Fane's depiction of the unusual, the "touches of nature, vivid sketches of high life, the subtle renderings of the phases and fancies of society, are also admirably done."

Wilde then considers the "remarkable volume," *Dreams and Dream-Stories* (1888) by the late Dr. Anna Kingsford, who was "one of the brilliant women of our day...." However, he expresses some disappointment in the way in which these tales came to her: "There is no reason whatsoever why the imagination should be finer in hours of dreaming than in its hours of waking." Though Kingsford quotes an author that the "night-time of the body is the day-time of the soul," Wilde contends that the "great masterpieces of literature and the great secrets of wisdom have not been communicated in this way; and even in Coleridge's case, though *Kubla Khan* is wonderful, it is not more wonderful, while it is certainly less complete, than the *Ancient Mariner*."

Amy Levy's *The Romance of a Shop* (1888), "a more mundane book," deals with the "adventures of some young ladies who open a photographic studio in Baker Street to the horror of some of their fashionable relatives. It is so brightly and pleasantly written that the sudden introduction of a tragedy into it seems violent and unnecessary." Wilde contends that the "most valuable faculty" for novelists is the power of observation, but when they "reflect and moralise, they are, as a rule, dull." Concluding this review, Wilde remarks that it would be, perhaps, "too much to say that Miss Levy has distinction; this is the rarest quality in modern literature, though not a few of its masters are modern; but she has many other qualities which are admirable."

Margaret Lee's *Faithful and Unfaithful* (1889), writes Wilde, is a "powerful but not very pleasing novel. However, the object of most modern fiction is not to give pleasure to the artistic instinct, but rather portray life vividly for us, to draw attention to social anomalies, and social forms of injustice." Many novelists, Wilde continues, are pamphleteers or reformers "masquerading as story-tellers, earnest sociologists seeking to mend as well as to mirror life." Lee's novel tells the story of a puritanical American girl, married at the age of 18 to a man whom she regards as a hero but who refuses to live up to her ideal. He eventually abandons her and secures a divorce without her consent. Wilde concludes with the observation that Lee's novel "seems to point to some coming change in the marriage-laws of America."

"SOME LITERARY NOTES"

Published: *Woman's World* 2 (March 1889): 277-80; rpt. in *Reviews* (1908). Signed reviews ("By the Editor").

Edith Nesbit, who, says Wilde, "has already made herself a name as a writer of graceful and charming verse...still fully maintains the high standard already achieved, and justifies the reputation of the author" in her *Leaves of Life* (1888). There is a "poignant note of passion" that "flashes across the song" here and there, "giving a new value to the delicate tints, and bringing the scheme of colour to a higher and more perfect key." She is "at her best when she sings of love and nature," when she gives "colour and form to the various dramatic moods that are either suggested by Nature herself or brought to Nature for interpretation."

Wilde's evaluation of Yeats's *The Wanderings of Oisin and Other Poems* (1889) is that it is "certainly full of promise." But, Wilde continues,

> many of the poems are too fragmentary, too incomplete. They read like stray scenes out of unfinished plays, like things only half remembered, or, at best, but dimly seen. But the architectonic power of construction, the power to build up and make perfect a harmonious whole, is nearly always the latest, as it certainly is the highest, development of the artistic temperament....

Wilde apprehends the "essentially Celtic" quality

of the verse, also strongly influenced by Keats, for Yeats is "more fascinated by the beauty of words than by the beauty of metrical music. The spirit that dominates the whole book is perhaps more valuable than any individual poem or particular passage.... It is impossible to doubt, after reading his present volume, that he will some day give us work of high import. Up to this he has been merely trying the strings of his instrument, running over the keys." (Wilde also reviewed Yeats's volume in the *Pall Mall Gazette*, 12 July 1889: see "Three New Poets.")

Lady Munster's *Dorinda* (1888) is "an exceedingly clever novel." The heroine, Wilde continues, is "a sort of well-born Becky Sharp, only much more beautiful than Becky, or at least than Thackeray's portraits of her, which, however, have always seemed to me rather ill-natured." Wilde describes Dorinda as a "kleptomaniac; that is to say, she is a member of the upper classes who spends her time in collecting works of art that do not belong to her." Lady Munster has a "very clever, bright style, and has a wonderful faculty of drawing in a few sentences the most lifelike portraits of social types and social exceptions." Wilde, in this review, again seizes the opportunity to criticize modern fiction's intent on reform – that is, in opposition to Aestheticism's focus on art for art's sake:

> The "novel of high life," as it used to be called, has of late years fallen into disrepute. Instead of duchesses in Mayfair, we have philanthropic young ladies in Whitechapel; and the fashionable and brilliant young dandies, in which Disraeli and Bulwer Lytton took such delight, have been entirely wiped out as heroes of fiction by hard-working curates in the East End. The aim of most of our modern novelists seems to be, not to write good novels, but to write novels that will do good....

Mrs. Walford's *Four Biographies from "Blackwood"* (1888) depicts the lives of "four remarkable women": Jane Taylor, Elizabeth Fry, Hannah More, and Mary Somerville (society ladies or authors). Mabel Wotton, says Wilde, has "invented a new form of picture-gallery" in her *Word Portraits of Famous Writers* (1887), extending from Chaucer to Mrs. Henry Wood, the prolific novel-

ist. Compared with Mrs. Wood and her "dazzling" complexion, many "'famous writers' seem to have been very ugly."

On this vexing issue, Wilde quotes Thomas Hardy that "ideal physical beauty is incompatible with mental development, and a full recognition of the evil of things...." Chatterton and Byron, Wilde remarks, were "splendidly handsome, and beauty of a high spiritual order may be claimed both for Milton and Shelley.... Though few of the word portraits," concludes Wilde, "can be said to have been drawn by a great artist," they are all "interesting, and Miss Wotton has certainly shown a wonderful amount of industry in collecting her reference and in grouping them." By means of such portraits, one may "raise the ghosts of the dead, at least as well as the Psychical Society can."

"SOME LITERARY NOTES"

Published: *Woman's World* 2 (April 1889): 333-36; rpt. in *Reviews* (1908). Signed reviews ("By the Editor").

Wilde begins his series of reviews with a quotation from Matthew Arnold: "In modern life, you cannot well enter a monastery; but you can enter the Wordsworth Society." Despite his use of this "somewhat uninviting description of this admirable and useful body," the essays of the Wordsworth Society in *Wordsworthiana*, ed. William Knight (1889) need not cause the public "any unnecessary alarm; and it is gratifying to note that, although the society is still in the first blush of enthusiasm, it has not yet insisted upon our admiring Wordsworth's inferior work."

An authority on modern Greek, Mrs. E. M. Edmonds has made her first attempt at writing fiction in *Mary Myles* (1888). Though her style has "a very pleasant literary flavour," her dialogues do not indicate a grasp of the distinction between spoken and written language. The heroine, a "sort of Nausicaa from Girton [College]," develops into the Pallas Athena in a provincial school, has a romance, "like her Homeric prototype, and her Odysseus returns to her at the close of the book. It is a nice story."

Following his faint praise of the Edmonds novel, Wilde turns to Lady Dilke's *Art in the Modern State* (1888), a book that "cannot fail to interest deeply every one who cares either for art or for history." The modern state in the title refers to that which emerged from 17th-century France, and

"SOME LITERARY NOTES"

Wilde poses the question "that naturally rises on one's lips, 'How can one dwell on the art of the seventeenth century? – it has no charm.'" Lady Dilke contends (in her own words) that

> the life of France wears, during the seventeenth century, a political aspect. The explanation of all changes in the social system, in letters, in the arts, in fashions even, has to be sought in the necessities of the political position; and the seeming caprices of taste take their rise from the same causes which went to determine the making of a treaty or the promulgation of an edict.

Finding the subject "extremely fascinating," Wilde then expresses, by way of contrast, a view of the Renaissance that he later developed in "The Soul of Man under Socialism":

> The Renaissance had for its object the development of great personalities. The perfect freedom of the temperament in matters of art, the perfect freedom of the intellect in intellectual matters, the full development of the individual, were the things it aimed at. As we study its history we find it full of great anarchies. It solved no political or social problems; it did not seek to solve them.

Wilde admires Lady Dilke's prose style for "its clearness, its sobriety, its fine and, at times, ascetic simplicity."

In a brief notice, Wilde regards Bret Harte's *Cressy* (1889) as "one of his most brilliant and masterly productions, and will take rank with the best of his Californian stories. Hawthorne recreated for us the America of the past with the incomparable grace of a very perfect artist, but Mr. Bret Harte's emphasised modernity has, in its own sphere, won equal, or almost equal, triumphs." Harte's "wit, pathos, humour, realism, exaggeration, and romance are in this marvellous story all blended together, and out of the very clash and chaos of these things comes life itself."

Richard Day, another American, is not, Wilde notes, a national poet but one "who tries to give expression to the literature that he loves rather than to the land in which he lives. The Muses care so little for geography!" His *Poems* (1888) lacks anything distinctively American: "...the spirit that animates the verse is simple and human, and there is hardly a poem in the volume that English lips might not have uttered."

Turning to Ella Curtis's *A Game of Chance* (1889), Wilde regards this novel as the best "that this clever young writer has as yet produced. If it has a fault, it is that it is crowded with too much incident, and often surrenders the study of character to the development of plot." Wilde then gives a lengthy account of the various plots, "which, in more economical hands, would have served as the basis of a complete story." The complications involving a clever lady's maid who is an adventuress and the subsidiary subplots of the novel lead Wilde to conclude that "no one could say that Miss Curtis's book is dull.... It is impossible, perhaps, not to be a little bewildered by the amount of characters, and by the crowded incidents; but, on the whole, the scheme of the construction is clear, and certainly the decoration is admirable."

"SOME LITERARY NOTES"

Published: *Woman's World* 2 (May 1889): 389-92; rpt. in *Reviews* (1908). Signed reviews ("By the Editor") of books published in 1889.

Noting that Caroline Fitz Gerald's *Venetia Victrix* is dedicated to Robert Browning, Wilde sees traces of Browning's influence in the title poem, a "powerful psychological study of a man's soul, a vivid presentation of a terrible, fiery-coloured moment in a marred and incomplete life." Modern poetry has the "marked tendency...to become obscure," which Wilde finds "curiously interesting":

> In Mr. Browning's poems, as in life itself which has suggested, or rather necessitated, the new method, thought seems to proceed not on logical lines, but on lines of passion. The unity of the individual is being expressed through its inconsistencies and its contradictions. In a strange twilight man is seeking for himself, and when he has found his own image, he cannot understand it. Objective forms of art, such as sculpture and the drama, sufficed one for the perfect presentation of life; they can no longer so suffice.

In Fitz Gerald's psychological poem, the "central motive...is the study of a man who to do a noble action wrecks his own soul, sells it to evil, and to the spirit of evil." Wilde comments: "Many martyrs have for a great cause sacrificed their physical life; the sacrifice of the spiritual life has a more poignant and a more tragic note." Her poem reveals a "new singer of considerable ability and vigour of mind...." (Wilde also reviewed another Fitz Gerald volume in the *Pall Mall Gazette*, 12 July 1889: see "Three New Poets.")

David Ritchie's *Darwinism and Politics*, Wilde remarks, "contains some very interesting speculations on the position and the future of women in the modern State." In this connection, Wilde quotes from Herbert Spencer's *Sociology*, which contends that, if women are admitted to political life, such a move might have an adverse effect by introducing family ethics into the State: "Under the ethics of the family the greatest benefits must be given where the merits are smallest; under the ethics of the State the benefits must be proportioned to the merits." Ritchie responds to this by asking whether any society rewards people in proportion to their merits and protests Spencer's divorce of family ethics from those of the State. Wilde comments on these views:

If something is right in a family, it is difficult to see why it is therefore, without any further reason, wrong in the State. If the participation of women in politics means that as a good family educates all its members, so must a good State, what better issue could there be? The family ideal of the State may be difficult of attainment, but as an ideal it is better than the policeman theory.

In countries where military service is compulsory for men, the argument has been that to give women "a voice in political matters...would be unjust and inexpedient." Ritchie, notes Wilde, responds to this point with a proposal that women be required to undergo training as nurses and be subject to a call in wartime. Such training, Ritchie states, "would be more useful to them and to the community in time of peace than his military training is to the peasant or artisan."

Pundita Ramabai Sarasvati's *The High-Caste Hindu Woman* is the story of the author, who was married, at the age of nine, to a "Brahman pundit." He taught her and gave her "the intellectual culture that had been always denied to women in India." Later, she travelled throughout India advocating

the cause of "female education." She is credited with suggesting the establishment of the profession of female doctors. Wilde finds this book "full of suggestion for the social reformer and the student of progress, and her book, which is wonderfully well written, is likely to produce a radical change in the educational schemes that at present prevail in India."

"SOME LITERARY NOTES"

Published: *Woman's World* 2 (June 1889): 446-48; rpt. in *Reviews* (1908). Signed reviews ("By the Editor") of *An Author's Love: Being the Unpublished Letters of Prosper Mérimée's "Inconnue"* and Graham R. Tomson's *The Bird-Bride: A Volume of Ballads and Sonnets* – both published in 1889.

"Inconnue," writes Wilde, was "undoubtedly a real person, and her letters in answer to those of Mérimée have just been published...under the title of *An Author's Love*." However, these are "such letters as she might have written." The publishers have issued "what is really a *jeu-d'esprit*, the first serious joke perpetrated by Messrs. Macmillan in their publishing capacity. Perhaps it is too much to call it a joke. It is a fine, delicate piece of fiction, an imaginative attempt to complete a real romance.... As for extracts from these fascinating forgeries, the letters should be read in conjunction with those of Mérimée himself." These letters contain not only acute observations but also political speculations, literary criticism, witty social scandal, and "a keen sense of humour." Wilde muses at the end of his review: "Perhaps the real letters will be published some day. When they are, how interesting to compare them!"

Tomson's *The Bird-Bride*, a "collection of romantic ballads, delicate sonnets, and metrical studies in foreign fanciful forms," contains in some poems a "curious combination of Scotch and Border dialect so much affected now by our modern poets." Wilde discusses at length the consequences of verse in dialect:

Sometimes one is tempted to look on dialect as expressing simply the pathos of provincialisms, but there is more in it than mere mispronunciations. With the revival of an antique form, often comes the revival of an antique spirit. Through limitations that are sometimes uncouth, and always narrow, comes Tragedy herself....

Tomson, Wilde concludes in his final contribution to *Woman's World*, has "certainly a very refined sense of form.... Some of the shorter poems are, to use a phrase made classical by Mr. Pater, 'little carved ivories of speech.' She is one of our most artistic workers in poetry, and treats language as a fine material."

"SOME NOVELS"
Published: *PMG*, 14 April 1886, 5; rpt. in *Reviews* (1908). Unsigned reviews of books published in 1886.

After "a careful perusal" of Tighe Hopkins's *'Twixt Love and Duty*, Wilde confesses that he is "unable to inform anxious inquirers who it is that is thus sandwiched, and how he (or she) got into so unpleasant a predicament." Nevertheless, the novel has "pleasant writing and clever character-drawing." As for the puzzling plot, "we brace up our nerves for a tragedy, and are treated instead to the mildest of marivaudage [subtle, elegant dialogue, as in the refined world of Pierre Marivaux's plays] – which is disappointing."

Antonio Gallenga has written "a tale without a murder" in *Jenny Jennet*, but since he has put "a pistol-ball diagonally through his hero's chest, and left him alive and hearty notwithstanding, he cannot be said to have produced a tale without a miracle." The novelist describes his heroine, who is 17, as "one of the Great Maker's masterpieces...a living likeness of the Dresden Madonna." To this Wilde comments: "One rather shudders to think of what she may become at forty, but this is an impertinent prying into futurity." The book's division into acts and scenes "is not justified by anything specially dramatic either in its structure or its method."

Mrs. H. Lovett Cameron's novel, *A Life's Mistake*, tells a tale that is very familiar, notes Wilde: "Its personages are the embarrassed squire, with his charming daughter, the wealthy and amorous mortgagee, and the sailor lover who is either supposed to be drowned or falsely represented to be fickle...." Since there is a stanza from Byron on the title page and poetical quotations at the beginning of each chapter, "we have possessed the discerning reader of all necessary information both as to the matter and the manner of Mrs. Cameron's performance."

Wilde facetiously hails Edward Oliver Pleydell-Bouverie's "new formula for the composition of titles" for the "novel-writing fraternity": "After *J.S.; or, Trivialities* there is no reason why we should not have *A.B.; or, Platitudes*, *M.N.; or, Sentimentalisms*, *Y.Z.; or, Inanities*." His novel tells of the "uninteresting fortunes of an insignificant person, one John Stiles, a briefless barrister.... The only point of interest presented by the book is the problem as to how it ever came to be written."

Wilde begins his notice of the final novel by alluding to Swinburne's proposal that there should be a penal offence against literature for any writer to use a proverb, a phrase or quotation to a novel, as a tag or title. Though Pen Oliver's *All But*, Wilde says, "is certainly an intolerable name to give any literary production," the story is "quite an interesting one," consisting of love, jealousy, and attempted murder. Wilde recommends this "charming tale" to those "who are tired of the productions of Mr. Hugh Conway's dreadful disciples" (see "One of Mr. Conway's Remainders").

"SOME NOVELS"
Published: *Saturday Review* 63 (7 May 1887): 663-64; rpt. in *Reviews* (1908). Unsigned reviews of books published in 1887.

Beginning with the witty remark that "the only form of fiction in which real characters do not seem out of place is history," Wilde condemns William Fraser Rae's *Miss Bayle's Romance* (published anonymously) for its introduction into the story of "a whole mob of modern celebrities and notorieties, including the Heir Apparent," who appears as "The Prince of Wales." The book, Wilde insists, "has really no claim to be regarded as a novel at all. It is simply a society paragraph expanded into three volumes, and, like most paragraphs of the kind, is in the worst possible taste."

Turning to Mrs. J. Hartley Perks's *From Heather Hills*, Wilde finds it "very pleasant reading indeed. It is healthy without being violent, subtle without being affected." Mrs. Perks has "a grace and delicacy of touch that is quite charming, and she can deal with nature without either botanizing or being blatant, which nowadays is a somewhat rare accomplishment." The story – concerning a Scotch girl who is brought to London and who takes everyone "by storm," then falls in love with an English peer, who is cautioned by a friend not to marry the outspoken young lady – has ironic reversals, as when the peer's friend himself falls in love with the young lady. Wilde concludes by hoping that in Mrs. Perks's next novel "she will not allow her hero to misquote English poetry. This is a privilege reserved for Mrs. Malaprop" (noted for her linguistic errors in Sheridan's *The Rivals*, 1775).

Of Mrs. Matilda Houston's *A Heart on Fire*, Wilde notes somewhat facetiously that "a constancy that lasts through three volumes is often rather tedious, so we are glad to make the acquaintance of Miss Lilian Ufford, the heroine of the novel. Despite the ironic turns in the plot, "all ends well, and the story is brightly and pleasantly told." Proceeding briskly to the next novel, George Manville Fenn's *A Bag of Diamonds*, Wilde writes that it "belongs to the Drury Lane school of fiction, and is a sort of fireside melodrama for the family circle...evidently written to thrill Bayswater, and no doubt Bayswater will be thrilled." He points to one scene in which a "kindly policeman assists two murderers to convey their unconscious victim into a four-wheeled cab, under the impression that they are a party of guests returning from a convivial supper in Bloomsbury...." This scene, he remarks, is "quite excellent of its kind, and on the whole not too improbable, considering that shilling literature is always making demands on our credulity without ever appealing to our imagination."

Frank Barrett's *The Great Hesper*, Wilde's next challenge, "has at least the merit of introducing into fiction an entirely new character. The villain is a Nyctalops [one affected by night blindness]...." Wilde notes that "pathology is rapidly becoming the basis of sensational literature, and in art, as in politics, there is a great future for monsters." This novel "belongs to a class of book that many people might read once for curiosity, but that nobody could read a second time for pleasure." William Cairns's *A Day after the Fair* is "an account of a holiday-tour through Scotland, taken by two young barristers, one of whom rescues a pretty girl from drowning, falls in love with her, and is rewarded for his heroism by seeing her married to his friend." The treatment, Wilde remarks, is "very satisfactory, and combines the triviality of the tourist with the dulness of good intentions."

Finally, Wilde reveals his previous reading of

novels by John Strange Winter (the pseudonym of Henrietta Vaughan Stannard), judging them "amusing and audacious, though we cannot say that we entirely approve of the names he gives to his stories." The title of the novel under review, *That Imp*, is "not much better." The writing, however, is "undoubtedly clever" and its "very brilliant description of a battle in the Soudan, and the account of barrack-life is of course admirable." However, he advises the author, whose name he puts in quotation marks to indicate that he is aware of the pseudonym, not to write "foolish prefaces about unappreciative critics; for it is only mediocrities and old maids who consider it a grievance to be misunderstood."

"SONNET ON APPROACHING ITALY"

Published: First appeared as "Salve Saturnia Tellus" in the *Irish Monthy* 5 (June 1877): 415, the title meaning "Hail, Land of Saturn," from Virgil's *Georgics* 2:173; rev. as "Sonnet Written at Turin," in the *Biograph and Review* 4 (Aug. 1880): 135; further rev. with the present title in *Poems* (1881) and (1882).

In wishing to celebrate Easter in the Holy City, Wilde departed for Rome in late March 1877, having written to his Oxford friend Reginald Harding (1857-1932): "This is an era in my life, a crisis. I wish I could look into the seeds of time and see what is coming" (*Letters* 34). The present poem was probably the first of several sonnets that he composed on his journey.

The speaker expresses the Romantic fascination with Italy when, on reaching the Alps, he exclaims: "...the soul within me burned, / Italia, my Italia, at thy name." When he sees the "land for which my life had yearned," he muses on the marvel of its fame as the day ends and the "turquoise sky to burnished gold was turned." But he then recalls that "far away at Rome / In evil bonds a second Peter lay [that is, Pope Pius IX, who, in 1871, considered himself to be "imprisoned" in the Vatican because of his refusal to acknowledge Italy as a united kingdom, which had freed Rome from the control of the Catholic Church]. The speaker concludes: "...I wept to see the land so very fair."

"SONNET. ON HEARING THE DIES IRAE SUNG IN THE SISTINE CHAPEL"
Published: First appeared as "Nay, Come Not

"SONNET. ON HEARING THE DIES IRAE"

Thus" in William MacIlwaine, ed., *Lyra Hibernica Sacra* (Belfast: M'Caw, Stevenson & Orr; Dublin: Hodges, Foster & Figgis; London: Geo Bell & Sons, 1878, 2nd ed. 1879), *not* listed in Mason; rev. with the present title in *Poems* (1881) and further rev. in (1882). The "Dies Irae" (Latin for "Day of Wrath") is a hymn that, as part of the Requiem Mass, poetically depicts the Last Judgment. In its concern for suffering souls, the "Dies Irae" celebrates neither joy nor triumph, though it presents death and judgment in dark and sombre tones.

The speaker in this sonnet pleads with the Lord to teach him more of His "life and love / Than terrors of red flame and thundering." He associates the Lord with "dear memories" of the "hillside vines" where the sparrows sing. He urges Him to appear on some autumn afternoon when the fields are aflame in splendid colors, an indication of His glory in the Second Coming: "Come when the splendid fulness of the moon / Looks down upon the rows of golden sheaves, / And reap Thy harvest: we have waited long."

Manuscript: The Clark Library has an early MS. of the poem, titled "Sonnet. (Written after hearing Mozart's 'Dies Irae' sung in Magdalen Chapel)," which was written before July 1877. The Jeremy Mason Collection contains a MS. with the present title.

"SONNET ON THE MASSACRE OF THE CHRISTIANS IN BULGARIA"

Published: *Poems* (1881), rev. in (1882).

Since the 14th century, when the Ottoman Empire absorbed Bulgaria, the oppressive rule by the Turks resulted in periodic rebellions against their attempt to suppress Bulgarian Christianity in favor of the authority of the Eastern Orthodox Church in Constantinople. A rebellion in March 1876 resulted in Turkish reprisals known as the "Bulgarian atrocities," which prompted the Russians to take advantage of their long-standing political antagonisms over the centuries to liberate Bulgaria in the Russo-Turkish War of 1877-78. While the poem reflects current political events, Wilde draws his inspiration for theme, title, and rhymes (such as *bones*, *stones*, and *groans*) from Milton's "On the Late Massacre in Piedmont."

In a letter posted around 12 May 1877, Wilde sent a draft of the poem (see *Letters* 37-38) to former Prime Minister Gladstone, who had voiced outrage over the event in such pamphlets as *The Bulgarian Horrors and the Question of the East* (1876) and *Lessons in Massacre* (1877). The poem is competent as political poetry, regarded in the 19th century as appropriate to the function of art – to instruct in a pleasing form. Progressively, Wilde turned away from such verse in favor of an ostensibly aesthetic rather than a discursively moral approach to art.

In his sonnet, Wilde calls upon Christ to save Christianity from the threat of Islam: "Christ, dost thou live indeed? or are thy bones / Still straitened in their rock-hewn sepulchre?" The priests who invoke his name are slain: "Dost thou not hear the bitter wail of pain / From those whose children lie upon the stones?" The sestet renews the call: "Come down, O Son of God!... / Over thy Cross a Crescent moon I see!" The concluding lines renew the plea: "Come down, O Son of Man! and show thy might, / Lest Mahomet be crowned instead of Thee!"

Manuscript: The British Library has a MS. of the poem titled "On the Recent Massacres of the Christians in Bulgaria."

"SONNET TO LIBERTY"

Published: *Poems* (1881).

Wilde's ambivalence towards the concept of political and personal liberty is here apparent, for liberty has given birth to those "Whose minds know nothing, nothing care to know" and "the roar of thy Democracies, / Thy reigns of Terror, thy great Anarchies, / Mirror my wildest passions like the sea...." Nevertheless, the speaker hails "Liberty!" despite its "dissonant cries" that "Delight my discreet soul," for without it, kings might "Rob nations of their rights inviolate / And I remain unmoved." The poem concludes on an equivocal note with the image of revolutionaries in a divinely sanctioned struggle for freedom: "These Christs that die upon the barricades, / God knows it I am with them, in some things."

On his American lecture tour, an interviewer in San Francisco asked Wilde, "Does the 'Sonnet to Liberty' voice your political creed?" He responded, "No; that is not my political creed. I wrote that when I was younger. Perhaps something of the fire of youth prompted it" (*Daily Examiner*, 27 March 1882; rpt. in Mikhail 1:62). The interviewer asked Wilde about another poem concerning Wilde's "political creed": see "Liberatatis Sacra Fames."

Manuscript: The Hyde Collection has a MS. of an early version.

"SONNET WRITTEN IN HOLY WEEK AT GENOA"

Published: First appeared as "Sonnet, Written During Holy Week" in the *Illustrated Monitor: A Monthly Magazine of Catholic Literature* (Dublin) 4 (July 1877): 186; rev. in *Poems* (1881) and (1882) with the present title. Wilde wrote this sonnet in late March 1877 while on a trip to Greece and Italy with his former Trinity College tutor, Rev. John Mahaffey (see entry) and David Hunter-Blair (1853-1939), an Oxford friend.

In a conventional Romantic style, the speaker contemplates natural beauty in the octave, "and life seemed very sweet." But, in the sestet, when a "young boy-priest" then passes singing "Jesus the son of Mary has been slain," the speaker is suddenly aware that the "dear Hellenic hours / Had drowned all memory of Thy bitter pain, / The Cross, the Crown, the Soldiers, and the Spear."

"SONNETS WRITTEN AT THE LYCEUM THEATRE"

The section title in *Poems* (1909) for "Portia" and "Queen Henrietta Maria."

"THE SOUL OF MAN UNDER SOCIALISM"

Published: *Fortnightly Review* 49 (Feb. 1891): 292-319; rpt. as *The Soul of Man* (London: Arthur L. Humphreys, 1895); rpt. in Volume 8 of the *Collected Edition* (1908).

Wilde opens his essay with the statement that the "chief advantage that would result from the establishment of Socialism is, undoubtedly, the fact that Socialism would relieve us from that sordid necessity of living for others which, in the present condition of things, presses so hardly upon almost everybody." Such great figures as Darwin, Keats, Flaubert, and Renan, "a fine critical spirit," have been able to isolate themselves and realize their perfection. (Ernest Renan's denial of Jesus's divinity in *La Vie de Jesus* [1863] was, remarks Guy Willoughby, "a particularly strong influence on Wilde," who, like Renan, regards Jesus as "an epoch-making humanitarian whose ministry was characterized by an inner strength...and a daunting belief in his own mission.... All these notably humanist qualities reappear in the great Individual-ist-Jesus of *The Soul of Man*," 52-53.) Most people, however, "spoil their lives by an unhealthy and exaggerated altruism – are forced, indeed, so to spoil them" (Wilde thus reveals his radical view of Socialism: not collectivism, which thinkers have regarded as central to the doctrine, but individualism, often associated in the late 19th century with Anarchism).

Most try, for example, "to solve the problem of poverty by keeping the poor alive," but this is not a solution: *"The proper aim is to try and re-construct society on such a basis that poverty will be impossible."* In present-day England, Wilde contends, those who do the most harm are those who attempt to do the most good. There are, at last, educated men living in the East End who are urging the community to "restrain its altruistic impulses of charity, benevolence and the like. They do so on the ground that such charity degrades and demoralises. They are perfectly right. Charity creates a multitude of sins." Later, Wilde says that "we are often told that the poor are grateful for charity. Some of them are, no doubt, *but the best amongst the poor are never grateful.* They are ungrateful, discontented, disobedient and rebellious." They are, Wilde remarks, "quite right to be so," for the "sentimentalist" distributing charity tyrannizes their private lives.

After depicting the miseries of poverty, which will be "altered" by Socialism, Wilde announces that *"Socialism itself will be of value simply because it will lead to Individualism"*:

Socialism, Communism, or whatever one chooses to call it, by converting private property into public wealth, and substituting co-operation for competition, will restore society to its proper condition of a thoroughly healthy organism, and ensure the material well-being of each member of the community.... But for the full development of Life to its highest mode of perfection something more is needed. What is needed is Individualism.

It follows, then, that "Authoritarian Socialism" – that is, a "form of compulsion" – will not do: "Every man must be left quite free to choose his own work." Furthermore, private property has "really harmed Individualism, and obscured it, by confusing a man with what he possesses.... *The true perfection of man lies, not in what man has, but in what man is....* With the abolition of private property, then, we shall have true, beautiful, healthy Individualism. Nobody will waste his life in accumulating things and the symbols for things."

In envisioning a brave new world, Wilde writes of the "true personality of man": "...it will not worry itself about the past, nor care whether things happened or did not happen. Nor will it admit any laws but its own laws; nor any authority but its own authority, yet it will love those who sought to intensify it, and speak often of them" (the influence of Emerson's essay, "Self-Reliance," is particularly noteworthy here). Introducing Jesus into this context, Wilde notes: "*When Jesus talks about the poor he simply means personalities, just as when he talks about the rich he simply means people who have not developed their personalities.*" He said to man: "You have a wonderful personality. Develop it. Be yourself. Don't imagine that your perfection lies in accumulating or possessing external things. Your perfection is inside of you."

Wilde then offers a paradoxical view of the wealthy, who, as a class, "are better than impoverished people, more moral, more intellectual, more well-behaved. *There is only one class in the community that thinks more about money than the rich, and that is the poor.* The poor can think of nothing else. That is the misery of being poor. What Jesus does say is that man reaches his perfection, not through what he has, not even through what he does, but entirely through what he is."

With the abolition of private property, Wilde continues, "marriage in its present form must disappear.... Individualism accepts this and makes it fine." With this freedom, the "full development of personality" is advanced in order to "make the love of man and woman more wonderful, more beautiful, and more ennobling." Jesus, Wilde asserts, rejected the claims of family life. Proceeding to an Anarchist position, Wilde argues that, as a result of Individualism, "the State must give up all idea of government.... *All modes of government are failures....* High hopes were once formed of democracy; but democracy means simply the bludgeoning of the people by the people for the people.... 'He who would be free,' says a fine thinker [that is, Emerson in "Self-Reliance," though Wilde is apparently quoting from memory], 'must not conform.'" (Emerson wrote: "Whoso

would be a man, must be a nonconformist.")

In a section on crime, Wilde follows previous Socialist utopias in envisioning the end of crime when private property is abolished: "Starvation, and not sin, is the parent of modern crime.... Jealousy, which is an extraordinary source of crime in modern life, is an emotion closely bound up with our conceptions of property, and under Socialism and Individualism will die out."

The machine, Wilde continues in his discussion of private property, inevitably results in widespread unemployment when, as a result of our system of competition, a factory fails, and "having no work to do, [the unemployed] become hungry and take to thieving.... Were that machine the property of all, every one would benefit by it.... *At present machinery competes against man. Under proper conditions machinery will serve man.*"

At one point, Wilde raises the question: "Is this Utopian? A map of the world that does not include Utopia is not worth even glancing at [an echo of "The Critic as Artist," Part II: "England will never be civilised till she has added Utopia to her dominions"], for it leaves out the one country at which Humanity is always landing. And when Humanity lands there, it looks out, and, seeing a better country, sets sail. Progress is the realisation of Utopias."

Wilde then moves to the artist's role in the Socialist state: when a community or a government

attempts to dictate to the artist what he is to do, Art either entirely vanishes, or becomes stereotyped, or degenerates into a low and ignoble form of craft. *A work of art is the unique result of a unique temperament. Its beauty comes from the fact that the author is what he is.*

Therefore, he cannot take notice of what others want, for "*Art is the most intense mode of individualism that the world has known.*" Though the public is continually pressing the artist to create popular art, Wilde insists that "*Art should never try to be popular. The public should try to make itself artistic.*" The public, however, dislikes novelty, Wilde insists, because it fears innovation: "Art is Individualism, and Individualism is a disturbing and disintegrating force."

When an artist is attacked in England for being immoral or unintelligible, his individuality, says

Wilde, is "intensified. He becomes more completely himself." The section that precedes and follows this remark is more concerned with the aesthetics of art than with Socialism – with such questions, for example, as to whether a work of art can be called "healthy" or "unhealthy" with respect to subject matter and style. Characteristically, Wilde launches a barb against those works that are "popular": "*In fact, the popular novel that the public calls healthy is always a thoroughly unhealthy production; and what the public calls an unhealthy novel is always a beautiful and healthy work of art.*" The confusion in judgment by the public "comes from the natural inability of a community corrupted by authority to understand or appreciate Individualism." Wilde regards the press as the disseminator of that "monstrous and ignorant thing that is called Public Opinion": "We are dominated by Journalism. In America the President reigns for four years and Journalism governs for ever and ever."

Much of the final section of this essay is a continuation of the preceding discussion on the nature of art and the artist's place in society. When Wilde raises the question of the most suitable form of government that the artist can live under, he restates his Anarchist position: "*The form of government that is most suitable to the artist is no government at all.* Authority over him and his art is ridiculous." Wilde then outlines the three kinds of despots that tyrannize over the body or the soul and over soul and body alike: "The first is called the Prince. The second is called the Pope. The third is called the People," whose authority is "a thing blind, deaf, hideous, grotesque, tragic, amusing, serious and obscene. It is impossible for the artist to live with the People."

Wilde admires the Renaissance, which he calls "great because it sought to solve no social problem, and busied itself not about such things, but suffered the individual to develop freely, beautifully and naturally, and so had great and individual artists, and great and individual men." Louis XIV, however, in creating the modern state, "destroyed the individualism of the artist, and made things monstrous in their monotony of repetition, and contemptible in their conformity to rule.... The error of Louis XIV was that he thought human nature would always be the same. The result of his error was the French Revolution."

Wilde adopts a Darwinian approach to Individu-

alism in his remark that "*Evolution is the law of life, and there is no evolution except towards Individualism.*" When one has realized Individualism, he will be capable of sympathy, which he will exercise "freely and spontaneously." Since man has sought "to live intensely, fully, perfectly," he will be "saner, healthier, more civilised, more himself" when he ceases to exert authority over others, for "Pleasure is Nature's text, her sign of approval." The Greeks sought for "perfect harmony": "...through it each man will attain to his perfection. The new Individualism is the new Hellenism."

References: William Buckler, "Oscar Wilde's Quest for Utopia: Persiflage with a Purpose in 'The Soul of Man under Socialism,'" *Victorians Institute Journal* 17 (1989); Isobel Murray, "Oscar Wilde and Individualism: Contexts for 'The Soul of Man Under Socialism,'" *Durham University Journal* (July 1991); Guy Willoughby, "The First Individualist: Jesus in *The Soul of Man under Socialism*," *Art and Christhood: The Aesthetics of Oscar Wilde* (1993); Horst Schroeder, "A Printing Error in 'The Soul of Man under Socialism,'" *N&Q* (March 1996); Lawrence Danson, "The Soul of Man under Socialism," *Wilde's Intentions: The Artist in His Criticism* (1997).

THE SPHINX

Written: According to Robert Sherard (238), *The Sphinx* was written in Paris in 1883, but Rupert Hart-Davis contends that Wilde began writing it while still an undergraduate at Oxford (*Letters* 144n3). Most scholars believe that the poem underwent final revision in the early 1890s. The poem consists of 87 couplets in sixteen-syllable lines, each containing internal rhyme: the rhyming word in the middle of one line rhyming with the last word in the other; indeed, Wilde had begun composing the poem by modeling his stanzas (with an *abba* rhyme scheme in iambic lines) after those in Tennyson's *In Memoriam*, then stretching them out into couplets.

Published: 11 June 1894 by Elkin Mathews and John Lane, At the Sign of the Bodley Head (London), and by Copeland and Day (Boston); rpt. in *Poems* (1908). Charles Ricketts designed the title page and the decorations in addition to 10 full-page illustrations. An unusual feature of the first edition is that the entire text is printed in capital letters. Wilde dedicated the poem to his friend, Marcel Schwob (see entry), "in friendship and in admiration."

Sources: Rodney Shewan has suggested that a principal source for Wilde's poem was either Dante Gabriel Rossetti's "The Burden of Nineveh" (1870), which combines Egyptian and Old Testament elements, or Flaubert's *La Tentation de Saint Antoine* (1874), which draws upon Egyptian mythology and which provided Wilde with such exotic words as *mandragores*, *oreichalch*, and *tragelaphos* (20). Indeed, Wilde noted in his essay "The Decay of Lying" (1889): "The solid stolid British intellect lies in the desert sands like the Sphinx in Flaubert's marvellous tale, and fantasy, *La Chimère*, dances round it, and calls to it with her false, flute-toned voice." Isobel Murray discusses other possible sources for *The Sphinx*: Baudelaire's several cat poems in *Les Fleurs du mal* (1857), with their explicit allusions to the sphinx; and Gautier's *Mademoiselle de Maupin* (1835), particularly Chapter 11, in which the hero, meditating on the "strange land" of his soul, alludes to "monstrous and fantastic animals" and in Chapter 13 to "the ambiguous and terrible beauty of the sphinx."

The Poem: The speaker, a student, contemplates the ancient history of the "beautiful and silent Sphinx," a small statue in a "dim corner" of the room: "Come forth you exquisite grotesque! half woman and half animal!" (Though Egyptian sphinxes were usually male, the famous Greek sphinx, associated with Oedipus, was female with the body of a lion and the wings of a bird. At Thebes, she could not resist posing riddles to passers-by, who were killed when they failed to respond with a solution. Only Oedipus succeeded in providing an answer, thereby dooming the sphinx to her self-imposed death.)

The speaker asks the Sphinx to recall its association with the Holy Family in Egypt: "Sing to me of the Jewish maid who wandered with the Holy Child, / And how you led them through the wild, and how they slept beneath your shade." The speaker, interested not only in biblical lore but also in this erotic whore, urges her to reveal her past: "Who were your lovers? who were they who wrestled for you in the dust?" Since she is a monster among monsters, the inevitable question arises: "Did gilt-scaled dragons writhe and twist with passion as you passed them by? ... / Or did you lure unto your bed the ivory-horned Tragela-

phos?"

Associating the Sphinx with the Mona Lisa (often regarded by late 19th-century Decadents as a *femme fatale*), the speaker exclaims: "How subtle-secret is your smile! Did you love none then? Nay I know / Great Ammon was your bedfellow! He lay with you beside the Nile!" (Ammon – also spelled Amon – was an Egyptian god, originally the principal god of Thebes, later known as the great Amon Ra, the supreme deity in the Egyptian pantheon and identified with the Greek god Zeus.) The speaker envisions Ammon "scattered here and there: deep hidden in the windy sand" and urges the Sphinx: "Go, seek his fragments on the moor and wash them in the evening dew, / And from their pieces make anew thy mutilated paramour!"

He assures her that "Only one God has ever died. / Only one God has let His side be wounded by a soldier's spear." But *her* lovers are not dead: "Back to your Nile!" And in a line reminiscent of some of Swinburne's shockers in *Poems and Ballads* (1866), the speaker urges that, if she has "grown sick of dead divinities," she can "hale [a lion] by the mane and bid him be your paramour!": "Couch by his side upon the grass and set your white teeth in his throat... / And toy with him in amorous jest, and when he turns, and snarls, and gnaws, / O smite him with your jasper claws! and bruise him with your agate breasts!"

Impatient with the monstrous Sphinx but fearful of her pagan sensuality, the speaker lashes out: "Get hence, you loathsome mystery! Hideous animal, get hence! / You wake in me each bestial sense, you make me what I would not be... / Go thou before, and leave me to my crucifix...." In the final stanza, Christ on the cross, "sick with pain, watches the world with wearied eyes.../ and weeps for every soul in vain" – a conclusion, suggests Kohl, of "weary resignation...deeply pessimistic" (203).

Early Reviews: The anonymous reviewer in the *Pall Mall Budget* (21 June 1894) voiced what other reviewers only distantly suggested, namely the sexual content of the poem:

There is a meaning underlying Mr. Wilde's poem – the keen olfactory nerves of the Nonconformist conscience would not, I fear, find it a difficult one to scent – its motive is mainly important as affording Mr. Wilde a theme for the display, in a sort of processional, of beautiful words strangely shaped and coloured, and far-sought pictures of ancient Egyptian luxury and legend. (rpt. in Beckson)

The reviewer (who may have been a friend of Wilde) recalls that, years before publication of *The Sphinx*, Wilde was asked why he had not published the poem, which "long had a reputation in MS." He allegedly replied, no doubt facetiously, that publication "would destroy domesticity in England."

In the *Pall Mall Gazette* (9 July), the poet and journalist W. E. Henley (writing anonymously), an ardent anti-Decadent, characterized Wilde as "the New Style, or Fin-de-Siècle, Minor Poet" who "is trading in a novel sort of fancy goods; and, vouchsafing unto him that smile of amazed amusement which it has ever been his chief ambition to win, you proceed to the examination of his wares. And wonderful wares you find they are." The irony is apparent when Henley describes such "wonderful wares" as the eccentric arrangement of the poem on the page: the couplets, he observes, are really a re-arrangement of the quatrains and metre of Tennyson's *In Memoriam*; the uneven distribution of couplets on the pages "is about as Fin-de-Siècle a business as you ever saw." The "whole thing," concludes Henley, is dedicated to M. Marcel Schwob – who deserves a vastly better fate" (rpt. in Beckson).

An unsigned review in the *Athenaeum* (25 Aug.) accuses Wilde of "cynical humour" in writing *The Sphinx* in the metre of *In Memoriam*. Alluding to "luscious lines" and "lewd imaginings" in the cataloguing of the Sphinx's lovers, never before known, the reviewer gives the "fullest credit" to the "ingenious fertility" in Wilde's "new conception of her." Admirers of his previous poems "will quarrel with such defects as the too frequent use of the word 'paramour' or the employment of 'curious' in a somewhat precious sense...but even they will not be able to deny the skilfulness with which the metre is handled..." (rpt. in Beckson).

Manuscripts: The Clark Library and the Hyde Collection have the earliest untitled MSS., which contain jottings or versions of stanzas, as well as fair copies (see Mason 396-97). The Clark Library also has a TS. prepared from an untitled MS. in the British Library, presented by Robert Ross in 1909, the so-called "final draft" of the poem in Wilde's

hand, though Wilde later provided some final revisions and additional lines.

References: Robert Sherard, *The Life of Oscar Wilde* (1906); Rodney Shewan, *Oscar Wilde: Art and Egotism* (1977); Isobel Murray, "Some Problems of Editing Wilde's Poem *The Sphinx*," *Durham University Journal* (Jan. 1990).

"THE SPHINX WITHOUT A SECRET"

Published: First appeared as "Lady Alroy" in the *World: A Journal for Men and Women* 26 (25 May 1887): 18-19; rpt. as "The Sphinx without a Secret: An Etching" in *Lord Arthur Savile's Crime and Other Stories* (1891). Wilde may have derived his title from Baudelaire's phrase – "*ce sphinx sans enigme*" – in *Notes Nouvelles sur Edgar Poe* (1857).

The Plot: The unnamed narrator, sitting outside the Café de la Paix in Paris and watching "the splendour and shabbiness of Parisian life," is hailed by a former Oxford classmate, Lord Murchison, who reveals his uncertainty concerning a woman he has loved. Examining a photograph, the narrator concludes that it was "the face of some one who had a secret, but whether the secret was good or evil I could not say": "...the faint smile that just played across the lips was far too subtle to be really sweet." Murchison tells him how he had seen this woman fleetingly; then suddenly, she appeared at a dinner party as Lady Alroy. At dinner, he fell "passionately, stupidly in love, and the indefinable atmosphere of mystery that surrounded her excited my most ardent curiosity." When she left, she agreed to meet him on the next day, but at the appointed hour, she was not at home. Days later, she received him and urged him not to write to her again: she gave him another name and address. After seeing her often throughout the season, he decided to ask her to marry him: "I was sick and tired of the incessant secrecy that she imposed on all my visits...."

By chance, he discovered the "mystery" by happening to see Lady Alroy, veiled, enter a house in a shabby street. That evening, when he visited her, he pressed her to tell him the truth, but she merely responded: "There is nothing to tell you." He rushed out, returned her letters unanswered, and left for a month abroad. On returning, he read of her death, caused by congestion of the lungs. He went to the house where he had seen her enter: the landlady told him that she used the rooms "merely to sit in my drawing-rooms now and then." No, the woman assured him, she met no one: "She simply sat in the drawing-room, sir, reading books, and sometimes had tea." The narrator assures Murchison that "Lady Alroy was simply a woman with a mania for mystery. She took these rooms for the pleasure of going there with her veil down, and imagining she was a heroine....she herself was merely a Sphinx without a secret."

As Shewan suggests, Lady Alroy is "a living exponant of Wildean mythopoeia fighting the good fight of fancy against annihilating fact." The "good fight" also occurs in Wilde's essay "The Decay of Lying" (26).

Reference: Rodney Shewan, *Oscar Wilde: Art and Egotism* (1977).

"THE STAR-CHILD"

Published: *A House of Pomegranates* (1891). Dedicated to Margot Tennant (1864-1945), who in 1894 married Herbert Henry Asquith, later Prime Minister, 1908-16.

The Plot: Two poor woodcutters, on their way home on a dark winter night, are saddened by their poverty, one of them saying: "Why did we make merry, seeing that life is for the rich, and not for such as we are?" The other, agreeing, remarks: "Injustice has parcelled out the world, nor is there equal division of aught save of sorrow." But as they speak, "a very bright and beautiful star" falls from heaven into a clump of willow trees. Believing that gold awaits them if they find it, they rush to the site.

But when they unwrap the "cloak of golden tissue," they find a sleeping child. One of the woodcutters suggests that they leave it there since they are poor and have children of their own to feed. The other, however, regards such indifference as evil and, though poor with "many mouths to feed," decides to take the child home. However, when the woodcutter arrives with the child, his wife angrily condemns her husband, for it may bring them "bad fortune." Moreover, there are other mouths to feed. However, she soon relents and welcomes the child, placing him in a bed with the youngest of her children. Into a chest, the woodcutter places the "curious cloak of gold" with the "chain of amber" that his wife took from the child's neck.

The Star-Child is brought up with the woodcutter's children as if he were his own. Though he grows into a strikingly beautiful child, he is also "proud, and cruel, and selfish," despising the other children because, he says, "they were of mean parentage, while he was noble, being sprung from a Star...." He regards himself as their master, and he calls them "his servants." Enamoured of his own beauty, he mocks the "weakly and ill-favoured, and [makes] jest of them." His companions follow him and learn to be as cruel as he is.

One day, when a poor beggar-woman, passes through the village and sits down to rest under a chestnut tree, the Star-Child tells his friends: "Come, let us drive her hence, for she is ugly and ill-favoured." Though he throws stones and mocks her, she remains seated, gazing in terror at him. The woodcutter then rebukes the Star-Child: "...what evil has this poor woman done to thee that thou should'st treat her in this wise?" When the woman hears that the woodcutter had found the Star-Child in the forest, she faints.

On her recovery, when the woodcutter tells her of his discovery of the Star-Child, she exclaims: "He is my little son whom I lost in the forest." But the Star-Child, at first filled with "wonder and great gladness" at the news that his mother awaits him, refuses to believe that the "vile beggar-woman" is his mother. Robbers, she insists, had stolen him and left him to die: "Come with me, my son, for I have need of thy love." If the woman's story is true, he responds, she should have stayed away rather than bring him shame as a beggar's child.

She leaves weeping bitterly, but when he rejoins his playmates, they mock him: "Why thou art as foul as the toad, and as loathsome as the adder." After they drive him out of the garden (Wilde's suggestive parable for the fall of mankind), he gazes into a well of water and sees himself as his playmates see him (a reversal of the Narcissus myth). He interprets his transformation as the result of his sin in driving away his mother. Aware of his cruelty, he resolves to search for her and achieve forgiveness.

During his three years of wandering in search of his mother, he is mocked by children in the villages, and he is denied shelter in barns by the peasants. On one evening, he comes to a walled city, where the soldiers deny him entrance. Passing by, "an old and evil-visaged man" buys the Star-Child, who is led to a dungeon. The old man, "the subtlest of the magicians of Libya," tells him that he is his slave and instructs him that in a nearby wood there are three pieces of gold, with which he must return.

When he reaches the wood, he cannot find the white gold despite an entire day's search. Weeping bitterly, he sees a hare caught in a trap and, pitying the animal, releases it: "I am myself but a slave, yet may I give thee thy freedom." Hearing the Star-Child's story concerning the white gold, the hare leads him to its site. At the gate of the city, the Star-Child encounters a leper who pleads that he is hungry and in need of money. Again filled with pity, the Star-Child gives him the white gold. When he tells the magician that he does not have the gold, he is beaten and flung into the dungeon.

The story continues with the same pattern: the magician demands on two further occasions that the Star-Child return with yellow, then red gold; each time, the hare leads him to the site of the gold, and each time the leper encounters the Star-Child at the gate demanding it. However, when the Star-Child gives the red gold to the leper, a transformation occurs: as he passes through the city's gates, the guards bow down to him, saying: "How beautiful is our lord!" and a crowd of citizens exclaims: "Surely there is none so beautiful in the whole world!" Finding himself in a great square, the Star-Child is approached by priests and city officers, who bow before him: "Thou art our lord for whom we have been waiting, and son of our King." Despite his protests, the Star-Child soon discovers that he has been restored to his former beauty.

When the priests and high officers kneel down and inform him that it was prophesied that on that day one would come who was to rule over them, the Star-Child protests: "I am not worthy, for I have denied the mother who bare me, nor may I rest till I have found her, and known her forgiveness." As he approaches the gate of the city to resume his search for her, the old beggar-woman and the leper appear. Joyfully, he kneels before her and kisses his mother's wounds, confessing that, in his pride, he had denied her. He then grasps the feet of the leper, saying: "Thrice did I give thee of my mercy. Bid my mother speak to me once." The woman and the leper bid the Star-Child to rise, and when he does, "lo! they were a King and a Queen." He is led to the palace and crowned as a ruler of the city.

The Star-Child banishes the magician, and he rewards the woodcutter and his wife by sending "many rich gifts" and honors to their children. He also rules over the poor with compassion. (Wilde, having employed the literary convention of "the Test," in which the Star-Child succeeds admirably, concludes the story with a brief final paragraph introducing an unconventional element in his fairy tale.) After only three years as king, the Star-Child dies, "so great had been his suffering, and so bitter the fire of his testing.... And he who came after him ruled evilly."

Manuscripts: The Beinecke Library and the Huntington Library have MSS. of this fairy tale.

Reference: David Monaghan, "The Literary Fairy-Tale: A Study of Oscar Wilde's 'The Happy Prince' and 'The Star-Child,'" *Canadian Review of Comparative Literature* (Spring 1974).

"SWEET I WENT OUT IN THE NIGHT"

Unpublished in Wilde's lifetime, this lyric poem consists of five quatrains. The epigraph – "Ah God it is a dreary thing / To sit at home with unkissed lips" – is, in fact, a paraphrase, despite the quotation marks, from Elizabeth Barrett Browning's *Aurora Leigh* (1857) 5:434-47, of which Wilde wrote on 26 July 1876 to an Oxford friend that it was "one of those books, that, written straight from the heart – and from such a large heart too – never weary one: because they are sincere. We tire of art but not of nature after all our aesthetic training. I look upon it as much the greatest work in our literature" (*Letters* 21).

The speaker tells of having waited "beneath the lamp's light, / For I knew I was fair to see." A young man with "eyes of fire" looked at him(?) with desire "And I knew that his name was Love." With his little white fingers and toes, "O he is lovely, this boy of mine." The final quatrain questions:

What do you say he's the child of sin,
    That God looks on him with angry eyes,
And never will let him enter in
    To the lilies and flowers and rivers
        of Paradise.

Wilde's poem anticipates Lord Alfred Douglas's "Two Loves," which also suggests a homoerotic encounter with a figure who is the "love that dare not speak its name."

Manuscript: The Clark Library has the MS. of

the poem.

SWINBURNE, ALGERNON CHARLES (1837-1909)

The poet and critic Algernon Swinburne described his meeting with Wilde in a letter, dated 4 April 1882, to the American poet E. C. Stedman:

> The only time I ever saw Mr. Oscar Wilde was in a crush at our acquaintance Lord Houghton's. I thought he seemed a harmless young nobody, and had no notion he was the sort of man to play the mountebank as he seems to have been doing. A letter which he wrote to me lately about Walt Whitman was quite a modest, gentlemanlike, reasonable affair, without any flourish or affectation of any kind in matter or expression. (*Swinburne Letters* 4:266)

Wilde wrote the letter to Swinburne after his meeting with Whitman on 18 January 1882 in Camden, New Jersey. Wilde then reported to Whitman what Swinburne wrote in response. In his letter to Wilde, Swinburne expressed his sincere interest and gratitude in Wilde's account of his visit to Whitman "and the assurance of his kindly friendly feeling towards me..." (*Swinburne Letters* 4:255). Grateful, Swinburne sent Wilde an inscribed copy of his *Studies in Song* (1880); in 1881, Wilde had sent him a copy of his *Poems*, which Swinburne called "an exquisitely pretty book," alluding to "Impressions: I. Les Silhouettes" as a poem he enjoyed reading (*More Letters* 35-36). Some of the other poems in Wilde's volume, such as "The Garden of Eros," echoed Swinburne closely in rhythm and imagery. However, when Wilde contributed an introduction to Rennell Rodd's volume of verse, published in 1882, Swinburne condemned the enterprise (see Rodd, Rennell).

Wilde reviewed only one of Swinburne's books, *Poems and Ballads*, Third Series (1889), in the *Pall Mall Gazette* (27 June 1889). Though acknowledging that Swinburne has "always been a great poet," Wilde points to "his limitations, the chief of which is, curiously enough, an entire lack of any sense of limit. His song is nearly always too loud for his subject" (see "Mr. Swinburne's Last Volume"). In the following year, Wilde was also critical of Swinburne in a letter to Michael Field

(see entry), who had sent him a copy of *The Tragic Mary* (1890), on Mary Queen of Scots: "She is closer to flesh and blood than the Mary of Swinburne's *Bothwell* [1876], who seems to me less real than the Mary of his *Chastelard* [1865]" (*Letters* 272).

While in Paris in late 1891, Wilde discovered that he was the subject of Edmond de Goncourt's journal entries for 1883, which were published in *L'Echo de Paris* (17 Dec. 1891). In one entry, Goncourt wrote that Wilde was an "individual of doubtful sex, with a ham-actor's language, and tall stories"; in another, Wilde allegedly spoke of Swinburne as "a flaunter of vice." Ignoring the remarks about himself, Wilde wrote to Goncourt to clarify the Swinburne remark. Swinburne, he wrote, was "our dear and noble English poet" who would be much surprised by the remark as reported by Goncourt since "he lives an austere life in a country dwelling, consecrated entirely to art and literature." Wilde continues:

> In Swinburne's work, we meet for the first time the cry of flesh tormented by desire and memory, joy and remorse, fecundity and sterility. The English public, as usual hypocritical, prudish, and philistine, has not known how to find the art in the work of art: it has searched for the man in it. Since it always confuses the man and his creations, it thinks that to create Hamlet you must be a little melancholy.... So it has built around M. Swinburne a legend of an ogre and a devourer of children. M. Swinburne, an aristocrat by birth and an artist by temperament, has merely laughed at these absurdities.... (trans. by Ellmann 352-53n/332n)

When Goncourt published his journals in book form, he omitted the passage about Swinburne as a "flaunter of vice" and about Wilde's doubtful sex.

In February 1892, Wilde addressed the Playgoers' Club, laying down an "axiom that the stage is only 'a frame furnished with a set of puppets.'" After reading the report of the meeting, Wilde sent a letter to *Daily Telegraph* (19 Feb. 1892) to clarify his remarks, in the course of which he contended that, in 19th-century England, the "only two great plays" were Shelley's *Cenci* and Swinburne's *Atalanta in Calydon*: "...neither of them is in any sense of the word an actable play. Indeed, the mere suggestion that stage representation is any test of a work of art is quite ridiculous" (*Letters* 310). Three years later, Wilde again expressed his high regard for Swinburne in a brief passage that he contributed to the *Idler* (April 1895), when the question was asked of 22 writers, "Who Should Be Laureate?" Wilde responded that Swinburne was "already the Poet Laureate of England." In that year, Swinburne remained silent in his letters on the subject of Wilde's debacle.

Reference: Cecil Y. Lang, ed., *The Swinburne Letters*, Vol. 4 (1960).

SYMONDS, JOHN ADDINGTON (1840-93)

A poet, critic, biographer, and noted historian, best known for his seven-volume work, *The Renaissance in Italy* (1875-86), Symonds is also well known for his early work with Havelock Ellis on the ground-breaking study of homosexuality, *Sexual Inversion* (1897), which, in its final form, included little of Symonds's contribution. Symonds and his family spent much of their lives in Switzerland, where he hoped a more suitable climate would control his tuberculosis. In August 1876, Wilde was writing a review essay on Symonds's second volume of *Studies of the Greek Poets*, but he never completed it. A MS. sold at the American Art Association on 25 April 1927 (see *Letters* 25n1) listed it with the title "The Women of Homer," after a chapter in Symonds's first volume of *Studies of the Greek Poets* (1873). An incomplete MS. of 45 leaves with the same title as that sold in 1927 is now in the Morgan Library.

In 1878, Symonds sent Wilde a copy of his translations of Michelangelo's sonnets; in the following year, Wilde bought Symonds's *Shelley*, marking a passage on "an intimate friendship of the adolescent Shelley with another boy" (Ellmann 33/31). When *Poems* (1881) appeared, Wilde sent him a copy with "affectionate admiration," accompanied by a letter (now apparently lost). To Horatio Forbes Brown, later his literary executor, Symonds wrote that Wilde's *Poems* "seems a caricature of himself in *Punch*. There are good things in the book, and he is a poet – undoubtedly, I think" (Symonds, *Letters* 2:686).

In the draft of a lengthy letter to Wilde, apparently never sent, Symonds excuses his silence since they had last exchanged letters: "These years I have spent in sickness, the seclusion of these

mountains, and studies." Acknowledging receipt of *Poems*, he praises the volume: "I feel the poet's gift in them.... Those wh[ich] I presume to have been written latest...seem to me the deepest and sincerest the most free from riot of luxuriant adolescence.... How few such volumes of new poems there are! Arise & shine! This [is] really what I want to say, & why I write" (qtd. in Ellmann 145/139).

In 1886, Wilde published four anonymous reviews in the *Pall Mall Gazette* of Symonds's books – see "Ben Jonson," "Mr. Symonds' History of the Renaissance," "Two Biographies of Sir Philip Sidney," and the recently identified review of *Sketches and Studies in Italy* (see entry below). Unaware that Wilde was the author of the last review, Symonds was deeply annoyed over some negative remarks – "put out," he told Edmund Gosse (Symonds, *Letters* 3:188). Ellmann remarks that at this time, "several writers had ceased to interest Wilde," among them Symonds (263/248), though, while in prison, Wilde requested books by him.

In 1890, Symonds unwittingly annoyed Wilde with a remark concerning "The Portrait of Mr W. H.," involving Shakespeare's love of Willie Hughes, a boy actor. In his essay "On Some Principles of Criticism," which appeared in Volume 1 of *Essays Speculative and Suggestive* (1890), Symonds remarks: "William Hughes had been in literary existence a century before Mr. Oscar Wilde resuscitated this hypothetical youth in a magazine of 1889" (118n). Wilde sent him a letter (now apparently lost) objecting to the remark; Symonds responded to Wilde on 13 July 1890, apologizing for the "pain" that his note on Wilde's story had given him, but the note was

> really left by carelessness in one of my essays.... It was by no means intended to imply that you imagined yourself to be the originator of the William Hughes theory [which had been advanced by Thomas Tyrwhitt, the 18th-century scholar]: I give you greater credit for your scholarship.... (3:472)

Symonds had meant the note for those without scholarship.

Shortly thereafter, Wilde sent a copy of the first version of *The Picture of Dorian Gray* to Symonds, who wrote to Brown on 22 July 1890 that

J. A. Symonds

it was "an odd and very audacious production, unwholesome in tone, but artistically and psychologically interesting. If the British public will stand this, they can stand anything. However, I resent the unhealthy, scented, mystic, congested touch which a man of this sort has on moral problems" (3:377). Symonds's reaction to the novel, with its suggestions of Decadence and homosexuality, echoes the reviews that were appearing at the time. Nevertheless, Symonds believed that Labouchere's Article XI to the Criminal Law Amendment Act (1885), under which Wilde was later imprisoned, was grossly unjust: privately he attempted to influence politicians to modify the law, but without success. In 1893, Symonds died of influenza.

References: Phyllis Grosskurth, *The Woeful Victorian: A Biography of John Addington Symonds* (1965); Herbert M. Schueller and Robert

L. Peters, eds., *The Letters of John Addington Symonds*, Vols. 2 and 3 (1968-69).

SYMONDS'S *SKETCHES AND STUDIES IN ITALY*, REVIEW OF

Published: *Athenaeum*, 14 June 1879, 754-55. This previously unidentified review is now authoritatively attributed to Wilde from the "marked file" of the *Athenaeum*, now in the library of the City University, London. As Oskar Wellens writes, "successive editors or their assistants identified each anonymous contributor" in each issue (364).

Wilde cites Symonds as "one of the foremost exponents" of that "rare power of painting and not merely a scene, a tendency to dwell constantly on the splendours and subtleties of colour, and a desire to develop...the emotional rather than the intellectual resources of language...." Though Symonds, Wilde continues, "possesses in a marked degree many of the noblest qualities of a writer of prose," he often lacks "that exquisite curb of an ever-present artistic sense which restrains Mr. Ruskin even in the highest flights of his eagle-like rhetoric." In the volume under review, Wilde senses a "false note," for example, when Symonds, in characterizing Lucretius, states that he "spanned the chasms of speculative insecurity with the masonry of hypotheses" – a metaphor that mars "the beauty of the whole."

Nevertheless, Symonds's essay on Lucretius is marked, writes Wilde, "by great appreciation both of the poet's creative genius and of his true relation to modern science," which has not surpassed his understanding of the world. Lucretius' poem *De Rerum Natura*, is "valuable not merely as anticipatory of the theory of molecular structure and the latest hypotheses of modern scientific men, but is in the highest degree representative of the true Roman spirit in its realism, its Positivism, its huge elemental conceptions of spiritual things, and its noble indifference to death...."

Wilde also points to the "peculiar tendencies of Mr. Symonds's mind...best appreciated in his slighter, less didactic essays, where, adopting a kind of 'Impressionist' attitude, he finds a motive for exquisite work in some slight incident of travel," as in his discovery in a shop of a crucifix, once belonging to the Franciscans, that contained a poisoned dagger hidden in the figure of Christ. Wilde concludes with praise for the opening essay on Amalfi and Paestum – "in every way worthy of

Mr. Symonds's reputation" – as "entirely delightful to those who love the peculiar qualities of Italian scenery."

Reference: Oskar Wellens, "A Hitherto Unnoticed Review by Wilde," *N&Q* (Sept. 1994).

SYMONS, ARTHUR (1865-1945)

A poet, translator, playwright, and critic, best known for his seminal work, *The Symbolist Movement in Literature* (1900), Symons thought little of Wilde's ability in the late 1880s, when he referred to him as "flighty-brained enthusiast and *poseur*" (*Selected Letters* 58). When Wilde was editing *Woman's World*, he published Symons's poem "Charity" in September 1888. He also asked him to contribute a critical article after having read his review of Walter Pater's *Imaginary Portraits* (1887). Symons's "Villiers de l'Isle Adam," his first article on a French Symbolist, appeared in October 1889, but Wilde had already left his post as editor.

In his only surviving letter to Symons, Wilde wrote in October 1890: "It was a great pleasure meeting you, as I had admired your work for a long time [in 1889, Symons had published his first volume of verse, *Days and Nights*]. I look forward to an evening together, and to a talk about French art, the one art now in Europe that is worth discussing – Verlaine's art especially" (*Letters* 276). In the 1890s, they saw each other infrequently. Whatever chance meetings occurred were at the Rhymers' Club, at the Café Royal, or in a theater: Symons's muted personality did not appeal to the more flamboyant Wilde, who once characterized him, according to Frank Harris, as "a sad example of an Egoist who had no Ego" (278).

With the publication of *Intentions* (1891), which contains some of Wilde's best critical writing, Symons revised his estimate of Wilde as a man of letters. Appreciative now of Wilde's versatility, Symons remarks in the *Speaker* (4 July 1891):

Mr. Wilde is much too brilliant to be ever believed; he is much too witty to be ever taken seriously. A passion for caprice, a whimsical Irish temperament, a love of art for art's sake – it is in qualities such as these that we find the origin of the beautiful farce of aestheticism, the exquisite echoes of the *Poems*, the subtle decadence of *Dorian Gray*, and the paradoxical truths, the perverted common

sense, of the *Intentions*. (rpt. in Beckson)

Suggesting that Wilde borrows from other writers, Symons states wittily that Wilde "can be admirable even when his eloquence reminds us of the eloquent writing of others. He is conscious of the charm of graceful echoes, and is always original in his quotations.... By constantly saying the opposite of sensible opinions he proves to us that opposites can often be equally true." Symons concludes with the observation that after "achieving a reputation by doing nothing, he is in a fair way to beat his own record by real achievements." He could be regarded, Symons contends, as the "perfect representative of all that is meant by the modern use of the word Decadence."

During the period of Wilde's criminal trials and imprisonment, Symons had little to say about the debacle. He stayed away from the trials, though his friends kept him informed of the proceedings. However, when *The Ballad of Reading Gaol* was

Arthur Symons

announced for publication, he wrote to Leonard Smithers, Wilde's publisher: "I need scarcely say that if I could do anything that would be of service to Wilde, now that he is making his first attempt to return to literature, I should be only too glad to do it" (qtd. in *Arthur Symons: A Life* 171). In his generous review of the poem in the *Saturday Review* (12 March 1898), Symons writes: "We see a great spectacular intellect, to which, at last, pity and terror have come in their own person, and no longer as puppets in a play" – the phrase "at last" implying Wilde's expression of deeply felt emotion instead of luxuriating in his dandiacal pose (rpt. in Beckson).

Though Wilde had admired Symons's early work, he became increasingly scornful of his voluminous journalistic writings. From his exile in France, Wilde thanked Smithers for sending him books, adding: "Your generosity in not including Symons is much appreciated" (*Letters* 629). But Symons's review of *The Ballad of Reading Gaol* delighted Wilde, who told Smithers that he was "greatly pleased": "It is admirably written, and most...artistic in its mode of approval..." (*Letters* 716). Vincent O'Sullivan recalled that Wilde now "felt obliged to rectify his attitude" towards Symons after the review appeared: "[Wilde] advanced the theory that there was a syndicate which produced a mass of printed matter under the corporate name of Arthur Symons. 'I have written to my solicitor to inquire about shares in Symons Ltd.' He added: 'Naturally in mass productions of that kind you can never be certain of the quality. But I think one might risk some shares in Symons'" (67-68).

When Wilde's *Collected Edition* appeared in 1908, Symons reviewed it at length in the *Athenaeum* (16 May 1908). Wilde, he said, was a "prodigious entertainer" who created an "artificial world" of art. One of Wilde's limitations had been "his egoism, his self-absorption, his self-admiration." His "sense of beauty was uncertain, his technique came and went," but his fairy tales, such as *A House of Pomegrantates* and *The Happy Prince and Other Tales*, suggest at times "the beating of a real heart under them." Citing *De Profundis*, Symons poses the question: "Beyond this one outburst, where shall we find in Wilde's work anything noble, permanent, or vital?"

Symons contends that "Wilde was never concerned with fundamental ideas, except perhaps in

'The Soul of Man under Socialism,' which contains his best and sanest and most valuable thinking, yet is almost as entertaining as *Intentions*...the most amusing book of criticism in English." Wilde's creation of a new form of drama ends with *The Importance of Being Earnest*, "a sort of sublime farce, meaningless and delightful...the most perfect" of his society plays. Thus, Symons concludes his tribute to the "most brilliant and entertaining wit of his time" (rpt. in Beckson).

Symons had never written or spoken about Wilde's homosexuality until after 1908. In that year, he suffered a severe mental breakdown that incapacitated him for almost two years. In the years following, he wrote autobiographical essays, frequently unpublishable because of their incoherence, the result of his mental affliction, which also involved his regression to the puritanism of his youthful upbringing by his minister father and devoutly religious mother. In one of his essays – unpublished in his lifetime – he wrote of Wilde:

If ever any man of my generation indulged in unreal passions, and to excess, and with a kind of Asiatic luxury – passions, to begin with for women; these passions, utterly extinguished, passion for men and boys; these, to the end, unextinguished, these leading him to an open proclamation of his peculiar and sinister Vice, to an obvious and evident, however carefully or carelessly concealed, advertisement of his Male Prostitution; who trailed with him, or after him, a series of painted boys, and with these was as shameless as Nero or Tiberius – it was Oscar Wilde. Unreal always, no seeker after unrealities, when his tragic death fell upon him he saw, I imagine, nothing before him but the unreal ghost of his unreal Passions. (*Memoirs* 132-33)

In 1930, Symons published *A Study of Oscar Wilde*, consisting of revised or cannibalized portions of his previously published reviews and articles on Wilde. The lingering effect of Symons's mental breakdown is obvious in this study, which suffers at times from incoherence and irrelevance, though occasionally revealing flashes of brilliance. In his final pages, Symons sums up his estimate of Wilde: "...for the most part, he was a personality rather than an artist, a personality certainly more interesting than any of his work..." (88). Such a

"SYMPHONY IN YELLOW"

view, common at the time, resulted in biographical rather than critical interest in Wilde for many years.

References: Vincent O'Sullivan, *Aspects of Wilde* (1936); Karl Beckson, ed., *The Memoirs of Arthur Symons: Life and Art in the 1890s* (1975); Karl Beckson, *Arthur Symons: A Life* (1987); Karl Beckson and John M. Munro, eds., *Arthur Symons: Selected Letters, 1880-1935* (1989).

"SYMPHONY IN YELLOW"

Published: *Centennial Magazine: An Australasian Monthly Illustrated* (Sydney) 1 (5 Feb. 1889): 437; rpt. in *Poems* (1908).

In an Australian publication, Wilde referred to his inspiration for the poem, calling Botany Bay, New South Wales, "the abode...of lost souls, whither criminals are transported to wear a horrible yellow livery [actually, such transportation of criminals to Australia had ceased years before]. Even they are called 'canaries.' So I have written for them a Symphony in Yellow – they will feel the homely touch. I rhyme 'elms' with 'Thames.' It is a venial offense in comparison with theirs" (qtd. in Ellmann 207n/196n). In late 1888, Wilde informed W. E. Henley, the editor of the *Scots Observer*, that he had sent his managing editor "a wicked little symphony in yellow, suggested by seeing an omnibus (yellow omnibus) crawl across Blackfriars Bridge one foggy day about a week ago" (*Letters* 233). The managing editor rejected it.

Wilde's title, suggesting such possible sources as Gautier's "Symphony in White Major" (1835) and Whistler's paintings in the 1870s called "symphonies in white," combines the transposition of music and poetry with suggestions of synaesthesia. Unity in the poem of three quatrains is achieved by the dominant color of yellow, as in the following:

Big barges full of yellow hay
   Are moved against the shadowy wharf,
   And, like a yellow silken scarf,
The thick fog hangs along the quay.

The final lines – "And at my feet the pale green Thames / Lies like a rod of rippled jade" – anticipate the hard, clear non-discursive verse of the early 20th-century Imagists.

T

"TAEDIUM VITAE"

Published: *Poems* (1881). The Latin title means "Weariness of Life."

Since Aesthetes and Decadents characteristically posed before their audience, this sonnet may be less than sincere in its protestations, though from our knowledge of Wilde's life, the posing here may be an artistic strategy revealing more than the author consciously intended. In Wilde's essay "The Decay of Lying," the "elect" – those who have rejected conventional Victorian virtues associated with an active life of moral earnestness and social responsibility – are the "Tired Hedonists," who wear faded roses when they meet.

The speaker in the poem protests that he has suffered from numerous indignities, such as

This paltry age's gaudy livery,
To let each base hand filch my treasury
To mesh my soul within a woman's hair,
And be mere Fortune's lackeyed groom,
– I swear I love it not!

He declares that it is "better to stand aloof / Far from these slanderous fools who mock my life / Knowing me not...." The poem concludes with the preference for the "lowliest roof / Fit for the meanest hind [a rustic] to sojourn in, / Than to go back to that coarse cave of strife / Where my white soul first kissed the mouth of sin."

"THE TEACHER OF WISDOM": *See* "POEMS IN PROSE"

TELENY; OR, THE REVERSE OF THE MEDAL

Published: Anonymously in 1893 by Leonard Smithers in a two-volume limited edition of 200 copies under the imprint "Cosmopoli" with an additional subtitle, *A Physiological Romance of To-Day*. The author or authors remain unknown, though Wilde is alleged to have had a hand in the writing or editing of the MS.

Peter Webb notes that *Teleny*

distinguishes itself from most Victorian pornography because it is not written to be enjoyed at the expense of women. The partners in the scenes of homosexual love are equals, enjoying a mutually pleasurable activity. There is no rape or flagellation, no partnership of dominance and submission. And the sexual scenes involve not merely activities but emotions and feelings. These scenes go into much more detail about the effects of sexual arousal than is usual, and show an attempt to escape from the usual hackneyed phraseology.

Webb contends that we can be "reasonably sure that Oscar Wilde edited and inspired *Teleny*, though whether he wrote any of it is less certain" (109-11). Webb does not clarify what he means by "reasonably sure." The only "evidence" that exists to support such a view is the preface to a French translation published in Paris in 1934 (over 40 years after the novel's first appearance). In the preface, Charles Hirsch, a French bookseller who had opened a bookshop in Coventry Street around 1889, recalls that Wilde would "order certain licentious works...euphemistically described as 'socratic'...." Certain obscene books from Amsterdam were so offensive that Wilde returned them to Hirsch.

In late 1890, Wilde allegedly brought a sealed package containing the MS. of *Teleny* to the bookshop and instructed Hirsch to give it to a friend who, showing Wilde's card, would ask for it. This friend subsequently took it with him, then returned it to Hirsch with instructions to pass it on to another friend. After three such transmissions, the package was returned unwrapped but tied with a ribbon. Unable to resist reading the MS., Hirsch noted that it was obviously written and revised by different hands, but he was convinced that Wilde had a hand in some of the revisions.

In the first published version, the setting of the novel was moved from London to Paris – Smithers allegedly told Hirsch when they met at the Paris Exhibition in 1900 – in order to spare his subscribers any distress. How Smithers obtained the MS. for publication remains a mystery.

In view of Wilde's fame as a writer and of the stormy reaction to the evident homoeroticism in the first version of *The Picture of Dorian Gray* when it appeared in 1890, it seems odd that he would have become so involved in the private circulation of pornography. Moreover, it seems unlikely (though not impossible) that such a secret could have been maintained after Wilde's death by those who had called for the MS. In 1906, Robert Ross, Wilde's closest friend and later literary executor, wrote to the journalist Clement Shorter (1857–1926) concerning the openly homosexual story "The Priest and the Acolyte" (which had been associated with Wilde at his trial but which had been written by John Bloxam, editor of the *Chameleon*, in which it appeared): "Much of Wilde's work is rather unwholesome in sentiment. Much of his prose is Asiatic and not Attic, as Arnold would have said. But whatever his faults may have been, he never wrote a deliberately obscene work, and if he had done so, even in his most foolish moments, he would never have allowed its publication" (Ross 119).

Most recent Wilde scholars are not convinced of the reliability of Hirsch's story, which may have been concocted to stimulate sales of *Teleny* (for many years after Wilde's death, spurious works attributed to Wilde continued to attract attention). Ellmann mentions neither the novel nor the bookseller in his biography, nor is either mentioned in any of Wilde's extant letters. Finally, none of the many memoirs of Wilde written by friends after his death or their private correspondence mentions the novel or the bookseller. Yet the alleged connection between Wilde and *Teleny* persists.

References: H. Montgomery Hyde, *A History of Pornography* (1965); Peter Webb, "Victorian Erotica," *The Sexual Dimension in Literature*, ed. Alan Bold (1982); Peter Mendes, "Hirsch's Memoirs of Oscar Wilde and Smithers," *Clandestine Erotic Fiction in English, 1800-1930: A Bibliographical Study,* Appendix D (1993).

TERRY, ELLEN (1847-1928)

The actress who became Henry Irving's leading lady at the Lyceum Theatre in 1878 continued her partnership with Irving until 1902.

When Wilde met Terry remains uncertain, but in June 1879, he was at the Lyceum to see Terry perform as the Queen in W. G. Wills's *Charles I,* resulting in his sonnet titled "Queen Henrietta Maria," which he published in the *World* (16 July 1879). Depicting the Queen in Act III in her "lone tent, waiting for victory," Wilde describes her "eyes marred by the mists of pain, / Like some wan lily overdrenched with rain." In her memoirs,

Terry writes of this moment in the play: "Some people thought me at my best in the camp scene in the third act, where I had even fewer lines to speak. I was proud of it myself when I found that it had inspired Oscar Wilde to write me this lovely sonnet.... That phrase 'wan lily' represented perfectly what I had tried to convey.... I hope that I thanked Oscar enough at the time" (140).

In November 1879, Wilde accompanied Ruskin to the Lyceum to see *The Merchant of Venice* with Terry as Portia, the occasion for another sonnet in her honor, titled "Portia," which also appeared in the *World* (14 Jan. 1880). This poem acclaims Terry's stage appearance – 'No woman Veronese looked upon / Was half so fair as thou whom I behold" – and Portia's triumph over Shylock's cruelty – "O Portia, take my heart! it is thy due." In a celebration of the 100th performance of the play on 14 February 1880, Wilde was invited to the Lyceum banquet.

When Wilde completed his melodrama *Vera; or, The Nihilists* in that year, he sent the script bound in dark red leather with her name stamped in gold on the binding with an inscription: "From her sincere admirer the Author" (qtd. in *Letters* 70n2). His accompanying letter modestly states: "Perhaps some day I shall be fortunate enough to write something worthy of your playing" (*Letters* 70), a hope never fulfilled.

In another instance of Wilde's devotion to Terry, Wilde wrote to her (addressing her as "Nellie") on 3 January 1881, the opening of Tennyson's verse play *The Cup* at the Lyceum with Terry and Irving performing the leads: "I write to wish you *every success* tonight. *You* could not do anything that would not be a mirror of the highest artistic beauty, and I am so glad to hear you have an opportunity of showing us that passionate power which *I know you have.* You will have a great success – perhaps one of your greatest" (*Letters* 74). For Terry, Wilde wrote a sonnet titled "Camma" (the leading role in the play, that of a priestess of Artemis), which was published in *Poems* (1881).

Apparently, the role did her little justice, for Wilde yearns to behold Terry as Cleopatra: "...methinks I'd rather see thee play / That serpent of old Nile..." (the phrase from *Antony and Cleopatra*, I.v.25). In the final extant letter to Terry, probably written in July 1887 on the occasion of her performance in the *The Merchant of Venice* at the Lyceum, Wilde writes appreciatively of her "love," which is "more wonderful even than a crystal caught in bent reeds of gold...." Looking forward with his wife, Constance, to seeing the "Goddess" perform, Wilde adds: " – and oh! dear Ellen, look sometimes in our direction, and let us come and pay due homage afterwards to the gracious lady and great artist we adore" (*More Letters* 68).

In her memoirs, Terry makes no mention of the Wilde debacle in 1895 or of any contact with Wilde that she may have had during or after that event. She does say that the "most remarkable men I have ever known were Whistler and Wilde.... There was something about both of them more instantaneously individual and audacious than it is possible to describe" (231). According to one of Terry's biographers, an indiscreet remark by Wilde to the actress Aimée Lowther in Terry's presence revealed the open secret of Wilde's homosexuality. To Lowther, Wilde reportedly said, "Aimée, if you were a boy I could adore you." To which Terry innocently responded: "Oscar, you really didn't mean it?" (qtd. in Steen 206). A silence ensued; later, Henry Irving explained Wilde's remark.

After Wilde's release from prison, Terry and Lowther came upon Wilde in Paris looking into a pastry shop window and biting his fingers. When they invited him to a meal, he talked quite splendidly. This was their last sight of Wilde (Steen 206n).

References: Ellen Terry, *Memoirs* (1908; 2nd ed. 1933); Marguerite Steen, *A Pride of Terrys: Family Saga* (1962); Roger Manvell, *Ellen Terry* (1968); Nina Auerbach, *Ellen Terry: Player in Her Time* (1987).

THEATER AUDIENCES IN THE 1890s

The audiences that Wilde wrote for were not, as George Rowell writes, coteries of "courtiers and courtesans," characteristic of theater audiences in earlier periods, such as the Restoration. By the 1890s, two of the most fashionable London theaters that staged Wilde's society plays – St. James's (*Lady Windermere's Fan* and *The Importance of Being Earnest*) and the Theatre Royal, Haymarket (*A Woman of No Importance* and *An Ideal Husband*) – still attracted aristocracy but also a more diversified audience. W. Macqueen-Pope, the historian of the St. James's, the "theatre of distinction," writes that under the direction of George Alexander, the actor-manager, the St. James's

became an aristocrat among theatres, and reflected in its heyday – the late Victorian and Edwardian epoch – all that was best in the life of this country. Elegant and rich people filled its stalls, its dress circle and its two boxes. People of substance but less social standing booked for the upper circle, and the rest of the playgoers made for the pit and the gallery. (16)

Hesketh Pearson, who had known many theatrical figures at the turn of the century, wrote in tribute to Alexander:

For the most part, his theatre mirrored to absolute perfection the people who patronized its stalls. He knew, none better, that the stalls enjoyed the gilded pill of romance about themselves, and that the gallery loved to see the stalls swallow it.... The light parts had to be charmingly playful, the serious parts had to be pleasantly sentimental, and the plot had to savour of scandal without being in any way truthfully objectionable....The working classes were seldom, if ever, introduced. Significant social problems were carefully avoided. It was the drama of the genteel – the Apotheosis of the Butterfly. (80-81)

Hence, Wilde's plays, tending towards sentimentality and offering social criticism clothed in the wit of dandies, succeeded brilliantly at the St. James's. Pearson remarks that Alexander "adhered to a principle": "correct riskiness," which accurately describes Wilde's dramatic writing (80). Those "good women" – "pillars of female respectability" – in the audience whether at the St. James's or the Theatre Royal, Haymarket, "confirmed the codes with which a broad, property-oriented section of the audience would identify.... Thus Wilde was able to satisfy the requirements of his audiences on two levels":

...the smart set enjoyed the elegance and luxury, as did the snobbish middle classes who were always partial to the glamour of great names, while characters such as Lord Illingworth [in *A Woman of No Importance*] confirmed their prejudices about the decadence of the aristocracy and about their own moral superiority. At the same time the aristocratic Establishment enjoyed the dismissal of norms adhered to by the middle class, which towards the end of the nineteenth century was bidding to take the place of the nobility. (Kohl 239)

In a history of the Haymarket under the direction of the actor-manager Herbert Beerbohm Tree, Macqueen-Pope writes that this "theatre of perfection"

became the smartest theatre in London in every sense of the word. It was not only the so-called "Smart Set" who went there, for the theatre became the centre of the social world of London, in so far as any theatre can, and remained so until Tree opened His Majesty's Theatre [in 1897]. His audiences were as brilliant as his plays.... Great people came to see a great man in a great production. The theatre was an aristocrat, and the audiences of the Haymarket, under Tree, were aristocratic playgoers from the gallery downwards. It is something which will never again be seen. (336)

In *A Woman of No Importance* at the Haymarket, such an attack as Hester Worsley's on the "rich people in England" rarely touches, in Wilde's society plays, on the foundations of English society: rather, only the individual behavior of the rich is criticized. Wilde reportedly said to Tree regarding the audience's preferences: "People love a wicked aristocrat who seduces a virtuous maiden, and they love a virtuous maiden for being seduced by a wicked aristocrat. I have given them what they like, so that they may learn to appreciate what I like to give them" (qtd. in Pearson, *Beerbohm Tree* 67).

Bernard Shaw, on the other hand, did not give them what they liked; hence, his problem plays did not find receptive audiences in the 1890s because he challenged them too directly. In the preface of his *Plays Unpleasant* (1898), which included the unproduced *Mrs. Warren's Profession*, Shaw remarked that "their dramatic power is used to force the spectator to face unpleasant facts" – in short, social problems that the audience had sought to escape in the theater. Only three of his plays were produced in the 1890s (*Widowers' Houses*, *Arms and the Man*, and *You Never Can Tell*) for a grand

total of only 78 performances. Of Wilde's four society plays, *Lady Windermere's Fan* alone had 197 performances.

References: Hesketh Pearson, *Modern Men and Mummers* (1921); W. Macqueen-Pope, *Haymarket: Theatre of Perfection* (1948); Hesketh Pearson, *Beerbohm Tree: His Life and Laughter* (1956); W. Macqueen-Pope, *St. James's: Theatre of Distinction* (1958); George Rowell, *The Victorian Theatre, 1792-1914*, 2nd ed. (1978).

"THE THEATRE AT ARGOS"

Published: *Pilot* (Boston) 40 (21 July 1877): 4; rpt. (with several textual emendations) in Bobby Fong, "Oscar Wilde: Five Fugitive Poems," *ELT* 22:1 (1979): 8-9. The *Pilot*, a weekly newspaper with Irish nationalist sympathies, had published Lady Wilde's contributions, and in the late 1880s and early 1890s, when the paper was known as the *Boston Pilot*, W. B. Yeats became a contributor. Robert Ross was apparently unaware of "The Theatre at Argos," for it does not appear in the *Collected Edition* (1908).

Written at Argos, when Wilde visited Greece in March-April 1877, the poem laments the death of Classical tragedy in the open-air theater where now "Nettles and poppy mar each rock-hewn seat" and where "No poet crowned with olive deathlessly / Chants his glad song, nor clamorous Tragedy / Startles the air...." Though the glory that was Greece has declined – "A nation's shipwreck on the rocks of Time" – it is not the season to mourn for such days of old: "For now the peoples clamor at our gate, / The world is full of plague and sin and crime, / And God Himself is half-dethroned for Gold!" Such undergraduate effusions by Wilde reveal his inclination to write rhetorical, discursive poetry filled with social and political concerns, later to be omitted in poems concerned with non-discursive, subjective expression.

Manuscript: The Clark Library has Mason's personal interleaved copy of his bibliography, which contains his transcription, opposite p. 177, of a MS. that remains unlocated.

"THEOCRITUS. A VILLANELLE"

Published: *Poems* (1881).

Probably born in Sicily, Theocritus was a Hellenistic Greek poet who lived in the early 3rd century BC. His extant work, usually referred to as

Idylls, originated many conventions of pastoral verse, traditionally involving figures drawn from mythology as well as shepherds and shepherdesses, who, relieved of the burdens of labor in a setting reminiscent of a mythical earthly paradise, indulge in such trivial pursuits as song contests and one another. These idealized fantasies have endured for centuries. For a brief discussion of the form of the villanelle, which derived its name from *villa*, a country house or farm, see "Pan. Double Villanelle."

Wilde's lyric of 38 lines is addressed to Theocritus – "O singer of Persephone" – the goddess of the Greek Underworld with the refrain alluding to the poet's native country and with allusions to various mythological figures. The concluding quatrain suggests that Theocritus has too often focused on the darker regions of the earth:

> Slim Lacon keeps a goat for thee,
> For thee the jocund shepherds wait;
> O Singer of Persephone!
> Dost thou remember Sicily?

Manuscript: The Clark Library has an untitled MS., an early draft of various lines written around 1878, when Wilde's immersion in Greek culture was extensive.

"THEORETIKOS"

Published: *Poems* (1881). The Greek title means "The Contemplative." (See "Amor Intellectualis" for its relationship with this poem.)

This sonnet reiterates a theme in several of Wilde's poems: England's glory has declined (see, for example, "To Milton" and "Quantum Mutata"), as evidenced in its policy of non-interference during the Balkan crisis of 1875-78, when Turkey was suppressing Christian rebellions. Thus, it opens with the now familiar lament: "This mighty empire hath but feet of clay: / Of all its ancient chivalry and might / Our little island is forsaken quite." Because "Wisdom and reverence are sold at mart" and "rude people rage with ignorant cries / Against an heritage of centuries," the speaker retreats to his "dreams of Art / And loftiest culture" where he will stand apart "Neither for God, nor for his enemies."

Manuscripts: The Clark Library has an untitled MS. For two early MS. versions, see Mason 292-93.

"A THOUGHT READER'S NOVEL"

Published: *PMG*, 5 June 1889, 2; rpt. in *Reviews* (1908). An unsigned review of Stuart Cumberland's *The Vasty Deep: A Strange Story of To-Day* (1889). "Stuart Cumberland" was the pseudonym of Charles Garner.

Wilde remarks that there is "a great deal to be said in favour of reading a novel backwards. The last page is, as a rule, the most interesting, and when one begins with the catastrophe or the *dénouement* one feels on pleasant terms of equality with the author." It is, says Wilde, like going behind the scenes in a theater: "One is no longer taken in, and hair-breadth escapes of the hero and the wild agonies of the heroine leave one absolutely unmoved." The final page of Cumberland's novel is "certainly thrilling", and makes us curious to know more about Dr. Josiah Brown, the eminent medium.

Wilde sets a scene from the book: "...a padded room in a madhouse in the United States. A gibbering lunatic [Dr. Brown, "haunted by the creations of his fancy"] discovered dashing wildly about the chamber, as if in the act of chasing invisible forms.... The lunatic makes a dash at the retreating form of his visitors.... A week later the lifeless body of Brown, the medium, is found suspended from the gas bracket in his cell." Impressed (but not without a touch of facetiousness), Wilde exclaims: "How clearly one sees it all! How forcible and direct the style is!" Concluding with an allusion to Dr. Brown's end by suicide in a madhouse, Wilde remarks: "Had we not known what was in store for him, we could hardly have got through the book.... [Cumberland's] chief fault is a tendency to low comedy, but some people like low comedy in fiction."

"THREE NEW POETS"

Published: *PMG*, 12 July 1889, 3; rpt. in *Reviews* (1908). An unsigned review of W. B. Yeats's *The Wanderings of Oisin and Other Poems*; Caroline Fitz Gerald's *Venetia Victrix*; and Richard Le Gallienne's *Volumes in Folio* – all published in 1889. In March, Wilde had reviewed Yeats's volume in *Woman's World* (see "Some Literary Notes") and, in the same magazine in May, Fitz Gerald's volume (see "Some Literary Notes").

Wilde's review of Yeats's early work reveals his recognition of the young poet's talent:

Books of poetry by young writers are usually promissory notes that are never met. Now and then, however, one comes across a volume that is so far above the average that one can hardly resist the fascinating temptation of recklessly prophesying a fine future for its author. Such a book Mr. Yeats's *Wanderings of Oisin* certainly is. Here we find nobility of treatment and nobility of subject matter, delicacy of poetic instinct, and richness of imaginative resource.

Aside from some "strange crudities and irritating conceits," Yeats "has at least something of that largeness of vision that belongs to the epical temper. He does not rob of their stature the great heroes of Celtic mythology. He is very naive, and very primitive, and speaks of his giants with the awe of a child." Quoting from the section of the poem where Oisin returns from the Island of Forgetfulness, Wilde concludes that "it is impossible not to feel in these stanzas the presence of the true poetic spirit."

Caroline Fitz Gerald's *Venetia Victrix*, "in many respects a fine poem," reveals her capacity, says Wilde, for "vigour, intellectual strength, and courage." After a brief account of the plot and a lengthy quotation from the poem, Wilde ends his notice of the volume by alluding to another poem with a somewhat less than enthusiastic comment: "Miss Fitz Gerald's volume is certainly worth reading."

Wilde then turns to Richard Le Gallienne's *Volumes in Folio* (Wilde had known Le Gallienne since 1887). The volume, as the review begins, is "full of dainty verse and delicate fancy." At the present time, says Wilde, Le Gallienne's "muse seems to devote herself entirely to the worship of books." He is "steeped in literary traditions, making Keats his model, and seeking to reproduce something of Keats's richness and affluence of imagery." Wilde has "no doubt that [Le Gallienne] will pass on to larger themes, and nobler subject-matter...."

"θPHNΩIΔIA" ("THRENODIA")

Published: *Kottabos* 2 (Michaelmas term 1876): 298-300; rpt. in *Poems* (1908). Below the title of this translation from Euripides' tragedy *Hecuba* (ca. 424 BC), 444-83, Wilde appended the follow-

ing: "Song sung by captive women of Troy on the sea beach at Aulis, while the Achaeans were there stormbound through the wrath of dishonoured Achilles, and waiting for a fair wind to bring them home." The Greek title means "Lamentation."

The translation of the Greek chorus is divided into strophes and antistrophes (indicating the movements forward and backward of the chorus in its formal dance as it sang each stanza, or strophe).

Manuscript: A MS. fragment, containing lines 52-67, is printed in Mason 94.

TITE STREET HOUSE

When Wilde married Constance Lloyd in May 1884, he leased the house in Chelsea (then No. 16, now No. 33) and engaged Edward Godwin (see entry) to redesign the interior. H. Montgomery Hyde has published Godwin's extensive descriptions of the plans for the various rooms, here modified and paraphrased:

Ground floor.

Dining room: All woodwork in white enamel; the walls in white and grey enamel "to the height of 5'-6," the remainder of walls and ceilings finished in lime-white with slight addition of black "to give the white a greyish tone."

Library: Walls to height of 5'-6" painted in dark blue. Upper portion of walls and ceiling in pale gold. Woodwork golden brown (russet). [Ellmann (257/242) writes of the library: "Over the doorway and along the sides of the room ran a heavy beam and an architrave bearing, in gilt, red, and blue, an inscription from Shelley." He then quotes the following:

Spirit of Beauty! Tarry still awhile,
They are not dead, thine ancient votaries,
Some few there are to whom thy radiant smile
Is better than a thousand victories.

"Spirit of Beauty" is from Shelley's "Hymn to Intellectual Beauty," but the entire passage is from Wilde's "The Garden of Eros," lines 103-06.]

Staircase: Walls and ceilings yellow. Woodwork white and "wall band to step with stair at intervals of 4 or 5 steps."

First floor.

Drawing room front: Woodwork ivory,

white walls mixed with "flesh pink from skirting to cornice," which is to be "gilded dull flat lemon colour gold and also the ceiling margin to Japanese leather which latter will be provided by Mr. Wilde...."

Drawing room back: Pale green ceiling and cornice walls in darker green. Fireplace and woodwork in brown pink. [Ellmann (257/242) writes that "on either side of the fireplace, filling the room's corners, were two three-cornered divans, very low, with cushions. On the mantelpiece was a small green bronze figure of Narcissus.... A portrait of Wilde by Harper Pennington" – now in the Clark Library – "was hung on one wall, and in a corner there was also the bust of Augustus Caesar which Wilde had received after the Newdigate Prize.... The ceiling originally had two gold dragons at opposite corners painted by Whistler.... Hung on the green walls were small white-framed lithographs by Whistler and Mortimer Menpes, a drawing by Beardsley (later), and the framed manuscript of Keats's sonnet given to Wilde in America."]

Second floor.

Bedroom front: Pink walls, woodwork ceiling and two feet of top of walls under cornice in apple green. [Constance's bedroom.]

Bedroom back: Dark blue walls; two feet of upper part cornice and ceiling pale blue with greenish tone added. [Originally Wilde's bedroom, adorned with a plaster cast of Hermes of Olympia, later the children's bedroom.]

Third floor.

"Mr. Oscar Wilde's room": "Greyish-pink-red ceiling & upper part of walls to depth of 4' 0" lower part of walls red russet brown." [Originally Wilde's study.]

Third floor front: White woodwork and walls with yellow ceilings. (175)

In addition to these specifications, Godwin's drawings include, Hyde writes, "an elaborate overmantel into which was set a bronze bas-relief by John Donoghue [1853-1903], an American sculptor, depicting a scene suggested by Wilde's poem 'Requiescat'" (175). Godwin also provided sketches showing how Whistler's etchings and Burne-Jones's drawings would be arranged along the walls "so as to form a deep frieze against a background of dull gold."

Godwin also designed some of the furniture. For the dining room, for example, he provided a suite in white, the chairs in various Grecian styles, and a strip of shelving round the walls for tea and buffet suppers. "By this arrangement," as one visitor to the house remarked, "the centre of the room was an open space instead of being absorbed by the customary huge table laden with refreshment, and gave an impression of greater size and lightness to the room" (qtd. in Hyde 175). Wilde was quite pleased with Godwin's "beautiful designs of the furniture. Each chair is a sonnet in ivory, and the table is a masterpiece in pearl" (*Letters* 172). For Wilde, Godwin remained the "builder of the 'house beautiful' and the creator of the only home that Wilde was ever able to call his own" (Hyde 176).

Reference: H. Montgomery Hyde, "Oscar Wilde and His Architect," *Architectural Review* (March 1951).

"TO M. B. J."

Published: Unpublished in Wilde's lifetime, this poem of three quatrains appeared in Bobby Fong, "Oscar Wilde: Five Fugitive Poems," *ELT* 22:1 (1979): 11.

Sometime in the 1880s, Wilde wrote this poem in a copy of his *Poems* (1881) as a gift for Margaret Burne-Jones (1866-1954), the daughter of the Pre-Raphaelite painter Edward Burne-Jones (see his entry). In September 1888, she married John W. MacKail (1859-1945), later professor of poetry at Oxford and biographer of William Morris.

The simple verses of the poem are obviously designed for a young person, as the first of three stanzas suggests:

Green are the summer meadows,
  Blue is the summer sky,
And the swallows like flickering shadows
  Over the tall corn fly.

In the final stanza the "morning dewdrops glisten" and the "lark is on the wing" (suitable clichés for a young mind), the poem ending: "Ah! how can you stop and listen / To what I have to sing."

Manuscripts: A facsimile of the MS. appeared in the Parke-Bernet Galleries catalogue for the Charles C. Auchincloss sale of 29-30 Nov. 1961,

"TO M. B. J."

p. 111. In 1882, while in New York during his lecture tour, Wilde presented Mrs. John Bigelow, wife of the former editor of the *Evening Post* and Minister to France, with an untitled autograph MS. of the poem, now in the Eisenhower Library at Johns Hopkins University.

"TO MILTON"

Published: *Poems* (1881).

The theme of this sonnet – England's decline – is echoed in "Sonnet on the Massacre of the Christians in Bulgaria" and in "Quantum Mutata," all of them expressing Wilde's response to the Balkan crisis between 1875 and 1878. Modeled after Wordsworth's "London, 1802" (1807) – "Milton! Thou should'st be living at this hour: / England hath need of thee" – Wilde's sonnet borrows the dramatic opening and image of England's glory having fallen into decay:

Milton! I think thy spirit hath passed away
From these white cliffs and high-embattled
    towers;
This gorgeous fiery-coloured world of ours
Seems fallen into ashes dull and grey...

England is ruled, the speaker laments, "By ignorant demagogues... / Who love her not," and her past glory "When Cromwell spake the word Democracy" is no more. (Wilde's association of Cromwell with democracy is perhaps odd, for many have regarded him a virtual dictator despite his championing of religious toleration and his contributions to the development of constitutional government.)

Manuscript: The Clark Library has an untitled rough draft, and the Hyde Collection has a MS. draft titled "Milton."

"TO MY WIFE: WITH A COPY OF MY POEMS"

Published: Gleeson White, ed., *Book-Song: An Anthology of Poems of Books and Bookmen from Modern Authors* (London: Elliot Stock, 1893), 156; rpt. in *Poems* (1908).

This lyric of three quatrains, written for Constance Wilde's autograph book, which guests of the Wildes were asked to sign, contains the expected sentiment of a poet presenting his poems to his wife:

For if of these fallen petals
    One to you seem fair,
Love will waft it till it settles
    On your hair.

Manuscript: A facsimile of the signed, untitled poem from Constance Wilde's autograph album appeared in Sotheby's sale catalogue, titled *English Literature and History* and dated 15 December 1987. The album is now owned by Frederick R. Koch.

"TO V. F."

Written: Wilde wrote the poem in a presentation copy of *Poems* (1881) for Mary Lamb Singleton (1843-1905), the author of poems, essays, and novels under the pseudonym of "Violet Fane." When Wilde became editor of *Woman's World*, he published two of her poems ("Hazely Heath" in Nov. 1887 and "The Mer-Baby" in Aug. 1888) and an article ("Records of a Fallen Dynasty" in May 1888).

Unpublished in Wilde's lifetime, this poem, consisting of a single quatrain, echoes Violet's name in the fourth line:

Through many loveless songless days
We have to seek the golden shrine,
But Venus taught you how to twine
Love's violets with Apollo's bays.

Manuscript: The copy of *Poems* (1881), with the autograph inscription, is in the Mark Samuels Lasner Collection.

"THE TOMB OF KEATS"

Published: *Irish Monthly* 5 (July 1877): 476-78; rpt. in *Miscellanies* (1908).

In his essay, Wilde initially describes the "first object that meets the eye" when one enters Rome from the Via Ostiensis by the Porta San Paolo: "...a marble pyramid which stands close at hand on the left...[a] gaunt, wedge-shaped pyramid standing here in this Italian city, unshattered amid the ruins and wrecks of time, looking older than the Eternal City itself...the tomb of one Caius Cestius, a Roman gentleman of small note, who died about 30 B.C." This pyramid, which houses one known only through his sepulchre, "will be ever dear to the eyes of all English-speaking people, because at evening its shadows fall on the tomb of one who walks with Spenser, and Shakespeare, and Byron, and Shelley, and Elizabeth Barrett Browning in the procession of the sweet singers of England. For at its foot there is a green, sunny slope, known as the Old Protestant Cemetery...."

Keats, buried there in "a common-looking grave" (rather than a "tomb," as Wilde's title implies), is only a "little distance off" from where "some tall gaunt cypresses rise, like burnt-out funeral torches, to mark the spot where Shelley's heart (that 'heart of hearts'!) lies in the earth; and, above all, the soil on which we tread is very Rome!" For Wilde's celebration of Keats's relation to the Religion of Art, complete with images of priest and martyred saint, central icons in late 19th-century Aestheticism, see "The Grave of Keats."

THE TOMB OF WILDE

On 1 December 1908, in the Ritz Hotel, over 200 dinner guests (including Edmund Gosse, Charles Ricketts, Robert Sherard, Frank Harris, William Archer, William Rothenstein, Max Beer-bohm, Roger Fry, Somerset Maugham, and H. G. Wells) celebrated the publication of the *Collected Edition of the Works of Oscar Wilde*, edited by Robert Ross, and acknowledged Ross's services to the Oscar Wilde Estate. In his speech, Ross announced that an unnamed donor had provided £2,000 to enable him to move Wilde's remains from Bagneux cemetery to Père Lachaise cemetery in Paris and, on Rothenstein's recommendation, to commission Jacob Epstein (1880-1959) to design the tomb over Wilde's grave site. The donor was one of Wilde's friends, Mrs. Helen Carew (d. 1947), to whom Ross dedicated Vol. 13, *Reviews*, of the *Collected Edition*:

The apparently endless difficulties against which I have contended, and am contending, in the management of Oscar Wilde's literary and dramatic property have brought me many valued friends; but only one friendship which seemed as endless; one friend's kindness which seemed to annul the disappointments of eight years.

During 1909-10 Epstein sketched possibilities for the tomb and completed a near life-size nude clay statue of Narcissus, with which Epstein had "tried to accommodate the wishes of Wilde's

admirers who wanted a classical monument," but, dissatisfied, he destroyed it (Silber, *The Sculpture of Epstein* 22). Epstein's long fascination with Assyrian and Egyptian art in the Louvre and in the British Museum, in addition to the possible influence of Wilde's *The Sphinx*, with its lustful figure, the Egyptian god Ammon, undoubtedly determined Epstein's final design for the tomb.

He went directly to Derbeyshire, purchased an immense block of stone of some 20 tons, transported it to his London studio, and began work on it immediately. Nine months later, the tomb was completed. In his autobiography, he wrote: "I carved a flying demon-angel across the face, a symbolic work of combined simplicity and ornate decoration, and no doubt influenced by antique carving" (51). Carved on the back of the tomb are the last four lines from Part IV of *The Ballad of Reading Gaol*, designed by Eric Gill (1882-1940), who also assisted Epstein in carving the wings of the figure in flight:

And alien tears will fill for him
    Pity's long-broken urn,
For his mourners will be outcast men,
    And outcasts always mourn.

Epstein opened his studio in Cheyne Walk to the public and the press in order to permit critics to view the monument for a month before its move to Paris. *The Evening Standard and St. James's Gazette* (3 June 1912) began its review:

Seldom in this country are we permitted to see such a dignified piece of monumental sculpture as Mr. Jacob Epstein has carved for the tomb of Oscar Wilde.... It is not executed but conceived in stone.... The face [of the figure in flight], remotely suggesting that of the dead writer, is a little upturned and blind to external light, the inner driving power being symbolised by little figures of Intellectual Pride and Luxury above the head. Fame, with her trumpet, is carved upon the forehead.

In the *Pall Mall Gazette* (6 June), the writer stresses Epstein's unconventional "notions of mortuary memorials":

...Mr. Epstein is not only a real sculptor – a carver, not a modeller – but he is also a Sculptor in Revolt, who is in deadly conflict with the ideas of current sculpture.... As the painter's idea lies, not in literary suggestion or imitation, but in the perfection of the paint, so the carver's idea must be born in the marble and spring directly from it. It is obvious that Mr. Epstein did not propose to be either a literary or a moral critic of Oscar Wilde.... The hand of the sculptor has groped in the block of marble impelled to the expression, without words or definitions, of the haunting tragedy of a great career.... "Go and see it at once" is my urgent advice to all who are interested in sculpture, and think of it...on a hill-top in Père Lachaise, dominating all those tawdry memorials of the easily-forgotten dead.

On 31 July 1912, Lytton Strachey organized a petition on behalf of Epstein to exempt him from the estimated £120 in customs duties in sending the tomb to France: "The monument is a serious and interesting work of art, destined for public position in Paris. It is dedicated to the memory of the famous English poet and author, Oscar Wilde.... The aesthetic merit of this work by Mr. Epstein and the public interest it has awakened lead us to hope that the artist could be freed from this onerous charge." The signatures included those of Bernard Shaw, H. G. Wells, John Lavery, and Robert Ross (Epstein, *Autobiography* 53-54). The petition failed.

When the tomb was in place at Père Lachaise in early September, Epstein arrived one morning to complete the carving of the head and discovered the entire sculpture covered with a tarpaulin. According to Epstein in a letter to a friend, the Préfet de la Seine and the keeper of the École des Beaux Arts had been "called in and decided that I must either castrate [the genitals that had been covered with plaster] or fig leaf the monument! ...I feel quite sick over it but ridicule will do the work I think. Imagine a bronze fig-leaf on the Oscar Wilde Tomb.... This is a mad world" (qtd. in Pennington 49). During the three weeks that Gill's assistant was carving the inscription on the back of the tomb, Epstein returned and attempted to remove the tarpaulin, but a gendarme standing beside it informed him that the tomb was "banned" and that he would not be permitted to work on it. Returning several days later with a group of French artists, Epstein again attempted to remove the covering but without success.

In the French press, protests (and ridicule, as Epstein had hoped) appeared: In the *Comoedia* (9 Oct. 1912), Georges Bazile voiced the opinion that, when Wilde died, he had "the right to believe that he was forever rid of all the petty annoyances he had suffered at the hands of the enemies of genius":

It became evident that Oscar Wilde was never to know true peace, even beyond the grave. He had not lain at rest more than a few years beneath the flower-decked tombstone at Bagneux when he was removed to be tossed under a slab of stone surrounded by chains at the cemetary of Père Lachaise. He was about to break these chains at last and take wing – in a halo of glory – no longer into the infinite but into immortality, Officialdom was on the watch...the prisoner of Reading Gaol is to-day the prisoner of M. le Conservateur du Père Lachaise.

Because of "a narrow-minded official, and of the obscene laughs and remarks of some gross-minded keepers and stone-masons," M. le Conservateur "would like the creator of *Salome* to have his fig-leaf." Instead, Bazile writes, Epstein discovered "a huge mass of plaster – a good kilo of it – covering up a certain part of the statue.... No doubt on that particular day M. le Conservateur did not have his fig-leaf handy.... Does M. le Conservateur mean to say he has never seen a man in his nakedness? Let him go the Luxembourg – the Museum as well as the Gardens – and his eyes will soon be edified."

On 21 March 1913, Bazile reported in *Comoedia* that a petition had been proposed "by workers with the pen, brush and chisel as a protest against the outrage on the liberty of Art contained in the decision of the Préfet de la Seine and of his Comité d'Esthétique regarding the Oscar Wilde monument." Bazile also included a letter to him from Epstein, who was en route to South Africa: "After having seen your courageous attack in *Comoedia*, I can leave this hemisphere with an easier mind. I leave it to Frenchmen like yourself to defend my work and the repose of the great soul who rests beneath it."

Epstein remarks that Ross, who had seen the work in progress and who approved of it, asked him to "modify" the allegedly "indecent" sexual organs of the flying demon-angel to pacify the authorities, but the sculptor refused. Ross then proceeded, without Epstein's approval or knowledge, to cover the body part with a fig-leaf-like bronze plaque, but, writes Epstein, "a band of artists and poets subsequently made a raid upon the monument and removed the plaque... (54). The "band" from the Latin Quarter, according to a news item in the *Times* (5 Nov. 1913), was led by the eccentric occultist and poet Aleister Crowley (1875-1947), who unveiled the monument in defiance of the Préfet of the Seine in the interest of "freedom of art." In a letter to the *Times* (8 Nov.), Epstein preferred the tarpaulin to remain until the "alleged improvements made against my express desires have been removed. I do not consider any unofficial unveiling a compliment to me, though no doubt a jolly occasion for Mr. Crowley and his companions." The monument, Epstein writes in his autobiography, "remained covered by the tarpaulin until the outbreak of the war" in August 1914 when it was removed without an official explanation (54).

References: *Epstein: An Autobiography* (1940; 2nd ed. 1955); Michael Pennington, *An Angel for a Martyr: Jacob Epstein's Tomb for Oscar Wilde* (1987); Evelyn Silber, *The Sculpture of Epstein* (1986); Evelyn Silber, "The Tomb of Oscar Wilde," *Jacob Epstein: Sculpture and Drawings* (1989).

TREE, HERBERT BEERBOHM (1853-1917)

The actor-manager and half-brother of Max Beerbohm, Tree acted in lampoons of Wilde in the early 1880s and in one in 1894 as characters who resembled the Aesthete: James Albery's *Where's the Cat?*, Francis Cowley's *The Colonel*, and Robert W. Buchanan's *The Charlatan* (see Parodies and Satires of Wilde). When he met Wilde in the mid-1880s, he instantly admired his genius. In the autumn of 1891, Wilde sent a script of *Salomé* to Tree, who responded: "I think, if you will allow me to criticize, that the dialogue is, here and there, somewhat redundant, and the heroine's passions struck me as too fluctuating – for *theatrical* purposes. But there is great force and picturesqueness in it all." Since the play would require a great deal of rewriting and since he had two "elaborate productions" already scheduled, Tree decided against accepting the play. He closes his letter with praise

for "Pen, Pencil & Poison" and "The Decay of Lying," which he has just read: "I think they are the most brilliantly written things of our time: – it was a real joy to read them" (qtd. in Small 83).

After *Lady Windermere's Fan* triumphed, Tree asked Wilde to write a play for the Haymarket Theatre. By the end of 1892, Wilde completed *A Woman of No Importance* for Tree, who performed the role of Lord Illingworth when the play opened on 19 April 1893. In later years, Tree gave the impression that he forbade Wilde access to the theater because of his interference with rehearsals. But apparently, Tree had confused Wilde with other playwrights with whom he had some difficulty; with Tree, Wilde agreed to cut and revise as requested. Hesketh Pearson recalled that Tree "always thought that authors should attend rehearsals solely for the pleasure of seeing how perfectly he produced their plays." Max Beerbohm remarked to Pearson: "I was at several of those rehearsals, and Oscar was always there. Herbert had known him for many years and, as you say, always delighted greatly in his company" (qtd. in Pearson 69).

While *A Woman of No Importance* was still in production, Wilde's blackmailers sent to Tree a copy of what turned out to be an incriminating letter to Alfred Douglas (*Letters* 441). During the time of the trials and imprisonment, Tree apparently did not correspond with Wilde. In a letter to Reginald Turner in October 1897, Wilde alludes to Tree in his characteristically ironic manner: "I am pleased to hear that [Max's] brother is still acting, and hope he will have a success, some day" (*Letters* 659). Early in 1900, Tree wrote to Wilde concerning payment for a performance of *A Woman of No Importance*. His letter, however, more concerned with Wilde's future as a dramatist, reveals Tree's kindness and compassion:

I am indeed glad, and we all shall be, to know that you are determined to resume your dramatic work, for no one did such distinguished work as you – it has been rumoured that you had already finished your play [probably the scenario for the later titled *Mr. and Mrs. Daventry*, written by Frank Harris] – but I suppose this was not true. – I do most sincerely hope that good luck may come to you and that your splendid talents may shine forth again.

I have a lively remembrance of your many acts of kindness and courtesy – and was one of those who devoutly hoped that misfortune would not submerge you. (qtd. in Small 95)

References: Max Beerbohm, ed., *Herbert Beerbohm Tree: Some Memories of Him and of His Art* (1920; rpt. 1969); Hesketh Pearson, *Beerbohm Tree: His Life and Laughter* (1956).

THE TRIALS, 1895

Between 3 April and 25 May, the three trials involving Wilde took place at the Central Criminal Court, known as the "Old Bailey" after the name of the street adjacent to the building: the first trial involved a libel suit brought by Wilde against the Marquess of Queensberry, Lord Alfred Douglas's father; in the second trial, Wilde was the defendant in a criminal trial brought against him by the Crown; and in the third trial, Wilde was again the defendant after the second trial ended in a hung jury. (For the events leading up to the trials, see entries on Queensberry and Douglas.)

When Queensberry left his personal card at Wilde's club with the charge that Wilde was "posing as Somdomite" (misspelling the offensive word), he published a possible libel, which was subject to prosecution. After Wilde was handed the card by the porter, he immediately sent notes to Robert Ross and Douglas, urging them to see him. To Ross, he wrote: "I don't see anything now but a criminal prosecution. My whole life seems ruined by this man" (*Letters* 384). Ross advised Wilde to ignore the insult and permit Queensberry and Douglas to settle their problems themselves instead of using him as an "expendable pawn in a lethal game" (Borland 43).

On the following day, with Douglas and Ross, Wilde consulted with the solicitor Charles Octavius Humphreys (1828-1902), who asked Wilde the pointed question whether there was any truth to Queensberry's charge. Wilde assured him of his complete innocence (indeed, he was not merely *posing* as a sodomite, though such an idea had presumably not occurred to the solicitor). Humphreys replied that if Wilde were innocent of the libel, his suit would succeed.

On a warrant requested by Wilde's solicitor, Queensberry was arrested at Carter's Hotel in Albemarle Street on 2 March and eventually brought to the court in Great Marlborough Street before the sitting magistrate. After hearing preliminary testimony from the porter of the Albemarle Club and from the inspector who had arrested Queensberry, the magistrate granted bail and adjourned the hearing for a week. On 9 March, in a crowded courtroom, Humphreys again appeared for Wilde, whereas Edward Carson (1854-1935) now appeared for Queensberry. Carson, who had attended Trinity College, Dublin, when Wilde was also a student, had initially refused to accept the brief but reversed himself after consulting a colleague concerning the nature of the case.

The intent of the hearing was to determine whether there was sufficient evidence available to warrant Queensberry's prosecution. The contents of letters written by Queensberry to Wilde were not permitted to be read aloud in court, such evidence being reserved for the trial. After Wilde signed his deposition, the magistrate turned to Queensberry to ask whether he had anything to say in response. "I wrote the card," Queensberry began, "simply with the intention of bringing matters to a head, having been unable to meet Mr. Wilde otherwise, and to save my son, and I abide by what I wrote" (qtd. in Hyde 86). The magistrate then committed him for trial.

On the following day, Humphreys went to the Temple to see the former Law Officer of the Crown, Sir Edward Clarke (1841-1931), whom Hyde calls "a veritable Titan at the Bar," one gifted with great forensic ability, to offer him the brief in the case. Clarke then asked Humphreys to bring Wilde to his chambers on the next day, at which time he asked Wilde the same pointed question that the solicitor had previously asked (such a question being proper since Wilde was prosecuting Queensberry, though improper if Wilde had been facing a criminal charge): "I can only accept this brief, Mr. Wilde, if you can assure me on your honour as an English [*sic*] gentleman that there is not and never has been any foundation for the charges that are made against you" (qtd. in Walker-Smith and Clarke 245). Wilde assured him that the charge made against him by Queensberry was absolutely false and groundless.

The First Trial: On 3 April, the courtroom in the Old Bailey filled up an hour before Mr. Justice Henn Collins (1842-1911) made his appearance. One of the spectators was heard to joke about "the importance of being early" – which provoked laughter (qtd. in Hyde 97-98). When all of the participants in the case were assembled, Queensberry was asked by the Clerk of Arraigns whether he was guilty of libeling Wilde: the defendant pleaded not guilty; the words on the calling card left by Queensberry were, he said, published for the public benefit. The trial then began.

Clarke's opening speech reviewed Wilde's friendship with Douglas, and one of Wilde's letters to him was quoted – a letter that Clarke believed would be used by the defense – in order to minimize its significance: "Your slim gilt soul walks between passion and poetry. I know Hyacinthus, whom Apollo loved so madly, was you in Greek days" (*Letters* 326). Clarke contended that Wilde had written "a prose sonnet...with no relation whatever to the hateful and repulsive suggestions put to it in the plea in this case" (qtd. in Hyde 101-02).

With Wilde in the witness box, Carson questioned him about his contribution to the *Chameleon* and the publication of *Dorian Gray*, many of the questions concerned with the relationship of morality to art. As one might expect, Wilde continually denied that a literary work could be moral or immoral; it could only be well or badly written. Questioning Wilde closely on certain passages in *Dorian Gray* that express Basil Hallward's devotion to Dorian, Carson asked repeatedly whether Wilde had ever had such feelings for a young man. Wilde denied that he had. Carson then turned to Wilde's relations with blackmailers and with young men with whom he had sexual contacts, particularly with the young clerk at the Bodley Head, Edward Shelley. The plea of justification charged that Wilde "did solicit and incite one Edward Shelley to commit sodomy and other acts of gross indecency with him...." Wilde denied that any improper conduct had occurred while he and Shelley were at the Albemarle Hotel.

On the second day, Carson resumed his cross-examination by asking questions about Alfred Taylor, whom Wilde admitted to being a friend for the past two and a half years and who, Queensberry alleged, was a procurer of young men for Wilde. When Carson mentioned that Taylor was "notorious for introducing young men to older men" and that he had been under surveillance by the police, Wilde responded that he was unaware of Taylor's notoriety. From Taylor, Carson went on to questions about Wilde's relationship with Charley Parker (both Taylor and Parker had been arrested with sixteen others – two of them in female dress – in a police raid on a club at 46 Fitzroy Street on 12 August 1894, but only two had been bound over; the others, including Taylor and Parker, were released).

Carson then alluded to several other young men cited in Queensberry's plea of justification until he mentioned a Walter Grainger, about 16 years of age, a servant at a house in Oxford, where Douglas had rooms. After several routine questions, Carson suddenly asked, "Did you ever kiss him?" Caught off-guard, Wilde blurted out, "Oh, dear no! He was a peculiarly plain boy. He was, unfortunately, extremely ugly. I pitied him for it." Instantly, Carson pressed his point: "Was that the reason why you did not kiss him?" Wilde, shaken by this question, responded: "Oh! Mr. Carson: you are pertinently insolent" (qtd. in Hyde 133-34). But Wilde became progressively unable to complete sentences as Carson aggressively asked why he had responded as he had.

Clarke closed the case for the prosecution without calling Douglas to testify, presumably to avoid worsening Wilde's position. Carson rose to deliver his opening speech for the defense, which stressed Queensberry's determination to save his son from Wilde's corrupting influence. But for the remainder of the hour, Carson announced that he would be calling as witnesses all of the young men cited in the plea of justification. Clarke now realized that Wilde was in imminent danger. Added to the lawyer's apprehension was Wilde's admission during the luncheon break that he and a boy had once been turned out of the Albemarle Hotel in the middle of the night: if revealed during the trial, the incident would seal his doom.

After the court adjourned for the day, Clarke concluded that he would advise Wilde to withdraw and consent to Queensberry's charge that he was posing as a sodomite. In his unpublished recollections, Clarke wrote:

> ...I said [to Wilde] that, if the case went to its end and the jury found that the accusations were justified, the judge would unquestionably order his arrest. He listened quietly and gravely, and then thanked me for my advice and said he was prepared to act upon it.... I hoped and expected that he would take the opportunity of escaping from the country, and I believe he would have found no difficulty in

doing so. (qtd in Hyde 145)

On the following day, 5 April, as Carson was continuing his speech on behalf of Queensberry, Clarke entered the courtroom and announced his client's decision. Accordingly, the judge instructed the jury to arrive at a verdict of "Not Guilty": the plea of justification was therefore "true in substance and in fact that the prosecutor had posed as a sodomite...[and] that the statement was published in such a manner as to be for the public benefit" (qtd. in Hyde 148). Wilde left the Old Bailey towards noon, accompanied by Douglas and Ross, who had been in court throughout the trial.

At a nearby hotel, Wilde wrote to the *Evening News* that it would have been impossible for him to have won the case without putting Douglas in the witness box. But because he refused to permit Douglas to testify against his father, he said in his letter to the editor, he decided to retire from the case and "to bear on my own shoulders whatever ignominy and shame might result from my prosecuting Lord Queensberry" (*Letters* 386). Meanwhile, Queensberry's solicitor wrote to the Director of Public Prosecutions that he was sending him a copy of the witnesses' statements. Informed of the nature of the statements, the Home Secretary directed that Wilde be found.

At about 3:30 p.m. a warrant for Wilde's arrest was requested from the Bow Street magistrate, who adjourned the court for more than a hour and a half without granting the request. Ever since, speculation has centered on the delay: that is, whether it was designed to enable Wilde to catch the last boat-train for the Continent or whether the magistrate delayed in order to read the documents. At the Cadogan Hotel in Sloane Street, Ross and other friends during the afternoon urged Wilde to leave for France, but he remained unable or unwilling to act on their advice. At about 6:30 p.m., Inspector Richards of Scotland Yard knocked at the door of Room 53 and arrested Wilde. The *Echo*, an evening paper, reported: "Lord Queensberry is triumphant, and Mr. Oscar Wilde is 'damned and done for.' He may now change places with Lord Queensberry and go into the dock himself. He appears to have illustrated in his life the beauty and truthfulness of his teachings."

The Second Trial: With Wilde in the prisoner's dock on 26 April, the second trial began, Sir Arthur Charles (1839-1921) presiding as judge.

Clarke, who was again Wilde's chief counsel, acted without fee, a gesture that pleased Wilde, who expressed "his deepest gratitude" for the kind offer. John Peter Grain (1839-1916) represented Taylor: to Wilde's disadvantage, both were tried together for the commission of "acts of gross indecency" under the Criminal Law Amendment Act of 1885, Article XI. In addition Taylor was charged as having been a procurer for Wilde.

The young men who were the prosecution's witnesses were led by Charles Gill to reveal – sometimes in rather graphic detail – Wilde's sexual behavior with them in various hotels, including the Savoy and Albemarle, as well as at Wilde's Tite Street home. In addition, a procession of landladies and chambermaids testified to what they witnessed, sometimes on entering a bedroom or in observing Wilde's arrival or departure from a visit to one of the young men. For most of the third day of the trial, Wilde's testimony given at the Queensberry trial was read into the record. By the fourth day, the conspiracy charges – at Gill's request – were dropped, but Clarke regretted that Gill had not decided earlier so that Wilde and Taylor could have been tried separately.

Clarke then put his client in the witness box: Wilde, during his testimony, was more restrained than he had been in the first trial, which had not included the accounts by the young men with whom he had been involved. After reviewing his client's career, Clarke then asked the pointed question: "Is there any truth in any of the allegations of indecent behaviour made against you in the evidence in the present case?" To which question, Wilde responded: "There is no truth whatever in any one of the allegations, no truth whatsoever" (qtd. in Hyde 198).

Gill then cross-examined Wilde by reading two of Douglas's poems, one of them, "Two Loves," ending with the line "I am the love that dare not speak its name." To Gill's question as to its meaning, Wilde responded:

"The love that dare not speak its name" in this century is such a great affection of an elder for a younger man as there was between David and Jonathan, such as Plato made the very basis of his philosophy, and such as you find in the sonnets of Michelangelo and Shakespeare. It is that deep, spiritual affection that is as pure as it is perfect.... It is in this century misunderstood, so much misunderstood that it may be described as the "Love that dare not speak its name," and on account of it I am placed where I am now. It is beautiful, it is fine, it is the noblest form of affection. There is nothing unnatural about it.... The world mocks at it and sometimes puts one in the pillory for it. (qtd. in Hyde 201)

The public gallery burst into applause, though accompanied by hisses, prompting the judge to warn that the court would be cleared if another such demonstration ensued. Hyde contends that Wilde's speech "undoubtedly contributed to the jury's failure to agree upon a verdict" (15).

After some further questions concerning Wilde's gifts to various young men, Gill called Alfred Taylor to the witness box. There followed an account of his background: his father, having died in 1874, was a cocoa manufacturer, who had left a fortune to his son; on coming of age in 1883, he inherited £45,000. Since then, he had lived a life of pleasure, apparently squandering the huge sum, as indicated in his remark that he had just gone through the Bankruptcy Court. All charges of improper conduct were "absolutely untrue," Taylor contended, though he conceded that "he had had a number of young men living in his rooms and sleeping in the same bed" (Hyde 205).

In his closing speech, Clarke reiterated his previous points that Fred Atkins, one of the "wretched gang of blackmailers," had perjured himself under close questioning, and Edward Shelley had "admitted that his mind was disordered at the time he wrote the letters that have been produced" (qtd. in Hyde 210). Thus, Wilde's counsel attempted to undermine the testimony of the prosecution's witnesses by attacking their credibility. For the Crown, Gill argued in his summation that the young witnesses "are accusing themselves, in accusing another, of shameful and infamous acts, and this they would hardly do if [it] were not the truth" (qtd. in Hyde 212). As for the Wilde-Douglas letters, they breathed "an unholy passion."

On the morning of the sixth day, 1 May, after the judge summed up the evidence, the jury – having deliberated for approximately four hours – sent a message to the judge that it was deadlocked on Wilde and Taylor. The jury dismissed, the judge granted bail to Wilde, who was directed to

give his personal security for £2,500, and to find two sureties of £1,250 each: they were Queensberry's eldest surviving son, Lord Douglas of Hawick (Alfred Douglas's brother) and the Rev. Stewart Headlam, who though not a friend, admired Wilde's bearing during the trial. Wilde was released on 7 May.

The Third Trial: For the trial that was to begin on 20 May, a new prosecutor was selected: Sir Frank Lockwood (1847-1897), the Solicitor-General, an indication that the Crown was determined to secure a conviction in the case. On the first day of the trial, with Sir Alfred Wills (1828-1912) sitting as judge, Clarke requested that the defendants be tried separately since conspiracy charges had been dropped in the previous trial. Wills granted the request, but Lockwood successfully prevailed on the judge to try Taylor first – to Wilde's disadvantage. Despite Clarke's protest, Wills decided that the prosecution should have its preference, though Taylor's trial should have no influence on Wilde's. Wills agreed that Wilde should remain free on bail.

Meanwhile, Wilde's friends were again urging him to flee the country: indeed, Lord Douglas of Hawick told his co-surety, Rev. Headlam, that he would willingly assume the entire loss if Wilde sought refuge abroad. Constance Wilde also pleaded with her husband to leave England, but Wilde refused. To Alfred Douglas, he wrote: "I decided that it was nobler and more beautiful to stay. We could not have been together. I did not want to be called a coward or a deserter. A false name, a disguise, a hunted life, all that is not for me..." (*Letters* 398). During Taylor's trial, which ended on 21 May, Lockwood pressed home some of the evidence previously explored in the preceding trial. Only 45 minutes after the jury retired, a guilty verdict was brought in on two principal counts of indecent sexual behavior. Sentencing was postponed until after Wilde's trial, which would be heard with a new jury. Since it was now past four in the afternoon, Wills agreed with Lockwood that the Wilde trial should formally begin on the following morning.

On 22 May, Wilde was in the prisoner's dock. The procession of young men, beginning with Edward Shelley, began with Lockwood's questioning that recalled material heard in the previous two trials. In his cross-examination, Clarke easily discredited much of the testimony of several

servants from the Savoy Hotel, for they had difficulty in identifying the young men associated with
Wilde and difficulty in recalling specific details of
their presence at the hotel. On the third morning of
the trial, Clarke called Wilde to the witness box.
The ordeal of three trials and of prison was evident
in his unkempt appearance. When asked whether
there was any truth in the accusations against him,
Wilde answered, "None whatever!" (qtd. in Hyde
243). In the cross-examination, Lockwood reviewed Wilde's relationship with Douglas, focusing on the "prose poem" letter quoted in the previous trials. In addition, he reviewed Wilde's relationships with Taylor and with the young men who
had also figured in the previous trials.

After lengthy closing speeches by Clarke and
Lockwood, Mr. Justice Wills presented the evidence in a manner, Hyde contends, that was not
"actually unfair" to Wilde but at the same time
"much less favourable to him than Mr. Justice
Charles's summing-up in the previous trial, particularly on the subject of the two letters to Lord
Alfred Douglas" (262). Moreover, Wills depicted
Queensberry as an "indignant father, a loving and
affectionate parent" who had been justified – as
the first trial revealed – in charging that Wilde was
posing as a sodomite. While the judge was evaluating Douglas's association with one of the blackmailers and with Wilde, the jury foreman rose to
ask a question: "In view of the intimacy between
Lord Alfred Douglas and Mr. Wilde, was a warrant ever issued for the apprehension of Lord
Alfred Douglas?" Wills responded curtly in the
negative, adding: "It may be that there is no evidence against Lord Alfred Douglas. But even
about that I know nothing. It is a thing we cannot
discuss..." (qtd. in Hyde 265-66).

Upon completion of the summation, the jury
retired at 3:30 p.m. for two hours, after which a
verdict of "Guilty" was rendered with respect to
Wilde's relationships with various young men but
"Not guilty" with respect to Edward Shelley. Since
Wills was convinced that the verdict was correct,
he passed sentence on both Taylor and Wilde: two
years at hard labor, the maximum under the Criminal Law Amendment Act. Taylor remained unmoved, but Wilde, swaying slightly with an expression of the utmost pain in his face, asked:
"And I? May I say nothing, my lord?" But the
judge merely waved his hand to the warders, who
hurried both convicts to the cells below to be

eventually transported to Pentonville Prison. Thus
ended the most notorious trials in 19th-century
England.

While the responses to the trials, during and
after, were generally virulent in the popular press,
the reactions of many writers reflected the distress
that the Wilde disaster evoked. For example, the
novelist George Gissing, who was not one of
Wilde's friends, wrote on 27 May to the writer
Morley Roberts:

> The Wilde business is frightfully depressing.
> I have a theory that he has got into this, not
> through natural tendency, but simply in delib-
> erate imitation of the old Greek vice.... But the
> catastrophe is awful, & one tries not to think
> of it overmuch. *(Collected Letters* 5:339)

(For other reactions to the Wilde trials, see the
entries on Henry James and Bernard Shaw.)

References: Derek Walker-Smith and Edward
Clarke, *The Life of Sir Edward Clarke* (1939); H.
Montgomery Hyde, *The Trials of Oscar Wilde*
(2nd ed., 1962; rpt. 1973); Thomas Mallon, "A
Boy of No Importance" [Edward Shelley], *Biogra-
phy* (Summer 1978); Paul F. Mattheisen, Arthur C.
Young, and Pierre Coustillas, eds., *The Collected
Letters of George Gissing*, Vol. 5 (1994); Michael
Foldy, *The Trials of Oscar Wilde: Deviance,
Morality, and Late Victorian Society* (1997).

TRINITY COLLEGE, DUBLIN

Trinity College (also called the "University of
Dublin") was founded in 1592 by Queen Elizabeth. On 10 October 1871, just before his 17th
birthday, Wilde matriculated on a Royal school
scholarship. Consisting of a campus of nearly 40
acres with approximately 1100 students, 90% of
them Protestant, the college – writes Davis
Coakley – resembled Oxford and Cambridge in its
"constitution and academic life." Moreover, from
its foundation, "it was linked with the Anglo-Irish
ascendancy, and many of its graduates held powerful positions in the country" (135). Among its
eminent alumni are Swift, Congreve, and Goldsmith as well as such noted patriots as Henry
Grattan, Robert Emmet, and Thomas Davis.

In 1872 Wilde distinguished himself with First
Class Honours in Classics in the Hilary, Trinity,
and Michaelmas Terms. In 1873, he also won a
Foundation Scholarship and, in his final year, the

Berkeley Gold Medal for Greek on an examination concerning *The Fragments of the Greek Comic Poets*, a scholarly work edited by Meineke. The award was presented annually from a fund established by George Berkeley (1685-1753), the Anglo-Irish philosopher and clergyman, whose works had been edited at Trinity College.

While at Trinity College, Wilde came under the influence of the Rev. John Pentland Mahaffy, a professor of ancient history (see entry), whose enthusiasm for ancient Greece resulted in Wilde's championing of the New Hellenism. Though Wilde left Trinity College in 1874 to attend Magdalen College, Oxford, between 1876 and 1879 he contributed several of his earliest poems to the Trinity College magazine, *Kottabos* (see index). Currently, there is an Oscar Wilde Society at the college.

Reference: Davis Coakley, "Trinity College Dublin," *Oscar Wilde: The Importance of Being Irish* (1994).

"THE TRUE KNOWLEDGE"

Published: *Irish Monthly* 4 (Sept. 1876): 594. Below the title, three lines in Greek are quoted from Euripides's *Hypsipile*, 6, translated by Gilbert Murray in *Euripides* (1902), 326, as follows: "...like the grassy leas / In the morning, Life is mown; and this man is, / And that man is not." Without the Greek epigraph, the poem was revised as "Unto One Dead" in William MacIlwaine, ed., *Lyra Hibernica Sacra* (Belfast: McCaw, Stevenson & Orr; London: Geo. Bell & Sons; Dublin: Hodges, Foster & Figgis, 1878, 2nd ed. 1879); rpt. with the original title and the Greek epigraph in *Poems* (1908).

In this lyric poem, the speaker, presumably Wilde, apparently addresses himself in the recurring refrain ("Thou knowest all") to his father, Sir William, who died on 19 April 1876 (see, also, "Lotus Leaves"). He concedes that all effort to seek "What lands to till or sow with seed" is fruitless, that he must "sit and wait / With blinded eyes and hands that fail, / Till the last lifting of the veil...." The struggle against doubt, a widespread Victorian theme, as in Tennyson's *In Memoriam* (1850), dramatizes but does not necessarily undermine faith:

Thou knowest all: – I cannot see;
   I trust I shall not live in vain:

I *know* that we shall meet again
In some divine eternity.

"THE TRUTH OF MASKS"

Published: First appeared in *Nineteenth Century* 17 (May 1885): 800-18, under the title "Shakespeare and Stage Costume"; rev. as "The Truth of Masks: A Note on Illusion" in *Intentions* (1891).

The Essay: Responding to Lord Lytton's article "Miss Anderson's Juliet" in *Nineteenth Century* (Dec.1884), which contends that Shakespeare had little concern about the costume wardrobe of his theater, Wilde writes: "...anybody who cares to study Shakespeare's method will see that there is absolutely no dramatist of the French, English, or Athenian stage who relies so much for his illusionist effects on the dress of his actors as Shakespeare does himself." Because the "artistic temperament is always fascinated by beauty of costume," Shakespeare includes in his plays such elements as masques and dances as well as stately processions with directions as to details of dress "purely for the pleasure which they give the eye...."

Clearly, Wilde argues, Shakespeare also "saw how important costume is as a means of producing certain dramatic effects." In *King Lear*, for example, Edgar conceals "his pride beneath an idiot's rags"; in *The Merchant of Venice*, Portia wears the costume of a lawyer; and Hamlet's black suit is "a kind of colour-motive in the piece." Though Shakespeare complains of the smallness of the Elizabethan stage "on which he has to produce big historical plays," he had a "most elaborate theatrical wardrobe" at his disposal, and he could rely "on the actors taking pains about their make-up."

Related to the introduction of authenticity into art, the passion for archeology during the Renaissance revival of interest in ancient Greece and Rome, was

not a mere science for the antiquarian; it was a means by which they could touch the dry dust of antiquity into the very breath and beauty of life, and fill with the new wine of romanticism forms that else had been old and outworn.... For the stage is not merely the meeting-place of all the arts, but is also the return of art to life.... Art, and art only, can make archaeology beautiful; and the theatric art can use it most directly and most vividly, for it can combine in one exquisite presentation the illusion of actual life with the wonder of the unreal world.

In turning to Lord Lytton's "proposal that the dresses should merely be beautiful without being accurate," Wilde regards it as a "misapprehension of the nature of costume, and of its value on the stage":

> This value is two fold, picturesque and dramatic; the former depends on the colour of the dress, the latter on its design and character. But so interwoven are the two that, whenever in our own day historical accuracy has been disregarded, and the various dresses in a play taken from different ages, the result has been that the stage has been turned into that chaos of costume, that caricature of the centuries, the Fancy Dress Ball, to the entire ruin of all dramatic and picturesque effect.

In short, "unless a dress is archaeologically correct, and artistically appropriate, it always looks unreal, unnatural, and theatrical in the sense of artificial." Wilde again stresses unity of artistic effect and the point "that archaeology is not a pedantic method, but a method of artistic illusion, and that costume is a means of displaying character without description...."

Wilde concludes with his characteristic penchant for irony and paradox by suggesting that he does not agree with everything that he has said in his own essay; indeed, there is much with which he entirely disagrees:

> The essay simply represents an artistic standpoint, and in aesthetic criticism attitude is everything. For in art there is no such thing as a universal truth. A Truth in art is that whose contradictory is also true. And just as it is only in art-criticism, and through it, that we can apprehend the Platonic theory of ideas, so it is only in art-criticism, and through it, that we can realise Hegel's system of contraries. The truths of metaphysics are the truths of masks.

Reference: Lawrence Danson, "The Truth of Masks," *Wilde's Intentions: The Artist in His Criticism* (1997).

TURNER, REGINALD (1869-1938)

A close friend of Wilde, a wit, journalist, and later a novelist, Turner (or "Reggie," as he was known) "always preferred to be remembered as a figure of the Nineties – as a disciple of Oscar Wilde and contributor to *The Yellow Book*" (Weintraub 3). The presumed illegitimate son of Lionel Lawson, Turner believed – or, perhaps, pretended to believe – that he was the son of Edward Levy-Lawson, later Lord Burnham, proprietor of the *Daily Telegraph*, and the nephew of Lionel Lawson. However, Edward Levy-Lawson became Turner's guardian when Lionel, a bachelor, had provided for the ten-year-old Reggie in his will before his death in 1879. In Turner's thinly disguised novels, Weintraub remarks, "The orphans and foundlings and long-lost parents recovered represent the fears and fantasies of a child whose background was as strange as the most far-fetched fiction popular in the Victorian world of his birth" (13).

At the age of 19, Turner matriculated at Merton College, Oxford, where he became the close friend of Max Beerbohm, both of whom charmed each other with wit and sophistication. Most likely, Beerbohm introduced Turner to Wilde in 1893, when Max's half-brother, Herbert Beerbohm Tree, the actor-manager, was performing in *A Woman of No Importance*. Thus, Max's first meeting with Wilde and Turner's introduction to him probably occurred sometime during late March or April of 1893, during rehearsals or just after the opening on 19 April.

After taking his BA (and leaving Beerbohm to complete his studies at Oxford), Turner spent the winter of 1893-94 in Egypt, where he ran into Alfred Douglas and Robert Hichens, who later satirized Wilde and his circle in *The Green Carnation* (1894). The character modeled after Douglas with the name "Lord Reggie" thereby includes Turner in the composite character. Sir Compton Mackenzie remarked that all of the "best cracks in *The Green Carnation* were noted down by Robert Hichens from Reggie Turner's conversation" (qtd. in Weintraub 52). On his return to London, Turner joined Wilde's entourage in 1894-95 so that, when *The Green Carnation* appeared, his status within the inner circle was enhanced by the recognition that his wit had contributed to the satire.

Concerned about Turner when the Marquess of Queensberry was arrested for allegedly libeling

Wilde, Beerbohm wrote to him from Chicago, where he had accompanied his half-brother on a theatrical tour: "Do not, I beg you, get mixed up in the scandal" (*Letters to Reggie* 100). But the loyal Turner, while not getting "mixed up" in the Wilde debacle, was present with Robert Ross at the Cadogan Hotel to urge Wilde to escape to the Continent. When the detectives arrived to escort Wilde to the Bow Street police station, Ross and Turner remained behind. But not for long: aware of possible implication, they immediately embarked for France, where Turner remained throughout 1895 and into 1896.

During Wilde's imprisonment, Turner sent him books and letters, though curiously, he made no attempt to visit him, possibly, as Weintraub suggests, "because of the Lawson family's uneasiness over his being identified in the press with Wilde" (74). When Wilde's prison sentence was nearing its end, Turner prepared for his release by purchasing a dressing case stamped with the initials "S.M." (for "Sebastian Melmoth," Wilde's adopted pseudonym) with a supply of toilet articles. Initially, Wilde preferred to have Turner meet him after his release. In a letter smuggled out of Reading Prison, Wilde set forth the arrangements:

I cannot tell you how good and dear it was of you [to purchase the dressing case] in my eyes.... You, dear Reggie, simply quietly and thoughtfully go and get me a beautiful and useful thing. You make no noise beforehand: you blow no lying trumpets like Frank Harris: you don't pose as the generous friend.... I can't tell you how touched I am: I shall never forget it.

Urging Turner to accompany him to France, Wilde adds: "I beg you, dear Reggie, to come with me. I shall never forget it if you do. I want someone whom I can trust" (*Letters* 552-53).

But Turner, concerned about the reaction of the Lawson family, which might cut off his yearly allowance if the press reported his association with Wilde, wrote that he would be unable to meet him but that others would. However, he and Robert Ross (whom Turner praised as Wilde's loyal and devoted friend) would be waiting for him in Dieppe on his arrival there. In closing, Turner assures him: "Dear Oscar, we all believe that the greatest triumphs of your life have yet to come.

You will be happy and renowned, but try, in this time, so terrible for your nerves, to be yourself, great, wonderful, noble" (qtd. in Weintraub 80). At 4:30 a.m. on 20 May 1897, Turner and Ross were on the pier when the night boat from Newhaven arrived in Dieppe.

Much of Turner's time was subsequently spent in London as a journalist. On yearly holidays, Turner tried to avoid Wilde (as he assured Beerbohm that he would perhaps because Wilde had become financially more desperate), but he accidentally encountered him in Paris in late September 1899. Writing to Ross, Wilde called Turner "wonderful...purple and perfect. The Boulevard, I regret to say, still talks of him" (*Letters* 810).

In late 1900, when Wilde, gravely ill, summoned Ross to Paris, Turner accompanied him. Near the end, Wilde confided that he had a horrible dream on the previous night: "I dreamt that I had died and that I was supping with the dead." Turner responded: "I am sure that you must have been the life and soul of the party" (qtd. in Behrman 186). Wilde's death, with Turner and Ross at his bedside, has resulted in contradictory stories from both witnesses: Ross's account, in a long letter to More Adey, dated December 14 (included in the "Epilogue" to *Letters*), was disputed in some of the details by Turner in *Two Worlds* (June 1926). Turner, Ross, Douglas, and others walked behind the hearse to the Church of St.-Germain-des-Prés for the Mass, then proceeded to Bagneaux cemetery.

As Weintraub writes, "Wilde's death freed Reggie from the most onerous responsibilities he had ever borne. But life seemed empty. He felt alienated from an England which had driven Oscar to his death..." (112). Between 1901 and 1911, he published 12 novels, though with little success. He had difficulty with Robert Ross during these years because of the publication of *De Profundis*, which Turner believed was "disgraceful" during Douglas's lifetime, but he attended the celebration of Ross's editing of Wilde's *Collected Edition* in 1908. Some of Turner's good friends at this time were H. G. Wells, Arnold Bennett, and Somerset Maugham, who regarded Turner as "on the whole the most amusing man I have known" (qtd. in Behrman 186). For most of his remaining years, Turner lived on the Continent, from 1912 in Florence, where he entertained many noted writers and artists who visited the city.

References: S. N. Behrman, *Conversations with Max* (1960); Stanley Weintraub, *Reggie: A Portrait of Reginald Turner* (1965); Rupert Hart-Davis, ed., *Max Beerbohm's Letters to Reggie Turner* (1965).

"'TWELFTH NIGHT' AT OXFORD"

Published: *Dramatic Review* 3 (20 Feb. 1886): 34-35; rpt. in *Reviews* (1908). A signed review of the University Dramatic Society's opening night performance at the New Theatre, Oxford.

Wilde praises the undergraduate society for having selected *Twelfth Night* since, unlike Shakespeare's tragedies, his comedies are not "made for a single star" but for "a galaxy of constellations." As to the various roles, Wilde remarks, "One may hate the villains of Shakespeare, but one cannot help loving his fools." Inevitably, a reviewer must confront Shakespeare's conception of Malvolio: "What a difficult part Malvolio is! Shakespeare undoubtedly meant us to laugh all through at the pompous steward, and to join in the practical joke upon him, and yet how impossible not to feel a good deal of sympathy with him! Perhaps in this century we are too altruistic to be really artistic." It is difficult, Wilde submits, "not to feel [that] Malvolio's treatment is unnecessarily harsh."

In concluding, Wilde expresses the hope that the university will someday have a theater of its own: "On the stage, literature returns to life and archaeology becomes art. A fine theatre is a temple where all the muses may meet, a second Parnassus, and the dramatic spirit, though she has long tarried at Cambridge, seems now to be migrating to Oxford."

"TWO BIOGRAPHIES OF KEATS"

Published: *PMG*, 27 Sept. 1887, 3; rpt. in *Reviews* (1908). An unsigned review of Sidney Colvin's *Keats* and William Michael Rossetti's *Life of John Keats* – both published in 1887.

Wilde begins by misquoting – no doubt from memory – the famous line from one of Keats's letters (written to Richard Woodhouse on 27 October 1818): "A poet is the most unpoetical of all God's creatures." (However, Keats's remark is that "A poet is the most unpoetical of anything in existence because he has no identity.") Wilde continues: "...whether the aphorism be universally true or not, this is certainly the impression produced by the two last biographies that have appeared of Keats himself. Neither Colvin nor Rossetti "makes us love Keats more, or understand him better." The reason is that nowadays "everybody pays a penalty for peeping through keyholes, and the keyhole and the back-stairs are essential parts of the method of the modern biographer."

Nevertheless, Colvin "has done his work much better than Mr. Rossetti." If Colvin "has not given us a very true picture of Keats's character" – Wilde remarks that "part of Keats's charm as a man is his fascinating incompleteness" – Colvin has told the story of Keats's life in "a pleasant and readable manner." On the other hand, Rossetti's biography is "a great failure," the result of his "grave mistake of separating the man from the artist. The facts of Keats's life are only interesting when they are shown in their relation to his creative activity. The moment they are isolated they are either uninteresting or painful." Wilde relentlessly pursues this point in his review, as in the following: "When Mr. Rossetti writes of the man he forgets the poet, and when he criticises the poet he shows that he does not understand the man."

Rossetti's "second error" – Wilde continues – is "his treatment of the work itself." For example, in "Ode to a Nightingale," with "all its marvellous magic of music, colour, and form," Rossetti regards as the "first point of weakness in the poem" the "'surfeit of mythological allusions,' a statement which is absolutely untrue, as out of the eight stanzas of the poem only three contain any mythological allusions at all...." With respect to Keats's line "Thou wast not born for death, immortal Bird!" Rossetti regards this address as a "'logical solecism,' as men live longer than nightingales." Since Colvin advances the same criticism, talking of "a breach of logic which is also a flaw in the poetry," Wilde expresses his disapproval of both Colvin and Rossetti by contending that, in the image of the "immortal Bird," Keats implies "the contrast between the permanence of beauty and the change and decay of human life, an idea which receives its fullest expression in the 'Ode on a Grecian Urn.'"

Finally, a critic "who can say that 'not many of Keats's poems are highly admirable' need not be too seriously treated. Mr. Rossetti is an industrious man, and a painstaking writer, but he entirely lacks the temper necessary for the interpretation of such poetry as was written by John Keats."

"TWO BIOGRAPHIES OF SIR PHILIP SIDNEY"

Published: *PMG*, 11 Dec. 1886, 5; *not* reprinted in *Reviews* (1908). An unsigned review of John Addington Symonds's *Sir Philip Sidney* (1886) and Edmund Gosse's "Sir Philip Sidney" in the *Contemporary Review* (Nov. 1886).

Both biographers, Wilde remarks, agree that Sidney was one "whose renown transcends his actual achievement." Symonds, more knowledgeable than Gosse on the subject, knows that Sidney was "an earnest and ardent politician, and one of the most remarkable statesmen of his day....that Sidney was fully conscious of the necessity of England maintaining her supremacy by means of her navy, and worked stoutly for that end," whereas Gosse "calmly informs us that 'it does not seem that he took any interest in politics,' which is really the most astounding statement ever made about Sidney by any writer."

Symonds, states Wilde, is "a high authority on all Elizabethan literature...quite aware of the reasons which led Spenser to celebrate Sidney in a pastoral elegy [*Astrophel*, published in 1595], and fully understands the significance of that form in literature, a subject which we fear Mr. Gosse has not sufficiently studied as he severely censures Spenser's verses on the ground that they 'falsify history,' Sidney never at any time of his life having been a merry shepherd...."

Despite his knowledge of Sidney's life and times, Symonds emphasizes the "picturesqueness of the background" and "omits many of the details of his central figure." In dismissing the "pseudo-classical school with brilliant eloquence and caustic wit," and with its emphasis on the unities, preferred by Sidney for the stage, Symonds omits much that is "so fertile in suggestion and so historically valuable," for it contrasts with the romantic method of Marlowe and Shakespeare, who triumphed when the "true Elizabethan drama was born" ("fortunately," says Wilde, "for our literature"). England, as Symonds points out, had "the good fortune to receive the Reformation and the Renaissance at the same epoch, and Sidney may be said to have summed up in himself all that in each movement was finest and most noble...."

"TWO NEW NOVELS"

Published: *PMG*, 15 May 1885, 5; rpt. in *Reviews* (1908). An unsigned review of Edna Lyall's *In the Golden Days* (1885) and Katherine S. Macquoid's *Louisa* (1885).

Wilde points to Lyall's "foolish preface," in which she expresses relief from "perpetual nineteenth-centuryism" by setting her novel in England two centuries before and appealing to her readers not to regard the book as an "historical novel," which might create terror in the reader. Yet, says Wilde, such historical novels as Thackeray's *Esmond* and Dumas's *The Hunchback of Notre Dame* are both popular successes. Nevertheless, Lyall has written "a very charming book" and the "picture of the time is well painted." Though it seems to have "a high purpose and a noble meaning...it is never dull."

Macquoid's fictional setting, Italy, "has been a good deal overdone in fiction. A little more Piccadilly and a little less Perugia would be a relief." The story – of a young English girl who marries an Italian nobleman, then out of boredom falls in love with an Englishman – is told with "a good deal of power, and ends properly and pleasantly. It can safely be recommended to young persons."

"TWO NEW NOVELS"

Published: *PMG*, Sept. 16, 1886, 5; rpt. in *Reviews* (1908). An unsigned review of George Manville Fenn's *The Master of the Ceremonies* (1886) and Emile Boucher's *A Statesman's Love* (1886).

Wilde observes that "most modern novels are more remarkable for their crime than for their culture." Fenn's work is "turbid, terrifying, and thrilling," containing such events as "an elopement, an abduction, a bigamous marriage, an attempted assassination, a duel, a suicide, and a murder. The murder, we must acknowledge, is a masterpiece." The novel "is a melancholy example of the fatal influence of Drury Lane [the location of the noted theater famous for its melodramas] on literature."

Though Fenn is "never dull, and his style is on the whole very good," Wilde wishes that Fenn "would not try to give articulate form to inarticulate exclamations. Such a passage as this is quite dreadful, and fails besides in producing the effect it aims at: 'He – he – he, hi – hi – hi, hec – hec – hec, ha – ha – ha! ho – ho! Bless my – hey – ha! hey – ha! hugh – hugh – hugh! Oh dear me! Oh – why don't you – heck – heck – heck – heck – heck!

shut the – ho – ho – ho – ho – hugh – hugh –
window before I – ho – ho – ho – ho!' This horrible jargon is supposed to convey the impression of
a lady coughing. It is, of course, a mere meaningless monstrosity, on a par with spelling a sneeze."

Boucher's novel is an "exaggerated psychological study of a modern woman, full of coarse
colours and violent contrasts, not by any means
devoid of cleverness but essentially false and
over-emphasised." The heroine takes three volumes to tell her story: "...we weary of the one
point of view. Life to be intelligible should be
approached from many sides, and valuable though
the permanent *ego* may be in philosophy, the
permanent *ego* in fiction soon becomes a bore."
Though the style of this historical romance is
"often original and picturesque," there is a "good
deal of pretense and a good deal of carelessness."

U

"UNDER THE BALCONY"

Published: J. S. Wood, ed., *Shakespearean Show Book* (Manchester: George Falkner & Sons, 1884), 23; rpt. in *Poems* (1908). The editor was Secretary of the Chelsea Hospital for Women, for whose benefit this volume was published as the official program for the Shakespearean Show held at the Royal Albert Hall, Kensington, on 29–31 May 1884.

In four eight-line stanzas, Wilde evokes the Romeo and Juliet scene (Act II, scene ii) under the balcony by the use of the vocative "O" and exclamation marks as well as echoing the image of the star in the first stanza: "O beautiful star with the crimson mouth! / O moon with the brows of gold! / Rise up, rise up, from the odorous south!" Wilde was obviously inviting parody. In Robert Hichens's satire of Wilde and Lord Alfred Douglas in *The Green Carnation* (1894), Esmé Amarinth (Wilde) declares that "The moon is the religion of the night" and recites the following:"Oh! beautiful moon with the ghostly face, / Oh! moon with the brows of snow, / Rise up, rise up from your slumbering place...."

Manuscript: Mason notes that a MS. version, titled "Rose Leaves" (apparently now lost), omits the third stanza and differs from the published text in several lines (199).

"THE UNITY OF THE ARTS: A LECTURE AND 'A FIVE O'CLOCK'"

Published: *PMG*, 12 Dec. 1887, 13; rpt. in *Miscellanies* (1908). An unsigned review of the first lecture by Selwyn Image in a series of four lectures on modern art at Willis's Rooms in King Street on 10 December.

Wilde focuses on the chief point made by Image: "the absolute unity of all the arts." By citing Shakespeare, Michelangelo, Veronese, and others, Image ultimately arrived at the following:

The Impressionists, with their frank artistic acceptance of form and colour, as things absolutely satisfying in themselves, have produced very beautiful work, but painting has something more to give us than the mere visible aspect of things. The lofty spiritual visions of William Blake, and the marvellous romance of Dante Gabriel Rossetti, can find their perfect expression in painting; every mood has its colour, and every dream has its form.

Wilde found the lecture "extremely suggestive," though it was sometimes difficult for him to know how Image was using the word *literary*. Adds Wilde: "The true unity of the arts is to be found, not in any resemblance of one art to another, but in the fact that to the really artistic nature all the arts have the same message, and speak the same language, though with different tongues." It is necessary, Wilde argues, that an art critic have a "nature receptive of beautiful impressions and sufficient intuition to recognize style, when he meets with it...but, if he does not possess these qualities, a reckless career of water-colour painting will not give them to him, for, if from the incompetent critic all things be hidden, to the bad painter nothing shall be revealed."

THE URANIANS

Though the term *homosexual* first appeared in the 1890s, the term preferred by late 19th-century homosexuals was *Uranian* (or the alternative *Urning*), derived from Plato's *Symposium* by the German lawyer and jurist Karl Heinrich Ulrichs (1825–95). The Greek myth of the god Uranus provided the source of Ulrichs's term, for the god's genitals were severed by his son, Cronus, and cast into the sea, the foam resulting in the birth of Aphrodite – hence the male's creative faculty without the female. In numerous pamphlets published with pseudonyms between 1864 and 1870, he contended that homosexuality was congenital, therefore natural.

Though these pamphlets were never translated, John Addington Symonds, himself homosexual (see entry), summarized Ulrichs's arguments in *A Problem in Modern Ethics* (1891) and in an appendix – with the pseudonym "Z" – to Havelock Ellis's *Sexual Inversion* (1897). Symonds preferred Ulrichs's term *Urning* for one who had a feminine soul in a male body. In a letter written in February 1893 to another Uranian, the poet and essayist Edward Carpenter (1844–1929), Symonds described a visit he had made to Ulrichs in Italy two years before: "He lives exiled & in great poverty.... There is a singular charm about the old man, great sweetness, the remains of refined beauty. His squalor was appalling...." Ulrichs, Symonds wrote, was "one of the men I prized & respected most in Europe" (Symonds, *Letters* 3:814–15).

Though homosexuality in England had been forbidden by the criminal law since 1533, the last executions for "buggery" – the legal term since the 16th century – occurred in the 1830s, but it took another 30 years for the death penalty to be abolished. The notorious Article XI, introduced by Henry Labouchere, into the Criminal Law Amendment Act of 1885 (see Labouchere) made criminal any male homosexual act, either private or public. As David Hilliard writes, the law resulted in "conditions within which men with homosexual feelings began to develop a conscious collective identity. For although a small homosexual subculture had existed in London and a few other cities in the British Isles since the early 18th century, the final development of a homosexual underground was essentially a phenomenon of the late 19th century" (183).

In 1880, among undergraduates at Oxford and Cambridge, the subject of boy love emerged in an "animated correspondence" in the *Oxford and Cambridge Undergraduate's Journal* in three issues in April and May after the appearance of an anonymous pamphlet written by Charles Edward Hutchinson, titled *Boy Worship*. Officials in both universities ended publication of such correspondence in the journal (Ellmann 60n/58n). Just three years before, Wilde, while still an undergraduate at Oxford, had submitted an essay and poem, "The Tomb of Keats," to the *Irish Monthly* commemorating his visit to Keats's grave in Rome: the editor, Rev. Matthew Russell, suggested that, in the essay, Wilde change the word *boy* to *youth* in such phrases as "this divine boy" (Keats) and "a lovely brown boy" (describing a painting of St. Sebastian, the favorite saint among Uranians), but Wilde declined to make the changes.

Within the homosexual subculture at the time were numerous Anglo-Catholic churchmen and adherents within the Church of England, for they found in Anglo-Catholicism a religion "freed from the respectability and the puritanism of the churches in which they had grown up" (McLeod 249). During the Oxford Movement of the 1860s,

ritualism performed by Anglican clergy was "increasingly subjected to hostile scrutiny" (189). Such clergymen of "extreme High Church proclivities," *Punch* (10 June 1865) noted, "are very fond of dressing like ladies. They are much addicted to wearing vestments diversified with smart and gay colours, and variously trimmed and embroidered." By the end of the century, such figures as Walter Pater and Gerard Manley Hopkins were attracted to ritualism as symbolic and aesthetic expressions of the church's authority (Hopkins converting to Roman Catholicism to enter the priesthood as a result), their Uranian impulses held discreetly in check. However, Pater's intimate friend, Brother à Becket, a lay brother at the priory of St. Austin's, wrote a poem for Pater's birthday:

> ...Your darling soul I say is enflamed with love
> for me;
> Your very eyes do move I cry with sympathy;
> Your darling feet and hands are blessings ruled
> by love.... (qtd. in Hilliard 193)

In the late 19th century, periodicals were generally available for Uranians to publish their works and establish a sense of solidarity. Charles Kains Jackson (1857–1933), during his editorship of the *Artist and Journal of Home Culture*, 1888–94, gave the periodical a distinctly Uranian orientation. He sent a copy to Symonds, who responded with enthusiasm and asked whether he could send poems or essays. At Oxford, Alfred Douglas, as editor of the *Spirit Lamp: An Aesthetic, Literary and Critical Magazine*, 1892–93, also provided Uranians with a haven for their work. Presumably at Douglas's urging, Wilde contributed a poem and two "poems in prose" (see entries): "The New Remorse" (with the suggestive beginning: "The sin was mine; I did not understand"); "The House of Judgment"; and "The Disciple."

When the periodical ceased publishing, Douglas urged Wilde to contribute to a new Oxford periodical, the *Chameleon* (1894), an appropriate title for a publication more obviously Uranian than the *Spirit Lamp*. To the first issue (which was its last), Wilde contributed "Phrases and Philosophies for the Use of the Young." The editor, John Francis Bloxam (see entry), contributed the startling story, "The Priest and the Acolyte," which was later brought up by the prosecution at Wilde's trials. In the early 20th century, the story was sometimes attributed to Wilde.

Another contributor, John Gambril Nicholson (1866–1931), who had appeared in the *Artist and Journal of Home Culture*, was the author of a volume of homosexual poems titled *Love in Earnest* (1892), the pun on "Earnest" – Ernest, a fourteen-year-old, is the love object – anticipating Wilde's pun in his play. Though it is unknown whether Wilde and Nicholson knew each other, it is likely that Wilde knew of Nicholson's *Love in Earnest*. Indeed, even Symonds, living in Switzerland, refers to the book in a letter to a friend (see Symonds, *Letters* 3:704). Also a contributor to the *Chameleon*, Nicholson wrote a prose poem in a pseudo-Biblical style, concerned with the loss of a sixteen-year-old Uranian love. Finally, one of Douglas's poems published in the *Chameleon* was "Two Loves," which contains the most famous line in Uranian literature: "I am the love that dare not speak its name."

In June 1892, at the Authors' Club Wilde met George Ives (see entry), who had established a secret society of Uranians that included such poets who were Anglican churchmen as Rev. Edwin Bradford (1860–1944), Rev. Ellsworth Cottam (1863–1945), and Rev. Montague Summers (1880–1948), but Wilde seems not to have been a member. Ives, who was impressed by Wilde's wit, was convinced that his friend was not committed to advancing the "Cause." In his diary, Ives wrote: "He seems to have no purpose, I am all purpose" (qtd. in Stokes 70-71). Because he had little confidence in Wilde's commitment, Ives was probably startled to read a letter from Wilde in March 1898 when *The Ballad of Reading Gaol* achieved success: "Yes: I have no doubt we shall win, but the road is long, and red with monstrous martyrdoms" (*Letters* 721).

References: Herbert M. Schueller and Robert L. Peters, eds., *Letters of John Addington Symonds*, Vol. 3 (1969); Timothy d'Arch Smith, *Love in Earnest: Some Notes on the Lives and Writings of English "Uranian" Poets from 1889 to 1930* (1970); Brian Reade, ed., *Sexual Heretics: Male Homosexuality in Literature from 1850 to 1900* (1970); Hugh McLeod, *Class and Religion in the Late Victorian City* (1974); Jeffrey Weeks, *Coming Out: Homosexual Politics in Britain from the Nineteenth Century to the Present* (1977); David Hilliard, "UnEnglish and Unmanly: Anglo-Catholicism and Homosexuality," *Victorian Studies*

(Winter 1982); Richard Dellamora, *Masculine Desire: The Sexual Politics of Victorian Aestheticism* (1990); Karl Beckson, "Love in Earnest: The Importance of Being Uranian," *London in the 1890s: A Cultural History* (1993); Alan Sinfield, *The Wilde Century: Effeminacy, Oscar Wilde, and the Queer Moment* (1994); Linda Dowling, *Hellenism and Homosexuality in Victorian Oxford* (1994); John Stokes, "Wilde at Bay: the Diary of George Ives," *Oscar Wilde: Myths, Miracles, and Imitations* (1996).

"URBS SACRA AETERNA"

Published: *Illustrated Monitor: A Monthly Magazine of Catholic Literature* (Dublin) 4 (June 1877): 130; rev. in *Poems* (1881) and (1882). The Latin title means "The Sacred, Eternal City."

This sonnet was written in Rome on Wilde's trip to Greece and Italy (returning via the Holy City) in March-April 1877 with Rev. John Mahaffey (see entry) and David Hunter-Blair, Wilde's Oxford friend. When Pope Pius IX received Wilde and Hunter-Blair, a Catholic, in a private audience, he turned to Wilde and urged that he follow his fellow student into the kingdom of God. On his return to the hotel, Wilde was so affected that he immediately locked himself in his room and wrote "Urbs Sacra Aeterna."

In this poem, Wilde celebrates the changes that Rome has seen: in the past, when "the wild nations shuddered at thy rod," but its true glory exists at "the present hour, / When pilgrims kneel before the Holy One, / The prisoned shepherd of the Church of God" (for the significance of the "prisoned shepherd," see entry: "Sonnet on Approaching Italy").

In following Hunter-Blair's memoir (see Mikhail 1:9), Ellmann errs (74/71): "Urbs Sacra Aeterna" was not published under the title "Graffiti d'Italia" (a different work entirely). Furthermore, "Urbs Sacra Aeterna" could not have appeared in 1876, as Ellmann states, since the event that Hunter-Blair describes occurred in 1877 (the date that Wilde gives for the writing of the poem).

V

"THE VALUE OF ART IN MODERN LIFE":
See LECTURES IN BRITAIN

"VARIOUS VERSIFIERS"

Published: *PMG*, 28 April 1887, 5. Unsigned reviews of books published in 1887. Mason, who had not listed "Various Versifiers" in his 1914 bibliography, identifies it as Wilde's in a notation in his personal copy at the Clark Library.

In the opening of this rather phlegmatic review of 12 books, Wilde employs an extended military metaphor to characterize the endless profusion of "awkward squads" of unimaginative poets plodding by:

Human nature is so inexhaustibly sanguine that even after countless disappointments one keeps hoping against hope for the appearance of a poet amid the poetasters. As each new "awkward squad" marches past, the reviewer watches with weary eyes for a single recruit who shows the faintest appearance of carrying a marshal's baton in his knapsack. Alas! the endless column drags along, some plodding heavily in measured time, others stumbling, halting, or indulging in quaint and grotesque caprioles; but none marching with the noble poise, and free, firm stride indicative of god-sent music in the soul.

Wilde proceeds with his inspection of John Stuart Blackie, no "raw recruit," who does not disappoint a reader, for his *Messis Vitae: Gleanings of Song from a Happy Life* contains what one expects: "...a cheerful, tolerant optimism, a healthy and breezy humour, and a gift teeming, with here and there a certain 'lilt' in his song...." The students of the Scotch universities, to whom Blackie dedicates his lays, "will get nothing but edification from them, only they should be warned not to accept as 'sonnets'...fourteen-line poems which the Professor so denominates." Quickly, Wilde turns to "the most promising of the poets now before us": Alfred Hayes, author of *The Last Crusade*,

who can write "excellent blank verse, not without pictorial vividness." He lacks, however, "that strong individuality without which no singer, in these days, can make himself clearly heard above the versifying throng."

Turning to H. D. Rawnsley's *Sonnets Round the English Coast*, Wilde notes that "'the sonnet's scanty plot of ground' has a fatal fascination for the modern rhymer. There are people who seem to go about building fourteen-line 'monuments' to every other 'moment' in their lives [an allusion to the first line of Dante Gabriel Rossetti's prefatory poem, "The Sonnet," in *The House of Life*, 1881: "A sonnet is a moment's monument"], until one would fain beg them to write an epic and have done with it." Wilde judges Rawnsley's sonnets as "very passable," but "the poet who deliberately sets himself to stud the coast with sonnets, like a contractor erecting martello towers, evidently proceeds on a false principle." Wilde's concluding remark leads him into a mere two sentences on J. Rutter's *Gordon's Songs and Sonnets*, "a solid volume [of] nearly sixty sonnets and a considerable number of other poems all dedicated to the honour and glory of General Gordon": "...it need only be said that they breathe a spirit of fervent piety and uncompromising patriotism."

Proceeding to Phillip Stewart's *Poems*, Wilde notes that this volume "evidently sets a high value on the lightest utterance of his muse...." Wilde quotes two lines from the volume, one of which mentions that "the poet [doth] lay aside his well": "If Mr. Stewart will take our advice, he himself will imitate this poet, and hasten to 'Lay aside his well.'" Of Joseph Sykes's *Poems*, Wilde has little to say beyond what Sykes himself tells the reader – that he has omitted from his collection "some compositions which seemed trivial or immature": Wilde adds that "since he says so we are bound to believe him." Of *Whims and Fantasies* by "Emeritus," Wilde has understandably little to say beyond quoting some lines from "Epitaph on a Favourite Red Spaniel, Killed by a Reaping Machine":

There lies, as dead as fallen log,
My humble friend, my faithful dog:
Twelve years of happiness he'd seen
When mangled by a damned machine.

With sparkling facetiousness, Wilde adds that Mrs. Leo Hunter's "Ode to an Expiring Frog" "contains nothing so true and tender as this."

Wilde mentions Francis Fahy, the author of *Irish Songs and Poems*, as "evidently qualifying to serve as the Laureate of liberated Erin...in the facility of his metres and the scantiness of his ideas; but he has a healthy hatred of the Saxon oppressor, and that should go a long way to furnish forth an Irish laureate." Wilde concludes with a brief notice of three American poets. Anna Katharine Green's *Risifi's Daughter: A Drama* is "an old-fashioned drama in blank verse," and Walter Campbell's *Civitas* is "a historico-political allegory in rhymed doggerel." Finally, G. L. Raymond's *Ballads of the Revolution* "are illustrated by copious footnotes giving chapter and verse for almost every line of the poems. Unfortunately the text is scarcely less prosaic than the footnotes."

"VENUS OR VICTORY?"

Published: *PMG*, 24 Feb. 1888, 2–3; rpt. in *Reviews* (1908). An unsigned review of W. J. Stillman's *On the Track of Ulysses: Together with an Excursion in Quest of the So-called Venus of Melos* (1888).

Wilde begins with the question of the identify of the "so-called Venus of Melos" (or Venus de Milo, discovered in Melos, Greece, in 1820): "Who is she, this marble mutilated goddess, whom Gautier loved, to whom Heine bent his knee?" This "fascinating subject...in a most interesting book recently published in America [by Stillman, an American artist, journalist, and art critic] claims that the work of art in question is no sea-born and foam-born Aphrodite, but that very Victory Without Wings that once stood in the little chapel outside the gates of the Acropolis at Athens." Six years after the discovery of the Venus of Melos, archeologists began arguing about its identity, Stillman following one line of thought that the statue is not that of Venus, "being far too heroic in character to correspond to the Greek conception of Aphrodite...but that it agrees distinctly with certain well-known statues of Victory...."

Though Stillman's basic argument is "on old ground," he has made a "real artistic discovery": while working about the Acropolis, he photographed the mutilated Victories in the Temple of Nikè Apteros, the "'Wingless Victory,' the little Ionic temple in which stood that statue of Victory of which it was said that '*the Athenians made her*

without wings that she might never leave Athens.'" He was struck, Wilde remarks, "with the close resemblance of the type to that of the Melian statue."

As for its discovery in Melos, Stillman "points out that Melos belonged to Athens as late as she had any Greek allegiance, and that it is probable that the statue was sent there for concealment on the occasion of some siege or invasion." Some will regret the "possibility of the disappearance of the old name, and as Venus not as Victory will still worship the stately goddess, but there are others who will be glad to see in her the image and ideal of that spiritual enthusiasm to which Athens owed her liberty, and by which alone can liberty be won."

VERA; OR, THE NIHILISTS

Privately Printed: September 1880 by Ranken & Co. (London); rpt., rev. in 1882 while Wilde was lecturing in America. Both editions have the words "Strictly Private" in square brackets at the top of the title page. (Richard D'Oyly Carte, who had organized Wilde's lecture tour, arranged for the printing of the 25 copies of the second, revised 1882 edition of *Vera*, which focuses on Vera in the prologue rather than on the Nihilists as a group, an indication why the title shifted to the singular *Nihilist* for the 1883 production.) Wilde continued revising the play after the second edition was printed in 1882, and, in preparation for the 1883 production, he revised further, renaming the Prologue as Act I and now referring to *Vera* as a play in five acts rather than with a Prologue and four acts.

The Aborted Production: In 1880, after having had only a few copies of *Vera* privately printed, Wilde sent them to some noted actresses, including Ellen Terry, in order to stimulate their interest in performing the leading role. Arrangements with Mrs. Bernard Beere to act the leading role in a morning performance of *Vera* at the Adelphi Theatre, London, on 17 December 1881, never came to pass, for three weeks before, the *World* (30 Nov. 1881) reported: "Considering the present state of political feeling in England, Mr. Oscar Wilde has decided on postponing, for a time, the production of his drama, *Vera*." The "political feeling" presumably involved the assassination by the Nihilists, in March, of Czar Alexander II (echoed in the murder of Czar Ivan in *Vera*).

Scholars have uniformly assumed that Wilde had withdrawn his play at the request of the Prince of Wales in order to spare the royal family undue discomfort (the new czar, Alexander III, was married to the sister of Alexandra, the Princess of Wales). However, George Rowell has argued convincingly that the assassination of Alexander II, some eight months before, was hardly news. Moreover, no evidence exists that the Prince of Wales had requested that the performance be cancelled. Finally, the Lord Chamberlain's papers do not indicate that a license had been issued for the performance. Rowell concludes that "the pretext for the postponement may have been the play's political content, but the real reason was surely lack of funds to put it on" (99).

The First Production: Prior to the production in 1883, Frank P. Hulette, the managing editor of the *Evening Observer* in Dunkirk, New York, and author of a play titled *Vera*, notified the managers of the Union Square Theatre, where the play was scheduled to be performed, of possible copyright infringement (Mason 268–69). In the event of any difficulty with the title, Marie Prescott, assigned to the role of Vera, inquired of Wilde whether he would change the title of his play to either *Vera Sabouroff* or *Vera – The Nihilist* (Mason 269). Subsequently, the title in the playbill was *Vera; or, The Nihilist*, the full title used to avoid litigation. (In Volume 2 of the 1908 *Collected Edition*, Ross merely reprinted the 1882 version with its plural *Nihilists* restored.)

On 11 August, Wilde arrived in New York for the première performance. Shortly before, Wilde had told Prescott: "My name signed to a play will excite some interest in London and America. Your name as the heroine carries great weight with it" (*Letters* 143). In another letter to her, he remarks that his play tries

to express within the limits of art that Titan cry of the peoples for liberty, which in the Europe of our day is threatening thrones, and making governments unstable from Spain to Russia.... But it is a play not of politics but of passion. It deals with no theories of government, but with men and women simply; and modern Nihilistic Russia, with all the terror of its tyranny and the marvel of its martyrdoms, is merely the fiery and fervent background in front of which the persons of my dream live

and love. (*Letters* 148–49)

As the production took shape, Wilde gave Prescott extensive directions concerning many details of scenery and costumes (see, for example, *Letters* 149).

Vera opened on 20 August 1883, at the Union Square Theatre in New York for a run of only one week. Marie Prescott suggested that Wilde join the company on tour in the role of Prince Paul, but he refused. Inaccurately, Mason remarks that she toured the United States with the play, appearing at the Detroit Opera House on 28 December and elsewhere (272); in fact, after two performances were given in Detroit, adverse reviews ended the prospect of any further performances in other cities.

Sources: In the late 19th century, English newspapers and periodicals reported extensively on Russian political events, particularly since the British involvement in the Russo-Turkish War, 1877–78, and in the conflict with the Russians in Afghanistan between 1878 and 1880. During this period, the Nihilists' subversive activities prompted Russian authorities to arrest 2,000 people on suspicion of treason. In the autumn and winter of 1877–78, 193 of this group were put on trial; in January, a Nihilist named Vera Zasulich shot a General Trepov, resulting in another widely covered trial by the British press. After the woman was acquitted, the Nihilists launched a "Wave of Terror," consisting of assassinations and attempts on the lives of the Czar and government officials.

On 14 December 1878, an article titled "Modern History and Tragedy" appeared in the *Era*, a theatrical publication, which had also been covering the Russian political situation. The paper, Reed writes, "called for contemporary history rather than matters of the distant past as the subject for new plays. Nihilism was not only contemporary history; it was fraught with intrigue, injustice, oppression, human conflict – in short, drama" (xxii). To Wilde, suggests Katharine Worth, the Nihilists were "congenial as an oppressed intellectual minority but above all, Nihilism would have appealed through its emphasis on freedom and the individual's right to express his individuality. Sexual freedom figured largely in the Nihilist manifesto and women's emancipation was a main plank in their programme" (25).

The Plot: In the 1882 version in the *Collected*

Edition, the play begins with a Prologue, in which the innkeeper Peter Sabouroff, Vera's father, is lamenting to Michael, one of Prince Paul Maraloffski's gamekeepers and secretly a Nihilist, that Dmitri, Peter's son, has been strangely silent (except for requests for more money) since he went to Moscow to study law. Though Dmitri is "a merry lad," Vera is serious – "she goes about as solemn as a priest for days at a time," her father says. Vera, who is present in the inn, expresses her misery concerning Dmitri's silence. Soldiers escorting chained prisoners, who are called "Nihilists," enter the inn.

When she bribes a soldier to permit the prisoners to rest and eat, she discovers that one of them is her brother, Dmitri, who had joined the revolutionaries. When their father, Peter, also recognizes Dmitri, he offers to pay for his release, but the colonel reminds him that Dmitri is a Nihilist. As Dmitri is led away, Vera picks up a slip of paper that her brother had surreptitiously dropped for her: It contains an address in Moscow and the Nihilists' oath, part of which follows: "To strangle whatever nature is in me; neither to love nor to be loved; neither to pity nor to be pitied; neither to marry nor to be given in marriage, till the end is come." She pledges to her brother, now gone, that she will keep this oath.

Act I opens five years later in Moscow with a gathering of Nihilists, who participate in rituals of obedience and allegiance to their oath, now extended: "...to stab secretly by night; to drop poison in the glass; to set father against son, and husband against wife; without fear, without hope, without future, to suffer, to annihilate, to revenge." They await the appearance of Vera, who has become their principal leader. Michael suspects that Alexis, a medical student, is a spy. When Vera arrives, after having attended a masked ball at the palace so that she might see the Czar and "all his cursed brood," she informs them that martial law is to be proclaimed on the next day: "The last right," she says, "to which the people clung has been taken from them.... It means the strangling of a whole nation."

Vera urges Alexis to return to his fellow students for fear that he will be missed: spies are prominent at the university. But Alexis affirms his solidarity with the Nihilists. Attracted to him, Vera broods to herself that she might have loved him had she not taken the oath. Reminding herself of

the oath, she concludes: "Remember what you are – a Nihilist, a Nihilist!" Michael, announcing that there is a traitor among them, points to Alexis, who had whispered the secret password to the guards at the palace and had let himself in by a private door with his own key. Michael had followed him and witnessed Alexis's treachery. They all cry: "Kill him! He is a spy!" But Vera defends him even before Alexis denies the allegations: "Spy? You know I am not. I am with you, my brothers, to the death."

Suddenly, soldiers knock at the door and demand that it be opened in the name of the Czar, an apparent confirmation that Alexis has betrayed them. They quickly don their masks as though they are actors rehearsing a tragedy. When the general, who has been searching for Vera, orders them to remove the masks, Alexis removes his to the surprise of the general, who exclaims: "His Imperial Highness the Czarevitch!" The Nihilists believe that all is over for them, but Alexis convinces the general that gipsies hate to be stared at, and he testifies that "these honest people" are his friends. He had joined them out of boredom at the palace, where his father, the Czar, had "imprisoned" him.

The general mentions that Vera Sabouroff, the leader of the Nihilists, had been seen in the city and that he had been hunting her for the last eighteen months. Recently, he caught sight of her outside Odessa, but she shot one of his horses as he was gaining on her. The Emperor has put 20,000 roubles on her head. When the soldiers depart, Vera exclaims: "Saved! and by you!" Clasping her hand, Alexis says to the others: "Brothers, you trust me now?"

Act II opens in the Council Chamber of the Emperor's Palace, where several courtiers are present. Entering, Alexis complains of his father's insistence that he remain in the palace. He has been sickened by the "bloody butchery" of some wretched Nihilists hanged that morning, though he says that "it was a noble thing to see how well these men can die." Responding to Alexis's remark concerning the lesson of experience, Prince Paul Maraloffski, the prime minister and the first of Wilde's sophisticates who speak in witty epigrams, says: "Experience, the name men give to their mistakes" (with a slight change in phraseology, Wilde recycled this remark in Act III of *Lady Windermere's Fan*). Soon, Alexis upbraids Prince Paul for mismanaging the Czar's business and embittering his nature, making him hated by the people as a tyrant.

When Prince Petrovitch remarks that the Nihilists have little interest in the Czar, Prince Paul says in an aside: "Indifference is the revenge the world takes on mediocrities," and when Prince Petrovitch confesses to being "bored with life," Prince Paul identifies such boredom as "The maladie du siècle! You want a new excitement, Prince." Alexis understands Prince Paul's Decadent sensibility: "He would stab his best friend for the sake of writing an epigram on his tombstone, or experiencing a new sensation." When the Czar enters, he is clearly driven by delusions of persecution, quick to hang anyone he suspects of plotting against him. When Alexis pleads with his father that the people's discontent is the result of tyranny and injustice, the Czar protests that he loves the people and warns his son: "Have a care, boy; have a care. You don't seem to be cured yet of your foolish tongue."

When the Czar asks Prince Paul whether Vera Sabouroff is still in Moscow, the prime minister vows to capture her. Alexis pleads with the Czar to give the people what they ask. In response, the Czar vows to have Vera in his power before the week has ended. Prince Paul urges the Czar to sign the proclamation establishing martial law so that he can "crush every Nihilist in Russia in six months...." When Alexis reminds his father of sacrifices made by the people on the battlefield, the Czar calls him an "insolent boy! Have you forgotten who is Emperor of Russia?" "No," says Alexis, "The people reign now, by the grace of God."

Furious, the Czar orders him removed, calling him "Devil! Assassin!" Alexis's response startles everyone at court: "Because I am a Nihilist!" All present call for his arrest. The cynical Prince Paul (never at a loss for a droll observation) remarks: "Heroics are out of place in a palace." Nevertheless, Alexis delivers a conventional Nihilist speech. Vowing war on the "people," the Czar tramples on Alexis's sword. Ordering his son to prison, he steps out on the balcony, where he is shot. Alexis cries out, "Father!" But the dying Czar calls him a murderer.

Act III opens with the same scene as that in Act I, the conspirators gathering once again, masked and cloaked, going through their secret rituals (Wilde modeled them after those he had learned as a Freemason: see Freemasonry). When the fifth conspirator fails to recite the creed, the others cry, "A spy! A spy! Unmask! Unmask!" The interloper is Prince Paul, who reveals that the new Czar, Alexis, has banished him. He has now joined the Nihilists to revenge himself for the loss of his estates and his office. The other conspirators, won over by Prince Paul, welcome him, though Vera is skeptical of his loyalty. Michael, who enters, is welcomed by the president of the group as the "man who has killed a king." Talk centers on the assassination of the new Czar, their former conspirator. Meanwhile, Vera is in a state of anxiety over Alexis's absence. When the group votes to kill him, Vera speaks in his defense. But they brandish daggers and shout, "To-night! to-night!" And Michael argues that Vera would betray them for a paramour. But she protests that she does not love Alexis, nor does he love her.

When Michael reminds her of Dmitri's fate, Vera calls for the lots to be drawn. (Since melodrama virtually demands that Vera choose the fatal lot, Wilde yields to the audience's expectations.) Vera opens her lot: "Dmitri, my brother, you shall have your revenge now." Prince Paul provides her with the key to the private door in the palace as well as the passwords for the guards.

Act IV takes place in the antechamber of the Czar's private room with the courtiers, who had appeared in Act II, commenting on how well the new Czar is doing. Unaware that the Czar has entered unobserved and is overhearing the conversation, the General announces that the Czar wishes the people to have deputies represent them in a parliament. During the conversation, the Czar bursts in, calling them "Traitors!" Determined to be merciful, he will spare their lives if they leave Russia immediately. Prince Petrovitch pleads, "Sire, we did but jest." The Czar responds: "Then I banish you for your bad jokes."

His thoughts turn to Vera: "Though I have broken my oath, she will have trust." After he lies down on a couch, Vera enters in a black cloak, and as she prepares to kill him, he seizes her hands, protesting that it was for her that he broke his oath and wore his father's crown. He then offers her the crown. He tells her that the Nihilists, including Dmitri, will be returned. Then, as conspirators murmur outside, the Czar suspects a plot against him and urges Vera to become the Empress. Freeing herself from him, she cries out: "I am a Nihilist! I cannot wear a crown!" But when she attempts to recite her oath, as though to fortify herself against the Czar's entreaties, she breaks down and confesses: "Oh, I am a woman! ...O Alexis! I too have broken my oath; I am a traitor. I love."

Meanwhile, loud murmurs of the conspirators are heard in the street. Vera, rushing across the room, stabs herself and rushes to the window. When the Czar snatches the dagger from her hand, Vera tells him that a bloody dagger is the sign to her fellow conspirators that the Czar is dead. She urges him to throw the poisoned dagger out of the window, but the Czar declares that they shall die together. Believing that Vera is in danger, the conspirators break in below, but while the Czar is distracted, she seizes the dagger and flings it out of the window. The Czar asks: "What have you done?" As though renouncing her former revolutionary ideals, Vera responds as she lies dying: "I have saved Russia."

Early Theater Reviews: The reviewer for the *New York Times* (21 Aug. 1883) regarded Nihilism in *Vera* as "a stupid and tiresome element of the work. These rabid fellows who talk like lunatics, swear the most preposterous oaths, and act like children give no dramatic force to the play." The play is "a kind of pulpit from which Mr. Wilde utters his declamatory dictum upon freedom and the rights of man.... Yet there is a great deal of good writing in *Vera*, and Mr. Wilde exhibits cleverness and wit in a character like Prince Paul....." Despite this favorable remark, the reviewer concludes that the play is "unreal, long-winded, and wearisome. It comes as near failure as an ingenious and able writer can bring it" (rpt. in Beckson).

In the *New York Daily Tribune* (21 Aug.), the reviewer remarks that public curiosity was "poorly rewarded...by a display of several queer scenes, picturesque at points, but mostly ugly, and by the exposition of a fanciful, foolish, highly peppered story of love, intrigue and politics, invested with the Russian accessories of fur and dark-lanterns, and overlaid with bantam gabble about freedom and the people...." Wilde has constructed his play "upon a central idea which is incredible and preposterous, but which, nevertheless, is useful as the motive or spring of climacteric situations." Though *Vera* is "high-stepping, wordy, and long-winded," it is "a practical piece of a common-place order..." (rpt. in Beckson).

In a review that departs radically from those preceding it, the *Dramatic Mirror* (25 Aug.) remarks that the audience had gathered at the Union Square Theatre to laugh, but "They remained to applaud." From a "literary, as well as a dramatic point of view, *Vera* is a work that takes rank among the highest order of plays." The subject, as the reviewer continues, "is masterly and it demanded masterly treatment. This the author has given it.... Just as it stands – making no allowance for the blunders – *Vera* is the noblest contribution to its literature the stage has received in many years."

Manuscripts: The Clark Library has the complete early draft of the play – with its original title of *Vera of the Nihilists* – in a notebook, with many differences from its 1880 printing, along with two pages of foolscap *not* in Wilde's autograph. The Clark Library also has a privately printed copy of *Vera* with corrections for the 1883 New York performance. The Berg Collection has a privately printed text of the play dated 1882 with a few revisions and additions for Act IV in Wilde's hand, presumably for the 1883 New York performance. The British Library holds an 1882 edition of *Vera* with emendations in Wilde's autograph on facing pages. The Beinecke Library has a draft of the close of Act II, consisting of 28 autograph pages (the autograph revisions and emendations printed in Mason 274–81), apparently used for the 1883 stage performance.

References: Katharine Worth, "A Revolutionary Start: 'Vera; or, The Nihilists,'" *Oscar Wilde* (1983); Frances Miriam Reed, ed., *Vera; or, The Nihilist* (1989); George Rowell, "The Truth about *Vera*," *Nineteenth Century Theatre* (Winter 1993).

VERLAINE, PAUL (1844–96)

The French Symbolist poet Verlaine first met Wilde in Paris early in 1883, but little is known of their relationship other than two or three brief encounters. An admirer of Verlaine's genius as a poet, Wilde invited Arthur Symons in October 1890 to dine with him and "to talk about French art, the one art now in Europe that is worth discussing – Verlaine's art especially" (*Letters* 276). In *De Profundis*, Wilde writes that "wherever there is a romantic movement in Art, there somehow, and under some form, is Christ, or the Soul of Christ." Among other writers, Wilde mentions "Verlaine and Verlaine's poems" (*Letters* 482), perhaps Wilde's allusion to Verlaine's return to Roman Catholicism as a result of his imprisonment from 1873 to 1875 for shooting Arthur Rimbaud during a turbulent homosexual relationship. Wilde called Verlaine "the one Christian poet since Dante" (*Letters* 488).

In November 1891, the French poet Yvanhoë Rambosson and Wilde joined Enrique Gomez Carrillo, a young Guatemalan writer who was also a diplomat, at the Café Harcourt. Verlaine, also present, was dressed shabbily. Discomforted by Verlaine's appearance, Wilde mentioned what he would later remark to Gide: "I have put only talent into my works. I have put all my genius into my life." Verlaine turned to Rambosson: "This man is a true pagan. He possesses the insouciance which is half of happiness, for he does not know penitence" (qtd. in Ellmann 341–42/322). After Verlaine's death, Wilde remarked in an interview concerning Verlaine that "the statue of heroes should be on the battlefield of his life" (see *Letters* 684n1) – perhaps an allusion to the Café François Premier, where Verlaine spent much of his time with other writers in aesthetic debate and where Wilde may have first met him in 1883.

"A VISION"

Published: First appeared as "A Night Vision" in *Kottabos* 2 (Hilary Term 1877): 331; rev. as "A Vision" in *Poems* (1881).

Dante's *Divine Comedy*, as the reference to Beatrice indicates in line 11, and Elizabeth Barrett Browning's "A Vision of Poets" (1844), in which Aeschylus, Sophocles, and Euripides appear, are the likely inspirations for Wilde's poem.

In this sonnet, the vision depicted by Wilde involves the three great Greek dramatists – two celebrated ("Two crowned Kings") but the third standing alone "with sad eyes as one uncomforted, / And wearied with man's never-ceasing moan...." When the speaker asks Beatrice, "Who are these?" she responds: "Aeschylos first, the second Sophokles, / And last (wide stream of tears!) Euripides." In his tragedies, Euripides departed from the conventions established by Aeschlyus and Sophocles by dressing his mythic figures in symbolic costumes reflecting their suffering; thus, in his *Telephus*, the hero is dressed in rags. He also employed contemporary language and gave prominence to women and slaves in the untraditional roles of tragic and noble figures. In his *Poetics*,

Aristotle called Euripides "the most tragic of the poets."

Manuscript: A MS. version, later than that published in *Kottabos*, is printed in Mason 96.

"VITA NUOVA"

Published: First appeared as "ΠΟΝΤΟΣ ΑΤΡΥΓΕΤΟΣ" (Greek: "The Unfruitful or Barren Sea," derived from Homer's *Odyssey* 2:370) in the *Irish Monthly* 5 (Dec. 1877): 746; rev. as "The Unvintageable Sea" in William MacIlwaine, ed., *Lyra Hibernica Sacra* (Belfast: M'Caw, Stevenson & Orr; Dublin: Hodges, Foster & Figgis; London: Geo. Bell & Sons, 1878, 2nd ed. 1879), 324 (unlisted in Mason); rev. as "Vita Nuova" in *Poems* (1881) and (1882). The present title is taken from Dante's similarly titled work, meaning "New Life," involving the vision that Dante has of Beatrice, who becomes in *The Divine Comedy* an instrument of his salvation.

The speaker, a fisherman standing by the "unvintageable sea," cries "'Alas!...my life is full of pain,' / And who can garner fruit or golden grain / From these waste fields which travail ceaselessly!'" But in his "final cast / Into the sea" (in Luke 5:5-6, Jesus tells his disciples to cast their empty nets once more, resulting in "a great multitude of fishes"), he sees "a sudden glory!": "...I saw / From the black waters of my tortured past / The argent splendour of white limbs ascend!"

Though the birth of Venus is implied, the lines also suggest Christ's resurrection, which confirms for his disciples their faith in his divine nature. In the earlier version of the poem in the *Irish Monthly*, Christ had been present in the final lines: "...and I saw / Christ walking on the waters: fear was past; / I knew that I had found my perfect friend."

W

"WASTED DAYS"

Published: *Kottabos* 3 (Michaelmas term 1877): 56. Below the title, there appears "(From a Picture Painted by Miss V.T.)." The picture, painted on a six-inch-square tile by Wilde's acquaintance Violet Troubridge (1858–1931), later Mrs. Walter Gurney, is reproduced in Mason, facing p. 96, with the text of "Wasted Days." For inclusion in *Poems* (1881), Wilde changed the title to "Madonna Mia," which Swinburne had used as a title in *Songs and Ballads* (1866). In addition to many revisions, Wilde changed the central figure, who becomes "a lily-girl" (taking on symbolic implications associated with death and resurrection as well as another possible allusion to Lillie Langtry) in contrast to the "fair slim boy" in "Wasted Days." Both poems appeared with separate titles in *Poems* (1908).

In this sonnet, the speaker describes the "fair slim boy not made for this world's pain" (echoing the first line of "The Grave of Keats"), whose pale cheeks have left no kiss's stain. There is a foreboding sense that his physical beauty may come to naught. The sestet depicts reapers in "weariest labour toiling wearily, / To no sweet sound of laughter, or of lute." But the boy "still dreams: nor knows that night is nigh: / And in the night-time no man gathers fruit" (the final phrase derived from the last line of Meleager's final speech in Swinburne's *Atalanta in Calydon*, 1865).

WELL-MADE PLAY

Though the term *well-made play* (or, in French, *pièce bien faite*) has been sometimes regarded as derogatory when referring to the devices used in constructing a play, in mid-19th-century France such drama was generally regarded with approval. The playwright who developed the popular form was Eugène Scribe (1791–1861), whose plots – such as that of his greatest success, *Adrienne Lecouvreur* (1849) – were designed to keep the audience in a constant state of suspense from beginning to end, no matter how seemingly improbable the action.

The formula included such devices as love intrigues and consequent misunderstandings among the characters with a reliance on theatrical props, such as letters, fans, and bracelets, which determine the direction of the plot by a series of ironic twists and turns. Often, the discovery of secrets in one or more characters' lives leads to the obligatory scene (*scène a faire*), which the audience expects to witness and which the playwright is obliged to present. As described by Jeffrey Huberman, such a scene is "the inevitable confrontation of misunderstandings that is at once the lowest and highest point in the protagonist's adventure" (40). The *dénouement* – or unravelling of the plot – involves a revelation hitherto withheld from one or more of the characters. The resolution concludes the play, in which a suspenseful reversal of circumstances often occurs. As John Russell Taylor remarks, 19th-century well-made plays were "held up by conservatives to proponents of the New Drama as models of craftsmanship" (17).

Scribe's best-known disciple was Victorien Sardou (1831–1908), whose versatile plays – such as *La Tosca* (1887), *Cléopatre* (1890), and *Madame Sans-Gêne* (1893) – contained a greater degree of craftsmanship than those by Scribe. Bernard Shaw, who had a low regard for the artificial devices of well-made plays, dubbed Sardou's work "Sardoodledom" (*Our Theatres* 1:133). Nevertheless, he borrowed various devices of the well-made play for his own works: in *Widowers' Houses* (1892), for example, Dr. Trench discovers to his horror that his income is derived from investments in slum housing, and in *Mrs. Warren's Profession* (1898), Vivie Warren discovers the secret of her mother's life of prostitution and her part-ownership of brothels. Other late 19th-century British playwrights, such as Henry Arthur Jones (1851–1929) and Arthur Wing Pinero (1855–1934), developed less artificial forms of the French well-made play by eliminating some of the more lurid elements for Victorian audiences.

Another practitioner of the well-made play, Dumas *fils* (1824–95), is best known for *La Dame aux Camélias* (1852) and *Le Demi-Monde* (1855), which could not be produced in England because of their questionable moral attitudes. Wilde, however, borrowed elements of plot and technique from several of Dumas's plays. In all of Wilde's dramas in the 1890s, secrets abound and theatrical props of various kinds have crucial roles to play: In *Lady Windermere's Fan*, for example, the fan has symbolic and theatrical functions; in *An Ideal Husband*, a bracelet leads to the resolution of the plot; and in *The Importance of Being Earnest*, the use of the handbag is crucial to the outcome of the action. Wilde's brilliant wit, however, injects vitality into much of the creaking machinery of the French well-made play, which provided much of the structural framework of his plays.

References: Bernard Shaw, *Our Theatres in the Nineties*, 3 vols. (1932); John Russell Taylor, *The Rise and Fall of the Well-Made Play* (1967); Jeffrey Huberman, *Late Victorian Farce* (1986).

WHAT NEVER DIES: *See SATYRICON*

WHISTLER, JAMES ABBOTT McNEILL (1834–1903)

Around 1879, the American painter and author, already famous in England and France, probably first met the little-known Wilde when the latter was living with the artist Frank Miles in Salisbury Street, just off the Strand. In 1877, while still an undergraduate at Oxford, Wilde had published a notice in the *Dublin University Magazine* (July), "The Grosvenor Gallery," which describes the opening exhibition of the London gallery. Wilde remarks that the two "most abused pictures in the whole Exhibition" are Whistler's *Nocturne in Black and Gold: The Falling Rocket* and the *Nocturne in Blue and Silver* (later known as the *Nocturne in Blue and Gold: Old Battersea Bridge*). *The Falling Rocket* was to be the object of John Ruskin's famous attack, which prompted Whistler to sue for libel.

Wilde writes facetiously that these pictures are "certainly worth looking at for about as long as one looks at a real rocket, that is, for somewhat less than a quarter of a minute." As for Whistler's portrait of Sir Henry Irving, *Arrangement in Black, No. 3* – "apparently some pseudonym for our greatest living actor" – Wilde is amused by its close approximation to the "original." The "one really good picture" – the portrait of Thomas Carlyle, *Arrangement in Grey and Black, No. 2* – shows Whistler "to be an artist of very great power when he likes."

Fortunately for Wilde, who was just beginning to publish reviews, Whistler probably never saw this notice since the journal circulated principally in Ireland. The aggressive Whistler – who once confessed, "My nature needs enemies" (qtd. in Weintraub 289) – was soon to encounter a younger version of himself, with whom he would engage in a public feud that became the talk of London. Indeed, George Du Maurier, who, as an art student, had lived with Whistler in Paris and whose cartoons in *Punch* in 1880 featured Maudle, the painter, and Jellaby Postlethwaite, the poet, modelled these figures after Whistler and Wilde when he saw his old friend with Wilde (Ellmann confuses Maudle with Postlethwaite: see 136/130).

When he was holding his first exhibition of Venice etchings, Whistler brought Wilde and Du Maurier together and asked, "I say, which one of you invented the other, eh?" (qtd. in Pennell 328). In the production of Gilbert and Sullivan's satire of Aestheticism, *Patience* (1881), the "fleshly" and "idyllic" Aesthetes contained elements of various figures but some of Wilde's qualities were present in both; the actor performing Bunthorne emphasized Whistler's physical appearance, including his monocle.

Wilde's admiration of Whistler's artistry resulted in poetic echoes in the early poems, particularly in "Impression du Matin" (1881), which opens with an allusion to Whistler's nocturnes mentioned in Wilde's Grosvenor Gallery notice: "The Thames nocturne of blue and gold / Changed to a Harmony in gray." During this period, Wilde and Whistler maintained their friendship, as indicated by their attendance together in Paris when the portrait of Whistler's mother was on show. While on his lecture tour of America in 1882, Wilde referred to Whistler as one of his "heroes" and extended an invitation to him to visit Japan and write a book together, but Whistler did not respond.

In November 1883, when *Punch* reported that Wilde and Whistler had been discussing the relative merits of Sarah Bernhardt and Mary Anderson as actresses, Wilde dispatched a telegram to Whistler: "*Punch* too ridiculous. When you and I are together we never talk about anything except ourselves." To which Whistler immediately replied: "No, no, Oscar, you forget. When you and I are together, we never talk about anything except me" (*Letters* 152 and n2). When Wilde married Constance Lloyd on 29 May 1884, Whistler sent the couple a comic telegram: "Fear I may not be able to reach you in time for the ceremony. Don't wait" (qtd. in Ellmann 295/234).

As a gift, he sent the Wildes some of his Venetian etchings.

In due course, however, Whistler's relationship with Wilde grew increasingly bitter as the younger man continually echoed the aesthetic theories of the older. Though Whistler's insistence on art for art's sake and the capacity of the imagination to transform our view of nature had been written about in France and England since the early 19th century, Wilde's trumpeting of the aesthetic ideal increasingly irritated Whistler, who now decided to deliver a lecture at Prince's Hall, Piccadilly, at the unusual hour of ten o'clock with the appropriate title "Ten 0'Clock." As Stanley Weintraub has written: "...Whistler might never have been provoked to the production of his *Ten O'Clock* credo had he not felt that Wilde was poaching dangerously upon his own intellectual preserve" (306–07).

On the evening of 20 February 1885, with such figures in the crowded auditorium as Wilde, George Moore, and Walter Sickert, a painter who was one of Whistler's "Followers," Whistler advanced notions that he had expounded over many dinner tables, sometimes in Wilde's presence, that art had "no desire to teach," that it did not "better [the viewer's] mental or moral state," and that nature was "usually wrong": that is, the artist, not nature, creates harmony by means of the transforming imagination, as in the famous passage:

> ...the evening mist clothes the riverside with poetry, as with a veil, and the poor buildings lose themselves in the dim sky, and the tall chimneys become campanili, and the warehouses are palaces in the night, and the whole city hangs in the heavens, and fairy-land is before us..., Nature, who for once, has sung in tune, sings her exquisite song to the artist alone, her son and her master.... (*Gentle Art* 144)

Directing a barb at Wilde, Whistler observes: "...the Dilettante stalks abroad. The amateur is loosed. The voice of the aesthete is heard in the land, and catastrophe is upon us."

Reviewing the lecture in the *Pall Mall Gazette* (21 Feb.) under the title "Mr. Whistler's 'Ten O'Clock,'" Wilde calls Whistler "a miniature Mephistopheles, mocking the majority," but he

J. A. M. Whistler

concludes that the lecture was a "masterpiece" and Whistler "one of the very greatest masters of painting.... And I may add that in this opinion Mr. Whistler himself entirely concurs." In a letter to Wilde, printed in the *World* (25 Feb.), Whistler refers to Wilde's "exquisite article" and to its remark that "the poet is the supreme artist...lord over all life and all arts": "...nothing is more delicate, in the flattery of 'the Poet' to 'the Painter' than the *naïveté* of 'the Poet'...."Wilde immediately replied: "Be warned in time, James; and remain, as I do, incomprehensible: to be great is to be misunderstood" (*Letters* 171) – the final statement from Emerson's "Self-Reliance" (1841).

Wilde, however, had risked his own incomprehensibility by lecturing on art and by joining the Committee of the National Art Exhibition, a reformist group to which Whistler had also been invited to join. Annoyed that Wilde was a member, Whistler wrote to the *World* (17 Nov. 1886) with mocking alliteration: "What has Oscar in common with Art? except that he dines at our tables and picks from our platters the plums for the pudding he peddles in the provinces?" The "amiable, irresponsible" Wilde, he said, had "the courage of the opinions – of others!" Wilde responded to this charge by writing to the *World* (24 Nov.): "With our James 'vulgarity begins at home,' and should be allowed to stay there" (*Letters* 191). In such exchanges, wit dwindled as bitterness increased. Whistler included a portion of the acrimonious correspondence as well as his "Ten O'Clock" lecture in his *Gentle Art of Making Enemies* (1890).

In "The Decay of Lying" (1889), Wilde again appropriates Whistler's aesthetic ideas but also extends them in his observation that "Life imitates Art far more than Art imitates Life." Characteristically, Whistler responded by sending a long letter for publication in *Truth* (2 Jan. 1890), calling Wilde "the all-pervading plagiarist" and addressing Wilde directly: "I had forgotten you – and so allowed your hair to grow over the sore place. And now, while I looked the other way, you have stolen your own scalp! and potted it in more of your pudding." Responding in *Truth* (9 Jan.), Wilde charges that Whistler "had the impertinence to attack me with both venom and vulgarity in your columns...." He insists that Whistler's assertions are "as deliberately untrue as they are deliberately offensive...and as for borrowing Mr. Whistler's ideas about art, the only thoroughly original ideas I have ever heard him express have had reference to his own superiority over painters greater than himself." Wilde concludes with the slashing remark that Whistler is "ill-bred and ignorant" (*Letters* 254).

Perhaps still smarting over his acrimonious exchange of letters with Whistler, Wilde echoed Whistler's famous "evening mist" passage in the "Ten O'Clock" lecture when he revised "The Decay of Lying" for publication in *Intentions* (1891). In Wilde's addition to the essay (bordering on parody), the allusion to the "master" is clearly to Whistler:

Where, if not from the Impressionists, do we get those wonderful brown fogs that come creeping down our streets, blurring the gas-

lamps and changing the houses into monstrous shadows? To whom, if not to them and their master, do we owe the lovely silver mists that brood over our river, and turn to faint forms of fading grace curved bridge and swaying barge? ...At present people see fogs, not because there are fogs, but because poets and painters have taught them the mysterious loveliness of such effects.

When Mallarmé wrote in December of the acclaim that Wilde was receiving in Paris, Whistler replied that the French had been seduced by someone who "pushes ingratitude as far as indecency. And all his old, worn out stories – he dares offer them to Paris as something new! – the tales of the sunflower – his promenades in the lilies – his trousers – his pink shirt-fronts – what else! And then 'Art' here – 'Art' there – It is really obscene – and will come to no good" (qtd. in Weintraub 306).

When Wilde went on trial in 1895, Whistler wrote from France to the publisher William Heinemann with apparent concern for his former follower: "What of Oscar? Did you go to the court? What does he look like now?" (qtd. in Weintraub 306). In April 1898, almost a year after being released from prison, Wilde encountered Whistler by chance in Paris – their final meeting, though apparently without a word exchanged – as he reported to Robert Ross: "Whistler and I met face to face the other night, as I was entering Pousset's to dine.... How old and weird he looks! Like Meg Merrilies" – the half-crazed gipsy woman in Sir Walter Scott's *Guy Mannering* (*Letters* 731).

References: Whistler, *The Gentle Art of Making Enemies* (2nd ed., 1892; rpt. 1967); E. R. and J. Pennell, *The Life of James McNeill Whistler* (1908; rpt. 1925); Roy McMullen, *Victorian Outsider: A Biography of J. A. M. Whistler* (1973); Stanley Weintraub, *Whistler: A Biography* (1974); Ronald Anderson and Ann Koval, *James McNeill Whistler: Beyond the Myth* (1994).

WHITMAN, WALT (1819–92)

By the late 19th century, Whitman had achieved such fame, if not notoriety, that Wilde, while in America on his lecture tour in 1882, was eager to meet him. When Wilde asked the publisher J. M. Stoddart to arrange such a meeting, Stoddart wrote to Whitman on 11 January: "Oscar Wilde has expressed his great desire to meet you socially. He will dine with me Saturday afternoon when I shall be most happy to have you join us" (MS., Library of Congress). Responding with a card, Whitman invited him and Wilde to his home in Camden, New Jersey, on 18 January between two and three-thirty in the afternoon.

On 17 January, the *Philadelphia Press* published a lengthy interview with Wilde, who expressed his admiration of Whitman: "Perhaps he is not widely read in England, but England never appreciates a poet until he is dead.... I admire him intensely – Dante Rossetti, Swinburne, William Morris and I often discuss him. There is something so Greek and sane about his poetry; it is so universal, so comprehensive" (qtd. in Lewis and Smith 65). On the following day, Stoddart and Wilde journeyed to Camden – the industrial city where Whitman is now buried – opposite Philadelphia on the Delaware River to visit the bearded, partly paralyzed Whitman, whose *Leaves of Grass* (1855) was still regarded with suspicion for its celebration of the body.

A reporter from the *Philadelphia Press*, having interviewed Whitman on the following day, reported on 19 January that the aging poet found Wilde "genuine, honest and manly...a great big, splendid boy." For two hours, talk between the two poets ranged from London literary circles to the "superiority of the masses of people in America." After expounding on Aestheticism, Wilde asked for a response from Whitman, who reportedly said: "I wish well to you, Oscar, and as to the aesthetes, I can only say that you are young and ardent, and the field is wide, and if you want my advice, I say 'go ahead.'" Wilde told him that Lady Wilde bought *Leaves of Grass* when it first appeared in Britain, presumably in the selected edition published by William Michael Rossetti in 1868; she used to read passages from the volume to Oscar; hence, he told Whitman: "I have come to you as to one with whom I have been acquainted almost from the cradle." Satiated with stimulating talk and "a big glass of milk punch," Wilde departed with Whitman's farewell in his ears: "Goodbye, Oscar; God bless you."

On his journey back to Philadelphia, Wilde was very silent (the reporter wrote) and seemed "deeply affected by the interview," speaking "admiringly of the 'grand old man' and of his struggles and triumphs" (qtd. in Lewis and Smith 75–77). Wilde was so delighted by the published account of his

meeting with Whitman that he asked Stoddart to send copies of the *Press* to Lady Wilde, Whistler, and others in England likely to be impressed. Of his meeting with Wilde, Whitman wrote to a friend with obvious levity: "Have you read about Oscar Wilde? He has been to see me and spent an afternoon – He is a fine large handsome youngster – had the *good sense* to take a great fancy to *me*!" (Whitman, *Correspondence* 3:264).

Their meeting was a huge success, for Wilde wrote to Whitman on 1 March with the salutation "My dear dear Walt," insisting that he "must" see him again: "There is no one in this wide great world of America whom I love and honour so much" (*Letters* 100). Wilde did visit him again in May. Wilde later told George Ives, who recorded the remark in his journal, that Whitman was open about his sexuality: "The kiss of Walt Whitman is still on my lips" (qtd. in Ellmann 171/163–64).

In reviewing Whitman's *November Boughs* in the *Pall Mall Gazette* (25 Jan. 1889), Wilde begins with a quotation from Whitman: "No one will get at my verses who insists upon viewing them as a literary performance...or as aiming mainly toward art and aestheticism." Despite this rejection of Aestheticism, Wilde nevertheless embraced Whitman's "joy and hope, and noble and unshaken faith in all that is fine and worthy of such faith" (see "The Gospel According to Walt Whitman").

References: "Oscar Wilde and Whitman," *Philadelphia Press* (19 Jan. 1882), rpt. in Mikhail 1:46–48; Whitman, *The Correspondence*, Vol. 3, ed. E. H. Miller (1964).

"WHO SHOULD BE LAUREATE?"

Published: *Idler Magazine* 7 (April 1895): 403 (unlisted in Mason).

After Tennyson's death in October 1892, debates on the appointment of the next Poet Laureate continued for several years until Alfred Austin was appointed in January 1896. In early 1895, the *Idler Magazine* invited 22 writers, among them Bernard Shaw, Israel Zangwill, W. B. Yeats, and the drama critic William Archer, to respond to the following: "Will you contribute about two hundred words on the man you think should be the next Poet Laureate, and the reasons for your choice?" Most of the contributors named Swinburne as the leading figure for the post. Wilde's brief response implies that to devote much space to defending Swinburne was unnecessary. His entire statement is as follows: "Mr. Swinburne is already the Poet Laureate of England. The fact that his appointment to this high post has not been degraded by official confirmation renders his position all the more unassailable. He whom all poets love is the Laureate Poet always."

Reference: Karl Beckson, "The Quest for a Poet Laureate," *London in the 1890s: A Cultural History* (1993).

A WIFE'S TRAGEDY

Written: The existing fragmentary draft of the play seems to have been written in the late 1880s after Wilde's early dramas (one character, for example, quotes from *The Duchess of Padua*, privately printed "as Manuscript" in 1883) and before the society comedies of the early 1890s – that is, between the romantic costume dramas with exotic settings and the critical, anti-romantic social comedies set in London, intended as vehicles for satirical, dandiacal expression, involving a "clash between aesthetic and moral values...perennial in Wilde's work." *A Wife's Tragedy* partakes of both romantic and un-romantic elements, perhaps a "trial run for *Lady Windermere's Fan*" (Shewan, "Facts" 85, 91).

The Plot: Because of the state of the MS., the following reconstructed plot, as Shewan states, has been "eked out by informed guesswork." In Act I, Gerald and Nellie Lovel, who have been married for four years, await the arrival of Gerald's college friend, Lord Arthur Merton, in their Venice home. Meanwhile, Gerald, a poet, has become infatuated with a comtesse, who embodies his poetic ideals associated with "the old Greek life." An admirer of his poetry, she is amused by his attention. When Arthur arrives, he appears to be the philistine whom Gerald had described.

In Act II, Arthur argues with Gerald about his relationship with the comtesse. An admirer of Walter Pater's view of life, Gerald talks of "fiery-coloured moments" and the necessity "to burn with some flame – that is the secret of life." Pitying Nellie, who shares nothing of Gerald's aesthetic interests, Arthur falls in love with her. However, she rejects his advances, shocked that he would betray his friend and her husband.

In Act III, the comtesse, who was given a present by her former husband of an heirloom consisting of diamonds valued at £27,000, is now required by a Parisian court to return them to the

family because she has borne no children. Since she has sold the diamonds to pay off her husband's debts, she faces disgrace and the seizure of her property. Desperate, she decides to obtain the money to buy back the diamonds by marrying Arthur after dropping Gerald. Disillusioned, Gerald nevertheless offers to obtain the money himself, but she urges him to return to his wife, who is the superior woman because she has the capacity to suffer.

In Act IV, Gerald attempts reconciliation with Nellie by writing to her, but he abandons the attempt by remarking that "words are common things!" Meanwhile, Arthur professes his love for Nellie when she encounters him writing a letter of farewell to her. Again, she rejects him. At home, Gerald and Nellie argue; she then leaves. The comtesse arrives in search of Arthur at the Lovels' home. A letter then arrives from Nellie announcing her elopement with Arthur. Gerald's marriage and romantic ideals are destroyed, while the comtesse is left without a husband or the £30,000 to purchase the diamonds. The play ends as Gerald banishes the comtesse from his sight.

Manuscript: The Clark Library has the fragmentary draft.

References: Rodney Shewan, "*A Wife's Tragedy*: An Unpublished Sketch for a Play by Oscar Wilde" and "Oscar Wilde and *A Wife's Tragedy*: Facts and Conjectures," *Theatre Research International* (Spring 1982) and (Summer 1983).

WILDE, CONSTANCE (1858–98)

Born Constance Lloyd into a family of lawyers who were English on her father's side (her mother was Irish), Constance first met Wilde at a young people's party given on 6 June 1881 by Lady Wilde for her two sons at Merrion Square in Dublin. A passionate reader of poetry, Constance discovered that Wilde had, like her, a deep admiration of Keats (indeed, he had already published a sonnet "The Grave of Keats," commemorating his visit to the Protestant Cemetery in Rome). On the following day, she wrote to her brother Otho:

O. W. came yesterday at about 5.30 (by which time I was shaking with fright!) and stayed for half an hour, begged me to come and see his mother again soon.... I can't help liking him, because when he's talking to me alone he's never a bit affected, and speaks naturally, excepting that he uses better language than most people. (qtd. in *Letters* 152n3)

In the ensuing months, her relatives were aware of her growing attachment to Wilde, but those who were English were unimpressed by Wilde's flamboyant personality and the notorious eccentricities of his parents.

It has been said that, because Constance's family was financially comfortable, Wilde was particularly interested in the possibility of marriage. Ann Clark Amor remarks, however, that "quite simply, he fell in love with her":

...she shared with Oscar a love of beauty and simplicity of form. Her high intelligence and deep knowledge of art and literature made her an ideal companion at theatres, art galleries and social gatherings, yet she combined this with a clinging trust in Oscar which was very endearing. (40)

Amor's view is perhaps simplistic, for Constance also had a darker view of life and a conventional view of art opposed to Wilde's. When Wilde brought a privately printed copy of *Vera; or, The Nihilists* (which had failed in New York) back with him to ask for her opinion, she wrote an extensive commentary on 11 November 1883 from Dublin:

...it seems to me to be a very good acting play and to have good dramatic situations. Also I like the passages on liberty and the impassioned parts, but I fancy that some of the minor parts of the dialogue strike me as being slightly halting or strained.... I cannot understand why you should have been so unfortunate in its reception unless either the acting was very inferior or the audience was unsympathetic to the political opinions expressed in it. The world surely is unjust and bitter to most of us; I think we must either renounce our opinions and run with the general stream or else totally ignore the world and go on our own regardless of all, there is not the slightest use in *fighting* against existing prejudices, for we are only worsted in the struggle....

She then disagrees with Wilde's aesthetic view on the relationship between art and morality: "...I hold that there is no perfect art without perfect morality, whilst you say that they are distinct and separate things..." (qtd. in Ellmann 244/230). Wilde saw her shortly after receiving this letter, for he gave a lecture in Dublin on 22 November on "The House Beautiful." Constance's relatives were delighted.

On 26 November, Constance wrote to her brother, Otho, that she was engaged to Wilde "and perfectly and insanely happy" (*Letters* 153), and Wilde wrote to Lillie Langtry in December: "...I am going to be married to a beautiful girl called Constance Lloyd, a grave, slight, violet-eyed little Artemis..." (*Letters* 154). In a letter to Wilde, Constance presented herself in a less flattering manner: "I am so cold and undemonstrative outwardly: you must read my heart and not my outward semblance if you wish to know how passionately I worship and love you" (qtd. in Ellmann 246/232). On 29 May 1884, at 2:30 p.m., Wilde and Constance were married in St. James's Church, Sussex Gardens, the witnesses including Lady Wilde and Oscar's brother, Willie. At 4 p.m., the couple were driven to Charing Cross Station, where friends were waiting to bid them *bon voyage* for Paris.

In the years before 1895, their relationship was based on their admiration of each other's unique qualities, as Amor writes:

He adored his shy young bride with her radiant beauty and slim form; he was proud of her, took infinite interest in her clothes (a rare quality in a husband) and loved going with her to choose more. He was her ideal mentor in matters of culture and taste, her professor in the art of love. He was the centre of her universe, till death and no doubt beyond. (46)

The dinner parties at their Tite Street home attracted such figures as Whistler, Sargent, Burne-Jones, Sarah Bernhardt, Ellen Terry, Lillie Langtry, Swinburne, Ruskin, and Browning. As a hostess, Constance was a success, though inevitably she was overshadowed by Oscar, as, indeed, almost everyone else was in his company.

Constance's pregnancies and births of Cyril and Vyvyan had an adverse effect on Wilde, for Constance was often unwell during this time. His social relationships now tended to exclude Constance, though they were still, on occasion, seen at a private view at the Grosvenor Gallery. She now turned to her writing, contributing anonymous articles on theater and fashion to the *Lady's Pictorial*, and when Wilde became editor of *Woman's World*, she undertook the task of inviting women to their home who might contribute to the periodical. Constance also contributed an article on "Children's Dress in this Century" (July 1888) and on "Muffs" (Feb. 1889).

In 1888, she became the editor of the *Rational Dress Society's Gazette*, its intent to advance the Society's protest "against the introduction of any fashion in dress that either deforms the figure, impedes the movements of the body, or in any way tends to injure the health." Because of her involvement in the Society, she was now called upon to lecture on its mission. At the same time, Constance was a member of various women's political associations; at one conference sponsored by the International Arbitration and Peace Association, she urged the group: "Children should be taught in the nursery to be against war" (qtd. in Ellmann 284/ 268), and she once brought Wilde to a Hyde Park demonstration supporting a dock strike. She also found time to publish a little book titled *There Was Once: Grandma's Stories* (1889), containing traditional fairy tales, and three years later another collection of children's stories titled *A Long Time Ago*.

By 1893, when the handsome Lord Alfred Douglas had begun to dominate Wilde's life, Constance had little suspicion that her husband was homosexual since she was characteristically Victorian in her conviction that two children were sufficient evidence of normal sexual behavior. Her attitude towards Douglas is difficult to evaluate since contradictions exist in his and in Wilde's views. For example, many years after the Wilde debacle, Douglas wrote: "I was always on the best of terms with Mrs. Wilde. I liked her and she liked me. She told me, about a year after I first met her, that she liked me better than any of Oscar's other friends" (59), but in prison Wilde wrote to Douglas in *De Profundis* that their friendship had always distressed her. Still, whatever confusion existed in Constance's mind before the trials concerning Douglas and Wilde, she was "wonderfully loyal," Wilde told Robert Ross from prison, adding: "She could not understand me, and I was bored to death with the married life" (*Letters* 516).

Aware of the financial difficulties that her husband was facing in 1894, the result of his relationship with Douglas, Constance decided to select her husband's epigrams from his writings and issue them as *Oscariana* (1895), the work published by Arthur Lee Humphreys (1865–1946), who was a senior partner and manager of Hatchard's bookshop in Piccadilly and whom – according to Joyce Bentley – she had met at Pre-Raphaelite Society meetings: "She was also in the habit of calling in at the shop to indulge in friendly arguments of a philanthropic nature" (149). As Amor writes: "Her selections show how well equipped she was intellectually to appreciate her husband's personal genius" (151). Within four months, the book's success resulted in a second printing of 200 copies despite Wilde's estimate of Constance's efforts. To Humphreys he had written in late November: "The book is, as it stands, so bad, so disappointing, that I am writing a set of new aphorisms.... The plays are particularly badly done. Long passages are quoted, where a single aphorism should have been extracted" (*Letters* 378).

New letters written by Constance in 1894 (offered in Sotheby's sale catalogue, dated 22–23 July 1985) reveal that she was in love with Humphreys: in a letter dated 1 June, running to eight pages, she writes that he is an "ideal husband, indeed I think you are not far short of being an ideal man!" (ironically, Wilde had rented rooms in St. James's Place from October 1893 to March 1894, when he wrote most of *An Ideal Husband*):

...I liked you & was interested in you, & I saw that you were good, and it is rarely that I come across a man that has that written in his face. And I stepped past the limits perhaps of good taste in the wish to be your friend and to have you for my friend. I spoke to you very openly about myself, & I confess that I should not like you to repeat what I said about my childhood....

By 11 August, she was addressing him as "My Darling Arthur," expressing how much she loved him and

how dear and delightful you have been to me to-day. I *have* been happy, and I *do* love you dear Arthur. Nothing in my life has ever made me so happy as this love of yours to me has done.... I love you just because you ARE, and because you have come into my life to fill it with love and make it rich....

She avows that she loves him also for being "dear to the children, and nice to Oscar too...." The letter closes:"Your always devotedly loving Constance." Though her husband's success in the theater had escalated in two productions – *An Ideal Husband* and *The Importance of Being Earnest* playing to packed houses early in 1895 – Constance seemed to feel "lonely and neglected" (Amor 154). What the course of her relationship with Humphreys was remains unknown.

Early in that year, she suffered a serious accident, which progressively developed into an apparent paralysis of the spine: she had tripped on a loose carpet on the stairs and had fallen to the bottom, injuring an arm as well as her back. In March 1895, forbidden to walk, she underwent an operation, which, however, resulted in little improvement. With the arrest of her husband, she removed the children from their schools, sent them with a governess to the Continent, and attempted to cope, in her difficult physical condition, with the legal and emotional demands that she now faced. She even consulted a palmist, Mrs. Robinson, from whom she and her husband had earlier sought advice in their marriage:

What is to become of my husband who has so betrayed and deceived me and ruined the lives of my darling boys?... As soon as this trial is over I have to get my judicial separation, or if possible my divorce in order to get the guardianship of the boys. What a tragedy for him who is so gifted. (qtd. in Amor 173)

After Wilde's conviction, Constance went to Switzerland to be with her children. Despite the change of their names to "Holland," which was a family name (it was her brother Otho's middle name), she remained uncertain whether to divorce her husband. On 21 September 1895, she visited Wilde at Wandsworth Prison (prior to his being transferred to Reading Prison) under the most adverse conditions since visitors and prisoners were separated by grills three feet apart, which prevented them from even seeing each other. Later, she wrote to Robert Sherard (his friend and later first biographer): "It was indeed awful, more so than I had any conception it could be. I could

not see him and I could not touch him, and I scarcely spoke. He has been mad the last three years, and he says that if he saw [Douglas] he would kill him" (qtd. in Sherard 201–02). And to a friend in October, she wrote: "I do not wish to sever myself entirely from Mr. Wilde who is in the very lowest depths of misery. And he is very repentant and minds most of all what he has brought on myself and the boys. It seems to me (and to many others too) that by sticking to him now, I may save him from even worse..." (qtd. in Amor 190).

Indeed, she wrote to Wilde constantly to convince him of her loyalty. When Lady Wilde died in 1896, Constance returned to England to inform him of his mother's death. He later wrote in *De Profundis*: "My wife, at that time kind and gentle to me, rather than that I should hear the news from indifferent or alien lips, travelled, ill as she was, all the way from Genoa to England to break to me herself the tidings of so irreparable, so irredeemable a loss" (*Letters* 458). Though appreciative, Wilde remained with the conviction that Constance had little interest in his art. When appointing Robert Ross his literary executor, he wrote on 1 April 1897: "My wife does not understand my art, nor could be expected to have any interest in it..." (*Letters* 512).

The approach of Wilde's release from prison inevitably required legal arrangements for a marriage settlement between Constance and Wilde. The provision of a yearly allowance from Constance became problematic to both parties, particularly when her husband rejoined Douglas, whom Constance called "that appalling individual" (qtd. in Amor 215). She obtained a legal separation from her husband to protect her assets and her children's futures, though she agreed to continue Wilde's allowance should she predecease him. She had also appointed Adrian Hope (1858–1904), related to her by marriage, as the children's official guardian. When he was informed of the arrangement, Wilde wrote to his solicitor: "He is an old friend of mine, and a man of the highest character, as well as of intellectual and literary sympathies" (*More Letters* 137).

When *The Ballad of Reading Gaol* was published in February 1898, Constance told her brother Otho after seeing extracts in a newspaper that she was "frightfully upset by this wonderful poem.... It is frightfully tragic and makes one cry" (qtd. in Amor 220–21). Wilde sent her and Otho copies. On 7 April, Constance died after undergoing another spinal operation, which was unsuccessful: she was buried in the Campo Santo cemetery in Genoa, her tombstone reading: "Constance Mary, daughter of Horace Lloyd, Q.C." When Wilde visited the grave site in February 1899, he broke down in tears and prayed for her soul. He described the visit to Ross: "It was very tragic seeing her name carved on a tomb – her surname, my name, not mentioned of course.... I brought some flowers. I was deeply affected – with a sense, also, of the uselessness of all regrets. Nothing could have been otherwise, and Life is a very terrible thing" (*Letters* 783). Long after Wilde's death, Constance's family had the words "Wife of Oscar Wilde" added to the stone.

References: Robert Sherard, *Oscar Wilde: The Story of an Unhappy Friendship* (1905; rpt. 1970); *The Autobiography of Lord Alfred Douglas* (1929; rpt. 1970); Anne Clark Amor, *Mrs. Oscar Wilde: A Woman of Some Importance* (1983); Joyce Bentley, *The Importance of Being Constance* (1983).

WILDE, CYRIL: *See* HOLLAND, CYRIL

WILDE, DOROTHY IERNE (1895–1941)

The only child of Lily and Willie Wilde, "Dolly" Wilde – as she was called by friends and family – bore "a striking resemblance to her famous uncle, a resemblance which only increased with age as her features and her figure grew heavier, and which she made no attempt to disguise" (Wickes 183). Indeed, she reportedly said: "I am more Oscar-like than he was like himself," and once she arrived at a masquerade party dressed to resemble her uncle, as Janet Flanner said, "looking both important and earnest" (qtd. in Wickes 183).

With the outbreak of World War I, Dolly rushed to France to volunteer as an ambulance driver; after the war, she moved in Parisian literary and artistic circles and became, for many years, a lover of the legendary American lesbian Natalie Barney, who characterized Dolly as "half androgyne and half goddess" (7). When H. G. Wells met Dolly at the Paris Pen Club, he exclaimed of her wit: "How exciting to meet at last a feminine Wilde!" (qtd. in Barney 15). Despite such a quality, as revealed in her personal correspondence, she never wrote for publication. Besides her indolence, her friends

noted her self-destructive tendencies: drink and drugs combined with two suicide attempts when Barney went off with an actress. Flanner recalled the extraordinary impression that Dolly, "a brilliant talker," had made on her: "She was not like anybody else or at any rate not like anybody else I have ever met..." (38).

In 1940, discovering that she had cancer, Dolly sought a cure at Lourdes, but she died in the following year in London. In her obituary in the London *Times* (14 April 1941), a friend (identified as "V. C.") remarked: "Epigram and paradox are the weapons of the Wilde family, and none of its members have used them more humanely nor more effectively than Dorothy."

References: [Natalie Barney, ed.,] *In Memory of Dorothy Ierne Wilde"* (1952); Janet Flanner, "Oscar Wilde's Niece," *Prose* (Spring 1973); George Wickes, "Dolly Wilde," *The Amazon of Letters: The Life and Loves of Natalie Barney* (1976).

WILDE, ISOLA (1857–1867)

The birth of Wilde's sister, Isola, brought joy to the family. Named Isola Francesca Emily ("Isola" after the Gaelic Iseult, "Francesca" after her mother's name, and Emily, an Elgee family name), "little Isola" was the subject of Lady Wilde's letter to a friend: "...[she] is now ten months old and is the pet of the house. She has fine eyes and promises to have a most acute intellect – these two gifts are enough for any woman" (qtd. in Melville 71).

But on 23 February 1967, two months short of her 10th birthday, Isola died of "a sudden effusion on the brain" following her recovery from a fever, as the devastated Lady Wilde described the day that she and the family were notified by Isola's uncle, to whose house, some 50 miles away, Isola had been sent: "...we were summoned by telegraph – and only arrived to see her die – such sorrows are hard to bear.... But *Isola* was the radiant angel of our home – and so bright and strong and joyous.... Sir William is crushed by sorrow. Isola was his idol – still, he goes on with his life work... (qtd. in Melville 109).

Years later, Wilde, who was 12 when Isola died, wrote a poem to commemorate her death (see "Requiescat").

Reference: Joy Melville, *Mother of Oscar: The Life of Jane Francesca Wilde* (1994).

WILDE, LADY JANE FRANCESCA: *See* **WILDE, SIR WILLIAM**

WILDE, VYVYAN: *See* **HOLLAND, VYVYAN**

WILDE, WILLIAM CHARLES KINGSBURY (1852–1899)

Oscar's elder brother, a journalist and poet, was educated, like Oscar, at Portora Royal School, Enniskillen, Ulster, where he was known for his conviviality. A former classmate described "Willie" (as everyone called him) as "clever, erratic and full of vitality." In 1871, when Oscar went on to Trinity College, Dublin, he joined Willie, who was already a student there, where they shared rooms in their second and third years. In 1876, Willie contributed poems to *Kottabos*, the college magazine that he also edited. One of his poems, "Salome," a favorite subject among 19th-century French writers and artists who depicted Salome as a *femme fatale*, may have aroused Oscar's early interest in her complex personality:

Fearless and reckless; for all maiden shame
Strange passion-poisons throbbing overcame
As every eye was riveted on me,
And every soul was mine, mine utterly –

Another of Willie's poems, "Faustine," fuses the eroticism and paganism associated with Swinburne (who, in 1862, had written a poem with that title). Willie's poetic gifts, however, were slender: "...bright jewels my fair bosom deck, / And Love's hot lips – close press'd – cling fast to mine...."

After graduating from Trinity College, Willie studied law, was called to the bar but apparently did not practice. After Sir William's death in 1876, Lady Wilde and Willie moved to London in early 1879, where he became a journalist, serving as drama critic for *Punch* and *Vanity Fair*, leader writer for the *Daily Telegraph*, and editor of Christmas numbers for several magazines. When Oscar married in 1884, Lady Wilde urged him to establish "a settled life at once. Literature and lectures and parliament – receptions 5 o'clock for the world – and small dinners of genius and culture at 8 o'clock. Charming this life, begin it at once – take warning by Willie" (qtd. in Melville 182). By this time, Willie, irresponsible about money, was fatally attracted to alcohol.

On 4 October 1891, now 39, Willie married Mrs. Frank Leslie, née Miriam Folline (1836–1914), proprietor of the Frank Leslie Publishing Co. in New York. It was she who had approached Oscar with the idea that he give a series of lectures in America. The brief courtship between Willie and Mrs. Leslie led to a brief marriage. Initially captivated by Willie's joviality and wit, Mrs. Leslie soon discovered his fondness for drink and his uselessness to her business. He spent much of his time at the Lotus Club on Fifth Avenue gossiping about London society or reciting parodies of Oscar's poetry (an indication of hostility towards his more successful brother). Within a year, Mrs. Leslie began divorce proceedings: on 10 June 1893, the divorce was granted on the grounds of drunkenness and adultery.

Willie, who had returned to London early in 1892, when Oscar was being hailed for his success in *Lady Windermere's Fan*, probably wrote the review that appeared, unsigned, in *Vanity Fair* (27 Feb.1892), for which he had been a theater reviewer: the play was "brilliantly unoriginal," he wrote, but the dialogue was "uniformly bright, graceful, and flowing." After running through the plot and pointing to some of its banalities, he nevertheless calls it "an undeniably clever piece of work; and even though it has its weaknesses, it reflects credit on its author." He concludes by declaring: "It is emphatically a play to see." Oscar, who apparently divined the author behind the anonymous mask, was currently writing *A Woman of No Importance*, in which one character remarks: "After a good dinner, one can forgive anybody, even one's own relations."

Oscar began giving Willie money, but antagonism between the brothers grew as Oscar learned that Willie was constantly asking their hard-pressed mother for money. To Max Beerbohm, they seemed to be mirror images, as indeed his cartoons of the brothers indicate. In a letter to the painter Will Rothenstein, Beerbohm writes: "...did I tell you that I saw a good deal of [Oscar's] brother Willie at Broadstairs? Quel monstre! Dark, oily, suspecte yet awfully like Oscar: he has Oscar's coy, carnal smile & fatuous giggle & not a little of Oscar's esprit. But he is awful – a veritable tragedy of family-likeness" (*Max and Will* 21).

In January 1894, Willie married Lily Lees (1859–1922), with whom he had been living. Kevin O'Brien characterizes her as "an emotional

413

woman with a tendency to early panic[;] she believed (incorrectly) that she was pregnant" and sought a powder to end the pregnancy (16). The marriage caused further grief to Lady Wilde when the couple moved in with her. She wrote to Oscar on 4 February 1894, to inform him of the marriage: "Miss Lees has but £50 a year and this just dresses her. She can give nothing to the house and Willie is always in a state of utter poverty. So all is left *upon me*" (qtd. in O'Brien 17). Willie and Lily had their only child in July 1895, Dorothy Ierne (see entry).

The relationship between Oscar and Willie found its way into *The Importance of Being Earnest*, which involves two characters pretending to be brothers (Jack, the protective guardian; Algy, the alleged spendthrift) who discover that they are, in fact, brothers. At the time that Oscar was writing the play, Lady Wilde wrote a lengthy letter urging him to be reconciled with Willie, who, she said, was "sickly and extravagant." She was "*miserable* at the present position of [her] two sons" and "at the general belief that you *hate your brother*." She then urges Oscar to hold out his hand to Willie, a gesture repeated several times in the letter: "Come then & offer him yr. hand in good faith – & begin a new course of action" (qtd. in Beckson, "Mutual Antagonism" 128–29). In *Earnest*, when Algernon, posing as the wicked "Ernest," arrives at Jack's country house, Cecily urges Jack: "However badly he may have behaved to you in the past he is still your brother. You couldn't be so heartless as to disown him....you will shake hands with him, won't you, Uncle Jack?" Though, at first, Jack refuses, he acquiesces shortly thereafter. If not in life, then in art, Oscar was willing to comply with his mother's wishes.

With Oscar's arrest and first trial in April 1895, Willie (according to his own account) provided shelter to his brother, who had been unable to find rooms in London, though Willie probably dramatized the scene: Willie reportedly said that Oscar "fell down on my threshold like a wounded stag" (qtd. in Sherard 358) – a brief moment of moral triumph for the elder brother. Willie, defending his brother, wrote to Bram Stoker (1847–1912), who had married Florence Balcombe (1858-1937), once courted by Oscar: "Bram, my friend, poor Oscar was *not* as bad as people thought him. He was led astray by his Vanity – & conceit, & he was so 'got at' that he was weak enough to be guilty – of

indiscretions and follies – that is *all*.... I believe this thing will help to *purify* him body & soul" (qtd. in Belford 245).

When Oscar was released from prison in 1897, Willie was not there to greet him. On 13 March 1899, alcoholism ended Willie's life. Informed of his brother's death by Robert Ross, Oscar, now living in self-imposed exile in France, pronounced his final words on him: "I suppose it had been expected for some time.... Between him and me there had been, as you know, wide chasms for many years. *Requiescat in Pace*" (*Letters* 785).

References: Robert Sherard, *The Life of Oscar Wilde* (1906); Madeleine Stern, *Purple Passage: The Life of Mrs. Frank Leslie* (1953); Mary M. Lago and Karl Beckson, eds., *Max and Will: Max Beerbohm and William Rothenstein, Their Friendship and Letters, 1893–1945* (1975); James Holroyd, "Brother to Oscar," *Blackwood's Magazine* (March 1979); Karl Beckson, "The Importance of Being Angry: The Mutual Antagonism of Oscar and Willie Wilde," *Blood Brothers: Siblings as Writers*, ed. Norman Kiell (1983); Kevin O'Brien, "Lily Wilde and Oscar's Fur Coat," *Journal of the Eighteen Nineties Society* 21 (1994); Joy Melville, *Mother of Oscar: The Life of Jan Francesca Wilde* (1994); Davis Coakley, *Oscar Wilde: The Importance of Being Irish* (1994); Barbara Belford, *Bram Stoker: A Biography of the Author of Dracula* (1996).

WILDE, SIR WILLIAM ROBERT WILLS (1815–76) and LADY JANE FRANCESCA WILDE (?1821–96)

In Dublin in 1851, Oscar Wilde's father, an ear and eye physician (Wilde's grandfather was also a doctor) and a Fellow of the College of Surgeons in Ireland, married the ardent Anglo-Irish patriot Jane Francesca Elgee, known as "Speranza," whose fiery poems had appeared in the *Nation* in the 1840s. When Sir William married her, he had already had at least three illegitimate children: Dr. Henry Wilson (1838–77), an ophthalmologist and Fellow of the Royal College of Surgeons, whom Oscar called "cousin," and two girls, who were born just two years before Sir William's marriage and brought up by Sir William's brother Ralph, a clergymen; in 1871, the two girls perished in a freakish accident when their gowns caught fire after a ball.

In addition to his distinguished medical career,

he wrote the standard textbook on aural surgery, established a clinic in Dublin, conducted an exhaustive medical census of Ireland, compiled a multi-volume catalogue of the antiquities in the Royal Irish Academy museum, and wrote books on a variety of other subjects, including archeology, folklore, and Jonathan Swift. In 1863, he was appointed Surgeon Oculist in Ordinary to Queen Victoria in Ireland, and in 1864, for his exhaustive work as Census Commissioner in compiling statistics for the Irish medical census, he was knighted.

In 1849, Lady Wilde had published a translation of Johann Meinhold's Gothic novel *Sidonia the Sorceress*; now, she continued her literary career by publishing volumes of Irish folk tales and superstitions. In the history of the 19th-century feminist movement, Lady Wilde also figures prominently in what Terence de Vere White calls her "ceaseless demand for recognition of woman's rights" (147). Moreover, writes Ellmann, Lady Wilde "had a sense of being destined for greatness, and imparted it. Her son subscribed to her view, and treated her with the utmost consideration and respect, almost as though he were her precursor rather than she his" (5/5).

Sir William, "full of vitality, with a lively personality," shared his wife's interests. Though a confirmed Unionist, he "was sympathetic to the cause of the Young Irelanders," the nationalists with whom Lady Wilde was associated (Melville 45). But a scandal that rocked Dublin in 1864, involving Sir William and the unstable Mary Josephine Travers, the daughter of a professor of medical jurisprudence at Trinity College, involved an accusation of libel lodged by her against Lady Wilde, who had attempted to protect Sir William against Mary Travers's attempts to impugn his reputation. Some ten years before, he had treated the young woman for an ear infection. Over the years, he established an apparently innocent friendship with her by guiding her reading and continuing to act as her doctor, even inviting her to exhibitions.

But concerned about the relationship, which had the appearance of an affair, Lady Wilde wrote to the young woman's father about his daughter's bizarre and provocative behavior. When Mary Travers discovered the letter, she brought a libel suit against Lady Wilde and, during the trial, accused Sir William of raping her while under

chloroform. The "whole sordid business," as White calls it, ended when the jury awarded her a farthing's damages (that is, a quarter of a penny – the estimated value, presumably, of her lost virginity). The court costs for Sir William, however, were considerable.

Early biographers have generally claimed that Sir William never recovered from the Travers case, that he progressively deteriorated in mind and body. Joy Melville, however, offers convincing evidence in opposition to such a view: Sir William "had not lost all his relish for life. The strain of the case over, he cheerfully embarked, with John Gilbert, on Part IV of the [Royal Irish] Academy Catalogue...as well as working enthusiastically on a new book about the whole area around Moytura..." (106).

Though Oscar's relationship to his father was apparently not close, he had the highest respect for him. When Sir William died, Oscar wrote poems alluding to his death (see entries on "Lotus Leaves" and "The True Knowledge"). Three months after Sir William's death, Oscar wrote to an Oxford friend that his father would have been pleased to hear of his having achieved a First in his examinations: "I think God has dealt very hardly with us" (*Letters* 15). For Lady Wilde, the future looked depressingly bleak: she discovered that Sir William had left her only debts and liabilities, the result of his poor health in his final three years.

However, Lady Wilde took solace in Oscar's great promise for notable achievements in his life. In the development of his personality, she exercised a profound hold on his imagination. Robert Sherard, Oscar's friend and first biographer, remarks that, for his mother, Oscar's "affection reached the degree of veneration" (6). She, too, wrote poems after her husband's death, the first of which was "The Soul's Questionings," a conventional (though deeply felt) response to the mystery of death:

> Tell us, O! mystic life-giver from the heights of
>   thy shrouded throne,
> Why the light must die from our eyes, our laughter be changed to a groan,
> And the spirit be crushed and broken, ere the task thou hast given is done? (qtd. in White 233)

Her eccentricity and narcissism had a major impact on Oscar, particularly her view of "domestic felicity," which, she contended, had the "best chance...when all the family are Bohemians, and all clever, and all enjoy thoroughly the erratic, impulsive, reckless life of work and glory, indifferent to everything save the intense moments of popular applause" (qtd. in White 147–48). In her justifiable pride in Oscar's scholarly achievements at Trinity College and at Oxford, she looked forward to a notable career for him in politics as well as literature. When Oscar won the prestigious Newdigate Prize at Oxford for *Ravenna* (1878), she responded with joy: "Oh Gloria, Gloria! Thank you a million times for the telegram – it is the first pleasant throb of joy I have had this year...well, after all we have *genius*....you have got *honour* and *recognition* – and this at only *22* [actually 23] is a grand thing" (qtd. in Melville 139).

For her elder son, Willie, however, she progressively had doubts about his life as a journalist, his attraction to alcohol, and his difficulty with women (she had hoped that he would marry into wealth): "Poor Willie – will he ever find the right woman?" she wrote to Oscar (qtd. in White 239). After Oscar returned from his American lecture tour in 1882, she urged him to establish himself at once as a writer and enter Parliament. To her, Willie served as a "warning" to Oscar.

The publication of the first version of *The Picture of Dorian Gray* (1890) confirmed Lady Wilde's estimate of her younger son's genius and her elder son's progressive decline. The novel, she wrote to Oscar, "is the most wonderful piece of writing in all the fiction of the day.... The story is tremendous; I nearly fainted at the last scene" (qtd. in Melville 219). In time, the antagonism between Oscar and Willie grew, the result of Willie's relying on his mother for financial support and, perhaps, Oscar's enormous success as a writer. Lady Wilde attempted to reconcile her sons but with little success (see Wilde, William).

In May 1879, Lady Wilde had settled in London with Willie and had completed, from notes, an article by Sir William for an archeological journal and resumed publishing her own writings, initially some Irish myths and legends for the *Dublin University Magazine*, material that she later included in *Ancient Legends of Ireland* (1887). Her work benefitted from notes gathered over a lifetime by Sir William, who had published an initial volume titled *Irish Popular Superstitions* (1852). She soon established herself as a hostess, as she had in Dublin, her "At Homes" providing a setting for sociable writers and actors (Shaw, for example, visited often and eventually met Oscar).

Lady Wilde was awed by her son's successes in the theater, which she read about in the notices (because of poor health, she never attended a performance of any of his plays). After *Lady Windermere's Fan* opened, she wrote to Oscar: "Truly you are a startling celebrity!" (qtd. in Melville 229). She also took the reviewers' criticisms seriously. For example, the success of *A Woman of No Importance* did not prevent her from suggesting how his future plays could overcome the critics' objections:

> You have had a brilliant success! ...they all want *more plot* and more human feelings. So in your part, strengthen the plot and heighten the human interest.... You are now the great sensation of London and I am very proud of you – you have made your name and taken your place and now hold a distinguished position in the circle of intellects.... Take care of yourself and your health and keep clear of suppers and late hours and champagne. Your health and *calm* of mind is most important. (qtd. in Melville 237)

But he ignored such motherly advice. When her son was arrested, Lady Wilde reportedly said to him: "If you stay, even if you go to prison, you will always be my son, it will make no difference to my affection, but if you go, I will never speak to you again" (qtd. in Yeats 192). Regardless of whether she actually said that, one can only imagine what her reaction was to her son's scandal and the destruction of her dreams. It is said that she turned to the wall during her final illness when she heard that Oscar could not leave prison to see her and said that "she hoped 'that prison would do him good.'" White expresses the irony that attended Lady Wilde's death in February 1896: "Had she died a year sooner she would have gone down before the sun, believing her mission accomplished" (269).

References: Robert Sherard, *The Life of Oscar Wilde* (1906); *The Autobiography of W. B. Yeats* (1965); Terence de Vere White, *The Parents of Oscar Wilde: Sir William and Lady Wilde* (1967);

Joy Melville, *Mother of Oscar: The Life of Jane Francesca Wilde* (1994); Davis Coakley, *Oscar Wilde: The Importance of Being Irish* (1994).

"WIND FLOWERS"

A half-title that appears in *Poems* (1882) as a section title for seven poems in the list of contents and with a separate page in the text preceding the seven poems.

"WITH A COPY OF 'THE HOUSE OF POMEGRANATES'"

Published: Gleeson White, ed., *Book-Song: An Anthology of Poems of Books and Bookmen from Modern Authors* (London: Elliot Stock, 1893), 157; rpt. in *Poems* (1908), with the correction from *The* to *A House of Pomegranates*.

In the traditional mode of sending one's book into the world, Wilde begins this poem of six lines with "Go, little book," urging it to bid the recipient ("him who, on a lute with horns of pearl, / Sang of the white feet of the Golden Girl") to look into its pages: "...it may hap that he / May find that golden maidens dance through thee." The phrase *Golden Girl* appears twice in Justin McCarthy's poem "The Gold Girl" in his *Serapion and Other Poems* (1883), the poem probably inspired by Whistler's painting entitled *Harmony in Yellow and Gold: The Gold Girl, Connie Gilchrist* (ca. 1876), which depicts the music-hall dancer (1865–1946) with her skipping rope (the painting now in the Metropolitan Museum of Art in New York).

Manuscript: The Clark Library has the presentation copy of *The Happy Prince and Other Tales*, in which Wilde inscribed an earlier version of this poem – preceded by the following: "To Justin Huntly McCarthy from his friend Oscar Wilde," apparently unaware that he was inscribing it in a different volume. McCarthy (1861–1936) was an Irish Nationalist M.P., dramatist, novelist, and historian. In Volume 1 of the 1907 unauthorized edition of Wilde's collected works, published by Keller-Farmer Co. (New York and London), a poem is included with the title "An Inscription: In a Presentation Copy of His Book 'A House of Pomegranates' to Richard Le Gallienne." The presentation copy remains unlocated, but oddly, the source of the poem is given as Gleeson White's edited *Book-Song*. The poem is a version of the McCarthy inscription, probably written from memory. Presumably, Wilde confused the volume presented to McCarthy with the one presented to Le Gallienne.

A WOMAN OF NO IMPORTANCE

Written: Wilde began work on the play around July or August 1892 for the actor-manager Herbert Beerbohm Tree (see entry). By September, he wrote to Tree from Grove Farm in Cromer that the first two acts were completed, the third act almost finished, and he hoped "to have it all ready in ten days or a fortnight at most. I am very pleased with it so far" (*Letters* 320). He completed the play at Babbacombe Cliff, Torquay, where he rented a house from November 1892 until March 1893. In a letter to Oswald Yorke (1866–1943), an out-of-work actor, Wilde wrote: "In my new play there are very few men's parts – it is a woman's play..." (*Letters* 335). At the end of March, Tree began rehearsals at the Haymarket Theatre.

First Productions: The play opened at the Haymarket on 19 April 1893 and closed on 16 August for a run of 113 performances. The leading roles were performed by Tree as Lord Illingworth, Mrs. Bernard Beere as Mrs. Arbuthnot, Mrs. Tree as Mrs. Allonby, Rose Leclercq as Lady Hunstanton, Fred Terry (the brother of Ellen) as Gerald Arbuthnot, and Julia Neilson (Fred Terry's wife) as Hester Worsley. With Maurice Barrymore (father of Ethel, John, and Lionel) in the role of Lord Illingworth, the New York production opened on 11 December 1893 at the Fifth Avenue Theater and closed on 13 January 1894.

Published: 9 October 1894, by John Lane at the Sign of the Bodley Head (London) in a printing of 500 copies (this first edition differs considerably from all previous versions, whether TS. or MS.); rpt. in the *Collected Edition* (1908) as Volume 4. The dedication reads: "To Gladys, Countess de Grey." The Countess (1859–1917) had married Lord de Grey in 1882 after the death of her first husband, the Earl of Lonsdale. In a letter in 1880, Wilde alludes to Lady Lonsdale and Lillie Langtry as "two beauties" (*Letters* 65).

Source: Again, Wilde turned to Alexandre Dumas *fils* (see the entries for *Lady Windermere's Fan* and *An Ideal Husband*) for the elements of plot suitable for his own play. In *Le Fils naturel* (1858), a characteristic noble-hearted woman – here a working girl – is seduced and betrayed by a charming young man. When a child is born, he argues that marriage or acknowledgement of the child is not possible because of his respectable family. Despite her effort to raise herself to his educational level, he ends their relationship, the young girl refusing to accept his offer of money. In later years, their son, a young man of sterling character, courts his father's niece. When the discovery is made that he is the illegitimate son, marriage is out of the question. When the son distinguishes himself in the diplomatic service, his father offers to legitimize him, but the son rejects the offer.

The Plot: The setting for Act I is the lawn in front of the terrace of Lady Hunstanton's country home. Lady Caroline Pontefract is querying Hester Worsley, a puritanical American heiress (whose Christian name echoes Hester Prynne's as Lord Illingworth's echoes Roger Chillingworth's in Hawthorne's *The Scarlet Letter* – Wilde's contrast of rigid American morality and England's casual view of sin). On this first visit to England, Hester harshly evaluates the guests who are invited to the house by Lady Hunstanton.

Lady Hunstanton and Gerald Arbuthnot enter, the latter announcing that Lord Illingworth has offered to make him his secretary – a post, says Lady Hunstanton, that will lead to a "very brilliant future." When Mrs. Allonby and Lady Stutfield enter, talk focuses on the "Woman Question." When Lady Stutfield remarks, "Ah! The world was made for men and not for women," Mrs. Allonby reacts with wit: "We have a much better time than they have. There are far more things forbidden to us than are forbidden to them." When Lord Illingworth overhears Lady Stutfield's remark that "the world says that Lord Illingworth is very, very wicked," he responds with dandiacal indifference: "But what world says that, Lady Stutfield? It must be the next world. This world and I are on excellent terms." When Lady Stutfield presses her point concerning his reputation, he retorts: "It is perfectly monstrous the way people go about, nowadays, saying things against one behind one's back that are absolutely and entirely true." After Illingworth leaves with Mrs. Allonby, the conversation continues.

At one point, Lord Alfred Rufford (the name suggesting Lord Alfred Douglas) enters but says nothing in this scene other than that he is in debt. Indeed, he soon vanishes from the play. (Is this Wilde's little joke in his portrayal of Lord Alfred Rufford as the fictional equivalent of the idle,

debt-ridden Lord Alfred Douglas? In a preliminary scenario for *The Importance of Being Earnest*, Lord Alfred Rufford appears again, though in the final version of the play he is renamed Algernon Moncrieff.)

Lord Illingworth and Mrs. Allonby return, chatting about relationships between men and women. When they go in for tea, Illingworth notices Mrs. Arbuthnot's letter on the table and looks at the envelope. He recognizes the handwriting as that of a woman he knew years ago. Mrs. Allonby asks who. "Oh, no one," he responds. "No one in particular. A woman of no importance." He throws the letter down and smiles at Mrs. Allonby as they pass up the steps of the terrace.

In response to the charge by critics that his plays were devoid of action, Wilde told an interviewer in the *Sketch* (9 Jan. 1895) that the first act of *A Woman of No Importance* was his answer to the critics who complained that *Lady Windermere's Fan* lacked action."In the act in question, there was absolutely no action at all. It was a perfect act" (rpt. in Mikhail 1:241). Noting that Wilde is always concerned with the unseen as well as the seen, Katharine Worth remarks that the various characters in the first act – "busily occupied in filling in the time, getting through the long spaces of an ordinary afternoon, creating a stage on which their existence will have more point, with the aid of wit and story-telling" – reveal "in their own way the patterns of their inner life" (99).

Act II opens in the drawing room of Lady Hunstantan's home. The ladies of the previous act are seated on sofas conducting what seems to be a continuation of their conversation on the relationships of men and women, particularly in marriage. When attention turns to Hester Worsley, who has been listening but not believing anything that has been said, she delivers a speech that denigrates English society in comparison to American life by attacking the English double standard in morality. (As Regenia Gagnier has remarked, "Wilde's world is precisely that twilight world of modern society where puritan values and cynical actions – two equally deplorable antitheses – operate in a symbiotic relationship," 123.)

Mrs. Arbuthnot, who arrives while Hester is speaking, is curious to know more about Lord Illingworth, whose elder brother had been killed while hunting, possibly while fishing. Lord Illingworth thus succeeded to the title. When some of the men, who had withdrawn to smoke after dinner, emerge, Mrs. Arbuthnot's son, Gerald, offers to introduce Illingworth to her; though she declines, he goes to Illingworth, who is startled when he sees her. Both Illingworth and Mrs. Arbuthnot are cold and formal towards each other.

When the guests withdraw to the music room to hear Hester play the violin, Mrs. Arbuthnot and Illingworth remain. His first words reveal the truth of their relationship: "So that is our son, Rachel! Well, I am very proud of him.... By the way, why Arbuthnot, Rachel?" Her response follows the 19th-century convention of the fallen woman, who adopts "Mrs.": "One name is as good as another, when one has no right to any name." Before their son was born, she had implored him to marry her, and she left Illingworth when he refused to give their son a name. He charges that she refused £600 from his mother.

When she refuses to permit Gerald to be his secretary, he is appalled that she would selfishly ruin a promising career by having him remain "an underpaid clerk in a provincial bank in a third-rate English town." But she pleads with Illingworth not to take away her only source of love. When Gerald approaches them, Illingworth proposes that her son make the final decision. But when Mrs. Arbuthnot cannot convince her son that he has no qualifications to be a private secretary and cannot offer any other objection to his taking the post, Illingworth regards the arrangement as settled. When he and Gerald leave, "she stands immobile, with a look of unutterable sorrow on her face."

Act III opens in the picture gallery at Hunstanton, where Lord Illingworth is "lolling on a sofa" while Gerald is sitting in a chair, their conversation following directly from the previous scene. When Gerald mentions that his mother is always going to church, Illingworth comments: "Ah! she is not modern, and to be modern is the only thing worth being nowadays.... A man who can dominate a London dinner-table can dominate the world. The future belongs to the dandy. It is the exquisites who are going to rule."

When several of the ladies join them, Illingworth's dandiacal talk continues. After some of the guests leave, Gerald asks his mother why she strenuously objects to his taking the position as secretary to Lord Illingworth. He also reveals that he is in love with Hester. With a position of substance, he could marry her. He accuses his mother

of always trying to crush his ambition, and he rejects her views that success is not worth having and that society is shallow. In fact, he would give anything to be just like Lord Illingworth.

When Gerald presses his mother as to the reasons why she objects to Illingworth, she tells the story of her own seduction and subsequent suffering at the hands of Illingworth, though she uses the third person in the narrative. But when Gerald does not make the connection between the young girl of 18 in the story and his own mother, he remarks that the girl was "just as much to blame as Lord Illingworth was." Mrs. Arbuthnot abruptly withdraws her objections to Gerald's wish to accept the post of secretary.

Suddenly, Hester is heard shouting, "Let me go! Let me go!" She enters in terror and, rushing over to Gerald, flings herself into his arms, shouting, "Oh! save me – save me from him!" When Gerald asks who has dared to "insult" her, Lord Illingworth enters, to whom Hester points. Threatening to kill him, Gerald rushes towards him, but he is restrained by his mother, who shouts, "Stop, Gerald, stop! He is your own father!" When Mrs. Arbuthnot "sinks slowly on the ground in shame," Gerald raises his mother up, puts his arm around her, and leads her from the room.

Act IV opens in Mrs. Arbuthnot's sitting room. Gerald informs Lady Hunstanton that he has decided not to accept Lord Illingworth's offer of a position, insisting that he is not suitable for the post. When the women leave, Mrs. Arbuthnot enters and discovers that Gerald has invited Illingworth to come that afternoon. She refuses to permit him to cross her threshold. When Gerald tells her that he has written to Illingworth that he must marry her, she repudiates her son's insistence that Illingworth must atone for his actions. It is she who refuses to marry him: "The woman suffers.... The man goes free." When Gerald argues that the marriage must take place "to take away the bitterness" from her life, she insists that it would be a travesty of religion to marry her seducer.

Hester enters but remains at a distance listening to Gerald and his mother arguing their points. Finally, she comes forward in support of Mrs. Arbuthnot's decision: "In her all women are martyred." Gerald blames himself for his insensitivity, and despite his illegitimacy and his mother's fallen state, Hester wishes to marry him and share her wealth with him. After Gerald and Hester go into the garden, Illingworth calls, but Mrs. Arbuthnot tells him that he must leave at once. He offers to marry her and leave Gerald his property if she agrees to an arrangement whereby Gerald would live with her for six months and with him for the other six. But she declines such an offer. Illingworth, on noticing a letter on the table addressed to him, reads it.

Convinced that all is over, he prepares to leave. When he utters a degrading remark concerning her being his mistress, she picks up his glove and strikes him across the face with it. When Gerald and Hester enter, Gerald notices a glove lying on the floor and asks whose it is. His mother responds: "Oh! no one. No one in particular. A man of no importance" – an ironic reversal of the title.

Early Theater Reviews: In general, reviewers could no longer regard Wilde as a playwright of no importance, no matter what his weaknesses might be. In the *World* (26 April 1893), William Archer established the standard for reviewers by announcing that "the one essential fact about Mr. Oscar Wilde's dramatic work is that it must be taken on the very highest plane of modern English drama, and furthermore, that it stands alone on that plane. In intellectual calibre, artistic competence – ay, and in dramatic instinct to boot – Mr. Wilde has no rival among his fellow-workers for the stage." The "prophet of the New Drama," as Archer has been called, may have sensed that Wilde might be the English Ibsen. Though he denied that either *Lady Windermere's Fan* or *A Woman of No Importance* could be regarded as masterpieces, he contended that "we are dealing with works of an altogether higher order than others which we may very likely have praised with much less reserve" (rpt. in Beckson).

In the *Speaker* (29 April), A. B. Walkley quotes what another dramatic critic "of credit and renown" confessed to him the other day:

"I have been spending the morning," he said, "in trying to write my notice of Oscar's new play, and I have found it jolly tough work. It's easy enough to point out scores of faults, and one has to point them out; but, hang it all, one can't help feeling that there is more in the fellow than in all the other beggars put together." That happens to be precisely my own experience.... Nine English playwrights out of ten, with all their technical skill, their knowl-

edge of "the sort of thing the public want, my boy," strike one as naive persons.... Wilde is the tenth man, sceptic, cynic, sophist, as well as artist, who moves at ease amid philosophical generalisations, and is the dupe of nothing – except a well-turned phrase (rpt. in Beckson).

In the *Saturday Review* (6 May), an unsigned review concurs with other reviews that Wilde "has more or less fairly earned his right to be taken seriously as a dramatist." As for the character of Lord Illingworth, the reviewer regards him as "not quite human, and is little more than a machine for the utterance of paradox and epigram, most of them, though by no means all, wonderfully clever, but bearing upon them the hall-mark of insincerity" (for the Victorians, *insincerity* was a critical term of denigration). The dialogue, the reviewer remarks, is "brilliant, epigrammatic, paradoxical, antithetical even to a fault.... The author is not always content to let well alone; and to work which is of his very best (and that is distinctly good) joins attempts at that kind of pseudo-paradox which is the distinguishing mark of a certain new school of machine-made humour" (rpt. in Beckson).

The review in the *Theatre* (1 June) is designed as an "open letter" to Wilde signed by "The Candid Friend," who, at first, seems to attack Wilde as a public figure and writer – "a man of genuine and brilliant talent who has made his success, not by the worthy culture and legitimate exhibition of that talent, but by the silliest kind of trick and quackery," advertising himself "as an insipid and pretentious dullard, whose motto was notoriety at any price.'" Gradually, however, the reviewer turns his "letter" into a favorable evaluation of his plays, though he regards *A Woman of No Importance* as less satisfactory than *Lady Windermere's Fan*, for Lord Illingworth is "too exclusively typical, and is very imperfectly individualised, less a cynic than a typification of cynicism. He talks vastly too much for effect, and one cannot help thinking that if the play lasted for another act he would be in grave danger of developing into a bore...." The writer concludes this "open letter" to Wilde with subdued admiration for his gifts: "Face, instead of evading, the difficulties of dramatic art, take its practice seriously, respect yourself and your audience, and you have in you the capacity to do good – it may be great – work" (rpt. in Beckson).

In the *Westminster Review* (June), an unsigned review asserts that, after *Lady Windermere's Fan*, "a well made, well written play of plot and incidents, rather than an incisive study of character, one had a right to hail in Oscar Wilde an English Sardou [see well-made play].... We call it a compliment to place Mr. Oscar Wilde on the same level as Sardou, the more as no other among our playwrights equals this distinguished Frenchman either in imagination or in brilliancy of style." After such an overture, the reviewer regrets that Wilde's *A Woman of No Importance* has "blighted some of our great expectations." Though it is a "play of distinction" with polished dialogue and "flashes of caustic wit," qualities that "are all too rare in native English plays," as a work of art the reviewer finds the play "unsatisfactory" (rpt. in Beckson).

Early Book Review: In the *Bookman* (March 1895), W. B. Yeats delights in the play's "famous paradoxes, the rapid sketches of men and women of society, the mockery of most things under heaven...while, on the other hand, the things which are too deliberate in their development, or too vehement and elaborate for a talker's inspiration, such as the plot, and the more tragic and emotional characters, do not rise above the general level of the stage." There is "something of heroism," Yeats continues, "in being always master enough of oneself to be witty.... Lord Illingworth and Mrs. Allonby have self-control and intellect; and to have these things is to have wisdom, whether you obey it or not." But, laments Yeats,

one puts the book down with disappointment. Despite its qualities, it is not a work of art, it has no central fire, it is not dramatic in any ancient sense of the word. The reason is that the tragic and emotional people, the people who are important to the story, Mrs. Arbuthnot, Gerald Arbuthnot, and Hester Worsley, are conventions of the stage.... (rpt. in Beckson)

Manuscripts: The Clark Library has notebooks containing the original TS. with Wilde's revisions, bearing the title *Mrs. Arbuthnot*. The British Library has the play in four separate MS. books, extensively revised, also with the title *Mrs. Arbuthnot*; in addition, the library has two TSS.

(bound together) of different acts written at different times bearing that title with Wilde's autograph corrections as well as a TS. with the final title, which was submitted to the Lord Chamberlain's office for licensing. Texas has the acting script, revised in Wilde's hand, among revisions by other unidentified figures (Tree initialed his notes for Act I). The Theatre Collection at the University of Bristol has various TSS. of the play used by Tree, some with revisions.

References: Elissa S. Guralnick and Paul M. Levitt, "Allusion and Meaning in Wilde's *A Woman of No Importance*," *Eire-Ireland* (Winter 1978); Ian Small, ed., *A Woman of No Importance* in *Two Society Comedies*, eds. Ian Small and Russell Jackson (1980); Katharine Worth, *Oscar Wilde* (1983); Regenia Gagnier, *Idylls of the Marketplace: Oscar Wilde and the Victorian Public* (1986); Russell Jackson and Ian Small, "Some New Drafts of a Wilde Play," *ELT* 30:1 (1987); Joseph Bristow, "Dowdies and Dandies: Oscar Wilde's Refashioning of Society Comedy," *Modern Drama* (Spring 1994); Karl Beckson, "Narcissistic Reflections in a Wilde Mirror," *Modern Drama* (Spring 1994).

WOMAN'S WORLD: *See* **NEWSPAPERS AND PERIODICALS**

Y

"YE SHALL BE GODS"

Unpublished in Wilde's lifetime, this poem derives its title from Genesis 3:5, when the serpent speaks to Eve about the forbidden fruit: "For God doth know that in the day ye eat thereof, then your eyes shall be opened, and ye shall be as gods, knowing good and evil."

In structuring his Classical ode of 60 lines, Wilde employs the traditional device derived from Pindar: four sections of the poem are called "Strophe" and "Antistrophe" (in Greek orthography), alluding to song and dance movements in one direction, followed by movements in the opposite direction. The poem's Classical structure suggests the romantic Hellenism of Swinburne, whose "Before the Beginning of Years" in his poetic drama *Atalanta in Calydon* (1865) probably provided the metrical and poetic model to the youthful Wilde. The opening lines fuse biblical and Classical imagery, God raising from the dust a "splendid and goodly thing":

> Man – from the womb of the land,
>   Man – from the sterile sod
> Torn with a terrible hand –
>   Formed in the image of God.

But then Wilde refers to the wrathful "gods... / Whose joy is in weeping of men." In the first antistrophe, man has overthrown the gods: "The spirit of man is arisen / And crowned as a mighty King." Love, symbolized by Aphrodite, "is the only religion, / And hers to entice and entwine." The poem ends with the establishment of a new order: "We kneel to the Cyprian mother [that is, Aphrodite, Cyprus's patron goddess], / We take up our lyres and sing...." The final lines are a modification of lines from Swinburne's "Hymn to Proserpine," which Wilde uses with quotation marks: "'Thou art crowned with the crown of another, / Thou art throned where another was King.'"

Manuscript: Written in the early 1870s in Lady Wilde's notebook (now in the Berg Collection)

when Wilde was a student at Trinity College, Dublin.

Yeats in the 1890s

YEATS, WILLIAM BUTLER (1865–1939)

The Anglo-Irish poet, playwright, and critic first met Wilde in September 1888 at the home of W. E. Henley, the editor of the *National Observer*. Almost 35 years later, Yeats recalled this first meeting as an "astonishment": "I never before heard a man talking with perfect sentences, as if he had written them all overnight with labour and yet all spontaneous" (*Autobiography* 87). When, later that year, Wilde invited Yeats to have Christmas dinner at his home in Tite Street, Wilde's talk again impressed him:

> I have never and shall never meet conversation that could match with his. Perplexed by my own shapelessness, my lack of self-possession and of easy courtesy, I was astonished by this scholar who as a man of the world was so perfect.... I saw nothing of the insolence that perhaps grew upon him later. "Ah, Yeats," he said that Christmas day – he had been reading to me from the proof sheets of his unpublished *Decay of Lying* – "we Irish are too poetical to be poets; we are a nation of brilliant failures." (*Memoirs* 21–22)

At about this time, Yeats said to Wilde, "I envy those men who become mythological while still living." Wilde's reply helped to shape his friend's aesthetic vision and Wilde's own self-image: "I think a man should invent his own myth" (qtd. in Ellmann 301/284). Ellmann contends that the "sense of living a myth was implicit in Yeats's defense of Wilde against the charge of being a poseur" ("Oscar and Oisin" 13).

In the first of two *Woman's World* reviews of Yeats's early works, Wilde calls *Fairy and Folk Tales of the Irish Peasantry* (1888), "a charming little book" and devotes more space to this edited volume than he customarily does to other books he reviewed (see "Some Literary Notes," Feb. 1889). In his review of *The Wanderings of Oisin and Other Poems* (1889), Wilde regards the volume as "certainly full of promise" (see "Some Literary Notes," March 1889). In the *Pall Mall Gazette* (12 July 1889), Wilde again briefly reviewed *The Wanderings of Oisin and Other Poems*, in which he mentions Yeats's "true poetic spirit" (see "Three New Poets"). Yeats, in turn, reviewed two of Wilde's works: *Lord Arthur Savile's Crime and Other Stories* and *A Woman of No Importance*: see both entries.

Yeats saw little of Wilde in the early 1890s (except at occasional meetings of the Rhymers' Club), for as Yeats became increasingly involved in founding the Irish Literary Society in London and the National Literary Society in Dublin, he moved in nationalist circles. Though political activism held little interest for Wilde, he joined the Irish Literary Society as a charter member and wrote, on occasion, in support of Home Rule. Yeats recalls that a few days after the première performance on 29 March 1894 of his play *The Land of Heart's Desire* (the curtain raiser before Shaw's *Arms and the Man*), Wilde entered the theater as the curtain fell and "overwhelmed" him with compliments, not about the play, which he had missed, but about a story by Yeats: "Your story in *The National Observer*, *The Crucifixion of the Outcast*, is sublime, wonderful, wonderful." That, says Yeats, was his last conversation with him (*Autobiography* 190–91).

Yeats's final connection with Wilde occurred when he returned to London in May 1895 during Wilde's criminal trials; he went to Lady Wilde's home with letters that the poet George Russell and others had written to Wilde expressing sympathy over his difficulties: "He had increased my admiration by his courage at the first trial...." But Wilde, then out on bail, had already left his mother's home to stay with Ada Leverson (see entry). When Wilde's brother, Willie, to whom Yeats gave the letters, asked, "Are you telling him 'to run away'?" Yeats replied: "No, I certainly would not advise him to run away." Yeats collected other letters that he brought to court, but, he concludes, "I never saw Wilde again" (*Memoirs* 79–80).

Years later, writing of the "Tragic Generation," Yeats was convinced that Wilde had made the "right decision" in not fleeing from England and that he owed "to that decision half of his renown" (*Autobiography* 192). Yet, as Edward Engelberg contends, the "hesitant and vacillating" Yeats regarded Wilde as having fallen short of the "tragic dimension because the personal passion was too much distilled, the irony too dominant, the comedy too obviously a grotesque distortion of the underlying tragedy" (85).

After Wilde's death, Yeats wrote in a note that Wilde was "an unfinished sketch of a great man" ("Oscar and Oisin" 24–25), but he continued to be absorbed by him and his work, though not always with admiration. For example, when he wrote in May 1906 to T. Sturge Moore, who was planning to stage *Salome* for the Literary Theatre Society, Yeats regarded the play as "thoroughly bad. The general construction is all right, is even powerful, but the dialogue is empty, sluggish and pretentious. It has nothing of drama of any kind, never working to any climax but always ending as it began.... Wilde was not a poet but a wit and critic and could not endure his limitations" (Bridge 8–9).

However, in a letter to his father in January 1909 concerning the current state of drama, Yeats praises Wilde's perception of the need for innovation: "Wilde wrote in his last book [*De Profundis*], 'I have made drama as personal as a lyric,' and I think, whether he has done so or not, that it is the only possible task now" (Wade 524). The weird power of Wilde's *Salome*, despite Yeats's earlier denigration of its dialogue and lack of drama, remained with him when he adapted some central images of the Salome legend in *A Full Moon in March* (1935), such as the severed head and erotic dance.

But this play was not the only attempt by Yeats to improve on Wilde: when Yeats decided to include *The Ballad of Reading Gaol* in his anthology *The Oxford Book of Modern Verse* (1936), he cut 71 stanzas from the poem, arguing in his introduction that the poem now "shows a stark realism akin to that of Thomas Hardy, the contrary to all its author deliberately sought." By removing some of Wilde's famous lines, such as those passages beginning with "Yet each man kills the thing he loves," Yeats eliminated what he regarded in the poem as "artificial, trivial, arbitrary," convinced that he had brought "into light a great, or almost great poem, as [Wilde] himself would have done had he lived" (vi–viii).

Finally, in *A Vision* (rev. ed., 1937), Yeats, who always regarded Wilde as a "man of action," places him in the 19th phase of the moon (with Byron), that of the "Assertive Man": "This phase is the beginning of the artificial, the abstract, the fragmentary, and the dramatic. Unity of Being is no longer possible, for the being is compelled to live in a fragment of itself and to dramatise that fragment" (148).

References: *The Autobiography of W. B. Yeats* (1938; rpt. 1965); Ursula Bridge, ed., *W. B. Yeats and T. Sturge Moore: Their Correspondence, 1901–1937* (1953); Allan Wade, ed., *The Letters of W. B. Yeats* (1954); Edward Engelberg, *The Vast Design: Patterns in W. B. Yeats's Aesthetic* (1964); Richard Ellmann, "Oscar and Oisin," *Eminent Domain: Yeats among Wilde, Joyce, Pound, Eliot, and Auden* (1967); W. B. Yeats, *Memoirs*, ed. Denis Donoghue (1972); *The Collected Letters of W. B. Yeats, 1865–1895*, Vol. 1, eds. John Kelly and Eric Domville (1986); Warwick Gould, "'The Crucifixion of the Outcasts': Yeats and Wilde in the Nineties," *Rediscovering Oscar Wilde*, ed. C. George Sandulescu (1994).

"THE YOUNG KING"

Published: *Lady's Pictorial* (Christmas number, 1888): 1–5; rpt. in *A House of Pomegranates* (1891), the story dedicated to Margaret, Lady Brooke (1849–1936), the Ranee of Sarawak, essayist and memoirist, the wife of the second Rajah of Sarawak. When Wilde saw Bernard Partridge's drawings for the tale in the *Lady's Pictorial*, he told the artist: "You have seen the Young King just as I hoped you would see him, and made him by delicate line and graceful design the most winsome and fascinating lad possible" (*Letters* 225). In *A House of Pomegranates*, Charles Shannon provided full-page illustrations for the tale.

The Plot: On the night before his coronation, the young King is lying on his couch "wild-eyed and open-mouthed, like a brown woodland Faun or some young animal of the forest newly snared by the hunters." Indeed, he had been found "bare-limbed and pipe in hand, following the flock of a poor goatherd who had brought him up, and whose son he had always fancied himself to be" (Wilde's adaptation of the Oedipus myth). The child of the King's only daughter by a secret marriage, he had been stolen (apparently by the King's order) and given to a peasant and his childless wife. Before the King's death, he summons his grandson and, before the Council, declares him as his heir.

The young King, from the "very first moment of his recognition" as heir to the throne, has shown a "strange passion for beauty that was destined to have so great an influence over his life" (in his prison letter to Lord Alfred Douglas, Wilde wrote that "The Young King" was one of his works that "prefigured" the "note of Doom" in his life: see *Letters* 475). Though he sometimes misses the "fine freedom of his forest life," he delights in the wonderful palace of Art called *Joyeuse*; wearied by affairs of state and court life, he runs down the great staircase and wanders from room to room," sometimes accompanied by the "slim, fair-haired Court pages, with their floating mantles, and gay fluttering ribands," though he discovers that "the secrets of art are best learned in secret, and that Beauty, like Wisdom, loves the lonely worshipper."

On one occasion he is seen "kneeling in real adoration before a great picture that had just been brought from Venice" (the Aesthete's devotion to the Religion of Art). Once he spends "a whole night in noting the effect of the moonlight on a silver image of Endymion" (the mythic figure in poems by Keats and by Wilde). He sends many merchants to Egypt to secure "that curious green turquoise which is found only in the tombs of kings," said to possess magical powers; he sends other merchants to Persia for silken carpets and painted pottery and still others to India for bracelets of jade and shawls of fine wool (in short, like Des Esseintes in Huysmans's *Against the Grain*, the young King seeks exotic, beautiful artifacts as an escape from the dull, commonplace world). The "rich tapestries" on the walls of his chamber represent the "Triumph of Beauty."

"THE YOUNG KING"

On one evening, when a "strange languor came over him," he feels as he had never felt or so keenly, "with such exquisite joy, the magic and the mystery of beautiful things." When he falls asleep, he dreams of a factory of many looms and weavers, "pale sickly-looking children crouched on the huge crossbeams." One of the weavers, not recognizing the young King, complains that his employer is no different from himself except that he wears fine clothes while he himself goes in rags. When the young King reminds him that no one is a slave in this free land, the weaver complains, "We have chains, though no eye beholds them; and are slaves, though men call us free." But, he says to the young King, "what are these things to you? Thou art not one of us. Thy face is too happy." When the youth asks what robe the weaver is at work on and discovers that it is for the young King's coronation, he cries out and awakens in his own chamber.

He falls asleep again and dreams that he is lying on the deck of a huge galley rowed by a hundred slaves, each chained to his neighbor. When the galley anchors in a bay, the youngest black dives for pearls. After his last dive, retrieving a magnificent pearl, he suddenly dies and his body is thrown overboard. Laughing, the master puts the pearl to his forehead: "It shall be for the sceptre of the young King." The young King again cries out and awakens.

Again falling asleep, he dreams of wandering through a wood containing "strange fruits" and poisonous flowers. Adders hiss at him, and "bright parrots" fly screaming from branch to branch. He comes to a dried-up river bed, where "an immense multitude of men" are toiling (in the various dreams, Guy Willoughby suggests, "Wilde is presenting a vision of the city that, owing much to John Ruskin and William Morris, insists on the interrelatedness of *all* members of society," 37). From a cavern, Death and Avarice (a characteristic allegorical device, to which Wilde was attracted) watch the laborers. Death says: "I am weary; give me a third of them and let me go," but Avarice responds by shaking her head: "They are my servants." Death, having asked her for a grain of corn to plant and having been refused, summons Ague, Plague, and Fever, who leave no man alive in the valley. The young King asks what these men were seeking. A pilgrim answers: "For rubies for a king's crown" and tells the young King to look in a mirror to see who the king is. Seeing his own face, the young King cries out once again and awakens.

On the day of the young King's coronation, the Chamberlain and high officers bring the young King a crown and a robe of tissued gold, but he tells them that he will not wear them: he says that "on the loom of Sorrow, and by the white hands of Pain, has this my robe been woven. There is Blood in the heart of the ruby, and Death in the heart of the pearl." He then tells them his three dreams. When they leave, he dons the sheepskin cloak that he had worn when watching the goatherd and takes his shepherd's staff. A young page asks him where his crown is. The young King plucks a "spray of wild briar," bends it into a circlet, and places it on his head (a fusion of pagan myth and Christian symbolism associated with Christ). On his way to the cathedral, a man in the crowd charges that the young King has nothing to do with the poor, and at the church the Bishop urges him to return to the palace and dress more fittingly: "The burden of this world is too great for one man to bear, and the world's sorrow too heavy for one heart to suffer."

The young King approaches the image of Christ and kneels in prayer. The nobles burst in with drawn swords, demanding to know where the King is, apparelled like a beggar who "brings shame upon our state." When, after prayer, the King faces them, sunlight comes streaming upon him, and sunbeams weave around him a brilliant tissued robe. His staff blossoms (a borrowing from the Tannhäuser myth), as does the briar thorn. From the monstrance on the altar shines "a marvellous and mystic light," and "the Glory of God" fills the church. The people fall to their knees, and the nobles sheath their swords and do homage. The Bishop exclaims: "A greater than I hath crowned thee," and he too kneels before the young King. On his return to the palace, "no man dared to look upon his face, for it was like the face of angel."

Reference: Guy Willoughby, "Christ's Vision in *A House of Pomegranates*," *Art and Christhood: The Aesthetics of Oscar Wilde* (1993).

GENERAL INDEX

Main entries are designated by page numbers in bold face. Reviews written by Wilde are cited after titles as (rev.). The abbreviations OW and AD refer to Oscar Wilde and Alfred Douglas.

Oscar Wilde" (with Bobby Fong), 95

Beerbohm, Max, 2, **24–27**, 34, 59, 73, 103, 104–05, 136, 139, 220, 224, 260, 310, 317, 319, 329, 342, 345, 377, 379, 386, 413; "Ballade de la Vie Joyeuse," 26; "A Defence of Cosmetics" (rev. as "The Pervasion of Rouge"), 25, 63; "The Happy Hypocrite," 26; "Oscar Wilde" (by "An American"), 24; "A Peep into the Past," 25, 259; *The Works of Max Beerbohm*, 25, 63

Beere, Mrs. Bernard, 396, 417

Beethoven, Ludwig van, 300

Behn, Mrs. Aphra, "A Song," 198

Beineke Library (MSS.), 400, 160, 250, 361

"Bella Donna della mia Mente, La," 18, **27–28**, 210

Bellair, Lady, *Gossips with Girls and Maidens Betrothed and Free*, 198

Belleau, Rémy de, 277

"Belle Gabrielle. (From the French), La," **28**

"'Belle Marguerite.' Ballade du Moyen Age, La" (early title of "Ballade de Marguerite"), 18

Benedict, St., 107

"Ben Jonson" (rev.), 28–29

Bennett, Arnold, 35, 139, 146, 387

Benson, Eugene, 126

Benson, William A.S., 222

Bentley, Joyce, 410

Beranger, G., 89

Béranger, Pierre-Jean de, *A Selection from the Songs of De Béranger*, ed. William Toynbee, 29

"Béranger in England" (rev.), 29

Berg Collection (MSS. and TSS.), 17, 18, 67, 75, 96, 159, 208, 255, 272, 330, 400, 423

Berggren, Ruth, 153–54

Bergonzi, Bernard, 307

Berkeley, George, 385

Berman, Jeffrey, 235

Bernard–Derosne, Léon, 329

Berners, Abbess Juliana, 91

Bernhardt, Sarah, **29–30**, 113, 209, 263, 309, 324, 331, 342, 404, 409

Bertrand, Aloysius, *Gaspard de la nuit*, 275

Besant (later Holland), Thelma, 140

Besant, Walter, 115

"Bevy of Poets, A" (rev.), 30

Beyle, Henri ("Stendhal," pseud.), 347

Bias (one of Seven Sages), 132

Bible (King James version), 114, 275; Genesis, 4, 423; Isaiah, 72; Job 11, 282; 2 Kings, 4; Luke, 49, 401; Mark, 326, 328; Matthew, 326, 328; Psalms, 70, 135, 315; 1 Samuel, 133

Bibliotheca Bodmeriana, 161, 164, 330

Bibliothèque Nationale, 66

Bierce, Ambrose, 274

Bigelow, Mrs. John, 376

Binyon, Laurence, 139; "Ode on Youth," 291; *Primavera*, 291

Bird, Alan, 148, 151, 326

Birnbaum, Martin, *Oscar Wilde: Fragments and Memories*, 163

"Birthday of the Infanta, The," **30–31**

"Birthday of the Little Princess, The" (early title of above story)

Blacker, Carlos, **31–32**

Blackie, John Stuart, *Messis Vitae*, 395

"Blackmailers' Charter": *see* Labouchere, Henry

Blackwood, William, 286–87, 290; publisher, *Blackwood's Edinburgh Magazine*

Blake, William, 92, 217, 262, 277, 308, 316, 329, 391; "The Little Girl Lost," 48; *The Marriage of Heaven and Hell*, 275

Blanche, Jacques-Émile, 294

Blind, Mathilde, 243

Block, Gordon A., 133

"Bloody Sunday" (13 Nov. 1887), 19, 116

Bloxam, John Francis, **32–33**; ed., *Chameleon*, 32, 33, 52, 98, 168, 370, 392; "The Priest and the Acolyte," 32–33, 52, 370, 392

Bloxham, Lady (in *The Importance of Being Earnest*), 33

Blunt, Wilfrid Scawen, *In Vinculus*, 276; *My Diaries: 1888–1900*, 324

Bodleian Library, Oxford (MSS. and TSS.), xii, 73

Bodley, J.E.C., 106

Bodley, Sir Thomas, 33

Bodley Head, 22, **33–35**, 83, 119, 194, 195, 274, 287, 325, 357, 381, 417

Bogue, David (publisher), 273, 274

Böhme, Jacob, 48

Boissier, Gaston, *Nouvelles Promenades Archéologiques: Horace et Virgile*, 203–04

Book of Kells, 89

Borland, Maureen, 316

Boucher, Emile, *A Statesman's Love*, 390

Boucicault, Darley George ("Dot" and "Dion Junior"), 36

Boucicault, Dion, **35–36**; *The Corsican Brothers*, 95, 166; *London Assurance*, 35, 97, 179; *Rescued*, 36

Boughton, George, 217

Bowen, Sir Charles, trans., *Virgil in English Verse*, 344

Bowling, E.W., *Sagittulae: Random Verses*, 30

Bracknell, Lady (in *The Importance of Being Earnest*), 33, 60–61, 149, 155–56, 158, 339, 340

Bradford, Rev. Edwin, 393

Bradley, Katherine: see "Field, Michael"

Brady, Matthew, 331

Brake, Laurel, 242

Bramston, Mary: *see* Yonge, Charlotte

Brancaster, Lady (later Lady Bracknell in *The Importance of Being Earnest*), 124

Brawne, Fanny, 250

Briel, Henri de: *see* Saix, Guillot de

Bristol, University of, (TSS.), 421

Bristow, Joseph, 122, 183

British Empire, 12, 106

British Library (MSS.), 73, 83, 89, 99, 153, 158, 184, 220, 359, 400, 421

British Museum, 11, 66, 70, 73, 89, 336, 377

British Secular Union, 297

Brodie, E.H., *Lyrics of the Sea*, 280

Brontë, Charlotte, 200, 308, 347

Brontë, Emily, 91, 198, 200, 308

Brooke, Stopford, 276

Brookfield, Charles, **36**, 258; *Dear Old Charlie*, 36; *Godpapa* (with F.C. Philips), 155; *The Poet and the Puppets: A Travestie Suggested by "Lady Windermere's Fan"* (with Charles Hawtrey and James Mackey Glover), 8, 36, 257

Brough, Fanny, 147

Broughton, Rhoda, *Betty's Visions*, 237

Brown, Horatio Forbes, 271, 363

Brown-Potter, Mrs. Cora, 5

Browne, Phyllis, *Mrs. Somerville and Mary Carpenter*, 199

Browning, Elizabeth Barrett, 198, 377; *Aurora Leigh*, 200, 281, 361;"The Dead Pan" in *Poems*, 331; *Sonnets from the Portuguese*, 91; "A Vision of Poets," 401

Browning, Oscar, 46, 274

Browning, Robert, 52, 54, 119, 138, 200, 201, 211, 240, 246, 262, 273, 278, 281, 308, 350, 409; *Sordello*, 7; *A Soul's Tragedy*, 284

Brummell, George "Beau," 59, 195

Bruno, Giordano, 231

Buchan, Alexander, *Joseph and His Brothers*, 280

Buchanan, Robert W., *The Blue Bells of Scotland*, 207; *The Charlatan* (with Henry Murray), 259, 379; "Fleshly School of Poetry," 3, 187, 259; *That Winter Night*, 21

Buckler, William, 16

"Buffalo Bill" (William Cody), 5

Bulwer-Lytton, Edward (lst Baron Lytton), 179, 252, 349; *Lucretia*, 262; *Pelham; or, The Adventures of a Gentleman*, 59

Bunbury (in *The Importance of Being Earnest*), 155

"Burden of Itys, The," **36–37**, 109

Burgess, Anthony, 307

Burke, Rev. Edmund, 61–62

Burlington Arcade, 122

Burnand, Francis Cowley, 136; *The Colonel*, 90; ed. *Punch*, 90

Burne-Jones, Edward, 21, **37–38**, 93, 125, 165, 185, 309, 314, 375, 409; *Annunciation*, 125; *Fides*, 37; *Spes*, 37; *Temperantia*, 37

Burne-Jones, Margaret, 37, 375

Burnett, Frances Hodgson, *The Real Little Lord Fauntleroy*, 313

Burns, Dawson, *Oliver Cromwell*, 279

Burns, Robert, 114, 217, 253, 333

Burnside, R.H., 154

"Butterfly's Boswell, The" (rev.), 38

Byron, George Gordon, Lord, 92, 95, 109, 165, 203, 273, 299, 306, 308, 336, 347, 349, 377, 425

"By the Arno," **38–39**, 331

C.3.3. (OW's cell number at Reading Prison), 15, 17, 18, **41**, 136, 305

Cadogan Hotel (where OW was arrested), 78, 382, 387

Café Royal, 25, 76, 118, 123, 143, 365

Caillavet, Mme Arman de, 295

Caine, T. Hall, *Life of Samuel Taylor Coleridge*, 121; ed., *Sonnets of Three Centuries*, 115

Cairns, William, *A Day after the Fair*, 353

Caius Cestius, 117, 376

"Calasaya, The" (Parisian café), 251

Caldecott, Randolph, *Gleanings from the "Graphic,"* 347

Cambridge University, 384, 388

Cameron, Mrs. H. Lovett, *A Life's Mistake*, 352

"Camma," **41–42**, 370

Campbell, Alan (in *The Picture of Dorian Gray*), 269, 270

Campbell, Lady Archibald, 10

Campbell, Lady Colin, 337, 338

Campbell, Mrs. Patrick, 22, **41**, 224, 325

Campbell, Patrick, 41

Can Grande della Scala, 11

Canninge, Mrs. George, 154

"Canterville Ghost, The," **42–43**

"Canzonet," **43**

Capel, John Mais, *Six Songs*, 95

Cardew, Cecily (in *The Importance of Being Earnest*), 155–56, 157, 236

Cardinal of Avignon, The, **43–44**

Carew, Mrs. Helen, 377

Carfax Gallery, 2, 317

Carillo, Enrique Gomez, 401

Carlyle, Thomas, 21, 125, 230

Carlyle, Mrs. Thomas, 198

Carnarvon, Earl of, trans., *The Odyssey of Homer*, 285

Caro, Elmé Marie, *George Sand*, trans. Gustave Masson, 211

Carpenter, Edward, 167, 391; ed., *Chants of Labour*, 276

Carpenter, Mary, 199

Carrington, Charles (publisher), 332

Carson, Edward, 380–82

Carte, Richard D'Oyly, 36, 160, 187, 188, 396

Catholicism: *see* Roman Catholicism

Catty, Charles, *Poems in the Modern Spirit*, 282

Cellini, Benvenuto, 162

"'The Cenci'" (rev.), 45

censorship, 167

Century Guild Hobby Horse, 46

Century Guild of Artists, 172

Ce qui ne meurt pas (*What Never Dies*): *see Satyricon*

Cevasco, G.A., 120; ed., *The 1890s: An Encyclopedia of British Literature, Art, and Culture*, xi

Chambers, John Graham, 297–98

Chameleon (periodical): *see* Bloxam, John Francis

Champion, Henry H., 19

Chancellor's English Essay Prize (Oxford), 311

"Chanson," 28, **45**

Chapman, Elizabeth Rachel, *The New Purgatory and Other Poems*, 200

Chapman, Frederick, 287

Charles, Sir Arthur, 382

"Charmides," 36, **45–46**, 144, 216

Chasuble, Rev. (in *The Importance of Being Earnest*), 154, 156

Chateaubriand, François René, vicomte de, 275

"Chatterton," **46–47**

Chatterton, Thomas, 46–47, 287, 335–36, 349

Chaucer, Geoffrey, 222, 228, 308, 349

"Cheap Edition of a Great Man, A" (rev.), 47

Chesson, Wilfred Hugh, 261

Chetwynd, Mrs. Henry, *Mrs. Dorriman*, 272

Cheveley, Mrs. (in *An Ideal Husband*), 60, 98, 148–51, 152

"Child-Philosopher, The," **47–48**

"Children of the Poets, The" (rev.), 48

Chiltern, Lady (in *An Ideal Husband*), 98, 148–51

Chiltern, Mabel (in *An Ideal Husband*), 148–51

Chiltern, Sir Robert (in *An Ideal Husband*), 147, 148–51, 152

"Chinese Sage, The" (rev.), 48–49, 56

"Choir Boy," **49**

"Chorus of Cloud-Maidens," **49**

Christ and Christianity, 17, **49–51**, 72, 89, 94, 127, 239, 250, 275–76, 298, 301, 302, 311, 327, 331, 354, 355, 356, 358, 400, 401, 426

Christian, Princess, trans., *Memoirs of Wilhelmine*, 198

Christie's (MSS.), 88, 218

Chuang Tzŭ, 48–49, 56

Church and Stage Guild, 132

Churchill, Winston, 80

Church of England, 276, 392

Clark, William Andrews, 105

Clark Library (MSS. and TSS.), 7, 10, 11, 18, 19, 23, 28, 37, 42, 44, 46, 49, 52, 57, 69, 73, 88, 89, 90, 93, 102, 105, 106, 130, 133, 135, 136, 153, 158, 159, 161, 163, 167, 184, 197, 204, 208, 210, 215, 221, 245, 249, 255, 264, 272, 303, 308, 312, 324, 330, 334, 335, 341, 354, 359, 361, 372, 373, 376, 400, 421

Clarke, Sir Edward, 78, 380–84

Clayton, Vista, 275

Clayworth, Anya and Ian Small, "'Amiel and Lord Beaconsfield': An Unpublished Review by Oscar Wilde," 7

Clement XII, Pope, 106

"Close of the 'Arts and Crafts': Mr. Walter Crane's Lecture on Design, The" (rev.), 51

Coakley, Davis, 163, 286, 384; *Oscar Wilde: The Importance of Being Irish*, 132

Cobden-Sanderson, T. J., 24

Cockle, John: *see* Mullner, Amand

Cole, Alan: *see* "Fascinating Book, A"

Coleridge, Christobel: *see* Yonge, Charlotte

Coleridge, Samuel Taylor, 2, 133; "The Eolian Harp," 133; "The Rime of the Ancient Mariner," 15, 16, 17, 348; "Kubla Khan," 348

Coleridge, Stephen, *Demetrius*, 113

Collected Edition of the Works of Oscar Wilde, ed., Robert Ross, **51–52**, 70, 83, 88, 103, 139, 306, 316, 317, 377, 387, 397

Collier, John, *A Manual of Oil Painting*, 52

Collins, Justice Henn, 380

Colvin, Sidney, *Keats*, 388

Comédie Française, 29, 263

comédie-proverbe, 155

"Commonplace Book" and "Notebook Kept at Oxford," **52**

"Common Sense in Art" (rev.), 52–53

Communism, 355

Conder, Charles, 2, **53**, 319

Confucius, 58

Congreve, William, 130, 132, 179, 341, 384

"Conqueror of Time, The" (early title of "Athanasia"), 10

Constable, John, 262

Constance (French version of *Mr. and Mrs. Daventry*), 224

Constant, Benjamin, *Journal intime*, 2

contemplative life ("being," not "doing"), 56, 230

"Conway, Hugh" (pseud. of Frederick John Fargus), *The Cardinal Sin*, 250

Cooper, Edith: *see* "Field, Michael"

Cooper, Elise, *The Queen's Innocent, with Other Poems*, 279

Corelli, Marie, 243

Corke, Hilary, 291

Corkran, Alice, *Margery Merton's Girlhood*, 201; *Meg's Friend*, 347

Corot, Jean Baptiste, 53, 56, 239

Correggio, Antonio, 141

Cottam, Rev. Ellsworth, 393

courtly love, 18, 28

Courtney, W.L., 224

Cousin, Victor, 2

Cowles, Virginia, *The Rothschilds: A Family of Fortune*, 218

Cowley, Francis, *The Colonel*, 379

Craig, Gordon, ed., *Mask* (Florence)

Craigie (later Holland), Violet, 140

Craik, Mrs. Dinah, 242; *John Halifax, Gentleman*, 199, 247; *Poems*, 247

Crane, Walter, 51, 125, 128, 243; (designs) Carpenter's *Chants of Labour*, 276; (illus.) Mrs. Molesworth's *A Christmas Posy*; *Flora's Feast*, 347; "The Prospects of Art under Socialism," 337

Crawford, John Martin: *see Kalevala, The*

"Crépuscule, La" (MS.), 161

Criminal Law Amendment Act, 168, 177, 240, 364, 382, 392

Cripps, Arthur, *Primavera*, 291

Criterion Theatre, 97

"Critic as Artist, The," 38, **53–57**, 82, 114, 132–33, 235, 256, 275, 304, 356

"Critic Who Had to Read Four Volumes of Modern Poetry, The" (letter by OW), 119

Cromwell, Oliver, 261, 376

Crosland, Thomas W.H., *The First Stone*, 80; ass't ed., *Academy*, 318

Cross and the Grail, The (anon.), 281

Cruso, Henry Alford Anthony: *see* Amery, Leopold Charles

Crowley, Aleister, 379

"Cumberland, Stuart" (pseud. of Charles Garner), *The Vasty Deep*, 373

Cundall, Joseph, *Annals of the Life of Shakespeare*, 252–53

Curling, Jonathan, 261

Currie, Sir Philip, 76

Curtis, Ella, *A Game of Chance*, 350

Curzon, George, *Delamere*, 273

Custance, Olive, 80

"Cypriots or Folk Making for Malta," **57**

Dalziel, George, *Pictures in the Fire*, 280

"Dame Jaune, La," **59**

Dandyism and dandies, **59–61**, 64, 97, 99, 119, 120, 123, 146, 148, 149, 150, 156, 182, 183, 189, 235, 256, 261–62, 263, 264, 268, 301, 340, 419

Danleigh, Prof. Thomas: *see* Peacock, Thomas Brower

Danson, Lawrence, 261

Dante Alighieri, 72, 203, 211, 299, 401; *The Divine Comedy*, 7, 8, 11, 28, 112, 253, 401; "Paradiso," 11; "Purgatory," 112; *Vita Nuova*, 401

D'Arcy, Ella, 35

Darnley, J.H.: *see* Fenn, George Manville

Dartmouth College (MSS.), 4, 44, 208

Darwin and Darwinism, 49, 109, 221, 247, 255–56, 355, 357

Daudet, Alphonse, 171, 215

David (Bible), 382

Davidson, John, 20

Davis, Cora, *Immortelles*, 285

Davis, Thomas, 166, 384

Davray, Henry-D., 15, 16, **61**, 305–06; trans., *The Ballad of Reading Gaol*, 61; *Oscar Wilde: La Tragédie finale*, 61; trans., "Poems in Prose," 61

Dawsons (publisher), 52

Day, F. Holland, 250

Day, Richard, *Poems*, 350

Death of Wilde, **61–63**

decadence (moral and artistic decline), 60, 63, 66,

Ugliness in Dress"
dress reform, 97, 199, 220–21, 300
Dryden, John, 308,
Duchess of Florence (early title of *The Duchess of Padua*), 88
Duchess of Padua, The, 5, 52, **83–88**, 103, 166, 297, 304, 333, 341, 408
Duffy, Bella, *Life of Madame de Staël*, 202
Duffy, Charles Gaven, 166
Dumas *fils*, Alexandre, 196; *L'Ami des femmes*, 147; *La Dame aux Camélias*, 219, 403; *Le Demi–Monde*, 403; *L'Etrangère*, 179 ; *Le Fils naturel*, 417–18; *Françillon*, 179
Dumas *père*, Alexandre, 95; *The Hunchback of Notre Dame*, 389
Du Maurier, George, 187, 257, 404
Dunn, Father Cuthbert, 61–62
Durant, Heloise, *Dante: A Dramatic Poem*, 285
Duret, Théodore, 113
Dyer, Rev. A. Saunders: *see* Guyon, Madame de la Mothe

"Early Christian Art in Ireland" (rev.), 89
"Easter Day," **89**, 94
Echo: *see* Narcissus and Narcissism
Echoes (attributed to OW), 4, **89–90**
Eckstein, Ernest, *Aphrodite*, 238–39
Edel, Leon, 169, 170, 171
Edison, Thomas, 157
Edmonds, Mrs. E. M., *Greek Lays, Idylls, Legends, etc.*, 219; *Mary Myles*, 349
Edward, Prince of Wales (later Edward VII), **90**, 185, 397
Edwards, Francis, 163
Edwards, Owen Dudley, "Oscar Wilde and Henry O'Neill," 226; ed., *The Fireworks of Oscar Wilde*, 100
Eglinton, J.Z., 33
Eisenhower Library (MS.), Johns Hopkins University, 376
"Eleutheria," **90**
Eliot, George, 198, 241, 295, 347; *Adam Bede*, 21
Eliot, T.S., 308
Elizabethan/Jacobean revenge tragedy, 84
Elliott, Fay and Geoffrey, 88, 94
Ellis, Havelock, *Sexual Inversion* (with John Addington Symonds), 363, 361
Ellmann, Richard, x, 21, 32, 37–38, 46–47, 62, 66, 76, 106, 110, 113, 117, 119, 122, 134, 171, 172, 186, 214, 216, 225, 256, 260, 286, 288, 293, 298, 303, 307, 320, 321, 363, 370, 374, 375,

393, 415, 424; *The Artist as Critic: Critical Writings of Oscar Wilde*, 48; *Oscar Wilde*, 122
Elton, Oliver, 273
embroidery and lace: *see* "A Fascinating Book"
"Emeritus" (unidentified), *Whims and Fantasies*, 395
Emerson, Ralph Waldo, 145; *Essays*, 70; "Self-Reliance," 356, 405
Emmet, Robert, 384
"Endymion. (For Music)," **90–91**, 249, 425
Endymion (the myth), 28, 90, 109
Engelberg, Edward, 424
England's moral decline: *see* "Quantum Mutata"
"English Poetesses," **91**
"English Renaissance, The," 9–10, 67, **91–93**, 94, 164, 189, 222
Englishwoman's Year-Book, 203
Enlightenment, the, 300
Enthoven, Gabrielle, 89, 303
Enthoven Collection (MSS.), Victoria and Albert Museum, 225
"Envoi, L'" (OW's intro. to Rodd's *Rose Leaf and Apple Leaf*), **93–94**, 315, 321, 362
Epicureanism, 260
Epistola: In Carcere et Vinculus (De Profundis), 70
Epstein, Jacob: *see* Tomb of Wilde, The
Era (theatrical publication), "Modern History and Tragedy," 397
Erigena, John Scotus, 48
Erlynne, Mrs. (in *Lady Windermere's Fan*), 5, 98, 178, 179–84, 258
Erlynne, Mrs. (in *The Picture of Dorian Gray*), 269
Erskine, George (in "The Portrait of Mr W.H."), 287–89
Erskine, Hughie (in "The Model Millionaire"), 218
Esterhazy, Major: *see* Walsin-Esterhazy, Ferdinand
"E Tenebris," **94**
Etherege, Sir George, 179
Euripides, 187, 212, 401; *Hecuba*, 374; *Hypsipile*, trans., Gilbert Murray, 385; *Telephus*, 401
Evans, W., *Caesar Borgia*, 281
Evelyn, John, *Life of Mrs. Godolphin*, 202–03
Ewing, Majl, 303
Examiner of Plays, Lord Chamberlain's office: *see* Piggott, Edward

Fabian Society, 278, 283, 337
"Fabien dei Franchi," **95**, 166

"Heart's Yearnings," **133**
"Heartsease" (unidentified), *God's Garden*, 281
Hedonism: *see* New Hedonism
Hegel, Georg Wilhelm, 52, 300, 386
Heine, Heinrich, 100, 396
Heinemann, William, 124
"Hélas!" **133–34**
Helen of Troy, 185, 237, 249
"Helena" (MS.), 42
"'Helena in Troas'" (rev.), 134
Helfand, Michael S.: *see* Smith, Philip E.
"Hellas! Hellas!" (early title of "Impression de Voyage"), 159
Hellenism, **134–35**; *also see* New Hellenism
Henderson, Philip, 221
Henley, William Ernest, 17, 115, **135–36**, 290, 316, 319, 359, 367, 423; "Ballade of a Toyokuni Colour-Print," 246; *A Book of Verses*, 135, 246–47; *In Hospital*, 136; ed., *New Review*, 135; ed., *Scots Observer* (later *National Observer*), 135, 258, 271
Henry, Lord (in *The Picture of Dorian Gray*): *see* Wotton, Lord Henry
"'Henry the Fourth' at Oxford" (rev.), 135
Herkomer, Hubert von, 126
Hermes of Olympia, 375
Herod (in *Salome*), 235, 325, 326–28, 329
Herodias (in *Salome*), 326–28
Herodotus, 311
Herrick, Robert, 225; "Ode on the Birth of Our Saviour," 48
Her Second Chance (early title of *Mr. and Mrs. Daventry*), 224
"Her Voice," 8, 112, **137**
"Heu Miserande Puer" (early title of "The Grave of Keats"), 117
Heywood, J.C., *Salome*, 281
Hichens, Robert, 220; *The Green Carnation*, 123–24, 386, 391; *Yesterday: The Autobiography*, 123
Higginson, Thomas Wentworth, 46, 144, 274
Hilliard, David, 391
Hird, Frank, 216
Hirsch, Charles, 369
Hirst, Francis Wrigley: *see* Amery, Leopold Charles
His Majesty's Theatre, 372
His Other Self, 264
Hole, W.G., *Procris and Other Poems*, 239–40
Holland, Cyril (OW's older son), 65, **137–38**, 138–39, 140, 371, 409

Holland, Lucian (OW's great grandson), 140
Holland, Merlin (OW's grandson), 62–63, 140; "Foreword," ix–x; *The Wilde Album*, xii; *also see* Gattégno, Jean
Holland, Vyvyan (OW's younger son) 5, 27, 65, 73, 105, 137, **138–40**, 187, 287, 317, 321, 409; ed., *Complete Works of Oscar Wilde*, 140, 287; ed., *De Profundis*, 70, 140; *An Explosion of Limericks*, 140; ed., *The Importance of Being Earnest*, 140; *Oscar Wilde: A Pictorial Biography*, 140; ed., *The Portrait of Mr W.H.*, 140, 287, 290; *Son of Oscar Wilde*, 90; trans., Barbusse's *Stalin*, 140; *Time Remembered: After Père Lachaise*, 140
Holloway Prison, 113
Holmes, Oliver Wendell, 189
Homer, *The Iliad*, 250; *The Odyssey*, 207, 208, 250 285
homosexuality, 289, 363, 364, 391–93
Hone, Joseph, 220
Honorius (Roman emperor), 299
Honorius (in *La Sainte Courtisane*), 323
Hood, Jacomb, 128
Hood, Thomas, "The Bridge of Sighs," 308; "The Dream of Eugene Aram," 15, 17; "The Song of the Shirt," 124
Hooley, Arthur ("Charles Vale," pseud.), 290
Hope, Adrian, 78, 411
Hopkins, Gerard Manley, 392
Hopkins, Tighe, *'Twixt Love and Duty*, 352
Horne, Herbert, ed., *Century Guild Hobby Horse*, 46
Hôtel d'Alsace (where OW died), 61
Houghton, Lord, 362
Houghton Library (MS.), Harvard University, 117
"House Beautiful, The," ix, 67, **140–42**, 189, 409
"House Decoration": *see* "House Beautiful, The" and "Decorative Arts, The" (first version)
House of Commons, 19, 239
"House of Judgment, The," 111, 392; *also see* "Poems in Prose"
"House of Pomegranates, A," 52, **142–43**, 309, 366
Housman, A.E., *A Shropshire Lad*, 15, 143
Housman, Laurence, **143–44**; *All-Fellows: Seven Legends of Lower Redemption*, 143
Houston, Mrs. Matilda, *A Heart on Fire*, 353
Howe, Julia Ward, **144–45**; "Battle Hymn of the Republic," 144; *Reminiscences, 1819–1899*, 145
Howells, William Dean, 153, 201, 305
How To Be Happy Though Married (anon. author

identified as the Rev. Edward J. Hardy), 127

Huberman, Jeffrey, 403

Hughes, Willie, 288–89

Hugh the Miller (in "The Devoted Friend"), 74–75

Hugo, Victor, 342; *Angelo*, 84, *Hernani*, 84; *Lucrèce Borgia*, 84, *Ruy Blas*, 31

Hulette, Frank P., *Vera*, 397

Humanism and humanists, 52, 232

"Humanitad," 36, 50, **145–46**

Hume, David, 52

Humphreys, Arthur Lee, 410–11

Humphreys, Charles Octavius, 380

Hunstanton, Lady (in *A Woman of No Importance*), 417

Hunt, Mrs. Alfred, *That Other Person*, 238

Hunt, Alfred William, 146

Hunt, H.J., trans., Balzac's *Ilusions perdues*, 72

Hunt, Leigh, 2

Hunt, Margaret Raine, 146

Hunt, Violet, **146**; *My Flurried Years*, 146; *My Oscar*, 146; *Their Lives*, 146

Hunt, William Holman, 92, 125

Hunter, Mrs. Leo, "Ode to an Expiring Frog," 395

Hunter-Blair, David, 117, 355, 393

Huntington Library (MSS. and TSS.), 42, 46, 93, 95, 96, 162, 171, 219, 256, 263, 274, 286, 315, 331, 361

Huret, Jules, 333

Hutchinson, Charles Edward, *Boy Worship*, 392

Hutchinson, Thomas, *Ballades and Other Rhymes*, 245

Huxley, T.H., 52, 301

Huysmans, Joris-Karl, *A Rebours* (*Against the Grain*), 63, 64, 268, 318, 326, 425

Hyde, H. Montgomery, 32, 78, 211–12, 225, 292, 374–75

Hyde Collection (MSS.), 37, 46, 57, 67, 88, 105, 130, 135, 146, 160, 161, 166, 250, 256, 315, 316, 331, 355, 359, 376

"I.S." (unidentified), *Rachel and Other Poems*, 203

Ibsen, Henrik, 95, 97, 115, 252, 305, 312, 328, 338, 420; *Brand*, 1; *A Doll's House*, 219, 223; *Hedda Gabler*, 313; *The Master Builder*, 313

Ideal Husband, An, 5, 8, 27, 33, 36, 52, 60, 90, 97, 98, 111, 131, **147–53**, 156, 170, 235, 294, 305, 309, 310, 338, 371, 404, 410

Idler (periodical), 407–08

Ignatius of Loyola, St., 231

Illingworth, Lord (in *A Woman of No Importance*),

44, 60, 197, 235, 371, 379, 418–21

Image, Selwyn, 10, 391

imagination, 66, 72

Imagism, anticipations of, 96, 159, 160, 161, 367

Importance of Being Earnest, The, xi, 5, 8, 27, 33, 35, 52, 54, 71, 78, 83, 121, 122, 124, 132, 149, **153–59**, 168, 170, 171, 177, 220, 236, 245, 298, 304, 305, 308, 309, 339, 341, 346, 366, 371, 404, 414, 418

"Impression: Le Réveillon," **159**

"Impression de Paris: Le Jardin des Tuileries" (MS.): *see* "Le Jardin des Tuileries," 96

"Impression de Voyage," 89, **159**

"Impression du Matin," 8, **160**, 404

"Impression du Soir" (MS.), 161

"Impression Japonais: Rose et Ivoire" (MS.), 96

Impressionism and the Impressionists, 55, 56, 64, 65, 67, 126, 159, 160, 219, 344, 391, 406

"Impressions: I. Le Jardin; II. La Mer," **160**

"Impressions: I. Les Silhouettes; II. La Fuite de la Lune," **161**; *also see* "Lotus Leaves"

"Impressions du Théâtre," **161**

Impressions of America, 7, **161–62**, 177, 193

Independent Theatre Society, 99, 118, 313

individualism, 10, 49, 50, 55, 56, 72, 256, 343, 355–56

Innocent IV, Pope, 97

"In the Forest," **162–63**

"In the Garden" (MS.), 160

"In the Gold Room: A Harmony," **163**

Intentions, 3, 52, **163–64**, 220, 242, 259, 278, 304–05, 309, 365, 366, 406

"Intentions: Aphorisms on Art," **164**

"Interior and Exterior House Decoration," 140–41

Iokanaan (in *Salome*), 235, 323, 327–28, 329

Ireland and England, the Relationship between, **164–65**, 225–26

Irish art, ancient and modern, 89

Irish Literary Society, 172, 424

Irish Poets and Poetry of the Nineteenth Century, 164, **165–66**, 189

Irving, Henry, 41, 95, 125, 127, **166–67**, 177, 249, 286, 321, 370, 371, 404

Irwin, Henry Crossly, *Rhymes and Renderings*, 278–79

Isaacson, Henry Bevan (Governor, Reading Prison), 293–94

Islam, threat of, 354

"Italia," **167**

"It is for Nothing" (MS.), 137

Ives, George, 33, **167–68**, 393, 407; *A Book of*

Morris, May, 223

Morris, William, 2, 19, 24, 29, 92, 93, 125, 141, **221–23**, 253, 273, 274, 276, 309, 334, 375, 407, 426; "Carpet and Tapestry Weaving," 227; *The Defence of Guenevere and Other Poems*, 18; *The Earthly Paradise*, 109, 165, 222; "The Eve of Crécy," 18; *News from Nowhere*, 120, 222–23; trans., Homer's *Odyssey*, 227–28, 228–29; "Praise of My Lady," 28; *A Tale of the House of the Wolfings*, 228; "The Unity of Art," 69

Morse, Colonel W.F., 188, 192, 331

Morton, Maddison, 157

Moulton, Louise Chandler, 99; *Ourselves and Our Neighbours*, 202

Mozart, Wolfgang Amadeus, 300, 343

Mr. and Mrs. Daventry, **223–25**, 346, 379; *also see* Harris, Frank

"Mr. Brander Matthews's Essays" (rev.), 225

"Mr. Froude's Blue Book" (rev.), 165, 225–26

"Mr. Henry O'Neill, Artist," **226**

"Mr. Mahaffy's New Book" (rev.), 226–27

"Mr. Morris on Tapestry" (rev.), 227

"Mr. Morris's Completion of the Odyssey" (rev.), 227–28

"Mr. Morris's Last Book" (rev.), 228

"Mr. Morris's Odyssey" (rev.), 228–29

"Mr. Pater's Imaginary Portraits" (rev.), 229

"Mr. Pater's Last Volume" (rev.), 229–30

"Mr. Swinburne's Last Volume" (rev.), 230–31, 362

"Mr. Symonds' History of the Renaissance" (rev.), 231–32

"Mr. Whistler's Ten O'Clock" (rev.), 232–33, 405

Mrs. Arbuthnot (MS. with an early title of *A Woman of No Importance*), 421

Mrs. Cheveley (MS. with an early title of *An Ideal Husband*), 153

"Mrs. Langtry" (rev.), 186, 233

"Mrs. Langtry as Hester Grazebrook": *see above*

Mudie's Select Library, 237

Mulholland, Rosa: *see* Gilbert, Lady

Mullner, Amand, *Guilt*, trans., John Cockle, 284

Munday, Luther, 160

Munster, Lady, *Dorina*, 349

Muntz, Lina, 325

Murby, Millicent, 326

Murchison, Lord (in "The Sphinx without a Secret"), 359–60

Murray, Gilbert, trans., Euripides' *Hypsipile*, 385

Murray, Henry: *see* Buchanan, Robert

Murray, Isobel, 48, 49, 53–54, 56, 70, 264, 275–76, 358

Murray, John Middleton, ed., *Athanaeum*, 27

Musset, Alfred de, 103; *Il ne faut jurer de rien*, 155

Myers, Frederick W.H., 237

Myrrhina (in *La Sainte Courtisane*), 323–24

"Myth of Wilde, The," 307

"My Voice," 8, 112, 137, **233**

Naden, Constance, *A Modern Apostle and Other Poems*, 198

Napoleon I, 97, 209

Narcissus and Narcissism, 28, 45, 49, 109, 150, **235–36**, 264, 265, 266, 267, 270, 275, 360, 375, 377, 416

Narraboth (in *Salome*), 326–27

Nash, Charles, *The Story of the Cross*, 282

Naturalism (French), 66, 220, 321

nature vs. artifice, 63–64, 212

"Nay, Come Not Thus" (early title of "Sonnet. On Hearing the Dies Irae Sung in the Sistine Chapel"), 354

Nelson, James G., 34

Nelson, Major James Osmond, 69, 70, 72, 294

Nelson, Julia, 147, 417

Neo-Platonism, 256, 289

Nero, 366

Nesbit, Edith, 91, 243: *Lays and Legends*, 283; *Leaves of Life*, 348

"New Book on Dickens, A" (rev.), 236–37

"New Calendar, A" (rev.), 237

New Culture, 259

Newdigate, Sir Roger, 212

Newdigate Prize (Oxford), 212, 291, 299, 314, 375, 416

New Drama, 403, 420

New English Players, 103

New Hedonism, 258, 259, 266, 268

"New Helen, The," 45, 185, 211, **237**, 249

New Hellenism, 36, 50, 89, 94, 110, 265, 357, 385, 423

New Journalism, 240

Newman, John Henry, Cardinal, 230, 260

"New Novels" (rev.): (28 Oct. 1886; 20 Aug. 1887), 237–38

"New Play, The" (rev.), 238–39

"New President, The" (rev.), 239

"New Remorse, The," **239**, 239

"News from Parnassus" (rev.), 239–40

Newspapers and Periodicals: Wilde's Contributions, **240–44**

Parodies and Satires, **257–59**

Partridge, John Bernard, 95, 96, 162, 425

pastoral literature, 43, 90, 95, l09, 245, 373

Pastoral Players, 10

Pater, Walter, 125, 129, 163, 169, 186, 195, **259–61**, 277, 301, 303, 321, 334, 352, 392, 408; *Appreciations*, 229, 260; *Imaginary Portraits*, 229, 260, 365; "The School of Giorgione," 93, 94; *Studies in the History of the Renaissance* (later, *The Renaissance*), 2, 55, 64, 93, 133, 134, 145, 230, 255, 259, 262, 266, 292; "Style," 2

Peacock (proposed periodical), 23

Peacock, Thomas Brower, *Poems of the Plains and Songs of the Solitudes* (preface by Prof. Thomas Danleigh), 283

Pearse, Mrs. Wodehouse (formerly Mrs. Chan Toon), 105

Pearson, Hesketh, 371, 379; *The Life of Oscar Wilde*, 122

Péladan, Joséphin, 325

Pembroke, Lord, 287

"Pen, Pencil and Poison," 122, **261–63**, 321, 379

Pennell, Joseph, 22

Pennington, Harper, 204, 375

Pentonville Prison, 2, 132, 292

Pepper, Robert D., 165

Père Lachaise cemetery: *see* Tomb of Wilde, The

Perks, Mrs. J. Hartley, *From Heather Hills*, 352–53

Personal Impressions of America: *see Impressions of America*

Petrarch, Francesco, 37, 203

Petronius Arbiter: *see Satyricon*

Peykenott, John Nott, *AEonial* (published anonymously), 280

Pfeiffer, Emily, *Women and Work*, 201

Pharaoh, **263**

"Phèdre," **263**

Philips, F.C.: *see* Brookfield, Charles

Philistinism and Philistines, 2, 6, 8, 72, 134, 135, 184, 186, 195, 204, 237, 246, 256, 290, 306, 320, 336, 343, 362

Phillimore, Mary, *Studies in Italian Literature*, 253

Phillips, Stephen, "Orestes," 291; *Primavera*, 291

Philo, 48

"Phrases and Philosophies for the Use of the Young," 33, 60, 64, 98, 150, 197, 235, **263–64**, 346, 392

Phryne, 252

Picture of Dorian Gray, The, ix, x, 3, 25, 31, 33,

42, 52, 56, 60, 64, 82, 83, 93, 96, 101, 110, 113, 118, 119, 123, 129, 130, 131, 133, 135, 163, 167, 169, 172, 182, 196, 205, 206, 214, 235, 243, 256, 258, **264–72**, 304, 309, 313, 318, 337, 342, 364, 365, 369, 381, 416

Picture's Secret, The, 264

pièce bien faite: *see* Well-Made Play

Pierce, J., *Stanzas and Sonnets*, 280

Piggott, Edward, 8, 257, 305, 324

Pimlico, Lord, *The Excellent Mystery*, 282

Pindar, 423

Pinero, Arthur Wing, 147, 207, 403; *The Cabinet Minister*, 147; *The Second Mrs. Tanqueray*, 8, 22, 41

Pinter, Harold, 326

Pius IX, Pope, 89, 117, 216, 353, 393

plagiarism, accusations of, 173, 273, 406

Plarr, Victor, 118

Plato and Platonism, 28, 48, 52, 65, 133, 289, 311, 312, 382, 386; *Charmides*, 45; *The Republic*, 66; *Symposium*, 59, 391

Playgoers' Club, 118, 362

"Pleasing and Prattling" (rev.), 272–73

Pleydell-Bouverie, Edward Oliver, *J.S.; or, Trivialities*, 352

Plutarch, 312

Podgers, Septimus R. (in "Lord Arthur Savile's Crime"), 205–06

Poe, Edgar Allan, 95, 166, 218, 260, 301, 336; "Annabel Lee," 48, "The Fall of the House of Usher," 129; "The Haunted Palace," 129; "The Oval Portrait," 264; "The Poetic Principle," 2; *The Raven*, trans., Stéphane Mallarmé

Poems (1881), 8, 27, 52, 106, 146, 163, 166, 216, 257, **273–74**, 304, 314, 362, 363, 365, 376

Poems (1882), 159, 166

Poems (1892), 34, 135, 194, **274**, 309

Poems (1908): *see Collected Edition*

"Poems in Prose": "The Artist," "The Doer of Good," "The Disciple," "The Master," "The House of Judgment," "The Teacher of Wisdom," **274–76**

"Poet, The": *see Echoes*

"Poetical Socialists" (rev.), 276

poetry, modern, 29

"Poetry and Prison" (rev.), 276–77

"Poetry of the People" (rev.), 277

"Poets and the People, The," 165, **277–78**, 285

"Poets' Corner, The" (rev.), (27 Sept. 1886–24 June 1889), 278–85

"Politician's Poetry, A," 285

Pollard, Alfred Williams, ed., *Odes from the Greek Dramatists*, 49

Pollock, W.H. 65

Polybius, 312

Πόντος Ἀτρύγετος (early title of "Vita Nuova"), 401

Pope, Alexander, 228, 253

"Portia," **286**, 355, 370

Portora Royal School, **286**

"Portrait of Mr W.H., The," 35, 102, 135, 243, 264, **286–91**, 309, 363

Positivism, 364

Potter, Mrs. Cora Brown, 224

Powell, Kerry, 155, 169, 264, 313

Praxiteles, 252

Pre-Raphaelite Society, 410

Pre-Raphaelitism and the Pre-Raphaelites, 2, 3, 18, 21, 28, 75, 92, 94, 146, 187, 211, 228, 233, 257, 258, 259, 321

Prescott, Marie, 397

Preston, Harriet Waters, *A Year in Eden*, 203

Prevost, Francis, *Fires of Green Wood*, 281

"Priest and the Acolyte, The": *see* Bloxam, John Francis

"Primavera" (American title of "Magdalen Walks"), 212

"'Primavera'" (rev.), 291

Princeton University (MSS.), 44, 79, 88, 134, 276

Pringle, Thomas, 284

"Printing and Printers: Lecture at the 'Arts and Crafts,'" (rev.), 291–92

Prism, Miss (in *The Importance of Being Earnest*), 153, 154, 156, 340

Prison Commission, 69, 70

prison reform, 70, 292, 294

Prison Years, 1895–97, **292–94**

progress: *see* sin and progress

Progressive Stage Society (NY), 326, 329

Protestant Cemetery (Rome), 109, 117, 377, 408

Protestant Reformation, 324, 389

Proust, Marcel, **294–95**; *Cities of the Plain*, 295; *Remembrance of Things Past*, 294, 295

proverbes dramatiques, 103, 155, 323

Psychical Society: *see* Society for Psychical Research

Punch, 2, 12; "Let Us Live Up to It," 257; "The Grosvenor Gallery," 257; "Punch's Fancy Portraits," 257, 304; "The Six-Mark Tea-Pot," 257

Puritanism and Puritans, 289

"Quantum Mutata," **297**, 373, 376

"Queen Henrietta Maria," **297**, 355, 370

Queensberry, 7th Marquess of (AD's grandfather), 76

Queensberry, 8th Marquess of (John Sholto Douglas, AD's father), ix, 33, 36, 71, 76, 78, 79, 110, 131, 135, 205, 209, 220, **297–98**, 316–17, 341, 380–84, 386; *The Spirit of the Matterhorn*, 297

"Queensberry Rules, The," 298

"Quia Multum Amavi," **298**

Quilter, Harry, 129; *Sententiae Artis: First Principles of Art*, 173

Quinn, John, 59

Quintus, John Allen, 50

Raby, Peter, 153, 179, 326, 327

"Rachel" (stage name of Élisa Félix), 113

"Rachilde" (pseud. of Marguerite Eymery), *Monsieur Venus*, 120

Racine, *Phèdre*, 29, 263

Raleigh, Sir Walter, 314

Rambosson, Yvanhoë, 401

Ramsay, Allan, *Poems* (preface by J. Logie Robertson), 253

Ransome, Arthur, 317; *Oscar Wilde: A Critical Study*, 62, 73, 80, 111, 318

Ravenna, 57, 184, 212, **299**

Rawnsley, H.D., *Sonnets Round the English Coast*, 395

Raymond, E.T., 306

Raymond, G.L., *Ballads of the Revolution*, 396

Reade, Brian, 216

Reading Prison, 41, 49, 72, 79, 132, 293–94, 309, 387

realism in the arts, 66, 67, 114, 126, 136–37, 201, 220

Reed, Frances Miriam, 397

Reformation: *see* Protestant Reformation

Reid, Wemyss, 243

Reinhardt, Max, 325

"Relation of Dress to Art," **299–300**

Religion of Art, 72, 117, 244–45, 250, 268, **300–02**, 335, 377, 425

"Remarkable Rocket, The," 236, **302–03**

Rembrandt van Rijn, 300, 301

"Remorse: (A Study in Saffron)," 59, **303**

Renaissance, the, 28, 43, 64, 92, 113, 231–32, 268, 289, 336, 350, 357, 385, 389

Renan, Ernest, 6; *La Vie de Jesus*, 355

Rénard, Jules, 110

Reni, Guido, 117

Toon, Mrs. Mabel Chan (née Cosgrave), 105

Toynbee, William, 29

Tragara Press, xii

"Tragic Generation," 424

Tree, Herbert Beerbohm, 24, 147, 313, 372, **379–80**, 386, 417

Tree, Mrs. Herbert Beerbohm, 417

Trevor, Alan (in "The Model Millionaire"), 218

Trepov, General, 397

Trials, 1895, The, **380–84**

Trinity College, Dublin, **384–85**

"Tristitiae" (MS.), 4

Trojan War, 111, 185, 207, 237, 311–12, 336, 374

Trollope, Anthony, 19, 200, 241

Troubridge, Laura (later Mrs. Adrian Hope), 171

Troubridge, Violet (later Mrs. Walter Gurney), 403

"True Function and Value of Criticism, The" (early title of "The Critic as Artist"), 53

"True Knowledge, The," **385**, 415

"Truth of Masks, The," 113, 257, **385–86**

truth vs. beauty in art, 202; *also see* "Decay of Lying, The"

Tucker, Benjamin, 15

Turgenev, Ivan, 20, 321; "A Fire at Sea" (OW's translation), 100

Turkish suppression in the Balkans: *see* "Sonnet on the Massacre of the Christians in Bulgaria," 354

Turner, G. Gladstone, *Errata*, 279

Turner, J.M.W., 126, 216, 262

Turner, Reginald, 1, 23, 24, 25, 26, 62, 78, 79, 123, 139, 220, 317, **386–87**

"Twain, Mark" (pseud. of Samuel Langhorne Clemens), 47–48, 138

"'Twelfth Night' at Oxford" (rev.), 388

"Two Biographies of Keats" (rev.), 388

"Two Biographies of Sir Philip Sidney" (rev.), 389

"Two New Novels" (rev.), (15 May 1885; 16 Sept. 1886), 389–90

"Two Tramps" (unidentified), *Low Down*, 278–79

Tyler, Louis, *Chess: A Christmas Masque*, 284

Tyndall, John, 301

Tyrrell, Christina: *see* Werner, E.

Tyrrell, Robert Yelverton, ed., *Kottabos*, 207

Tyrwhitt, Thomas, 290, 363

Ulrichs, Karl Heinrich, 391–92

"Under the Balcony," **391**

"Unity of the Arts, The" (rev.), 10, 231, 391

University Dramatic Society (Oxford), 136, 388

"Unto One Dead" (revised title of "The True Knowledge"), 385

"Unvintageable Sea, The" (early title of "Vita Nuova"), 401

Uranians, The, 117, 122, 167–68, 177, 209, 265, 267, 268, 316, 366, **391–93**

"Urbs Sacra Aeterna," 94, 167, **393**

Urning: *see* Uranians, The

Utopia, 356

Vale, the, 308–09

"Vale, Charles": *see* Hooley, Charles

Valéry, Paul, 110, 209

Vanbrugh, Sir John, 179

Vanbrugh, Irene, 154

"Value of Art in Modern Life," 321; *also see* Lectures in Britain, 1883–85

Vane, James (in *The Picture of Dorian Gray*), 264, 266, 270

Vane, Sibyl (in *The Picture of Dorian Gray*), 42, 235, 264, 266–67

"Various Versifiers" (rev.), 395–96

Vatican, 12, 117

Veiled Picture, The, 264

Veitch, John, *The Feeling for Nature in Scottish Poetry*, 333

Veitch, Sophie, *James Hepburn*, 238

Velásquez, Diego, 301

Venus de Milo, 162, 396

"Venus or Victory?" (rev.), 396

Vera; or, The Nihilists, 35, 52, 57, 90, 106, 166, 188, 197, 304, 330, 370, **396–400**, 409

Vera of the Nihilists (MS.), 400

Verdi, Giuseppi, *Luisa Miller*, 219

Vere, Aubrey de, 166

Verlaine, Paul, 72, 209, 303, 365, **400–01**; "Langueur," 63, 64

Victoria, Queen, 12, 29, 78–79, 90, 215, 224, 303

Victoria and Albert Museum, Enthoven Collection (MS.), 225

Viessy (periodical), 103

Vigilance Society, 304

villanelle: *see* French fixed forms

Villiers de l'Isle Adam, Philippe Auguste, Comte de, 243

Vincent, H.H., 154

Vincentio (scribe), 291

"Vinkvooms, Van" (pseud. of Thomas Griffiths Wainewright), 261

Virgil, 203; *Aeneid*, 117; *Georgics*, 353

er), x, 25, 286, 326, 337, 339, 409, **413–14**, 416, 424; "Faustine," 413; "Salome," 413

Wilde, Dr. (later Sir) William Robert Wills (OW's father), x, 35, 89, 106, 208, 249, 385, 412; *Irish Popular Superstitions*, 416; *Memoir of G. Beranger*, 89

Wilhelmine, Memoirs of, trans., Princess Christian, 198

Wildenbruch, Ernst von, *The Master of Tanagra*, trans., Baroness von Lauer, 252

Wilkinson, L.P., 63

Willard, Edward Smith, 105

Williams, F. Harald, *Women Must Weep*, 280

Williamson, David, *Poems of Nature and Life*, 284

Willis, E. Cooper, *Tales and Legends in Verse*, 284

Willoughby, Guy, 50, 128, 275, 355, 426

Wills, Sir Alfred, 383–84

Wills, W.G., *Charles I*, 297, 370; *Melchior*, 218–19

Wilmost, Alexander, ed., *The Poetry of South Africa*, 284

Wilson, Daniel, *Chatterton: A Biographical Study*, 46

Wilson, Ernest: *see* Sheridan, Richard Brinsley

Wilson, Dr. Henry (OW's half-brother), 414

"Wilson, William" (pseud. of More Adey), 1

Winckelmann, Johann, 268; *also see* Pater, Walter

Windermere, Lady (in *Lady Windermere's Fan*), 98, 179–84, 196, 258

Windermere, Lady (in "Lord Arthur Savile's Crime"), 205–06

Windermere, Lord (in *Lady Windermere's Fan*), 98, 179–83

"Wind Flowers," **417**

Wing, Donald G., "The Katherine S. Dreier Collection of Oscar Wilde," 250

"Winter, John Strange" (pseud. of Henrietta Vaughan Stannard), *That Imp*, 353

Winter, William, 158

"With a Copy of 'The House of Pomegranates," **417**

"With Can Grande at Verona" (early MS. version of "At Verona"), 11

women in politics, 351

Woman of No Importance, A, 8, 24, 27, 35, 44, 52, 90, 98, 111, 151, 170, 179, 209, 214, 220, 235, 305, 309, 338, 346, 371, 379, 386, 416, **417–21**, 424

"Woman Question," 242, 418

"woman's work," 203

Woman's World (OW's contributions), 96–97, 198–203, 246–47

women and the Victorian theater, 313

"Women of Homer, The" (MS.), 363

Wood, Mrs. Henry, 349

Wood, J.S., ed., *Shakespearean Show Book*, 391

Woods, Margaret L., *A Village Tragedy*, 198

Wooldridge, William Lestocq: *see* "Lestocq, W."

Wooldridge, Charles Thomas, 15

Wordsworth, William, 52, 246, 308, 333; "London, 1802," 376; "My Heart Leaps Up," 256; "Ode: Intimations of Immortality," 145, 256; "Tintern Abbey," 255

Wordsworth Society, *Wordsworthiana*, ed., William Knight, 349

World: A Journal for Men and Women, ed., Edmund Yates, 240

Worsley, Hester (in *A Woman of No Importance*), 98, 372, 417, 418–21

Worth Katharine, 87, 155, 223, 328, 340, 397, 418

Worthing, Jack (in *The Importance of Being Earnest*), 5, 33, 153, 155–56, 157, 168, 236, 340

Wotton, Lord Henry (in *The Picture of Dorian Gray*), 60, 64, 110, 196, 216, 235, 259, 260, 265–70

Wotton, Mabel, *Word Portraits of Famous Writers*, 349

Wratislaw, Theodore, 194

Wyndham, Charles, 147

Wyndham, George, 78

Wyndham, Hon. Percy, 78

Yale University Library Gazette, 250

Yates, Edmund: *see World*

"Ye Shall Be Gods," **423**

Yeats, William Butler, 33, 35, 64, 81, 135, 136, 172, 185, 206–07, 259, 269, 271, 301, 304, 337, 372, 407, 421, **423–25**; "The Autumn of the Body," 301; *A Book of Irish Verse*, 308; "The Crucifixion of the Outcast," 301; *Fairy and Folk Tales of the Irish Peasantry*, 347–48, 424; *A Full Moon in March*, 424; *The Land of Heart's Desire*, 424; ed., *Oxford Book of Modern Verse*, 424–25; *A Vision*, 425; *The Wanderings of Oisin and Other Poems*, 348–49, 373–74, 424

Yellow Book, 23, 25, 33, 34, 41, 63, 80, 258, 259, 345, 386

Yonge, Charlotte M., *Astray* (with Mary Bramston, Christabel Coleridge, Esmé Stuart), 237

Yorke, Oswald, 417

Young Ireland, 166, 415